Lecture Notes in Computer Science

T0238659

Commenced Publication in 1973
Founding and Former Series Editors:
Gerhard Goos, Juris Hartmanis, and Jan van Leeuwen

Editorial Board

Advanced Research in Computing and Software Science

Subline of Lectures Notes in Computer Science

Subline Series Editors

Subline Advisory Board

Matthias Felleisen   Philippa Gardner (Eds.)

Programming Languages and Systems

22nd European Symposium on Programming, ESOP 2013
Held as Part of the European Joint Conferences
on Theory and Practice of Software, ETAPS 2013
Rome, Italy, March 16-24, 2013
Proceedings

 Springer

Volume Editors

Matthias Felleisen
Northeastern University
College of Computer Science
Boston, MA 02115, USA
E-mail: matthias@ccs.neu.edu

Philippa Gardner
Imperial College
Department of Computing
London, SW7 2AZ, UK
E-mail: p.gardner@imperial.ac.uk

ISSN 0302-9743   e-ISSN 1611-3349
ISBN 978-3-642-37035-9   e-ISBN 978-3-642-37036-6
DOI 10.1007/978-3-642-37036-6
Springer Heidelberg Dordrecht London New York

Library of Congress Control Number: 2013932559

CR Subject Classification (1998): D.2.1-5, D.3.1-4, D.1.3, D.1.0, D.4.1-2
F.3.1-3, F.1.2

LNCS Sublibrary: SL 2 – Programming and Software Engineering

Typesetting: Camera-ready by author, data conversion by Scientific Publishing Services, Chennai, India

Printed on acid-free paper

Springer is part of Springer Science+Business Media (www.springer.com)

Foreword

ETAPS 2013 is the sixteenth instance of the European Joint Conferences on Theory and Practice of Software. ETAPS is an annual federated conference that was established in 1998 by combining a number of existing and new conferences. This year it comprised six sister conferences (CC, ESOP, FASE, FOSSACS, POST, TACAS), 20 satellite workshops (ACCAT, AiSOS, BX, BYTECODE, CerCo, DICE, FESCA, GRAPHITE, GT-VMT, HAS, Hot-Spot, FSS, MBT, MEALS, MLQA, PLACES, QAPL, SR, TERMGRAPH and VSSE), three invited tutorials (*e-education*, by John Mitchell; *cyber-physical systems*, by Martin Fränzle; and *e-voting* by Rolf Küsters) and eight invited lectures (excluding those specific to the satellite events).

The six main conferences received this year 627 submissions (including 18 tool demonstration papers), 153 of which were accepted (6 tool demos), giving an overall acceptance rate just above 24%. (ETAPS 2013 also received 11 submissions to the software competition, and 10 of them resulted in short papers in the TACAS proceedings). Congratulations therefore to all the authors who made it to the final programme! I hope that most of the other authors will still have found a way to participate in this exciting event, and that you will all continue to submit to ETAPS and contribute to making it the best conference on software science and engineering.

The events that comprise ETAPS address various aspects of the system development process, including specification, design, implementation, analysis, security and improvement. The languages, methodologies and tools that support these activities are all well within its scope. Different blends of theory and practice are represented, with an inclination towards theory with a practical motivation on the one hand and soundly based practice on the other. Many of the issues involved in software design apply to systems in general, including hardware systems, and the emphasis on software is not intended to be exclusive.

ETAPS is a confederation in which each event retains its own identity, with a separate Programme Committee and proceedings. Its format is open-ended, allowing it to grow and evolve as time goes by. Contributed talks and system demonstrations are in synchronised parallel sessions, with invited lectures in plenary sessions. Two of the invited lectures are reserved for 'unifying' talks on topics of interest to the whole range of ETAPS attendees. The aim of cramming all this activity into a single one-week meeting is to create a strong magnet for academic and industrial researchers working on topics within its scope, giving them the opportunity to learn about research in related areas, and thereby to foster new and existing links between work in areas that were formerly addressed in separate meetings.

ETAPS 2013 was organised by the *Department of Computer Science of 'Sapienza' University of Rome*, in cooperation with

▷ European Association for Theoretical Computer Science (EATCS)
▷ European Association for Programming Languages and Systems (EAPLS)
▷ European Association of Software Science and Technology (EASST).

The organising team comprised:

General Chair: *Daniele Gorla;*
Conferences: *Francesco Parisi Presicce;*
Satellite Events: *Paolo Bottoni* and *Pietro Cenciarelli;*
Web Master: *Igor Melatti;*
Publicity: *Ivano Salvo;*
Treasurers: *Federico Mari* and *Enrico Tronci.*

Overall planning for ETAPS conferences is the responsibility of its Steering Committee, whose current membership is:

Vladimiro Sassone (Southampton, chair), Martín Abadi (Santa Cruz), Erika Ábrahám (Aachen), Roberto Amadio (Paris 7), Gilles Barthe (IMDEA-Software), David Basin (Zürich), Saddek Bensalem (Grenoble), Michael O'Boyle (Edinburgh), Giuseppe Castagna (CNRS Paris), Albert Cohen (Paris), Vittorio Cortellessa (L'Aquila), Koen De Bosschere (Gent), Ranjit Jhala (San Diego), Matthias Felleisen (Boston), Philippa Gardner (Imperial College London), Stefania Gnesi (Pisa), Andrew D. Gordon (MSR Cambridge and Edinburgh), Daniele Gorla (Rome), Klaus Havelund (JLP NASA Pasadena), Reiko Heckel (Leicester), Holger Hermanns (Saarbrücken), Joost-Pieter Katoen (Aachen), Paul Klint (Amsterdam), Jens Knoop (Vienna), Steve Kremer (Nancy), Gerald Lüttgen (Bamberg), Tiziana Margaria (Potsdam), Fabio Martinelli (Pisa), John Mitchell (Stanford), Anca Muscholl (Bordeaux), Catuscia Palamidessi (INRIA Paris), Frank Pfenning (Pittsburgh), Nir Piterman (Leicester), Arend Rensink (Twente), Don Sannella (Edinburgh), Zhong Shao (Yale), Scott A. Smolka (Stony Brook), Gabriele Taentzer (Marburg), Tarmo Uustalu (Tallinn), Dániel Varró (Budapest) and Lenore Zuck (Chicago).

The ordinary running of ETAPS is handled by its management group comprising: Vladimiro Sassone (chair), Joost-Pieter Katoen (deputy chair and publicity chair), Gerald Lüttgen (treasurer), Giuseppe Castagna (satellite events chair), Holger Hermanns (liaison with local organiser) and Gilles Barthe (industry liaison).

I would like to express here my sincere gratitude to all the people and organisations that contributed to ETAPS 2013, the Programme Committee chairs and members of the ETAPS conferences, the organisers of the satellite events, the speakers themselves, the many reviewers, all the participants, and Springer-Verlag for agreeing to publish the ETAPS proceedings in the ARCoSS subline.

Last but not least, I would like to thank the organising chair of ETAPS 2013, Daniele Gorla, and his Organising Committee, for arranging for us to have ETAPS in the most beautiful and historic city of Rome.

My thoughts today are with two special people, profoundly different for style and personality, yet profoundly similar for the love and dedication to our discipline, for the way they shaped their respective research fields, and for the admiration and respect that their work commands. Both are role-model computer scientists for us all.

ETAPS in Rome celebrates *Corrado Böhm*. Corrado turns 90 this year, and we are just so lucky to have the chance to celebrate the event in Rome, where he has worked since 1974 and established a world-renowned school of computer scientists. Corrado has been a pioneer in research on programming languages and their semantics. Back in 1951, years before FORTRAN and LISP, he defined and implemented a *metacircular compiler* for a programming language of his invention. The compiler consisted of just 114 instructions, and anticipated some modern list-processing techniques.

Yet, Corrado's claim to fame is asserted through the breakthroughs expressed by the *Böhm-Jacopini Theorem* (CACM 1966) and by the invention of *Böhm-trees*. The former states that any algorithm can be implemented using only sequencing, conditionals, and while-loops over elementary instructions. Böhm trees arose as a convenient data structure in Corrado's milestone proof of the decidability inside the λ-calculus of the equivalence of terms in β-η-normal form.

Throughout his career, Corrado showed exceptional commitment to his roles of researcher and educator, fascinating his students with his creativity, passion and curiosity in research. Everybody who has worked with him or studied under his supervision agrees that he combines an outstanding technical ability and originality of thought with great personal charm, sweetness and kindness. This is an unusual combination in problem-solvers of such a high calibre, yet another reason why we are ecstatic to celebrate him. *Happy birthday from ETAPS, Corrado!*

ETAPS in Rome also celebrates the life and work of *Kohei Honda*. Kohei passed away suddenly and prematurely on December 4th, 2012, leaving the saddest gap in our community. He was a dedicated, passionate, enthusiastic scientist and –more than that!– his enthusiasm was contagious. Kohei was one of the few theoreticians I met who really succeeded in building bridges between theoreticians and practitioners. He worked with W3C on the standardisation of web services choreography description languages (WS-CDL) and with several companies on *Savara* and *Scribble*, his own language for the description of application-level protocols among communicating systems.

Among Kohei's milestone research, I would like to mention his 1991 epoch-making paper at ECOOP (with M. Tokoro) on the treatment of asynchrony in message passing calculi, which has influenced all process calculi research since. At ETAPS 1998 he introduced (with V. Vasconcelos and M. Kubo) a new concept in type theories for communicating processes: it came to be known as 'session types,' and has since spawned an entire research area, with practical and multi-disciplinary applications that Kohei was just starting to explore.

Kohei leaves behind him enormous impact, and a lasting legacy. He is irreplaceable, and I for one am proud to have been his colleague and glad for the opportunity to arrange for his commemoration at ETAPS 2013.

— ∎ —

My final ETAPS '*Foreword*' seems like a good place for a short reflection on ETAPS, what it has achieved in the past few years, and what the future might have in store for it.

On April 1st, 2011 in Saarbrücken, we took a significant step towards the consolidation of ETAPS: the establishment of *ETAPS e.V.* This is a *non-profit association* founded under German law with the immediate purpose of supporting the conference and the related activities. ETAPS e.V. was required for practical reasons, e.g., the conference needed (to be represented by) a legal body to better support authors, organisers and attendees by, e.g., signing contracts with service providers such as publishers and professional meeting organisers. Our ambition is however to make of '*ETAPS the association*' more than just the organisers of '*ETAPS the conference*'. We are working towards finding a voice and developing a range of activities to support our scientific community, in cooperation with the relevant existing associations, learned societies and interest groups. The process of defining the structure, scope and strategy of ETAPS e.V. is underway, as is its first ever membership campaign. For the time being, ETAPS e.V. has started to support community-driven initiatives such as open access publications (LMCS and EPTCS) and conference management systems (Easychair), and to cooperate with cognate associations (European Forum for ICT).

After two successful runs, we continue to support POST, *Principles of Security and Trust*, as a candidate to become a permanent ETAPS conference. POST was the first addition to our main programme since 1998, when the original five conferences met together in Lisbon for the first ETAPS. POST resulted from several smaller workshops and informal gatherings, supported by IFIP WG 1.7, and combines the practically important subject of security and trust with strong technical connections to traditional ETAPS areas. POST is now attracting interest and support from prominent scientists who have accepted to serve as PC chairs, invited speakers and tutorialists. I am very happy about the decision we made to create and promote POST, and to invite it to be a part of ETAPS.

Considerable attention was recently devoted to our *internal processes* in order to streamline our procedures for appointing Programme Committees, choosing invited speakers, awarding prizes and selecting papers; to strengthen each member conference's own Steering Group, and, at the same time, to strike a balance between these and the ETAPS Steering Committee. A lot was done and a lot remains to be done.

We produced a *handbook* for local organisers and one for PC chairs. The latter sets out a code of conduct that all the people involved in the selection of papers, from PC chairs to referees, are expected to adhere to. From the point of view of the authors, we adopted a *two-phase submission* protocol, with fixed deadlines in the first week of October. We published a *confidentiality policy* to set high standards for the handling of submissions, and a *republication policy* to clarify what kind of material remains eligible for submission to ETAPS after presentation at a workshop. We started an *author rebuttal phase*, adopted by most of the conferences, to improve the author experience. It is important to acknowledge that – regardless of our best intentions and efforts – the quality of reviews is not always what we would like it to be. To remain true to our commitment to the authors who elect to submit to ETAPS, we must endeavour to improve our standards of refereeing. The rebuttal phase is a step in that direction and, according to our experience, it seems to work remarkably well at little cost, provided both authors and PC members use it for what it is. ETAPS has now reached a healthy paper acceptance rate around the 25% mark, essentially uniformly across the six conferences. This seems to me to strike an excellent balance between being selective and being inclusive, and I hope it will be possible to maintain it even if the number of submissions increases.

ETAPS signed a favourable three-year publication contract with Springer for publication in the ARCoSS subline of LNCS. This was the result of lengthy negotiations, and I consider it a good achievement for ETAPS. Yet, publication of its proceedings is possibly the hardest challenge that ETAPS – and indeed most computing conferences – currently face. I was invited to represent ETAPS at a most interesting Dagstuhl Perspective Workshop on the '*Publication Culture in Computing Research*' (seminar 12452). The paper I gave there is available online from the workshop proceedings, and illustrates three of the views I formed also thanks to my experience as chair of ETAPS, respectively on open access, bibliometrics, and the roles and relative merits of conferences versus journal publications. Open access is a key issue for a conference like ETAPS. Yet, in my view it does not follow that we can altogether dispense with publishers – be they commercial, academic, or learned societies – and with their costs. A promising way forward may be based on the '*author-pays*' model, where publications fees are kept low by resorting to learned-societies as publishers. Also, I believe it is ultimately in the interest of our community to de-emphasise the perceived value of conference publications as viable – if not altogether superior – alternatives to journals. A large and ambitious conference like ETAPS ought to be able to rely on quality open-access journals to cover its entire spectrum of interests, even if that means promoting the creation of a new journal.

Due to its size and the complexity of its programme, hosting ETAPS is an increasingly challenging task. Even though excellent candidate *locations* keep being volunteered, in the longer run it seems advisable for ETAPS to provide more support to local organisers, starting e.g., by taking direct control of the organisation of satellite events. Also, after sixteen splendid years, this may be a good time to start thinking about exporting ETAPS to other continents. The US East Coast would appear to be the obvious destination for a first ETAPS outside Europe.

The strength and success of ETAPS comes also from presenting – regardless of the natural internal differences – a homogeneous interface to authors and participants, i.e., to look like one large, coherent, well-integrated conference rather than a mere co-location of events. I therefore feel it is vital for ETAPS to regulate the centrifugal forces that arise naturally in a 'union' like ours, as well as the legitimate aspiration of individual PC chairs to run things their way. In this respect, we have large and solid foundations, alongside a few relevant issues on which ETAPS has not yet found agreement. They include, e.g., submission by PC members, rotation of PC memberships, and the adoption of a rebuttal phase. More work is required on these and similar matters.

January 2013

Vladimiro Sassone
ETAPS SC Chair
ETAPS e.V. President

Preface

This volume contains the proceedings of the 22nd European Symposium on Programming (ESOP 2013). The conference took place in Rome, Italy, during March 20–22, 2013, as part of the European Joint Conferences on Theory and Practice of Software (ETAPS).

ESOP is an annual conference devoted to the art and science of programming. The conference solicits contributions on fundamental issues concerning the specification, analysis, and implementation of systems and programming languages.

The 2013 conference attracted 150 abstracts and 120 full submissions, including two tool demo papers. For each submission, we solicited at least three reviews from the Program Committee members and external reviewers, and for most submissions, one of us authored a summary review to help the authors understand the final decision. After an intensive electronic meeting over two weeks, the Program Committee accepted 31 papers for presentation, two of which focus on tools.

In addition, this volume also contains the invited paper, "Distributed Electonic Rights in JavaScript." Mark Miller presented the paper as the ESOP invited talk in Rome.

We greatly appreciate the work of the Program Committee members, who read the papers, solicited expert reviews, studied the author responses, and intensively discussed every submission. Together with our colleagues on the Program Committee, we also wish to thank the numerous external reviewers, without whom running such a large conference would be impossible. Finally, we thank the authors of all submissions for entrusting us with their work and the authors of the accepted papers for their diligent work in preparing their final versions and their conference presentations.

We acknowledge the use of the EasyChair conference system and the support of the ETAPS Steering committee and its Chair, Vladimiro Sassone, with regard to all the administrative work.

January 2013

Matthias Felleisen
Philippa Gardner

Organization

Program Committee

Luca Aceto	Reykjavik University, Iceland
Véronique Benzaken	Université Paris Sud 11, France
Derek Dreyer	MPI-SWS, Germany
Matthias Felleisen	Northeastern University, USA
Philippa Gardner	Imperial College, UK
Giorgio Ghelli	Università di Pisa, Italy
Holger Hermanns	Universität des Saarlandes, Germany
Suresh Jagannathan	Purdue University, USA
Andy King	University of Kent, UK
Akash Lal	Microsoft Research, India
Cosimo Laneve	Università di Bologna, Italy
Gary Leavens	University of Central Florida, USA
Xavier Leroy	INRIA, France
Annie Liu	SUNY at Stony Brook, USA
Aleksandar Nanevski	The IMDEA Software Institute
Michael Norrish	National ICT Australia
Nate Nystrom	University of Lugano, Switzerland
Joel Ouaknine	University of Kent, UK
Scott Owens	University of Cambridge, UK
Jens Palsberg	UCLA, USA
Simon Peyton-Jones	Microsoft Research, Cambridge, UK
Xavier Rival	INRIA, France
Sukyoung Ryu	KAIST, South Korea
Zhong Shao	Yale University, USA
Yannis Smaragdakis	University of Athens, Greece
Geoff Smith	Florida International University, USA
Eran Yahav	Technion, Israel

Additional Reviewers

Ahmed, Amal	Carbone, Marco
Andrade, Diego	Carbonell, Enric
Balabonski, Thibaut	Cerny, Pavol
Berdine, Josh	Chang, Bor-Yuh Evan
Botincan, Matko	Chin, Wei-Ngan
Boyland, John	Chitil, Olaf
Braud, Laurent	Costanzo, David
Cachera, David	Dal Lago, Ugo

Demange, Delphine
Denielou, Pierre-Malo
Dezani, Mariangiola
Dijkstra, Atze
Dimoulas, Christos
Dodds, Mike
Drachsler, Dana
Drossopoulou, Sophia
Dunfield, Joshua
Effinger-Dean, Laura
Escardó, Martín
Felleien, Matthias
Felleisen, Matthias
Feng, Xinyu
Ferrara, Pietro
Ferrer Fioriti, Luis MarÃa
Filiot, Emmanuel
Filliatre, Jean-Christophe
Fu, Ming
Galmiche, Didier
Garg, Deepak
Gawlitza, Thomas Martin
Genaim, Samir
Gesbert, Nils
Giachino, Elena
Gibbons, Jeremy
Giunti, Marco
Given-Wilson, Thomas
Gorbovitski, Michael
Goriac, Eugen-Ioan
Gorla, Daniele
Gotsman, Alexey
Gray, Kathryn
Gueta, Guy
Habermehl, Peter
Hartmanns, Arnd
Hoffmann, Jan
Howe, Jacob
Hur, Chung-Kil
Igarashi, Atsushi
Jacobs, Bart
Janssens and Verdoolaege,
    Gerda and Sven
Jobin, Arnaud
Jérôme, Feret

Kennedy, Andrew
Kolanski, Rafal
Koutavas, Vasileios
Krishnaswami, Neelakantan
Krivine, Jean
Lanese, Ivan
Levy, Paul Blain
Liang, Hongjin
Lin, Bo
Lindley, Sam
Lins, Rafael
Lippmeier, Ben
Liu, Yang
Lluch Lafuente, Alberto
Loreti, Michele
Lux, Wolfgang
Maffeis, Sergio
Mandel, Louis
Maneth, Sebastian
Marmar, Michael
Martignon, Fabio
Mauborgne, Laurent
Mazza, Damiano
Merro, Massimo
Meshman, Yuri
Meyer, Roland
Miculan, Marino
Neis, Georg
Niehren, Joachim
Noble, James
Okasaki, Chris
Padovani, Luca
Park, Sungwoo
Partush, Nimrod
Petri, Gustavo
Philippou, Anna
Pitts, Andrew
Potop Butucaru, Dumitru
Pottier, François
Pérez, Jorge A.
Qiu, Xiaokang
Rajan, Kaushik
Ramalingam, Ganesan
Rayside, Derek
Remy, Didier

Rinetzky, Noam
Rosu, Grigore
Rothamel, Tom
Sacerdoti Coen, Claudio
Sack, Joshua
Schmitt, Alan
Seidl, Helmut
Sergey, Ilya
Sewell, Thomas
Shan, Chung-Chieh
Shoham, Sharon
Simmons, Robert
Slepak, Justin
Smith, Gareth
Song, Lei
Sotin, Pascal

Spieler, David
Spiwack, Arnaud
Stampoulis, Antonis
Staton, Sam
Strichman, Ofer
Strub, Pierre-Yves
Struth, Georg
Suenaga, Kohei
Svendsen, Kasper
Talpin, Jean-Pierre
Thiemann, Peter

Tiezzi, Francesco
Tiu, Alwen
Tobin-Hochstadt, Sam
Toninho, Bernardo
Toronto, Neil
Toubhans, Antoine
Tov, Jesse
Tozawa, Akihiko
Turon, Aaron
Turrini, Andrea
Tzevelekos, Nikos
Ulidowski, Irek
Uustalu, Tarmo
Vafeiadis, Viktor
Van Cutsem, Tom
Vaswani, Kapil
Versari, Cristian
Voigt, Janina
Vytiniotis, Dimitrios
Wachter, Björn
Wadler, Philip
Weirich, Stephanie
Weng, Shu-Chun
Worrell, James
Zavattaro, Gianluigi
Zeilberger, Noam
Zhang, Lijun

Table of Contents

Session IV: Gradual Typing

Session V: Shared-Memory Concurrency and Verification

Session VI: Process Calculi

Session VII: Taming Concurrency

Session VIII: Model Checking and Verification

Session IX: Weak-Memory Concurrency and Verification

Session X: Types, Inference, and Analysis

Distributed Electronic Rights in JavaScript

Mark S. Miller[1], Tom Van Cutsem[2], and Bill Tulloh

[1] Google, Inc.
[2] Vrije Universiteit Brussel

Abstract. Contracts enable mutually suspicious parties to cooperate safely through the exchange of rights. Smart contracts are programs whose behavior enforces the terms of the contract. This paper shows how such contracts can be specified elegantly and executed safely, given an appropriate distributed, secure, persistent, and ubiquitous computational fabric. JavaScript provides the ubiquity but must be significantly extended to deal with the other aspects. The first part of this paper is a progress report on our efforts to turn JavaScript into this fabric. To demonstrate the suitability of this design, we describe an escrow exchange contract implemented in 42 lines of JavaScript code.

Keywords: security, distributed objects, object-capabilities, smart contracts.

1 Smart Contracts for the Rest of Us

The fabric of the global economy is held together by contracts. A contract is an agreed framework for the rearrangement of rights between mutually suspicious parties. But existing contracts are ambiguous, jurisdictions-specific, and written, interpreted, and adjudicated only by expensive experts. *Smart contracts* are contract-like arrangements expressed in program code, where the behavior of the program enforces the terms of the "contract"[1]. Though not a substitute for legal contracts, they can provide some of the benefits of contracts for fine-grain, jurisdiction-free, and automated arrangements for which legal contracts are impractical.

To realize this potential, smart contracts need a distributed, secure, persistent, and ubiquitous computational fabric. To avoid merely substituting one set of expensive experts for another, non-experts should be able to write smart contracts understandable by other non-experts. We[1] are working towards turning JavaScript into such a fabric. JavaScript is already understood and used by many non-expert programmers. We call our target JavaScript platform *Dr. SES* for *Distributed Resilient Secure EcmaScript.*[2]

Dr. SES is not specifically tied to electronic rights (erights) or smart contracts per se. Its focus is to make distributed secure programming in JavaScript as effortless as possible. But much of the design of Dr. SES and its predecessors [2,3,4] was shaped by examining what we need to express smart contracts simply. Taking a rights-based approach to local and distributed computing, we believe, has led us to building a better general purpose platform as well as one naturally suited for expressing new kinds of erights and contracts.

---

[1] Including many collaborators over many years. See the acknowledgements.
[2] The official standards name for JavaScript is "ECMAScript".

M. Felleisen and P. Gardner (Eds.): ESOP 2013, LNCS 7792, pp. 1–20, 2013.
© Springer-Verlag Berlin Heidelberg 2013

The first half of this paper, section 2, explains the design of Dr. SES and our progress building it. After section 2.2, the rest can be skipped on a first read. Section 3 explains how rights help organize complexity in society in a decentralized manner, addressing many of the problems we face building distributed systems. Section 4 examines an implementation of "money". Section 5 examines an escrow exchange contract. Section 6 examines a generic contract host, able to host this contract and others. Together, they demonstrate the simplicity and expressiveness of Dr. SES.

2 Dr. SES: Distributed Resilient Secure EcmaScript

Dr. SES is a platform for distributed, resilient, and secure computing, layered on JavaScript. How do these ingredients support erights and contracts?

The participants in a contract are typically represented by mutually suspicious machines communicating over open networks. JavaScript is not a distributed programming language. In the browser, a large number of APIs are available to scripts to communicate with servers and other frames, but these APIs do not operate at the level of individual objects. Dr. SES builds on the Q library[3] to extend the JavaScript language with a handful of features to support distributed programming at the level of objects and messages.

In an architecture that aims to express erights or contracts, security must play a key role. Dr. SES uses the Q library to support distributed cryptographic capabilities, and builds on the SES library to support local object-capabilities. The latter allows Dr. SES programs to safely execute mobile code from untrusted parties. This is especially relevant in the context of JavaScript, where mobile code is routinely sent from servers to clients. In Section 6, we will show an example that depends on the ability to safely execute third-party code on servers.

Finally, the resilience aspect of Dr. SES deals with the unavoidable issues of failure handling that come up in distributed systems. Server-side Dr. SES programs periodically checkpoint their state, so that in the event of a failure, the program can always recover from a previously consistent state. Such Dr. SES programs can survive failures without effort on the part of the programmer. Dr. SES builds on the *NodeKen* project, which is layering the Node.js server-side JavaScript platform onto the Ken system [6] for distributed orthogonal persistence—resilient against many failures.

2.1 Just Enough JavaScript

JavaScript is a complex language, but this paper depends only on a small subset with two core constructs, *functions* and *records*. As of this writing, the standard and ubiquitous version of JavaScript is ECMAScript 5 (ES5). For the sake of brevity, this paper borrows one syntactic convenience proposed for ES6, *arrow functions* ("=>"), and one proposed for ES7, the *eventual-send operator* ("!"). Expanding away these conveniences, all the code here is working ES5 code, and is available at `code.google.com/p/es-lab/source/browse/trunk/src/ses/#ses` and its `contract` subdirectory.

---

[3] Once the `es-lab.googlecode.com/svn/trunk/src/ses/makeQ.js`, [5], and `https://github.com/kriskowal/q` implementations of Q are reconciled.

Arrow functions. The following four lines all define a one parameter function which returns double its parameter. All bind a local variable named "twice" to this function. This paper uses only the arrow function syntax of the last three lines.

```
var twice = function(n) { return n+n; };      // old function expr
var twice = (n) => { return n+n; };           // ES6 arrow function
var twice = (n) => n+n;             // non-"{" expr implicitly returned
var twice = n => n+n;               // parens optional if one param
```

Records. The record syntax $\{x: 3, y: 4\}$ is an expression that evaluates to a record with two named properties initialized to the values shown. Records and functions compose together naturally to give objects:

```
var makePoint = (x, y) => {
  return {
    getX: () => x,
    getY: () => y,
    add: other => makePoint(x + other.getX(), y + other.getY())
  };
};

var pt = makePoint(3, 5).add(makePoint(2, 7));
```

A record of functions hiding variables serves as an object of methods (getX, getY, add) hiding instance variables (x, y). The makePoint function serves as a class-like factory for making new point instances.

2.2   Basic Concepts of Dr. SES

Dr. SES extends this object model across time and space (persistence and distribution), while relieving programmers of many of the typical worries associated with building secure distributed resilient systems. The non-expert programmer can begin with the following oversimplified understanding of Dr. SES:

SES. Don't worry about script injection. Mobile code can't do anything it isn't authorized to do. Functions and objects are encapsulated. Objects can invoke objects they have a reference to, but cannot tamper with those objects.

Q. Don't worry about memory races or deadlocks, they can't happen. Objects can be local or remote. The familiar infix dot (".") in pt.getX() accesses the pt object *immediately*. Q adds the bang "!" to access an object *eventually*. Anywhere you can write a dot, you can use "!" as in pt ! getX(). Eventual operations return promises for what the answer will be. If the object is remote or a promise, you can only use "!" on it.

NodeKen. Don't worry about network partitions or machine crashes. Once the machine comes back up, everything keeps going, so a crash and restart is just a very long (possibly infinite) pause. Likewise, a partitioned network is just a slow network waiting to heal. Once things come back up, every message ever sent will be delivered in order exactly once.

The above should be adequate to understand the functionality of the smart contract code when things go well. Of course, much of the point of erights and smart contracts is to limit the damage when things go badly. Understanding these risks does require a careful reading of the following sections.

2.3   SES: Securing JavaScript

In a memory-safe object language with unforgeable object references (protected pointers) and encapsulated objects, an object reference grants the right to invoke the public interface of the object it designates. A message sent on a reference both exercises this right and grants to the receiving object the right to invoke the passed arguments.

In an *object-capability* (ocap) language [7], an object can cause effects on the world outside itself *only* by using the references it holds. Some objects are transitively immutable or *powerless* [8], while others might cause effects. An object must not be given any powerful references by default; any references it has implicit access to, such as language-provided global variables, must be powerless. Under these rules, granted references are the *sole* representation of permission.

Secure EcmaScript (SES) is an ocap subset of ES5. SES is lexically scoped, its functions are encapsulated, and only the global variables on its whitelist (including all globals defined by ES5) are accessible. Those globals are unassignable, and all objects transitively reachable from them are immutable, rendering all implicit access powerless.

SES supports *defensive consistency* [7]. An object is *defensively consistent* when it can defend its own invariants and provide correct service to its well behaved clients, despite arbitrary or malicious misbehavior by its other clients. SES has a formal semantics supporting automated verification of some security properties of SES code [9]. The code in this paper uses the following functions from the SES library:

def(obj) *def*ines a *def*ensible object. To support defensive consistency, the def function makes the properties of its argument read-only, likewise for all objects transitively reachable from there by reading properties. As a result, this subgraph of objects is effectively tamper proof. A *tamper-proof* record of *encapsulated* functions hiding *lexical* variables is a *defensible object*. In SES, if makePoint called def on the points it returns by saying "return def({...})", it would make defensively consistent points.

confine(exprSrc, endowments) enables safe mobile code. The confine function takes the source code string for a SES expression and an endowments record. It evaluates the expression in a new global environment consisting of the SES whitelisted (powerless) global variables and the properties of this endowments record. For example, confine('x + y', {x: 3, y: 6}) returns 9.

Nat(allegedNumber) tests whether allegedNumber is indeed a primitive number, and whether it is a non-negative integer (a natural number) within the contiguous range of exactly representable integers in JavaScript. If so, it returns allegedNumber. Otherwise it throws an error.

var m = WeakMap() assigns to m a new empty weak map. WeakMaps are an ES6 extension (emulated by SES on ES5 browsers) supporting *rights amplification* [10]. Ignoring space usage, m is simply an object-identity-keyed table.

`m.set(obj,val)` associates `obj`'s identity as key with `val` as value, so `m.get(obj)` returns `val` and `m.delete(obj)` removes this entry. These methods use only `obj`'s identity without interacting with `obj`.

2.4 Q: Distributed JavaScript Objects

To realize erights, we need a distributed, secure, and persistent computational fabric. We have just seen how SES can secure a local JavaScript environment. Here, we focus on how to link up multiple secured JavaScript environments into a distributed system.

Communicating Event-Loop Concurrency. JavaScript's de-facto concurrency model, on both the browser and the server, is "shared nothing" *communicating event loops*. In the browser, every frame of a web page has its own event loop, which is used both for updating the UI (i.e. rendering HTML) and for executing scripts. Node.js, the most widespread server-side JavaScript environment, is based on a similar model, although on the server the issue is asynchronous networking and file I/O rather than UI.

In its most general form, an event loop consists of an event queue and a set of event handlers. The event loop processes events one by one from its queue by dispatching to the appropriate event handler. In JavaScript, event handlers are usually functions registered as callbacks on certain events (e.g. button clicks or incoming XHR responses).

The processing of a single event is called a *turn* of the event loop. Processing an event usually entails calling a callback function, which then runs to completion without interruption. Thus, turns are the smallest unit of interleaving.

A system of communicating event loops consists of multiple event loops (in the same or distributed address spaces) that communicate with each other solely by means of asynchronous message passing. The Web Workers API enables such communication among multiple isolated event loops within the same browser. A JavaScript webpage communicating with a Node.js server using asynchronous XHR requests is an example of two distributed communicating event loops.

Communicating event loop concurrency makes it manageable for objects to maintain their invariants in the face of concurrent (interleaved) requests made by multiple clients [11]. While JavaScript environments already support event loop concurrency, the JavaScript language itself has no support for concurrent or distributed programming. Q thus extends JavaScript with a handful of features that enable programmers to more directly express distributed interactions between individual objects.

Promises. We introduce a new type of object, a promise, to represent both the outcome of asynchronous operations as well as remote references [12]. A normal JavaScript direct reference may only designate an object within the same event loop. Only promises designate objects in other event loops. A promise may be in one of several states:

Pending. When it is not yet determined what object the promise designates,
Resolved. When it is either fulfilled or rejected,

> **Fulfilled.** When it is resolved to successfully designate some object,
> **Rejected.** When it will never designate an object, for an alleged reason represented by an associated error.

var tP = Q(target) assigns to tP a promise for target. If target is already a promise, that same promise is assigned. Otherwise, tP is a fulfilled promise designating target.

Q.promise((resolve,reject) => (...)) returns a fresh promise which is initially pending. It immediately calls the argument function with two functions, conventionally named resolve and reject, that can be used to either resolve or reject this new promise explicitly.

var resultP = tP.then((v) => result1, (e) => result2) provides eventual access to tP's resolution. The .then method takes two callback arguments, a success callback and an optional failure callback. It registers these callbacks to be called back in a later turn after tP is resolved. If tP was fulfilled with a value v, then success(v) is called. If tP was rejected with an error e, then failure(e) is called. resultP is a promise for the invoked callback's result value.

If the callback invoked by .then throws an error, that error is used to reject resultP. This propagation of errors along chains of dependent promises is called rejected promise contagion [11], and it is the asynchronous analogue of propagating exceptions up the call stack. If the failure callback is missing, rejecting tP will eventually reject resultP with the same reason. If pointP is a promise for a local point object, we may construct a derived point promise as follows:

var newP = pointP.then((point) => point.add(makePoint(1,2)));

Just like it is useful to compose individual functions into a composite function, it is often useful to compose individual promises into a single promise whose outcome depends on the individual promises. The Q library provides some useful combinator[4] functions we use later in the escrow exchange contract:

Q.race(answerPs) takes an array of promises, answerPs, and returns a promise for the resolution of whichever promise we notice has resolved first. For example, Q.race([xP,yP]).then(v => print(v)) will cause either the value of xP or yP to be printed, whichever resolves first. If neither resolves, then neither does the promise returned by Q.race. If the first promise to resolve is rejected, the promise returned by Q.race is rejected with the same reason.

Q.all(answerPs) takes an array of promises and returns a promise for an array of their fulfilled values. We often need to collect several promised answers, in order to react either when *all* the answers are ready or when *any* of them become rejected. Given var sumP = Q.all([xP,yP]).then(([x,y]) => x+y), if both xP and yP are fulfilled with numbers, sumP is fulfilled with their sum. If neither resolves, neither does sumP. If either xP or yP is rejected, sumP is rejected with the same reason.

Q.join(xP,yP) takes two promises and returns a promise for the one object they both designate. Q.join is our eventual equality operation. Any messages sent to the joined promise are only delivered if xP and yP eventually come to designate

---

[4] These are easily built from the above primitives. Their implementation can be found at wiki.ecmascript.org/doku.php?id=strawman:concurrency.

the same target. In this case, all messages are eventually delivered to that target and the joined promise itself eventually becomes fulfilled to designate that target. Otherwise, all these messages are discarded with the usual rejected promise contagion.

Immediate call and eventual send. Promises may designate both local objects, and remote objects belonging to another event loop. If the promise comes to designate a local object (or a primitive value), that value can be accessed via the .then method.

However, if the promise comes to designate a remote object, it is not possible to resolve the promise to a local reference. Instead, one must interact with the remote object via the promise. Any such interaction must be asynchronous, to ensure that interaction between the event loops as a whole remains asynchronous.

JavaScript provides many operators to interact with an object. Here, we will focus on only three: method calls, function calls, and reading the value of a property. JavaScript has the familiar dot operator to express local, immediate method calls, such as point.getX(). We introduce a corresponding infix "!" operator (named the *eventually*) operator, which designates asynchronous, possibly remote interactions.

The ! operator can be used anywhere the dot operator can be used. If pointP is a promise for a point, then pointP ! getX() denotes an eventual send, which enqueues a request to call the getX() method in the event loop of point. The syntax fP ! (x,y), where fP is a promise designating a function f, enqueues a request to call f(x,y) in the event loop of f. The ! operator is actually syntactic sugar for calling a method on the promise object itself:

Immediate syntax	Eventual syntax	Expansion
p.m(x,y)	p ! m(x,y)	Q(p).send("m",x,y)
p(x,y)	p ! (x,y)	Q(p).fcall(x,y)
p.m	p ! m	Q(p).get("m")

Remote object references. A local reference to an object is guaranteed to be unique and unforgeable, and only grants access to the public interface of the designated object. When a promise comes to designate a remote object, the promise effectively becomes a remote object reference. A remote reference only carries eventual message sends, not immediate method calls. Whereas local references are unforgeable, for remote references over open networks, we use unguessability to approximate unforgeability.

Primitive values such as strings and numbers are *pass-by-copy*—when passed as arguments or returned as results in remote messages, their contents are serialized and unserialized. JavaScript arrays default to pass-by-copy. All other objects and functions default to *pass-by-reference*—when passed as an argument or returned result, information needed to access them is serialized, which is unserialized into a remote reference for sending messages back to this object itself.

Over the RESTful transport [5], we serialize pass-by-reference objects using unguessable HTTPS URLs (also called web-keys [13]). Such a reference may look like https://www.example.com/app/#mhbqcmmva5ja3, where the fragment (everything after the #) is a random character string that uniquely identifies an object on the example.com server. We use unguessable secrets for remote object references because of a key similarity between secrets and object references: If you do not know an unguessable secret, you can only come to know it if somebody else who knows the secret chooses to share it with you.

`Q.passByCopy(record)` will override the pass-by-reference default, marking `record` as pass-by-copy. The record will then be shallow-copied to the destination, making a record with the same property names. The values of these properties get serialized according to these same argument passing rules.

2.5   NodeKen: Distributed Orthogonal Persistence

Rights, to be useful, must persist over time. Since object-references are our representation of rights, object references and the objects they designate must persist as well. We have already covered the distributed and secure aspects of Dr. SES. Here, we cover resilience against failures.

To introduce resilience, Dr. SES builds upon the Ken platform [6]. Ken applications are distributed communicating event loops, which aligns well with JavaScript's de-facto execution model. The event loop of a Ken process invokes application-level code to process incoming messages (one turn, i.e., one event loop iteration, per message). In addition, Ken provides:

Distributed Consistent Snapshots. Ken provides a persistent heap for storing application data. All objects stored in this heap are persistent. Ken ensures that the snapshots of two or more communicating processes cannot grow inconsistent, by recording messages in flight as part of a process' snapshot.

Reliable Messaging. Under the assumption that all Ken processes eventually recover, all messages transmitted between Ken processes are delivered exactly once, in FIFO order. A permanently crashed Ken process is indistinguishable from a very slow process. To deal with such situations, applications may still want to do their own failure handling using time-outs.

A set of Ken processes can tolerate arbitrary failures in such a way that when a process is restarted after a crash, it is always restored to a previously consistent state. To the crashed process itself, it is as if the crash had never happened. To any of the process's communication partners, the process just seemed slow to respond. A crash will never cause messages to be dropped or delivered twice.

To achieve orthogonal persistence of JavaScript programs, the Ken platform must be integrated with the JavaScript runtime. NodeKen is our attempt at layering the Node.js runtime on top of Ken.[5] NodeKen can then be used as a stand-alone JavaScript environment to run persistent server-side Dr. SES programs. It is not our aim to embed Ken into the browser. This leads to two types of Dr. SES environments: Dr. SES in the browser runs in an ephemeral environment that ceases to exist when the user navigates to a different page, or closes the page. Objects and object references in such environments are not persistent.

---

[5] At the time of writing, NodeKen does not yet exist. We are actively working on integrating Ken with the v8 JavaScript virtual machine, upon which Node.js is based. See `https://github.com/supergillis/v8-ken`.

By contrast, Dr. SES on NodeKen runs in a persistent environment. JavaScript objects born in such an environment are persistent by default, as are object references spanning two persistent Dr. SES environments. Eventual message sends made using the "!" operator over persistent references are reliable.

Following the philosophy of Waterken [4], the persistent Java web server where the Ken ideas originated, we expect it to be common for ephemeral and persistent Dr. SES environments to communicate with each other, The ephemeral environment (inside the browser) primarily deals with UI and the persistent environment stores durable application state, a distributed form of the Model-View-Controller pattern. In the remainder of this paper, we assume that all Dr. SES code runs in persistent Dr. SES environments.

Implementation. Ken achieves distributed consistent snapshots as follows:

- During a turn, accumulate all outgoing messages in an outgoing message queue. These messages are not yet released to the network.
- At the end of each turn, make an (incremental) checkpoint of the persistent heap and of all outgoing messages.
- After the end-of-turn checkpoint is made, release any new outgoing messages to the network and acknowledge the incoming message processed by this turn.
- Number outgoing messages with a sequence number (for duplicate detection and message ordering).
- Periodically retry sending unacknowledged outgoing messages (with exponential back-off) until an acknowledgement is received.
- Check incoming messages for duplicates. When a duplicate message is detected, it is dropped (not processed) and immediately acknowledged.

The key point is that outgoing messages are released, and incoming messages are acknowledged, only *after* the message has been fully processed by the receiver *and* the heap state has been checkpointed. The snapshot of a Ken process consists of both the heap and the outgoing message queue. It does not include the runtime stack (which is always empty between turns) nor the incoming message queue.

Checkpointing a program's entire state after every event loop turn may be considered costly. Ken takes care to only store those parts of the heap to disk that are updated during a turn. Further, the availability of cheap low-latency non-volatile memory (such as solid-state drives) has driven down the cost of writing state to "disk" to the point that making micro-snapshots after every turn becomes practical.

Ken and security. The Ken protocol guarantees distributed snapshots even among mutually suspicious machines. An adversarial process cannot corrupt the distributed snapshots of benign processes.

The implementation of Ken underlying NodeKen currently does not use an encrypted communications channel to deliver messages between Ken processes. Hence, the authenticity, integrity or confidentiality of incoming messages cannot be guaranteed. In NodeKen, our plan is to actively secure the communications channels between NodeKen processes using a cryptographic library.[6]

---

[6] An outline of such a design, due to Brian Warner, is available online:
   eros-os.org/pipermail/cap-talk/2012-September/015386.html

Now that we've seen the elements of Dr. SES, we can proceed to explain how to use it to build erights and smart contracts.

3   Toward Distributed Electronic Rights

The elements of Dr. SES demonstrate how JavaScript can be transformed into a distributed, secure, and resilient system. At its core is the recognition that object references represent a right to perform a set of operations on a specific, designated resource. This emphasis on distributed rights has its counterpart in society: a system of rights is society's answer to creating distributed, secure, and resilient commercial systems.

Global commerce rests on tradeable rights. This system is: *"the product of thousands of years of evolution. It is highly complex and embraces a multitude of actions, objects, and individuals. ... With minor exceptions, rights to take almost all conceivable actions with virtually all physical objects are fixed on identifiable individuals or firms at every instant of time. The books are kept up to date despite the burden imposed by dynamic forces, such as births and deaths, dissolutions, and new technology."* [14]

Rights help people coordinate plans and resolve conflicts over use of resources. Rights partition the space of actions to avoid interference between separately formulated plans, thus enabling cooperative relationships despite mutual suspicion and competing goals [15]. This rights-based perspective can shed light on the problem of securing distributed computational systems.

All computational systems must address the problem of open access. Global mutable state creates a tragedy of the commons: since anyone can access and change it, no one can safely rely on it. Use conflicts arise from both intentional (malicious) and unintentional (buggy) actions. Preventing use conflicts over shared state is one of the main challenges designers face in building computational systems.

Historically, two broad strategies for avoiding the tragedy of the commons have emerged: a governance strategy and a property rights strategy [16]. The governance approach solves the open access problem by restricting access to members and regulating each member's use of the shared resource. The property rights approach divides ownership of the resource among the individuals and creates abstract rules that govern the exchange of rights between owners. These approaches have their analogues in computational systems: ocap systems pursue a property rights strategy, while access control lists implement a governance strategy.

Access control lists solve the open access problem by denying unauthorized users access, and specifying access rights for authorized users. Great effort is put into perimeter security (firewalls, antivirus, intrusion detection, and the like) to keep unauthorized users out, while detailed access control lists regulate use by authorized users.

Governance regimes have proved successful in managing shared resources in many situations [17]. However, they tend to break down under increasing complexity. As the number of users and types of use increases, the ability of governance systems to limit external access and manage internal use breaks down. Perimeter security can no longer cope with the pressure for increased access, and access control lists cannot keep up with dynamic requests for changes in access rights.

The property rights strategy deals with increasing complexity by implementing a decentralized system of individual rights. Rights are used to partition the commons into separate domains under the control of specific agents who can decide its use, as long as the use is consistent with the rights of others. Instead of excluding non-members at the perimeter, the property strategy brings all agents under a common set of abstract rules that determine how rights are initially acquired, transferred, and protected [18]. Individual rights define the boundaries within which agents can act free of interference from others. Contracts enable the exchange of rights across these protected domains.

The ocap approach can be seen as analogous to an individual rights approach to coordinating action in society. The local unforgeable object reference and the remote unguessable reference represent one kind of eright—the right to invoke the public interface of the object it designates. In ocap systems, references bundle authority with designation [19]. Like property rights, they are possessory rights: possession of the reference is all that is required for its use, its use is at the discretion of the possessing entity, and the entity holding the reference is free to transfer it to others [20].

The private law system of property, contract, and tort brings resources into a system of rights. Property law determines the initial acquisition of rights; contract law governs the transfer of rights; and tort law protects rights from interference [21]. Ocap systems follow a similar logic: the rules of object creation make it easy to create objects with only the rights they need, the message passing rules govern the transfer of rights, and encapsulation protects rights from interference [7].

While object references represent a kind of eright, they differ in several respects from more familiar rights in society. For example, object references are typically shared. When Alice gives Bob a reference to an object, she is transferring a copy of the reference thereby sharing access to the object. In society, transfers of rights usually take the form of a transfer of exclusive access due to the rivalrous nature of physical objects. I give up my access to my car when I transfer title to you. Exclusive rights is the default in the physical world; complex legal frameworks are needed to enable sharing (partnerships, corporations, easements, and so forth). Computational systems face the opposite tradeoff: sharing is easy, but exclusivity is hard.

In the next sections, we will show how, by building on object references as erights, we can create new kinds of erights at a new level of abstraction. We look first at how money can be implemented as a smart contract. Money differs from other forms of property in several ways [22]. Here, we identify four dimensions in which money differs from object references as rights. Object references are shareable, specific, opaque, and exercisable, whereas money is exclusive, fungible, measurable, and symbolic.

By contrast with object references that are shareable, money needs to be exclusive to serve as medium of exchange. Bob does not consider himself paid by Alice until he knows that he has exclusive access to the funds. Object references are also specific; they designate a particular object. Money, on the other hand, is fungible. You care about having a certain quantity of a particular currency, not having a specific piece of currency. One dollar is as good as another.

Objects are opaque. The clients of an object can invoke it but don't necessarily know how it will react—that information is private to the object. By contrast, money is measurable. Bob must be able to determine that he really has a certain quantity of a particular currency. Finally, money, unlike object references, is never exercisable. The right you have when you have an object reference is the right to do something: the right to invoke the behavior of the object it designates. Money, however, has no direct use value; its value is symbolic. It has value only in exchange.

Contracts manipulate rights. The participants in a contract each bring to it those rights the contract will manipulate [23]. The logic of the contract together with the decisions of the participants determines which derived rights they each walk away with. The simplest example is a direct trade. Since half the rights exchanged in most trades are money, we start with money.

4   Money as an Electronic Right

Figure 1 is our implementation of a money-like rights issuer, using only elements of Dr. SES explained above. To explain how it works, it is best to start with how it is used. Say Alice wishes to buy something from Bob for $10. The three parties involved would be Alice, Bob, and a $ issuer, which we will informally call a bank. The starting assumptions are that Alice and Bob do not trust each other, the bank does not trust either Alice or Bob, and Alice and Bob trust the bank with their money but with nothing else. In this scenario, Alice is willing to risk her $10 on the possibility of Bob's non-delivery. But Bob wants to be sure he's been paid before he releases the good in exchange.

What do these relationships mean in terms of a configuration of persistent objects? Say Alice owns (or is) a set of objects on machine A, Bob on machine B, and the bank on machine C. In order for Alice to make a buy request of Bob, we assume one of Alice's objects already has a remote reference to one of Bob's objects. Alice's trust of the bank with her money is represented by a remote reference to an object within the bank representing Alice's account at the bank. We refer to such objects as *purses*. The one for Alice's account is Alice's *main purse*. And likewise for Bob. Where do these initial account purses come from?

For each currency the bank wishes to manage, the bank calls makeMint() once to get a mint function for making purses holding units of that currency. When Alice opens an account with, say $100 in cash, the bank calls mint(100) on its $ mint, to make Alice's main purse. The bank then gives Alice a persistent remote reference to this purse object within the bank.

For Alice to pay Bob, she sets up a *payment purse*, deposits $10 into it from her main purse, and sends it to Bob in a buy request, together with a description of what she wishes to buy.

```
var paymentP = myPurse ! makePurse();
var ackP = paymentP ! deposit(10, myPurse);
var goodP = ackP.then(_ => bobP ! buy(desc, paymentP));
```

On the diagram in Figure 1, each makeMint call creates a layer with its own (mint, m) pair representing a distinct currency. Each mint call creates a nested layer with its

```
1  var makeMint = () => {
2    var m = WeakMap();
3    var makePurse = () => mint(0);

4    var mint = balance => {
5      var purse = def({
6        getBalance: () => balance,
7        makePurse: makePurse,
8        deposit: (amount, srcP) =>
9          Q(srcP).then(src => {
10           Nat(balance + amount);
11           m.get(src)(Nat(amount));
12           balance += amount;
13         })
14     });
15     var decr = amount => { balance = Nat(balance - amount); };
16     m.set(purse, decr);
17     return purse;
18   };
19   return mint;
20 };
```

Fig. 1. The Mint Maker

own (purse, decr, balance) triple. On line 16 of the code, each purse to decr mapping is also entered into the m table shared by all purses of the same currency. Alice's main purse is on the bottom purse layer. Bob's is on the top layer. Alice's payment purse, being sent to Bob in the buy message, is in the middle layer.

Bob receives this request at the following buy method:

```
buy: (desc, paymentP) => {
  // do whatever with desc, look up $10 price
  return (myPurse ! deposit(10, paymentP)).then(_ => good);
}
```

Bob's buy method handles a message from untrusted clients such as Alice, and thus it does not know what object Alice actually provided as the payment argument. At this point, the purse provided by Alice is *specific*—it is the specific object Alice designated, but to Bob it also is *opaque*. In particular, Bob has no idea if his paymentP parameter actually designates a purse, whether it is a purse at this bank, of this currency, and with adequate funds. Even if he knew all these conditions were true at the moment, due to the *shareable* nature of argument passing, Bob wouldn't know the funds would still be there by the time he deposits it. Alice may have retained a reference to it. He delegates all these problems to the bank with the deposit request above.

If the bank's deposit method acknowledges a successful deposit, by fulfilling the promise for the result of the deposit, then Bob knows he has obtained *exclusive* access to a *fungible* and *measurable* quantity of a given currency at a given bank. In this case, the success callback of the .then above gets called, returning the good, fulfilling Alice's pending goodP promise.

The interesting work starts on line 11, where deposit looks up the alleged payment purse in the m table. If this is anything other than a purse of the same currency at the same bank, this lookup will instead return undefined, causing the following function call to throw an error, rejecting Bob's promise for the result of the deposit, rejecting Alice's goodP. If this lookup succeeds, it finds the decr function for decrementing that purse's balance, which it calls with the amount to withdraw. If the payment has insufficient funds, balance - amount would be negative and Nat would throw.

We have now arrived at the commit point. All the tests that might cause failure have already passed, and no side effects have yet happened. Now we perform all side effects, all of which will happen since no locally observable failure possibilities remain. The assignment decrements the payment purse's balance by amount, and decr returns. Line 12 increments the balance of the purse being deposited into.

The success callback in the deposit method implicitly returns undefined, fulfilling Bob's promise for the result of the deposit request, triggering Bob to release the good to Alice in exchange.

5   The Escrow Exchange Contract

In the mint maker scenario, Alice must risk her $10 on the possibility of Bob's non-delivery. We now introduce an escrow exchange contract that implements an *all or nothing* trade. We explain the escrow exchange contract in terms of a scenario among five players: Alice, Bob, a money issuer (running the code of Figure 1), a stock issuer (also running the code of Figure 1 but with the units representing shares of some particular stock), and an escrow exchange agent (running the code of Figure 2). The diagram at the top of Figure 3 shows the initial relationships, with the escrow exchange agent in the role of contract host.

Alice and Bob again do not trust each other. They wish to trade $10 of Alice's money for 7 shares of Bob's stock, but in this case, neither is willing to risk their assets on the possibility of the other's non-delivery. They both trust the same money issuer with their money, the same stock issuer with their stock, and the same escrow exchange agent with the rights to be traded. The money issuer, the stock issuer, and the escrow exchange agent each have no prior knowledge or trust in the others. Additionally, none of these trust Alice or Bob. The rest of the scenario as presented below examines only the consequences of Alice or Bob's misbehavior and assumes the other three run the code shown honestly. A full analysis of vulnerabilities should consider all combinations.

Since the situation is now symmetric, we explain the progression of events from Alice's perspective. Alice's prior trust in each issuer is represented as before—Alice holds a persistent reference to her main purse at each issuer. Alice's prior trust in the escrow exchange agent is represented as the ability to provide the first "a" argument in the call to escrowExchange (Figure 2, line 12) for which Bob is able to provide the second "b" argument.

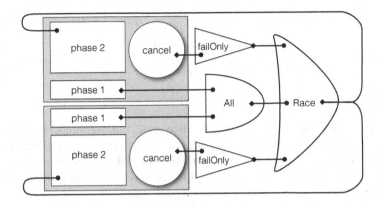

```
1  var transfer = (decisionP, srcPurseP, dstPurseP, amount) => {
2    var makeEscrowPurseP = Q.join(srcPurseP ! makePurse,
3                                   dstPurseP ! makePurse);
4    var escrowPurseP = makeEscrowPurseP ! ();

5    Q(decisionP).then(                                      // setup phase 2
6      _ => { dstPurseP ! deposit(amount, escrowPurseP); },
7      _ => { srcPurseP ! deposit(amount, escrowPurseP); });

8    return escrowPurseP ! deposit(amount, srcPurseP); // phase 1
9  };

10 var failOnly = cancellationP => Q(cancellationP).then(
11   cancellation => { throw cancellation; });

12 var escrowExchange = (a, b) => {              // a from Alice, b from Bob
13   var decide;
14   var decisionP = Q.promise(resolve => { decide = resolve; });

15   decide(Q.race([Q.all([
16     transfer(decisionP, a.moneySrcP, b.moneyDstP, b.moneyNeeded),
17     transfer(decisionP, b.stockSrcP, a.stockDstP, a.stockNeeded)
18   ]),
19   failOnly(a.cancellationP),
20   failOnly(b.cancellationP)]));
21   return decisionP;
22 };
```

Fig. 2. The Escrow Exchange Contract

Alice might create this argument as follows:

```
var cancel;
var a = Q.passByCopy({
  moneySrcP: myMoneyPurse ! makePurse(),
  stockDstP: myStockPurse ! makePurse(),
  stockNeeded: 7,
  cancellationP: Q.promise(r => { cancel = r; })
});
a.moneySrcP ! deposit(10, myMoneyPurse);
```

By a protocol whose details appear below, Alice sends this "a" object to the escrow exchange agent, for it to use as the first argument in a call to `escrowExchange`, which initiates this specific contract between Alice and Bob. The `escrowExchange` function returns a promise for the outcome of the contract, which the escrow exchange agent returns to Alice.

If this outcome promise becomes fulfilled, the exchange succeeded, she should expect her `a.moneySrcP` to be drained, and 7 shares of stock to be deposited into her `a.stockDstP` promptly.[7] If this promise becomes rejected, the exchange failed, and she should expect her $10 to reappear in her `a.moneySrcP` promptly. In the meantime, if she gets impatient and would rather not continue waiting, she can call her `cancel` function with her alleged reason for walking away. Once she does so, the exchange will then either succeed or fail promptly.

On lines 13 and 14 of Figure 2 the `escrowExchange` contract makes a `decisionP` promise whose fulfillment or rejection represents its decision about whether the exchange must succeed or fail. It makes this decision by calling `decide` with the outcome of a race between a `Q.all` and two calls to `failOnly`. Until a player cancels the exchange, the `Q.race` can only be won by the `Q.all`, where the exchange is proceeding.

The arguments to `Q.all` are the results of two calls to `transfer`. The first call to `transfer` sets up an arrangement of objects whose purpose is to transfer money from Alice to Bob. The second call's purpose is to transfer stock from Bob to Alice. Each call to transfer returns a promise whose fulfillment or rejection indicates whether it has become confident that this one-way transfer of erights would succeed. If both transfers become confident (before any cancellations win the race), then the overall decision is to proceed. If either transfer indicates failure, by rejecting the promise it has returned, then, via `Q.all`, `decisionP` becomes rejected.[8]

We do not feed the cancellation promises directly into the race, as Alice could then fulfill the cancellation promise, causing the race to signal a decision to proceed with the exchange, even though Alice's money has not been escrowed, potentially giving Bob's stock to Alice for free. Instead, once the cancellation promise has been either fulfilled

---

[7] By "promptly" we mean, once the relevant machines are up, processes running, and reachable to each other over the network.

[8] This pattern implements two phase commit enhanced with the possibility of cancellation, where the call to `escrowExchange` creates a transaction coordinator, and each of its calls to `transfer` creates a participant.

or rejected, the promise returned by `failOnly` will only become rejected. Only the `Q.all` can win the race with a success.

Since the two calls to `transfer` are symmetric, we examine only the first. The first phase of the transfer, on line 8 of Figure 2, attempts to deposit Alice's money into an escrow purse mentioned only within this transfer. If this deposit succeeds, Alice's money has been escrowed, so the money portion of the exchange is now assured. If this deposit fails, then the exchange as a whole should be cancelled. So `transfer` simply returns the promise for the outcome of this first deposit.

The `transfer` function sets up the second phase on lines 5, 6, and 7. If the overall decision is that the exchange should succeed, the success callback deposits Alice's escrowed money into Bob's account. Otherwise it refunds Alice's money.

Only one mystery remains. How does the escrow agent obtain a fresh escrow purse at this money issuer, in order to be confident that it has obtained exclusive access to the money at stake? Since the escrow exchange agent has no prior knowledge or trust in the money issuer, it cannot become confident that the issuer is honest or even that the money it issues means anything. The question is meaningless. Instead, it only needs to obtain a fresh escrow purse whose veracity is *mutually acceptable* to Alice and Bob.

If the escrow contract simply asks Alice's purse for a new empty purse (`srcPurseP ! makePurse()`), Alice could return a dishonest purse that acknowledges deposit without transferring anything. Alice would then obtain Bob's stock for free. If it simply asks Bob's purse, then Bob could steal Alice's money during phase 1. Instead, it checks if their `makePurse` methods have the same object identity by using `Q.join` on promises for these two methods. This is why, on lines 3 and 7 of Figure 1, all purses of the same currency at the same bank share the same function as their `makePurse` method. If the `Q.join` of these two methods fails, then either Alice was dishonest, Bob was dishonest, or they simply didn't have prior agreement on the same currency at the same money issuer.

6   The Contract Host

Once Alice and Bob agree on a contract, how do they arrange for it to be run in a mutually trusted manner?

To engage in the escrow exchange contract, Alice and Bob had to agree on the issuers, which is unsurprising since they need to agree on the nature of rights exchanged by the contract. And they had to agree on an escrow exchange agent to honestly run this specific escrow exchange contract. For a contract as reusable as this, perhaps that is not a problem. But if Alice and Bob negotiate a custom contract specialized to their needs, they should not expect to find a mutually trusted third party specializing in running this particular contract. Rather, it should be sufficient for them to agree on:

- The issuers of each of the rights at stake.
- The source code of the contract.
- Who is to play which side of the contract.
- A third party they mutually trust to run their agreed code, *whatever it is*, honestly.

```
 1  var makeContractHost = () => {
 2    var m = WeakMap();

 3    return def({
 4      setup: contractSrc => {
 5        contractSrc = ''+contractSrc
 6        var tokens = [];
 7        var argPs = [];
 8        var resolve;
 9        var resultP = Q.promise(r => { resolve = r; });
10        var contract = confine(contractSrc, {Q: Q});

11        var addParam = (i, token) => {
12          tokens[i] = token;
13          var resolveArg;
14          argPs[i] = Q.promise(r => { resolveArg = r; });
15          m.set(token, (allegedSrc, allegedI, arg) => {
16            if (contractSrc !== allegedSrc) {
17              throw new Error('unexpected contract: '+contractSrc);
18            }
19            if (i !== allegedI) {
20              throw new Error('unexpected side: '+i);
21            }
22            m.delete(token);
23            resolveArg(arg);
24            return resultP;
25          });
26        };
27        for (var i = 0; i < contract.length; i++) {
28          addParam(i, def({}));
29        }
30        resolve(Q.all(argPs).then(
31          args => contract.apply(undefined, args)));
32        return tokens;
33      },
34      play: (tokenP, allegedSrc, allegedI, arg) => Q(tokenP).then(
35        token => m.get(token)(allegedSrc, allegedI, arg))
36    });
37  };
```

Fig. 3. The Contract Host

Figure 3 shows the code for a generic contract host. It is able to host any contract formulated, as our escrow exchange contract is, as a function, taking one argument from each player and returning the outcome of the contract as a whole. Setting up a contract involves a necessary asymmetry among the players. One of the players, say Bob, must initiate a new live contract instance by sending the contract's code to the contract host. At this point, only Bob knows both this contract instance and that he'd like to invite Alice to participate in *this* instance. If Bob simply sent to Alice references to those objects on the contract host that enable Alice to play, Alice would not know what she's received, since she received it from Bob whom she does not trust. She does trust the contract host, and these objects are on the contract host, but so are the objects corresponding to other contracts this host is initiating or running. Only Bob can connect Alice to this contract instance, but Alice's confidence that she's playing the contract she thinks she is must be rooted in her prior trust in the contract host.

Our contract host is an object with two methods, `setup` and `play`. Bob sets up the contract instance by calling `setup` with the source code for the contract function in question, e.g., `escrowExchange`. At line 32, `setup` returns an array of unique unforgeable tokens, one for each contract parameter. Bob's invitation to Alice includes this token, the source for the contract he wishes Alice to play, the argument index indicating what side of the contract Alice is to play, and the contract host in question.

If Alice decides she'd like to play this contract, she formulates her argument object as above, and sends it in a `play` request to the contract host along with the token, the alleged contract source code, and the alleged side she is to play. If all of this checks out and this token has not previously been redeemed, then this token gets used up, Alice's argument is held until the arguments for the other players arrive, and Alice receives a promise for the outcome of the contract. Once all arguments arrive, the contract function is called and its result is used to resolve the previously returned promise.

By redeeming the token, Alice obtains the exclusive right to play a specific contract whose logic she knows, and whose play she expects to cause external effects. This eright is exclusive, specific, measurable, and exercisable.

7 Conclusions

In human society, rights are a scalable means for organizing the complex cooperative interactions of decentralized agents with diverse interests. This perspective is helping us shape JavaScript into a distributed resilient secure programming language. We show how this platform would enable the expression of new kinds of rights and smart contracts *simply*, supporting new forms of cooperation among computational agents.

Acknowledgements. Many people contributed to the progress reported here, including the e-lang community for refining ocap-based smart contracting, the Google Caja group for SES's growth and deployment, TC39 for making ES5 and successors friendly to ocaps, Tyler Close for the first Ken and Q, Terence Kelly for the new Ken, and Kris Kowal for the new Q.

Tom Van Cutsem is a post-doctoral fellow of the Research Foundation, Flanders. Thanks to Terry Stanley, Kevin Reid, and Terence Kelly for suggestions improving this paper.

References

1. Szabo, N.: Formalizing and securing relationships on public networks. First Monday 2(9) (1997)
2. Tribble, E.D., Miller, M.S., Hardy, N., Krieger, D.: Joule: Distributed Application Foundations. Technical Report ADd03.4P, Agorics Inc., Los Altos (December 1995), `erights.org/history/joule/`
3. Miller, M.S., Morningstar, C., Frantz, B.: Capability-Based Financial Instruments. In: Frankel, Y. (ed.) FC 2000. LNCS, vol. 1962, pp. 349–378. Springer, Heidelberg (2001), `www.erights.org/elib/capability/ode/index.html`
4. Close, T.: Waterken Server: capability-based security for the Web (2004), `waterken.sourceforge.net`
5. Close, T.: web_send, `waterken.sourceforge.net/web_send/`
6. Yoo, S., Killian, C., Kelly, T., Cho, H.K., Plite, S.: Composable reliability for asynchronous systems. In: Proceedings of the 2012 USENIX Conference on Annual Technical Conference, USENIX ATC 2012, p. 3. USENIX Association, Berkeley (2012)
7. Miller, M.S.: Robust Composition: Towards a Unified Approach to Access Control and Concurrency Control. PhD thesis, Johns Hopkins University, Baltimore, Maryland, USA (May 2006)
8. Mettler, A.: Language and Framework Support for Reviewably-Secure Software Systems. PhD thesis, EECS Department, University of California, Berkeley (December 2012)
9. Taly, A., Erlingsson, U., Mitchell, J.C., Miller, M.S., Nagra, J.: Automated analysis of security-critical javascript apis. In: 2011 IEEE Symposium on Security and Privacy (SP), pp. 363–378. IEEE (2011)
10. Jones, A.K.: Protection in Programmed Systems. PhD thesis, Department of Computer Science, Carnegie-Mellon University (June 1973)
11. Miller, M.S., Tribble, E.D., Shapiro, J.: Concurrency Among Strangers: Programming in E as Plan Coordination. In: De Nicola, R., Sangiorgi, D. (eds.) TGC 2005. LNCS, vol. 3705, pp. 195–229. Springer, Heidelberg (2005)
12. Liskov, B., Shrira, L.: Promises: Linguistic Support for Efficient Asynchronous Procedure Calls in Distributed Systems. In: PLDI 1988: Proc. ACM SIGPLAN 1988 Conference on Programming Language Design and Implementation, pp. 260–267. ACM Press, New York (1988)
13. Close, T.: Web-key: Mashing with permission. In: W2SP 2008 (2008)
14. Jensen, M.C., Meckling, W.H.: Specific and general knowledge and organizational structure. Journal of Applied Corporate Finance 8(2), 4–18 (1995)
15. Steiner, H.: An Essay on Rights. Wiley-Blackwell (1994)
16. Smith, H.E.: Exclusion versus governance: two strategies for delineating property rights. Journal of Legal Studies 31 (2002)
17. Ostrom, E.: Governing the Commons: The Evolution of Institutions for Collective Action. Cambridge University Press (1990)
18. Hayek, F.A.: Law, Legislation and Liberty. Rules and Order, vol. 1. University of Chicago Press (1973)
19. Hardy, N.: The Confused Deputy. Operating Systems Review (October 1988)
20. Mossoff, A.: What is property-putting the pieces back together. Arizona Law Review 45, 371 (2003)
21. Epstein, R.A.: Simple Rules for a Complex World. Harvard University Press (1995)
22. Fox, D.: Property rights in money. Oxford University Press (2008)
23. Barnett, R.E.: A consent theory of contract. Columbia Law Review 86, 269 (1986)

The Compiler Forest

Mihai Budiu[1], Joel Galenson[1,2], and Gordon D. Plotkin[1,3]

[1] Microsoft Research, Silicon Valley
[2] University of California, Berkeley
[3] University of Edinburgh

Abstract. We address the problem of writing compilers targeting *complex execution environments*, such as computer clusters composed of machines with multi-core CPUs. To that end we introduce *partial compilers*. These compilers can pass sub-programs to several child (partial) compilers, combining the code generated by their children to generate the final target code. We define a set of high-level polymorphic operations manipulating both compilers and partial compilers as first-class values. These mechanisms provide a software architecture for modular compiler construction. This allows the building of a forest of compilers, providing a structured treatment of multistage compilers.

1 Introduction

Today's computers are routinely composed of multiple computational units: multi-core processors, hyperthreaded processors, graphics processors, and multi-processors; we use the term "execution engine" for these computational resources. The work presented in this paper was motivated by the DryadLINQ compiler [27]. DryadLINQ translates programs written in the LINQ programming language (Language INtegrated Query) [17] into distributed computations that run on shared-nothing computer clusters, using multiple cores on each machine. The core DryadLINQ compilation is structured as a three-stage process: (1) translating a cluster-level computation into a set of interacting machine-level computations, (2) translating each machine-level computation into a set of CPU core-level computations, and (3) implementing each core-level computation.

Modifying a compiler stage requires deep understanding of both the compiler architecture and its implementation. We would prefer to be able to experiment easily, replacing some stages without knowing the implementation of others. Our goal is therefore to develop a general modular software architecture enabling compilers for distributed execution environments to be factored into a *hierarchy* of completely independent compilers, or "pieces" of compilers that cooperate via well-defined interfaces; the architecture should allow different pieces to be mixed and matched, with no access to source code or knowledge of internals.

To this end we propose a novel architecture employing a standard type-theoretical interface. In Section 2 we present *partial compilers*, a formalization of a "piece" of a compiler: partial compilers need "help" from one or more *child* compilers to produce a complete result. The resulting composite compilers form *compiler forests*. Formally, one uses *polymorphic composition operations* on compilers and partial compilers. The interface between component compilers is surprisingly simple and succinct. Traditional compiler stages can be recast as partial compilers.

M. Felleisen and P. Gardner (Eds.): ESOP 2013, LNCS 7792, pp. 21–40, 2013.

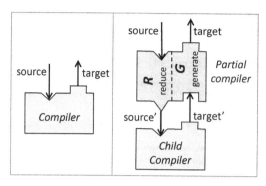

Fig. 1. L: A compiler translates sources to targets. **R:** A partial compiler invokes the service of a child compiler.

We present other natural polymorphic composition operations on compilers and partial compilers in Sections 2 and 3. Taken together, these operations can be seen as a form of "structured programming" manipulating compilers and partial compilers as first-class values. We thereby support dynamic compiler construction and extension, enabling sophisticated users to construct, customize, and extend compilers by mixing predefined and custom-built compiler components.

The theoretical foundations we establish have immediate practical applications. To demonstrate this, we revisit the original problem of compiling LINQ for computer clusters. In order to expose the fundamental ideas without undue detail, we use a stylized version of LINQ, called μLINQ. This language is rich enough to express many interesting computations, including the popular MapReduce [6] large-scale computation model. In Section 4 we build a fully functional compiler for μLINQ that executes programs on a computer cluster with multi-core machines.

Remarkably, partial compliers have their origins in work on categorical logic and on computer-assisted theorem proving, specifically de Paiva and Hyland's Dialectica categories [5,12] and Milner's tactics [10,19], the building blocks of his approach to computer-aided theorem proving. Section 5 treats the mathematical foundations of partial compilers in terms of a slight variant of the Dialectica category incorporating compile-time effects via a suitable monad. The morphisms of this category can be viewed as providing (the semantics of) a typed version of Milner's tactics. The polymorphic operations on partial compilers and compilers that we use to manipulate them as first-class objects were inspired by categorical considerations. For example, the composition and tensor operations of Section 2 correspond to compositions and tensors of morphisms.

We have also validated the partial compiler architecture with two proof-of-concept compiler implementations: a (simplified) reimplementation of DryadLINQ, and a compiler for large-scale matrix expressions. They are described briefly in Section 6. Finally, Sections 7 and 8 discuss related work and conclude.

2   Compilers and Partial Compilers

We call the program fed as input to a compiler a *"source"* (usually denoted by S), and the output generated by the compiler a *"target"* (usually denoted by T). The intuition behind partial compilers is shown on the right of Figure 1. There a partial compiler *reduces* the source program to a source' program, to be handled by a *child* compiler. Given a target' result obtained from the source' program by the child compiler, the partial compiler then *generates* the target for the original source program.

More generally, a partial compiler may use several child compilers. For example, given a source, a cluster-level partial compiler may generate a target to distribute input data among many machines, of various types, instructing each machine to perform a computation on its local data. In order to generate the target code running on each machine, the cluster-level compiler creates machine-level source programs source', which are handed to machine-level child compilers, one for each type of machine; these, in turn, generate the needed machine-level target's. The global, cluster-level target contains code to (1) move data between machines and (2) invoke machine-level target's of appropriate types on cluster machines and their local data.

2.1 Definitions

With these intuitions in mind, we can now give a theory of partial compilers. We take a call-by-value typed lambda calculus as our *compiler* language, and use it to define partial compilers and operations on them. We do not detail the calculus, but we make use of product and function types, labeled sum types (see [22]), list types, and base types. Our theory permits the lambda calculus to be effectful, i.e., we permit *compile-time effects*; it also permits recursion. However neither our examples nor our implementations make use of either of these two possibilities.

Formally, we take the calculus to be a suitable extension of Moggi's computational lambda calculus [20,21,1] to allow for compile-time effects. For its semantics we assume available a Cartesian closed category equipped with a strong *"compile-time"* monad T_{comp} and suitable extra structure to accommodate the sum types, etc. As our examples and implementations use neither compile-time effects nor recursion, the reader can assume there that the category is that of sets and functions, so that types denote sets and terms denote elements of them.

Compilers transform sources into targets so they are terms C typed as:

$$C : \text{source} \longrightarrow \text{target}$$

as pictured on the left of Figure 1. We do not specify the relationship between source and target; in particular, the target type of some compiler may be the source type of some other compiler.

Rather than making specific choices of target languages, we use a lambda calculus to define the semantics $[\![T]\!]$ of targets T output by compilers. We assume that the target computations output by compilers act on a type "data" so that this semantics has the form:

$$[\![T]\!] : \text{data} \to \text{data}$$

As in the case of the compiler language, we do not detail such a *run-time* lambda calculus, but, in particular, it may have *run-time effects*. In general, target languages may differ in both the data their targets handle and the run-time effects they create; however, for simplicity, we keep both fixed in the examples.

Formally, we (again) use the computational lambda calculus, but for the semantics we now use *"run-time"* monads T_{run} to account for run-time effects. As it suffices for the examples at hand, we work in the category of sets, but nothing depends on that.

We define (unary) partial compilers to be terms of type:

$$PC : \text{source} \to (\text{source}' \times (\text{target}' \to \text{target}))$$

As discussed above, the idea is that, given a source program, a partial compiler "reduces" it to a source$'$ program, to be handled by a child compiler, and also produces a "generation" function that, given a target$'$ obtained from the child, returns the required target. With this type, compile-time effects can occur at two points: when reducing the original source, and when computing the target.

To make formulas more readable we employ syntactic sugar for both types and terms. We write

$$(\text{source}, \text{target}) \multimap (\text{source}', \text{target}')$$

for the above partial compiler type, reading the type as "going from source to source$'$ and then back from target$'$ to target"; and we write

$$\begin{aligned}
&Compiler \ \ S: \text{source}. \\
&Reduction \ \ R, \\
&Generation \ \ T': \text{target}'. G
\end{aligned}$$

for the partial compiler

$$\lambda S: \text{source.\ let } S': \text{source}' \text{ be } R \text{ in } (S', \lambda T': \text{target}'. G)$$

Note that S is bound in both the reduction and generation clauses.

Figure 1 (right) shows a simple compiler tree, consisting of a parent partial compiler invoking the services of a child compiler. We model this by a polymorphic *composition* operation, which returns a compiler, given a (parent) partial compiler and a (child) compiler. Let PC be a partial compiler, as above, and $C : \text{source}' \to \text{target}'$ be a compiler. We write their composition using angle brackets:

$$PC\langle\!\langle C \rangle\!\rangle : \text{source} \to \text{target}$$

and define it to be:

$$\lambda S: \text{source.\ let } (S', G) \text{ be } PC(S) \text{ in } G(C(S'))$$

If there are no compile-time effects, we can view the operation of the compiler $PC\langle\!\langle C \rangle\!\rangle$ on a source S' as going through a sequence of compiler stages or passes:

$$S \xrightarrow{\ \text{fsto}PC\ } S' \xrightarrow{\ \ C\ \ } T' \xrightarrow{\ \text{snd}(PC(S))\ } T$$

where the last pass $\text{snd}(PC(S))$ is a function of the initial source. In contrast, the operation of the partial compiler PC is a "partial" sequence of passes:

$$S \xrightarrow{\ \text{fsto}PC\ } S' \xrightarrow{\ \ ?\ \ } T' \xrightarrow{\ \text{snd}(PC(S))\ } T$$

The core function of our methodology is to generate useful patterns of such passes in a structured way, including combining partial passes. We define the composition

$$PC\langle\!\langle PC' \rangle\!\rangle : (\text{source}, \text{target}) \multimap (\text{source}'', \text{target}'')$$

of a partial compiler PC with a partial compiler

$$PC' : (\text{source}', \text{target}') \multimap (\text{source}'', \text{target}'')$$

to be:

$$\lambda S: \text{source.\ let } (S', G) \text{ be } PC(S) \text{ in let } (S'', G') \text{ be } PC'(S') \text{ in } (S'', G \circ G')$$

In terms of a partial sequence of passes this is:

$$S \xrightarrow{\text{fsto}PC} S' \xrightarrow{\text{fsto}PC'} S'' \xrightarrow{?} T'' \xrightarrow{\text{snd}(PC'(S'))} T' \xrightarrow{\text{snd}(PC(S))} T$$

Certain *equations* hold in the computational lambda calculus, for all compiler-time effects. Partial compiler composition is *associative*:

$$PC\langle\!\langle PC'\langle\!\langle PC''\rangle\!\rangle\rangle\!\rangle = PC\langle\!\langle PC'\rangle\!\rangle\langle\!\langle PC''\rangle\!\rangle$$

and the two compositions are compatible, as shown by the *action* equation:

$$PC\langle\!\langle PC'\langle\!\langle C\rangle\!\rangle\rangle\!\rangle = PC\langle\!\langle PC'\rangle\!\rangle\langle\!\langle C\rangle\!\rangle$$

The partial compiler Id $=_{\text{def}} (\lambda S.S, \lambda(S,T).T)$ passes a given source to its child and then passes back the target generated by its child unchanged. It is the identity element for composition, i.e., the following *identity* equations hold:

$$\text{Id}\langle\!\langle PC\rangle\!\rangle = PC = PC\langle\!\langle \text{Id}\rangle\!\rangle \qquad \text{Id}\langle\!\langle C\rangle\!\rangle = C$$

Unary partial compilers can be generalized to n-ary terms PC^n of type

$$\text{source} \longrightarrow ((\text{source}'_1 \times \ldots \times \text{source}'_n) \times (\text{target}'_1 \times \ldots \times \text{target}'_n) \rightarrow \text{target})$$

One can reduce such n-ary partial compilers to unary partial compilers by taking source$'$ to be source$'_1 \times \ldots \times$ source$'_n$ and target$'$ to be target$'_1 \times \ldots \times$ target$'_n$. Compilers can be thought of as 0-ary partial compilers. The ability to write n-ary partial compilers that can communicate with several children, which may be addressing different execution engines, is crucial to our approach.

To define composition on n-ary partial compilers we iterate two pairing operations, which are both called *tensor*, on compilers and partial compilers. For the first, given compilers $C_i : \text{source}_i \rightarrow \text{target}_i$ (for $i = 1, 2$), we define their tensor

$$C_1 \otimes C_2 : (\text{source}_1 \times \text{source}_2) \rightarrow (\text{target}_1 \times \text{target}_2)$$

to be:

$$C_1 \otimes C_2 = \lambda(S_1, S_2). (C_1(S_1), C_2(S_2))$$

Given an n-ary partial compiler PC^n and n compilers $C_i : \text{source}'_i \rightarrow \text{target}'_i$ (for $i = 1, \ldots, n$) the n-ary composition $PC^n\langle\!\langle C_1, \ldots, C_n\rangle\!\rangle$ is an abbreviation for the unary composition $PC^n\langle\!\langle C_1 \otimes \ldots \otimes C_n\rangle\!\rangle$. The n-fold tensor is the iterated binary one, associated to the left; it is the trivial compiler for $n = 0$.

Next, we define the binary tensor

$$PC_1 \otimes PC_2 : (\text{source}_1 \times \text{source}_2, \text{target}_1 \times \text{target}_2) \multimap$$
$$(\text{source}'_1 \times \text{source}'_2, \text{target}'_1 \times \text{target}'_2)$$

of two partial compilers

$$PC_i : (\text{source}_i, \text{target}_i) \multimap (\text{source}'_i, \text{target}'_i)$$

to be:

$$\lambda S_1, S_2. \ \text{let } (S'_1, G_1) \text{ be } PC_1(S_1) \text{ in}$$
$$\text{let } (S'_2, G_2) \text{ be } PC_2(S_2) \text{ in}$$
$$((S'_1, S'_2), \lambda T_1, T_2. \text{ let } T'_2, T'_1 \text{ be } G_2(T_2), G_1(T_1) \text{ in } (T'_1, T'_2))$$

The reason for the "twist" in the order of the G's is explained in Section 5. Intuitively, G_2's effects are "well-bracketed" by G_1's.

Using this tensor, one defines the composition of an n-ary partial compiler with n partial compilers via iterated tensors, analogously to the case of compilers. One then obtains suitable n-ary generalizations of the above unary associativity, action, and unit equations for the two n-ary compositions. These hold when there are no compile-time effects; Section 5 discusses the general case.

2.2 An Example: The Sequential Partial Compiler

We give an example of a binary partial compiler and its composition with two compilers; Section 3.4 makes use of the composition of partial compilers. We consider compiling source programs S obtained from the composition of two simpler sources prefix(S) and suffix(S), where:

$$\text{prefix}, \text{suffix} : \text{source} \longrightarrow \text{source}$$

The binary partial compiler

$$PC^2_{\text{SEQ}} : (\text{source}, \text{target}) \multimap (\text{source} \times \text{source}, \text{target} \times \text{target})$$

generates (partial) sources from the source prefix and suffix, and the targets obtained for these two sources are composed:

> $Compiler\ \ S : \text{source}.$
> $Reduction\ \ (\text{prefix}(S), \text{suffix}(S)),$
> $Generation\ \ T_{\text{prefix}} : \text{target}, T_{\text{suffix}} : \text{target}.\text{Comp}(T_{\text{suffix}}, T_{\text{prefix}})$

where Comp is an assumed available composition operation with semantics:

$$[\![\text{Comp}(T_{\text{suffix}}, T_{\text{prefix}})]\!] = \lambda d : \text{data}.\ [\![T_{\text{suffix}}]\!]([\![T_{\text{prefix}}]\!](d))$$

Suppose we wish to run our computation on a computer with a CPU and a graphics card (GPU). Assume we have compilers C_{GPU}, generating a GPU target', and C_{CPU}, generating a CPU target, and a term $\text{run}_{\text{GPU}} : \text{target}' \rightarrow \text{target}$ that, given T', produces a T with the same semantics that loads T' on the GPU and then runs it on the data supplied to T, returning the result to the CPU. The composition of C_{GPU} with run_{GPU} then defines a compiler $C_{\text{G}} : \text{source} \rightarrow \text{target}$ such that, for all source's S and data d:

$$[\![C_{\text{G}}(S)]\!](d) = [\![\text{run}_{\text{GPU}}(C_{\text{GPU}}(S))]\!](d) = [\![C_{\text{GPU}}(S)]\!](d)$$

Given a source program, we can then run its prefix on the GPU and its suffix on the CPU, using the binary composition $PC^2_{\text{SEQ}}\langle\!\langle C_{\text{G}}, C_{\text{CPU}} \rangle\!\rangle$ of the binary partial compiler PC^2_{SEQ} with the two compilers C_{G} and C_{CPU}.

3   Compilers and Partial Compilers as First-Class Objects

While composition and tensor are the main operations on compilers and partial compilers, we now discuss five more, shown in Table 1.

Table 1. Generic compiler operations described in this paper

Operation	Symbol	Compilers	Partial Compilers	Section
Composition	$\langle\!\langle\rangle\!\rangle$	Yes	Yes	2.1
Tensor	$\otimes$	Yes	Yes	2.1
Star	$*$	Yes	No	3.1
Conditional	$COND$	Yes	Yes	3.2
Cases	$CASES$	Yes	Yes	3.3
Functor	PC_{Func}	No	Yes	3.4
Iteration	DO	No	Yes	3.5

3.1 Star

So far we have considered partial compilers whose arity is constant. We generalize, defining partial compilers that operate with lists of sources and targets. For any compiler C : source $\rightarrow$ target, we define C^* : source* $\rightarrow$ target*, the *star* of C, to be the pointwise application of C to all elements of a given list l of sources:

$$C^*(l) = \mathrm{map}(C, l)$$

Consider the partial compiler PC_{SEQ} : (source, target) $\multimap$ (source*, target*) that generalizes the sequential compiler PC_{SEQ}^2 from Section 2.2 by decomposing a source S that is function composition into a list $[S_1, \ldots, S_n]$ of its components. Given a compiler C : source $\rightarrow$ target for simple sources, the composition $PC_{\text{SEQ}} \langle\!\langle C^* \rangle\!\rangle$ is a compiler for queries that are an arbitrary composition of simple sources. A practical example involving the star operation is given in Section 4.2.

3.2 Conditionals

The partial compiler operations we have constructed so far are all independent of the sources involved; by allowing dependence we obtain a richer class of compiler composition operations. For example, it may be that one compiler is better suited to handle a given source than another, according to some criterion:

$$Pred : \text{source} \rightarrow \text{bool}$$

We define a natural conditional operation to choose between two compilers

$$\text{COND} : (\text{source} \rightarrow \text{bool}) \times (\text{source} \rightarrow \text{target})^2 \rightarrow (\text{source} \rightarrow \text{target})$$

by:

$$\text{COND} = \lambda(p, (C_1, C_2)). \lambda S. \text{ if } p(S) \text{ then } C_1(S) \text{ else } C_2(S)$$

We may write *IF Pred THEN C_1 ELSE C_2* instead of $\text{COND}(Pred, (C_1, C_2))$. There is an evident analogous conditional operation on partial compilers.

We can use the conditional to "patch" bugs in a compiler without access to its implementation. Assume we have a predicate bug : source $\rightarrow$ bool that describes (a superset of) the sources for which a specific complex optimizing compiler C_{OPT} generates an incorrect target. Let us also assume that we have a simple (non-optimizing) compiler C_{SIMPLE} that always generates correct targets. Then the compiler

$$IF \text{ bug } THEN \ C_{\text{SIMPLE}} \ ELSE \ C_{\text{OPT}}$$

"hides" the bugs in C_{OPT}.

3.3   Cases

Similar to the * operation, but replacing list types by labeled sum types, we can define a "cases" operation, a useful generalization of conditional composition. Given n individual compilers $C_i : \text{source}_i \to \text{target}$ (for $i = 1, \ldots, n$) together with a function $W : \text{source} \to l_1 : \text{source}_1 + \ldots + l_n : \text{source}_n$, we define

$$CASES \ W \ OF \ l_1 : C_1, \ldots, l_n : C_n$$

to be the compiler $C : \text{source} \to \text{target}$ where:

$$C(S) = cases \ W(S) \ of \ l_1 : C_1(S), \ldots, l_n : C_n(S)$$

We give a practical example using $CASES$ in Section 4.2.

There is an evident analogous cases operation on partial compilers. Given two partial compilers $PC_i : (\text{source}_i, \text{target}) \multimap (\text{source}', \text{target}')$, we define

$$CASES \ W \ OF \ l_1 : PC_1, \ldots, l_n : PC_n$$

to be the partial compiler $PC : (\text{source}, \text{target}) \multimap (\text{source}', \text{target}')$ given by:

$$\lambda S. \ cases \ W(S) \ of \ l_1 : PC_1(S), \ldots, l_n : PC_n(S)$$

3.4   Functor

Given functions $f : \text{source} \to \text{source}'$ and $g : \text{target}' \to \text{target}$, we define the partial compiler

$$PC_{\text{Func}}(f, g) : (\text{source}, \text{target}) \multimap (\text{source}', \text{target}')$$

to be:

> $Compiler \ \ S : \text{source}.$
> $Reduction \ \ f(S),$
> $Generation \ \ T' : \text{target}'. \ g(T')$

This operation is *functorial*, meaning that this equation holds:

$$PC_{\text{Func}}(f, g) \langle\!\langle PC_{\text{Func}}(f', g') \rangle\!\rangle = PC_{\text{Func}}(f' {\circ} f, g {\circ} g')$$

We describe two useful applications in which g is the identity $\text{id}_{\text{target}}$ on target.

Traditional compilers usually include a sequence of optimizing passes, given by optimizing transformation functions $\text{Opt} : \text{source} \to \text{source}$. Such passes correspond to partial compilers of the form $PC_{\text{Func}}(\text{Opt}, \text{Id}_{\text{target}})$.

Staged compilers (e.g., [13,24]) are frequently built from a sequence of transformations between (progressively lower-level) intermediate representations, followed by a
final compilation step:

$$\text{source}_1 \xrightarrow{\text{Trans}_1} \ldots \xrightarrow{\text{Trans}_{n-1}} \text{source}_n \xrightarrow{C} \text{target}$$

One can model this structure by composing partial compilers $PC_{\text{Func}}(\text{Trans}_i, \text{Id}_{\text{target}})$,
obtaining a partial compiler $PC_{\text{Stage}} : (\text{source}_1, \text{target}) \multimap (\text{source}_n, \text{target})$, where

$$PC_{\text{Stage}} =_{\text{def}} PC_{\text{Func}}(\text{Trans}_1, \text{Id})\langle\!\langle \ldots \langle\!\langle PC_{\text{Func}}(\text{Trans}_{n-1}, \text{Id})\rangle\!\rangle \ldots \rangle\!\rangle$$

The final compiler is then $PC_{\text{Stage}}\langle\!\langle C \rangle\!\rangle$. This integrates staged compilation into our
framework in a straightforward way.

3.5   Iteration

The iteration operation iterates a partial compiler

$$PC : (\text{source}, \text{target}) \multimap (\text{source}, \text{target})$$

up to n times, stopping if a given predicate $Pred : \text{source} \to \text{bool}$ becomes true. We
define

$$H_{PC} : \text{nat} \to ((\text{source}, \text{target}) \multimap (\text{source}, \text{target}))$$

to be:

$$\begin{aligned} H_{PC}(0) &= \text{Id} \\ H_{PC}(n+1) &= \textit{IF Pred THEN } \text{Id} \textit{ ELSE } PC\langle\!\langle H_{PC}(n)\rangle\!\rangle \end{aligned}$$

(We assume the λ-calculus has a facility for primitive recursion.) Applying H_{PC} to
$Num : \text{nat}$, one obtains the partial compiler

$$\text{DO } PC \text{ UNTIL } Pred \text{ FOR } Num \text{ TIMES}$$

This could be used to repeatedly apply an optimizing compiler PC until a fixed-point
is reached, as detected by $Pred$.

4   Application to Query Processing

In this section we return to our motivating problem: compiling LINQ. We introduce
essential aspects of LINQ and give a much simplified version, called μLINQ, that is
small enough to be tractable in a paper, but rich enough to express interesting computations. We develop a hierarchy of partial compilers that, composed together, provide
increasingly more powerful μLINQ compilers. In the LINQ terminology, inherited from
databases, source programs are called "queries" and target programs are called "plans".

4.1   LINQ and μLINQ

LINQ was introduced in 2008 as a set of extensions to traditional .Net languages such
as C# and F#. It is essentially a functional, strongly-typed language, inspired by the
database language SQL (or relational algebra) and comprehension calculi [3]. Much as
in LISP, the main datatype manipulated by LINQ computations is that of lists of values;
these are thought of as *(data) collections*.

LINQ operators transform collections to other collections. Queries (source programs) are (syntactic) compositions of LINQ operators. For example, the query `C.Select(e => f(e))`, where `e => f(e)` is the LINQ syntax for the lambda expression $\lambda e.f(e)$, uses the `Select` operator (called *map* in other programming languages) to apply `f` to every element `e` of a collection `C`. The result is a collection of the same size as the input collection. The elements `e` can have any .Net type, and `f(e)` can be any .Net computation returning a value. The core LINQ operators are named after SQL. All LINQ operators are second-order, as their arguments include functions.

μLINQ Syntax. The *basic datatypes* are ranged over by I, O, and K (which stand for "input", "output" and "key"); they are given by the grammar:

$$\text{I} ::= \text{B} \mid \text{I}^*$$

where B ranges over a given set of *primitive* datatypes, such as `int`, the type of integers. The type I* stands for the type of collections (taken to be finite lists) of elements of type I. The corresponding .NET type is `IEnumerable⟨I⟩`.

μLINQ queries (source programs) consist of sequences of operator applications; they are not complete programs as the syntax does not specify the input data collection (in contrast to LINQ). They are specified by the grammar

$$\text{Query} ::= \text{OpAp}_1; \ldots; \text{OpAp}_n \qquad (n \geq 0)$$
$$\text{OpAp} ::= \text{SelectMany<I,O>(FExp)} \mid$$
$$\text{Aggregate<I>(FExp,Exp)} \mid$$
$$\text{GroupBy<I,K>(FExp)}$$

Here Exp and FExp range over given sets of *expressions* and *function expressions*, of respective given types I or $\text{I}_1 \times \ldots \times \text{I}_n \to \text{O}$. The details of the given primitive types, expressions, and function expressions are left unspecified.

Only well-formed operator applications and queries are of interest. The following rules specify these and their associated types:

$$\text{SelectMany<I,O>(FExp)} : \text{I}^* \to \text{O}^* \text{ (if FExp has type I} \to \text{O}^*)$$
$$\text{Aggregate<I>(FExp,Exp)} : \text{I}^* \to \text{I}^*$$
$$\text{(if FExp has type I} \times \text{I} \to \text{I}, \text{ and Exp has type I)}$$
$$\text{GroupBy<I,K>(FExp)} : \text{I}^* \to \text{I}^{**} \qquad \text{(if FExp has type I} \to \text{K})$$

$$\frac{\text{OpAp}_i : \text{I}_i \to \text{I}_{i+1} \qquad (i = 1, \ldots, n)}{\text{OpAp}_1; \ldots; \text{OpAp}_n : \text{I}_1 \to \text{I}_{n+1}}$$

μLINQ Semantics. We begin with an informal explanation of the semantics. A query of type $\text{I}^* \to \text{O}^*$ denotes a function from I collections to O collections. We begin with operator applications and then consider composite queries.

`SelectMany<I,O>(FExp)` applied to a collection returns the result of applying FExp to all its elements and concatenating the results. So, for example, the query `SelectMany<int,int>(n => [n,n+1])` applied to $C =_{\text{def}} [1,2,3,4,5]$ results in the list $[1,2,2,3,3,4,4,5,5,6]$.

`Aggregate<I>(FExp,Exp)` applied to a collection produces a singleton list containing the result of a fold operation [11] performed using FExp and Exp. So, for example, $\text{Aggregate<int,int>}((\text{m,n}) \Rightarrow \text{m+n},6)$ applied to C results in the list $[1 + (2 + (3 + (4 + (5 + 6))))] = [21]$. Some of the compilers we construct require that such aggregations are *(commutatively) monoidal*, i.e., that FExp is associative (and commutative) with unit Exp.

$\text{GroupBy<I,K>}(\text{FExp})$ groups all the elements of a collection into a collection of sub-collections, where each sub-collection consists of all the elements in the original collection sharing a common key; the key of a value is computed using FExp. The sub-collections in the result occur in the order of the occurrences of their keys, via FExp, in the original collection, and the elements in the sub-collections occur in their order in the original collection. So, for example, $\text{GroupBy}(\text{n} \Rightarrow \text{n mod 2})$ applied to C results in the list [[1,3,5],[2,4]].

Composite queries are constructed with semicolons and represent the composition, from left to right, of the functions denoted by their constituent operator applications.

The formal definition of μLINQ is completed by giving it a denotational semantics. We only show the semantics for a language fragment; it is easy, if somewhat tedious, to spell it out for the full language. First we assign a set $[\![\text{I}]\!]$ to every μLINQ type I, assuming every primitive type already has such a set assigned:

$$[\![\text{I}_1 \times \ldots \times \text{I}_n]\!] =_{\text{def}} [\![\text{I}_1]\!] \times \ldots \times [\![\text{I}_n]\!]$$

Next, to any well-typed operator application $\text{OpApp} : \text{I} \to \text{O}$ we assign a function $[\![\text{OpApp}]\!] : [\![\text{I}]\!] \to [\![\text{O}]\!]$, given a denotation $[\![\text{Exp}]\!] \in [\![\text{I}]\!]$ for each expression Exp : I. For example:

$$[\![\text{Aggregate<T>}(\text{FExp},\text{Exp})]\!](d) =_{\text{def}} [\text{fold}([\![\text{FExp}]\!], [\![\text{Exp}]\!], d)]$$

Finally, to any well-typed query $\text{S} : \text{I} \to \text{O}$ we assign a function $[\![\text{S}]\!] : [\![\text{I}]\!] \to [\![\text{O}]\!]$

$$[\![\text{OpAp}_1; \ldots; \text{OpAp}_n]\!] =_{\text{def}} [\![\text{OpAp}_n]\!] \circ \ldots \circ [\![\text{OpAp}_1]\!] \qquad (n \geq 0)$$

μLINQ and MapReduce. The popular MapReduce [6] distributed computation programming model can be succinctly expressed in μLINQ:

$$\text{MapReduce}(\text{map, reduceKey, reduce}) : \text{I}^* \to \text{O}^*$$

is the same as

$$\text{SelectMany}(\text{map}); \text{GroupBy}(\text{reduceKey}); \text{SelectMany}(1 \Rightarrow [\text{reduce}(1)])$$

where $\text{map} : \text{I} \to \text{O}$ is the map function, $\text{reduceKey} : \text{O} \to \text{K}$ computes the key for reduction, and $\text{reduce} : \text{O}^* \to \text{O}$ is the reduction function. (Since we use SelectMany for applying the reduction function, the result of reduce is embedded into a list with a single element.)

4.2 Compiling μLINQ

A Single-Core Compiler. We start by defining the types for sources (queries) and targets (plans). Let us assume we are given a type FExp corresponding to the set of function expressions, and a type Exp for constants. Then we define types OpAp and MLSource, corresponding to the sets of μLINQ operator applications and queries by setting:

$$
\begin{aligned}
\text{OpAp} \quad &= \textit{SelectMany} : \text{FExp} +\\
&\quad \textit{Aggregate} : \text{FExp} \times \text{Exp} +\\
&\quad \textit{GroupBy} : \text{FExp}\\
\text{MLSource} &= \text{OpAp}^*
\end{aligned}
$$

We assume we have a type MLTarget of μLINQ targets (plans) T with semantics $[\![T]\!]$: MLData $\longrightarrow$ MLData, where MLData consists of lists of items, where items are either elements of (the semantics of) a basic μLINQ type B, or lists of such items.

As a basic building block for constructing μLINQ compilers, we start from three very simple compilers, each of which can only generate a plan for a query consisting of just one of the operators:

$$
\begin{aligned}
C_{\text{SelectMany}} &: \text{FExp} \longrightarrow \text{MLTarget}\\
C_{\text{Aggregate}} &: \text{FExp} \times \text{Exp} \longrightarrow \text{MLTarget}\\
C_{\text{GroupBy}} &: \text{FExp} \longrightarrow \text{MLTarget}
\end{aligned}
$$

The denotational semantics of μLINQ operators (Section 4.1) gives a blueprint for a possible implementation of these compilers.

We use the *CASES* operation from Section 3.3 to combine these three elementary compilers into a compiler that can handle simple one-operator queries:

$$
\begin{aligned}
C_{\text{OO}} = \textit{CASES}\ (\lambda S : \text{OpAp}.\ S)\ \textit{OF}\\
\textit{SelectMany} : C_{\text{SelectMany}},\\
\textit{Aggregate} : C_{\text{Aggregate}},\\
\textit{GroupBy} : C_{\text{GroupBy}}
\end{aligned}
$$

Finally, we use the generalized sequential partial compiler PC_{SEQ} and the star operation, both introduced in Section 3.1, to construct a compiler

$$
C_{\mu\text{LINQ}} : \text{MLSource} \to \text{MLTarget}
$$

for arbitrary μLINQ queries, where

$$
C_{\mu\text{LINQ}} = PC_{\text{SEQ}} \langle\!\langle C_{\text{OO}}^* \rangle\!\rangle
$$

A Multi-core Compiler. In this example we construct a partial compiler PC_{MC} to allow our single-core compiler to target a multi-core machine whose cores can execute plans independently. The most obvious way to take advantage of the available parallelism is to decompose the work by splitting the input data into disjoint parts, performing the work in parallel on each part using a separate core, and then merging the results.

Table 2. Compiling a query S for a dual-core computer

S	$\text{collate}(S, l, r)$	$\text{part}(S, d)$
SelectMany(FExp)	$l \cdot r$	$\text{prefix}(d)$
Aggregate(FExp,Exp)	$[\![\text{FExp}]\!](\text{head}_{\text{Exp}}(l), \text{head}_{\text{Exp}}(r))$	$\text{prefix}(d)$
GroupBy(FExp)	$l \cdot r$	$[x \in d \mid [\![\text{FExp}]\!](x) \in \text{prefix}(\text{setr}(\text{map}([\![\text{FExp}]\!], d)))]$

A partial compiler $PC_{\mathrm{MC}} : (\mathrm{OpAp}, \mathrm{MLTarget}) \multimap (\mathrm{OpAp}, \mathrm{MLTarget})$ for operator applications for multi-core machines with cores c_1 and c_2 can be given by:

$$\begin{aligned}
&Compiler \ \ S : \mathrm{OpAp}. \\
&Reduction \ \ S, \\
&Generation \ \ T : \mathrm{MLTarget}. \ G_{\mathrm{MC}}(S, T)
\end{aligned}$$

where, for any OpAp S, MLTarget T:

$$\begin{aligned}
\llbracket G_{\mathrm{MC}}(S,T) \rrbracket(d) = \lambda d : \mathrm{MLData}. \ &let \ d' \ be \ \mathrm{part}(S, d) \ in \\
&\mathrm{collate}(S, \llbracket \mathrm{run}_{c_1}(T) \rrbracket(d'), \llbracket \mathrm{run}_{c_2}(T) \rrbracket(d \backslash d'))
\end{aligned}$$

The definition of the semantics of G_{MC}, which we now explain, provides a blueprint for its intended parallel implementation. First, the functions $\mathrm{run}_{c_1}, \mathrm{run}_{c_2}$ ensure that their argument MLTarget is run on the specified core; they act as the identity on the semantics. Next, for any list d, $\mathrm{part}(S, d)$ and $d \backslash \mathrm{part}(S, d)$ constitute a division of d into two parts in a query-dependent manner; here $d \backslash d'$ is chosen so that $d = d' \cdot (d \backslash d')$, if possible (we use $\cdot$ for list concatenation). The function "collate" assembles the results of the computations together, also in a query-dependent manner.

There are many possible ways to define part and collate and one reasonable specification is shown in Table 2. There, $\mathrm{prefix}(d)$ gives a prefix of d, $\mathrm{head}_{\mathrm{Exp}}(d)$ is the first element of d, assuming d is non-empty, and $\llbracket \mathrm{Exp} \rrbracket$ otherwise, and $\mathrm{setr}(d)$, which is used to ensure that a given key is in only one partition, consists of d with all repetitions of an element on its right deleted.

The `SelectMany` operator is homomorphic w.r.t. concatenation. It can be computed by partitioning the collection d into an arbitrary prefix and suffix, applying `SelectMany` recursively on the parts, and concatenating the results.

Similarly, if monoidal, `Aggregate(FExp,Exp)` is homomorphic w.r.t. the aggregation function FExp, so it can be applied to an arbitrary partition of d, combining the two results using FExp.

Finally, `GroupBy` partitions the input collection d so that values with the same key end up in the same partition. (It does so by splitting the codomain of the key function FExp into two arbitrary disjoint sets.) The results of recursively applying `GroupBy` on these partitions can be concatenated as the groups from both parts will also be disjoint.

The complete multi-core μLINQ compiler is given by

$$PC_{\mathrm{SEQ}} \langle\!\langle PC_{\mathrm{MC}} \langle\!\langle C_{\mathrm{OO}} \rangle\!\rangle^* \rangle\!\rangle$$

It is straightforward to generalize this to machines with n cores by suitably modifying part and collate.

Note that we have achieved a non-trivial result: we have built a real μLINQ compiler targeting multi-cores by writing just a few lines of code, combining several simple compilers. This implementation is certainly not optimal as it repartitions the data around each operation, but we can transform it into a smarter compiler by using the same techniques. The functionality it provides is essentially that of PLINQ [7], the parallel LINQ implementation.

Compilation for Distributed Execution. The strategy employed for the multi-core compiler for parallelizing μLINQ query evaluations across cores can be used to parallelize further, across multiple machines, in a manner similar to the DryadLINQ compiler. We add one additional twist by including resource allocation and scheduling in the plan language. Consider an example of a cluster of machines, and suppose we are dealing with a large input collection, stored on a distributed filesystem (e.g., [9]) by splitting the collection into many partitions resident on different cluster machines (each machine may have multiple partitions). The goal of the generated plan is to process the partitioned collections in an efficient way, ideally having each piece of data be processed by the machine where it is stored. In the following simple example we just use two machines.

We define the operator application unary partial compiler PC_{Cluster} to be:

$$\begin{aligned}
&Compiler \ \ S : \text{OpAp}. \\
&Reduction \ \ S, \\
&Generation \ \ T : \text{MLTarget}. \ \text{G}_{\text{CL}}(S, T)
\end{aligned}$$

where, for any OpAp S and MLTarget T,

$$\begin{aligned}
[\![\text{G}_{\text{CL}}(S, T)]\!](d) = \lambda d : \ &\text{MLData}. \\
&let \ m_1, m_2 : \text{Machine} \ be \ \text{getm}, \text{getm} \ in \\
&let \ d' \ be \ \text{mpart}(S, d, m_1, m_2) \ in \\
&\text{collate}(S, [\![\text{run}(m_1, T)]\!](d'), [\![\text{run}(m_2, T)]\!](d \backslash d'))
\end{aligned}$$

Here, Machine is the type of cluster machines and the constant getm:Machine nondeterministically schedules a new machine. When applied to S, d, m_1, m_2, the function mpart returns the first part of a partition of d into two, using a policy not detailed here; as in the case of part, when S is a GroupBy the two parts should contain no common keys. Note that the run functions are now parametrized on machines. The relative location of data and machines on the cluster is important. In particular, the partition policy for mpart may depend on that; we also assume that the code run(m, T) first loads remote data onto m. As before, the semantics of G_{CL} provides a blueprint for a parallel implementation.

Formally we assume given a set Sch of scheduler states, and as run-time monad T_{run} take $\mathcal{F}^+(\text{Sch} \times X)^{\text{Sch}}$, the standard combination of side-effect and nondeterminism monads ($\mathcal{F}^+(X)$ is the collection of non-empty finite subsets of X); for $[\![\text{getm}]\!]$ we assume an allocation function $\text{Sch} \to \mathcal{F}^+(\text{Sch} \times [\![\text{Machine}]\!])$.

The cluster-level operator application compiler is then obtained by composing the cluster partial compiler with the multi-core compiler described previously

$$PC_{\text{Cluster}} \langle\!\langle PC_{\text{MC}} \langle\!\langle C_{\text{OO}} \rangle\!\rangle \rangle\!\rangle$$

and then the complete compiler is:

$$PC_{\text{SEQ}} \langle\!\langle PC_{\text{Cluster}} \langle\!\langle PC_{\text{MC}} \langle\!\langle C_{\text{OO}} \rangle\!\rangle \rangle\!\rangle^* \rangle\!\rangle$$

The cluster-level compiler is structurally similar to the multi-core compiler, but the collections themselves are already partitioned and the compiler uses the collection structure to allocate the computation's run-time resources.

This compiler is in some respects more powerful than MapReduce, because (1) it can handle more complex queries, including chains of MapReduce computations and

(2) it parallelizes the computation across both cores and machines. With a tiny change we obtain a compiler that only parallelizes across machines:

$$PC_{\text{SEQ}}\langle\!\langle PC_{\text{Cluster}}\langle\!\langle C_{\text{OO}}\rangle\!\rangle^{*}\rangle\!\rangle.$$

With a little more work one can also add the only important missing MapReduce optimization, namely early aggregation in the map stage.

5   Mathematical Foundations

We now turn to a semantical account of partial compilers in terms of a category of *tactics*. We then discuss the categorical correlates of our polymorphic operations on compilers and partial compilers, and the relationships with the Dialectica category and Milner's tactics. We work with a cartesian closed category $\mathbf{K}$ with a strong monad T. This supports Moggi's computational lambda calculus [20]: each type σ denotes an object $[\![\sigma]\!]$ of $\mathbf{K}$, and every term

$$x_1 : \sigma_1, \ldots, x_n : \sigma_n \vdash M : \tau$$

denotes a morphism of $\mathbf{K}$

$$[\![M]\!] : [\![\sigma_1]\!] \times \ldots \times [\![\sigma_n]\!] \to [\![\tau]\!]$$

As is common practice, we may confuse terms and their denotations, writing M instead of $[\![M]\!]$; in particular we make free use of the definitions and notation of Section 2. In doing so, we can use types and terms as notations for objects and morphisms, and treat objects x as type constants denoting themselves and morphisms $f : x \to y$ as constants denoting elements of the corresponding function type $x \to y$. We can also use the proof rules of the computational lambda calculus to establish relations between morphisms.

The objects of our category of tactics are pairs (P, S) of objects of $\mathbf{K}$; we call P and S (objects of) *problems* and *solutions*, respectively. The morphisms from (P, S) to (P', S') are morphisms of $\mathbf{K}$ of the form

$$f : P \longrightarrow \mathrm{T}(P' \times (S' \Rightarrow \mathrm{T}(S)))$$

and it is these that are called tactics.

The identity on (P, S) is $\mathrm{Id}_{(P,S)} = \lambda x : P.(x, \lambda y : S.y)$ and the composition $(P, S) \xrightarrow{gf} (P'', S'')$ of $(P, S) \xrightarrow{f} (P', S')$ and $(P', S') \xrightarrow{g} (P'', S'')$ is $gf = f\langle\!\langle g \rangle\!\rangle$ (note the order reversal), making use of the definition in Section 2. Using Moggi's laws for the computational lambda calculus, one can show that composition is associative with the identity as unit, and so this does indeed define a category.

Rather than speaking of sources, targets and partial compilers, we have chosen here to speak more neutrally of problems, solutions and tactics. We follow Blass [2] for problems and solutions, and Milner for tactics: one can think of tactics as tactics for reducing problems to subproblems. Compilers are simply modelled as Kleisli morphisms $P \to \mathrm{T}(S)$.

We now consider the categorical operations corresponding to some of the operations on partial compilers and compilers that we defined above. We define the action of a given tactic $f : (P, S) \longrightarrow (P', S')$ on a Kleisli morphism $h : P' \longrightarrow \mathrm{T}(S')$ by:

$$h \cdot f = f \langle\!\langle h \rangle\!\rangle : P \longrightarrow S$$

using the composition operation of partial compilers with compilers of Section 2. In terms of this "right action" notation the action equations of Section 2 become:

$$(h \cdot g) \cdot f = h \cdot gf \qquad h \cdot \mathrm{Id} = \mathrm{Id}$$

We define tensors of Kleisli morphisms and tactics similarly, again making use of the definitions in Section 2. The expected functorial laws

$$\mathrm{Id} \otimes \mathrm{Id} = \mathrm{Id} \qquad (f' \otimes g')(f \otimes g) = (f'f \otimes g'g)$$

for the tensors of tactics hold if the monad is *commutative* [14], for example when there are no compile-time effects, or for nondeterminism, probabilistic choice, or non-termination (so having recursion is fine); typical cases where they fail are exceptions or side-effects. When they hold, so too do the expected associativity, action, and unit laws for the n-ary compositions defined in Section 2.

In general one obtains only a premonoidal structure [23] with weaker laws:

$$\mathrm{Id} \otimes \mathrm{Id} = \mathrm{Id} \qquad (f \otimes g) = (g \otimes \mathrm{Id})(\mathrm{Id} \otimes f)$$

$$(f' \otimes \mathrm{Id})(f \otimes \mathrm{Id}) = (f'f \otimes \mathrm{Id}) \qquad (\mathrm{Id} \otimes g')(\mathrm{Id} \otimes g) = (\mathrm{Id} \otimes g'g)$$

The "twist" in the definition of the tensor in Section 2 of two tactics is needed to obtain these laws. The weaker laws yield correspondingly weaker laws for the n-ary compositions.

Turning to Section 3, the cases operation arises from the fact that categorical sums exist when the solution objects are the same, i.e., $(P_1, S) + (P_2, S) = (P_1 + P_2, S)$, and the functorial operation arises from the evident functor from $\mathbf{K}_T^{\mathrm{op}} \times \mathbf{K}_T$ to the category of tactics ($\mathbf{K}_T$ is the Kleisli category of T). The literature on Dialectica categories contains further functorial constructions that may also prove useful—for example, the sequential construction of Blass [2] is intriguing.

The Dialectica category has the same objects as the tactics category. A morphism $(f, g) : (P, S) \longrightarrow (P', S')$ consists of a *reduction* function $f : P \longrightarrow P'$ and a *solution* function $g : P \times S' \longrightarrow S$. This is essentially the same as a tactic, in the case of the identity monad, and the Dialectica category is then equivalent to the category of tactics. To incorporate compile-time effects in the Dialectica category, one might alternatively try $f : P \longrightarrow \mathrm{T}(P')$ and $g : P \times S' \longrightarrow \mathrm{T}(S)$. However this does not give a category: the evident composition is not associative.

As we have said, partial compilers also arose by analogy with Milner's tactics. Milner cared about sequents and theorems, whereas we care about sources and targets. His tactics produce lists and have the form:

$$\text{sequent} \to (\text{sequent}^* \times (\text{theorem}^* \to \text{theorem}))$$

But these are nothing but partial compilers of type:

$$(\text{sequent}, \text{theorem}) \multimap (\text{sequent}^*, \text{theorem}^*)$$

Our methods of combining partial compilers correspond, more or less, to his tacticals, e.g., we both use a composition operation, though his is adapted to lists, and the composition of two tactics may fail. He also makes use of an OR tactical, which tries a tactic and, if that fails (by raising a failure exception), tries an alternate; we have replaced that by our conditional partial compiler.

6 Implementations

Section 4 describes a compiler for a stylized language. We used the compiler forest architecture to implement two proof-of-concept compilers for (essentially) functional languages targeting a computer cluster: one for LINQ and one for matrix computations. The implementations reuse multiple partial compilers.

Our compiler forest implementations closely parallel the examples in this paper. The lowest layer implements "tactics" (see Section 5): computations on abstract problems and solutions that provide the basic composition operation. On top of this we build a partial compiler abstraction, where problems are source programs and solutions are targets. We then implement a combinator library for the operations described in Sections 2 and 3. A set of abstract base classes for partial compilers, programs, data, optimization passes, and execution engines provide generic useful operations. A set of libraries provides support for manipulating .Net System.Linq.Expressions objects, which are the core of the intermediate representation used by all our compilers. To implement partial compilers one writes source reduction functions R and target generation functions G, exactly as described in Section 2.

Compiling LINQ. The LINQ compiler structure closely parallels the description from Section 4, but handles practically the entire LINQ language, with a cluster-level compiler (PC_{Cluster}), a machine multi-core compiler (PC_{MC}), and a core-level compiler based on native LINQ-to-objects. We also implemented a simple GPU compiler C_{GPU} based on Accelerator [26]. A conditional partial compiler steers queries to either C_{GPU} or PC_{MC}, since C_{GPU} handles only a subset of LINQ, and operates on a restricted set of data types.

While our implementation is only preliminary, it performs well and has served to validate the architectural design. For example, when running MapReduce queries, our multi-core compiler produces a speed-up of 3.5 using 4 cores. We tested our compiler on a cluster with 200 machines; at this size the performance of MapReduce computations is essentially the same as with DryadLINQ, since I/O is the dominant cost in such applications.

Compiling Matrix Algebra. We have defined a simple functional language for computing on matrices, with operations such as addition, multiplication, transposition, solving linear systems, Cholesky factorization, and LU decomposition. All these operations are naturally parallelizable. The matrices are modeled as two-dimensional collections of tiles, where the tiles are smaller matrices. Large-scale matrices are distributed collections of tiles, each of which is a matrix composed of smaller tiles. This design is useful for dense matrices; by making tiles very small it can also accommodate sparse matrices.

The top-level partial compiler translates matrix operations into operations on collections of tiles. The collection operations are translated by a second-level partial compiler into LINQ computations on collections of tiles, where the functions FExp applied to the elements are also tile/matrix operations. The collection computations are then passed to the distributed LINQ compiler of Section 6 to generate code running on a cluster. The basic distributed matrix compiler is:

$$PC_{\text{SEQ}} \langle\!\langle PC_{\text{Matrix}} \langle\!\langle C_{\text{Tile}}, C_{\text{Cluster}} \rangle\!\rangle^* \rangle\!\rangle$$

where PC_{Matrix} is a binary partial compiler that rewrites an operation on matrices in terms of a LINQ computation (compiled by its second child) applying functions to a set of tiles (compiled by its first child), and C_{Cluster} is the distributed LINQ compiler described previously.

Figure 2 illustrates how the work of compiling the expression $M1 \times M2 + M3$ is partitioned between the compilers involved. In this example we do not use a multi-core LINQ compiler as part of C_{Cluster}.

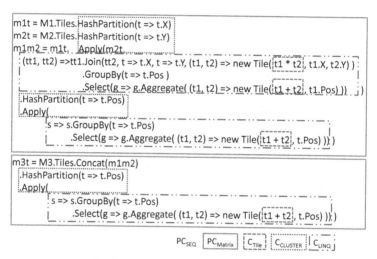

Fig. 2. Intermediate result produced when compiling the expression M1 * M2 + M3 using the distributed matrix compiler. The colored dotted lines indicate how various parts of the program are generated or assigned to various compilers; PC_{SEQ} is responsible for the complete program. We show the logical program state just before the leaf compilers C_{Tile} and C_{LINQ} (which is a part of C_{Cluster}) are invoked. HashPartition implements the "part" partitioning construct, while Apply corresponds to the "run$_m$" construct that executes a program on one partition, and Concat is concatenation.

7   Related Work

Federated and heterogeneous distributed databases also decompose computations between multiple computation engines. In the former, queries are converted into queries against component databases using wrappers [25,15], and most work concentrates on optimizations. Partial compilers serve a similar, but more general, role as they can have multiple children while wrappers operate on a single database. Regarding the latter, systems such as Dremel [18] that use a tree of databases to execute queries could be implemented in a principled way using a hierarchy of partial compilers.

The authors of [16] use graph transformations to allow multiple analyses to communicate. In [4] cooperating decompilers are proposed, where individual abstract interpretations share information. Our approach supports these applications using the iteration operation.

As we have seen, multistage compilers, e.g., [13,24], fit within our framework. However our formalism is more general than standard practice, as non-unary partial compilers enable branching partial multistage compilation, dividing sources between different engines, or parallelizing data computations.

8   Discussion and Conclusions

We made several simplifications so as to concentrate on the main points: partial compilers and their compositions. For example, μLINQ does not have a join operator, and function expressions were left unspecified; in particular they did not contain nested queries. Adding join leads to tree-shaped queries rather than lists, and nested queries lead to DAG's: indeed DryadLINQ plans are DAG's. (There seems to be no natural treatment of operator-labeled DAG's for functional programming in the literature, though there is related work on graphs [8].) There is a version of the star operator of Section 3.1 for trees, which enables the compiler of Section 4.2 to be extended to joins; there should also be a version for DAG's.

A well-known shortcoming of modularity is that it hides information that could potentially be useful across abstraction boundaries thereby impacting performance (see for example the micro-kernel/monolithic operating system debate); in our context, it may prevent cooperating partial compilers from sharing analysis results. A way to "cheat" to solve this problem is to use a partial compiler whose source language is the same as the intermediate language of its parent — a much richer language than the source alone. Whether this approach is practical remains to be validated by more complex compiler implementations.

The benefits of structuring compilers as we do may extend beyond modularity: since partial compilers are now first-class values, operations for compiler creation, composition and extensibility can be exposed to users, allowing compilers to be customized, created and invoked at run-time.

Partial compilers were motivated by the desire to discover the "right" interface between a set of cooperating compilers (the components of DryadLINQ described in the introduction). We were surprised when we stumbled on the partial compiler methodology, because it is extremely general and very simple. A partial compiler *provides a compilation service* to the upper layers (as do traditional compilers), but also *invokes the same, identical service* from the lower layers. While this structure looks overly simple, it is surprisingly powerful; one reason is that the objects that cross the interface between compilers are quite rich (source and target programs).

Acknowledgements. We are grateful to Martin Abadi, Gavin Bierman, Valeria de Paiva, Robert Harper, Martin Hyland, Michael Isard, Frank McSherry, and Phil Scott for their comments and suggestions.

References

1. Benton, N., Hughes, J., Moggi, E.: Monads and Effects. In: Barthe, G., Dybjer, P., Pinto, L., Saraiva, J. (eds.) APPSEM 2000. LNCS, vol. 2395, pp. 42–122. Springer, Heidelberg (2002)
2. Blass, A.: Questions and answers – a category arising in linear logic, complexity theory, and set theory. In: Advances in Linear Logic. London Math. Soc. Lecture Notes, vol. 222, pp. 61–81 (1995)
3. Buneman, P., et al.: Comprehension syntax. SIGMOD Record 23(1), 87–96 (1994)
4. Chang, B.-Y.E., Harren, M., Necula, G.C.: Analysis of low-level code using cooperating decompilers. In: Proc. 13th SAS, pp. 318–335. ACM (2006)
5. de Paiva, V.: The Dialectica categories. In: Proc. Cat. in Comp. Sci. and Logic, 1987. Cont. Math., vol. 92, pp. 47–62. AMS (1989)
6. Dean, J., Ghemawat, S.: MapReduce: Simplified data processing on large clusters. In: Proc. 6th OSDI, pp. 137–150. ACM (2004)
7. Duffy, J.: Concurrent Programming on Windows. Addison Wesley (2008)
8. Erwig, M.: Inductive graphs and functional graph algorithms. J. Funct. Program. 11(5), 467–492 (2001)
9. Ghemawat, S., Gobioff, H., Leung, L.: The Google file system. In: Proc. 19th SOSP, pp. 29–43. ACM (2003)
10. Gordon, M.J., Milner, A.J., Wadsworth, C.P.: Edinburgh LCF. LNCS, vol. 78. Springer, Heidelberg (1979)
11. Hutton, G.: A tutorial on the universality and expressiveness of fold. J. Funct. Program. 9(4), 355–372 (1999)
12. Hyland, J.M.E.: Proof theory in the abstract. APAL 114(1-3), 43–78 (2002)
13. Kelsey, R., Hudak, P.: Realistic compilation by program transformation. In: Proc. 16th POPL, pp. 281–292. ACM (1989)
14. Kock, A.: Commutative monads as a theory of distributions. Theory and Applications of Categories 26(4), 97–131 (2012)
15. Kossmann, D.: The state of the art in distributed query processing. ACM Comput. Surv. 32, 422–469 (2000)
16. Lerner, S., et al.: Composing dataflow analyses and transformations. In: Proc. 29th POPL, pp. 270–282. ACM (2002)
17. Meijer, E., et al.: LINQ: reconciling object, relations and XML in the .NET framework. In: Proc. SIGMOD Int. Conf. on Manage. Data, p. 706. ACM (2006)
18. Melnik, S., et al.: Dremel: interactive analysis of web-scale datasets. Proc. VLDB Endow. 3, 330–339 (2010)
19. Milner, R., Bird, R.: The use of machines to assist in rigorous proof. Phil. Trans. R. Soc. Lond. A 312(1522), 411–422 (1984)
20. Moggi, E.: Computational lambda-calculus and monads. In: Proc. 4th LICS, pp. 14–23. IEEE Computer Society (1989)
21. Moggi, E.: Notions of computation and monads. Inf. Comput. 93(1), 55–92 (1991)
22. Pierce, B.C.: Types and programming languages. MIT Press (2002)
23. Power, J., Robinson, E.: Premonoidal categories and notions of computation. MSCS 7(5), 453–468 (1997)
24. Sarkar, D., Waddell, O., Dybvig, R.K.: Educational pearl: A nanopass framework for compiler education. J. Funct. Program. 15(5), 653–667 (2005)
25. Sheth, A., Larson, J.: Federated database systems for managing distributed, heterogeneous, and autonomous databases. ACM Comput. Surv. 22, 183–236 (1990)
26. Tarditi, D., Puri, S., Oglesby, J.: Accelerator: using data parallelism to program GPU's for general-purpose uses. In: Proc. 12th. ASPLOS, pp. 325–335. ACM (2006)
27. Yu, Y., et al.: DryadLINQ: A system for general-purpose distributed data-parallel computing using a high-level language. In: Proc. 8th OSDI, pp. 1–14. ACM (2008)

Pretty-Big-Step Semantics

Arthur Charguéraud

Inria Saclay – Île-de-France & LRI, Université Paris Sud, CNRS
arthur.chargueraud@inria.fr

Abstract. In spite of the popularity of small-step semantics, big-step semantics remain used by many researchers. However, big-step semantics suffer from a serious duplication problem, which appears as soon as the semantics account for exceptions and/or divergence. In particular, many premises need to be copy-pasted across several evaluation rules. This duplication problem, which is particularly visible when scaling up to full-blown languages, results in formal definitions growing far bigger than necessary. Moreover, it leads to unsatisfactory redundancy in proofs. In this paper, we address the problem by introducing pretty-big-step semantics. Pretty-big-step semantics preserve the spirit of big-step semantics, in the sense that terms are directly related to their results, but they eliminate the duplication associated with big-step semantics.

1 Introduction

There are two traditional approaches to formalizing the operational semantics of a programming language: small-step semantics [11], and big-step semantics [7]. In small-step semantics, the subterm in evaluation position is reduced step by step and these transitions are reflected at the top level. In big-step semantics, a term is directly related to its result, and the behavior of a term is expressed in terms of the behavior of its subterms. While provably equivalent, these two approaches are fundamentally different in terms of how evaluation rules are stated and how proofs are conducted.

This paper describes and proposes a solution to a severe limitation of big-step semantics: the fact that a number of rules and premises need to be duplicated in order to handle exceptions and divergence. In particular, this limitation typically discourages the use of big-step semantics in mechanized definitions of large-scale languages. Before trying to address this limitation of the big-step semantics, we may ask ourselves: Why should we care about big-step semantics? Why not just use small-step semantics all the time?

To find out whether big-step semantics are still being used, we opened up proceedings from recent programming language conferences. We counted the number of research papers making use of a big-step semantics. In ICFP'11, 5 papers were describing results based on a big-step semantics, out of 8 papers that had an operational semantics. In POPL'11, there were 7 out of 23. In ICFP'12, there were 5 out of 9. An immediate conclusion that we can draw from these rough statistics is that *big-step is not dead.*

M. Felleisen and P. Gardner (Eds.): ESOP 2013, LNCS 7792, pp. 41–60, 2013.

A closer look at the papers involved reveals that the choice of the operational semantics usually depends on the topic covered by the paper. Papers on type systems nearly always use a small-step semantics to conduct a soundness proof in Wright and Felleisen's style [12]. Papers describing a machine-level language typically use a small-step relation to describe transitions between pairs of machine configurations. Papers concerned with concurrent languages are also almost exclusively described using small-step semantics. Furthermore, a majority of the mechanized definitions of full-blown programming languages that have been developed in recent years were based on small-step semantics.

There are, however, topics for which the use of a big-step semantics appears to prevail. Cost semantics, which associate a cost to the evaluation of every expression, are mainly presented as big-step relations. Program logics often have soundness and completeness proofs that are easier to conduct with respect to a big-step relation. In particular, there are cases of completeness proofs, such as that developed in the author's thesis [1], that need to be conducted by induction over a big-step derivation; any attempt to build the completeness proof with respect to a small-step semantics amounts to re-proving on-the-fly the equivalence between small-step and big-step semantics. Moreover, there are compiler transformations that are easier to prove correct with respect to big-step semantics, in particular for transformations introducing so-called "administrative redexes", which typically clutter simulation diagrams based on small-step semantics.

Big-step semantics are also widely used in informal descriptions. For example, the reference manual of a programming language typically contain sentences of the form "to evaluate if $e1$ then $e2$ else $e3$, first evaluate $e1$; if the result is true, then evaluate $e2$; otherwise, evaluate $e3$." None of the many reference manuals that we have looked at contains a sentence of the form "if $e1$ takes a step to expression $e1'$ then if $e1$ then $e2$ else $e3$ takes a step to if $e1'$ then $e2$ else $e3$." Thus, we speculate that it would be easier to convince the standards committee in charge of a given programming language of the adequacy of a big-step formalization than to convince them of the adequacy of a small-step formalization.

Given that there are a number of important applications for which big-step semantics seem to have an edge on small-step semantics, any significant improvement to big-step semantics should be considered as a valuable contribution.

In this paper, we focus on a critical issue associated with big-step semantics: the amount of duplication involved in the statement of the evaluation rules. To illustrate the extent of the problem, consider a C-style for-loop of the form "for (; t_1 ; t_2) { t_3 }", that is, a for-loop where the initialization expression has already been executed. We use the notation "for $t_1 \, t_2 \, t_3$" to describe such a loop. We next formalize its big-step semantics. For terminating executions, the evaluation judgment takes the form $t_{/m_1} \Rightarrow v_{/m_2}$, asserting that, in a store m_1, the evaluation of t terminates on the value v in a store m_2. The two rules at the top of Figure 1 describe the regular execution of a loop. When the loop condition t_1 evaluates to false, the loop terminates. Otherwise, if t_1 evaluates to true, we evaluate the body t_3 of the loop, and obtain the unit value, written tt. We then evaluate the stepping expression t_2, and start over.

$$\frac{t_{1/m_1} \Rightarrow \mathsf{false}_{/m_2}}{\mathsf{for}\, t_1\, t_2\, t_{3/m_1} \Rightarrow t\!\!t_{/m_2}}$$

$$\frac{t_{1/m_1} \Rightarrow \mathsf{true}_{/m_2} \quad t_{3/m_2} \Rightarrow t\!\!t_{/m_3} \quad t_{2/m_3} \Rightarrow t\!\!t_{/m_4} \quad \mathsf{for}\, t_1\, t_2\, t_{3/m_4} \Rightarrow t\!\!t_{/m_5}}{\mathsf{for}\, t_1\, t_2\, t_{3/m_1} \Rightarrow t\!\!t_{/m_5}}$$

$$\frac{t_{1/m_1} \Rightarrow^{\mathsf{exn}}{}_{/m_2}}{\mathsf{for}\, t_1\, t_2\, t_{3/m_1} \Rightarrow^{\mathsf{exn}}{}_{/m_2}} \qquad\qquad \frac{t_{1/m_1} \Rightarrow^{\infty}}{\mathsf{for}\, t_1\, t_2\, t_{3/m_1} \Rightarrow^{\infty}} \, \text{co}$$

$$\frac{t_{1/m_1} \Rightarrow \mathsf{true}_{/m_2} \quad t_{3/m_2} \Rightarrow^{\mathsf{exn}}{}_{/m_3}}{\mathsf{for}\, t_1\, t_2\, t_{3/m_1} \Rightarrow^{\mathsf{exn}}{}_{/m_3}} \qquad \frac{t_{1/m_1} \Rightarrow \mathsf{true}_{/m_2} \quad t_{3/m_2} \Rightarrow^{\infty}}{\mathsf{for}\, t_1\, t_2\, t_{3/m_1} \Rightarrow^{\infty}} \, \text{co}$$

$$\frac{\begin{array}{c} t_{1/m_1} \Rightarrow \mathsf{true}_{/m_2} \quad t_{3/m_2} \Rightarrow t\!\!t_{/m_3} \\ t_{2/m_3} \Rightarrow^{\mathsf{exn}}{}_{/m_4} \end{array}}{\mathsf{for}\, t_1\, t_2\, t_{3/m_1} \Rightarrow^{\mathsf{exn}}{}_{/m_4}} \qquad \frac{\begin{array}{c} t_{1/m_1} \Rightarrow \mathsf{true}_{/m_2} \quad t_{3/m_2} \Rightarrow t\!\!t_{/m_3} \\ t_{2/m_3} \Rightarrow^{\infty} \end{array}}{\mathsf{for}\, t_1\, t_2\, t_{3/m_1} \Rightarrow^{\infty}} \, \text{co}$$

$$\frac{\begin{array}{c} t_{1/m_1} \Rightarrow \mathsf{true}_{/m_2} \quad t_{3/m_2} \Rightarrow t\!\!t_{/m_3} \\ t_{2/m_3} \Rightarrow t\!\!t_{/m_4} \quad \mathsf{for}\, t_1\, t_2\, t_{3/m_4} \Rightarrow^{\mathsf{exn}}{}_{/m_5} \end{array}}{\mathsf{for}\, t_1\, t_2\, t_{3/m_1} \Rightarrow^{\mathsf{exn}}{}_{/m_5}} \qquad \frac{\begin{array}{c} t_{1/m_1} \Rightarrow \mathsf{true}_{/m_2} \quad t_{3/m_2} \Rightarrow t\!\!t_{/m_3} \\ t_{2/m_3} \Rightarrow t\!\!t_{/m_4} \quad \mathsf{for}\, t_1\, t_2\, t_{3/m_4} \Rightarrow^{\infty} \end{array}}{\mathsf{for}\, t_1\, t_2\, t_{3/m_1} \Rightarrow^{\infty}} \, \text{co}$$

Fig. 1. Big-step rules for C loops of the form "for (; t_1 ; t_2) { t_3 }", written "for $t_1\, t_2\, t_3$"

The four rules at the bottom-left of Figure 1 describe the case of an exception being raised during the execution of the loop. These rules are expressed using another inductive judgment, written $t_{/m_1} \Rightarrow^{\mathsf{exn}}{}_{/m_2}$. They capture the fact that the exception may be triggered during the evaluation of any of the subexpressions, or during the subsequent iterations of the loop. The four rules at the bottom-right of Figure 1 describe the case of the loop diverging. These rules rely on a coinductive big-step judgment, written $t_{/m} \Rightarrow^{\infty}$ [2,8]. "Coinductive" means that a derivation tree for a judgment of the form $t_{/m} \Rightarrow^{\infty}$ may be infinite.

The amount of duplication in Figure 1 is overwhelming. There are two distinct sources of duplication. First, the rules for exceptions and the rules for divergence are extremely similar. Second, a number of evaluation premises are repeated across many of the rules. For example, even if we ignore the rules for divergence, the premise $t_{1/m_1} \Rightarrow \mathsf{true}_{/m_2}$ appears 4 times. Similarly, $t_{3/m_2} \Rightarrow t\!\!t_{/m_3}$ appears 3 times and $t_{2/m_3} \Rightarrow t\!\!t_{/m_4}$ appears 2 times. This pattern is quite typical in big-step semantics for constructs with several subterms.

One may wonder whether the rules from Figure 1 can be factorized. The only obvious factorization consists of merging the regular evaluation judgment $(t_{/m_1} \Rightarrow v_{/m_2})$ with the judgment for exceptions $(t_{/m_1} \Rightarrow^{\mathsf{exn}}{}_{/m_2})$, using a single evaluation judgment that relates a term to a *behavior*, which consists of either a value or an exception. This factorization, quite standard in big-step semantics, here only saves one evaluation rule: the second rule from the top of Figure 1 would be merged with the rule at the bottom-left corner. It is, however, not easy to factorize the evaluation judgment with the divergence judgment, because one is inductive while the other is coinductive. Another trick sometimes used to reduce the amount of duplication is to define the semantics of a for-loop in terms of other language constructs, using the encoding "if t_1 then (t_3 ; t_2 ; for t_1 t_2 t_3) else tt". Yet, this approach does not support *break* and *continue* instructions, so it cannot be applied in general. In summary, just to define the semantics of for-loops, even if we merge the two inductive judgments, we need at least 9 evaluation rules with a total number of 21 evaluation premises. We will show how to achieve a much more concise definition, using only 6 rules with 7 evaluation premises.

With the *pretty-big-step semantics* introduced in this paper, we are able to eliminate the two sources of duplication associated with big-step definitions. First, we eliminate the duplication of premises. To that end, we break down evaluation rules into simpler rules, each of them evaluating at most one subterm. This transformation introduces a number of intermediate terms and increases the number of evaluation rules, but it eliminates the need for duplicating premises across several rules. Overall, the size of the formal definitions usually decreases.

Second, we set up the set of evaluation rules in such a way that it characterizes either *terminating* executions or *diverging* executions, depending on whether we consider an *inductive* or a *coinductive* interpretation for this set of rules. In contrast to Cousot and Cousot's bi-inductive semantics [3,4], which are based on the construction of a least fixed point of the set of evaluation rules with respect to a non-standard ordering that corresponds neither to induction nor coinduction, our definitions are based on the standard notions of induction and coinduction (as provided, e.g., by Coq).

Furthermore, we show that, when adding traces to the pretty-big-semantics, the coinductive judgment suffices to describe both terminating and diverging executions. Our definitions syntactically distinguish finite traces from infinite traces. This approach leads to rules that are, in our opinion, simpler to understand and easier to reason about than rules involving possibly-infinite traces (coinductive lists), as used by Nakata and Uustalu [10] and Danielsson [5].

In theory, the fact that we are able to capture the semantics through a single judgment means that we should be able to establish, through a *single* proof, that a program transformation correctly preserves both terminating and diverging behaviors. Unfortunately, the guard condition implemented in existing proof assistants such as Coq or Agda prevents us from conducting such reasoning. Workarounds are possible, but the encodings involved are so tedious that it would not be realistic to use them in practice. For this reason, we have to postpone the construction of proofs based on pretty-big-step trace semantics.

In this paper, we also investigate the formalization of type soundness proofs. Interestingly, the pretty-big-step semantics allows for a *generic error rule* that replaces all the error rules that are typically added manually to the semantics. This generic error rule is based on a *progress judgment*, whose definition can be derived in a simple and very systematic way from the set of evaluation rules.

To demonstrate the ability of the pretty-big-step to accommodate realistic languages, we formalized a large fragment of Caml Light. Compared with the big-step semantics, the pretty-big-step semantics has a size reduced by about 40%.

This paper is organized as follows. In §2, we explain how to turn a big-step semantics into its pretty-big-step counterpart. In §3, we discuss error rules and type soundness proofs. In §4, we show how to extend the semantics with traces. In §5, we explain how to handle more advanced language constructs and report on the formalization of core-Caml. We then discuss related work (§6), and conclude (§7). All the definitions and proofs from this paper have been formalized in Coq and put online at: `http://arthur.chargueraud.org/research/2012/pretty`.

2 Pretty-Big-Step Semantics

2.1 Decomposition of Big-Step Rules

We present the pretty-big-step semantics using the call-by-value λ-calculus. The grammar of values and terms are as follows.

$$v := \mathsf{int}\, n \mid \mathsf{abs}\, x\, t \qquad\qquad t := \mathsf{val}\, v \mid \mathsf{var}\, x \mid \mathsf{app}\, t\, t$$

Thereafter, we leave the constructor val implicit, writing simply v instead of $\mathsf{val}\, v$ whenever a term is expected. (In Coq, we register val as a coercion.) We recall the definition of the standard big-step judgment, which is written $t \Rightarrow v$.

$$\frac{}{v \Rightarrow v} \qquad\qquad \frac{t_1 \Rightarrow \mathsf{abs}\, x\, t \qquad t_2 \Rightarrow v \qquad [x \to v]\, t \Rightarrow v'}{\mathsf{app}\, t_1\, t_2 \Rightarrow v'}$$

The rules of the pretty-big-step semantics are obtained by decomposing the rules above into more atomic rules that consider the evaluation of at most one subterm at a time. A first attempt at such a decomposition consists of replacing the evaluation rule for applications with the following three rules.

$$\frac{t_1 \Rightarrow v_1 \quad \mathsf{app}\, v_1\, t_2 \Rightarrow v'}{\mathsf{app}\, t_1\, t_2 \Rightarrow v'} \quad \frac{t_2 \Rightarrow v_2 \quad \mathsf{app}\, v_1\, v_2 \Rightarrow v'}{\mathsf{app}\, v_1\, t_2 \Rightarrow v'} \quad \frac{[x \to v]\, t \Rightarrow v'}{\mathsf{app}\, (\mathsf{abs}\, x\, t)\, v \Rightarrow v'}$$

These rules, without further constraints, suffer from an overlapping problem. For example, consider the term $\mathsf{app}\, v_1\, t_2$. This term is subject to the application of the second rule, which evaluates t_2. However, it is also subject to application of the first rule, whose first premise would reduce v_1 to itself and whose second premise would be identical to the conclusion of the rule. The fact that two different rules can be applied to a same term means that the evaluation judgment is not syntax-directed and thus not very convenient to work with. Even worse, the fact that an evaluation rule can be applied without making progress is problematic when considering a coinductive interpretation of the evaluation rules; typically, one could prove, by applying the first reduction rule infinitely many times, that any term of the form $\mathsf{app}\, v_1\, t_2$ diverges.

Cousot and Cousot [3,4], who use a similar decomposition of the big-step rules· as shown above, prevent the overlapping of the rules by adding side-conditions. For example, the evaluation rule that reduces $\mathsf{app}\, t_1\, t_2$ has a side-condition enforcing t_1 to not be already a value. However, such side-conditions are numerous and they need to be discharged in formal proofs.

Instead of using side-conditions, we ensure that the three evaluation rules introduced above are always applied one after the other by introducing *intermediate terms*, whose grammar is shown below. Observe that intermediate terms are not defined as an extension of the grammar of regular terms, but as a new grammar that embeds that of regular terms. This presentation avoids polluting the syntax of source terms with purely-semantical entities.

$$e := \mathsf{trm}\, t \mid \mathsf{app1}\, v\, t \mid \mathsf{app2}\, v\, v$$

We extend the evaluation judgment to intermediate terms, defining an inductive judgment of the form $e \Downarrow v$. In the particular case where e describes a regular term, the judgment takes the form $(\mathsf{trm}\, t) \Downarrow v$. Thereafter, we leave the constructor trm implicit and thus simply write $t \Downarrow v$. The predicate $e \Downarrow v$ is defined inductively by the rules shown below. The evaluation of an application $\mathsf{app}\, t_1\, t_2$ takes three step. First, we reduce t_1 into v_1 and obtain the term $\mathsf{app1}\, v_1\, t_2$. Second, we reduce t_2 into v_2 and obtain the term $\mathsf{app2}\, v_1\, v_2$. Third, assuming v_1 to be of the form $\mathsf{abs}\, x\, t$, we proceed to the β-reduction and evaluate $[x \to v]\, t$ in order to obtain some final result v'.

$$\frac{}{v \Downarrow v} \qquad\qquad \frac{t_1 \Downarrow v_1 \qquad \mathsf{app1}\, v_1\, t_2 \Downarrow v'}{\mathsf{app}\, t_1\, t_2 \Downarrow v'}$$

$$\frac{t_2 \Downarrow v_2 \qquad \mathsf{app2}\, v_1\, v_2 \Downarrow v'}{\mathsf{app1}\, v_1\, t_2 \Downarrow v'} \qquad\qquad \frac{[x \to v]\, t \Downarrow v'}{\mathsf{app2}\, (\mathsf{abs}\, x\, t)\, v \Downarrow v'}$$

The definitions above provide an adequate reformulation of the big-step semantics by which complex rules have been decomposed into a larger number of more elementary rules. This decomposition avoids the duplication of premises when adding support for exceptions and divergence. Observe that the intermediate terms introduced in the process correspond to the intermediate states of an interpreter. For example, the form $\mathsf{app1}\, v_1\, t_2$ corresponds to the state of the interpreter after the evaluation of the first let-binding in the code "$\mathsf{let}\, v_1 = \mathsf{eval}\, t_1\, \mathsf{in}\, \mathsf{let}\, v_2 = \mathsf{eval}\, t_2\, \mathsf{in}\, \mathsf{let}\, (\mathsf{abs}\, x\, t) = v_1\, \mathsf{in}\, \mathsf{eval}\, ([x \to v_2]\, t)$".

2.2   Treatment of Exceptions

We now extend the source language with value-carrying exceptions and exception handlers. The term $\mathsf{raise}\, t$ builds an exception and throws it. The term $\mathsf{try}\, t_1\, t_2$ is an exception handler with body t_1 and handler t_2. Its semantics is as follows. If t_1 produces a regular value, then $\mathsf{try}\, t_1\, t_2$ returns this value. However, if t_1 raises an exception carrying a value v_1, then $\mathsf{try}\, t_1\, t_2$ reduces to $\mathsf{app}\, t_2\, v_1$.

To describe the fact that a term can produce either a regular value or an exception carrying a value, the evaluation judgment is generalized to the form $e \Downarrow b$, where b denotes a *behavior*, built according to the grammar below.

$$b := \mathsf{ret}\, v \mid \mathsf{exn}\, v$$

Because we generalize the form of the judgment, we also need to generalize the form of the intermediate terms. For example, consider the evaluation of an application $\mathsf{app}\, t_1\, t_2$. First, we evaluate t_1 into a behavior b_1. We then obtain the intermediate term $\mathsf{app1}\, b_1\, t_2$. To evaluate this later term, we need to distinguish two cases. On the one hand, if b_1 is of the form $\mathsf{ret}\, v_1$, then we should evaluate the second branch t_2. On the other hand, if b_1 is of the form $\mathsf{exn}\, v$, then we should directly propagate $\mathsf{exn}\, v$. The updated grammar of intermediate terms, augmented with intermediate forms for raise and try, is as follows.

$$e := \mathsf{trm}\, t \mid \mathsf{app1}\, b\, t \mid \mathsf{app2}\, v\, b \mid \mathsf{raise1}\, b \mid \mathsf{try1}\, b\, t$$

The definition of $e \Downarrow b$ follows a similar pattern as previously. It now also includes rules for propagating exceptions. For example, $\mathsf{app1}\, (\mathsf{exn}\, v)\, t$ evaluates to $\mathsf{exn}\, v$. Moreover, the definition includes rules for evaluating raise and try. For example, to evaluate $\mathsf{try}\, t_1\, t_2$, we first evaluate t_1 into a behavior b_1, and then we evaluate the term $\mathsf{try1}\, b_1\, t_2$. In the rules shown below, the constructor ret is left implicit.

$$\frac{}{v \Downarrow v} \qquad \frac{t_1 \Downarrow b_1 \qquad \mathsf{app1}\, b_1\, t_2 \Downarrow b}{\mathsf{app}\, t_1\, t_2 \Downarrow b} \qquad \frac{}{\mathsf{app1}\, (\mathsf{exn}\, v)\, t \Downarrow \mathsf{exn}\, v}$$

$$\frac{t_2 \Downarrow b_2 \qquad \mathsf{app2}\, v_1\, b_2 \Downarrow b}{\mathsf{app1}\, v_1\, t_2 \Downarrow b} \qquad \frac{}{\mathsf{app2}\, v\, (\mathsf{exn}\, v) \Downarrow \mathsf{exn}\, v} \qquad \frac{[x \to v]\, t \Downarrow b}{\mathsf{app2}\, (\mathsf{abs}\, x\, t)\, v \Downarrow b}$$

$$\frac{t \Downarrow b_1 \qquad \mathsf{raise1}\, b_1 \Downarrow b}{\mathsf{raise}\, t \Downarrow b} \qquad \frac{}{\mathsf{raise1}\, v \Downarrow \mathsf{exn}\, v} \qquad \frac{}{\mathsf{raise1}\, (\mathsf{exn}\, v) \Downarrow \mathsf{exn}\, v}$$

$$\frac{t_1 \Downarrow b_1 \qquad \mathsf{try1}\, b_1\, t_2 \Downarrow b}{\mathsf{try}\, t_1\, t_2 \Downarrow b} \qquad \frac{}{\mathsf{try1}\, v\, t \Downarrow v} \qquad \frac{\mathsf{app}\, t\, v \Downarrow b}{\mathsf{try1}\, (\mathsf{exn}\, v)\, t \Downarrow b}$$

2.3 Treatment of Divergence

The above set of rules only describes terminating evaluations. To specify diverging evaluations, we are going to generalize the grammar of behaviors and to consider a coinductive interpretation of the same set of rules as that describing terminating evaluations.

First, we introduce the notion of *outcome*: the outcome of an execution is either to terminate on a behavior b (i.e., to return a value or an exception), or to diverge. We explicitly materialize the divergence outcome with a constant, called div. An outcome, written o, is thus described as follows: $o := \mathsf{ter}\, b \mid \mathsf{div}$.

We update accordingly the grammar of intermediate terms. For example, consider the evaluation of an application $\mathsf{app}\, t_1\, t_2$. First, we evaluate t_1 into some outcome o_1 (a value, an exception, or divergence). We then consider the term $\mathsf{app1}\, o_1\, t_2$, whose evaluation depends on o_1. If o_1 describes a value v_1, we can continue as usual by evaluating t_2. However, if o_1 describes an exception or the constant div, then the term $\mathsf{app1}\, o_1\, t_2$ directly propagates the outcome o_1.

$$b := \mathsf{ret}\, v \mid \mathsf{exn}\, v \qquad o := \mathsf{ter}\, b \mid \mathsf{div} \qquad e := \mathsf{trm}\, t \mid \mathsf{app1}\, o\, t \mid \mathsf{app2}\, v\, o \mid \mathsf{raise1}\, o \mid \mathsf{try1}\, o\, t$$

$$\frac{}{\mathsf{abort}\,(\mathsf{exn}\, v)} \qquad \frac{}{\mathsf{abort}\,\mathsf{div}} \qquad \frac{}{v \Downarrow v} \qquad \frac{t_1 \Downarrow o_1 \qquad \mathsf{app1}\, o_1\, t_2 \Downarrow o}{\mathsf{app}\, t_1\, t_2 \Downarrow o}$$

$$\frac{\mathsf{abort}\, o}{\mathsf{app1}\, o\, t \Downarrow o} \qquad \frac{t_2 \Downarrow o_2 \qquad \mathsf{app2}\, v_1\, o_2 \Downarrow o}{\mathsf{app1}\, v_1\, t_2 \Downarrow o} \qquad \frac{\mathsf{abort}\, o}{\mathsf{app2}\, v\, o \Downarrow o} \qquad \frac{[x \to v]\, t \Downarrow o}{\mathsf{app2}\,(\mathsf{abs}\, x\, t)\, v \Downarrow o}$$

$$\frac{t \Downarrow o_1 \qquad \mathsf{raise1}\, o_1 \Downarrow o}{\mathsf{raise}\, t \Downarrow o} \qquad \frac{\mathsf{abort}\, o}{\mathsf{raise1}\, o \Downarrow o} \qquad \frac{}{\mathsf{raise1}\, v \Downarrow \mathsf{exn}\, v} \qquad \frac{t_1 \Downarrow o_1 \qquad \mathsf{try1}\, o_1\, t_2 \Downarrow o}{\mathsf{try}\, t_1\, t_2 \Downarrow o}$$

$$\frac{}{\mathsf{try1}\, v\, t \Downarrow v} \qquad \frac{\mathsf{app}\, t\, v \Downarrow o}{\mathsf{try1}\,(\mathsf{exn}\, v)\, t \Downarrow o} \qquad \frac{\mathsf{abort}\, o \qquad \forall v.\, o \neq \mathsf{exn}\, v}{\mathsf{try1}\, o\, t \Downarrow o}$$

Fig. 2. Pretty-big-step semantics: $e \Downarrow o$ (inductive) and $e \Downarrow^{co} \mathsf{div}$ (coinductive), with the constructors val, trm, ret and ter left implicit in the rules

To capture the fact that $\mathsf{app1}\, o_1\, t_2$ returns o_1 both when o_1 describes divergence or an exception, we use an auxiliary predicate, called abort. The predicate $\mathsf{abort}\, o_1$ asserts that o_1 "breaks the normal control flow" in the sense that o_1 is either of the form $\mathsf{exn}\, v$ or is equal to div. We are then able to factorize the rules propagating exceptions and divergence into a single *abort rule*, as shown below.

$$\frac{\mathsf{abort}\, o_1}{\mathsf{app1}\, o_1\, t_2 \Downarrow o_1}$$

For describing terminating evaluations, we use an inductive judgment of the form $e \Downarrow o$. The particular form $e \Downarrow \mathsf{ter}\, b$, simply written $e \Downarrow b$, corresponds to the same evaluation judgment as that defined previously. For describing diverging evaluations, we use a *coevaluation* judgment, written $e \Downarrow^{co} o$, which is defined by taking a coinductive interpretation of the same set of rules as that defining the inductive judgment $e \Downarrow o$. The particular form $e \Downarrow^{co} \mathsf{div}$ asserts that the execution of e diverges.

The complete set of rules defining both $e \Downarrow o$ and $e \Downarrow^{co} o$ appears in Figure 2. One novelty is the last rule, which is used to propagate divergence out of exception handlers. The rule captures the fact that $\mathsf{try1}\,\mathsf{div}\, t$ produces the outcome div, but it is stated in a potentially more general way that will be useful when adding errors as a new kind of behavior. Remark: in Coq, we currently need to copy-paste all the rules in order to build one inductive definition and one coinductive definition, however it would be easy to implement a Coq plug-in to automatically generate the coinductive definition from the inductive one.

2.4 Properties of the Judgments

While we are ultimately only interested in the forms $e \Downarrow b$ and $e \Downarrow^{co} \mathsf{div}$, our definitions syntactically allow for the forms $e \Downarrow \mathsf{div}$ and $e \Downarrow^{co} b$. It is worth clarifying their interpretation. For the former, the situation is quite simple: the form $e \Downarrow$ div is derivable only when e is an intermediate term that carries a div. In particular, $t \Downarrow$ div is never derivable.

Lemma 1. *For any term* t, $\quad t \Downarrow div \rightarrow False$.

The interpretation of the form $e \Downarrow^{co} b$ is more subtle. On the one hand, the coinductive judgment contains the inductive one, because any finite derivation is also a potentially-infinite derivation. It is trivial to prove the following lemma.

Lemma 2. *For any term e and outcome o,* $\quad e \Downarrow o \rightarrow e \Downarrow^{co} o$.

On the other hand, due to coinduction, it is sometimes possible to derive $e \Downarrow^{co} b$ even when e diverges. For example, consider $\omega = $ app $\delta\,\delta$, where $\delta = $ abs x (app $x\,x$); one can prove by coinduction that, for any outcome o, the relation $\omega \Downarrow^{co} o$ holds. Nevertheless, the coevaluation judgment is relatively well-behaved, in the sense that if $e \Downarrow^{co} o$ holds, then either e terminates on some behavior b, or e diverges. This property is formalized in the next lemma.

Lemma 3. *For any term e and outcome o,* $\quad e \Downarrow^{co} o \rightarrow e \Downarrow o \lor e \Downarrow^{co} div$.

We have proved in Coq that the pretty-big-step semantics shown in Figure 2 yields an operational semantics adequate with respect to the standard big-step evaluation judgment for terminating programs ($t \Rightarrow b$) and with respect to the coinductive big-step evaluation judgment ($t \Rightarrow^{\infty}$) introduced by Leroy and Grall [8,9] for diverging programs. (The proof requires the excluded middle.)

Theorem 1 (Equivalence with big-step semantics). *For any term t, and for any behavior b (describing either a value or an exception),*

$$t \Downarrow b \text{ if and only if } t \Rightarrow b \qquad \text{and} \qquad t \Downarrow^{co} div \text{ if and only if } t \Rightarrow^{\infty}.$$

All the results presented so far can be generalized to non-deterministic semantics. In the particular case of a deterministic semantics, such as our call-by-value λ-calculus, we can express the determinacy property as follows.

Lemma 4 (Determinacy). $\quad \forall e o_1 o_2. \; e \Downarrow o_1 \land e \Downarrow^{co} o_2 \rightarrow o_1 = o_2$

As corollaries, we can prove that if a given term e evaluates to a behavior o_1, then it cannot evaluate to a different behavior o_2 and it cannot diverge.

3   Error Rules and Type Soundness Proofs

3.1   Explicit Error Rules

When considering a deterministic language, one can express the type soundness theorem in the form "if a term is well-typed, then it either terminates or diverges". However, for a non-deterministic language, such a statement does not ensure soundness, because a term could execute safely in some execution but get stuck in other executions. For a non-deterministic big-step semantics, the traditional approach to proving type soundness consists of adding explicit *error rules* to the semantics, and then proving a theorem of the form "if a term is well-typed, then it cannot evaluate to an error".

Adding error rules to a pretty-big-step semantics turns out to be much easier than for a big-step semantics, because we are able to reuse the abort rules for propagating errors to the top level. To describe stuck terms in our language, it suffices to add a behavior err, to state that it satisfies the predicate abort, and to add two error rules, one for variables and one for stuck applications.

$$b := \ldots \mid \text{err} \qquad \frac{}{\text{abort err}} \qquad \frac{}{\text{var } x \Downarrow \text{err}} \qquad \frac{\forall x t.\ v_1 \neq \text{abs } x\, t}{\text{app2 } v_1\, v_2 \Downarrow \text{err}}$$

3.2   The Generic Error Rule

A classic problem with the introduction of explicit error rules for proving type soundness is that the theorem can be compromised if an error rule is missing. Indeed, if we remove a few error rules, then it makes it *easier* to prove that "if a term is well-typed, then it cannot evaluate to an error". So, the omission of an error rule may hide a flaw in the type system that we want to prove sound.

For a language as simple as the λ-calculus, the error rules are few. However, for a more realistic language, they can be numerous. In such a case, it becomes fairly easy to forget a rule and thereby compromise the adequacy of the type soundness theorem. One could hope to be able to prove (say, in Coq) that a semantics is not missing any error rules. Yet, as far as we know, there is no way of formally stating this property. (The formulation "every term either evaluates to a value or to an error, or diverges" is not appropriate, due to non-determinism.)

In what follows, we explain how a pretty-big-step semantics can be equipped with a *generic error rule*, which directly captures the intuition that "a term should evaluate to an error if no other evaluation rule can be applied". Remark: this intuition was at the source of the work by Gunter and Rémy [6] on *partial proof semantics*, which consists of a specialized proof theory that allows describing derivation trees with exactly one unproved leaf; our approach at handling error rules in a generic manner can be viewed as a realization of Gunter and Rémy's idea of partial proofs within a standard proof theory.

The generic error rule is defined in terms of the *progress judgment*, written $e \downarrow$, which asserts that there exists at least one pretty-big-step evaluation rule whose conclusion matches the term e. The rules defining the progress judgment can be derived in a systematic manner from the pretty-big-step evaluation rules, as described next. An evaluation rule has a conclusion of the form $e \Downarrow o$, a number of evaluation premises and some other premises. The corresponding *progress rule* is obtained by changing the conclusion to $e \downarrow$ (i.e., dropping the outcome o) and by removing all the evaluation premises. The progress judgment associated with the semantics described in Figure 2 is defined in Figure 3.

Then, the generic error rule, shown below, simply asserts that "if a term e cannot make progress ($e \downarrow$ is false) then e should evaluate to an error".

$$\frac{\neg\ (e \downarrow)}{e \Downarrow \text{err}}$$

$$\frac{}{v \downarrow} \qquad \frac{}{\mathsf{app}\, t_1\, t_2 \downarrow} \qquad \frac{\mathsf{abort}\, o}{\mathsf{app1}\, o\, t_2 \downarrow} \qquad \frac{}{\mathsf{app1}\, v_1\, t_2 \downarrow} \qquad \frac{\mathsf{abort}\, o}{\mathsf{app2}\, v\, o \downarrow}$$

$$\frac{}{\mathsf{app2}\,(\mathsf{abs}\, x\, t)\, v \downarrow} \qquad \frac{}{\mathsf{raise}\, t \downarrow} \qquad \frac{\mathsf{abort}\, o}{\mathsf{raise1}\, o \downarrow} \qquad \frac{}{\mathsf{raise1}\, v \downarrow} \qquad \frac{}{\mathsf{try}\, t_1\, t_2 \downarrow}$$

$$\frac{}{\mathsf{try1}\, v\, t \downarrow} \qquad \frac{}{\mathsf{try1}\,(\mathsf{exn}\, v)\, t \downarrow} \qquad \frac{\mathsf{abort}\, o \qquad \forall v.\, o \neq \mathsf{exn}\, v}{\mathsf{try1}\, o\, t \downarrow}$$

Fig. 3. Progress judgment

We have proved in Coq that using the generic error rule yields evaluation and coevaluation judgments that are equivalent to those obtained with the traditional approach to introducing explicit error rules.

There are two main benefits to using the generic error rule. First, deriving the progress rules from the evaluation rules is easier than deriving explicit error rules. Indeed, instead of having to find out which rules are needed to complete the semantics, we can apply to each of the evaluation rules a very systematic process —so systematic that we believe it could be automated by a Coq plug-in. Second, forgetting a progress rule does not compromise the type soundness theorem. Indeed, omitting a progress rule makes it *easier* to prove that a term evaluates to an error, and therefore makes it *harder* (if not impossible) to prove the statement of the type soundness theorem. To be fair, it should be acknowledged that adding arbitrary progress rules can compromise type soundness. That said, we believe that it is much more unlikely for a researcher to add arbitrary progress rules than to omit a few legitimate rules.

3.3 Type Soundness Proofs

To give an example of a type soundness proof, we equip our λ-calculus with simple types. For simplicity, we enforce exceptions to carry only values of type int. A source program can be typed using the standard typing judgment, of the form $E \vdash t : T$. We write $\vdash t : T$ when the typing context E is empty. The typing rules for terms are standard, so we do not show them.

To prove type soundness, we first need to consider a typing judgment for intermediate terms, written $\vdash e : T$, and another one for outcomes, written $\vdash o : T$. The proposition $\vdash o : T$ asserts that the outcome o describes either a value of type T, or an exception carrying a value of type int, or the outcome div. Note that err, the error outcome, is never well-typed. The rules defining the new typing judgments appear in Figure 4. The type soundness theorem states that "if a closed term is well-typed, then it cannot evaluate to an error".

Theorem 2 (Type soundness). *For any t and T,* $\vdash t : T \;\rightarrow\; \neg\, t \Downarrow err$.

The proof is conducted by induction on the preservation property: $(e \Downarrow o) \rightarrow (\vdash e : T) \rightarrow (\vdash o : T)$. To see why the above proposition implies the type

$$\frac{\vdash v \,:\, T}{\vdash \mathsf{ret}\, v \,:\, T} \qquad \frac{\vdash v \,:\, \mathsf{int}}{\vdash \mathsf{exn}\, v \,:\, T} \qquad \frac{}{\vdash \mathsf{div} \,:\, T} \qquad \frac{\vdash t \,:\, T}{\vdash \mathsf{trm}\, t \,:\, T} \qquad \frac{\vdash o \,:\, S \to T \quad \vdash t \,:\, S}{\vdash \mathsf{appl}\, o\, t \,:\, T}$$

$$\frac{\vdash v \,:\, S \to T \quad \vdash o \,:\, S}{\vdash \mathsf{app2}\, v\, o \,:\, T} \qquad \frac{\vdash o \,:\, \mathsf{int}}{\vdash \mathsf{raisel}\, o \,:\, T} \qquad \frac{\vdash o \,:\, T \quad \vdash t \,:\, \mathsf{int} \to T}{\vdash \mathsf{tryl}\, o\, t \,:\, T}$$

Fig. 4. Typing rules for outcomes and intermediate terms

soundness theorem, it suffices to instantiate e with t, instantiate o with err, and observe that $\vdash$ err $:\, T$ is equivalent to False. There are two particularly interesting cases in the proof. First, when the evaluation rule is an abort rule, we need to exploit the fact that a well-typed outcome satisfying abort admits any type. Formally: $(\vdash o \,:\, T) \wedge (\mathsf{abort}\, o) \to (\vdash o \,:\, T')$. Second, when the evaluation rule is the error rule, we need to establish that if a term is well-typed then it must satisfy the progress judgment. Formally: $(\vdash e \,:\, T) \to (e \downarrow)$.

All the other proof cases are straightforward. Compared with the big-step semantics, the pretty-big-step semantics leads to a type soundness proof that involves a slightly larger number of cases, however these proof cases are typically simpler, due to the fact that the evaluation rules have at most two premises. In practice, we have found that having simpler proof cases makes the proofs easier to complete and easier to automate.

In summary, the pretty-big-step semantics, by reusing its abort rules, reduces the amount of work needed for adding error behaviors. It also allows for a generic error rule that makes it faster and less error-prone to add all the error rules. Moreover, even though it requires additional typing rules for intermediate terms, it leads to proofs that involve cases that are simpler and easier to automate.

4   Traces

Traces are typically used to record the interactions of a program with its environment, for example i/o operations. In what follows, we show how to extend the pretty-big-step evaluation rules with traces. A trace describes a sequence of *effects*. Here, an effect, written α, describes a read operation $(\mathsf{in}\, n)$, or a write operation $(\mathsf{out}\, n)$, or the absence of an operation (ϵ). We use the ϵ effect to make the evaluation rules *productive* with respect to traces. Productivity is needed in particular to ensure that a diverging program that does not perform any i/o cannot be associated with arbitrary traces. A trace can be finite or infinite. A finite trace, written τ, consists of a list of effects. An infinite trace, written σ, consists of a stream of effects (i.e., an infinite list). The outcome of a program can be either "termination on a value with a finite trace" or "divergence with an infinite trace". These definitions are summarized below.

$$\alpha := \epsilon \mid \mathsf{in}\, n \mid \mathsf{out}\, n \qquad o := \mathsf{ter}\, \tau\, b \mid \mathsf{div}\, \sigma \qquad (\tau \text{ list of } \alpha, \text{ and } \sigma \text{ stream of } \alpha)$$

In several evaluation rules, we need to append a finite trace to the head of a finite or an infinite trace. We write $\tau \cdot \tau'$ and $\tau \cdot \sigma$ the corresponding concatenation

$$\frac{}{\text{abort } (\text{ter } \tau \, (\text{exn } v))} \qquad \frac{}{\text{abort } (\text{div } \sigma)}$$

$$\frac{}{v \Downarrow \text{ter } [\epsilon] \, v} \qquad \frac{t_1 \Downarrow o_1 \quad \text{app1} \, o_1 \, t_2 \Downarrow o}{\text{app } t_1 \, t_2 \Downarrow [\epsilon] \cdot o} \qquad \frac{\text{abort } o}{\text{app1} \, o \, t \Downarrow [\epsilon] \cdot o}$$

$$\frac{t_2 \Downarrow o_2 \quad \text{app2} \, v_1 \, o_2 \Downarrow o}{\text{app1} \, (\text{ter } \tau \, v_1) \, t_2 \Downarrow [\epsilon] \cdot \tau \cdot o} \qquad \frac{\text{abort } o}{\text{app2} \, v \, o \Downarrow [\epsilon] \cdot o} \qquad \frac{[x \to v] \, t \Downarrow o}{\text{app2} \, (\text{abs } x \, t) \, (\text{ter } \tau \, v) \Downarrow [\epsilon] \cdot \tau \cdot o}$$

$$\frac{t \Downarrow o_1 \quad \text{read1} \, o_1 \Downarrow o}{\text{read } t \Downarrow [\epsilon] \cdot o} \qquad \frac{\text{abort } o}{\text{read1} \, o \Downarrow [\epsilon] \cdot o} \qquad \frac{}{\text{read1} \, (\text{ter } \tau \, tt) \Downarrow \text{ter } ([\epsilon] \cdot \tau \cdot [\text{in } n]) \, n}$$

$$\frac{t \Downarrow o_1 \quad \text{write1} \, o_1 \Downarrow o}{\text{write } t \Downarrow [\epsilon] \cdot o} \qquad \frac{\text{abort } o}{\text{write1} \, o \Downarrow [\epsilon] \cdot o} \qquad \frac{}{\text{write1} \, (\text{ter } \tau \, n) \Downarrow \text{ter } ([\epsilon] \cdot \tau \cdot [\text{out } n]) \, tt}$$

Fig. 5. Pretty-big-step semantics with traces

operations. By extension, we define an operation, written $\tau \cdot o$, to concatenate a finite trace τ to the trace contained in the outcome o. The updated definition for abort and the evaluation rules appear in Figure 5. ($[\cdot]$ denotes a singleton list.)

With traces, the inductive interpretation of the rules is no longer needed because, thanks to the productivity of the rules with respect to the trace, a diverging expression cannot coevaluate to a terminating behavior. We have:

Lemma 5. *For any finite trace* τ, $\quad (e \Downarrow^{co} \text{ter } \tau \, v) \; \Leftrightarrow \; (e \Downarrow \text{ter } \tau \, v)$.

An important consequence of Lemma 5 is that, when the semantics includes traces, we do not need the inductive judgment $(e \Downarrow o)$ anymore. In theory, all our reasoning can be conducted using solely the coevaluation judgment. In particular, we should be able to prove a program transformation correct with respect to both terminating and diverging programs through a single coinductive proof. In practice, though, coinductive reasoning in proof assistants such as Coq or Agda remains problematic because they only accept statement of theorems whose conclusion is a coinductive judgment and where all applications of the coinduction hypothesis are guarded by constructors. As soon as we fall out of this basic pattern, we need to resort to heavy encodings in order to transform the statement and the proof in the appropriate form.

The verification of program transformations, one important applications of formal semantics, almost systematically departs from the basic pattern. Their correctness proof typically relies on a simulation diagram establishing that any behavior exhibited by the compiled code is indeed a behavior of the original code. Consider for example a source-to-source translation, written $[\![\cdot]\!]$. Its correctness would typically be captured by a statement of the form $([\![t]\!] \Downarrow^{co} o) \to \exists o'. (o' \approx o) \wedge (t \Downarrow^{co} o')$, where $o' \approx o$ asserts that o' and o describe the same behavior and contain traces that are bisimilar up to insertion or deletion of a finite number of ϵ between every two items of the traces. (The equivalence relation $\approx$ is defined coinductively, by a single rule with premise $o \approx o'$ and with conclusion

$\epsilon^n \cdot [\alpha] \cdot o \approx \epsilon^m \cdot [\alpha] \cdot o'$.) Intuitively, such a statement could be established by coinduction, performing a case analysis on the derivation of $[\![t]\!] \Downarrow^{co} o$ and, in each case, picking the right o' to build the proof of $t \Downarrow^{co} o'$.

Unfortunately, this form of reasoning currently cannot be mechanized in Coq because the conclusion of the statement is not just a coinductive judgment; indeed, the conclusion starts with an existential quantifier and a conjunction. One possible work-around consists in defining o' as a function of o and t (this definition is non-constructive), and then proving $o' \approx o$ and $t \Downarrow^{co} o'$, through two independent proofs. These two proofs have a chance of satisfying the guard condition because they conclude on coinductive judgments. Yet, overall, the work-around described here is extremely unpleasant. First, defining the function that produces o' amounts to building the core of a proof term by hand. Second, the process requires one to go three times over the structure of the intended proof: once for the function definition, and once for each of the two coinductive proofs.

We must therefore acknowledge that, with the support for coinduction currently provided by Coq, mechanizing proofs based on pretty-big-step trace semantics appears to be unrealistic in practice. Nevertheless, we hope that further developments of proof assistants could allow us to conduct the intended reasoning without resorting to painful encodings, either by automating the generation of the encoding, or by somehow relaxing the guard condition. We should then be able to reason about both terminating and diverging programs in a single pass.

5   Scaling Up to Real Languages

So far, we have only considered a toy λ-calculus with exceptions. In this section, we explain how to set up pretty-big-step rules for more advanced programming language constructs, such as effectful operations, tuples of arbitrary arity, and C-style for loops. We also show how to handle constructs for which the order of evaluation of the subterms needs to remain deliberately unspecified.

5.1   Factorization of the Abort Evaluation Rules

The pretty-big-step semantics of a realistic language may involve a fair number of intermediate terms. For each intermediate term, we typically need to introduce an abort rule, i.e., a rule with a premise of the form abort o, to propagate exceptions, divergence and errors. Fortunately, it is possible to factorize all the abort rules using the *generic abort rule*. This rule formalizes the following intuition: if an intermediate term e is not an exception handler and if one of its arguments is an outcome o that satisfies the predicate abort, then e should directly evaluate to o. The definition of the generic abort rule relies on an auxiliary function, called getout. It is defined in such a way that getout e returns the outcome contained in e (there is at most one), except for exception handlers, which are treated specially. Formally:

$$
\begin{array}{ll}
\text{getout } (\text{appl } o\,t) \equiv \text{Some } o & \qquad \text{getout } (\text{trm } t) \;\equiv \text{None} \\
\text{getout } (\text{app2 } v\,o) \equiv \text{Some } o & \qquad \text{getout } (\text{try1 } o\,t) \equiv \text{None} \\
\text{getout } (\text{raise1 } o) \;\equiv \text{Some } o &
\end{array}
$$

The generic abort rule, shown below, replaces the three abort rules from Figure 2.

$$\frac{\text{getout}\, e = \text{Some}\, o \qquad \text{abort}\, o}{e \Downarrow o}$$

Throughout the rest of this section, when we introduce new intermediate terms, we assume the definition of getout to be extended accordingly.

5.2   Side Effects

We now extend the source language with side effects. When the evaluation of a term terminates, it produces not just a value or an exception, but also an updated memory store. We therefore update the grammar of outcomes as follows.

$$o := \text{ter}\, m\, b \mid \text{div}$$

The pretty-big-step evaluation judgment now takes the form $e_{/m} \Downarrow o$, asserting that the evaluation of the term e in the store m has o for outcome. In particular, the proposition $t_{/m} \Downarrow \text{ter}\, m'\, b$ corresponds to the traditional big-step judgment $t_{/m} \Rightarrow b_{/m'}$ and, similarly, the proposition $t_{/m} \Downarrow \text{div}$ corresponds to $t_{/m} \Rightarrow^{\infty}$. The evaluation rules are extended so as to take memory stores into account. For example, the first rules for reducing applications are as shown below. Observe that the intermediate term $\text{app1}\, o_1\, t_2$ is evaluated in the store m in which t_1 was evaluated, and not yet in the store produced by t_1. Indeed, at this point, we do not yet know whether the evaluation of t_1 terminates or diverges. In the particular case where t_1 terminates, the store produced by the evaluation of t_1 can be pulled out of the outcome o_1 and used for the evaluation of t_2.

$$\frac{t_1\,_{/m} \Downarrow o_1 \qquad \text{app1}\, o_1\, t_2\,_{/m} \Downarrow o}{\text{app}\, t_1\, t_2\,_{/m} \Downarrow o} \qquad \frac{t_2\,_{/m} \Downarrow o_2 \qquad \text{app2}\, v_1\, o_2\,_{/m} \Downarrow o}{\text{app1}\, (\text{ter}\, m\, v_1)\, t_2\,_{/m'} \Downarrow o}$$

We end this section with an example of a rule that modifies the store. Consider a term $\text{ref}\, t_1$. Its evaluation goes through an intermediate term $\text{ref1}\, o_1$. If o_1 is a value, then a memory cell is allocated at a fresh location. The updated store is then returned together with the address of the new memory cell.

$$\frac{t_1\,_{/m} \Downarrow o_1 \qquad \text{ref1}\, o_1\,_{/m} \Downarrow o}{\text{ref}\, t_1\,_{/m} \Downarrow o} \qquad \frac{l \notin \text{dom}(m)}{\text{ref1}\, (\text{ter}\, m\, v)\,_{/m'} \Downarrow \text{ter}\, (m[l \mapsto v])\, l}$$

Other rules accessing and updating the memory store follow a similar pattern.

5.3   C-Style for Loops

We now come back to the example of C-style for loops described in the introduction, revisiting the evaluation rules from Figure 1 using a pretty-big-step semantics. We introduce a single intermediate term, written "for $i\, o\, t_1\, t_2\, t_3$", where $i \in \{1, 2, 3\}$. The pretty-big-step evaluation rules, shown below, are significantly more concise than their big-step counterpart. Note that we included an abort rule, even though it would typically be covered by the generic abort rule (§5.1).

$$\frac{t_1 \,_{/m} \Downarrow o_1 \quad \text{for } 1 \, o_1 \, t_1 \, t_2 \, t_3 \,_{/m} \Downarrow o}{\text{for } t_1 \, t_2 \, t_3 \,_{/m} \Downarrow o} \qquad \frac{}{\text{for } 1 \, (\text{ret } m \, \text{false}) \, t_1 \, t_2 \, t_3 \,_{/m'} \Downarrow \text{ret } m \, \mathit{tt}}$$

$$\frac{t_3 \,_{/m} \Downarrow o_3 \quad \text{for } 2 \, o_3 \, t_1 \, t_2 \, t_3 \,_{/m} \Downarrow o}{\text{for } 1 \, (\text{ret } m \, \text{true}) \, t_1 \, t_2 \, t_3 \,_{/m'} \Downarrow o} \qquad \frac{t_2 \,_{/m} \Downarrow o_2 \quad \text{for } 3 \, o_2 \, t_1 \, t_2 \, t_3 \,_{/m} \Downarrow o}{\text{for } 2 \, (\text{ret } m \, \mathit{tt}) \, t_1 \, t_2 \, t_3 \,_{/m'} \Downarrow o}$$

$$\frac{\text{for } t_1 \, t_2 \, t_3 \,_{/m} \Downarrow o}{\text{for } 3 \, (\text{ret } m \, \mathit{tt}) \, t_1 \, t_2 \, t_3 \,_{/m'} \Downarrow o} \qquad \frac{\text{abort } o}{\text{for } i \, o \, t_1 \, t_2 \, t_3 \,_{/m} \Downarrow o}$$

5.4   List of Subterms

Consider a tuple expression, written $\text{tuple}\,\bar{t}$, where $\bar{t}$ denotes a list of terms of arbitrary length, and assume a left-to-right evaluation order. The semantics needs to describe the fact that if one of the subterms of the tuple raises an exception or diverge, then the remaining subterms should not be evaluated. In what follows, we describe a technique for evaluating an ordered list of subterms in a way that is not specific to tuples, so that we are able to reuse the same rules for reducing other language constructs that involve lists of subterms (e.g., records).

We introduce an intermediate term, written $\text{list1}\,\bar{t}\,\bar{v}\,K$, where $\bar{v}$ represents the list of values that have already been produced, $\bar{t}$ represents the list of terms remaining to be evaluated, and K denotes the continuation describing what term to transition to once all the subterms have been evaluated. Here, K is a logical function that takes a list of values as arguments and produces an intermediate term. In practice, K is usually a partially-applied constructor.

To evaluate $\text{tuple}\,\bar{t}$, we evaluate $\text{list1}\,\bar{t}\,\text{nil}\,(\text{tuple1})$, where the continuation tuple1 indicates that, when we get the list of values $\bar{v}$ describing the results of the terms $\bar{t}$, we should evaluate the term $\text{tuple1}\,\bar{v}$. This latter term will immediately evaluate to the value $\text{vtuple}\,\bar{v}$. The corresponding evaluation rules are:

$$\frac{\text{list1}\,\bar{t}\,\text{nil}\,(\text{tuple1}) \,_{/m} \Downarrow o}{\text{tuple}\,\bar{t}\,_{/m} \Downarrow o} \qquad \frac{}{\text{tuple1}\,\bar{v}\,_{/m} \Downarrow \text{ter } m \, (\text{vtuple}\,\bar{v})}$$

It remains to describe the rules involved in the evaluation of $\text{list1}\,\bar{t}\,\bar{v}\,K$. If $\bar{t}$ is empty, we apply (in the logic) the continuation K to $\bar{v}$ and obtain the term from which to continue the evaluation. Otherwise, $\bar{t}$ is of the form $t_1 :: \bar{t}$. In this case, we evaluate the head term t_1, obtaining some outcome o, and we then evaluate the term $\text{list2}\,o\,\bar{t}\,\bar{v}\,K$. If o corresponds to a value, we can save this value at the tail of the list $\bar{v}$ and continue. Otherwise, we can apply the generic abort rule to propagate this outcome directly, skipping the evaluation of the remaining terms $\bar{t}$. The corresponding evaluation rules are shown below.

$$\frac{(K\,\bar{v}) \,_{/m} \Downarrow o}{\text{list1}\,\text{nil}\,\bar{v}\,K\,_{/m} \Downarrow o} \qquad \frac{t_1 \,_{/m} \Downarrow o_1 \quad \text{list2}\,o_1\,\bar{t}\,\bar{v}\,K\,_{/m} \Downarrow o}{\text{list1}\,(t_1 :: \bar{t})\,\bar{v}\,K\,_{/m} \Downarrow o} \qquad \frac{\text{list1}\,\bar{t}\,(\bar{v} \mathbin{+\!\!+} [v_1])\,K\,_{/m} \Downarrow o}{\text{list2}\,(\text{ter } m\,v_1)\,\bar{t}\,\bar{v}\,K\,_{/m'} \Downarrow o}$$

5.5   Unspecified Order of Evaluation

Some programming languages choose to deliberately *not* specify the order of evaluation of the subterms of particular language constructs. For example, Caml does not specify the order of evaluation of the arguments of a function call. In what follows, we explain how to describe the semantics of a list of subterms without specifying the order of evaluation. We use a list $\bar{r}$ whose items are either values or unevaluated terms. Formally, $r := \mathsf{Trm}\, t \mid \mathsf{Val}\, v$, and $\bar{r} := \mathsf{list}\, r$.

We start from an intermediate term $\mathsf{ulist1}\,\bar{t}\, K$, where, as previously, $\bar{t}$ denotes the list of subterms and K is a logical function that denotes the continuation. To evaluate $\mathsf{ulist1}\,\bar{t}\, K$, we evaluate another intermediate term, $\mathsf{ulist2}\,\bar{r}\, K$, where $\bar{r}$ is obtained by mapping the constructor Trm to all the elements of $\bar{t}$. Then, we pick any unevaluated term from the list $\bar{r}$ and evaluate it. We repeat this process until either the evaluation of one of the term diverges or produces an exception, or until all the items in $\bar{r}$ are values. The rules, shown below, involve an intermediate term of the form $\mathsf{ulist3}\,\overline{r_1}\, o\, \overline{r_2}\, K$, where o denotes the outcome that has just been produced, and where $\overline{r_1}$ and $\overline{r_2}$ denote the prefix and the suffix of $\bar{r}$, respectively.

$$\frac{\mathsf{ulist2}\,(\mathsf{map}\,(\mathsf{Trm})\,\bar{t})\, K\, _{/m} \Downarrow o}{\mathsf{ulist1}\,\bar{t}\, K\, _{/m} \Downarrow o} \qquad \frac{t_1\, _{/m} \Downarrow o_1 \qquad \mathsf{ulist3}\,\overline{r_1}\, o_1\, \overline{r_2}\, K\, _{/m} \Downarrow o}{\mathsf{ulist2}\,(\overline{r_1} + [\mathsf{Trm}\, t_1] + \overline{r_2})\, K\, _{/m} \Downarrow o}$$

$$\frac{\mathsf{ulist2}\,(\overline{r_1} + [\mathsf{Val}\, v_1] + \overline{r_2})\, K\, _{/m} \Downarrow o}{\mathsf{ulist3}\,\overline{r_1}\,(\mathsf{ter}\, m\, v_1)\,\overline{r_2}\, K\, _{/m'} \Downarrow o} \qquad \frac{(K\,\bar{v})\, _{/m} \Downarrow o}{\mathsf{ulist2}\,(\mathsf{map}\,(\mathsf{Val})\,\bar{v})\, K\, _{/m} \Downarrow o}$$

5.6   Formalization of Core-Caml

To assess the ability of the pretty-big-step semantics to scale up to a realistic programming language, we formalized the semantics of *core-Caml*, both in big-step and in pretty-big-step style. By core-Caml, we refer to the subset of Caml Light made of booleans, integers, tuples, algebraic data types, mutable records, boolean operators (lazy and, lazy or, negation), integer operators (negation, addition, subtraction, multiplication, division), comparison operator, functions, recursive functions, applications, sequences, let-bindings, conditionals (with optional *else* branch), *for* loops and *while* loops, pattern matching (with nested patterns, *as* patterns, *or* patterns, and *when* clauses), *raise* construct, *try-with* construct with pattern matching, and assertions. (The features missing from Caml Light are: floats, mutual recursion, recursive values, *with* construct for records, and arrays. Objects and modules are not covered either.)

Translating the big-step semantics into a pretty-big-step one following the ideas described in this paper was straightforward and took little time. Apart from adapting the rules, the only extra work required consisted of the definition of outcomes and of the abort predicate (4 lines), the definition of the 28 intermediate terms, and the definition of the auxiliary function getout using a simple pattern matching with 22 cases (one case per intermediate term carrying an outcome).

The table shown below quantifies the improvement. It reports on the number of evaluation rules, the number of evaluation premises, and the number of tokens (excluding head quantified variables, which are typically omitted in paper definitions). It shows that switching to the pretty-big-step semantics reduced the number of the evaluation rules by 38%, reduced the total number of evaluation premises by more than a factor of 2, and reduced the total size of the evaluation rules (as counted by the number of tokens) by 40%.

	rules	premises	tokens
Big-step without divergence	71	83	1540
Big-step with divergence	113	143	2263
Pretty-big-step	70	60	1361

6   Related Work

Cousot and Cousot [2] proposed a coinductive big-step characterization of divergence for λ-terms. Leroy and Grall [8,9] showed how to represent coinductive big-step semantics in a theorem prover such as Coq, and used this semantics to prove that nontrivial program transformations preserve diverging behaviors. They justify the need to introduce separate coinductive rules by observing that naively taking the coinductive interpretation of the standard evaluation rules yields a coevaluation judgment that does not properly characterizes diverging terms. Indeed, there exist terms that diverge but do not coevaluate. Leroy and Grall also explained how to extend their semantics with traces, using two judgments: $t \Rightarrow v/\tau$ asserts that the execution of t produces the value v and a finite trace τ (a list), and $t \Rightarrow^\infty/\sigma$ asserts that the execution of t diverges producing an infinite trace σ (a stream). We have shown in this paper, among other things, how to factorize these two separate judgments into a single one.

Following up on earlier work [2], Cousot and Cousot further developed the notion of bi-inductive semantics [3,4]. These semantics are able to characterize both terminating and diverging executions using a common set of inference rules. Their approach is based on the construction of a least fixed point of a set of evaluation rules with respect to a non-standard ordering, which corresponds neither to induction nor coinduction. By contrast, we have shown in this paper how to achieve the same goal using only the standard notions of induction and coinduction. In their work, Cousot and Cousot also decompose the evaluation rule for application in separate rules. However, their decomposition does not go as far as ours. For example, two of their rules perform the evaluation of the left branch of an application, whereas with the pretty-big-step semantics we only need one such rule.

Nakata and Uustalu [10] propose a coinductive relation that provides a big-step semantics for both terminating and diverging programs, using possibly-infinite traces (coinductive lists) that record all the intermediate memory states of an execution. Formally, they define traces coinductively: $\phi := \langle m \rangle \mid m ::: \phi$. Their (coinductive) big-step evaluation judgment takes the form $t_{/m} \Rightarrow \phi$. Its definition, whose key rules are shown below, is mutually-recursive with another judgment, $t/\phi \overset{*}{\Rightarrow} \phi'$. The definition is quite subtle. It is explained next.

$$\frac{t_{1/m} \Rightarrow \phi \quad t_2/(m ::: \phi) \overset{*}{\Rightarrow} \phi'}{(t_1 \,;\, t_2)_{/m} \Rightarrow \phi'} \qquad \frac{t_{/m} \Rightarrow \phi}{t/\langle m \rangle \overset{*}{\Rightarrow} \phi} \qquad \frac{t/\phi \overset{*}{\Rightarrow} \phi'}{t/(m ::: \phi) \overset{*}{\Rightarrow} (m ::: \phi')}$$

To evaluate a sequence $(t_1 ; t_2)$, we first evaluate t_1 and obtain a trace ϕ. Using the relation $t_2/(m ::: \phi) \stackrel{*}{\Rightarrow} \phi'$, we ensure that the trace ϕ produced by t_1 corresponds to the prefix of the trace ϕ' associated with the term $(t_1 ; t_2)$. If the trace ϕ is finite, then we reach the judgment $t_2/\langle m'\rangle \stackrel{*}{\Rightarrow} \phi''$, where m' denotes the state produced by t_1 and where ϕ'' corresponds to what remains of the trace ϕ' after stripping its prefix ϕ. We can then proceed to the evaluation of t_2 in m'. Otherwise, if the trace ϕ is infinite, then the third rule shown above applies indefinitely, ensuring that the trace ϕ' associated with the term $(t_1 ; t_2)$ is equal (up to bisimilarity) to the trace ϕ produced by t_1.

The manipulation of traces involved with the pretty-big-step semantics is, in our opinion, much simpler for several reasons. First, instead of working with potentially-infinite lists, we use a syntactic disjunction between finite traces and infinite traces, so it is always clear whether we are describing a finite or an infinite execution. Second, we do not need to use an auxiliary, mutually-coinductive judgment to traverse traces; instead, we use a simpler concatenation operation that only needs to traverse finite traces. Third, applying Nakata and Uustalu's approach to a λ-calculus instead of a simple imperative language would require all the rules to be stated in continuation-passing style, because the judgment $t/\phi \stackrel{*}{\Rightarrow} \phi'$ would need to be generalized to the form $K/\phi \stackrel{*}{\Rightarrow} \phi'$, where K denotes a continuation that expects the result of the previous computation (that is, the result stored at the end of the trace ϕ) and produces the term to continue the evaluation from. Such a systematic use of continuations would likely result in fairly obfuscated rules.

Danielsson [5] revisits Nakata and Uustalu's work by defining a corecursive function that yields a big-step semantics for both terminating and diverging programs. This function produces a value of type $(\mathsf{Maybe}\,\mathsf{Value})_\perp$, where the Maybe indicates the possibility of an error and where the bottom represents the partiality monad. The partiality monad involves two constructors: one that carries a value, and one that "delays" the exhibition of a value. Formally, the coinductive definition is $A_\perp := \mathsf{now}\,A \mid \mathsf{later}\,(A_\perp)$. The partiality monad thus corresponds to a degenerated version of potentially-infinite traces, where the spine of a trace does not carry any information; only the tail of a trace, if any, carries a value. Note that, to accommodate non-deterministic semantics, the type $(\mathsf{Maybe}\,\mathsf{Value})_\perp$ needs to be further extended with the non-determinism monad.

In summary, Danielsson's semantics for the λ-calculus consists of a reference interpreter, defined in a formal logic. (It is actually not so straightforward to convince the checker of the guard condition that the definition of the interpreter indeed yields a productive function.) Note that this interpreter should only be used for specification, not for execution, because it is quite inefficient: each bind operation needs to traverse the trace that carries the result that it is binding. Specifying the semantics of a language via an interpreter departs quite significantly from the traditional statement of a big-step semantics as a relation between a term and a result. We find that pretty-big-step semantics remains much more faithful to big-step semantics, and is thus more likely to be accepted as the reference semantics of a programming language. Moreover, some forms of reasoning, such as reasoning by inversion, are typically easier to conduct when the definition is a relation than when it is a function.

7   Conclusion

In this paper, we addressed the duplication problem associated with big-step semantics by introducing pretty-big-step semantics. Pretty-big-semantics rely on four key ingredients: (1) a breakdown of complex rules into a larger number of simpler rules, (2) a grammar of intermediate terms for ensuring that rules are applied in the appropriate order, (3) an explicit constant div to represent divergence, and (4) an inductive and a coinductive interpretation of the same set of reduction rules. Pretty-big-step semantics accommodate the introduction of a generic error rule for conducting type soundness proofs, and they scale up to realistic programming languages. Moreover, they can easily be extended with traces, in which case the behavior of both terminating and diverging programs is adequately captured by the coinductive evaluation judgment alone.

Acknowledgments. I am grateful to Xavier Leroy for very useful feedback.

References

1. Charguéraud, A.: Characteristic Formulae for Mechanized Program Verification. PhD thesis, Université Paris-Diderot (2010)
2. Cousot, P., Cousot, R.: Inductive definitions, semantics and abstract interpretation. In: POPL, pp. 83–94 (1992)
3. Cousot, P., Cousot, R.: Bi-inductive structural semantics: (extended abstract). Electronic Notes Theoretical Computer Sciences 192(1), 29–44 (2007)
4. Cousot, P., Cousot, R.: Bi-inductive structural semantics. Information and Computation 207(2), 258–283 (2009)
5. Danielsson, N.A.: Operational semantics using the partiality monad. In: ICFP, pp. 127–138. ACM (2012)
6. Gunter, C.A., Rémy, D.: A proof-theoretic assessment of runtime type errors. Research Report 11261-921230-43TM, AT&T Bell Laboratories (1993)
7. Kahn, G.: Natural Semantics. In: Brandenburg, F.J., Wirsing, M., Vidal-Naquet, G. (eds.) STACS 1987. LNCS, vol. 247, pp. 22–39. Springer, Heidelberg (1987)
8. Leroy, X.: Coinductive Big-Step Operational Semantics. In: Sestoft, P. (ed.) ESOP 2006. LNCS, vol. 3924, pp. 54–68. Springer, Heidelberg (2006)
9. Leroy, X., Grall, H.: Coinductive big-step operational semantics. CoRR, abs/0808.0586 (2008)
10. Nakata, K., Uustalu, T.: Trace-Based Coinductive Operational Semantics for While. In: Berghofer, S., Nipkow, T., Urban, C., Wenzel, M. (eds.) TPHOLs 2009. LNCS, vol. 5674, pp. 375–390. Springer, Heidelberg (2009)
11. Plotkin, G.D.: A structural approach to operational semantics. Internal Report DAIMI FN-19, Department of Computer Science, Aarhus University (1981)
12. Wright, A.K., Felleisen, M.: A syntactic approach to type soundness. Information and Computation 115(1), 38–94 (1994)

Language Constructs
for Non-Well-Founded Computation

Jean-Baptiste Jeannin[1], Dexter Kozen[1], and Alexandra Silva[2]

[1] Cornell University, Ithaca, NY 14853-7501, USA
{jeannin,kozen}@cs.cornell.edu
[2] Institute for Computing and Information Sciences, Radboud University Nijmegen,
Postbus 9010, 6500 GL Nijmegen, The Netherlands
alexandra@cs.ru.nl

Abstract. Recursive functions defined on a coalgebraic datatype C may not converge if there are cycles in the input, that is, if the input object is not well-founded. Even so, there is often a useful solution. Unfortunately, current functional programming languages provide no support for specifying alternative solution methods. In this paper we give numerous examples in which it would be useful to do so: free variables, α-conversion, and substitution in infinitary λ-terms; halting probabilities and expected running times of probabilistic protocols; abstract interpretation; and constructions involving finite automata. In each case the function would diverge under the standard semantics of recursion. We propose programming language constructs that would allow the specification of alternative solutions and methods to compute them.

Keywords: coalgebraic types, functional programming, recursion.

1 Introduction

Coalgebraic datatypes have become popular in recent years in the study of infinite behaviors and non-terminating computation. One would like to define functions on coinductive datatypes by structural recursion, but such functions may not converge if there are cycles in the input; that is, if the input object is not well-founded. Even so, there is often a useful solution that we would like to compute.

For example, consider the problem of computing the set of free variables of a λ-term. In pseudo-ML, we might write

```
type term =                    let rec fv = function
  | Var of string                | Var v -> {v}
  | App of term * term           | App (t1,t2) -> (fv t1) ∪ (fv t2)
  | Lam of string * term         | Lam (x,t) -> (fv t) − {x}
```

and this works provided the argument is an ordinary (well-founded) λ-term. However, if we call the function on an infinitary term (λ-coterm), say

```
let rec t = App (Var "x", App (Var "y", t))
```

M. Felleisen and P. Gardner (Eds.): ESOP 2013, LNCS 7792, pp. 61–80, 2013.

$$\text{(1)}$$

then the function will diverge, even though it is clear the answer should be $\{x, y\}$. Note that this is not a corecursive definition: we are not asking for a greatest solution or a unique solution in a final coalgebra, but rather a least solution in a different ordered domain from the one provided by the standard semantics of recursive functions. The standard semantics gives us the least solution in the flat Scott domain $(\mathcal{P}(\mathbf{string})_\bot, \sqsubseteq)$ with bottom element $\bot$ representing nontermination, whereas we would like the least solution in a different CPO, namely $(\mathcal{P}(\mathbf{string}), \subseteq)$ with bottom element $\varnothing$.

The coinductive elements we consider are always *regular*, that is, they have a finite but possibly cyclic representation. This is different from a setting in which infinite elements are represented lazily. A few of our examples, like substitution, could be computed by lazy evaluation, but most of them, for example free variables, could not.

Theoretically, the situation is governed by diagrams of the form

$$
\begin{array}{ccc}
C & \xrightarrow{\;\;h\;\;} & A \\
{\scriptstyle\gamma}\downarrow & & \uparrow{\scriptstyle\alpha} \\
FC & \xrightarrow[Fh]{} & FA
\end{array}
\qquad\text{(2)}
$$

describing a recursive definition of a function $h : C \to A$. Here F is a functor describing the structure of the recursion. To apply h to an input x, the function $\gamma : C \to FC$ identifies the base cases, and in the recursive case prepares the arguments for the recursive calls; the function $Fh : FC \to FA$ performs the recursive calls; and the function $\alpha : FA \to A$ assembles the return values from the recursive calls into final value $h(x)$.

A canonical example is the usual factorial function

```
let rec factorial = function
  | 0 -> 1
  | n -> n * factorial (n-1)
```

Here the abstract diagram (2) becomes

$$
\begin{array}{ccc}
\mathbb{N} & \xrightarrow{\;\;h\;\;} & \mathbb{N} \\
{\scriptstyle\gamma}\downarrow & & \uparrow{\scriptstyle\alpha} \\
\mathbb{1} + \mathbb{N} \times \mathbb{N} & \xrightarrow[\mathrm{id}_\mathbb{1} + \mathrm{id}_\mathbb{N} \times h]{} & \mathbb{1} + \mathbb{N} \times \mathbb{N}
\end{array}
\qquad\text{(3)}
$$

where the functor is $FX = \mathbb{1} + \mathbb{N} \times X$ and γ and α are given by:

$$\gamma(0) = \iota_0() \qquad\qquad \alpha(\iota_0()) = 1$$
$$\gamma(n+1) = \iota_1(n+1, n) \qquad\qquad \alpha(\iota_1(c, d)) = cd$$

where ι_0 and ι_1 are injectors into the coproduct. The fact that there is one recursive call is reflected in the functor by the single X occurring on the right-hand side. The function γ determines whether the argument is the base case 0 or the inductive case $n+1$, and in the latter case prepares the recursive call. The function α combines the result of the recursive call with the input value by multiplication. In this case we have a unique solution, which is precisely the factorial function.

Theoretical accounts of this general idea have been well studied [1,2,3,9]. Most of this work is focused on conditions ensuring unique solutions, primarily when C is well-founded or when A is a final coalgebra. The account most relevant to this study is the work of Adámek et al. [2], in which a canonical solution can be specified even when it is not unique, provided various desirable conditions are met; for example, when A is a complete CPO and α is continuous, or when A is a complete metric space and α is contractive. Also closely related are the work of Widemann [10] on coalgebraic semantics of recursion and cycle detection algorithms and the work of Simon et al. [7,8] on coinductive logic programming, which addresses many of the same issues in the context of logic programming.

Ordinary recursion over inductive datatypes corresponds to the case in which C is well-founded. In this case, the solution h exists and is unique: it is the least solution in the standard flat Scott domain. For example, the factorial function is uniquely defined by (3) in this sense. If C is not well-founded, there can be multiple solutions, and the one provided by the standard semantics of recursion is typically not be the one we want. Nevertheless, the diagram (2) can still serve as a valid definitional scheme, provided we are allowed to specify a desired solution. In the free variables example, the codomain of the function (sets of variables) is indeed a complete CPO under the usual set inclusion order, and the constructor α is continuous, thus the desired solution can be obtained by a least fixpoint computation.

The example (1) involving free variables of a λ-coterm fits this scheme with the diagram

$$
\begin{array}{ccc}
\text{Term} & \xrightarrow{\ \ \text{fv}\ \ } & \mathcal{P}(\text{Var}) \\
\gamma \downarrow & & \uparrow \alpha \\
F(\text{Term}) & \xrightarrow[\text{id}_{\text{Var}} + \text{fv}^2 + \text{id}_{\text{Var}} \times \text{fv}]{} & F(\mathcal{P}(\text{Var}))
\end{array}
$$

where $FX = \text{Var} + X^2 + \text{Var} \times X$ and

$$
\begin{aligned}
\gamma(\text{Var } x) &= \iota_0(x) & \alpha(\iota_0(x)) &= \{x\} \\
\gamma(\text{App }(t_1, t_2)) &= \iota_1(t_1, t_2) & \alpha(\iota_1(u, v)) &= u \cup v \\
\gamma(\text{Lam }(x, t)) &= \iota_2(x, t) & \alpha(\iota_2(x, v)) &= v \setminus \{x\}.
\end{aligned}
$$

Here the domain of fv (regular λ-coterms) is not well-founded and the codomain (sets of variables) is not a final coalgebra, but the codomain is a complete CPO under the usual set inclusion order with bottom element $\varnothing$, and the desired solution is the least solution in this order; it is just not the one that would be computed by the standard semantics of recursive functions.

Unfortunately, current programming languages provide little support for specifying alternative solutions. One must be able to specify a canonical method for solving systems of equations over an F-algebra (the codomain) obtained from the function definition and the input. We will demonstrate through several examples that such a feature would be extremely useful in a programming language and would bring coinduction and coinductive datatypes to a new level of usability in accordance with the elegance already present for algebraic datatypes. Our examples include free variables, α-conversion, and substitution in infinitary terms; halting probabilities, expected running times, and outcome functions of probabilistic protocols; and abstract interpretation. In each case, the function would diverge under the standard semantics of recursion.

In this paper we propose programming language constructs that would allow the specification of alternative solutions and methods to compute them. These examples require different solution methods: iterative least fixpoint computation, Gaussian elimination, structural coinduction. We describe how this feature might be implemented in a functional language and give mock-up implementations of all our examples. In our implementation, we show how the function definition specifies a system of equations and indicate how that system of equations might be extracted automatically and then passed to an equation solver. In many cases, we suspect that the process can be largely automated, requiring little extra work on the part of the programmer.

Current functional languages are not particularly well suited to the manipulation of coinductive datatypes. For example, in OCaml one can form coinductive objects with **let rec** as in (1), but due to the absence of mutable variables, such objects can only be created and not dynamically manipulated, which severely limits their usefulness. One can simulate them with references, but this negates the elegance of algebraic manipulation of inductively defined datatypes, for which the ML family of languages is so well known. It would be of benefit to be able to treat coinductive types the same way.

Our mock-up implementation with all examples and solvers is available from [5].

2   Motivating Examples

In this section we present a number of motivating examples that illustrate the usefulness of the problem. Several examples of well-founded definitions that fit the scheme (2) can be found in the cited literature, including the Fibonacci function and various divide-and-conquer algorithms such as quicksort and mergesort, so we focus on non-well-founded examples: free variables and substitution in λ-coterms, probabilistic protocols, and abstract interpretation.

2.1   Substitution

We now describe another function on infinitary λ-terms: substitution. A typical implementation for well-founded terms would be

```
let rec subst t y = function
  | Var x -> if x = y then t else Var x
  | App (t1,t2) -> App (subst t y t1, subst t y t2)
  | Lam (x,s) -> if x = y then Lam (x,s)
                 else if x ∈ fv t then
                   let w = fresh ()
                   in Lam (w, subst t y (rename w x s))
                 else Lam (x, subst t y s)
```

where `fv` is the free variable function defined above and **rename w x s** is a function that substitutes a fresh variable `w` for `x` in a term `s`.

```
let rec rename w x = function
  | Var z -> Var (if z = x then w else z)
  | App (t1,t2) -> App (rename w x t1, rename w x t2)
  | Lam (z,s) -> if z = x then Lam (z,s)
                 else Lam (z, rename w x s)
```

Applied to a λ-coterm with a cycle, for example attempting to substitute a term for y in (1), the computation would never finish. Nevertheless, this computation fits the scheme (2) with $C = A = \mathbf{term}$ (the set of λ-coterms), functor

$$FX = \mathbf{term} + X^2 + \mathbf{string} \times X \qquad Fh = \mathrm{id}_{\mathbf{term}} + h^2 + \mathrm{id}_{\mathbf{string}} \times h$$

and γ and α defined by

$$\gamma(\mathbf{Var}\ x) = \begin{cases} \iota_0(t) & \text{if } x = y \\ \iota_0(\mathbf{Var}\ x) & \text{otherwise} \end{cases}$$

$$\gamma(\mathbf{App}\ (t_1, t_2)) = \iota_1(t_1, t_2)$$

$$\gamma(\mathbf{Lam}\ (x, s)) = \begin{cases} \iota_0(\mathbf{Lam}\ (x, s)) & \text{if } x = y \\ \iota_2(w, \mathbf{rename}\ w\ x\ s) & \text{if } x \neq y \text{ and } x \in \mathbf{fv}\ t, \text{ where } w \text{ is fresh} \\ \iota_2(x, s) & \text{otherwise} \end{cases}$$

$$\alpha(\iota_0(s)) = s$$
$$\alpha(\iota_1(s_1, s_2)) = \mathbf{App}\ (s_1, s_2)$$
$$\alpha(\iota_2(x, s)) = \mathbf{Lam}\ (x, s)$$

In this case, even though the domain is not well-founded, the solution nevertheless exists and is unique up to observational equivalence. This is because the definition of the function is corecursive and takes values in a final coalgebra.

2.2 Probabilistic Protocols

In this section, we present a few examples in the realm of probabilistic protocols. Imagine one wants to simulate a biased coin, say a coin with probability 2/3 of heads, with a fair coin. Here is a possible solution: flip the fair coin. If it comes up heads, output heads, otherwise flip again. If the second flip is tails, output tails, otherwise repeat from the start. This protocol can be represented succinctly by the following probabilistic automaton:

$$(4)$$

Operationally, starting from states s and t, the protocol generates series that converge to 2/3 and 1/3, respectively.

$$\mathsf{Pr}_H(s) = \tfrac{1}{2} + \tfrac{1}{8} + \tfrac{1}{32} + \tfrac{1}{128} + \cdots = \tfrac{2}{3}$$
$$\mathsf{Pr}_H(t) = \tfrac{1}{4} + \tfrac{1}{16} + \tfrac{1}{64} + \tfrac{1}{256} + \cdots = \tfrac{1}{3}.$$

However, these values can also be seen to satisfy a pair of mutually recursive equations:

$$\mathsf{Pr}_H(s) = \tfrac{1}{2} + \tfrac{1}{2} \cdot \mathsf{Pr}_H(t) \qquad\qquad \mathsf{Pr}_H(t) = \tfrac{1}{2} \cdot \mathsf{Pr}_H(s).$$

This gives rise to a contractive map on the unit interval, which has a unique solution. It is also monotone and continuous with respect to the natural order on the unit interval, therefore has a unique least solution.

One would like to define the probabilistic automaton (4) by

```
type pa = H | T | Flip of float * pa * pa
let rec s = Flip (0.5,H,t) and t = Flip (0.5,T,s)
```

and write a recursive program, say something like

```
let rec pr_heads = function
  | H -> 1.
  | T -> 0.
  | Flip (p,u,v) -> p *. (pr_heads u) +. (1 -. p) *. (pr_heads v)
```

and specify that the extracted equations should be solved exactly by Gaussian elimination, or by iteration until achieving a fixpoint to within a sufficiently small error tolerance ε. We give implementations using both methods.

The *von Neumann trick* for simulating a fair coin with a coin of arbitrary bias is a similar example. In this protocol, we flip the coin twice. If the outcome is HT, we output heads. If the outcome is TH, we output tails. These outcomes occur with equal probability. If the outcome is HH or TT, we repeat.

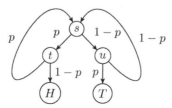

Here we would define

```
let rec s = Flip (p,t,u) and t = Flip (p,s,H) and u = Flip (p,T,s)
```

but the typing and recursive function `pr_heads` are the same. Markov chains and Markov decision processes can be modeled the same way.

Other functions on probabilistic automata can be computed as well. The expected number of steps starting from state s is the least solution of the equation

$$E(s) = \begin{cases} 0 & \text{if } s \in \{\text{H}, \text{T}\} \\ 1 + p \cdot E(u) + (1 - p) \cdot E(v) & \text{if } s = \text{Flip}(p, u, v). \end{cases}$$

We would like to write simply

```
let rec ex = function
 | H -> 0.
 | T -> 0.
 | Flip (p,u,v) -> 1. +. p *. (ex u) +. (1 -. p) *. (ex v)
```

and specify that the extracted equations should be solved by Gaussian elimination or least fixpoint iteration from 0.

The coinflip protocols we have discussed all fit the abstract definitional scheme (2) in the form

$$\begin{array}{ccc} S & \xrightarrow{\;h\;} & \mathbb{R} \\ \gamma \downarrow & & \uparrow \alpha \\ FS & \xrightarrow[Fh]{} & F\mathbb{R} \end{array}$$

where S is the set of states (a state can be either H, T, or a triple (p, u, v), where $p \in \mathbb{R}$ and $u, v \in S$, the last indicating that it flips a p-biased coin and moves to state u with probability p and v with probability $1 - p$), and F is the functor

$$FX = \mathbb{1} + \mathbb{1} + \mathbb{R} \times X^2 \qquad\qquad Fh = \text{id}_{\mathbb{1}} + \text{id}_{\mathbb{1}} + \text{id}_{\mathbb{R}} \times h^2.$$

For both the probability of heads and expected running times examples, we can take

$$\gamma(s) = \begin{cases} \iota_0() & \text{if } s = \text{H} \\ \iota_1() & \text{if } s = \text{T} \\ \iota_2(p, u, v) & \text{if } s = (p, u, v). \end{cases}$$

For the probability of heads, we can take

$$\alpha(\iota_0()) = 1 \qquad \alpha(\iota_1()) = 0 \qquad \alpha(\iota_2(p, a, b)) = pa + (1 - p)b.$$

For the expected running time, we can take

$$\alpha(\iota_0()) = \alpha(\iota_1()) = 0 \qquad \alpha(\iota_2(p, a, b)) = 1 + pa + (1 - p)b.$$

The desired solution in all cases is a least fixpoint in an appropriate ordered domain.

2.3   Abstract Interpretation

In this section we present our most involved example: abstract interpretation of a simple imperative language. Our example follows Cousot and Cousot [6] as inspired by lecture notes of Stephen Chong [4].

Consider a simple imperative language of while programs with integer expressions a and commands c. Let Var be a countable set of variables.

$$a ::= n \in \mathbb{Z} \mid x \in \mathsf{Var} \mid a_1 + a_2$$
$$c ::= \mathsf{skip} \mid x := a \mid c_1 \; ; \; c_2 \mid \mathsf{if} \; a \; \mathsf{then} \; c_1 \; \mathsf{else} \; c_2 \mid \mathsf{while} \; a \; \mathsf{do} \; c$$

For the purpose of tests in the conditional and while loop, an integer is considered true if and only if it is nonzero. Otherwise, the operational semantics is standard, in the style of [11]. A store is a partial function from variables to integers, an arithmetic expression is interpreted relative to a store and returns an integer, and a command is interpreted relative to a store and returns an updated store.

Abstract interpretation defines an abstract domain that approximates the values manipulated by the program. We define an abstract domain for integers that abstracts an integer by its sign. The set of abstract values is $\mathsf{AbsInt} = \{\mathsf{neg}, \mathsf{zero}, \mathsf{pos}, \top\}$, where neg, zero, and pos represent negative, zero, and positive integers, repectively, and $\top$ represents an integer of unknown sign. The abstract values form a join semilattice with join $\sqcup$ defined by the following diagram:

$$\begin{array}{c} \top \\ \diagup \mid \diagdown \\ \mathsf{neg} \quad \mathsf{zero} \quad \mathsf{pos} \end{array} \tag{5}$$

The abstract interpretation of an arithmetic expression is defined relative to an abstract store $\sigma : \mathsf{Var} \rightharpoonup \mathsf{AbsInt}$, used to interpret the abstract values of variables. We write $\mathsf{AS} = \mathsf{Var} \rightharpoonup \mathsf{AbsInt}$ for the set of abstract stores. The abstract interpretation of arithmetic expressions is given by:

$$\mathcal{A}[\![n]\!]\sigma = \begin{cases} \mathsf{pos} & \text{if } n > 0 \\ \mathsf{zero} & \text{if } n = 0 \\ \mathsf{neg} & \text{if } n < 0 \end{cases}$$

$$\mathcal{A}[\![x]\!]\sigma = \sigma(x)$$

$$\mathcal{A}[\![a_1 + a_2]\!] = \begin{cases} \mathcal{A}[\![a_1]\!]\sigma & \text{if } \mathcal{A}[\![a_2]\!]\sigma = \mathsf{zero} \\ \mathcal{A}[\![a_2]\!]\sigma & \text{if } \mathcal{A}[\![a_1]\!]\sigma = \mathsf{zero} \\ \mathcal{A}[\![a_1]\!]\sigma \sqcup \mathcal{A}[\![a_2]\!]\sigma & \text{otherwise.} \end{cases}$$

The abstract interpretation of commands returns an abstract store, which is an abstraction of the concrete store returned by the commands. Abstract stores form a join semilattice, where the join $\sqcup$ of two abstract stores just takes the join of each variable: $(\sigma_1 \sqcup \sigma_2)(x) = \sigma_1(x) \sqcup \sigma_2(x)$. Commands other than the while loop are interpreted as follows:

$$\mathcal{C}[\![\mathsf{skip}]\!]\sigma = \sigma \quad \mathcal{C}[\![x := a]\!]\sigma = \sigma[x \mapsto \mathcal{A}[\![a]\!]\sigma] \quad \mathcal{C}[\![c_1 \; ; \; c_2]\!]\sigma = \mathcal{C}[\![c_2]\!](\mathcal{C}[\![c_1]\!]\sigma)$$

$$\mathcal{C}[\![\text{if } a \text{ then } c_1 \text{ else } c_2]\!]\sigma = \begin{cases} \mathcal{C}[\![c_1]\!]\sigma & \text{if } \mathcal{A}[\![a]\!]\sigma \in \{\text{pos, neg}\} \\ \mathcal{C}[\![c_2]\!]\sigma & \text{if } \mathcal{A}[\![a]\!]\sigma = \text{zero} \\ \mathcal{C}[\![c_1]\!]\sigma \sqcup \mathcal{C}[\![c_2]\!]\sigma & \text{otherwise.} \end{cases}$$

We would ideally like to define

$$\mathcal{C}[\![\text{while } a \text{ do } c]\!]\sigma = \begin{cases} \sigma & \text{if } \mathcal{A}[\![a]\!]\sigma = \text{zero} \\ \sigma \sqcup \mathcal{C}[\![\text{while } a \text{ do } c]\!](\mathcal{C}[\![c]\!]\sigma) & \text{otherwise.} \end{cases}$$

Unfortunately, when $\mathcal{A}[\![a]\!]\sigma \neq \text{zero}$, the definition is not well-founded, because it is possible for σ and $\mathcal{C}[\![c]\!]\sigma$ to be equal. However, it is a correct definition of $\mathcal{C}[\![\text{while } a \text{ do } c]\!]$ as a least fixpoint in the join semilattice of abstract stores. The existence of the least fixpoint can be obtained in a finite time by iteration because the join semilattice of abstract stores satisfies the ascending chain condition (ACC), that is, it does not contain any infinite ascending chains.

Given $\mathcal{A}[\![a]\!]$ and $\mathcal{C}[\![c]\!]$ previously defined, $\mathcal{C}[\![\text{while } a \text{ do } c]\!]$ satisfies the following instantiation of (2):

$$\begin{array}{ccc} \mathsf{AS} & \xrightarrow{\quad \mathcal{C}[\![\text{while } a \text{ do } c]\!] \quad} & \mathsf{AS} \\ {\scriptstyle \gamma}\downarrow & & \uparrow{\scriptstyle \alpha} \\ \mathsf{AS} + \mathsf{AS} \times \mathsf{AS} & \xrightarrow[\ \mathrm{id}_{\mathsf{AS}} + \mathrm{id}_{\mathsf{AS}} \times \mathcal{C}[\![\text{while } a \text{ do } c]\!] \ ]{} & \mathsf{AS} + \mathsf{AS} \times \mathsf{AS} \end{array}$$

where the functor is $FX = \mathsf{AS} + \mathsf{AS} \times X$ and

$$\gamma(\sigma) = \begin{cases} \iota_1(\sigma) & \text{if } \mathcal{A}[\![a]\!]\sigma = \text{zero} \\ \iota_2(\sigma, \mathcal{C}[\![c]\!]\sigma) & \text{otherwise} \end{cases} \qquad \begin{aligned} \alpha(\iota_1(\sigma)) &= \sigma \\ \alpha(\iota_2(\sigma, \tau)) &= \sigma \sqcup \tau \end{aligned}$$

The function $\mathcal{C}[\![\text{while } a \text{ do } c]\!]$ is the least function in the pointwise order that makes the above diagram commute.

This technique allows us to define $\mathcal{C}[\![c]\!]$ inductively on the structure of c. An inductive definition can be used here because the set of abstract syntax trees is well-founded.

The literature on abstract interpretation explains how to compute the least fixpoint, and much research has been done on techniques for accelerating convergence to the least fixpoint. This body of research can inform compiler optimization techniques for computation with coalgebraic types.

2.4 Finite Automata

We conclude this section with a brief example involving finite automata. Suppose we want to construct a deterministic finite automaton (DFA) over a two-letter alphabet accepting the intersection of two regular sets given by two other DFAs over the same alphabet. We might define states coalgebraically by

```
type state = State of bool * state * state
```

where the first component specifies whether the state is an accepting state and the last two components give the states to move to under the two input symbols. The standard product construction is defined coalgebraically simply by

```
let rec product (s : state) (t : state) : state =
  match s, t with
  | State (b1,s1,t1), State (b2,s2,t2) ->
      State (b1 && b2, product s1 t1, product s2 t2)
```

and we can compute it, provided we can solve the generated equations.

3   A Framework for Non-Well-Founded Computation

In this section we discuss our proposed framework for incorporating language constructs to support non-well-founded computation. At a high level, we wish to specify a function h uniquely using a finite set E of structural recursive equations. The function is defined in much the same way as an ordinary recursive function on an inductive datatype. However, the value $h(x)$ of the function on a particular input x is computed not by calling the function in the usual sense, but by generating a system of equations from the function definition and then passing the equations to a specified equation solver to find a solution. The equation solver is either a standard library function or programmed by the user according to an explicit interface.

The process is partitioned into several tasks as follows.

1. The left-hand sides of the clauses in the function definition determine syntactic terms representing equation schemes. These schemes are extracted by the compiler from the abstract syntax tree of the left-hand side expressions. This determines (more or less, subject to optimizations) the function γ in the diagram (2).

2. The right-hand sides of the clauses in the function definition determine the function α in the diagram (2) (again, more or less, subject to optimizations). These expressions essentially tell how to evaluate terms extracted in step 1 in the codomain. As in 1, these are determined by the compiler from the abstract syntax trees of the right-hand sides.

3. At runtime, when the function is called with a coalgebraic element c, a finite system of equations is generated from the schemes extracted in steps 1 and 2, one equation for each element of the coalgebra reachable from c. In fact, we can take the elements reachable from c as the variables in our equations. Each such element matches exactly one clause of the function body, and this determines the right-hand side of the equation that is generated.

4. The equations are passed to a solver that is specified by the user. This will presumably be a module that is programmed separately according to a fixed interface and available as a library function. There should be a simple syntactic mechanism for specifying an alternative solution method (although we do not specify here what that should look like).

Let us illustrate this using our initial example of the free variables. Recall the infinitary λ-term below and the definition of the free variables function from the introduction:

```
let rec fv = function
  | Var v -> {v}                                    (6)
  | App (t1,t2) -> (fv t1) ∪ (fv t2)
  | Lam (x,t) -> (fv t) − {x}
```

Steps 1 and 2 would analyze the left-and right-hand sides of the three clauses in the body at compile time to determine the equation schemes. Then at runtime, if the function were called on the coalgebraic element pictured, the runtime system would generate four equations, one for each node reachable from the top node:

$$\texttt{fv t = (fv x)} \cup \texttt{(fv u)} \qquad \texttt{fv u = (fv y)} \cup \texttt{(fv t)} \qquad \texttt{fv x = \{x\}} \qquad \texttt{fv y = \{y\}}$$

where t and u are the unlabeled top and right nodes of the term above.

As noted, these equations have many solutions. In fact, any set containing the variables x and y will be a solution. However, we are interested in the least solution in the ordered domain $(\mathcal{P}(\mathsf{Var}), \subseteq)$ with bottom element $\varnothing$. In this case, the least solution would assign $\{x\}$ to the leftmost node, $\{y\}$ to the lowest node, and $\{x,y\}$ to the other two nodes.

With this in mind, we would pass the generated equations to an iterative equation solver, which would produce the desired solution. In many cases, such as this example, the codomain is a complete partial order and we have default solvers to compute least fixpoints, leaving to the programmer the simple task of indicating that this is the desired solution method. That would be an ideal situation: the defining equations of (6) plus a simple tag would be enough to obtain the desired solution.

3.1   Generating Equations

The equations are generated from the recursive function definition and the input c, a coalgebraic element, in accordance with the abstract definitional scheme (2). The variables can be taken to be the elements of the coalgebraic object reachable from c. There are finitely many of these, as no infinite object can ever exist in a running program. More accurately stated, the objects of the final coalgebra represented by coalgebraic elements during program execution are all *regular* in the sense that they have a finite representation. These elements are first collected into a data structure (in our implementation, simply a list) and the right-hand sides of the equations are determined by the structure of the object using pattern matching. The object matches exactly one of the terms extracted in step 1.

4   Implementation

The examples of §2 show the need for new program constructs that would allow the user to manipulate corecursive types with the same ease and elegance as we are used to for algebraic datatypes. It is the goal of this section to provide language constructs that allow us to provide the intended semantics to the examples above in a functional language like OCaml.

The general idea behind the implementation is as follows. We want to keep the overhead for the programmer to a minimum. We want the programmer to specify the function in the usual way, then at runtime, when the function is evaluated on a given argument, a set of equations is generated and passed on to a solver, which will find a solution according to the specification. In an ideal situation, the programmer only has to specify the solver. For the examples where a CPO structure is present in the codomain, such as the free variables example, or when we have a complete metric space and a contractive map, we provide the typical solution methods (least and unique fixpoint) and the programmer only needs to tag the codomain with the intended solver. In other cases, the programmer needs to implement the solver.

4.1 Equations and Solvers

Our mock-up implementation aims to allow the programmer to encode a particular instantiation of the general diagram (2) as an OCaml module. This module can then be passed to an OCaml functor, `Corecursive`, that builds the desired function. We discuss the structure of `Corecursive` later in this section.

The functor F is represented by a parameterized type `'b f`. The structures (C, γ) and (A, α), which form a coalgebra and an algebra, respectively, for the functor F, are defined by types `coalgebra` and `algebra`, respectively. This allows us to specify γ naturally as a function from `coalgebra` to `coalgebra f` and α as a function from `algebra f` to `algebra`. In the free variables example, if `VarSet` is a module implementing sets of strings, this is done as:

```
type 'b f = I1 of string | I2 of 'b * 'b | I3 of string * 'b
type coalgebra = Var of string
               | App of coalgebra * coalgebra
               | Lam of string * coalgebra
type algebra = VarSet.t

let gamma (c:coalgebra) : coalgebra f =
  match c with
    | Var v -> I1 v
    | App(c1, c2) -> I2(c1, c2)
    | Lam(x, c) -> I3(x, c)
let alpha (s:algebra f) : algebra =
  match s with
    | I1 v -> VarSet.singleton v
    | I2(s1, s2) -> VarSet.union s1 s2
    | I3(x, s) -> VarSet.remove x s
```

Variables are represented by strings and fresh variables are generated with a counter. Equations are of the form `variable = t`, where the variables on the left-hand side are elements of the domain and the terms on the right side are built up from the constructors of the datatype, constants and variables.

In the `fv` example, the domain was specified by the following datatype:

```
type term =
  | Var of string
  | App of term * term
  | Lam of string * term
```

Recall the four equations above defining the free variables of the λ-term (1) from the introduction:

$$\texttt{fv t} = (\texttt{fv x}) \cup (\texttt{fv u}) \qquad \texttt{fv u} = (\texttt{fv y}) \cup (\texttt{fv t}) \qquad \texttt{fv x} = \{\texttt{x}\} \qquad \texttt{fv y} = \{\texttt{y}\}$$

A variable name is generated for each element of the coalgebra encountered. For example, here we write `v1` for the unknown corresponding to the value of `fv t`; `v2` for `x`; `v3` for `u`; and `v4` for `y`. An equation is represented as a pair of a variable and an element of type `f variable`. The intuitive meaning of a pair (v, w) is the equation $v = \alpha(w)$. In the example above, we would have

`("v1", I2("v2", "v3"))`	representing $\texttt{v1} = \texttt{v2} \cup \texttt{v3}$
`("v2", I1("x"))`	representing $\texttt{v2} = \{\texttt{x}\}$
`("v3", I2("v4", "v1"))`	representing $\texttt{v3} = \texttt{v4} \cup \texttt{v1}$
`("v4", I1("y"))`	representing $\texttt{v4} = \{\texttt{y}\}$

The function `solve` can now be described. Its arguments are a variable v for which we want a solution and a system of equations in which v appears. It returns a value for v that satisfies the equations. In most cases the solution is not unique, and the `solve` method determines which solution is returned.

For technical reasons, two more functions need to be provided. The function `equal` provides an equality test on the coalgebra, which allows the equation generator to know when it has encountered a loop. In most cases, this equality is just the OCaml physical equality `==`; this is necessary because the OCaml equality `=` on coinductive objects does not terminate. In some other cases the function `equal` is an equality function built from both `=` and `==`.

The function `fh` can be seen either as an iterator on the functor `f` in the style of folding and mapping on lists or as a monadic operator on the functor `f`. It allows the lifting of a function from `'c` (typically `coalgebra`) to `'a` (typically `algebra`) to a function from `'c f` to `'a f`, while folding on an element of type `'e`. It works by destructing the element of type `'c f` to get some number (perhaps zero) elements of type `'c`, successively applying the function on each of them while passing through the element of type `'e`, and reconstructing an element of type `'a f` with the same constructor used in `'c f`, returned with the final value of the element of type `'e`. In the example on free variables, the function `fh` is defined as:

```
let fh (h: 'c * 'e -> 'a * 'e) : 'c f * 'e -> 'a f * 'e = function
  | I1 v, e -> I1 v, e
  | I2(c1, c2), e -> let a1, e1 = h (c1, e) in
                     let a2, e2 = h (c2, e1) in
                     I2(a1, a2), e2
  | I3(x, c), e -> let a, e1 = h (c, e) in
                   I3(x, a), e1
```

If we had access to an abstract representation of the functor f, analyzing it allows to automatically generate the function fh. This is what we do in §5.

All this is summarized in the signature of a type SOLVER, used to specify one of those functions:

```
module type SOLVER = sig
  type 'b f
  type coalgebra
  type algebra

  val gamma : coalgebra -> coalgebra f
  val alpha : algebra f -> algebra

  type variable = string
  type equation = variable * (variable f)

  val solve : variable -> equation list -> algebra

  val equal : coalgebra -> coalgebra -> bool
  val fh : ('c * 'e -> 'a * 'e) -> 'c f * 'e -> 'a f * 'e
end
```

Let us now define the OCaml functor Corecursive. From a specification of a function as a module S of type SOLVER, it generates the equations to be solved and sends them to S.solve. Here is how it generates the equations: starting from an element c of the coalgebra, it gathers all the elements of the coalgebra that are reachable from c, recursively descending with gamma and fh, and stopping when reaching an element that is equal—in the sense of the function equal—to an element that has already been seen. For each of those elements, it generates an associated fresh variable and an associated equation based on applying gamma to that element.

From an element c, generating the equations and solving them with solve returns an element a in the coalgebra, the result of applying the function we defined to c.

```
module Corecursive :
  functor (S: SOLVER) -> sig
    val main : S.coalgebra -> S.algebra
  end
```

We will now explain the default solvers we have implemented and which are available for the programmer to use. These solvers cover the examples we have shown before: a least fixpoint solver, a solver that generates coinductive elements and is used for substitution, and a Gaussian elimination solver.

4.2   Least Fixpoints

If the algebra A is a CPO, then every monotone function f on A has a least fixpoint, by the Knaster–Tarski theorem. Moreover, if the CPO satisfies the *ascending chain condition* (ACC), that is, if there does not exist an infinite ascending chain, then this least fixpoint can be computed in finite time by iteration, starting from $\perp_A$. Even if the ACC is not satisfied, an approximate least fixpoint may suffice.

In the free variables example, the codomain $(\mathcal{P}(\mathsf{Var}), \subseteq)$ is a CPO, and its bottom element is $\perp_A = \varnothing$. It satisfies the ACC as long as we restrict ourselves to the total set of variables appearing in the term. This set is finite because the term is regular and thus has a finite representation.

To implement this, first consider the set of equations: each variable is defined by one equation relating it to the other variables. We keep a guess for each variable, initially set at $\perp_A$, and compute a next guess based on the equation for each variable. This eventually converges and we can return the value of the desired variable. Note that to implement this, the programmer needs to know that A is a CPO satisfying the ACC, and needs to provide two things: a bottom element $\perp_A$, and an equality relation on A that determines when a fixpoint is achieved.

The same technique can be used to implement the solver for the abstract interpretation example, as it is also a least fixpoint in a CPO. This CPO is the subset of the join semilattice of abstract domains containing only the elements greater than or equal to the initial abstract domain. The ACC is ensured by the fact that the abstract domain is always of finite height. The bottom element is the initial abstract domain. Much of the code is shared with the free variables example. As pointed out before, only the bottom element of A and the equality on A change.

More suprisingly, this technique can also be used in the probability examples. Here the system of equations looks more like a linear system of equation on $\mathbb{R}$. Except in trivial extreme cases, the equations are contracting, thus we can solve them by iterative approximation until getting close enough to a fixpoint. The initial element $\perp_A$ is 0. The equality test on A is the interesting part: since it determines when to stop iterating, two elements of A are considered equal if and only if they differ by less than ε, the precision of the approximation. This is specified by the programmer in the definition of equality on A. Of course, such a linear system could also be solved with Gaussian elimination, as presented below in §4.4.

It can be seen from these examples that the least fixpoint solver is quite generic and works for a large class of problems. We need only parameterize with a bottom element to use as an initial guess and an equality test.

4.3   Generating Coinductive Elements and Substitution

Let us return to the substitution example. Suppose we wanted to replace y in Fig. 1(b) by the term of Fig. 1(a) to obtain Fig. 1(c). The extracted equations would be

```
v1 = App(v2, v3)
v2 = Var("x")
v3 = App(v4, v1)
```

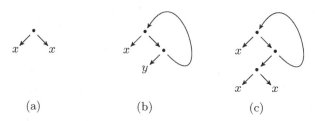

Fig. 1. A substitution example

```
v4 = App(Var "x", Var "x")
```

and we are interested in the value of v1. Finding such a v1 is easily done by executing the following code in OCaml:

```
let rec v1 = App(v2, v3)
    and v2 = Var("x")
    and v3 = App(v4, v1)
    and v4 = App(Var "x", Var "x")
in v1
```

This code can be easily generated (as a string of text) from the equations. Unfortunately, there is no direct way of generating the element that this code would produce. One workaround is to use the module `Toploop` of OCaml that provides the ability to dynamically execute code from a string, like `eval` in Javascript. But that is not a satisfying solution.

Another solution is to allow the program to manipulate terms by making all subterms mutable using references:

```
type term =
  | Var of string
  | App of term ref * term ref
  | Lam of string * term ref
```

This type allows the creation of the desired term by going down the equations and building the terms progressively, backpatching if necessary when encountering a loop. But this is also unsatisfactory, as we had to change the type of `term` to allow references.

The missing piece is mutable variables, which are currently not supported in the ML family of languages. A variable is mutable if it can be dynamically rebound, as with the Scheme `set!` feature or ordinary assignment in imperative languages. In ML, variables are only bound once when they are declared and cannot be rebound.

References can simulate mutable variables, but this corrupts the typing and forces the programmer to work at a lower pointer-based level. Moreover, there are subtle differences in the aliasing behavior of references and mutable variables. The language constructs we propose should ideally be created in a programming language with mutable variables.

4.4   Gaussian Elimination

In many of the examples on probabilities and streams, a set of linear equations is generated. One of the examples on probabilistic protocols of §2.2 requires us to find a float var1 such that

```
var1 = 0.5 + 0.5 * var2
var2 = 0.5 * var1
```

In the case where the equations are contractive, we have already seen that the solution is unique and we can approximate it by iteration. We have also implemented a Gaussian elimination solver that can be used to get a more precise answer or when the map is not contractive but the solution is still unique.

But what happens when the linear system has no solution or an infinite number of solutions? If the system does not have a solution, then there is no fixpoint for the function, and the function is undefined on that input. If there are an infinite number of solutions, it depends on the application. For example, in the case of computing the probability of heads in a probabilistic protocol, we want the least such solution such that all variables take values between 0 and 1.

For example, let us consider the following probabilistic protocol: Flip a fair coin. If it comes up heads, output heads, otherwise flip again. Ignore the result and come back to this last state, effectively flipping again forever. This protocol can be represented by the following probabilistic automaton:

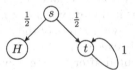

The probability of heads starting from s and t, respectively, is given by:

$$\Pr_H(s) = \tfrac{1}{2} + \tfrac{1}{2} \cdot \Pr_H(t) \qquad\qquad \Pr_H(t) = 1 \cdot \Pr_H(t).$$

The set of solutions for these equations for $\Pr_H(t)$ is the interval $[0,1]$, thus the set of solutions for $\Pr_H(s)$ is the interval $[\tfrac{1}{2}, 1]$. The desired result, however, is the least of those solutions, namely $1/2$ for $\Pr_H(s)$, because the protocol halts with result heads only with probability $1/2$.

Again, the Gaussian solver is quite generic and would be applicable to a large class of problems involving linear equations.

5   Future Work: Automatic Partitioning

In §4, we described a mock-up implementation that demonstrates the feasibility of our approach. In this implementation, the programmer needs to provide the elements of the SOLVER module. We now describe our ideas for future work, and in particular, ideas to make the task of the programmer easier by automatically generating some of those elements.

Providing all the elements to a SOLVER module requires from the programmer a good understanding of the concepts explained in this paper and a method to solve equations. On the other hand, examples show that the same solving techniques arise again and again. Ideally, we would like the programmer to have to write only:

```
type term =                    let rec[...] fv = function
  | Var of string                | Var v -> {v}
  | App of term * term           | App (t1,t2) -> (fv t1) ∪ (fv t2)
  | Lam of string * term         | Lam (x,t) -> (fv t) − {x}
```

where the keyword **rec** has been parameterized by the name of a module implementing the **SOLVER** interface for a particular codomain, such as a generic iteration solver for CPOs or contractive maps or a Gaussian elimination solver for linear equations.

This definition is almost enough to generate the **SOLVER** module. Only three more things need to be specified by the programmer:

– the function **equal** on coalgebras, which is just **==** in most cases; and
– the two elements needed in the least fixpoint algorithm: a bottom element $\perp_A$ and an equality test $=_A$ on the algebra A, written **algebra** in the code.

The other elements can be directly computed from a careful analysis of the function definition:

– The function can be typed with the usual typing rules for recursive functions. Then **algebra** is defined as its input type and **coalgebra** as its output type.
– An analysis of the abstract syntax trees of the clauses of the function definition can determine what is executed before the recursive calls, which comprises γ, and what is executed after the recursive calls, which comprises α. An analysis of the arguments that are passed to the recursive calls, as well as the variables that are still alive across the boundary between **gamma** and **alpha**, determine the functor **f**.
– The function **fh** can be defined by induction on the structure of the abstract syntax tree defining **'a f**. The only difficult case is the product, where we apply **h** to every element of type **'a** in the product, passing through the element of type **'e**, and returning a reconstructed product of the results.
– The type **equation** is always defined in the same way.
– Finally, the **solve** function is generic for all functions solved as a least fixpoint by iteration, just depending on the bottom element and the equality on the algebra.

6   Conclusion

Coalgebraic (coinductive) datatypes and algebraic (inductive) datatypes are similar in many ways. Nevertheless, there are some important distinctions. Algebraic types have a long history, are very well known, and are heavily used in modern applications, especially in the ML family of languages. Coalgebraic types, on the other hand, are the subject of more recent research and are less well known. Not all modern languages support coalgebraic types—for example, Standard ML and F# do not—and even those that do may not do so adequately.

The most important distinction is that coalgebraic objects can be cyclic, whereas algebraic objects are always well-founded. Functions defined by structural recursion on well-founded data always terminate and yield a value under the standard semantics of recursion, but not so on coalgebraic data. A more subtle distinction is that constructors can be interpreted as functions under the algebraic interpretation, as they are in Standard ML, but not under the coalgebraic interpretation as in OCaml.

Despite these differences, there are some strong similarities. They are defined in the same way by recursive type equations, algebraic types as initial solutions and coalgebraic types as final solutions. Because of this similarity, we would like to program with them in the same way, using constructors and destructors and writing recursive definitions using pattern matching.

In this paper we have shown through several examples that this approach to computing with coalgebraic types is not only useful but viable. For this to be possible, it is necessary to circumvent the standard semantics of recursion, and we have demonstrated that this obstacle is not insurmountable. We have proposed new programming language features that would allow the specification of alternative solutions and methods to compute them, and we have given mock-up implementations that demonstrate that this approach is feasible.

The chief features of our approach are the interpretation of a recursive function definition as a scheme for the specification of equations, a means for extracting a finite such system from the function definition and its (cyclic) argument, a means for specifying an equation solver, and an interface between the two. In many cases, such as an iterative fixpoint on a codomain satisfying the ascending chain condition, the process can be largely automated, requiring little extra work on the part of the programmer.

We have mentioned that mutable variables are essential for manipulating coalgebraic data. Current functional languages in the ML family do not support mutable variables; thus true coalgebraic data can only be constructed explicitly using **let rec**, not programmatically. Moreover, once constructed, a coalgebraic object cannot be changed dynamically. These restrictions currently constitute a severe restriction the use of coalgebraic datatypes. One workaround is to simulate mutable variables with references, but this is a grossly unsatisfactory alternative, because it confounds algebraic elegance and forces the programmer to work at a lower pointer-based level. A future endeavor is to provide a smoother and more realistic implementation of these ideas in an ML-like language with mutable variables.

Acknowledgments. We are grateful to Bob Constable, Edgar Friendly, Nate Foster, Helle Hvid Hansen, Bart Jacobs, Jonathan Kimmitt, Xavier Leroy, Andrew Myers, Stefan Milius, Ross Tate, and the anonymous referees for helpful comments. Part of this work was done while the first two authors were visiting Radboud University Nijmegen and the CWI Amsterdam.

References

1. Adámek, J., Lücke, D., Milius, S.: Recursive coalgebras of finitary functors. Theoretical Informatics and Applications 41, 447–462 (2007)
2. Adámek, J., Milius, S., Velebil, J.: Elgot algebras. Log. Methods Comput. Sci. 2(5:4), 1–31 (2006)
3. Capretta, V., Uustalu, T., Vene, V.: Corecursive Algebras: A Study of General Structured Corecursion. In: Oliveira, M.V.M., Woodcock, J. (eds.) SBMF 2009. LNCS, vol. 5902, pp. 84–100. Springer, Heidelberg (2009)
4. Chong, S.: Lecture notes on abstract interpretation. Harvard University (2010), http://www.seas.harvard.edu/courses/cs152/2010sp/lectures/lec20.pdf
5. CoCaml project (December 2012), http://www.cs.cornell.edu/Projects/CoCaml/
6. Cousot, P., Cousot, R.: Abstract interpretation: a unified lattice model for static analysis of programs by construction or approximation of fixpoints. In: 4th ACM SIGPLAN-SIGACT Symp. Principles of Programming Languages, pp. 238–252. ACM Press, New York (1977)
7. Simon, L., Mallya, A., Bansal, A., Gupta, G.: Coinductive Logic Programming. In: Etalle, S., Truszczyński, M. (eds.) ICLP 2006. LNCS, vol. 4079, pp. 330–345. Springer, Heidelberg (2006)
8. Simon, L., Bansal, A., Mallya, A., Gupta, G.: Co-Logic Programming: Extending Logic Programming with Coinduction. In: Arge, L., Cachin, C., Jurdziński, T., Tarlecki, A. (eds.) ICALP 2007. LNCS, vol. 4596, pp. 472–483. Springer, Heidelberg (2007)
9. Taylor, P.: Practical Foundations of Mathematics. Cambridge Studies in Advanced Mathematics, vol. 59. Cambridge University Press (1999)
10. y Widemann, B.T.: Coalgebraic semantics of recursion on circular data structures. In: Cirstea, C., Seisenberger, M., Wilkinson, T. (eds.) CALCO Young Researchers Workshop (CALCO-jnr 2011), pp. 28–42 (August 2011)
11. Winskel, G.: The Formal Semantics of Programming Languages: An Introduction. MIT Press, Cambridge (1993)

Laziness by Need

Stephen Chang

Northeastern University
stchang@ccs.neu.edu

Abstract. Lazy functional programming has many benefits that strict functional languages can simulate via lazy data constructors. In recognition, ML, Scheme, and other strict functional languages have supported lazy stream programming with `delay` and `force` for several decades. Unfortunately, the manual insertion of `delay` and `force` can be tedious and error-prone.

We present a semantics-based refactoring that helps strict programmers manage manual lazy programming. The refactoring uses a static analysis to identify where additional `delays` and `forces` might be needed to achieve the desired simplification and performance benefits, once the programmer has added the initial lazy data constructors. The paper presents a correctness argument for the underlying transformations and some preliminary experiences with a prototype tool implementation.

1 Laziness in a Strict World

A lazy functional language naturally supports the construction of reusable components and their composition into reasonably efficient programs [12]. For example, the solution to a puzzle may consist of a generator that produces an easily-constructed stream of all *possible* solutions and a filter that extracts the desired *valid* solutions. Due to laziness, only a portion of the possible solutions are explored. Put differently, lazy composition appears to naturally recover the desired degree of efficiency without imposing a contorted programming style.

Unfortunately, programming in a lazy language comes at a cost. Not only are data constructors lazy, but all functions are as well. This pervasiveness of laziness makes it difficult to predict the behavior and time/space performance of lazy programs. As several researchers noticed [2,6,15,16,23], however, most programs need only a small amount of laziness. In response, people have repeatedly proposed lazy programming in strict functional languages [1,8,20,25,27]. In fact, Scheme [22] and ML [3] have supported manual stream programming with `delay` and `force` for decades. Using `delay` and macros, a programmer can easily turn an eager, Lisp-style list `constructor` into a lazy one [11], while `force` retrieves the value from a delayed computation.

However, merely switching from eager constructors to lazy ones is often not enough to achieve the performance benefits of laziness. The insertion of one `delay` tends to require additional `delays` elsewhere in the program to achieve the desired lazy behavior. Since these additional `delay` insertions depend on

M. Felleisen and P. Gardner (Eds.): ESOP 2013, LNCS 7792, pp. 81–100, 2013.

the value flow of the program, it can be difficult to determine where to insert them, especially in the presence of higher-order functions. In short, manual lazy programming is challenging and error-prone.

In response, we introduce a static analysis-based refactoring that assists programmers with the task of inserting `delays` and accompanying `forces`. We imagine a programmer who wishes to create a lazy generator and starts using lazy constructs in the obvious places. Our transformation then inserts additional `delays` and `forces` to achieve the desired lazy performance benefit.

The paper is organized as follows. The second section introduces some motivating examples. Section 3 presents the analysis-based program transformation, and section 4 argues its correctness. Section 5 sketches a prototype implementation, and section 6 describes real-world applications. Section 7 compares our approach with other attempts at taming laziness. Finally, section 8 lists some ideas for future work.

2   Motivating Examples

Nearly every modern strict programming language supports laziness, either via `delay` and `force`, or in the form of a streams or other lazy data structure library. None of these languages offer much help, however, in figuring out the right way to use these forms. To illustrate the problems, this section presents three examples in three distinct languages, typed and untyped. The first one, in Racket [10], shows how conventional program reorganizations can eliminate the performance benefits of laziness without warning. The second, in Scala [19], demonstrates how laziness propagates across function calls. The third example illustrates the difficulties of developing an idiomatic lazy n-queens algorithm in a strict language like OCaml [14]. That is, the problems of programming lazily in a strict language are universal across many languages.

2.1   Reorganizations Interfere with Laziness

Using `delay` and `force` occasionally confuses even the most experienced programmers. This subsection retells a recent story involving a senior Racket developer. A game tree is a data structure representing all possible sequences of moves in a game. It is frequently employed in AI algorithms to calculate an optimal next move, and it is also useful for game developers wishing to experiment with the rules of a game. For anything but the simplest games, however, the multitude of available moves at each game state results in an unwieldy or even infinite game tree. Thus, laziness is frequently utilized to manage such trees.

The Racket code to generate a game tree might roughly look like this:

```
;; A GameTree (short: GT) is one of:
;; -- (GT-Leaf GameState)
;; -- (GT-Node GameState Player [ListOf Move])

;; A Move is a (Move Name Position GameTree)
```

```
;; gen-GT : GameState Player -> GameTree
(define (gen-GT game-state player)
  (if (final-state? game-state)
      (GT-Leaf game-state)
      (GT-Node game-state player (calc-next-moves game-state player))))

;; calc-next-moves : GameState Player -> [ListOf Move]
(define (calc-next-moves game-state player)
  ⟨⟨for each possible attacker and target in game-state:⟩⟩
    (define new-state ...)
    (define new-player ...)
    (Move attacker target (gen-GT new-state new-player)))
```

A game tree is created with the gen-GT function, which takes a game state and the current active player. If the given state is a final state, then a GT-Leaf node is created. Otherwise, a GT-Node is created with the current game state, the current player, and a list of moves from the given game state. The calc-next-moves function creates a list of Move structures, where each move contains a new game tree starting from the game state resulting from the move.

An upcoming, Racket-based programming book utilizes such a game tree. Initially, only a small game is implemented, so Move is defined as a strict constructor. As the book progresses, however, the game tree becomes unwieldy as more features are added to the game. In response, the third argument of the Move structure is changed to be lazy, meaning the call to the Move constructor implicitly wraps the third argument with a delay.[1] With the lazy Move constructor, the code above generates only the first node of a game tree.

To prepare the book for typesetting, an author reorganized the definition of calc-next-moves in a seemingly innocuous fashion to fit it within the margins of a page:

```
;; calc-next-moves : GameState Player -> [ListOf Move]
(define (calc-next-moves game-state player)
  ⟨⟨for each possible attacker and target in game-state:⟩⟩
    (define new-state ...)
    (define new-player ...)
    (define new-gt (gen-GT new-state new-player))
    (Move attacker target new-gt))
```

The underlined code above pulls the generation of the game tree into a separate definition. As the astute reader will recognize, the new game tree is no longer created lazily. Even though the Move constructor is lazy in the third position, the benefits of laziness are lost. Even worse, such a performance bug is easily unnoticed because the program still passes all unit tests.

In contrast, our laziness transformation recognizes that the new-gt variable flows into the lazy position of the Move constructor, and in turn, proposes a delay around the construction of the new game tree.

---

[1] Specifically, Move becomes a macro that expands to a private constructor call where the third argument is delayed. This is a common idiom in Lisp-like languages [11].

2.2   Laziness Must Propagate

A 2009 blog post[2] illustrates a related tricky situation in the following Scala [19] example. Scala delays method arguments whose type is marked with =>, as in:[3]

```
def foo[A,B](a: A, b: => B): B = ...
```

When foo is called, its second argument is not evaluated until its value is needed inside the function body. However, if another function, bar, calls foo:

```
def bar[C,A,B](c: C, a: A, b: B): B = {  ...  foo(a, b) }
```

the b argument is evaluated when bar is called, thus negating the benefit of laziness in foo. To recover it, we must delay the third argument to bar:

```
def bar[C,A,B](c: C, a: A, b: => B): B = ...
```

If yet another function calls bar then that function must delay its argument as well. For programs with complex call graphs, the required delay points may be scattered throughout the program, making programmer errors more likely. Our transformation is designed to help with just such situations.

2.3   Idiomatic Lazy Programming in a Strict Language

The n-queens problem makes an illustrative playground for advertising lazy programming. An idiomatic lazy solution to such a puzzle may consist of just two parts: a part that places n queens at arbitrary positions on an n by n chess board, and a part for deciding whether a particular placement is a solution to the puzzle. Given these two components, a one-line function calculates a solution:

```
let nqueens n = hd (filter isValid all_placements)
```

The all_placements variable stands for a stream of all possible placements of n queens; filter isValid eliminates placements with conflicting queens; and hd picks the first valid one. Lazy evaluation guarantees that filter isValid traverses all_placements for just enough placements to find the first solution.

The approach cleanly separates two distinct concerns. While all_placements may ignore the rules of the puzzle, it is the task of isValid to enforce them. If the components were large, two different programmers could tackle them in parallel. All they would have to agree on is the representation of queen placements, for which we choose a list of board coordinates (r, c). The rest of the section explains how an OCaml [14] programmer may develop such a lazy algorithm. Here is all_placements: :

```
let process_row r qss_so_far =
  foldr (fun qs new_qss -> (map (fun c -> (r,c)::qs) (rng n)) @ new_qss)
        [] qss_so_far

let all_placements = foldl process_row [[]] (rng n)
```

---

[2] http://pchiusano.blogspot.com/2009/05/
optional-laziness-doesnt-quite-cut-it.html

[3] The => syntax specifies "by-name" parameter passing for this position but the distinction between "by-name" and "lazy" is inconsequential here.

Brackets denote lists, rng n is [1...n], :: is infix cons, and @ is infix append. All possible placements are generated by adding one coordinate at a time. The process_row function, given a row r and a list of placements qss_so_far, duplicates each placement in qss_so_far n times, adding to each copy a new coordinate of r with a different column c, and then appends all these new placements to the final list of all placements. The process_row function is called n times, once per row. The result of evaluating all_placements looks like this:

```
[[(n,1);(n-1,1);  ...  ;(1,1)];
 ...;
 [(n,n);(n-1,n);  ...  ;(1,n)]]
```

where each line represents one possible placement.

Since OCaml is strict, however, using all_placements with the nqueens function from earlier generates all possible placements before testing each one of them for validity. This computation is obviously time consuming and performs far more work than necessary. For instance, here is the timing for $n = 8$ queens:[4]

```
real 0m52.122s   user 0m51.399s   sys 0m0.468s
```

If the programmer switches to lazy lists to represent all_placements, then only a portion of the possible placements should be explored. Specifically, all instances of cons (::) are replaced with its lazy variant, represented with ::$_{lz}$ below. In this setting, lazy cons is defined using OCaml's Lazy module and is cons with a delayed rest list. It is also necessary to add forces where appropriate.[5] For example, here is append (@) and map with lazy cons ([] also represents the empty lazy list):[6]

```
let rec (@) lst1 lst2 =
  match force lst1 with
  | [] -> lst2
  | x::lzxs -> x::lzdelay (xs @ lst2)

let rec map f lst =
  match force lst with
  | [] -> []
  | x::lzxs -> f x::lzdelay (map f xs)
```

Running this program, however, surprises our lazy-strict programmer:

```
real 1m3.720s   user 1m3.072s   sys 0m0.352s
```

With lazy cons and force, the program runs even slower than the strict version. Using lazy cons naïvely does not seem to generate the expected performance gains. Additional delays and forces are required, though it is not immediately obvious where to insert them. This step is precisely where our analysis-based refactoring transformation helps a programmer. In this particular case, our transformation would insert a delay in the foldr function:

---

[4] Run on an Intel i7-2600k, 16GB memory machine using the Linux time command.

[5] "Appropriate" here means we avoid Wadler et al.'s [27] "odd" errors.

[6] OCaml's delaying construct is lazy but for clarity and consistency with the rest of the paper we continue to use delay. Also, in ML languages, the delay is explicit.

```
let rec foldr f base lst =
  match force lst with
  | [] -> base
  | x::lzxs -> f x (delay (foldr f base xs))
```

This perhaps unobvious `delay` is needed because `f`'s second argument eventually flows to a lazy `cons` in append (`@`). Without this `delay`, the list of all queen placements is evaluated prematurely. With this refactoring, and an appropriate insertion of `force`s, the lazy-strict programmer sees a dramatic improvement:

```
real 0m3.103s    user 0m3.068s    sys 0m0.024s
```

Lazy programmers are already familiar with such benefits, but our refactoring transformation enables strict programmers to reap the same benefits as well.

3 Refactoring For Laziness

The heart of our refactoring is a whole-program analysis that calculates where values may flow. Our transformation uses the results of the analysis to insert `delay`s and `force`s. Section 3.1 describes the core of our strict language. We then present our analysis in three steps: section 3.2 explains the analysis rules for our language; section 3.3 extends the language and analysis with lazy forms: `delay`, `force`, and lazy `cons` (`lcons`); and section 3.4 extends the analysis again to calculate the potential insertion points for `delay` and `force`. Finally, section 3.5 defines the refactoring transformation function.

3.1 Language Syntax

Our starting point is an untyped[7] functional core language. The language is *strict* and uses a standard expression notation:

$$e \in Exp = n \mid b \mid x \mid \lambda(x\ldots).e \mid e\,e\ldots \mid o\,e\,e \mid \text{zero? } e \mid \text{not } e \mid \text{if } e\,e\,e$$
$$\mid \text{let } x = e \text{ in } e \mid \text{null} \mid \text{cons } e\,e \mid \text{first } e \mid \text{rest } e \mid \text{null? } e$$
$$n \in \mathbb{Z}, \quad b \in Bool = \text{true} \mid \text{false}, \quad x \in Var, \quad o \in Op = + \mid - \mid * \mid / \mid < \mid > \mid = \mid \text{or} \mid \text{and}$$

There are integers, booleans, variables, λs, applications, boolean and arithmetic primitives, conditionals, (non-recursive) lets, and eager lists and list operations. Here are the values, where both components of a non-empty list must be values:

$$v \in Val = n \mid b \mid \lambda(x\ldots).e \mid \text{null} \mid \text{cons } v\,v$$

A program p consists of two pieces: a series of mutually referential function definitions and an expression that may call the functions:

$$p \in Prog = d\ldots e \qquad\qquad d \in Def = \text{define } f(x\ldots) = e$$

---

[7] Standard type systems cannot adequately express the flow of laziness and thus cannot solve the `delay`-insertion problems from section 2. A type error can signal a missing `force`, but a type system will not suggest where to add performance-related `delay`s. Thus we omit types for this first step in our research.

3.2   Analysis Step 1: 0-CFA

Our initial analysis is based on 0-CFA [13,24,26]. The analysis assumes that each subexpression has a unique label ℓ, also drawn from Var, but that the set of labels and the set of variables in a program are disjoint. The analysis computes an abstract environment $\widehat{\rho}$ that maps elements of Var to sets of abstract values:

$$\widehat{\rho} \in Env = Var \to \mathcal{P}(\widehat{v}) \qquad \ell \in Var \qquad \widehat{v} \in \widehat{Val} = \mathtt{val} \mid \lambda(x\ldots).\ell \mid \mathtt{cons}\ \ell\ \ell$$

A set $\widehat{\rho}(x)$ or $\widehat{\rho}(\ell)$ represents an approximation of all possible values that can be bound to x or observed at ℓ, respectively, during evaluation of the program.

The analysis uses abstract representations of values, $\widehat{v}$, where $\mathtt{val}$ stands for all literals in the language. In addition, $\lambda(x\ldots).\ell$ are abstract function values where the body is represented with a label, and $(\mathtt{cons}\ \ell\ \ell)$ are abstract list values where the ℓ's are the labels of the respective pieces. We overload the $\widehat{}$ notation to denote a function that converts a concrete value to its abstract counterpart:

$$\widehat{n} = \mathtt{val} \qquad \widehat{b} = \mathtt{val} \qquad \widehat{\mathtt{null}} = \mathtt{val} \qquad \boxed{\widehat{} : Val \to \widehat{Val}}$$

$$\widehat{\lambda(x\ldots).e^\ell} = \lambda(x\ldots).\ell \qquad \widehat{\mathtt{cons}\ v_1^{\ell_1}\ v_2^{\ell_2}} = \mathtt{cons}\ \ell_1\ \ell_2$$

We present our analysis with a standard [18], constraints-based specification, where notation $\widehat{\rho} \models p$ means $\widehat{\rho}$ is an acceptable approximation of program p. Figures 1 and 2 show the analysis for programs and expressions, respectively.

The [prog] rule specifies that environment $\widehat{\rho}$ satisfies program $p = d\ldots e$ if it satisfies all definitions $d\ldots$ as well as the expression e in the program. The [def] rule says that $\widehat{\rho}$ satisfies a definition if the corresponding abstract λ-value is included for variable f in $\widehat{\rho}$, and if $\widehat{\rho}$ satisfies the function body as well.

In figure 2, the [num], [bool], and [null] rules show that $\mathtt{val}$ represents these literals in the analysis. The [var] rule connects variables x and their labels ℓ, specifying that all values bound to x should also be observable at ℓ. The [lam] rule for an ℓ-labeled λ says that its abstract version must be in $\widehat{\rho}(\ell)$ and that $\widehat{\rho}$ must satisfy its body. The [app] rule says that $\widehat{\rho}$ must satisfy the function and arguments in an application. In addition, for each possible λ in the function position, the arguments must be bound to the corresponding parameters of that λ and the result of evaluating the λ's body must also be a result for the application itself. The [let] rule has similar constraints. The [op], [zero?], [not], and [null?] rules require that $\widehat{\rho}$ satisfy a primitive's operands and uses $\mathtt{val}$ as the result. The [if] rule requires that $\widehat{\rho}$ satisfy the test expression and the two branches, and that any resulting values in the branches also be a result for the entire

$$\widehat{\rho} \models d\ldots e \text{ iff} \qquad [prog]$$
$$\widehat{\rho} \models_d d \ \wedge\ \ldots\ \wedge\ \widehat{\rho} \models_e e$$

$$\widehat{\rho} \models_d \mathbf{define}\ f(x\ldots) = e^\ell \text{ iff} \qquad [def]$$
$$\lambda(x\ldots).\ell \in \widehat{\rho}(f)\ \wedge\ \widehat{\rho} \models_e e^\ell$$

Fig. 1. 0-CFA analysis on programs

$$\widehat{\rho} \models_e n^\ell \text{ iff } \mathbf{val} \in \widehat{\rho}(\ell) \qquad [num]$$

$$\widehat{\rho} \models_e b^\ell \text{ iff } \mathbf{val} \in \widehat{\rho}(\ell) \qquad [bool]$$

$$\widehat{\rho} \models_e x^\ell \text{ iff } \widehat{\rho}(x) \subseteq \widehat{\rho}(\ell) \qquad [var]$$

$$\widehat{\rho} \models_e (\lambda(x \ldots).e_0^{\ell_0})^\ell \text{ iff } \qquad [lam]$$
$$\lambda(x \ldots).\ell_0 \in \widehat{\rho}(\ell) \ \wedge \ \widehat{\rho} \models_e e_0^{\ell_0}$$

$$\widehat{\rho} \models_e (e_f^{\ell_f} \ e_1^{\ell_1} \ldots)^\ell \text{ iff } \qquad [app]$$
$$\widehat{\rho} \models_e e_f^{\ell_f} \ \wedge \ \widehat{\rho} \models_e e_1^{\ell_1} \ \wedge \ \ldots \ \wedge$$
$$(\forall \lambda(x_1 \ldots).\ell_0 \in \widehat{\rho}(\ell_f) :$$
$$\widehat{\rho}(\ell_1) \subseteq \widehat{\rho}(x_1) \ \wedge \ \ldots \ \wedge$$
$$\widehat{\rho}(\ell_0) \subseteq \widehat{\rho}(\ell))$$

$$\widehat{\rho} \models_e (\mathbf{let} \ x = e_1^{\ell_1} \ \mathbf{in} \ e_0^{\ell_0})^\ell \text{ iff } \qquad [let]$$
$$\widehat{\rho} \models_e e_1^{\ell_1} \ \wedge \ \widehat{\rho}(\ell_1) \subseteq \widehat{\rho}(x) \ \wedge$$
$$\widehat{\rho} \models_e e_0^{\ell_0} \ \wedge \ \widehat{\rho}(\ell_0) \subseteq \widehat{\rho}(\ell)$$

$$\widehat{\rho} \models_e (o \ e_1^{\ell_1} \ e_2^{\ell_2})^\ell \text{ iff } \qquad [op]$$
$$\widehat{\rho} \models_e e_1^{\ell_1} \ \wedge \ \widehat{\rho} \models_e e_2^{\ell_2} \ \wedge \ \mathbf{val} \in \widehat{\rho}(\ell)$$

$$\widehat{\rho} \models_e (\mathbf{zero?} \ e_1^{\ell_1})^\ell \text{ iff } \qquad [zero?]$$
$$\widehat{\rho} \models_e e_1^{\ell_1} \ \wedge \ \mathbf{val} \in \widehat{\rho}(\ell)$$

$$\widehat{\rho} \models_e (\mathbf{not} \ e_1^{\ell_1})^\ell \text{ iff } \qquad [not]$$
$$\widehat{\rho} \models_e e_1^{\ell_1} \ \wedge \ \mathbf{val} \in \widehat{\rho}(\ell)$$

$$\widehat{\rho} \models_e (\mathbf{if} \ e_1^{\ell_1} \ e_2^{\ell_2} \ e_3^{\ell_3})^\ell \text{ iff } \qquad [if]$$
$$\widehat{\rho} \models_e e_1^{\ell_1} \ \wedge \ \widehat{\rho} \models_e e_2^{\ell_2} \ \wedge \ \widehat{\rho}(\ell_2) \subseteq \widehat{\rho}(\ell)$$
$$\wedge \ \widehat{\rho} \models_e e_3^{\ell_3} \ \wedge \ \widehat{\rho}(\ell_3) \subseteq \widehat{\rho}(\ell)$$

$$\widehat{\rho} \models_e \mathbf{null}^\ell \text{ iff } \mathbf{val} \in \widehat{\rho}(\ell) \qquad [null]$$

$$\widehat{\rho} \models_e (\mathbf{null?} \ e_1^{\ell_1})^\ell \text{ iff } \qquad [null?]$$
$$\widehat{\rho} \models_e e_1^{\ell_1} \ \wedge \ \mathbf{val} \in \widehat{\rho}(\ell)$$

$$\widehat{\rho} \models_e (\mathbf{cons} \ e_1^{\ell_1} \ e_2^{\ell_2})^\ell \text{ iff } \qquad [cons]$$
$$\widehat{\rho} \models_e e_1^{\ell_1} \ \wedge \ \widehat{\rho} \models_e e_2^{\ell_2} \ \wedge \ (\mathbf{cons} \ \ell_1 \ \ell_2) \in \widehat{\rho}(\ell)$$

$$\widehat{\rho} \models_e (\mathbf{first} \ e_1^{\ell_1})^\ell \text{ iff } \ \widehat{\rho} \models_e e_1^{\ell_1} \ \wedge \qquad [first]$$
$$(\forall (\mathbf{cons} \ \ell_2 \ \_) \in \widehat{\rho}(\ell_1) : \ \widehat{\rho}(\ell_2) \subseteq \widehat{\rho}(\ell))$$

$$\widehat{\rho} \models_e (\mathbf{rest} \ e_1^{\ell_1})^\ell \text{ iff } \ \widehat{\rho} \models_e e_1^{\ell_1} \ \wedge \qquad [rest]$$
$$(\forall (\mathbf{cons} \ \_ \ \ell_2) \in \widehat{\rho}(\ell_1) : \ \widehat{\rho}(\ell_2) \subseteq \widehat{\rho}(\ell))$$

Fig. 2. Step 1: 0-CFA analysis on expressions

expression. The [cons] rule for an ℓ-labeled, eager cons requires that $\widehat{\rho}$ satisfy both arguments and that a corresponding abstract cons value be in $\widehat{\rho}(\ell)$. Finally, the [first] and [rest] rules require satisfiability of their arguments and that the appropriate piece of any cons arguments be a result of the entire expression.

3.3   Analysis Step 2: Adding delay and force

Next we extend our language and analysis with lazy forms:

$$e \in Exp = \ldots \mid \mathbf{delay} \ e \mid \mathbf{force} \ e \mid \mathbf{lcons} \ e \ e$$
$$\text{where } \mathbf{lcons} \ e_1 \ e_2 \ \stackrel{df}{=} \ \mathbf{cons} \ e_1 \ (\mathbf{delay} \ e_2)$$

The language is still strict but delay introduces promises. A force term recursively forces all nested delays. Lazy cons (lcons) is only lazy in its rest argument and first and rest work with both lcons and cons values so that rest (lcons v e) results in (delay e).

We add promises and lazy lists to the sets of values and abstract values, and $\widehat{\cdot}$ is similarly extended. The abstract representation of a delay replaces the labeled delayed expression with just the label and the abstract lcons is similar.

$$v \in Val = \ldots \mid \text{delay } e \mid \text{lcons } v\ e$$

$$\widehat{v} \in \widehat{Val} = \ldots \mid \text{delay } \ell \mid \text{lcons } \ell\ \ell$$

$$\ldots \quad \widehat{\text{delay } e^\ell} = \text{delay } \ell \quad \widehat{\text{lcons } v_1^{\ell_1}\ e_2^{\ell_2}} = \text{lcons } \ell_1\ \ell_2 \quad \boxed{\widehat{\cdot} : Val \to \widehat{Val}}$$

Figure 3 presents the new and extended analysis rules. The [*delay*] rule specifies that for an ℓ-labeled delay, the corresponding abstract delay must be in $\widehat{\rho}(\ell)$ and $\widehat{\rho}$ must satisfy the delayed subexpression. In addition, the values of the delayed subexpression must also be in $\widehat{\rho}(\ell)$. This means that the analysis approximates evaluation of a promise with both a promise and the result of forcing that promise. We discuss the rationale for this constraint below. The [*force*] rule says that $\widehat{\rho}$ must satisfy the argument and that non-delay arguments are propagated to the outer ℓ label. Since the [*delay*] rule already approximates evaluation of the delayed expression, the [*force*] rule does not have any such constraints.

We also add a rule for lcons and extend the [*first*] and [*rest*] rules to handle lcons values. The [*lcons*] rule requires that $\widehat{\rho}$ satisfy the arguments and requires a corresponding abstract lcons at the expressions's ℓ label. The [*first*] rule handles lcons values just like cons values. For the [*rest*] rule, a delay with the lcons's second component is a possible result of the expression. Just like the [*delay*] rule, the [*rest*] rule assumes that the lazy component of the lcons is both forced and unforced, and thus there is another constraint that propagates the values of the (undelayed) second component to the outer label.

Implicit Forcing. In our analysis, delays are both evaluated and unevaluated. We assume that during evaluation, a programmer does not want an unforced delay to appear in a strict position. For example, if the analysis discovers an unforced delay as the function in an application, we assume that the programmer forgot a force and analyze that function call anyway. This makes our analysis quite conservative but minimizes the effect of any laziness-related errors in the computed control flow. On the technical side, implicit forcing also facilitates the proof of a safety theorem for the transformation (see subsection 4.3).

$\widehat{\rho} \models_e (\text{delay } e_1^{\ell_1})^\ell$ iff   [*delay*]

$\quad (\text{delay } \ell_1) \in \widehat{\rho}(\ell) \wedge \widehat{\rho} \models_e e_1^{\ell_1} \wedge \widehat{\rho}(\ell_1) \subseteq \widehat{\rho}(\ell)$

$\widehat{\rho} \models_e (\text{force } e_1^{\ell_1})^\ell$ iff   [*force*]

$\quad \widehat{\rho} \models_e e_1^{\ell_1} \wedge (\forall \widehat{v} \in \widehat{\rho}(\ell_1), \widehat{v} \notin \text{delay} : \widehat{v} \in \widehat{\rho}(\ell))$

$\widehat{\rho} \models_e (\text{lcons } e_1^{\ell_1}\ e_2^{\ell_2})^\ell$ iff   [*lcons*]

$\quad \widehat{\rho} \models_e e_1^{\ell_1} \wedge \widehat{\rho} \models_e e_2^{\ell_2} \wedge (\text{lcons } \ell_1\ \ell_2) \in \widehat{\rho}(\ell)$

$\widehat{\rho} \models_e (\text{first } e_1^{\ell_1})^\ell$ iff $\ldots \wedge$ [*first*]

$\quad (\forall (\text{lcons } \ell_2\ \_) \in \widehat{\rho}(\ell_1) :$

$\qquad \widehat{\rho}(\ell_2) \subseteq \widehat{\rho}(\ell))$

$\widehat{\rho} \models_e (\text{rest } e_1^{\ell_1})^\ell$ iff $\ldots \wedge$ [*rest*]

$\quad (\forall (\text{lcons } \_\ \ell_2) \in \widehat{\rho}(\ell_1) :$

$\qquad (\text{delay } \ell_2) \in \widehat{\rho}(\ell) \wedge$

$\qquad \widehat{\rho}(\ell_2) \subseteq \widehat{\rho}(\ell))$

Fig. 3. Step 2: Analysis with lazy forms

$$(\widehat{\rho}, \widehat{\mathcal{D}}) \models_e (e_f^{\ell_f}\, e_1^{\ell_1} \ldots)^\ell \text{ iff} \qquad [app]$$
$$(\widehat{\rho}, \widehat{\mathcal{D}}) \models_e e_f^{\ell_f} \,\wedge\, (\widehat{\rho}, \widehat{\mathcal{D}}) \models_e e_1^{\ell_1} \wedge \ldots \wedge$$
$$(\forall \lambda(x_1 \ldots).\ell_0 \in \widehat{\rho}(\ell_f):$$
$$\widehat{\rho}(\ell_1) \subseteq \widehat{\rho}(x_1) \,\wedge\, \ldots \,\wedge$$
$$\boxed{(\text{arg } \ell_1) \in \widehat{\rho}(x_1) \,\wedge\, \ldots}_1 \wedge$$
$$\boxed{(\forall \widehat{v} \in \widehat{\rho}(\ell_0), \widehat{v} \notin \text{arg}: \widehat{v} \in \widehat{\rho}(\ell))}_2)$$

$$(\widehat{\rho}, \widehat{\mathcal{D}}) \models_e (\text{delay } e_1^{\ell_1})^\ell \text{ iff} \qquad [delay]$$
$$(\text{delay } \ell_1) \in \widehat{\rho}(\ell) \,\wedge$$
$$(\widehat{\rho}, \widehat{\mathcal{D}}) \models_e e_1^{\ell_1} \,\wedge\, \widehat{\rho}(\ell_1) \subseteq \widehat{\rho}(\ell) \,\wedge$$
$$(\forall x \in fv(e_1): (\forall(\text{arg } \ell_2) \in \widehat{\rho}(x):$$
$$\boxed{\ell_2 \in \widehat{\mathcal{D}}}_3 \wedge \boxed{(\text{darg } \ell_2) \in \widehat{\rho}(x)}_4))$$

$$(\widehat{\rho}, \widehat{\mathcal{D}}) \models_e (\text{let } x = e_1^{\ell_1} \text{ in } e_0^{\ell_0})^\ell \text{ iff} \quad [let]$$
$$(\widehat{\rho}, \widehat{\mathcal{D}}) \models_e e_1^{\ell_1} \,\wedge\, \widehat{\rho}(\ell_1) \subseteq \widehat{\rho}(x) \,\wedge$$
$$\boxed{(\text{arg } \ell_1) \in \widehat{\rho}(x)}_1 \wedge (\widehat{\rho}, \widehat{\mathcal{D}}) \models_e e_0^{\ell_0} \,\wedge$$
$$\boxed{(\forall \widehat{v} \in \widehat{\rho}(\ell_0), \widehat{v} \notin \text{arg}: \widehat{v} \in \widehat{\rho}(\ell))}_2$$

$$(\widehat{\rho}, \widehat{\mathcal{D}}) \models_e (\text{lcons } e_1^{\ell_1}\, e_2^{\ell_2})^\ell \text{ iff} \quad [lcons]$$
$$(\widehat{\rho}, \widehat{\mathcal{D}}) \models_e e_1^{\ell_1} \,\wedge\, (\widehat{\rho}, \widehat{\mathcal{D}}) \models_e e_2^{\ell_2} \,\wedge$$
$$(\text{lcons } \ell_1\, \ell_2) \in \widehat{\rho}(\ell) \,\wedge$$
$$(\forall x \in fv(e_2): (\forall(\text{arg } \ell_3) \in \widehat{\rho}(x):$$
$$\boxed{\ell_3 \in \widehat{\mathcal{D}}}_3 \wedge \boxed{(\text{darg } \ell_3) \in \widehat{\rho}(x)}_4))$$

Fig. 4. Step 3a: Calculating flow to lazy positions

3.4   Analysis Step 3: Laziness Analysis

Our final refinement revises the analysis to calculate three additional sets, which are used to insert additional `delay`s and `force`s in the program:

$$\widehat{\mathcal{D}} \in DPos = \mathcal{P}(Var), \quad \widehat{\mathcal{S}} \in SPos = \mathcal{P}(Var), \quad \widehat{\mathcal{F}} \in FPos = \mathcal{P}(Var \cup (Var \times Var))$$

Intuitively, $\widehat{\mathcal{D}}$ is a set of labels representing function arguments that flow to lazy positions and $\widehat{\mathcal{S}}$ is a set of labels representing arguments that flow to strict positions. Our transformation then delays arguments that reach a lazy position but not a strict position. Additionally, $\widehat{\mathcal{F}}$ collects the labels where a delayed value may appear—both those manually inserted by the programmer and those suggested by the analysis—and is used by the transformation to insert `force`s.

We first describe how the analysis computes $\widehat{\mathcal{D}}$. The key is to track the flow of arguments from an application into a function body and for this, we introduce a special abstract value $(\text{arg } \ell)$, where ℓ labels an argument in a function call.

$$\widehat{v} \in \widehat{Val} = \ldots \mid \text{arg } \ell$$

Figure 4 presents revised analysis rules related to $\widehat{\mathcal{D}}$. To reduce clutter, we express the analysis result as $(\widehat{\rho}, \widehat{\mathcal{D}})$, temporarily omitting $\widehat{\mathcal{S}}$ and $\widehat{\mathcal{F}}$. In the new [app] and [let] rules, additional constraints (box 1) specify that for each labeled argument, an `arg` abstract value with a matching label must be in $\widehat{\rho}$ for the corresponding parameter. We are only interested in the flow of arguments within a function's body, so the result-propagating constraint filters out `arg` values (box 2).

Recall that $\widehat{\mathcal{D}}$ is to contain labels of arguments that reach lazy positions. Specifically, if an $(\text{arg } \ell)$ value flows to a `delay` or the second position of an

$$(\widehat{\rho},\widehat{\mathcal{D}},\widehat{\mathcal{S}},\widehat{\mathcal{F}}) \models_e (\texttt{force } e_1^{\ell_1})^\ell \text{ iff} \qquad [force]$$

$$(\widehat{\rho},\widehat{\mathcal{D}},\widehat{\mathcal{S}},\widehat{\mathcal{F}}) \models_e e_1^{\ell_1} \wedge$$

$$(\forall \widehat{v} \in \widehat{\rho}(\ell_1), \widehat{v} \notin \texttt{delay} : \widehat{v} \in \widehat{\rho}(\ell)) \wedge$$

$$\boxed{(\forall(\texttt{arg } \ell_2) \in \widehat{\rho}(\ell_1) : \ell_2 \in \widehat{\mathcal{S}})}_5$$

$$(\widehat{\rho},\widehat{\mathcal{D}},\widehat{\mathcal{S}},\widehat{\mathcal{F}}) \models_e S[e^\ell] \text{ iff} \quad \dots \wedge \quad [strict]$$

$$\boxed{(\forall(\texttt{arg } \ell_1) \in \widehat{\rho}(\ell) : \ell_1 \in \widehat{\mathcal{S}})}_5 \wedge$$

$$\boxed{(\exists \texttt{delay} \in \widehat{\rho}(\ell) \Rightarrow \ell \in \widehat{\mathcal{F}})}_6 \wedge$$

$$\boxed{(\forall(\texttt{darg } \ell_2) \in \widehat{\rho}(\ell) : (\ell, \ell_2) \in \widehat{\mathcal{F}})}_7$$

where $S \in SCtx = [\,] \; e \dots \mid o\,[\,] \; e \mid o \; v\,[\,] \mid \texttt{if }[\,] \; e_1 \; e_2$
$\mid \texttt{zero? }[\,] \mid \texttt{not }[\,] \mid \texttt{null? }[\,] \mid \texttt{first }[\,] \mid \texttt{rest }[\,]$

Fig. 5. Step 3b: Calculating flow to strict positions

$\texttt{lcons}$, then ℓ must be in $\widehat{\mathcal{D}}$ (box 3) ($fv(e)$ calculates free variables in e). If an ℓ-labeled argument reaches a lazy position, the transformation *may* decide to delay that argument, so the analysis must additionally track it for the purposes of inserting $\texttt{forces}$. To this end, we introduce another abstract value ($\texttt{darg } \ell$),

$$\widehat{v} \in \widehat{Val} = \dots \mid \texttt{darg } \ell$$

and insert it when needed (box 4). While ($\texttt{arg } \ell$) can represent any argument, ($\texttt{darg } \ell$) only represents arguments that reach a lazy position (i.e., $\ell \in \widehat{\mathcal{D}}$).

Figure 5 presents revised analysis rules involving $\widehat{\mathcal{S}}$ and $\widehat{\mathcal{F}}$. These rules use the full analysis result $(\widehat{\rho},\widehat{\mathcal{D}},\widehat{\mathcal{S}},\widehat{\mathcal{F}})$. Here, $\widehat{\mathcal{S}}$ represents arguments that reach a strict position so the new [*force*] rule dictates that if an ($\texttt{arg } \ell$) is the argument of a $\texttt{force}$, then ℓ must be in $\widehat{\mathcal{S}}$ (box 5). However, a $\texttt{force}$ is not the only expression that requires the value of a promise. There are several other contexts where a $\texttt{delay}$ should not appear and the [*strict*] rule deals with these strict contexts S: the operator in an application, the operands in the primitive operations, and the test in an $\texttt{if}$ expression. Expressions involving these strict positions have three additional constraints. The first specifies that if an ($\texttt{arg } \ell_1$) appears in any of these positions, then ℓ_1 should also be in $\widehat{\mathcal{S}}$ (box 5). The second and third additional constraints show how $\widehat{\mathcal{F}}$ is computed. Recall that $\widehat{\mathcal{F}}$ determines where to insert $\texttt{forces}$ in the program. The second [*strict*] constraint says that if any $\texttt{delay}$ flows to a strict position ℓ, then ℓ is added to $\widehat{\mathcal{F}}$ (box 6). This indicates that a programmer-inserted $\texttt{delay}$ has reached a strict position and should be forced. Finally, the third constraint dictates that if a ($\texttt{darg } \ell_2$) value flows to a strict label ℓ, then a pair (ℓ, ℓ_2) is required to be in $\widehat{\mathcal{F}}$ (box 7), indicating that the analysis *may* insert a $\texttt{delay}$ at ℓ_2, thus requiring a $\texttt{force}$ at ℓ.

3.5   The Refactoring Transformation

Figure 6 specifies our refactoring as a function φ that transforms a program p using analysis result $(\widehat{\rho},\widehat{\mathcal{D}},\widehat{\mathcal{S}},\widehat{\mathcal{F}})$. The φ_e function wraps expression e^ℓ with

$$\boxed{\varphi : Prog \times Env \times DPos \times SPos \times FPos \rightarrow Prog}$$

$$\varphi[\![(\texttt{define } f(x\ldots) = e_1)\ldots e]\!]_{\widehat{\rho}\widehat{\mathcal{D}}\widehat{\mathcal{S}}\widehat{\mathcal{F}}} = (\texttt{define } f(x\ldots) = \varphi_e[\![e_1]\!]_{\widehat{\rho}\widehat{\mathcal{D}}\widehat{\mathcal{S}}\widehat{\mathcal{F}}})\ldots\varphi_e[\![e]\!]_{\widehat{\rho}\widehat{\mathcal{D}}\widehat{\mathcal{S}}\widehat{\mathcal{F}}}$$

$$\boxed{\varphi_e : Exp \times Env \times DPos \times SPos \times FPos \rightarrow Exp}$$

$$\varphi_e[\![e^\ell]\!]_{\widehat{\rho}\widehat{\mathcal{D}}\widehat{\mathcal{S}}\widehat{\mathcal{F}}} = (\texttt{delay}^* \ (\varphi_e[\![e]\!]_{\widehat{\rho}\widehat{\mathcal{D}}\widehat{\mathcal{S}}\widehat{\mathcal{F}}})^\ell)^{\ell_1}, \quad \text{if } \ell \in \widehat{\mathcal{D}},\ \ell \notin \widehat{\mathcal{S}},\ \ell_1 \notin dom(\widehat{\rho}) \tag{†}$$

$$\varphi_e[\![e^\ell]\!]_{\widehat{\rho}\widehat{\mathcal{D}}\widehat{\mathcal{S}}\widehat{\mathcal{F}}} = (\texttt{force} \ (\varphi_e[\![e]\!]_{\widehat{\rho}\widehat{\mathcal{D}}\widehat{\mathcal{S}}\widehat{\mathcal{F}}})^\ell)^{\ell_1}, \quad \text{if } \ell \in \widehat{\mathcal{F}},\ \ell_1 \notin dom(\widehat{\rho}), \tag{‡}$$

$$\text{or } \exists \ell_2.(\ell,\ell_2) \in \widehat{\mathcal{F}},\ \ell_2 \in \widehat{\mathcal{D}},\ \ell_2 \notin \widehat{\mathcal{S}},\ \ell_1 \notin dom(\widehat{\rho})$$

$$\ldots$$

Fig. 6. Transformation function φ

delay* if ℓ is in $\widehat{\mathcal{D}}$ and not in $\widehat{\mathcal{S}}$. In other words, e is delayed if it flows to a lazy position but not a strict position. With the following correctness section in mind, we extend the set of expressions with delay*, which is exactly like delay and merely distinguishes programmer-inserted delays from those inserted by the our transformation. The new delay* expression is given a fresh label ℓ_1. In two cases, φ_e inserts a force around an expression e^ℓ. First, if ℓ is in $\widehat{\mathcal{F}}$, it means ℓ is a strict position and a programmer-inserted delay reaches this strict position and must be forced. Second, an expression e^ℓ is also wrapped with force if there is some ℓ_2 such that (ℓ,ℓ_2) is in $\widehat{\mathcal{F}}$ and the analysis says to delay the expression at ℓ_2, i.e., $\ell_2 \in \widehat{\mathcal{D}}$ and $\ell_2 \notin \widehat{\mathcal{S}}$. This ensures that transformation-inserted delay*s are also properly forced. All remaining clauses in the definition of φ_e, represented with ellipses, traverse the structure of e in a homomorphic manner.

4   Correctness

Our refactoring for laziness is not semantics-preserving. For example, non-terminating programs may be transformed into terminating ones or exceptions may be delayed indefinitely. Nevertheless, we can prove our analysis sound and the φ transformation safe, meaning that unforced promises cannot cause exceptions.

4.1   Language Semantics

To establish soundness, we use Flanagan and Felleisen's [9] technique, which relies on a reduction semantics. The semantics is based on evaluation contexts, which are expressions with a hole in place of one subexpression:

$$E \in Ctx = [\,] \mid v\ldots E\,e\ldots \mid o\,E\,e \mid o\,v\,E \mid \texttt{let } x = E \texttt{ in } e \mid \texttt{if } E\,e\,e \mid \texttt{zero? } E$$
$$\mid \texttt{not } E \mid \texttt{null? } E \mid \texttt{force } E \mid \texttt{cons } E\,e \mid \texttt{cons } v\,E \mid \texttt{lcons } E\,e \mid \texttt{first } E \mid \texttt{rest } E$$

A reduction step $\longmapsto$ is defined as follows, where $\rightarrow$ is specified in figure 7:

$$E[e] \longmapsto E[e'] \quad \text{iff} \quad e \rightarrow e'$$

A conventional δ function evaluates primitives and is elided. We again assume that subexpressions are uniquely labeled but since labels do not affect evaluation, they are implicit in the reduction rules, though we do mention them explicitly in the theorems. Since our analysis does not distinguish memoizing promises from non-memoizing ones, neither does our semantics. To evaluate complete programs, we parameterize $\longmapsto$ over definitions $d \ldots$, and add a look-up rule:

$$E[f] \longmapsto_{d\ldots} E[\lambda(x \ldots).e], \quad \text{if } (\text{define } f(x \ldots) = e) \in d \ldots$$

Thus, the result of evaluating a program $p = d \ldots e$ is the result of reducing e with $\longmapsto_{d\ldots}$. We often drop the $d \ldots$ subscript to reduce clutter.

Exceptions

Our $\rightarrow$ reduction thus far is partial, as is the (elided) δ function. If certain expressions show up in the hole of the evaluation context, e.g., `first null` or division by 0, we consider the evaluation stuck. To handle stuck expressions, we add an exception **exn** to our semantics. We assume that δ returns **exn** for invalid operands of primitives and we extend $\rightarrow$ with the exception-producing reductions in figure 8.

The (apx) rule says that application of non-λs results in an exception. The (fstx) and (rstx) rules state that reducing `first` or `rest` with anything but a non-empty list is an exception as well. The (strictx) and (strictx*) reductions partially override some reductions from figure 7 and specify that an exception occurs when an unforced promise appears in a context where the value of that promise is required. These contexts are exactly the strict contexts S from figure 5. We introduce **dexn** and **dexn*** to indicate when a `delay` or `delay*` causes an exception; otherwise these tokens behave just like **exn**. We also extend $\longmapsto$:

$$E[\text{exn}] \longmapsto \text{exn}$$

A conventional well-definedness theorem summarizes the language's semantics.

$(\lambda(x \ldots).e)\ v \ldots \rightarrow e\{x := v, \ldots\}$	(ap)	`null?` `null` $\rightarrow$ `true`	(nuln)
$o\ v_1\ v_2 \rightarrow \delta\ o\ v_1\ v_2$	(op)	`null?` $v \rightarrow$ `false`, $v \neq$ `null`	(nul)
`let` $x = v$ `in` $e \rightarrow e\{x := v\}$	(let)	`first` (`cons` $v_1\ v_2$) $\rightarrow v_1$	(fstc)
`if` `false` $e_1\ e_2 \rightarrow e_2$	(iff)	`first` (`lcons` $v\ e$) $\rightarrow v$	(fstlc)
`if` $v\ e_1\ e_2 \rightarrow e_1$, $v \neq$ `false`	(if)	`rest` (`cons` $v_1\ v_2$) $\rightarrow v_2$	(rstc)
`zero?` $0 \rightarrow$ `true`	(z0)	`rest` (`lcons` $v\ e$) $\rightarrow$ `delay` e	(rstlc)
`zero?` $v \rightarrow$ `false`, $v \neq 0$	(z)	`force` (`delay` e) $\rightarrow$ `force` e	(ford)
`not` `false` $\rightarrow$ `true`	(notf)	`force` $v \rightarrow v$, $v \neq$ `delay` e	(forv)
`not` $v \rightarrow$ `false`, $v \neq$ `false`	(not)		

Fig. 7. Call-by-value reduction semantics

$$v\ v_1 \ldots \to \mathtt{exn}, \text{ if } v \neq \lambda(x \ldots).e \quad \text{(apx)} \qquad S[\![\mathtt{delay}\ e]\!] \to \mathtt{dexn} \quad \text{(strictx)}$$

$$\mathtt{first}\ v \to \mathtt{exn}, \text{ if } v \notin \mathtt{cons} \text{ or } \mathtt{lcons} \quad \text{(fstx)} \qquad S[\![\mathtt{delay}^*\ e]\!] \to \mathtt{dexn}^* \quad \text{(strictx}^*\text{)}$$

$$\mathtt{rest}\ v \to \mathtt{exn}, \text{ if } v \notin \mathtt{cons} \text{ or } \mathtt{lcons} \quad \text{(rstx)}$$

Fig. 8. Exception producing reductions

Theorem 1 (Well-Definedness). *A program p either reduces to a value v; starts an infinitely long chain of reductions; or reduces to* **exn**.

4.2   Soundness of the Analysis

Before stating the soundness theorem, we first extend our analysis for exceptions:

$$(\widehat{\rho}, \widehat{\mathcal{D}}, \widehat{\mathcal{S}}, \widehat{\mathcal{F}}) \models_e \mathtt{exn}^\ell \qquad\qquad\qquad \text{[exn]}$$

Lemma 1 states that $\longmapsto$ preserves $\models_e$. We use notation $\widehat{\rho} \models_e e$ when we are not interested in $\widehat{\mathcal{D}}$, $\widehat{\mathcal{S}}$, and $\widehat{\mathcal{F}}$, which are only used for transformation. This means $\widehat{\rho}$ satisfies only the constraints from sections 3.2 and 3.3.

Lemma 1 (Preservation). *If $\widehat{\rho} \models_e e$ and $e \longmapsto e'$, then $\widehat{\rho} \models_e e'$.*

We now state our soundness theorem, where $\longmapsto\!\!\!\!\!\to$ is the reflexive-transitive closure of $\longmapsto$. The theorem says that if an expression in a program reduces to an ℓ-labeled value, then any acceptable analysis result $\widehat{\rho}$ correctly predicts that value.

Theorem 2 (Soundness). *For all $\widehat{\rho} \models p$, $p = d \ldots e$, if $e \longmapsto\!\!\!\!\!\to_{d\ldots} E[v^\ell]$, $\widehat{v} \in \widehat{\rho}(\ell)$.*

4.3   Safety of Refactoring

We show that refactoring for laziness cannot raise an exception due to a `delay` or `delay`* reaching a strict position. To start, we define a function ξ that derives a satisfactory abstract environment for a φ-transformed program:

$$\xi[\![\widehat{\rho}]\!]_p = \widehat{\rho}', \text{ where} \qquad\qquad \boxed{\xi : Env \times Prog \to Env}$$

$$\forall \ell, x \in dom(\widehat{\rho}) : \widehat{\rho}'(\ell) = \widehat{\rho}(\ell) \cup \{(\mathtt{delay}^*\ \ell_1) \mid (\mathtt{darg}\ \ell_1) \in \widehat{\rho}(\ell), (\mathtt{delay}^*\ e_1^{\ell_1}) \in p\} \quad (1)$$

$$\widehat{\rho}'(x) = \widehat{\rho}(x) \cup \{(\mathtt{delay}^*\ \ell_1) \mid (\mathtt{darg}\ \ell_1) \in \widehat{\rho}(x), (\mathtt{delay}^*\ e_1^{\ell_1}) \in p\}$$

$$\forall (\mathtt{delay}^*\ e_1^{\ell_1})^\ell \in p, \ell \notin dom(\widehat{\rho}) : \qquad\qquad\qquad\qquad\qquad\qquad\qquad\qquad (2)$$

$$\widehat{\rho}'(\ell) = \widehat{\rho}(\ell_1) \cup \{(\mathtt{delay}^*\ \ell_1)\} \cup \{(\mathtt{delay}^*\ \ell_2) \mid (\mathtt{darg}\ \ell_2) \in \widehat{\rho}(\ell_1), (\mathtt{delay}^*\ e_2^{\ell_2}) \in p\}$$

$$\forall (\mathtt{force}\ e_1^{\ell_1})^\ell \in p, \ell \notin dom(\widehat{\rho}) : \widehat{\rho}'(\ell) = \{\widehat{v} \mid \widehat{v} \in \widehat{\rho}(\ell_1), \widehat{v} \notin \mathtt{delay}\} \quad (3)$$

The ξ function takes environment $\widehat{\rho}$ and a program p and returns a new environment $\widehat{\rho}'$. Part 1 of the definition copies $\widehat{\rho}$ entries to $\widehat{\rho}'$, except `darg` values are replaced with `delay`*s when there is a corresponding `delay`* in p. Parts 2 and 3 add new $\widehat{\rho}'$ entries for `delay`*s and `force`s not accounted for in $\widehat{\rho}$. When the given p is a φ-transformed program, then the resulting $\widehat{\rho}'$ satisfies that program.

Lemma 2. *If* $(\widehat{\rho}, \widehat{\mathcal{D}}, \widehat{\mathcal{S}}, \widehat{\mathcal{F}}) \models p$, *then* $\xi[\![\widehat{\rho}]\!]_{\varphi[\![p]\!]_{\widehat{\rho}\widehat{\mathcal{D}}\widehat{\mathcal{S}}\widehat{\mathcal{F}}}} \models \varphi[\![p]\!]_{\widehat{\rho}\widehat{\mathcal{D}}\widehat{\mathcal{S}}\widehat{\mathcal{F}}}$.

Finally, theorem 3 states the safety property. It says that evaluating a transformed program cannot generate an exception due to **delay**s or **delay***s.

Theorem 3 (Safety). *For all* p *and* $(\widehat{\rho}, \widehat{\mathcal{D}}, \widehat{\mathcal{S}}, \widehat{\mathcal{F}}) \models p$, *if* $\varphi[\![p]\!]_{\widehat{\rho}\widehat{\mathcal{D}}\widehat{\mathcal{S}}\widehat{\mathcal{F}}} = d \dots e$, *then* $e \not\longmapsto_{d\dots}$ ***dexn***, *and* $e \not\longmapsto_{d\dots}$ ***dexn****.

Proof. (Sketch) Using Soundness, the analysis rules in figure 5, and Lemma 2.

4.4 Idempotency

Our transformation is not idempotent. Indeed, it may be necessary to refactor a program multiple times to get the "right" amount of laziness. For example:

```
let x = ⟨long computation⟩ in let y = ⟨short computation involving x⟩
in (delay y)
```

The long computation should be delayed but applying our transformation once only delays the short computation. To delay the long computation, a second transformation round is required. In practice, we have observed that one round of laziness refactoring suffices to handle the majority of cases. However, section 6 presents a real-world example requiring multiple transformations so our tool currently allows the programmer to decide how often to apply the refactoring.

5   A Prototype Implementation

We have implemented refactoring for laziness as a tool for Racket [10], in the form of a plugin for the DrRacket IDE. It uses laziness analysis to automatically insert **delay** and **force** expressions as needed, with graphical justification.

5.1   Constraint Solving Algorithm

Computing our laziness analysis requires two stages: (1) generate a set of constraints from a program, and (2) solve for the least solution using a conventional worklist algorithm [18]. The graph nodes are the variables and labels in the program, plus one node each for $\widehat{\mathcal{D}}$, $\widehat{\mathcal{S}}$, and $\widehat{\mathcal{F}}$. Without loss of generality, we use only labels for the nodes and $\widehat{\rho}$ for the analysis result in our description of the algorithm. There exists an edge from node ℓ_1 to ℓ_2 if there is a constraint where $\widehat{\rho}(\ell_2)$ depends on $\widehat{\rho}(\ell_1)$; the edge is labeled with that constraint. Thus one can view a node ℓ as the endpoint for a series of data flow paths. To compute $\widehat{\rho}(\ell)$, it suffices to traverse all paths from the leaves to ℓ, accumulating values according to the constraints along the way.

The analysis result is incrementally computed in a breadth-first fashion by processing constraints according a worklist of nodes. Processing a constraint entails adding values to $\widehat{\rho}$ so the constraint is satisfied. The algorithm starts by processing all constraints where a node depends on a value, e.g., $val \in \widehat{\rho}(\ell)$; the nodes on the right-hand side of these constraints constitute the initial work-list. Nodes are then removed from the worklist, one at a time. When a node is removed, the constraints on the out-edges of that node are processed and a neighbor ℓ of the node is added to the worklist if $\widehat{\rho}(\ell)$ was updated while processing a constraint. A node may appear in the worklist more than once, but only a finite number of times, as shown by the following termination argument.

Termination and Complexity of Constraint Solving

Inspecting the constraints from section 3 reveals that an expression requires recursive calls only for subexpressions. Thus, a finite program generates a finite number of constraints. For a finite program with finitely many labels and variables, the set of possible abstract values is also finite. Thus, a node can only appear in the worklist a finite number of times, so algorithm must terminate.

We observe in the constraint-solving algorithm that, (1) a node ℓ is added to the worklist only if $\widehat{\rho}(\ell)$ is updated due to a node on which it depends being in the worklist, and (2) values are only ever added to $\widehat{\rho}$; they are never removed. For a program of size n, there are $O(n)$ nodes in the dependency graph. Each node can appear in the worklist $O(n)$ times, and a data flow path to reach that node could have $O(n)$ nodes, so it can take $O(n^2)$ node visits to compute the solution at a particular node. Multiplying by $O(n)$ total nodes, means the algorithm may have to visit $O(n^3)$ nodes to compute the solution for all nodes.

5.2   Laziness Refactoring Tool

Our prototype tool uses the result of the analysis and the φ function from section 3.5 to insert additional `delay`s and `force`s. In contrast to the mathematical version of φ, its implementation avoids inserting `delay`s and `force`s around values and does not insert duplicate `delay`s or `force`s.

We evaluated a number of examples with our tool including the n-queens problem from section 2. Figure 9 (top) shows the program in Racket, including timing information and a graphical depiction of the answer. Despite the use of `lcons`,[8] the program takes as long as an eager version of the same program (not shown) to compute an answer. Figure 9 (bot) shows the program after our tool applies the laziness transformation. When the tool is activated, it: (1) computes an analysis result for the program, (2) uses the result to insert `delay`s and `force`s, highlighting the added `delay`s in yellow and the added `force`s in blue, and (3) adds arrows originating from each inserted `delay`, pointing to the source of the laziness, thus explaining its decision to the programmer in an intuitive manner. Running the transformed program exhibits the desired performance.

---

[8] Though `lcons` is not available in Racket, to match the syntax of our paper, we simulate it with a macro that wraps a `delay` around the second argument of a `cons`.

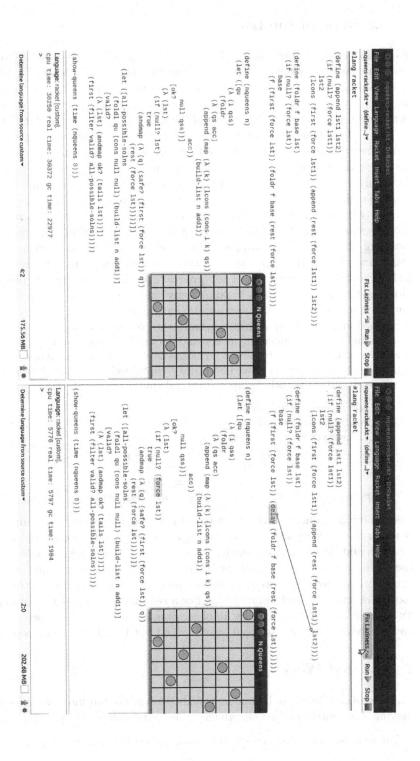

Fig. 9. Evaluating n-queens in Racket: only lazy cons (top), after refactoring (bot)

6   Laziness in the Large

To further evaluate our idea and our tool, we examined the Racket code base and some user-contributed packages for manual uses of laziness. We found several erroneous attempts at adding laziness and we verified that our tool would have prevented many such errors.[9] We consider this investigation a first confirmation of the usefulness of our tool. The rest of the section describes two of the examples.

The DMdA languages [5] allow students to write contracts for some data structures. These contracts are based on Findler et al.'s lazy contracts [8]. The contracts are primarily implemented via a constructor with a few lazy fields. Additionally, several specialized contract constructors for various data structures call the main constructor. However, since the specialized constructors are implemented with ordinary strict functions, to preserve the intended lazy behavior, the programmer must manually propagate the laziness to the appropriate arguments of these functions, similar to the Scala example from section 2. Thus, a small amount of laziness in the main contract constructor requires several more `delays` scattered all throughout the program. Adding these `delays` becomes tedious as the program grows in complexity and unsurprisingly, a few were left out. Our tool identified the missing `delays`, which the author of the code has confirmed and corrected with commits to the code repository.

A second example concerns queues and deques [21] based on implicit recursive slowdown [20, Chapter 11], where laziness enables fast amortized operations and simplifies the implementation. The library contained several performance bugs, as illustrated by this code snippet from a deque enqueue function:

```
define enqueue(elem dq) =  ...
  let strictprt = ⟨extract strict part of dq⟩
      newstrictprt = ⟨combine elem and strictprt⟩
      lazyprt = force ⟨extract lazy part of dq⟩
      lazyprt1 = ⟨extracted from lazyprt⟩
      lazyprt2 = ⟨extracted from lazyprt⟩
  in Deque newstrictprt (delay ⟨combine lazyprt1 and lazyprt2⟩)
```

The function enqueues `elem` in deque `dq`, which has a lazy part and a strict part. In one execution path, the lazy part is extracted, forced, and separated into two additional pieces. Clearly, the forcing is unnecessary because neither of the pieces are used before they are inserted back into the new deque. Worse, the extra forcing slows the program significantly. For this example, activating our tool *twice* fixes the performance bug. For a reasonably standard benchmark, the fix reduced the running time by an order of magnitude. The authors of the code have acknowledged the bug and have merged our fix into the code repository.

7   Related Work

The idea of combining strict and lazy evaluation is old, but most works involve removing laziness from lazy languages. We approach strict-lazy programming

---

[9] The examples were first translated to work with the syntax in this paper.

from the other, relatively unexplored, end of the spectrum, starting with a strict language and then only adding laziness as needed. This seems worthwhile since empirical studies indicate that most promises in a lazy language are unneeded [6,15,16,23]. Starting with a strict language also alleviates many disadvantages of lazy evaluation such as difficulty reasoning about space/time consumption.

The most well-known related work is strictness analysis [4,17], which calculates when to eagerly evaluate arguments without introducing non-termination. With our work, calculating divergence properties is not sufficient since even terminating programs may require additional laziness, as seen in examples from this paper. Hence we take a different, flow-analysis-based approach.[10] Researchers have also explored other static [7] and dynamic [2,6,15] laziness-removal techniques. However, these efforts all strive to preserve the program's semantics. We focus on the problem of strict programmers trying to use laziness, but doing so *incorrectly*. Thus our transformation necessarily allows the semantics of the program to change (i.e., from non-terminating to terminating), but hopefully in a way that the programmer intended in the first place.

Sheard [25] shares our vision of a strict language that is also practical for programming lazily. While his language does not require explicit `forces`, the programmer must manually insert all required `delay` annotations.

8   Future Work

This paper demonstrates the theoretical and practical feasibility of a novel approach to assist programmers with the introduction of laziness into a strict context. We see several directions for future work. The first is developing a modular analysis. Our transformation requires the whole program and is thus unsatisfactory in the presence of libraries. Also, we intend to develop a typed version of our transformation and tool, so typed strict languages can more easily benefit from laziness as well. We conjecture that expressing strictness information via types may also provide a way to enable a modular laziness-by-need analysis.

Acknowledgements. Partial support provided by NSF grant CRI-0855140. Thanks to Matthias Felleisen, Eli Barzilay, David Van Horn, and J. Ian Johnson for feedback on earlier drafts.

References

1. Abelson, H., Sussman, G.J., Sussman, J.: Structure and Interpretation of Computer Programs. MIT Press (1984)
2. Aditya, S., Arvind, Augustsson, L., Maessen, J.W., Nikhil, R.S.: Semantics of pH: A parellel dialect of Haskell. In: Proc. Haskell Workshop, pp. 34–49 (1995)

---

[10] Interestingly, we conjecture that our approach would be useful to lazy programmers trying to insert strictness *annotations*, such as Haskell's `seq`, to their programs.

3. Appel, A., Blume, M., Gansner, E., George, L., Huelsbergen, L., MacQueen, D., Reppy, J., Shao, Z.: Standard ML of New Jersey User's Guide (1997)
4. Burn, G.L., Hankin, C.L., Abramsky, S.: Strictness analysis for higher-order functions. Sci. Comput. Program. 7, 249–278 (1986)
5. Crestani, M., Sperber, M.: Experience report: growing programming languages for beginning students. In: Proc. 15th ICFP, pp. 229–234 (2010)
6. Ennals, R., Peyton Jones, S.: Optimistic evaluation: an adaptive evaluation strategy for non-strict programs. In: Proc. 8th ICFP, pp. 287–298 (2003)
7. Faxén, K.F.: Cheap eagerness: speculative evaluation in a lazy functional language. In: Proc. 5th ICFP, pp. 150–161 (2000)
8. Findler, R.B., Guo, S.-Y., Rogers, A.: Lazy Contract Checking for Immutable Data Structures. In: Chitil, O., Horváth, Z., Zsók, V. (eds.) IFL 2007. LNCS, vol. 5083, pp. 111–128. Springer, Heidelberg (2008)
9. Flanagan, C., Felleisen, M.: Modular and polymorphic set-based analysis: Theory and practice. Tech. Rep. TR96-266, Rice Univ. (1996)
10. Flatt, M., PLT: Reference: Racket. Tech. Rep. PLT-TR-2012-1, PLT Inc. (2012), http://racket-lang.org/tr1/
11. Friedman, D., Wise, D.: Cons should not evaluate its arguments. In: Proc. 3rd ICALP, pp. 257–281 (1976)
12. Hughes, J.: Why functional programming matters. Comput. J. 32, 98–107 (1989)
13. Jones, N.D.: Flow analysis of lambda expressions. Tech. rep., Aarhus Univ. (1981)
14. Leroy, X., Doligez, D., Frisch, A., Garrigue, J., Rémy, D., Vouillon, J.: The OCaml system, release 3.12, Documentation and user's manual. INRIA (July 2011)
15. Maessen, J.W.: Eager Haskell: resource-bounded execution yields efficient iteration. In: Proc. Haskell Workshop, pp. 38–50 (2002)
16. Morandat, F., Hill, B., Osvald, L., Vitek, J.: Evaluating the Design of the R Language. In: Noble, J. (ed.) ECOOP 2012. LNCS, vol. 7313, pp. 104–131. Springer, Heidelberg (2012)
17. Mycroft, A.: Abstract interpretation and optimising transformations for applicative programs. Ph.D. thesis, Univ. Edinburgh (1981)
18. Nielson, F., Nielson, H.R., Hankin, C.: Principles of Program Analysis. Springer (2005)
19. Odersky, M.: The Scala Language Specification, Version 2.9. EPFL (May 2011)
20. Okasaki, C.: Purely Functional Data Structures. Cambridge Univ. Press (1998)
21. Hari Prashanth, K.R., Tobin-Hochstadt, S.: Functional data structures for Typed Racket. In: Proc. Scheme Workshop (2010)
22. Rees, J., Clinger, W. (eds.): Revised[3] Report on the Algorithmic Language Scheme. ACM SIGPLAN Notices (December 1986)
23. Schauser, K.E., Goldstein, S.C.: How much non-strictness do lenient programs require? In: Proc. 7th FPCA (1995)
24. Sestoft, P.: Replacing function parameters by global variables. Master's thesis, Univ. Copenhagen (1988)
25. Sheard, T.: A pure language with default strict evaluation order and explicit laziness. In: 2003 Haskell Workshop: New Ideas Session (2003)
26. Shivers, O.: Control-flow analysis in scheme. In: Proc. PLDI, pp. 164–174 (1988)
27. Wadler, P., Taha, W., MacQueen, D.: How to add laziness to a strict language, without even being odd. In: Proc. Standard ML Workshop (1998)

FliPpr: A Prettier Invertible Printing System

Kazutaka Matsuda[1] and Meng Wang[2]

[1] The University of Tokyo
[2] Chalmers University of Technology

Abstract. When implementing a programming language, we often write a parser and a pretty-printer. However, manually writing both programs is not only tedious but also error-prone; it may happen that a pretty-printed result is not correctly parsed. In this paper, we propose FliPpr, which is a program transformation system that uses program inversion to produce a CFG parser from a pretty-printer. This novel approach has the advantages of fine-grained control over pretty-printing, and easy reuse of existing efficient pretty-printer and parser implementations.

1   Introduction

In this paper, we will discuss the implementation of a programming language, say the following one

$$
\begin{aligned}
prog &::= rule_1; \ldots; rule_n \\
rule &::= f\ p_1\ \ldots\ p_n = e \\
p &::= x \mid C\ p_1\ \ldots\ p_n \\
e &::= x \mid C\ e_1\ \ldots\ e_n \mid e_1 \oplus e_2 \mid f\ e_1\ \ldots\ e_n
\end{aligned}
$$

which is a standard first-order functional language with data constructors C, functions f and binary operators $\oplus$. Ignoring the semantics of the language for the time being, we start with writing a parser and a pretty-printer to deal with the syntax: the parser converts textual representations of programs into the AST, and the pretty-printer converts the AST to nicely laid-out programs. Though not often measured objectively, the prettiness of printing results is important: a pretty-printer is central to the communication between a compiler and the programmers, and the quality of it directly contributes to the productivity and satisfaction of the users of the language.

Despite being developed separately, the parser and the pretty-printer are always expected to be consistent to each other: very informally, parsing a pretty-printed program should succeed, and produces the same AST that is pretty-printed. It is common knowledge that consistency properties like this between a pair of tightly-coupled programs are hard to produce and maintain; and perhaps less widely known that they are difficult to be tested effectively too, due to the complexity of AST data [5].

In this paper, we are going to discuss the implementation of a language, which has a more elaborated version of the above-presented syntax. The language can be used to program pretty-printers, and at the same time through program inversion techniques, obtain a consistent parser. We, as usual, manually implemented

M. Felleisen and P. Gardner (Eds.): ESOP 2013, LNCS 7792, pp. 101–120, 2013.
© Springer-Verlag Berlin Heidelberg 2013

a parser and a pretty-printer for the language, but with the hope that we, and many others who read this paper, will not need to do it again for their own language implementations.

Prior to this work, there has been a rich body of literature on exploring correctness-by-construction techniques to automatically generate one or both programs of the printer/parser pair, notably [2, 4, 17] . We have intentionally omitted the prefix "pretty-" from the mentioning of printers here because few of the existing work is actually producing pretty-printers in the sense of Hughes [10] and Wadler [22].[1]

To be more precise about what we mean by "prettiness", let us consider a subtraction language $e ::= 1 \mid e_1 - e_2$ that has a constant (1) and a left-associative binary operator $(-)$. We represent the syntax with the following AST datatype.

$$\textbf{data } E \ = \textsf{One} \mid \textsf{Sub } E \ E$$

Using the language we propose in this paper, which is based on Wadler's library [10], one can define a pretty-printer as below.

ppr One $= text$ "1"
ppr (Sub e_1 e_2) $= group$ (ppr e_1 <> $nest$ 2 ($line$ <> $text$ "-" <> $text$ " " <> $pprP$ e_2))
-- The suffix P in $pprP$ stands for parentheses.
$pprP$ One $= text$ "1"
$pprP$ (Sub e_1 e_2) =
        $text$ "(" <> $group$ (ppr e_1 <> $nest$ 2 ($line$
                        <> $text$ "-" <> $text$ " " <> $pprP$ e_2)) <> $text$ ")"

The pretty-printing library functions are shown in *slant sans serif*. Roughly speaking, *text s* converts a string s to a layout, $d_1 <> d_2$ is an infix binary operator that concatenates two layouts d_1 and d_2, which binds looser than prefix applications, and *line* starts a new line, but its behavior can be affected by surrounding *nest* and *group* applications: *nest n d* inserts n-spaces after each *line*s in d, and *group d* smartly chooses between the layout d and other layouts derivable from d by selectively interpreting *line*s as single spaces. (In this paper, we write "space" for the space character and write "whitespace" for the space character and the newline character. Other kinds of spaces such as horizontal tabs are not discussed as they do not yield new insight.) The function ppr pretty-prints Sub (Sub One One) (Sub One One) as

```
                                              1 - 1
                              1 - 1             - (1
        1 - 1 - (1 - 1)   or    - (1 - 1)  or      - 1)
```

depending on the screen width that is used to render the result. This fine-grained control from users over bracketing, spacing and indentation is clearly beyond any technique based on mechanical traversals of ASTs, which is likely to rigidly

---

[1] The Syn system [2] is capable of handling non-contextual layouts, which can be seen as a limited form of prettiness.

produce 1 - 1 - (1 - 1) (with arbitrary line-wrapping) or even (1 - 1) - (1 - 1) as the only printing result.

Knowing that prettiness cannot be generated automatically, in this paper we propose a novel approach: the programmer provides a carefully turned pretty-printer (which is slightly annotated with some additional information for parsing), and our system invert it to obtain a consistent parser. We claim the following benefits of our approach:

- **Fine-Grained Control over Pretty-Printing.** Our language based on Wadler's library [22] offers the possibility of refined control over different aspects of pretty-printing: spacing can be tuned; redundant bracketing can be eliminated through the passing of fixity and precedence information; indentation can be designed by nesting lines; and wrapping of lines can be performed smartly.
- **Efficiency.** FliPpr is efficient in the sense that we can reuse existing efficient implementation of pretty-printers and parsers. For pretty-printing, we can use Wadler's library [22]. For parsing, we can use any parser generator that supports full CFG.

The technique of program inversion used in FliPpr is not new; it is a direct consequence of our previous work [15]. The novelty of this paper lies in the design of the pretty-printing system, which makes the program inversion possible. Specifically, in this work:

- We propose an invertible pretty-printing technique based on grammar-based inversion [15], by which we can obtain a consistent parser from a pretty-printer.
- We give a surface language such that a pretty-printer written in it can be converted to a linear and treeless form by deforestation [21] which is suitable for inversion [15].
- We implemented our idea as a program transformation tool that generates parsers in Haskell[2].

2   Overview

In this section, we present an overview of our technique using the subtraction language from the introduction as the running example. Figure 1 shows the overall picture of FliPpr. A user of our system programs a pretty-printer in a surface language, which is translated to a core language that can be inverted. The example pretty-printer for the subtraction language is simple enough not to require any advanced features that the surface

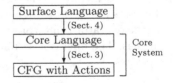

Fig. 1. Architecture of FliPpr

---

[2] Available at http://www-kb.is.s.u-tokyo.ac.jp/~kztk/FliPpr/

language provides, and the translation from the surface language to the core language is the identity operation in this case. Therefore, we focus on the core system in this section and postpone the discussion of the surface language to Sect. 4.

As a start, let's revisit the pretty-printer *ppr* defined in the previous section. If the function is inverted as it is, we can hope for no more than a parser that only recognizes pretty strings. This is neither the fault of function *ppr* nor of the inverter: a pretty-printer *ppr* (correctly) produces only pretty layouts, and an inverter cannot invent information that is not already carried by the function to be inverted. To remedy this information mismatch, we instrument the pretty-printer with additional information about non-pretty but nevertheless valid layouts.

2.1   Introducing Ugliness

Reinterpretation of line. A common source of prettiness is the clever interpretation of *lines* either as a single space or a nicely indented new line depending on the environment. This effect can be simply eliminated by reinterpreting *line* as one or more whitespaces. Using this new interpretation in the derivation of a parser enables us to parse certain non-pretty layouts. For example, now the inverse of the pretty-printer can parse the following strings.

$$1 \quad - 1 \quad \text{or} \quad \begin{matrix} 1 \\ - 1 \end{matrix}$$

These strings do not satisfy our notion of prettiness defined by *ppr*, and will not be produced by the pretty-printer, but will be accepted by the generated parser through the reinterpretation of *lines*. Also note that this reinterpretation also means that we can safely ignore **group** and **nest** during inversion, because their sole purpose is to affect the behavior of *lines*.

Still, this solution alone is not enough. Strings like `1 -    1` and `(1)- ((1))` remain unparsable: the pretty-printer has dictated that there is only a single space between the operator and the second operand by using **text** `" "` instead of *line*, and that there shouldn't be redundant parentheses. We need to find a way to alter these behaviors in parsing without losing pretty-printing.

Biased Choice. To annotate pretty-printers with information about non-pretty layouts, we introduce the choice operator <+. In pretty-printing the operator behaves as $e_1 \mathbin{<\!\!+} e_2 = e_1$, ignoring the non-pretty alternative e_2; in parser derivation the operator is interpreted as a nondeterministic choice, which accepts both branches. The operator <+ binds looser than <> and has the following algebraic properties.

Associativity	$e_1 \mathbin{<\!\!+} (e_2 \mathbin{<\!\!+} e_3) = (e_1 \mathbin{<\!\!+} e_2) \mathbin{<\!\!+} e_3$
Distributivity-L	$(e_1 \mathbin{<\!\!+} e_2) \mathbin{<\!\!>} e_3 = e_1 \mathbin{<\!\!>} e_3 \mathbin{<\!\!+} e_2 \mathbin{<\!\!>} e_3$
Distributivity-R	$e_1 \mathbin{<\!\!>} (e_2 \mathbin{<\!\!+} e_2) = e_1 \mathbin{<\!\!>} e_2 \mathbin{<\!\!+} e_1 \mathbin{<\!\!>} e_3$

For example, one can define variants of (white)spaces with the choice operator as follows.

$$nil\ \ \ = \text{text}\ ""\ \texttt{<+}\ space \qquad\qquad \text{-- (zero-or-more whitespaces in parsing)}$$
$$space = (\text{text}\ "\ "\ \texttt{<+}\ \text{text}\ "\backslash n")\ \texttt{<>}\ nil\quad \text{-- (one-or-more whitespaces in parsing)}$$

Here, nil and $space$ pretty-print "" and " " respectively, but represent zero-or-more and one-or-more whitespaces in parsing. We can now refactor our pretty-printer ppr with the aim of obtaining more robust parsers.

$$ppr\ x = ppr\_\ x\ \texttt{<+}\ \text{text}\ "("\ \texttt{<>}\ nil\ \texttt{<>}\ ppr\ x\ \texttt{<>}\ nil\ \texttt{<>}\ \text{text}\ ")"$$
$$ppr\_\ \text{One}\qquad\ = \text{text}\ "1"$$
$$ppr\_\ (\text{Sub}\ e_1\ e_2) = group\ (ppr\ e_1\ \texttt{<>}\ nest\ 2\ (line'\ \texttt{<>}\ \text{text}\ "-"\ \texttt{<>}\ space'\ \texttt{<>}\ pprP\ e_2))$$

$$pprP\ x = pprP\_\ x\ \texttt{<+}\ \text{text}\ "("\ \texttt{<>}\ nil\ \texttt{<>}\ pprP\ x\ \texttt{<>}\ nil\ \texttt{<>}\ \text{text}\ ")"$$
$$pprP\_\ \text{One}\qquad\ = \text{text}\ "1"$$
$$pprP\_\ (\text{Sub}\ e_1\ e_2) =$$
$$\qquad\text{text}\ "("\ \texttt{<>}\ nil\ \texttt{<>}\ group\ (ppr\ e_1\ \texttt{<>}\ nest\ 2\ (line'$$
$$\qquad\qquad\qquad\qquad\quad \texttt{<>}\ \text{text}\ "-"\ \texttt{<>}\ space'\ \texttt{<>}\ pprP\ e_2))\ \texttt{<>}\ nil\ \texttt{<>}\ \text{text}\ ")"$$

$$space' = space\ \texttt{<+}\ \text{text}\ ""\ \text{-- (zero-or-more whitespaces in parsing)}$$
$$line'\ \ = line\ \texttt{<+}\ \text{text}\ ""\quad \text{-- (zero-or-more whitespaces in parsing)}$$

Note that we have separated the original definitions of ppr and $pprP$ into two parts: the top level definitions introduce annotations for optional parentheses, and the actual pretty-printing is handled by worker functions that are subscripted. Optional whitespaces are also introduced by replacing $\text{text}\ "\ "$ and $line$ with $space'$ and $line'$ respectively in the definitions.

This refactoring is semantic preserving with respect to pretty-printing, and at the same time brings in necessary information for robust parsing. For example, we can now expect the inverse program to parse strings like `1   - 1`, `(1)-((1))`, and `(1 - (1))` correctly.[3]

2.2   Construction of CFG with Actions

So far, we have discussed how a user can provide a refactored pretty-printer that behaves like the original, but with additional information for non-pretty strings embedded. Our system FliPpr further transforms the program by removing the layouting and replacing $\texttt{<+}$ with a nondeterministic choice $?$ to create an ugly-printer solely for inversion.

$$ppr\ x = ppr\_\ x\ ?\ "("\ \texttt{++}\ nil\ \texttt{++}\ ppr\ x\ \texttt{++}\ nil\ \texttt{++}\ ")"$$
$$ppr\_\ \text{One}\qquad\ = "1"$$
$$ppr\_\ (\text{Sub}\ e_1\ e_2) = ppr\ e_1\ \texttt{++}\ line'\ \texttt{++}\ "-"\ \texttt{++}\ space'\ \texttt{++}\ pprP\ e_2$$
$$\cdots$$

We postpone a detailed discussion of the transformation to Sect. 3. For now, it is sufficient to know that the above program nondeterministically produces a string that is valid for parsing, but not necessarily pretty.

---

[3] To also make strings like `" 1-1"` parsable, we can add a declaration $f\ x = nil\ \texttt{<>}$ $ppr\ x\ \texttt{<>}\ nil$. However this addition does not post any new insight, and is omitted for simplicity.

$$\begin{array}{lll} prog & ::= rule_1; \ldots; rule_n \\ rule & ::= f \ p_1 \ \ldots \ p_n = e \\ p & ::= x \mid \mathsf{C} \ p_1 \ \ldots \ p_n \\ e & ::= \textit{text} \ \texttt{"string"} \mid e_1 <> e_2 \mid \textit{line} \mid \textit{nest} \ n \ e \mid \textit{group} \ e & \text{(Wadler's Combinators)} \\ & \quad \mid \ e_1 \mathrel{<\!\!+} e_2 & \text{(Biased Choice)} \\ & \quad \mid \ f \ x_1 \ \ldots \ x_n & \text{(Treeless Call)} \end{array}$$

Fig. 2. Syntax of the core language: f ranges over function, C ranges over constructors, x and x_is range over variables and n range over natural numbers

Then, using our previous work on grammar-based inversion [15], the program can be inverted to construct the following grammar with actions (simplified for presentation).

$$\begin{array}{lll} Ppr & \to Ppr_- & \{\$1\} \\ & \mid \ \texttt{"("} \ Nil \ Ppr \ Nil \ \texttt{")"} & \{\$3\} \\ Ppr_- & \to 1 & \{\mathsf{One}\} \\ & \mid \ Ppr \ Line' \ \texttt{"-"} \ Space' \ PprP & \{\mathsf{Sub} \ \$1 \ \$5\} \\ & \ldots \end{array}$$

The correctness of the parser construction comes from our previous work [15]. Since FliPpr produces a CFG with actions, users have the choice of using any parser generator that supports full CFG. In our implementation, we use Frost *et al.* [8]'s top-down parser.

3 Core Language and Parser Construction

In this section, we give the formal definition of the core language of FliPpr, and discuss parser construction by program inversion.

3.1 Syntax and Semantics

Figure 2 shows the syntax of our core language, a first-order functional language similar to one found in the introduction. We include Wadler's pretty-printing combinators [22] and the biased choice as primitive operators, and place two restrictions for later inversion:

- Function calls must be *treeless* [21]: they take only variables as arguments.
- Variable use must be *linear*: every bound variable in a rule is used *exactly once* on the right-hand side. A notable exception is with <+. For $e_1 <\!\!+ e_2$, the two branches are supposed to be both linear. Thus, they contain the same set of free variables. For example, assuming f is linear, then $g \ x = f \ x <\!\!+ f \ x$ is linear, but $h \ x = \textit{line} <\!\!+ f \ x$ and $k \ x = \textit{line} <\!\!+ \textit{text} \ \texttt{"s"}$ are not.

For simplicity, we often omit the rule separator ";" if no confusion would arise. We use vector notation $\widetilde{x}$ for a sequence $x_1, \ldots, x_n$. We abuse the notation to write $f \ \widetilde{x}$ for $f \ x_1 \ \ldots \ x_n$.

$$\frac{\exists (f\ \widetilde{p} = e).\ \widetilde{p}\Gamma' = \widetilde{x}\Gamma \quad \Gamma' \vdash e \Downarrow v}{\Gamma \vdash f\ \widetilde{x} \Downarrow v} \qquad \frac{\Gamma \vdash e_1 \Downarrow v_1}{\Gamma \vdash e_1 \leftnotf... }$$

$$\frac{\exists (f\ \widetilde{p} = e).\ \widetilde{p}\Gamma' = \widetilde{x}\Gamma \quad \Gamma' \vdash e \Downarrow v}{\Gamma \vdash f\ \widetilde{x} \Downarrow v} \qquad \frac{\Gamma \vdash e_1 \Downarrow v_1}{\Gamma \vdash e_1 \leftplus e_2 \Downarrow v_1}$$

$$\frac{\{\Gamma \vdash e_i \Downarrow v_i\}_{i=1,2}}{\Gamma \vdash \textit{text } \texttt{"s"} \Downarrow \textit{text } \texttt{"s"} \qquad \Gamma \vdash e_1 \diamond e_2 \Downarrow v_1 \diamond v_2 \qquad \Gamma \vdash \textit{line} \Downarrow \textit{line}}$$

$$\frac{\Gamma \vdash e \Downarrow v}{\Gamma \vdash \textit{nest } n\ e \Downarrow \textit{nest } n\ v} \qquad \frac{\Gamma \vdash e \Downarrow v}{\Gamma \vdash \textit{group } e \Downarrow \textit{group } v}$$

Fig. 3. The call-by-value pretty-printing semantics of the language

$$\frac{\exists (f\ \widetilde{p} = e).\ \widetilde{p}\Gamma' = \widetilde{x}\Gamma \quad \Gamma' \vdash e \Downarrow_{\text{ND}} s}{\Gamma \vdash f\ \widetilde{x} \Downarrow_{\text{ND}} s} \qquad \frac{\Gamma \vdash e_i \Downarrow_{\text{ND}} s_i}{\Gamma \vdash e_1 \leftplus e_2 \Downarrow_{\text{ND}} s_i}\ i = 1,2$$

$$\frac{\{\Gamma \vdash e_i \Downarrow_{\text{ND}} s_i\}_{i=1,2} \qquad s \in \bigcup_{1 \leq i} S_i}{\Gamma \vdash \textit{text } \texttt{"s"} \Downarrow_{\text{ND}} \texttt{"s"} \qquad \Gamma \vdash e_1 \diamond e_2 \Downarrow_{\text{ND}} s_1 \mathbin{+\!\!+} s_2 \qquad \Gamma \vdash \textit{line} \Downarrow_{\text{ND}} s}$$

$$\frac{\Gamma \vdash e \Downarrow_{\text{ND}} s}{\Gamma \vdash \textit{nest } n\ e \Downarrow_{\text{ND}} s} \qquad \frac{\Gamma \vdash e \Downarrow_{\text{ND}} s}{\Gamma \vdash \textit{group } e \Downarrow_{\text{ND}} s}$$

Fig. 4. Nondeterministic printing semantics of the language

The formal pretty-printing semantics of the language is shown in Fig. 3. We write $\Gamma \vdash e \Downarrow v$ if under environment Γ, expression e evaluates to value v. Values are closed expressions that only consist of Wadler's combinators (*i.e.*, we don't evaluate Wadler's combinators). The environment Γ is a mapping from variables to terms (*i.e.*, expressions or patterns). We write $t\Gamma$ for the term obtained from t by replacing free variables x in t with $\Gamma(x)$. Pattern matching is nondeterministic in this semantics.

We do not define formally the semantics of Wadler's combinators, as our discussion in this paper is not dependent on it. However, we define the reinterpretation of the combinators and the biased choice $\leftplus$ for parser generation, firstly mentioned in Sect. 2, where *lines* are seen as one-or-more whitespaces and $\leftplus$ as a true nondeterministic choice. As shown in Fig. 4, the reinterpretation is defined similarly to the pretty-printing semantics; the main difference is that it returns a string nondeterministically, pretty or not. We write $\Gamma \vdash e \Downarrow_{\text{ND}} s$ if, under the environment Γ, e nondeterministically evaluates to a string s. Here, S_i is the set of i-long consecutive whitespaces, inductively defined by: $S_1 = \{$ " " $,$ "\n" $\}$ and $S_{n+1} = \{s_1 \mathbin{+\!\!+} s_2 \mid s_1 \in S_1, s_2 \in S_n\}$, and $\mathbin{+\!\!+}$ is the concatenation of two strings. The possible evaluation results of the nondeterministic semantics, which covers both pretty and non-pretty strings, is a super set of what Wadler's combinators may produce if evaluated in the original semantics. Thanks to treelessness and linearity, the sets of strings defined by $L_e = \{s \mid \Gamma \vdash e \Downarrow_{\text{ND}} s\}$ for expressions e are exactly those that are expressible by CFGs. This fact enables us to use CFG-parsers for inverses, which will be shown in the rest of this section. Also note that due to linearity, call-by-value and call-by-name coincide for the language, even with nondeterminism (assuming that Wadler's combinators and string operations are strict). This is handy later when we require a call-by-value semantics for program inversion [15], and a call-by-name semantics for fusion [21] in the surface language (Sect. 4).

3.2 Parser Construction by Inversion

To invert programs written in the core language, we firstly perform a semantic-preserving transformation to remove the pretty-printing combinators, and obtain a syntax that is recognizable by our grammar-based inversion system [15].

Converting to Nondeterministic Programs. This step is done by "forgetting smart layouting mechanism", through the following rewriting rules.

$$
\begin{array}{lll}
\textit{text } "\texttt{s}" \longrightarrow "\texttt{s}" & \textit{group } e \longrightarrow e & e_1 <> e_2 \longrightarrow e_1 +\!\!+ e_2 \\
\textit{nest } n\ e \longrightarrow e & \textit{line} \quad \longrightarrow \textit{space} & e_1 <\!\!+ e_2 \longrightarrow e_1\ ?\ e_2
\end{array}
$$

Here, *space* is a rewritten version (according to the rules above) of its definition in Sect. 2, *i.e.* the function defined by

$$
\textit{space} = (\texttt{"\ "}\ ?\ \texttt{"\textbackslash n"}) +\!\!+ \textit{nil} \qquad \textit{nil} = \texttt{""}\ ?\ \textit{space}
$$

and the operator ? is a nondeterministic choice.

The formal semantics of the obtained nondeterministic programs is defined straightforwardly by adding the following rules.

$$
\frac{}{\Gamma \vdash "\texttt{s}" \Downarrow "\texttt{s}"} \qquad \frac{\Gamma \vdash e_i \Downarrow v}{\Gamma \vdash e_1\ ?\ e_2 \Downarrow v}\ i = 1, 2 \qquad \frac{\{\Gamma \vdash e_i \Downarrow v_i\}_{i=1,2}}{\Gamma \vdash e_1 +\!\!+ e_2 \Downarrow v_1 +\!\!+ v_2}
$$

Their behaviors of "s", ? and +\!+ are the same as the reinterpretations of *text* "s", <+ and <>, respectively; we use different symbols to clarify that the conversion discards the pretty-printing semantics. Note that, since the language is linear and treeless, the call-time choice and the run-time choice [19] do not differ.

We write $\underline{f}$ and $\underline{e}$ as the rewritten version of f and e. The following lemma states that the rewriting is semantic preserving.

Lemma 1 (Semantic Preservation). $\Gamma \vdash e \Downarrow_{\text{ND}} s$ *iff* $\Gamma \vdash \underline{e} \Downarrow s$.   □

Grammar-Based Inversion. The rewritten programs can be processed to obtain a grammar with actions[4] that computes the inverse of the rewritten program by using grammar-based inversion [15]. The basic idea of the inversion is to read a rule of a program as a production rule of a grammar, and to use semantic actions to track how variables (*i.e.*, inputs) are passed.

In the inversion, we construct two sorts of non-terminals: F_f for functions $\underline{f}$ and E_e for expressions $\underline{e}$. For a function $\underline{f}$ that takes $t_1, \ldots, t_n$ and returns s, F_f is used to parse string s, and the semantic action returns original inputs

---

[4] In the original paper [15], transformations on parse trees (or more precisely, derivation trees of productions) are used, instead of semantic actions.

Rules of F_f

For function f, we generate:

$$F_f \rightarrow E_{e_1} \ \{\textbf{let } \Gamma = \$1 \textbf{ in } (\widetilde{p}_1)\Gamma\}$$
$$\cdots \qquad\qquad \text{if } f \text{ has rules } f \ \widetilde{p} = \underline{e_1}; \ldots; f \ \widetilde{p}_n = \underline{e_n}.$$
$$| \quad E_{e_n} \ \{\textbf{let } \Gamma = \$1 \textbf{ in } (\widetilde{p}_n)\Gamma\}$$

Rules of E_e

For expression $\underline{e}$, we generate:

$$E_e \rightarrow F_f \quad \begin{Bmatrix} \textbf{let } (t_1, \ldots, t_n) = \$1 \\ \textbf{in } \{x_1 \mapsto t_1, \ldots, x_n \mapsto t_n\} \end{Bmatrix} \quad \text{if } \underline{e} = f \ x_1 \ \ldots \ x_n$$

$$E_e \rightarrow E_{e_1} E_{e_2} \quad \{\$1 \uplus \$2\} \qquad\qquad\quad \text{if } \underline{e} = \underline{e_1} + \!\!+ \ \underline{e_2}$$

$$E_e \rightarrow \texttt{"s"} \quad \{\emptyset\} \qquad\qquad\qquad\quad\; \text{if } \underline{e} = \texttt{"s"}$$

$$E_e \rightarrow E_{e_1} \quad \{\$1\} \qquad\qquad\qquad\quad \text{if } \underline{e} = \underline{e} = \underline{e_1} \ ? \ \underline{e_2}$$
$$| \quad E_{e_2} \quad \{\$1\}$$

Here, $\uplus$ merges two environments assuming that their domains are disjoint. Note that this disjoint property is guaranteed by linearity.

Fig. 5. Construction of CFG with actions

$(t_1, \ldots, t_n)$. For an expression $\underline{e}$ such that $\Gamma \vdash \underline{e} \Downarrow s$, E_e is used to parse string s, and the semantic action returns the original environment Γ. The generation of the production rules and semantics actions are presented in Fig. 5. The grammar in Sect. 2 is a simplified version of the grammar obtained by this generation.

We write $[\![N]\!]_\mathrm{P}(s)$ for the set of results returned by the semantics actions, when s is parsed with start symbol N (the subscript P means "parse"). The following lemma holds.

Lemma 2 (Correctness of Inversion)

- $\Gamma \vdash \underline{e} \Downarrow s$ and $\mathsf{dom}(\Gamma) = \mathsf{fv}(\underline{e})$ iff $\Gamma \in [\![E_e]\!]_\mathrm{P}(s)$,
- $\{x_1 \mapsto t_1, \ldots, x_n \mapsto t_n\} \vdash \underline{f} \ x_1 \ \ldots \ x_n \Downarrow s$ iff $(t_1, \ldots, t_n) \in [\![F_f]\!]_\mathrm{P}(s)$.

Proof. Follows from [15]. $\qquad\qquad\qquad\qquad\qquad\qquad\qquad\qquad\qquad\qquad$ □

Let ppr be a single-argument function defined in the core language, and $parse$ be a function defined by $parse \ s = [\![F_{ppr}]\!]_\mathrm{P}(s)$. Then, the following theorem is a special case of the above lemma.

Theorem 1. $\{x \mapsto t\} \vdash ppr \ x \Downarrow_\mathrm{ND} s$ *iff* $t \in parse \ s$. $\qquad\qquad\qquad$ □

The set $parse \ s$ contains at most one element if $\underline{ppr}$ is injective. Note that the inversion can produce arbitrary CFGs, and therefore FliPpr requires parser generators that support *full* CFGs.

4   Surface Language: Making It More Flexible

The core language is restricted to be linear and treeless, which is expressive enough for CFG parsing, but may be cumbersome to program in at times. In this section, we present a surface language that has a relaxed form of the restrictions, and through fusion techniques (specifically deforestation [21] or supercompilation [20]), programs written in the surface language are transformed to treeless and linear programs in the core language.

4.1 Problems with Programming in the Core Language

Let us consider extending the subtraction language with division and variables.

$$\textbf{data } E = \cdots \mid \text{Div } E\ E \mid \text{Var } \textit{String}$$

Recall that we used two mutually recursive functions ppr and $pprP$ to control bracketing issues around "−". In general, when there are many operators with different precedence levels, it suffices to use a function for each precedence level. For example, assuming "−" has precedence-level 6 and "/" has precedence-level 7 as they do in Haskell, a pretty-printer can be written as follows.

$$ppr\ x = ppr_5\ x \qquad \text{-- 5 is the lowest precedence level}$$
$$\dots$$
$$ppr_5\ (\text{Sub } x\ y) = \dots ppr_6\ x \dots text\ \texttt{"-"} \dots ppr_7\ y \dots \qquad \text{-- (1)}$$
$$ppr_5\ (\text{Div } x\ y) = \dots ppr_5\ x \dots text\ \texttt{"/"} \dots ppr_6\ y \dots \qquad \text{-- (2)}$$
$$\dots$$
$$ppr_6\ (\text{Sub } x\ y) = text\ \texttt{"("}\ <> nil\ <> \dots \{\text{- the RHS of (1) -}\} \dots <> nil\ <> text\ \texttt{")"}$$
$$ppr_6\ (\text{Div } x\ y) = \dots \{\text{- the RHS of (2) -}\} \dots$$
$$\dots$$
$$ppr_7\ (\text{Sub } x\ y) = text\ \texttt{"("}\ <> nil\ <> \dots \{\text{- the RHS of (1) -}\} \dots <> nil\ <> text\ \texttt{")"}$$
$$ppr_7\ (\text{Div } x\ y) = text\ \texttt{"("}\ <> nil\ <> \dots \{\text{- the RHS of (2) -}\} \dots <> nil\ <> text\ \texttt{")"}$$

There are a lot of undesirable repetitions in the above definition largely due to the treeless restriction.

Another problem that it is non-trivial to separate variable names with pre-defined names. For example, let us consider pretty-printing for Var x. One may be tempted to write $ppr_-\ (\text{Var } x) = text\ x$ but a parser derived from the above will parse "−" as Var $\texttt{"-"}$, because there is no information in the above definition that specifies valid variable names. We can improve the pretty-printer as follows.

$$ppr_-\ (\text{Var } x) = f\ x \qquad\qquad g\ [] \quad = \quad text\ \texttt{""}$$
$$f\ (\texttt{'a'} : x) = \quad text\ \texttt{"a"}\ <> g\ x \qquad g\ (\texttt{'a'} : x) = \quad text\ \texttt{"a"}\ <> g\ x$$
$$\dots \qquad\qquad\qquad\qquad \dots$$
$$f\ (\texttt{'z'} : x) = \quad text\ \texttt{"z"}\ <> g\ x \qquad g\ (\texttt{'z'} : x) = \quad text\ \texttt{"z"}\ <> g\ x$$

Note that strings are represented as lists of characters as in Haskell. This function ppr_- is partial and intentionally undefined for Var $\texttt{"-"}$. In this definition, we have successfully restricted variable names to range over lower-case English alphabets, but in a very cumbersome way.

4.2 An Overview

To reduce the programming effort, we propose a surface language, which has relaxed linearity and treelessness restrictions, and is equipped with a shorthand notation for expressing name ranges. In this language, a pretty-printer for the extended subtraction language can be written as follows.

$$ppr\ x = go\ 5\ x$$
$$go\ i\ x = manyPars\ (go\_\ i\ x)$$
$$go\_\ i\ \mathsf{One} \qquad\quad = text\ \mathtt{"1"}$$
$$go\_\ i\ (\mathsf{Var}\ x) \qquad = text\ (x\ \mathbf{as}\ \mathtt{[a\text{-}z]}+)$$
$$go\_\ i\ (\mathsf{Sub}\ x\ y) =$$
$$\quad parIf\ (i \geq 6)\ (group\ (go\ 5\ e_1 <> nest\ 2\ (line' <> text\ \mathtt{"-"} <> space' <> go\ 6\ e_2)))$$
$$go\_\ i\ (\mathsf{Div}\ x\ y) =$$
$$\quad parIf\ (i \geq 7)\ (group\ (go\ 6\ e_1 <> nest\ 2\ (line' <> text\ \mathtt{"/"} <> space' <> go\ 7\ e_2)))$$

Here, *manyPars* and *parIf* are defined as:

$$parIf\ b\ d = \mathbf{if}\ b\ \mathbf{then}\ par\ d\ \mathbf{else}\ d$$
$$manyPars\ d = d \nleftrightarrow par\ (manyPars\ d)$$
$$par\ d = text\ \mathtt{"("} <> nil <> d <> nil <> text\ \mathtt{")"}$$

This program differs from the one in the core language in the following ways:

1. The auxiliary functions *manyPars*, *parIf* and *par* are used and applied to non-variable arguments, which enable users to avoid duplicating frequently-occurring patterns such as *text* $\mathtt{"("} <> nil <> \ldots <> nil <> text\ \mathtt{")"}$.
2. Instead of embedding precedence-levels into function names, we pass them as arguments and inspect them by **if** and $\leq$ for bracketing. (These were previously impossible due to the linearity and treelessness restrictions.)
3. A new construct *text* $(x\ \mathbf{as}\ r)$ is used to avoid explicit recursion on strings.

Item 3 of the above is relatively easy to deal with. For Item 1, we borrow the idea of program fusion [14,20,21] to make sure that these auxiliary functions are fused away. For Item 2, we use partial evaluation to erase statically-computable arguments such as precedence-levels. The statically-computable arguments are separated from the rest through types.

4.3 Surface Language

Figure 6 shows the syntax of the surface language. The treeless restriction is replaced by a relaxed one that will be discussed towards the end of this subsection. The language has constants as expressions, such as the precedence levels of operations found in the previous subsection. Used as arguments, such constants can be eliminated at compilation time through partial evaluation; we call such constants *static information*. The **if** branchings inspect static information, and are eliminable statically as well.

We use a type system to distinguish static information (of type St) from other kinds of values such as the input ASTs (of type AST) and the pretty-printing results (of type Doc). The type system ensures that static information are eliminable through partial-evaluation, and variable uses are linear. Formally, primitive types τ and function types σ are defined by:

$$\tau ::= \mathsf{AST}\ |\ \mathsf{St}\ |\ \mathsf{Doc} \qquad\qquad \sigma ::= \tau_1 \rightarrow \cdots \rightarrow \tau_n \rightarrow \tau$$

$$
\begin{aligned}
prog &::= rule_1 \ldots rule_n \\
rule &::= f\ p_1\ \ldots\ p_n = e \\
e &::= \textbf{\textit{text}}\ \texttt{"s"} \mid e_1 <> e_2 \mid \textbf{\textit{line}} \mid \textbf{\textit{nest}}\ n\ e \mid \textbf{\textit{group}}\ e \mid e_1 <+ e_2 \quad \text{(Combinators)} \\
&\quad\mid\ \textbf{\textit{text}}\ (x\ \textbf{as}\ r) \qquad\qquad\qquad\qquad\qquad\qquad\quad \text{(Annotated Text)} \\
&\quad\mid\ x \qquad\qquad\qquad\qquad\qquad\qquad\qquad\qquad\qquad\ \text{(Variable)} \\
&\quad\mid\ f\ e_1\ \ldots\ e_n \qquad\qquad\qquad\qquad\qquad\qquad\qquad\ \text{(Call)} \\
&\quad\mid\ \textbf{if}\ pred\ e_1\ \ldots\ e_n\ \textbf{then}\ e_t\ \textbf{else}\ e_f \qquad\qquad \text{(Static Branching)} \\
&\quad\mid\ c \qquad\qquad\qquad\qquad\qquad\qquad\qquad\qquad\qquad\ \text{(Constant)} \\
c &::= \ldots \text{ any constants } \ldots \\
r &::= \ldots \text{ regular expression } \ldots
\end{aligned}
$$

Fig. 6. Syntax of the surface language: *pred* are Boolean predicates

$$\boxed{\Theta, \Gamma, \Delta \vdash e : \tau}$$

$$
\overline{\Theta, \Gamma, \{x : \tau\} \vdash x : \tau} \quad \overline{\Theta, \Gamma, \emptyset \vdash x : \Gamma(x)} \quad \overline{\Theta, \Gamma, \emptyset \vdash c : \mathsf{St}}
$$

$$
\frac{\Theta, \Gamma, \Delta \vdash e : \mathsf{Doc}}{\Theta, \Gamma, \Delta \vdash \textbf{\textit{nest}}\ n\ e : \mathsf{Doc}} \quad \frac{\{\Theta, \Gamma, \Delta_i \vdash e_i : \mathsf{Doc}\}_{1 \le i \le n} \quad op = \textbf{\textit{text}}\ \texttt{"s"}, \textbf{\textit{group}}, (<>), \textbf{\textit{line}}}{\Theta, \Gamma, \biguplus_{1 \le i \le n} \Delta_i \vdash op\ e_1\ \ldots\ e_n : \mathsf{Doc}}
$$

$$
\frac{\{\Theta, \Gamma, \Delta \vdash e_i : \mathsf{Doc}\}_{i=1,2}}{\Theta, \Gamma, \Delta \vdash e_1 <+ e_2 : \mathsf{Doc}} \quad \overline{\Theta, \Gamma, \{x : \mathsf{AST}\} \vdash \textbf{\textit{text}}\ (x\ \textbf{as}\ r) : \mathsf{Doc}}
$$

$$
\frac{\{\Theta, \Gamma, \emptyset \vdash e_i : \mathsf{St}\}_{1 \le i \le n} \quad \{\Theta, \Gamma, \Delta \vdash e_b : \tau\}_{b = t, f}}{\Theta, \Gamma, \Delta \vdash \textbf{if}\ pred\ e_1\ \ldots\ e_n\ \textbf{then}\ e_t\ \textbf{else}\ e_f : \tau}
$$

$$
\frac{\{\Theta, \Gamma, \Delta_i \vdash e_i : \tau_i\}_{1 \le i \le n} \quad \Theta(f) = \tau_1 \to \cdots \to \tau_n \to \mathsf{Doc}}{\Theta, \Gamma, \biguplus_{1 \le i \le n} \Delta_i \vdash f\ e_1\ \ldots\ e_n : \mathsf{Doc}}
$$

$$\boxed{\Theta \vdash f\ p_1\ \ldots\ p_n = e}$$

$$
\frac{\Theta(f) = \tau_1 \to \cdots \to \tau_n \to \mathsf{Doc}}{\exists \Gamma, \Delta_1, \ldots, \Delta_n \quad \{\Gamma, \Delta_i \vdash p_i : \tau_i\}_{1 \le i \le n} \quad \mathrm{dom}(\Gamma) \subseteq \biguplus_{1 \le i \le n} \mathrm{fv}(p_i)}{\Theta, \Gamma, \biguplus_{1 \le i \le n} \Delta_i \vdash e : \mathsf{Doc}}
$$
$$
\frac{}{\Theta \vdash f\ p_1\ \ldots\ p_n = e}
$$

$$\boxed{\Gamma, \Delta \vdash p : \tau}$$

$$
\frac{\Gamma(x) = \mathsf{St}}{\Gamma, \emptyset \vdash x : \mathsf{St}} \quad \frac{\tau \in \{\mathsf{AST}, \mathsf{Doc}\}}{\Gamma, \{x : \tau\} \vdash x : \tau} \quad \frac{\{\Gamma, \Delta_i \vdash p_i : \tau\}_{1 \le i \le n} \quad \tau \in \{\mathsf{AST}, \mathsf{St}\}}{\Gamma, \biguplus_{1 \le i \le n} \Delta_i \vdash \mathsf{C}\ p_1\ \ldots\ p_n : \tau}
$$

Fig. 7. Typing rules: here $\biguplus$ represents disjoint union

Typing judgment $\Theta, \Gamma, \Delta \vdash e : \tau$ reads that under function-type environment Θ, non-linear type environment Γ and linear type environment Δ, e has type τ. Similarly, we define $\Gamma, \Delta \vdash p : \tau$ and $\Theta \vdash f\ p_1\ \ldots\ p_n = e$ for patterns and declarations. Figure 7 shows the typing rules, which are mostly self-explanatory. Notably, the uses of variables of type AST and Doc have to be linear, as dictated by the rules. The linearity restriction of AST variables is inherited from the core language, while that of Doc variables is required for the correctness of fusion; it is known that the deforestation is not correct for non-linear *and* non-deterministic programs [1]. A program is assumed to have a distinguished entry point function of type AST → Doc. The type Doc is treated as a black box in the language; nothing except Wadler's combinators can handle Doc data. Only variables can have type AST.

Treeless Restriction. We replace the universal treeless restriction of the core language to a typed one: only arguments of type AST or Doc are restricted to be variables. Moreover, we view programs in the surface language as *multi-tier* systems [14]: every function is associated to a natural number called *tier*, and every function call occurring in the body of a tier-i function must be to a tier-j ($\leq i$) function. Tiers of functions are easily inferred by topologically sorting of the call-graph. A program is called *tiered-treeless* if for every call of a tier-k function f occurring in the body of a tier-k function, the arguments (of type AST or Doc) passed to the call must be variables. The pretty-printer defined in Sect. 4.2 is tiered-treeless: functions *ppr*, *go* and *go_* belong to tier 3, function *manyPars* belongs to tier 2, and other functions belong to tier 1.

We omit a formal semantics of the surface language, as it is a straightforward extension of the core language. Similar to the case of the core language, the evaluation results of the call-by-value and the call-by-name semantics coincide in the surface language due to linearity.

4.4   Conversion to the Core Language

The surface language is elaborated to the core language through a number of program transformations: (1) desugaring expressions of the form *text* (x **as** r), (2) partial-evaluating static information, (3) fusing higher-tier functions. Steps (1) and (2) above are straightforward adaptation of existing technologies, while step (3) is new and uses a property specific to our surface language. In what follows, we discuss the steps one by one.

Desugaring *text* (x **as** r)**.** We firstly convert r to a deterministic automaton. Then, we replace *text* (x **as** r) with f_{q_0} x where q_0 is an initial state of the automaton, and, for each state q, a function f_q is defined as follows: function f_q has a rule f_q ('a' : x) = $f_{q'}$ x if the automaton has a transition rule (q, a, q'), and has a rule f_q [] = *text* "" if q is a final state of the automaton. For the example in Sect. 4.2, the regular expression [a-z]+ can be expressed in a deterministic automaton with two states, and the functions f and g correspond to the two states.

Partial-Evaluating St-Expressions. A role of our type system is to perform binding-time analysis; the expressions of type St can be statically evaluated, assuming that predicate applications are terminating. Thus, a standard partial evaluation suffices to eliminate all the St-expressions and thus we omit the details. For the example in Sect. 4.2, we obtain the partially evaluated functions as below.

$$ppr\ x = go_5\ x$$

$$\ldots$$

$$go_5\ (\mathsf{Sub}\ x\ y) = \ldots go_5\ x \ldots go_6\ y \ldots$$
$$go_5\ (\mathsf{Div}\ x\ y) = \ldots go_6\ x \ldots go_7\ y \ldots$$

$$\ldots$$

$$go_6\ (\mathsf{Sub}\ x\ y) = \ldots go_5\ x \ldots go_6\ y \ldots$$
$$go_6\ (\mathsf{Div}\ x\ y) = par\ (\ldots go_6\ x \ldots go_7\ y \ldots)$$

$$\ldots$$

$$go_7\ (\mathsf{Sub}\ x\ y) = par\ (\ldots go_5\ x \ldots go_6\ y \ldots)$$
$$go_7\ (\mathsf{Div}\ x\ y) = par\ (\ldots go_6\ x \ldots go_7\ y \ldots)$$

Roughly speaking, thanks to the type $\mathsf{AST} \to \mathsf{Doc}$ of the entry point function, the type system guarantees that every St-type expression must be a constant itself or a part of some constant obtained by pattern-matching, and thus can eliminated by partial-evaluation.

Fusing Functions to Obtain 1-Tier Programs. We show the transformation of 2-tiered programs to 1-tiered programs, with the understanding that the procedure can be applied iteratively to transform m-tiered programs to 1-tiered programs.

The transformation is done by deforestation [21]. Roughly speaking, deforestation (or, supercompilation [20][5]) performs call-by-name evaluation of expressions; but instead of computing a value, it produces a new expression that has the same behavior as the original one but with intermediate data structures eliminated. Without loss of generality, we assume that AST arguments appear before Doc arguments in function calls. The deforestation procedure $\mathcal{D}[\![e]\!]$ is defined as follows.

- $\mathcal{D}[\![op\ e_1\ \ldots\ e_n]\!] = op\ \mathcal{D}[\![e_1]\!]\ \ldots\ \mathcal{D}[\![e_n]\!]$, where op ranges over *text* `"s"`, (<>), *line*, *nest* i, *group* and (<+).
- $\mathcal{D}[\![f\ \widetilde{x}\ \widetilde{e}]\!] = f_{\widetilde{e}}\ \widetilde{x}\ \widetilde{z}$. Assuming $\widetilde{x}$ have type AST (recall that only variables have type AST), $\widetilde{e}$ have type Doc, and $\{\widetilde{z}\}$ are the free variables in $\widetilde{e}$, the newly generated function $f_{\widetilde{e}}$ is defined as $f_{\widetilde{e}}\ \widetilde{p}\ \widetilde{z} = \mathcal{D}[\![e[\widetilde{y} \mapsto \widetilde{e}]]\!]$ for each corresponding rule $f\ \widetilde{p}\ \widetilde{y} = e$ in the definition of f (with proper α-renaming). Here, we do not repeatedly generate rules of $f_{\widetilde{e}}$ if they are already generated (up to renaming of the free variables in $\widetilde{e}$).

The above procedure follows from the original one [21], and is simplified to suit the restricted surface language. The procedure terminates if the number of functions $f_{\widetilde{e}}$ generated in the latter case is finite. By using $\mathcal{D}[\![e]\!]$, we replace every tier-2 rule $f\ \widetilde{p}\ \widetilde{y} = e$ with $f\ \widetilde{p}\ \widetilde{y} = \mathcal{D}[\![e]\!]$.

Example 1. We deforest the pretty-printer defined in Sect. 4.2.

---

[5] Because of the linearity, Wadler's deforestation [21] and (positive) supercompilation [20] coincide for the surface language.

The tier-2 function *manyPars* is transformed into the following.

$$manyPars \; d \quad = d \mathbin{<\!\!+} par_{manyPars \; d} \; d$$
$$par_{manyPars \; d} \; d = text \text{ "("} <> nil <> manyPars \; d <> nil <> text \text{ ")"}$$

And iteratively, we can now apply the procedure to the function go_5 (reproduced below), which is in tier-2 after the above transformation.

$$go_5 \; x = manyPars \; (go_5 \; x)$$

After renaming $par_{manyPars \; d}$ to *parMP*, we obtain the following tier-1 functions

$$go_5 \; x \qquad\qquad = manyPars_{go_5 \; x} \; x$$
$$manyPars_{go_5 \; x} \; x = go_5 \; x \mathbin{<\!\!+} parMP_{go_5 \; x} \; x$$
$$parMP_{go_5 \; x} \; x \quad = text \text{ "("} <> nil <> go_5 \; x <> nil <> text \text{ ")"}$$

assuming calls $go_5 \; x$ are transformed too. This behavior is similar to inlining except that the deforestation handles recursive functions such as *manyPars*. □

Theorem 2 (Termination). *For tier-2 expression e, $\mathcal{D}[\![e]\!]$ terminates.*

Proof (Sketch). All expressions $\tilde{e}$ in $\mathcal{D}[\![f \; \tilde{x} \; \tilde{e}]\!]$ must be tier-2 expressions in the original program or just variables, which implies the finiteness of the number of functions $f_{\tilde{e}}$ generated in the deforestation process. □

Theorem 3. *The resulting tier-1 program is treeless and linear.* □

The correctness of the deforestation is known for call-by-name languages [18]. Note again that call-by-value and call-by-name coincide in our surface language.

In the deforestation process, we treat Wadler's combinators as constructors because Doc-values are black boxes. This is key to termination; if we allow pattern-matching on Doc-values, then we can make a tiered-treeless program for which deforestation runs infinitely. As a result, Theorem 2 can be generalized and $\mathcal{D}[\![e]\!]$ terminates for tier-n expression e. Also, since deforestation (supercompilation) is a sort of partial-evaluation, the steps (2) and (3) of the transformation can be performed at once. We omit a formal discussion on this for space reason.

5   An Involved Example

In the introduction, we advertised that *"we, and many others who read this paper, will not need to do it [writing both parser and pretty-printer] for their own language implementations."*. In this section, we demonstrate the feasibility of this goal by writing a pretty-printer for the core language in the surface language, which, if fed to FliPpr, will generate a parser for the core language.

The ASTs of the core language can be expressed by the following datatype.

```
type Prog = [Rule]
data Rule = Rule String [Pat] Exp
data Exp = ECon String [Exp] | EOp Op Exp Exp | EVar String [Exp]
data Pat = PVar String | PCon String [Pat]
data Op = OCat | OAlt     -- <> and <+
```

We leave out *nest* and *text* "s" for simplicity. In the datatype, we use EVar both for variables and function calls to avoid ambiguity in grammars.

The overall principle of our pretty-printing is to insert breaks after =, and before <> and <+, with 2-space indentation. We start with lists of rules, and insert separators with optional whitespaces *nil* <> *text* ";" <> *line'* between individual rules.

$$ppr\ x = pprRules\ x$$

$$pprRules\ [] \qquad = nil$$
$$pprRules\ (r:rs) = nil <> pRules\ r\ rs <> nil$$

$$pRules\ r'\ [] \qquad = pprRule\ r'$$
$$pRules\ r'\ (r:rs) = pprRule\ r' <> nil <> text\ ";" <> line' <> pRules\ r\ rs$$

For each rule, its right-hand side may start a new line.

$$pprRule\ (\text{Rule}\ f\ ps\ e) =$$
$$\quad group\ (var\ f <> space <> pprPats\ ps <> space' <> text\ "=" <> nest\ 4\ (line' <> pprExp\ e))$$
$$var\ x = text\ (x\ \text{as}\ [a\text{-}z]\ [\_a\text{-}zA\text{-}Z0\text{-}9]*'*)$$

A list of patterns is treated in a similar way to a list of rules.

$$pprPats\ [] \qquad = text\ ""$$
$$pprPats\ (p:ps) = pPats\ p\ ps$$

$$pPats\ p'\ [] \qquad = pprPat\ p'$$
$$pPats\ p'\ (p:ps) = pprPat\ p' <> space <> pPats\ p\ ps$$

Redundant parentheses in patterns are admissible to the generated parser, but will not be produced by the pretty-printer.

$$pprPat\ p = manyPars\ (pprPat\_\ p)$$
$$pprPat\_\ (\text{PVar}\ x) \qquad = var\ x$$
$$pprPat\_\ (\text{PCon}\ c\ []) \qquad = con\ c$$
$$pprPat\_\ (\text{PCon}\ c\ (p:ps)) = par\ (con\ c <> space <> pPats\ p\ ps)$$
$$con\ f = text\ (x\ \text{as}\ [A\text{-}Z]\ [\_a\text{-}zA\text{-}Z0\text{-}9]*'*)$$

Expressions are printed according to the precedence-levels and associativities of the operators.

$$pprExp\ e = go\ 4\ e$$

$$go\ i\ e = manyPars\ (go\_\ i\ e)$$
$$go\_\ i\ (\text{ECon}\ c\ []) \qquad = con\ c$$
$$go\_\ i\ (\text{ECon}\ c\ (e:es)) = parIf\ (i \geq 9)\ (con\ c <> space <> pExps\ e\ es)$$
$$go\_\ i\ (\text{EOp}\ \text{OAlt}\ e_1\ e_2) =$$
$$\qquad parIf\ (i \geq 5)\ (group\ (go\ 5\ e_1 <> nest\ 2\ (line' <> text\ "<+" <> space' <> go\ 4\ e_2)))$$
$$go\_\ i\ (\text{EOp}\ \text{OCat}\ e_1\ e_2) =$$
$$\qquad parIf\ (i \geq 6)\ (group\ (go\ 6\ e_1 <> nest\ 2\ (line' <> text\ "<>" <> space' <> go\ 5\ e_2)))$$
$$go\_\ i\ (\text{EVar}\ f\ []) \qquad = var\ f$$
$$go\_\ i\ (\text{EVar}\ f\ (e:es)) = parIf\ (i \geq 9)\ (var\ f <> space <> pExps\ e\ es)$$

Finally, a list of expressions printed in a similar way to a list of patterns.

$$pExps\ e'\ [] \qquad = go\ 9\ e'$$
$$pExps\ e'\ (e:es) = go\ 9\ e' <> space <> pExps\ e\ es$$

6   Discussion

We discuss limitations and extensions of FliPpr.

Non-Structured Values in AST. ASTs may contain non-structured values such as Int. It is easy to extend the core system to handle the issue. For example, our implementation supports the syntax *text* (f x **as** r) where f is a bijection between a non-structured value and a string representation of it. The bijections can be read bidirectionally for either pretty-printing and parsing.

Higher-Order Functions. Higher-order functions, such as map, foldr and foldr1 are useful in writing pretty-printers. For example, *pprRules* and *pprPats* in Sect. 5 can be more conveniently implemented by map and foldr1. However, general use of higher-order functions in pretty-printing may produce grammars that go beyond CFG. The linearity restriction is also affected, most of the higher-order functions use the functional arguments more than once on the right-hand sides.

In line with the spirit of the surface language, a way forward is to use higher-order functions only when they can be fused away. A sufficient condition for fusion is the absence of λ-abstractions and partial-applications. In other words, functions must be *treeless* in the sense that intermediate function values are prohibited, and all the higher-order values must be variables (function names). We leave this extension as future work.

Spacing. We have demonstrated that careful use of whitespaces in the definition of the pretty-printer is an effectively way to control the behavior of the generated parser. For example, for pretty-printing constructor application in Sect. 5, we wrote (*con c* <> *space* <> *pExps e es*); the use of *space* (representing one-or-more whitespaces) allows us to parse "S Z" or "S Z" as valid strings. However, it is difficult to express the use of spaces that are dynamically dependent on the printing results of adjacent expressions, especially with nondeterminism. In the above example, if we were to know that the argument of the application is printed in parentheses as "(Z)", then in some syntax the space between the constructor and the argument can be omitted as in "S(Z)". On the other hand, we cannot simply replace *space* with *space'*, because we don't want to accept "SZ" as a valid constructor application. One possible solution to the problem is to try to extend the generate parsers with a lexing phase. But it may require some major surgery to the current system.

Non-Linearity. In the literature of tree transducers [9], the discussion of linearity can be separated into input- and output-linearity. In our case, variables of type AST can be seen as inputs, and those of type Doc can be seen as outputs.

For AST variables, sometimes we want to pretty-print the same AST twice; for example, an element e in XML is printed as <e>...</e>. A naive solution to admit this behavior is to check the equivalence of values of duplicated variables in semantic actions. More concretely, we relax ⊎ to allow overlapping domains in the operands, and define $\{x \mapsto v\} \uplus \{x \mapsto v\} = \{x \mapsto v\}$. This naive solution works effectively for XML, because the number of possible ASTs is usually finite. However, in general parsing becomes undecidable with non-linear use of AST variables, as shown in [13] (Theorem 4.4). Thus, for this kind of non-linear uses, a method that checks the finiteness of parse trees is required.

The non-linearity of Doc values has non-trivial interaction with nondeterminism. In the absence of linearity, the call-by-value and the call-by-name semantics may cease to coincide. This is a problem because call-by-value is suitable for grammar-based inversion [15], but call-by-name is suitable for deforestation [18]. We also need to resort to grammars beyond CFGs, which may pose difficulties in inversion. It is a challenging problem to find a sweet spot between obtaining efficient inverses and supporting fusion in the surface language.

7   Related Work

Different approaches have been proposed to simultaneously derive a parser and a printer from some intermediate descriptions. In particularly, one could start from an annotated CFG specification to derive both a parser and a pretty-printer [2]. Compared to these systems, FliPpr offers finer control over pretty-printing. In particular, we are able to deal with contextual information and to define auxiliary functions like *par* in printing, which is made conveniently available by the surface language. Other approaches include invertible syntax descriptions [17] based on invertible programming, and BNFC-meta [4] based on meta programming. Both work recognizes the importance of good printing, but is not able to support pretty-printing.

There are also general-purpose bidirectional languages [3, 6, 11] that in theory can be used to build the printer/parser pair from the definition of one of them. Notably quotient lenses [7] are designed to include a representative of a quotient before performing bidirectional conversions; in our case, roughly speaking this quotient operation is the erasure of redundant whitespaces and parentheses. However, there is a gap between the theoretical possibility and practically execution. In particular, the pretty-printing libraries of Wadler [22] and Hughes [10] are not only user-friendly but also highly optimized. Moreover, for efficient parsing we have to perform whole-program analysis (as in conventional parsing algorithms like LR-k) or use sophisticated data structures and memoization [8,16]. It is not obvious how these sophisticated implementations can be packed into a bidirectional program. In our approach, we avoid this problem by using grammar-based inversion [15], which generates grammars and outsources the parsing algorithms to selected parser generators.

There are a lot of discussions on how to make deforestation (supercompilation) terminate (*e.g.*, [12]) for Turing-complete languages. These approaches use conditions to give up fusion, and reuse the already-generated deforested functions. As a result, these approaches may fail to fuse some functions, and thus are not suitable for our purpose. The completeness of deforestation, in the sense whether all the nested calls are fused away, has not been the focus of study in the literature. Notable exceptions are Wadler's original work [21] and tree transducer fusion [1, 9, 14]. However, there is a gap between treeless functions and tree transducers; especially, treeless functions can take multiple inputs. It is not obvious how existing results can be directed applied in our case.

8   Conclusion

In this paper, we proposed a method to derive parsers from pretty-printers. We start with a program written in a language equipped with Wadler's pretty-printing combinators [22], and an additional "choice" operator. The choice operator allows us to enrich the pretty-printer with information about valid but yet non-pretty strings, without changing the pretty-printing behavior. This enriched pretty-printer can be transformed and inverted using grammar-based inversion [15] to produce a CFG parser. For the inversion to be possible, the language is restricted to be linear and treeless [21]. We also provide a surface language that has relaxed restrictions, which eases programming. The surface language is transformed into the linear and treeless language through fusion.

We feel that the specific problem we addressed in this paper has much wider implications. It suggests a general framework for program inversion problems with "information mismatch". A compression/decompression pair is another example of this kind. For the example of runlength encoding, we want to decode both A3B1 and A1A2B1 as AAAB, but an encoder "prefers" the former. Our result for pretty-printing/parsing benefits from Wadler's combinators, in which the "preference" is encapsulated in the combinators in a compositional way. It is an interesting problem to see how the technique may apply in different contexts.

Acknowledgments. We thank Nils Anders Danielsson for his critical yet constructive comments on an earlier version of this work, without which the surface language probably would not exist. We also thank Janis Voigtländer and Akimasa Morihata for their insightful comments on deforestation. This work was partially supported by JSPS KAKENHI Grant Number 24700020. Part of this research was done when the first author was visiting Chalmers Univeristy of Technology supported by Study Program at the Overseas Universities by Graduate School of Information Science and Technology, the University of Tokyo.

References

1. Baker, B.S.: Composition of Top-down and Bottom-up Tree Transductions. Information and Control 41(2), 186–213 (1979)
2. Boulton, R.J.: Syn: A Single Language for Specifiying Abstract Syntax Tress, Lexical Analysis, Parsing and Pretty-Printing. Technical Report UCAM-CL-TR-390, University of Cambridge Computer Laboratory (1996)
3. Brabrand, C., Møller, A., Schwartzbach, M.I.: Dual Syntax for XML Languages. Inf. Syst. 33(4-5), 385–406 (2008)
4. Duregård, J., Jansson, P.: Embedded Parser Generators. In: Haskell 2011: Proceedings of the 2011 ACM SIGPLAN Haskell Symposium, pp. 107–117. ACM (2011)

5. Duregård, J., Jansson, P., Wang, M.: Feat: Functional Enumeration of Algebraic Types. In: Haskell 2012: Proceedings of the 2012 ACM SIGPLAN Haskell Symposium, pp. 61–72. ACM (2012)

6. Foster, J.N., Greenwald, M.B., Moore, J.T., Pierce, B.C., Schmitt, A.: Combinators for Bidirectional Tree Transformations: A Linguistic Approach to the View-Update Problem. ACM Trans. Program. Lang. Syst. 29(3) (2007)

7. Foster, J.N., Pilkiewicz, A., Pierce, B.C.: Quotient Lenses. In: ICFP 2008: Proceedings of the 13th ACM SIGPLAN International Conference on Functional Programming, pp. 383–396. ACM (2008)

8. Frost, R.A., Hafiz, R., Callaghan, P.: Parser Combinators for Ambiguous Left-Recursive Grammars. In: Hudak, P., Warren, D.S. (eds.) PADL 2008. LNCS, vol. 4902, pp. 167–181. Springer, Heidelberg (2008)

9. Fülöp, Z., Vogler, H.: Syntax-Directed Semantics: Formal Models Based on Tree Transducers, 1st edn. Springer-Verlag New York, Inc., Secaucus (1998)

10. Hughes, J.: The Design of a Pretty-Printing Library. In: Jeuring, J., Meijer, E. (eds.) AFP 1995. LNCS, vol. 925, pp. 53–96. Springer, Heidelberg (1995)

11. Jansson, P., Jeuring, J.: Polytypic Data Conversion Programs. Sci. Comput. Program. 43(1), 35–75 (2002)

12. Jonsson, P.A., Nordlander, J.: Positive Supercompilation for a Higher Order Call-by-Value Language. In: POPL 2009: Proceedings of the 36th ACM SIGPLAN-SIGACT Symposium on Principles of Programming Languages, pp. 277–288. ACM (2009)

13. Kobayashi, N., Tabuchi, N., Unno, H.: Higher-Order Multi-Parameter Tree Transducers and Recursion Schemes for Program Verification. In: POPL 2010: Proceedings of the 37th ACM SIGPLAN-SIGACT Symposium on Principles of Programming Languages, pp. 495–508. ACM (2010)

14. Kühnemann, A., Glück, R., Kakehi, K.: Relating Accumulative and Non-accumulative Functional Programs. In: Middeldorp, A. (ed.) RTA 2001. LNCS, vol. 2051, pp. 154–168. Springer, Heidelberg (2001)

15. Matsuda, K., Mu, S.-C., Hu, Z., Takeichi, M.: A Grammar-Based Approach to Invertible Programs. In: Gordon, A.D. (ed.) ESOP 2010. LNCS, vol. 6012, pp. 448–467. Springer, Heidelberg (2010)

16. Might, M., Darais, D., Spiewak, D.: Parsing with Derivatives: A Functional Pearl. In: ICFP 2011: Proceeding of the 16th ACM SIGPLAN International Conference on Functional Programming, pp. 189–195. ACM (2011)

17. Rendel, T., Ostermann, K.: Invertible Syntax Descriptions: Unifying Parsing and Pretty Printing. In: Haskell 2010: Proceedings of the 2010 ACM SIGPLAN Haskell Symposium, pp. 1–12. ACM (2010)

18. Sands, D.: Proving the Correctness of Recursion-Based Automatic Program Transformations. Theor. Comput. Sci. 167(1&2), 193–233 (1996)

19. Søndergaard, H., Sestoft, P.: Non-Determinism in Functional Languages. Comput. J. 35(5), 514–523 (1992)

20. Sørensen, M.H., Glück, R., Jones, N.D.: A Positive Supercompiler. J. Funct. Program. 6(6), 811–838 (1996)

21. Wadler, P.: Deforestation: Transforming Programs to Eliminate Trees. Theor. Comput. Sci. 73(2), 231–248 (1990)

22. Wadler, P.: A Prettier Printer. In: Gibbons, J., de Moor, O. (eds.) The Fun of Programming. Palgrave Macmillan (2003)

Slicing-Based Trace Analysis of Rewriting Logic Specifications with iJULIENNE[*]

María Alpuente[1], Demis Ballis[2], Francisco Frechina[1], and Julia Sapiña[1]

[1] DSIC-ELP, Universitat Politècnica de València,
Camino de Vera s/n, Apdo 22012, 46071 Valencia, Spain
{alpuente,ffrechina,jsapina}@dsic.upv.es
[2] DIMI, Università degli Studi di Udine,
Via delle Scienze 206, 33100 Udine, Italy
demis.ballis@uniud.it

Abstract. We present iJULIENNE, a trace analyzer for conditional rewriting logic theories that can be used to compute abstract views of Maude executions that help users understand and debug programs. Given a Maude execution trace and a slicing criterion which consists of a set of target symbols occurring in a selected state of the trace, iJULIENNE is able to track back reverse dependences and causality along the trace in order to incrementally generate highly reduced program and trace slices that reconstruct all and only those pieces of information that are needed to deliver the symbols of interest. iJULIENNE is also endowed with a trace querying mechanism that increases flexibility and reduction power and allows program runs to be examined at the appropriate level of abstraction.

1 Introduction

Execution traces are an important source of information for program understanding and debugging. Standard tracers usually present execution histories that mainly consist of low-level execution steps so that the relationship between the executed program and the execution history is not easy to derive because some key dependences that are naturally expressed at the programming language level can be either scattered or omitted in the trace. This is particularly true for those systems that are specified in Rewriting Logic (RWL) —a logic of change that can deal naturally with highly nondeterministic concurrent computations.

Rewriting logic is efficiently implemented in the high-performance language Maude. Execution traces generated by Maude are complex objects to deal with. The traces typically include thousands of rewrite steps that are obtained by applying the equations and rules of the considered specification (including all the internal rewrite steps for evaluating the conditions of such equations/rules).

---

[*] This work has been partially supported by the EU (FEDER) and the Spanish MEC project ref. TIN2010-21062-C02-02, and Generalitat Valenciana ref. PROMETEO2011/052, and was carried out during the tenure of D. Ballis' ERCIM "Alain Bensoussan" Postdoctoral Fellowship. The research leading to these results has received funding from the EU 7th Framework Programme (FP7/2007-2013) under agreement n. 246016. F. Frechina is supported by FPU-ME grant AP2010-5681.

M. Felleisen and P. Gardner (Eds.): ESOP 2013, LNCS 7792, pp. 121–124, 2013.

In addition, Maude traces are incomplete because algebraic axiom applications, which implicitly occur in an equational simplification process that is hidden within Maude's *matching modulo* algorithm, are not recorded at all in the trace. This provides a very low-level blueprint of program execution whose manual inspection is frequently unfeasible or, in the best case, is an extremely labor-intensive and time-consuming task.

This paper describes *i*JULIENNE, a slicing-based trace analysis tool that assists the user in the comprehension and debugging of RWL theories that are encoded in Maude. *i*JULIENNE is built on top of a trace slicer that implements the backward conditional trace slicing algorithm described in [2,3,4]. Roughly speaking, the trace slicing mechanism included in *i*JULIENNE rolls back the program execution (making *all* the rewrite and equational simplification steps explicit) while tracking back only and all data in the trace that are needed to accomplish the selected *slicing criterion* —that is, the data that contribute to producing the set of *target symbols* that occur in the observed state of the trace. The core trace slicer included within *i*JULIENNE is a totally redesigned implementation of our slicing technique in [2,3] that supersedes and greatly improves the preliminary system presented in [4]. In particular, the new trace analyzer *i*JULIENNE is equipped with an *incremental* backward trace slicing algorithm that supports stepwise refinements of the trace slice and achieves huge reductions in the size of the trace. Starting from a Maude execution trace $\mathcal{T}$, a slicing criterion $\mathcal{S}$ can be attached to any given state of the trace and the computed trace slice $\mathcal{T}^*$ can be repeatedly refined by applying backward trace slicing w.r.t. increasingly restrictive versions of $\mathcal{S}$. Furthermore, the system supports a cogent form of *dynamic program slicing* [7] as follows. Given a Maude program $\mathcal{M}$ and a trace slice $\mathcal{T}^*$ for $\mathcal{M}$, *i*JULIENNE is able to infer the minimal fragment of $\mathcal{M}$ (i.e., the *program slice*) that is needed to reproduce $\mathcal{T}^*$. Finally, *i*JULIENNE is endowed with a powerful and intuitive Web user interface that allows the slicing criteria to be easily defined by either highlighting the chosen target symbols or by applying a user-defined filtering pattern. A browsing facility is also provided that enables forward and backward navigation through the trace (and the trace slice) and allows the user to examine each state transition (and its corresponding sliced counterpart) at different granularity levels.

2   *i*JULIENNE at Work

The *i*JULIENNE system is written in Maude and consists of about 250 Maude function definitions. It can be invoked as a Maude command or used online through a Java Web service. The tool is publicly available at [6] together with several case studies which consider large execution traces, such as the counter-examples delivered by the Maude LTLR model-checker [1]. A thorough experimental evaluation of our slicing methodology can be found in [5].

To illustrate how *i*JULIENNE works in practice, we show a typical trace slicing session on a Maude implementation of *Blocks World* —one of the most popular planning problems in artificial intelligence. We assume that there are some blocks, placed on a table, that can be moved by means of a robot arm; the

```
mod BLOCKS-WORLD is inc INT .
  sorts Block Prop State .
  subsort Prop < State .
  ops a b c : -> Block .
  op table : Block -> Prop .      *** block is on the table
  op on : Block Block -> Prop .   *** first block is on the second block
  op clear : Block -> Prop .      *** block is clear
  op hold : Block -> Prop .       *** robot arm holds the block
  op empty : -> Prop .            *** robot arm is empty
  op _&_ : State State -> State [assoc comm] .
  op size : Block -> Nat .
  vars X Y : Block .

  eq [sizeA] : size(a) = 1 .
  eq [sizeB] : size(b) = 2 .
  eq [sizeC] : size(c) = 3 .

  rl [pickup]  : clear(X) & table(X) => hold(X) .
  rl [putdown] : hold(X) => empty & clear(X) & table(X) .
  rl [unstack] : empty & clear(X) & on(X,Y) => hold(X) & clear(Y) .
  crl [stack]  : hold(X) & clear(Y) => empty & clear(X) & on(X,Y) if size(X) < size(Y) .
endm
```

Fig. 1. BLOCKS-WORLD faulty Maude specification

goal of the robot arm is to produce one or more vertical stacks of blocks. In our specification, which is shown in the Maude module BLOCKS-WORLD of Figure 1, we define a Blocks World system with three different kinds of blocks that are defined by means of the operators a, b, and c of sort Block. Different blocks have different sizes that are described by using the unary operator size. We also consider some operators that formalize block and robot arm properties whose intuitive meanings are given in the accompanying program comments.

The states of the system are modeled by means of associative and commutative lists of properties of the form $prop_1 \& prop_2 \& \ldots \& prop_n$, which describe any possible configuration of the blocks as well as the status of the robot arm. The system behavior is formalized by four, simple rewrite rules that control the robot arm. Specifically, the pickup rule describes how the robot arm grabs a block from the table, while putdown rule corresponds to the inverse move. The stack and unstack rules respectively allow the robot arm to drop one block on top of another block and to remove a block from the top of a stack. Note that the conditional stack rule forbids a given block B_1 from being piled on a block B_2 if the size of B_1 is greater than the size of B_2.

Barely perceptible, the Maude specification of Figure 1 fails to provide a correct Blocks World implementation. By using the BLOCKS-WORLD module, it is indeed possible to derive system states that represent erroneous configurations. For instance, the initial state

$s_i = $ empty & clear(a) & table(a) & clear(b) & table(b) & clear(c) & table(c)

describes a simple configuration where the robot arm is empty and there are three blocks a, b, and c on the table. It can be rewritten in 7 steps to the state

$s_f = \boxed{\text{empty}}$ & $\boxed{\text{empty}}$ & table(b) & table(c) & clear(a) & clear(c) & $\boxed{\text{on(a,b)}}$

which clearly indicates a system anomaly, since it shows the existence of two empty robot arms!

To find the cause of this wrong behavior, we feed iJULIENNE with the faulty rewrite sequence $\mathcal{T} = s_i \rightarrow^* s_f$, and we initially slice $\mathcal{T}$ w.r.t. the slicing criterion that observes the two anomalous occurrences of the empty property and the stack on(a, b) in State s_f. This task can be easily performed in iJULIENNE by first highlighting the terms that we want to observe in State s_f with the mouse pointer and then starting the slicing process. Alternatively, we can also query the trace using an appropriate pattern, which extracts the considered target data by means of pattern-matching, to State s_f. iJULIENNE yields a trace slice which only records those data that are strictly needed to produce the considered slicing criterion. Also, it automatically computes the corresponding program slice, which consists of the equations defining the size operator together with the pickup and stack rules. This allows us to deduce that the malfunction is located in one or more rules and equations that are included in the computed program slice.

The generated trace slice is then browsed backwards using the iJULIENNE's navigation facility in search of a possible explanation for the wrong behavior. During this phase, we found an inconsistent state that models a robot arm that is holding block a and is empty at the same time. Therefore, we further refine the trace slice by incrementally applying backward trace slicing to the detected, inconsistent state w.r.t. the slicing criterion hold(a). This way, we achieve a trace reduction of ~90% in which we can easily observe that hold(a) only depends on the clear(a) and table(a) properties. Furthermore, the computed program slice includes the single pickup rule. Thus, we can conclude that: (i) the malfunction is certainly located in the pickup rule (since the computed program slice only contains that rule); (ii) the pickup rule does not depend on the status of the robot arm (this is witnessed by the fact that hold(a) only relies on the clear(a) and table(a) properties); (iii) by (i) and (ii), we can deduce that the pickup rule is incorrect, as it never checks the emptiness of the robot arm before grasping a block.

References

1. Alpuente, M., Ballis, D., Espert, J., Romero, D.: Model-Checking Web Applications with WEB-TLR. In: Bouajjani, A., Chin, W.-N. (eds.) ATVA 2010. LNCS, vol. 6252, pp. 341–346. Springer, Heidelberg (2010)
2. Alpuente, M., Ballis, D., Espert, J., Romero, D.: Backward Trace Slicing for Rewriting Logic Theories. In: Björner, N., Sofronie-Stokkermans, V. (eds.) CADE 2011. LNCS, vol. 6803, pp. 34–48. Springer, Heidelberg (2011)
3. Alpuente, M., Ballis, D., Frechina, F., Romero, D.: Backward Trace Slicing for Conditional Rewrite Theories. In: Björner, N., Voronkov, A. (eds.) LPAR-18 2012. LNCS, vol. 7180, pp. 62–76. Springer, Heidelberg (2012)
4. Alpuente, M., Ballis, D., Frechina, F., Romero, D.: JULIENNE: A Trace Slicer for Conditional Rewrite Theories. In: Giannakopoulou, D., Méry, D. (eds.) FM 2012. LNCS, vol. 7436, pp. 28–32. Springer, Heidelberg (2012)
5. Alpuente, M., Ballis, D., Frechina, F., Romero, D.: Using Conditional Trace Slicing for Improving Maude Programs. Science of Comp. Progr. (to appear, 2013)
6. The iJULIENNE website (2013), http://safe-tools.dsic.upv.es/iJulienne
7. Korel, B., Laski, J.: Dynamic Program Slicing. Inf. Process. Lett. 29(3), 155–163 (1988)

Why3 — Where Programs Meet Provers

Jean-Christophe Filliâtre[1,2] and Andrei Paskevich[1,2]

[1] Lab. de Recherche en Informatique, Univ. Paris-Sud, CNRS, Orsay, F-91405
[2] INRIA Saclay – Île-de-France, Orsay, F-91893

Abstract. We present Why3, a tool for deductive program verification, and WhyML, its programming and specification language. WhyML is a first-order language with polymorphic types, pattern matching, and inductive predicates. Programs can make use of record types with mutable fields, type invariants, and ghost code. Verification conditions are discharged by Why3 with the help of various existing automated and interactive theorem provers. To keep verification conditions tractable and comprehensible, WhyML imposes a static control of aliases that obviates the use of a memory model. A user can write WhyML programs directly and get correct-by-construction OCaml programs via an automated extraction mechanism. WhyML is also used as an intermediate language for the verification of C, Java, or Ada programs. We demonstrate the benefits of Why3 and WhyML on nontrivial examples of program verification.

1 Introduction

Why3 is a platform for deductive program verification [1]. It provides a rich language of specification and programming, called WhyML, and relies on external theorem provers, both automated and interactive, to discharge verification conditions. The tool comes with a standard library of logical theories (integer and real arithmetic, sets and maps, etc.) and of basic programming data structures. WhyML is used as an intermediate language for the verification of C, Java, or Ada programs [2], in a similar fashion to the Boogie language [3]. Besides, WhyML strives to be comfortable as a primary programming language and inherits numerous high-level features from ML, listed below.

The specification component of WhyML, used to write program annotations and background logical theories, is presented in [4], and here we only mention the most essential features. Why3 is based on first-order logic with rank-1 polymorphic types and several extensions: recursive definitions, algebraic data types, and (co-)inductive predicates. Pattern matching, let-expressions, and conditional expressions are allowed both in terms and in formulas. A type, a function, or a predicate can be given a definition or just declared as abstract symbols and then axiomatized. The specification language of Why3 does not depend on any features of the programming language, and can serve as a rich common format for theorem proving problems, readily suitable (via Why3) for multiple automated and interactive provers, such as Alt-Ergo, CVC3, Z3, E, SPASS, Vampire, Coq, or PVS. When a proof obligation is dispatched to a prover that does not support some language features, Why3 applies a series of encoding transformations to, for example, eliminate pattern matching or polymorphic types [5].

M. Felleisen and P. Gardner (Eds.): ESOP 2013, LNCS 7792, pp. 125–128, 2013.

2   Programming Language

WhyML can be seen as an ML dialect, with two important restrictions. Firstly, in order to generate first-order proof obligations, WhyML is also limited to the first order: Nested function definitions and partial application are supported, but higher-order functions are not. Secondly, in order to keep proof obligations more tractable for provers and more readable (hence debuggable) for users, WhyML uses no memory model and imposes a static control of aliases instead. Every l-value in a program must have a finite set of names and all these names must be known statically, at the time of generation of verification conditions. In particular, recursive data types cannot have mutable components. This restriction is not as limiting as it may seem, and we show in the next section that it does not preclude us from writing and verifying complex algorithms and data structures.

WhyML functions are annotated with pre- and post-conditions for normal and exceptional termination, and WhyML loops are annotated with invariants. Recursive functions and while-loops can be given variants (*i.e.* values that decrease at each recursive call or iteration) to ensure termination. Statically checked assertions can be inserted at arbitrary points in a program. Verification conditions are generated using a standard weakest-precondition procedure. Every pure type, function or predicate introduced in the logical component can be used in a WhyML program. For instance, the type of integers and basic arithmetic operations are shared between specifications and programs.

The mutable state of a computation is embodied in mutable fields of record data types. Mutable data types can be nested. For example, a polymorphic resizable array can be modeled by a record with a mutable field containing an ordinary fixed-size array:

```
type rarray 'a = { mutable data: array 'a; mutable size: int }
    invariant { 0 ≤ size ≤ data.length }
```

Here, the type is accompanied by an invariant, *i.e.* a logical property imposed on any value of that type. Why3 assumes that any rarray passed as an argument to a program function satisfies the invariant and it produces a proof obligation every time an rarray is created or modified in a program. Notice that this requires that types with invariants not be used in recursive data structures, just as mutable types.

An important feature of WhyML is ghost code, *i.e.* computations that only serve to facilitate verification and that can be safely removed from a program without affecting its final result. A ghost expression cannot be used in a non-ghost computation, it cannot modify a non-ghost mutable value, and it cannot raise exceptions that would escape into non-ghost code. However, a ghost expression can use non-ghost values and its result can be used in program annotations. A classical use case for ghost code is that of step counters to prove time complexity of an algorithm. It also serves to equip a data structure with a ghost field containing a pure logical "view" for specification purposes.

3   Case Studies

We have used WhyML to verify a lot of non-trivial data structures and algorithms. Our gallery (http://proval.lri.fr/gallery/why3.en.html) currently contains 67 case studies. In this section, we illustrate three different kinds of verification.

Verification of an Algorithm. Let us consider the Knuth-Morris-Pratt algorithm for string searching [6]. A string is simply an array of characters. Arrays are imported from the Why3 standard library. Conversely, the type of characters is declared as an abstract, uninterpreted type `character`. The Knuth-Morris-Pratt algorithm is then implemented as a function that receives two strings p and t and that returns, if any, the position of the first occurrence of p in t and, otherwise, the length of t:

```
let kmp (p a: array character)
   requires { 1 ≤ length p ∧ 0 ≤ length a }
   ensures  { first_occur p a result }        = ...
```

where `first_occur` is a predicate introduced earlier in the specification. To get an executable code, Why3 translates WhyML to OCaml. In the process, uninterpreted WhyML types are either mapped to existing OCaml types or left as abstract data types. In the example above, this results into the following OCaml function:

```
val kmp: character array → character array → Num.t
```

where `array` is the OCaml built-in type, `character` is an abstract data type, and `Num.t` is the type of arbitrary precision integers from OCaml library. Such a mapping can be customized at the user level. The key point here is *genericity*. Extracted code is parameterized w.r.t. uninterpreted symbols, such as the `character` type from the above example. It is then possible to instantiate the extracted code in different ways, for example by wrapping it into an OCaml functor.

Verification of a Data Structure. Let us implement hash tables (associative arrays) in WhyML, using an uninterpreted type key for keys:

```
type t 'a = { mutable size: int;   (* total number of elements *)
              mutable data: array (list (key, 'a)); (* buckets *) }
```

where arrays and lists are imported from the Why3 standard library. Field `data` is declared mutable, in order to allow dynamic resizing, for the case when the array holding the buckets is replaced by a new, larger array. This operation changes the current set of aliases and the type system of WhyML can detect and safely handle it. In particular, after the resize, one cannot use any stale pointer to the old value of `data`. Also, the new value of `data` must be fresh. The key point here is *modularity*: One can implement resizing in a separate function and call it, for instance, from the add function that inserts a new element in the table.

Specification of a Data Structure. There are data structures that cannot be implemented in WhyML. Simply speaking, these are pointer-based data structures where mutable nodes are arbitrarily nested, *e.g.* doubly-linked lists or mutable trees. Still we can easily *model* such data structures and then verify the programs that use them. Let us consider, for instance, a program building a perfect maze using a union-find data structure, as proposed in the VACID-0 benchmark [7]. A union-find can be implemented in WhyML using arrays. However, a more flexible implementation, with chains of pointers, is beyond the scope of WhyML, and is simply modeled as follows:

```
type uf model { mutable contents: uf_pure }
```

There are three ideas here. First, the keyword **model** replaces the equal sign. This means that type uf is not a record, as far as programs are concerned, but an abstract data type. Inside specifications, though, it is a record and its field contents may be accessed. Second, field contents is declared mutable, to account for the fact that uf is a mutable data structure. Last, a pure data type uf_pure represents the immutable snapshot of the contents of the union-find data structure.

We then declare and specify operations over type uf. For instance, the function find that returns the representative of the class of a given element and may modify the structure (*e.g.* for path compression) can be specified as follows:

```
val find (u : uf) (x : elt) : elt  writes {u}
  ensures { result = repr u x ∧ same_repr u (old u) }
```

The key point here is *encapsulation*: Though we cannot implement the union-find data structure, we can declare an interface data type to model it and then verify a client code (in this case, a program building a maze). Any implementation of union-find could be used without compromising the proof of the client code.

4   Future Work

The most immediate direction of our future development is the ability to verify that a given implementation conforms to an interface. This amounts to establishing a refinement relation between WhyML modules, their data types and their functions, be they defined or merely specified. We also plan to introduce some higher-order features in the specification language, *e.g.* set comprehensions and sum-like operations, together with suitable encodings to first-order logic. A more ambitious goal would be to accept higher-order programs in WhyML, in order to bring it closer to functional programming. Finally, our long-term goal is to merge the specification and programming languages, in the spirit of PVS and ACL2. The challenge is two-fold. We want to allow imperative constructions in pure functions, provided they do not break referential transparency. Even more importantly, we want to state and prove theorems about WhyML programs, beyond what is possible to express using pre- and postconditions.

References

1. Why3, a tool for deductive program verification, GNU LGPL 2.1, http://why3.lri.fr
2. Guitton, J., Kanig, J., Moy, Y.: Why Hi-Lite Ada? In: Boogie, pp. 27–39 (2011)
3. Barnett, M., Chang, B.-Y.E., DeLine, R., Jacobs, B., Leino, K.R.M.: Boogie: A Modular Reusable Verifier for Object-Oriented Programs. In: de Boer, F.S., Bonsangue, M.M., Graf, S., de Roever, W.-P. (eds.) FMCO 2005. LNCS, vol. 4111, pp. 364–387. Springer, Heidelberg (2006)
4. Bobot, F., Filliâtre, J.C., Marché, C., Paskevich, A.: Why3: Shepherd your herd of provers. In: Boogie, pp. 53–64 (2011)
5. Bobot, F., Paskevich, A.: Expressing Polymorphic Types in a Many-Sorted Language. In: Tinelli, C., Sofronie-Stokkermans, V. (eds.) FroCoS 2011. LNCS, vol. 6989, pp. 87–102. Springer, Heidelberg (2011)
6. Knuth, D.E., Morris, J.H., Pratt, V.R.: Fast pattern matching in strings. SIAM Journal on Computing 6, 323–350 (1977)
7. Leino, K.R.M., Moskal, M.: VACID-0: Verification of ample correctness of invariants of datastructures, edition 0. In: VSTTE (2010)

Compositional Invariant Checking for Overlaid and Nested Linked Lists*

Constantin Enea, Vlad Saveluc, and Mihaela Sighireanu

Univ Paris Diderot, Sorbonne Paris Cite, LIAFA CNRS UMR 7089, Paris
{cenea,sighirea}@liafa.univ-paris-diderot.fr,
vlad.saveluc@gmail.com

Abstract. We introduce a fragment of separation logic, called *NOLL*, for automated reasoning about programs manipulating overlaid and nested linked lists, where overlaid means that the lists share the same set of objects. The distinguishing features of *NOLL* are: (1) it is parametrized by a set of user-defined predicates specifying nested linked list segments, (2) a "per-field" version of the separating conjunction allowing to share object locations but not record field locations, and (3) it can express sharing constraints between list segments. We prove that checking the entailment between two *NOLL* formulas is co-NP complete using a small model property. We also provide an effective procedure for checking entailment in *NOLL*, which first constructs a Boolean abstraction of the two formulas in order to infer all the implicit constraints, and then, it checks the existence of a homomorphism between the two formulas, viewed as graphs. We have implemented this procedure and applied it on verification conditions generated from several interesting case studies that manipulate overlaid and nested data structures.

1 Introduction

Reasoning about behaviors of programs that manipulate dynamic data structures is a challenging problem because of the difficulty of representing (potentially infinite) sets of configurations, and of manipulating these representations for the analysis of the execution of program statements. For instance, pre/post-condition reasoning requires being able, given pre- and post-conditions ϕ resp. ψ, and a straight-line code P, (1) to compute the (strongest) post-condition of executing P starting from ϕ, denoted $\mathrm{post}(P,\phi)$, and (2) to check that it entails ψ. Therefore, an important issue is to investigate logic-based formalisms where pre/post conditions are expressible for the class of programs under interest, and for which it is possible to compute effectively post-conditions, and to efficiently check the entailment. The latter can be done either using theorem provers, where user-provided tactics are needed to guide the proof system, or using decision procedures, when the given annotations are in a decidable fragment. An essential ingredient in order to scale to large programs is being able to perform compositional reasoning and, in this context, Separation Logic [17] (SL) has emerged as a fundamental approach. Its main tool is the frame rule, which states that if the Hoare triple $\{\phi\}P\{\psi\}$ holds and P does not alter free variables in σ then $\{\phi * \sigma\}P\{\psi * \sigma\}$ also holds, where $*$ denotes the

---

* This work has been partially supported by the French ANR project Veridyc and by FSMP.

M. Felleisen and P. Gardner (Eds.): ESOP 2013, LNCS 7792, pp. 129–148, 2013.

separating conjunction. Therefore, when reasoning about P one has to manipulate only specifications for the heap region altered by P.

In this paper, we define a fragment of SL, called *NOLL*, suitable for compositional reasoning about programs that manipulate *overlaid and nested* linked lists, built with an arbitrary set of fields. Such data structures are used in low-level code to link objects with respect to different aspects. For example, the network monitoring software Nagios (www.nagios.com) manipulates hash-tables with closed addressing, implemented as arrays of linked lists, where all the elements in the lists are also linked in the order of their insertion time. Here, we have two overlaid data structures, i.e., which share a set of objects: an array of linked lists and a singly-linked list.

To specify such data structures, *NOLL* is parametrized by a fixed, but arbitrary, set of recursive predicates defined in a higher-order extension of *NOLL* and which are expressive enough to specify various types of (nested) linked lists, e.g., singly-linked lists of singly-linked lists, where all the elements point to some fixed object.

To specify that these list segments are overlapped, *NOLL* includes, besides the classical operator $*$, that we will call object separating conjunction, a field separating conjunction operator $*_w$. Both operators separate the heap into disjoint regions, the only difference being the granularity of the separated heap cells. For $*$, a heap cell corresponds to a heap object. For $*_w$, a heap cell corresponds to a field from a heap object. Thus, the $*_w$ operator allows to specify data structures sharing sets of objects as long as they are built over disjoint sets of fields. In the example above, if ArrOfSl and Sl are formulas specifying the array of lists, resp. the list, then ArrOfSl $*_w$ Sl expresses the fact that the two structures share some objects.

However, $*w$ alone is not enough to describe precisely overlaid data structures. In the example above, we would also need to express the fact that the objects of the list described by Sl are exactly *all* the list objects in ArrOfSl; let Sl_type be their type. To this, we index each atomic formula specifying list segments by a variable, called a *set of locations variable* and interpreted as the set of all heap objects in the list segment. The values of these new variables can be constrained in a logic that uses classical set operators $\subseteq$ and $\cup$. For example, the specification ArrOfSl$_\alpha$ $*_w$ Sl$_\beta$ $\wedge$ α(Sl_type) $= \beta$ constrains the set of objects in the linked list to be exactly the set of objects of type Sl_type in the array of linked lists. (A *NOLL* formula φ can also put constrains over some set of locations variables, which are not associated to atomic formulas in φ.)

The semantics of the field separating conjunction $*_w$ allows us to establish another frame rule, which is essential for compositional reasoning about overlaid data structures: if the Hoare triple $\{\phi\}$ P $\{\psi\}$ holds then $\{\phi *_w \sigma\}$ P $\{\psi *_w \sigma\}$ also holds, where P is a straight-line code that does not alter fields described by σ, and the set of locations variables in σ are not bound to atomic formulas in ϕ or ψ. The consequences of this frame rule are that, to reason about a program fragment P, one has to provide only specifications for the data structures built with fields altered by P.

We prove that checking satisfiability of *NOLL* formulas is NP-complete and that the problem of checking entailments between *NOLL* formulas is co-NP complete. The upper bound on the complexity of checking satisfiability/entailment is first proved using a small model argument, and subsequently, following the approach in [8]. The second proof provides also an effective decision procedure for proving the validity of an entailment $\varphi \Rightarrow \psi$ by (1) computing a normal form for the two formulas and (2) checking the existence of a homomorphism from the graph representation of the normal form of ψ to the graph representation of the normal form of φ. The main advantages of this decision procedure are: (i) by defining a Boolean abstraction for *NOLL* formulas, the construction of the normal form is reduced to (un)satisfiability queries to a SAT solver and (ii) checking the existence of a homomorphism between graph representations of formulas can be done in polynomial time.

To summarize, this work makes the following contributions:

- defines a fragment of SL, called *NOLL*, that can be used to perform compositional reasoning about overlaid and nested linked structures,
- proves that checking satisfiability, resp. entailment, of *NOLL* formulas is NP-complete, resp. co-NP complete,
- defines effective procedures for checking satisfiability and entailment of *NOLL* formulas based on SAT solvers, which are implemented in a prototype tool and proven to be efficient in practice.

Related Work. SL has been widely used in the literature for the analysis and the verification of programs with dynamic data structures [1–8, 12, 13, 17, 19].

The *NOLL* fragment incorporates several existing features of SL: the separating conjunction $*$ introduced in [12], the separating conjunction $*_w$ introduced in [6], and the inductive predicates describing nested linked structures introduced in [1]. The set of location variables are an abstraction of the sequences defined in [17]. However, [1, 6] use these features in order to define abstract domains for program analysis. The (partial) order relation on elements of these abstract domains can be seen as a sound, but not complete, decision procedure for entailment.

The works in [2, 5, 8] introduce results concerning the decidability/complexity of the satisfiability/entailment problem in fragments of SL. Berdine et al. [2] defines a fragment that allows to reason about programs with singly-linked lists and proves that the satisfiability of a formula can be decided in NP and that checking the validity of an entailment between two formulas belongs to the co-NP complexity class. A decision procedure for entailments in the same fragment is introduced in [16], which combines SL inference rules with a superposition calculus to deal with (in)equalities between variables. These complexity results were improved in [8] where it is proved that the satisfiability/entailment problem for the previous fragment can be solved in polynomial time. In fact, the procedure for checking entailments of *NOLL* formulas based on normal forms and graph homomorphism is inspired by the work in [8]. The differences are that (a) the procedure for computing the normal form of a *NOLL* formula is based on a new approach that uses Boolean abstractions (the procedure in [8] works only for singly-linked lists and can not be extended to *NOLL*) and (b) the notion of graph homomorphism is extended in order to handle the two versions of the separating conjunction, the constraints on set of locations variables, and more general recursive predicates.

The (sound) decision procedures for satisfiability/entailment introduced in [18, 15] are also based on Boolean abstractions of formulas. As in our case, the Boolean abstractions are used to transform logical validity into simpler decidable problems. However, they concern different types of logics: algebraic data types specifications for reasoning about functional programs in [18] and a recursive extension of first-order logic for reasoning about programs manipulating tree data structures in [15].

Semi-automatic frameworks for reasoning about programs within SL, based on theorem provers, have been defined in [7, 4, 13]. In this paper, we target a completely automatic framework based on decision procedures.

2 Overview

In general, *NOLL* formulas have the form $\Pi \wedge \Sigma \wedge \Lambda$, where Π is the pure part, i.e., a conjunction of equalities and inequalities between program variables expressing aliasing constraints, Σ is the spatial part specifying the data structures and the separation properties, and Λ specifies the sharing constraints between the data structures. The objects building the data structures in the heap are sets of record fields, called simply fields in the following.

$$\varphi := x \neq \text{NULL} \wedge Hash_\alpha(x, y, \text{NULL}) *_w List_\beta(z, \text{NULL}) \wedge \alpha(\text{SI\_type}) = \beta \tag{1}$$

$$Hash(in, out, dest) \triangleq (in = out) \vee (\exists u, v. \; in \mapsto \{(g, u); (h, v)\} * LowList(v, dest) \\ * Hash(u, out, dest)) \tag{2}$$

$$LowList(in, out) \triangleq (in = out) \vee (\exists u. \, in \mapsto \{(s, u)\} * LowList(u, out)) \tag{3}$$

$$List(in, out) \triangleq (in = out) \vee (\exists u. \, in \mapsto \{(f, u)\} * List(u, out)) \tag{4}$$

Fig. 1. *NOLL* specification of a hash table whose elements are shared with a list

Examples of *NOLL* Formulas: Fig. 1 contains a *NOLL* formula φ describing a list of lists, using the predicate $Hash_\alpha(x, y, \text{NULL})$, such that the elements of the nested lists are shared with another list, represented by the predicate $List_\beta(z, \text{NULL})$. This is an abstraction of the hash table sharing all its elements with a singly-linked list, presented in Sec. 1, in the sense that we use a linked list to represent the array structure.

The predicate $Hash_\alpha(in, out, dest)$ has a recursive definition, written in a higher-order extension of *NOLL*: either $in = out$, which means that the nested list segment is empty, or in contains a field h pointing to an inner singly-linked list $(in \mapsto \{\ldots; (h, v)\} * LowList(v, dest))$ and also a field g pointing to a new location u $(in \mapsto \{(g, u); \ldots\})$, which is the starting point of another nested list segment. Note that the elements of the lists described by $LowList(v, dest)$ are linked by the field s. In general, we suppose that variables and fields are typed. Thus, if SI_type is the type of the variables used in the predicate *LowList*, all the objects in the nested lists are of type SI_type. Moreover, the use of the object separating conjunction $*$ implies that all the nested lists are disjoint.

The overlapping property is expressed using two features of this logic. The first one is the field separating conjunction operator $*_w$ which allows to share object locations but not the locations of fields in these objects. The second feature is the ability to speak about the set of all object locations in a list segment. This set of locations is given by the interpretation of the variable that indexes some recursive predicate, e.g., α in $Hash_\alpha(\ldots)$. These variables are constrained in the Λ part of a formula. For example, $\alpha(\text{SI\_type}) = \beta$ says that all the locations of type SI_type in the list of lists are also present in the list starting in z (β stands for the set of locations in $List_\beta(z, \text{NULL})$).

The operators $*$ and $*_w$ can be nested. This is essential to specify a similar data structure (considered in [11]) where the elements stored in a hash table are shared between two disjoint linked lists (using the predicates from Fig. 1):

$$x \neq \text{NULL} \wedge Hash_\alpha(x, y, \text{NULL}) *_w (List_\beta(z, \text{NULL}) * List_\gamma(u, \text{NULL})) \wedge \alpha(\text{SI\_type}) = \beta \cup \gamma,$$

where $*$ is used to specify the disjointness of the linked lists starting in z and u.

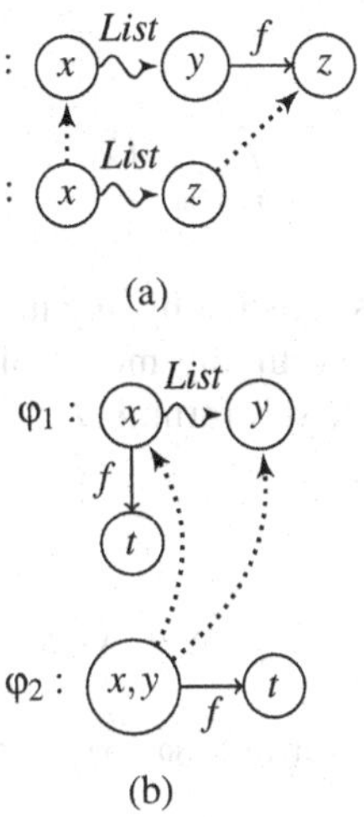

(a)

(b)

Fig. 2.

Decision Procedure for Entailment: We define a procedure for checking entailments of *NOLL* formulas, which is based on the graph homomorphism approach in [8]. The basic idea is to think of formulas as graphs, where nodes represent variables (sets of equal variables) and edges represent list segments, and then, given φ_1 and φ_2 two formulas, if there exists a homomorphism from φ_2 to φ_1 then $\varphi_1 \Rightarrow \varphi_2$ holds. Roughly, the homomorphism is a function mapping each node of φ_2 to a node of φ_1 representing at least the same set of variables. It is required that this function defines a mapping from edges of φ_2 to disjoint paths in φ_1. (Note that the homomorphism is unique.) For example, there exists such a homomorphism from φ_2 to φ_1 in Fig. 2(a), where a snaked edge labeled by *List* from x to y denotes a predicate $List(x, y)$, a straight edge labeled by f from y to z denotes a points-to constraint $y \mapsto \{(f, z)\}$, all these constraints are supposed to be separated by $*$, and the dotted edges represent the homomorphism.

In order to be complete, this procedure needs that the formulas of an entailment contain the maximum number of equalities and inequalities; in this case, we say that the formula is in *normal form*. Also, if it contains an equality $u = v$ then, it contains no spatial constraint defining a list segment from u to v (as usual in separation logic, $u = v \wedge List(u, v)$ is equivalent to $u = v$). For example, although the entailment $\varphi_1 \Rightarrow \varphi_2$ in Fig. 2(b) holds, there exists no homomorphism from φ_2 to φ_1. (Because the field f is already defined in x, the list segment using this field and starting in x is empty. Thus, φ_1 implies $x = y$, which is needed to show that $\varphi_1 \Rightarrow \varphi_2$.)

Boolean Abstractions of *NOLL* Formulas: Our first insight in defining such a decision procedure is that the normal form of a *NOLL* formula $\varphi = \Pi \wedge \Sigma \wedge \Lambda$ can be constructed through a boolean abstraction of φ, denoted $F(\varphi)$. For the moment, let us consider the case when $\Lambda = true$. Then, the formula $F(\varphi)$ is defined over a set of boolean variables denoting (in)equalities between variables and atomic formulas from the spatial part Σ.

We illustrate the definition of $F(\varphi)$ on the formula:

$$\varphi := List(x, y) * List(x, z) * y \mapsto \{(f, t)\} * List(y, s). \tag{5}$$

The set of boolean variables in $F(\varphi)$ consists of:
- a variable $[u = v]$, for every two variables u and v in φ,
- a variable $[y, t, f]$ to represent the points-to constraint $y \mapsto \{(f, t)\}$, and
- a variable $[List(u, v)]$, for every spatial constraint $List(u, v)$ in φ.

In this case, the formula $F(\varphi) \triangleq F_{eq} \wedge F(\Sigma)$, where F_{eq} encodes the reflexivity and the transitivity of the equality relation, i.e.,

$$\bigwedge_{u,v,w \text{ variables in } \varphi} [u = u] \quad \wedge \quad ([u = v] \wedge [v = w]) \Rightarrow [u = w],$$

and $F(\Sigma)$ models the spatial part of φ, i.e.,

$$F(\Sigma) \triangleq [y,t,f] \quad \wedge \quad \bigwedge_{List(u,v) \text{ atom in } \varphi} [List(u,v)] \oplus [u = v] \quad \wedge \quad \bigwedge_{A,B \text{ atoms in } \Sigma} F_*(A,B).$$

The sub-formula $[y,t,f]$ ensures that the points-to constraint is satisfied by any model of φ; the sub-formula $[List(u,v)] \oplus [u = v]$ models the fact that in any model of φ, either $u = v$ or $List(u,v)$ describes a non-empty list segment. The sub-formula $F_*(A,B)$ contains the in(equalities) implied by the use of $*$, i.e,

$$F_*(y \mapsto \{(f,t)\}, List(u,v)) \triangleq \neg[y = u] \vee [u = v], \text{ for any } u,v,$$
$$F_*(List(u_1,v_1), List(u_2,v_2)) \triangleq \neg[u_1 = u_2] \vee [u_1 = v_1] \vee [u_2 = v_2], \text{ for any } u_1,v_1,u_2,v_2.$$

In general, the size of $F(\varphi)$ is polynomial in the size of the formula φ. Also, φ is satisfiable iff $F(\varphi)$ is satisfiable.

Computing the Normal Form: The formula $F(\varphi)$ can be used to compute the normal form of φ since $\varphi \Rightarrow (u = v)$ iff $F(\varphi) \Rightarrow [u = v]$, for any u and v. Thus, for any valid entailment $F(\varphi) \Rightarrow [u = v]$, the equality $u = v$ is added to φ, and all predicates describing list segments between u and v are removed. For example, the normal form of φ in (5) is $y = s \wedge x = z \wedge List(x,y) * y \mapsto \{(f,t)\}$ (the formula $F(\varphi)$ implies $[y = s]$ and $[x = z]$).

Handling Sharing Constraints: For *NOLL* formulas with sharing constraints, computing the normal form before checking the existence of a graph homomorphism is not enough. Besides (in)equalities, we may have implicit spatial constraints which are not exposed in some formula. Consider the entailment $\varphi_1 \Rightarrow \varphi_2$, where:

$$\varphi_1 := List_\alpha(x,y) *_w LowList_\beta(n,m) \wedge \beta \subseteq \alpha \tag{6}$$
$$\varphi_2 := (List_\delta(x,n) * List_\gamma(n,y)) *_w LowList_{\beta'}(n,m) \wedge \beta' \subseteq \delta \cup \gamma \tag{7}$$

Note that $\beta \subseteq \alpha$ implies that n is a location on the list segment described by $List_\alpha(x,y)$ and thus $\varphi_1 \Rightarrow \varphi_2$ holds. In this case, $F(\varphi_1)$ includes constraints over a set of boolean variables $[u \in \varepsilon]$ representing the fact that u is a location in the set of locations denoted by ε, for any u and $\varepsilon \in \{\alpha, \beta\}$ (we defer the reader to Sec. 5 for more details).

In general, if the formula $F(\varphi)$ implies $[u \in \varepsilon]$, for some u and ε, then the graph representation of φ includes some additional edges induced by the fact that u is a location on the list segment indexed by ε. In this case, $F(\varphi_1) \Rightarrow [n \in \alpha]$ and the graph representation of φ_1 completed with these additional edges is the graph $\overline{G}(\varphi_1)$ in Fig. 3. Now, it is easy to see that there exists a homomorphism from $G(\varphi_2)$ to $\overline{G}(\varphi_1)$ (the homomorphism must satisfy additional constraints explained in Sec. 6.3).

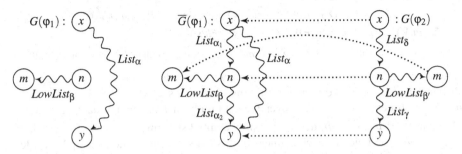

Fig. 3. The graph representations $G(\varphi_1)$ resp. $G(\varphi_2)$ of the (normal forms of the) formulas in eq. (6–7). $\overline{G}(\varphi_1)$ is the graph representation of φ_1 that includes the implicit spatial constraints. Dotted edges represent the homomorphism proving that $\varphi_1 \Rightarrow \varphi_2$.

3   Logic *NOLL*

The logic *NOLL* is a multi-sorted fragment of Separation Logic [17]. Let $\mathcal{T}$ be a set of sorts (corresponding to record types defined in the program), *Flds* a set of field names, and τ a typing function mapping each field name into a function type over $\mathcal{T}$. A field $f \in Flds$ is called recursive iff $\tau(f) = R \rightarrow R$ with $R \in \mathcal{T}$ and non-recursive, otherwise. The set of recursive fields is denoted by $Flds_{rec}$.

Syntax: Let *LVars* and *SetVars* be two sets of variables, called *location variables* and *set of locations variables*, respectively. We assume that the typing function τ associates a sort, resp. a set of sorts, to every variable in *LVars*, resp. *SetVars*. For simplicity, we assume that *LVars* contains the constant NULL. The syntax of *NOLL* is given in Fig. 4.

$x, y, y_i \in LVars$	location variables	$\overrightarrow{z} \in LVars^+$	tuples of location variables
$f, f_i \in Flds$	field names	$\alpha \in SetVars$	set of locations variables
$R \in \mathcal{T}$	sort	$P \in \mathcal{P}$	list segment predicates

$$\varphi ::= \Pi \wedge \Sigma \wedge \Lambda \qquad\qquad\qquad \textit{NOLL formula}$$
$$\Pi ::= true \mid x \neq y \mid x = y \mid \Pi \wedge \Pi \qquad\qquad \text{pure constraints}$$
$$\Sigma ::= emp \mid x \mapsto \{(f_1, y_1); \ldots; (f_k, y_k)\} \mid P_\alpha(x, y, \overrightarrow{z}) \mid \Sigma * \Sigma \mid \Sigma *_w \Sigma \qquad \text{spatial constraints}$$
$$\Lambda ::= true \mid t \subseteq t' \mid x \in t \mid x \notin t \mid \Lambda \wedge \Lambda \qquad\qquad \text{sharing constraints}$$
$$t ::= \{x\} \mid \alpha \mid \alpha(R) \mid t \cup t' \qquad\qquad\qquad \text{set of locations terms}$$

Fig. 4. Syntax of *NOLL* formulas

An atomic *points-to constraint* $x \mapsto \{(f_1, y_1); \ldots; (f_k, y_k)\}$ is used to specify the values of fields $f_1, \ldots, f_k$ in the location denoted by x: the value stored by the field f_i is y_i, for all $1 \leq i \leq k$. The fields shall be pairwise disjoint and the formula shall be well typed, i.e., for any f_i, $\tau(f_i) = \tau(x) \rightarrow \tau(y_i)$.

In every *list segment constraint* $P_\alpha(x, y, \overrightarrow{z})$, P is a predicate from a fixed, but arbitrary, set $\mathcal{P}$. The predicates in $\mathcal{P}$ have recursive definitions with the following syntax:

$$P(in, out, \overrightarrow{nhb}) \triangleq (in = out) \vee$$
$$(\exists u, \overrightarrow{v}. \Sigma_0(in, u \cup \overrightarrow{v} \cup \overrightarrow{nhb}) * \Sigma_1(\overrightarrow{v}, \overrightarrow{nhb}) * P(u, out, \overrightarrow{nhb}))$$
$$\Sigma_0(in, V) ::= in \mapsto \theta, \text{ where } \theta \subseteq \{(f, w) \mid f \in Flds, w \in V\}$$
$$\Sigma_1(\overrightarrow{v}, \overrightarrow{nhb}) ::= emp \mid Q(v, b, \overrightarrow{b}) \mid \Sigma_1(\overrightarrow{v}, \overrightarrow{nhb}) * \Sigma_1(\overrightarrow{v}, \overrightarrow{nhb}) \text{ with } b, \overrightarrow{b} \subseteq \overrightarrow{nhb}, \text{ and } Q \in \mathcal{P}$$

where $in, out, u \in LVars$ and $\overrightarrow{nhb}, \overrightarrow{v}, \overrightarrow{b} \in LVars^+$. The definition of every $P \in \mathcal{P}$ is well typed and satisfies the additional typing constraints $\tau(in) = \tau(out) = \tau(u)$, and $\tau(in) \neq \tau(v)$, for every $v \in \overrightarrow{v}$. Moreover, the definitions in $\mathcal{P}$ are not mutually recursive.

A predicate $P(in, out, \overrightarrow{nhb})$ defines possibly empty list segments starting from in and ending in out. The fields of each element in this list segment are defined by Σ_0 while the nested lists to which it points to are defined by Σ_1. The parameters $\overrightarrow{nhb}$ are used to define the "boundaries" of the nested list segment described by P, in the sense that every location described by P belongs to a path between in and some location in $out \cup \overrightarrow{nhb}$ (this path may be defined by more than one field). Every element of the list segment described by P points to several nested lists, each one of them being described by a predicate Q in $\mathcal{P}$. The use of $*$ in the definition of P implies that the inner list segments are disjoint. The typing constraints ensure bounded nesting.

For simplicity of the presentation, we have restricted ourselves to such inductive definitions, which are not expressive enough to describe doubly-linked lists or nested lists containing cyclic lists on their inner levels. However, our techniques can be extended to cover such cases. For example, to describe doubly-linked lists, one must allow further points-to constraints and use a special type of existential variables representing the next to last location in a doubly-linked list segment like, e.g., in [1].

For any predicate P, $\Sigma_0(P)$, resp. $\Sigma_1(P)$, denotes the sub-formula Σ_0, resp. Σ_1 of P. Moreover, $Flds_0(P)$ denotes the set of fields of in that point to u according to the formula $\Sigma_0(P)$, i.e., $f \in Flds_0(P)$ iff $\Sigma_0(P) = in \mapsto \theta$ and $(f, u) \in \theta$.

In every spatial constraint $P_\alpha(x, y, \overrightarrow{z})$, α is a set of locations variable, which is said to *be bounded to* or to *index* the spatial constraint. The constraint Λ may contain set of locations variables which are not bounded to some spatial constraint. For simplicity, we assume that a variable in *SetVars* appears in Σ at most once. Also, we consider that all atomic constraints in Λ are well typed, i.e., for any $t \subseteq t'$ in Λ, $\tau(t) \subseteq \tau(t')$ and for any $(x \in t)$ in Λ, $\tau(x) \in \tau(t)$, where τ is extended to set of locations terms as usual.

In the following, we denote by $LVars(\varphi)$ (and $SetVars(\varphi)$) the set of location variables (resp. set of locations variables) used in φ. Also, $atoms(\varphi)$ denotes the set of atomic formulas in φ. Two atoms in Σ are *object separated*, resp. *field separated*, if their least common ancestor in the syntactic tree of φ is $*$, resp. $*_w$.

Semantics: Let *Loc* be a multi-sorted set of *locations* typed by the typing function τ, and let Loc_R denote the set of locations in *Loc* of sort R.

A *program heap* is modeled by a pair $C = (S, H)$, where $S : LVars \rightarrow Loc$ maps location variables to locations in *Loc* and $H : Loc \times Flds \rightharpoonup Loc$ defines values of fields for a subset of locations. Intuitively, each allocated object is denoted by a location in *Loc* and then, H defines the fields for the allocated objects and S gives for each variable, the object it points to. The set of locations l for which there exists f s.t. $H(l, f)$ is defined is called the set of locations in C, and denoted by $Loc(C)$. The component S (resp. H) of a heap C is denoted by S^C (resp. H^C).

$$(C,J) \models \varphi_1 \wedge \varphi_2 \qquad \text{iff } (C,J) \models \varphi_1 \text{ and } (C,J) \models \varphi_2$$

$$(C,J) \models x = y \qquad \text{iff } S(x) = S(y)$$

$$(C,J) \models x \mapsto \cup_{i \in I}\{(f_i, y_i)\} \quad \text{iff } H(S(x), f_i) = S(y_i) \text{ for all } i \in I$$

$$(C,J) \models P_\alpha(x,y,\vec{z}) \qquad \text{iff there exists } k \in \mathbb{N} \text{ s.t. } (C,J) \models P_\alpha^k(x,y,\vec{z})$$

$$(C,J) \models P_\alpha^0(x,y,\vec{z}) \qquad \text{iff } S(x) = S(y) \text{ and } J(\alpha) = \emptyset$$

$$(C,J) \models P_\alpha^{k+1}(x,y,\vec{z}) \qquad \text{iff } S(x) \neq S(y) \text{ and there exists } \rho : \{u\} \cup \vec{v} \to Loc \text{ and } J' \text{ s.t.}$$
$$(C[S \mapsto S \cup \rho], J') \models \Sigma_0(x, u \cup \vec{v} \cup \vec{z}) * \Sigma_1(\vec{v}, \vec{z}) * P_\alpha^k(u, y, \vec{z}),$$
$$\text{img}(\rho) \cap \text{img}(S) = \emptyset,$$
$$J'(\alpha) = J(\alpha) \setminus (\{S(x)\} \cup \rho(\vec{v})), \text{ and } J'(\beta) = J(\beta), \text{ for any } \beta \neq \alpha$$

$$(C,J) \models \Sigma_1 * \Sigma_2 \qquad \text{iff there exist program heaps } C_1 \text{ and } C_2 \text{ s.t. } C = C_1 * C_2,$$
$$(C_1,J) \models \Sigma_1, \text{ and } (C_2,J) \models \Sigma_2$$

$$(C,J) \models \Sigma_1 *_w \Sigma_2 \qquad \text{iff there exist program heaps } C_1 \text{ and } C_2 \text{ s.t. } C = C_1 *_w C_2,$$
$$(C_1,J) \models \Sigma_1, \text{ and } (C_2,J) \models \Sigma_2$$

$$(C,J) \models x \in t \qquad \text{iff } S(x) \in [t]_J$$

$$(C,J) \models t \subseteq t' \qquad \text{iff } [t]_J \subseteq [t']_J$$

Separation operators over program heaps:

$$C = C' * C'' \text{ iff } Loc(C) = Loc(C') \cup Loc(C'') \text{ and } Loc(C') \cap Loc(C'') = \varnothing,$$
$$S^{C'} = S^C |_{Loc(C')} \text{ and } S^{C''} = S^C |_{Loc(C'')}$$

$$C = C' *_w C'' \text{ iff } \text{dom}(H^C) = \text{dom}(H^{C'}) \cup \text{dom}(H^{C''}) \text{ and } \text{dom}(H^{C'}) \cap \text{dom}(H^{C''}) = \varnothing,$$
$$S^{C'} = S^C |_{Loc(C')} \text{ and } S^{C''} = S^C |_{Loc(C'')}$$

Interpretation of a term t, $[t]_J$:

$$[\{x\}]_J = \{S(x)\}, \quad [\alpha]_J = J(\alpha), \quad [\alpha(R)]_J = J(\alpha) \cap Loc_R, \quad [t \cup t']_J = [t]_J \cup [t']_J.$$

Fig. 5. Semantics of *NOLL* formulas. $\text{dom}(F)$ denotes the domain of the function F and $S \cup \rho$ denotes a new mapping $K : \text{dom}(S) \cup \text{dom}(\rho) \to Loc$ s.t. $K(x) = \rho(x)$, $\forall x \in \text{dom}(\rho)$ and $K(y) = S(y)$, $\forall y \in \text{dom}(S)$).

NOLL interpretations are pairs (C,J), where $C = (S,H)$ is a program heap and $J : SetVars \to 2^{Loc}$ interprets variables in *SetVars* to finite subsets of *Loc*. We assume that S, H, and J are well-typed w.r.t. τ. A *NOLL* interpretation (C,J) is a model of a formula φ iff $(C,J) \models \varphi$, where $\models$ is defined in Fig. 5 for its non trivial cases. For simplicity, we consider the intuitionistic semantics of SL [17]: if a formula is true on a model then it remains true for any extension of that model with more locations. Our techniques can be adapted to work also for the non-intuitionistic semantics [10].

Note the difference between the two kinds of separation of heaps: $C = C' * C''$ holds iff the set of locations in C' and C'' are disjoint while $C = C' *_w C''$ holds iff the domains of the H component in C' and C'' are disjoint.

W.l.o.g., we suppose that the sharing constraints in Λ are in a simplified form obtained as follows. First, inclusion constraints are put in the form $\alpha \subseteq t$, where t contains at most two set of locations variables. Second, for any atomic formula $\alpha \subseteq t$ in Λ such that α is bound to some spatial constraint $P_\alpha(x,y,\vec{z})$, we remove from t (1) all the variables α' such that α and α' are bound to object separated spatial constraints and (2) all the terms of the form $\{x\}$ such that φ contains a points-to constraint $x \mapsto \theta$, which is object separated from the spatial constraint indexed by α. If t becomes empty then, the equality $x = y$ is added to φ.

We denote by $[\varphi]$ the set of pairs (C, J) which are models of φ. The entailment between two *NOLL* formulas is denoted by $\Rightarrow$ and it is defined by $\varphi \Rightarrow \psi$ iff $[\varphi] \subseteq [\psi]$.

Fragment *MOLL*: To illustrate some constructions in this paper, we consider the fragment *MOLL* which does not allow to specify nested lists, but only overlaid multi-linked lists. Formally, the fragment *MOLL* contains all the *NOLL* formulas defined over a set of predicates $\mathcal{P}$ such that, for any $P \in \mathcal{P}$, $\Sigma_1(P) = emp$, i.e., P is defined by $P(in, out, \overrightarrow{nhb}) \triangleq (in = out) \vee (\exists u. \Sigma_0(in, u \cup \overrightarrow{nhb}) * P(u, out, \overrightarrow{nhb}))$.

4   A Model-Theoretic Procedure for Checking Entailment

We prove that satisfiability, resp. entailment checking, of *NOLL* formulas is NP-complete, resp. co-NP complete. The upper bound for the complexity of satisfiability is proved using a small model property: if $\varphi \in NOLL$ has a model, then it has also a model of size polynomial in the size of φ and $\mathcal{P}$ (the size of $\mathcal{P}$ is defined as the size of all recursive definitions for predicates in $\mathcal{P}$). The co-NP upper bound for entailment checking is obtained by proving a small model property for formulas of the form $\varphi \not\Rightarrow \psi$ (a model for this formula corresponds to a counter-example for $\varphi \Rightarrow \psi$).

4.1   Satisfiability Problem

The NP lower bound of the satisfiability problem for *NOLL* formulas is given by the next theorem. The proof is based on a reduction of 3SAT, the satisfiability problem for CNF formulas with three literals in each clause, to the satisfiability problem for *MOLL* formulas. The proof of this result is detailed in [10].

Theorem 1. *The satisfiability problem for NOLL (MOLL) is NP-hard.*

To prove the small model property for the NP upper bound, we use an abstraction of the models of *NOLL* formulas by *colored heap graphs*. Intuitively, a model (C, J) of a *NOLL* formula is represented by a colored graph where each location ℓ from C is represented by a set of graph nodes V_ℓ. V_ℓ is a singleton when ℓ is the interpretation of a location variable or it is not shared between list segments described in φ. Otherwise, each node in V_ℓ represents a subset of fields at location ℓ such that two nodes in V_ℓ represent disjoint sets of fields. All nodes in V_ℓ are colored by ℓ and are called *sibling nodes*. The abstraction is built such that the sub-graphs corresponding to list segments defined using different atoms of φ share only nodes which are interpretations of location variables. Thus, we can collapse in these sub-graphs most of nodes and still obtain a model of φ. The collapsed nodes shall not be colored by the interpretation of a location variable, i.e., they are *anonymous* nodes. We show that for any model (C, J), one can identify a set of anonymous nodes, whose size is polynomial in the size of φ and $\mathcal{P}$, called *crucial nodes*, such that by collapsing all the non-crucial anonymous nodes one can still obtain a model of φ. Formally,

Definition 1 (Colored heap graph). *A* colored heap graph *over LVars, Flds, and SetVars is a tuple* $G = (V, E, \mathcal{P}, \mathcal{L}, \mathcal{S})$, *where (1)* V *is a finite set of nodes, (2)* $E :$ $V \times Flds \rightharpoonup V$ *is a set of edges, (3)* $\mathcal{P} : LVars(\varphi) \rightarrow V$ *is a labeling of nodes with location variables, (4)* $\mathcal{L} : V \rightarrow Loc$ *is a coloring of nodes with locations, and (5)* $\mathcal{S} : SetVars \rightarrow 2^V$ *is an interpretation of variables in SetVars to sets of nodes.*

Fig. 6 pictures a model of φ in eq. (1) and its colored heap graph abstraction. We denote the components of a colored heap graph G using superscripts, e.g., the set V in G is denoted by V^G. The semantics of *NOLL* formulas on colored heap graphs is defined similarly to the one on *NOLL* interpretations, except for $*$ and the constraints in Λ. A colored heap graph G satisfies a formula $\varphi_1 * \varphi_2$ iff G can be split into two disjoint graphs G_1 and G_2 such that $G_1 \models \varphi_1$, $G_2 \models \varphi_2$, and for any two nodes $v_1 \in V^{G_1}$ and $v_2 \in V^{G_2}$, $\mathcal{L}^{G_1}(v_1) \neq \mathcal{L}^{G_2}(v_2)$. Also, for any constraint $P_\alpha(x, y, \vec{z})$, $\mathcal{S}(\alpha)$ is interpreted as the union of $\mathcal{L}(v)$, for all nodes v in the unique subgraph defined by P_α.

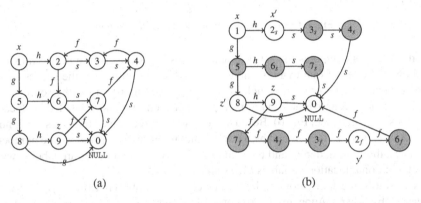

(a)   (b)

Fig. 6. A program heap satisfying φ in (1) and its colored heap graph. For any $0 \leq n \leq 9$, the nodes n_s and n_f in (b) are colored by the location n from (a). Primed variables x', y', z' label crucial nodes. A small model is obtained by collapsing filled nodes in (b).

Lemma 1. *If a NOLL formula* φ *has a model* (C, J) *then it also has a model* (C_s, J_s) *of size polynomial in the size of* φ *and* $\mathcal{P}$.

Proof. (Idea) The proof builds a small model following the steps given in Fig. 7a. Roughly, we show that anonymous locations from (C, J) can be collapsed until the list segments are of bounded length. The bounds are determined by the sharing constraints in φ and the levels of nesting in the definition of the recursive predicates. To collapse anonymous locations on list segments, we use the colored heap graph abstraction. However, some distinguished set of *crucial* anonymous nodes shall not be collapsed because this will invalidate spatial or sharing constraints in φ (an example is shown below). Also, to preserve the truth value of sharing constraints, if a node is found crucial on some list segment, then all its sibling nodes are also marked as crucial (this corresponds to the fact that the small model contains all the fields for that location).

The procedure purify removes from (C, J) all the locations not involved in spatial constraints from φ. This is possible because the minimal part of C satisfying some spatial constraint is unique. splitLocations builds the colored heap graph abstraction of (C', J') by splitting the nodes not labeled by location variables but shared between several list segments described by predicates in φ. An example is given in Fig. 6.

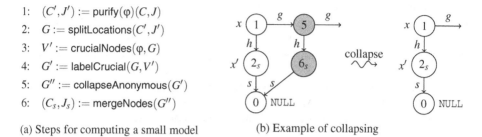

1:   $(C', J') := \text{purify}(\varphi)(C, J)$
2:   $G := \text{splitLocations}(C', J')$
3:   $V' := \text{crucialNodes}(\varphi, G)$
4:   $G' := \text{labelCrucial}(G, V')$
5:   $G'' := \text{collapseAnonymous}(G')$
6:   $(C_s, J_s) := \text{mergeNodes}(G'')$

(a) Steps for computing a small model   (b) Example of collapsing

Fig. 7. Computing a small model for *NOLL* formulas

crucialNodes computes the set of crucial nodes V' as the closure under the sibling relation of the set of (anonymous) nodes in G which are either (1) the successor of a labeled node by a non recursive field (e.g., node 2_s in Fig. 6), or (2) the source or the target of a non recursive field on a fixed path between two nodes labeled by location variables (e.g., node 8 in Fig. 6). Because the nesting of recursive predicates is bounded, the size of the set V' is bounded by a polynomial in the size of φ and $\mathcal{P}$ (the number of variables, the nesting depth, and the size of *Flds*). The crucial nodes are labeled with a set of additional location variables *LVars'* in labelCrucial.

Afterwards, the anonymous nodes (not labeled by variables in $LVars(\varphi) \cup LVars'$) are collapsed by collapseAnonymous in a bottom up manner, i.e., starting from the inner list segments to the upper ones. Roughly, the collapsing removes a node (and the sub-graph representing the nested, anonymous structure) if it is between two recursive fields (see Fig. 7b). Intuitively, this process preserves a model of φ because no edges are added and the nodes marked as important for the satisfaction of the spatial and sharing constraints are kept. Due to the special syntax of predicates in $\mathcal{P}$, we can compute for each list segment the minimal number of anonymous nodes that must be preserved in order to satisfy some given spatial constraint. This number depends only on the size of $\mathcal{P}$ and it is obtained when all the spatial constraints in the predicate definition are interpreted as list segments of length one. Thus, we obtain a colored heap graph G'' where all labeled nodes are preserved and with them some sub-graphs with a bounded number of anonymous nodes. Finally, from G'', a (small) model (C_s, J_s) of φ is built, by applying mergeNodes, which roughly merges sibling nodes in locations.   □

Since the complexity of the model-checking problem for *NOLL* formulas is polynomial, the following result holds.

Theorem 2. *The satisfiability problem for NOLL is NP-complete.*

4.2 Entailment Problem

The colored heap graph abstraction is also used to prove a small counter-example property for entailments $\varphi \Rightarrow \psi$ when φ and ψ are in *NOLL*. The proof is similar to the proof of Lemma 1, with two main differences. Let (C, J) be a counter-example for $\varphi \Rightarrow \psi$. First, in purify, the locations not used in φ are removed from (C, J) except for locations that are witnesses for some unsatisfied sharing constraint in ψ. It is enough to keep one location per sharing constraint in ψ and thus, their number is bounded by the size of ψ. We label these locations with variables from some set $LVars''$. Second, crucialNodes marks some additional nodes as crucial, in order to keep track if two list segments are sharing at least one location and in order to distinguish between list segments of size 1 and list segments of size at least 2. However, this process adds at most one more node per constraint, and thus the bound on the number of nodes is increased by a linear term in the size of φ and ψ. This property and the NP-completeness of satisfiability imply:

Theorem 3. *Checking the validity of an entailment between two NOLL formulas is co-NP complete.*

5 Computing the Normal Form

This section makes a first step towards the effective procedure for checking entailments of *NOLL* formulas by presenting the procedure for computing the normal form of a *NOLL* formula. We say that a *NOLL* formula is in *normal form* if it contains the maximum set of equalities and disequalities between location variables and the minimum set of list segment constraints. Formally,

Definition 2 (Normal form). *A NOLL formula $\varphi = \Pi \wedge \Sigma \wedge \Lambda$ is in normal form iff:*

- *for any $x, y \in LVars(\varphi)$, if $\varphi \Rightarrow x = y$, resp. $\varphi \Rightarrow x \neq y$, then Π contains the atom $x = y$, resp. $x \neq y$, and*
- *for any atomic formula $P_\alpha(x, y, \overrightarrow{z})$ in Σ, there exists a model (C, J) of φ such that $S^C(x) \neq S^C(y)$.*

The normal form of φ is a formula φ' in normal form and equivalent to φ.

We now describe the main ideas behind the procedure that computes the normal form and to this, we must define the class of reduced, explicit *NOLL* formulas.

A *NOLL* formula is called *explicit* if it contains $x = y$ or $x \neq y$, for any constraint $P_\alpha(x, y, \overrightarrow{z})$ in φ, and $x \in \alpha$ or $x \notin \alpha$, for any x and α in φ. Then, an explicit formula ψ is called *reduced* if it does not contain both the atoms $x = y$ and $P_\alpha(x, y, \overrightarrow{z})$.

Any *NOLL* formula φ is equivalent to a disjunction of reduced, explicit formulas $\psi_1 \vee \ldots \vee \psi_n$. The formulas ψ_i are obtained from φ by (1) adding in all possible ways atoms $x = y$, $x \neq y$, $x \in \alpha$, and $x \notin \alpha$ until the obtained formula is explicit and then, (2) if a formula contains $x = y$, by removing atoms $P_\alpha(x, y, \overrightarrow{z})$ together with all occurrences of α in the sharing constraints (e.g., every atom $x \in \alpha$ or $\beta \subseteq \alpha$, where β indexes a constraint $Q_\beta(u, v, \overrightarrow{w})$ and $u \neq v$ belongs to the formula, is replaced by *false*).

The equivalent formula $\psi_1 \vee \ldots \vee \psi_n$ can be used to compute the normal form of φ as follows. An atom $x = y$ or $x \neq y$ is implied by φ iff this atom is included in all the *satisfiable* formulas ψ_i. Also, for any $P(x,y,\overrightarrow{z})$ in φ, there exists a model (C,J) of φ s.t. $S^C(x) \neq S^C(y)$ iff this atom is included in some satisfiable ψ_i.

In general, the number of satisfiable formulas in the disjunction $\psi_1 \vee \ldots \vee \psi_n$ may be exponential w.r.t. the size of φ. However, all these formulas can be represented symbolically as the satisfying assignments of a boolean formula, denoted by $F(\varphi)$.

In order to simplify the presentation, we give below the construction of $F(\varphi)$ only for *MOLL* formulas where variables are of the same type; [10] gives the general case. $F(\varphi)$ is defined over the set of boolean variables $BVars(F(\varphi))$ defined in Tab. 1.

Table 1. Definition of the set $BVars(F(\varphi))$ of boolean variables used in $F(\varphi)$

$[x = y]$	for every $x,y \in LVars(\varphi)$
$[x,y,f]$	for every atom $x \mapsto \theta$ of φ with $(f,y) \in \theta$
$[P_\alpha(x,y,\overrightarrow{z})]$	for every atom $P_\alpha(x,y,\overrightarrow{z})$ of φ
$[x \in \alpha]$	for every $x \in LVars(\varphi)$ and $\alpha \in SetVars(\varphi)$

Given a satisfying assignment $\sigma : BVars(F(\varphi)) \to \{0,1\}$ for $F(\varphi)$ such that $\sigma([x,y,f]) = 1$, for any $[x,y,f] \in BVars(F(\varphi))$, we define the *MOLL* formula ψ_σ to be φ to which the following transformations are applied:

- if $\sigma([x = y])$ is 0, resp. 1, then ψ_σ includes the pure constraint $x \neq y$, resp. $x = y$,
- if $\sigma([P_\alpha(x,y,\overrightarrow{z})]) = 0$ then $P_\alpha(x,y,\overrightarrow{z})$ and α are removed from φ,
- if $\sigma([x \in \alpha])$ is 0, resp. 1, then $x \notin \alpha$, resp. $x \in \alpha$, is added to ψ_σ.

Let $\varphi = \Pi \wedge \Sigma \wedge \Lambda$ be a *MOLL* formula. The formula $F(\varphi)$ is defined by:

$$F(\varphi) = F(\Pi) \wedge F_{eq} \wedge F(\Sigma) \wedge F_{det} \wedge F(\Lambda) \wedge F_\in, \tag{8}$$

where $F(\Pi)$, $F(\Sigma)$, and $F(\Lambda)$ encode the semantics of the atomic formulas of φ, F_{eq} encodes the reflexivity and the transitivity of the equality relation in Π, F_{det} encodes the semantics of the field separating conjunction, and $F_\in$ encodes the properties of the membership relation $\in$. These sub-formulas are defined inductively on the syntax of *MOLL* formulas. Most of them are not difficult to follow. We provide here some intuition for the most interesting ones.

In $F(\Sigma)$, an atom $P_\alpha(x,y,\overrightarrow{z})$ is translated into $F(P_\alpha(x,y,\overrightarrow{z})) = [P_\alpha(x,y,\overrightarrow{z})] \oplus [x = y]$, where $\oplus$ is the exclusive or. This expresses the fact that the atom is kept in a reduced, explicit *MOLL* formula only if its endpoints are not equal.

The separation of fields (defined for locations which are interpretations of location variables) induced by the use of the field separating conjunction is expressed in the formula F_{det} in Fig. 8. Thus, F_{det} states that for any location variable x and any field $f \in Flds$, at most one of the following conditions is true:

1. the reduced, explicit formula contains the equality $x = x'$ and a points-to constraint $x' \mapsto \theta$ such that $(f,y) \in \theta$, for some y,
2. the reduced, explicit formula contains the atoms $x \in \alpha$ and $P_\alpha(x',y,\overrightarrow{z})$ (therefore it also includes $x' \neq y$), for some y and $\overrightarrow{z}$, such that $f \in Flds_0(P_\alpha)$.

$$F_{det} = \bigwedge \text{ for any } [x_1,y_1,f],[x_2,y_2,f] \in BVars(F(\varphi)) \text{ different variables}$$

$$[x_1 = x_2] \wedge [x_1,y_1,f] \;\Rightarrow\; \neg[x_2,y_2,f] \tag{9}$$

$$\bigwedge \text{ for any } [x_1,y_1,f],[P_\alpha(x_2,y_2,\vec{z_2})] \in BVars(F(\varphi)) \text{ s.t. } f \in Flds_0(P) \text{ and } x \in LVars(\varphi)$$

$$[x_1 = x] \wedge [x \in \alpha] \wedge [x_1,y_1,f] \;\Rightarrow\; \neg[P_\alpha(x_2,y_2,\vec{z_2})] \tag{10}$$

$$\bigwedge \text{ for any } [P_\alpha(x_1,y_1,\vec{z_1})],[Q_\beta(x_2,y_2,\vec{z_2})] \in BVars(F(\varphi)) \text{ different variables}$$

$$\text{s.t. } Flds_0(P) \cap Flds_0(Q) \neq \emptyset \text{ and } x, x' \in LVars(\varphi)$$

$$[x \in \alpha] \wedge [x' \in \beta] \wedge [x = x'] \wedge [P_\alpha(x_1,y_1,\vec{z_1})] \;\Rightarrow\; \neg[Q_\beta(x_2,y_2,\vec{z_2})] \tag{11}$$

Fig. 8. Definition of F_{det} for a *MOLL* formula $\varphi = \Pi \wedge \Sigma \wedge \Lambda$

Fig. 9 gives the main definitions of $F(\Lambda)$. For instance, $F(\alpha_1 \subseteq \alpha_2)$ in eq. (14) expresses the fact that if there exists some variable x such that $x \in \alpha_1$ is true then $x \in \alpha_2$ also holds. In eq. (15), $F_\in$ encodes the closure of $\in$ under the equality, the fact that if a boolean variable $[x_1 \in \alpha]$ is true then the list segment bound to α in φ, if any, is not empty, and if α is bound to a non-empty list segment $P_\alpha(x,y,\vec{z})$ in φ, then α contains the first element of the segment, i.e., x.

$$F(x \in \alpha_1) = [x \in \alpha_1] \tag{12}$$

$$F(x \in \bigcup_{1 \leq i \leq n} \{u_i\}) = \bigvee_{1 \leq i \leq n} [x = u_i] \tag{13}$$

$$F(\alpha_1 \subseteq \alpha_2) = \bigwedge_{x \in LVars(\varphi)} [x \in \alpha_1] \Rightarrow [x \in \alpha_2] \tag{14}$$

$$F_\in = \bigwedge_{u,v,\alpha \text{ in } \varphi} \big([u = v] \wedge [u \in \alpha]\big) \Rightarrow [v \in \alpha] \tag{15}$$

$$\wedge \bigwedge_{x_1,P_\alpha(x,y,\vec{z}) \text{ in } \varphi} \big([x_1 \in \alpha] \Rightarrow [P_\alpha(x,y,\vec{z})]\big) \;\wedge\; \big([P_\alpha(x,y,\vec{z})] \Rightarrow [x \in \alpha]\big)$$

Fig. 9. Main definitions of $F(\Lambda)$ and $F_\in$ for a *MOLL* formula $\varphi = \Pi \wedge \Sigma \wedge \Lambda$

Proposition 1. *The size of $F(\varphi)$ is polynomial in the size of φ.*

Proposition 2. *Let φ be a NOLL formula. For any satisfying assignment σ of $F(\varphi)$, ψ_σ is an explicit, reduced, and satisfiable formula. Also, φ is equivalent to the disjunction of ψ_σ, for all satisfying assignments σ of $F(\varphi)$.*

Theorem 4. *The problem of computing the normal form of a formula φ is in co-NP.*

Proof. To compute the maximum set of (in)equalities that should be included in the normal form of φ, we iterate over every pair of location variables x, y in φ and check if $F(\varphi) \Rightarrow [x = y]$ or $F(\varphi) \Rightarrow \neg[x = y]$ is valid. In the first (resp., second) case, $x = y$ (resp., $x \neq y$) is included in the normal form. When some equality $x = y$ is added to the normal form, the atoms $P_\alpha(x,y,\vec{z})$ in φ are removed, and all occurrences of α are interpreted as the empty set. Since we need to perform a polynomial number of Boolean formula validity tests, the overall complexity of this procedure is co-*NP* time. $\square$

6   An Effective Procedure for Checking Entailment

The procedure for checking the validity of the entailments $\varphi \Rightarrow \psi$ between two *NOLL* formulas is detailed in Fig. 10. It has three main steps: (a) compute (lines 1–2) the normal form of φ and ψ, denoted by φ' and ψ', respectively, (b) compute (line 3) additional spatial constraints, which are implied by φ, and (c) check (lines 3–6) if the graph representation of ψ' is *homomorphic* to the graph representation of both φ' and the additional constraints computed in the previous step.

```
procedure CheckEntl(φ ⇒ ψ)
1: φ′ := the normal form of φ
2: ψ′ := the normal form of ψ
3: G₁ := the complete NOLL graph of φ′
4: G₂ := the NOLL graph of ψ′
5: h := the function h : V(G₂) ⇀ V(G₁) s.t.
       vars_G₂(n) ⊆ vars_G₁(h(n)), ∀n ∈ V(G₂)
6: return (h is total) and
       (h is a homomorphism)
```

Fig. 10.

In the following, we first describe the step (b) above, then we define graph representations for *NOLL* formulas, called (complete) *NOLL* graphs, and finally, we define the notion of homomorphism between *NOLL* graphs. *Moreover, we assume that φ and ψ are satisfiable.* Otherwise, Proposition 2 implies that a formula φ is satisfiable iff $F(\varphi)$ is satisfiable, which allows to decide in co-NP time entailments of the form $\varphi \Rightarrow \psi$ when φ or ψ is unsatisfiable.

6.1   Inferring Additional Spatial Constraints

In order to give an intuition about the additional spatial constraints deduced from φ, recall the entailment $\varphi_1 \Rightarrow \varphi_2$, where φ_1 and φ_2 are defined in eq. (6–7) at page 134. The entailment holds because the list segments linking x to n and n to y, and described by $List_\delta(x,n) * List_\gamma(n,y)$, exist in every model of φ_1. To obtain a complete decision procedure for entailment, such constraints must be made explicit before checking the existence of a homomorphism between the two formulas viewed as graphs.

Observe that φ_1 does not imply $\varphi_1 *_w (List_\delta(x,n) * List_\gamma(n,y))$ but, $\varphi_1 \wedge (List_\delta(x,n) * List_\gamma(n,y))$. Thus, these implicit constraints will be added only to the graph representation of *NOLL* formulas and not to the formula itself, as explained in Sec. 6.2.

For simplicity, we give the definition only for *MOLL* formulas φ. Let ξ be a set of atoms in φ of the form $Q_\beta(u,v,\vec{w})$. For any such ξ, $\mathcal{P}(\xi)$ denotes the set of recursive predicates in ξ, $SetVars(\xi)$ denotes the set of variables $\beta \in SetVars$ bounded to atoms in ξ, and t_ξ is the term defined as the union of all variables in $SetVars(\xi)$.

An atom $P_\alpha(x,y,\vec{z})$ is called *implicit in* ξ iff one of the following holds:

– ξ consists of one atom $P_\beta(u,v,\vec{z})$, the source of P_α is the same as the source of P_β, i.e., $\varphi \Rightarrow x = u$, and the destination of P_α is included in the list segment defined by P_β, i.e., $\varphi \Rightarrow y \in \beta$;

– (1) $\varphi \Rightarrow x \in t_\xi$, (2) t_ξ is a minimal term t such that $\varphi \Rightarrow x \in t$, i.e., for every other term t', which is the union of the variables from a strict subset of $SetVars(\xi)$, $\varphi \not\Rightarrow x \in t'$, (3) $Flds_0(P) = \bigcap_{Q \in \mathcal{P}(\xi)} Flds_0(Q)$, and (4) $\varphi \Rightarrow \bigwedge_{Q_\beta(u,v,\vec{z}) \in \xi} y = v$.

Similarly, an atom $x \mapsto \{(f,y)\}$ is called implicit in ξ iff the conditions (1) and (2) above hold, (3′) an atom $u \mapsto \theta_i$ with $(f,d_i) \in \theta_i$ is included in the definition of Q, for all $Q \in \mathcal{P}(\xi)$, and (4′) $\varphi \Rightarrow \bigwedge_{1 \leq i \leq n} y = d_i$.

For example, for $\xi = \{List_\alpha(x,y)\}$ a set of atoms in φ_1 from eq. (6), the atom $List_\delta(x,n)$ is implicit in ξ because $\beta \subseteq \alpha$ in φ_1 implies that $n \in \alpha$ and the equality $x = x$ is trivially implied by φ_1. Also, the atom $List_\gamma(n,y)$ is implicit in ξ because the conditions (1–4) above hold.

By definition, the Boolean abstraction $F(\varphi)$ defined in Sec. 5 can be used to check that φ implies the equalities and the sharing constraints in the above conditions. The conditions (3) and (3′) can be checked syntactically. Thus, the computation of the implicit spatial constraints for a formula is co-NP complete.

6.2 NOLL Graphs

We define *NOLL graphs*, a graph representation for *NOLL* formulas. Roughly, the nodes of these graphs represent sets of equal location variables and the edges represent spatial or difference constraints. The object separated spatial constraints are represented by a binary relation Ω_* over edges while the sharing constraints are kept unchanged.

Definition 3 (*NOLL graph*). *Given a NOLL formula $\varphi = \Pi \wedge \Sigma \wedge \Lambda$ over a set of predicates $\mathcal{P}$, the NOLL graph of φ, denoted $G(\varphi)$, is a tuple $(V, E_P, E_R, E_D, \ell, \Omega_*, \Lambda)$ or the error graph $\bot$, where:*

- *each node in V denotes an equivalence class over elements of LVars w.r.t. the equality relation defined in Π; the equivalence class of x is denoted by $[x]$. If Π contains both $x \neq y$ and $x = y$ then G is the error graph $\bot$;*
- *$E_P \subseteq V \times Flds \times V$ represents the points-to constraints: $([x], f, [y]) \in E_P$ iff $x \mapsto \theta$ with $(f,y) \in \theta$ is an atomic formula in Σ;*
- *$E_R \subseteq V \times \mathcal{P} \times V^+ \times V$ represents list segment constraints: $([x], P_\alpha, [\overrightarrow{z}], [y]) \in E_R$ iff $P_\alpha(x, y, \overrightarrow{z})$ is an atomic formula in Σ;*
- *$E_D \subseteq V \times V$ represents inequalities: $([x], [y]) \in E_D$ iff $x \neq y$ is an atom in Π;*
- *$\ell : LVars \to V$, called variable labeling, it is defined by $\ell(x) = [x]$, for any $x \in LVars$;*
- *Ω_* contains all pairs of edges in $E_P \cup E_R$ denoting object separated atoms in Σ.*

In the following, $V(G)$, denotes the set of nodes in the *NOLL* graph G. We use a similar notation for all the other components of G. Also, for any $n \in V(G)$, $vars_G(n)$ denotes the set of all the variables labeling the node n in G. The graph $G(\varphi_2)$ in Fig. 3 represents the *NOLL* graph of φ_2, where $V = \{x,y,n,m\}$, $E_P = E_D = \emptyset$, E_R contains the three edges corresponding to the three list segments, Ω_* contains only one pair $\langle([x], List_\alpha, [n]), ([n], List_{\beta'}, [y])\rangle$, and Λ is $\beta' \subseteq \delta \cup \gamma$.

A graph representation for φ which includes an edge for each implicit spatial constraint of φ is called a *complete NOLL graph*. This representation has an additional attribute Δ, which identifies the set of atoms where a spatial constraint is implicit in.

Definition 4 (**complete** *NOLL graph*). *Given a NOLL formula $\varphi = \Pi \wedge \Sigma \wedge \Lambda$, the complete NOLL graph of φ, denoted by $\overline{G}(\varphi)$ is a tuple (G, Δ) where:*

- *G is a NOLL graph where all components except E_R, E_P, Ω_*, and Λ are equal to the components of $G(\varphi)$;*
- *$E_R(G)$ (resp. $E_P(G)$) includes $E_R(G(\varphi))$ (resp. $E_P(G(\varphi))$) and, for any atom $P_\alpha(x, y, \overrightarrow{z})$ (resp. $x \mapsto \{(f,y)\}$) which is implicit in some set of atoms ξ, $e = ([x], P_\alpha, [\overrightarrow{z}], [y]) \in E_R(G)$ (resp. $e = ([x], f, [y]) \in E_P(G)$);*

- $\Omega_*(G)$ consists of $\Omega_*(G(\varphi))$ plus all pairs (e,e') s.t. e represents an implicit constraint in ξ and $(e',e'') \in \Omega_*(G)$ for some e'' representing an atom in ξ;
- $\Delta \subseteq (E_P \cup E_R) \times 2^{E_R}$ represents the relation between edges and the sets of list segments where they are implicit in, i.e., for every $P_\alpha(x,y,\overrightarrow{z})$ (resp. $x \mapsto \{(f,y)\}$) implicit in ξ, $(([x],P_\alpha,[\overrightarrow{z}],[y]),E_\xi) \in \Delta$ (resp. $(([x],f,[y]),E_\xi) \in \Delta$), where E_ξ is the set of edges representing the atoms in ξ;
- if $P_{\alpha_1}(x,y,\overrightarrow{z})$ and $P_{\alpha_2}(y,t,\overrightarrow{z})$ are implicit in $\xi = \{P_\alpha(x,t,\overrightarrow{z})\}$ then, $\alpha = \alpha_1 \cup \alpha_2$ is added to Λ.

The graph in the middle of Fig. 3 represents the complete *NOLL* graph of φ_1, $\overline{G}(\varphi_1)$, where $V = \{x,y,n,m\}$, $E_P = E_D = \Omega_* = \emptyset$, and E_P contains the four edges: two edges represent the spatial constraints in φ_1, and the edges $([x],List_{\alpha_1},[n])$ and $([n],List_{\alpha_2},[m])$ represent implicit constraints in $\xi = \{List_\alpha(x,y)\}$. Λ is $\beta \subseteq \alpha \wedge \alpha = \alpha_1 \cup \alpha_2$ and Δ is the relation $\{(([x],List_{\alpha_1},[n]),\xi),(([n],List_{\alpha_2},[m]),\xi)\}$.

6.3 *NOLL* Graph Homomorphism

Given a *NOLL* graph G_1 and a complete *NOLL* graph G_2, a *homomorphism from G_1 to G_2* is a mapping $h : V(G_1) \mapsto V(G_2)$, which:

1. preserves the labeling with location variables, i.e., $vars_{G_1}(n) \subseteq vars_{G_2}(h(n))$, for any $n \in V(G_1)$,
2. maps each difference, resp., points-to, edge of G_1 to a difference, resp., points-to, edge of G_2, (e.g., for any $(n,f,n') \in E_P(G_1)$, $(h(n),f,h(n')) \in E_P(G_2)$),
3. maps each edge representing a list segment in G_1 to a path in G_2 formed of edges in $E_P(G_2) \cup E_R(G_2)$, and
4. satisfies the constraints required by the semantics of the separating conjunctions, the special status of the implicit spatial constraints, and the sharing constraints.

To explain the mapping of edges in $E_R(G_1)$ to paths of G_2, let us consider the case of an edge $(n,P_\alpha,m,p) \in E_R(G_1)$, where $n,m,p \in V(G_1)$ and P is a *MOLL* predicate, i.e., $P(in,out,b) \triangleq (in = out) \vee (\exists u. \Sigma_0(in,u \cup b) * P(u,out,b))$. The definition of h requires that there exists a sequence of nodes $\pi = \pi_1 \ldots \pi_k$, $k \geq 1$, in G_2 s.t. $\pi_1 = h(n)$, $\pi_k = h(p)$, and for every two consecutive nodes π_i and π_{i+1}, either

- $E_P(G_2)$ contains some set of edges between π_i, π_{i+1}, and $h(m)$, which prove that $\Sigma_0(x_i,x_{i+1} \cup x_{h(m)})$ holds, where x_i, x_{i+1}, and $x_{h(m)}$ are some variables labeling π_i, π_{i+1}, and $h(m)$, respectively, or
- there exists an edge $(\pi_i,P'_\beta,\overrightarrow{q},\pi_{i+1})$ in $E_R(G_2)$, representing a stronger predicate than P_α, i.e., $h(m) \in \overrightarrow{q}$ and $P'_\beta(x_i,x_{i+1},\overrightarrow{z}) \Rightarrow P_\alpha(x_i,x_{i+1},x_{h(m)})$, where x_i, x_{i+1}, and $x_{h(m)}$ are as above, and $\overrightarrow{z}$ is a set of variables labeling $\overrightarrow{q}$ s.t. $x_{h(m)} \in \overrightarrow{z}$ (this is possible because $h(m) \in \overrightarrow{q}$). The entailment between recursive predicates can be checked syntactically in polynomial time.

In the following, we explain the constraints required by the 4th item in the definition of the homomorphism. For any edge e in $E_P(G_1) \cup E_R(G_1)$, we define a set $used(e) \subseteq E_P(G_2) \cup 2^{(E_R(G_2) \times Flds)}$, which represents all the edges/fields used in the path from G_2 to which e is mapped by h. If $e \in E_P(G_1)$ then $used(e) = \{e'\}$, where e' is the edge of

G_2 to which e is mapped by h. If $e \in E_R(G_1)$ represents a list segment P_α then, $used(e)$ consists of (1) the set of points-to edges in the path associated to e and (2) the set of pairs (e', f), where e' represents a list segment Q_β from the same path, if such an edge exists, and $f \in Flds_0(P) \cap Flds_0(Q)$. When the path associated to $e \in E_R(G_1)$ labeled by P_α (resp. $e \in E_P(G_1)$ labeled by f) contains an edge e' representing a constraint implicit in some ξ, i.e., $(e', E_\xi) \in \Delta(G_2)$, then $used(e)$ includes all pairs (e'', f) with $e'' \in E_\xi$ labeled by $Q_\beta \in \xi$, and $f \in Flds_0(P) \cap Flds_0(Q)$ (resp. $f \in Flds_0(Q)$).

Then, to express the semantics of $*_w$, we require that $used(e_1) \cap used(e_2) = \emptyset$, for any two edges e_1 and e_2 in $E_P(G_1) \cup E_R(G_1)$. Concerning $*$, it is required that for any two edges e_1 and e_2 in $E_P(G_1) \cup E_R(G_1)$ s.t. $(e_1, e_2) \in \Omega_*(G_1)$, we have that $(e'_1, e'_2) \in \Omega_*(G_2)$, for any e'_1 an edge appearing in $used(e_1)$ and e'_2 an edge appearing in $used(e_2)$.

Finally, for the sharing constraints, the mapping by h of edges in $E_R(G_1)$ to paths in G_2 defines a substitution Γ for set of locations variables in $\Lambda(G_1)$ to terms over set of locations variables in $\Lambda(G_2)$. For example, the homomorphism in Fig. 3 defines the substitution $\Gamma(\delta) = \alpha_1$, $\Gamma(\gamma) = \alpha_2$, and $\Gamma(\beta') = \beta$. Then, it is required that $\Lambda(G_2) \Rightarrow \Lambda(G_1)[\Gamma]$. Such a formula belongs for instance, to the fragment of BAPA [14], and thus its validity can be decided in NP-time. For the example in Fig. 3, we obtain the trivial entailment $\beta \subseteq \alpha \wedge \alpha = \alpha_1 \cup \alpha_2 \Rightarrow \beta \subseteq \alpha_1 \cup \alpha_2$.

6.4 Checking Entailments of *NOLL* Formulas

The following theorem states the correctness and the complexity of the procedure CheckEntl given in Fig. 10; the proof is given in [10].

Theorem 5. *Given two NOLL formulas φ and ψ, $\varphi \Rightarrow \psi$ holds iff* CheckEntl$(\varphi \Rightarrow \psi)$ *returns* true. *Moreover, the complexity of* CheckEntl *is co-NP time.*

7 Experimental Results

We have implemented the procedure for entailment checking in a solver which takes as input the specification of predicates in $\mathcal{P}$ and two formulas $\varphi, \psi \in NOLL$ defined over $\mathcal{P}$ and returns as result either the homomorphism found when $\varphi \Rightarrow \psi$ or a diagnosis explaining why the entailment is not valid. The diagnosis is given as a list of variables or atomic spatial constraints in φ and ψ for which the conditions for the homomorphism are not satisfied. The solver is implemented in C. It uses MiniSat [9] to compute normal forms and an ad-hoc solver for the sharing constraints.

We have used this solver to check verification conditions generated for procedures working on singly linked lists, doubly linked lists, and overlaid hash tables and lists in the Nagios network monitoring example. We have considered mainly the procedures for inserting or moving elements in these data structures. The post-condition computation follows the standard approach: introducing primed variables to denote old values and unfolding recursive predicates for statements that involve fields. To generate simpler verification conditions, we use the frame rules for the separating conjunction operators. In this way, the graph representations for the *NOLL* formulas have less than ten vertices and twenty edges (including the inferred edges), and less than five set of locations variables. Each verification condition is decided in less than 0.1 seconds.

References

1. Berdine, J., Calcagno, C., Cook, B., Distefano, D., O'Hearn, P.W., Wies, T., Yang, H.: Shape Analysis for Composite Data Structures. In: Damm, W., Hermanns, H. (eds.) CAV 2007. LNCS, vol. 4590, pp. 178–192. Springer, Heidelberg (2007)
2. Berdine, J., Calcagno, C., O'Hearn, P.W.: A Decidable Fragment of Separation Logic. In: Lodaya, K., Mahajan, M. (eds.) FSTTCS 2004. LNCS, vol. 3328, pp. 97–109. Springer, Heidelberg (2004)
3. Berdine, J., Calcagno, C., O'Hearn, P.W.: Smallfoot: Modular Automatic Assertion Checking with Separation Logic. In: de Boer, F.S., Bonsangue, M.M., Graf, S., de Roever, W.-P. (eds.) FMCO 2005. LNCS, vol. 4111, pp. 115–137. Springer, Heidelberg (2006)
4. Bobot, F., Filliâtre, J.-C.: Separation Predicates: A Taste of Separation Logic in First-Order Logic. In: Aoki, T., Taguchi, K. (eds.) ICFEM 2012. LNCS, vol. 7635, pp. 167–181. Springer, Heidelberg (2012)
5. Calcagno, C., Yang, H., O'Hearn, P.W.: Computability and Complexity Results for a Spatial Assertion Language for Data Structures. In: Hariharan, R., Mukund, M., Vinay, V. (eds.) FSTTCS 2001. LNCS, vol. 2245, pp. 108–119. Springer, Heidelberg (2001)
6. Chang, B.-Y.E., Rival, X.: Relational inductive shape analysis. In: POPL, pp. 247–260. ACM (2008)
7. Chlipala, A.: Mostly-automated verification of low-level programs in computational separation logic. In: PLDI, pp. 234–245. ACM (2011)
8. Cook, B., Haase, C., Ouaknine, J., Parkinson, M., Worrell, J.: Tractable Reasoning in a Fragment of Separation Logic. In: Katoen, J.-P., König, B. (eds.) CONCUR 2011. LNCS, vol. 6901, pp. 235–249. Springer, Heidelberg (2011)
9. Eén, N., Sörensson, N.: An Extensible SAT-solver. In: Giunchiglia, E., Tacchella, A. (eds.) SAT 2003. LNCS, vol. 2919, pp. 502–518. Springer, Heidelberg (2004)
10. Enea, C., Saveluc, V., Sighireanu, M.: Composite invariant checking for nested, overlaid linked lists (2012), Extended version available as HAL-00768389 report
11. Hawkins, P., Aiken, A., Fisher, K., Rinard, M.C., Sagiv, M.: Data representation synthesis. In: PLDI, pp. 38–49. ACM (2011)
12. Ishtiaq, S., O'Hear, P.W.: BI as an assertion language for mutable data structures. In: POPL, pp. 14–26. ACM (2001)
13. Jacobs, B., Smans, J., Piessens, F.: A Quick Tour of the VeriFast Program Verifier. In: Ueda, K. (ed.) APLAS 2010. LNCS, vol. 6461, pp. 304–311. Springer, Heidelberg (2010)
14. Kuncak, V., Nguyen, H.H., Rinard, M.: An Algorithm for Deciding BAPA: Boolean Algebra with Presburger Arithmetic. In: Nieuwenhuis, R. (ed.) CADE 2005. LNCS (LNAI), vol. 3632, pp. 260–277. Springer, Heidelberg (2005)
15. Madhusudan, P., Qiu, X., Stefanescu, A.: Recursive proofs for inductive tree data-structures. In: POPL, pp. 123–136. ACM (2012)
16. Navarro Pérez, J.A., Rybalchenko, A.: Separation logic + superposition calculus = heap theorem prover. In: PLDI, pp. 556–566. ACM (2011)
17. Reynolds, J.C.: Separation logic: A logic for shared mutable data structures. In: LICS, pp. 55–74. IEEE Computer Society (2002)
18. Suter, P., Dotta, M., Kuncak, V.: Decision procedures for algebraic data types with abstractions. In: POPL, pp. 199–210. ACM (2010)
19. Yang, H., Lee, O., Berdine, J., Calcagno, C., Cook, B., Distefano, D., O'Hearn, P.W.: Scalable Shape Analysis for Systems Code. In: Gupta, A., Malik, S. (eds.) CAV 2008. LNCS, vol. 5123, pp. 385–398. Springer, Heidelberg (2008)

A Discipline for Program Verification Based on Backpointers and Its Use in Observational Disjointness

Ioannis T. Kassios[1,*] and Eleftherios Kritikos[2]

[1] ETH Zurich, Switzerland
`ioannis.kassios@inf.ethz.ch`
[2] National Technical University of Athens, Greece
`eleftherios.kritikos@gmail.com`

Abstract. In the verification of programs that manipulate the heap, logics that emphasize *localized reasoning*, such as separation logic, are being used extensively. In such logics, state conditions may only refer to parts of the heap that are reachable from the stack. However, the correct implementation of some data structures is based on state conditions that depend on unreachable locations. For example, reference counting depends on the invariant that *"the number of nodes pointing to a certain node is equal to its reference counter"*. Such conditions are cumbersome or even impossible to formalize in existing variants of separation logic.

In the first part of this paper, we develop a minimal programming discipline that enables the programmer to soundly express *backpointer conditions*, i.e., state conditions that involve heap objects that *point* to the reachable part of the heap, such as the above-mentioned reference counting invariant.

In the second part, we demonstrate the expressiveness of our methodology by verifying the implementation of *concurrent copy-on-write lists* (CCoWL). CCoWL is a data structure with *observational disjointness*, i.e., its specification *pretends* that different lists depend on disjoint parts of the heap, so that separation logic reasoning is made easy, while its implementation uses sharing to maximize performance. The CCoWL case study is a very challenging problem, to which we are not aware of any other solution.

1 Introduction

The advent of *separation logic* [1] has revolutionized reasoning about programs with rich heap structure. The main motivation behind this line of work is *localized reasoning* (also referred to as *"reasoning in the small"*). In particular, the specifier is only allowed to talk about the locations of the heap s/he has explicit permission to, completely ignoring the rest of the heap. In separation logic, a state condition *contains its own permissions*. For example, $x \mapsto 3$ is a condition

---

* The first author was funded by the Hasler Foundation.

M. Felleisen and P. Gardner (Eds.): ESOP 2013, LNCS 7792, pp. 149–168, 2013.

that not only expresses the fact that 3 is the content of memory location x, but also that the programmer is permitted to read and write to x.

State conditions that contain their own permissions are called *self-framing* [2–4]. A self-framing assertion has the important property that it *cannot be falsified by an unknown program*. As a result, the *localized* verification of our program cannot be falsified when this program is composed (sequentially, parallelly, through method call, or through thread forking) with other programs. In concurrent variants of separation logic, permissions can be split [5] (e.g., in fractions [6]), thus enabling shared resources without data races. These well-known extensions of separation logic, maintain this important property: all expressible state conditions are self-framing.

Self-framing conditions cannot talk about objects that are unreachable by the pointers of the program under verification. However, there are cases when such conditions would be desirable.

For example, assume that we have a concurrent program operating on a graph. Normally, none of its threads has access to the whole graph, because that would mean that only one thread can perform changes, which defeats the purpose of concurrency. Consider now the following examples of *node invariants*:

- *Reference counting.* The value of the reference counter of a node N is equal to the number of nodes N' such that $N'.f = N$.
- *Priority Inheritance Protocol* [7]. The priority of a node is the minimum of its initial priority and the priority of the node pointing to it (see also [8]).
- *The union-find structure.* In this structure each node represents a set of nodes. The set represented by a node N is $\{N\}$ unioned with the sets represented by all nodes that point to N.

Assume that a thread T has access to a node N. The invariant of N involves nodes that are unreachable from N, and therefore inaccessible to T. This makes the invariant of N non-self-framing, and therefore inexpressible in existing variants of separation logic.

All the examples of node invariants that we mentioned are *conditions which may involve unreachable heap objects that point to reachable heap objects*. We call such conditions *backpointer conditions*. Our purpose is to enable the "reasoning in the small" style of separation logic, in verification problems that involve backpointer conditions.

1.1 Contributions

In this paper, we propose an extension of separation logic with a minimal programming discipline that makes it possible to express backpointer conditions in a self-framing way. Our methodology enables the verification, in the localized style of separation logic, of data structures with backpointer node invariants.

Furthermore, we use our technique to verify the case study of *concurrent copy-on-write lists* (hence CCoWL). This is a challenging problem of *observational disjointness*: the structure pretends that it supports mutually disjoint mutable sequences of integers, even though it uses data sharing under the hood, to enhance performance. The clients are happy to use the facilities of separation logic to verify their programs as if the lists were actually heap-disjoint, but the verifier of the implementation is faced with a challenging reference counting mechanism. We are not aware of other solutions to the CCoWL verification problem.

1.2 Structure of the Paper

The paper is organized as follows: In Sect. 2, we motivate and introduce the discipline of backpointers. In Sect. 3, we show how the discipline can be used to verify CCoWLs, highlighting the most important parts of the implementation and the correctness proof. In Sect. 4, we discuss the relationship of our methodology to related work and point out some possibilities for future work. Sect. 5 concludes.

Our online technical report [9] contains an appendix with the full specification, implementation and correctness proof of the CCoWL example.

2   The Backpointers Discipline

In this section, we introduce the discipline of backpointers. We start by introducing the background (Sect. 2.1) on which we work, a framework for locking, monitor invariants, and deadlock avoidance borrowed from Chalice [10]. We then extend our language with the backpointer formalism (Sect. 2.2) and provide an argument about the soundness of this extension (Sect. 2.3).

2.1 Background

Records and Locking. Our language supports mutable records. A *monitor* is associated with each record and a *monitor invariant* is also associated with each monitor. The monitor invariant is an expression written in separation logic with fractional permissions.

Consider the following definition:

```
struct  Pair
{
  x,y : int
  invariant  ∃X,Y ∈ ℤ· this.x↦X  *  this.y⟶̲0.5 Y ∧ X>0
}
```

The definition introduces a set Pair. The members of Pair are: (a) the special record **null** and (b) records r such that $r.x$ and $r.y$ are heap locations that store integers.

Assume that this is a non-null record of type Pair. The monitor invariant associated with this asserts that this.x stores a positive value. It also grants write (full) access permission to this.x and 50% permission to this.y. In general, when we write monitor invariants, this refers to the current record and may be omitted when referring to its fields.

We are interested in thread-modular verification. From the point of view of the current thread, a record can be in one of the following three conditions: (a) local, (b) shared and not held by the current thread, (c) shared and held by the current thread. Fig. 1 shows all these conditions, together with the commands that perform the transitions between them.

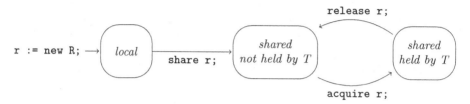

Fig. 1. A record's life cycle from the point of view of thread T

The invariant of a monitor is always true when the associated record is shared but not held by any thread. To hold a record, a thread must *acquire* it. As long as it holds the record, the thread may invalidate the monitor invariant but must ensure that the invariant holds before it *releases* the record. Similarly, a thread that *shares* a record must first ensure that the associated invariant holds.

Sharing and releasing means that the current thread loses all permissions that are contained in the invariant. Acquiring means that the thread gains these permissions and that it may furthermore assume that the invariant holds immediately after the record is acquired.

The Chalice locking model has a simple mechanism to prevent cyclic dependencies between "acquire" requests, and thus to prevent deadlock [10]. Assume that **Ord** is a set equipped with a strict partial ordering $\sqsubset$. We furthermore assume that $\sqsubset$ is *dense* in the sense that if $a \sqsubset b$ then there exists $c \in$ **Ord** such that $a \sqsubset c \sqsubset b$. Every shared record is associated with a value in **Ord** called its *lock-level*. A thread is allowed to acquire a record, only when that record is greater in $\sqsubset$ than all the other records that the thread holds.

The rules that govern record creation, sharing, releasing and acquiring are shown in Fig. 2. In it:

- local and shared are abstract predicates that indicate that a record is local or shared resp. The second argument of shared equals the lock-level of the record.
- Both predicates imply that their first argument, the record, is non-null:

$$\text{shared}(r,\_) \ \lor \ \text{local}(r) \quad \Rightarrow \quad r \neq \textbf{null}$$

- shared is infinitely divisible, i.e.,

$$\mathsf{shared}\,(r,\mu) \iff \mathsf{shared}\,(r,\mu) \;*\; \mathsf{shared}\,(r,\mu)$$

This means that, unlike in Chalice, the lock-level of an object is immutable.
- Each shared record has a single lock-level:

$$\mathsf{shared}\,(r,\mu) \;*\; \mathsf{shared}\,(r,\mu') \;\Rightarrow\; \mu{=}\mu'$$

- If r, r' are records, the notation $r \sqsubset r'$ is a shorthand for:

$$\exists \mu, \mu' \in \mathbf{Ord} \cdot \; \mathsf{shared}\,(r,\mu) \;*\; \mathsf{shared}\,(r',\mu') \;*\; \mu \sqsubset \mu'$$

We extend this notation to "compare" a record r to a set of records:

$$R \sqsubset r \iff \forall r' \in R \cdot r' \sqsubset r$$

- Note that $R \sqsubset r \;\Rightarrow\; r \notin R$
- $Inv(r)$ is the monitor invariant of record r
- held is a thread-local variable whose value is the set of all records held by the current thread
- newRec is an abstract predicate describing the situation directly after a new record is created. It gives access to all fields f_i of the new record r, initializes them to the default value of their type and asserts that r is local:

$$\mathsf{newRec}(r) \iff r.f_1 \mapsto d_1 \;*\; \ldots \;*\; r.f_n \mapsto d_n \;*\; \mathsf{local}\,(r)$$

- The default value of all record types is **null**

The **share** command can specify bounds for the lock-level of the record being shared. We omit the rules for these variants of **share** for brevity.

Counting Permissions. *Counting permissions* are an important alternative to fractional permissions. The idea is as follows. A counting permission is a natural number n, or -1. At any given execution time, there is one thread that holds a non-negative counting permission n to a heap location and n threads that hold a -1 counting permission. We call the holder of counting permission n the *main thread* for that heap location.

The main thread can give away -1 counting permissions, increasing its own counting permission accordingly. The holders of -1 counting permissions may return their counting permission to the main thread, decreasing its counting permission accordingly. If $n = 0$, then the main thread is the only thread that can access the location and thus has write privileges. Otherwise, all involved threads have read-only access.

We do not need to invent new notation for counting permissions. Instead, we introduce an infinitesimal fractional permission ϵ to stand for the -1 counting permission. Then the counting permission n corresponds to fractional permission $1 - n\epsilon$. This approach is taken in the current Chalice permission model [11].

$$\{\mathsf{emp}\}$$
$$\quad \mathsf{r} := \mathbf{new} \ \ \mathsf{R}$$
$$\{\mathsf{newRec}(\mathsf{r})\}$$

$$\{\mathsf{local}(\mathsf{r}) \ * \ \mathit{Inv}(\mathsf{r}) \ * \ \mathsf{held} \mapsto O \ \wedge \ \mathsf{r} \not\in O\}$$
$$\quad \mathbf{share} \ \ \mathsf{r}$$
$$\{\mathsf{shared}(\mathsf{r}, \_) \ * \ \mathsf{held} \mapsto O\}$$

$$\{\mathsf{shared}(\mathsf{r}, \mu) \ * \ \mathsf{held} \mapsto O \ * \ O \sqsubseteq \mathsf{r}\}$$
$$\quad \mathbf{acquire} \ \ \mathsf{r}$$
$$\{\mathsf{shared}(\mathsf{r}, \mu) \ * \ \mathsf{held} \mapsto O \cup \{\mathsf{r}\} \ * \ \mathit{Inv}(\mathsf{r})\}$$

$$\{\mathsf{shared}(\mathsf{r}, \mu) \ * \ \mathsf{held} \mapsto O \ * \ \mathit{Inv}(\mathsf{r}) \ \wedge \ \mathsf{r} \in O\}$$
$$\quad \mathbf{release} \ \ \mathsf{r}$$
$$\{\mathsf{shared}(\mathsf{r}, \mu) \ * \ \mathsf{held} \mapsto O - \{\mathsf{r}\}\}$$

Fig. 2. Commands on records

2.2   Backpointers

To make the backpointer properties self-framing, we impose a restriction on the assignments which may potentially invalidate such properties.

Tracked Fields. Our first step is to identify those reference-valued fields, whose value influences backpointer invariants. We mark these fields as *tracked*, because we want to track assignments to them.

struct C { **tracked** $f : D$; }

Backpointer Definitional Axiom. Suppose now that a record type C has a tracked field f of type D (where C, D are not necessarily different). To express backpointer properties, it should be possible to refer to "all allocated records of type C that point to the record d of type D through the field f". We write $d.(C.f)^{-1}$ to refer to that set. In other words, the *definitional axiom* of backpointers is (for every state σ):

$$\llbracket \forall c \in \alpha C, d \in \alpha D \cdot \ c \in d.(C.f)^{-1} \ \Leftrightarrow \ c.f = d \rrbracket (\sigma) \tag{1}$$

where

- $\llbracket E \rrbracket (\sigma)$ evaluates expression E in state σ
- αT is the set of all non-null allocated records of type T in a given state

If C is clear from the context, we simply write $d.f^{-1}$.

Backpointer Fields. The value of the expression $(C.f)^{-1}$ is not associated with any permission, which is what makes it non-self-framing. To fix this, we turn $(C.f)^{-1}$ into *a field* of D. This field has access permissions like any regular field. However, it is a *ghost* field: it does not appear in the actual program; it is only part of its specification annotation. Furthermore, even explicit "ghost assignments" to it are forbidden[1].

Tracked Assignments. Assume now that record r points to record q through a tracked field f. Consider the assignment:

$$r.f := p$$

Notice that this assignment changes not only the value of $r.f$, but also that of $q.f^{-1}$ and $p.f^{-1}$. The situation is depicted graphically in Fig. 3. Since the values of two backpointer fields are changed, the thread that executes the assignment *must have full permission to those fields*. In the case q or p are the **null** reference, then, of course, we do not require access to their backpointer fields.

We introduce two axiomatic rules for tracked assignments[2]. First, for the case $p \neq q$:

$$
\begin{aligned}
&\{ \\
&\quad r{=}R{\neq}\mathbf{null} \;\wedge\; p{=}P{\neq}Q \;\wedge\; r.f \mapsto Q \\
&\quad * \;(p{\neq}\mathbf{null} \;\Rightarrow\; p.f^{-1} \mapsto S_1) \;*\; (Q{\neq}\mathbf{null} \;\Rightarrow\; Q.f^{-1} \mapsto S_2) \\
&\} \\
&\quad r.f := p \\
&\{ \\
&\quad r{=}R{\neq}\mathbf{null} \;\wedge\; p{=}P{\neq}Q \;\wedge\; r.f \mapsto p \\
&\quad * \;(p{\neq}\mathbf{null} \;\Rightarrow\; p.f^{-1} \mapsto S_1 - \{r\}) \;*\; (Q{\neq}\mathbf{null} \;\Rightarrow\; Q.f^{-1} \mapsto S_2 \cup \{r\}) \\
&\}
\end{aligned}
$$

and second, for the contrived case $p = q$

$$
\begin{aligned}
&\{ \; r{=}R{\neq}\mathbf{null} \;\wedge\; p{=}P \;\wedge\; r.f \mapsto P \;*\; (P{\neq}\mathbf{null} \;\Rightarrow\; P.f^{-1} \mapsto S) \; \} \\
&\quad r.f := p \\
&\{ \; r{=}R{\neq}\mathbf{null} \;\wedge\; p{=}P \;\wedge\; r.f \mapsto P \;*\; (P{\neq}\mathbf{null} \;\Rightarrow\; P.f^{-1} \mapsto S) \; \}
\end{aligned}
$$

Example 1. In this simple example, we will show how the backpointers discipline makes it possible to express reference counting, and how we can use reference counting to protect shared data from mutation.

Suppose that we have two types Cell and Client. Clients have a reference field f to cells. Many clients may share a cell and we are interested in keeping track of them. Therefore f is a tracked field:

```
struct Client { tracked f : Cell; }
```

---

[1] In this sense, backpointer fields are like JML's model fields [12]. Unlike model fields however, backpointer fields are associated with permissions.

[2] For simplicity, assume that r and p are local variables.

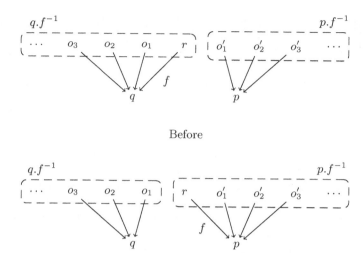

Fig. 3. Assignment to a tracked field $r.f := p$. This diagram depicts the case where p is not equal to the original value q of $r.f$ and where both p and q are non-null.

A cell has an integer field data and a reference counter refCount. If n clients point to the cell, then each of them holds ϵ permission and $1 - n\epsilon$ remains in the monitor invariant of the cell. The reference counter must be equal to n. Using the ghost field f^{-1}, the requirement is stably expressible:

```
struct Cell
{
    data , refCount : int ;
    invariant ∃B· f⁻¹↦B  *  refCount↦|B|  *  data⟼^{1−|B|ε}_
}
```

It is impossible for a client to add/remove a reference to a cell c without first acquiring it (because one needs write access to $c.\,f^{-1}$ to perform such an assignment). After acquiring c, if the client wishes to release c, it must also update the reference counter appropriately, since otherwise the monitor invariant of c will not hold. Here is an example of a client which correctly adds a reference to a cell:

```
acquire c;
cl:=new Client;
cl.f:=c;
c.refCount := c.refCount+1;
release c;
```

Every client that references c holds an ϵ permission to $c.\mathtt{data}$. For example, in the above code, the client has gained an ϵ permission to $c.\mathtt{data}$, because it added a new reference to c.

A holder of an ϵ permission to $c.\mathtt{data}$ can probe the reference counter of c, to see if it shares the cell with any other client. If the reference counter is 1, then the holder may acquire the cell, combine its ϵ permission with the $1 - \epsilon$ permission to $c.\mathtt{data}$, and obtain write permission to $c.\mathtt{data}$. Here is a client that does this correctly:

```
//  here:  c.data↦_
acquire c;
if (c.refCounter=1)
{
    //  here we can  prove  c.data↦_
  c.data:=42;
}
```

So long as the reference counter is greater than 1, it is not possible for a client to gain write access to the data.   □

2.3   Soundness

In this subsection, we give an brief informal argument to explain why the back-pointers discipline is sound.

The extension of a specification and programming language with backpointers imposes the soundness requirement that the definitional axiom of backpointers (1) is a *system invariant*, i.e., a property that holds at any given state during the execution of the program.

Consider a programming language that supports all the features that we have introduced so far: mutable records, locking, assignment, conditionals, procedures, sequential and parallel composition. Assume a standard small step semantics for that programming language. The rule for field assignment in this language is

$$[\![e_1 \neq \mathbf{null}]\!](\sigma) \;\;\Rightarrow\;\; \langle e_1.f := e_2, \; \sigma \rangle \rightsquigarrow \sigma[\,([\![e_1]\!](\sigma).f) \rightarrow [\![e_2]\!](\sigma)\,] \quad (2)$$

where $\langle s, \sigma \rangle$ is a configuration, $\rightsquigarrow$ is the operational semantics relation and $[\cdot \rightarrow \cdot]$ is the update notation.

The introduction of backpointers entails the following change to the operational semantic rules:

- Rule (2) applies only when f is a non-tracked field
- Backpointers are introduced as ghost fields. Explicit assignments to them are forbidden.
- If f is a tracked field, then (2) is replaced by the following rule

$$[\![e_1 \neq \mathbf{null}]\!](\sigma) \;\;\Rightarrow\;\; \langle e_1.f := e_2, \; \sigma \rangle \rightsquigarrow \sigma'[\,o.f \rightarrow [\![e_2]\!](\sigma)\,] \quad (3)$$

where

$$o = [\![e_1]\!](\sigma)$$

$$\sigma' = \begin{cases} \sigma''[\ o.f^{-1} \twoheadrightarrow [\![e_1.f.f^{-1}]\!]\,(\sigma) - \{o\}\ ] & if\ [\![e_1.f \neq \mathbf{null}]\!]\,(\sigma) \\ \sigma'' & otherwise \end{cases}$$

$$\sigma'' = \begin{cases} \sigma[\ [\![e_2]\!]\,(\sigma).f^{-1} \twoheadrightarrow [\![e_2.f^{-1}]\!]\,(\sigma) \cup \{o\}\ ] & if\ [\![e_2 \neq \mathbf{null}]\!]\,(\sigma) \\ \sigma & otherwise \end{cases}$$

– The rule for the creation of new records is revised as follows:
  - The new record can only be assigned to a local variable[3]
  - All reference-typed fields of the new record are initialized to **null** and all backpointer fields of the new record are initialized to $\emptyset$

To prove that (1) is a system invariant, we perform a standard induction on the structure of the statements of the language. Notice that (1) can only be falsified by rule (3) and by the creation of new records.

It is easy to see that (3) does not falsify (1). For the creation of new records, we also assume that there are no dangling pointers, as is the case with languages that support garbage collection. Under this assumption, the creation of new records as described above does not falsify (1).

3   Concurrent Copy-on-Write Lists

We now turn our attention to a hard verification problem, that of concurrent copy-on-write lists (CCoWL). We discuss how backpointers help us verify this data structure.

In this section, we highlight the most important aspects of the verification. As we commented above, the specifications, implementations, and proof outlines for all the procedures can be found in [9].

3.1   Description of the Problem

A CCoWL data structure supports a record called list, which represents a mutable sequence of integers. One can create new empty sequences, insert items at the beginning of an existing sequence, update an item at a specific index, and copy one sequence to another. For simplicity, we restrict ourselves to the operations mentioned here, which can already generate all possible graphs in the underlying data structure.

The clients of lists, which may be one or more threads, are given the impression that every list is completely heap-disjoint from all the others and thus can reason about mutations using ordinary separation logic. The specification of the procedures that are available to the clients is shown in Fig. 4. In it, $\mathsf{list}\,(l,L)$ is an abstract predicate that expresses the fact that the list record l represents the integer sequence L, the operator $++$ denotes concatenation, and the expression $L[i \twoheadrightarrow v]$ denotes the sequence L with the content of index i updated to value v. Indexes are zero-based.

---
[3] Assignment to a field is considered syntactic sugar.

$$\{\mathsf{newRec(this)} \; * \; \mathsf{held} \mapsto O\}$$
$$\quad \mathsf{initEmpty(this)}$$
$$\{\mathsf{list(this}, \; []) \; * \; \mathsf{held} \mapsto O \; * \; O \sqsubseteq \mathsf{this}\}$$

$$\{\mathsf{newRec(this)} \; * \; \mathsf{list(other}, \; L) \; * \; \mathsf{held} \mapsto O \; * \; O \sqsubseteq \mathsf{other}\}$$
$$\quad \mathsf{copy(this, other)}$$
$$\{\quad \mathsf{list(this}, \; L) \; * \; \mathsf{list(other}, \; L) \; * \; \mathsf{held} \mapsto O$$
$$* \; O \sqsubseteq \mathsf{this} \; * \; O \sqsubseteq \mathsf{other}\}$$

$$\{\mathsf{list(this}, \; L) \; * \; \mathsf{held} \mapsto O \; * \; O \sqsubseteq \mathsf{this}\}$$
$$\quad \mathsf{insert(this, newValue)}$$
$$\{\mathsf{list(this}, \; [\mathsf{newValue}] +\!\!+ L) \; * \; \mathsf{held} \mapsto O\}$$

$$\{\mathsf{list(this}, \; L) \; * \; \mathsf{held} \mapsto O \; * \; O \sqsubseteq \mathsf{this} \; \wedge \; 0 \leq \mathsf{index} < |L| \;\; \}$$
$$\quad \mathsf{set(this, index, value)}$$
$$\{\mathsf{list(this}, \; L[\mathsf{index} \rightarrow \mathsf{value}]) \; * \; \mathsf{held} \mapsto O\}$$

Fig. 4. Public Specification of CCoWLs

For example, consider the following client:

```
list1 := new List ;
initEmpty ( list1 );
insert ( list1 , 3); insert ( list1 , 2); insert ( list1 , 1);
list2 := new List ;
copy ( list2 , list1 );
set ( list1 , 1, 4);
```

We can use ordinary separation logic and the specifications of Fig. 4 to prove that, at the end of the execution, list1 contains the sequence $[1, 4, 3]$, and list2 contains $[1, 2, 3]$.

Behind the scenes however, the data structure performs *lazy copying*: all operations are implemented with reference manipulations *as long as this does not influence the clients' disjointness illusion*. Copying happens only when necessary.

The underlying representation uses linearly linked lists of node records. First the implementation creates such a linked list to represent that list1 contains the sequence [1,2,3] (Fig. 5a). After that, a new list list2 is created and it is initialized by copying list1. The client may pretend that the lists are disjoint, but the implementation is being lazy: it just sets the head node reference of list2 to point to the head node of list1, producing the situation in Fig. 5b. Finally, the client sets the item 1 of list1 to 4. The change must influence only list1 and not list2. The implementation must now copy the first two nodes of the common underlying structure, and then perform the set operation in a way that ensures that list2 is not affected. The last node remains shared. The final situation is shown in Fig. 5c.

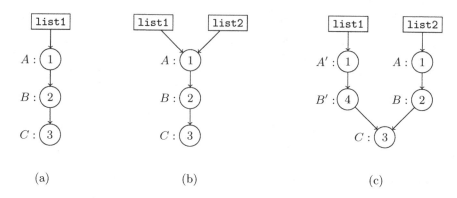

Fig. 5. An example of CCoWL history

To achieve this copy-on-write effect, the nodes are equipped with a reference counter. When a `set` operation occurs, then the affected list is traversed from the head to the index where the update should happen. During the traversal, the reference counter of all the nodes is examined. As long as the reference count equals 1, the procedure knows that only one list is affected. As soon as the procedure meets a reference count greater than 1, it knows that, from that point on, more than one lists are affected. At that point, the procedure copies the nodes of the list all the way to the index where the update should happen.

Starting from Fig. 5c, a `set(list1 , 1, 10)` operation will only find reference counts of 1 in its way and will perform no copying. On the contrary, `set(list1 , 2, 10)` will find that the reference count of the node it is trying to mutate is 2, thus it must copy this node, separating the two lists completely.

3.2   Record Definitions, Abstract Predicates, and Invariants

Our implementation contains `List` and `Node` records. A `List` record contains a reference to a *head node*. The reference should be tracked, because it should be counted in the reference count of the head node.

```
struct List { tracked head : Node }
```

If `head` points to `null`, then the list record represents the empty sequence.

A `Node` record contains a value, a tracked reference to the next node, and a reference count. We defer the monitor invariant of nodes for later.

```
struct Node
{
  value , refCount : int ;
  tracked  next : Node;
  invariant  ...
}
```

We now define the abstract predicate list. The definition uses the auxiliary abstract predicate node:

```
predicate list(this:List, L:ℤ*)
{
    ∃H ∈Node· shared(this,_) * this.head↦H
        * ((node(H,L) * this⊏H) ∨ (H=null ∧ L=[]))
}


predicate node(this:Node, L:ℤ*)
{
    L≠[] ∧
    ∃N ∈Node·
        this.value↦ᵉL[0] * this.next↦ᵉN * shared(this,_)
        * ((node(N,L[1..]) * this⊏N) ∨ (N=null ∧ |L|=1))
}
```

The predicate node traverses the structure following recursively the next references of the node records it encounters. The represented sequence is not empty. The first item L[0] of the sequence is stored in field value. The rest of the sequence L[1..] is represented by the node pointed to by field next, if one exists. The lock-order of node n is below that of n.next, because we intend to acquire monitors of nodes in the order in which we traverse the structure. Similarly, the lock-order of a list l is below that of l.head.

If a node record n is reachable from a list record l, then it contributes to the value of the sequence that l represents. We then say that l is *interested* in n.

Note that each holder of a list(l, L) predicate has ϵ access to all the value and next fields of the nodes in which l is interested. The rest of the permissions to these fields are in the monitors of their respective records. So, if a node record interests n different lists, then it stores in its monitor $1 - n\epsilon$ permission to its fields value and next.

So far, this pattern is exactly the same as the one we have seen in Ex. 1. There is however a complication: the reference counter of a node does *not* indicate how many lists are interested in it. For example, consider Fig. 6, in which a possible state of a CCoWL structure is shown. Both nodes A and B interest three lists, however their reference counters are 2 and 1 respectively.

To deal with this problem, we introduce a *ghost* field in Node. This field counts how many lists are interested in the current node. We call it transRefCount (for *transitive reference counter*). In Fig. 6, we see not only the reference counters but also the transitive reference counters of all the nodes.

We now know the following about the monitor invariant of the Node type:

− It grants permission $1 - T\epsilon$ to the fields value and next, where T is the value of the transitive reference counter:

$$value\xmapsto{1-T\epsilon} V * next\xmapsto{1-T\epsilon} N$$

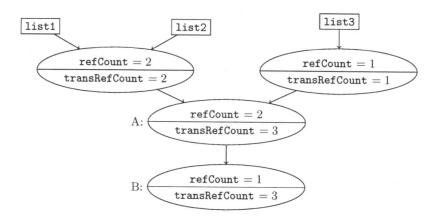

Fig. 6. Reference and Transitive Reference Counters in a CCoWL

- It grants full access to the fields head^{-1} and next^{-1}:

$$\mathsf{head}^{-1} \mapsto B_1 \ * \ \mathsf{next}^{-1} \mapsto B_2$$

- The value of the reference counter is equal to $|B_1| + |B_2|$. The field $\mathsf{refCount}$ is granted full access, as it should be possible for the thread that acquires the node to update the reference counter correctly:

$$\mathsf{refCount} \mapsto |B_1| + |B_2|$$

Notice that the value of the transitive reference counter is equal to the sum of *the transitive reference counters of all nodes that point to the current node* plus the number of list records that point directly to the current node. In order to be able to express this condition, we must grant to the monitor invariant of the current node *read access* to the $\mathsf{transRefCount}$ field of *all the nodes that point to the current node*. We give them 0.5 permission:

$$\exists F \in \mathsf{Node} \rightarrow \mathbb{Z} \cdot \circledast n \in B_2 \cdot n . \mathsf{transRefCount} \xrightarrow{0.5} F(n)$$

The value of the field $\mathsf{transRefCount}$ is given by

$$T = |B_1| + \sum n \in B_2 \cdot F(n)$$

The permission to the field $\mathsf{transRefCount}$ cannot be 1, since, as we have discussed above, the node N that follows the current one has 0.5 permission to it. Therefore, the invariant conjunct that relates $\mathsf{transRefCount}$ to its value is:

$$\mathsf{transRefCount} \xrightarrow{0.5} T$$

The final detail: if N is **null**, then there is no other node that has 0.5 permission to the current node's $\mathsf{transRefCount}$ field. In this case, the monitor invariant of the current node should include the extra permission:

$$N=\textbf{null} \implies \text{transRefCount} \overset{0.5}{\longmapsto} T$$

Putting it all together, the definition of Node, together with the monitor invariant, is:

```
struct Node
{
    value , refCount : int ;
    ghost transRefCount : int ;
    tracked next : Node ;
    invariant ∃T ∈ ℤ, N ∈ Node, B₁ ∈ 2^Head, B₂ ∈ 2^Node, F ∈ Node → ℤ ·
        value ^{1−Tε}↦ _ * next ^{1−Tε}↦ N * head⁻¹↦B₁ * next⁻¹↦B₂
      * refCount↦|B₁|+|B₂| * transRefCount ^{0.5}↦ T
      * ( ⊛n ∈ B₂·n.transRefCount ^{0.5}↦ F(n))
      * (N=null ⇒ transRefCount ^{0.5}↦ T )
      ∧  T =  |B₁| + ∑n ∈ B₂·F(n)
}
```

3.3   Some Highlights of the Implementation

In this section, we discuss three interesting aspects of the implementation: how lists gain and lose interest to nodes and how the updating procedure decides how to substitute in-place update by copy-and-update.

Gaining Interest. In our procedures, the only place where a list gains interest to new nodes is lazy list copying. When a list is copied, only the head reference of the target list changes. The target list gains interest to all the nodes of the source list. To ensure that our bookkeeping is correct, we must update the transitive reference counters of all these nodes. We do this with a *ghost* procedure[4] addOneToTransRefCount, which traverses the whole list and adds 1 to all transitive reference counters.

Losing Interest. Our copy-and-update procedure node_copy_set takes as parameters (besides the obvious index/value pair) a *source* node this and a *target* node new_node. The precondition of node_copy_set asserts that the caller has a predicate node(this , L). Its postcondition returns a predicate node(new_node, L[index→value]). The predicate node(this , L) of the precondition is lost. Indeed, the permissions node(this , L) are taken away from the thread. Those monitors of the nodes to which the source list loses interest obtain an extra ε permission to the corresponding value and next field. For the nodes to which no interest is lost, the thread maintains its ε permissions, but they are now part of the node(new_node, L[index→value]) predicate. In this way, no permission to fields value and next is ever lost.

---

[4] A ghost procedure updates the state by assigning only to ghost fields, and therefore is not executed in the actual program.

For example, consider the situation in Fig. 5b. The permission to the value and next fields that is stored in the monitor of nodes A, B, C is $1 - 2\epsilon$. There is a thread that holds a list(list1, [1,2,3]) predicate, that grants ϵ permission to the value and next fields of these nodes. Now set(list1, 1, 4) is called. Since the reference count of A is 2, a new node A' is created and the node_copy_set procedure is called with source A and target A'. The procedure takes away the node(A, [1,2,3]) predicate of the caller and returns a new node(A', [1,4,3]) predicate. The final state is shown in Fig. 5c.

List list1 lost interest in nodes A, B. The ϵ permissions to their value and next fields are returned from the node(A, [1,2,3]) predicate back to their monitor, which now maintains $1-\epsilon$ permission to these fields. The list maintained interest to node C, so an ϵ permission to the value and next fields of C is transferred from node(A, [1,2,3]) to node(A', [1,4,3]). The monitor of C has $1 - 2\epsilon$ permission to those fields, as before. The predicate node(A', [1,4,3]) has ϵ permission to the value and next fields of the newly generated A' and B' nodes. There was no loss of permission; only permission transfer.

Setting without Copying. As we have explained, the algorithm decides to start the copy-and-update procedure once it sees a reference counter greater than 1. To verify that this policy is indeed correct, we include a precondition to our update-in-place procedure node_set that the transitive reference counter of the node it is applied to equals 1.

The algorithm calls node_set on the next node, under the circumstance "I have not yet seen a reference counter greater than 1 and the reference counter of the next node is 1". In our formalism, this is translated into:

$$\text{this.refCount} \mapsto 1 \ * \ \text{this.transRefCount} \overset{0.5}{\mapsto} 1$$
$$* \ \text{this.next} \mapsto N \ * \ N.\text{refCount} \mapsto 1 \ \wedge \ N \neq \textbf{null}$$

From this condition, together with the fact that $Inv(\text{this})$ and $Inv(N)$ hold, one must prove that the value of the transitive reference counter of N is 1. In the following, we explain how we prove this property.

Let B_1 be the value of $N.\text{head}^{-1}$ and B_2 be the value of $N.\text{next}^{-1}$. By the definitional axiom, we know that $\text{this} \in B_2$. By $Inv(N)$, we conclude that $B_2 = \{\text{this}\}$ and $B_1 = \emptyset$. Again by $Inv(N)$, we get that the value of $N.\text{transRefCount}$ is equal to the value of $\text{this.transRefCount}$, which is 1.

The above argument applies when node_set recursively calls itself. Initially however, it is procedure set (the update procedure on lists) that decides whether it should call node_set or node_copy_set on its head node. The argument for this decision is similar.

4   Discussion

4.1   Related Work

Invariant Disciplines. An *invariant discipline* is a set of rules that specifiers and programmers have to follow to ensure that some state (or history) conditions remain true throughout a computation (or at specific states thereof). Some such conditions are independent of the program, for example, our methodology guarantees that the backpointer definitional axiom (1) holds in any state σ. We call these conditions *system invariants*. Some other conditions are given by the programmer, for example *object* or *monitor invariants*. There are several flavors of treating program-specific invariants, mostly focusing on the special case of object invariants [13]. Various forms of ownership [14, 15] are popular invariant disciplines.

Parkinson [16] comments that object invariants are inflexible, in comparison to the use of abstract predicates. Summers et al. [8] answer by making the case for object invariants as an independent specification tool. Most of their arguments have to do with the usefulness of object invariants in practical software engineering contexts; but they also provide an example (the priority inheritance protocol [7]) as one in which object invariants can turn a seemingly global property (in our terminology, a backpointer property) into a local one. It seems, the authors argue, that the priority inheritance protocol example is not easy to handle with abstract predicates alone.

Our paper provides a monitor invariant discipline that can handle such backpointer examples. The discipline consists of restricting the use of assignments to tracked fields. We have expressed our discipline not as a set of rules, as is common, but by using permissions in the separation logic style. Our proposal makes it possible to treat backpointer conditions as special cases of separation logic conditions, turning them into local properties, which supports the argument of [8], in the concurrent case.

Our verification of CCoWLs is influenced by *considerate reasoning* [17], a framework in which it is possible for a procedure to "notify" via specification annotations all interested parties about the object invariants that it might break. Our specification and implementation of addOneToTransRefCount is a direct adaptation of their addToTotal method.

Observational Disjointness. While separation logic has been a revolution in the specification of heap-intensive computations, it has been observed, especially in the context of concurrency, that the association of separating conjunction with actual heap separation is too restrictive: sometimes we want the client(s) to "observe" disjointness, but, at the same time, allow the implementers the opportunity to share heap under the hood.

In our work, we make use of a standard solution to loosen the heap disjointness requirement: fractional and counting permissions. Furthermore, our use of backpointers permits us to maintain bookkeeping information about the clients of observationally disjoint data structures. These two ingredients together suffice for the verification of the CCoWL case study.

Concurrent abstract predicates [18] support the hidden sharing of state with the use of *capabilities*, i.e., special predicates that allow exclusive access to a shared region. This idea has been successfully applied to the specification and verification of indexing structures [19]. The work presented here cannot substitute for capabilities. On the other hand, it is not clear how one would handle the CCoWL example with CAPs. It seems that backpointers and CAPs are orthogonal tools and could be integrated into a single specification language.

Fictional Separation Logic [20] is an ambitious mathematical framework that allows the implementer to *choose* their own separation algebra as part of the implementation. This idea completely decouples heap disjointness from separating conjunction. The use of fractional permissions as well as other examples of observational disjointness are shown to be special cases of this very general methodology. The generality comes at the price of complexity at the part of the implementer, so it remains an open question if this idea scales up to reasonably-sized programs. Furthermore, it seems that fictional separation logic has no provision for object and monitor invariants, nor does it provide the means of mentioning unreachable parts of the heap, like we do.

In [21], the verification of *snapshotable trees* is proposed as a challenge. The problem is very similar to the CCoWLs: the clients see a mutable tree and immutable snapshots of previous states of that tree. A snapshot can be created at any time. All snapshots and the tree appear to be heap-disjoint, but, in fact, the implementation uses lazy copying and shares as much as possible. There are four different versions of the structure, one of which is verified by the authors, using whole-heap predicates (and therefore restricting it to sequential programs).

The fact that snapshots are immutable is a very crucial difference compared to the CCoWL example, in which all lists are mutable. In the terminology of [22] snapshotable trees are *partially persistent*, while CCoWLs are *fully persistent*. The implementers of snapshotable trees need no permission accounting, because they do not wish to reclaim write permissions to the part of the structure that becomes immutable. Contrary to that, we ensure that no permissions are lost. For example, suppose that exactly two lists l_1, l_2 are interested in a node n. At this state, no thread can change the fields of n. Suppose now that l_2 loses interest. The fields of n become mutable again: the list l_1 may gain write permissions to them. To achieve this, the bookkeeping of backpointers is essential (see also Sect. 3.3, "losing interest").

4.2   Evaluation and Work in Progress

Two significant questions that have not been answered so far are (a) how expressive is the new specification language and (b) how automatable it is.

Expressiveness. In the Introduction, we have mentioned three examples, in which backpointers seem useful. From these examples, we have focused on reference counting, which we have used in a very complex example, CCoWLs, which we have specified, implemented and verified.

It is worth mentioning that our CCoWL example is a fully-persistent data structure [22]. It is a further research direction to investigate how much our proof technique generalizes to fully-persistent data structures in general.

Besides reference counting and the CCoWLs, we have also specified, implemented, and verified the priority inheritance protocol. We are currently working on specifying union-find structures; a challenging problem for which backpointers seem to be particularly promising.

We believe that the potential of the methodology has not yet been fully explored and we expect new interesting case studies to be revealed as experience accumulates.

Automation. We have implemented a prototype verifier for backpointers as an extension of Chalice. We have tested it on a suite of 20 unit tests, observing significant variation in verification times, which is undesirable.

To counter the problem we have experimented with various degrees of restricting the automation. For example, we have given the programmer the possibility to control the triggering of backpointer and set theoretic axioms. We have also introduced explicit annotations for the application of the frame rule, for the framing of aggregate expressions.

The automation of the CCoWL case study has been extremely challenging. At the time of this writing, our tool has verified all but one of the procedures of the present example. The verification of most procedures happens within less than 5 minutes, which is satisfactory. The procedure `node_set_copy` verifies in 90 minutes. The verification of one of the branches of the procedure `node_set` unfortunately seems not to terminate.

To conclude, the automation of the discipline does not yet deliver consistently low verification times and seems to diverge in some cases. Much improvement has been achieved since the beginning of the project, but further research is required to achieve consistently satisfactory performance and less annotation.

5   Conclusion

We have introduced an invariant discipline to enhance the expressiveness of separation logic with backpointer conditions. We have used our methodology to specify and verify concurrent copy-on-write lists, a challenging case study of observational disjointness, which, to the best of our knowledge, has not been tackled before.

Acknowledgements. The authors are deeply grateful to P. Müller and to the three anonymous ESOP reviewers, whose deep and insightful comments significantly helped improve the quality of the paper.

References

1. Reynolds, J.: Separation logic: A logic for shared mutable data structures. In: LICS 2002, pp. 55–74. IEEE Computer Society (2002)
2. Parkinson, M.J., Summers, A.J.: The Relationship between Separation Logic and Implicit Dynamic Frames. In: Barthe, G. (ed.) ESOP 2011. LNCS, vol. 6602, pp. 439–458. Springer, Heidelberg (2011)
3. Smans, J., Jacobs, B., Piessens, F.: Implicit Dynamic Frames: Combining Dynamic Frames and Separation Logic. In: Drossopoulou, S. (ed.) ECOOP 2009. LNCS, vol. 5653, pp. 148–172. Springer, Heidelberg (2009)

4. Kassios, I.T.: Dynamic Frames: Support for Framing, Dependencies and Sharing Without Restrictions. In: Misra, J., Nipkow, T., Sekerinski, E. (eds.) FM 2006. LNCS, vol. 4085, pp. 268–283. Springer, Heidelberg (2006)
5. Bornat, R., Calcagno, C., O'Hearn, P., Parkinson, M.: Permission accounting in separation logic. In: POPL 2005, pp. 259–270 (2005)
6. Boyland, J.: Checking Interference with Fractional Permissions. In: Cousot, R. (ed.) SAS 2003. LNCS, vol. 2694, pp. 55–72. Springer, Heidelberg (2003)
7. Sha, L., Rajkumar, R., Lehoczky, J.P.: Priority inheritance protocols: An approach to real-time synchronization. IEEE Trans. Comput. 39(9), 1175–1185 (1990)
8. Summers, A., Drossopoulou, S., Müller, P.: The need for flexible object invariants. In: IWACO 2009, pp. 1–9. ACM (2009)
9. Kassios, I.T., Kritikos, E.: A discipline for program verification based on back-pointers and its use in observational disjointness. Technical Report 772, Dept. of Computer Science, ETH Zurich (2012),
   http://pm.inf.ethz.ch/publications/getpdf.php?bibname
   =Own&id=KassiosKritikos12.pdf
10. Leino, K.R.M., Müller, P.: A Basis for Verifying Multi-threaded Programs. In: Castagna, G. (ed.) ESOP 2009. LNCS, vol. 5502, pp. 378–393. Springer, Heidelberg (2009)
11. Heule, S., Leino, K.R.M., Müller, P., Summers, A.: Fractional permissions without the fractions. In: FTfJP 2011 (2011)
12. Leavens, G., Baker, A.L., Ruby, C.: JML: a notation for detailed design. In: Kilov, I., Rumpe, B., Simmonds, I. (eds.) Behavioral Specifications of Businesses and Systems, pp. 175–188. Kluwer (1999)
13. Drossopoulou, S., Francalanza, A., Müller, P., Summers, A.J.: A Unified Framework for Verification Techniques for Object Invariants. In: Vitek, J. (ed.) ECOOP 2008. LNCS, vol. 5142, pp. 412–437. Springer, Heidelberg (2008)
14. Leino, K.R.M., Müller, P.: Object Invariants in Dynamic Contexts. In: Odersky, M. (ed.) ECOOP 2004. LNCS, vol. 3086, pp. 491–515. Springer, Heidelberg (2004)
15. Müller, P.: Modular Specification and Verification of Object-Oriented Programs. LNCS, vol. 2262. Springer, Heidelberg (2002)
16. Parkinson, M.: Class invariants: the end of the road? In: IWACO 2007 (2007)
17. Summers, A.J., Drossopoulou, S.: Considerate Reasoning and the Composite Design Pattern. In: Barthe, G., Hermenegildo, M. (eds.) VMCAI 2010. LNCS, vol. 5944, pp. 328–344. Springer, Heidelberg (2010)
18. Dinsdale-Young, T., Dodds, M., Gardner, P., Parkinson, M.J., Vafeiadis, V.: Concurrent Abstract Predicates. In: D'Hondt, T. (ed.) ECOOP 2010. LNCS, vol. 6183, pp. 504–528. Springer, Heidelberg (2010)
19. da Rocha Pinto, P., Dinsdale-Young, T., Dodds, M., Gardner, P., Wheelhouse, M.: A simple abstraction for complex concurrent indexes. In: OOPSLA 2011, pp. 845–864. ACM (2011)
20. Jensen, J.B., Birkedal, L.: Fictional Separation Logic. In: Seidl, H. (ed.) ESOP 2012. LNCS, vol. 7211, pp. 377–396. Springer, Heidelberg (2012)
21. Mehnert, H., Sieczkowski, F., Birkedal, L., Sestoft, P.: Formalized Verification of Snapshotable Trees: Separation and Sharing. In: Joshi, R., Müller, P., Podelski, A. (eds.) VSTTE 2012. LNCS, vol. 7152, pp. 179–195. Springer, Heidelberg (2012)
22. Driscoll, J.R., Sarnak, N., Sleator, D.D., Tarjan, R.E.: Making data structures persistent. In: STOC 1986, pp. 109–121. ACM (1986)

Modular Reasoning about Separation of Concurrent Data Structures

Kasper Svendsen[1], Lars Birkedal[1], and Matthew Parkinson[2]

[1] IT University of Copenhagen
{kasv,birkedal}@itu.dk
[2] Microsoft Research Cambridge
mattpark@microsoft.com

Abstract. In a concurrent setting, the usage protocol of standard separation logic specifications are not refinable by clients, because standard specifications abstract all information about potential interleavings. This breaks modularity, as libraries cannot be verified in isolation, since the appropriate specification depends on how clients intend to use the library.

In this paper we propose a new logic and a new style of specification for thread-safe concurrent data structures. Our specifications allow clients to refine usage protocols and associate ownership of additional resources with instances of these data structures.

1 Introduction

Why? One of the challenges of specifying the abstract behavior of a library is that the appropriate specification depends on the context in which the library is going to be used. Consider a simple bag library with operations to push and pop elements from the bag. In a sequential setting the standard separation logic specification is:

$$\{\mathsf{bag}_e(\mathsf{x}, X)\}\ \mathsf{x.Push(y)}\ \{\mathsf{bag}_e(\mathsf{x}, X \cup \{\mathsf{y}\})\}$$
$$\{\mathsf{bag}_e(\mathsf{x}, X)\}\ \ \mathsf{x.Pop()}\ \ \{\mathsf{ret.}\ (X = \emptyset \wedge \mathsf{ret} = \mathsf{null} \wedge \mathsf{bag}_e(\mathsf{x}, X)) \vee$$
$$(\exists Y.\ X = Y \cup \{\mathsf{ret}\} \wedge \mathsf{bag}_e(\mathsf{x}, Y))\}$$

$$\mathsf{bag}_e(\mathsf{x}, X) * \mathsf{bag}_e(\mathsf{x}, Y) \Rightarrow \bot$$

Here bag_e is an abstract predicate, i.e., implicitly existentially quantified, so that clients cannot depend on its definition [2], x is a reference to a bag object, and X and Y range over multisets of elements. The implication in the third line expresses that the bag_e predicate cannot be duplicated. Hence this specification enforces that clients follow a strict usage protocol, with a single exclusive owner of the bag object. On the other hand, this specification allows the owner of the bag to track the exact contents of the bag. In other words, $\mathsf{bag}_e(\mathsf{x}, X)$ asserts full ownership of the bag and that the bag contains exactly the objects in the multiset X.

Now consider a client of the bag library and suppose this client wants to implement a bag of independent tasks scheduled for execution. This client might

M. Felleisen and P. Gardner (Eds.): ESOP 2013, LNCS 7792, pp. 169–188, 2013.
© Springer-Verlag Berlin Heidelberg 2013

not care about the exact contents of the bag, only that each task in the bag owns the resources necessary to perform its task. In addition, this client might wish to share the bag to allow multiple users to schedule tasks for execution. Thus this client might prefer the following specification for shared bags:

$$\{bag_s(x, P) * P(y)\}\ x.Push(y)\ \{bag_s(x, P)\}$$
$$\{bag_s(x, P)\}\ x.Pop()\ \{ret.\ bag_s(x, P) * (ret = null\ \lor\ P(ret))\}$$
$$bag_s(x, P) \Rightarrow bag_s(x, P) * bag_s(x, P)$$

This specification allows more sharing, but it does not track the exact contents of the bag. Instead, it allows clients to associate additional resources with each element of the bag using the P predicate, and to freely share the bag as expressed by the implication in the third line. Clients thus transfer P(y) to the bag when pushing y, and receive P(ret) from the bag, when pop returns a non-null element.

In a sequential first-order setting without reentrancy, the standard separation logic specification suffices. Using techniques from fictional separation logic [11], clients can refine the standard specification to allow the additional sharing of the shared bag specification. However, in a concurrent setting, it is easy to come up with a non-thread-safe implementation (without synchronization), that satisfies the standard specification (as it enforces a single exclusive owner), but not the shared bag specification. Hence, in a higher-order concurrent setting with reentrancy, this type of refinement is unsound!

What?   The key challenge is to provide a logic that enables clients to refine the specifications to their requirements in a concurrent setting. In this paper we propose such a logic, called Higher-Order Concurrent Abstract Predicates (HOCAP), and a new style of specification for thread-safe concurrent data structures.[1] This style of specification allows clients to refine the usage protocol and associate ownership of additional resources with instances of the data structure, in a concurrent higher-order setting.

How?   Observe first that while it is not sound to refine specifications to allow *more sharing* in a concurrent setting, it is sound to refine specifications to permit *less sharing*. Thus we will start with a weak specification that allows unrestricted sharing of instances of the data structure, and then let clients refine this specification as needed.

To reason about sharing we partition the state into *regions*, with *protocols* governing how the state in each region is allowed to evolve, following earlier work on concurrent abstract predicates [5]. Our new program logic, HOCAP, also uses *phantom fields* – a logical construct akin to auxiliary variables, that only occur in the logic.

To support abstract refinement of library specifications, we propose to verify the implementation using a region to share the concrete state of the implementation, with a fixed protocol that *relates* the concrete state of the implementation

---

[1] We consider a concurrent data structure thread-safe if each of its methods has one *or more* synchronization points, where the abstract effects of the method appear to take affect. See Related Work for a discussion of the relation to linearizability.

with an abstract description of the state of the data structure. To refine this specification, clients define a region of their own, with a protocol on the *abstract state*
of the data structure. For soundness, these two regions must evolve in lock-step
and *synchronize* when the abstract state changes (in synchronization points).
We do so by giving each region a half permission to a shared phantom field;
synchronization can then be enforced since updating a phantom field requires
full permission. Half permissions have previously been used to synchronize local
and shared state [14]; here we are using it to synchronize two shared regions.

For the bag example, we introduce a phantom field cont that contains the
abstract state of the bag: a multiset of references to the elements in the bag.
The bag constructor also returns a half permission to the phantom field cont:

$$\{\mathsf{emp}\}\mathsf{new\ Bag()}\{\mathsf{ret.\ bag(ret)} * \mathsf{ret_{cont}} \xmapsto{1/2} \emptyset\}$$

Here $\mathsf{ret_{cont}} \xmapsto{1/2} \emptyset$ asserts partial ownership of the phantom cont field. Since the
client obtains half the cont permission upon calling the constructor, the library
cannot update the cont field on its own.

The protocol governing the bag x thus relates the concrete state of the bag
with its abstract state (the value of the cont field):

$$(\exists X.\ \mathsf{x_{cont}} \xmapsto{1/2} X \ * \ \mathsf{list(x, X)}) \quad \rightsquigarrow \quad (\exists X.\ \mathsf{x_{cont}} \xmapsto{1/2} X \ * \ \mathsf{list(x, X)})$$

This protocol permits any atomic update to the region containing the internal
state of bag x from a state satisfying the left side of $\rightsquigarrow$ to a state satisfying the
right side.

To allow the library to update cont in synchronization points, we therefore
transfer the library's half-permission to the client and require the client to update
the phantom field with the abstract effects of the method, and then transfer a
half-permission back to the library. When the client updates the phantom field,
the client is forced to prove that the abstract effects of the method is permitted
by whatever protocols the client may have imposed on the abstract state.

We express the update to the phantom cont field using a *view-shift* [4]. Conceptually, a view-shift corresponds to a step in the instrumented semantics that does
not change the concrete machine state. View-shifts, written $P \sqsubseteq Q$, thus generalize assertion implication by allowing updates to phantom fields (given sufficient
permission) and ownership transfer between the local state and shared regions.

The bag push method thus requires the client to provide a view-shift, to
update the abstract state from X to $X \cup \{y\}$ in the synchronization point:

$$\frac{\forall X.\ \mathsf{x_{cont}} \xmapsto{1/2} X * P \sqsubseteq \mathsf{x_{cont}} \xmapsto{1/2} X \cup \{y\} * Q}{\{\mathsf{bag(x)} * P\}\mathsf{x.Push(y)}\{\mathsf{bag(x)} * Q\}}$$

Here, P and Q are universally quantified and thus picked by the client. Hence,
the client can use P and Q to perform further updates of the instrumented state
in the synchronization point and relate the new abstract state with its local
state. We thus refer to P and Q as synchronization pre- and postconditions.

Likewise, the bag pop operation requires two view-shifts; one, in case the bag is empty in the synchronization point, and another, in case the bag is non-empty in the synchronization point:

$$\frac{x_{cont} \overset{1/2}{\longmapsto} \emptyset * P \sqsubseteq x_{cont} \overset{1/2}{\longmapsto} \emptyset * Q(null)}{\forall X. \ \forall y. \ x_{cont} \overset{1/2}{\longmapsto} X \cup \{y\} * P \sqsubseteq x_{cont} \overset{1/2}{\longmapsto} X * Q(y)}$$
$$\{bag(x) * P\}x.Pop()\{bag(x) * Q(ret)\}$$

Finally, the bag predicate is freely duplicable:

$$bag(x) \Rightarrow bag(x) * bag(x)$$

Note that since P and Q are universally quantified — our logic is *higher order* — the client could potentially pick instantiations referring to the library's region, thus introducing self-referential region assertions. We can illustrate this problem by instantiating P with an assertion that itself refers to the bag in the specification of Push. Since bag(x) asserts that there exists a shared region that owns half the x_{cont} field, it follows that $bag(x) * x_{cont} \mapsto \_ \Rightarrow false$. Hence, by instantiating P with $bag(x) * x_{cont} \overset{1/2}{\longmapsto} \_$, we can derive the postcondition false from the specification of Push.

To prevent this, we introduce a notion of *region type* and a notion of *support*, as an over-approximation of the types of regions a given assertion refers to. Our formal bag specification (presented in Section 3) thus imposes support restrictions on P and Q to ensure the client does not introduce self-referential region assertions.

Another key challenge we address is higher-order protocols. Higher-order protocols are crucial to allow clients to associate ownership of additional resources with shared data structures. For example, to derive the shared bag specification from the generic specification, we use a second region with a protocol that requires clients to transfer ownership of P(x), when pushing x into the bag:

$$(\exists X. \ x_{cont} \overset{1/2}{\longmapsto} X \ * \ \circledast_{y \in x} P(y)) \quad \leadsto \quad (\exists X. \ x_{cont} \overset{1/2}{\longmapsto} X \ * \ \circledast_{y \in x} P(y))$$

Again, P is a predicate variable and could be instantiated to refer to the state and protocol of this and other regions – making the above protocol a higher-order protocol. We also use region types to break a circularity introduced by higher-order protocols. In particular, instead of assigning protocols to individual regions, we assign parameterized protocols to region types. This allows us to reason about higher-order protocols that refer to the region types – and thus, implicitly, the protocol – of other regions. We show that this well-behaved subset of higher-order protocols, called *state-independent* protocols, suffices for sophisticated libraries, such as the Joins library [16].

To summarize, our new logic and specification methodology allows clients to refine the usage protocol of the bag. It also allows clients to transfer ownership of resources to the bag, by transferring them to a client region synchronized with the abstract state of the bag.

More details and examples can be found in the extended version of this article, which is available at http://www.itu.dk/people/kasv/hocap-ext.pdf.

Related Work. Jacobs and Piessens introduced the idea of parameterizing the specification of concurrent methods with ghost code, to be executed in synchronization points [10]. Here we build on their idea, using a much stronger logic based on CAP [5], to address the main problem with their approach.

Instead of regions with protocols, Jacobs and Piessens use ghost objects – data structures built from ghost variables – with handles that represent partial information about the data structure and permissions to modify it. While these handles provide support for reasoning about the state of shared ghost objects, they lack the ability to associate ownership of additional state with ghost objects. Instead, Jacobs and Piessens use the lock invariant of the lock protecting the concurrent data structure to associate ownership of additional state.

However, this approach is problematic without proper storable locks. In particular, Jacobs and Piessens logic and model of storable locks only supports lock labels parameterized over simple types (i.e., not assertions). This forces the *client* to create the synchronization primitive, so that the *client* can pick a lock invariant containing both the state of the concurrent data structure and any additional resources the client may wish to associated with the data structure. This breaks abstraction, by exposing internal implementation details to the client (the synchronization primitive used) and it requires the client to reprove the shared bag specification every time it is needed. Hence, Jacobs and Piessens cannot derive the shared bag specification. We solve this problem using higher-order protocols.

CAP was designed to verify concurrent data structures [5]. However, the original specifications and proofs are non-modular in the sense that implementations have been verified against unrefinable specifications with fixed usage protocols.

Recently, Dodds et. al. introduced a higher-order variant of CAP to give a generic specification for a library for deterministic parallelism [6]. While their proofs make explicit use of nested region assertions and higher-order protocols, the authors failed to recognize the semantic difficulties these features introduce. Consequently, their reasoning is unsound. In particular, their higher-order representation predicates are not stable.

Another approach for achieving modular reasoning is to prove concurrent implementations to be contextual refinements of coarse-grained counterparts – thus taking the coarse-grained counterparts as specifications. Previous efforts for proving such contextual refinements have mostly focused on indirect proofs through a linearizability property on traces of concurrent libraries [9,7]. So far, this approach lacks support for transfer of ownership of resources between client and library. More recently, there has been work on proving such contextual refinements directly, using logical relations [20]. Unless combined with a program logic, both of these approaches restrict all reasoning to statements about contextual refinement or contextual equivalence. As our approach demonstrates, if a Hoare-style specification is what we are ultimately interested in, then contextual refinement is unnecessary; what we really want is a generic specification that is refinable by clients.

Conceptually, linearizability aims to provide a fiction of atomicity to clients of concurrent libraries. Our approach does not. Instead, we aim to allow clients to reason about changes of the abstract state in synchronization points *inside* concurrent libraries. To illustrate the distinction, consider an extension of the bag library with a Push2(x, y) method that takes two elements and pushes them one at a time (i.e., with the implementation Push(x); Push(y)). This method is not linearizable, as it has two synchronization points. However, it still has a natural specification expressed in terms of two view-shifts, one for each synchronization point:

$$\frac{\forall X.\ x_{cont} \xmapsto{1/2} X * P \sqsubseteq x_{cont} \xmapsto{1/2} X \cup \{y\} * Q \qquad \forall X.\ x_{cont} \xmapsto{1/2} X * Q \sqsubseteq x_{cont} \xmapsto{1/2} X \cup \{z\} * R}{\{bag(x) * P\}x.Push2(y,z)\{bag(x) * R\}}$$

From this specification, a client can derive a natural shared bag specification:

$$\{bag_s(x, P) * P(y) * P(z)\}x.Push2(y, z)\{bag_s(x, P)\}$$

Contributions. We propose a new style of specification for thread-safe concurrent data structures. Using protocol synchronization, this style of specification allows clients to refine the usage protocol of concurrent data structures. Moreover, using nested region assertions and state-independent higher-order protocols, our specification style allows clients to associate additional resources with the data structure.

Technically, we realize the ideas by developing HOCAP, a higher-order separation logic for a subset of C♯ featuring named delegates and fork concurrency. The logic allows two or more protocols to be synchronized and evolve in lock-step. In addition, we support nested region assertions, state-independent higher-order protocols, and guarded recursive assertions. We present a step-indexed model of the logic and use it to prove the logic sound. We emphasize that unlike earlier versions of CAP, our logic includes sufficient proof rules for carrying out all proofs (including stability proofs) of examples *in the logic*, i.e., without passing to the semantics.

Lastly, in the extended version we demonstrate the power and utility of the logic by verifying a library for executing tasks in parallel, based on Doug Lea's Fork/Join framework [12]. We have also used the logic to specify and verify the Joins library [16] and clients thereof, which will be described in a separate paper.

2   The Logic

Our logic is a general program logic for a subset of C♯, featuring delegates referring to named methods[2] and an atomic compare-and-swap statement. New threads are

---

[2] Anonymous delegates in C♯ may capture the *l*-values of free variables and hence the semantics and logic for anonymous methods is non-trivial, see our earlier paper [18]. Those semantic issues are orthogonal to what we discuss in the present paper and hence we omit anonymous delegates here.

allocated via a fork statement that forks a delegate. Each thread has a private stack, but all threads share a common heap. We use an interleaving semantics.

The specification logic is an intuitionistic higher-order logic over a simply typed term language, and the assertion logic an intutionistic higher-order separation logic over the same simply typed term language. Types are closed under the usual type constructors, $\rightarrow$, $\times$, and $+$. Basic types include the type of assertions, Prop, the type of specifications, Spec, the type of $C^\sharp$ values, Val, and the type of fractional permissions, Perm.

2.1   Concurrent Abstract Predicates

Recall that the basic idea behind CAP is to provide an abstraction of possible interference from concurrently executing threads, by partitioning the state into regions, with protocols governing how the state in each region is allowed to evolve. Requiring all assertions to be *stable* – i.e., closed under protocols – and proving all specifications with respect to arbitrary stable frames, then achieves thread-local reasoning about shared mutable state.

Following earlier work on CAP [5], we use a shared region assertion, written $\boxed{\mathsf{P}}^{r,t,a}$, which asserts that r is a region and that the resources in region r satisfy the assertion P. Unlike earlier versions, the region assertion is also annotated with a region type t and a protocol argument a, since we assign parameterized protocols to region types instead of regions, as mentioned above. Region assertions are freely duplicable and thus satisfy,

$$\boxed{\mathsf{P}}^{r,t,a} \Leftrightarrow \boxed{\mathsf{P}}^{r,t,a} * \boxed{\mathsf{P}}^{r,t,a} \tag{1}$$

Protocols consist of *named actions* and updates to a shared region require *ownership* of a named action justifying the update. Protocols are specified using protocol assertions, written $\mathsf{protocol}(t, I)$. Here t is a region type and I is a parametric protocol. We use the following notation for a parametric protocol I with parameter a and named actions $\alpha_1, ..., \alpha_n$:

$$I(a) = (\alpha_1 : (\Delta_1). \; \mathsf{P}_1 \rightsquigarrow \mathsf{Q}_1; \cdots ; \alpha_n : (\Delta_n). \; \mathsf{P}_n \rightsquigarrow \mathsf{Q}_n)$$

Here Δ_i is a context of logical variables relating the action precondition P_i with the action postcondition Q_i. The action α_i thus allows updates from states satisfying P_i to states satisfying Q_i. We use $I(a)[\alpha_i]$ to refer to the definition of the α_i action in protocol I applied to argument a. Hence, $I(a)[\alpha_i] = (\Delta_i). \; \mathsf{P}_i \rightsquigarrow \mathsf{Q}_i$. We use $\boxed{\mathsf{P}}_I^{r,t,a}$ as shorthand for $\boxed{\mathsf{P}}^{r,t,a} * \mathsf{protocol}(t, I)$.

We can distinguish different client roles in protocols through ownership of named actions. An action assertion $[\alpha]_\pi^r$ asserts fractional ownership of the named action α on region r with fraction π. Fractions are used to allow multiple clients to use the same action. We can split or reassemble action assertions using the following property,

$$[\alpha]_{p+q}^r \Leftrightarrow [\alpha]_p^r * [\alpha]_q^r \tag{2}$$

where $p, q, p + q$ are terms of type Perm – permissions in $(0, 1]$.

An assertion p is *stable* if it is closed under interference from the environment. In the absence of self-referential region assertions and higher-order protocols, the region assertion, $\boxed{P}_I^{r,t,a}$ is stable if P is closed under all $I(a)$ actions:[3]

$$\forall \tilde{y}.\ \mathsf{valid}(P \wedge P_i(\tilde{y}) \Rightarrow \bot) \vee \mathsf{valid}(Q_i(\tilde{y}) \Rightarrow P)$$

for all i, where $I(a)[\alpha_i] = (\tilde{x}).\ P_i(\tilde{x}) \rightsquigarrow Q_i(\tilde{x})$.

Example. To illustrate reasoning about sharing, consider a counter with read and increment methods. Since the count can only be increased, this counter satisfies the specification of a monotonic counter [15]:

$$\{\mathsf{counter}(x,n)\}\ x.\mathsf{Increment}()\ \{\mathsf{counter}(x,n+1)\}$$
$$\{\mathsf{counter}(x,n)\}\quad x.\mathsf{Read}()\quad \{\mathsf{ret}.\ \mathsf{counter}(x,\mathsf{ret}) * n \leq \mathsf{ret}\}$$
$$\mathsf{counter}(x,n) \Rightarrow \mathsf{counter}(x,n) * \mathsf{counter}(x,n)$$

Here $\mathsf{counter}(x,n)$ asserts that n is a lower-bound on the current count. Hence we expect that this predicate can be freely duplicated, as expressed by the third line above.

To verify a counter implementation against this specification, we place the current count in a shared region, with a protocol that allows the current count to be increased. Assertions about lower bounds are thus invariant under the protocol. If the counter implementation maintains the current count in field count, then we can specify the counter protocol as follows:

$$\mathsf{counter}(x,n) \stackrel{\mathrm{def}}{=} \exists r, \pi.\ [\mathrm{INCR}]_\pi^r * \boxed{\exists m.\ n \leq m * x.\mathsf{count} \mapsto m}^{r,\mathsf{Counter},x}$$

where I is a parametric protocol with parameter x and a single action INCR, that allows the count field of x to be increased:

$$I(x) = (\mathrm{INCR} : (m,k : \mathsf{N}).\ x.\mathsf{count} \mapsto m * m \leq k \rightsquigarrow x.\mathsf{count} \mapsto k)$$

Here we have used a fixed region type Counter for the counter region r. Since fractional permissions can always be split (2), and region assertions always duplicated (1), it follows that $\mathsf{counter}(x,n) \Rightarrow \mathsf{counter}(x,n) * \mathsf{counter}(x,n)$, as required by the specification. Since the shared region assertion in $\mathsf{counter}(x,n)$ contains no self-referential region assertions or higher-order protocols, to prove it stable, it suffices to show that,

$$\forall m, k.\ \mathsf{valid}((\exists m : \mathsf{N}.\ n \leq m * x.\mathsf{count} \mapsto m) \wedge (x.\mathsf{count} \mapsto m * m \leq k) \Rightarrow \bot) \vee$$
$$\mathsf{valid}(x.\mathsf{count} \mapsto k \Rightarrow (\exists m : \mathsf{N}.\ n \leq m * x.\mathsf{count} \mapsto m))$$

This follows easily by case analysis on $n \leq k$. Lastly, to verify the implementation of Increment and Read, we have to prove they satisfy the protocol, namely that they do not decrease the current count. This is easy.

---

[3] This is a formula in the specification logic; P and Q are assertions and for an assertion P, $\mathsf{valid}(P)$ is the specification that expresses that P is valid in the assertion logic.

2.2 Higher-Order Concurrent Abstract Predicates

As the above example illustrates, we can use CAP to reason about a shared counter by imposing a protocol on the shared count field. Since this is a protocol on a primitive resource (the count field), first-order CAP suffices. To reason about examples, such as the shared bag, which associates ownership of general resources – through the P predicate – with a shared bag, we need Higher-Order CAP. In particular, to define the bag_s predicate requires region and protocol assertions containing the predicate variable P.

To support modular reasoning about region and protocol assertions containing predicate and assertion variables, ideally, we want to treat predicate and assertion variables as black boxes. For instance, consider the assertion,

$$Q \stackrel{\mathrm{def}}{=} \boxed{P}^{r,t,-} * \mathsf{protocol}(t, I) \qquad (3)$$

where I is the parametric protocol $I(-) = (\tau : P \rightsquigarrow P)$ expressed in terms of the assertion variable P. Treating P as a black box, Q is clearly stable if P is stable, as Q asserts that P holds of the resources in region r, which is clearly closed under the protocol I. However, in general P could itself be instantiated with region and protocol assertions, introducing the possibility of *self-referential region assertions* and turning I into a *higher-order protocol*. This makes reasoning significantly more challenging. In particular, some self-referential region assertions do not admit modular stability proofs: it is possible to instantiate P with stable assertions for which Q is not stable. Furthermore, higher-order protocols introduce a circularity in the definition of the model.

Self-referential Region Assertions. To see how self-referential region assertions can break the modularity of stability proofs, consider assertion P below:

$$P \stackrel{\mathrm{def}}{=} x \mapsto 0 * \boxed{y \mapsto 0}^{r',t',-} * \mathsf{protocol}(t', J),$$

where J is the protocol with a single α action that allows the y variable to be changed from 0 to 1, provided region r owns variable x and x is zero:

$$J(-) = \left(\alpha : \boxed{x \mapsto 0}^{r,t,-} * y \mapsto 0 \rightsquigarrow \boxed{x \mapsto 0}^{r,t,-} * y \mapsto 1 \right)$$

Then P is stable, because P asserts full ownership of the x variable, ensuring that the environment cannot perform the α action, as x cannot also be owned by region r. However, the region assertion Q defined above is not stable when instantiated with this P, as $\boxed{P}^{r,t,-}$ asserts that region r *does* own x, thus allowing the environment to perform the α action. As this example illustrates, some self-referential region assertions thus do not admit modular stability proofs. A similar problem occurs when reasoning about atomic updates to shared regions.

Support. To ensure modular reasoning about stability and atomic updates to shared regions, we require clients to explicitly prove that their instantiations of predicate variables do not introduce self-referential region assertions. To facilitate these proofs, we introduce a notion of support, which gives an over-approximation of the types of regions a given assertion refers to.

An assertion P is supported by a set of region types A, if P is invariant under arbitrary changes to the state and protocol of any region of a region type not in A. To support modular reasoning about hierarchies of concurrent libraries, instead of reasoning directly in terms of sets of regions, we introduce a partial order on region types and reason in terms of upwards-closed sets of region types. More formally, we introduce a new type, RType, of region types with a partial order $\leq$: RType $\times$ RType $\rightarrow$ Spec, with a bottom element $\bot$: RType and finite meets. We say that an assertion P is dependent on region type t if it is supported by the set of region types greater than or equal to t. We introduce two new specification assertions, dep, indep : RType $\times$ Prop $\rightarrow$ Spec for asserting that an assertion is dependent and independent of a given region type, respectively. The inference rules for dep and indep are fairly natural. For instance, if P is dependent on region type t_1, then $\boxed{\text{P}}^{r,t_2,a}$ is dependent on the greatest lower bound, of t_1 and t_2.

Whenever we reason about region assertions, $\boxed{\text{P}}^{r,t,a}$ we thus require that P is independent of the region type t. This excludes self-referential region assertions through protocols (such as in (3)), and through nested region assertions (such as $\boxed{\boxed{\text{P}}^{r,t,a}}^{r,t,a}$).

Stability. General higher-order protocols would introduce a circularity in the definition of the model. We break this circularity by exploiting the indirection of region types – i.e., that we assign protocols to region types instead of individual regions. This allows us to support protocols with assertions about the region types of regions, but without assertions about the protocols assigned to those region types. Technically, we enforce this restriction by ignoring protocol assertions in action pre- and postconditions when interpreting protocols. The parameterized higher-order protocol I,

$$\text{I}(x) = (x \mapsto 0 * \text{protocol}(t, J) \rightsquigarrow x \mapsto 1 * \text{protocol}(t, J))$$

is thus interpreted as $\text{I}(x) = (x \mapsto 0 \rightsquigarrow x \mapsto 1)$. The interpretation simply ignores the protocol(t, J) assertion (See definition of *act* in the technical report [19]).

In the absence of self-referential region assertions, a region assertion $\boxed{\text{P}}_I^{r,t,a}$ is stable under the α action, if P is closed under the action pre- and postcondition of the α action of I(a) and I is a first-order protocol. If I is a higher-order protocol, then the assertion $\boxed{\text{P}}_I^{r,t,a}$ is stable under the α action, if P is closed under the action pre- and postcondition of the α action of $I(a)$ and P is also *protocol-pure*. We thus have the following proof rule for stability:

$$\frac{I(a)[\alpha] = (\bar{x}).I_p(\bar{x}) \rightsquigarrow I_q(\bar{x}) \quad \forall \bar{x}.\ \mathsf{valid}(P \wedge I_p(\bar{x}) \Rightarrow \bot) \vee \mathsf{valid}(I_q(\bar{x}) \Rightarrow P)}{\mathsf{indep}_t(P) \quad \mathsf{indep}_t(Q) \quad \mathsf{stable}(P * Q) \quad \mathsf{pure}_{\mathsf{protocol}}(P) \quad \mathsf{pure}_{\mathsf{state}}(Q)}{\mathsf{stable}_\alpha^r\left(\boxed{P}_I^{r,t,a} * Q\right)}\ \mathrm{SA}$$

Here $\mathsf{pure}_{\mathsf{protocol}}$ and $\mathsf{pure}_{\mathsf{state}}$ are propositions in the specification logic; $\mathsf{pure}_{\mathsf{protocol}}(P)$ expresses that P is invariant under any changes to protocols and $\mathsf{pure}_{\mathsf{state}}(P)$ expresses that P is invariant under any change to the local or shared state. The SA proof rule thus allows us to prove stability of region assertions, by first "pulling out" any protocol assertions, Q, from the region assertion. We say that an assertion is *expressible using state-independent protocols* if the protocol assertions can be "pulled out" in this sense. Formally,

$$\mathsf{sip} \stackrel{\mathsf{def}}{=} \lambda P : \mathsf{Prop}.\ \exists Q, R : \mathsf{Prop}.\ \mathsf{valid}(P \Leftrightarrow Q * R) \wedge \mathsf{pure}_{\mathsf{protocol}}(Q) \wedge \mathsf{pure}_{\mathsf{state}}(R)$$

In particular, if $P \Leftrightarrow Q * R$ and $\mathsf{pure}_{\mathsf{state}}(R)$, then $\boxed{P}_I^{r,t,a} \Leftrightarrow \boxed{Q}_I^{r,t,a} * R$. Thus, if $\mathsf{sip}(P)$, then $\boxed{P}_I^{r,t,a}$ can be rewritten to a form that satisfies the $\mathsf{pure}_{\mathsf{protocol}}$ premise of the SA rule. Expressibility using state-independent protocols is closed under conjunction and separating conjunction, but in general not under disjunction or existential quantification. To achieve closure under existential quantification, $\exists x : X.\ P(x)$, we have to impose a stronger restriction on the predicate family P. Namely, P has to be uniformly expressible using state-independent protocols:

$$\mathsf{usip}_X \stackrel{\mathsf{def}}{=} \lambda P : X \rightarrow \mathsf{Prop}.\ \exists R : \mathsf{Prop}.\ \exists Q : X \rightarrow \mathsf{Prop}.\ \mathsf{pure}_{\mathsf{state}}(R) \wedge$$
$$\forall x \in X.\ (P(x) \Leftrightarrow Q(x) * R) \wedge \mathsf{pure}_{\mathsf{protocol}}(Q(x))$$

Then we have that $\mathsf{usip}_X(P) \Rightarrow \mathsf{sip}(\exists x \in X.\ P(x))$.

2.3 View-Shifts

Phantom State. Proofs in Hoare logic often employ auxiliary variables [13], as an abstraction of the history of execution and state. To support this style of reasoning, without changing the formal operational semantics, we instrument our abstract semantics with phantom fields.

We thus extend our logic with a phantom points-to assertion, written $x_f \overset{p}{\mapsto} v$, which asserts partial ownership, with fraction p, of the phantom field f on object x, and that the current value of the phantom field is v.

Phantom fields live in the instrumented state and are thus updated through view-shifts. Updating a phantom field requires full ownership of the field ($x_f \overset{1}{\mapsto} v_1 \sqsubseteq_\bot x_f \overset{1}{\mapsto} v_2$).[4] A fractional phantom field permission can be split and re-assembled arbitrarily. As a partial fraction only confers read-only ownership, two

---

[4] The view-shift is annotated with the $\bot$ region type; we explain the reason for such annotations on view-shifts in the following.

partial fractional assertions must agree on the current value of a given phantom field ($x_f \overset{p_1}{\mapsto} v_1 * x_f \overset{p_2}{\mapsto} v_2 \Rightarrow v_1 = v_2$). To create a phantom field f we require that the field does not already exist, so that we can take full ownership of the field. We thus require all phantom fields of an object o to be created simultaneously when o is first constructed (in the proof rule for constructors, see the technical report [19]).

Simultaneous Updates. To support synchronization of two regions by splitting ownership of a common phantom field, we need to update the value of the phantom field in both regions *simultaneously*. Previous versions of CAP have only supported sequences of *independent* updates to *single* regions. To support synchronization of protocols we thus extend CAP with support for simultaneous updates of *multiple* regions.

We have chosen a semantics that requires that updates of regions have the same action granularity (you cannot have one simultaneous update of two regions, where the update of one region is justified by one action, and the update of the other region is justified by two actions). This is a choice; it simplifies stability proofs, but it means that we must explicitly track the regions that may have been updated by a view-shift. We thus index the view-shift relation with a region type t. The indexed view-shift relation, $\sqsubseteq_t$, thus describes a *single* update that, in addition to updating the local state, may update *multiple* shared regions with region types not greater than or equal to t, where each update must be justified by a *single* action. The indexed view-shift relation is thus *not* transitive.

Figure 1 contains a selection of proof rules for view-shifts. The two main rules, VSNOPEN and VSOPEN, are used to open a region, to allow access to the resources in that shared region. Both rules allow us to open a region and perform a nested view-shift on the contents of that region. This is how we reason about simultaneous updates to multiple regions in the logic. Rule VSNOPEN allows the nested view-shift to modify further regions, while VSOPEN does not (note the use of region type $\perp$ on the nested view shift in VSOPEN). Both rules require a proof the update is possible –

$$P_1 * P_2 \sqsubseteq_{t_1 \sqcap t_2} Q_1 * Q_2 \qquad \text{and} \qquad P_1 * P_2 \sqsubseteq_\perp Q_1 * Q_2,$$

respectively – and a proof that the update is allowed by the protocol, denoted

$$\boxed{P_1}^{r,t_1,a} * P_2 \rightsquigarrow^{r,t_2} \boxed{Q_1}^{r,t_1,a} * Q_2$$

and explained below.

Since actions owned by shared regions cannot be used to perform updates to shared regions, the VSNOPEN rule further requires that P_1 does not assert ownership of any local action permissions ($\mathsf{pure}_{\mathsf{perm}}(P_1)$). This ensures that no local action permissions from P_1 were used to justify any actions performed in the nested view-shift. Since VSOPEN does not allow the nested view-shift to update any regions, this restriction is unnecessary for the VSOPEN rule.

$$\frac{\text{pure}_{\text{perm}}(P_1) \quad \text{indep}_{t_1 \sqcap t_2}(P_1, P_2, Q_1, Q_2) \quad t_2 \nleq t_1}{\boxed{P_1}^{r,t_1,a} * P_2 \leadsto^{r,t_2} \boxed{Q_1}^{r,t_1,a} * Q_2 \quad P_1 * P_2 \sqsubseteq_{t_1 \sqcap t_2} Q_1 * Q_2} \quad \text{VSNOPEN}}{\boxed{P_1}^{r,t_1,a} * P_2 \sqsubseteq_{t_2} \boxed{Q_1}^{r,t_1,a} * Q_2}$$

$$\frac{\text{indep}_{t_1 \sqcap t_2}(P_1, P_2, Q_1, Q_2) \quad t_2 \nleq t_1}{\boxed{P_1}^{r,t_1,a} * P_2 \leadsto^{r,t_2} \boxed{Q_1}^{r,t_1,a} * Q_2 \quad P_1 * P_2 \sqsubseteq_{\perp} Q_1 * Q_2} \quad \text{VSOPEN}}{\boxed{P_1}^{r,t_1,a} * P_2 \sqsubseteq_{t_2} \boxed{Q_1}^{r,t_1,a} * Q_2}$$

$$\frac{P \sqsubseteq_t Q \quad \text{stable}(R)}{P * R \sqsubseteq_t Q * R} \quad \text{VSFRAME} \qquad\qquad \frac{P \sqsubseteq_{t_1} Q \quad t_1 \leq t_2}{P \sqsubseteq_{t_2} Q} \quad \text{VSWEAKEN}$$

Fig. 1. Selected view-shift proof rules

Update Allowed. The update allowed relation, $P \leadsto^{r,t} Q$, asserts that the update described by P and Q to region r is justified by an action owned by P.

Thus the basic proof rule for the update allowed relation is:

$$\frac{\text{indep}_{t_2}(P(\tilde{v}), Q(\tilde{v})) \quad t_2 \nleq t_1 \quad I(a)[\alpha] = (\tilde{x}).\ P(\tilde{x}) \leadsto Q(\tilde{x})}{\boxed{P(\tilde{v})}^{r,t_1,a} * [\alpha]_\pi^r \leadsto^{r,t_2} \boxed{Q(\tilde{v})}^{r,t_1,a} * [\alpha]_\pi^r} \quad \text{UAACT}$$

Since the update allowed relation simply asserts that any update described by P and Q is allowed, it satisfies a slightly non-standard rule of consequence, that allows strengthening of both the pre- and postcondition. From this non-standard rule-of-consequence, it follows that the update allowed relation satisfies a frame rule that allows arbitrary changes to the context:

$$\frac{P \Rightarrow P' \quad P' \leadsto^{r,t} Q' \quad Q \Rightarrow Q'}{P \leadsto^{r,t} Q} \quad \text{UACONSEQ} \qquad\qquad \frac{P \leadsto^{s,t} Q}{P * R_1 \leadsto^{s,t} Q * R_2} \quad \text{UAF}$$

3 Concurrent Bag

We now return to the concurrent bag from the introduction, and show how to formalize the informal specification from the introduction. Next, we show how to derive the two bag specifications from the introduction, using protocol synchronization, nested region assertions, and higher-order protocols.

Specification. In the introduction we proposed a refineable bag specification with phantom variables to force protocol synchronization and with view-shifts to synchronize client and library in synchronization points. In the formal specification we restrict the synchronization pre- and postconditions, P and Q, using region types, to ensure that the client's instantiation does not introduce self-referential region assertions. Upon creation of new bag instances, the client picks a region type t for that bag instance and the client is then required to prove that all its synchronization pre- and postconditions are independent of region type t. The formal refinable bag specification is:

$$\{\mathsf{emp}\}\mathsf{new}\ \mathsf{Bag}()\{\mathsf{ret}.\ \mathsf{bag}(t,\mathsf{ret}) * \mathsf{ret}_{\mathsf{cont}} \xmapsto{1/2} \emptyset\}$$

$$\frac{\mathsf{stable}(P) \quad \mathsf{stable}(Q) \quad \mathsf{indep}_t(P) \quad \mathsf{indep}_t(Q) \\ \forall x.\ x_{\mathsf{cont}} \xmapsto{1/2} \emptyset * P(x) \sqsubseteq_t x_{\mathsf{cont}} \xmapsto{1/2} \emptyset * Q(x,\mathsf{null}) \\ \forall X.\ \forall x,y.\ x_{\mathsf{cont}} \xmapsto{1/2} X \cup \{y\} * P(x) \sqsubseteq_t x_{\mathsf{cont}} \xmapsto{1/2} X * Q(x,y)}{\{\mathsf{bag}(t,x) * P(x)\}x.\mathsf{Pop}()\{\mathsf{ret}.\ \mathsf{bag}(t,x) * Q(x,\mathsf{ret})\}}$$

$$\frac{\mathsf{stable}(P) \quad \mathsf{stable}(Q) \quad \mathsf{indep}_t(P) \quad \mathsf{indep}_t(Q) \\ \forall X.\ \forall x,y.\ x_{\mathsf{cont}} \xmapsto{1/2} X * P(x,y) \sqsubseteq_t x_{\mathsf{cont}} \xmapsto{1/2} X \cup \{y\} * Q(x,y)}{\{\mathsf{bag}(t,x) * P(x,y)\}x.\mathsf{Push}(y)\{\mathsf{bag}(t,x) * Q(x,y)\}}$$

$$\overline{\mathsf{bag}(t,x) \Leftrightarrow \mathsf{bag}(t,x) * \mathsf{bag}(t,x)} \qquad \overline{\mathsf{dep}_t(\mathsf{bag}(t,x))}$$

The indep_t assumptions on the synchronization pre- and postconditions ensure that P and Q do not introduce self-referential region assertions. Furthermore, the index on the view-shifts, $\sqsubseteq_t$, ensures that the granularity of actions match between the library and any client protocols.

Exclusive Owner. We now show how to derive the standard specification with a single exclusive owner. This specification is very simple to derive; we simply let the exclusive owner of the bag keep the 1/2 permission of the phantom field containing the abstract state of the bag: $\mathsf{bag}_e(t,x,X) \overset{\mathsf{def}}{=} \mathsf{bag}(t,x) * x_{\mathsf{cont}} \xmapsto{1/2} X$.

Shared Bag. The derivation of the shared bag specification is more interesting, as it uses both protocol synchronization and higher-order protocols. We begin by formalizing the shared bag specification in our logic:

$$\frac{\mathsf{dep}_r(P)}{\mathsf{dep}_{r \sqcap t}(\mathsf{bag}_s(t,x,P))} \qquad \frac{\mathsf{stable}(P) \quad \mathsf{indep}_t(P) \quad \mathsf{usip}_{\mathsf{Val}}(P)}{\{\mathsf{emp}\}\mathsf{new}\ \mathsf{Bag}()\{\mathsf{ret}.\ \mathsf{bag}_s(t,\mathsf{ret},P)\}}$$

$$\overline{\{\mathsf{bag}_s(t,x,P) * P(y)\}x.\mathsf{Push}(y)\{\mathsf{bag}_s(t,x,P)\}}$$

$$\overline{\{\mathsf{bag}_s(t,x,P)\}x.\mathsf{Pop}()\{\mathsf{ret}.\ \mathsf{bag}_s(t,x,P) * (\mathsf{ret} = \mathsf{null}\ \vee\ P(\mathsf{ret}))\}}$$

$$\overline{\mathsf{bag}_s(t,x,P) \Leftrightarrow \mathsf{bag}_s(t,x,P) * \mathsf{bag}_s(t,x,P)}$$

This corresponds to the specification from the introduction, except with restrictions on predicate $\mathbb{P}$ to ensure it is expressible using state-independent protocols and does not introduce self-referential protocol or region assertions.

With these restrictions on P we can now derive the shared bag specification from our generic specification. The idea is to introduce a new region containing the state associated with each element currently in the bag:

$$\mathsf{bag}_s(t, x, P) \overset{\mathsf{def}}{=} \exists r : \mathrm{RId}.\ \exists \pi : \mathrm{Perm}.\ \exists t_1, t_2 : \mathrm{RType}.$$

$$t \leq t_1 \wedge t \leq t_2 \wedge t_1 \not\leq t_2 \wedge t_2 \not\leq t_1 \wedge \mathsf{indep}_t(P) \wedge \mathsf{usip}(P) \wedge$$

$$\mathsf{bag}(t_1, x) * \boxed{\mathsf{q}(x, P)}_{\mathsf{I}(P)}^{r, t_2, x} * [\mathrm{Upd}]_\pi^r$$

$$\mathsf{q}(x, P) \overset{\mathsf{def}}{=} \exists X : \mathcal{P}_m(\mathrm{Val}).\ x_{\mathsf{cont}} \overset{1/2}{\longmapsto} X * \circledast_{y \in X} P(y)$$

$$\mathsf{I}(P)(x) \overset{\mathsf{def}}{=} (\mathrm{Upd} : \mathsf{q}(x, P) \rightsquigarrow \mathsf{q}(x, P))$$

The parametric protocol $\mathsf{I}(P)$ allows the bag to be changed arbitrarily, provided the region still contains the state associated with each element currently in the bag. From the assumption that each $P(x)$ is stable and that $\mathsf{usip}_{\mathrm{Val}}(P)$ it follows that $\mathsf{q}(x, P)$ is stable and $\mathsf{sip}(\mathsf{q}(x, P))$. Hence, there exists $R, S : \mathsf{Prop}$ such that $\mathsf{q}(x, P) \Leftrightarrow R * S$, $\mathsf{pure}_{\mathsf{protocol}}(S)$ and $\mathsf{pure}_{\mathsf{state}}(R)$. Thus, $\mathsf{bag}_s(t, x, P)$ is equivalent to the following assertion:

$$\exists r, \pi, t_1, t_2.\ t \leq t_1 \wedge t \leq t_2 \wedge t_1 \not\leq t_2 \wedge t_2 \not\leq t_1 \wedge \mathsf{bag}(t_1, x) * \boxed{S}_{\mathsf{I}(P)}^{r, t_2, x} * R * [\mathrm{Upd}]_\pi^r$$

Hence, to prove $\mathsf{bag}_s(t, x, P)$ stable, it suffices to prove stability of $\boxed{S}_{\mathsf{I}(P)}^{r, t_2, x} * R$. Applying rule SA, it thus suffices to prove,

$$\mathsf{valid}(\mathsf{q}(x, P) \wedge S \Rightarrow \bot) \vee \mathsf{valid}(\mathsf{q}(x, P) \Rightarrow S)$$

and the right disjunct follows easily from the assumption that $\mathsf{q}(x, P) \Leftrightarrow R * S$.

To derive the shared bag specification for **push**, we thus have to transfer the resources associated with the element being pushed, $P(y)$, to the client region containing the element resources. We thus instantiate P and Q in the generic bag specification with $P(y) * \boxed{\mathsf{q}(x, P)}_{\mathsf{I}(P)}^{r, t_2, x} * [\mathrm{Upd}]_\pi^r$ and $\boxed{\mathsf{q}(x, P)}_{\mathsf{I}(P)}^{r, t_2, x} * [\mathrm{Upd}]_\pi^r$, respectively.

We thus have to provide a view-shift to synchronize the abstract state of the library protocol with our client protocol r:

$$\forall X : \mathcal{P}_m(\mathrm{Val}).\ x_{\mathsf{cont}} \overset{1/2}{\longmapsto} X * P(y) * \boxed{\mathsf{q}(x, P)}_{\mathsf{I}(P)}^{r, t_2, x} * [\mathrm{Upd}]_\pi^r \sqsubseteq_{t_1}$$

$$x_{\mathsf{cont}} \overset{1/2}{\longmapsto} (X \cup \{y\}) * \boxed{\mathsf{q}(x, P)}_{\mathsf{I}(P)}^{r, t_2, x} * [\mathrm{Upd}]_\pi^r$$

Since $x_{\mathsf{cont}} \overset{1/2}{\longmapsto} X * P(y) * [\mathrm{Upd}]_\pi^r$ and $\mathsf{q}(x, P)$ are all independent of region type t, by rule VSOPEN it suffices to prove that the change to region r is allowed and possible. The update is easily shown to be allowed by the UPD action, using the UAACT rule and update action frame rule (UAF). To show the possibility of the view shift it suffices to prove that:

$$x_{\mathsf{cont}} \overset{1/2}{\longmapsto} X * P(y) * \exists Z : \mathcal{P}_m(\mathrm{Val}).\ x_{\mathsf{cont}} \overset{1/2}{\longmapsto} Z * \circledast_{z \in Z} P(z) * [\mathrm{Upd}]_\pi^r \sqsubseteq_\bot$$

$$x_{\mathsf{cont}} \overset{1/2}{\longmapsto} (X \cup \{y\}) * \exists Z : \mathcal{P}_m(\mathrm{Val}).\ x_{\mathsf{cont}} \overset{1/2}{\longmapsto} Z * \circledast_{z \in Z} P(z) * [\mathrm{Upd}]_\pi^r$$

which follows easily, as $x_{\mathsf{cont}} \overset{1/2}{\longmapsto} X * x_{\mathsf{cont}} \overset{1/2}{\longmapsto} Z \Rightarrow X = Z$.

Note that to provide a view-shift to synchronize the abstract state of the library protocol with the client protocol, we were essentially forced to update the phantom field cont in the client region, which in turn forced us to transfer ownership of $P(y)$ to the client region.

4 Semantics

In this section we sketch the model and the interpretation of our logic. Due to lack of space, we focus on parts presented in Section 2. The full model, interpretation and accompanying soundness proof can be found in the technical report [19].

The presentation of the model is strongly inspired by the Views framework presentation [4]. The model is an instance of the Views framework extended with step-indexing to model guarded recursion, and thread local state to model dynamic allocation of threads.

The basic structure of the model is defined below. Assertions are modeled as step-indexed predicates on instrumented states ($\mathcal{M}$). Instrumented states consist of three components, a local state, a shared state and an action model. The local state specifies the current local resources. The shared state is further partitioned into regions and each region consists of a local state, a region type and a protocol parameter. The action model maps region types to parameterized protocols, which are functions from a tuple containing a protocol argument, a region identifier and an action identifier to an action. Lastly, actions are modeled as certain step-indexed relations on shared states. In particular, actions are *not* relations on shared states *and* action models, and thus do not support general higher-order protocols. Actions do however support state-independent protocols, through the region type indirection.

$$\text{LState} \stackrel{\text{def}}{=} \text{Heap} \times \text{PHeap} \times \text{Cap} \qquad \text{SState} \stackrel{\text{def}}{=} \text{RId} \rightharpoonup (\text{LState} \times \text{RType} \times \text{Val})$$

$$\mathcal{M} \stackrel{\text{def}}{=} \text{LState} \times \text{SState} \times \text{AMod} \qquad \text{AMod} \stackrel{\text{def}}{=} \text{RType} \rightharpoonup ((\text{Val} \times \text{RId} \times \text{AId}) \rightarrow \text{Act})$$

$$\text{Cap} \stackrel{\text{def}}{=} \{f \in \text{RId} \times \text{AId} \rightarrow [0,1] \mid \exists R \subseteq_{fin} \text{RId}. \ \forall r \in \text{RId} \setminus R. \ \forall \alpha \in \text{AId}. \ f(r, \alpha) = 0\}$$

$$\text{Act} \stackrel{\text{def}}{=} \{R \in \mathcal{P}(\text{N} \times \text{SState} \times \text{SState}) \mid$$
$$\forall (i, s_1, s_2) \in R. \ \forall j \leq i. \ \forall r \in \text{RId} \setminus dom(s_2). \ \forall n \in \text{RType}. \ \forall l, l' \in \text{LState}.$$
$$s_1 \leq s_2 \wedge (j, s_1, s_2) \in R \wedge (j, s_1, s_2[r \mapsto (l', n)]) \in R \wedge$$
$$(j, s_1[r \mapsto (l, n)], s_2[r \mapsto (l', n)]) \in R\}$$

$$\text{Prop} \stackrel{\text{def}}{=} \{U \in \mathcal{P}(\text{N} \times \mathcal{M}) \mid \forall (i, m_1) \in U. \ \forall j \leq i. \ \forall m_2 \in \mathcal{M}.$$
$$(m_1 =_j m_2 \vee m_1 \leq m_2) \Rightarrow (j, m_2) \in U\}$$

$$\text{Spec} \stackrel{\text{def}}{=} \{U \in \mathcal{P}(\text{N}) \mid \forall i \in U. \ \forall j \leq i. \ j \in U\}$$

The semantics of both the assertion logic and specification logic is step-indexed. The specification logic is step-indexed to allow reasoning about mutual recursion. The assertion logic is step-indexed to support nested triples (which embed specifications in the assertion logic) [17] and guarded recursive predicates [1,3]. Specifications are thus modeled as downwards closed subsets of numbers, and assertions are modeled as step-indexed predicates on instrumented states, that are downwards closed in the step-index and upwards closed in $\mathcal{M}$. The upwards closure in $\mathcal{M}$ ensures that assertions are closed under allocation of new regions and protocols (the ordering $\leq$ on $\mathcal{M}$ is defined as expected). To define guarded recursive functions and predicates, the types of our logic are modeled as sets with a step-indexed equivalence relation, $=_i$, and terms and predicates are modeled as non-expansive functions. However, as this part of the model is mostly orthogonal to CAP, we will elide the details, which can be found in the technical report [19].

Comparison with Previous Models of CAP. The original model of (first-order) CAP [5] employed a syntactic treatment of actions to break a circularity in the definition of worlds. Our model follows the previous model of higher-order CAP (without higher-order protocols) [6] in treating actions semantically. However, to support higher-order protocols we introduce a new indirection, in the form of region types. Actions are thus relations on shared states, which include the region types of allocated regions. Actions can thus implicitly refer to the protocol on regions through the region type indirection. While previous work has only considered CAP for a *first-order programming language*, our HOCAP is for a *higher-order programming language*. We thus step-index both the specification and assertion logic, instead of just the specification logic.

Model Operations. Separating conjunction is interpreted as the lifting of the partial commutative $\bullet_{\mathcal{M}}$ function to Prop (point-wise in the step-index). The $\bullet_{\mathcal{M}}$ function expresses how to compose two instrumented states. Two instrumented states are combinable if they agree on the shared state and action model, by combining their local states, using $\bullet_{\text{LState}}$. Local states are combined using the standard combination function, $\bullet_{\uplus}$, on disjoint partial functions, on the heap and phantom heap component, and by point-wise summing up the action permissions.

While assertions are modeled as step-indexed predicates on instrumented states, which include phantom fields, protocols, and regions, the operational semantics operates on concrete states, which are simply heaps. The main soundness theorem (Theorem 1) expresses that any step in the concrete semantics has a corresponding step in the instrumented semantics. This is expressed in terms of an erasure function, $\lfloor - \rfloor \in \mathcal{M} \rightharpoonup \text{Heap}$, that erases the instrumentation from an instrumented state. The erasure of an instrumented state is simply the combination of the local state and all shared regions.

$$\lceil (l, s) \rceil \overset{\text{def}}{=} l \bullet_{\text{LState}} \prod_{r \in dom(s)} s(r).l$$

$$\lfloor (l, s, \varsigma) \rfloor \overset{\text{def}}{=} \begin{cases} h & \text{if } (h, ph, c) = \lceil (l, s) \rceil \text{ and } \pi_1(dom(ph)) \subseteq objs(h) \\ \text{undef} & \text{otherwise} \end{cases}$$

Interference. The interference relation $R_i^A \subseteq \mathcal{M} \times \mathcal{M}$ describes possible interference from the environment. It is defined as the reflexive, transitive closure of the single-action interference relation, $\hat{R}_i^A$ (defined below), that describes possible environment interference using at most one action on each region. Defining

R_i^A as the reflexive, transitive closure of $\hat{R}_i^A$ forces a common action granularity on updates to multiple regions with protocols referring to each other. In addition to the step-index $i \in \mathbb{N}$, the single-action interference relation is also indexed by a set $A \in \mathcal{P}(\text{RType})$ of region types of those regions that are allowed to change and that actions justifying those changes are allowed to depend on.

$$(l_1, s_1, \varsigma_1) \; \hat{R}_i^A \; (l_2, s_2, \varsigma_2) \quad \text{iff} \quad l_1 = l_2 \wedge s_1 \leq s_2 \wedge \varsigma_1 \leq \varsigma_2 \wedge \lceil (l_1, s_1) \rceil \text{ defined } \wedge$$
$$(\forall r \in dom(s_1). \; s_1(r) = s_2(r) \vee (\exists \alpha. \; s_1(r).t \in A \; \wedge$$
$$(\lceil (l_1, s_1) \rceil .c)(r, \alpha) < 1 \wedge (i, s_1|_A, s_2|_A) \in \varsigma_1(s_1(r).t)(s_1(r).a, r, \alpha)))$$

$$s|_A \stackrel{\text{def}}{=} \lambda r \in \text{RId}. \begin{cases} s(r) & \text{if } r \in dom(s) \text{ and } s(r).t \in A \\ \text{undef} & \text{otherwise} \end{cases}$$

In particular, the $\hat{R}_i^A$ relation expresses that the environment is not allowed to change the local state ($l_1 = l_2$), but it is allowed to allocate new regions and protocols ($s_1 \leq s_2$ and $\varsigma_1 \leq \varsigma_2$). Furthermore, the environment is allowed to update the resources of any region r with a region type in A ($s_1(r).t \in A$), provided the update is justified by an action α that is partially owned by the environment ($\lceil (l_1, s_1) \rceil (r, \alpha) < 1$).

An assertion is stable if it is closed under interference to all region types:

$$stable(p) \stackrel{\text{def}}{=} \{i \in \mathbb{N} \mid \forall j \leq i. \; \forall (m_1, m_2) \in R_j^{\text{RType}}. \; (j, m_1) \in p \Rightarrow (j, m_2) \in p\}$$

Previous models of CAP have only permitted multiple independent updates, whereas our model supports multiple dependent updates. Previous models thus lack the A-index that we use to enforce a common action granularity on updates to multiple dependent regions.

View-Shifts. View-shifts describe a step in the instrumented semantics that correspond to a no-op in the concrete semantics. To perform a view-shift from p to q we thus have to prove that for every concrete state c in the erasure of some instrumented state $m \in p$ there exists an instrumented state $m' \in q$ such that c is in the erasure of m'.

$$p \sqsubseteq_t q \stackrel{\text{def}}{=} \{i \in \mathbb{N} \mid \forall m \in \mathcal{M}. \; \forall j \in \mathbb{N}. \; 0 \leq j \leq i \Rightarrow$$
$$\lfloor p * \{(j, m)\} \rfloor_j \subseteq \lfloor q * \{(j, m') \mid m \; \hat{R}_j^{\{t' \mid t \not\leq t'\}} \; m'\} \rfloor_j\}$$

To allow framing on view-shifts (rule VSFRAME in Section 2.3) we bake in framing under certain stable frames. The frames in question depend on the region index $t \in \text{RType}$. In particular, $\sqsubseteq_t$ permits a single simultaneous update of multiple regions with region types not greater than or equal to t, each justified by a single action. Hence, we require that $\sqsubseteq_t$ is closed under arbitrary frames that are stable under a single simultaneous update of multiple regions with region types not greater than or equal to t, each justified by a single action, i.e., $\hat{R}^{\{t' \mid t \not\leq t'\}}$.

Support. In Section 2.2 we introduced specification logic assertions indep and dep, to internalize a notion of region type support in the logic, to allow explicit proofs of the absence of self-referential region assertions. Their meaning is defined in terms of the following supp assertion, which asserts that p is supported by the set of region types $A \in \mathcal{P}(\mathsf{RType})$. Formally, $\mathsf{supp}_A(p)$ asserts that p is closed under arbitrary shared states that agree on all regions of type A ($s|_A = s'|_A$) and arbitrary action models that are A equivalent ($\varsigma \equiv_A \varsigma'$).

$$\mathsf{supp}_A(p) \stackrel{\mathrm{def}}{=} \{i \in \mathsf{N} \mid \forall j \leq i. \; \forall (j, (l, s, \varsigma)) \in p. \; \forall s'. \; \forall \varsigma'.$$
$$s|_A = s'|_A \wedge \varsigma \equiv_A \varsigma' \Rightarrow (j, (l, s', \varsigma')) \in p\}$$

Intuitively, two action models are considered A-equivalent if they agree on the regions of types in A (but they are allowed to differ on regions of types not in A). An assertion p is then dependent on region type $t \in \mathsf{RType}$ if p is supported by the set of region types greater than or equal to t, and independent if it is supported by the set of region types not greater than or equal to t:

$$\mathsf{dep}_t(p) \stackrel{\mathrm{def}}{=} \mathsf{supp}_{\{t' \mid t \leq t'\}}(p) \qquad\qquad \mathsf{indep}_t(p) \stackrel{\mathrm{def}}{=} \mathsf{supp}_{\{t' \mid t \not\leq t'\}}(p)$$

Purity. To reason about state-independent protocols and nested view-shifts we have introduced several types of purity; namely, state, protocol and permission purity. Since our assertion logic is intuitionistic, we interpret purity as closure under arbitrary changes to the state, protocols, and permissions, respectively. For instance, $pure_{prot}(p) \stackrel{\mathrm{def}}{=} \{i \in \mathsf{N} \mid \forall j \leq i. \; \forall (j, (l, s, \varsigma)) \in p. \; \forall \varsigma'. \; (j, (l, s, \varsigma')) \in p\}$.

Soundness. The main soundness theorem expresses that for any derivable Hoare triple, $\{p\}\bar{c}\{q\}$, if $\bar{c}$ is executed with a local stack s as thread t, with a global heap h that is in the erasure of some instrumented state in $p(s)$, then, if t (and any threads t may have forked) terminates, then the terminal heap h' is in the erasure of some instrumented state in $q(s')$, where s' is the terminal stack of t.

Theorem 1. *If* $\Gamma \vdash (\Delta).\{P\}\bar{c}\{Q\}$ *then for all* $\vartheta \in \llbracket \Gamma \rrbracket$, *thread identifiers* $t \in$ *TId, stacks* $s \in \llbracket \Delta \rrbracket$, *and heaps* $h \in \lfloor \llbracket \Gamma; \Delta \vdash P : \mathit{Prop} \rrbracket(\vartheta, s) \rfloor$, *if*

$$(h, \{(t, s, \bar{c})\}) \rightarrow (h', \{(t, s', skip)\} \uplus T')$$

and T' *is irreducible then* $h' \in \lfloor \llbracket \Gamma; \Delta \vdash Q : \mathit{Prop} \rrbracket(\vartheta, s') \rfloor$.

5   Conclusion and Future Work

We have proposed a new style of specification for thread-safe data structures that allows the client to refine the specification with a usage protocol, in a concurrent setting. We have shown how to apply it to the bag and concurrent runner example. To realize this style of specification we have presented a new higher-order separation logic with Concurrent Abstract Predicates, that supports state-independent higher-order protocols and synchronization of multiple regions. We have also used the logic to specify and verify Joins, a sophisticated library implemented using higher-order code and shared mutable state.

We have demonstrated that our logic and style of specification scales to implementations of fine-grained concurrent data structures without helping [8]. Future work includes investigating concurrent data structures that use helping.

References

1. Appel, A., Melliès, P.-A., Richards, C., Vouillon, J.: A very modal model of a modern, major, general type system. In: Proc. of POPL (2007)
2. Biering, B., Birkedal, L., Torp-Smith, N.: BI-Hyperdoctrines, Higher-order Separation Logic, and Abstraction. ACM TOPLAS (2007)
3. Birkedal, L., Møgelberg, R., Schwinghammer, J., Støvring, K.: First Steps in Synthetic Guarded Domain Theory: Step-Indexing in the Topos of Trees. In: Proc. of LICS (2011)
4. Dinsdale-Young, T., Birkedal, L., Gardner, P., Parkinson, M., Yang, H.: Views: Compositional Reasoning for Concurrent Programs. In: Proceedings of POPL (2013)
5. Dinsdale-Young, T., Dodds, M., Gardner, P., Parkinson, M.J., Vafeiadis, V.: Concurrent Abstract Predicates. In: D'Hondt, T. (ed.) ECOOP 2010. LNCS, vol. 6183, pp. 504–528. Springer, Heidelberg (2010)
6. Dodds, M., Jagannathan, S., Parkinson, M.J.: Modular reasoning for deterministic parallelism. In: Proceedings of POPL, pp. 259–270 (2011)
7. Filipović, I., O'Hearn, P., Rinetzky, N., Yang, H.: Abstraction for Concurrent Objects. In: Castagna, G. (ed.) ESOP 2009. LNCS, vol. 5502, pp. 252–266. Springer, Heidelberg (2009)
8. Herlihy, M., Shavit, N.: The Art of Multiprocessor Programming. Morgan Kaufmann (2008)
9. Herlihy, M.P., Wing, J.M.: Linearizability: a correctness condition for concurrent objects. ACM TOPLAS 12, 463–492 (1990)
10. Jacobs, B., Piessens, F.: Expressive modular fine-grained concurrency specification. In: Proceedings of POPL, pp. 271–282 (2011)
11. Jensen, J.B., Birkedal, L.: Fictional Separation Logic. In: Seidl, H. (ed.) ESOP 2012. LNCS, vol. 7211, pp. 377–396. Springer, Heidelberg (2012)
12. Lea, D.: A java fork/join framework. In: Proceedings of the ACM 2000 Conference on Java Grande, JAVA 2000, pp. 36–43. ACM (2000)
13. Owicki, S.S.: Axiomatic Proof Techniques for Parallel Programs. PhD thesis, Cornell (1975)
14. Parkinson, M., Bornat, R., O'Hearn, P.: Modular verification of a non-blocking stack. SIGPLAN Not. 42(1) (2007)
15. Pilkiewicz, A., Pottier, F.: The essence of monotonic state. In: Proceedings of TLDI, pp. 73–86 (2011)
16. Russo, C.V.: The Joins Concurrency Library. In: Hanus, M. (ed.) PADL 2007. LNCS, vol. 4354, pp. 260–274. Springer, Heidelberg (2007)
17. Schwinghammer, J., Birkedal, L., Reus, B., Yang, H.: Nested Hoare Triples and Frame Rules for Higher-Order Store. LMCS 7(3:21) (2011)
18. Svendsen, K., Birkedal, L., Parkinson, M.: Verifying Generics and Delegates. In: D'Hondt, T. (ed.) ECOOP 2010. LNCS, vol. 6183, pp. 175–199. Springer, Heidelberg (2010)
19. Svendsen, K., Birkedal, L., Parkinson, M.: Higher-order Concurrent Abstract Predicates. Technical report, IT University of Copenhagen (2012), http://www.itu.dk/people/kasv/hocap-tr.pdf
20. Turon, A., Thamsborg, J., Ahmed, A., Birkedal, L., Dreyer, D.: Logical Relations for Fine-Grained Concurrency. In: Proceedings of POPL (2013)

Ribbon Proofs for Separation Logic

John Wickerson[1], Mike Dodds[2], and Matthew Parkinson[3]

[1] Technische Universität Berlin, Germany
[2] University of York, United Kingdom
[3] Microsoft Research Cambridge, United Kingdom

Abstract. We present *ribbon proofs*, a diagrammatic system for proving program correctness based on separation logic. Ribbon proofs emphasise the structure of a proof, so are intelligible and pedagogical. Because they contain less redundancy than proof outlines, and allow each proof step to be checked locally, they may be more scalable. Where proof outlines are cumbersome to modify, ribbon proofs can be visually manoeuvred to yield proofs of variant programs. This paper introduces the ribbon proof system, proves its soundness and completeness, and outlines a prototype tool for validating the diagrams in *Isabelle*.

1   Introduction

A program proof should not merely certify *that* a program is correct; it should explain *why* it is correct. A proof should be more than 'true': it should be informative, and it should be intelligible. This paper does not contribute new methods for proving more properties of more programs, but rather, a new way to present such proofs. Building on work by Bean [2], we present a system that produces program proofs in separation logic that are readable, scalable, and easily modified.

A program proof in Hoare logic [15] is usually presented as a *proof outline*, in which the program's instructions are interspersed with 'enough' assertions to allow the reader to reconstruct the derivation tree. Since emerging circa 1971, the proof outline has become the de facto standard in the literature on both Hoare logic (e.g. [1, 16, 25, 28]) and its recent descendant, separation logic (e.g. [3, 8–11, 14, 17, 18, 20, 27, 31]). Its great triumph is what might be called *instruction locality*: that one can verify each instruction in isolation (by confirming that the assertions immediately above and below it form a valid Hoare triple) and immediately deduce that the entire proof is correct.

Yet proof outlines also suffer several shortcomings, some of which are manifested in Fig. 1a. This proof outline concerns a program that writes to three memory cells, which separation logic's $*$-operator deems distinct. First, it is highly repetitive: '$x \mapsto 1$' appears three times. Second, it is difficult to interpret the effect of each instruction, there being no distinction between those parts of an assertion that are actively involved and those that are merely in what separation logic calls the *frame*. For instance, line 4 affects only the second conjunct of its preceding assertion, but it is difficult to deduce the assignment's effect because two unchanged conjuncts are also present. Of course, these are only minor problems in our toy example, but they quickly become devastating when scaled to serious programs.

M. Felleisen and P. Gardner (Eds.): ESOP 2013, LNCS 7792, pp. 189–208, 2013.

1 $\{x \mapsto 0 * y \mapsto 0 * z \mapsto 0\}$
2 $[x] := 1;$
3 $\{x \mapsto 1 * y \mapsto 0 * z \mapsto 0\}$
4 $[y] := 1;$
5 $\{x \mapsto 1 * y \mapsto 1 * z \mapsto 0\}$
6 $[z] := 1;$
7 $\{x \mapsto 1 * y \mapsto 1 * z \mapsto 1\}$

(a) A proof outline

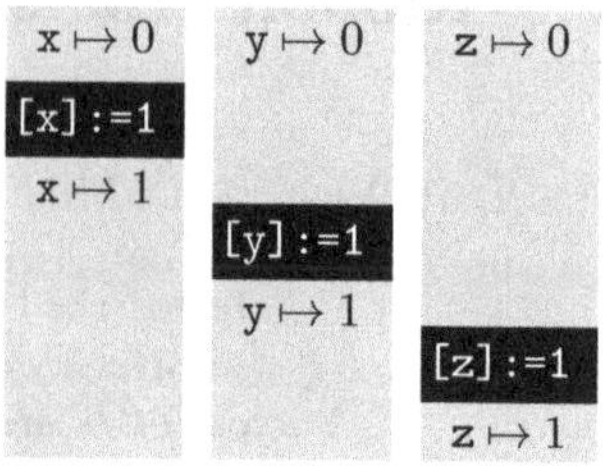

(b) A ribbon proof

Fig. 1. A simple example

The crux of the problem is what might be called *resource locality*. Separation logic [18, 27] specialises in this second dimension of locality. One can use separation logic's *small axioms* to reason about each instruction as if it were executing in a state containing only the resources (i.e. memory cells) that it needs, and immediately deduce its effect on the entire state using the *frame rule*. The proof outline below depicts this mechanism for line 4 of Fig. 1a.

$$\text{frame} \quad x \mapsto 1 * z \mapsto 0 \left[\begin{array}{l} \{x \mapsto 1 * y \mapsto 0 * z \mapsto 0\} \\ \quad \{y \mapsto 0\} \\ \qquad [y] := 1; \\ \quad \{y \mapsto 1\} \\ \{x \mapsto 1 * y \mapsto 1 * z \mapsto 0\} \end{array} \right] \begin{array}{l} \text{small axiom} \\ \text{for heap update} \end{array}$$

Showing such detail throughout a proof outline would clarify the effect of each instruction, but escalate the repetition. Cleverer use of the frame rule can help, but only a little – see Sect. 6. Essentially, we need a new proof representation to harness the new technology separation logic provides, and we propose the **ribbon proof**.

Figure 1b gives an example. The repetition has disappeared, and each instruction's effect is now clear: it affects exactly those assertions directly above and below it, while framed assertions (which must not mention variables written by the instruction) pass unobtrusively to the left or right. Technically, we are still invoking the frame rule at each instruction, but crucially in a ribbon proof, such invocations are implicit and do not complicate the diagram.

A bonus of this particular ribbon proof is that it emphasises that the three assignments update different memory cells. They are thus independent, and amenable to reordering or parallelisation. One can imagine obtaining a proof of the transformed program by simply sliding the left-hand column downward and the right-hand column upward. The corresponding proof outline neither suggests nor supports such manoeuvres.

Where a proof outline essentially flattens a proof to a list of assertions and instructions, our system produces geometric objects that can be navigated and modified by leveraging human visual intuition, and whose basic steps correspond exactly to separation logic's small axioms. A ribbon proof de-emphasises the program's shallow syntax, such as the order of independent instructions, and illuminates instead the deeper structure, such as the flow of resources through the code. Proof outlines focus on Hoare triples $\{p\} c \{q\}$, and often neglect the details of entailments between assertions, $p \Rightarrow q$, even though such entailments often encode important insights about the program being verified. Ribbon proofs treat both types of judgement equally, within the same system.

There are many recent extensions of separation logic (e.g. [7–11, 14, 17, 20, 23, 31]) to which our ribbon proof technology can usefully be applied; indeed, ribbons have already aided the development of a separation logic for relaxed memory [5]. All of these program logics are based on increasingly complex reasoning principles, of which clear explanations are increasingly vital. We propose ribbon proofs as the ideal device for providing them.

Comparison with Bean's System. Bean [2] introduced ribbon proofs as an extension of Fitch's *box proofs* [12] to handle the propositional fragment of bunched implications logic (BI) [24]. BI being the basis of separation logic's assertion language [18], his system can be used to prove entailments between propositional separation logic assertions. Our system expands Bean's into a full-blown program logic by adding support for commands and existentially-quantified variables. It is further distinguished by its treatment of ribbon proofs as graphs, which gives our diagrams an appealing degree of flexibility.

Contributions and Paper Outline. We describe a diagrammatic proof system that enables a natural presentation of separation logic proofs. We prove it sound and complete with respect to separation logic (Sect. 3). We also give an alternative, graphical formalisation (Sect. 4), which is sound in the absence of the frame rule's side-condition.

We describe a prototype tool (Sect. 5) for mechanically checking ribbon proofs with the *Isabelle* proof assistant. Given a small proof script for each basic step, our tool assembles a script that verifies the entire diagram. Such tediums as the associativity and commutativity of $*$ are handled in the graphical structure, leaving the user to focus on the interesting parts of the proof.

We discuss (Sect. 6) extensions to handle concurrent separation logic, possible applications to parallelisation, and connections to proof nets, bigraphs and string diagrams.

We begin by introducing our ribbon proof system with the aid of an example. Further examples can be found in Wickerson's PhD dissertation [33]. Of those, our ribbon proof of the Version 7 Unix memory manager demonstrates that our system can present readable proofs of more complex programs than those considered in this paper.

2   An Example

Let us consider a simple program for in-place reversal of a linked list.

Figure 3a presents a proof of this program as a proof outline (adapted from [27]). For a binary relation r, we write $x \mathbin{\dot{r}} y$ for $x \mathrel{r} y \wedge emp$, where emp describes an empty heap. We write ϵ for the empty sequence, $(-)^{\dagger}$ for sequence reversal, and $\cdot$ for cons and concatenation. We define the $list\ \alpha\ x$ predicate by induction on the length of the sequence α:

$$list\ \epsilon\ x \stackrel{\text{def}}{=} (x \mathbin{\dot{=}} \texttt{nil}) \qquad list\ (i \cdot \alpha')\ x \stackrel{\text{def}}{=} (\exists x'.\ x \mapsto i, x' * list\ \alpha'\ x'),$$

where $x \mapsto y, z$ abbreviates $(x \mapsto y) * (x + 1 \mapsto z)$.

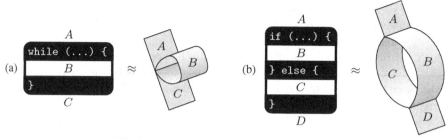

Fig. 2. While-loops and if-statements, pictorially

The invariant (line 5) states that x and y are linked lists representing two sequences α and β such that the initial sequence α_0 is obtained by concatenating the reverse of β onto α. Our proof outline seeks to clarify the proof by making minimal changes between successive assertions, despite this making the proof large and highly redundant. Alternatively, intermediate assertions can be elided, but this can make the proof hard to follow. Either way, proof outlines do not make the structure of the proof clear.

Figure 3b presents a ribbon proof for the same program. It comprises

- *steps*, each labelled with an instruction (black) or a justification of an entailment (dark grey),
- *ribbons* (light grey), each labelled with an assertion, and
- *existential boxes*, which delimit the scope of logical variables.

The ribbon proof advances vertically, and the resources (memory cells) being operated upon are distributed horizontally across the ribbons. Instructions are positioned according to the resources they access, not merely according to the syntax of the program, as in the proof outline. Horizontal separation between ribbons corresponds to the separating conjunction of the assertions on those ribbons; that is, parallel ribbons refer to disjoint sets of memory cells. Because * is commutative, we can 'twist' one ribbon over another. The resource distribution is not only unordered, but also non-uniform, so the width of a ribbon is not proportional to the amount of resource it describes. In particular, the assertion 'x $\neq$ nil' obtained upon entering the while-loop describes no memory cells at all; it merely states that the program variable x is not the null pointer. A gap in the diagram (e.g. above the 'y:=nil' step) corresponds to the '*emp*' assertion.

While-loops are special steps that contain further nested steps. The loop invariant is the collection of ribbons and existential boxes entering the top of the loop. This collection must be recreated at the end of the loop body, so that one could roll the proof into the shape drawn in Fig. 2a. If-statements are not depicted in our example, but appear in Wickerson's PhD dissertation [33]. They are treated straightforwardly: the ribbons and boxes entering the then-branch must match those entering the else-branch, and likewise at the two exit points, so that the proof could be cut and folded into the three-dimensional shape suggested in Fig. 2b.

After the 'z:=[x+1]' step, the assertion '*list* α z' is not needed for a while. In a proof outline, this assertion would either be temporarily removed via an explicit application of the frame rule or, as is done in Fig. 3a, redundantly repeated at every intermediate

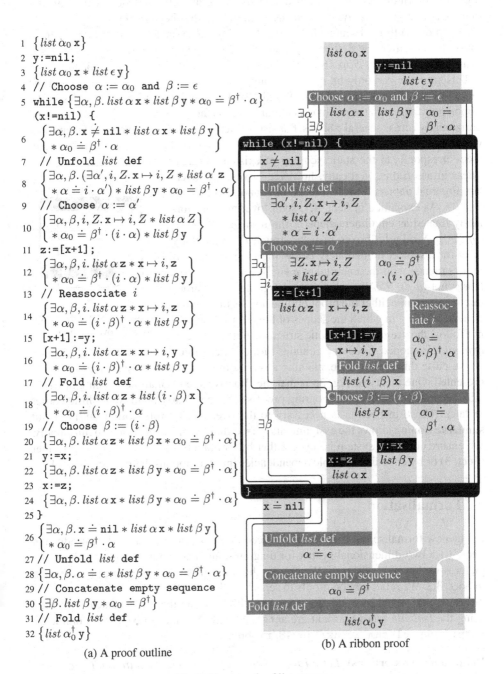

1 $\{list\ \alpha_0\ \mathtt{x}\}$
2 `y:=nil;`
3 $\{list\ \alpha_0\ \mathtt{x} * list\ \epsilon\ \mathtt{y}\}$
4 `// Choose` $\alpha := \alpha_0$ `and` $\beta := \epsilon$
5 `while` $\{\exists\alpha,\beta.\ list\ \alpha\ \mathtt{x} * list\ \beta\ \mathtt{y} * \alpha_0 \doteq \beta^\dagger \cdot \alpha\}$
  `(x!=nil) {`
6 $\left\{\begin{array}{l}\exists\alpha,\beta.\ \mathtt{x} \not\doteq \mathbf{nil} * list\ \alpha\ \mathtt{x} * list\ \beta\ \mathtt{y} \\ {} * \alpha_0 \doteq \beta^\dagger \cdot \alpha\end{array}\right\}$
7 `// Unfold` $list$ `def`
8 $\left\{\begin{array}{l}\exists\alpha,\beta.\ (\exists\alpha',i,Z.\ \mathtt{x} \mapsto i, Z * list\ \alpha'\ \mathtt{z} \\ {} * \alpha \doteq i \cdot \alpha') * list\ \beta\ \mathtt{y} * \alpha_0 \doteq \beta^\dagger \cdot \alpha\end{array}\right\}$
9 `// Choose` $\alpha := \alpha'$
10 $\left\{\begin{array}{l}\exists\alpha,\beta,i,Z.\ \mathtt{x} \mapsto i, Z * list\ \alpha\ Z \\ {} * \alpha_0 \doteq \beta^\dagger \cdot (i \cdot \alpha) * list\ \beta\ \mathtt{y}\end{array}\right\}$
11 `z:=[x+1];`
12 $\left\{\begin{array}{l}\exists\alpha,\beta,i.\ list\ \alpha\ \mathtt{z} * \mathtt{x} \mapsto i, \mathtt{z} \\ {} * \alpha_0 \doteq \beta^\dagger \cdot (i \cdot \alpha) * list\ \beta\ \mathtt{y}\end{array}\right\}$
13 `// Reassociate` i
14 $\left\{\begin{array}{l}\exists\alpha,\beta,i.\ list\ \alpha\ \mathtt{z} * \mathtt{x} \mapsto i, \mathtt{z} \\ {} * \alpha_0 \doteq (i \cdot \beta)^\dagger \cdot \alpha * list\ \beta\ \mathtt{y}\end{array}\right\}$
15 `[x+1]:=y;`
16 $\left\{\begin{array}{l}\exists\alpha,\beta,i.\ list\ \alpha\ \mathtt{z} * \mathtt{x} \mapsto i, \mathtt{y} \\ {} * \alpha_0 \doteq (i \cdot \beta)^\dagger \cdot \alpha * list\ \beta\ \mathtt{y}\end{array}\right\}$
17 `// Fold` $list$ `def`
18 $\left\{\begin{array}{l}\exists\alpha,\beta,i.\ list\ \alpha\ \mathtt{z} * list\ (i \cdot \beta)\ \mathtt{x} \\ {} * \alpha_0 \doteq (i \cdot \beta)^\dagger \cdot \alpha\end{array}\right\}$
19 `// Choose` $\beta := (i \cdot \beta)$
20 $\{\exists\alpha,\beta.\ list\ \alpha\ \mathtt{z} * list\ \beta\ \mathtt{x} * \alpha_0 \doteq \beta^\dagger \cdot \alpha\}$
21 `y:=x;`
22 $\{\exists\alpha,\beta.\ list\ \alpha\ \mathtt{z} * list\ \beta\ \mathtt{y} * \alpha_0 \doteq \beta^\dagger \cdot \alpha\}$
23 `x:=z;`
24 $\{\exists\alpha,\beta.\ list\ \alpha\ \mathtt{x} * list\ \beta\ \mathtt{y} * \alpha_0 \doteq \beta^\dagger \cdot \alpha\}$
25 `}`
26 $\left\{\begin{array}{l}\exists\alpha,\beta.\ \mathtt{x} \doteq \mathbf{nil} * list\ \alpha\ \mathtt{x} * list\ \beta\ \mathtt{y} \\ {} * \alpha_0 \doteq \beta^\dagger \cdot \alpha\end{array}\right\}$
27 `// Unfold` $list$ `def`
28 $\{\exists\alpha,\beta.\ \alpha \doteq \epsilon * list\ \beta\ \mathtt{y} * \alpha_0 \doteq \beta^\dagger \cdot \alpha\}$
29 `// Concatenate empty sequence`
30 $\{\exists\beta.\ list\ \beta\ \mathtt{y} * \alpha_0 \doteq \beta^\dagger\}$
31 `// Fold` $list$ `def`
32 $\{list\ \alpha_0^\dagger\ \mathtt{y}\}$

(a) A proof outline

(b) A ribbon proof

Fig. 3. Two proofs of list reverse

point. In the ribbon proof, it slides discreetly down the left-hand side. This indicates that the assertion is *inactive* without suggesting that it has been *removed*.

The proof outline obscures the usage of the logical variables α and β. The witness for α changes after line 8, then stays the same until line 24; meanwhile, β's witness is constant through lines 5 to 18 before becoming the previous witness prepended with i. This structure can only be spotted through careful examination of the proof outline (aided by the textual hints on lines 9 and 19). The scoping of logical variables in the ribbon proof, through the use of existential boxes, is far more satisfactory. Boxes extend horizontally across several ribbons, but also vertically to indicate the range of steps over which the same witness is used. Horizontally, existential boxes must be well-nested; this corresponds to the static scoping of existential quan-

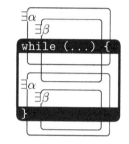

tifiers in assertions. Vertically, however, boxes may over-lap. Figure 4 depicts how the boxes for α and β overlap in Fig. 3b. As explained in Sect. 3.1, such 'overlaps' are for-mally treated as entailment steps of the form $\exists x.\,\exists y.\,p \Rightarrow \exists y.\,\exists x.\,p$. Similarly, boxes may be stretched horizontally (see, for instance, immediately below the loop in Fig. 3b) in accordance with the entailment $p * (\exists x.\,q) \Rightarrow \exists x.\,p * q$ (for x not in p). We thus obtain an intriguing proof struc-ture – present in neither the proof outline nor the underlying derivation tree – in which the scopes of logical variables do not follow the program's syntactic structure, but are instead *dynamically* scoped. Section 6 contains further discussion.

Fig. 4. Existential boxes, vertically overlapping

We close this section by explaining a shortcoming in the proof system as currently presented. One nicety of Fig. 3b is that the 'Reassociate i' entailment, being horizon-tally separated from its neighbouring proof steps, can clearly be moved a little earlier or later. (Close inspection is necessary to discover this from the proof outline.) But similar reasoning allows the assignments 'y:=x' and 'x:=z' to be swapped, unsoundly. We ensure our proof system is sound either by forbidding such manoeuvres altogether (Sect. 3) or by encoding variable dependencies into the ribbons themselves (Sect. 4).

3   Formalisation

Let us now formalise the concepts introduced in the previous section. We introduce in Sect. 3.1 a two-dimensional syntax for diagrams, and explain how it can generate the pictures we have already seen. We present the rules of our diagrammatic proof system in Sect. 3.2. We relate ribbon proofs to separation logic in Sect. 3.3.

Proofs performed by hand are annotated with □, while those mechanically verified using the *Isabelle* proof assistant are annotated with 🐸, and can be viewed online at: http://www.cl.cam.ac.uk/~jpw48/ribbons.html

Definition 1 (Assertions). *Let p range over a set of ordinary separation logic asser-tions, containing at least the following constructions:*

$$\text{Assertion} \stackrel{\text{def}}{=} \{p ::= emp \mid p * p \mid \exists x.\,p \mid \ldots\}.$$

$$\frac{\vdash_{\mathsf{SL}} \{p\}\, c\, \{q\} \qquad wr(c) \cap rd(r) = \emptyset}{\vdash_{\mathsf{SL}} \{p * r\}\, c\, \{q * r\}} \qquad \frac{(p, c, q) \in \mathsf{Axioms}}{\vdash_{\mathsf{SL}} \{p\}\, c\, \{q\}} \qquad \frac{\vdash_{\mathsf{SL}} \{p\}\, c\, \{q\}}{\vdash_{\mathsf{SL}} \{\exists x.\, p\}\, c\, \{\exists x.\, q\}}$$

$$\frac{\vdash_{\mathsf{SL}} \{p_1\}\, c\, \{q_1\} \\ \vdash_{\mathsf{SL}} \{p_2\}\, c\, \{q_2\}}{\vdash_{\mathsf{SL}} \{p_1 \vee p_2\}\, c\, \{q_1 \vee q_2\}} \qquad \frac{\vdash_{\mathsf{SL}} \{p'\}\, c\, \{q'\} \qquad p \Rightarrow p' \quad q' \Rightarrow q}{\vdash_{\mathsf{SL}} \{p\}\, c\, \{q\}} \qquad \frac{\vdash_{\mathsf{SL}} \{p\}\, c_1\, \{q\} \\ \vdash_{\mathsf{SL}} \{p\}\, c_2\, \{q\}}{\vdash_{\mathsf{SL}} \{p\}\, c_1 \text{ or } c_2\, \{q\}}$$

$$\frac{\vdash_{\mathsf{SL}} \{p\}\, c_1\, \{q\} \qquad \vdash_{\mathsf{SL}} \{q\}\, c_2\, \{r\}}{\vdash_{\mathsf{SL}} \{p\}\, c_1 ; c_2\, \{r\}} \qquad \frac{}{\vdash_{\mathsf{SL}} \{p\} \, \mathtt{skip}\, \{p\}} \qquad \frac{\vdash_{\mathsf{SL}} \{p\}\, c\, \{p\}}{\vdash_{\mathsf{SL}} \{p\} \, \mathtt{loop}\, c\, \{p\}}$$

Fig. 5. Proof rules for commands

Definition 2 (Commands). *Let c range over the commands of a sequential programming language, containing at least sequential composition (which is associative),* skip *(the unit of sequential composition), and non-deterministic choice and looping:*

$$\text{Command} \overset{\text{def}}{=} \{c ::= c \, ; c \mid \mathtt{skip} \mid c \text{ or } c \mid \mathtt{loop}\, c \mid \ldots\}.$$

If a primitive 'assume b' command is available (where b is a *pure* assertion; that is, independent of the heap) then standard if-statements and while-loops can be derived:

$$\text{if } b \text{ then } c_1 \text{ else } c_2 \overset{\text{def}}{=} (\mathtt{assume}\, b \, ; c_1) \text{ or } (\mathtt{assume}\, \neg b \, ; c_2)$$

$$\text{while } b \text{ do } c \overset{\text{def}}{=} \mathtt{loop}(\mathtt{assume}\, b \, ; c) \, ; \mathtt{assume}\, \neg b.$$

We assume a separation logic comprising the rules given in Fig. 5 plus a set of Axioms. In the first rule, the *frame rule*, the rd and wr functions respectively extract the sets of program variables read and written.

Remark 1. We do not consider Hoare logic's conjunction rule in this paper. Conjunction and universal quantification can still appear inside individual ribbon assertions. We could design graphical analogues (which would resemble our treatment of disjunction and existential quantification) but this would complicate our graphical language with constructs that are seldom used in separation logic proofs.

3.1 Syntax of Diagrams

We present a syntax that can generate the pictures seen in the preceding section. Each diagram is built up as a sequence of rows, each containing a single proof step. We thus refer to such diagrams as 'stratified'. (Section 4 will present an alternative formalisation that does not impose such strict sequentiality.) We begin by introducing *interfaces*, which are the top and bottom boundaries through which diagrams can be composed.

Definition 3 (Interfaces). *An interface is either a single ribbon labelled with an assertion, an empty interface (shown as whitespace in pictures), two interfaces side by side, or an existential box wrapped around an interface:*

$$\text{Interface} \overset{\text{def}}{=} \{P ::= \boxed{p} \mid \varepsilon \mid P\,P \mid \exists x P \mid \}.$$

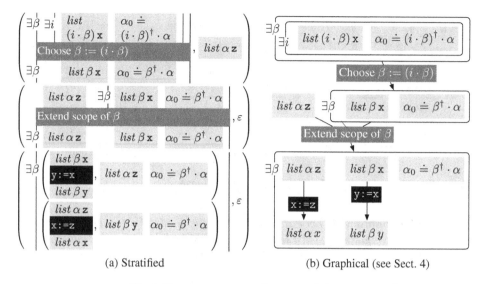

(a) Stratified   (b) Graphical (see Sect. 4)

Fig. 6. Two ways to parse a fragment of Fig. 3b

The *asn* function maps an interface to the assertion it represents:

$$asn\ p\ =\ p \qquad\qquad asn\ (P\,Q)\ =\ asn\ P * asn\ Q$$
$$asn\ \varepsilon\ =\ emp \qquad\qquad asn\ {}^{\exists x}_{\ }P|\ =\ \exists x.\ asn\ P.$$

When clarity demands it, we shall write $P \otimes Q$ instead of $P\,Q$, and hence $\otimes_{i \in I} P_i$ for iterated composition. We equate interfaces up to $(P\,Q)\,R = P\,(Q\,R)$, $P\,\varepsilon = \varepsilon\,P = P$ and $P\,Q = Q\,P$. Since $\otimes$ commutes, ribbon 'twisting' is merely a presentational artefact.

A *diagram* can be thought of as a mapping between two interfaces.

Definition 4 (Diagrams). *A diagram $D \in$ Diagram is a non-empty list of* rows $\rho \in$ Row. *When space permits, we align the list elements in a single column without punctuation. A* row *is a pair (γ, F) comprising a* cell $\gamma \in$ Cell *and a* frame $F \in$ Interface. *The syntax of cells is as follows:*

$$\text{Cell} \stackrel{\text{def}}{=} \{\gamma ::= P \mid \begin{array}{c} P \\ \boxed{c} \\ P \end{array} \mid {}^{\exists x}_{\ }D| \mid \begin{array}{c} P \\ \boxed{\begin{array}{c}D \\ \text{or} \\ D\end{array}} \\ P \end{array} \mid \begin{array}{c} P \\ \boxed{\begin{array}{c}\text{loop} \\ D\end{array}} \\ P \end{array} \}.$$

To illustrate how this syntax is used, Fig. 6a shows a term of Diagram that corresponds to a fragment of the picture in Fig. 3b. Note that the cell in each row is always pushed to the left-hand side. In the concrete pictures, it can be moved to allow corresponding ribbons in different rows to be aligned, and hence for redundant labels to be removed. Each entailment $p \Rightarrow q$ is handled as the basic step $\{p\}\ \texttt{skip}\ \{q\}$. Rather than write 'skip', we label such a step with a justification of the entailment, and colour it dark grey to emphasise those steps that actually contain program instructions. Concerning

RIBBON

$$\vdash^{cel} P : P \to P$$

BASIC

$$\vdash_{\mathsf{SL}} \{asn\ P\}\ c\ \{asn\ Q\}$$

$$\vdash^{cel} \boxed{\ c\ } : P \to Q$$

(cell with P above and Q below c)

EXISTS

$$\vdash^{dia} D : P \to Q$$

$$\vdash^{cel} \exists x D| : \exists x P| \to \exists x Q|$$

CHOICE

$$\vdash^{dia} D : P \to Q$$
$$\vdash^{dia} E : P \to Q$$

$$\vdash^{cel} \boxed{\begin{array}{c} D \\ \mathbf{or} \\ E \end{array}} : P \to Q$$

(with P above and Q below)

LOOP

$$\vdash^{dia} D : P \to P$$

$$\vdash^{cel} \boxed{\begin{array}{c} \mathbf{loop} \\ D \end{array}} : P \to P$$

(with P above and P below)

ROW

$$\vdash^{cel} \gamma : P \to Q$$
$$wr(\gamma) \cap rd(F) = \emptyset$$

$$\vdash^{row} (\gamma, F) : P \otimes F \to Q \otimes F$$

MAIN

$$\forall i \le k.\ \vdash^{row} \rho_i : P_i \to P_{i+1}$$

$$\vdash^{dia} [\rho_0, \dots, \rho_k] : P_0 \to P_{k+1}$$

Fig. 7. Proof rules for stratified ribbon diagrams

existential boxes: the operations of extending, contracting and commuting are really the entailments depicted informally below. Having to show these entailments explicitly would make Fig. 3b much more repetitive. (We are working on an improved formalisation that supports these operations directly – see Sect. 6 for further discussion.)

3.2 Proof Rules for Diagrams

There are two pertinent questions to be asked of a given ribbon diagram. The first question is: is it a valid proof? This subsection develops a *provability* judgement to answer this. The second question – if this ribbon diagram *is* deemed valid, what does it prove? – is addressed in the next subsection.

The rules given in Fig. 7 define provability judgements for cells ($\vdash^{cel}$), for rows ($\vdash^{row}$) and for diagrams ($\vdash^{dia}$). Each judgement ascribes a type, which comprises the top and bottom interfaces of that object.

The ROW and MAIN rules recall Hoare logic's sequencing rule and separation logic's frame rule. They embody the 'locally checkable' nature of ribbon proofs: that the entire diagram is valid if each row is valid in isolation, and that a row is valid if its active cell is valid and writes no program variable that is read elsewhere in the row.

The BASIC rule corresponds to an ordinary separation logic judgement $\vdash_{\mathsf{SL}} \{p\}\ c\ \{q\}$. This judgement may be arbitrarily complex, so a ribbon diagram may be no easier to check than a traditional proof outline. This is intentional. Our formalisation *allows* p and q to be minimised, by framing common fragments away, but does not *demand* this. The command c *can* be reduced to skip or some primitive command, but this may not be desirable if one requires only a high-level overview proof. A ribbon diagram can

$$com\,[(\gamma_0, F_0), \ldots, (\gamma_k, F_k)]\qquad com\,P = \texttt{skip}\qquad com\,\left|\begin{smallmatrix}\exists x\\ D\end{smallmatrix}\right| = com\,D$$
$$= com\,\gamma_0\;;\;\cdots\;;\;com\,\gamma_k$$

$$com\;\begin{array}{c}P\\ \blacksquare\,c\\ Q\end{array} = c \qquad com\;\begin{array}{c}P\\ \boxed{\begin{array}{c}\texttt{loop}\\ D\end{array}}\\ Q\end{array} = \texttt{loop}(com\,D) \qquad com\;\begin{array}{c}P\\ \boxed{\begin{array}{c}D\\ \texttt{or}\\ E\end{array}}\\ Q\end{array} = \begin{array}{l}(com\,D)\\ \texttt{or}(com\,E)\end{array}$$

Fig. 8. Extracting a command from a stratified diagram

thus be viewed as a flexible combination of diagrammatic and traditional proofs, with the BASIC rule as the interface between these two levels.

We remark that these proof rules provide only limited mechanisms for building new diagrams from old. Diagrams can be wrapped in existential boxes, or put inside choice or loop diagrams, but not stacked vertically or placed side by side. One can define operations for composing elements of Diagram in sequence or in parallel, and hence additional proof rules for diagrams so composed. The process is straightforward, and described in Wickerson's PhD dissertation [33].

3.3 Semantics of Diagrams

A stratified ribbon diagram denotes a Hoare triple. The pre- and postconditions of this triple are the assertions represented by the diagram's top and bottom interfaces. The command being proved is extracted by composing the labels on all of the proof steps in top-to-bottom order. Figure 8 defines the function responsible for this extraction. We hence obtain the following soundness result for ribbon proofs.

Theorem 1 (Soundness – stratified diagrams). *Separation logic can encode any provable ribbon diagram.*

$$\vdash^{\mathrm{dia}} D : P \to Q \implies \vdash_{\mathsf{SL}} \{asn\,P\}\;com\,D\;\{asn\,Q\}.$$

Proof. By mutual rule induction on $\vdash^{\mathrm{cel}}$, $\vdash^{\mathrm{row}}$, and $\vdash^{\mathrm{dia}}$.   ❧

Ribbon diagrams are trivially complete, because the BASIC rule can be invoked right at the root of the proof tree. In fact, ribbon diagrams remain complete even when the BASIC rule can occur only immediately beneath an axiom or the rule of consequence.

Theorem 2 (Completeness – stratified diagrams). *A strengthened ribbon proof system in which the* BASIC *rule is replaced by*

$$\dfrac{(asn\,P, c, asn\,Q) \in \mathsf{Axioms}}{\vdash^{\mathrm{cel}} \begin{array}{c}P\\ \blacksquare\,c\\ Q\end{array} : P \to Q} \qquad and \qquad \dfrac{asn\,P \Rightarrow asn\,Q}{\vdash^{\mathrm{cel}} \begin{array}{c}P\\ \boxed{\texttt{skip}}\\ Q\end{array} : P \to Q}$$

can encode any separation logic proof.

$$\vdash_{\mathsf{SL}} \{p\}\,c\,\{q\} \implies \exists D, P, Q.\, c \in com\,D \wedge p = asn\,P \wedge q = asn\,Q \wedge \vdash^{\mathrm{dia}} D : P \to Q$$

Proof. By rule induction on $\vdash_{\mathsf{SL}}$.   □

The main problem with the formalisation given in this section is that it sacrifices much of the flexibility we expect in our ribbon diagrams. It is often sound to tweak the layout of a diagram by sliding steps up or down or reordering ribbons, but by thinking of our diagrams as sliced into a sequence of rows, we rule out *all* such manoeuvres.

4   Graphical Formalisation

We now give an alternative formalisation, in which diagrams are represented not as a sequence of rows, but as graphs.

Our 'graphical' diagrams are more flexible than their 'stratified' cousins, but extra precautions must be taken to ensure soundness. The core difficulty is the side-condition on the frame rule: that the command writes no program variable in the frame. With stratification, the frame is clearly delimited, so this condition is easily checked. Without it, this check would become more global: a command may affect a ribbon that appears far above or below itself in a laid-out diagram. Our simple solution is to require henceforth that the frame rule has no side-condition. This requirement could be met by abolishing program variables altogether, leaving only the heap and numerical constants. A more practical alternative, explored later in this section, is to use the *variables-as-resource* paradigm [4].

Our graphs are nested, directed, acyclic hypergraphs. Ribbons correspond to nodes, and basic steps to hyperedges. Existential boxes are represented as single nodes that contain a nested graph. Likewise, choice diagrams and loop diagrams are represented by single hyperedges that contain, respectively, one or two nested graphs.

Definition 5 (Graphical diagrams, assertion-gadgets and command-gadgets). *Let $\mathcal{V}$ be an infinite set of node-identifiers. We define a language of* assertion-gadgets, command-gadgets *and graphical diagrams as follows.*

$$\mathsf{AsnGadget} = \{A ::= \boxed{p} \mid \boxed{\exists x\, G}\} \qquad \mathsf{ComGadget} = \{C ::= \boxed{c} \mid \boxed{\substack{G \\ \mathrm{or} \\ G}} \mid \boxed{\substack{\mathrm{loop} \\ G}}\}$$

$$\mathsf{GDiagram} = \{G \mid \Lambda_G \in V_G \to \mathsf{AsnGadget},\ E_G \subseteq_{\mathrm{fin}} \mathcal{P}(V_G) \times \mathsf{ComGadget} \times \mathcal{P}(V_G),$$
$$V_G \subseteq_{\mathrm{fin}} \mathcal{V},\ acyclic(G)\ and\ linear(G),\ where\ G = (V_G, \Lambda_G, E_G)\}$$

The definitions are mutually recursive, and are well-formed because the definienda (left-hand sides) appear only positively in the definientia (right-hand sides).[1] The first of these equations defines an assertion-gadget $A \in \mathsf{AsnGadget}$ to be either a ribbon or an existential box. The second defines a command-gadget $C \in \mathsf{ComGadget}$ to be either a basic step, a choice diagram, or a loop diagram. The third equation defines a graphical diagram $G \in \mathsf{GDiagram}$ to be a triple (V_G, Λ_G, E_G) that comprises:

- *a finite set $V_G \subseteq_{\mathrm{fin}} \mathcal{V}$ of node identifiers;*
- *a labelling $\Lambda_G : V_G \to \mathsf{AsnGadget}$ that associates each node identifier with an assertion-gadget; and*

---

[1] This is true even for the occurrence of ComGadget in the definiens of GDiagram, because the set in which it appears is finite.

– *a finite set $E_G \subseteq_{fin} \mathcal{P}(V_G) \times \mathsf{ComGadget} \times \mathcal{P}(V_G)$ of hyperedges $(\mathbf{v}, C, \mathbf{w})$, each comprising a set $\mathbf{v}$ of tail identifiers, a command-gadget C, and a set $\mathbf{w}$ of head identifiers,*

and which satisfies the following two properties.

ACYCLICITY: *Let us write $v \rightarrow w$ if $v \in \mathbf{v}$ and $w \in \mathbf{w}$ for some $(\mathbf{v}, C, \mathbf{w}) \in E_G$. Then define $acyclic(G)$ to hold iff the transitive closure of $\rightarrow$ is irreflexive.*

LINEARITY: *Define $linear(G)$ to hold iff the hyperedges in E_G have no common heads and no common tails. (This forbids the duplication or merging of ribbons, in accordance with $p \Rightarrow p * p$ and $p * p \Rightarrow p$ being invalid in separation logic.)*

Remark 2. We could represent our diagrams by a single graph, with dedicated 'parent' edges to simulate the nesting hierarchy. However, mindful of our *Isabelle* formalisation, and that "reasoning about graphs [. . .] can be a real hassle in HOL-based theorem provers" [34], we prefer to use an algebraic datatype to depict the hierarchy.

Figure 6b presents a term of GDiagram that corresponds to a fragment of the picture in Fig. 3b. Unlike Fig. 6a, this representation does not impose a strict ordering between the 'y:=x' and 'x:=z' instructions. As such, this proof is *invalid*; the figure serves merely to demonstrate how the graphical syntax is used.

The problem is that the graph does not take into account dependencies on program variables. To address this, let us remove the side-condition on the frame rule in our axiomatisation $\vdash_{\mathsf{SL}}$ of separation logic (Fig. 5). The new proof system thus obtained shall be written as $\vdash_{\mathsf{SL}}^{*}$. We shall now develop proof rules for graphical diagrams, and show them to be sound and complete with respect to $\vdash_{\mathsf{SL}}^{*}$. Section 4.3 describes the application of ribbon proofs to variables-as-resource, which is one instance of $\vdash_{\mathsf{SL}}^{*}$.

4.1 Proof Rules for Graphical Diagrams

Proof rules for graphical diagrams, command-gadgets and assertion-gadgets are defined in Fig. 9, which refers to the *top* and *bot* functions defined below. The judgement $\vdash^{\mathrm{gra}} G : P \rightarrow Q$ means that the diagram G, precondition P, and postcondition Q form a valid proof. The interfaces P and Q are always equal to $top(G)$ and $bot(G)$ respectively, so we sometimes omit them. The judgements for command-gadgets and assertion-gadgets are similar, the latter without interfaces.

Definition 6 (Top and bottom interfaces). *These functions extract interfaces from assertion-gadgets and from diagrams. For assertion-gadgets:*

$$top\ p = p \qquad bot\ p = p \qquad top\ \boxed{\exists x\, G} = \exists_{\mathsf{i}}^{x} top\, G| \qquad bot\ \boxed{\exists x\, G} = \exists_{\mathsf{i}}^{x} bot\, G|.$$

For diagrams:

$$top(G) = \otimes_{v \in initials\, G}\, top(\Lambda_G\, v) \qquad bot(G) = \otimes_{v \in terminals\, G}\, bot(\Lambda_G\, v)$$

where $initials(G) = V_G \setminus \bigcup_{(\_,\_,\mathbf{v}) \in E_G} \mathbf{v}$ and $terminals(G) = V_G \setminus \bigcup_{(\mathbf{v},\_,\_) \in E_G} \mathbf{v}$.

As was the case for stratified diagrams, one can define operations for composing elements of GDiagram in sequence or parallel, and hence additional proof rules for graphical diagrams so composed [33].

GRIBBON

$$\frac{}{\vdash^{asn} \boxed{p}}$$

GBASIC

$$\frac{\vdash^*_{SL}\{asn\,P\}\,c\,\{asn\,Q\}}{\vdash^{com}\boxed{\blacksquare\,c\,\blacksquare}:P\to Q}$$

GEXISTS

$$\frac{\vdash^{gra} G}{\vdash^{asn} \boxed{\exists x G}}$$

GCHOICE

$$\frac{\vdash^{gra} G_1 : P \to Q \qquad \vdash^{gra} G_2 : P \to Q}{\vdash^{com} \boxed{\begin{array}{c} G_1 \\ \text{or} \\ G_2 \end{array}} : P \to Q}$$

GLOOP

$$\frac{\vdash^{gra} G : P \to P}{\vdash^{com} \boxed{\begin{array}{c}\text{loop}\\ G\end{array}} : P \to P}$$

GMAIN

$$\frac{\forall v \in V_G.\,\vdash^{asn} \Lambda_G\,v \qquad \forall(\mathbf{v}, C, \mathbf{w}) \in E_G.\,\vdash^{com} C : \otimes_{v\in\mathbf{v}} bot(\Lambda_G\,v) \to \otimes_{w\in\mathbf{w}} top(\Lambda_G\,w)}{\vdash^{gra} G : top(G) \to bot(G)}$$

Fig. 9. Proof rules for graphical diagrams

$$coms(G) = \{c_0 ; \cdots ; c_{k-1} ; \text{skip} \mid \exists [x_0, \ldots, x_{k-1}] \in lin\,G.\,\forall i < k.\,c_i \in coms\,x_i\}$$

$$coms\,\boxed{p} = \{\text{skip}\} \qquad coms\,\boxed{\exists x G} = coms\,G \qquad coms\,\boxed{\blacksquare\,c\,\blacksquare} = \{c\}$$

$$coms\,\boxed{\begin{array}{c} G_1 \\ \text{or} \\ G_2 \end{array}} = \begin{array}{l}\{c_1 \text{ or } c_2 \mid \\ c_1 \in coms\,G_1, \\ c_2 \in coms\,G_2\}\end{array} \qquad coms\,\boxed{\begin{array}{c}\text{loop}\\ G\end{array}} = \{\text{loop}\,c \mid c \in coms\,G\}$$

Fig. 10. Extracting commands from a diagram

4.2 Semantics of Graphical Diagrams

Since graphical diagrams have a parallel nature, but our language is only sequential, it follows that each graphical diagram proves not a single command, but a set of commands, each one a linear extension of the partial order imposed by the diagram. The *coms* function defined in Fig. 10 is responsible for extracting this set from a given diagram. Each command is obtained by picking an ordering of command- and assertion-gadgets that is compatible with the partial order defined by the edges (this is the purpose of the *lin* function defined below), then recursively extracting a command from each gadget and sequentially composing the results.

Definition 7 (Linear extensions). *For a diagram G, we define lin G as the set of all lists* $[x_0, \ldots, x_{k-1}]$ *of* AsnGadgets *and* ComGadgets, *for which there exists a bijection* $\pi : k \to V_G \cup E_G$ *that satisfies, for all* $(\mathbf{v}, C, \mathbf{w}) \in E_G$:

$$\forall v \in \mathbf{v}.\,\pi^{-1}(v) < \pi^{-1}(\mathbf{v}, C, \mathbf{w}) \qquad \forall w \in \mathbf{w}.\,\pi^{-1}(\mathbf{v}, C, \mathbf{w}) < \pi^{-1}(w)$$

and where, for all $i < k$: $x_i = \Lambda_G(v)$ *if* $\pi(i) = v$, *and* $x_i = C$ *if* $\pi(i) = (\mathbf{v}, C, \mathbf{w})$.

By ACYCLICITY, every diagram admits at least one linear extension.

Theorem 3 (Soundness – graphical diagrams). *Separation logic without the side-condition on the frame rule can encode any provable ribbon diagram:*

$$\vdash^{gra} G : P \to Q \implies \forall c \in coms\,G.\,\vdash^*_{SL}\{asn\,P\}\,c\,\{asn\,Q\}.$$

Proof. By mutual induction on $\vdash^{gra}$, $\vdash^{com}$ and $\vdash^{dia}$. See [33] for details.   ☙

Theorem 4 (Completeness – graphical diagrams). *A strengthened ribbon proof system in which the* GBASIC *rule is replaced by*

$$\frac{(asn\ P, c, asn\ Q) \in \mathsf{Axioms}}{\vdash^{\mathrm{com}}\ \boxed{c}\ : P \to Q} \quad and \quad \frac{asn\ P \Rightarrow asn\ Q}{\vdash^{\mathrm{com}}\ \boxed{\mathtt{skip}}\ : P \to Q}$$

can encode any proof in separation logic without the side-condition on the frame rule.

$$\vdash^*_{\mathsf{SL}} \{p\}\, c \,\{q\} \implies \exists G, P, Q.\, c \in coms\ G \land p = asn\ P \land q = asn\ Q \land \vdash^{\mathrm{gra}} G : P \to Q$$

Proof. By rule induction on $\vdash^*_{\mathsf{SL}}$. $\qquad\qquad\qquad\qquad\qquad\qquad\qquad\qquad\qquad\qquad$ □

4.3   Using Variables-as-Resource

The variables-as-resource paradigm [4] treats program variables a little like separation logic treats heap cells. Each program variable x is associated with a piece of resource, all of which (written $Own_1(x)$) must be held to write to x, and some of which ($Own_\pi(x)$ for some $0 < \pi \le 1$) must be held to read it. This treatment replaces the use of *rd* and *wr* sets in Fig. 5. The variables-as-resource proof system is an instance of separation logic without the side-condition on the frame rule, and can be obtained from $\vdash^*_{\mathsf{SL}}$ simply by selecting an appropriate Axioms set.

Figure 11 exhibits a ribbon proof, conducted using variables-as-resource, of the list-reversal program from Sect. 2. Variables-as-resource dictates that every assertion in the proof is accompanied by one *Own* predicate per program variable it mentions. For instance, the precondition *list* α_0 x is paired with some of x's resource. The extra shading is merely syntactic sugar; for instance:

$$\boxed{\mathtt{x}, \tfrac{1}{2}\mathtt{y}\ \ \mathtt{x} \mapsto i, \mathtt{y}} \quad \overset{\mathrm{def}}{=} \quad Own_1(\mathtt{x}) * Own_{.5}(\mathtt{y}) * \mathtt{x} \mapsto i, \mathtt{y} .$$

The other preconditions – the resources associated with y and z – entitle the program to write to these program variables in due course. Note that at the entry to the while loop, part of x's resource is required in order to carry out the test of whether x is zero. At various points in the proof, variable resources are split or combined, but their total is always conserved.

Figure 11 introduces a couple of novel visual features: ribbons may pass 'underneath' basic steps to reduce the need for twisting (see the three 'Choose ...' steps), and horizontal space is conserved by writing some assertions sideways. The diagram can be laid out in several ways, unconstrained by the stratification strategy of the previous section, so there exists the potential to use the same diagram to justify several variations of a program. Recall the shortcoming of Fig. 3b: that it misleadingly suggested that 'y:=x' and 'x:=z' could be safely permuted. Figure 11 forbids this by inserting a ribbon between them labelled 'x'. On the other hand, both figures agree that the 'Reassociate i' step can be safely manoeuvred up or down a little.

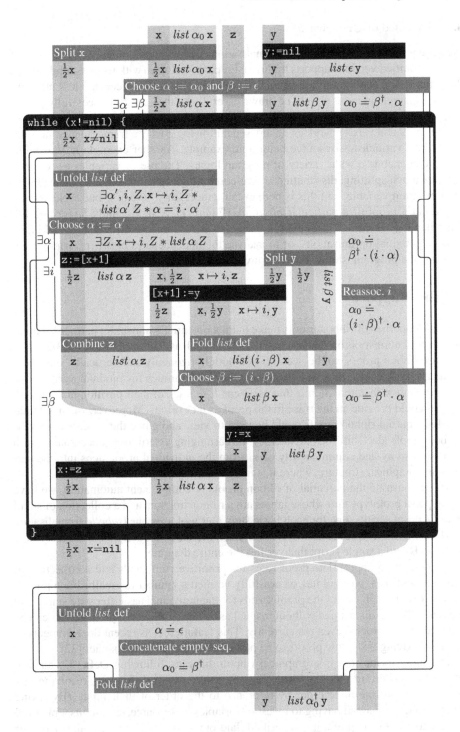

Fig. 11. A ribbon proof of list reverse using variables-as-resource

4.4   Stratified or Graphical?

We have presented two alternative formalisations of ribbon diagrams.

The stratified version supports traditional separation logic (with its side-condition on the frame rule), and the formalisation is simpler, but its proof objects are less manoeuvrable. Concrete pictures should be drawn carefully so they can be successfully parsed into a sequence of rows.

The graphical version works with any separation logic whose frame rule has no side-conditions, variables-as-resource being one example. Another example is Views [7], which can encode a wide variety of program logics. The use of variables-as-resource requires much splitting, distributing and re-combining of the resources associated with each program variable, and this is perhaps an unnecessary burden if one seeks merely to present a proof of a particular program. (Figure 11 is significantly larger and fiddlier than Fig. 3b, which does not use variables-as-resource.) However, one seeking to explore potential optimisations, or to analyse the dependencies between various components of a program, should consider investing in variables-as-resource.

5   Tool Support

Several properties of ribbon proofs make them a potentially appealing partner for automatic verification tools based on separation logic, such as *Bedrock* [6] and *VeriFast* [19]. Because ribbon proofs can be decomposed both horizontally and vertically, into independent proof blocks, they may suggest more opportunities for modular verification. One problem with automation is that users can lose track of their position in the proof: ribbons could provide an interface to the proof as it develops. Moreover, when automation fails, partial ribbon proofs could be used to view and guide the process manually. Ribbon proofs also shift the bureaucracy of rearranging assertions (in accordance with the associativity and commutativity of $*$) from the individual proof steps into the surrounding graphical structure, where it is more naturally handled.

To demonstrate the potential of ribbon proofs to complement automation, we have developed a prototype tool whose inputs are a ribbon diagram and a collection of small *Isabelle* proof scripts, one for each basic step. Our tool uses our *Isabelle* formalisation of Thm. 1 and the proof rules of Fig. 7 to assemble the proof scripts for the individual commands into a single script that verifies the entire diagram.

Supplied with appropriate proof rules for primitive commands and a collection of axioms about lists, our tool has successfully verified a number of small ribbon proofs, among them Fig. 3b. All of the proof scripts for the individual basic steps are small, and they can often be discharged without manual assistance. Individual proof scripts can be checked in any order – even concurrently. This feature recalls recent developments in theorem proving that allow proofs to be processed in a non-serial manner [32].

The input to the tool is a graphical ribbon diagram, following Defn. 5. Our tool begins by converting this graphical diagram into a stratified diagram, resolving any ambiguity about the node order by reference to the order of their input. (By taking this approach, we avoid having to invest in variables-as-resource.) It outputs a pictorial representation of the graph it has verified, laid out using the *dot* tool in the *Graphviz* library. Clicking on any basic step loads the corresponding proof script, which can then

(a)

$$\{x \mapsto 0 * y \mapsto 0 * z \mapsto 0\}$$
$$[x] := 1;$$
$$\{x \mapsto 1 * y \mapsto 0 * z \mapsto 0\}$$
$$\left.\begin{array}{l}\{y \mapsto 0 * z \mapsto 0\}\\ [y] := 1;\\ \{y \mapsto 1 * z \mapsto 0\}\\ [z] := 1;\\ \{y \mapsto 1 * z \mapsto 1\}\end{array}\right] \begin{array}{l}\text{frame}\\ x \mapsto 1\end{array}$$
$$\{x \mapsto 1 * y \mapsto 1 * z \mapsto 1\}$$

(b)

$$\{x \mapsto 0 * y \mapsto 0 * z \mapsto 0\}$$
$$\left.\begin{array}{l}\{x \mapsto 0 * y \mapsto 0\}\\ [x] := 1;\\ \{x \mapsto 1 * y \mapsto 0\}\\ [y] := 1;\\ \{x \mapsto 1 * y \mapsto 1\}\end{array}\right] \begin{array}{l}\text{frame}\\ z \mapsto 0\end{array}$$
$$\{x \mapsto 1 * y \mapsto 1 * z \mapsto 0\}$$
$$[z] := 1;$$
$$\{x \mapsto 1 * y \mapsto 1 * z \mapsto 1\}$$

Fig. 12. Two alternatives to the proof outline in Fig. 1a

be edited. When a step's proof is admitted by *Isabelle*, the corresponding node in the pictorial representation is marked with a tick; a failed or incomplete proof is marked with a cross. The picture below illustrates this on a snippet of Fig. 6b, and also shows the proof script for one of the steps.

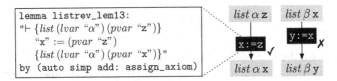

In the current prototype, the user must supply the input in textual form, but in the future, we intend to enable direct interaction with the graphical representation, perhaps through a framework for diagrammatic reasoning such as *Diabelli* [30]. We envisage an interactive graphical interface for exploring and modifying proofs, that allows steps to be collapsed or expanded to the desired granularity – whether that is the fine details of every rule and axiom, or a coarse bird's-eye view of the overall structure of the proof.

The ribbon proofs in this paper have all been laid out manually (and we are preparing a public release of the LATEX macros we use to do this) but there is scope for additional tool support for discovering pleasing layouts automatically.

6   Related and Further Work

Ribbon proofs are more than just a pretty syntax; they are a sound and complete proof system. Proof outlines have previously been promoted from a notational device to a formal system by Schneider [28], and by Ashcroft, who remarks that "the essential property of [proof outlines] is that each piece of program appears *once*" [1]. Very roughly speaking, ribbon proofs extend this property to each piece of assertion.

When constructing a proof outline, one can reduce the repetition by 'framing off' state that is unused for several instructions. For instance, Fig. 12a depicts one variation of Fig. 1a obtained by framing off x during the latter two instructions; another option is to frame off z during the first two (Fig. 12b). It is unsatisfactory that there are several different proof outlines for what is essentially the same proof. More pragmatically, deciding among these options can be difficult with large proof outlines. Happily, each of

```
while true {
  x:=new();
  with buff when !full {
    full:=true;
    c:=x;
  }
}
```

(a) Code for 'producer' thread

```
while true {
  with buff when full {
    full:=false;
    y:=c;
  }
  dispose(y);
}
```

(b) Code for 'consumer' thread

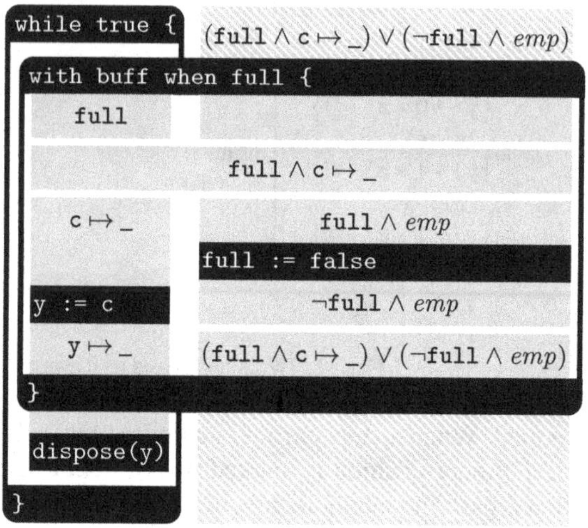

(c) Ribbon proof for 'consumer' thread (mock-up)

Fig. 13. Concurrency example: a single-cell buffer

these options yields the same ribbon proof (Fig. 1b). We note a parallel here with *proof nets* [13], which are a graphical mechanism for unifying proofs in linear logic that differ only in uninteresting ways, such as the order of rule applications.

The graphical structures in Defn. 5 resemble Milner's *bigraphs* [22]. Assertions and commands are nodes, the deductions of the proof form the *link graph*, and existential boxes, choices and loops form the *place graph*. In fact, our diagrams correspond to *binding* bigraphs, in which links may not cross place boundaries. Relaxing this restriction may enable a model of the 'dynamic' scoping of existential boxes exhibited in Fig. 4, which our current formalisation dismisses as a purely syntactic artefact.

Ribbon proofs can be understood as objects of a symmetric monoidal category, and our pictures as *string diagrams*, which are widely used as graphical languages for such categories [29]. In future work we intend to investigate this categorical semantics of ribbon proofs; in particular, the use of *traces* [21] to model the loop construction depicted in Fig. 2a, and coproducts to model if-statements and existential boxes.

Another avenue for future work is the connection between ribbon proofs and Raza et al.'s *labelled separation logic* [26]. Labelled separation logic seeks to justify compiler reorderings by analysing the dependencies between program statements, and checking that these are not violated. The dependencies are detected by first labelling each component of each assertion with the commands that access it, and then propagating these labels through program proofs. Raza's labels recall the *columns* in our ribbon diagrams: each ribbon and each command occupies one or more columns of a diagram, and commands that occupy common columns (modulo twisting) may share a dependency.

We have so far considered only sequential programs, but our proofs have a distinctly concurrent flavour. It may be possible to extend ribbon proofs to *concurrent separation logic* [23] as follows. Figure 13 gives a program (adapted from [23]) in which two threads communicate through a shared buffer at location c. The *resource invariant* (full ∧ c ↦ _) ∨ (¬full ∧ *emp*) protected by the lock buff signifies that c is shared exactly when full is set. Figure 13c imagines a ribbon proof of the 'consumer' thread. The resource invariant is initially in a protected ribbon, inaccessible to the thread (as suggested by the hatching). Upon entering the critical region, the ribbon becomes available, and upon leaving it, the resource invariant is re-established and the ribbon is inaccessible once again.

Beyond concurrent separation logic, we intend to apply our system to more advanced separation logics. It has already aided the development of a logic for relaxed memory [5]; other candidates handle fine-grained concurrency [8, 10, 11, 31], dynamic threads [9], storable locks [14], loadable modules [20] and garbage collection [17]. Increasingly complicated logics for increasingly complicated programming features make techniques for intuitive construction and clear presentation ever more crucial.

7 Conclusion

Ribbon proofs are an attractive and practical approach for constructing and presenting proofs in separation logic or any derivative thereof. They contain less redundancy than a proof outline, and express the intent of the proof more clearly. Each step of the proof can be checked locally, by focusing only on the relevant resources. They are useful pedagogically for explaining how a simple proof is constructed, but also scale to more complex programs (as demonstrated in [33]), and have aided the development of a separation logic for relaxed memory [5]. They show graphically the distribution of resource in a program, and in particular, which parts of a program operate on disjoint resources, and this may prove useful for exploring parallelisation opportunities.

Acknowledgements. Wickerson was supported by a DAAD postdoctoral scholarship and EPSRC grant F019394/1. Dodds was supported by EPSRC grants EP/H005633/1 and EP/F036345. Figure 2 was drawn by Rasmus Petersen. We thank him, Nick Benton, Richard Bornat, Matko Botinčan, Daiva Naudžiūnienė, Peter O'Hearn, Andy Pitts, Noam Rinetzky and the anonymous reviewers for suggestions and encouragement.

References

[1] Ashcroft, E.A.: Program verification tableaus. Technical Report CS-76-01, University of Waterloo (1976)

[2] Bean, J.: Ribbon Proofs - A Proof System for the Logic of Bunched Implications. PhD thesis, Queen Mary University of London (2006)

[3] Bornat, R., Calcagno, C., O'Hearn, P.W., Parkinson, M.J.: Permission accounting in separation logic. In: POPL 2005. ACM Press (2005)

[4] Bornat, R., Calcagno, C., Yang, H.: Variables as resource in separation logic. In: MFPS XXI. ENTCS, vol. 155 (2006)

[5] Bornat, R., Dodds, M.: Abducing barriers for Power and ARM. Draft (2012)

[6] Chlipala, A.: Mostly-automated verification of low-level programs in computational separation logic. In: PLDI 2011. ACM Press (2011)

[7] Dinsdale-Young, T., Birkedal, L., Gardner, P., Parkinson, M.J., Yang, H.: Views: Compositional reasoning for concurrent programs. In: POPL 2013. ACM Press (2013)

[8] Dinsdale-Young, T., Dodds, M., Gardner, P., Parkinson, M.J., Vafeiadis, V.: Concurrent Abstract Predicates. In: D'Hondt, T. (ed.) ECOOP 2010. LNCS, vol. 6183, pp. 504–528. Springer, Heidelberg (2010)

[9] Dodds, M., Feng, X., Parkinson, M., Vafeiadis, V.: Deny-Guarantee Reasoning. In: Castagna, G. (ed.) ESOP 2009. LNCS, vol. 5502, pp. 363–377. Springer, Heidelberg (2009)

[10] Feng, X.: Local rely-guarantee reasoning. In: POPL 2009. ACM Press (2009)

[11] Feng, X., Ferreira, R., Shao, Z.: On the Relationship Between Concurrent Separation Logic and Assume-Guarantee Reasoning. In: De Nicola, R. (ed.) ESOP 2007. LNCS, vol. 4421, pp. 173–188. Springer, Heidelberg (2007)

[12] Fitch, F.B.: Symbolic Logic: An Introduction. Ronald Press Co. (1952)

[13] Girard, J.-Y.: Linear logic. Theor. Comput. Sci. 50 (1987)

[14] Gotsman, A., Berdine, J., Cook, B., Rinetzky, N., Sagiv, M.: Local Reasoning for Storable Locks and Threads. In: Shao, Z. (ed.) APLAS 2007. LNCS, vol. 4807, pp. 19–37. Springer, Heidelberg (2007)

[15] Hoare, C.A.R.: An axiomatic basis for computer programming. Communications of the ACM 12(10) (1969)

[16] Hoare, C.A.R.: Proof of a program: Find. Communications of the ACM 14(1) (1971)

[17] Hur, C.-K., Dreyer, D., Vafeiadis, V.: Separation logic in the presence of garbage collection. In: LICS 2011. IEEE Computer Society (2011)

[18] Ishtiaq, S., O'Hearn, P.W.: BI as an assertion language for mutable data structures. In: POPL 2001. ACM Press (2001)

[19] Jacobs, B., Smans, J., Philippaerts, P., Vogels, F., Penninckx, W., Piessens, F.: VeriFast: A Powerful, Sound, Predictable, Fast Verifier for C and Java. In: Bobaru, M., Havelund, K., Holzmann, G.J., Joshi, R. (eds.) NFM 2011. LNCS, vol. 6617, pp. 41–55. Springer, Heidelberg (2011)

[20] Jacobs, B., Smans, J., Piessens, F.: Verification of Unloadable Modules. In: Butler, M., Schulte, W. (eds.) FM 2011. LNCS, vol. 6664, pp. 402–416. Springer, Heidelberg (2011)

[21] Joyal, A., Street, R., Verity, D.: Traced monoidal categories. Math. Proc. of the Cambridge Philosophical Society 119(3) (1996)

[22] Milner, R.: The Space and Motion of Communicating Agents. Cambridge University Press (2009)

[23] O'Hearn, P.W.: Resources, concurrency and local reasoning. Theor. Comput. Sci. 375(1-3) (2007)

[24] O'Hearn, P.W., Pym, D.J.: The logic of bunched implications. B. Symb. Log. 5(2) (1999)

[25] Owicki, S., Gries, D.: An axiomatic proof technique for parallel programs I. Acta Informatica 6 (1976)

[26] Raza, M., Calcagno, C., Gardner, P.: Automatic Parallelization with Separation Logic. In: Castagna, G. (ed.) ESOP 2009. LNCS, vol. 5502, pp. 348–362. Springer, Heidelberg (2009)

[27] Reynolds, J.C.: Separation logic: A logic for shared mutable data structures. In: LICS 2002. IEEE Computer Society (2002)

[28] Schneider, F.B.: On Concurrent Programming, ch. 4. Springer (1997)

[29] Selinger, P.: A survey of graphical languages for monoidal categories. In: New Structures for Physics, vol. 813, ch. 4. Springer (2011)

[30] Urbas, M., Jamnik, M.: Diabelli: A Heterogeneous Proof System. In: Gramlich, B., Miller, D., Sattler, U. (eds.) IJCAR 2012. LNCS, vol. 7364, pp. 559–566. Springer, Heidelberg (2012)

[31] Vafeiadis, V., Parkinson, M.: A Marriage of Rely/Guarantee and Separation Logic. In: Caires, L., Vasconcelos, V.T. (eds.) CONCUR 2007. LNCS, vol. 4703, pp. 256–271. Springer, Heidelberg (2007)

[32] Wenzel, M.: Asynchronous proof processing with Isabelle/Scala and Isabelle/jEdit. In: UITP 2010. ENTCS, vol. 285 (2012)

[33] Wickerson, J.: Concurrent Verification for Sequential Programs. PhD thesis, University of Cambridge (2013)

[34] Wu, C., Zhang, X., Urban, C.: A Formalisation of the Myhill-Nerode Theorem Based on Regular Expressions (Proof Pearl). In: van Eekelen, M., Geuvers, H., Schmaltz, J., Wiedijk, F. (eds.) ITP 2011. LNCS, vol. 6898, pp. 341–356. Springer, Heidelberg (2011)

Abstract Refinement Types

Niki Vazou[1], Patrick M. Rondon[2], and Ranjit Jhala[1]

[1] UC San Diego
[2] Google

Abstract. We present *abstract refinement types* which enable quantification over the refinements of data- and function-types. Our key insight is that we can avail of quantification while preserving SMT-based decidability, simply by encoding refinement parameters as *uninterpreted* propositions within the refinement logic. We illustrate how this mechanism yields a variety of sophisticated means for reasoning about programs, including: *parametric* refinements for reasoning with type classes, *index-dependent* refinements for reasoning about key-value maps, *recursive* refinements for reasoning about recursive data types, and *inductive* refinements for reasoning about higher-order traversal routines. We have implemented our approach in a refinement type checker for Haskell and present experiments using our tool to verify correctness invariants of various programs.

1 Introduction

Refinement types offer an automatic means of verifying semantic properties of programs by decorating types with predicates from logics efficiently decidable by modern SMT solvers. For example, the refinement type `{v: Int | v > 0}` denotes the basic type `Int` refined with a logical predicate over the "value variable" `v`. This type corresponds to the set of `Int` values `v` which additionally satisfy the logical predicate, *i.e.*, the set of positive integers. The (dependent) function type `x:{v:Int| v > 0} -> {v:Int | v < x}` describes functions that take a positive argument `x` and return an integer less than `x`. Refinement type checking reduces to *subtyping* queries of the form $\Gamma \vdash \{\tau : \nu \mid p\} \preceq \{\tau : \nu \mid q\}$, where p and q are refinement predicates. These subtyping queries reduce to logical *validity* queries of the form $[\![\Gamma]\!] \wedge p \Rightarrow q$, which can be automatically discharged using SMT solvers [6].

Several groups have shown how refinement types can be used to verify properties ranging from partial correctness concerns like array bounds checking [27,23] and data structure invariants [16] to the correctness of security protocols [2], web applications [14] and implementations of cryptographic protocols [10].

Unfortunately, the automatic verification offered by refinements has come at a price. To ensure decidable checking with SMT solvers, the refinements are quantifier-free predicates drawn from a decidable logic. This significantly limits expressiveness by precluding specifications that enable abstraction over the refinements (*i.e.*, invariants). For example, consider the following higher-order for-loop where `set i x v` returns the vector `v` updated at index `i` with the value `x`.

M. Felleisen and P. Gardner (Eds.): ESOP 2013, LNCS 7792, pp. 209–228, 2013.

```
for :: Int -> Int -> a -> (Int -> a -> a) -> a
for lo hi x body      = loop lo x
  where loop i x
          | i < hi    = loop (i+1) (body i x)
          | otherwise = x

initUpto :: Vec a -> a -> Int -> Vec a
initUpto a x n = for 0 n a (\i -> set i x)
```

We would like to verify that `initUpto` returns a vector whose *first* n elements are equal to x. In a first-order setting, we could achieve the above with a loop invariant that asserted that at the ith iteration, the first i elements of the vector were already initalized to x. However, in our higher-order setting we require a means of *abstracting* over possible invariants, each of which can *depend on* the iteration index i. Higher-order logics like Coq and Agda permit such quantification over invariants. Alas, validity in such logics is well outside the realm of decidability, and hence their use precludes automatic verification.

In this paper, we present *abstract refinement types* which enable abstraction (quantification) over the refinements of data- and function-types. Our key insight is that we can preserve SMT-based decidable type checking by encoding abstract refinements as *uninterpreted* propositions in the refinement logic. This yields several contributions:

- First, we illustrate how abstract refinements yield a variety of sophisticated means for reasoning about high-level program constructs (§2), including: *parametric* refinements for type classes, *index-dependent* refinements for key-value maps, *recursive* refinements for data structures, and *inductive* refinements for higher-order traversal routines.
- Second, we demonstrate that type checking remains decidable (§3) by showing a fully automatic procedure that uses SMT solvers, or, to be precise, decision procedures based on congruence closure [19], to discharge logical subsumption queries over abstract refinements.
- Third, we show that the crucial problem of *inferring* appropriate instantiations for the (abstract) refinement parameters boils down to inferring (non-abstract) refinement types (§3), which we have previously automated via the abstract interpretation framework of Liquid Types [23].
- Finally, we have implemented abstract refinements in HSOLVE, a new Liquid Type-based verifier for Haskell. We present experiments using HSOLVE to concisely specify and verify a variety of correctness properties of several programs ranging from microbenchmarks to some widely-used libraries (§4).

2   Overview

We start with a high level overview of abstract refinements, by illustrating how they can be used to uniformly specify and automatically verify various kinds of invariants.

2.1 Parametric Invariants

Parametric Invariants via Type Polymorphism. Suppose we had a generic comparison `(<=) :: a -> a -> Bool` as in OCAML. We could use it to write:

```
max       :: a -> a -> a
max x y = if x <= y then y else x

maximum :: [a] -> a
maximum (x:xs) = foldr max x xs
```

In essence, the type given for `maximum` states that *for any* a, if a list of a values is passed into `maximum`, then the returned result is also an a value. Hence, for example, if a list of *prime* numbers is passed in, the result is prime, and if a list of *even* numbers is passed in, the result is even. Thus, we can use refinement types [23] to verify

```
type Even = {v:Int | v % 2 = 0 }

maxEvens :: [Int] -> Even
maxEvens xs = maximum (0 : xs')
    where xs' = [ x | x <- xs, x `mod` 2 = 0]
```

Here the % represents the modulus operator in the refinement logic [6] and we type the primitive `mod :: x:Int -> y:Int -> {v: Int | v = x % y}`. Verification proceeds as follows. Given that `xs :: [Int]`, the system has to verify that `maximum (0 : xs') :: Even`. To this end, the type parameter of `maximum` is instantiated with the *refined* type `Even`, yielding the instance:

```
maximum :: [Even] -> Even
```

Then, `maximum`'s argument should be proved to have type `[Even]`. So, the type parameter of `(:)` is instantiated with `Even`, yielding the instance:

```
(:) :: Even -> [Even] -> [Even]
```

Finally, the system infers that `0 :: Even` and `xs' :: [Even]`, *i.e.*, the arguments of `(:)` have the expected types, thereby verifying the program. The refinement type instantiations can be inferred from an appropriate set of logical qualifiers using the abstract interpretation framework of Liquid Types [23]. Here, once `v%2 = 0` is added to the set of qualifiers, either manually or (as done by our implementation) by automatically scraping predicates from refinements appearing in specification signatures, the refinement type instantiations, and hence verification, proceed automatically. Thus, parametric polymorphism offers an easy means of encoding second-order invariants, *i.e.*, of quantifying over or parametrizing the invariants of inputs and outputs of functions.

Parametric Invariants via Abstract Refinements. Instead, suppose that the comparison operator was monomorphic, and only worked for `Int` values. The resulting (monomorphic) signatures

```
max       :: Int -> Int -> Int
maximum :: [Int] -> Int
```

preclude the verification of maxEvens (*i.e.,* typechecking against the signature shown earlier). This is because the new type of maximum merely states that *some* Int is returned as output, and not necessarily one that enjoys the properties of the values in the input list. This is a shame, since the property clearly still holds. We could type

```
max :: forall t <: Int. t -> t -> t
```

but this route would introduce the complications that surround bounded quantification which could render checking undecidable [22].

To solve this problem, we introduce *abstract refinements* which let us quantify or parameterize a type over its constituent refinements. For example, we can type max as

```
max :: forall <p::Int->Bool>. Int<p> -> Int<p> -> Int<p>
```

where Int<p> is an abbreviation for the refinement type {v:Int | p(v)}. Intuitively, an abstract refinement p is encoded in the refinement logic as an *uninterpreted function symbol*, which satisfies the *congruence* axiom [19]

$$\forall \overline{X}, \overline{Y} : (\overline{X} = \overline{Y}) \Rightarrow P(\overline{X}) = P(\overline{Y})$$

Thus, it is trivial to verify, with an SMT solver, that max enjoys the above type: the input types ensure that both p(x) and p(y) hold and hence the returned value in either branch satisfies the refinement {v:Int | p(v)}, thereby ensuring the output type. By the same reasoning, we can generalize the type of maximum to

```
maximum :: forall <p :: Int -> Bool>. [Int<p>] -> Int<p>
```

Consequently, we can recover the verification of maxEvens. Now, instead of instantiating a *type* parameter, we simply instantiate the *refinement* parameter of maximum with the concrete refinement {\v -> v % 2 = 0}, after which type checking proceeds as usual [23]. Later, we show how to retain automatic verification by inferring refinement parameter instantiations via liquid typing (§ 3.4).

Parametric Invariants and Type Classes. The example above regularly arises in practice, due to type classes. In Haskell, the functions above are typed

```
(<=)    :: (Ord a) => a -> a -> Bool
max     :: (Ord a) => a -> a -> a
maximum :: (Ord a) => [a] -> a
```

We might be tempted to ignore the typeclass constraint and treat maximum as [a] -> a. This would be quite unsound, as typeclass predicates preclude universal quantification over refinement types. Consider the function sum :: (Num a)=> [a] -> a which adds the elements of a list. The Num class constraint implies that numeric operations occur in the function, so if we pass sum a list of odd numbers, we are *not* guaranteed to get back an odd number.

Thus, how do we soundly verify the desired type of maxEvens without instantiating class predicated type parameters with arbitrary refinement types? First, via the same analysis as the monomorphic Int case, we establish that

```
max:: forall <p::a->Bool>. (Ord a)=> a<p> -> a<p> -> a<p>
maximum:: forall <p::a ->Bool>. (Ord a) => [a<p>] -> a<p>
```

Next, at the call-site for maximum in maxEvens we instantiate the type variable a with Int, and the abstract refinement p with { \v -> v % 2 = 0} after which, the verification proceeds as described earlier (for the Int case). Thus, abstract refinements allow us to quantify over invariants without relying on parametric polymorphism, even in the presence of type classes.

2.2 Index-Dependent Invariants

Next, we illustrate how abstract invariants allow us to specify and verify index-dependent invariants of key-value maps. To this end, we develop a small library of *extensible vectors* encoded, for purposes of illustration, as functions from Int to some generic range a. Formally, we specify vectors as

```
data Vec a <dom :: Int -> Bool, rng :: Int -> a -> Bool>
   = V (i:Int<dom> -> a <rng i>)
```

Here, we are parameterizing the definition of the type Vec with *two* abstract refinements, dom and rng, which respectively describe the *domain* and *range* of the vector. That is, dom describes the set of *valid* indices, and r specifies an invariant relating each Int index with the value stored at that index.

Creating Vectors. We can use the following basic functions to create vectors:

```
empty :: forall <p::Int->a->Bool>.Vec<{\_ -> False}, p> a
empty = V (\_ -> error "Empty Vec")

create :: x:a -> Vec <{\_ -> True}, {\_ v -> v = x}> a
create x = V (\_ -> x)
```

The signature for empty states that its domain is empty (*i.e.*, is the set of indices satisfying the predicate **False**), and that the range satisfies any invariant. The signature for create, instead, defines a *constant* vector that maps every index to the constant x.

Accessing Vectors. We can write the following get function for reading the contents of a vector at a given index:

```
get :: forall <d :: Int -> Bool, r :: Int -> a -> Bool>
          i:Int<d> -> Vec<d, r> a -> a<r i>
get i (V f) = f i
```

The signature states that for any domain d and range r, if the index i is a valid index, *i.e.*, is of type, Int<d> then the returned value is an a that additionally satisfies the range refinement at the index i. The type for set, which *updates* the vector at a given index, is even more interesting, as it allows us to *extend* the domain of the vector:

```
set :: forall <d :: Int -> Bool, r :: Int -> a -> Bool>
          i:Int<d>
       -> a<r i>
       -> Vec<d && {\k -> k != i}, r> a
       -> Vec<d, r> a
set i v (V f) = V (\k -> if k == i then v else f k)
```

The signature for `set` requires that (a) the input vector is defined everywhere at d *except* the index i, and (b) the value supplied must be of type a<r i>, *i.e.*, satisfy the range relation at the index i at which the vector is being updated. The signature ensures that the output vector is defined at d and each value satisfies the index-dependent range refinement r. Note that it is legal to call `get` with a vector that is *also* defined at the index i since, by contravariance, such a vector is a subtype of that required by (a).

Initializing Vectors. Next, we can write the following function, `init`, that "loops" over a vector, to `set` each index to a value given by some function.

```
initialize :: forall <r :: Int -> a -> Bool>.
              (z: Int -> a<r z>)
           -> i: {v: Int | v >= 0}
           -> n: Int
           -> Vec <{\v -> 0 <= v && v < i}, r> a
           -> Vec <{\v -> 0 <= v && v < n}, r> a

initialize f i n a
  | i >= n    = a
  | otherwise = initialize f (i+1) n (set i (f i) a)
```

The signature requires that (a) the higher-order function f produces values that satisfy the range refinement r, and (b) the vector is initialized from 0 to i. The function ensures that the output vector is initialized from 0 through n. We can thus verify that

```
idVec  :: Vec <{\v -> 0<=v && v<n}, {\i v -> v=i}> Int
idVec n = initialize (\i -> i) 0 n empty
```

i.e., `idVec` returns a vector of size n where each key is mapped to itself. Thus, abstract refinement types allow us to verify low-level idioms such as the incremental initialization of vectors, which have previously required special analyses [12,15,5].

Null-Terminated Strings. We can also use abstract refinements to verify code which manipulates C-style null-terminated strings, represented as `Char` vectors for ease of exposition. Formally, a null-terminated string of size n has the type

```
type NullTerm n
  = Vec <{\v -> 0<=v<n}, {\i v -> i=n-1 => v='\0'}> Char
```

The above type describes a length-n vector of characters whose last element must be a null character, signalling the end of the string. We can use this type in the specification of a function, `upperCase`, which iterates through the characters of a string, uppercasing each one until it encounters the null terminator:

```
upperCase :: n:{v: Int| v>0} -> NullTerm n -> NullTerm n
upperCase n s = ucs 0 s where
  ucs i s = case get i s of
              '\0' -> s
              c    -> ucs (i + 1) (set i (toUpper c) s)
```

Note that the length parameter n is provided solely as a "witness" for the length of the string s, which allows us to use the length of s in the type of upperCase; n is not used in the computation. In order to establish that each call to get accesses string s within its bounds, our type system must establish that, at each call to the inner function ucs, i satisfies the type {v: Int | 0 <= v && v < n}. This invariant is established as follows. First, the invariant trivially holds on the first call to ucs, as n is positive and i is 0. Second, we assume that i satisfies the type {v: Int | 0 <= v && v < n}, and, further, we know from the types of s and get that c has the type {v: Char | i = n - 1 => v = '\0'}. Thus, if c is non-null, then i cannot be equal to n - 1. This allows us to strengthen our type for i in the else branch to {v: Int | 0 <= v && v < n - 1} and thus to conclude that the value i + 1 recursively passed as the i parameter to ucs satisfies the type {v: Int | 0 <= v && v < n}, establishing the inductive invariant and thus the safety of the upperCase function.

Memoization. Next, let us illustrate how the same expressive signatures allow us to verify memoizing functions. We can specify to the SMT solver the definition of the Fibonacci function via an uninterpreted function fib and an axiom:

```
measure fib :: Int -> Int
axiom: forall i. fib(i) = i<=1 ? 1 : fib(i-1) + fib(i-2)
```

Next, we define a type alias FibV for the vector whose values are either 0 (*i.e.*, undefined), or equal to the Fibonacci number of the corresponding index.

```
type FibV = Vec<{\_->True},{\i v-> v!=0 => v=fib(i)}> Int
```

Finally, we can use the above alias to verify fastFib, an implementation of the Fibonacci function which uses a vector to memoize intermediate results

```
fastFib :: n:Int -> {v:Int | v = fib(n)}
fastFib n = snd $ fibMemo (create 0) n

fibMemo :: FibV -> i:Int -> (FibV, {v: Int | v = fib(i)})
fibMemo t i
   | i <= 1    = (t, 1)
   | otherwise = case get i t of
                    0 -> let (t1, n1) = fibMemo t  (i-1)
                             (t2, n2) = fibMemo t1 (i-2)
                             n        = n1 + n2
                         in (set i n t2,  n)
                    n -> (t, n)
```

Thus, abstract refinements allow us to define key-value maps with index-dependent refinements for the domain and range. Quantification over the domain and range refinements allows us to define generic access operations (*e.g.*, get, set, create, empty) whose types enable us establish a variety of precise invariants.

2.3 Recursive Invariants

Next, we turn our attention to recursively defined datatypes, and show how abstract refinements allow us to specify and verify high-level invariants that relate the elements of a recursive structure. Consider the following refined definition for lists:

```
data [a] <p :: a -> a -> Bool> where
  []  :: [a]<p>
  (:) :: h:a -> [a<p h>]<p> -> [a]<p>
```

The definition states that a value of type [a]<p> is either empty ([]) or constructed from a pair of a *head* h::a and a *tail* of a list of a values *each* of which satisfies the refinement (p h). Furthermore, the abstract refinement p holds recursively within the tail, ensuring that the relationship p holds between *all* pairs of list elements.

Thus, by plugging in appropriate concrete refinements, we can define the following aliases, which correspond to the informal notions implied by their names:

```
type IncrList a = [a]<{\h v -> h <= v}>
type DecrList a = [a]<{\h v -> h >= v}>
type UniqList a = [a]<{\h v -> h != v}>
```

That is, IncrList a (resp. DecrList a) describes a list sorted in increasing (resp. decreasing) order, and UniqList a describes a list of *distinct* elements, *i.e.,* not containing any duplicates. We can use the above definitions to verify

```
[1, 2, 3, 4] :: IncrList Int
[4, 3, 2, 1] :: DecrList Int
[4, 1, 3, 2] :: UniqList Int
```

More interestingly, we can verify that the usual algorithms produce sorted lists:

```
insertSort :: (Ord a) => [a] -> IncrList a
insertSort []     = []
insertSort (x:xs) = insert x (insertSort xs)

insert :: (Ord a) => a -> IncrList a -> IncrList a
insert y []       = [y]
insert y (x:xs)
  | y <= x        = y : x : xs
  | otherwise     = x : insert y xs
```

Thus, abstract refinements allow us to *decouple* the definition of the list from the actual invariants that hold. This, in turn, allows us to conveniently reuse the same underlying (non-refined) type to implement various algorithms unlike, say, singleton-type based implementations which require up to three different types of lists (with three different "nil" and "cons" constructors [24]). This, makes abstract refinements convenient for verifying complex sorting implementations like that of Data.List.sort which, for efficiency, use lists with different properties (*e.g.,* increasing and decreasing).

Multiple Recursive Refinements. We can define recursive types with multiple parameters. For example, consider the following refined version of a type used to encode functional maps (`Data.Map`):

```
data Tree k v <l :: k->k->Bool, r :: k->k->Bool>
    = Bin { key   :: k
          , value :: v
          , left  :: Tree <l, r> (k <l key>) v
          , right :: Tree <l, r> (k <r key>) v }
      | Tip
```

The abstract refinements `l` and `r` relate each `key` of the tree with *all* the keys in the *left* and *right* subtrees of `key`, as those keys are respectively of type `k <l key>` and `k <r key>`. Thus, if we instantiate the refinements with the following predicates

```
type BST k v     = Tree<{\x y -> x> y},{\x y-> x< y}> k v
type MinHeap k v = Tree<{\x y -> x<=y},{\x y-> x<=y}> k v
type MaxHeap k v = Tree<{\x y -> x>=y},{\x y-> x>=y}> k v
```

then `BST k v`, `MinHeap k v` and `MaxHeap k v` denote exactly binary-search-ordered, min-heap-ordered, and max-heap-ordered trees (with keys and values of types k and v). We demonstrate in (§ 4) how we use the above types to automatically verify ordering properties of complex, full-fledged libraries.

2.4 Inductive Invariants

Finally, we explain how abstract refinements allow us to formalize some kinds of structural induction within the type system.

Measures. First, let us formalize a notion of *length* for lists within the refinement logic. To do so, we define a special `len` measure by structural induction

```
measure len :: [a] -> Int
len []     = 0
len (x:xs) = 1 + len(xs)
```

We use the measures to automatically strengthen the types of the data constructors[16]:

```
data [a] where
    []  :: forall a.{v:[a] | len(v) = 0}
    (:) :: forall a.a -> xs:[a] -> {v:[a]|len(v)=1+len(xs)}
```

Note that the symbol `len` is encoded as an *uninterpreted* function in the refinement logic, and is, except for the congruence axiom, opaque to the SMT solver. The measures are guaranteed, by construction, to terminate, and so we can soundly use them as uninterpreted functions in the refinement logic. Notice also, that we can define *multiple* measures for a type; in this case we simply conjoin the refinements from each measure when refining each data constructor.

With these strengthened constructor types, we can verify, for example, that `append` produces a list whose length is the sum of the input lists' lengths:

```
append :: l:[a] -> m:[a] -> {v:[a]|len(v)=len(l)+len(m)}
append []      zs = zs
append (y:ys) zs = y : append ys zs
```

However, consider an alternate definition of `append` that uses `foldr`

$$\text{append ys zs = foldr (:) zs ys}$$

where `foldr :: (a -> b -> b)-> b -> [a] -> b`. It is unclear how to give `foldr` a (first-order) refinement type that captures the rather complex fact that the fold-function is "applied" all over the list argument, or, that it is a catamorphism. Hence, hitherto, it has not been possible to verify the second definition of `append`.

Typing Folds. Abstract refinements allow us to solve this problem with a very expressive type for `foldr` whilst remaining firmly within the boundaries of SMT-based decidability. We write a slightly modified fold:

```
foldr :: forall <p :: [a] -> b -> Bool>.
            (xs:[a] -> x:a -> b <p xs> -> <p (x:xs)>)
         -> b<p []>
         -> ys:[a]
         -> b<p ys>
foldr op b []     = b
foldr op b (x:xs) = op xs x (foldr op b xs)
```

The trick is simply to quantify over the relationship p that `foldr` establishes between the input list xs and the output b value. This is formalized by the type signature, which encodes an induction principle for lists: the base value b must (1) satisfy the relation with the empty list, and the function op must take (2) a value that satisfies the relationship with the tail xs (we have added the xs as an extra "ghost" parameter to op), (3) a head value x, and return (4) a new folded value that satisfies the relationship with x:xs. If all the above are met, then the value returned by `foldr` satisfies the relation with the input list ys. This scheme is not novel in itself [3] — what is new is the encoding, via uninterpreted predicate symbols, in an SMT-decidable refinement type system.

Using Folds. Finally, we can use the expressive type for the above `foldr` to verify various inductive properties of client functions:

```
length :: zs:[a] -> {v: Int | v = len(zs)}
length = foldr (\_ _ n -> n + 1) 0

append :: l:[a] -> m:[a] -> {v:[a]| len(v)=len(l)+len(m)}
append ys zs = foldr (\_ -> (:)) zs ys
```

The verification proceeds by just (automatically) instantiating the refinement parameter p of `foldr` with the concrete refinements, via Liquid typing:

```
{\xs v -> v = len(xs)}                    -- for length
{\xs v -> len(v) = len(xs) + len(zs)}   -- for append
```

Expressions	$e ::= x \mid c \mid \lambda x : \tau.e \mid e\, e \mid \Lambda \alpha.e \mid e\,[\tau] \mid \Lambda \pi : \tau.e \mid e\,[e]$
Abstract Refinements	$p ::= \mathit{true} \mid p \wedge \pi\, \overline{e}$
Basic Types	$b ::= \mathtt{int} \mid \mathtt{bool} \mid \alpha$
Abstract Refinement Types	$\tau ::= \{v : b\langle p \rangle \mid e\} \mid \{v : (x : \tau) \rightarrow \tau \mid e\}$
Abstract Refinement Schemas	$\sigma ::= \tau \mid \forall \alpha.\sigma \mid \forall \pi : \tau.\sigma$

Fig. 1. Syntax of Expressions, Refinements, Types and Schemas

3 Syntax and Semantics

Next, we present a core calculus λ_P that formalizes the notion of abstract refinements. We start with the syntax (§ 3.1), present the typing rules (§ 3.2), show soundness via a reduction to contract calculi [17,1] (§ 3.3), and inference via Liquid types (§ 3.4).

3.1 Syntax

Figure 1 summarizes the syntax of our core calculus λ_P which is a polymorphic λ-calculus extended with abstract refinements. We write b, $\{v : b \mid e\}$, and $b\langle p \rangle$ to abbreviate $\{v : b\langle \mathit{true} \rangle \mid \mathit{true}\}$, $\{v : b\langle \mathit{true} \rangle \mid e\}$, and $\{v : b\langle p \rangle \mid \mathit{true}\}$ respectively. We say a type or schema is *non-refined* if all the refinements in it are *true*. We write $\overline{z}$ to abbreviate a sequence $z_1 \ldots z_n$.

Expressions. λ_P expressions include the standard variables x, primitive constants c, λ-abstraction $\lambda x : \tau.e$, application $e\, e$, type abstraction $\Lambda \alpha.e$, and type application $e\,[\tau]$. The parameter τ in the type application is a *refinement type*, as described shortly. The two new additions to λ_P are the refinement abstraction $\Lambda \pi : \tau.e$, which introduces a refinement variable π (together with its type τ), which can appear in refinements inside e, and the corresponding refinement application $e\,[e]$.

Refinements. A *concrete refinement* e is a boolean valued expression e drawn from a strict subset of the language of expressions which includes only terms that (a) neither diverge nor crash, and (b) can be embedded into an SMT decidable refinement logic including the theory of linear arithmetic and uninterpreted functions. An *abstract refinement* p is a conjunction of refinement variable applications of the form $\pi\, \overline{e}$.

Types and Schemas. The basic types of λ_P include the base types $\mathtt{int}$ and $\mathtt{bool}$ and type variables α. An *abstract refinement type* τ is either a basic type refined with an abstract and concrete refinements, $\{v : b\langle p \rangle \mid e\}$, or a dependent function type where the parameter x can appear in the refinements of the output type. We include refinements for functions, as refined type variables can be replaced by function types. However, type-checking ensures these refinements are trivially true. Finally, types can be quantified over refinement variables and type variables to yield abstract refinement schemas.

Well-Formedness
$$\boxed{\Gamma \vdash \sigma}$$

$$\frac{}{\Gamma \vdash true(v)} \; \text{WF-TRUE} \qquad \frac{\Gamma \vdash p(v) \quad \Gamma \vdash \pi\,\bar{e}\,v : \texttt{bool}}{\Gamma \vdash (p \wedge \pi\,\bar{e})(v)} \; \text{WF-RAPP}$$

$$\frac{\Gamma, v : b \vdash e : \texttt{bool} \quad \Gamma, v : b \vdash p(v) : \texttt{bool}}{\Gamma \vdash \{v : b\langle p\rangle \mid e\}} \; \text{WF-BASE}$$

$$\frac{\Gamma \vdash e : \texttt{bool} \quad \Gamma \vdash \tau_x \quad \Gamma, x : \tau_x \vdash \tau}{\Gamma \vdash \{v : (x : \tau_x) \to \tau \mid e\}} \; \text{WF-FUN}$$

$$\frac{\Gamma, \pi : \tau \vdash \sigma}{\Gamma \vdash \forall \pi : \tau.\sigma} \; \text{WF-ABS-}\pi \qquad \frac{\Gamma, \alpha \vdash \sigma}{\Gamma \vdash \forall \alpha.\sigma} \; \text{WF-ABS-}\alpha$$

Subtyping
$$\boxed{\Gamma \vdash \sigma_1 \preceq \sigma_2}$$

$$\frac{\text{SMT-Valid}(\llbracket \Gamma \rrbracket \wedge \llbracket p_1\,v \rrbracket \wedge \llbracket e_1 \rrbracket \Rightarrow \llbracket p_2\,v \rrbracket \wedge \llbracket e_2 \rrbracket)}{\Gamma \vdash \{v : b\langle p_1\rangle \mid e_1\} \preceq \{v : b\langle p_2\rangle \mid e_2\}} \; \preceq\text{-BASE}$$

$$\frac{\Gamma \vdash \tau_2 \preceq \tau_1 \quad \Gamma, x_2 : \tau_2 \vdash \tau_1'[x_2/x_1] \preceq \tau_2'}{\Gamma \vdash \{v : (x_1 : \tau_1) \to \tau_1' \mid e_1\} \preceq \{v : (x_2 : \tau_2) \to \tau_2' \mid true\}} \; \preceq\text{-FUN}$$

$$\frac{\Gamma, \pi : \tau \vdash \sigma_1 \preceq \sigma_2}{\Gamma \vdash \forall \pi : \tau.\sigma_1 \preceq \forall \pi : \tau.\sigma_2} \; \preceq\text{-RVAR} \qquad \frac{\Gamma \vdash \sigma_1 \preceq \sigma_2}{\Gamma \vdash \forall \alpha.\sigma_1 \preceq \forall \alpha.\sigma_2} \; \preceq\text{-POLY}$$

Type Checking
$$\boxed{\Gamma \vdash e : \sigma}$$

$$\frac{\Gamma \vdash e : \sigma_2 \quad \Gamma \vdash \sigma_2 \preceq \sigma_1 \quad \Gamma \vdash \sigma_1}{\Gamma \vdash e : \sigma_1} \; \text{T-SUB} \qquad \frac{}{\Gamma \vdash c : tc(c)} \; \text{T-CONST}$$

$$\frac{x : \{v : b\langle p\rangle \mid e\} \in \Gamma}{\Gamma \vdash x : \{v : b\langle p\rangle \mid e \wedge v = x\}} \; \text{T-VAR-BASE} \qquad \frac{x : \tau \in \Gamma}{\Gamma \vdash x : \tau} \; \text{T-VAR}$$

$$\frac{\Gamma, x : \tau_x \vdash e : \tau \quad \Gamma \vdash \tau_x}{\Gamma \vdash \lambda x : \tau_x.e : (x : \tau_x) \to \tau} \; \text{T-FUN} \qquad \frac{\Gamma \vdash e_1 : (x : \tau_x) \to \tau \quad \Gamma \vdash e_2 : \tau_x}{\Gamma \vdash e_1 \, e_2 : \tau[e_2/x]} \; \text{T-APP}$$

$$\frac{\Gamma, \alpha \vdash e : \sigma}{\Gamma \vdash \Lambda \alpha.e : \forall \alpha.\sigma} \; \text{T-GEN} \qquad \frac{\Gamma \vdash e : \forall \alpha.\sigma \quad \Gamma \vdash \tau}{\Gamma \vdash e \, [\tau] : \sigma[\tau/\alpha]} \; \text{T-INST}$$

$$\frac{\Gamma, \pi : \tau \vdash e : \sigma \quad \Gamma \vdash \tau}{\Gamma \vdash \Lambda \pi : \tau.e : \forall \pi : \tau.\sigma} \; \text{T-PGEN} \qquad \frac{\Gamma \vdash e : \forall \pi : \tau.\sigma \quad \Gamma \vdash \lambda \overline{x : \tau_x}.e' : \tau}{\Gamma \vdash e \, [\lambda \overline{x : \tau_x}.e'] : \sigma[\pi \triangleright \lambda \overline{x : \tau_x}.e']} \; \text{T-PINST}$$

Fig. 2. Static Semantics: Well-formedness, Subtyping and Type Checking

3.2 Static Semantics

Next, we describe the static semantics of λ_P by describing the typing judgments and derivation rules. Most of the rules are standard [21,23,17,2]; we discuss only those pertaining to abstract refinements.

Judgments. A type environment Γ is a sequence of type bindings $x : \sigma$. We use environments to define three kinds of typing judgments:

- **Wellformedness judgments** ($\Gamma \vdash \sigma$) state that a type schema σ is well-formed under environment Γ, that is, the refinements in σ are boolean expressions in the environment Γ.

- **Subtyping judgments** ($\Gamma \vdash \sigma_1 \preceq \sigma_2$) state that the type schema σ_1 is a subtype of the type schema σ_2 under environment Γ, that is, when the free variables of σ_1 and σ_2 are bound to values described by Γ, the set of values described by σ_1 is contained in the set of values described by σ_2.
- **Typing judgments** ($\Gamma \vdash e : \sigma$) state that the expression e has the type schema σ under environment Γ, that is, when the free variables in e are bound to values described by Γ, the expression e will evaluate to a value described by σ.

Wellformedness Rules. The wellformedness rules check that the concrete and abstract refinements are indeed `bool`-valued expressions in the appropriate environment. The key rule is WF-BASE, which checks, as usual, that the (concrete) refinement e is boolean, and additionally, that the abstract refinement p applied to the value v is also boolean. This latter fact is established by WF-RAPP which checks that each refinement variable application $\pi \, \bar{e} \, v$ is also of type `bool` in the given environment.

Subtyping Rules. The subtyping rules stipulate when the set of values described by schema σ_1 is subsumed by the values described by σ_2. The rules are standard except for $\preceq$-VAR, which encodes the base types' abstract refinements p_1 and p_2 with conjunctions of *uninterpreted predicates* $[\![p_1 \, v]\!]$ and $[\![p_2 \, v]\!]$ in the refinement logic as follows:

$$[\![true \, v]\!] \doteq true$$
$$[\![(p \wedge \pi \, \bar{e}) \, v]\!] \doteq [\![p \, v]\!] \wedge \pi([\![e_1]\!], \ldots, [\![e_n]\!], v)$$

where $\pi(\bar{e})$ is a term in the refinement logic corresponding to the application of the uninterpreted predicate symbol π to the arguments $\bar{e}$.

Type Checking Rules. The type checking rules are standard except for T-PGEN and T-PINST, which pertain to abstraction and instantiation of abstract refinements. The rule T-PGEN is the same as T-FUN: we simply check the body e in the environment extended with a binding for the refinement variable π. The rule T-PINST checks that the concrete refinement is of the appropriate (unrefined) type τ, and then replaces all (abstract) applications of π inside σ with the appropriate (concrete) refinement e' with the parameters $\bar{x}$ replaced with arguments at that application. Formally, this is represented as $\sigma[\pi \triangleright \lambda \overline{x : \tau}.e']$ which is σ with each base type transformed as

$$\{v : b\langle p \rangle \mid e\}[\pi \triangleright z] \doteq \{v : b\langle p'' \rangle \mid e \wedge e''\}$$
$$\text{where} \quad (p'', e'') \doteq \mathsf{Apply}(p, \pi, z, true, true)$$

Apply replaces each application of π in p with the corresponding conjunct in e'', as

$$\mathsf{Apply}(true, \cdot, \cdot, p', e') \doteq (p', e')$$
$$\mathsf{Apply}(p \wedge \pi' \, \bar{e}, \pi, z, p', e') \doteq \mathsf{Apply}(p, \pi, z, p' \wedge \pi' \, \bar{e}, e')$$
$$\mathsf{Apply}(p \wedge \pi \, \bar{e}, \pi, \lambda \overline{x : \tau}.e'', p', e') \doteq \mathsf{Apply}(p, \pi, \lambda \overline{x : \tau}.e'', p', e' \wedge e''[\bar{e}, v/\bar{x}])$$

In other words, the instantiation can be viewed as two symbolic reduction steps: first replacing the refinement variable with the concrete refinement, and then "beta-reducing" concrete refinement with the refinement variable's arguments. For example,

$$\{v : \mathtt{int}\langle \pi\, y \rangle \mid v > 10\}[\pi \rhd \lambda x_1 : \tau_1.\lambda x_2 : \tau_2.x_1 < x_2] \doteq \{v : \mathtt{int} \mid v > 10 \land y < v\}$$

3.3   Soundness

As hinted by the discussion about refinement variable instantiation, we can intuitively think of abstract refinement variables as *ghost* program variables whose values are boolean-valued functions. Hence, abstract refinements are a special case of higher-order contracts, that can be statically verified using uninterpreted functions. (Since we focus on static checking, we don't care about the issue of blame.) We formalize this notion by translating λ_P programs into the contract calculus F_H of [1] and use this translation to define the dynamic semantics and establish soundness.

Translation. We translate λ_P schemes σ to F_H schemes $\langle\!| \sigma |\!\rangle$ as by translating abstract refinements into contracts, and refinement abstraction into function types:

$$\langle\!| true\; v |\!\rangle \doteq true \qquad\qquad \langle\!| \forall \pi : \tau.\sigma |\!\rangle \doteq (\pi : \langle\!| \tau |\!\rangle) \to \langle\!| \sigma |\!\rangle$$
$$\langle\!| (p \land \pi\, \overline{e})\; v |\!\rangle \doteq \langle\!| p\, v |\!\rangle \land \pi\, \overline{e}\, v \qquad\qquad \langle\!| \forall \alpha.\sigma |\!\rangle \doteq \forall \alpha.\langle\!| \sigma |\!\rangle$$
$$\langle\!| \{v : b\langle p \rangle \mid e\} |\!\rangle \doteq \{v : b \mid e \land \langle\!| p\, v |\!\rangle\} \qquad\qquad \langle\!| (x : \tau_1) \to \tau_2 |\!\rangle \doteq (x : \langle\!| \tau_1 |\!\rangle) \to \langle\!| \tau_2 |\!\rangle$$

Similarly, we translate λ_P terms e to F_H terms $\langle\!| e |\!\rangle$ by converting refinement abstraction and application to λ-abstraction and application

$$\langle\!| x |\!\rangle \doteq x \qquad\qquad \langle\!| c |\!\rangle \doteq c$$
$$\langle\!| \lambda x : \tau.e |\!\rangle \doteq \lambda x : \langle\!| \tau |\!\rangle.\langle\!| e |\!\rangle \qquad\qquad \langle\!| e_1\, e_2 |\!\rangle \doteq \langle\!| e_1 |\!\rangle\, \langle\!| e_2 |\!\rangle$$
$$\langle\!| \Lambda\alpha.e |\!\rangle \doteq \Lambda\alpha.\langle\!| e |\!\rangle \qquad\qquad \langle\!| e\, [\tau] |\!\rangle \doteq \langle\!| e |\!\rangle\, \langle\!| \tau |\!\rangle$$
$$\langle\!| \Lambda\pi : \tau.e |\!\rangle \doteq \lambda\pi : \langle\!| \tau |\!\rangle.\langle\!| e |\!\rangle \qquad\qquad \langle\!| e_1\, [e_2] |\!\rangle \doteq \langle\!| e_1 |\!\rangle\, \langle\!| e_2 |\!\rangle$$

Translation Properties. We can show by induction on the derivations that the type derivation rules of λ_P *conservatively approximate* those of F_H. Formally,

- If $\Gamma \vdash \tau$ then $\langle\!| \Gamma |\!\rangle \vdash_H \langle\!| \tau |\!\rangle$,
- If $\Gamma \vdash \tau_1 \preceq \tau_2$ then $\langle\!| \Gamma |\!\rangle \vdash_H \langle\!| \tau_1 |\!\rangle <: \langle\!| \tau_2 |\!\rangle$,
- If $\Gamma \vdash e : \tau$ then $\langle\!| \Gamma |\!\rangle \vdash_H \langle\!| e |\!\rangle : \langle\!| \tau |\!\rangle$.

Soundness. Thus rather than re-prove preservation and progress for λ_P, we simply use the fact that the type derivations are conservative to derive the following preservation and progress corollaries from [1]:

- **Preservation:** If $\emptyset \vdash e : \tau$ and $\langle\!| e |\!\rangle \longrightarrow e'$ then $\emptyset \vdash_H e' : \langle\!| \tau |\!\rangle$
- **Progress:** If $\emptyset \vdash e : \tau$, then either $\langle\!| e |\!\rangle \longrightarrow e'$ or $\langle\!| e |\!\rangle$ is a value.

Note that, in a contract calculus like F_H, subsumption is encoded as a *upcast*. However, if subtyping relation can be statically guaranteed (as is done by our conservative SMT based subtyping) then the upcast is equivalent to the identity function and can be eliminated. Hence, F_H terms $\langle\!| e |\!\rangle$ translated from well-typed λ_P terms e have no casts.

3.4   Refinement Inference

Our design of abstract refinements makes it particularly easy to perform type inference via Liquid typing, which is crucial for making the system usable by eliminating the tedium of instantiating refinement parameters all over the code. (With value-dependent refinements, one cannot simply use, say, unification to determine the appropriate instantiations, as is done for classical type systems.) We briefly recall how Liquid types work, and sketch how they are extended to infer refinement instantiations.

Liquid Types. The Liquid Types method infers refinements in three steps. First, we create refinement *templates* for the unknown, to-be-inferred refinement types. The *shape* of the template is determined by the underlying (non-refined) type it corresponds to, which can be determined from the language's underlying (non-refined) type system. The template is just the shape refined with fresh refinement variables κ denoting the unknown refinements at each type position. For example, from a type $(x : \mathtt{int}) \to \mathtt{int}$ we create the template $(x : \{v : \mathtt{int} \mid \kappa_x\}) \to \{v : \mathtt{int} \mid \kappa\}$. Second, we perform type checking using the templates (in place of the unknown types.) Each wellformedness check becomes a wellformedness constraint over the templates, and hence over the individual κ, constraining which variables can appear in κ. Each subsumption check becomes a subtyping constraint between the templates, which can be further simplified, via syntactic subtyping rules, to a logical implication query between the variables κ. Third, we solve the resulting system of logical implication constraints (which can be cyclic) via abstract interpretation — in particular, monomial predicate abstraction over a set of logical qualifiers [9,23]. The solution is a map from κ to conjunctions of qualifiers, which, when plugged back into the templates, yields the inferred refinement types.

Inferring Refinement Instantiations. The key to making abstract refinements practical is a means of synthesizing the appropriate arguments e' for each refinement application $e\,[e']$. Note that for such applications, we can, from e, determine the non-refined type of e', which is of the form $\tau_1 \to \ldots \to \tau_n \to \mathtt{bool}$. Thus, e' has the template $\lambda x_1 : \tau_1.\ldots.\lambda x_n : \tau_n.\kappa$ where κ is a fresh, unknown refinement variable that must be solved to a boolean valued expression over $x_1, \ldots, x_n$. Thus, we generate a *wellformedness* constraint $x_1 : \tau_1, \ldots, x_n : \tau_n \vdash \kappa$ and carry out typechecking with template, which, as before, yields implication constraints over κ, which can, as before, be solved via predicate abstraction. Finally, in each refinement template, we replace each κ with its solution e_κ to get the inferred refinement instantiations.

4   Evaluation

In this section, we empirically evaluate the expressiveness and usability of abstract refinement types by exploring the process of typechecking a set of challenging benchmark programs using a prototype type checker for Haskell. (We defer the task of extending the metatheory to a call-by-name calculus to future work.)

HSOLVE. We have implemented abstract refinement in HSOLVE, a refinement type checker for Haskell. HSOLVE verifies Haskell source one module (.hs file) at a time. It takes as input:

Table 1. (**LOC**) is the number of non-comment Haskell source code lines as reported by *sloccount*, (**Specs**) is the number of lines of type specifications, (**Annot**) is the number of lines of other annotations, including refined datatype definitions, type aliases and measures, required for verification, (**Time**) is the time in seconds taken for verification.

Program	LOC	Specs	Annot	Time (s)
Micro	32	19	4	2
Vector	56	56	2	14
ListSort	29	4	1	3
Data.List.sort	71	3	1	8
Data.Set.Splay	136	15	11	15
Data.Map.Base	1399	119	31	235
Total	1723	216	50	277

- A *target* Haskell source file, with the desired refinement types specified as a special form of comment annotation,
- An (optional) set of type specifications for imported definitions; these can either be put directly in the source for the corresponding modules, if available, or in special .spec files otherwise. For imported functions for which no signature is given, HSOLVE conservatively uses the non-refined Haskell type.
- An (optional) set of logical qualifiers, which are predicate templates from which refinements are automatically synthesized [23]. Formally, a logical qualifier is a predicate whose variables range over the program variables, the special value variable ν, and *wildcards* $\star$, which HSOLVE instantiates with the names of program variables. Aside from the qualifiers given by the user, HSOLVE also uses qualifiers mined from the refinement type annotations present in the program.

After analyzing the program, HSOLVE returns as output:

- Either SAFE, indicating that all the specifications indeed verify, or UNSAFE, indicating there are refinement type errors, together with the positions in the source code where type checking fails (*e.g.,* functions that do not satisfy their signatures, or callsites where the inputs don't conform to the specifications).
- An HTML file containing the program source code annotated with inferred refinement types for all sub-expressions in the program. The inferred refinement type for each program expression is the strongest possible type over the given set of logical qualifiers. When a type error is reported, the programmer can use the inferred types to determine why their program does not typecheck: they can examine what properties HSOLVE *can* deduce about various program expressions and add more qualifiers or alter the program as necessary so that it typechecks.

Implementation. HSOLVE verifies the contents of a single file (module) at a time as follows. First, the Haskell source is fed into GHC, which desugars the program to GHC's "core" intermediate representation [26]. Second, the desugared program, the type signatures for the module functions (which are to be verified) and the type signatures for externally imported functions (which are assumed to hold) are sent to the constraint generator, which traverses the core bindings in a syntax-directed manner to generate subtyping constraints. The resulting constraints are simplified via our sub-typing rules (§ 3) into simple logical implication constraints. Finally, the implication constraints, together with the logical qualifiers provided by the user and harvested from the type signatures, are sent into an SMT- and abstract interpretation-based fixpoint computation procedure that determines if the constraints are satisfiable [13,9]. If so, the program is reported to be *safe*. Otherwise, each unsatisfiable constraint is mapped back to the corresponding program source location that generated it and a potential error is reported at that line in the program.

Benchmarks. We have evaluated HSOLVE over the following list of benchmarks which, in total, represent the different kinds of reasoning described in § 2. While we can prove, and previously have proved [16], many so-called "functional correctness" properties of these data structures using refinement types, in this work we focus on the key invariants which are captured by abstract refinements.

- `Micro`, which includes several functions demonstrating parametric reasoning with base values, type classes, and higher-order loop invariants for traversals and folds, as described in § 2.1 and § 2.4;
- `Vector`, which includes the domain- and range-generic `Vec` functions and several "clients" that use the generic `Vec` to implement incremental initialization, null-terminated strings, and memoization, as described in § 2.2;
- `ListSort`, which includes various textbook sorting algorithms including insert-, merge- and quick-sort. We verify that the functions actually produce sorted lists, *i.e.*, are of type `IncrList` a, as described in § 2.3;
- `Data.List.sort`, which includes three non-standard, optimized list sorting algorithms, as found in the `base` package. These employ lists that are increasing and decreasing, as well as lists of (sorted) lists, but we can verify that they also finally produce values of type `IncrList` a;
- `Data.Set.Splay`, which is a purely functional, top-down splay set library from the `llrbtree` package. We verify that all the interface functions take and return binary search trees;
- `Data.Map.Base`, which is the widely-used implementation of functional maps from the `containers` package. We verify that all the interface functions preserve the crucial binary search ordering property and various related invariants.

Table 1 quantitatively summarizes the results of our evaluation. We now give a qualitative account of our experience using HSOLVE by discussing what the specifications and other annotations look like.

Specifications are Usually Simple. In our experience, abstract refinements greatly simplify writing specifications for the *majority* of interface or public functions. For example, for `Data.Map.Base`, we defined the refined version of the `Tree` ADT (actually called `Map` in the source, we reuse the type from § 2.3 for brevity), and then instantiated it with the concrete refinements for binary-search ordering with the alias `BST k v` as described in § 2.3. Most refined specifications were just the Haskell types with the `Tree` type constructor replaced with the alias `BST`. For example, the type of `fromList` is refined from `(Ord k)=> [(k, a)] -> Tree k a` to `(Ord k)=> [(k, a)] -> BST k a`. Furthermore, intra-module Liquid type inference permits the automatic synthesis of necessary stronger types for private functions.

Auxiliary Invariants Are Sometimes Difficult. However, there are often rather thorny *internal* functions with tricky invariants, whose specification can take a bit of work. For example, the function `trim` in `Data.Map.Base` has the following behavior (copied verbatim from the documentation): "`trim blo bhi t` trims away all subtrees that surely contain no values between the range `blo` to `bhi`. The returned tree is either empty or the key of the root is between `blo` and `bhi`." Furthermore `blo` (resp. `bhi`) are specified as option (*i.e.*, `Maybe`) values with **Nothing** denoting $-\infty$ (resp. $+\infty$). Fortunately, refinements suffice to encode such properties. First, we define measures

```
measure isJust       :: Maybe a -> Bool
isJust (Just x)      = true
isJust (Nothing)     = false

measure fromJust     :: Maybe a -> a
fromJustS (Just x) = x

measure isBin        :: Tree k v -> Bool
isBin (Bin _ _ _ _)  = true
isBin (Tip)          = false

measure key :: Tree k v -> k
key (Bin k _ _ _)    = k
```

which respectively embed the `Maybe` and `Tree` root value into the refinement logic, after which we can type the `trim` function as

```
trim :: (Ord k) => blo:Maybe k
                 -> bhi:Maybe k
                 -> BST k a
                 -> {v:BST k a | bound(blo, v, bhi)}
```

where bound is simply a refinement alias

```
refinement bound(lo, v, hi)
   = isBin(v) => isJust(lo) => fromJust(lo) < key(v)
   && isBin(v) => isJust(hi) => fromJust(hi) > key(v)
```

That is, the output refinement states that the root is appropriately lower- and upper-bounded if the relevant terms are defined. Thus, refinement types allow one to formalize the crucial behavior as machine-checkable documentation.

Code Modifications. On a few occasions we also have to change the code slightly, typically to make explicit values on which various invariants depend. Often, this is for a trivial reason; a simple re-ordering of binders so that refinements for *later* binders can depend on earlier ones. Sometimes we need to introduce "ghost" values so we can write the specifications (*e.g.*, the `foldr` in § 2.4). Another example is illustrated by the use of list append in `quickSort`. Here, the append only produces a sorted list if the two input lists are sorted and such that each element in the first is less than each element in the second. We address this with a special `append` parameterized on `pivot`

```
append :: pivot:a
       -> IncrList {v:a | v < pivot}
       -> IncrList {v:a | v > pivot}
       -> IncrList a
append pivot [] ys     = pivot : ys
append pivot (x:xs) ys = x : append pivot xs ys
```

5 Related Work

The notion of type refinements was introduced by Freeman and Pfenning [11], with refinements limited to restrictions on the structure of algebraic datatypes, for which inference is decidable. Our present notion of refinement types has its roots in the *indexed types* of Xi and Pfenning [27], wherein data types' ranges are restricted by *indices*, analogous to our refinement predicates, drawn from a decidable domain; in the example case explored by Xi and Pfenning, types were indexed by terms from Presburger arithmetic. Since then, several approaches to developing richer refinement type systems and accompanying methods for type checking have been developed. Knowles and Flanagan [17] allow refinement predicates to be arbitrary terms of the language being typechecked and present a technique for deciding some typing obligations statically and deferring others to runtime. Findler and Felleisen's [8] higher-order contracts, which extend Eiffel's [18] first-order contracts — ordinary program predicates acting as dynamic pre- and post-conditions — to the setting of higher-order programs, eschew any form of static checking, and can be seen as a dynamically-checked refinement type system. Bengtson et al. [2] present a refinement type system in which type refinements are drawn from a decidable logic, making static type checking tractable. Greenberg et al. [1] gives a rigorous treatment of the metatheoretic properties of such a refinement type system.

Refinement types have been applied to the verification of a variety of program properties [27,7,2,10]. In the most closely related work to our own, Kawaguchi et al. [16] introduce *recursive* and *polymorphic* refinements for data structure properties. The present work unifies and generalizes these two somewhat ad-hoc notions into a single, strictly and significantly more expressive mechanism of abstract refinements.

A number of higher-order logics and corresponding verification tools have been developed for reasoning about programs. Example of systems of this type include NuPRL [4], Coq [3], F* [25] and Agda [20] which support the development and verification of higher-order, pure functional programs. While these systems are highly expressive, their expressiveness comes at the cost of making logical validity checking undecidable. To help automate validity checking, both built-in and user-provided tactics are used to attempt to discharge proof obligations; however, the user is ultimately responsible for manually proving any obligations which the tactics are unable to discharge.

References

1. Belo, J.F., Greenberg, M., Igarashi, A., Pierce, B.C.: Polymorphic Contracts. In: Barthe, G. (ed.) ESOP 2011. LNCS, vol. 6602, pp. 18–37. Springer, Heidelberg (2011)
2. Bengtson, J., Bhargavan, K., Fournet, C., Gordon, A.D., Maffeis, S.: Refinement types for secure implementations. ACM TOPLAS 33(2), 8 (2011)
3. Bertot, Y., Castéran, P.: Interactive Theorem Proving and Program Development. Coq'Art: The Calculus of Inductive Constructions. Texts in Theoretical Computer Science. Springer (2004)
4. Constable, R.L.: Implementing Mathematics with the Nuprl Proof Development System. Prentice-Hall (1986)
5. Cousot, P., Cousot, R., Logozzo, F.: A parametric segmentation functor for fully automatic and scalable array content analysis. In: POPL, pp. 105–118 (2011)
6. de Moura, L., Bjørner, N.: Z3: An Efficient SMT Solver. In: Ramakrishnan, C.R., Rehof, J. (eds.) TACAS 2008. LNCS, vol. 4963, pp. 337–340. Springer, Heidelberg (2008)
7. Dunfield, J.: A Unified System of Type Refinements. PhD thesis, Carnegie Mellon University, Pittsburgh, PA, USA (2007)
8. Findler, R.B., Felleisen, M.: Contracts for higher-order functions. In: ICFP, pp. 48–59 (2002)
9. Flanagan, C., Joshi, R., Leino, K.R.M.: Annotation inference for modular checkers. Information Processing Letters (2001)
10. Fournet, C., Kohlweiss, M., Strub, P.-Y.: Modular code-based cryptographic verification. In: CCS, pp. 341–350 (2011)
11. Freeman, T., Pfenning, F.: Refinement types for ML. In: PLDI (1991)
12. Gopan, D., Reps, T.W., Sagiv, S.: A framework for numeric analysis of array operations. In: POPL, pp. 338–350 (2005)
13. Graf, S., Saïdi, H.: Construction of Abstract State Graphs with PVS. In: Grumberg, O. (ed.) CAV 1997. LNCS, vol. 1254, pp. 72–83. Springer, Heidelberg (1997)
14. Guha, A., Fredrikson, M., Livshits, B., Swamy, N.: Verified security for browser extensions. In: IEEE Symposium on Security and Privacy, pp. 115–130 (2011)
15. Jhala, R., McMillan, K.L.: Array Abstractions from Proofs. In: Damm, W., Hermanns, H. (eds.) CAV 2007. LNCS, vol. 4590, pp. 193–206. Springer, Heidelberg (2007)
16. Kawaguchi, M., Rondon, P., Jhala, R.: Type-based data structure verification. In: PLDI, pp. 304–315 (2009)
17. Knowles, K.W., Flanagan, C.: Hybrid type checking. ACM TOPLAS 32(2) (2010)
18. Meyer, B.: Eiffel: the language. Prentice-Hall, Inc., Upper Saddle River (1992)
19. Nelson, G.: Techniques for program verification. Technical Report CSL81-10, Xerox Palo Alto Research Center (1981)
20. Norell, U.: Towards a practical programming language based on dependent type theory. PhD thesis, Chalmers, SE-412 96 Göteborg, Sweden (September 2007)
21. Ou, X., Tan, G., Mandelbaum, Y., Walker, D.: Dynamic Typing with Dependent Types. In: Levy, J.-J., Mayr, E.W., Mitchell, J.C. (eds.) TCS 2004. IFIP, vol. 155, pp. 437–450. Springer, Boston (2004)
22. Pierce, B.C.: Types and Programming Languages. MIT Press (2002)
23. Rondon, P., Kawaguchi, M., Jhala, R.: Liquid types. In: PLDI (2008)
24. Sheard, T.: Type-level computation using narrowing in omega. In: PLPV (2006)
25. Swamy, N., Chen, J., Fournet, C., Strub, P.-Y., Bhargavan, K., Yang, J.: Secure distributed programming with value-dependent types. In: ICFP, pp. 266–278 (2011)
26. Vytiniotis, D., Peyton Jones, S.L., Magalhães, J.: Equality proofs and deferred type errors: a compiler pearl. In: ICFP, pp. 341–352 (2012)
27. Xi, H., Pfenning, F.: Eliminating array bound checking through dependent types. In: PLDI (1998)

Constraining Delimited Control with Contracts*

Asumu Takikawa[1], T. Stephen Strickland[2], and Sam Tobin-Hochstadt[1]

[1] Northeastern University
[2] University of Maryland, College Park

Abstract. Most programming languages provide abstractions for non-local control flow and access to the stack by using continuations, coroutines, or generators. However, their unrestricted use breaks the local reasoning capability of a programmer. Gradual typing exacerbates this problem because typed and untyped code co-exist. We present a contract system capable of protecting code from control flow and stack manipulations by unknown components. We use these contracts to support a gradual type system, and we prove that the resulting system cannot blame typed components for errors.

1 Ubiquitous Continuations

Delimited continuations [6, 10, 12, 18, 19, 26, 27] enable the expression of many useful programming constructs such as coroutines, engines, and exceptions as libraries. Their expressive power stems from three key operations on the control stack: (1) marking a stack frame with a *prompt*; (2) *jumping* to a marked frame, discarding the context in between; and (3) *re-attaching* the slice of the control stack that the jump discarded. Continuations are not the only operations that manipulate the stack. In particular, continuation marks [4] provide the ability to (4) *annotate* a stack frame with data that can be dynamically accessed and updated from subsequent frames. They are used to implement features like general stack inspection for debugging, dynamic binding, and aspect-oriented programming as libraries [4, 22, 23].

Many dynamically-typed languages support delimited continuations and related control operators such as coroutines or generators [15, 20], and some also support continuation marks [5, 15]. Their lack of static typing, however, implies that a programmer could easily misuse manipulations of the stack to jump to the wrong place or annotate a frame with the wrong kind of data. Gradual typing addresses just these kinds of problems. Gradually typed languages allow programmers to type parts of their programs statically but leave other parts untyped. Even better, they provide strong dynamic guarantees about the safety of the combination of typed and untyped code [24, 32]. In particular, a gradually typed language does not allow untyped code to cause a run-time violation of the type invariants in the typed code.

Unfortunately, naïvely combining delimited continuations, continuation marks, and gradual typing fails to maintain the benefits of gradual typing. The numerous type systems proposed for delimited continuations [2, 6, 11, 18, 20, 21] can prevent an ill-typed

---

* Supported in part by NSF CRI-0855140, SHF-1064922, CCF-0915978, the Mozilla Foundation, and the DARPA CRASH program.

M. Felleisen and P. Gardner (Eds.): ESOP 2013, LNCS 7792, pp. 229–248, 2013.

re-attachment of a continuation or an ill-typed continuation jump. However, these type systems alone are not sufficient for gradual typing, because of the need for *dynamic enforcement*. Ordinarily, gradual type systems dynamically protect a typed component from its untyped context with a contract [14] that monitors the flow of values across the boundary [31]. Continuations, however, allow an untyped component to *bypass* the contract protection at the component boundary by jumping over the contract. After the jump, the untyped code could arrive in the middle of a typed component on the control stack and deliver an ill-typed value. Similarly, a continuation mark allows untyped code to update a stack annotation in typed code with an ill-typed value. In other words, continuations and continuation marks establish illicit communication channels between components. For the invariants of the typed language to hold, these channels require additional protection [9].

In this paper, we equip a gradually typed language with typed delimited control operators and continuation marks while maintaining the soundness of the entire system. To support this gradual type system, we introduce and formalize *control contracts* that mediate continuation jumps between prompts and their clients. We implement them in the Racket programming language [15] using *control chaperones* based on Strickland et al. [28]'s chaperone framework. Control chaperones allow a programmer to redirect communication between a prompt and a corresponding jump, inserting contract checks in between. For continuation marks, we offer an analogous pair of *continuation mark key contracts* and *continuation mark key chaperones*.

We also prove a soundness theorem for the combined language using Dimoulas et al's *complete monitoring* [9] technique. The key idea is to split a program into typed and untyped components via ownership annotations on values. Using these annotations, we impose a single owner policy which ensures that, at any given point, all of the values in the program are owned *only* by the typed or untyped portion of the program. Components may transfer ownership of a value only through the use of a contract, guaranteeing that no value changes hands without being checked. We prove that our contract system is a complete monitor and use this result to show that the gradual type system is sound.

2 Types and Contracts for Control Operators

To illustrate how delimited continuations and continuation marks cause problems for gradual typing, we present a series of examples using Sitaram's % and fcontrol operators [26]. The following example illustrates a simple use of the % operator to install a prompt and then a use of fcontrol to jump to that prompt, aborting part of the stack. The diagram on the right depicts the control flow of the example on the stack:

```
> (+ 2 (% (+ 1 (fcontrol 7))
          (λ (nat con) (+ 1 nat))))
10
```

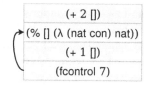

The evaluation of this example starts at (fcontrol 7), which immediately discards the current continuation up to the prompt (i.e., the third frame in the diagram). After discarding the continuation, fcontrol calls the handler, the λ expression argument to %, with two arguments: the value passed to fcontrol (i.e., 7) and the discarded continuation reified as a function, i.e., (λ (x) (+ 1 x)). In this case, the handler just increments the first argument by one and returns, ignoring the reified continuation. The % operator then returns the result of the handler to its context.

The handler in this example is simple, but in general prompt handlers allow the programmer to specify arbitrary computations. The correspondence between the prompt handler and fcontrol matches the correspondence between exception handlers and throwing an exception [26]. In other words, continuation operators like fcontrol generalize exceptions [18].

One major difference between fcontrol and most exception interfaces is that instead of throwing the continuation away, the handler can also re-install the continuation:

```
> (% (+ 1 (fcontrol 2))
     (λ (v k) (+ v (k 8)))))
11
```

(% [] (λ (v k) (+ v (k 8))))
(+ 1 [])
(fcontrol 2)

Here the handler calls its second argument, the reified continuation, instead of ignoring it. Since the continuation is a value, the handler just calls it like any other function. In fact, the handler could choose to return the continuation or apply it multiple times. The presence of the reified continuation makes fcontrol a *higher-order* control operator, as opposed to exceptions, which usually only provide *first-order* control

2.1 Types for Delimited Control

To implement a type system for delimited control, we must provide a means to type-check % and fcontrol. Each handler, however, may provide a different interface to its corresponding fcontrol. That is, they expect different types of input from a jump. In order to give a precise type for these handlers, we need to keep different logical uses of fcontrol separate and type-check them separately.[1]

To distinguish prompts with conflicting uses, control operators in the literature often allow the programmer to annotate prompts with *prompt tags* [11, 16, 18, 26]. For example, an implementation of coroutines and an implementation of exceptions might both install prompts on the stack. However, the stack changes coordinated by these libraries are "logically different" [26], even if they use the same operators, and should not interfere with one another.

Prompt tags also provide a convenient means to type-check separate uses of fcontrol [18]. The type of a prompt tag determines the valid types of values that an application of fcontrol can send to the corresponding prompt's handler. The prompt tag type also specifies the return type of the handler and the prompt's body. The % and fcontrol operators can be used with prompt tags to allow fine-grained control over what prompt is targeted:

---

[1] A type and effect system for delimited control [2, 6] could provide more precise types. However, an effect system would require intrusive run-time monitoring to enforce with contracts.

```
(define handler-1 (λ (v k) (string-append v "0")))
(define handler-2 (λ (v k) (k 1)))


> (% (number->string (% (+ 1 (fcontrol "10" prompt-tag-1))
                        handler-2 prompt-tag-2))
     handler-1 prompt-tag-1)
"100"
```

Since the call to fcontrol uses prompt-tag-1, the jump arrives at the outermost prompt, which is tagged with prompt-tag-1. The jump triggers handler-1, associated with the outer prompt. Notably, the jump does *not* invoke handler-2. It is vital that the programmer does not use the wrong prompt tag here, because the handlers expect different types: a string for handler-1 and an integer for handler-2.

Using a type system for prompt tags, we could declare that prompt-tag-1 has the type (Prompt String (Integer -> String) String). The first two types mean that the handler expects to receive a string and a function that takes integers and returns strings. The third type corresponds to the return type of the body and handler. This matches our example, since fcontrol sends the string "10" and the continuation from fcontrol to the outer prompt expects an integer and produces a string. Both the body (using number->string) and the handler clearly produce strings as well.

2.2 Gradual Typing, the Broken Variant

In a language with gradual typing, a typed component may import unknown functions from an untyped component:

```
#lang typed/racket
(require/typed [g : Integer -> String] from "untyped.rkt")

(% (string-length (g 2))
   (λ ([v : Integer] [k : Integer -> Integer])
      (+ v (k 8))))
```

In this example, the typed component imports a function g that is specified to have the type Integer -> String, which is valid for its use in the prompt expression. The gradual type system enforces the type for g with the generated contract (-> integer? string?). It blames the untyped component if its export fails to uphold the contract. Imports from untyped components and exports to untyped components are always protected with contracts translated from the corresponding type [31]. The type system prevents the typed component from misapplying the function.

Unfortunately, this naïve model of interaction fails in the presence of control operators, as demonstrated by the following *untyped* component:

```
#lang racket
(provide g)
(define (g x) (fcontrol "bad"))
```

The use of the `fcontrol` operator in the body of g immediately transfers control to the handler function when the typed module invokes g. Since this control transfer bypasses the contract boundary, the string `"bad"` is passed to the + operation, which causes a run-time failure that the type system should have prevented. The failure stems from the lack of protection on the communication channel between `fcontrol` and %.

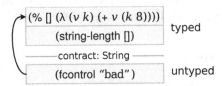

Generally speaking, the usual strategy of applying contracts to just the component imports and exports does not adequately protect the typed code from invalid uses of control operators within untyped code. In particular, the abort-like behavior of `fcontrol` allows it to directly communicate with the handler in the typed code, without first passing through a contract check at the component boundary.

With higher-order programming, the illicit communication may also take place using control operators in the opposite direction, as in the following pair of components:

```
#lang typed/racket
(provide g)

(define: (g) : Void (fcontrol h))
(define: (h [y : Integer]) : Integer (+ 1 y))
```

```
#lang racket
(require g from "typed.rkt")
(% (+ 1 (g)) (λ (v k) (v "bad")))
```

Here, the typed component exports a function g that uses a control operator to jump to the prompt, passing its handler a function. The untyped component calls g inside of a prompt whose handler misapplies the returned function to the string `"bad"` instead of an integer. Again, we depict this situation with a diagram:

$$
\begin{array}{|c|}
\hline
(\% \; [] \; (\lambda \; (v) \; (v \; \text{``bad''}))) \\
\hline
(+ \; 1 \; []) \\
\hline
\end{array} \quad \text{untyped}
$$

——— contract: Void ———

$$
\begin{array}{|c|}
\hline
(\text{fcontrol} \; (\lambda \; (y) \; (+ \; y \; 2))) \\
\hline
\end{array} \quad \text{typed}
$$

This stack illustrates a situation similar to the last diagram except that the typed and untyped components have swapped roles. Furthermore, notice that the contract on the stack is `Void` because the contract system checks the return value of g, because exports from typed components are wrapped with a contract.

On the surface, this may not seem like a problem; after all, the untyped component is free to do anything it likes with values since it is not beholden to a type system.

Unfortunately, f control has smuggled the *function* h across the contract boundary. Since h originates from typed code, applying it should not cause an error that the type system could prevent. In the top frame, however, the untyped component applies h to a value "bad" that the function does not expect, causing the addition (+ 1 y) to fail. This shows that higher-order programming requires protection for communication in *both* directions between typed and untyped components. To make gradual typing work, we must account for and protect all extra channels of communication.

2.3 Gradual Typing, Fixed

In order to fix our naïve gradual type system, we reuse the key insight from the gradual typing literature: the dynamic semantics must protect *all* possible channels of communication between typed and untyped components [9]. We instantiate this research insight for stack abstractions by installing contract checks on prompt tags that activate when control operators cross component boundaries. A prompt tag is a *capability* for communicating between two stack frames in a program. Thus, only components that have access to a given tag are allowed to communicate with the matching prompt, enabling the programmer to leverage lexical scope to limit access. However, the capability nature of prompt tags only determines *who* can communicate over the channel, but not *what* can be communicated across the channel.

To enable prompt tags to protect the data communicated via control operators, we equip prompt tags with contracts that trigger when a control operator transfers a value to the matching prompt. Since prompt tags function as capabilities, a component can be assured that *only* components with access to the corresponding prompt tag can jump to its prompts. Thus, as long as typed prompt tags are always exported with appropriate contracts, other components cannot jump to them without incurring contract checks. We formally characterize the translation of types to contracts in section 4.

For the problematic example from before, we revise the typed component to create and export a prompt tag. The untyped component can import and use the tag to jump to the typed component's prompt:

```
#lang typed/racket
(require/typed [g : Integer -> Integer] from "untyped.rkt")
(provide pt)

(pt : (Prompt Integer (Integer -> String) Integer))
(define pt (make-prompt-tag))

(% (string-length (g 2))
   (λ ([v : Integer] [k : Integer -> Integer])
     (+ v (k 8)))
   pt)
```

As before, the prompt tag type describes the type of the two values that f control sends to the handler and the result type of the handler. In the untyped code, the call to f control uses the prompt tag from the typed code:

```
#lang racket
(require pt from "typed.rkt")
(provide g)
(define (g x) (fcontrol "bad" pt))
```

Now, the type system installs a contract on uses of the exported tag in untyped code that corresponds to the type (Prompt Integer (Integer -> Integer)). When the function g aborts the continuation using the fcontrol operator, the "bad" value is checked with the Integer contract. The contract check fails and blames the untyped component for not providing an Integer to the prompt's handler. Pictorially, the fix adds a second contract boundary between the use of fcontrol and its matching prompt:

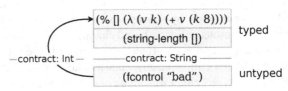

With the second contract boundary, all possible paths between the untyped and typed components are protected. This ensures that no unmonitored communication can occur between the components. In other words, the contract system completely monitors all communication between components, thus ensuring the safety of typed code that uses continuation operations.

2.4 Continuation Marks

The stack also offers non-local data storage to the programmer. Continuation marks are a language feature that enables this view, allowing the association of a key-value storage cell with each of the continuation frames that make up the stack. In turn, continuation marks enable other language features and tools such as debuggers, dynamic binding, and aspect-oriented programming [3, 4, 33].

A continuation mark is added to the current continuation frame with the wcm form (short for with-continuation-mark) and accessed with the ccm form (short for current-continuation-marks):

```
> (wcm 'key 7 (+ 1 (first (ccm 'key))))
8
```

Continuation marks consist of a key and an associated value, which are passed to the wcm operation. The ccm operation returns a list of the marks stored in the continuation associated with some key. The previous example demonstrates a simple case of setting and accessing a mark. As with continuations, continuation marks allow non-local communication of data through the stack, and thus require new forms of protection from the contract system. More concretely, continuation marks can be set in an untyped component and then accessed later in a typed component:

```
#lang racket
(require g from "typed.rkt")
(define key (make-continuation-mark-key))
(wcm key "bad" (g 7))
```

```
#lang typed/racket
(require/typed [key : (Mark Integer)] from "untyped.rkt")
(provide g)
(define (g x) (+ x (first (ccm key))))
```

In this example, the untyped component stores a string in the continuation mark with a new continuation mark key. The typed component imports the key with a type that requires integers in the mark storage for the key. However, the untyped component has already violated this assumption by storing a string in the mark. This demonstrates another example of an unprotected stack-based channel of communication.

Our solution for continuation mark protection is similar to the solution for delimited continuations. First, instead of allowing any value as a key for marks, we require the use of a prompt-tag-like key type, which we call a *continuation mark key*. This key acts as a capability for accessing the data contained in the mark. Using the same technique as prompt tags, we attach contracts to this key so that the continuation mark operations can introduce contract checks based on the key's contract. The following diagram illustrates the example above (on the left) and our solution (right):

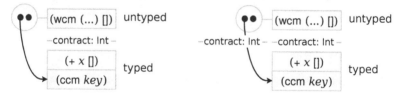

The new circle attached to the top stack frame illustrates a storage cell for the continuation mark on that frame. The cell might store many values, up to one for each key. The arrow from the cell depicts the flow of a value from the cell to the continuation frame that requests it using the ccm operation. As with continuations, this flow bypasses the ordinary contract boundary on the stack. The diagram on the right shows the fix in the form of an extra contract boundary that is established for accesses to the continuation mark store. In short, the contract system must protect all possible channels of interaction between the typed and untyped portions of the program.

From a contract system design perspective, continuation marks are similar to mutable reference; both enable non-local communication. Moreover, contracts for references and marks have related semantics. Mutable references need specialized support from the contract system to ensure that all access to the reference is protected by a contract [9, 28]. This extra protection amounts to wrapping the reference with a guard that redirects reads or writes to the reference and injects appropriate contract checking. Similarly, continuation mark key contracts wrap the key with a guard that redirects reads or writes to the continuation mark. Our formal model characterizes these guards and contracts more precisely.

3 Formalizing Contracts for Stack Abstractions

To explain our design and to validate its soundness, we present a formal model of a gradually typed λ-calculus extended with low-level operations on stacks. The low-level operators faithfully macro-express [13] the high-level operators. We chose our model's operators to match the production libraries used in both Racket [16] and in Guile [17] in order to demonstrate the model's practical applicability. Further details are available in a technical report [30].

Dybvig et al. [11] identify a template of five key operations that are necessary for delimited continuations: (1) construction of a delimiter, (2) delimiting a continuation, (3) capturing a continuation, (4) aborting a continuation, and (5) re-instating a continuation. Our model provides each of the elements in the template above. In our case, (1) corresponds to prompt tag creation and (5) to function application. The remaining three are provided as distinct operations %, call/comp, and abort, detailed below.

Our language is Dimoulas et al's CPCF [8], extended with Flatt et al's continuation operators [16]. We augment this model with an adaptation of Gunter et al. [18]'s type system for delimited control and a type system for continuation marks based on similar ideas. For dynamic invariant enforcement, we add contracts for delimited continuations and continuation marks.

Figure 1 presents the core grammar of the model. Programs consist of a tuple with an expression and a store. The store tracks the allocation of prompt tags and continuation mark keys. Expressions include straightforward PCF operations, list operations, and a set of control operators. The language is parameterized over a set of basic data types and primitive unary and binary operations such as addition, subtraction, and so on.

The key control operators are $(\% \, e_1 \, e_2 \, v)$, $(\text{abort} \, e_1 \, e_2)$, and $(\text{call/comp} \, v \, e)$, which correspond to delimiting the continuation, aborting the continuation, and capturing the continuation respectively. For continuation marks, the $(\text{call/cm} \, e_1 \, e_2 \, e_3)$ and $(\text{ccm} \, e)$ operations model the setting of continuation marks and access of marks respectively.

$$
\begin{array}{ll}
P ::= \, <e, \sigma> & t ::= B \mid (\to t\,t) \mid (\text{Prompt}\,t\,t) \\
\sigma ::= \varnothing \mid (key\,\sigma) \mid (tag\,\sigma) & \quad\mid (\text{Mark}\,t) \mid (\text{List}\,t) \\
e ::= x \mid v \mid (e\,e) \mid (\text{if}\,e\,e\,e) \mid (\mu\,(x:t)\,e) & pt ::= tag \\
\quad\mid (unop\,e) \mid (binop\,e\,e) \mid (\text{cons}\,e\,e) & mk ::= key \\
\quad\mid (\text{case}\,e\,(\text{null}=e)\,((\text{cons}\,x\,x)=e)) & E ::= M \mid (\text{wcm}\,w\,M) \\
\quad\mid (\text{prompt-tag}) \mid (\text{cm-key}) & M ::= [] \mid (\text{if}\,E\,e\,e) \mid (E\,e) \mid (v\,E) \\
\quad\mid (\%\,e\,e\,v) \mid (\text{abort}\,e\,e) & \quad\mid (unop\,E) \mid (binop\,E\,e) \mid (binop\,v\,E) \\
\quad\mid (\text{wcm}\,w\,e) \mid (\text{ccm}\,e) & \quad\mid (\text{case}\,E\,(\text{null}=e)\,((\text{cons}\,x\,x)=e)) \\
\quad\mid (\text{call/comp}\,e\,e) \mid (\text{call/cm}\,e\,e\,e) & \quad\mid (\text{cons}\,E\,e) \mid (\text{cons}\,v\,E) \\
\quad\mid (\text{update}\,mk\,e);e & \quad\mid (\text{update}\,mk\,E);e \\
\quad\mid (\text{error}) & \quad\mid (\%\,e\,E\,v) \mid (\%\,E\,pt\,v) \\
v ::= b \mid (\lambda\,(x:t)\,e) \mid pt \mid mk & \quad\mid (\text{abort}\,E\,e) \mid (\text{abort}\,v\,E) \\
\quad\mid (\text{cons}\,v\,v) \mid \text{null} & \quad\mid (\text{call/comp}\,E\,e) \mid (\text{call/comp}\,v\,E) \\
\quad\mid \text{call/comp} \mid \text{call/cm} & \quad\mid (\text{call/cm}\,E\,e\,e) \mid (\text{call/cm}\,v\,E\,e)
\end{array}
$$

Fig. 1. Core grammar and evaluation contexts

$$\frac{\Gamma \mid \Sigma \vdash e_2 : t_1 \qquad \Gamma \mid \Sigma \vdash e_1 : (\text{Prompt } t_1\ t_2)}{\Gamma \mid \Sigma \vdash (\text{abort } e_1\ e_2) : t} \text{[TAbort]}$$

$$\frac{\Gamma \mid \Sigma \vdash e_1 : (\to (\to t_3\ t_2)\ t_3) \qquad \Gamma \mid \Sigma \vdash e_2 : (\text{Prompt } t_1\ t_2)}{\Gamma \mid \Sigma \vdash (\text{call/comp } e_1\ e_2) : t_3} \text{[TCallComp]}$$

$$\frac{\Gamma \mid \Sigma \vdash e_1 : (\text{Mark } t_1) \qquad \Gamma \mid \Sigma \vdash e_2 : t_1 \qquad \Gamma \mid \Sigma \vdash e_3 : t_2}{\Gamma \mid \Sigma \vdash (\text{call/cm } e_1\ e_2\ e_3) : t_2} \text{[TCallCM]}$$

$$\frac{\Gamma \mid \Sigma \vdash e : (\text{Mark } t)}{\Gamma \mid \Sigma \vdash (\text{ccm } e) : (\text{List } t)} \text{[TCCM]}$$

$$\frac{\Gamma \mid \Sigma \vdash e_1 : t_2 \qquad \Gamma \mid \Sigma \vdash v : (\to t_1\ t_2) \qquad \Gamma \mid \Sigma \vdash e_2 : (\text{Prompt } t_1\ t_2)}{\Gamma \mid \Sigma \vdash (\%\ e_1\ e_2\ v) : t_2} \text{[TPrompt]}$$

$$\frac{\Gamma \mid \Sigma \vdash e : t \qquad \Gamma \mid \Sigma \vdash mk : (\text{Mark } t_1) \quad \cdots \quad \Gamma \mid \Sigma \vdash v : t_1 \quad \cdots}{\Gamma \mid \Sigma \vdash (\text{wcm } ((mk\ v)\ ...)\ e) : t} \text{[TWCM]}$$

Fig. 2. Typing rules

Our continuation operators suffice to encode high-level operators such as % and fcontrol. For example, here is a macro encoding of fcontrol:

```
(fcontrol v p) = (call/comp (λ (k) (abort v k)) p)
```

The static semantics of the model is straightforward. For delimited continuations, we adapt the prompt types of Gunter et al.'s cupto system [18]. The major type judgments are shown in figure 2. A judgment $\Gamma \mid \Sigma \vdash e : t$ separates the environment typing Γ from the store typing Σ. The store typing straightforwardly keeps track of the types of allocated prompt tags and mark keys. Prompt tag types (Prompt $t_1\ t_2$) are parameterized by two types: t_1 for the argument type expected by the handler function and t_2 for the body of the prompt. The rule for prompt expressions requires that, given an appropriate prompt tag, the body and the handler both produce a result of type t_2 and that the handler accepts an argument of type t_1. Conversely, an abort must carry a value of type t_2 for a given prompt tag and may result in any type, since control never returns.

Meanwhile, the call/comp operator captures a continuation up to a prompt with the given prompt tag and passes it to its handler. The return type t_3 of call/comp is the return type of its argument function. Since the current continuation has a hole of type t_3, and since the type of the expression up to the prompt is dictated by the prompt tag type t_2, the type rule also requires that call/comp's argument expects an argument type of ($\to t_3\ t_2$).

Continuation mark keys have a type (Mark t) where t is type of the value to be stored in the mark. The rule for wcm requires that all of the key-value pairs it stores are consistently typed; that is, the value stored is well-typed with respect to the mark key's type parameter. Similarly, call/cm requires that the specified mark key and value match and that its result type is the result type of its body. The ccm operation, used to extract the mark values, returns a list containing the values of the type stored in the mark.

$$
\begin{aligned}
e ::= & \;.... \\
 & |\ (\text{mon}_{l}^{l'}\ ctc\ e) \\
 & |\ (\text{ctc-error}_{l}) \\
 & |\ (\text{check}_{l}\ e\ v) \\
pt ::= & \;.... \\
 & |\ (\text{PG}_{l}^{l'}\ ctc\ pt) \\
mk ::= & \;.... \\
 & |\ (\text{MG}_{l}^{l'}\ ctc\ mk) \\
ctc ::= & \;(\text{flat}\ (\lambda\ (x : t)\ e)) \\
 & |\ (\mapsto ctc\ ctc) \\
 & |\ (\text{prompt-tag/c}\ ctc) \\
 & |\ (\text{mark/c}\ ctc) \\
 & |\ (\text{list/c}\ ctc) \\
t ::= & \;.... \\
 & |\ (\text{Con}\ t) \\
M ::= & \;.... \\
 & |\ (\text{mon}_{l}^{l'}\ ctc\ E) \\
 & |\ (\text{check}_{l}\ E\ v)
\end{aligned}
$$

$$(\text{mon}_{j}^{k,l}\ (\text{flat}\ v_f)\ v) \longrightarrow (\text{check}_{j}^{k}\ (v_f\ v)\ v)$$

$$(\text{mon}_{j}^{k,l}\ (\mapsto ctc_a\ ctc_r)\ v) \longrightarrow$$
$$(\lambda\ (x_1 : t)$$
$$((\lambda\ (x_2 : t)\ (\text{mon}_{j}^{k,l}\ ctc_r\ (v\ x_2)))$$
$$(\text{mon}_{j}^{l,k}\ ctc_a\ x_1)))$$
$$\text{where}\ v = (\lambda\ (x : t)\ e)$$

$$(\text{mon}_{j}^{k,l}\ (\text{list/c}\ ctc)\ \text{null}) \longrightarrow \text{null}$$

$$(\text{mon}_{j}^{k,l}\ (\text{list/c}\ ctc)\ (\text{cons}\ v_1\ v_2)) \longrightarrow$$
$$(\text{cons}\ (\text{mon}_{j}^{k,l}\ ctc\ v_1)\ (\text{mon}_{j}^{k,l}\ (\text{list/c}\ ctc)\ v_2))$$

$$(\text{mon}_{j}^{k,l}\ (\text{prompt-tag/c}\ ctc)\ v_p) \longrightarrow (\text{PG}_{j}^{k,l}\ ctc\ v_p)$$

$$(\text{mon}_{j}^{k,l}\ (\text{mark/c}\ ctc)\ v_m) \longrightarrow (\text{MG}_{j}^{k,l}\ ctc\ v_m)$$

$$(\text{check}_{j}\ \#t\ v) \longrightarrow v$$

$$(\text{check}_{j}\ \#f\ v) \longrightarrow (\text{ctc-error}_{j})$$

Fig. 3. Contracts and monitors

We specify the dynamic semantics in an operational style using evaluation contexts [12], omitting straightforward rules for conventional operations. The evaluation contexts, shown in figure 1, follow the form of the expression grammar. The contexts are stratified into two non-terminals E and M to ensure that adjacent wcm frames in the context are merged before further reduction. These merge steps simplify the rest of the operational rules and have precedent in the continuation mark literature [4, 16].

The contract system, based on CPCF, adds additional constructs to the language. The additional constructs and reduction rules for contracts are shown in figure 3. Contracts are applied using both monitors and guards. A monitor $(\text{mon}_{j}^{k,l}\ ctc\ e)$ represents a term e protected by a contract ctc. The labels k and l indicate the server and client parties, respectively, that entered into the contract. The final label j indicates the component that the contract belongs to [9]. Since monitored terms are not values, we need additional guard terms for prompt tags and continuation mark keys, because guarded tags and keys may appear in positions that expect values. Guards, like monitors, include a contract and server, client, and contract labels for the involved parties. A monitor or guard and its labels delineate the boundary between two components: server and client. Boundaries play a key role when we prove that no values pass between components (i.e., across a monitor or guard) without appropriate contract protection.

Monitors with a flat contract, i.e., one that the contract system can immediately check, reduce to a check expression that runs the contract predicate and either raises a contract error or returns the checked value. Monitors for functions reduce to a wrapped function that checks both the domain and range contracts. For prompt tags and mark contracts, the monitors respectively reduce to a prompt tag or mark key guard.

Figure 4 shows the key rules for continuations and continuation marks, which warrant additional explanation. The make-prompt-tag and make-cm-key terms reduce to fresh prompt tag and mark key values, respectively, allocating them in the store. A prompt that contains a value reduces to the value itself.

When a prompt contains an abort, the reduction relation takes the prompt's handler and applies it to the aborted value (via [abort]). The notation E_{pt} means that the context E does *not* contain a prompt tagged with the prompt tag pt. The rule additionally wraps the aborted value with any necessary contracts using the wrap+ and wrap- metafunctions. Respectively, these metafunctions wrap the values with the contract checks that are necessitated by the prompt tag of the prompt and the tag used by the abort. This rule only triggers when the prompt tag on the prompt side and the abort side are equivalent modulo any contract guards. An abort where the surrounding context contains no matching prompt tag gets stuck. Like Gunter et al. [18], we isolate this error case, which is difficult to rule out without a type and effect system, in our theorems.

Within a prompt, call/comp reifies the continuation as (λ (x : t) $E_{pt}[x]$) and applies v to this function. As with aborts, the rule only triggers when the prompt tags on both sides are the same.

Continuation mark frames (wcm w v) are discarded when the body is a value and reduce to the value itself. When two continuation mark frames are directly adjacent in the form (wcm w_1 (wcm w_2 e)), the frames are merged. The metafunction takes the innermost value for any given continuation mark key for the resulting store.

For continuation captures and setting a continuation mark, a continuation mark frame is allocated unless one already exists in the continuation. These are used to ensure that subsequent updates to the marks can be carried out. A call/cm operation that sets or updates a continuation mark reduces to an intermediate update term that first applies any necessary contract checks and then sets or updates the mark value. Continuation marks are actually updated via the [wcm/update/set] and [wcm/update/add] rules. The values stored in a continuation mark are extracted with the ccm expression for a given mark key. If the key is unguarded, the reduction rule uses a metafunction to retrieve the relevant values stored in the continuation's mark frames. If a guard exists, the ccm term reduces to a contract check wrapped around a new ccm term.

Notice that the only rules that involve both contracts and control operators are those that potentially cross into another component across a monitor or guard. Specifically, these are the [abort], [ccm/guard], and [call/cm] rules. None of the other control rules involve contracts, demonstrating the one key intuition behind our formalism: only the operations that set up communication across component boundaries need additional attention from the contract system. The proof technique in the next section justifies this intuition.

4   Complete Monitoring and the Blame Theorem

To show that our contract system comprehensively protects all of the communication channels in the language, we prove that the contract system satisfies the *complete monitoring* property [9]. Essentially, this property requires that the values in the language are always owned and manipulated by a single component at a time. Values only flow to a different component under the auspices of the contract system. Expressions that attempt to smuggle values without the contract system's knowledge would get stuck. We prove that the reduction relation is a complete monitor in order to show the blame theorem, which informally states that the contract system does not find the typed component at fault for any violation of types turned into contracts.

$<E[(\text{prompt-tag})], \sigma> \implies <E[tag], (tag\ \sigma)>$ [prompt-tag]
$\qquad\qquad\qquad$ where $tag \notin \sigma$

$(\%\ v_1\ pt\ v_2) \longrightarrow v_1$ [prompt]

$(\%\ E_{pt}[(\text{abort}\ pt\ v)]\ pt_1\ v_h) \longrightarrow (v_h\ E_+[E_-[v]])$ [abort]
$\qquad\qquad$ where $E_+ = \text{wrap+}[\![pt_1]\!],\ E_- = \text{wrap-}[\![pt, []]\!],\ pt =_{pt} pt_1$

$(\%\ E_{pt}[(\text{wcm}\ w\ (\text{call/comp}\ v\ pt))] \longrightarrow (\%\ E_{pt}[(\text{wcm}\ w\ (v\ (\lambda\ (x:t)\ E_{pt}[x])))]$ [call/comp]
$\quad pt_1\ v_h) \qquad\qquad\qquad\qquad\qquad pt_1\ v_h)$
$\qquad\qquad\qquad\qquad\qquad$ where $pt =_{pt} pt_1$

$<E[(\text{cm-key})], \sigma> \implies <E[key], (key\ \sigma)>$ [mark-key]
$\qquad\qquad\qquad$ where $key \notin \sigma$

$(\text{wcm}\ w\ v) \longrightarrow v$ [wcm/v]

$(\text{wcm}\ w_1\ (\text{wcm}\ w_2\ e)) \longrightarrow (\text{wcm}\ (w_1 \oplus w_2)\ e)$ [wcm/merge]

$<E[(\text{call/cm}\ v_1\ v_2\ e)], \sigma> \implies <E[(\text{wcm}\ ()\ (\text{call/cm}\ v_1\ v_2\ e))], \sigma>$ [wcm/intro/cm]
$\qquad\qquad\qquad$ where $E \neq E_1[(\text{wcm}\ w\ [])]$

$(\text{wcm}\ w\ (\text{call/cm}\ mk\ v\ e)) \longrightarrow (\text{wcm}\ w\ (\text{update}\ mk_1\ e_1);\ e\ )$ [call/cm]
$\qquad\qquad\qquad$ where $(mk_1\ e_1) = \text{push}[\![mk, v]\!]$

$(\text{wcm}\ ((key_1\ v_1)\ ... \qquad\qquad \longrightarrow (\text{wcm}\ ((key_1\ v_1)\ ...$ [wcm/set]
$\quad (key_2\ v_2)\ (key_3\ v_3)\ ...) \qquad\qquad (key_2\ v_4)\ (key_3\ v_3)\ ...)$
$\quad (\text{update}\ key_2\ v_4);\ e\ ) \qquad\qquad e)$

$(\text{wcm}\ ((key_1\ v_1)\ ...) \qquad\qquad \longrightarrow (\text{wcm}\ ((key_1\ v_1)\ ...\ (key_2\ v_2))\ e)$ [wcm/add]
$\quad (\text{update}\ key_2\ v_2);\ e\ )$
$\qquad\qquad\qquad$ where $key_2 \notin (key_1\ ...)$

$<E[(\text{ccm}\ key)], \sigma> \implies <E[\text{marks}[\![E, key, \text{null}]\!]], \sigma>$ [ccm]

$(\text{ccm}\ (\text{MG}_j^{k,l}\ ctc\ mk)) \longrightarrow (\text{mon}_j^{k,l}\ (\text{list/c}\ ctc)\ (\text{ccm}\ mk))$ [ccm/guard]

$\text{wrap+}[\![(\text{PG}_j^{k,l}\ ctc\ pt)]\!] = (\text{mon}_j^{k,l}\ ctc\ \text{wrap+}[\![pt]\!]) \qquad \text{wrap-}[\![(\text{PG}_j^{k,l}\ ctc\ pt), E]\!] = \text{wrap-}[\![pt, (\text{mon}_j^{l,k}\ ctc\ E)]\!]$
$\text{wrap+}[\![tag]\!] \qquad\qquad = [] \qquad\qquad\qquad\qquad \text{wrap-}[\![tag, E]\!] \qquad\qquad = E$

Fig. 4. Control reductions

Judgment	Description
$\Gamma;\ \Sigma;\ l \Vdash e$	Well-formed source terms
$\Gamma;\ \Sigma;\ (l\ ...);\ (l\ ...);\ l \rhd ctc$	Well-formed contracts
$\Gamma;\ \Sigma;\ l \vDash e$	Loosely well-formed terms
$\Sigma \sim \sigma$	Well-formed store
$S,\ S^v\ \vert\ G \vdash e : t$	Well-typed mixed terms (sec. 5)
$S,\ S^v\ \vert\ G \vdash e$	Well-formed mixed terms (sec. 5)

Fig. 5. Judgments

$$\frac{l = \Sigma(tag)}{\Sigma; \Gamma; l \Vdash tag} \; [\text{WPromptTag}] \qquad \frac{l = \Sigma(key)}{\Sigma; \Gamma; l \Vdash key} \; [\text{WKey}] \qquad \frac{\Sigma; \Gamma; l \Vdash e}{\Sigma; \Gamma; l \Vdash |e|^l} \; [\text{WOwn}]$$

$$\frac{\Sigma; \Gamma; k \Vdash e \quad \Sigma; \Gamma; (k); (l); j \rhd ctc}{\Sigma; \Gamma; l \Vdash (\text{mon}_j^{k,l} \, ctc \, |e|^k)} \; [\text{WMon}] \qquad \frac{\Sigma; \Gamma; k \Vdash v \quad \Sigma; \Gamma; (k\,l); (k\,l); j \rhd ctc}{\Sigma; \Gamma; l \Vdash (\text{PG}_j^{k,l} \, ctc \, v)} \; [\text{WPromptGuard}]$$

$$\frac{\Sigma; \Gamma; l \Vdash e \quad \Sigma; \Gamma; \Sigma(key) \Vdash v \quad \dots}{\Sigma; \Gamma; l \Vdash (\text{wcm} \, ((key \, v) \dots) \, e)} \; [\text{WWCM}] \qquad \frac{\Sigma; \Gamma; k \Vdash key \quad \Sigma; \Gamma; k \Vdash v \quad \Sigma; \Gamma; l \Vdash e}{\Sigma; \Gamma; l \Vdash (\text{update} \, k \, key \, v); e} \; [\text{WUpdate}]$$

$$\frac{\Sigma; \Gamma; j \Vdash e}{\Sigma; \Gamma; (k \dots); (l \dots); j \rhd \lfloor (\text{flat} \, |e|^j) \rfloor^{k \dots}} \; [\text{WCFlat}] \qquad \frac{\Sigma; \Gamma; (l \dots); (k \dots); j \rhd ctc_1 \quad \Sigma; \Gamma; (k \dots); (l \dots); j \rhd ctc_2}{\Sigma; \Gamma; (k \dots); (l \dots); j \rhd (\mapsto ctc_1 \, ctc_2)} \; [\text{WCFun}]$$

Fig. 6. Selected well-formed source program and contract rules

A proof of complete monitoring requires an annotation of values and expressions with ownership labels, using the component labels that contracts already use. In addition, we annotate contracts with obligation labels to show which components are responsible for which parts of the contract:

$$e ::= \dots \qquad\qquad v ::= \dots \qquad ctc ::= \dots$$
$$|\;|e|^l \qquad\qquad\quad |\;|v|^l \qquad\qquad |\;\lfloor(\text{flat} \, (\lambda \, (x : t) \, e))\rfloor^{l\dots}$$
$$|\;(\text{update} \, l \, mk \, e); e$$

The proof that our reduction relation is a complete monitor utilizes the traditional subject reduction technique. First, we describe how to set up the subject. We use several judgments, listed in figure 5, to enforce the necessary properties from the contract system. The judgment $\Gamma; \Sigma; l \Vdash e$ checks that source programs are well-formed with respect to the ownership annotations. We omit the details of several judgments; see the separate appendix for additional rules. Figure 6 presents a key subset of the rules for our model. Essentially, the judgment ensures that terms that set up a contract boundary, i.e., monitors, guards, and so on, contain sub-terms with matching ownership. For example, a monitor must be well-formed under its server label and its sub-term must be well-formed under the monitor's client label with an appropriate annotation. Guards set up a contract boundary in a similar fashion.

The judgment also features a store environment Σ. We use this environment to statically track the ownership of prompt tags and continuation mark keys. Since these values are unique and originate in a single component, we say that their ownership is determined purely by their mapping in the store. This ensures that any given tag or mark key appears only in the component that created them *unless* transported to another component via a contract.

$$(\|(\lambda\ (x : t)\ e)\|^l\ \|v\|^l) \longrightarrow |e[x := |v|^l]|^l \qquad\qquad [\beta]$$

$$(\%\ E^k_{pt}[(\text{wcm}\ w\ (\text{call/comp}\ \|v\|^k\ \|pt\|^k))] \longrightarrow (\%\ E^k_{pt}[(\text{wcm}\ w\ (|v|^k\ |(\text{cont}\ E)|^k))] \quad [\text{call/comp}]$$
$$\|pt_1\|^l\ \|v_h\|^l) \qquad\qquad\qquad\qquad\qquad \|pt_1\|^l\ \|v_h\|^l)$$
$$\text{where } pt =_{pt} pt_1$$

$$(\%\ E^k[(\text{abort}\ \|pt\|^k\ \|v\|^k)]\ \|pt_1\|^l\ \|v_h\|^l) \longrightarrow (|v_h|^j\ E^j_+[E^k[|v|^k]]) \qquad\qquad [\text{abort}]$$
$$\text{where } E^j_+ = \text{wrap+}[\![pt_1]\!],\ E^k = \text{wrap-}[\![pt,\ []]\!],\ pt =_{pt} pt_1$$

$$(\text{wcm}\ w\ (\text{call/cm}\ \|mk\|^l\ \|v\|^l\ e)) \longrightarrow (\text{wcm}\ w\ (\text{update}\ k\ key\ e_1);\ e\ ) \quad [\text{call/cm}]$$
$$\text{where } (key\ e_1\ k) = \text{push}[\![mk, v]\!]$$

Fig. 7. Select reduction rules with annotations

In the case of monitors and guards, we also require that their contract is well-formed using the judgment $\Gamma;\ \Sigma;\ (k\ ...);\ (l\ ...);\ j \triangleright ctc$. The third and fourth parts of the judgment indicate the components that should be responsible for the positive and negative parts of a contract, respectively. The fifth label indicates the component that should own the contract. Flat contracts are well-formed when their obligations match up with the positive parties and their code matches the contract party. Function contracts swap the positive and negative obligations for the domain contract. In all other cases, we require that sub-contracts are appropriately well-formed.

For some terms in a reduction sequence, the well-formedness condition is too strict. Most commonly, terms that reduce to monitored expressions can cause well-formedness to fail, even though a few additional steps of reduction corrects this failure. To handle this situation, we extend well-formedness to a *loose* well-formedness judgment $\Gamma;\ \Sigma;\ l \vDash e$, which is preserved by reduction.

Finally, we require with the judgment $\Sigma \sim \sigma$ that the program store is well-formed with respect to the store environment, meaning all of the statically known tags and keys are allocated with the correct owners. This requirement prevents a situation where unallocated tags or keys appear in an expression or where the environment records the wrong ownership.

To guarantee that the preservation lemma actually holds, we also modify the reduction rules to propagate the ownership annotations appropriately. Figure 7 shows a subset of the revised reduction rules. We rely on the notation $\|v\|^l$, which means the value v may be wrapped with zero or more ownership annotations, all with the label l. In the rules, we take any possibly annotated values and replace them in the contractum with the value wrapped in a single annotation, ensuring the annotation remains in future steps. One interesting case is the [call/cm] rule. The rule utilizes a modified push metafunction that guides the value v through several contract boundaries to reach the component that the mark key lives in. Each boundary traversal wraps the value with an additional monitor. The modified metafunction additionally returns the final owner of the component v after wrapping, which we need to annotate the update term.

With the judgments in mind, we formalize the complete monitoring property.

Definition 1. *A reduction relation is a complete monitor if for all well-typed terms e_0 such that $\Sigma; \varnothing; l_0 \Vdash e_0$,*

- *$<e_0, \varnothing> \rightarrow^* <v, \sigma>$, or*
- *for all e_1 and stores σ_1 such that $<e_0, \varnothing> \rightarrow^* <e_1, \sigma_1>$, there exists an e_2 and σ_2 such that $<e_1, \sigma_1> \rightarrow <e_2, \sigma_2>$, or*
- *$<e_0, \varnothing> \rightarrow^* <E_{pt}[(\text{abort } v \, pt)], \sigma_1>$, or*
- *$<e_0, \varnothing> \rightarrow^* <e_1, \sigma_1> \rightarrow^* <(\text{ctc-error}_j^k), \sigma_2>$ where e_1 is of the form $E^l[(\text{mon}_j^{k,l} \lfloor (\text{flat } v) \rfloor^{l \cdots} |v|^k)]$ and $k \in (l \ldots)$.*

Theorem 1. *The reduction relation $\rightarrow$ is a complete monitor.*

The proof follows a standard subject reduction strategy with two main lemmas: progress and preservation. We list the key lemmas below but omit details of the proof cases, which are similar to those presented by Dimoulas et al. [9].

Lemma 1. *For all e_0, σ_0, and Σ_0 such that $\Sigma_l; \varnothing; 0 \Vdash e_1$ and $\Sigma_0 \sim \sigma_0$, then either*

- *$e_0 = v$,*
- *$e_0 = (\text{ctc-error}_j^k)$,*
- *there exists an e_1 and σ_1 such that $<e_0, \sigma_0> \rightarrow <e_1, \sigma_1>$, or*
- *$<e_0, \sigma_0> = <E_{pt}[(\text{abort } v \, pt)], \sigma_0>$.*

Lemma 2. *For all $<e_0, \sigma_0> \rightarrow <e_1, \sigma_1>$ and there exists Σ_0 such that $\Sigma_l; \varnothing; Q \Vdash e_1$ and $\Sigma_0 \sim \sigma_0$, then for some $\Sigma_1 \supseteq \Sigma_0, \Sigma_1; \varnothing; l \Vdash e_1$.*

The culmination of the formalism is the Blame Theorem. Informally, the key idea of the Blame Theorem is that the contract system never blames the typed components of a mixed program for a contract error. Again, we first require some setup in order to state the theorem. The technique that we use here is detailed in Dimoulas et al. [9].

First, we set up an untyped sister language of our original typed language in order to have mixed programs. The untyped language shares the syntax and current operational semantics, but omits type annotations. Second, we isolate any stuck states that occur due to type errors and reduce them to contract errors blaming the component. For the contract system, we also require that flat contracts are picked from a pool of built-in contracts that exactly correspond to the base datatypes we use: integers, strings, etc.

In the mixed language, monitors allow the embedding of expressions from other components as before. We now limit the server and client labels to τ and υ for typed and untyped components. In other words, untyped components are embedded in a typed component with server and client labels υ and τ, respectively. For embedding in the other direction, the labels are reversed.

To ensure that components are well-formed, we require that the typed portions of any mixed program are well-typed and require that all components respect the ownership annotations as before. Furthermore, we need to guarantee that all component boundaries are protected by the correct contracts. We formalize this notion in the judgments $S, S^\upsilon \mid G \vdash e$ and $S, S^\upsilon \mid G \vdash e : t$ with store typing S, an environment S^υ for tracking untyped locations, and type environment G. Our notion of store consistency requires that untyped and typed locations are tracked disjointly [7]. These judgments rely on the mapping between types and contracts, presented in figure 8.

Finally, we can state and prove the Blame Theorem:

$$T[(\mapsto ctc_1\ ctc_2)] = (\to T[ctc_1]\ T[ctc_2])$$
$$T[(\text{prompt-tag/c}\ ctc)] = (\text{Prompt}\ T[ctc])$$
$$T[(\text{mark/c}\ ctc)] = (\text{Mark}\ T[ctc])$$
$$T[(\text{list/c}\ ctc)] = (\text{List}\ T[ctc])$$

Fig. 8. Contract-type translation

Theorem 2. *For all untyped terms e_0 such that $\varnothing, \varnothing \mid \varnothing \vdash e_0$ and $\varnothing; \varnothing; \upsilon \Vdash e_0$, $<e_0, \varnothing>$ does not reduce to a configuration of the form $<(\text{ctc-error}\ \math}{j}\ ), \sigma>$.*

The proof follows by subject reduction, again with two main lemmas [7, 9].

5   Implementing Stack Protection

In addition to demonstrating the theoretical soundness of our design, we also describe its implementation in a production language.[2] Our implementation technique builds on Strickland et al's chaperone framework [28]. Chaperones act as proxies for values that behave the same as the originals, modulo additional exceptions. This allows the enforcement of a desirable property of contracts: a contracted value should behave the same as the uncontracted value except for the possibility of contract errors.

To implement our control contracts, we modified the Racket runtime system to provide additional primitive operations such as `chaperone-continuation-prompt-tag` and `chaperone-continuation-mark-key`. Both prompt tag and mark key chaperones take two function arguments that are called when continuation and continuation mark operations are used, respectively. For the prompt tag case, one function is interposed on the application of a prompt handler and the other is interposed on a continuation abort. For continuation marks, one function is interposed on retrieval from a mark and the other is interposed on insertion into a mark.

Prompt and mark operations in the runtime coordinate with chaperones by checking if the prompt tag or mark key, respectively, is a chaperone and then using the appropriate interposition function if so. The interposition function receives the aborted value in the continuation case and the stored mark value in the case of continuation marks. The result of the interposition function is then used in place of the original value. If the prompt tag or mark key is not chaperoned, the operation proceeds normally.

6   Related Work

Types for delimited control. We use a variation of Gunter et al. [18]'s type system for the `cupto` delimited control operator. Although their type system does not support continuation marks, it inspired our solution. The main difference is our choice of primitives:

---

[2] Contracts for control are available in Racket 5.3 and higher. A development version of Typed Racket supports delimited control and continuation marks.

abort and call/comp are lower-level than cupto [15]. In addition, our type constructors for prompt tags take two arguments instead of one. This allows the handler to return a different type than its argument.

Many type systems for delimited control, following Danvy and Filinksi, use a type and effect system [2, 6]. These type systems support result type modification and statically eliminating continuation jumps to missing prompts. Our design choices make different compromises, based on two pragmatic considerations: simplicity of the system and the difficulty of dynamically enforcing effect typing with contracts.

Gradual typing and the Blame Theorem. Many researchers have constructed models of gradual typing: both functional and object-oriented [1, 24, 25, 29, 31]. The soundness theorem for gradual typing originates from Tobin-Hochstadt and Felleisen [31] and was christened the "Blame Theorem" in Wadler and Findler [34]. Our proof technique for this central theorem of gradual typing comes from Dimoulas et al. [9]. In general, the idea of complete monitoring also provides the intuition for the design of a contract system for gradual typing.

7   Conclusion

Virtually every modern programming language provides facilities for accessing and manipulating the stack, with exceptions, generators, and stack inspection as just a few examples. However, these facilities add non-local flows to programs, defeating the invariants programmers expect of their code. This problem is particularly acute in gradually typed languages, where type invariants are enforced with software contracts.

In this paper, we show that contracts, originally designed to mediate between caller and receiver, extend naturally to these non-local constructs. We equip Racket's delimited control and continuation mark operations with a gradual type system enforced at the boundaries by contracts. This system maintains type soundness in arbitrary composition with untyped code, as proved via the blame theorem. The implementation of control contracts in Racket leverages the existing chaperone framework for implementing contracts.

Acknowledgments. The authors wish to thank Aaron Turon and Stephen Chang for comments on early drafts. Christos Dimoulas gave valuable advice on the formalism. Matthias Felleisen also provided his feedback and insight on continuations.

References

[1] Ahmed, A., Findler, R.B., Siek, J.G., Wadler, P.: Blame for All. In: Proc. ACM Sym. Principles of Programming Languages, pp. 201–214 (2011)

[2] Asai, K., Kameyama, Y.: Polymorphic Delimited Continuations. In: Shao, Z. (ed.) APLAS 2007. LNCS, vol. 4807, pp. 239–254. Springer, Heidelberg (2007)

[3] Clements, J.: Portable and High-level Access to the Stack with Continuation Marks. PhD dissertation, Northeastern University (2006)

[4] Clements, J., Flatt, M., Felleisen, M.: Modeling an Algebraic Stepper. In: Proc. European Sym. on Programming, pp. 320–334 (2001)

[5] Clements, J., Sundaram, A., Herman, D.: Implementing Continuation Marks in Javascript. In: Proc. Wksp. Scheme and Functional Programming (2008)

[6] Danvy, O., Filinski, A.: Abstracting Control. In: Proc. LISP and Functional Programming, pp. 151–160 (1990)

[7] Dimoulas, C.: Foundations for Behavioral Higher-Order Contracts. PhD dissertation, Northeastern University (2012)

[8] Dimoulas, C., Felleisen, M.: On Contract Satisfaction in a Higher-Order World. Trans. Programming Languages and Systems 33(5), 16:1–16:29 (2011)

[9] Dimoulas, C., Tobin-Hochstadt, S., Felleisen, M.: Complete Monitors for Behavioral Contracts. In: Proc. European Sym. on Programming, pp. 214–233 (2012)

[10] Draves, R.P.: Control Transfer in Operating System Kernels. PhD dissertation, Carnegie Mellon University (1994)

[11] Dybvig, K., Peyton-Jones, S., Sabry, A.: A Monadic Framework for Delimited Continuations. J. Functional Programming 17(6), 687–730 (2007)

[12] Felleisen, M.: The Theory and Practice of First-Class Prompts. In: Proc. ACM Sym. Principles of Programming Languages, pp. 180–190 (1988)

[13] Felleisen, M.: On the Expressive Power of Programming Languages. Science of Computer Programming 17(1-3), 35–75 (1991)

[14] Findler, R.B., Felleisen, M.: Contracts for Higher-Order Functions. In: Proc. ACM Intl. Conf. Functional Programming, pp. 48–59 (2002)

[15] Flatt, M., PLT: Reference: Racket. PLT Inc., PLT-TR-2010-1 (2010), http://racket-lang.org/tr1/

[16] Flatt, M., Yu, G., Findler, R.B., Felleisen, M.: Adding Delimited and Composable Control to a Production Programming Environment. In: Proc. ACM Intl. Conf. Functional Programming, pp. 165–176 (2007)

[17] Free Software Foundation. Guile Reference Manual: Prompts (2012), http://www.gnu.org/software/guile/manual/html_node/Prompts.html

[18] Gunter, C.A., Didier, R., Riecke, J.G.: A Generalization of Exceptions and Control in ML-like Languages. In: Proc. ACM Intl. Conf. Functional Programming Languages and Computer Architecture, pp. 12–23 (1995)

[19] Hieb, R., Kent Dybvig, R., Anderson, C.W.: Subcontinuations. In: LISP and Symbolic Computation, pp. 83–110 (1994)

[20] James, R.P., Sabry, A.: Yield: Mainstream Delimited Continuations. In: Proc. Theory and Practice of Delimited Continuations, pp. 20–32 (2011)

[21] Kiselyov, O., Shan, C.-C.: A Substructural Type System for Delimited Continuations. In: Della Rocca, S.R. (ed.) TLCA 2007. LNCS, vol. 4583, pp. 223–239. Springer, Heidelberg (2007)

[22] Kiselyov, O., Shan, C.-C., Sabry, A.: Delimited Dynamic Binding. In: Proc. ACM Intl. Conf. Functional Programming, pp. 26–37 (2006)

[23] Pettyjohn, G., Clements, J., Marshall, J., Krishnamurthi, S., Felleisen, M.: Continuations from Generalized Stack Inspection. In: Proc. ACM Intl. Conf. Functional Programming, pp. 216–227 (2005)

[24] Siek, J.G., Taha, W.: Gradual Typing for Functional Languages. In: Proc. Wksp. Scheme and Functional Programming (2006)

[25] Siek, J.G., Taha, W.: Gradual Typing for Objects. In: Ernst, E. (ed.) ECOOP 2007. LNCS, vol. 4609, pp. 2–27. Springer, Heidelberg (2007)

[26] Sitaram, D.: Handling Control. In: Proc. ACM Conf. Programming Language Design and Implementation, pp. 147–155 (1993)

[27] Sitaram, D., Felleisen, M.: Control Delimiters and their Hierarchies. In: LISP and Symbolic Computation, pp. 67–99 (1990)

[28] Stephen Strickland, T., Tobin-Hochstadt, S., Findler, R.B., Flatt, M.: Chaperones and Impersonators: Run-time Support for Reasonable Interposition. In: Proc. ACM Conf. Object-Oriented Programming, Systems, Languages and Applications (2012)

[29] Takikawa, A., Stephen Strickland, T., Dimoulas, C., Tobin-Hochstadt, S., Felleisen, M.: Gradual Typing for First-Class Classes. In: Proc. ACM Conf. Object-Oriented Programming, Systems, Languages and Applications (2012)

[30] Takikawa, A., Stephen Strickland, T., Tobin-Hochstadt, S.: Constraining Delimited Control with Contracts. Northeastern University, NU-CCIS-13-01 (2013)

[31] Tobin-Hochstadt, S., Felleisen, M.: Interlanguage Migration: from Scripts to Programs. In: Proc. Dynamic Languages Symposium, pp. 964–974 (2006)

[32] Tobin-Hochstadt, S., Felleisen, M.: The Design and Implementation of Typed Scheme. In: Proc. ACM Sym. Principles of Programming Languages, pp. 395–406 (2008)

[33] Tucker, D.B., Krishnamurthi, S.: Pointcuts and Advice in Higher-Order Languages. In: Proc. Intl. Conf. on Aspect-Oriented Software Development, pp. 158–167 (2003)

[34] Wadler, P., Findler, R.B.: Well-typed Programs Can't be Blamed. In: Proc. European Sym. on Programming, pp. 1–15 (2009)

Verifying Concurrent Memory Reclamation Algorithms with Grace

Alexey Gotsman, Noam Rinetzky, and Hongseok Yang

[1] IMDEA Software Institute
[2] Tel-Aviv University
[3] University of Oxford

Abstract. Memory management is one of the most complex aspects of modern concurrent algorithms, and various techniques proposed for it—such as hazard pointers, read-copy-update and epoch-based reclamation—have proved very challenging for formal reasoning. In this paper, we show that different memory reclamation techniques actually rely on the same implicit synchronisation pattern, not clearly reflected in the code, but only in the form of assertions used to argue its correctness. The pattern is based on the key concept of a *grace period*, during which a thread can access certain shared memory cells without fear that they get deallocated. We propose a modular reasoning method, motivated by the pattern, that handles all three of the above memory reclamation techniques in a uniform way. By explicating their fundamental core, our method achieves clean and simple proofs, scaling even to realistic implementations of the algorithms without a significant increase in proof complexity. We formalise the method using a combination of separation logic and temporal logic and use it to verify example instantiations of the three approaches to memory reclamation.

1 Introduction

Non-blocking synchronisation is a style of concurrent programming that avoids the blocking inherent to lock-based mutual exclusion. Instead, it uses low-level synchronisation techniques, such as compare-and-swap operations, that lead to more complex algorithms, but provide a better performance in the presence of high contention among threads. Non-blocking synchronisation is primarily employed by concurrent implementations of data structures, such as stacks, queues, linked lists and hash tables.

Reasoning about concurrent programs is generally difficult, because of the need to consider all possible interactions between concurrently executing threads. This is especially true for non-blocking algorithms, where threads interact in subtle ways through dynamically-allocated data structures. In the last few years, great progress has been made in addressing this challenge. We now have a number of logics and automatic tools that combat the complexity of non-blocking algorithms by verifying them *thread-modularly*, i.e., by considering every thread in an algorithm in isolation under some assumptions on its environment and thus avoiding explicit reasoning about all thread interactions. Not only have such efforts increased our confidence in the correctness of the algorithms, but they have often resulted in human-understandable proofs that elucidated the core design principles behind these algorithms.

M. Felleisen and P. Gardner (Eds.): ESOP 2013, LNCS 7792, pp. 249–269, 2013.

However, one area of non-blocking concurrency has so far resisted attempts to give proofs with such characteristics—that of *memory management*. By their very nature, non-blocking algorithms allow access to memory cells while they are being updated by concurrent threads. Such optimistic access makes memory management one of the most complex aspects of the algorithms, as it becomes very difficult to decide when it is safe to reclaim a memory cell. Incorrect decisions can lead to errors such as memory access violations, corruption of shared data and return of incorrect results. To avoid this, an algorithm needs to include a protocol for coordinating between threads accessing the shared data structure and those trying to reclaim its nodes. Relying on garbage collection is not always an option, since non-blocking algorithms are often implemented in languages without it, such as C/C++.

In recent years, several different methods for explicit memory reclamation in non-blocking algorithms have been proposed:

- *Hazard pointers* [12] let a thread publish the address of a node it is accessing as a special global pointer. Another thread wishing to reclaim the node first checks the hazard pointers of all threads.
- *Read-copy-update (RCU)* [11] lets a thread mark a series of operations it is performing on a data structure as an RCU critical section, and provides a command that waits for all threads currently in critical sections to exit them. A thread typically accesses a given node inside the same critical section, and a reclaimer waits for all threads to finish their critical sections before deallocating the node.
- *Epoch-based reclamation* [5] uses a special counter of epochs, approximating the global time, for quantifying how long ago a given node has been removed from the data structure. A node that has been out of the data structure for a sufficiently long time can be safely deallocated.

Despite the conceptual simplicity of the above methods, their implementations in non-blocking algorithms are extremely subtle. For example, as we explain in §2, the protocol for setting a hazard pointer is more involved than just assigning the address of the node being accessed to a global variable. Reasoning naturally about protocols so subtle is very challenging. Out of the above algorithms, only restricted implementations of hazard pointers have been verified [14,6,3,16], and even in this case, the resulting proofs were very complicated (see §6 for discussion).

The memory reclamation algorithms achieve the same goal by intuitively similar means, yet are very different in details. In this paper, we show that, despite these differences, the algorithms actually rely on the same synchronisation pattern that is *implicit*—not clearly reflected in the code, but only in the form of assertions used to argue its correctness. We propose a modular reasoning method, formalising this pattern, that handles all three of the above approaches to memory reclamation in a uniform way. By explicating their fundamental core, we achieve clean and simple proofs, scaling even to realistic implementations of the algorithms without a significant increase in proof complexity.

In more detail, we reason about memory reclamation algorithms by formalising the concept of a *grace period*—the period of time during which a given thread can access certain nodes of a data structure without fear that they get deallocated. Before deallocating a node, a reclaimer needs to wait until the grace periods of all threads that could have had access to the node pass. Different approaches to memory reclamation define

```
 1  int *C = new int(0);
 2  int inc() {
 3      int v, *s, *n;
 4      n = new int;
 5      do {
 6          s = C;
 7          v = *s;
 8          *n = v+1;
 9      } while
10          (!CAS(&C,s,n));
11      // free(s);
12      return v;
13  }
```

(a)

```
14  int *C = new int(0);
15  int *HP[N] = {0};
16  Set detached[N] = {∅};
17  int inc() {
18      int v, *n, *s, *s2;
19      n = new int;
20      do {
21          do {
22              s = C;
23              HP[tid-1] = s;
24              s2 = C;
25          } while (s != s2);
26          v = *s;
27          *n = v+1;
28      } while(!CAS(&C,s,n));
29      reclaim(s);
30      return v; }
```

(b)

```
31  void reclaim(int *s) {
32      insert(detached[tid-1],s);
33      if (nondet()) return;
34      Set in_use = ∅;
35      while (!isEmpty(
36          detached[tid-1])) {
37          bool my = true;
38          int *n =
39          pop(detached[tid-1]);
40          for (int i = 0;
41              i < N && my; i++)
42              if (HP[i] == n)
43                  my = false;
44          if (my) free(n);
45          else insert(in_use, n);
46      }
47      moveAll(detached[tid-1],
48          in_use); }
```

(c)

Fig. 1. A shared counter: (a) an implementation leaking memory; (b)-(c) an implementation based on hazard pointers. Here tid gives the identifier of the current thread.

the grace period in a different way. However, we show that, for the three approaches above, the duration of a grace period can be characterised by a temporal formula of a fixed form "η since μ", e.g., "the hazard pointer has pointed to the node since the node was present in the shared data structure". This allows us to express the contract between threads accessing nodes and those trying to reclaim them by an invariant stating that a node cannot be deallocated during the corresponding grace period for any thread. The invariant enables modular reasoning: to prove the whole algorithm correct, we just need to check that separate threads respect it. Thus, a thread accessing the data structure has to establish the assertion "η since μ", ensuring that it is inside a grace period; a thread wishing to reclaim a node has to establish the *negation* of such assertions for all threads, thus showing that all grace periods for the node have passed. Different algorithms just implement code that establishes assertions of the same form in different ways.

We formalise such correctness arguments in a modular program logic, combining one of the concurrent versions of separation logic [17,4] with temporal logic (§3). We demonstrate our reasoning method by verifying example instantiations of the three approaches to memory reclamation—hazard pointers (§4), RCU (§5) and epoch-based reclamation [7, §D]. In particular, for RCU we provide the first specification of its interface that can be effectively used to verify common RCU-based algorithms. Due to space constraints, the development for epochs is deferred to [7, §D]. As far as we know, the only other algorithm that allows explicitly returning memory to the OS in non-blocking algorithms is the Repeat-Offender algorithm [8]. Our preliminary investigations show that our method is applicable to it as well; we leave formalisation for future work.

2   Informal Development

We start by presenting our reasoning method informally for hazard pointers and RCU, and illustrating the similarities between the two.

2.1   Running Example

As our running example, we use a counter with an increment operation inc that can be called concurrently by multiple threads. Despite its simplicity, the example is representative of the challenges that arise when reasoning about more complex algorithms.

The implementation shown in Figure 1a follows a typical pattern of non-blocking algorithms. The current value of the counter is kept in a heap-allocated node pointed to by the global variable C. To increment the counter, we allocate a new memory cell n (line 4), atomically read the value of C into a local pointer variable s (line 6), dereference s to get the value v of the counter (line 7), and then store v's successor into n (line 8). At that point, we try to change C so that it points to n using an atomic *compare-and-swap* (CAS) command (line 10). A CAS takes three arguments: a memory address (e.g., &C), an expected value (s) and a new value (n). It atomically reads the memory address and updates it with the new value if the address contains the expected value; otherwise, it does nothing. The CAS thus succeeds only if the value of C is the same as it was when we read it at line 6, thus ensuring that the counter is updated correctly. If the CAS fails, we repeat the above steps all over again. The algorithm is *memory safe*, i.e., it never accesses unallocated memory cells. It is also functionally correct in the sense that every increment operation appears to take effect atomically. More formally, the counter is *linearizable* with respect to the expected sequential counter specification [9]. Unfortunately, the algorithm leaks memory, as the node replaced by the CAS is never reclaimed. It is thus not appropriate for environments without garbage collection.

A Naive Fix. One can try to prevent memory leakage by uncommenting the free command in line 11 of Figure 1a, so that the node previously pointed to by C is deallocated by the thread that changed C's value (in this case we say that the thread *detached* the node). However, this violates both memory safety and linearizability. To see the former, consider two concurrent threads, one of which has just read the value x of C at line 6, when the other executed inc to completion and reclaimed the node at the address x. When the first thread resumes at line 7 it will access an unallocated memory cell.

The algorithm also has executions where a memory fault does not happen, but inc just returns an incorrect value. Consider the following scenario: a thread t_1 running inc gets preempted after executing line 7 and, at that time, C points to a node x storing v; a thread t_2 executes inc, deallocating the node x and incrementing the counter to $v + 1$; a thread t_3 calls inc and allocates x, recycled by the memory system; t_3 stores $v + 2$ into x and makes C point to it; t_1 wakes up, its CAS succeeds, and it sets the counter value to $v + 1$, thereby decrementing it! This is a particular instance of the well-known *ABA problem*: if we read the value A of a global variable and later check that it has the value A, we cannot conclude, in general, that in the meantime it did not change to another value B and then back to A. The version of the algorithm without free in line 11 does not suffer from this problem, as it always allocates a fresh cell. This algorithm is also correct when executed in a garbage-collected environment, as in this case the node x in the above scenario will not be recycled as long as t_1 keeps the pointer s to it.

2.2   Reasoning about Hazard Pointers

Figure 1b shows a correct implementation of inc with explicit memory reclamation based on *hazard pointers* [12]. We assume a fixed number of threads with identifiers from 1 to N. As before, the thread that detaches a node is in charge of reclaiming it. However, it delays the reclamation until it is assured that no other thread requested that the node be protected from reclamation. A thread announces a request for a node to be protected using the array HP of shared hazard pointers indexed by thread identifiers. Every thread is allowed to write to the entry in the array corresponding to its identifier and read all entries. To protect the location s, a thread writes s into its entry of the hazard array (line 23) and then checks that the announcement was not too late by validating that C still points to s (line 25). Once the validation succeeds, the thread is assured that the node s will not be deallocated as long as it keeps its hazard pointer equal to s. In particular, it is guaranteed that the node s remains allocated when executing lines 26–28, which ensures that the algorithm is memory safe. This also guarantees that, if the CAS in line 28 is successful, then C has not changed its value since the thread read it at line 24. This prevents the ABA problem and makes the algorithm linearizable.

The protection of a node pointed to by a hazard pointer is ensured by the behaviour of the thread that detaches it. Instead of invoking free directly, the latter uses the reclaim procedure in Figure 1c. This stores the node in a thread-local detached set (line 32) and occasionally performs a batched reclamation from this set (for clarity, we implemented detached as an abstract set, rather than a low-level data structure). To this end, the thread considers every node n from the set and checks that no hazard pointer points to it (lines 40–43). If the check succeeds, the node gets deallocated (line 44).

Reasoning Challenges. The main idea of hazard pointers is simple: threads accessing the shared data structure set hazard pointers to its nodes, and threads reclaiming memory check these pointers before deallocating nodes. However, the mechanics of implementing this protocol in a non-blocking way is very subtle.

For example, when a thread t_1 deallocates a node x at line 44, we may actually have a hazard pointer of another thread t_2 pointing to x. This can occur in the following scenario: t_2 reads the address x from C at line 22 and gets preempted; t_1's CAS detaches x and successfully passes the check in lines 40–43; t_2 wakes up and sets its hazard pointer to x; t_1 deallocates x at line 44. However, such situations do not violate the correctness, as the next thing t_2 will do is to check that C still points to x at line 25. Provided x has not yet been recycled by the memory system, this check will fail and the hazard pointer of t_2 will have no force. This shows that the additional check in line 25 is indispensable for the algorithm to be correct.

It is also possible that, before t_2 performs the check in line 25, x is recycled, allocated at line 19 by another thread t_3 and inserted into the shared data structure at line 28. In this case, the check by t_2 succeeds, and the element can safely be accessed. This highlights a subtle point: when t_3 executes the CAS at line 28 to insert x, we might already have a hazard pointer pointing to x. This, however, does not violate correctness.

Our Approach. We achieve a natural reasoning about hazard pointers and similar patterns by formalising the main intuitive concept in their design—that of a *grace period*. As follows from the above explanation, a thread t can only be sure that a node x its hazard pointer points to is not deallocated after a moment of time when both the hazard pointer was set and the node was pointed to by C. The grace period for the node x and thread t starts from this moment and lasts for as long as the thread keeps its hazard pointer pointing to x. Informally, this is described by the following temporal judgement:

"the hazard pointer of thread t has pointed to x <u>since</u> C pointed to x",   (1)

where <u>since</u> is a temporal connective with the expected interpretation: both of the facts connected were true at some point, and since then, the first fact has stayed true. We can thus specify the contract between threads accessing nodes and those trying to reclaim them by the following invariant that all threads have to respect:

"for all t and x, if the hazard pointer of thread t has pointed to x <u>since</u>
C pointed to x, then x is allocated."   (2)

It is this invariant that justifies the safety of the access to a shared node at line 26. On the other hand, a thread that wants to deallocate x when executing `reclaim` checks that the hazard pointers of other threads do not point to x (lines 40–43) only after detaching the node from the shared data structure, and it keeps the node in the `detached` set until its deallocation. Thus, even though threads can set their hazard pointers to x after the reclaimer executes the check in lines 40–43, they cannot do this at the same time as C points to x. Hence, when the reclaimer deallocates x at line 44, we know that

"for all t, C has not pointed to x <u>since</u> the hazard pointer of t did not
point to x."   (3)

Clearly, (3) is inconsistent with (1). Therefore, no thread is inside a grace period for x at the time of its deallocation, and the command in line 44 does not violate invariant (2).

More formally, let us denote the property "the hazard pointer of thread t points to node x" by $\eta_{t,x}$, "C points to node x" by μ_x, and "x is allocated" by λ_x. Then (1) is $(\eta_{t,x}$ since $\mu_x)$, (2) is $(\forall t, x. (\eta_{t,x}$ since $\mu_x) \implies \lambda_x)$, and (3) is $(\forall t. \neg\mu_x$ since $\neg\eta_{t,x})$. The combination of (1) and (3) is inconsistent due to the following tautology:

$$\forall \eta, \mu. (\eta \text{ since } \mu) \wedge (\neg\mu \text{ since } \neg\eta) \implies \text{false}. \quad (4)$$

The above argument justifies the memory safety of the algorithm, and (as we show in §4) the absence of memory leaks. Moreover, (2) guarantees to a thread executing `inc` that, when the CAS in line 28 succeeds, the node s has not been reallocated, and so the ABA problem does not occur.

We have achieved a simple reasoning about the algorithm by defining the duration of a grace period (1), the protocol all threads follow (2), and the fact a reclaimer establishes before deallocating a node (3) as temporal formulas of particular forms. We find that the above reasoning with temporal facts of these forms is applicable not only to our example, but also to uses of hazard pointers in other data structures [7, §B], and in fact, to completely different approaches to memory reclamation, as we now illustrate.

2.3   Reasoning about Read-Copy-Update

Read-Copy-Update (RCU) [11] is a non-standard synchronisation mechanism used in Linux to ensure safe memory deallocation in data structures with concurrent access. So far, there have been no methods for reasoning about programs with RCU. We now show that we can use our temporal reasoning principle based on grace periods to this end.

```
1  bool rcu[N] = {0};
2  rcu_enter() {⟨rcu[tid-1]=1⟩RCU_tid;}
3  rcu_exit() {⟨rcu[tid-1]=0⟩RCU_tid;}
4  sync() {
5    bool r[N] = {0};
6    for(int i = 0; i < N; i++)
7      ⟨r[i] = rcu[i]⟩_ld;
8    for(int i = 0; i < N; i++)
9      if(r[i]) {while(⟨rcu[i]⟩_ld);}
10 }
```

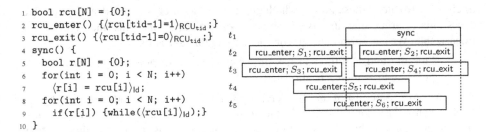

Fig. 2. An abstract RCU implementation and an illustration of the semantics of sync. Blocks represent the time spans of RCU critical sections or an execution of sync.

```
1  int *C = new int(0);                    15  int inc() {
2  bool rcu[N] = {0};                       16    int v, *n, *s;
3  Set detached[N] = {∅};                   17    n = new int; rcu_enter();
4                                           18    do {
5  void reclaim(int* s) {                   19      rcu_exit(); rcu_enter();
6    insert(detached[tid-1], s);            20      s = C; v = *s; *n = v+1;
7    if (nondet()) return;                  21    } while (!CAS(&C,s,n));
8    sync();                                22    rcu_exit();
9    while (!isEmpty(detached[tid]))        23    reclaim(s);
10     free(pop(detached[tid])); }          24    return v; }
```

Fig. 3. Counter with RCU-based memory management

RCU Primer. RCU provides three commands: rcu_enter, rcu_exit and sync. The rcu_enter and rcu_exit commands delimit an RCU *critical section*. They do *not* ensure mutual exclusion, so multiple threads can be in their critical sections simultaneously. Instead of enforcing mutual exclusion, RCU provides the sync command, which records the identifiers of the threads currently in critical sections and waits until all of them exit the sections. Note that if a new thread enters a critical section while sync is waiting, the command does not wait for the completion of its section. For example, when t_1 calls sync in the execution in Figure 2, it has to wait for critical sections S_1, S_5 and S_6 to finish. However, it does not wait for S_2 or S_4, as they start after sync was called.

Figure 2 shows an *abstract* implementation of the RCU primitives, formalising the above description of their semantics (for now, the reader should disregard the annotations in the figure). A *concrete* optimised RCU implementation would simulate the abstract one. Whether every thread is inside or outside an RCU critical section is determined by its entry in the rcu array.

RCU-Based Counter. Figure 3 gives the implementation of the running example using RCU. Its overall structure is similar to the implementation using hazard pointers. In inc, we wrap an RCU critical section around the commands starting from the read of the global variable C at line 20 and including all memory accesses involving the value read up to the CAS at line 21. The correctness of the algorithm is ensured by having reclaim call sync at line 8, before deallocating the detached nodes. This blocks the thread until all critical sections that existed at the time of the call to sync finish. Since, when sync is called, the nodes to be deallocated have already been moved to the thread-local detached set, newly arriving inc operations have no way of gaining a reference to one of these nodes, which guarantees the safety of their deallocation. We can similarly argue that an ABA problem does not occur, and thus, the algorithm is linearizable. We can formulate the contract among threads as follows:

"for all t and x, if thread t has stayed in a critical section <u>since</u> it saw C pointing to x, then x is allocated," $\qquad(5)$

which is of the same form as (2). Here, a grace period for a thread, specified by the 'since' clause, lasts for as long as the thread stays in its critical section. During the time span of sync, every thread passes through a point when it is not in a critical section. Hence, after executing line 8, for every node x to be deallocated we know:

"for all t, C has not pointed to x <u>since</u> t was not in a critical section," $\qquad(6)$

which is of the same form as (3). As before, this is inconsistent with the 'since' clause of (5), which guarantees that deallocating x will not violate (5).

Pattern. The algorithms using hazard pointers and read-copy-update fundamentally rely on the same synchronisation pattern, where a potentially harmful race between threads accessing nodes and those trying to reclaim them is avoided by establishing an assertion of the form $(\eta_{t,x}$ since $\mu_x)$ before every access, and $(\neg\mu_x$ since $\neg\eta_{t,x})$ before every deallocation. This *implicit* pattern is highlighted not by examining the syntactic structure of different memory management implementations, but by observing that the arguments about their correctness have the same form, as can be seen in our proofs.

3   Abstract Logic

Reasoning about highly concurrent algorithms, such as the example in §2, is convenient in logics based on rely-guarantee [10,15], which avoids direct reasoning about all possible thread interactions in a concurrent program by specifying a relation (the *guarantee* condition) for every thread restricting how it can change the program state. For any given thread, the union of the guarantee conditions of all the other threads in the program (its *rely* condition) restricts how those threads can interfere with it, and hence, allows reasoning about this thread in isolation.

The logic we use to formalise our verification method for memory reclamation algorithms uses a variant of rely-guarantee reasoning proposed in SAGL [4] and RGSep [17]—logics for reasoning about concurrent programs that combine rely-guarantee reasoning with separation logic. These partition the program heap into several *thread-local* parts (each of which can only be accessed by a given thread) and the *shared* part (which can be accessed by all threads). The partitioning is defined by proofs in the logic: an assertion in the code of a thread restricts its local state and the shared state. Thus, while reasoning about a thread, we do not have to consider local states of other threads. Additionally, the partitioning is dynamic, meaning that we can use ownership transfer to move some part of the local state into the shared state and vice versa. Rely and guarantee conditions are then specified as relations *on the shared state* determining how the threads change it. This is in contrast with the original rely-guarantee method, in which rely and guarantee conditions are relations *on the whole program state*. We use RGSep [17] as the basis for the logic presented in this section. Our logic adds just enough temporal reasoning to RGSep to formalise the verification method for algorithms based on grace periods that we explained in §2.

3.1 Preliminaries

Programming Language. We formalise our results for a simple language:

$$C ::= \alpha \mid C; C \mid C + C \mid C^* \mid \langle C \rangle \qquad \mathcal{P} ::= C_1 \parallel \ldots \parallel C_N$$

A program $\mathcal{P}$ is a parallel composition of N threads, which can contain primitive commands $\alpha \in \mathsf{PComm}$, sequential composition $C; C'$, nondeterministic choice $C + C'$, iteration C^* and atomic execution $\langle C \rangle$ of C. We forbid nested atomic blocks. Even though we present our logic for programs in the above language, for readability we use a C-like notation in our examples, which can be easily desugared [7, §A].

Separation Algebras. To reason about concurrent algorithms, we often use *permissions* [1], describing ways in which threads can operate on an area of memory. We present our logic in an abstract form [2] that is parametric in the kind of permissions used. A *separation algebra* is a set Σ, together with a partial commutative, associative and cancellative operation $*$ on Σ and a unit element $\varepsilon \in \Sigma$. The property of cancellativity says that for each $\theta \in \Sigma$, the function $\theta * \cdot : \Sigma \rightharpoonup \Sigma$ is injective. In the rest of the paper we assume a separation algebra State with the operation $*$. We think of elements $\theta \in \mathsf{State}$ as *portions* of program states and the $*$ operation as combining such portions.

Primitive Commands. We assume that the semantics of every primitive command $\alpha \in \mathsf{PComm}$, executed by thread t, is given by a transformer $f_\alpha^t : \mathsf{State} \rightarrow \mathcal{P}(\mathsf{State})^\top$. Here $\mathcal{P}(\mathsf{State})^\top$ is the set of subsets of State with a special element $\top$ used to denote an error state, resulting, e.g., from dereferencing an invalid pointer. For our logic to be sound, we need to place certain standard restrictions on f_α^t, deferred to [7, §A].

Notation. We write $g(x)\downarrow$ to mean that the function g is defined on x, and $g(x)\uparrow$ that it is undefined on x. We also write $\_$ for an expression whose value is irrelevant.

3.2 Assertion Language

Assertions in the logic describe sets of *worlds*, comprised of the *local state* of a thread and a *history* of the *shared* state. Local states are represented by elements of a separation algebra (§3.1), and histories, by sequences of those. Our assertion language thus includes three syntactic categories, for assertions describing states, histories and worlds.

Logical Variables. Our logic includes logical variables from a set $\mathsf{LVar} = \mathsf{LIVar} \uplus \mathsf{LSVar}$; variables from $\mathsf{LIVar} = \{x, y, \ldots\}$ range over integers, and those from $\mathsf{LSVar} = \{X, Y, \ldots\}$, over memory states. Let $\mathsf{LVal} = \mathsf{State} \cup \mathbb{Z}$ be the set of values of logical variables, and $\mathsf{LInt} \subseteq \mathsf{LVar} \rightarrow \mathsf{LVal}$, the set of their type-respecting interpretations.

Assertions for States. We assume a language for denoting subsets of $\mathsf{State} \times \mathsf{LInt}$:

$$p, q ::= \mathsf{true} \mid \neg p \mid p \Rightarrow q \mid X \mid \exists x.\, p \mid \exists X.\, p \mid \mathsf{emp} \mid p * q \mid \ldots$$

The interpretation of interesting connectives is as follows:

$$\theta, \mathbf{i} \models \mathsf{emp} \iff \theta = \varepsilon \qquad\qquad \theta, \mathbf{i} \models X \iff \theta = \mathbf{i}(X)$$
$$\theta, \mathbf{i} \models p * q \iff \exists \theta', \theta''.\, (\theta' * \theta'' = \theta) \wedge (\theta', \mathbf{i} \models p) \wedge (\theta'', \mathbf{i} \models q)$$

The assertion emp denotes an empty state; X, the state given by its interpretation; and $p * q$, states that can be split into two pieces such that one of them satisfies p and the other, q. We assume that $*$ binds stronger than the other connectives.

Assertions for Histories. A history is a non-empty sequence recording all shared states that arise during the execution of a program: $\xi \in \mathsf{History} = \mathsf{State}^+$. We denote the length of a history ξ by $|\xi|$, its i-th element by ξ_i, and its i-th prefix, by $\xi|_i$ (so that $|\xi|_i| = i$.) We refer to the last state $\xi_{|\xi|}$ in a history ξ as the *current* state. We define assertions denoting subsets of $\mathsf{History} \times \mathsf{LInt}$:

$$\tau, \Upsilon ::= \mathsf{true} \mid \neg\tau \mid \tau_1 \Rightarrow \tau_2 \mid \exists x.\, \tau \mid \exists X.\, \tau \mid \boxed{p} \mid \tau_1 \text{ since } \tau_2 \mid \tau \lhd \boxed{p}$$

$$\xi, \mathbf{i} \models \boxed{p} \iff \xi_{|\xi|}, \mathbf{i} \models p$$
$$\xi, \mathbf{i} \models \tau_1 \text{ since } \tau_2 \iff \exists i \in \{1, ..., |\xi|\}.\, (\xi|_i, \mathbf{i} \models \tau_2) \wedge \forall j \in \{i, ..., |\xi|\}.\, (\xi|_j, \mathbf{i} \models \tau_1)$$
$$\xi, \mathbf{i} \models \tau \lhd \boxed{p} \iff \exists \xi', \theta.\, (\xi = \xi'\theta) \wedge (\xi', \mathbf{i} \models \tau) \wedge (\theta, \mathbf{i} \models p)$$

The assertion $\boxed{p}$ denotes the set of histories of shared states, whose last state satisfies p; the box signifies that the assertion describes a shared state, as opposed to a thread-local one. The assertion $(\tau_1 \text{ since } \tau_2)$ describes those histories where both τ_1 and τ_2 held at some point in the past, and since then, τ_1 has held continuously. The assertion $\tau \lhd \boxed{p}$ (τ *extended with* $\boxed{p}$) describes histories obtained by appending a state satisfying p to the end of a history satisfying τ. It is easy to check that (4) from §2 is indeed a tautology.

Assertions for Worlds. A world consists of a thread-local state and a history of shared states such that the combination of the local state and the current shared state is defined:

$$\omega \in \mathsf{World} = \{(\theta, \xi) \in \mathsf{State} \times \mathsf{History} \mid (\theta * \xi_{|\xi|})\!\downarrow\}. \tag{7}$$

We define assertions denoting subsets of $\mathsf{World} \times \mathsf{LInt}$:

$$P, Q ::= p \mid \tau \mid \mathsf{true} \mid \neg P \mid P \Rightarrow Q \mid \exists x.\, P \mid \exists X.\, P \mid P * Q$$

$$\theta, \xi, \mathbf{i} \models p \iff \theta, \mathbf{i} \models p \qquad\qquad \theta, \xi, \mathbf{i} \models \tau \iff \xi, \mathbf{i} \models \tau$$
$$\theta, \xi, \mathbf{i} \models P * Q \iff \exists \theta', \theta''.\, (\theta = \theta' * \theta'') \wedge (\theta', \xi, \mathbf{i} \models P) \wedge (\theta'', \xi, \mathbf{i} \models Q)$$

An assertion $P * Q$ denotes worlds in which the local state can be divided into two parts such that one of them, together with the history of the shared partition, satisfies P and the other, together with the same history, satisfies Q. Note that $*$ does not split the shared partition, p does not restrict the shared state, and τ does not restrict the thread-local one.

3.3 Rely/Guarantee Conditions and the Temporal Invariant

Actions. The judgements of our logic include *guarantee* G and *rely* R conditions, determining how a thread or its environment can change the shared state, respectively. Similarly to RGSep [17], these are sets of *actions* of the form $l \mid p * X \rightsquigarrow q * X$, where l, p and q are assertions over states, and X is a logical variable over states. An action denotes a relation in $\mathcal{P}(\mathsf{State} \times \mathsf{State} \times \mathsf{State})$:

$$[\![l \mid p * X \rightsquigarrow q * X]\!] = \{(\theta_l, \theta_p, \theta_q) \mid \exists \mathbf{i}.\, (\theta_l, \mathbf{i} \models l) \wedge (\theta_p, \mathbf{i} \models p * X) \wedge (\theta_q, \mathbf{i} \models q * X)\},$$

and a rely or a guarantee denotes the union of their action denotations. We write $R \Rightarrow R'$ for $[\![R]\!] \subseteq [\![R']\!]$. Informally, the action $l \mid p * X \rightsquigarrow q * X$ allows a thread to change the part of the shared state that satisfies p into one that satisfies q, while leaving the rest of the shared state X unchanged. The assertion l is called a *guard*: it describes a piece of state that has to be in the local partition of the thread for it to be able to perform the action. We omit l when it is emp. Our actions refer explicitly to the unchanged part X of the shared state, as we often need to check that a command performing an action

$$\frac{f_\alpha^{\text{tid}}(\llbracket p \rrbracket) \subseteq \llbracket q \rrbracket}{R, G, \Upsilon \vdash_{\text{tid}} \{p\}\, \alpha \,\{q\}} \ \text{LOCAL} \qquad \frac{P \wedge \Upsilon \Rightarrow P' \quad R \Rightarrow R' \quad G' \Rightarrow G \quad Q' \wedge \Upsilon \Rightarrow Q}{R', G', \Upsilon \vdash_{\text{tid}} \{P'\}\, C \,\{Q'\}}{R, G, \Upsilon \vdash_{\text{tid}} \{P\}\, C \,\{Q\}} \ \text{CONSEQ}$$

$$\frac{R, G, \Upsilon \vdash_{\text{tid}} \{P\}\, C \,\{Q\} \quad F \text{ is stable under } R \cup G \text{ and } \Upsilon}{R, G, \Upsilon \vdash_{\text{tid}} \{P * F\}\, C \,\{Q * F\}} \ \text{FRAME} \qquad \frac{Q \Rightarrow \Upsilon \quad P, Q \text{ are stable under } R \text{ and } \Upsilon \quad \emptyset, G, \text{true} \vdash_{\text{tid}} \{P\}\, \langle C \rangle_a \,\{Q\}}{R, G, \Upsilon \vdash_{\text{tid}} \{P\}\, \langle C \rangle_a \,\{Q\}} \ \text{SHARED-R}$$

$$\frac{p \Rightarrow l * \text{true} \quad \{l \mid p_s \leadsto q_s\} \Rightarrow \{a\} \quad a \in G \quad \emptyset, \emptyset, \text{true} \vdash_{\text{tid}} \{p * p_s\}\, C \,\{q * q_s\}}{\emptyset, G, \text{true} \vdash_{\text{tid}} \{p \wedge \tau \wedge \boxed{p_s}\}\, \langle C \rangle_a \,\{q \wedge ((\tau \wedge \boxed{p_s}) \lhd \boxed{q_s})\}} \ \text{SHARED}$$

$$\frac{R_1, G_1, \Upsilon \vdash_1 \{P_1\}\, C_1 \,\{Q_1\} \quad \dots \quad R_n, G_n, \Upsilon \vdash_n \{P_n\}\, C_n \,\{Q_n\}}{\vdash \{P_1 * \dots * P_n\}\, C_1 \parallel \dots \parallel C_n \,\{Q_1 * \dots * Q_n\}} \ \text{PAR}$$
$$R_{\text{tid}} = \bigcup \{G_k \mid 1 \leq k \leq n \wedge k \neq \text{tid}\} \qquad P_1 * \dots * P_n \Rightarrow \Upsilon \qquad P_k, Q_k \text{ stable under } R_k \text{ and } \Upsilon$$

Fig. 4. Proof rules of the logic

preserves global constraints on it (see §4.3). We require that p and q in $l \mid p * X \leadsto q * X$ be precise. An assertion r for states is *precise* [13], if for every state θ and interpretation $\mathbf{i}$, there exists at most one substate θ_1 satisfying r, i.e., such that $\theta_1, \mathbf{i} \models r$ and $\theta = \theta_1 * \theta_2$ for some θ_2. Informally, a precise assertion carves out a unique piece of the heap.

Temporal Invariant. Rely/guarantee conditions describe the set of actions that threads can perform at any point, but do not say anything about temporal protocols that the actions follow. We describe such protocols using a *temporal invariant*, which is an assertion Υ over histories of the shared state. Every change to the shared state that a thread performs using one of the actions in its guarantee has to preserve Υ; in return, a thread can rely on the environment not violating the invariant. We require that Υ be insensitive to logical variables, i.e., $\forall \xi, \mathbf{i}, \mathbf{i}'. \, (\xi, \mathbf{i} \models \Upsilon) \iff (\xi, \mathbf{i}' \models \Upsilon)$.

Stability. When reasoning about the code of a thread in our logic, we take into account the interference from the other threads in the program, specified by the rely R and the temporal invariant Υ, using the concept of stability. An assertion over worlds P is *stable* under an action $l \mid p_s \leadsto q_s$ and a temporal invariant Υ, if it is insensitive to changes to the shared state permitted by the action that preserve the invariant:

$$\forall \theta, \theta_s, \theta'_s, \theta_l, \mathbf{i}, \xi. \, ((\theta, \xi\theta_s, \mathbf{i} \models P) \wedge (\xi\theta_s, \mathbf{i} \models \Upsilon) \wedge (\xi\theta_s\theta'_s, \mathbf{i} \models \Upsilon) \wedge$$
$$(\theta_l, \theta_s, \theta'_s) \in \llbracket l \mid p_s \leadsto q_s \rrbracket \wedge (\theta * \theta_l * \theta_s)\!\downarrow \wedge (\theta * \theta'_s)\!\downarrow) \implies (\theta, \xi\theta_s\theta'_s, \mathbf{i} \models P). \quad (8)$$

This makes use of the guard l: we do not take into account environment transitions when the latter cannot possibly own the guard, i.e., when θ_l is inconsistent with the current thread-local state θ and the current shared state θ_s. An assertion is stable under R and Υ, when it is stable under every action in R together with Υ. We only consider assertions that are closed under stuttering on histories: $(\theta, \xi\theta_s\xi', \mathbf{i} \models P) \Rightarrow (\theta, \xi\theta_s\theta_s\xi', \mathbf{i} \models P)$.

3.4 Proof System

The judgements of the logic are of the form $R, G, \Upsilon \vdash_{\text{tid}} \{P\}\, C \,\{Q\}$. Here P and Q are the pre- and postcondition of C, denoting sets of worlds; G describes the set of atomic changes that the thread tid executing C can make to the shared state; R, the changes to the shared state that its environment can make; and Υ, the temporal invariant that both have to preserve. The judgement guarantees that the command C is safe, i.e., it does not dereference any invalid pointers when executed in an environment respecting R and Υ.

The proof rules of our logic are given in Figure 4. We have omitted the more standard rules [7, §A]. We have a single axiom for primitive commands executing on the local state (LOCAL), which allows any pre- and postconditions consistent with their semantics. The axiom uses the expected pointwise lifting of the transformers f_α^t from §3.1 to assertion denotations, preserving the interpretation of logical variables. The CON-SEQ rule looks as usual in rely/guarantee, except it allows strengthening the pre- and postcondition with the information provided by the temporal invariant Υ.

By convention, the only commands that can operate on the shared state are atomic blocks, handled by the rules SHARED-R and SHARED. The SHARED-R rule checks that the atomic block meets its specification in an empty environment, and then checks that the pre- and postcondition are stable with respect to the actual environment R, and that the postcondition implies the invariant Υ. Note that to establish the latter in practice, we can always add Υ to the precondition of the atomic block using CONSEQ.

SHARED handles the case of an empty rely condition, left by SHARED-R. It is the key rule in the proof system, allowing an atomic command C to make a change to the shared state according to an action $l \mid p_s \rightsquigarrow q_s$. The action has to be included into the *annotation* a of the atomic block, which in its turn, has to be permitted by the guarantee G. The annotations are part of proofs in our logic. For the logic to be sound, we require that every atomic command in the program be annotated with the same action throughout the proof. SHARED also requires the thread to have a piece of state satisfying the guard l in its local state p. It combines the local state p with the shared state p_s, and runs C as if this combination were in the thread's local state. The rule then splits the resulting state into local q and shared q_s parts. Note that SHARED allows the postcondition of the atomic block to record how the shared state looked like before its execution: the previous view $\boxed{p_s}$ of the shared state and the assertion τ about its history are extended with the new shared state $\boxed{q_s}$ with the aid of $\lhd$ (§3.1).

The FRAME rule ensures that if a command C is safe when run from states in P, then it does not touch an extra piece of state described by F. Since F can contain assertions constraining the shared state, we require it to be stable under $R \cup G$ and Υ.

PAR combines judgements about several threads. Their pre- and postconditions in the premises of the rule are $*$-conjoined in the conclusion, which composes the local states of the threads and enforces that they have the same view of the shared state.

3.5 Soundness

Let us denote by Prog the set of programs $\mathcal{P}$ with an additional command done, describing a completed computation. The language of §3.1 has a standard small-step operational semantics, defined by a relation $\longrightarrow$: Config $\times$ Config, which transforms configurations from the set Config $=$ (Prog $\times$ State) $\cup \{\top\}$. (Note that this semantics ignores the effects of weak memory consistency models, which are left for future work.) We defer the definition of $\longrightarrow$ to [7, §A]. The following theorem is proved in [7, §E].

Theorem 1 (Soundness). *Assume* $\vdash \{P\}\, \mathcal{P}\, \{Q\}$ *and take* θ_l, θ_s *and* $\mathbf{i}$ *such that* $\theta_l, \theta_s, \mathbf{i} \models P$. *Then* $(\mathcal{P}, \theta_l * \theta_s) \not\longrightarrow^* \top$ *and, whenever* $(\mathcal{P}, \theta_l * \theta_s) \longrightarrow^*$ (done $\parallel$ $\dots \parallel$ done, θ')*, for some* θ'_l, θ'_s *and* ξ *we have* $\theta' = \theta'_l * \theta'_s$ *and* $\theta'_l, \xi\theta'_s, \mathbf{i} \models Q$.

4   Logic Instantiation and Hazard Pointers

As explained in §2, proofs of algorithms based on grace periods, use only a restricted form of temporal reasoning. In this section, we describe an instantiation of the abstract logic of §3 tailored to such algorithms. This includes a particular form of the temporal invariant (§4.2) and a specialised version of the SHARED rule (SHARED-I below) that allows us to establish that the *temporal* invariant is preserved using standard *state-based* reasoning. We present the instantiation by the example of verifying the concurrent counter algorithm with hazard pointers from §2.

4.1   Assertion Language

Permissions. We instantiate State to $\mathsf{RAM}_e = \mathbb{N} \rightharpoonup_{fin} ((\mathbb{Z} \times \{1, \mathsf{m}\}) \cup \{\mathsf{e}\})$. A state thus consists of a finite partial function from memory locations allocated in the heap to the values they store and/or permissions. The permission 1 is a *full* permission, which allows a thread to perform any action on the cell; the permission m is a *master* permission, which allows reading and writing the cell, but not deallocating it; and e is an *existential* permission, which only allows reading the cell and does not give any guarantees regarding its contents. The transformers f_α^t over RAM_e are given in [7, §A].

We define $*$ on cell contents as follows: $(u, \mathsf{m}) * \mathsf{e} = (u, 1)$; undefined in all other cases. This only allows a full permission to be split into a master and an existential one, which is enough for our purposes. For $\theta_1, \theta_2 \in \mathsf{RAM}_e$, $\theta_1 * \theta_2$ is undefined, if for some x, we have $\theta_1(x){\downarrow}, \theta_2(x){\downarrow}$, but $(\theta_1(x) * \theta_2(x)){\uparrow}$. Otherwise,

$$\theta_1 * \theta_2 = \{(x, w) \mid (\theta_1(x) = w \wedge \theta_2(x){\uparrow}) \vee (\theta_2(x) = w \wedge \theta_1(x){\uparrow}) \vee (w = \theta_1(x) * \theta_2(x))\}.$$

State Assertions. To denote elements of RAM_e, we extend the assertion language for predicates over states given in §3.2: $p ::= \ldots \mid E \mapsto F \mid E \mapsto_\mathsf{m} F \mid E \mapsto_\mathsf{e} \_$, where E, F range over expressions over integer-valued logical variables. The semantics is as expected; e.g., $[\![E]\!]_\mathsf{i} : ([\![F]\!]_\mathsf{i}, 1)], \mathsf{i} \models E \mapsto F$ and $x \mapsto u \Leftrightarrow x \mapsto_\mathsf{m} u * x \mapsto_\mathsf{e} \_$.

Conventions. We assume that logical variables $t, t', \ldots$ range over thread identifiers in $\{1, \ldots, N\}$. We write $\mathsf{A}[k]$ for $\mathsf{A} + k$, and true_e for $\exists A. \circledast_{x \in A} x \mapsto_\mathsf{e} \_$, where $\circledast$ is the iterated version of $*$. We adopt the convention that global variables are constants, and local variables are allocated at fixed addresses in memory. For a local variable var of thread tid, we write $var \Vdash P$ for $\exists var. (\&\mathsf{var} + \mathsf{tid} - 1) \mapsto var * P$, where $\&\mathsf{var}$ is the address of the variable. Note that here var is a program variable, whereas var is a logical one. We use a similar notation for lists of variables V.

4.2   Actions and the Temporal Invariant

The actions used in the proof of the running example and the rely/guarantee conditions constructed from them are given in Figure 5. Id allows reading the contents of the shared state, but not modifying it, and HP_tid allows modifying the contents of the t-th entry in the hazard pointer array. The rely R_tid and the guarantee G_tid are set up in such a way that only thread tid can execute HP_tid.

Inc allows a thread to change the node pointed to by C from x to y, thus detaching the old node x. Note that $y \mapsto \_$ occurs on the right-hand side of Inc, but not on its

$$X \rightsquigarrow X \quad \text{(Id)} \qquad x \mapsto_m \_ \mid x \mapsto_e \_ * X \rightsquigarrow X \quad \text{(Take)}$$

$$\mathsf{HP}[\mathsf{tid}-1] \mapsto \_ * X \rightsquigarrow \mathsf{HP}[\mathsf{tid}-1] \mapsto \_ * X \qquad (\mathsf{HP}_{\mathsf{tid}})$$

$$\mathsf{C} \mapsto x * x \mapsto \_ * X \rightsquigarrow \mathsf{C} \mapsto y * y \mapsto \_ * x \mapsto_e \_ * X \qquad (\mathsf{Inc})$$

$$G_{\mathsf{tid}} = \{\mathsf{HP}_{\mathsf{tid}}, \mathsf{Inc}, \mathsf{Take}, \mathsf{Id}\}; \qquad R_{\mathsf{tid}} = \bigcup \{G_k \mid 1 \le k \le N \wedge k \ne \mathsf{tid}\}$$

$$\varUpsilon_{\mathsf{HP}} \iff \forall x, t. \left(\left(\boxed{\mathsf{HP}[t-1] \mapsto x * \mathsf{true}} \text{ since } \boxed{\mathsf{C} \mapsto x * x \mapsto \_ * \mathsf{true}} \right) \Rightarrow \boxed{x \mapsto_e \_ * \mathsf{true}} \right)$$

Fig. 5. Rely/guarantee conditions and the temporal invariant used in the proof of the counter algorithm with hazard pointers

left-hand side. Hence, the thread executing the action transfers the ownership of the node y (in our example, initially allocated in its local state) into the shared state. Since $x \mapsto \_$ occurs on the left-hand side of Inc, but only $x \mapsto_e \_$ occurs on its right-hand side, the thread gets the ownership of $x \mapsto_m \_$. This is used to express the protocol that the thread detaching the node will be the one to deallocate it. Namely, Take allows a thread to take the remaining existential permission from the shared state only when it has the corresponding master permission in its local state. The existential permission left in the shared state after a thread executes Inc lets concurrently running threads access the detached node until it is deallocated.

Threads can only execute Take and other actions when these do not violate the temporal invariant $\varUpsilon_{\mathsf{HP}}$ in Figure 5. Temporal invariants used for proofs of algorithms based on grace periods are of the form "$\forall x, t. (\boxed{g} \text{ since } \boxed{r}) \Rightarrow \boxed{c}$", where "$\boxed{g} \text{ since } \boxed{r}$" defines the duration of the grace period for a thread t and a location x, and $\boxed{c}$ gives the property that has to be maintained during the grace period. In our example, the invariant formalises (2): if a hazard pointer of t has pointed to a node x continuously since C pointed to x, then an existential permission for x is present in the shared state.

4.3 Proof Outlines and a Derived Rule for Grace Periods

The proof outline for the running example is shown in Figures 6 and 7. In the figure, we write $\mathsf{CAS}_{a,b}(\texttt{addr},\texttt{v1},\texttt{v2})$ as a shorthand for the following, where the assume command "assumes" its parameter to be non-zero [7, §A]:

```
if (nondet()) {⟨assume(*addr == v1); *addr = v2⟩ₐ; return 1; }
else { ⟨assume(*addr != v1)⟩ᵦ; return 0; }
```

The bulk of the proof employs standard state-based reasoning of the kind performed in RGSep [17]. Temporal reasoning is needed, e.g., to check that every command changing the shared state preserves the temporal invariant $\varUpsilon_{\mathsf{HP}}$ (the premiss $Q \Rightarrow \varUpsilon$ in SHARED-R). We start by discussing the proof outline of inc in Figure 6 in general terms; we then describe the handling of commands changing the shared state in detail.

Verifying inc. Let $H \iff (\circledast_t \mathsf{HP}[t-1] \mapsto \_)$ and $I \iff \boxed{H * \exists y. \mathsf{C} \mapsto y * y \mapsto \_ * \mathsf{true}_e}$. The pre- and postcondition of inc in Figure 6 thus state that the shared state always contains the hazard pointer array, the pointer at the address C and the node it identifies. Additionally, we can have an arbitrary number of existential permissions for nodes that threads leave in the shared state in between executing Inc and Take. We also have an assertion F_{tid}, defined later, which describes the thread-local $\texttt{detached}$ set.

```
1  int *C = new int(0), *HP[N] = {0};            18         (HP[tid − 1] ↦ s * true
2  Set detached[N] = {∅};                        19          since C ↦ s2 * s2 ↦ _ * true)}
3  int inc() {                                   20       } while (s != s2);
4    int v, *n, *s, *s2;                         21       {V ⊩ n ↦ _ * Ftid ∧ I ∧ s ↦e _ * true ∧
5    {V ⊩ Ftid ∧ I}                             22        (HP[tid − 1] ↦ s * true
6    n = new int;                                23          since C ↦ s * s ↦ _ * true)}
7    do {                                        24       ⟨v = *s⟩ld ;
8      {V ⊩ n ↦ _ * Ftid ∧ I}                   25       *n = v+1;
9      do {                                      26       {V ⊩ n ↦ _ * Ftid ∧ I ∧ s ↦e _ * true ∧
10       {V ⊩ n ↦ _ * Ftid ∧ I}                 27        (HP[tid − 1] ↦ s * true
11       ⟨s = C⟩ld ;                             28          since C ↦ s * s ↦ _ * true)}
12       {V ⊩ n ↦ _ * Ftid ∧ I}                 29       } while (!CASInc,ld(&C, s, n));
13       ⟨HP[tid−1] = s⟩HPtid ;                  30       {V ⊩ s ↦m _ * Ftid ∧ I ∧ s ↦e _ * true}
14       {V ⊩ n ↦ _ * Ftid ∧ I ∧                31       reclaim(s);
15        HP[tid − 1] ↦ s * true}               32       {V ⊩ Ftid ∧ I}
16       ⟨s2 = C⟩ld ;                            33       return v; }
17       {V ⊩ n ↦ _ * Ftid ∧ I ∧
```

Fig. 6. Proof outline for `inc` with hazard pointers. Here V is $v, n, s, s2, my, in\_use, i$.

At line 11 of `inc`, the current thread reads the value of C into the local variable s. For the postcondition of this command to be stable, we do not maintain any correlation between the values of C and s, as other threads might change C using Inc at any time. The thread sets its hazard pointer to s at line 13. The postcondition includes $\boxed{\text{HP}[\text{tid} − 1] \mapsto s * \text{true}}$, which is stable, as R_{tid} and G_{tid} (Figure 5) allow only the current thread to execute HP_{tid}.

At line 16, the thread reads the value of C into s2. Right after executing the command, we have $\boxed{\text{HP}[\text{tid} − 1] \mapsto s * \text{true}} \wedge \boxed{C \mapsto s2 * s2 \mapsto \_ * \text{true}}$. This assertion is unstable, as other threads may change C at any time using Inc. We therefore weaken it to the postcondition shown by using the tautology $(\eta \wedge \mu) \Rightarrow (\eta \text{ since } \mu)$. It is easy to check that an assertion $(\eta \text{ since } \mu)$ is stable if η is. Since $\boxed{\text{HP}[\text{tid} − 1] \mapsto s * \text{true}}$ is stable, so is the postcondition of the command in line 16. After the test s != s2 in line 20 fails, the since clause in this assertion characterises the grace period of the thread tid for the location s, as stated by Υ_{HP}. This allows us to exploit Υ_{HP} at line 23 using CONSEQ, establishing $\boxed{s \mapsto_e \_ * \text{true}}$. This assertion allows us to access the node at the address s safely at line 24.

If the CAS in line 29 is successful, then the thread transfers the ownership of the newly allocated node n to the shared state, and takes the ownership of the master permission for the node s; the existential permission for s stays in the shared state. The resulting assertion $s \mapsto_m \_ \wedge \boxed{s \mapsto_e \_ * \text{true}}$ is stable, because the only action that can remove $s \mapsto_e \_$ from the shared state, Take, is guarded by $s \mapsto_m \_$. Since the current thread has the ownership of $s \mapsto_m \_$ and $s \mapsto_m \_ * s \mapsto_m \_$ is inconsistent, the condition $(\theta * \theta_l * \theta_s) \!\downarrow$ in (8), checking that the guard is consistent with the local state, implies that the action cannot be executed by the environment, and thus, the assertion is stable.

Derived Rule for Grace Periods. To check that the commands in lines 13 and 29 of `inc` preserve Υ_{HP}, we use the following rule SHARED-I, derived from SHARED [7, §A]:

$$\frac{\begin{array}{cccc} p \Rightarrow l * \mathsf{true} & a = (l \mid p'_s \rightsquigarrow q'_s) \in G & p_s \Rightarrow p'_s & q_s \Rightarrow q'_s \\ \emptyset, \emptyset, \mathsf{true} \vdash_{\mathsf{tid}} \{p * (p_s \wedge \neg(g \wedge r))\} \, C \, \{q * (q_s \wedge (g \wedge r \Rightarrow c))\} \\ \emptyset, \emptyset, \mathsf{true} \vdash_{\mathsf{tid}} \{p * (p_s \wedge g \wedge c)\} \, C \, \{q * (q_s \wedge (g \Rightarrow c))\} \end{array}}{\emptyset, G, \mathsf{true} \vdash_{\mathsf{tid}} \{p \wedge \boxed{p_s} \wedge ((\boxed{g} \text{ since } \boxed{r}) \Rightarrow \boxed{c})\} \langle C \rangle_a \{q \wedge \boxed{q_s} \wedge ((\boxed{g} \text{ since } \boxed{r}) \Rightarrow \boxed{c})\}}$$

This gives conditions under which $\langle C \rangle$ preserves the validity of an assertion of the form

$$(\boxed{g} \text{ since } \boxed{r}) \Rightarrow \boxed{c} \tag{9}$$

and thus allows us to prove the preservation of a temporal invariant of the form (9) using standard Hoare-style reasoning. In the rule, p_s describes the view of the shared partition that the current thread has before executing C, and q_s, the state in which C leaves it. The rule requires that the change from p_s to q_s be allowed by the annotation $a = (l \mid p'_s \rightsquigarrow q'_s)$, i.e., that $p_s \Rightarrow p'_s$ and $q_s \Rightarrow q'_s$. It further provides two Hoare triples to be checked of C, which correspond, respectively, to the two cases for why $(\boxed{g} \text{ since } \boxed{r}) \Rightarrow \boxed{c}$ may hold before the execution of C: $\neg(\boxed{g} \text{ since } \boxed{r})$ or $(\boxed{g} \text{ since } \boxed{r}) \wedge \boxed{c}$.

As in SHARED, the two Hoare triples in the premiss allow the command inside the atomic block to access both local and shared state. Consider the first one. We can assume $\neg(g \wedge r)$ in the precondition, as it is implied by $\neg(\boxed{g} \text{ since } \boxed{r})$. Since $\boxed{g} \text{ since } \boxed{r}$ does not hold before the execution of C, the only way to establish it afterwards is by obtaining $g \wedge r$. In this case, to preserve (9), we have to establish c, which motivates the postcondition. Formally: $((\neg(\boxed{g} \text{ since } \boxed{r})) \lhd \boxed{g \wedge r \Rightarrow c}) \Rightarrow ((\boxed{g} \text{ since } \boxed{r}) \Rightarrow \boxed{c})$.

Consider now the second Hoare triple. Its precondition comes from the tautology $((\boxed{g} \text{ since } \boxed{r}) \wedge \boxed{c}) \Rightarrow \boxed{g \wedge c}$. We only need to establish c in the postcondition when $\boxed{g} \text{ since } \boxed{r}$ holds there, which will only be the case if g continues to hold after C executes: $(((\boxed{g} \text{ since } \boxed{r}) \wedge \boxed{c}) \lhd \boxed{g \Rightarrow c}) \Rightarrow ((\boxed{g} \text{ since } \boxed{r}) \Rightarrow \boxed{c})$.

Preserving the Temporal Invariant. We illustrate the use of SHARED-I on the command in line 29 of Figure 6; the one in line 13 is handled analogously. We consider the case when the CAS succeeds, i.e., C is $\{\texttt{assume(C == s); C = n;}\}$. Let P and Q be the pre- and postconditions of this command in lines 26 and 30, respectively. We thus need to prove $R_{\mathsf{tid}}, G_{\mathsf{tid}}, \varUpsilon \vdash_{\mathsf{tid}} \{P\} \langle C \rangle_{\mathsf{Inc}} \{Q\}$. We first apply CONSEQ to strengthen the precondition of the CAS with $\varUpsilon$, and then apply SHARED-R. This rule, in particular, requires us to show that the temporal invariant is preserved: $\emptyset, G_{\mathsf{tid}}, \mathsf{true} \vdash_{\mathsf{tid}} \{P \wedge \varUpsilon\} \, C \, \{Q \wedge \varUpsilon\}$. Let us first strip the quantifiers over x and t in $\varUpsilon$ using a standard rule of Hoare logic. We then apply SHARED-I with

$$g = (\mathtt{HP}[t-1] \mapsto x * \mathsf{true}); \qquad r = (\mathtt{C} \mapsto x * x \mapsto \_ * \mathsf{true}); \qquad c = (x \mapsto_{\mathsf{e}} \_ * \mathsf{true});$$
$$p_s = (H * \exists y.\, \mathtt{C} \mapsto y * y \mapsto \_ * \mathsf{true}_{\mathsf{e}}); \qquad\qquad p = n \mapsto \_;$$
$$q_s = (H * \exists y.\, \mathtt{C} \mapsto y * y \mapsto \_ * s \mapsto_{\mathsf{e}} \_ * \mathsf{true}_{\mathsf{e}}); \qquad\qquad q = s \mapsto_{\mathsf{m}} \_.$$

We consider only the first Hoare triple in the premiss of SHARED-I, which corresponds to $\boxed{g} \text{ since } \boxed{r}$ being false before the atomic block. The triple instantiates to

$$\{n \mapsto \_ * ((H * \exists y.\, \mathtt{C} \mapsto y * y \mapsto \_ * \mathsf{true}_{\mathsf{e}}) \wedge \neg(\mathtt{HP}[t-1] \mapsto x * \mathsf{true} \wedge \mathtt{C} \mapsto x * x \mapsto \_ * \mathsf{true}))\}$$
$$\texttt{assume(C == s); C = n;} \, \{s \mapsto_{\mathsf{m}} \_ * (H * \exists y.\, \mathtt{C} \mapsto y * y \mapsto \_ * s \mapsto_{\mathsf{e}} \_ * \mathsf{true}_{\mathsf{e}}) \wedge$$
$$(((\mathtt{HP}[t-1] \mapsto x * \mathsf{true}) \wedge (\mathtt{C} \mapsto x * x \mapsto \_ * \mathsf{true})) \Rightarrow (x \mapsto_{\mathsf{e}} \_ * \mathsf{true}))\}$$

Recall that when the CAS at line 29 inserts a node into the shared data structure, we already might have a hazard pointer set to the node (§2). The postcondition of the above

```
1  void reclaim(int *s) { {V ⊩ s ↦ₘ _ * Fₜᵢd ∧ |s ↦ₑ _ * true| ∧ I}
2    insert(detached[tid-1], s);
3    if (nondet()) return;
4    Set in_use = ∅;
5    while (!isEmpty(detached[tid-1])) {
6      {V ⊩ ∃A. detached[tid − 1] ↦ A * D(A) * D(in_use) ∧ A ≠ ∅ ∧ I}
7      bool my = true;
8      Node *n = pop(detached[tid-1]);
9      {V ⊩ my ∧ ∃A. detached[tid − 1] ↦ A * D(A) * D(in_use) * n ↦ₘ _ ∧ |n ↦ₑ _ * true| ∧ I}
10     for (int i = 0; i < N && my; i++) {
11       {V ⊩ my ∧ ∃A. detached[tid − 1] ↦ A * D(A) * D(in_use) * n ↦ₘ _ * |n ↦ₑ _ * true| ∧
12        0 ≤ i < N ∧ I ∧ |H * ∃y. y ≠ n ∧ C ↦ y * y ↦ _ * trueₑ| ∧
13        ∀0 ≤ j < i. (|∃y. y ≠ n ∧ C ↦ y * y ↦ _ * trueₑ| since |∃x. x ≠ n ∧ HP[j] ↦ x * true|)}
14       if (⟨HP[i] == n⟩ₗd) my = false;
15     }
16     if (my) {
17       {V ⊩ ∃A. detached[tid − 1] ↦ A * D(A) * D(in_use) * n ↦ₘ _ ∧ |n ↦ₑ _ * true| ∧ I ∧
18        ∀t. ¬|C ↦ n * true| since ¬|HP[t − 1] ↦ n * true|}
19       ⟨ ; ⟩ₜake
20       {V ⊩ ∃A. detached[tid − 1] ↦ A * D(A) * D(in_use) * n ↦ _ ∧ I}
21       free(n);
22     } else { insert(in_use, n); }
23   } {V ⊩ detached[tid − 1] ↦ ∅ * D(in_use) ∧ I}
24   moveAll(in_use, detached[tid-1]); {V ⊩ Fₜᵢd ∧ I}
25 }
```

Fig. 7. Proof outline for `reclaim` with hazard pointers. V is $v, n, s, s2, my, in\_use, i$.

triple states that, in this case, we need to establish the conclusion of the temporal invariant. This is satisfied, as $x \mapsto _ \Leftrightarrow x \mapsto_m \_ * x \mapsto_e \_$.

Verifying `reclaim`. We now explain the proof outline in Figure 7. The predicate F_{tid} describes the `detached` set of thread tid:

$$D(A) \iff \circledast_{x \in A}(x \mapsto_m \_ \wedge \boxed{x \mapsto_e \_ * \mathsf{true}});$$
$$F_{tid} \iff \exists A. \, \mathrm{detached}[tid-1] \mapsto A * D(A). \tag{10}$$

F_{tid} asserts that thread tid owns the tid-th entry of the `detached` array, which stores the set A of addresses of detached nodes; $D(A)$ asserts that, for every $x \in A$, the thread has the master permission for x in its local state, and the shared state contains the existential permission for x. The assertion F_{tid} is stable, since, as we explained above, so is $x \mapsto_m \_\wedge \boxed{x \mapsto_e \_ * \mathsf{true}}$. We assume the expected specifications for set operations.

The core of `reclaim` is the loop following the pop operation in line 8, which checks that the hazard pointers do not point to the node that we want to deallocate. The assertion in line 13 formalises (3) and is established as follows. If the condition on the pointer HP[i] in line 14 fails, then we know that $\boxed{\exists x. x \neq n \wedge \mathrm{HP}[i] \mapsto x * \mathsf{true}}$. Recall that, according to (7), §3.2, the combination of the local and the shared states has to be consistent. Then, since we have $n \mapsto_m \_$ in our local state, we cannot have C pointing to n: in this case the full permission $n \mapsto \_$ would be in the shared state, and $n \mapsto \_ * n \mapsto_m \_$ is inconsistent. Hence, $\boxed{\exists y. y \neq n \wedge C \mapsto y * y \mapsto \_ * \mathsf{true}}$. By the tautology $(\eta \wedge \mu) \Rightarrow (\eta \text{ since } \mu)$, we obtain the desired assertion:

$$\boxed{\exists y. y \neq n \wedge C \mapsto y * y \mapsto \_ * \mathsf{true}} \text{ since } \boxed{\exists x. x \neq n \wedge \mathrm{HP}[i] \mapsto x * \mathsf{true}}. \tag{11}$$

Since $n \mapsto_m \_ \wedge \boxed{\exists y.\, y \neq n \wedge C \mapsto y * y \mapsto \_ * \mathsf{true}}$ is stable, so is the loop invariant. At line 19, we use (11) and (4) to show that the existential permission for the node n can be safely removed from the shared state. After this, we recombine it with the local master permission to obtain $n \mapsto \_$, which allows deallocating the node.

Absence of Memory Leaks. According to Theorem 1, the above proof establishes that the algorithm is memory safe. In fact, it also implies that the algorithm does not leak memory. Indeed, let $\mathcal{P}$ be the program consisting of any number of inc operations running in parallel. From our proof, we get that $\mathcal{P}$ satisfies the following triple:

$$\vdash \{L * (\circledast_t \mathtt{detached}[t-1] \mapsto \emptyset) \wedge \boxed{(\circledast_t \mathtt{HP}[t-1] \mapsto 0) * \exists y.\, C \mapsto y * y \mapsto 0}\}$$
$$\mathcal{P}\ \{L * (\circledast_t F_t) \wedge \boxed{(\circledast_t \mathtt{HP}[t-1] \mapsto \_) * \exists y.\, C \mapsto y * y \mapsto \_ * \mathsf{true}_e}\},$$

where L includes the local variables of all threads. The assertion true_e in the postcondition describes an arbitrary number of existential permissions for memory cells. However, physical memory cells are denoted by full permissions; an existential permission can correspond to one of these only when the corresponding master permission is available. Every such master permission comes from some F_t, and hence, the corresponding cell belongs to $\mathtt{detached}[t-1]$. Thus, at the end of the program, any allocated cell is reachable from either C or one of the $\mathtt{detached}$ sets.

Extensions. Even though we illustrated our proof technique using the idealistic example of a counter, the technique is also applicable both to other algorithms based on hazard pointers and to different ways of optimising hazard pointer implementations. In [7, §B], we demonstrate this on the example of a non-blocking stack with several optimisations of hazard pointers used in practice [12]: e.g., the pointers are dynamically allocated, `reclaim` scans the hazard list only once, and the `detached` sets are represented by lists with links stored inside the detached elements themselves. The required proof is not significantly more complex than the one presented in this section.

In [7, §C], we also present an adaptation of the above proof to establish the linearizability of the algorithm following the approach in [17] (we leave a formal integration of the two methods for future work). The main challenge of proving linearizability of this and similar algorithms lies in establishing that the ABA problem described in §2 does not occur, i.e., when the CAS in line 29 of Figure 6 is successful, we can be sure that the value of C has not changed since we read it at line 16. In our proof this is easy to establish, as between lines 16 and 29, all assertions are stable and contain $\boxed{s \mapsto_e \_ * \mathsf{true}}$, which guarantees that s cannot be recycled.

5   Formalising Read-Copy-Update

RCU Specification. We start by deriving specifications for RCU commands in our logic from the abstract RCU implementation in Figure 2; see Figure 8. The formula $S(\mathsf{tid}, 1)$ states that the thread tid is in a critical section, and $S(\mathsf{tid}, 0)$, that it is outside one. We use the identity action Id and an action $\mathsf{RCU}_{\mathsf{tid}}$ allowing a thread tid to enter or exit a critical section. The latter is used to derive the specification for rcu_enter and rcu_exit (see Figure 2). To satisfy the premises of the SHARED-R rule in these derivations, we require certain conditions ensuring that the RCU client will not corrupt

Let $S(\text{tid}, k) = \boxed{\text{rcu}[\text{tid} - 1] \mapsto k * \text{true}}$ and

$$X \rightsquigarrow X \quad (\text{Id}) \qquad \text{rcu}[\text{tid} - 1] \mapsto \_ * X \rightsquigarrow \text{rcu}[\text{tid} - 1] \mapsto \_ * X \quad (\text{RCU}_{\text{tid}})$$

Then, $\quad R, \{\text{RCU}_{\text{tid}}\}, \varUpsilon \vdash_{\text{tid}} \{S(\text{tid}, 0) \wedge \text{emp}\} \, \text{rcu\_enter}() \, \{S(\text{tid}, 1) \wedge \text{emp}\};$
$\qquad R, \{\text{RCU}_{\text{tid}}\}, \varUpsilon \vdash_{\text{tid}} \{S(\text{tid}, 1) \wedge \text{emp}\} \, \text{rcu\_exit}() \, \{S(\text{tid}, 0) \wedge \text{emp}\};$
$\qquad R, \{\text{Id}\}, \varUpsilon \vdash_{\text{tid}} \{p \wedge \tau\} \, \text{sync}() \, \{p \wedge \forall t. \tau \text{ since } S(t, 0)\},$

where $\quad$ 1. $R \Rightarrow \{(\text{rcu}[\text{tid} - 1] \mapsto x * \text{true}) \rightsquigarrow (\text{rcu}[\text{tid} - 1] \mapsto x * \text{true})\};$
$\qquad$ 2. $\varUpsilon$ is stable under $\{\text{Id}, \text{RCU}_{\text{tid}}\}$ and true; and
$\qquad$ 3. $p \wedge \tau$ is stable under $R \cup \{\text{Id}\}$ and $\varUpsilon$.

Fig. 8. Specification of RCU commands

the rcu array. First, we require that the rely R does not change the element of the rcu array for the thread tid executing the RCU function (condition 1). In practice, R includes the actions RCU_k for $k \neq \text{tid}$ and actions that do not access the rcu array. Second, we require that $\varUpsilon$ be preserved under the actions that RCU functions execute (condition 2).

The specification for sync is the most interesting one. The precondition $p \wedge \tau$ is required to be stable (condition 3), and thus holds for the whole of sync's duration. Since, while sync is executing, every thread passes through a point when it is not in a critical section, we obtain $\forall t. \tau$ since $S(t, 0)$ in the postcondition. (We mention the local state p in the specification, as it helps in checking stability; see below.) The derivation of the specification from Figure 2 is straightforward: e.g., the invariant of the loop in line 8 is $r, i \Vdash p \wedge \forall t. (t < i + 1 \vee r[t - 1] = 0) \Rightarrow (\tau \text{ since } S(t, 0))$. As usual, here we obtain the since clause by weakening: $(\tau \wedge S(\text{tid}, 0)) \Rightarrow (\tau \text{ since } S(\text{tid}, 0))$.

Verification of the RCU-Based Counter. Since this RCU-based algorithm is similar to the one using hazard pointers, most actions in relies and guarantees are reused from that proof (Figure 5): we let $G_{\text{tid}} = \{\text{Id}, \text{Inc}, \text{Take}, \text{RCU}_{\text{tid}}\}$ and $R_{\text{tid}} = \bigcup\{G_k \mid 1 \leq k \leq N \wedge k \neq \text{tid}\}$. The following invariant formalises (5):

$$\varUpsilon_{\text{RCU}} \iff \forall x, t. (S(t, 1) \text{ since } \boxed{C \mapsto x * x \mapsto \_ * \text{true}}) \Rightarrow \boxed{x \mapsto_e \_ * \text{true}}.$$

The proof outline for the RCU-based counter is given in Figure 9. The assertion F_{tid} is the same as for hazard pointers and is defined by (10) in §4. The assertion I describes the state invariant of the algorithm:

$$I \iff \boxed{(\circledast_t \text{rcu}[t - 1] \mapsto \_) * \exists y. C \mapsto y * y \mapsto \_ * \text{true}_e}.$$

The key points are as follows. After reading C at line 12, we obtain an unstable assertion $S(\text{tid}, 1) \wedge \boxed{C \mapsto s * s \mapsto \_ * \text{true}}$, which we weaken to a stable one $(S(\text{tid}, 1) \text{ since } \boxed{C \mapsto s * s \mapsto \_ * \text{true}})$. Then $\varUpsilon_{\text{RCU}}$ yields $\boxed{s \mapsto_e \_ * \text{true}}$, which justifies the safety of dereferencing s at line 15. The same assertion in line 17 would let us rule out the ABA problem in a linearizability proof. We get the assertion in line 35 from the tautology $x \mapsto_m \_ \Rightarrow \boxed{\neg C \mapsto x * x \mapsto \_ * \text{true}}$. At line 36, we apply the specification of sync with $\tau = \boxed{(\circledast_{x \in A} x \mapsto_e \_) * \text{true}} \wedge (\circledast_{x \in A} \boxed{\neg C \mapsto x * x \mapsto \_ * \text{true}})$ and $p = (\circledast_{x \in A} x \mapsto_m \_)$. The resulting since clause formalises (6) and allows us to justify that the Take action in line 41 does not violate $\varUpsilon_{\text{RCU}}$.

```
1  int *C=new int(0); bool rcu[N]={0};
2  Set detached[N]={∅};
3  int inc() {
4    int v, *n, *s;
```
5    $\{V \Vdash F_{\mathsf{tid}} \wedge I \wedge S(\mathsf{tid}, 0)\}\}$
```
6    n = new int;
```
7    $\{V \Vdash n \mapsto \_ * F_{\mathsf{tid}} \wedge I \wedge S(\mathsf{tid}, 0)\}\}$
```
8    rcu_enter();
```
9   do { $\{V \Vdash n \mapsto \_ * F_{\mathsf{tid}} \wedge I \wedge S(\mathsf{tid}, 1)\}$
```
10     rcu_exit();
11     rcu_enter();
```
12     $\langle s = C \rangle_{\mathsf{ld}};$
13     $\{V \Vdash n \mapsto \_ * F_{\mathsf{tid}} \wedge I \wedge \boxed{s \mapsto_e \_ * \mathsf{true}} \wedge$
14     $(S(\mathsf{tid}, 1) \text{ since } \boxed{C \mapsto s * s \mapsto \_ * \mathsf{true}})\}$
15     $\langle v = *s \rangle_{\mathsf{ld}};$
```
16     *n = v+1;
```
17     $\{V \Vdash n \mapsto \_ * F_{\mathsf{tid}} \wedge I \wedge \boxed{s \mapsto_e \_ * \mathsf{true}}$
18     $(S(\mathsf{tid}, 1) \text{ since } \boxed{C \mapsto s * s \mapsto \_ * \mathsf{true}})\}$
```
19   } while (!CAS_Inc,ld(&C, s, n));
20   rcu_exit();
```
21   $\{V \Vdash s \mapsto_m \_ * F_{\mathsf{tid}} \wedge I \wedge S(\mathsf{tid}, 0) \wedge$
22   $\boxed{s \mapsto_e \_ * \mathsf{true}}\}$
```
23   reclaim(s);
```
24   $\{V \Vdash F_{\mathsf{tid}} \wedge I \wedge S(\mathsf{tid}, 0)\}$
```
25   return v; }
```

```
26  void reclaim(int* s) {
```
27   $\{V \Vdash s \mapsto_m \_ * F_{\mathsf{tid}} \wedge I \wedge S(\mathsf{tid}, 0) \wedge$
28   $\boxed{s \mapsto_e \_ * \mathsf{true}}\}$
```
29   insert(detached[tid-1], s);
30   if (nondet()) return;
```
31   $\{V \Vdash I \wedge S(\mathsf{tid}, 0) \wedge$
32   $\exists A. \mathsf{detached}[\mathsf{tid} - 1] \mapsto A *$
33   $(\circledast_{x \in A} x \mapsto_m \_) \wedge$
34   $\boxed{(\circledast_{x \in A} x \mapsto_e \_) * \mathsf{true}} \wedge$
35   $(\circledast_{x \in A} \boxed{\neg C \mapsto x * x \mapsto \_ * \mathsf{true}})\}$
```
36   sync();
```
37   $\{V \Vdash I \wedge S(\mathsf{tid}, 0) \wedge$
38   $\exists A. \mathsf{detached}[\mathsf{tid} - 1] \mapsto A *$
39   $\circledast_{x \in A}((x \mapsto_m \_ \wedge \boxed{x \mapsto_e \_ * \mathsf{true}}) \wedge \forall t.$
40   $\boxed{\neg C \mapsto x * x \mapsto \_ * \mathsf{true}} \text{ since } S(t, 0))\}$
41   $\langle \; ; \; \rangle_{\mathsf{Take}}$
42   $\{V \Vdash I \wedge S(\mathsf{tid}, 0) \wedge$
43   $\exists A. \mathsf{detached}[\mathsf{tid} - 1] \mapsto A *$
44   $(\circledast_{x \in A} x \mapsto \_)\}$
```
45   while (!isEmpty(detached[tid]))
46     free(pop(detached[tid]));
```
47   $\{V \Vdash F_{\mathsf{tid}} \wedge I \wedge S(\mathsf{tid}, 0)\}$
```
48  }
```

Fig. 9. Counter with an RCU-based memory management. Here V is v, n, s.

Like for hazard pointers, this proof implies that the algorithm does not leak memory, and that the ABA problem does not occur.

6   Related Work

Out of the three techniques for memory reclamation that we consider in this paper, only restricted versions of the non-blocking stack with hazard pointers that we handle in [7, §B] have been verified: in concurrent separation logic [14], a combination of separation logic and temporal logic [6], a reduction-based tool [3] and interval temporal logic [16]. These papers use different reasoning methods from the one we propose, none of which has been grounded in a pattern common to different algorithms.

Among the above-mentioned verification efforts, the closest to us technically is the work by Fu et al. [6], which proposed a combination of separation logic and temporal logic very similar to the one we use for formalising our method. We emphasise that we do not consider the logic we present in §3 as the main contribution of this paper, but merely as a *tool* for formalising our reasoning method. It is this method that is the main difference of our work in comparison to Fu et al. The method used by Fu et al. to verify a non-blocking stack with hazard pointers leads to a complicated proof that embeds a lot of implementation detail into its invariants and rely/guarantee conditions. In contrast, our proofs are conceptually simple and technically straightforward, due to the use of a strategy that captures the essence of the algorithms considered. Fu et al. also handle only an idealistic implementation of hazard pointers, where deallocations are not batched, and many assertions in the proof inherently rely on this simplification. We do not think that their proof would scale easily to the implementation that batches deallocations (§2), let alone other extensions we consider [7, §B].

Having said that, we fully acknowledge the influence of the work by Fu et al. In particular, we agree that a combination of temporal and separation logics provides a useful means of reasoning about non-blocking algorithms. We hope that our formalisation of powerful proof patterns in such a combined logic will motivate verification researchers to adopt the pattern-based approach in verifying other complex concurrent algorithms.

Acknowledgements. We thank the following people for discussions and comments: Richard Bornat, Sungkeun Cho, Byron Cook, Wonchan Lee, Paul McKenney, Peter O'Hearn, Matthew Parkinson, Mooly Sagiv, Viktor Vafeiadis, Jonathan Walpole, Eran Yahav and Kwangkeun Yi.

References

1. Boyland, J.: Checking Interference with Fractional Permissions. In: Cousot, R. (ed.) SAS 2003. LNCS, vol. 2694, pp. 55–72. Springer, Heidelberg (2003)
2. Calcagno, C., O'Hearn, P., Yang, H.: Local action and abstract separation logic. In: LICS (2007)
3. Elmas, T., Qadeer, S., Tasiran, S.: A calculus of atomic actions. In: POPL (2009)
4. Feng, X., Ferreira, R., Shao, Z.: On the Relationship Between Concurrent Separation Logic and Assume-Guarantee Reasoning. In: De Nicola, R. (ed.) ESOP 2007. LNCS, vol. 4421, pp. 173–188. Springer, Heidelberg (2007)
5. Fraser, K.: Practical lock-freedom. PhD Thesis. University of Cambridge (2004)
6. Fu, M., Li, Y., Feng, X., Shao, Z., Zhang, Y.: Reasoning about Optimistic Concurrency Using a Program Logic for History. In: Gastin, P., Laroussinie, F. (eds.) CONCUR 2010. LNCS, vol. 6269, pp. 388–402. Springer, Heidelberg (2010)
7. Gotsman, A., Rinetzky, N., Yang, H.: Verifying concurrent memory reclamation algorithms with grace. Technical Report 7/13, School of Computer Science, Tel-Aviv University (2013), http://www.cs.tau.ac.il/~maon
8. Herlihy, M., Luchangco, V., Moir, M.: The Repeat Offender Problem: A Mechanism for Supporting Dynamic-Sized, Lock-Free Data Structures. In: Malkhi, D. (ed.) DISC 2002. LNCS, vol. 2508, pp. 339–353. Springer, Heidelberg (2002)
9. Herlihy, M.P., Wing, J.M.: Linearizability: a correctness condition for concurrent objects. TOPLAS (1990)
10. Jones, C.B.: Specification and design of (parallel) programs. In: IFIP Congress (1983)
11. McKenney, P.: Exploiting deferred destruction: an analysis of read-copy-update techniques in operating system kernels. PhD Thesis. OGI (2004)
12. Michael, M.M.: Hazard pointers: Safe memory reclamation for lock-free objects. IEEE Trans. Parallel Distrib. Syst. (2004)
13. O'Hearn, P.: Resources, concurrency and local reasoning. TCS (2007)
14. Parkinson, M., Bornat, R., O'Hearn, P.: Modular verification of a non-blocking stack. In: POPL (2007)
15. Pnueli, A.: In transition from global to modular temporal reasoning about programs. In: Logics and Models of Concurrent Systems (1985)
16. Tofan, B., Schellhorn, G., Reif, W.: Formal Verification of a Lock-Free Stack with Hazard Pointers. In: Cerone, A., Pihlajasaari, P. (eds.) ICTAC 2011. LNCS, vol. 6916, pp. 239–255. Springer, Heidelberg (2011)
17. Vafeiadis, V.: Modular fine-grained concurrency verification. PhD Thesis. University of Cambridge (2008)

Interleaving and Lock-Step Semantics
for Analysis and Verification of GPU Kernels[*]

Peter Collingbourne[1],[**], Alastair F. Donaldson[1], Jeroen Ketema[1], and Shaz Qadeer[2]

[1] Imperial College London
peter@pcc.me.uk, {afd,jketema}@imperial.ac.uk
[2] Microsoft Research
qadeer@microsoft.com

Abstract. We study semantics of GPU kernels — the parallel programs that run on Graphics Processing Units (GPUs). We provide a novel lock-step execution semantics for GPU kernels represented by *arbitrary* reducible control flow graphs and compare this semantics with a traditional interleaving semantics. We show for terminating kernels that either both semantics compute identical results or both behave erroneously.

The result induces a method that allows GPU kernels with arbitrary reducible control flow graphs to be verified via transformation to a sequential program that employs predicated execution. We implemented this method in the GPUVerify tool and experimentally evaluated it by comparing the tool with the previous version of the tool based on a similar method for *structured programs*, i.e., where control is organised using **if** and **while** statements. The evaluation was based on a set of 163 open source and commercial GPU kernels. Among these kernels, 42 exhibit unstructured control flow which our novel method can handle fully automatically, but the previous method could not. Overall the generality of the new method comes at a modest price: Verification across our benchmark set was 2.25 times slower overall; however, the median slow down across all kernels was 0.77, indicating that our novel technique yielded faster analysis in many cases.

1 Introduction

Graphics Processing Units (GPUs) have recently found application in accelerating general-purpose computations, e.g., in image retrieval [23] and machine learning [3]. If an application exhibits significant parallelism it may be possible to extract the computational core of the application as a *kernel* and offload this kernel to run across the parallel hardware of a GPU, sometimes beating CPU performance by orders of magnitude. Writing kernels for massively parallel GPUs is challenging, requiring coordination of a large number of threads. Data races and mis-synchronisation at barriers (known as *barrier divergence*) can lead to erroneous and non-deterministic program behaviours. Worse, they can lead to bugs which manifest only on some GPU architectures.

Substantial effort has been put into the design of tools for rigorous analysis of GPU kernels [7,16,8,17,15]. In prior work [7], we presented a verification technique and tool, GPUVerify, for analysis of data races and barrier divergence in OpenCL [13] and

---

[*] This work was supported by the EU FP7 STREP project CARP (project number 287767).
[**] Peter Collingbourne is currently employed at Google.

M. Felleisen and P. Gardner (Eds.): ESOP 2013, LNCS 7792, pp. 270–289, 2013.

CUDA [21] kernels. GPUVerify achieves scalability by reducing verification of a parallel kernel to a *sequential* program verification task. This is achieved by transforming kernels into a form where all threads execute in *lock-step* in a manner that still facilitates detection of data races and barrier divergence arising due to arbitrary thread interleavings.

Semantics and program transformations for lock-step execution have been formally studied for *structured* GPU kernels where control flow is described by **if** and **while** constructs [7]. In this setting, the hierarchical structure of a program gives rise to a simple, recursive algorithm for transforming control flow into *predicated* form so that all threads execute the same sequence of statements. Lock-step semantics for GPU kernels where control flow is described by an *arbitrary* reducible control flow graph (CFG),[1] has *not* been studied. Unlike structured programs, arbitrary CFGs do not necessarily exhibit a hierarchical structure, thus the existing predication-based approach cannot be directly extended. Furthermore, it is not possible in to efficiently pre-process an arbitrary CFG into a structured form [9].

The restriction to structured programs poses a serious limitation to the design of GPU kernel analysis techniques: kernels frequently exhibit unstructured control flow, either directly, e.g., through **switch** statements, or indirectly, through short-circuit evaluation of Boolean expressions. Dealing with CFGs also enables analysis of GPU kernels after compiler optimisations have been applied, bringing the analysis closer to the code actually executed by the GPU. It allows for the reuse of existing compiler infrastructures, such as Clang/LLVM, which use CFGs as their intermediate representation. Reusing compiler infrastructures hugely simplifies tool development, removing the burden of writing a robust front-end for C-like languages.

We present a traditional interleaving semantics and a novel lock-step semantics for GPU kernels described by CFGs. We show that if a GPU kernel is guaranteed to terminate then the kernel is correct with respect to the interleaving semantics if and only if it is correct with respect to the lock-step semantics, where *correct* means that all execution traces are free from data races, barrier divergence, and assertion failures. Our novel lock-step semantics enables the strategy of reducing verification of a multithreaded GPU kernel to verification of a sequential program to be applied to arbitrary GPU kernels, and we have implemented this method in the GPUVerify tool. We present an experimental evaluation, applying our new tool to a set of 163 open source and commercial GPU kernels. In 42 cases these kernels exhibited unstructured control flow either (a) explicitly (e.g., through **switch** statements), or (b) implicitly due to short-circuit evaluation. In the case of (a), these kernels had to be manually simplified to be amenable to analysis using the original version of GPUVerify. In the case of (b), it turned out that the semantics of short-circuit evaluation of logical operators was not handled correctly in GPU-Verify. Our new, more general implementation handles all these kernels accurately and automatically. Our results show that GPUVerify continues to perform well: compared to the original version that was limited to structured kernels [7], verification across our

---

[1] Henceforth, whenever we refer to a CFG we shall always mean a reducible CFG. For a definition of reducibility we refer the reader to [1]. We note that irreducibility is uncommon in practice. In particular, we have never encountered a GPU kernel with an irreducible control flow graph, and whether irreducible control flow is supported at all is implementation-defined in OpenCL [13].

```
__kernel void                          __kernel void
scan(__global int *sum) {              scan(__global int *sum) {
  int offset = 1, temp;                  int offset = 1, temp;
  while (offset < TS) {                  while (offset <= tid) {
    if (tid >= offset)                     temp = sum[tid - offset];
      temp = sum[tid - offset];            barrier();
    barrier();                             sum[tid] = sum[tid] + temp;
    if (tid >= offset)                     barrier();
      sum[tid] = sum[tid] + temp;          offset *= 2;
    barrier();                           }
    offset *= 2;                        }
  }
}
```

(a) A correct kernel   (b) A kernel with barrier divergence

Fig. 1. Two OpenCL kernels

benchmark set was 2.25 times slower overall, but the median slow down across all kernels was 0.77, indicating that our novel technique yields faster analysis in many cases.

In summary, our main contributions are:

- A novel operational semantics for lock-step execution of GPU kernels with arbitrary reducible control flow.
- A proof-sketch that this semantics is equivalent to a traditional interleaving semantics for terminating GPU kernels.
- A revised implementation of GPUVerify which uses our lock-step semantics to reduce verification of a multithreaded kernel to a sequential verification task.

After presenting a small example to provide some background on GPU kernels and illustrate the problems of data races and barrier divergence (Sect. 2), we present the interleaving semantics (Sect. 3), our novel lock-step semantics (Sect. 4) and a proof-sketch showing that the semantics are equivalent for terminating kernels (Sect. 5). We then discuss the implementation in GPUVerify, and present our experimental results (Sect. 6). We end with related work and conclusions (Sect. 7).

2 A Background Example

We use an example to illustrate the key concepts from GPU programming and provide an informal description as to how predicated lock-step execution works for structured programs. We return to this example when presenting interleaving and lock-step semantics for kernels described as CFGs in Sects. 3 and 4.

Threads, Barriers, and Shared Memory. Figure 1a shows an OpenCL kernel[2] to be executed by TS threads, where TS is a power of two. The kernel implements a *scan* (or *prefix-sum*) operation on the sum array so that at the end of the kernel we have, for all $0 \leq i < TS$, $\text{sum}[i] = \Sigma_{j=0}^{i} \text{old}(\text{sum})[j]$, where $\text{old}(\text{sum})$ refers to the sum array at the start of the kernel. All threads execute this kernel function in parallel,

---

[2] For ease of presentation we use a slightly simplified version of OpenCL syntax, and we assume that all threads reside in the same work group and that this work group is one dimensional. Our implementation, described in Sect. 6, supports OpenCL in full.

and threads may follow different control paths or access distinct data by querying their unique thread id, `tid`. Communication is possible via shared memory; the `sum` array is marked as residing in global shared memory via the `__global` qualifier. Threads synchronise using a `barrier`-statement, a collective operation that requires all threads to reach the same syntactic barrier before any thread proceeds past the barrier.

Data Races and Barrier Divergence. Two common defects from which GPU kernels suffer are *data races* and *barrier divergence*. In Fig. 1a, accesses to `sum` inside the loop are guarded so that on loop iteration i only threads with id at least 2^{i-1} access the `sum` array. If either of the barriers in the example were omitted the kernel would be prone to a *data race* arising due to thread t_1 reading from sum$[t_1 -$ `offset`$]$, while thread t_2 writes to sum$[t_2]$, where $t_2 = t_1 -$ `offset`. The kernel of Fig. 1b aims to optimise the original example by reducing branches inside the loop: threads are restricted to only execute the loop body if their id is sufficiently large. This optimisation is *erroneous*; given a barrier inside a loop, the OpenCL standard requires that either all threads or zero threads reach the barrier during a given loop iteration, otherwise *barrier divergence* occurs and behaviour is undefined. In Fig. 1b, thread 0 will not enter the loop at all and thus will *never* reach the first barrier, while all other threads will enter the loop and reach the barrier. Unfortunately, on an NVIDIA 9400M the kernel of Fig. 1b behaves identically to the kernel of Fig. 1a, meaning that this barrier divergence bug would not be detected on this platform. This is problematic because the erroneous kernel code is not portable across architectures which support OpenCL (e.g., the kernel fails to produce correct results with Intel's SDK for OpenCL).

Lock-Step Predicated Execution. We informally describe lock-step execution for structured programs as used by GPUVerify [7] and which we here generalise to CFGs.

To achieve lock-step execution, GPUVerify transforms kernels into *predicated* form [2]. The example of Fig. 2 illustrates the effect of applying predication to the kernel of Fig. 1a. A statement of the form $e \Rightarrow stmt$ is a *predicated* statement which is a no-op if e is false, and has the same effect as $stmt$ if e is true. Observe that the `if` statements in the body of the loop have been predicated: the condition (which is the same for both statements) is evaluated into a Boolean variable q, the conditional statements are removed and the statements previously inside the conditionals are predicated by the associated Boolean variable. Predication of the `while` loop is achieved by evaluating the loop condition into a Boolean variable p, pred-

```
__kernel void
scan(__global int *sum) {
  bool p, q;
  int offset = 1, temp;
  p = (offset < TS);
  while (∃ t :: t.p) {
    q = (p && tid >= offset);
    q ⇒ temp = sum[tid - offset];
    p ⇒ barrier();
    q ⇒ sum[tid] = sum[tid] + temp;
    p ⇒ barrier();
    p ⇒ offset *= 2;
    p ⇒ p = (offset < TS);
  }
}
```

Fig. 2. Lock-step predicated execution for structured kernel of Fig. 1a

icating all statements in the loop body by p, and recomputing p at the end of the loop body. The loop condition is replaced by a guard which evaluates to false if and only if the predicate variable p is false for *every* thread. Thus all threads continue to execute the loop until each thread is ready to leave the loop; when the loop condition becomes false for a given thread the thread simply performs no-ops during subsequent loop iterations.

In predicated form, the threads do not exhibit any diverging behaviour due to execution of different branches, and thus the kernel can be regarded as a *sequential*, vector program. GPUVerify exploits this fact to reduce GPU kernel verification to a sequential program verification task. The full technique, described in [7], involves considering lock-step execution of an arbitrary *pair* of threads, rather than all threads.

The example illustrates that predication is easy to perform at the level of structured programs built hierarchically using **if** and **while** statements. However, predication does not directly extend to the unstructured case, and unstructured control flow cannot be efficiently pre-processed into structured form [9]. Hence, we present a program transformation for predicated execution of GPU kernels described as CFGs.

3   Interleaving Semantics for GPU Kernels

We introduce a simple language for describing GPU kernels as CFGs.

3.1   Syntax

A kernel is defined over a set of variables $Var = V_s \uplus V_p$ with V_s the *shared* variables and V_p the *private* variables. Variables take values from a domain D. Kernels are expressed using a syntax that is identical to the core of the Boogie programming language [5], except that it includes an additional **barrier** statement:

$Program ::= Block^+$

$\quad Block ::= BlockId : Stmts \textbf{ goto } BlockId^+ ;$

$\quad Stmts ::= \varepsilon \mid Stmt ; Stmts$

$\quad Stmt ::= Var := Expr \mid \textbf{havoc } Var \mid \textbf{assume } Expr \mid \textbf{assert } Expr \mid \textbf{skip} \mid \textbf{barrier}$

Here, ε is an empty sequence of statements. The form of expressions is irrelevant, except that we assume (a) *equality testing* ($=$), (b) the standard Boolean operators, and (c) a ternary operator $Expr_1 ? Expr_2 : Expr_3$, which — like the operator from C — evaluates to the result of $Expr_2$ if $Expr_1$ is *true* and to the result of $Expr_3$ otherwise.

Thus, a kernel consists of a number of *basic blocks*, with each block consisting of a number of *statements* followed by a **goto** that non-deterministically chooses which block to execute next based on the provided *BlockId*s; non-deterministic choice in combination with **assume**s at the beginning of blocks is used to model branching.

Because gotos only appear at the end of blocks there is a one-to-one correspondence between kernels and CFGs. We assume that all kernels have reducible CFGs, which means that cycles in a CFG are guaranteed to form *natural loops*. A natural loop has a unique *header* node, the single entry point to the loop, and one or more *back edges* going from a loop node to the header [1].

We assume that each block in a kernel is uniquely labelled and that there is a block labelled *Start*. This is the block from which execution of each thread commences. Moreover, no block is labelled *End*; instead the occurrence of *End* in a **goto** signifies that the program may terminate at this point. The first statement of a block is always an **assume** and only variables from V_p appear in the guard of the **assume**. No other **assume**s occur in blocks and the first statement of *Start* is **assume** *true*. Observe that any kernel can be easily pre-processed to satisfy these restrictions.

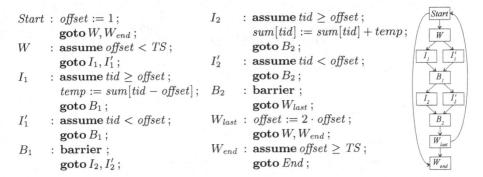

$Start$: $offset := 1$;
  goto W, W_{end} ;
W : assume $offset < TS$;
  goto I_1, I_1' ;
I_1 : assume $tid \geq offset$;
  $temp := sum[tid - offset]$;
  goto B_1 ;
I_1' : assume $tid < offset$;
  goto B_1 ;
B_1 : barrier ;
  goto I_2, I_2' ;

I_2 : assume $tid \geq offset$;
  $sum[tid] := sum[tid] + temp$;
  goto B_2 ;
I_2' : assume $tid < offset$;
  goto B_2 ;
B_2 : barrier ;
  goto W_{last} ;
W_{last} : $offset := 2 \cdot offset$;
  goto W, W_{end} ;
W_{end} : assume $offset \geq TS$;
  goto End ;

Fig. 3. The kernel of Fig. 1a encoded in our kernel language and its CFG

Figure 3 shows the kernel of Fig. 1a encoded in our simple programming language, where we omit **assume** *true* for brevity. Remark that an array is being used; we could easily add arrays to our GPU kernel semantics but, again for brevity, we do not.

3.2 Operational Semantics

We now define a small-step operational semantics for our kernel programming language, which is based on interleaving the steps taken by individual threads.

Individual Threads. The behaviour of individual threads and the non-barrier statements executed by these threads is presented in Figs. 4a and 4b.

The operational semantics of a thread t is defined in terms of triples $\langle \sigma, \sigma_t, b_t \rangle$, where $\sigma : V_s \to D$ is the *shared* store, $\sigma_t : V_p \to D$ is the *private* store of thread t, and b_t is the statement or sequence of statements the thread will *reduce* (i.e., execute) next.

In Fig. 4a, $(\sigma, \sigma_t)[v \mapsto val]$ denotes a pair of stores equal to (σ, σ_t) except that v (which we assume occurs in either σ or σ_t) has been updated and is equal to val. The evaluation of an expression e given (σ, σ_t) is denoted $(\sigma, \sigma_t)(e)$. The labels on arrows allow us to observe (a) changes to stores and (b) the state of stores upon termination. A label is omitted when the stores do not change, e.g., in the case of the SKIP rule.

The symbols $\sqrt{}$, $\mathcal{E}$, and $\perp$ indicate, resp., *termination*, *error*, and *infeasible*. These are *termination statuses* which signify that a thread (or later kernel) has terminated with that particular status. Below, termination always means termination with status *termination*; termination with status *error* or *infeasible* is indicated explicitly.

The ASSIGN and SKIP rules of Fig. 4a are standard. The HAVOC rule updates the value of a variable v with an arbitrary value from the domain D of v. The ASSERT$_T$ and ASSUME$_T$ rules are no-ops if the assumption or assertion $(\sigma, \sigma_t)(e)$ holds. If the assumption or assertion does not hold, ASSERT$_F$ and ASSUME$_F$ yield, resp., $\mathcal{E}$ and $\perp$.

In Fig. 4b, s denotes a statement and b denotes the *body of a block*, i.e., a sequence of statements followed by a **goto**. The SEQ$_B$ and SEQ$_{E,I}$ rules define reduction of s ; b in terms of reduction of s. The GOTO and BLOCK rules specify how reduction continues once the end of a block is reached. The END rule specifies termination of a thread.

$$\frac{val = (\sigma, \sigma_t)(e)}{P \vdash \langle \sigma, \sigma_t, v := e \rangle \overset{(\sigma, \sigma_t)}{\to} (\sigma, \sigma_t)[v \mapsto val]} \text{ ASSIGN}$$

$$\frac{val \in D}{P \vdash \langle \sigma, \sigma_t, \textbf{havoc } v \rangle \overset{(\sigma, \sigma_t)}{\to} (\sigma, \sigma_t)[v \mapsto val]} \text{ HAVOC}$$

$$\frac{a \in \{\textbf{assert}, \textbf{assume}\} \quad (\sigma, \sigma_t)(e)}{P \vdash \langle \sigma, \sigma_t, a\, e \rangle \to (\sigma, \sigma_t)} \begin{array}{l} \text{ASSERT}_\text{T} \\ \text{ASSUME}_\text{T} \end{array} \qquad \frac{\neg(\sigma, \sigma_t)(e)}{P \vdash \langle \sigma, \sigma_t, \textbf{assume } e \rangle \overset{(\sigma, \sigma_t)}{\to} \bot} \text{ ASSUME}_\text{F}$$

$$\frac{\neg(\sigma, \sigma_t)(e)}{P \vdash \langle \sigma, \sigma_t, \textbf{assert } e \rangle \overset{(\sigma, \sigma_t)}{\to} \mathcal{E}} \text{ ASSERT}_\text{F} \qquad \frac{}{P \vdash \langle \sigma, \sigma_t, \textbf{skip} \rangle \to (\sigma, \sigma_t)} \text{ SKIP}$$

(a) Statement rules

$$\frac{P \vdash \langle \sigma, \sigma_t, s \rangle \overset{(\sigma, \sigma_t)}{\to} (\tau, \tau_t)}{P \vdash \langle \sigma, \sigma_t, s \, ; \, b \rangle \overset{(\sigma, \sigma_t)}{\to} \langle \tau, \tau_t, b \rangle} \text{ SEQ}_\text{B} \qquad \frac{P \vdash \langle \sigma, \sigma_t, s \rangle \overset{(\sigma, \sigma_t)}{\to} e \quad e \in \{\mathcal{E}, \bot\}}{P \vdash \langle \sigma, \sigma_t, s \, ; \, b \rangle \overset{(\sigma, \sigma_t)}{\to} e} \text{ SEQ}_\text{E,I}$$

$$\frac{1 \le i \le n}{P \vdash \langle \sigma, \sigma_t, \textbf{goto } B_1, \ldots, B_n \, ; \rangle \to \langle \sigma, \sigma_t, B_i \rangle} \text{ GOTO} \qquad \frac{(B : b) \in P}{P \vdash \langle \sigma, \sigma_t, B \rangle \to \langle \sigma, \sigma_t, b \rangle} \text{ BLOCK}$$

$$\frac{}{P \vdash \langle \sigma, \sigma_t, End \rangle \overset{\sigma, \sigma_t}{\to} \surd} \text{ END}$$

(b) Thread rules

$$\frac{T_{\vec{\sigma}}|_t = \langle \sigma_t, b_t \rangle \quad P \vdash \langle \sigma, \sigma_t, b_t \rangle \overset{(\sigma, \sigma_t)}{\to} \langle \tau, \tau_t, c_t \rangle}{P \vdash \langle \sigma, T_{\vec{\sigma}} \rangle \overset{(\sigma, \vec{\sigma})}{\to} \langle \tau, T_{\vec{\sigma}}[\langle \tau_t, c_t \rangle]_t \rangle} \text{ THREAD}_\text{B}$$

$$\frac{T_{\vec{\sigma}}|_t = \langle \sigma_t, b_t \rangle \quad P \vdash \langle \sigma, \sigma_t, b_t \rangle \overset{(\sigma, \sigma_t)}{\to} \surd}{P \vdash \langle \sigma, T_{\vec{\sigma}} \rangle \overset{(\sigma, \vec{\sigma})}{\to} \langle \sigma, T_{\vec{\sigma}}[\langle \sigma_t, \surd \rangle]_t \rangle} \text{ THREAD}_\text{T}$$

$$\frac{T_{\vec{\sigma}}|_t = \langle \sigma_t, b_t \rangle \quad P \vdash \langle \sigma, \sigma_t, b_t \rangle \overset{(\sigma, \sigma_t)}{\to} s \quad s \in \{\mathcal{E}, \bot\}}{P \vdash \langle \sigma, T_{\vec{\sigma}} \rangle \overset{(\sigma, \vec{\sigma})}{\to} s} \text{ THREAD}_\text{E,I}$$

$$\frac{\forall\, 1 \le t \le TS : T_{\vec{\sigma}}|_t = \langle \sigma_t, \surd \rangle}{P \vdash \langle \sigma, T_{\vec{\sigma}} \rangle \overset{(\sigma, \vec{\sigma})}{\to} \surd} \text{ TERMINATION}$$

(c) Interleaving rules

$$\frac{T_{\vec{\sigma}}|_t = \langle (\beta_t, \sigma_t), \textbf{barrier } e_t \, ; \, b_t \rangle \wedge \neg(\sigma, \sigma_t)(e_t)}{P \vdash \langle \sigma, T_{\vec{\sigma}} \rangle \to \langle \sigma, T_{\vec{\sigma}}[\langle (\beta_t, \sigma_t), b_t \rangle]_t \rangle} \text{ BARRIER}_\text{SKIP}$$

$$\frac{\forall\, t : T_{\vec{\sigma}}|_t = \langle (\beta_t, \sigma_t), \textbf{barrier } e_t \, ; \, b_t \rangle \wedge (\sigma, \sigma_t)(e_t) \quad \forall\, t_1, t_2 : \beta_{t_1} = \beta_{t_2}}{P \vdash \langle \sigma, T_{\vec{\sigma}} \rangle \to \langle \sigma, \langle (\beta_1, \sigma_1), b_1 \rangle, \ldots, \langle (\beta_{TS}, \sigma_{TS}), b_{TS} \rangle \rangle} \text{ BARRIER}_\text{S}$$

$$\frac{\forall\, t : T_{\vec{\sigma}}|_t = \langle (\beta_t, \sigma_t), \textbf{barrier } e_t \, ; \, b_t \rangle \wedge (\sigma, \sigma_t)(e_t) \quad \exists\, t_1, t_2 : \beta_{t_1} \ne \beta_{t_2}}{P \vdash \langle \sigma, T_{\vec{\sigma}} \rangle \overset{(\sigma, \vec{\sigma})}{\to} \mathcal{E}} \text{ BARRIER}_\text{F}$$

(d) Synchronisation rules; barrier variables β_{t_1} and β_{t_2} enforce OpenCL conditions **B1** and **B2**

Fig. 4. Interleaving operational semantics

Interleaving. Fig. 4c, we give our interleaving semantics for a kernel P given thread count TS. The semantics is defined over tuples $\langle \sigma, \langle \sigma_1, b_1 \rangle, \ldots, \langle \sigma_{TS}, b_{TS} \rangle \rangle$, where σ is the *shared store*, σ_t is the *private store* of thread t, and b_t is the statement or sequence of statements thread t will reduce next. A thread *cannot* access the private store of any other thread, while the shared store is accessible by *all* threads. In the figure, $T_{\vec{\sigma}}$ denotes $(\langle \sigma_1, b_1 \rangle, \ldots, \langle \sigma_{TS}, b_{TS} \rangle)$, where $\vec{\sigma} = (\sigma_1, \ldots, \sigma_{TS})$. Moreover, $T_{\vec{\sigma}}|_t$ denotes $\langle \sigma_t, b_t \rangle$ and $T_{\vec{\sigma}}[\langle \sigma', b \rangle]_t$ denotes $T_{\vec{\sigma}}$ with the t-th element replaced by $\langle \sigma', b \rangle$.

The THREAD$_B$ rule defines how a single step is performed by a single thread, cf. the rules in Fig. 4b. The THREAD$_T$ rule defines termination of a single thread, where the thread enters the termination state $\sqrt{}$ from which no further reduction is possible. The THREAD$_{E,I}$ rule specifies that a kernel terminates with status *error* or *infeasible* if one of the threads terminates as such. The TERMINATION rule specifies that a kernel terminates once all threads have terminated. As steps might be possible in multiple threads, the THREAD rules are non-deterministic and, hence, define an interleaving semantics.

We define a *reduction* of a kernel P as sequence of applications of the operational rules where each thread starts reduction from *Start* and where the *initial* shared store is some σ and the *initial* private store of thread t is some σ_t. A reduction is *maximal* if it is either infinite or if termination with status *termination*, *error*, or *infeasible* has occurred.

Our interleaving semantics effectively has a sequentially consistent memory model, which is not the case for GPUs in practice. However, because our viewpoint is that GPU kernels that exhibit data races should be regarded as erroneous, this is of no consequence.

Barrier Synchronisation. When we define lock-step predicated execution of barriers in Sect. 4 we will need to model execution of a barrier by a thread in a *disabled* state. In preparation for this, let us say that a barrier statement has the form **barrier** e, where e is a Boolean expression. In Sect. 4, e will evaluate to *true* if and only if the barrier is executed in an enabled state. The notion of thread-enabledness is not relevant to our interleaving semantics: we can view a thread as *always* being enabled. Thus we regard the **barrier** syntax of our kernel programming language as short for **barrier** *true*.

Figure 4d defines the rules for (mis-)synchronisation between threads at barriers. Our aim here is to formalise the conditions for correct barrier synchronisation in OpenCL, which are stated informally in the OpenCL specification as follows [13]:

B1. If **barrier** is inside a conditional statement, then all [threads] must enter the conditional if any [thread] enters the conditional statement and executes the barrier.
B2. If **barrier** is inside a loop, all [threads] must execute the barrier for each iteration of the loop before any are allowed to continue execution beyond the barrier.

The rules of Fig. 4d capture these conditions using a number of special *barrier variables* that we assume are implicit in definition of each kernel:

- Every thread has a private variable v_{barrier}. We assume that each barrier appearing in the kernel has a unique id. The variable v_{barrier} of each thread t is initialised to a special value $(-)$ different from every barrier id. When t reaches a barrier, v_{barrier} is set to the id of that barrier, and it is reset to $(-)$ after reduction of the barrier.
- For every loop L in the kernel, every thread has a private *loop counter* variable v_L. The variable v_L of each thread t is initialised to zero, incremented each time the header node for L is reduced by t, and reset to zero on exit from L.

The variable v_{barrier} codifies that each thread is synchronising on the same barrier, capturing condition **B1** above. The loop counters codify that each thread must have executed the same number of loop iterations upon synchronisation, capturing **B2**.

In Fig. 4d, we express the private store of a thread t as a pair (β_t, σ_t), where β_t records the barrier variables for the thread and σ_t the values of all other private variables. The $\text{BARRIER}_{\text{SKIP}}$ rule specifies that **barrier** e is a no-op if e is *false*. Although this can never occur for kernels written directly in our kernel programming language, our equivalence proof in Sect. 5 requires this detail to be accounted for.

The $\text{BARRIER}_{\text{S}}$ rule specifies that reduction continues beyond a barrier if all threads are at a barrier and the barrier variables agree across threads. The $\text{BARRIER}_{\text{F}}$ rule specifies that a kernel should terminate with *error* if the threads have reached barriers with disagreeing barrier variables: this means that one of **B1** or **B2** has been violated and thus *barrier divergence* has occurred.

Data Races. We say that a thread t is *responsible* for a step in a reduction if a THREAD rule (see Fig. 4c) was employed in the step and the premise of the rule was instantiated with t. Moreover, we say that a thread t *accesses* a variable v in a step if t is responsible for the step and if in the step either (a) the value of v is used to evaluate an expression or (b) v is updated. The definition is now as follows:

Definition 3.1. *Let P be a kernel. Then, P has data race if there is a maximal reduction ρ of P, distinct threads t and t', and a shared variable v such that: ρ does not end in the infeasible status $\perp$; t updates v during ρ; t' accesses v during ρ; no application of $\text{BARRIER}_{\text{S}}$ occurs between the accesses (i.e., no barrier separates them).*

Terminating and Race Free Kernels. We say that a kernel P is *(successfully) terminating* with respect to the interleaving semantics if all maximal reductions of P are finite and do not end with status *error*. We say that P is *race free* with respect to the interleaving semantics if P has no data races according to Definition 3.1.

4   Lock-Step Semantics for GPU Kernels

We define lock-step execution semantics for GPU kernels represented as arbitrary CFGs in two stages. First, in Sect. 4.1, we present a transformation which turns the program executed by a single thread into a form where control flow is *flattened*: all branches, except for loop back edges, are eliminated. Then, in Sect. 4.2, we use the transformation to express lock-step execution of all threads in a kernel as a sequential *vector* program.

To avoid many corner cases we assume that kernels always synchronise on a barrier immediately preceding termination. This is without loss of generality, as threads implicitly synchronise on kernel termination. In addition, if a block B ends with $\mathbf{goto}\, B_1, \ldots, B_n$ then at most one of $B_1, \ldots, B_n$ is a loop head. A kernel can be trivially preprocessed to satisfy these restrictions.

Sort Order. Predication of CFGs involves flattening control flow, rewriting branches by predicating blocks and executing these blocks in a linear order. Intuitively, for a kernel exhibiting control flow corresponding to an **if-then-else** statement s, this linear order must arrange blocks such that statements preceding s occur before the statements inside s, which in turn must precede the statements occurring after s. However, if statements s_1 and s_2 occur, resp., in the **then** and **else** branches of s, then the order in which the blocks associated with s_1 and s_2 appear does not matter.

For arbitrary CFGs without loops any topological sort gives a suitable order: it ensures that if block B is a predecessor of C in the original CFG then B will be executed before C in the predicated program. In the presence of loops the order must ensure that once execution of the blocks in a loop commences this loop will be executed completely before any node outside the loop is executed.

Formally, we require a total order $\leq$ on blocks satisfying the following conditions:

- For all blocks B and C, if there is a path from B to C in the CFG, then $B \leq C$ unless a back edge occurs on the path.
- For all loops L, if $B \leq D$ and $B, D \in L$, then $C \in L$ for all $B \leq C \leq D$.

A total order satisfying the above conditions always can always be computed: Consider any innermost loop of the kernel and perform a topological sort of the blocks in the loop body (disregarding back edges). Replace the loop body by an abstract block. Repeat until no loops remain and perform a topological sort of resulting CFG. The sort order is now the order obtained by the final topological sort where one recursively replaces each abstract node by the nodes it represents, i.e., if $B \leq L \leq D$ with L an abstract node, then for any $C \leq C'$ in the loop body represented by L one defines $B \leq C \leq C' \leq D$.

Considering the kernel of Fig. 3, we have that $L = \{W, I_1, I'_1, B_1, I_2, I'_2, B_2, W_{last}\}$ is a loop and that $Start \leq W \leq I_1 \leq I'_1 \leq B_1 \leq I_2 \leq I'_2 \leq B_2 \leq W_{last} \leq W_{end}$ satisfies our requirements; reversing I_1 and I'_1, and also I_2 and I'_2, is possible.

In what follows we assume that a total order satisfying the above conditions has been chosen, and we refer to this order as the *sort order*. For a block B we use $next(B)$ to denote the block that follows B in the sort order. If B is the final block in the sort order we define $next(B)$ to be End, the block label denoting thread termination.

4.1 Predication of a Single Thread

We now describe how predication of the body of a kernel thread is performed.

Predication of Statements. To predicate statements, we introduce a fresh private variable v_{active} for each thread, to which we assign *BlockIds*; the assigned *BlockId* indicates the block that needs to be executed. If the value of v_{active} is not equal to the block that is currently being executed, all statements in the block will effectively be no-ops. In the case of **barrier** this follows by the BARRIER$_{SKIP}$ rule of Fig. 4d.

Assuming the *BlockId* of current block is B, predication of statements is defined in Table 1,

Table 1. Predication of statements

Original form	Predicated form
$v := e$;	$v := (v_{active} = B) ? e : v$;
havoc v;	**havoc** v_{havoc};
	$v := (v_{active} = B) ? v_{havoc} : v$;
assert e;	**assert** $(v_{active} = B) \Rightarrow e$;
skip;	**skip**;
barrier;	**barrier** $(v_{active} = B)$;

except for **assume** statements which are dealt with below at the level of blocks. In the case of **havoc**, the variable v_{havoc} is fresh and private.

Table 2. Predication of blocks

Original form	Predicated form
B : **assume** $guard(B)$; ss **goto** $B_1, \ldots, B_n$; (B *is not* the last node of a loop according to the sort order)	B : $\pi(ss)$ $v_{\text{next}} :\in \{B_1, \ldots, B_n\}$; **assume** $(v_{\text{active}} = B)$ $\qquad \Rightarrow \bigwedge_{i=1}^{n}((v_{\text{next}} = B_i) \Rightarrow guard(B_i))$; $v_{\text{active}} := (v_{\text{active}} = B)$? $v_{\text{next}} : v_{\text{active}}$; **goto** $next(B)$;
B : **assume** $guard(B)$; ss **goto** $B_1, \ldots, B_n$; (B *is* the last node of a loop according to the sort order)	B : $\pi(ss)$ $v_{\text{next}} :\in \{B_1, \ldots, B_n\}$; **assume** $(v_{\text{active}} = B)$ $\qquad \Rightarrow \bigwedge_{i=1}^{n}((v_{\text{next}} = B_i) \Rightarrow guard(B_i))$; $v_{\text{active}} := (v_{\text{active}} = B)$? $v_{\text{next}} : v_{\text{active}}$; **goto** $B_{\text{back}}, B_{\text{exit}}$; B_{back} : **assume** $v_{\text{active}} = B_{\text{head}}$; **goto** B_{head}; B_{exit} : **assume** $v_{\text{active}} \neq B_{\text{head}}$; **goto** $next(B)$;

Predication of Blocks. Let $\pi(s)$ denote the predicated form of a single statement s, and $\pi(ss)$ the pointwise extension to a sequence of statements ss. Predication of blocks is defined by default as in the top row of Table 2 (see also Fig. 5). Here, v_{next} is a fresh, private variable, and $v_{\text{next}} :\in \{B_1, \ldots, B_n\}$ is shorthand for **havoc** v_{next}; **assume** $\bigvee_{i=1}^{n}(v_{\text{next}} = B_i)$. Furthermore, $guard(B)$ denotes the expression that occurs in the **assume** that is required to occur at the beginning of block B.

At the end of the predicated block, v_{active} is set to the value of the block to be reduced next, while actual reduction continues with block $next(B)$, as specified by the sort order. The **assume** that 'guards' the block to be reduced next is moved into the block currently being reduced. Moving guards does not affect behaviour, but only shortens traces that end in *infeasible*; this is needed to properly handle barrier divergence in lock-step kernels.

The above method does not deal correctly with loops: no block can be executed more than once as no back-edges are occur. As such, we predicate block a B in a special manner if B belongs to a loop L and B occurs last in the sort order among all the blocks of L. Assume B_{head} is the header of L. The block B is predicated as in the bottom row of Table 2, where B_{back} and B_{exit} are fresh (see again Fig. 5). Our definition of the sort order guarantees that B_{head} is always sorted first among the blocks of L. By the introduction of B_{back}, reduction jumps back to B_{head} if L needs to be reduced again, otherwise reduction will continue beyond L by definition of B_{exit}.

Predication of Kernels. Predicating a complete kernel P now consists of three steps: (1) Compute a sort order on blocks as detailed above; (2) Predicate every block with respect to the sort order, according to the rules of Table 2; (3) Insert the assignment $v_{\text{active}} := Start$ at the beginning of $\pi(Start)$. The introduction of $v_{\text{active}} := Start$ ensures that the statements from $\pi(Start)$ are always reduced first.

B_2 : **barrier** $(v_{\text{active}} = B_2)$;
$\qquad v_{\text{next}} :\in \{W_{last}\}$;
$\qquad v_{\text{active}} := (v_{\text{active}} = B_2) \;?\; v_{\text{next}} : v_{\text{active}}$;
$\qquad$ **goto** W_{last} ;

W_{last} : *offset* :=
$\qquad\qquad (v_{\text{active}} = W_{last}) \;?\; (2 \cdot \text{offset}) : \text{offset}$;
$\qquad v_{\text{next}} :\in \{W, W_{end}\}$;
$\qquad v_{\text{active}} := (v_{\text{active}} = W_{last}) \;?\; v_{\text{next}} : v_{\text{active}}$;
$\qquad$ **assume** $(v_{\text{active}} = W_{last}) \Rightarrow (((v_{\text{next}} = W) \Rightarrow (\text{offset} < TS))$
$\qquad\qquad\qquad\qquad\qquad\qquad\qquad \wedge ((v_{\text{next}} = W_{end}) \Rightarrow (\text{offset} \geq TS)))$

$\qquad$ **goto** $W_{\text{back}}, W_{\text{exit}}$;
W_{back} : **assume** $v_{\text{active}} = W$;
$\qquad$ **goto** W ;
W_{exit} : **assume** $v_{\text{active}} \neq W$;
$\qquad$ **goto** W_{end} ;
W_{end} : **goto** End ;

Fig. 5. Predication of part of the kernel of Fig. 3

4.2 Lock-Step Execution of All Threads

We now use the predication scheme of Sect. 4.1 to define a lock-step execution semantics for kernels. We achieve this by encoding the kernel as a sequential program, each statement of which is a *vector* statement that performs the work of all threads simultaneously. To enable this, we first extend our programming language with these vector statements.

Vector Statements. We extend our language as follows:

$$Stmt ::= \cdots \mid Var^* := Expr^* \mid \textbf{havoc } Var^* \mid Var := \psi((Expr \times Expr)^*)$$

The vector assignment simultaneously assigns values to multiple variables, where the variables assigned to are assumed to be distinct and where the number of expressions is equal to the number of variables. Similarly, the vector **havoc** havocs multiple variables, which are are assumed to be distinct. The ψ-assignment is used to model simultaneous writes to a shared variable by all threads. It takes a sequence $(e_1, e_1'), \ldots, (e_n, e_n')$, with each e_i a Boolean, and non-deterministically assigns to the variable v a value from the set $\{\sigma(e_i') \mid 1 \leq i \leq n \wedge \sigma(e_i)\}$ (if the set is empty, v is left unchanged).

The semantics for the new statements is presented in Fig. 6, where $\langle e_i \rangle_{i=1}^n$ denotes $(e_1), \ldots, (e_n)$ and $[v_i \mapsto val_i]_{i=1}^n$ denotes $[v_1 \mapsto val_1] \cdots [v_n \mapsto val_n]$.

Lock-Step Execution. To encode a kernel P as a single-threaded program $\phi(P)$ which effectively executes all threads in lock-step, we assume for every *private* variable v from P that there exists a variable v_t in $\phi(P)$ for each $1 \leq t \leq TS$. For each *shared* variable v from P we assume there exists an identical variable in $\phi(P)$. Construction of a lock-step program for P starts from $\pi(P)$ — the predicated version of P.

Statements. The construction for the predicated statements from Table 1 is presented in Table 3a. In the table, ϕ_t denotes a map over expressions which replaces each private variable v by v_t. Note that for every thread t, there exists a variable $v_{\text{active},t}$, as variables

$$\frac{\forall i : val_i = (\sigma, \sigma_t)(e_i)}{P \vdash \langle (\sigma, \sigma_t), \langle v_i \rangle_{i=1}^n := \langle e_i \rangle_{i=1}^n \rangle \stackrel{(\sigma, \sigma_t)}{\rightarrow} (\sigma, \sigma_t)[v_i \mapsto val_i]_{i=1}^n} \text{ ASSIGNS}$$

$$\frac{\forall i : val_i \in D}{P \vdash \langle (\sigma, \sigma_t), \mathbf{havoc} \langle v_i \rangle_{i=1}^n \rangle \stackrel{(\sigma, \sigma_t)}{\rightarrow} (\sigma, \sigma_t)[v_i \mapsto val_i]_{i=1}^n} \text{ HAVOCS}$$

$$\frac{\exists i : \sigma(e_i) \wedge val = (\sigma, \sigma_t)(e_i')}{P \vdash \langle \sigma, v := \psi(\langle e_i, e_i' \rangle_{i=1}^n) \rangle \stackrel{(\sigma, \sigma_t)}{\rightarrow} \sigma[v \mapsto val]} \psi_T$$

$$\frac{\forall i : \neg(\sigma, \sigma_t)(e_i)}{P \vdash \langle (\sigma, \sigma_t), v := \psi(\langle e_i, e_i' \rangle_{i=1}^n) \rangle \rightarrow (\sigma, \sigma_t)} \psi_F$$

Fig. 6. Operational semantics for vector statements

freshly introduced by the predication scheme of Sect. 4.1 are private. Hence, we always know for each thread which block to reduce next. We discuss each statement in turn.

With respect to assignments, we distinguish between assignments to private and shared variables. For a private variable v, the assignment is replaced by a vector assignment to the variables v_t, where ϕ_t is applied to e as appropriate. For a shared variable v, it is not obvious which value needs to be assigned to v, as there might be multiple threads t with $v_{\text{active},t} = B$; we non-deterministically pick the value from one of the threads with $v_{\text{active},t} = B$, employing a ψ-assignment.

In the case of a **havoc** followed by an assignment, there is again a case distinction between private and shared variables. For a private variable, the **havoc** and assignment are simply replaced by corresponding vector statements. For a shared variable, a vector havoc is used to produce an arbitrary value for each thread, and then the value associated with one of the threads t with $v_{\text{active},t} = B$ is non-deterministically assigned employing ψ.

In the case of **assert**, we test whether $(v_{\text{active},t} = B) \Rightarrow \phi_t(e)$ holds for each thread $1 \leq t \leq TS$. The **skip** statement remains a no-op.

Lock-step execution of a **barrier** statement with condition $v_{\text{active}} = B$ translates to an assertion checking that if $v_{\text{active},t} = B$ holds for *some* thread t then it must hold for *all* threads. We call these assertions *barrier assertions*. We shall sketch in Sect. 5 that checking for barrier divergence in this manner is equivalent to checking for barrier divergence in the interleaving semantics of Sect. 3. However, contrary to the interleaving case, there is no need to consider barrier variables in the lock-step case.

The last three rows of Table 3a consider statements that do not originate from Table 1 but that do occur in blocks: Initially, each $v_{\text{active},t}$ is assigned to $Start$; assignments to v_{active} are vectorised, where $:\in$ is extended in the obvious way to non-deterministically assign values from multiple sets to multiple variables; **assume** is dealt with as **assert**.

Blocks. The lock-step construction for blocks is presented in Table 3b, where $\phi(ss)$ denotes the lock-step form of a sequence of statements.

If a block *is not* sorted last among the blocks of a loop (see the top row of Table 3b), we simply apply the lock-step construction to the statements in the block. If a block *is* sorted last among blocks in a loops L (see the bottom row of Table 3b) then the

Table 3. Lock-step construction

(a) Statements

Predicated form	Lock-step form	
$v := (v_{\text{active}} = B) \; ? \; e : v;$	v private	$\langle v_t \rangle_{t=1}^{TS} := \langle (v_{\text{active},t} = B) \; ? \; \phi_t(e) : v_t \rangle_{t=1}^{TS};$
	v shared	$v := \psi(\langle v_{\text{active},t} = B, \phi_t(e) \rangle_{t=1}^{TS});$
havoc $v_{\text{havoc}};$ $v := (v_{\text{active}} = B) \; ? \; v_{\text{havoc}} : v;$	v private	**havoc** $\langle v_{\text{havoc},t} \rangle_{t=1}^{TS};$ $\langle v_t \rangle_{t=1}^{TS} := \langle (v_{\text{active},t} = B) \; ? \; v_{\text{havoc},t} : v_t \rangle_{t=1}^{TS};$
	v shared	**havoc** $\langle v_{\text{havoc},t} \rangle_{t=1}^{TS};$ $v := \psi(\langle v_{\text{active},t} = B, v_{\text{havoc},t} \rangle_{t=1}^{TS});$
assert $(v_{\text{active}} = B) \Rightarrow e;$	**assert** $\bigwedge_{t=1}^{TS}((v_{\text{active},t} = B) \Rightarrow \phi_t(e))$	
skip;	**skip**;	
barrier $(v_{\text{active}} = B);$	**assert** $\left(\bigvee_{t=1}^{TS}(v_{\text{active},t} = B)\right) \Rightarrow \left(\bigwedge_{t=1}^{TS}(v_{\text{active},t} = B)\right);$	
$v_{\text{active}} := Start;$	$\langle v_{\text{active},t} \rangle_{t=1}^{TS} := \langle Start \rangle_{t=1}^{TS};$	
$v_{\text{next}} :\in \{B_1, \dots, B_n\};$	$\langle v_{\text{next},t} \rangle_{t=1}^{TS} :\in \langle \{B_1, \dots, B_n\} \rangle_{t=1}^{TS};$	
assume $(v_{\text{active}} = B) \Rightarrow e;$	**assume** $\bigwedge_{t=1}^{TS}((v_{\text{active},t} = B) \Rightarrow \phi_t(e))$	

(b) Blocks

Predicated form		Lock-step form	
B	: ss $\quad$ **goto** $next(B);$	B	: $\phi(ss)$ $\quad$ **goto** $next(B);$
B	: ss $\quad$ **goto** $B_{\text{back}}, B_{\text{exit}};$	B	: $\phi(ss)$ $\quad$ **goto** $B_{\text{back}}, B_{\text{exit}};$
B_{back}	: **assume** $v_{\text{active}} = B_{\text{head}};$ $\quad$ **goto** $B_{\text{head}};$	B_{back}	: **assume** $\bigvee_{t=1}^{TS}(v_{\text{active},t} = B_{\text{head}});$ $\quad$ **goto** $B_{\text{head}};$
B_{exit}	: **assume** $v_{\text{active}} \neq B_{\text{head}};$ $\quad$ **goto** $next(B);$	B_{exit}	: **assume** $\bigwedge_{t=1}^{TS}(v_{\text{active},t} \neq B_{\text{head}});$ $\quad$ **goto** $next(B);$

successors of the block in the predicated program are B_{back}, which leads to the loop header, and B_{exit}, which leads to a node outside the loop. Our goal is to enforce the rule that *no* thread should leave the loop until *all* threads are ready to leave the loop, as discussed informally in Sect. 2 and illustrated for structured programs by the guard of the **while** loop in Fig. 2. To achieve this, the bottom row of Table 3b employs an **assume** in B_{back} requiring that $v_{\text{active}} = B_{\text{head}}$ for *some* thread, and an **assume** in B_{exit} requiring $v_{\text{active}} \neq B_{\text{head}}$ for *all* threads. A concrete example is given in Fig. 7.

Lock-Step Semantics and Data Races. Having completed our definition of the lock-step construction $\phi(P)$ for a kernel P, we now say that the lock-step semantics for P is the *interleaving* semantics for $\phi(P)$, with respect to a *single* thread (i.e., with $TS = 1$). Barrier divergence is captured via the introduction of *barrier assertions*. This leaves to define data races in lock-step execution traces.

Say that thread t is *enabled* during a reduction step if the statement being reduced occurs in block B and $v_{\text{active},t} = B$ holds at the point of reduction and let v be a variable. A thread t *reads* v during a reduction step if t is enabled during the step and if the step involves evaluating an expression containing v. A thread t *writes* v during a

B_2 : **assert** $\left(\bigvee_{t=1}^{TS}(v_{\text{active},t} = B_2)\right) \Rightarrow \left(\bigwedge_{t=1}^{TS}(v_{\text{active},t} = B_2)\right)$;
$\langle v_{\text{next},t}\rangle_{t=1}^{TS} :\in \langle\{W_{last}\}\rangle_{t=1}^{TS}$;
$\langle v_{\text{active},t}\rangle_{t=1}^{TS} := \langle(v_{\text{active},t} = B_2)\ ?\ v_{\text{next},t} : v_{\text{active},t}\rangle_{t=1}^{TS}$;
goto W_{last} ;

W_{last} : $\langle offset_t\rangle_{t=1}^{TS} := \langle(v_{\text{active},t} = W_{last})\ ?\ (2 \cdot offset_t) : offset_t\rangle_{t=1}^{TS}$;
$\langle v_{\text{next},t}\rangle_{t=1}^{TS} :\in \langle\{W, W_{end}\}\rangle_{t=1}^{TS}$;
assume $\bigwedge_{t=1}^{TS}((v_{\text{active},t} = W_{last}) \Rightarrow (((v_{\text{next},t} = W) \Rightarrow (offset_t < TS))$
$\wedge ((v_{\text{next},t} = W_{end}) \Rightarrow (offset_t \geq TS))))$;
$\langle v_{\text{active},t}\rangle_{t=1}^{TS} := \langle(v_{\text{active},t} = W_{last})\ ?\ v_{\text{next},t} : v_{\text{active},t}\rangle_{t=1}^{TS}$;
goto $W_{\text{back}}, W_{\text{exit}}$;

W_{back} : **assume** $\bigvee_{t=1}^{TS}(v_{\text{active},t} = W)$;
goto W ;

W_{exit} : **assume** $\bigwedge_{t=1}^{TS}(v_{\text{active},t} \neq W)$;
goto W_{end} ;

W_{end} : **goto** End ;

Fig. 7. Part of the lock-step program for the kernel of Fig. 3

reduction step if t is enabled during the step and if the statement being reduced is an assignment to v. In the case of a write, if multiple threads are enabled then v will be updated non-deterministically using one of the values supplied by the enabled threads. Nevertheless, we regard *all* enabled threads as having written to v.

A data race in a lock-step program is defined as follows:

Definition 4.1. *Let $\phi(P)$ be the lock-step form of a kernel P. Then, $\phi(P)$ has a data race if there is a maximal reduction ρ of $\phi(P)$, distinct threads t and t', and a shared variable v such that: ρ does not end in* infeasible; *t writes v during ρ and t' either reads or writes v during ρ; the accesses are not separated by a* barrier assertion *(i.e., no barrier is reduced between the accesses).*

Terminating and Race Free Kernels. We say that a kernel P is *terminating* with respect to the lock-step semantics if all maximal reductions of $\phi(P)$ are finite and do not end with status *error*. We say that P is *race free* with respect to the lock-step semantics if $\phi(P)$ has no data races according to Definition 4.1.

5   Equivalence between Interleaving and Lock-Step Semantics

We can now prove our main result, an equivalence between the interleaving semantics of Sect. 3 and lock-step semantics of Sect. 4. Our result applies to *well-formed* kernels:

Definition 5.1. *A kernel P is* well-formed *if for every block B in P if B ends with* **goto** $B_1, \ldots, B_n$, *then $\bigvee_{i=1}^{n} guard(B_i)$ is a tautology.*

Well-formedness implies that whenever a thread reduces a **goto**, the guard of *at least one* block that can be reached via the **goto** is guaranteed to hold. Recall from Sect. 3.1 that guards of assume statements refer only to private variables, thus it is not possible for another thread to invalidate the guard of an **assume** between reduction of a **goto** and evaluation of the guard. Well-formedness is guaranteed to hold if the CFG for P is obtained from a kernel written in a C-like language such as OpenCL or CUDA.

Theorem 5.2. *Let* P *be a well-formed kernel and let* $\phi(P)$ *be the lock-step version of* P. *Then,* P *is race free and terminating with respect to the interleaving semantics iff* P *is race free and terminating with respect to the lock-step semantics. Moreover, if race-freedom holds then for every terminating reduction of* P *there exists a terminating reduction of* $\phi(P)$, *and vice versa, such that every shared variable* v *has the same value at the end of both reductions.*

To see why well-formedness is required, consider the following kernel, where each thread t has a private variable tid whose value is t and where v is shared and v' is private:

$Start$:	**assume** $true$	B_1 :	**assume** $tid = 1 \wedge v' = 5$;	B_2 :	**assume** $tid \neq 1$;
	$v := 4$; $v' := v$;		**goto** End;		$v := 5$;
	goto B_1, B_2;				**goto** End;

The interleaving semantics allows for reduction of **assume** $tid = 1 \wedge v' = 5$ after all assignments in all threads have taken place. Hence, if the assignment of 4 to v by thread 1 is not last among the assignments to v, then $v' = 5$ evaluates to $true$, and eventually termination occurs with a data race. In the case of lock-step execution and assuming the sort order $Start \leq B_1 \leq B_2$, we have that **assume** $tid = 1 \wedge v' = 5$ is always reduced immediately after $v := 4$; $v' := v$;. Hence, reduction always terminates with *infeasible* and no data race occurs.

That termination is required follows by adapting the counterexamples from [12,11] showing that CUDA hardware does not necessarily schedule threads from a non-terminating kernel in a way that that is fair from an interleaving point-of-view.

The proof of the theorem proceeds by showing that P and its predicated form $\pi(P)$ are stutter equivalent, and then establishing a relationship between $\pi(P)$ and $\phi(P)$.

Equivalence of P *and* $\pi(P)$. To show that P and $\pi(P)$ are stutter equivalent [14], we define a denotational semantics of kernels in terms of *execution traces* [5], i.e., sequences of tuples $(\sigma, \vec{\sigma}) = (\sigma, \sigma_1, \ldots, \sigma_{TS})$ with σ the shared store and σ_t the private store of thread t.

Definition 5.3. *Let* ρ *be a maximal reduction. The* denotation *or* execution trace $\mathcal{D}(\rho)$ *of* ρ *is the sequence of* $\to$-*labels of* ρ *together with the termination status of* ρ *if* ρ *terminates. Let* $(b_1, \ldots, b_{TS})$ *be a tuple of block labels. The denotation* $\mathcal{D}(b_1, \ldots, b_{TS})$ *of* $(b_1, \ldots, b_{TS})$ *is the set of denotations of all maximal reductions of* $(b_1, \ldots, b_{TS})$ *for all initial stores* $\sigma, \sigma_1, \ldots, \sigma_t$ *not* terminating as infeasible. *Let* P *be a kernel. The denotation* $\mathcal{D}(P)$ *of* P *is* $\mathcal{D}(Start, \ldots, Start)$.

Observe that *infeasible* traces are *not* included in the denotations of $(b_1, \ldots, b_{TS})$ and P; these traces do not constitute actual program behaviour.

Stutter equivalence is defined on subsets of variables, where a *restriction* of a store σ to a set of variables V is denoted by $\sigma\lceil_V$ and, where given a tuple $(\sigma, \vec{\sigma}) = (\sigma, \sigma_1, \ldots, \sigma_{TS})$, the restriction $(\sigma, \vec{\sigma})\lceil_V$ is $(\sigma, \vec{\sigma})\lceil_V = (\sigma\lceil_V, \sigma_1\lceil_V, \ldots, \sigma_{TS}\lceil_V)$.

Definition 5.4. *Let* V *be a set of variables. Define the map* δ_V *over execution traces as the map that replaces every maximal subsequence* $(\sigma_1, \vec{\sigma}_1)(\sigma_2, \vec{\sigma}_2) \cdots (\sigma_n, \vec{\sigma}_n) \cdots$ *where* $(\sigma_1, \vec{\sigma}_1)\lceil_V = (\sigma_2, \vec{\sigma}_2)\lceil_V = \ldots = (\sigma_n, \vec{\sigma}_n)\lceil_V = \ldots$ *by* $(\sigma_1, \vec{\sigma}_1)$.

Let Σ and T be execution traces. The traces are stutter *equivalent with respect to V, denoted $\Sigma \sim_{st}^V T$, iff:*

- *Σ and T are both finite with equal termination statuses and $\delta_V(\Sigma) = \delta_V(T)$;*
- *Σ and T are both infinite and $\delta_V(\Sigma) = \delta_V(T)$.*

Let P and Q be kernels. The kernels are stutter *equivalent with respect to V, denoted $P \sim_{st}^V Q$, iff for every $\Sigma \in \mathcal{D}(P)$ there is a $T \in \mathcal{D}(Q)$ with $\Sigma \sim_{st}^V T$, and vice versa.*

Theorem 5.5. *If P is a kernel with variables V, then $\pi(P) \sim_{st}^V P$, where $\pi(P)$ is the predicated form of P. A data race occurs in P iff a data race occurs in $\pi(P)$ where, during reduction of neither of the two statements causing the data race, $v_{active} \neq B$ with B is the block containing the statement.*

The above result follows immediately by a case distinction on the statements that may occur in kernels once we establish the following lemma, which is a direct consequence of our construction and the first requirement on the sort order of blocks.

Lemma 5.6. *Let P be a kernel with variables V. For any thread t and each block B of P, if (σ, σ_t) is a store of t and $(\hat{\sigma}, \hat{\sigma}_t)$ is a store of in t in $\pi(P)$ such that $\hat{\sigma}\!\restriction_V = \sigma$ and $\hat{\sigma}(v_{active}) = B$, then*

1. *if the reduction of B is immediately followed by the reduction of a block C, then there exists a reduction of $\pi(B)$ such that v_{active} is equal to C at the end of $\pi(B)$ and eventually $\pi(C)$ is reduced with v_{active} equal to C;*
2. *if the reduction of $\pi(B)$ ends with v_{active} equal to C, then there exists a reduction of B that is immediately followed by the reduction of a block C.*

Soundness and Completeness. Theorem 5.2 is now proved as follows.

Proof (Sketch). For termination and race-freedom of $\phi(P)$, it suffices by Theorem 5.5 to consider $\pi(P)$ — the predicated form of P. Reason by contradiction and construct for a reduction of $\phi(P)$ which is either infinite or has data race, a reduction of $\pi(P)$ that also is either infinite or has a data race: Replace each statement and **goto** from the right-hand columns of Table 3 by a copy of the statement or **goto** in the left-hand column and reduce, where we introduce a copy for each thread. That a reduction of a barrier assertion can be replaced by BARRIER$_S$ follows as no statements from outside loops can be reduced while we are inside a loop (cf. the second requirement on sort order of blocks) and by the guards of blocks having been moved during predication to the end of the block preceding it in execution. The remainder of the theorem follows by permuting steps of different threads so the reverse transformation from above can be applied.   □

6   Implementation and Experiments

Implementation in GPUVerify. We have implemented the predication technique described here in GPUVerify [7], a verification tool for OpenCL and CUDA kernels built on top of the Boogie verification engine [6] and Z3 SMT solver [19]. GPUVerify previously employed a predication technique for structured programs. Predication for CFGs has allowed us to build a new front-end for GPUVerify which takes LLVM intermediate representation (IR) as input; IR directly corresponds to a CFG. This allows us to compile OpenCL and CUDA kernels using the Clang/LLVM framework and perform analysis on the resulting IR. Hence, tricky syntactic features of C-like languages are taken care of by Clang/LLVM. Analysing kernels after compilation and optimisation also increases the probity of verification, opening up the opportunity to discover compiler-related bugs.

Experimental Evaluation. To assess the performance overhead in terms of verification time for our novel predication scheme and associated tool chain we compared our new implementation (GPUVerify II) with the original structured one (GPUVerify I).

We compared the tool versions using 163 OpenCL and CUDA kernels drawn from the AMD Accelerated Parallel Processing SDK v2.6 [4] (71 OpenCL kernels), the NVIDIA GPU Computing SDK v2.0 [20] (20 CUDA kernels), Microsoft C++ AMP Sample Projects [18] (20 kernels translated from C++ AMP to CUDA) and Rightware's Basemark CL v1.1 suite [22] (52 OpenCL kernels, provided to us under an academic license). These kernels were used for analysis of GPUVerify I in [7], where several of the kernels had to be manually modified before they could be subjected to analysis: 4 kernels exhibited unstructured control flow due to **switch** statements, and one featured a **do-while** loop which was beyond the scope of the predication scheme of [7]. Furthermore, unstructured control flow arising from short-circuit evaluation of logical operators had been overlooked in GPUVerify I, which affected 30 kernels. In GPUVerify II all kernels are handled uniformly as a consequence of our novel predication scheme in combination with the use of Clang/LLVM, which encodes short-circuit evaluation using unstructured control flow.

All experiments were performed on a PC with a 3.6 GHz Intel i5 CPU, 8 GB RAM running Windows 7 (64-bit), using Z3 v4.1. All times reported are averages over 3 runs. Both tool versions and all our benchmarks, except the commercial Basemark CL kernels, are available online to make our results reproducible.[3]

The majority of our benchmark kernels could be automatically verified by both GPUVerify I and GPUVerify II; 22 kernels were beyond the scope of both tools and resulted in a failed proof attempt. Key to the usability of GPUVerify is its *response time*, the time the tool takes to either report successful verification vs. a failed proof attempt. Comparing GPUVerify I and GPUVerify II we found that across the entire benchmark set the analysis time taken by GPUVerify II was 2.25 times that of GPUVerify I, with GPUVerify II taking on average 2.53 times longer than GPUVerify per kernel. However, the median slow down associated with GPUVerify II was 0.77, i.e., a speed up of 1.3.

The average, median and longest analysis time across all kernels were 4.3, 1.7 and 157 seconds, resp., for GPUVerify I, and 9.6, 1.4 and 300 seconds, resp., for GPUVerify II. For 124 of the 163 kernels (76%), GPUVerify II was marginally (though not significantly) faster than GPUVerify I. For a further 21 kernels (13%) GPUVerify II was up to 50% slower than GPUVerify I. The remaining 18 kernels (11%) caused the slow

---

[3] http://multicore.doc.ic.ac.uk/tools/GPUVerify

down on average. In each case the difference lay in constraint solving times; the SMT queries generated by our CFG-based tool chain can be somewhat more complex than in the structured case. The most dramatic example is a kernel which was verified by GPU-Verify I and GPUVerify II in 3 and 202 seconds, resp., a slow-down for GPUVerify II of 70 times. This kernel exhibits a large number of shared memory accesses. In the LLVM IR processed by GPUVerify II these accesses are expressed as many separate, contiguous loads and stores, requiring reasoning about race-freedom between many pairs of operations. The structured approach of GPUVerify I captures these accesses at the abstract syntax tree level, allowing a load/store from/to a contiguous region to be expressed as a single access, significantly simplifying reasoning. This illustrates that there are benefits to working at the higher level of abstract syntax trees, and suggests that optimisations in GPUVerify II to automatically identify and merge contiguous memory accesses might be beneficial.

7 Related Work and Conclusion

Related Work. Interleaving semantics for GPU kernels has been defined by [15,17,12]. These are similar to our semantics except that [15,12] do not give a semantics for barriers. Contrary to our lock-step approach, [15,17] battle the state space explosion due to arbitrary interleavings of threads by considering one particular schedule.

In [11,12], a semantics of CUDA kernels is defined that tries to model NVIDIA hardware as faithfully as possible. The focus is not on predicated execution (although it does figure briefly in [11]), but on so-called *immediate post-dominator re-convergence* [10], a method to continue lock-step execution of threads as soon as possible after branch divergence has occurred between threads.

In addition to the above and similar to us, [12] shows for terminating kernels that CUDA execution of kernels can be faithfully simulated by certain interleaving thread schedules. The reverse is not shown; our analysis is that such a result is difficult to establish due to data races that occur in the examples of [12].

Conclusion. Our lock-step semantics for GPU kernels expressed as arbitrary reducible CFGs enables automated analysis of a wider class of GPU kernels than previous techniques for structured programs, and allows for the analysis of compiled kernel code, after optimisations have been applied. Our soundness and completeness result establishes an equivalence between our lock-step semantics and a traditional semantics based on interleaving, and our implementation in GPUVerify and associated experimental evaluation demonstrate that our approach is practical.

Because our kernel programming language supports non-deterministic choice and havocking of variables it can express an over-approximation of a concrete kernel. In future work we plan to exploit this, investigating the combination of source-level abstraction techniques such as predicate abstraction with our verification method.

The well-formedness restriction of Definition 5.1 means that our equivalence result does not apply to kernels that exhibiting 'dead end' paths. This is relevant if such paths are introduced through under-approximation, e.g., unwinding a loop by a fixed number of iterations in the style of bounded model checking. We plan to investigate whether it is possible to relax these well-formedness conditions under certain circumstances.

References

1. Aho, A.V., Lam, M.S., Sethi, R., Ullman, J.D.: Compilers: Principles, Techniques, and Tools. Pearson Education, 2nd edn. (2007)
2. Allen, J., Kennedy, K., Porterfield, C., Warren, J.: Conversion of control dependence to data dependence. In: POPL 1983, pp. 177–189 (1983)
3. Alshawabkeh, M., Jang, B., Kaeli, D.: Accelerating the local outlier factor algorithm on a GPU for intrusion detection systems. In: GPGPU-3, pp. 104–110 (2010)
4. AMD: AMD Accelerated Parallel Processing (APP) SDK, http://developer.amd.com/sdks/amdappsdk/pages/default.aspx
5. Barnett, M., Leino, K.R.M.: Weakest-precondition of unstructured programs. In: PASTE 2005, pp. 82–87 (2005)
6. Barnett, M., Chang, B.-Y.E., DeLine, R., Jacobs, B., Leino, K.R.M.: Boogie: A Modular Reusable Verifier for Object-Oriented Programs. In: de Boer, F.S., Bonsangue, M.M., Graf, S., de Roever, W.-P. (eds.) FMCO 2005. LNCS, vol. 4111, pp. 364–387. Springer, Heidelberg (2006)
7. Betts, A., Chong, N., Donaldson, A.F., Qadeer, S., Thomson, P.: GPUVerify: a verifier for GPU kernels. In: OOPSLA 2012, pp. 113–132 (2012)
8. Collingbourne, P., Cadar, C., Kelly, P.H.J.: Symbolic Testing of OpenCL Code. In: Eder, K., Lourenço, J., Shehory, O. (eds.) HVC 2011. LNCS, vol. 7261, pp. 203–218. Springer, Heidelberg (2012)
9. DeMillo, R.A., Eisenstat, S.C., Lipton, R.J.: Space-time trade-offs in structured programming: An improved combinatorial embedding theorem. J. ACM 27(1), 123–127 (1980)
10. Fung, W.W., Sham, I., Yuan, G., Aamodt, T.M.: Dynamic warp formation and scheduling for efficient GPU control flow. In: MICRO 2007, pp. 407–418 (2007)
11. Habermaier, A.: The model of computation of CUDA and its formal semantics. Tech. Rep. 2011-14, University of Augsburg (2011)
12. Habermaier, A., Knapp, A.: On the Correctness of the SIMT Execution Model of GPUs. In: Seidl, H. (ed.) ESOP 2012. LNCS, vol. 7211, pp. 316–335. Springer, Heidelberg (2012)
13. Khronos Group: The OpenCL specification, version 1.2 (2011)
14. Lamport, L.: What good is temporal logic? In: Information Processing 1983, pp. 657–668 (1983)
15. Leung, A., Gupta, M., Agarwal, Y., Gupta, R., Jhala, R., Lerner, S.: Verifying GPU kernels by test amplification. In: PLDI 2012, pp. 383–394 (2012)
16. Li, G., Gopalakrishnan, G.: Scalable SMT-based verification of GPU kernel functions. In: FSE 2010, pp. 187–196 (2010)
17. Li, G., Li, P., Sawaya, G., Gopalakrishnan, G., Ghosh, I., Rajan, S.P.: GKLEE: concolic verification and test generation for GPUs. In: PPoPP 2012, pp. 215–224 (2012)
18. Microsoft Corporation: C++ AMP sample projects for download, http://blogs.msdn.com/b/nativeconcurrency/archive/2012/01/30/c-amp-sample-projects-for-download.aspx
19. de Moura, L., Bjørner, N.: Z3: An Efficient SMT Solver. In: Ramakrishnan, C.R., Rehof, J. (eds.) TACAS 2008. LNCS, vol. 4963, pp. 337–340. Springer, Heidelberg (2008)
20. NVIDIA: CUDA Toolkit Release Archive, http://developer.nvidia.com/cuda/cuda-toolkit-archive
21. NVIDIA: NVIDIA CUDA C Programming Guide, Version 4.2 (2012)
22. Rightware Oy: Basemark CL, http://www.rightware.com/en/Benchmarking+Software/Basemark%99+CL
23. Zhu, F., Chen, P., Yang, D., Zhang, W., Chen, H., Zang, B.: A GPU-based high-throughput image retrieval algorithm. In: GPGPU-5, pp. 30–37 (2012)

Verifying Concurrent Programs against Sequential Specifications[*]

Ahmed Bouajjani, Michael Emmi, Constantin Enea, and Jad Hamza

LIAFA, Université Paris Diderot
{abou,mje,cenea,jhamza}@liafa.univ-paris-diderot.fr

Abstract. We investigate the algorithmic feasibility of checking whether concurrent implementations of shared-memory objects adhere to their given sequential specifications; sequential consistency, linearizability, and conflict serializability are the canonical variations of this problem. While verifying sequential consistency of systems with unbounded concurrency is known to be undecidable, we demonstrate that conflict serializability, and linearizability with fixed linearization points are EXPSPACE-complete, while the general linearizability problem is undecidable.

Our (un)decidability proofs, besides bestowing novel theoretical results, also reveal novel program explorations strategies. For instance, we show that every violation to conflict serializability is captured by a conflict cycle whose length is bounded independently from the number of concurrent operations. This suggests an incomplete detection algorithm which only remembers a small subset of conflict edges, which can be made complete by increasing the number of remembered edges to the cycle-length bound. Similarly, our undecidability proof for linearizability suggests an incomplete detection algorithm which limits the number of "barriers" bisecting non-overlapping operations. Our decidability proof of bounded-barrier linearizability is interesting on its own, as it reduces the consideration of all possible operation serializations to numerical constraint solving. The literature seems to confirm that most violations are detectable by considering very few conflict edges or barriers.

1 Introduction

A key class of correctness criteria for concurrent systems is adherence to better established sequential specifications. Such criteria demand that each concurrent execution of operations corresponds, at the level of abstraction described by the operations' specification, to some serial sequence of the same operations permitted by the specification. For instance, given a conventional specification of a mathematical set, a concurrent execution in which the operations $add(a), remove(b), is\_empty(true), remove(a), add(b)$ overlap could be permitted, though one with only the operations $add(a)$ and $remove(b)$ could not.

Variations on this theme of criteria are the accepted correctness conditions for various types of concurrent systems. In the context of processor memory architectures, *sequential consistency (SC)* [24] allows only executions of memory access

---

[*] The proofs to many of our technical results appear in an extended report [7].

M. Felleisen and P. Gardner (Eds.): ESOP 2013, LNCS 7792, pp. 290–309, 2013.
© Springer-Verlag Berlin Heidelberg 2013

operations for which the same operations taken serially adhere to the specification of individual memory registers—i.e., where each load reads the last-written value. Additionally, any two operations of the serialization carried out by the same process must occur in the same order as in the original concurrent execution. In the context of concurrent data structure implementations, *linearizability* [21] demands additionally that two operations which do not overlap in the original concurrent execution occur in the same order in any valid serialization.

The same kinds of criteria are also used in settings where operation specifications are less abstract. For transactional systems (e.g., databases, and runtime systems which provide atomic sections in concurrent programs), *(strict) serializability* [28] allows only executions for which the same transactions taken serially adhere to the specification of an entire (random-access) memory observable by the transactions; additionally, transactions executed by the same process (or which did not overlap, in the *strict* case) are obliged to occur in the same order in any valid serialization. Practical considerations, such as the complexity of determining whether a given trace is serializable, have generated even more restrictive notions of serializability. *Conflict serializability* (Papadimitriou [28] calls this property "DSR") demands additionally—viewing a serialization as a reordering of actions which untangles the operations of a concurrent execution— that no two *conflicting* actions are reordered in the serialization. The typical definition of "conflict" relates accesses to the same memory location or region, with at least one being a store.

In this work we investigate the fundamental questions about the algorithmic feasibility of verifying concurrent programs with respect to sequential specifications. While our results consider programs with unbounded concurrency arising from, e.g., dynamic thread-creation, they, as do most other (un)decidability results concerning concurrent program analysis, apply to programs where the domain of data values is either finite, or reduced by a finitary abstraction.

While the problem of determining whether a given concurrent system is sequentially consistent with respect to a given sequential specification is known to be undecidable, even when the number of concurrent processes is bounded [1], the decidability of the analogous questions for (conflict) serializability and linearizability, for unbounded systems of concurrent processes, remains open. (Alur et al. [1] have proved both of these problems decidable[1], resp., in PSPACE and EXPSPACE, when the number of concurrent processes is bounded.) In this work we establish these decidability and complexity results for unbounded systems, and as byproduct, uncover program exploration strategies which prioritize the discovery of naturally-occurring property violations.

Our first result, of Section 3, is that conflict serializability is decidable, and complete for exponential space. Since existing techniques rely on cycle detection in an exhaustive exploration of possible conflict relations (graphs) among concurrent operations [17], allowing for an unbounded number of concurrent operations renders these techniques inapplicable to verification, since the unbounded set of possible conflict graphs cannot generally be enumerated in finite time. Contrarily, here we

---

[1] The correct decidability proof for serializability is due to Farzan and Madhusudan [17].

demonstrate that every cyclic conflict graph contains a cycle which is bounded independently of the number of concurrent operations; this cycle length is instead bounded as a linear function in the number of memory locations. This suggests that an incomplete cycle detection algorithm which only remembers a small subset of conflict edges can be made complete by increasing the number of remembered edges to the given cycle-length bound. Even so, we expect that most violations to conflict serializability can be efficiently detected by remembering very few conflict edges: those we have seen reported in the literature are expressed with length 2 cycles [13, 19], and for systems satisfying certain supposedly-common symmetry conditions, any violation *must* occur with only two threads [19].

Our second result, of Section 4, is that the *static linearizability problem*, in which the so-called "linearization points" of operations which modify the shared-object state are fixed to particular implementation actions, is also decidable, and complete for exponential space. Informally, a *linearization point* of an operation in an execution is a point in time where the operation is conceptually effectuated; given the linearization points of each operation, the only valid serialization is the one which takes operations in order of their linearization points. Although static linearizability is a stronger criterion than linearizability, it is based on a fairly-well established proof technique [21] which is sufficiently weak to prove linearizability of many common concurrent data-structure algorithms [31].

Turning to the general problem, in Section 5, we show that verifying linearizability for unbounded concurrent systems is undecidable. Our proof is a reduction from a reachability problem on counter machines, and relies on imposing an unbounded number of "barriers" which bisect non-overlapping operations in order to encode an unbounded number of zero-tests of the machines' counters. Informally, a barrier is a temporal separation between two non-overlapping operations, across which valid serializations are forbidden from commuting those operations.

Besides disarming our proof of undecidability, bounding the amount of barriers reveals an incomplete algorithm for detecting linearizability violations, by exploring only those expressed with few barriers. Similarly to the small-cycle case in conflict serializability, we expect that most violations to linearizability are detectable with very few barriers; indeed the naturally-occurring bugs we are aware of, including the infamous "ABA" bug [26], induce violations with zero or one barrier. Our decidability proof of bounded-barrier linearizability in Section 6 is interesting on its own, since it effectively reduces the problem of considering all possible serializations of an unbounded number of operations to a numerical constraint solving problem. Using a simple prototype implementation leveraging SMT-based program exploration, we use this reduction to quickly discover bugs known in or injected into textbook concurrent algorithms.

To summarize, the contributions of this work are the first known (un)decidability results for (§3) conflict serializability, (§4) static linearizability, (§5) linearizability, and (§6) bounded-barrier linearizability, for systems with unbounded concurrency. Furthermore, besides substantiating these theoretical results our proofs reveal novel prioritized exploration strategies, based on cycle- and barrier-bounding. Since most known linearizable systems are also static-linearizable, combining static-linearizability with bounded-barrier exploration ought to provide a promising approach for proving either correctness or violation for many practically-occurring systems.

2 Preliminaries

In this work we consider a program model in which an unbounded number of *operations* concurrently access finite-domain shared data. Operations correspond to invocations of a finite *library* of *methods*. Here, methods correspond to the implementations of application programming interface (API) entries of concurrent or distributed data structures, and less conventionally, to the atomic code sections of concurrent programs, or to the SQL implementations of database transactions. A library is then simply the collection of API implementations, or transactional code. Usually concurrent data structure libraries and transactional runtime systems are expected to ensure that executed operations are logically equivalent to some understood serial behavior, regardless of how *clients* concurrently invoke their methods or transactions; the implication is that such systems should function correctly for a *most-general client* which concurrently invokes an unbounded number of methods with arbitrary timing. In what follows we formalize these notions as a basis for formulating our results.

2.1 Unbounded Concurrent Systems

A *method* is a finite automaton $M = \langle Q, \Sigma, I, F, \hookrightarrow \rangle$ with labeled transitions $\langle m_1, v_1 \rangle \xrightarrow{a} \langle m_2, v_2 \rangle$ between method-local states $m_1, m_2 \in Q$ paired with finite-domain shared-state valuations $v_1, v_2 \in V$. The initial and final states $I, F \subseteq Q$ represent the method-local states passed to, and returned from, M. A *library* L is a finite set of methods, and we refer to the components of a particular method (resp., library) by subscripting, e.g., the states and symbols Q_M and Σ_M (resp., Q_L and Σ_L). Though here we suppose an abstract notion of shared-state valuations, in later sections we interpret them as valuations to a finite set of finite-domain variables.

A *client* of a library L is a finite automaton $C = \langle Q, \Sigma, \ell_0, \hookrightarrow \rangle$ with initial state $\ell_0 \in Q$ and transitions $\hookrightarrow \subseteq Q \times \Sigma \times Q$ labeled by the alphabet $\Sigma = \{M(m_0, m_f) : M \in L, m_0, m_f \in Q_M\}$ of library method calls; we refer to a client C's components by subscripting, e.g., the states and symbols Q_C and Σ_C. The *most general client* $C^\star = \langle Q, \Sigma, \ell_0, \hookrightarrow \rangle$ of a library L nondeterministically calls L's methods in any order: $Q = \{\ell_0\}$ and $\hookrightarrow = Q \times \Sigma \times Q$.

We consider *unbounded concurrent systems* $L[C]$ in which the methods of a library L are invoked by an arbitrary number of concurrent *threads* executing a copy of a given client C; note that any shared memory program with an unbounded number of finite-state threads can be modeled using a suitably-defined client C. A *configuration* $c = \langle v, u \rangle$ of $L[C]$ is a shared memory valuation $v \in V$, along with a map u mapping each thread $t \in \mathbb{N}$ to a tuple $u(t) = \langle \ell, m_0, m \rangle$,

INTERNAL
$$u_1(t) = \langle \ell, m_0, m_1 \rangle$$
$$\langle m_1, v_1 \rangle \xrightarrow{a} \langle m_2, v_2 \rangle$$
$$u_2 = u_1 (t \mapsto \langle \ell, m_0, m_2 \rangle)$$
$$\langle v_1, u_1 \rangle \xrightarrow[L[C]]{\langle a, t \rangle} \langle v_2, u_2 \rangle$$

CALL
$$u_1(t) = \langle \ell_1, \bot, \bot \rangle$$
$$m_0 \in I_M \quad \ell_1 \xrightarrow{M(m_0, m_f)}_C \ell_2$$
$$u_2 = u_1 (t \mapsto \langle \ell_1, m_0, m_0 \rangle)$$
$$\langle v, u_1 \rangle \xrightarrow[L[C]]{\mathsf{call}(M, m_0, t)} \langle v, u_2 \rangle$$

RETURN
$$u_1(t) = \langle \ell_1, m_0, m_f \rangle$$
$$m_f \in F_M \quad \ell_1 \xrightarrow{M(m_0, m_f)}_C \ell_2$$
$$u_2 = u_1 (t \mapsto \langle \ell_2, \bot, \bot \rangle)$$
$$\langle v, u_1 \rangle \xrightarrow[L[C]]{\mathsf{ret}(M, m_f, t)} \langle v, u_2 \rangle$$

Fig. 1. The transition relation $\to_{L[C]}$ for the library-client composition $L[C]$

composed of a client-local state $\ell \in Q_C$, along with initial and current method states $m_0, m \in Q_L \cup \{\bot\}$; $m_0 = m = \bot$ when thread t is not executing a library method. In this way, configurations describe the states of arbitrarily-many threads executing library methods. The transition relation $\to_{L[C]}$ of $L[C]$ is listed in Figure 1 as a set of operational steps on configurations. A configuration $\langle v, u \rangle$ of $L[C]$ is called v_0-*initial* for a given $v_0 \in V$ when $v = v_0$ and $u(t) = \langle \ell_0, \bot, \bot \rangle$ for all $t \in \mathbb{N}$, where ℓ_0 is the initial state of client C. An *execution* of $L[C]$ is a sequence $\rho = c_0 c_1 \ldots$ of configurations such that $c_i \to_{L[C]} c_{i+1}$ for all $0 \le i < |\rho|$, and ρ is called v_0-*initial* when c_0 is.

We associate to each concurrent system $L[C]$ a *canonical vector addition systems with states (VASS)*,[2] denoted $\mathcal{A}_{L[C]}$, whose states are the set of shared-memory valuations, and whose vector components count the number of threads in each thread-local state; a transition of $\mathcal{A}_{L[C]}$ from $\langle v_1, \boldsymbol{n}_1 \rangle$ to $\langle v_2, \boldsymbol{n}_2 \rangle$ updates the shared-memory valuation from v_1 to v_2 and the local state of some thread t from $u_1(t)$ to $u_2(t)$ by decrementing the $u_1(t)$-component of $\boldsymbol{n}_1$, and incrementing the $u_2(t)$-component, to derive $\boldsymbol{n}_2$. Several of our proof arguments in the following sections invoke the canonical VASS simulation of a concurrent system, which we define fully in our extended report [7].

A *call action of thread* t is a symbol $\mathsf{call}(M, m, t)$, a *return action* is a symbol $\mathsf{ret}(M, m, t)$, and an *internal action* is a symbol $\langle a, t \rangle$. We write σ to denote a sequence of actions, and τ to denote a *trace*—i.e., a sequence of actions labeling some execution. An $M[m_0, m_f]$-*operation* θ (or more simply, M-*operation*, or just *operation*) of a sequence σ is a maximal subsequence of actions of some thread t beginning with a call action $\mathsf{call}(M, m_0, t)$, followed by a possibly-empty sequence of internal actions, and possibly ending with a return action $\mathsf{ret}(M, m_f, t)$; $m_f = *$ when θ does not end in a return action. When θ ends with a return action, we say θ is *completed*, and otherwise θ is *pending*; a sequence σ is *complete* when all of its operations are completed. Two operations θ_1 and θ_2 of σ *overlap* when the minimal subsequence of σ containing both θ_1 and θ_2 is neither $\theta_1 \cdot \theta_2$ nor $\theta_2 \cdot \theta_1$. Two non-overlapping operations θ_1 followed by θ_2 in σ are called *serial* when θ_1 is completed; note that all operations of the same thread are serial. A sequence σ is *(quasi) serial* when no two (completed) operations of σ overlap.

A *(strict) permutation* of an action sequence σ containing operations Θ is an action sequence π with operations Θ such that every two same-thread operations

---

[2] See our extended report [7] for a standard definition of VASS.

(resp., every two serial operations) of σ occur in the same serial order in π. Note that π itself is not necessarily a trace of a system from which σ may be a trace.

2.2   Conflict Serializability

The notion of "conflict serializability" is a restriction to the more liberal "serializability" [28]: besides requiring that each concurrent execution of operations corresponds to some serial sequence, a "conflict relation," relating the individual actions of each operation, must be preserved in deriving that serial sequence from a permutation of actions in the original concurrent execution. Both notions are widely accepted correctness criteria for transactional systems.

We fix a symmetric[3] relation $\prec$ on the internal library actions Σ_L called the *conflict relation*. Although here we assume an abstract notion of conflict, in practice, two actions conflict when both access the same memory location, and at least one affects the value stored in that location; e.g., two writes to the same shared variable would conflict. A permutation π of a trace τ is *conflict-preserving* when every pair $\langle a_1, t_1 \rangle$ and $\langle a_2, t_2 \rangle$ of actions of τ appear in the same order in π whenever $a_1 \prec a_2$. Intuitively, a conflict-preserving permutation w.r.t. the previously-mentioned notion of conflict is equally executable on a sequentially-consistent machine.

Definition 1 (Conflict Serializability [28]). *A trace τ is* conflict serializable *when there exists a conflict-preserving serial permutation of τ.*

This definition extends to executions, to systems $L[C]$ whose executions are all conflict serializable, and to libraries L when C is the most general client $C^\star$.

2.3   Linearizability

Contrary to (conflict) serializability, linearizability [21] is more often used in contexts, such as concurrent data structure libraries, in which an abstract specification of operations' serial behavior is given explicitly. For instance, linearizability with respect to a specification of a concurrent stack implementation would require the abstract push($\cdot$) and pop($\cdot$) operations carried out in a concurrent trace τ correspond to some serial sequence σ of push($\cdot$)s and pop($\cdot$)s, in which each pop(a) can be matched to a previous push(a); Figure 2 illustrates an automaton-based specification of a two-element unary stack. Note that linearizability does not require that a corresponding reordering of the trace τ can actually be executed by this stack implementation, nor that the implementation could have even executed these operations serially.

A *specification* S of a library L is a language over the *specification alphabet*

$$\Sigma_S \stackrel{\text{def}}{=} \{ M[m_0, m_f] : M \in L, m_0, m_f \in Q_M \}.$$

In this work we assume specifications are regular languages; in practice, specifications are prefix closed. We refer to the alphabet containing both symbols

---

[3] All definitions of conflict that we are aware of assume symmetric relations.

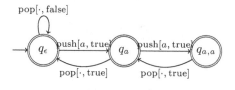

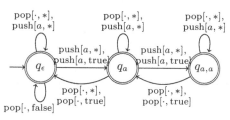

Fig. 2. The sequential specification of two-element stacks containing the (abstract) value a, given as the language of a finite automaton, whose operation alphabet indicates both the argument and return values.

Fig. 3. The pending closure of the stack specification from Figure 2

$M[m_0, m_f]$ and $M[m_0, *]$ for each $M[m_0, m_f]$ occurring in Σ_S as the *pending-closed* alphabet of S, denoted $\overline{\Sigma}_S$.

Informally, a library L is linearizable w.r.t. a specification S when the operations of any concurrent trace can be serialized to a sequence of operations belonging to S, which must preserve the order between non-overlapping operations. However, the presence of pending operations introduces a subtlety: a trace may be considered linearizable by supposing that certain pending operations have already been effectuated—e.g., a trace of a concurrent stack implementation in which push(a) is pending and pop(a) has successfully completed *is* linearizable—while simultaneously supposing that other pending operations are ignored—e.g., a trace in which push(a) is pending and pop(a) returned false is also linearizable. To account for the possible effects of pending operations, we define a *completion* of a (quasi) serial sequence $\sigma = \theta_1 \theta_2 \dots \theta_i$ of operations to be any sequence $f(\sigma) = f(1)f(2) \dots f(i)$ for some function f preserving completed operations (i.e., $f(j) = \theta_j$ when θ_j is completed), and either deleting (i.e., $f(j) = \varepsilon$) or completing (i.e., $f(j) = \theta_j \cdot \mathsf{ret}(M, m_f, t)$, for some $m_f \in Q_M$) each $M[m_0, *]$ operation of some thread t. Note that a completion of a (quasi) serial sequence σ is a complete serial sequence. Finally, the S-*image* of a serial sequence σ, denoted $\sigma \mid S$, maps each $M[m_0, m_f]$-operation θ to the symbol $M[m_0, m_f] \in \overline{\Sigma}_S$.

Definition 2 (Linearizability [21]). *A trace τ is S-linearizable when there exists a completion[4] π of a strict, quasi-serial permutation of τ such that $(\pi \mid S) \in S$.*

This notion extends naturally to executions of a system $L[C]$, to the system $L[C]$ itself, and to L when C is the most general client C^*.

Example 1. The trace pictured in Figure 4 can be strictly permuted into a quasi-serial sequence whose completion (shown) excludes the pending push operation, and whose S-image

$$\text{push}[a, \text{true}] \ \text{pop}[\cdot, \text{true}] \ \text{pop}[\cdot, \text{false}] \ \text{push}[a, \text{true}]$$

belongs to the stack specification from Figure 2.

---

[4] Some works give an alternative yet equivalent definition using the completion of a strict, quasi-serial permutation of the S-image, rather than the S-image of a completion.

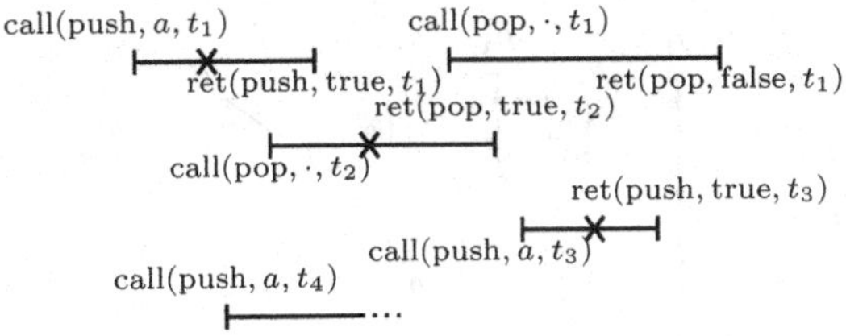

$\mathsf{call}(\mathrm{push}, a, t_1) \cdot \mathsf{ret}(\mathrm{push}, \mathrm{true}, t_1)$
$\cdot\, \mathsf{call}(\mathrm{pop}, \cdot, t_2) \cdot \mathsf{ret}(\mathrm{pop}, \mathrm{true}, t_2)$
$\cdot\, \mathsf{call}(\mathrm{pop}, \cdot, t_1) \cdot \mathsf{ret}(\mathrm{pop}, \mathrm{false}, t_1)$
$\cdot\, \mathsf{call}(\mathrm{push}, a, t_3) \cdot \mathsf{ret}(\mathrm{push}, \mathrm{true}, t_3)$

Fig. 4. The visualization of a trace τ with four threads executing four completed and one pending operation, along with a completion of a strict, quasi-serial permutation of τ (ignoring internal actions)

2.4 Linearizability with Pending-Closed Specifications

In fact, even though the subtlety arising from pending operations is a necessary complication to the definition of linearizability, for the specifications we consider in this work given by regular languages, this complication can be "compiled away" into the specification itself. This leads to an equivalent notion of linearizability without the need to find a completion of a given quasi-serial operation sequence.

The *pending closure* of a specification S, denoted $\overline{S}$ is the set of S-images of serial sequences which have completions whose S-images are in S:

$$\overline{S} \stackrel{\text{def}}{=} \{(\sigma \mid S) \in \overline{\Sigma}_S^* : \exists \sigma' \in \Sigma_S^*. \ (\sigma' \mid S) \in S \text{ and } \sigma' \text{ is a completion of } \sigma\}.$$

The language of the automaton of Figure 3 is the pending closure of the specification from Figure 2; looping transitions labeled from $\overline{\Sigma}_S \setminus \Sigma_S$ correspond to deleting a pending operation in the completion, while non-loop transitions labeled from $\overline{\Sigma}_S \setminus \Sigma_S$ correspond to completing a pending operation.

The following straightforward results allow us to suppose that the complication of closing serializations of each trace is compiled away, into the specification.

Lemma 1. *The pending closure $\overline{S}$ of a regular specification S is regular.*

Lemma 2. *A trace τ is S-linearizable if and only if there exists a strict, quasi-serial permutation π of τ such that $(\pi \mid S) \in \overline{S}$.*

3 Deciding Conflict Serializability

Existing procedures for deciding conflict serializability (e.g., of individual traces, or finite-state systems) essentially monitor executions using a "conflict graph" which tracks the conflict relation between concurrent operations; an execution remains conflict serializable as long as the conflict graph remains acyclic, while a cyclic graph indicates a violation to conflict serializability. While the conflict graph can be maintained in polynomial-space when the number of concurrent threads is bounded [17], this graph becomes unbounded as soon as the number of threads does. In this section we demonstrate that there exists an alternative structure witnessing non-conflict-serializability, whose size remains bounded

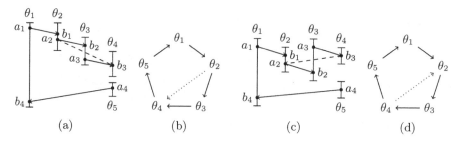

Fig. 5. Conflict-violation witness embeddings and their corresponding conflict graph cycles over five operations $\theta_1, \theta_2, \theta_3, \theta_4, \theta_5$. (a) The witness $\langle a_1, b_1 \rangle \langle a_2, b_2 \rangle \langle a_3, b_3 \rangle \langle a_4, b_4 \rangle$ is not minimal when $b_2 = b_3$, since $\langle a_1, b_1 \rangle \langle a_2, b_3 \rangle \langle a_4, b_4 \rangle$ is also a witness. (c) The witness $\langle a_1, b_1 \rangle \langle a_2, b_2 \rangle \langle a_3, b_3 \rangle \langle a_4, b_4 \rangle$ is not minimal when $b_2 = b_3$, since $\langle b_3, a_2 \rangle \langle a_2, b_2 \rangle \langle a_3, b_3 \rangle$ is also a witness. The conflict graphs of (a) and (c) are shown in (b) and (d).

independently of the number of concurrent threads, and which we use to prove EXPSPACE-completeness of conflict-serializability.

Definition 3 (Conflict-Graph [28]). *The* conflict graph *of a trace* τ *is the directed graph* $G_\tau = \langle \Theta, E \rangle$ *whose nodes* Θ *are the operations of* τ, *and which contains an edge from* θ_1 *to* θ_2 *when either:*

- θ_1 *and* θ_2 *are serial and* θ_1 *occurs before* θ_2 *in* τ, *or*
- *there exist a* conflicting pair *of actions* a_1 *and* a_2 *of* θ_1 *and* θ_2, *resp., such that* $a_1 \prec a_2$ *and* a_1 *occurs before* a_2 *in* τ.

Although a trace is serializable if and only if its conflict graph is acyclic [17], the size of the conflict graph grows with the number of concurrent operations.

An *embedding* of a sequence of conflicting action pairs $\langle a_1, b_1 \rangle \ldots \langle a_k, b_k \rangle$, into a trace τ, is a function f from $\{a_i, b_i : 1 \leq i \leq k\}$ to the actions of τ, such that:

- each $f(a_i)$ is executed by a different thread,
- $f(b_i)$ and $f(a_{\eta(i)})$ are actions of the same thread,
- $f(a_i)$ precedes $f(b_i)$ in τ, and
- $f(b_i)$ precedes $f(a_{\eta(i)})$ in τ when $f(b_i)$ and $f(a_{\eta(i)})$ are of different operations,

for each $1 \leq i \leq k$, where $\eta(i) = (i \bmod k) + 1$. A *conflict-violation witness* for a trace τ is a sequence w for which there exists an embedding into τ.

Example 2. Figure 5a pictures the embeddings of two conflict-violation witnesses containing 4 action pairs, corresponding to a cycle $\theta_1 \theta_2 \theta_3 \theta_4 \theta_5 \theta_1$ in the conflict graph of Figure 5c associated to the same trace.

The key to decidability of conflict-serializability is that any conflict cycle constructed from two occurrences of the same conflicting action $a \in \Sigma_L$ can be short-circuited into a smaller conflict cycle.

Lemma 3. *A trace* τ *of a library* L *(w.r.t. some client* C*) is not conflict serializable iff there exists a conflict-violation witness for* τ *of size at most* $|\Sigma_L| + 1$.

Proof. As a direct consequence of our definition, τ is not conflict serializable iff there exists a witness w embedded into τ by some f. (Each w embedded in τ defines a conflict graph cycle, and vice-versa). We show that if some b_i besides b_1 repeats in w, then there exists an even smaller witness w'.

For any $i, j \in \mathbb{N}$ such that $1 < i < j \leq |w|$ and $b_i = b_j$, we consider the two possibilities:

- Suppose $f(b_j)$ occurs after $f(a_i)$ in τ. Then there exists a smaller conflict-violation witness for τ:

$$w' = \langle a_1, b_1 \rangle \ldots \langle a_i, b_i \rangle \langle a_{j+1}, b_{j+1} \rangle \ldots \langle a_k, b_k \rangle.$$

  The illustration of Figure 5a exemplifies this case when $b_2 = b_3$.
- Suppose $f(b_j)$ occurs before $f(a_i)$ in τ. Then, leveraging the fact that $\prec$ is symmetric, there exists a smaller conflict-violation witness for τ:

$$w' = \langle b_j, a_i \rangle \langle a_i, b_i \rangle \ldots \langle a_j, b_j \rangle.$$

  The illustration of Figure 5b exemplifies this case when $b_2 = b_3$.

In either case w is not minimal unless $|w| \leq |\Sigma_L| + 1$. $\qquad\qquad\square$

As we have considered an abstraction notion of actions which constitute a finite set Σ_L, Lemma 3 would hold equally well for libraries accessing an unbounded shared memory, given an equivalence relation whose quotient set is finite—e.g., by partitioning memory into a finite number of regions—which is obtained in practice by abstraction.

As soon as conflict cycles are bounded, the set of all possible cycles is finitely enumerable. We use this fact to prove that conflict serializability is decidable in exponential space by reduction to state-reachability in VASS, using an extension to the canonical VASS $\mathcal{A}_{L[C]}$ of a given system $L[C]$ (see Section 2.1). We augment the states of $\mathcal{A}_{L[C]}$ to store a (bounded) conflict violation witness w, which is chosen nondeterministically, and incrementally validated as $\mathcal{A}_{L[C]}$ simulates the behavior of $L[C]$. This algorithm is asymptotically optimal, since state-reachability in VASS is also polynomial-time reducible to checking conflict serializability. Our full proof is listed in an extended report [7].

Theorem 1. *The conflict serializability problem for unbounded concurrent systems is EXPSPACE-complete.*

Although exploring all possible conflict cycles up to the bound $|\Sigma_L| + 1$ yields a complete procedure for deciding conflict serializability, we believe that in practice incomplete methods—e.g., based on constraint solving—using much smaller bounds could be more productive. The existing literature on verification of conflict serializability seems to confirm that violations are witnessed with very small cycles; for instance, two different violations on variations to the Transactional Locking II transactional memory algorithm reported by Guerraoui et al. [19] and Dragojević et al. [13] are witnessed by cycles formed by just two pairs of conflicting actions between two operations. Furthermore, Guerraoui et al. [19] show that any violation to conflict serializability in practically-occurring transactional memory systems must occur in an execution with only two threads.

4 Deciding Static Linearizability

Due to the intricacy of checking whether a system is linearizable according to
the general notion, of Definition 2, Herlihy and Wing [21] have introduced a
stricter criterion, where the so-called "linearization points"—i.e., the points at
which operations' effects become instantaneously visible—are specified manually.
Though it is sometimes possible to map linearization points to atomic actions
in method implementations, generally speaking, the placement of an operation's
linearization point can be quite complicated: it may depend on other concurrently executing operations, and it may even reside outside of the operation's
execution. Vafeiadis [31] observed that in practice such complicated linearization
points arise mainly for "read-only" operations, which do not modify a library's
abstract state; a typical example being the contains-operation of an optimistic
set [27], whose linearization point may reside in a concurrently executing add-
or remove-operation when the contains-operation returns, resp., true or false.

In this section we demonstrate that the *static linearizability* problem, in which
the linearization points of non-read-only operations can be statically fixed to
implementation actions, is decidable, and complete for exponential space.

Given a method M of a library L and $m_0, m_f \in Q_M$, an $M[m_0, m_f]$-operation
θ is *read-only* for a specification S if and only if for all $w_1, w_2, w_3 \in \Sigma_S^*$,

1. If $w_1 \cdot M[m_0, m_f] \cdot w_2 \in S$ then $w_1 \cdot M[m_0, m_f]^k \cdot w_2 \in S$ for all $k \geq 0$, and
2. If $w_1 \cdot M[m_0, m_f] \cdot w_2 \in S$ and $w_1 \cdot w_3 \in S$ then $w_1 \cdot M[m_0, m_f] \cdot w_3 \in S$.

The first condition is a sort of idempotence of $M[m_0, m_f]$ w.r.t. S, while the
second says that $M[m_0, m_f]$ does not disable other operations.

Remark 1. Whether an operation is read-only can be derived from the specification. Roughly, an operation $M[m_0, m_f]$ is read-only for a specification given by
a finite automaton $\mathcal{A}$ if every transition of $\mathcal{A}$ labeled by $M[m_0, m_f]$ is a self-loop.
For instance, the specification in Fig. 2 dictates that pop$[\cdot, \text{false}]$ is read-only.

The *control graph* $G_M = \langle Q_M, E \rangle$ is the quotient of a method M's transition
system by shared-state valuations V: $\langle m_1, a, m_2 \rangle \in E$ iff $\langle m_1, v_1 \rangle \hookrightarrow_M^a \langle m_2, v_2 \rangle$
for some $v_1, v_2 \in V$. A function $\mathsf{LP} : L \to \wp(\Sigma_L)$ is called a *linearization-point
mapping* when for each $M \in L$:

1. each symbol $a \in \mathsf{LP}(M)$ labels at most one transition of M,
2. any directed path in G_M contains at most one symbol of $\mathsf{LP}(M)$, and
3. all directed paths in G_M containing $a \in \mathsf{LP}(M)$ reach the same $m_a \in F_M$.

An action $\langle a, i \rangle$ of an M-operation is called a *linearization point* when $a \in \mathsf{LP}(M)$,
and operations containing linearization points are said to be *effectuated*; $\mathsf{LP}(\theta)$
denotes the unique linearization point of an effectuated operation θ. A *read-
points mapping* $\mathsf{RP} : \Theta \to \mathbb{N}$ for an action sequence σ with operations Θ maps
each read-only operation θ to the index $\mathsf{RP}(\theta)$ of an internal θ-action in σ.

Remark 2. One could also define linearization points which depend on predicates
involving, e.g., shared-state valuations, loop iteration counts, and return values.

An action sequence σ is called *effectuated* when every completed operation of σ is either effectuated or read-only, and an effectuated completion σ' of σ is *effect preserving* when each effectuated operation of σ also appears in σ'. Given a linearization-point mapping LP, and a read-points mapping RP of an action sequence σ, we say a permutation π of σ is *point preserving* when every two operations of π are ordered by their linearization/read points in σ.

Definition 4. *A trace τ is $\langle S, \mathsf{LP}\rangle$-linearizable when τ is effectuated, and there exists a read-points mapping RP of τ, along with an effect-preserving completion π of a strict, point-preserving, and serial permutation of τ such that $(\pi \mid S) \in S$.*

This notion extends naturally to executions of a system $L[C]$, to the system $L[C]$ itself, and to L when C is the most general client $C^\star$.

Definition 5 (Static Linearizability). *The system $L[C]$ is S-static linearizable when $L[C]$ is $\langle S, \mathsf{LP}\rangle$-linearizable for some mapping LP.*

Example 3. The execution of Example 1 is $\langle S, \mathsf{LP}\rangle$-linearizable with an LP which assigns points denoted by ×s in Figure 4; the completion of a strict, point-preserving, and serial permutation which witnesses this fact is also shown.

Lemma 4. *Every S-static linearizable library is S-linearizable.*

To decide $\langle \mathsf{LP}, S\rangle$-static-linearizability we reduce to a reachability problem on an extension of the given system $L[C]$. The extension simulates the specification automaton $\mathcal{A}_S$, updating its state when operations are effectuated—i.e., at linearization points. Besides ensuring that the method corresponding to each read-only operation θ is enabled in $\mathcal{A}_S$ at some point during θ's execution, our reachability query ensures that each effectuated operation corresponds to an enabled transition in $\mathcal{A}_S$; otherwise the current execution is not S-linearizable, w.r.t. the mapping LP. Technically, we discharge this reachability query via state-reachability on the canonical VASS of $L[C]$'s extension (see Section 2.1), which yields an exponential-space procedure. As the set of possible linearization-point mappings is finite, this procedure is hoisted to an exponential-space procedure for static-linearizability, leveraging Savitch's Theorem. Our proof in our extended report [7] also demonstrates asymptotic optimality, since VASS state-reachability is also polynomial-time reducible to static linearizability.

Theorem 2. *The static linearizability problem for unbounded concurrent systems with regular specifications is EXPSPACE-complete.*

5   Undecidability of Linearizability in the General Case

Though verifying linearizability is decidable for finite-state systems [1], allowing for an unbounded number of concurrent operations lends the power, e.g., to encode unbounded counters. In this section we demonstrate how to harness this power via a reduction from the undecidable state-reachability problem of counter machines to linearizability of unbounded concurrent systems. Technically, given a counter machine $\mathcal{A}$, we construct a library $L_{\mathcal{A}}$ and a specification $S_{\mathcal{A}}$ such that $L_{\mathcal{A}}[C^\star]$ is *not* $S_{\mathcal{A}}$-linearizable exactly when $\mathcal{A}$ has an execution reaching the given target state. In what follows we outline our simulation of $\mathcal{A}$, ignoring several details in order to highlight the crux of our reduction. Our full proof is listed in an extended report [7].

In our simulation of $\mathcal{A}$ the most general client $C^\star$ invokes an arbitrary sequence of methods from the library $L_{\mathcal{A}}$ containing a *transition method* T[t] for each transition t of $\mathcal{A}$, and an *increment method* I[c_i], a *decrement method* D[c_i], and a *zero-test method* Z[c_i], for each counter c_i of $\mathcal{A}$. As our simulation should allow only concurrent traces which correspond to executions of $\mathcal{A}$, and $C^\star$ is a priori free to invoke operations at arbitrary times, we are faced with constructing the library $L_{\mathcal{A}}$ and specification $S_{\mathcal{A}}$ so that only certain well-formed concurrent traces are permitted. Our strategy is essentially to build $L_{\mathcal{A}}$ to allow only those traces corresponding to valid sequences of $\mathcal{A}$-transitions, and to build $S_{\mathcal{A}}$ to allow only those traces, which either do not reach the target state of $\mathcal{A}$, or which erroneously pass some zero-test—i.e., on a counter whose value is non-zero.

Figure 6 depicts the structure of our simulation, on an $\mathcal{A}$-execution where two increments are followed by two decrements and a zero test, all on the same counter c_1. Essentially we simulate each execution by a trace in which:

1. A sequence $t_1 t_2 \ldots t_i$ of $\mathcal{A}$-transitions is modeled by a pairwise-overlapping sequence of T[t_1] $\cdot$ T[t_2] $\cdots$ T[t_i] operations.
2. Each T[t]-operation has a corresponding I[c_i], D[c_i], or Z[ci] operation, depending on whether t is, resp., an increment, decrement, or zero-test transition with counter c_i.
3. Each I[c_i] operation has a corresponding D[c_i] operation.
4. For each counter c_i, all I[c_i] and D[c_i] between Z[c_i] operations overlap.
5. For each counter c_i, no I[c_i] nor D[c_i] operations overlap with a Z[c_i] operation.
6. The number of I[c_i] operations between two Z[c_i] operations matches the number of D[c_i] operations.

The library $L_{\mathcal{A}}$ ensures Properties 1–4 using rendezvous synchronization, with six types of signals: a T/T signal between T[$\cdot$]-operations, and for each counter c_i, T/I, T/D, and T/Z signals between T[$\cdot$]-operations and, resp., I[c_i], D[c_i], and Z[c_i] operations, an I/D signal between I[c_i] and D[c_i] operations, and a T/C signal between T[t] operations and I[c_i] or D[c_i] operations, for zero-testing transitions t. An initial operation (not depicted in Figure 6) initiates a T/T rendezvous with some T[t] operation. Each T[t] operation then performs a rendezvous sequence: when t is an increment or decrement of counter c_i, then T[t] performs a T/T rendezvous, followed by a T/I, resp., T/D for counter c_i, followed by a final T/T rendezvous; when t is a zero-test of counter c_i, T[t] performs a T/T rendezvous, followed by some arbitrary number of T/Cs for c_i, followed by a T/Z for c_i, and finally a last T/T rendezvous. Each I[c_i] operation performs T/I, then I/D, and finally T/C rendezvous for counter c_i, while each D[c_i] operation performs I/D, then T/D, and finally T/C rendezvous for c_i; the Z[c_i] operations

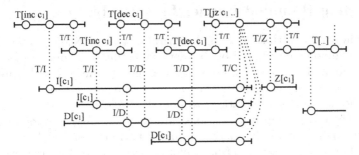

Fig. 6. The $L_\mathcal{A}$ simulation of an $\mathcal{A}$-execution with two increments followed by two decrements and a zero-test of counter c_1. Operations are drawn as horizontal lines containing rendezvous actions drawn as circles. Matching rendezvous actions are connected by dotted lines labeled by rendezvous type. Time advances to the right.

perform a single T/Z rendezvous for c_i. T/T rendezvousing ensures Property 1, T/I, T/D, and T/Z rendezvousing ensures Property 2, I/D rendezvousing ensures Property 3, and T/C rendezvousing ensures Property 4. Note that even in the case where not all pending $I[c_i]$ and $D[c_i]$ operations perform T/C rendezvous with a concurrent $T[t]$ operation, where t is a zero-test transition, at the very least, they overlap with all other pending $I[c_i]$ and $D[c_i]$ operations having performed T/I, resp., T/D, rendezvous since the last $Z[c_i]$ operation.

The trickier part of our proof is indeed ensuring Properties 5 and 6. There we leverage Property 4: when all $I[c_i]$ and $D[c_i]$ operations between two $Z[c_i]$ operations overlap, every permutation of them, including those alternating between $I[c_i]$ and $D[c_i]$ operations, is strict, i.e., is permitted by the definition of linearizability. Our specification $S_\mathcal{A}$ takes advantage of this in order to match the unbounded number of $I[c_i]$ and $D[c_i]$ operations using only bounded memory.

Lemma 5. *The specification $S_\mathcal{A}$ accepting all sequences which either do not end with a transition to the target state, or in which the number of alternating $I[c_i]$ and $D[c_i]$ operations between two $Z[c_i]$ operations are unequal, is regular.*

Lemma 5 gives a way to ensure Properties 5 and 6, since any trace which is $S_\mathcal{A}$-linearizable either does not encode an execution to $\mathcal{A}$'s target state, or respects Property 5 while violating Property 6—i.e., the number of increments and decrements between zero-tests does not match—or violates Property 5: in the latter case, where some $I[c_i]$ or $D[c_i]$ operation θ_1 overlaps with an $Z[c_i]$ operation θ_2, θ_1 can always be commuted over θ_2 to ensure that the number of $I[c_i]$ and $D[c_i]$ operations does not match in some interval between $Z[c_i]$ operations. Thus any trace which is *not* $S_\mathcal{A}$-linearizable must respect both Properties 5 and 6. It follows that any trace of $L_\mathcal{A}$ which is not $S_\mathcal{A}$-linearizable guarantees Properties 1–6, and ultimately corresponds to a valid execution of $\mathcal{A}$, and visa versa, thus reducing counter machine state-reachability to $S_\mathcal{A}$-linearizability.

Theorem 3. *The linearizability problem for unbounded concurrent systems with regular specifications is undecidable.*

6   Deciding Bounded Barrier Linearizability

Our proof in Section 5 that verifying linearizability is undecidable relies on constructing an unbounded amount of "barriers" bisecting serial operations in order to encode unboundedly-many zero-tests of a counter machine. Besides disarming our undecidability proof, bounding the number of barriers leads to an interesting heuristic for detecting violations to linearizability, based on the hypothesis that many violations occur in executions expressed with few barriers. In this section we demonstrate not only that the bounded-barrier linearizability problem is decidable, but that when restricting exploration to bounded-barrier executions, checking linearizability reduces to a constraint solving problem on the valuations of counters counting the number of each operation occurring in a finite number of barrier-separated intervals. Similarly to how context-bounding reduces the problem of exploring concurrent program *interleavings* to sequential program behaviors [22], barrier-bounding reduces the problem of exploring concurrent operation *serializations* to counter-constraint solving.

Formally, a *barrier* of a trace τ is an index $0 < B < |\tau|$ such that $\tau(B)$ is a call action, and the nearest preceding non-internal action of τ is a return action. An *interval* is a maximal integer interval $I = [i_1, i_2]$ of τ-indices containing no barriers except i_1, in the case that $i_1 > 0$; we index the intervals of a trace sequentially from 0, as $I_0, I_1, \ldots, I_k$. The *span* of an operation θ of τ is the pair $\langle I_i, I_j \rangle$ of intervals such that θ begins in I_i and ends in I_j—and $I_j = \omega$ when θ is pending. The trace τ of Example 1 contains two barriers, B_1 and B_2, where $\tau(B_1) = \mathsf{call}(\mathsf{pop}, \cdot, t_1)$ and $\tau(B_2) = \mathsf{call}(\mathsf{push}, a, t_3)$, thus dividing τ into three intervals, $I_0 = [0, B_1 - 1]$, $I_1 = [B_1, B_2 - 1]$, and $I_2 = [B_2, |\tau| - 1]$; the span of, e.g., the operation of threads t_2 and t_4 are, resp., $\langle I_0, I_1 \rangle$ and $\langle I_0, \omega \rangle$. Note that the spans of two serial operations of a trace are disjoint.

Definition 6. *The system $L[C]$ is $\langle S, k \rangle$-linearizable when every trace of $L[C]$ with at most k barriers is S-linearizable.*

In what follows we develop the machinery to reduce this bounded-barrier linearizability problem to a reachability problem on systems which count the number of each operation spanning each pair of intervals.

An *interval-annotated alphabet* $\dot{\Sigma} \stackrel{\text{def}}{=} \Sigma \times \mathbb{N} \times (\mathbb{N} \cup \{\omega\})$ attaches (non-zero) interval indices to each symbol of Σ, and an *interval-annotated sequence* $\dot{\sigma} \in \dot{\Sigma}^*$ is k-bounded when $i_1 \leq k$ and either $i_2 \leq k$ or $i_2 = \omega$ for each symbol $\langle a, i_1, i_2 \rangle$ of $\dot{\sigma}$. The homomorphism $\dot{h} : \dot{\Sigma} \to \Sigma$ maps each symbol $\langle a, \_, \_ \rangle$ to $h(\langle a, \_, \_ \rangle) = a$. An interval-annotated sequence $\dot{\sigma}$ is *timing consistent* when $i_1 \leq i_2$, $i_3 \leq i_4$, and $i_1 \leq i_4$ for any symbol $\langle \_, i_1, i_2 \rangle$ occurring before $\langle \_, i_3, i_4 \rangle$ in $\dot{\sigma}$.

We say that the sequence over the interval-annotated (and pending closed, see Section 2.4) specification alphabet $\dot{\sigma} \in \dot{\Sigma}_S^*$ is *consistent* when $\dot{\sigma}$ is timing consistent, and $i_2 = \omega$ iff $m_f = *$, for all symbols $\langle M[m_0, m_f], i_1, i_2 \rangle$ of $\dot{\sigma}$. The *(k-bounded) interval-annotated specification* $\dot{S}$ of a specification S is the language containing all consistent interval-annotated sequences $\dot{\sigma}$ such that $h(\dot{\sigma}) \in S$. For example, we obtain the 1-bounded interval-annotated specification from the specification of Figure 3 by attaching the interval indices $\langle 1, \omega \rangle$ to each pop$[\cdot, *]$ and push$[a, *]$ symbol, and $\langle 1, 1 \rangle$ to each pop$[\cdot, \text{false}]$, pop$[\cdot, \text{true}]$, and push$[a, \text{true}]$ symbol.

Lemma 6. *The k-bounded interval-annotated specification $\dot{S}$, of a regular specification S, is also regular.*

Proof. For any given $k > 0$ the set $W \subseteq \dot{\Sigma}_S^*$ of k-bounded consistent interval-annotated sequences is regular. As regular languages are closed under inverse homomorphism and intersection, $\dot{S} = W \cap h^{-1}(S)$ is also regular. $\square$

To relate traces to an interval-annotated specification $\dot{S}$, we define the *interval-annotated S-image* $\dot{\sigma}$ of an action sequence σ as the multiset $\dot{\sigma} : \dot{\Sigma}_S \rightarrow \mathbb{N}$ mapping each $\langle M[m_0, m_f], i_1, i_2 \rangle \in \dot{\Sigma}_S$ to the number of occurrences of $M[m_0, m_f]$-operations in σ with span $\langle i_1, i_2 \rangle$.

Example 4. The interval-annotated image $\dot{\tau}$ of the trace τ from Example 1 maps the interval-annotated symbols

$$\text{push}[a, \text{true}][1,1], \ \text{push}[a, *][1, \omega], \ \text{pop}[\cdot, \text{true}][1, 2],$$
$$\text{pop}[\cdot, \text{false}][2, 3], \ \text{and} \ \text{push}[a, \text{true}][3, 3]$$

to 1, and the remaining symbols of $\dot{\Sigma}_S$ to zero.

Annotating operations with the intervals in which they occur allows a compact representation of specifications' ordering constraints, while abstracting away the order of same-interval operations—as they are free to commute. To realize this abstraction, we recall that the *Parikh image* of a sequence $\sigma \in \Sigma^*$ is the multiset $\Pi(\sigma) : \Sigma \rightarrow \mathbb{N}$ mapping each symbol $a \in \Sigma$ to the number of occurrences of a in σ. The *Parikh image* of a language $L \subseteq \Sigma^*$ are the images $\Pi(L) \stackrel{\text{def}}{=} \{\Pi(\sigma) : \sigma \in L\}$ of sequences in L. We prove the following key lemma in our extended report [7].

Lemma 7. *A trace τ with at most k barriers is S-linearizable iff $\dot{\tau} \in \Pi(\dot{S})$, where $\dot{S}$ is the $(k+1)$-bounded interval-annotated specification of S.*

Lemma 7 essentially allows us to reduce the bounded-barrier linearizability problem to a reachability problem: given a trace τ with at most k barriers, τ is linearizable so long as its image $\dot{\tau}$ is included in the Parikh image of the $(k+1)$-bounded specification $\dot{S}$. In effect, rather than considering all possible serializations of τ, it suffices to keep count of the number of pending and completed operations over each span of intervals, and ensure that these counts continually remain within the semi-linear set of counts allowed by the specification. For the purposes of our results here, we keep these counts by increasing the dimension of the canonical vector addition system $\mathcal{A}_{L[C]}$ (see Section 2.1) of a given system $L[C]$. Furthermore, since Bouajjani and Habermehl [6] prove that checking whether reachable VASS configurations lie within a semi-linear set is itself reducible to VASS reachability, and the Parikh image of a regular set is a semi-linear, ensuring these counts continually remain within those allowed by the specification is therefore reducible to VASS reachability. In fact, our proof in our extended report [7] shows this reduction-based procedure is asymptotically optimal, since VASS reachability is also polynomial-time reducible to to $\langle S, k \rangle$-linearizability.

Theorem 4. *The bounded-barrier linearizability problem for unbounded concurrent systems with regular specifications is decidable, and asymptotically equivalent to VASS reachability.*

Theorem 4 holds for any class of specifications with semi-linear Parikh images, including, e.g., context-free languages. Furthermore, though Theorem 4 leverages our reduction from serializations to counting operations for decidability with unbounded concurrent systems, in principle this reduction applies to any class of concurrent systems, including infinite-data systems—without any guarantee of decidability—provided the ability to represent suitable constraints on the counters of annotated specification alphabet symbols. We believe this reduction is valuable whether or not data and/or concurrency are bounded, since we avoid the explicit enumeration of possible serializations.

As a proof of concept, we have implemented a prototype of our reduction. First we instrument a given library implementation (written in Boogie) with (1) auxiliary counters, counting the number of each operation within each bounded span, (2) with Presburger assertions over these counters, encoding the legal specification images, and (3) with a client nondeterministically invoking methods with arbitrary arguments. As a second step we translate this instrumented (concurrent) program to a sequential (Boogie) program, encoding a subset of delay-bounded executions [16], then discover assertion violations using an SMT-based sequential reachability engine [23]. Note that the bounded-barrier reduction, which treats operation serialization, composes naturally with the bounded-delay reduction, which treats operation interleaving. Furthermore, the reduction to SMT allows us to analyze infinite-data implementations; e.g., we analyze an unbounded stack with arbitrary data values, according to a specification which ensures each pop is preceded by a matching push—which is context-free, thus has a semi-linear Parikh image—while ignoring the pushed and popped values.

We have applied our prototype to discover bugs known in or manually-injected into several textbook concurrent data structure algorithms; the resulting linearizability violations are discovered within a few seconds to minutes. Besides evidence to the practical applicability of our reduction algorithm, our small set of experiments suggests that many linearizability violations occur with very few barriers; we discover violations arising from the infamous "ABA" bug [26], along with bugs injected into a 2-lock queue, a lock-coupling set, and Treiber's stack, in executions *without any* barriers. For instance, in an improperly-synchronized Treiber-style stack algorithm, two concurrent pop(a) operations may erroneously remove the same element added by one concurrent push(a) operation; however, no serialization of pop(a), pop(a), and push(a) is included in our stack specification.

Of course, some violations do require barriers. A very simple example is a violation involving one pop(a) serial with one push(a) operation, though since pop(a) and push(a) are not concurrent, a bug causing this violation is unlikely. More interestingly, a lost update due to improper synchronization between two concurrent inc() operations in a zero-initialized counter can only be observed as a linearizability violation when a barrier prevents, e.g., a subsequent read(1) operation from commuting over an inc() operation.

7 Related Work

Papadimitriou [28] and Gibbons and Korach [18] studied variations on the problems of deciding serializability, sequential consistency, and linearizability for single concurrent traces, finding the general problems to be NP-complete, and pointing out several PTIME variants, e.g., when serializations must respect a suitable conflict-order. Alur et al. [1] studied the complexity of similar decision problems for *all* traces of finite-state concurrent systems: while sequential consistency already becomes undecidable for finite-state systems—though Bingham [4] proposes certain decidable pathology-omitting variations—checking conflict serializability is declared PSPACE-complete[5] while linearizability is shown to be in EXPSPACE. Our work considers the complexity of these problems for systems where the number of concurrent operations is unbounded.

Though many have developed techniques for proving linearizability [33, 2, 32, 3, 25, 14, 27, 31, 34, 10], we are not aware of decidability or complexity results for the corresponding linearizability and static linearizability verification problems for unbounded systems. While a few works propose testing-based detection of linearizability violations [9, 11, 10], they rely on explicit enumeration of possible serializations; prioritizing the search for violations with few barriers, and the resulting reduction to numerical constraint solving, are novel.

Several works have also developed techniques for verifying sequential consistency [20, 29, 5, 8] and serializability [12, 30, 17, 19, 15]; Farzan and Madhusudan [17] demonstrate a complete technique for verifying conflict serializability with a bounded number of concurrent operations, and while Guerraoui et al. [19] identify symmetry conditions on transactional systems with which conflict serializability can be verified completely, for an unbounded number of concurrent operations, they propose no means of *checking* that these symmetry conditions hold on any given system. On the contrary, we show that verifying conflict serializability without bounding the number of concurrent operations is EXPSPACE-complete.

References

[1] Alur, R., McMillan, K.L., Peled, D.: Model-checking of correctness conditions for concurrent objects. Inf. Comput. 160(1-2), 167–188 (2000)

[2] Amit, D., Rinetzky, N., Reps, T., Sagiv, M., Yahav, E.: Comparison Under Abstraction for Verifying Linearizability. In: Damm, W., Hermanns, H. (eds.) CAV 2007. LNCS, vol. 4590, pp. 477–490. Springer, Heidelberg (2007)

[3] Berdine, J., Lev-Ami, T., Manevich, R., Ramalingam, G., Sagiv, M.: Thread Quantification for Concurrent Shape Analysis. In: Gupta, A., Malik, S. (eds.) CAV 2008. LNCS, vol. 5123, pp. 399–413. Springer, Heidelberg (2008)

[4] Bingham, J.: Model Checking Sequential Consistency and Parameterized Protocols. PhD thesis, The University of British Columbia (August 2005)

---

[5] The correct proof of PSPACE-completeness is given by Farzan and Madhusudan [17].

[5] Bingham, J.D., Condon, A., Hu, A.J., Qadeer, S., Zhang, Z.: Automatic Verification of Sequential Consistency for Unbounded Addresses and Data Values. In: Alur, R., Peled, D.A. (eds.) CAV 2004. LNCS, vol. 3114, pp. 427–439. Springer, Heidelberg (2004)

[6] Bouajjani, A., Habermehl, P.: Constrained Properties, Semilinear Systems, and Petri Nets. In: Sassone, V., Montanari, U. (eds.) CONCUR 1996. LNCS, vol. 1119, pp. 481–497. Springer, Heidelberg (1996)

[7] Bouajjani, A., Emmi, M., Enea, C., Hamza, J.: Verifying concurrent programs against sequential specifications. Technical report (January 2013)

[8] Burckhardt, S., Alur, R., Martin, M.M.K.: CheckFence: checking consistency of concurrent data types on relaxed memory models. In: PLDI 2007: Proc. ACM SIGPLAN 2007 Conf. on Programming Language Design and Implementation, pp. 12–21. ACM (2007)

[9] Burckhardt, S., Dern, C., Musuvathi, M., Tan, R.: Line-up: a complete and automatic linearizability checker. In: PLDI 2010: Proc. 2010 ACM SIGPLAN Conf. on Programming Language Design and Implementation, pp. 330–340. ACM (2010)

[10] Burckhardt, S., Gotsman, A., Musuvathi, M., Yang, H.: Concurrent Library Correctness on the TSO Memory Model. In: Seidl, H. (ed.) ESOP 2012. LNCS, vol. 7211, pp. 87–107. Springer, Heidelberg (2012)

[11] Burnim, J., Necula, G.C., Sen, K.: Specifying and checking semantic atomicity for multithreaded programs. In: ASPLOS 2011: Proc. 16th Intl. Conf. on Architectural Support for Programming Languages and Operating Systems, pp. 79–90. ACM (2011)

[12] Cohen, A., O'Leary, J.W., Pnueli, A., Tuttle, M.R., Zuck, L.D.: Verifying correctness of transactional memories. In: FMCAD 2007: Proc. 7th Intl. Conf. on Formal Methods in Computer-Aided Design, pp. 37–44. IEEE Computer Society (2007)

[13] Dragojević, A., Guerraoui, R., Kapalka, M.: Dividing transactional memories by zero. In: TRANSACT 2008: Proc. 3rd ACM SIGPLAN Workshop on Transactional Computing. ACM (2008)

[14] Elmas, T., Qadeer, S., Sezgin, A., Subasi, O., Tasiran, S.: Simplifying Linearizability Proofs with Reduction and Abstraction. In: Esparza, J., Majumdar, R. (eds.) TACAS 2010. LNCS, vol. 6015, pp. 296–311. Springer, Heidelberg (2010)

[15] Emmi, M., Majumdar, R., Manevich, R.: Parameterized verification of transactional memories. In: PLDI 2010: Proc. 2010 ACM SIGPLAN Conf. on Programming Language Design and Implementation, pp. 134–145. ACM (2010)

[16] Emmi, M., Qadeer, S., Rakamaric, Z.: Delay-bounded scheduling. In: POPL 2011: Proc. 38th ACM SIGPLAN-SIGACT Symp. on Principles of Programming Languages, pp. 411–422. ACM (2011)

[17] Farzan, A., Madhusudan, P.: Monitoring Atomicity in Concurrent Programs. In: Gupta, A., Malik, S. (eds.) CAV 2008. LNCS, vol. 5123, pp. 52–65. Springer, Heidelberg (2008)

[18] Gibbons, P.B., Korach, E.: Testing shared memories. SIAM J. Comput. 26(4), 1208–1244 (1997)

[19] Guerraoui, R., Henzinger, T.A., Singh, V.: Model checking transactional memories. Distributed Computing 22(3), 129–145 (2010)

[20] Henzinger, T.A., Qadeer, S., Rajamani, S.K.: Verifying Sequential Consistency on Shared-Memory Multiprocessor Systems. In: Halbwachs, N., Peled, D.A. (eds.) CAV 1999. LNCS, vol. 1633, pp. 301–315. Springer, Heidelberg (1999)

[21] Herlihy, M., Wing, J.M.: Linearizability: A correctness condition for concurrent objects. ACM Trans. Program. Lang. Syst. 12(3), 463–492 (1990)

[22] Lal, A., Reps, T.W.: Reducing concurrent analysis under a context bound to sequential analysis. Formal Methods in System Design 35(1), 73–97 (2009)

[23] Lal, A., Qadeer, S., Lahiri, S.K.: A Solver for Reachability Modulo Theories. In: Madhusudan, P., Seshia, S.A. (eds.) CAV 2012. LNCS, vol. 7358, pp. 427–443. Springer, Heidelberg (2012)

[24] Lamport, L.: How to make a multiprocessor computer that correctly executes multiprocess programs. IEEE Trans. Computers 28(9), 690–691 (1979)

[25] Liu, Y., Chen, W., Liu, Y.A., Sun, J.: Model Checking Linearizability via Refinement. In: Cavalcanti, A., Dams, D.R. (eds.) FM 2009. LNCS, vol. 5850, pp. 321–337. Springer, Heidelberg (2009)

[26] Michael, M.M.: ABA prevention using single-word instructions. Technical Report RC 23089, IBM Thomas J. Watson Research Center (January 2004)

[27] O'Hearn, P.W., Rinetzky, N., Vechev, M.T., Yahav, E., Yorsh, G.: Verifying linearizability with hindsight. In: PODC 2010: Proc. 29th Annual Symp. on Principles of Distributed Computing, pp. 85–94. ACM (2010)

[28] Papadimitriou, C.H.: The serializability of concurrent database updates. J. ACM 26(4), 631–653 (1979)

[29] Qadeer, S.: Verifying sequential consistency on shared-memory multiprocessors by model checking. IEEE Trans. Parallel Distrib. Syst. 14(8), 730–741 (2003)

[30] Taşıran, S.: A compositional method for verifying software transactional memory implementations. Technical Report MSR-TR-2008-56, Microsoft Research (April 2008)

[31] Vafeiadis, V.: Automatically Proving Linearizability. In: Touili, T., Cook, B., Jackson, P. (eds.) CAV 2010. LNCS, vol. 6174, pp. 450–464. Springer, Heidelberg (2010)

[32] Vechev, M.T., Yahav, E.: Deriving linearizable fine-grained concurrent objects. In: PLDI 2008: Proc. ACM SIGPLAN 2008 Conf. on Programming Language Design and Implementation, pp. 125–135. ACM (2008)

[33] Wang, L., Stoller, S.D.: Static analysis of atomicity for programs with non-blocking synchronization. In: PPOPP 2005: Proc. ACM SIGPLAN Symp. on Principles and Practice of Parallel Programming, pp. 61–71. ACM (2005)

[34] Zhang, S.J.: Scalable automatic linearizability checking. In: ICSE 2011: Proc. 33rd Intl. Conf. on Software Engineering, pp. 1185–1187. ACM (2011)

On Distributability in Process Calculi*

Kirstin Peters[1], Uwe Nestmann[1], and Ursula Goltz[2]

[1] TU Berlin, Germany
[2] TU Braunschweig, Germany

Abstract. We present a novel approach to compare process calculi and their synchronisation mechanisms by using synchronisation patterns and explicitly considering the degree of distributability. For this, we propose a new quality criterion that (1) measures the preservation of distributability and (2) allows us to derive two synchronisation patterns that separate several variants of pi-like calculi. Precisely, we prove that there is no good and distributability-preserving encoding from the synchronous pi-calculus with mixed choice into its fragment with only separate choice, and neither from the asynchronous pi-calculus (without choice) into the join-calculus.

1 Introduction

The pi-calculus is a well-known and frequently used process calculus to model concurrent systems. Therein, intuitively, the *degree of distributability* corresponds to the amount of parallel components that can act independently. Practical experience has shown that it is not possible to implement every pi-calculus term—not even every asynchronous one—in an asynchronous setting while preserving its degree of distributability. To overcome these problems, the join-calculus was introduced as a model of distributed computation [12]. It employs a *locality* principle by ensuring that there is always exactly one immobile receiver for each communication channel. More precisely, for every name, exactly one receiver is defined at the time of the name's creation, and communication occurs only on so-defined channels [7].

Most of the existing approaches that analyse the distributability of concurrent systems use special formalisms often equipped with an explicit notion of location, e.g. [2] in Petri nets or the distributed pi-calculus [9]. In contrast to these approaches, we analyse (similarly to [17,25]) the potential of a formalism to describe distributed systems without an explicit allocation of locations to processes. Instead, we abstract from a particular distribution and consider *distributability* and, thus, all possible explicitly-located variants of a calculus. We do so, because we consider the expressive power of languages, not just individual terms. Moreover, we obtain results for a larger number of process calculi.

In order to measure whether an encoding respects the degree of distribution, usually the homomorphic translation of the parallel operator, i.e., $[\![P \mid Q]\!] =$

---

* Supported by the DFG (German Research Foundation), grants NE-1505/2-1 and GO-671/6-1.

M. Felleisen and P. Gardner (Eds.): ESOP 2013, LNCS 7792, pp. 310–329, 2013.

[[P]] | [[Q]], is used as a criterion (see e.g. [17,5,11]). Such an encoding naturally preserves the parallel structure of terms and, thus (at least for process calculi such as CSP or the pi-calculus), the degree of distribution. However, the opposite is not true. In [19], the first two authors present an encoding that preserves the degree of distribution although it does not translate the parallel operator homomorphically. In this sense, the homomorphic translation of the parallel operator is too strict—at least for separation results. It rightly forbids the introduction of coordinators that reduce the degree of distribution. But it also forbids protocols that handle communications of parallel components without sequentialising them or reducing the degree of distribution in another sense. Moreover, the homomorphic translation of the parallel operator is not always suited to reason about distribution in process calculi as, for example, the join-calculus: there, it is not always possible to separate distributable subterms by means of a parallel operator (see the discussion in Section 3). To overcome this problem, [19] presents a first formulation of a new criterion to more succinctly measure the preservation of distributability in process calculi like the pi-calculus. We generalise this criterion to reason about arbitrary process calculi. Moreover, we show that the distributability of processes implies also distributability of executions. This leads to a new proof method for separation results.

As a result, we obtain a difference between the distributability of the asynchronous pi-calculus (π_a) and the join-calculus (J), elucidated by the non-existence of a good and distributability-preserving encoding from π_a into J. Interestingly, the difference between these two calculi is captured by a synchronisation pattern that was already used in [25] when studying the distributability of Petri nets. Moreover, we shed more light on the difference between the synchronous pi-calculus with mixed choice (π_m) and its fragment with only separate choice (π_s) already considered in [17,8,19] by capturing this difference within a novel synchronisation pattern. Hence, these calculi, although they all have the same abstract expressive power [7,16,19], embody different levels of synchronisation.

Overview. We start with some general definitions on process calculi in §2. In §3, we propose a new criterion to reason about the preservation of distributability. §4 then introduces the first synchronisation pattern and separates π_a and J. A second synchronisation pattern and separation between π_m and π_s is presented in §5. We conclude with §6. Proofs and additional material can be found in [20].

2   Process Calculi

Within this paper we compare different variants of the pi-calculus and the join-calculus as they are described e.g. in [14,13] and [7], respectively. We provide a short introduction into process calculi in general and these variants in particular.

Assume a countably-infinite set $\mathcal{N}$, whose elements are called *names*. We use lower case letters $a, b, c, \ldots, a', a_1, \ldots$ to range over names. Moreover, let $\tau \notin \mathcal{N}$ and $\overline{\mathcal{N}} = \{ \overline{n} \mid n \in \mathcal{N} \}$ be the set of co-names (used in the pi-calculus). A *process calculus* is a language $\mathcal{L} = \langle \mathcal{P}, \longmapsto \rangle$ that consists of a set of process terms $\mathcal{P}$ (its syntax) and a relation $\longmapsto : \mathcal{P} \times \mathcal{P}$ on process terms (its semantics). We often refer to process terms also simply as processes or as terms and use upper case letters $P, Q, R, \ldots, P', P_1, \ldots$ to range over them.

The *syntax* is usually defined by a context-free grammar defining operators, i.e., functions op : $\mathcal{N}^n \times \mathcal{P}^m \to \mathcal{P}$. An operator of arity 0, i.e., $m = 0$, is a *constant*. The arguments that are again process terms are called *subterms* of P.

Definition 1 (Subterms). *Let* $\langle \mathcal{P}, \longmapsto \rangle$ *be a process calculus and* $P \in \mathcal{P}$. *The set of* subterms *of* $P = \mathrm{op}\,(x_1, \ldots, x_n, P_1, \ldots, P_m)$ *is defined recursively as* $\{P\} \cup \{ P' \mid \exists i \in \{1, \ldots, m\} \,.\, P'$ *is a subterm of* $P_i \}$.

Hence every term is a subterm of itself and constants have no further subterms. We require that each process calculus defines at least the *empty process* as constant and the *parallel operator* as binary operator. Moreover, we add the special constant ✓ to each process calculus. Its purpose is to denote *success* (or *successful termination*) which allows us to compare the abstract behaviour of terms in different process calculi as described in Section 2.1. Another typical operator is the restriction of scopes of names. A *scope* defines an area in which a particular name is known and can be used. For several reasons, it can be useful to restrict the scope of a name. For instance to forbid interaction between two processes or with an unknown and, hence, potentially untrusted environment. Names whose scope is restricted such that they cannot be used from outside the scope are denoted as *bound names*. The remaining names are called *free names*. Accordingly, we assume three sets—the sets of names $\mathsf{n}(P)$ and its subsets of free names $\mathsf{fn}(P)$ and bound names $\mathsf{bn}(P)$—with each term P. In the case of bound names, their syntactical representation as lower case letters serves as a place holder for any fresh name, i.e., any name that does not occur elsewhere in the term. To avoid name capture or clashes, i.e., to avoid confusion between free and bound names or different bound names, bound names can be mapped to fresh names by α-*conversion*. We write $P \equiv_\alpha Q$ if P and Q differ only by α-conversion.

We use $\sigma, \sigma', \sigma_1, \ldots$ to range over substitutions. A substitution is a finite mapping from names to names defined by a set $\{ y_1/x_1, \ldots, y_n/x_n \}$ of renamings, where the $x_1, \ldots, x_n$ are pairwise distinct. The application of a substitution on a term $\{ y_1/x_1, \ldots, y_n/x_n \}\,(P)$ is defined as the result of simultaneously replacing all free occurrences of x_i by y_i for $i \in \{1, \ldots, n\}$, possibly applying α-conversion to avoid capture or name clashes. For all names $\mathcal{N} \setminus \{x_1, \ldots, x_n\}$ the substitution behaves as the identity mapping. We sometimes omit the parentheses, i.e., $\sigma(P) = \sigma P$. We naturally extend substitutions to co-names, i.e., $\forall \overline{n} \in \overline{\mathcal{N}} \,.\, \sigma(\overline{n}) = \overline{\sigma(n)}$ for all substitutions σ.

To reason about environments of process terms, we use functions on process terms called contexts. More precisely, a *context* $\mathcal{C}\,([\cdot]_1, \ldots, [\cdot]_n) : \mathcal{P}^n \to \mathcal{P}$ with n holes is a function from n process terms into a process term, i.e., given $P_1, \ldots, P_n \in \mathcal{P}$, the term $\mathcal{C}\,(P_1, \ldots, P_n)$ is the result of inserting $P_1, \ldots, P_n$ in that order into the n holes of $\mathcal{C}$.

We consider three variants of the pi-calculus—the full pi-calculus π_m including mixed choice, its subcalculus π_s with only separate choice, and the asynchronous pi-calculus π_a—, and the join-calculus J. Their process terms are given by the sets $\mathcal{P}_\mathrm{m}, \mathcal{P}_\mathrm{s}, \mathcal{P}_\mathrm{a},$ and $\mathcal{P}_\mathrm{J}$, respectively.

Definition 2 (Syntax). *The sets of process terms are given by*

$$\mathcal{P}_m ::= P_1 \mid P_2 \quad \mid \quad \checkmark \quad \mid \quad (\nu n)\,P \quad \mid \quad !P \quad \mid \quad \sum_{i \in I} \pi_i.P_i$$
$$\pi ::= \overline{y}\langle z \rangle \quad \mid \quad y(x) \quad \mid \quad \tau$$

$$\mathcal{P}_s ::= P_1 \mid P_2 \quad \mid \quad \checkmark \quad \mid \quad (\nu n)\,P \quad \mid \quad !P \quad \mid \quad \sum_{i \in I} \pi_i^O.P_i \quad \mid \quad \sum_{i \in I} \pi_i^I.P_i$$
$$\pi^O ::= \overline{y}\langle z \rangle \quad \mid \quad \tau \quad and \quad \pi^I ::= y(x) \quad \mid \quad \tau$$

$$\mathcal{P}_a ::= 0 \quad \mid \quad P_1 \mid P_2 \quad \mid \quad \checkmark \quad \mid \quad (\nu n)\,P \quad \mid \quad !P \quad \mid \quad \overline{y}\langle z \rangle \quad \mid \quad y(x)\,.P \quad \mid \quad \tau.P$$

$$\mathcal{P}_J ::= 0 \quad \mid \quad P_1 \mid P_2 \quad \mid \quad \checkmark \quad \mid \quad y\,\langle z \rangle \quad \mid \quad \mathsf{def}\,D\,\mathsf{in}\,P$$
$$J ::= y\,(x) \quad \mid \quad J_1 \mid J_2 \quad and \quad D ::= J \triangleright P \quad \mid \quad D_1 \wedge D_2$$

for some names $n, x, y, z \in \mathcal{N}$ *and a finite index set* I.

The interpretation of the defined terms is as usual. In all languages the *empty process* is denoted by 0 and $P_1 \mid P_2$ defines *parallel composition*. Within the pi-calculi *restriction* $(\nu n)\,P$ restricts the scope of the name n to the definition of P and $!P$ denotes *replication*. The process term $\sum_{i \in I} \pi_i.P_i$ represents *finite guarded choice*; as usual, the sum $\sum_{i \in \{1,\dots,n\}} \pi_i.P_i$ is sometimes written as $\pi_1.P_1 + \dots + \pi_n.P_n$ and 0 abbreviates the empty sum, i.e., where $I = \emptyset$. The input prefix $y(x)$ is used to describe the ability of receiving the value x over link y and, analogously, the output prefix $\overline{y}\langle z \rangle$ describes the ability to send a value z over link y. The prefix τ describes the ability to perform an internal, not observable action. The choice operators of π_m and π_s require that all branches of a choice are guarded by one of these prefixes. We omit the match prefix, because it does not influence the results.

In $\mathcal{P}_s$ within a single choice term either there are no input or no output guards, i.e., we have input- and output-guarded choice, but no mixed choice. Apart from that, $\mathcal{P}_m$ and $\mathcal{P}_s$ define the same processes. π_m and π_s represent synchronous variants of the pi-calculus. Asynchronous variants were introduced independently by [10] and [3]. In asynchronous communication, a process has no chance to directly determine (without a hint by another process) whether a value sent by it was already received or not. Hence, output actions are not allowed to guard a process different from 0. Also, the interpretation of output guards within a choice construct is delicate. We use the standard variant of π_a, where choice is not allowed at all. Since $\mathcal{P}_a$ has no choice, we include 0 as a primitive.

In $\mathcal{P}_J$ the operator $y\,\langle z \rangle$ describes an output prefix similar to $\mathcal{P}_a$. A *definition* $\mathsf{def}\,D\,\mathsf{in}\,P$ defines a new receiver on fresh names, where D consists of one or several elementary definitions $J \triangleright P$ connected by $\wedge$, J potentially joins several reception patterns $y\,(x)$ connected by $\mid$, and P is a process. Note that $\mathsf{def}\,D\,\mathsf{in}\,P$ unifies the concepts of restriction, input prefix, and replication of the pi-calculus. Moreover, [7] define the *core join-calculus* cJ as a subcalculus of J that restricts definitions to the form $\mathsf{def}\,y_1\,(x_1) \mid y_2\,(x_2) \triangleright P_1\,\mathsf{in}\,P_2$, i.e., in cJ definitions consist of a single elementary definition of exactly two reception patterns.

As usual, the continuation 0 is often omitted, so e.g. $y(x).0$ becomes $y(x)$. In addition, for simplicity in the presentation of examples, we sometimes omit an action's object when it does not effectively contribute to the behaviour of a term, e.g. $y(x)\,.0$ is written as $y.0$ or just y, and $\mathsf{def}\,y\,(x) \triangleright 0\,\mathsf{in}\,y\,\langle z \rangle$ is abbreviated as $\mathsf{def}\,y \triangleright 0\,\mathsf{in}\,y$. Moreover, let $(\nu\tilde{x})\,P$ abbreviate the term $(\nu x_1)\dots(\nu x_n)\,P$.

The definitions of free and bound names are completely standard, i.e., names are bound by restriction and as parameter of input and $n(P) = fn(P) \cup bn(P)$ for all P. In the join-calculus the definition $\mathsf{def}\,D\,\mathsf{in}\,P$ binds for all elementary definitions $J_i \triangleright P_i$ in D and all join pattern $y_{i,j}\,(x_{i,j})$ in J_i the *received variables* $x_{i,j}$ in the corresponding P_i and the *defined variables* $y_{i,j}$ in P. By convention, the received variables of composed join patterns have to be pairwise distinct.

To compare process terms, process calculi usually come with different well-studied equivalence relations (see [23] for an overview). A special kind of equivalence with great importance to reason about processes are *congruences*, i.e., the closure of an equivalence with respect to contexts. Process calculi usually come with a special congruence $\equiv\, \subseteq \mathcal{P} \times \mathcal{P}$ called *structural congruence*. Its main purpose is to equate syntactically different process terms that model quasi-identical behaviour. In the pi-calculus structural congruence is usually provided by a set of equivalence equations. For the above variants we have:

$$P \equiv Q \text{ if } P \equiv_\alpha Q \quad P \mid 0 \equiv P \quad P \mid Q \equiv Q \mid P \quad P \mid (Q \mid R) \equiv (P \mid Q) \mid R \quad !P \equiv P \mid !P$$
$$(\nu n)\,0 \equiv 0 \quad (\nu n)\,(\nu m)\,P \equiv (\nu m)\,(\nu n)\,P \quad P \mid (\nu n)\,Q \equiv (\nu n)\,(P \mid Q) \text{ if } n \notin fn(P)$$

The entanglement of input prefix and restriction within the definition operator of the join-calculus limits the flexibility of relations defined by sets of equivalence equations. Instead structural congruence is given by an extension of the chemical approach in [1] by the heating and cooling rules. They operate on so-called solutions $\mathcal{R} \vdash \mathcal{M}$, where $\mathcal{R}$ and $\mathcal{M}$ are multisets. We have (1) $\vdash P \mid Q \rightleftharpoons \vdash P, Q$, (2) $D \wedge E \vdash\, \rightleftharpoons D, E \vdash$, and (3) $\vdash \mathsf{def}\,D\,\mathsf{in}\,P \rightleftharpoons \sigma_{dv}(D) \vdash \sigma_{dv}(P)$, where only elements—separated by commas—that participate in the rule are mentioned and σ_{dv} instantiates the defined variables in D to distinct fresh names. Then $P \equiv Q$ if P and Q differ only by applications of the $\rightleftharpoons$-rules, i.e., if $\vdash P \rightleftharpoons\, \vdash Q$.

We assume that the *semantics* is given as an *operational semantics* consisting of inference rules defined on the operators of the language [22]. For many process calculi, the semantics is provided in two forms, as *reduction semantics* and as *labelled semantics*. We assume that at least the reduction semantics $\longmapsto$ is given as part of the definition, because its treatment is easier in the context of encodings. A single application of the reduction semantics is called a *(reduction) step* and is written as $P \longmapsto P'$. If $P \longmapsto P'$ we say P' is a *derivative* of P. Moreover, let $P \longmapsto$ (or $P \longmapsto\!\!\!/$) denote the existence (absence) of a step from P, i.e., $P \longmapsto\, \triangleq\, \exists P' \in \mathcal{P}\,.\,P \longmapsto P'$ and $P \longmapsto\!\!\!/\, \triangleq\, \neg(P \longmapsto)$, and let $\Longmapsto$ denote the reflexive and transitive closure of $\longmapsto$. A sequence of reduction steps is called a *reduction*. We write $P \longmapsto^\omega$ if P has an infinite sequence of steps. We also use *execution* to refer to a reduction starting from a particular term. A *maximal execution* of a process P is a reduction starting from P that cannot be further extended, i.e., that is either infinite or of the form $P \Longmapsto P' \longmapsto\!\!\!/$.

The semantics of the above variants of the pi-calculus is given by the axioms
$$(\ldots + \tau.P + \ldots) \longmapsto P \quad (\ldots + y(x).P + \ldots) \mid (\ldots + \overline{y}\langle z\rangle.Q + \ldots) \longmapsto \{z/x\}\,P \mid Q$$
for π_m and π_s, the axioms
$$\tau.P \longmapsto P \quad y(x).P \mid \overline{y}\langle z\rangle \longmapsto \{z/x\}\,P$$
for π_a, and the three rules

$$\frac{P \longmapsto P'}{P \mid Q \longmapsto P' \mid Q} \qquad \frac{P \longmapsto P'}{(\nu n)\,P \longmapsto (\nu n)\,P'} \qquad \frac{P \equiv Q \quad Q \longmapsto Q' \quad Q' \equiv P'}{P \longmapsto P'}$$

that hold for all three variants π_m, π_s, and π_a. The operational semantics of J is given by the heating and cooling rules (see structural congruence) and the reduction rule $J \triangleright P \vdash \sigma_{rv}(J) \longmapsto J \triangleright P \vdash \sigma_{rv}(P)$, where σ_{rv} substitutes the transmitted names for the distinct received variables.

We distinguish between *dynamic* and *static* operators. Intuitively, dynamic operators define terms that can perform steps, while static operators define connections between terms and side conditions on the reductions of their respective subterms. Moreover, we denote the parts of a term that are removed in reduction steps as *capabilities*. Usually, the reduction of dynamic operators is described by the axioms of the reduction semantics, while the remaining inference rules and the structural congruence describe the interplay with static operators. Accordingly, the dynamic operators of the above calculi are prefix and choice, because these operators are removed in the axioms of the respective reductions semantics, while 0, $\checkmark$, parallel composition, restriction, and replication are static operators. Note that we consider the definition operator of the join-calculus as dynamic, because e.g. a reduction of def $J \triangleright P'$ in P copies the elementary definition $J \triangleright P'$ and removes J if P contains the required outputs.

Furthermore, we distinguish between operators that allow for reductions of their subterms and those that require to be reduced first. We denote an operator as *guard* if at least one of its subterms cannot be used to perform a step before the guard itself is reduced. Its subterm(s) that cannot perform steps before the guard is reduced are denoted as *guarded* subterms. The other subterms, if there are any, as well as the subterms of operators that are not guards are denoted as *unguarded* subterms. Guards model sequential behaviour. To our intuition a purely sequential component cannot be cut into pieces to occupy different locations. Hence guarded subterms are not distributable until their guards are removed. However, there are process calculi, as the join-calculus, where a single operator combines different needs and guards only some of its subterms. Section 3 explains how we deal with such operators in the definition of distributability.

The capabilities of the pi-calculus are the prefixes, where the capability of a choice is the conjunction of the prefixes of all its branches—considered as single capability. Prefixes and thus also choice are guards, and all their subterms are guarded. The capabilities of the join-calculus are outputs and (compositions of) reception pattern, where the capability of a definition def D in P is the conjunction of all compositions of reception patterns in D. In def $(J_1 \triangleright P_1) \wedge \ldots \wedge (J_n \triangleright P_n)$ in P the subterms $P_1, \ldots, P_n$ are guarded while P is an unguarded subterm. Reception patterns are matched against outputs in order to instantiate and unguard an instance of a guarded subterm. Note that the distinction into static and dynamic operators, guards, and capabilities are decisions made with the design of a process calculus. We use guards and capabilities to define distributability in Section 3. Hence, we require that all process calculi explicitly distinguish their guards, guarded subterms, and capabilities.

Replication or recursion can be provided by dynamic or static operators, e.g. def D in P in J is a dynamic and $!P$ in π_m a static operator. Also the semantics can be given by a reduction rule or a rule of structural congruence. In both cases, recursion or replication distinguishes itself from other operators by the fact that (one of) its subterms can be copied within rules of structural congruence or by reduction rules while the operator itself is usually never removed during reductions. We call such operators and capabilities *recurrent*.

In order to formalise the identification of sequential components, we assume for each process calculus a so-called *labelling* on the capabilities of processes. The labelling has to ensure that (1) each capability has a label (2) no label occurs more than once in a labelled term, (3) a label disappears only when the corresponding capability is reduced in a reduction step, and (4), once it has disappeared, it will not appear in the execution any more. A labelling method that satisfies these conditions for processes of the pi-calculus is presented in [4] (cf. [20]). Note that such a labelling can be derived from the syntax tree of processes. We require that, once the labelling of a term is fixed, the labels are preserved by the rules of structural congruence as well as by the reduction semantics of the respective calculus. Because of recurrent operators, new subterms with fresh labels for their capabilities may arise from applications of structural congruence or reduction rules. Since we need the labels only to distinguish syntactically similar components of a term, and to track them alongside reductions, we do not restrict the domain of the labels nor the method used to obtain them as long as the resulting labelling satisfies the above properties for all terms and all their derivatives in the respective calculus. Due to space constraints, and in order not to clutter the development with the details of labelling, we prefer to argue at the corresponding informal level. More precisely, we assume that **all** processes in the following are implicitly labelled. Remember that we need these labels only to distinguish between syntactical equivalent capabilities, e.g. to distinguish between the left and the right $\overline{y}$ in $\overline{y} \mid \overline{y}$.

2.1   Encodings and Quality Criteria

Let $\mathcal{L}_S = \langle\, \mathcal{P}_S, \longmapsto_S \,\rangle$ and $\mathcal{L}_T = \langle\, \mathcal{P}_T, \longmapsto_T \,\rangle$ be two process calculi, denoted as *source* and *target language*. An *encoding* from $\mathcal{L}_S$ into $\mathcal{L}_T$ is a function $[\![\, \cdot \,]\!] : \mathcal{P}_S \to \mathcal{P}_T$. Encodings often translate single source term steps into a sequence or pomset of target term steps. We call such a sequence or pomset an *emulation* of the corresponding source term step.

To analyse the quality of encodings and to rule out trivial or meaningless encodings, they are augmented with a set of quality criteria. In order to provide a general framework, Gorla in [8] suggests five criteria well suited for language comparison. Accordingly, we consider an encoding to be "good", if it satisfies the following conditions:

(1) *Compositionality*: The translation of an operator **op** is the same for all occurrences of that operator in a term, i.e., it can be captured by a context.

(2) *Name Invariance*: The encoding does not depend on particular names.

(3) *Operational Correspondence*: Every computation of a source term can be emulated by its translation, i.e., $S \Longmapsto_S S'$ implies $[\![\, S \,]\!] \Longmapsto_T \asymp [\![\, S' \,]\!]$ (completeness), and every computation of a target term corresponds to some computation of the corresponding source term (soundness).

(4) *Divergence Reflection*: The encoding does not introduce divergence.

(5) *Success Sensitiveness*: A source term and its encoding answer the tests for success in exactly the same way, i.e., $S \Downarrow_\checkmark$ iff $[\![S]\!] \Downarrow_\checkmark$.

Note that the second criterion is not necessary to derive the separation results of this paper. Also note that a behavioural equivalence $\asymp$ on the target language is assumed for the definition of name invariance and operational correspondence. Its purpose is to describe the abstract behaviour of a target process, where abstract refers to the behaviour of the source term. By [8] the equivalence $\asymp$ is often defined in the form of a barbed equivalence (as described e.g. in [15]) or can be derived directly from the reduction semantics and is often a congruence, at least with respect to parallel composition. We require only that $\asymp$ is a weak reduction bisimulation, i.e., for all $T_1, T_2 \in \mathcal{P}_T$ such that $T_1 \asymp T_2$, for all $T_1 \Longmapsto_T T_1'$ there exists a T_2' such that $T_2 \Longmapsto_T T_2'$ and $T_1' \asymp T_2'$.

We choose may-testing to instantiate the test for success in success sensitiveness, i.e., $P \Downarrow_\checkmark$, if it is reducible to a process containing a top-level unguarded occurrence of $\checkmark$. However, as we claim, this choice is not crucial. We have $\mathsf{n}(\checkmark) = \mathsf{fn}(\checkmark) = \mathsf{bn}(\checkmark) = \emptyset$. Moreover, we write $P \Downarrow_{\checkmark!}$, if P reaches success in every finite maximal execution. Note that success sensitiveness only links the behaviours of source terms and their literal translations, but not of their derivatives. To do so, Gorla relates success sensitiveness and operational correspondence by requiring that the equivalence on the target language never relates two processes with different success behaviours, i.e., $P \Downarrow_\checkmark$ and $Q \not\Downarrow_\checkmark$ implies $P \not\asymp Q$.

3 Distributability

Within this section, we discuss and fix the notions of distributability and preservation of distributability in the context of process calculi. Intuitively, a distribution of a process means the extraction (or: separation) of its (sequential) components and their association to different locations. However, we do not consider locations explicitly; we just focus on the possible division of a process term into components. Accordingly, a process P is *distributable into* $P_1, \ldots, P_n$, if we find some distribution that extracts $P_1, \ldots, P_n$ from within P onto different locations. Preservation of distributability then means that the target term is at least as distributable as the source term.

3.1 Distributable Processes

The most important operator to implement distributability is the parallel operator. Indeed we consider distributability as a special case of parallel composition with a stricter notion of independence, which becomes visible if we compare calculi. So, first of all, two subterms are distributable if they are parallel.

Unfortunately, the converse of that statement—two subterms are not distributable if they are not parallel—is usually not true. The main reason for this is scoping of names. Consider for example the term $(\nu x)(P \mid Q)$ in the pi-calculus. Although the outermost operator is not the parallel operator, the processes

P and Q are nonetheless distributable. More precisely, for all considered variants of the pi-calculus, two subterms are distributable if they are (modulo $\equiv$) composed in parallel under some restrictions; see the notion of *standard form* of the pi-calculus [13]. Hence, (1) we consider distributability modulo structural congruence, and (2) we allow to remove toplevel restrictions and parallel operators to separate the distributable components.

In the case of the join-calculus, the situation is worse. Again, the problematic operator is responsible for scoping of names. But in the case of the join-calculus scoping is realised by definitions that at the same time represent the input capabilities of the calculus. Consider the term $R = \mathsf{def}\, a \triangleright 0 \,\mathsf{in}\, (\mathsf{def}\, b \triangleright c \langle a \rangle \,\mathsf{in}\, (a \mid b))$. It is constructed of two nested definitions. Intuitively, it represents the combination of the two processes $\mathsf{def}\, a \triangleright 0 \,\mathsf{in}\, a$ and $\mathsf{def}\, b \triangleright c \langle a \rangle \,\mathsf{in}\, b$ but, because of $c \langle a \rangle$, we cannot get rid of the nesting of the definitions—not even modulo structural congruence. The best we can achieve is $R \equiv \mathsf{def}\, a \triangleright 0 \,\mathsf{in}\, ((\mathsf{def}\, b \triangleright c \langle a \rangle \,\mathsf{in}\, b) \mid a)$. Note that $\mathsf{def}\, b \triangleright c \langle a \rangle \,\mathsf{in}\, b$ is not guarded within R. Because of that, the cooling and heating rules, which model structural congruence of the join-calculus, allow us to derive $\vdash R \rightleftharpoons b \triangleright c \langle a \rangle \vdash \mathsf{def}\, a \triangleright 0 \,\mathsf{in}\, a, b$ as well as $\vdash R \rightleftharpoons a \triangleright 0 \vdash \mathsf{def}\, b \triangleright c \langle a \rangle \,\mathsf{in}\, b, a$. This reason is enough for us to consider $\mathsf{def}\, a \triangleright 0 \,\mathsf{in}\, a$ and $\mathsf{def}\, b \triangleright c \langle a \rangle \,\mathsf{in}\, b$ as distributable within R. Formally, each J-term J is distributable into the terms $J_1, \ldots, J_n \in \mathsf{J}$ if, for all $1 \leq i \leq n$, there exists some multisets $\mathcal{R}, \mathcal{M}$ such that $\vdash J \rightleftharpoons \mathcal{R} \vdash J_i, \mathcal{M}$ and there are no two capabilities in $J_1, \ldots, J_n$ with the same label. Note that we can define structural congruence for all process calculi by a chemical abstract machine, but that this kind of special consideration is only necessary because definitions in the join-calculus are guards that have unguarded subterms. Hence, we assume that, (at least) for all process calculi that contain a guard with unguarded subterms, structural congruence is given by a chemical abstract machine.

Note that this example on the join-calculus illuminates that we consider distributability as an irreversible predicate. There is no possibility to restore from a given set of distributable components the original process term, because by the separation of the components we irreversibly loose their original connections. Thus, we cannot beyond doubt conclude that the terms $\mathsf{def}\, a \triangleright 0 \,\mathsf{in}\, a$ and $\mathsf{def}\, b \triangleright c \langle a \rangle \,\mathsf{in}\, b$ originally belong to R. Similarly, we cannot conclude that the terms P and Q were originally subterms of the pi-calculus term $(\nu x)\,(P \mid Q)$, because we lost the information about the restriction. However, these lost information, i.e., the connections between distributable components in the original term, are already captured by the other criteria on the quality of an encoding.

Another important observation is that, because of $!P \equiv P \mid !P$, different copies of a recursive term are distributable in the pi-calculus, whereas there is no such $\equiv$-rule for definitions in the join-calculus. This reflects a fundamental design decision in the join-calculus, namely that the receptors of a given channel are forced to reside at the same location [7,12]. Note that this design decision marks the main difference between the join-calculus and the asynchronous pi-calculus. Accordingly, we require that this design decision is made explicit within the structural congruence of the calculus. A recurrent operator is called distributable if such a $\equiv$-rule is provided and, otherwise, as not distributable, i.e., $!P$ is distributable but J-term definitions are not distributable.

Definition 3 (Distributability). *Let* $\langle\, \mathcal{P}, \longmapsto \,\rangle$ *be a process calculus,* $\equiv$ *be its structural congruence, and* $P \in \mathcal{P}$. P *is* distributable *into* $P_1, \ldots, P_n \in \mathcal{P}$ *if there exists* $P' \in \mathcal{P}$ *with* $P' \equiv P$ *such that*

1. *for all* $1 \leq i \leq n$, P_i *contains at least one capability or constant different from* 0 *and* P_i *is an unguarded subterm of* P' *or, in case* $\equiv$ *is given by a chemical approach,* $\vdash P' \rightleftharpoons \mathcal{R} \vdash P_i, \mathcal{M}$ *for some multisets* $\mathcal{R}, \mathcal{M}$,
2. *in* $P_1, \ldots, P_n$ *there are no two occurrences of the same capability, i.e., no label occurs twice, and*
3. *each guarded subterm and each constant (different from* 0) *of* P' *is a subterm of at least one of the terms* $P_1, \ldots, P_n$.

The degree of distributability *of* P *is the maximal number of distributable subterms of* P.

Hence, we can split a process into its sequential components or larger subterms, e.g. each term is distributable into itself. This allows us to analyse the behaviour of distributable subterms. Note that we do not allow to distribute the empty process, because otherwise usually every process is distributable into infinitely many empty processes. The same holds for subterms not containing any capability or constant different from 0, as e.g. in the term $0 \mid 0$. Of course, $!P$ is distributable into arbitrary many copies of P (and one $!P$). However, since none of the later counterexamples contains replication, this decision is not crucial.

Hence a pi-term P is distributable into $P_1, \ldots, P_n$ if $P \equiv (\nu\tilde{a})\,(P_1 \mid \ldots \mid P_n)$. The $\mathcal{P}_{\mathrm{J}}$-term $\mathsf{def}\, a \vartriangleright 0\, \mathsf{in}\, (\mathsf{def}\, b \vartriangleright c\,\langle a\rangle\, \mathsf{in}\, (a \mid b))$ is distributable into $\mathsf{def}\, a \vartriangleright 0\, \mathsf{in}\, a$ and $\mathsf{def}\, b \vartriangleright c\,\langle a\rangle\, \mathsf{in}\, b$, but e.g. also into $\mathsf{def}\, a \vartriangleright 0\, \mathsf{in}\, 0$, $\mathsf{def}\, b \vartriangleright c\,\langle a\rangle\, \mathsf{in}\, 0$, a, and b, because $\vdash \mathsf{def}\, a \vartriangleright 0\, \mathsf{in}\, (\mathsf{def}\, b \vartriangleright c\,\langle a\rangle\, \mathsf{in}\, (a \mid b)) \rightleftharpoons \mathsf{def}\, a\, \mathsf{in}\, 0, \mathsf{def}\, b\, \mathsf{in}\, c\,\langle a\rangle \vdash a \mid b \rightleftharpoons \mathsf{def}\, a\, \mathsf{in}\, 0, \mathsf{def}\, b\, \mathsf{in}\, c\,\langle a\rangle \vdash a, b \rightleftharpoons \vdash \mathsf{def}\, a \vartriangleright 0\, \mathsf{in}\, 0, \mathsf{def}\, b \vartriangleright c\,\langle a\rangle\, \mathsf{in}\, 0, a, b$.

3.2 Preservation of Distributability

Note that an encoding can always trivially ensure that the encoding has at least as much distributable components by introducing new subterms without any behaviour. Hence, it does not suffice to reason only about the degree of distributability, i.e., about the number of distributable components. Instead we require that the encodings of distributable source term parts and their corresponding parts in the encoding are related by $\asymp$. By doing so we relate the definition of the preservation of distributability to operational completeness, i.e., a semantical criterion that ensures the preservation of the behaviour of the source term (part). We require that each target term part has to be able to emulate at least all behaviour of the respective source part. As a side effect we require that whenever a part of a source term can solve a task independently of the other parts—i.e., it can reduce on its own—then the respective part of its encoding must also be able to emulate this reduction independently of the rest of the encoded term. This reflects the intuition that distribution adds some additional requirements on the independence of parallel terms.

Definition 4 (Preservation of Distributability). *An encoding $[\![\cdot]\!] : \mathcal{P}_S \to \mathcal{P}_T$ preserves distributability if for every $S \in \mathcal{P}_S$ and for all terms $S_1, \ldots, S_n \in \mathcal{P}_S$ that are distributable within S there are some $T_1, \ldots, T_n \in \mathcal{P}_T$ that are distributable within $[\![S]\!]$ such that $T_i \asymp [\![S_i]\!]$ for all $1 \leq i \leq n$.*

In essence, this requirement is a distributability-enhanced adaptation of operational completeness. It respects both the intuition on distribution as separation on different locations—an encoded source term is at least as distributable as the source term itself—as well as the intuition on distribution as independence of processes and their executions—implemented by $T_i \asymp [\![S_i]\!]$.

To ensure that the new criterion is not in conflict with the framework of Gorla, it suffices to show the existence of encodings that satisfy all six criteria. Such encodings are presented in [16] and [19]. Moreover, [19] shows that in case of the pi-calculus every good encoding that translates the parallel operator and restriction homomorphically and preserves structural congruence also preserves distributability. Not surprisingly, the most crucial requirement here is the homomorphic translation of the parallel operator. However, this holds only in case of process calculi as the pi-calculus, where distributable terms can be separated modulo $\equiv$ by parallel operators.

Thus, the (semantic) criterion formalised in Definition 4 can be considered to be at most as hard as the (syntactic) criterion on the homomorphic translation of the parallel operator. To see that it is not an equivalent requirement, but indeed strictly weaker, [19] refers to an encoding from π_m (without replication) into π_a^2, the asynchronous pi-calculus augmented with a two-level polyadic synchronisation by Carbone and Maffeis [5]. This encoding is good and preserves distributability but it does not translate the parallel operator homomorphically. Moreover, [5] proves that there is no good encoding from π_m into π_a^2 that translates the parallel operator homomorphically; this separation result does not rely on replication, i.e., it also implies that there is no such encoding from π_m without replication into π_a^2.

3.3 Distributable Reductions

As discussed above, the criterion in Definition 4 requires not only the preservation of the distributability of processes but also the preservation of the distributability of steps or executions of the respective distributable processes. In order to obtain an alternative way to prove the preservation of distributability, we make this intuition explicit. More precisely, we show that an operationally complete encoding that preserves distributability always also preserves the distributability between sequences of source term steps. To do so, we define first what it means for two steps or executions to be distributable.

If a single process—of an arbitrary process calculus—can perform two different steps, i.e., steps on capabilities with different labels, then we call these steps alternative to each other. Two alternative steps can either be in conflict or not; in the latter case, it is possible to perform both of them in parallel, according to some assumed step semantics.

Definition 5 (Distributable Steps). *Let* $\langle\,\mathcal{P}, \longmapsto\,\rangle$ *be a process calculus and* $P \in \mathcal{P}$ *a process. Two alternative steps of* P *are in* conflict, *if performing one step disables the other step, i.e., if both reduce the same not recurrent capability. Otherwise they are* parallel. *Two parallel steps of* P *are* distributable, *if each recurrent capability reduced by both steps is distributable, else the steps are* local.

Remember that the "same" means "with the same label", i.e., in $\overline{y} \mid y.P_1 \mid y.P_2$ the two steps on y are in conflict but $\overline{y} \mid y.P_1 \mid y.P_2 \mid \overline{y}$ and $\overline{y} \mid !y.P_1 \mid \overline{y}$ can both perform two parallel steps on y. Moreover, the reductions on channel a and b are parallel in $\overline{a} \mid \overline{b} \mid a.P_1 \mid b.P_2$, but they are in conflict in $\overline{a} \mid \overline{b} \mid a.P_1 + b.P_2$, because choice counts as a single capability which is reduced in both steps.

Also note that in contrast to parallel steps, distributable steps can reduce the same recurrent capability only if it is distributable. In many process calculi such as π_a, two steps are distributable iff they are parallel, because all recurrent capabilities are distributable. However, there are also process calculi as J in which these notions indeed refer to quite different situations. Thus, for the comparison with these calculi, their intuitive distinction is useful.

In the join-calculus, two alternative steps that reduce the same definition but do not compete for some output, as e.g. the reduction of $x\langle u \rangle$ and $x\langle v \rangle$ in def $x(z) \triangleright y\langle z \rangle$ in $(x\langle u \rangle \mid x\langle v \rangle)$, can be considered as *parallel* steps; they do not compete for the input capability, because it is recurrent. However, we can *not* consider these two steps as distributable, as this would imply that the definition itself is distributable which—by design—is not intended in J: there is always exactly one receiver for each defined name [7].

Next we define parallel and distributable sequences of steps.

Definition 6 (Distributable Executions). *Let* $\langle\,\mathcal{P}, \longmapsto\,\rangle$ *be a process calculus,* $P \in \mathcal{P}$, *and let* A *and* B *denote two executions of* P. A *and* B *are in* conflict, *if a step of* A *and a step of* B *are in conflict, else* A *and* B *are* parallel.

Two parallel sequences of steps A *and* B *are* distributable, *if each pair of a step of* A *and a step of* B *is distributable.*

In π_a, two sequences of steps A and B of a process P are parallel iff $P \equiv (\nu\tilde{x})\,(P_1 \mid P_2)$ such that P_1 can perform A while P_2 can perform B, i.e., if $A : P \longmapsto P_{A,1} \longmapsto \dots \longmapsto P_{A,n}$ and $B : P \longmapsto P_{B,1} \longmapsto \dots \longmapsto P_{B,m}$ then, for all $1 \leq i \leq n$ and all $1 \leq j \leq m$, there exists $P'_{A,i}, P'_{B,j} \in \mathcal{P}$ such that $P_{A,i} \equiv (\nu\tilde{x})\,(P'_{A,i} \mid P_2)$ and $P_{B,j} \equiv (\nu\tilde{x})\,(P_1 \mid P'_{B,j})$. Again, two sequences of steps are distributable iff they are parallel. Unfortunately, in the join-calculus two processes able to perform parallel sequences of steps cannot always be separated by a parallel operator in this way; even if they do not reduce the same definition. The reason is again the restriction caused by definitions. In the term def $a \triangleright P_1$ in (def $b \triangleright c\langle a \rangle$ in $(a \mid b)$) the reduction of a is independent of the reduction of b. Hence, these two steps are parallel and even distributable. But, because of $c\langle a \rangle$, we cannot get rid of the nesting of these two definitions.

Although the definitions of distributable processes in Definition 3 and distributable executions in Definition 6 are quite different, they are closely related. Two executions of a term P are distributable iff P is distributable into two

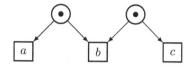

Fig. 1. A fully reachable pure M in Petri nets

subterms such that each performs one of these executions. Hence, an operationally complete encoding is distributability-preserving only if it preserves the distributability of sequences of source term steps. The proofs of this and the following results can be found in [20].

Lemma 1 (Distributability-Preservation). *An operationally complete encoding $[\![\cdot]\!] : \mathcal{P}_S \to \mathcal{P}_T$ that preserves distributability also preserves distributability of executions, i.e., for all source terms $S \in \mathcal{P}_S$ and all sets of pairwise distributable executions of S, there exists an emulation of each execution in this set such that all these emulations are pairwise distributable in $[\![S]\!]$.*

4   Separation by the Synchronisation Pattern M

[24] analyses the possibility to implement a (synchronous) Petri net specification within an asynchronous setting. They find a semi-structural property called M that distinguishes distributable Petri nets from those nets that may only under additional assumptions on the underlying system structure be implemented in a fully asynchronous and distributed setting.

An M, as visualised in Figure 1, describes a Petri net that consists of two parallel transitions and one transition that is in conflict with both of the former. In other words, it describes a situation where either two parts of the net can proceed independently or they synchronise to perform a single transition together. We denote such descriptions of special situations of synchronisation as *synchronisation pattern*. [24,25] states that a Petri net specification can be implemented in an asynchronous, fully distributed setting iff it does not contain a fully reachable pure M. Accordingly, they denote such Petri nets as distributable. They also present a description of a fully reachable pure M as a property of a step transition system which allows us to directly use this pattern to reason about process calculi.

A first analysis shows that we find the M also in the asynchronous pi-calculus (see Example 1 below). This reflects earlier observations in [12]: it is not possible to implement the pi-calculus and even its asynchronous fragment in an asynchronous and fully distributed setting. To overcome these problems the join-calculus was introduced as a model of distributed computation [7,12]. Mutual encodings between the (core) join-calculus and the asynchronous pi-calculus have shown that they have the same expressive power [7]. Here, we show a difference with respect to the degree of distributability. Hence, we explain what exactly distinguishes both calculi. It turns out that this distinction is well described by the synchronisation pattern M, i.e., what distinguishes the asynchronous pi-calculus and the join-calculus is the ability to express conflicts between distributable steps. This lack in expressiveness in turn allows fully distributed implementations of the join-calculus.

4.1   The Synchronisation Pattern M

If we compare the asynchronous pi-calculus and the join-calculus, the most obvious difference is that in J any channel can appear only once in input position. As a consequence, two conflicting steps in the join-calculus can only compete for different output messages but not for different input capabilities, as it is the case in π_a. Repeating this argument, all steps of a chain of conflicting steps in the join-calculus are tied to the same definition, i.e., are not distributable.

Lemma 2. *For all $P \in \mathcal{P}_J$ and all lists $S = [s_1, \ldots, s_n]$ of steps of P such that for all $1 \le i < n$ the step s_i is in conflict with the step s_{i+1}, all steps in S are pairwise local and reduce the same definition.*

In contrast, in π_a, it is very easy to find such a list of conflicting steps of which some are distributable, by combining conflicts on outputs and inputs.

Example 1. Consider $P = \overline{y}\langle u \rangle \mid y(x).P_1 \mid \overline{y}\langle v \rangle \mid y(x).P_2$ with $P \in \mathcal{P}_a$. P can perform four different alternative steps modulo structural congruence:

$$P \longmapsto \{ u/x \} P_1 \mid \overline{y}\langle v \rangle \mid y(x).P_2 \tag{s_1}$$

$$P \longmapsto y(x).P_1 \mid \overline{y}\langle v \rangle \mid \{ u/x \} P_2 \tag{s_2}$$

$$P \longmapsto \overline{y}\langle u \rangle \mid y(x).P_1 \mid \{ v/x \} P_2 \tag{s_3}$$

$$P \longmapsto \overline{y}\langle u \rangle \mid \{ v/x \} P_1 \mid y(x).P_2 \tag{s_4}$$

The step s_1 is in conflict with step s_2, since both compete for the first output $\overline{y}\langle u \rangle$. Similarly, step s_2 and s_3 compete for the second input $y(x).P_2$, and step s_3 and step s_4 compete for the second output, i.e., P has a chain $S = [s_1, \ldots, s_4]$ of conflicting steps. But s_1 and s_3 as well as s_2 and s_4 are distributable in P.

Thus, the ability to express distributable conflicts separates the asynchronous pi-calculus from the join-calculus. However, the preservation of distributability in Definition 4 does not require to preserve the distributability of conflicts but only of processes and their executions. On the other side, the structure used in [24] to identify distributable Petri nets strongly relies on the notion of conflict. More precisely, an M arises from the combination of two parallel steps and a third step that is in conflict with both of the former.

Definition 7 (Synchronisation Pattern M). *Let $\langle \mathcal{P}, \longmapsto \rangle$ be a process calculus and $P \in \mathcal{P}$ such that:*
1. *P can perform at least three alternative reduction steps $a : P \longmapsto P_a$, $b : P \longmapsto P_b$, and $c : P \longmapsto P_c$ such that P_a, P_b, and P_c are pairwise different.*
2. *Moreover, the steps a and c are parallel in P.*
3. *But b is in conflict with both a and c.*

In this case, we denote the process P as M. *If the steps a and c are distributable in P, then we call the* M *non-local. Otherwise, the* M *is called* local.

We observe, that the P of Example 1 represents a *non-local* M in π_a, because we can choose the step s_1 as a, s_2 as b, and s_3 as c. In contrast, the term $Q = $ def $x\,(z) \mid y\,(z') \triangleright z\,\langle z' \rangle$ in $(x\,\langle u \rangle \mid x\,\langle v \rangle \mid y\,\langle u \rangle \mid y\,\langle v \rangle)$ is a *local* M in the (core) join-calculus. Indeed, all M in the join-calculus are local, because, by Lemma 2, the step b forces its conflicting counterparts to reduce the same definition.

Lemma 3. *All* M *in the join-calculus are local.*

Thus, the asynchronous pi-calculus and the join-calculus do also differ by the ability to express a non-local M. As described in [24], a language that cannot express a non-local M can be considered as distributable. Accordingly, as intended by its design, the join-calculus is distributable. We show that the pi-calculus is not distributable—not even in its asynchronous and choice-free fragment.

4.2   Distributability of the Pi-calculus

To show that the examined difference forbids distributability-preserving encodings, we have to show that it is not possible to express the abstract behaviour of all non-local M in the join-calculus with respect to our requirements on good and distributability-preserving encodings. We use the M of Example 1 as running counterexample S. In the framework of Gorla, source terms and their encodings are compared by their ability to reach success. To distinguish the conflicting step $b = s_2$ from the parallel steps $a = s_1$ and $c = s_3$, we instantiate P_1 with $\overline{x}$, P_2 with $\overline{x} \mid \overline{x}$, and place the observer $O = u.v.v.\checkmark$ in parallel to P. Hence,

$$S = (\overline{y}\langle u \rangle \mid y(x)\,.\overline{x}) \mid (\overline{y}\langle v \rangle \mid y(x)\,.\,(\overline{x} \mid \overline{x}) \mid u.v.v.\checkmark) \qquad (\text{E1})$$

reaches success iff S performs both of the distributable steps a and c. Note that any good encoding that preserves distributability has to translate E1 such that the emulations of the steps a and c are again distributable. However, the encoding can translate these two steps into sequences of steps, which allows to emulate the conflicts with the emulation of b by two different distributable steps. We show that every distributability-preserving encoding has to distribute b and, afterwards, that this distribution of b violates the criteria of a good encoding.

Lemma 4. *Every encoding $[\![\cdot]\!] : \mathcal{P}_a \to \mathcal{P}_J$ that is good (except for compositionality) and distributability-preserving has to split up the conflict in S given by E1 of b with a and c such that there exists a maximal execution in $[\![S]\!]$ in which a is emulated but not c, and vice versa.*

Lemma 4 describes a partial deadlock. If the emulation of b and with it the conflicts with the emulation of a and c are distributed, the encoded term can make the wrong decision and, thus, result in one successful emulation (of a or c) but two deadlocked emulation attempts of the respective other two steps. Since there is no maximal execution of E1 with a but not c (or vice versa), such an encoding cannot be considered as a good encoding. In the setting used so far, we cannot observe the difference in the abstract behaviour of E1 and $[\![\, E1 \,]\!]$.

One reason is the weak requirements on $\asymp$. A success respecting bisimulation, in its simplest case, cannot distinguish between more than three different cases: success is not reachable, success is always reachable, and success is reachable in some but not all maximal executions. To prove non-existence of distribution-preserving encodings it suffices to require that $\asymp$ is not trivial, e.g. by requiring that it distinguishes more than two observables. In this case, we have to modify E1, i.e., choose a suitable instantiation of P_1, P_2, and the observer, such that $[\![\, S_a \,]\!]$, $[\![\, S_b \,]\!]$, $[\![\, S_c \,]\!]$, and $[\![\, S_{ac} \,]\!]$ are pairwise distinguished by $\asymp$, where S_{ac} is the result of performing a and c in S. Then, the maximal execution that emulates a but not c contradicts operational correspondence. Note that in this case we do not need compositionality at all.

Another way is to make use of compositionality. Remember that the best known encoding from the asynchronous pi-calculus into the join-calculus in [7] is not compositional, but consists of an inner, compositional encoding surrounded by a fixed context—the implementation of so-called firewalls—that is parametrised on the free names of the source term. Actually, it is this surrounding context that reduces the degree of distributability, because different steps on the same channel name have to synchronise on a firewall. The following result captures this and similar encodings.

Theorem 1. *There is no good and distributability-preserving encoding from π_a into J. There is no distributability-preserving encoding from π_a into J that is good except for compositionality but consists of an inner compositional encoding surrounded by a fixed context parametrised on the free names of the source term.*

4.3 Distributability in Other Calculi

Above, first an absolute result, i.e., a result that refers to the properties of a single language, is derived in Lemma 2. It clarifies which property distinguishes the source and the target language, i.e., the reason why the target language does not contain the synchronisation pattern M. Then, the existence of the M in the source language is shown by an example, which is subsequently used as counterexample. Lemma 4 uses properties of the target language—basically the absolute result in Lemma 2—to show that any encoding has to split the conflict in the counterexample. Finally, Theorem 1 reasons about some properties of the source language to show that the split of the conflict in the encoded counterexample violates the criteria of a good encoding. This argumentation provides a guideline for similar considerations in other languages.

Note that the synchronisation pattern does not only describe the difference between two languages as an abstraction of a particular situation of synchronisation but it also serves as an abstract description of the properties of the counterexample. This allows us to separate more clearly between the argumentation for the source and the target language in the above proofs. Hence, to change the source language it usually suffices to find an example with the properties required by the synchronisation pattern. In case of the target language we have to revise the absolute result and Lemma 4, i.e., we have to show why the new target language can not express the synchronisation pattern modulo the criteria required on an encoding. As example, we exhibit a separation between two simple variants of CSP in [20,18]. The splitting of arguments on the source and the target languages simplifies also the comparison of multiple languages, because not every pair has to be checked.

5 Another Synchronisation Pattern

In the last section we compare different process calculi by their ability to express the synchronisation pattern M. We learn that the different synchronisation mechanisms of the calculi lead to differences in the expressive power with respect to specific kinds of conflicts. By [17,8,21,19], we also know that the restriction in the choice operator leads to a separation result between π_m and π_s. However, in [17] and [8] the homomorphic translation of the parallel operator was used to derive this separation result and in [21,19] the proof was unsatisfactory, because it reveals not much intuition on why the counterexamples lead to the difference. In order to provide more intuition on this separation result and on the difference in the expressive power of π_m and π_s with respect to conflicts, we show that the calculi can be distinguished by a new synchronisation pattern similar to the M. Not surprisingly, the new pattern combines again conflicting and distributable steps. Interestingly, it reflects a well-known standard problem in the area of distributed systems, namely the problem of the dining philosophers [6].

We start with a simple observation on the asynchronous pi-calculus. Without choice each reduction step reduces exactly one output and one input. So all conflicts in π_a are on steps on the same link. With separate choice a single step can reduce more than a single out- or input. But if we consider steps between two distributable subprocesses then each reduction step reduces only outputs in one subprocess and only inputs in the other. As a consequence, a chain of conflicting steps can build an M by alternating input and output capabilities as visualised in Example 1. But, by this method, no circle of odd length can be constructed as it is represented by the synchronisation pattern $\star$.

Definition 8 (Synchronisation Pattern $\star$). *Let $\langle\,\mathcal{P}, \longmapsto\,\rangle$ be a process calculus and $P \in \mathcal{P}$ such that:*

1. *P can perform at least five alternative reduction steps $i : P \longmapsto P_i$ for $i \in \{\,a,b,c,d,e\,\}$ such that the P_i are pairwise different.*
2. *Moreover, the steps a, b, c, d, and e form a circle such that a is in conflict with b, b is in conflict with c, c is in conflict with d, d is in conflict with e, and e is in conflict with a. Finally,*
3. *every pair of steps in $\{\,a,b,c,d,e\,\}$ that is not in conflict is parallel in P.*

In this case, we denote the process P as $\star$. The synchronisation pattern $\star$ is visualised by the Petri net in Figure 2. If all pairs of parallel steps in $\{\,a,b,c,d,e\,\}$ are distributable in P, then we call the $\star$ non-local. Otherwise, it is called local.

Note that in the pi-calculus every $\star$ and every M is non-local. To see the connection with the dining philosophers problem, consider the places in Figure 2 as the

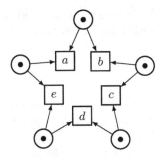

Fig. 2. The Synchronisation Pattern $\star$ in Petri nets

chopsticks of the philosophers, i.e., as resources, and the transitions as eating operations, i.e., as steps consuming resources. Each step needs mutually exclusive access to two resources and each resource is shared among two subprocesses. If both resources are allocated simultaneously, eventually exactly two steps are performed. As shown in the following, a fully distributable implementation of that pattern requires the expressive power of mixed choice.

By Example 1 we know that π_s can express distributable conflicts, but π_s cannot express a circle of such conflicts that is of odd degree greater than four as it is depicted by $\star$. Note that smaller circles do not have parallel, i.e., distributable, steps. Hence, $\star$ represents the smallest example of the problematic structure but separation can principally be proved for any such structure of odd degree and at least five steps. The main argument is that π_s can build chains of conflicts by alternating conflicts between output and input capabilities, but without mixed choice no cycle of odd degree can be obtained this way.

Lemma 5. *There is no $\star$ in π_s.*

In contrast to π_s, π_m can express the synchronisation pattern $\star$ as the example

$$S = \overline{a} + b.S_1 \mid \overline{b} + c.S_2 \mid \overline{c} + d.S_3 \mid \overline{d} + e.S_4 \mid \overline{e} + a.S_5 \qquad \text{(E3)}$$

shows. We use this example as counterexample. Similar to Section 4.2, we show that each encoding of the counterexample requires that at least one conflict has to be distributed and that this violates the requirements on a good encoding.

Theorem 2. *No good encoding from π_m into π_s preserves distributability.*

Note that we could derive the same result if, as in Section 4.2, we allow for a not compositional encoding that consists of an inner compositional encoding surrounded by a fixed context parametrised on the free names of the source term. Moreover, since the synchronisation pattern $\star$ includes the pattern M—more precisely it consists of three cyclic overlapping M—separation results derived on these two patterns (with respect to the same quality criteria) automatically lead to a lattice. Here, by Theorem 1 and Theorem 2, no good encoding from π_m into J preserves distributability.

Also note, that the E3 is in fact a CCS-term. Hence, we can apply the same line of argument to show separation between the corresponding variants of CCS.

Moreover, we can show that there is no good and distributability-preserving encoding from π_a into CCS with mixed choice.

6   Conclusion

As main contributions, we (1) propose a new criterion to reason about the degree of distribution which is better suited than the common homomorphic translation of the parallel operator. Then, (2) we present a new separation result that clarifies the difference between the asynchronous pi-calculus and the join-calculus. Moreover, we (3) show that the proof method of this result is in general well suited to reason about the expressive power of synchronisation mechanisms by discussing how it can be transferred with little effort to compare other source and target languages (cf. [20,18]). And (4) we present two generally formulated synchronisation patterns that expose the power of different synchronisation mechanisms in the pi-calculus family but can be used in a similar manner to reason about and to classify synchronisation mechanisms in other process calculi.

Note that [16] presents a good encoding from π_s into π_a that translates the parallel operator homomorphically, i.e., that preserves distributability. Moreover, [7,19] present good (but not distributability-preserving) encodings between J and π_a, and from π_m into π_a. Combining these positive results and the new separation results on the two synchronisation patterns, we obtain a hierarchy of distributability between pi-like calculi. The synchronous pi-calculus (π_m), the asynchronous pi-calculus (π_a), and the join-calculus (J) all have the same abstract expressive power, but there exists no good and distributability-preserving encoding from π_m into π_a, and neither from π_a into J.

Of course we do not believe that these two patterns already capture all kinds of synchronisation mechanisms in process calculi. In further research we want to analyse e.g. what kind of synchronisation patterns are expressed by polyadic synchronisation in [5] or by the synchronisation mechanisms described in [11].

In case of separation results, a natural next step to improve the results is to go back to particular distributions in terms, in order to examine the problematic set of distributed terms in the source language. This way a positive result for a sublanguage of the source language can be derived. An exhaustive analysis may even lead to an exact borderline between distributable and not distributable languages. Note that the results in [25] go in this direction for the area of Petri nets. This kind of consideration is beyond the scope of this paper but another interesting topic of further research.

References

1. Berry, G., Boudol, G.: The Chemical Abstract Machine. In: Proc. of POPL. SIGPLAN-SIGACT, pp. 81–94 (1990)
2. Best, E., Darondeau, P.: Petri Net Distributability. In: Clarke, E., Virbitskaite, I., Voronkov, A. (eds.) PSI 2011. LNCS, vol. 7162, pp. 1–18. Springer, Heidelberg (2012)

3. Boudol, G.: Asynchrony and the π-calculus (note). Note, INRIA (1992)
4. Cacciagrano, D., Corradini, F., Palamidessi, C.: Explicit fairness in testing semantics. Logical Methods in Computer Science 5(2), 1–27 (2009)
5. Carbone, M., Maffeis, S.: On the Expressive Power of Polyadic Synchronisation in π-Calculus. Nordic Journal of Computing 10(2), 70–98 (2003)
6. Dijkstra, E.W.: Hierarchical Ordering of Sequential Processes. Acta Informatica 1(2), 115–138 (1971)
7. Fournet, C., Gonthier, G.: The Reflexive CHAM and the Join-Calculus. In: Proc. of POPL. SIGPLAN-SIGACT, pp. 372–385 (1996)
8. Gorla, D.: Towards a Unified Approach to Encodability and Separation Results for Process Calculi. Information and Computation 208(9), 1031–1053 (2010)
9. Hennessy, M.: A Distributed Pi-Calculus. Cambridge University Press (2007)
10. Honda, K., Tokoro, M.: An Object Calculus for Asynchronous Communication. In: America, P. (ed.) ECOOP 1991. LNCS, vol. 512, pp. 133–147. Springer, Heidelberg (1991)
11. Laneve, C., Vitale, A.: The Expressive Power of Synchronizations. In: Proc. of LICS, pp. 382–391 (2010)
12. Lévy, J.-J.: Some Results in the Join-Calculus. In: Ito, T., Abadi, M. (eds.) TACS 1997. LNCS, vol. 1281, pp. 233–249. Springer, Heidelberg (1997)
13. Milner, R.: Communicating and Mobile Systems: The π-Calculus. Cambridge University Press, New York (1999)
14. Milner, R., Parrow, J., Walker, D.: A Calculus of Mobile Processes, Part I and II. Information and Computation 100(1), 1–77 (1992)
15. Milner, R., Sangiorgi, D.: Barbed Bisimulation. In: Kuich, W. (ed.) ICALP 1992. LNCS, vol. 623, pp. 685–695. Springer, Heidelberg (1992)
16. Nestmann, U.: What is a "Good" Encoding of Guarded Choice? Information and Computation 156(1-2), 287–319 (2000)
17. Palamidessi, C.: Comparing the Expressive Power of the Synchronous and the Asynchronous π-calculus. Mathematical Structures in Computer Science 13(5), 685–719 (2003)
18. Peters, K.: Translational Expressiveness. PhD thesis, TU Berlin (2012), http://nbn-resolving.de/urn:nbn:de:kobv:83-opus-37495
19. Peters, K., Nestmann, U.: Is It a "Good" Encoding of Mixed Choice? In: Birkedal, L. (ed.) FOSSACS 2012. LNCS, vol. 7213, pp. 210–224. Springer, Heidelberg (2012)
20. Peters, K., Nestmann, U., Goltz, U.: On Distributability in Process Calculi (Appendix). Technical Report, TU Berlin (2013), http://www.mtv.tu-berlin.de/fileadmin/a3435/pubs/distProcCal.pdf
21. Peters, K., Schicke-Uffmann, J.-W., Nestmann, U.: Synchrony vs Causality in the Asynchronous Pi-Calculus. In: Proc. of EXPRESS. EPTCS, vol. 64, pp. 89–103 (2011)
22. Plotkin, G.D.: A structural approach to operational semantics. Journal of Logic and Algebraic Programming 60, 17–140 (2004); (An earlier version of this paper was published as technical report at Aarhus University in 1981)
23. van Glabbeek, R.: The Linear Time – Branching Time Spectrum I: The Semantics of Concrete, Sequential Processes. Handbook of Process Algebra, 3–99 (2001)
24. van Glabbeek, R., Goltz, U., Schicke, J.-W.: On Synchronous and Asynchronous Interaction in Distributed Systems. In: Ochmański, E., Tyszkiewicz, J. (eds.) MFCS 2008. LNCS, vol. 5162, pp. 16–35. Springer, Heidelberg (2008)
25. van Glabbeek, R., Goltz, U., Schicke-Uffmann, J.-W.: On Distributability of Petri Nets. In: Birkedal, L. (ed.) FOSSACS 2012. LNCS, vol. 7213, pp. 331–345. Springer, Heidelberg (2012)

Behavioral Polymorphism and Parametricity in Session-Based Communication

Luís Caires[1], Jorge A. Pérez[1], Frank Pfenning[2], and Bernardo Toninho[1,2]

[1] CITI and Departamento de Informática, FCT, Universidade Nova de Lisboa
[2] Computer Science Department, Carnegie Mellon University

Abstract. We investigate a notion of behavioral genericity in the context of session type disciplines. To this end, we develop a logically motivated theory of parametric polymorphism, reminiscent of the Girard-Reynolds polymorphic λ-calculus, but casted in the setting of concurrent processes. In our theory, polymorphism accounts for the exchange of abstract communication protocols and dynamic instantiation of heterogeneous interfaces, as opposed to the exchange of data types and dynamic instantiation of individual message types. Our polymorphic session-typed process language satisfies strong forms of type preservation and global progress, is strongly normalizing, and enjoys a relational parametricity principle. Combined, our results confer strong correctness guarantees for communicating systems. In particular, parametricity is key to derive non-trivial results about internal protocol independence, a concurrent analogous of representation independence, and non-interference properties of modular, distributed systems.

1 Introduction

Modern distributed systems are typically conceived as decentralized collections of software artifacts which execute intricate communication protocols. These large-scale systems must meet strict correctness and trustworthiness requirements. Emerging technologies—such as service-oriented computing and subscription-based, cost-sharing platforms (e.g. cloud computing)—promise to be effective towards achieving these goals, while reducing costs and enhancing business agility. They also pose new challenges for system construction: communicating systems should behave properly even when deployed in open, highly dynamic environments, such as third-party infrastructures.

In this communication-oriented context, *genericity*—one of the fundamental principles in software engineering—is a most relevant concern. Indeed, genericity promotes modular protocol specifications, therefore facilitating system verification and evolution/maintenance. It allows for convenient representations of, for instance, families of protocols which differ only in the format of the exchanged messages (as in, e.g., protocols for file distribution which behave correctly independently of the transferred items). This "message genericity" is most useful and appears to be well-understood.

Nevertheless, and partly due to the widespread adoption of technologies such as those hinted at above, distributed systems nowadays exhibit fairly sophisticated incarnations of genericity, which often go well beyond message genericity. Indeed, systems are increasingly generic with respect to *arbitrary communication protocols*, which may be known and instantiated only at runtime. Here we refer to this kind of genericity as *behavioral genericity*; we find it to be a very common concept in several settings:

M. Felleisen and P. Gardner (Eds.): ESOP 2013, LNCS 7792, pp. 330–349, 2013.
© Springer-Verlag Berlin Heidelberg 2013

– *Critical web applications* (such as banking portals) are increasingly being deployed into service-oriented architectures. As such, upgrade actions (e.g., replacing a service provider) often involve the dynamic reconfiguration of communication interfaces/protocols. These changes should be transparent to clients. To this end, web applications should be conceived as generic with respect to such interfaces/protocols.
– *Online application stores* are infrastructures for the distribution of software applications. They should concurrently interact with (i) *developers* willing to add new (i.e. unknown) applications to the store and (ii) *clients* wishing to remotely execute/buy/download available applications. In order to operate securely and reliably, the store needs to be generic with respect to the behavior of clients and applications.
– *Cloud-based services* admit highly dynamic, flexible architectures. In fact, these services are *elastic*, for they acquire computing resources when demand is high, and release them when they are no longer needed. For such scaling policies to be effective, services need to be generic with respect to their underlying coordination protocols, as these may well depend on the system's architecture at a given time.

Many other distributed software systems exhibit forms of behavioral genericity in the context of disciplined, structured communications. Reasoning about these systems and their correctness is extremely hard, essentially because the required abstractions should enforce independence with respect to arbitrary complex behaviors, and not just over messages. Models and techniques for data/message genericity are thus simply inadequate for this task. This calls for novel reasoning techniques, which may effectively support the analysis of behavioral genericity in complex distributed protocols.

Here we rise to this challenge in the context of *session-based concurrency* [17,18], a foundational approach to communication correctness. In session-based concurrency, dialogues between participants are structured into *sessions*, the basic units of communication; interaction patterns are abstracted as *session types*, which are statically checked against specifications. Session types ensure protocols in which actions always occur in dual pairs: when one partner sends, the other receives; when one partner offers a selection, the other chooses; when a session terminates, no further interaction may occur.

In this paper, we develop a session types discipline able to cope with behavioral genericity. Our system includes *impredicative* universal and existential quantification over *sessions*: this results in *parametric polymorphism*—in the sense of the Girard-Reynolds polymorphic λ-calculus [23,13]—defined in a session-based, concurrent setting. In our theory, universal and existential quantification correspond to the input and output of a session type, respectively. As session types may describe arbitrarily complex communication protocols, our theory of polymorphic processes enables an expressive form of *abstract protocol communication*. As a key distinguishing feature, our developments follow naturally from the interpretation of session types as *intuitionistic* linear logic propositions given in [6,7]. This allows us to obtain central technical results for polymorphic, session-typed processes in a remarkably elegant way:

1. Polymorphic processes respect session typed specifications in a deadlock-free way. These two central—and non trivial—correctness guarantees follow from our *type preservation* and *global progress* results (Theorems 1 and 2).
2. Polymorphic processes never engage into infinite internal behavior. In fact, well-typed processes are *strongly normalizing* (Theorem 5). The proof of this important

(and arguably expected) result is via the reducibility candidates technique, by relying on an elegant generalization of the linear logical relations of [20].

3. Polymorphic processes enjoy a principle of *relational parametricity* in the context of a behavioral type theory (Theorem 8). In Section 6, we illustrate how parametricity allows us to formally justify properties of behavioral genericity and representation independence, which in our case means behavioral independence on representation protocols. Parametricity also enables a sound and complete characterization of *typed contextual equivalence* (Theorem 9).

To our knowledge, relational parametricity (in the sense of Reynolds [24]) has not been previously investigated in the context of a rich behavioral type theory for processes, such as session types. In the realm of concurrent processes, genericity via (existential) polymorphism was first investigated by Turner [27], in the context of a simply-typed π-calculus. Berger et al. [1,2] were the first to study a π-calculus with parametric polymorphism based on universal and existential quantification over types. In the setting of session types, support for genericity has been obtained mainly via *bounded polymorphism* [12,10,9], which extends session types with a form of (universal) quantification over types, controlled via subtyping. While useful to reason about protocols with message genericity, bounded polymorphism is insufficient to support behavioral genericity. Recently, Wadler [28] proposed a logic-based session type theory which includes the natural typing rules for second-order quantifiers and may support polymorphism of the kind we consider here; however, no analysis of behavioral genericity is identified. Our results thus provide substantial evidence of how a logically motivated approach offers appropriate, powerful tools for actually reasoning about behavioral genericity in complex protocols. In passing, we establish rather strong connections between well-known foundational results and polymorphically typed concurrent processes.

In the remainder of this introduction, we briefly describe the logical interpretation of [6] and illustrate the potential of our model of polymorphic sessions with an example. Our ongoing research program on logical foundations for session-based concurrency [6,26,21,7,20,8] builds upon an interpretation of intuitionistic linear logical propositions as session types, sequent proofs as π-calculus processes [25], and cut elimination as process communication. In the resulting Curry-Howard correspondence, well-typed processes enjoy strong forms of type preservation and global progress [6,7], and are strongly normalizing [20]. The interpretation endows channel names with types (logic propositions) that describe their session protocol. This way, e.g., an assignment $x{:}A\multimap B$ denotes a session x that first *inputs* a name of type A, and then behaves as type B on x; dually, $x{:}A \otimes B$ denotes a session x that first *outputs* a name of type A and then behaves as type B on x. Other constructors are given compatible interpretations; in particular, $!A$ is the type of a shared server offering sessions of type A. Given a *linear* environment Δ and an *unrestricted* environment Γ, a type judgment in our system is of the form $\Gamma; \Delta \vdash P :: z{:}C$, where Γ, Δ, and $z{:}C$ have pairwise disjoint domains. Such a judgment is intuitively read as: process P offers session C along channel z, provided it is placed in a context providing the sessions declared in Γ and Δ.

Here we uniformly extend the system of [6] with two new kinds of session types, $\forall X.A$ and $\exists X.A$, corresponding to impredicative universal and existential quantification over sessions. As mentioned above, they are interpreted as the input and output of a session type, respectively. As an example, consider the polymorphic session type:

$$\mathsf{CloudServer} \triangleq \forall X.!(\mathsf{api}{\multimap}X){\multimap}!X$$

which represents a simple interface for a *cloud-based application server*. In our theory, this is the session type of a system which first *inputs* an arbitrary type (say GMaps); then inputs a shared service of type api $\multimap$ GMaps. Each instance of this service yields a session that when provided with the implementation of an API will provide a behavior of type GMaps; finally becoming a persistent (shared) server of type GMaps. Our application server is meant to interact with developers who, by building upon the services it offers, implement their own applications. In our framework, the dependency between the cloud server and applications may be expressed by the typing judgment

$$\cdot\,; \; x{:}\mathsf{CloudServer} \vdash \mathit{DrpBox} :: z{:}\mathsf{dbox} \qquad (1)$$

Intuitively, (1) says that to offer behavior dbox on z, the file hosting service represented by process DrpBox relies on a linear behavior described by type CloudServer provided on x (no shared behaviors are required). The rôle of behavioral genericity should be clear from the following observation: to support interaction with developers such as DrpBox—which implement all kinds of behaviors, such as dbox above—any process realizing type CloudServer should necessarily be *generic* on such expected behaviors.

The above example illustrates how the combination of polymorphism and linearity enables very fine-grained specifications of interactive behavior via types. Indeed, as just discussed, impredicative quantification enforces that every cloud server implementation must be agnostic to the specific behavior of the actual applications it will provide, whereas linearity allows us to reason precisely about behavior and session usage (e.g., the only way the server can provide the behavior X is by making use of session api$\multimap X$). In Section 3 we develop this example further, demonstrating how the expressiveness and flexbility of polymorphic session types is captured in process specifications. Then, in Section 6 we illustrate how to exploit parametricity, strong normalization, and other properties of well-typed processes to reason about such specifications. In fact, we show how by merely exploiting the shape of its (polymorphic) type, we are able to analyze the observable behavior of a generic cloud-based server.

For space reasons, most proofs are omitted. An associated technical report [5] gives full technical details, and reports further developments which connect our work with impredicative polymorphism in the functional setting via an encoding of System F.

2   Polymorphic Session Types

We consider a synchronous π-calculus [25] extended with binary guarded choice, channel links, and prefixes for type input/output. The syntax of processes/types is as follows:

Definition 1 (Processes, Session Types). *Given an infinite set Λ of names (x, y, z, u, v), the set of* processes (P, Q, R) *and session types* (A, B, C) *is defined by*

$$P ::= \overline{x}\langle y\rangle.P \;\mid\; x(y).P \;\mid\; !x(y).P \;\mid\; P\mid Q \;\mid\; (\nu y)P \;\mid\; \mathbf{0}$$
$$\mid\; \overline{x}\langle A\rangle.P \;\mid\; x(X).P \;\mid\; x.\mathtt{inl}; P \;\mid\; x.\mathtt{inr}; P \;\mid\; x.\mathtt{case}(P, Q) \;\mid\; [x \leftrightarrow z]$$

$$A ::= \mathbf{1} \;\mid\; A{\multimap}B \;\mid\; A\otimes B \;\mid\; A\,\&\,B \;\mid\; A\oplus B \;\mid\; !A \;\mid\; X \;\mid\; \forall X.A \;\mid\; \exists X.A$$

The guarded choice mechanism and the channel link construct are as in [6,26,20]. Informally, channel links "re-implement" an ambient session on a different channel name, thus defining a renaming operation (see below). Moreover, channel links allow a simple interpretation of the identity rule. Polymorphism is represented by prefixes for input and output of types, denoting the exchange of abstract communication protocols.

We identify processes up to consistent renaming of bound names, writing $\equiv_\alpha$ for this congruence. We write $P\{x/y\}$ for the process obtained from P by capture avoiding substitution of x for y in P, and $fn(P)$ for the free names of P. Session types are directly generated from the language of linear propositions. Structural congruence expresses basic identities on the structure of processes, reduction expresses internal behavior of processes, and labeled transitions define interaction with the environment.

Definition 2. Structural congruence *is the least congruence relation generated by the following laws:* $P \mid \mathbf{0} \equiv P$; $P \equiv_\alpha Q \Rightarrow P \equiv Q$; $P \mid Q \equiv Q \mid P$; $P \mid (Q \mid R) \equiv (P \mid Q) \mid R$; $(\boldsymbol{\nu}x)(\boldsymbol{\nu}y)P \equiv (\boldsymbol{\nu}y)(\boldsymbol{\nu}x)P$; $x \notin fn(P) \Rightarrow P \mid (\boldsymbol{\nu}x)Q \equiv (\boldsymbol{\nu}x)(P \mid Q)$; $(\boldsymbol{\nu}x)\mathbf{0} \equiv \mathbf{0}$; *and* $[x \leftrightarrow y] \equiv [y \leftrightarrow x]$.

Definition 3. Reduction *($P \rightarrow Q$) is the binary relation on processes defined by:*

$$\overline{x}\langle y\rangle.Q \mid x(z).P \rightarrow Q \mid P\{y/z\} \qquad \overline{x}\langle A\rangle.Q \mid x(Y).P \rightarrow Q \mid P\{A/Y\}$$
$$\overline{x}\langle y\rangle.Q \mid !x(z).P \rightarrow Q \mid P\{y/z\} \mid !x(z).P \qquad x.\mathsf{inl}; P \mid x.\mathsf{case}(Q,R) \rightarrow P \mid Q$$
$$(\boldsymbol{\nu}x)([x \leftrightarrow y] \mid P) \rightarrow P\{y/x\} \ (x \neq y) \qquad x.\mathsf{inr}; P \mid x.\mathsf{case}(Q,R) \rightarrow P \mid R$$
$$Q \rightarrow Q' \Rightarrow P \mid Q \rightarrow P \mid Q' \qquad P \rightarrow Q \Rightarrow (\boldsymbol{\nu}y)P \rightarrow (\boldsymbol{\nu}y)Q$$
$$P \equiv P', P' \rightarrow Q', Q' \equiv Q \Rightarrow P \rightarrow Q$$

A transition $P \xrightarrow{\alpha} Q$ denotes that P may evolve to Q by performing the action represented by label α. In general, an action α ($\overline{\alpha}$) requires a matching $\overline{\alpha}$ (α) in the environment to enable progress. Labels include: the silent internal action τ, output and bound output actions $\overline{x}\langle y\rangle$ and $\overline{(\nu z)x\langle z\rangle}$, respectively, and input action $x(y)$. Also, they include labels pertaining to the binary choice construct ($x.\mathsf{inl}$, $\overline{x.\mathsf{inl}}$, $x.\mathsf{inr}$, and $\overline{x.\mathsf{inr}}$), and labels describing output and input of types (denoted $\overline{x\langle A\rangle}$ and $x(A)$, respectively).

Definition 4 (Labeled Transition System). *The relation* labeled transition *($P \xrightarrow{\alpha} Q$) is defined by the rules in Fig. 1, subject to the side conditions: in rule* (res), *we require* $y \notin fn(\alpha)$; *in rule* (par), *we require* $bn(\alpha) \cap fn(R) = \emptyset$; *in rule* (close), *we require* $y \notin fn(Q)$. *We omit the symmetric versions of rules* (par), (com), *and* (close).

We write $\rho_1\rho_2$ for the composition of relations ρ_1, ρ_2. Weak transitions are defined as usual: we write $\Longrightarrow$ for the reflexive, transitive closure of $\xrightarrow{\tau}$. Given $\alpha \neq \tau$, notation $\xoverset{\alpha}{\Longrightarrow}$ stands for $\Longrightarrow \xrightarrow{\alpha} \Longrightarrow$ and $\xoverset{\tau}{\Longrightarrow}$ stands for $\Longrightarrow$.

Type System. Our type system assigns session types to communication channels. Our session type language (cf. Definition 1) corresponds exactly to second-order linear logic, and our typing rules capture this correspondence in a precise way. We define two judgments: $\Omega; \Gamma; \Delta \vdash P :: x{:}A$ and $\Omega \vdash A$ type. Context Ω keeps track of type variables that can be introduced by the polymorphic type constructors; Γ records persistent sessions $u{:}B$, which can be invoked arbitrarily often along channel u; Δ maintains the sessions $x{:}B$ that can be used exactly once on channel x. When empty, Γ, Δ, and (out)   (in)   (outT)   (inT)

$$\overline{x}\langle y\rangle.P \xrightarrow{\overline{x}\langle y\rangle} P \quad x(y).P \xrightarrow{x(z)} P\{z/y\} \quad \overline{x}\langle A\rangle.P \xrightarrow{\overline{x}\langle A\rangle} P \quad x(Y).P \xrightarrow{x(B)} P\{B/Y\}$$

(par)   (com)   (res)

(id)
$$(\nu x)([x \leftrightarrow y] \mid P) \xrightarrow{\tau} P\{y/x\} \qquad \dfrac{P \xrightarrow{\alpha} Q}{P \mid R \xrightarrow{\alpha} Q \mid R} \qquad \dfrac{P \xrightarrow{\overline{\alpha}} P' \quad Q \xrightarrow{\alpha} Q'}{P \mid Q \xrightarrow{\tau} P' \mid Q'} \qquad \dfrac{P \xrightarrow{\alpha} Q}{(\nu y)P \xrightarrow{\alpha} (\nu y)Q}$$

(open)   (close)

(rep)
$$!x(y).P \xrightarrow{x(z)} P\{z/y\} \mid !x(y).P \qquad \dfrac{P \xrightarrow{\overline{x}\langle y\rangle} Q}{(\nu y)P \xrightarrow{\overline{(\nu y)x}\langle y\rangle} Q} \qquad \dfrac{P \xrightarrow{\overline{(\nu y)x}\langle y\rangle} P' \quad Q \xrightarrow{x(y)} Q'}{P \mid Q \xrightarrow{\tau} (\nu y)(P' \mid Q')}$$

(lout)   (rout)   (lin)   (rin)

$$x.\mathtt{inl}; P \xrightarrow{\overline{x.\mathtt{inl}}} P \quad x.\mathtt{inr}; P \xrightarrow{\overline{x.\mathtt{inr}}} P \quad x.\mathtt{case}(P,Q) \xrightarrow{x.\mathtt{inl}} P \quad x.\mathtt{case}(P,Q) \xrightarrow{x.\mathtt{inr}} Q$$

Fig. 1. π-calculus Labeled Transition System

Ω are often denoted by '·'. Judgment $\Omega \vdash A$ type defines well-formedness of types: it denotes that A is a well-formed type with free variables registered in Ω. The rules for type well-formedness are straightforward (see [5]). Our main typing judgment thus states that process P implements a session of type A along channel x, provided it is composed with processes providing sessions linearly in Δ and persistently in Γ, such that the types occurring in the judgment are well-formed according to Ω.

The typing rules for our polymorphic session calculus are given in Fig. 2. We use T, S for right-hand-side singleton environments (e.g., $z{:}C$). Rules pertaining to the propositional fragment extend those introduced in [6] with context Ω. The rules in the last two rows of Fig. 2 explain how to *provide* and *use* sessions of a polymorphic type. More precisely, rule (T∀R) describes the offering of a session of universal type $\forall X.A$ by inputing an arbitrary type, bound to X, and proceeding as A, which may bind the type variable X, regardless of what the actual received type is. Rule (T∀L) says that the use of type $\forall X.A$ consists of the output of a type B—well-formed under type context Ω—which then warrants the use of the session as $A\{B/X\}$. The existential type is dual: providing an existentially typed session $\exists X.A$ (cf. rule (T∃R)) is accomplished by outputting a well-formed type B and then providing a session of type $A\{B/X\}$. Using an existential session $\exists X.A$ (cf. rule (T∃L)) implies inputing a type and then using the session as A, agnostic to what the actual received type can be. Note that in the presence of polymorphism the identity rule (Tid) (not present in [6,7], but used in [26,21,20]) is necessary, since it is the only way of typing a session with a type variable.

As usual, in the presence of type annotations in binders, type-checking is decidable in our system (these are omitted for readability). We consider π-calculus terms up to structural congruence, and so typability is closed under $\equiv$ by definition. The system enjoys the usual properties of equivariance, weakening, and contraction in Γ, as well as *name coverage* (free names of a process are bound by the contexts or the right-hand-side) and *regularity* (free variables of types are bound in the type variable context).

Correspondence with Second-Order Linear Logic. Our type system exhibits a tight correspondence with a sequent calculus presentation of intuitionistic second-order linear logic. Informally, if we erase the processes and channel names from the typing

(Tid)

$$\Omega; \Gamma; x{:}A \vdash [x \leftrightarrow z] :: z{:}A$$

(T1L)

$$\dfrac{\Omega; \Gamma; \Delta \vdash P :: T}{\Omega; \Gamma; \Delta, x{:}\mathbf{1} \vdash P :: T}$$

(T1R)

$$\Omega; \Gamma; \cdot \vdash \mathbf{0} :: x{:}\mathbf{1}$$

(T⊗L)

$$\dfrac{\Omega; \Gamma; \Delta, y{:}A, x{:}B \vdash P :: T}{\Omega; \Gamma; \Delta, x{:}A \otimes B \vdash x(y).P :: T}$$

(T⊗R)

$$\dfrac{\Omega; \Gamma; \Delta \vdash P :: y{:}A \quad \Omega; \Gamma; \Delta' \vdash Q :: x{:}B}{\Omega; \Gamma; \Delta, \Delta' \vdash (\nu y)\overline{x}\langle y\rangle.(P \mid Q) :: x{:}A \otimes B}$$

(T⊸L)

$$\dfrac{\Omega; \Gamma; \Delta \vdash P :: y{:}A \quad \Omega; \Gamma; \Delta', x{:}B \vdash Q :: T}{\Omega; \Gamma; \Delta, \Delta', x{:}A{\multimap}B \vdash (\nu y)\overline{x}\langle y\rangle.(P \mid Q) :: T}$$

(T⊸R)

$$\dfrac{\Omega; \Gamma; \Delta, y{:}A \vdash P :: x{:}B}{\Omega; \Gamma; \Delta \vdash x(y).P :: x{:}A{\multimap}B}$$

(Tcut)

$$\dfrac{\Omega; \Gamma; \Delta \vdash P :: x{:}A \quad \Omega; \Gamma; \Delta', x{:}A \vdash Q :: T}{\Omega; \Gamma; \Delta, \Delta' \vdash (\nu x)(P \mid Q) :: T}$$

(Tcut!)

$$\dfrac{\Omega; \Gamma; \cdot \vdash P :: y{:}A \quad \Omega; \Gamma, u{:}A; \Delta \vdash Q :: T}{\Omega; \Gamma; \Delta \vdash (\nu u)(!u(y).P \mid Q) :: T}$$

(T!L)

$$\dfrac{\Omega; \Gamma, u{:}A; \Delta \vdash P\{u/x\} :: T}{\Omega; \Gamma; \Delta, x{:}!A \vdash P :: T}$$

(Tcopy)

$$\dfrac{\Omega; \Gamma, u{:}A; \Delta, y{:}A \vdash P :: T}{\Omega; \Gamma, u{:}A; \Delta \vdash (\nu y)\overline{u}\langle y\rangle.P :: T}$$

(T!R)

$$\dfrac{\Omega; \Gamma; \cdot \vdash Q :: y{:}A}{\Omega; \Gamma; \cdot \vdash !x(y).Q :: x{:}!A}$$

(T⊕L)

$$\dfrac{\Omega; \Gamma; \Delta, x{:}A \vdash P :: T \quad \Omega; \Gamma; \Delta, x{:}B \vdash Q :: T}{\Omega; \Gamma; \Delta, x{:}A \oplus B \vdash x.\mathsf{case}(P,Q) :: T}$$

(T&R)

$$\dfrac{\Omega; \Gamma; \Delta \vdash P :: x{:}A \quad \Omega; \Gamma; \Delta \vdash Q :: x{:}B}{\Omega; \Gamma; \Delta \vdash x.\mathsf{case}(P,Q) :: x{:}A \,\&\, B}$$

(T&L₁)

$$\dfrac{\Omega; \Gamma; \Delta, x{:}A \vdash P :: T}{\Omega; \Gamma; \Delta, x{:}A \,\&\, B \vdash x.\mathtt{inl}; P :: T}$$

(T⊕R₁)

$$\dfrac{\Omega; \Gamma; \Delta \vdash P :: x{:}A}{\Omega; \Gamma; \Delta \vdash x.\mathtt{inl}; P :: x{:}A \oplus B}$$

(T∀L)

$$\dfrac{\Omega \vdash B \text{ type} \quad \Omega; \Gamma; \Delta, x : A\{B/X\} \vdash P :: T}{\Omega; \Gamma; \Delta, x : \forall X.A \vdash \overline{x}\langle B\rangle.P :: T}$$

(T∀R)

$$\dfrac{\Omega, X; \Gamma; \Delta \vdash P :: z{:}A}{\Omega; \Gamma; \Delta \vdash z(X).P :: z{:}\forall X.A}$$

(T∃L)

$$\dfrac{\Omega, X; \Gamma; \Delta, x{:}A \vdash P :: T}{\Omega; \Gamma; \Delta, x : \exists X.A \vdash x(X).P :: T}$$

(T∃R)

$$\dfrac{\Omega \vdash B \text{ type} \quad \Omega; \Gamma; \Delta \vdash P :: x{:}A\{B/X\}}{\Omega; \Gamma; \Delta \vdash \overline{x}\langle B\rangle.P :: x{:}\exists X.A}$$

Fig. 2. The Type System. Rules (T&L₂)-(T⊕R₂), analogous to (T&L₁)-(T⊕R₁), are omitted.

derivations we obtain precisely sequent proofs in intuitionistic second-order linear logic. This correspondence (detailed in [5]) is made precise by defining a faithful proof term assignment for the sequent calculus and a typed extraction function that maps these proof terms to process typing derivations, as reported in [6] for the propositional case.

Notice that the correspondence goes beyond the mapping of proof inferences to typing derivations. We can show that process reductions can be mapped to proof conversions arising from the standard proof-theoretic cut elimination procedure. This induces a strong form of subject reduction on well-typed processes (see below). Furthermore, we can classify *all* proof conversions arising in this manner as reductions, structural congruences, or as observational equivalences on well-typed processes. See [6,20] for details of the correspondence of proof conversions and their process interpretation.

Subject Reduction and Progress. The deep logical foundations allow us to establish strong properties of process behavior through typing. We now discuss and state *subject reduction* and *global progress* for our system. Subject reduction (Theorem 1) follows from a simulation between reductions in the typed π-calculus and proof conversions that arise naturally in proof theory. This ensures that our interpretation is not arbitrary, but rather captures the actual dynamics of proofs. Subject reduction, together with linear typing, ensures session fidelity; the proof follows closely that of [6,7], extending it with lemmas that characterize process/proof reductions at universal and existential types.

Theorem 1 (Subject Reduction/Type Preservation). *If* $\Omega; \Gamma; \Delta \vdash P :: z{:}A$ *and* $P \rightarrow Q$ *then* $\Omega; \Gamma; \Delta \vdash Q :: z{:}A$.

As for global progress (Theorem 2), also in this case the proof is an orthogonal extension from that of [6,7], requiring a series of inversion lemmas and the following notion of *live* process. For any P, define $live(P)$ if and only if $P \equiv (\nu\tilde{n})(\pi.Q \mid R)$, for some process R, a sequence of names $\tilde{n}$, and a *non-replicated* guarded process $\pi.Q$.

Theorem 2 (Progress). *If* $\cdot; \cdot; \cdot \vdash P :: x{:}\mathbf{1}$ *and* $live(P)$ *then* $\exists Q$ *s.t.* $P \rightarrow Q$.

3   The Cloud Application Server, Revisited

To illustrate the expressiveness and flexibility that we obtain via polymorphic sessions, here we present concurrent specifications associated to the cloud-based application server described in the Introduction. Below, for the sake of clarity, we abbreviate bound outputs $(\nu y)\overline{x}\langle y\rangle$ as $\overline{x}\langle y\rangle$. Recall the type for the cloud-based application server: $\mathsf{CloudServer} \triangleq \forall X.!(\mathsf{api} \multimap X) \multimap !X$. Then, following the logic interpretation just introduced, a process which realizes type $\mathsf{CloudServer}$ on name x is the following:

$$CS_x \triangleq x(X).x(y).!x(w).\overline{y}\langle v\rangle.\overline{v}\langle a\rangle.(P_a \mid [w \leftrightarrow v])$$

where P_a is a process implementing the server API along channel a. Process CS_x expects a protocol description X (a session type) and a session y, which is a persistent implementation of X that requires the API provided by the server. CS_x will then create a replicated service that can provide the behavior X after delivering to y the API implementation that is represented by process P_a.

What does an application to be published in the cloud server look like? Let us assume a simple process, noted $Conv_w$, representing a *file conversion service* which, by using a suitable API, takes a file and generates its PDF version (e.g., performing OCR on images and generating the PDF of the text): $a{:}\mathsf{api} \vdash Conv_w :: w{:}\mathsf{file}\multimap(\mathsf{pdf} \otimes \mathbf{1})$.

In order to publish the conversion service into our application server, developers need to harmonize its requirements (as described by the left-hand side typing) with those of the server infrastructure CS_x. To this end, we define a "wrapper" process which contains $Conv_w$ and is compatible with CS_x (where conv $\triangleq \mathsf{file}\multimap(\mathsf{pdf} \otimes \mathbf{1})$):

$$x{:}\mathsf{CloudServer} \vdash PubConv_z :: z{:}!\mathsf{conv}$$
$$PubConv_z \triangleq \overline{x}\langle\mathsf{conv}\rangle.\overline{x}\langle y\rangle.(!y(w).w(a).Conv_w \mid [x \leftrightarrow z])$$

Process $PubConv_z$ first sends protocol/type conv to the cloud server, followed by a session y that consists of a persistent service, that when given the API will produce a session of type conv. After these communication steps, the cloud server session now provides the full behavior of conv along x, and so the client forwards x along the endpoint channel z, thus providing !conv along z by making use of the functionality provided by the server. By combining the above processes, we obtain:

$$\cdot; \cdot \vdash (\nu x)(CS_x \mid PubConv_z) :: z : \text{!conv} \tag{2}$$

representing the publication of our file conversion service in the cloud-based infrastructure. Behavioral genericity is in the fact that publishing *any* other service would require following exactly the same above procedure. Assume, for instance, a service $Maps_n$:

$$a{:}\text{api} \vdash Maps_n :: n{:}\text{addr} \multimap (\text{AMaps} \,\&\, \text{GMaps})$$

which when provided a value of type addr (representing an address), it offers a choice between map services AMaps (vector-based maps) and GMaps (raster-based maps). Let maps $\triangleq$ addr $\multimap$ (AMaps $\&$ GMaps). Clearly, the behavior described by types conv and maps is very different. Still, their relationship with the server at x is exactly the same—they are equally independent. Indeed, by proceeding exactly as we showed above for process $Conv_w$, we can produce a wrapper process $PubMaps_z$ and then obtain:

$$\cdot; \cdot \vdash (\nu x)(CS_x \mid PubMaps_z) :: z : \text{!maps} \tag{3}$$

The parametric behavior of CS_x can be thus witnessed by comparing (2) and (3) above. In Section 6 we illustrate how to use parametricity to formally justify properties of behavioral genericity/representation independence for processes such as those above.

The above example can be extended to illustrate the interplay of behavioral genericity and concurrency. A more realistic cloud-based platform is one which is always available on a certain name u. This can be represented in our framework by stating

$$\cdot; \cdot \vdash !u(x).CS_x :: u : \text{!CloudServer}$$

and by slightly modifying our assumptions on processes $PubConv_z$ and $PubMaps_z$, in such a way that they become two clients of the persistent server on u:

$$u{:}\text{CloudServer}; \cdot \vdash \overline{u}\langle x\rangle.PubConv_z :: z : \text{!conv}$$

(The client for $PubMaps_z$ is similar.) Our typing system ensures that interactions between the server $!u(x).CS_x$ and clients such as the two above will be consistent, safe, and finite. Moreover, these interactions exploit behavioral genericity without interfering with each other, and respecting resource usage policies declared by typing.

Above we have considered a very simple interface type for the cloud-based server. Our framework allows us to represent much richer interfaces. For instance, the type CloudServerAds $\triangleq \forall X.!(\text{api} \multimap X) \multimap !(X \,\&\, \text{AdListings})$ captures a more sophisticated server which provides its API but forces the resulting system to feature an advertisement service. Type AdListings encodes a listing of advertisements that the application server "injects" into the service—this injection is represented with a choice $\&$, so as to model the ability of a client to choose to watch an advertisement. It is not difficult to extend this mechanism with further functionalities, such as providing the server developers/clients with an administrator service not exposed to the external clients.

Having illustrated the expressiveness of polymorphic session-typed processes, it is legitimate to investigate the correctness guarantees they enjoy. In the next section, we establish strong normalization, a desirable liveness property for mobile code. Then, in Section 5, we develop a theory of relational parametricity for session-typed processes.

4   Polymorphic Session-Typed Processes Are Strongly Normalizing

In this section, we show that well-typed processes of our polymorphic language are (compositionally) strongly normalizing (terminating). Hence, in addition to adhering to the behavior prescribed by session types in a deadlock-free way (cf. Theorems 1 and 2), our well-typed, polymorphic processes never engage into infinite computations (Theorem 5). This property is practically meaningful in the context of distributed computing, as it may be used to certify that mobile polymorphic code will not attempt, e.g., a denial-of-service attack by exhausting the resources of a remote service.

Our proof builds on the well-known reducibility candidates technique [14], and generalizes the linear logical relations for session typed processes given in [20] to the *impredicative* polymorphic setting. Technically, the proof is in two stages: we first define a logical predicate inductively on the linear type structure; then, we show that all well-typed processes are in the predicate.

Below, we say that a process P *terminates* (written $P{\Downarrow}$) if there is no infinite reduction sequence starting with P. The logical predicate uses the following extension to structural congruence with the so-called *sharpened replication axioms* [25].

Definition 5. *We write $\equiv_!$ for the least congruence relation on processes which results from extending structural congruence $\equiv$ (Def. 2) with the following axioms:*

1. $(\nu u)(!u(z).P \mid (\nu y)(Q \mid R)) \equiv_! (\nu y)((\nu u)(!u(z).P \mid Q) \mid (\nu u)(!u(z).P \mid R))$

2. $(\nu u)(!u(y).P \mid (\nu v)(!v(z).Q \mid R))$
$$\equiv_! (\nu v)((!v(z).(\nu u)(!u(y).P \mid Q)) \mid (\nu u)(!u(y).P \mid R))$$

3. $(\nu u)(!u(y).Q \mid P) \equiv_! P \quad if\ u \notin fn(P)$

Intuitively, $\equiv_!$ allows us to properly "split" processes: axioms (1) and (2) represent the distribution of shared servers among processes, while (3) formalizes the garbage collection of shared servers which can no longer be invoked by any process. It is worth noticing that $\equiv_!$ expresses sound behavioral equivalences in our typed setting (see [6]).

We now define a notion of *reducibility candidate* at a given type: this is a predicate on well-typed processes which satisfies some crucial closure conditions. As in Girard's proof, the idea is that one of the particular candidates is the "true" logical predicate. Below and henceforth, $\cdot \vdash P :: z{:}A$ stands for a process P which is well-typed under the empty typing environment.

Definition 6 (Reducibility Candidate). *Given a type A and a name z, a reducibility candidate at $z{:}A$, written $R[z{:}A]$, is a predicate on all processes P such that $\cdot \vdash P :: z{:}A$ and satisfy the following:*

(1) If $P \in R[z{:}A]$ then $P{\Downarrow}$.   (2) If $P \in R[z{:}A]$ and $P \Longrightarrow P'$ then $P' \in R[z{:}A]$.
(3) If for all P_i such that $P \Longrightarrow P_i$ we have $P_i \in R[z{:}A]$ then $P \in R[z{:}A]$.

As in the functional case, the properties required for our reducibility candidates are termination (1), closure under reduction (2), and closure under backward reduction (3).

The Logical Predicate. Intuitively, the logical predicate captures the terminating behavior of processes as induced by typing. This way, e.g., the meaning of a terminating process of type $z{:}\forall X.A$ is that after inputing an arbitrary type B, a terminating process of type $z{:}A\{B/X\}$ is obtained. As we consider impredicative polymorphism, the main technical issue is that $A\{B/X\}$ may be larger than $\forall X.A$, for any measure of size.

The logical predicate is defined inductively, and is parameterized by two mappings, denoted ω and η. Given a context Ω, we write $\omega : \Omega$ to denote that ω is an assignment of closed types to variables in Ω. We write $\omega[X \mapsto A]$ to denote the extension of ω with a new mapping of X to A. We use a similar notation for extensions of η. We write $\hat{\omega}(P)$ (resp. $\hat{\omega}(A)$) to denote the application of the mapping ω to free type-variables in P (resp. in A). We write $\eta : \omega$ to denote that η is an assignment of functions taking names to reducibility candidates, to type variables in Ω (at the types in ω).

It is instructive to compare the key differences between our development and the notion of logical relation for functional languages with impredicative polymorphism, such as System F. In that context, types are assigned to terms and thus one maintains a mapping from type variables to reducibility candidates at the appropriate types. In our setting, since types are assigned to channel names, we need the ability to refer to reducibility candidates at a given type at channel names which are *yet to be determined*. Therefore, when we quantify over all types and all reducibility candidates at that type, intuitively, we need to "delay" the choice of the actual name along which the candidate must offer the session type. A reducibility candidate at type A which is "delayed" in this sense is denoted as $R[-{:}A]$, where '$-$' stands for a name to be instantiated later on.

We thus define a sequent-indexed family of process predicates: a set of processes $\mathcal{T}_\eta^\omega[\Gamma; \Delta \vdash T]$ satisfying some conditions is assigned to any sequent of the form $\Omega; \Gamma; \Delta \vdash T$, provided both $\omega{:}\Omega$ and $\eta{:}\omega$. The predicate is defined inductively on the structure of the sequents: the base case considers sequents with an empty left-hand side typing (abbreviated $\mathcal{T}_\eta^\omega[T]$), whereas the inductive case considers arbitrary typing contexts and relies on principles for process composition (cf. rules (Tcut) and (Tcut!)).

Definition 7 (Logical Predicate - Base Case). *For any type A and name z, the logical predicate $\mathcal{T}_\eta^\omega[z{:}A]$ is inductively defined by the set of all processes P such that $\cdot \vdash \hat{\omega}(P) :: z{:}\hat{\omega}(A)$ and satisfy the conditions in Figure 3.*

Definition 8 (Logical Predicate - Inductive Case). *For any sequent $\Omega; \Gamma; \Delta \vdash T$ with a non-empty left hand side environment, we define $\mathcal{T}_\eta^\omega[\Gamma; \Delta \vdash T]$ (with $\omega : \Omega$ and $\eta : \omega$) as the set of processes inductively defined as follows:*

$$P \in \mathcal{T}_\eta^\omega[\Gamma; y{:}A, \Delta \vdash T] \text{ iff } \forall R \in \mathcal{T}_\eta^\omega[y{:}A].(\nu y)(\hat{\omega}(R) \mid \hat{\omega}(P)) \in \mathcal{T}_\eta^\omega[\Gamma; \Delta \vdash T]$$
$$P \in \mathcal{T}_\eta^\omega[u{:}A, \Gamma; \Delta \vdash T] \text{ iff } \forall R \in \mathcal{T}_\eta^\omega[y{:}A].(\nu u)(!u(y).\hat{\omega}(R) \mid \hat{\omega}(P)) \in \mathcal{T}_\eta^\omega[\Gamma; \Delta \vdash T]$$

Definitions 7 and 8 are the natural extension of the linear logical relations in [20] to the case of impredicative polymorphic types. Notice how the interpretation of the variable type includes the instantiation at name z of the reducibility candidate given by $\eta(X)$.

$$P \in \mathcal{T}_\eta^\omega[z{:}X] \text{ iff } P \in \eta(X)(z)$$
$$P \in \mathcal{T}_\eta^\omega[z{:}\mathbf{1}] \text{ iff } \forall P'.(P \Longrightarrow P' \wedge P' \not\longrightarrow) \Rightarrow P' \equiv_! \mathbf{0}$$
$$P \in \mathcal{T}_\eta^\omega[z{:}A{\multimap}B] \text{ iff } \forall P'y.(P \overset{z(y)}{\Longrightarrow} P') \Rightarrow \forall Q \in \mathcal{T}_\eta^\omega[y{:}A].(\nu y)(P' \mid Q) \in \mathcal{T}_\eta^\omega[z{:}B]$$
$$P \in \mathcal{T}_\eta^\omega[z{:}A \otimes B] \text{ iff } \forall P'y.(P \overset{\overline{(\nu y)z\langle y\rangle}}{\Longrightarrow} P') \Rightarrow$$
$$\exists P_1, P_2.(P' \equiv_! P_1 \mid P_2 \wedge P_1 \in \mathcal{T}_\eta^\omega[y{:}A] \wedge P_2 \in \mathcal{T}_\eta^\omega[z{:}B])$$
$$P \in \mathcal{T}_\eta^\omega[z{:}!A] \text{ iff } \forall P'.(P \Longrightarrow P') \Rightarrow \exists P_1.(P' \equiv_! !z(y).P_1 \wedge P_1 \in \mathcal{T}_\eta^\omega[y{:}A])$$
$$P \in \mathcal{T}_\eta^\omega[z{:}\forall X.A] \text{ iff } (\forall B, P', \mathsf{R}[-{:}B].\ (B\ \text{type} \wedge P \overset{z(B)}{\Longrightarrow} P') \Rightarrow P' \in \mathcal{T}_{\eta[X\mapsto\mathsf{R}[-{:}B]]}^{\omega[X\mapsto B]}[z{:}A])$$
$$P \in \mathcal{T}_\eta^\omega[z{:}\exists X.A] \text{ iff } (\exists B, \mathsf{R}[-{:}B].(B\ \text{type} \wedge P \overset{\overline{z(B)}}{\Longrightarrow} P') \Rightarrow P' \in \mathcal{T}_{\eta[X\mapsto\mathsf{R}[-{:}B]]}^{\omega[X\mapsto B]}[z{:}A])$$

Fig. 3. Logical predicate (base case). Definitions for $\mathcal{T}_\eta^\omega[z{:}A \oplus B]$ and $\mathcal{T}_\eta^\omega[z{:}A \& B]$ are as expected; see [5] for details.

The clause for the universal $\forall X.A$ denotes that a terminating session of universal type must be able to input *any* type and then be terminating at the open type A, where the meaning of the type variable can be any possible candidate of appropriate type (which includes the actual logical predicate). The clause for the existential is dual.

Proving Strong Normalization. Using the above logical predicate, the proof of strong normalization of well-typed processes follows the one presented in [20]. Roughly, the idea is to define a notion of logical representatives of the dependencies specified in the left-hand side typing. Such representatives simplify reasoning, as they allow to move from predicates for sequents with non empty left-hand side typings to predicates with an empty left-hand side typing, provided processes have been appropriately closed.

The theorem below ensures that $\mathcal{T}_\eta^\omega[\Gamma; \Delta \vdash T]$ is indeed a reducibility candidate, and thus it implies termination.

Theorem 3 (The Logical Predicate is a Reducibility Candidate). *If $\Omega \vdash A$ type, $\omega : \Omega$, and $\eta : \omega$ then $\mathcal{T}_\eta^\omega[z{:}A]$ is a reducibility candidate at $z{:}\hat\omega(A)$.*

With the technical machinery appropriately defined, we can show the Fundamental Theorem, stating that all well-typed processes belong to the logical predicate.

Theorem 4 (Fundamental Theorem). *If $\Omega; \Gamma; \Delta \vdash P :: T$ then, for all $\omega : \Omega$ and $\eta : \omega$, we have that $\hat\omega(P) \in \mathcal{T}_\eta^\omega[\Gamma; \Delta \vdash T]$.*

We state the main result of this section, which follows as a consequence of the Fundamental Theorem above: all well-typed polymorphic processes terminate.

Theorem 5 (Strong Normalization). *If $\Omega; \Gamma; \Delta \vdash P{::}T$ then $\hat\omega(P)\Downarrow$, for every $\omega{:}\Omega$.*

5   Relational Parametricity for Session-Typed Processes

The cloud-based server given in Section 3 calls for the need for formally asserting that a server with type $u :\ !\mathsf{CloudServer}$ must behave "the same" independently of the arbitrary types of its clients. In general, the characterization of any well-behaved notion of type genericity has been captured by some kind of parametricity property, in particular *relational parametricity*, as introduced by Reynolds [24]. The principle of relational parametricity allows us to formally support reasoning about non-trivial properties of processes, such as observational equivalence under changes of representation, which have important consequences on our setting, where types actually denote process behaviors, and the abstraction result implies observational equivalence of a composite system under change of some internal (representation) *protocol* (not just *data*) types.

In this section we thus establish for the first time a relational parametricity result for a session-typed process calculus, based on our underlying logically founded approach.

We first introduce a form of logical equivalence, noted $\approx_L$, which formalizes a relational parametricity principle (Theorem 8) along the lines of Reynolds' abstraction theorem [24] (see [16]). Logical equivalence also allows us to characterize *barbed congruence*, noted $\cong$, in a sound and complete way (Theorem 9). Notice that while $\approx_L$ corresponds to the natural extension of $\mathcal{T}_\eta^\omega[\Gamma; \Delta \vdash T]$ (cf. Definition 8) to the binary setting, $\cong$ represents the form of contextual equivalence typically used in concurrency.

Barbed Congruence. We begin by introducing barbed congruence. It is defined as the largest equivalence relation on typed processes that is (i) closed under internal actions; (ii) preserves barbs— arguably the most basic observable on the behavior of processes; and is (iii) *contextual*, i.e., preserved by every admissible process context. We make these three desiderata precise, defining first a suitable notion of *type-respecting relations* in our setting. Below, we use $\mathcal{S}$ to range over sequents of the form $\Omega; \Gamma; \Delta \vdash T$.

Definition 9 (Type-respecting relations). *A (binary) type-respecting relation over processes, written $\{\mathcal{R}_\mathcal{S}\}_\mathcal{S}$, is defined as a family of relations over processes indexed by $\mathcal{S}$. We often write $\mathcal{R}$ to refer to the whole family. Also, $\Omega; \Gamma; \Delta \vdash P \mathcal{R} Q :: T$ stands for*

$$(i)\ \Omega; \Gamma; \Delta \vdash P :: T \text{ and } \Omega; \Gamma; \Delta \vdash Q :: T \quad \text{and} \quad (ii)\ (P, Q) \in \mathcal{R}_{\Omega; \Gamma; \Delta \vdash T}.$$

We omit the definitions of reflexivity, transitivity, and symmetry for type-respecting relations; we will say that a type-respecting relation that enjoys the three properties is an equivalence. In what follows, we will often omit the adjective "type-respecting".

We now define τ-closedness, barb preservation, and contextuality.

Definition 10 (τ-closed). *Relation $\mathcal{R}$ is τ-closed if $\Omega; \Gamma; \Delta \vdash P\mathcal{R}Q :: T$ and $P \to P'$ imply there exists a Q' such that $Q \Longrightarrow Q'$ and $\Omega; \Gamma; \Delta \vdash P' \mathcal{R} Q' :: T$.*

The following definition of observability predicates, or barbs, extends standard presentations with observables for labeled choice and selection, and type input and output:

Definition 11 (Barbs). *Let $O_x = \{\overline{x}, x, \overline{x.\mathsf{inl}}, \overline{x.\mathsf{inr}}, x.\mathsf{inl}, x.\mathsf{inr}\}$ be the set of basic observables under name x. Given a well-typed process P, we write: (i) $\mathsf{barb}(P, \overline{x})$, if $P \xrightarrow{\overline{(\nu y)x\langle y\rangle}} P'$; (ii) $\mathsf{barb}(P, \overline{x})$, if $P \xrightarrow{\overline{x\langle A\rangle}} P'$, for some A, P'; (iii) $\mathsf{barb}(P, x)$, if $P \xrightarrow{x(A)} P'$, for some A, P'; (iv) $\mathsf{barb}(P, x)$, if $P \xrightarrow{x(y)} P'$, for some y, P'; (v) $\mathsf{barb}(P, \alpha)$, if $P \xrightarrow{\alpha} P'$, for some P' and $\alpha \in O_x \setminus \{x, \overline{x}\}$. Given some $o \in O_x$, we write $\mathsf{wbarb}(P, o)$ if there exists a P' such that $P \Longrightarrow P'$ and $\mathsf{barb}(P', o)$ holds.*

Definition 12 (Barb preserving relation). *Relation $\mathcal{R}$ is a* barb preserving *if, for every name x, $\Omega; \Gamma; \Delta \vdash P \mathcal{R} Q :: T$ and* barb(P, o) *imply* wbarb(Q, o), *for any $o \in O_x$.*

In an untyped setting, a relation is said to be *contextual* if it is closed under any well-formed process context C (i.e., a process with a hole). In our case, contexts are typed, and the set of well-formed process contexts (i.e., processes with a typed hole) can be mechanically derived from the typing rules, by exhaustively considering all possibilities for typed holes. This way, e.g., rules (Tcut) and (Tcut$^!$) are the basis for defining parallel contexts. The operation of "filling in" the hole of a context with a process can be handled by an additional typing rule available to contexts, which checks that the type of the process matches that of the hole. For space reasons, we refrain from reporting the complete formal definition of typed process contexts; see [5] for details. Based on these intuitions, we define a contextual relation as follows:

Definition 13 (Contextuality). *Relation $\mathcal{R}$ is* contextual *if $\Omega; \Gamma; \Delta \vdash P \mathcal{R} Q :: T$ implies $\Omega; \Gamma; \Delta' \vdash C[P] \mathcal{R} C[Q] :: T'$, for every Δ', T' and typed context C.*

Definition 14 (Barbed Congruence). Barbed congruence, *noted $\cong$, is the largest equivalence on well-typed processes that is τ-closed, barb preserving, and contextual.*

Logical Equivalence. We now define our notion of logical equivalence for well-typed processes: it arises as a natural extension of the logical predicate of Definition 8 to the relational setting. We begin by defining the crucial notion of equivalence candidate: an equivalence relation on well-typed processes satisfying certain basic closure conditions.

Definition 15 (Equivalence Candidate). *Let A, B be types. An* equivalence candidate $\mathcal{R}$ at $z{:}A$ and $z{:}B$, noted $\mathcal{R} :: z{:}A \Leftrightarrow B$, *is a binary relation on processes such that, for every $(P, Q) \in \mathcal{R} :: z{:}A \Leftrightarrow B$ both $\cdot \vdash P :: z{:}A$ and $\cdot \vdash Q :: z{:}B$ hold, together with the following conditions:*

1. *If $(P, Q) \in \mathcal{R} :: z{:}A \Leftrightarrow B$, $\cdot \vdash P \cong P' :: z{:}A$, and $\cdot \vdash Q \cong Q' :: z{:}B$ then $(P', Q') \in \mathcal{R} :: z{:}A \Leftrightarrow B$.*
2. *If $(P, Q) \in \mathcal{R} :: z{:}A \Leftrightarrow B$ then, for all P_0 such that $P_0 \Longrightarrow P$, we have $(P_0, Q) \in \mathcal{R} :: z{:}A \Leftrightarrow B$. Similarly for Q: If $(P, Q) \in \mathcal{R} :: z{:}A \Leftrightarrow B$ then, for all Q_0 such that $Q_0 \Longrightarrow Q$ then $(P, Q_0) \in \mathcal{R} :: z{:}A \Leftrightarrow B$.*

We often write $(P, Q) \in \mathcal{R} :: z{:}A \Leftrightarrow B$ as $P \mathcal{R} Q :: z{:}A \Leftrightarrow B$.

While item (1) says that equivalence candidates are closed with respect to $\cong$, item (2) can be shown to be redundant. As in our definition of logical predicate, we require some auxiliary notation. We recall that $\omega : \Omega$ denotes a type substitution ω that assigns a closed type to type variables in Ω. Given two type substitutions $\omega : \Omega$ and $\omega' : \Omega$, we define an equivalence candidate assignment η between ω and ω' as a mapping of a delayed (in the sense of the mapping η of Section 4) equivalence candidate $\eta(X) :: -{:}\omega(X) \Leftrightarrow \omega'(X)$ to the type variables in Ω. We write $\eta(X)(z)$ for the instantiation of the (delayed) equivalence candidate with the name z. We write $\eta : \omega \Leftrightarrow \omega'$ to denote that η is a (delayed) equivalence candidate assignment between ω and ω'.

We define a sequent-indexed family of process relations, that is, a set of pairs of processes (P, Q), written $\Gamma; \Delta \vdash P \approx_L Q :: T[\eta : \omega \Leftrightarrow \omega']$, satisfying some conditions,

$$P \approx_L Q :: z{:}X[\eta : \omega \Leftrightarrow \omega'] \text{ iff } (P, Q) \in \eta(X)(z)$$

$$P \approx_L Q :: z{:}\mathbf{1}[\eta : \omega \Leftrightarrow \omega'] \text{ iff } \forall P', Q'. \ (P \Longrightarrow P' \wedge P' \nrightarrow \wedge Q \Longrightarrow Q' \wedge Q' \nrightarrow) \Rightarrow$$
$$(P' \equiv_! \mathbf{0} \wedge Q' \equiv_! \mathbf{0})$$

$$P \approx_L Q :: z{:}A{\multimap}B[\eta : \omega \Leftrightarrow \omega'] \text{ iff } \forall P', y. \ (P \xrightarrow{z(y)} P') \Rightarrow \exists Q'.Q \overset{z(y)}{\Longrightarrow} Q' \text{ s.t.}$$
$$\forall R_1, R_2. \ R_1 \approx_L R_2 :: y{:}A[\eta : \omega \Leftrightarrow \omega']$$
$$(\nu y)(P' \mid R_1) \approx_L (\nu y)(Q' \mid R_2) :: z{:}B[\eta : \omega \Leftrightarrow \omega']$$

$$P \approx_L Q :: z{:}A \otimes B[\eta : \omega \Leftrightarrow \omega'] \text{ iff } \forall P', y. \ (P \xrightarrow{\overline{(\nu y)z\langle y\rangle}} P') \Rightarrow \exists Q'.Q \overset{\overline{(\nu y)z\langle y\rangle}}{\Longrightarrow} Q' \text{ s.t.}$$
$$\forall R_1, R_2, n. \ y{:}A \vdash R_1 \approx_L R_2 :: n{:}\mathbf{1}[\eta : \omega \Leftrightarrow \omega']$$
$$(\nu y)(P' \mid R_1) \approx_L (\nu y)(Q' \mid R_2) :: z{:}B[\eta : \omega \Leftrightarrow \omega']$$

$$P \approx_L Q :: z{:}!A[\eta : \omega \Leftrightarrow \omega'] \text{ iff } \forall P'. \ (P \xrightarrow{z(y)} P') \Rightarrow \exists Q'.Q \overset{z(y)}{\Longrightarrow} Q' \wedge$$
$$\forall R_1, R_2, n. \ y{:}A \vdash R_1 \approx_L R_2 :: n{:}\mathbf{1}[\eta : \omega \Leftrightarrow \omega']$$
$$(\nu y)(P' \mid R_1) \approx_L (\nu y)(Q' \mid R_2) :: z{:}!A[\eta : \omega \Leftrightarrow \omega']$$

$$P \approx_L Q :: z{:}\forall X.A[\eta : \omega \Leftrightarrow \omega'] \text{ iff } \forall B_1, B_2, P', \mathcal{R} :: -{:}B_1 \Leftrightarrow B_2. \ (P \xrightarrow{z(B_1)} P') \Rightarrow$$
$$\exists Q'.Q \overset{z(B_2)}{\Longrightarrow} Q', \ P' \approx_L Q' :: z{:}A[\eta[X \mapsto \mathcal{R}] : \omega[X \mapsto B_1] \Leftrightarrow \omega'[X \mapsto B_2]]$$

$$P \approx_L Q :: z{:}\exists X.A[\eta : \omega \Leftrightarrow \omega'] \text{ iff } \exists B_1, B_2, \mathcal{R} :: -{:}B_1 \Leftrightarrow B_2. \ (P \xrightarrow{\overline{z\langle B\rangle}} P') \Rightarrow$$
$$\exists Q'.Q \overset{\overline{z\langle B\rangle}}{\Longrightarrow} Q', \ P' \approx_L Q' :: z{:}A[\eta[X \mapsto \mathcal{R}] : \omega[X \mapsto B_1] \Leftrightarrow \omega'[X \mapsto B_2]]$$

Fig. 4. Logical equivalence (base case). Definitions for $P \approx_L Q :: z{:}A \ \& \ B[\eta : \omega \Leftrightarrow \omega']$ and $P \approx_L Q :: z{:}A \oplus B[\eta : \omega \Leftrightarrow \omega']$ are as expected; see [5] for details.

is assigned to any sequent of the form $\Omega; \Gamma; \Delta \vdash T$, with $\omega : \Omega$, $\omega' : \Omega$ and $\eta : \omega \Leftrightarrow \omega'$. As in the definition of the logical predicate, logical equivalence is defined inductively on the structure of the sequents: the base case considers empty left-hand side typings, whereas the inductive case which considers arbitrary typing contexts.

Definition 16 (Logical Equivalence - Base Case). *Given a type A and mappings ω, ω', η, we define logical equivalence, noted $P \approx_L Q :: z{:}A[\eta : \omega \Leftrightarrow \omega']$, as the largest binary relation containing all pairs of processes (P, Q) such that (i) $\cdot \vdash \hat{\omega}(P) :: z{:}\hat{\omega}(A)$; (ii) $\cdot \vdash \hat{\omega}'(Q) :: z{:}\hat{\omega}'(A)$; and (iii) satisfies the conditions in Figure 4.*

Definition 17 (Logical Equivalence - Inductive Case). *Let Γ, Δ be non empty typing environments. Given the sequent $\Omega; \Gamma; \Delta \vdash T$, the binary relation on processes $\Gamma; \Delta \vdash P \approx_L Q :: T[\eta : \omega \Leftrightarrow \omega']$ (with $\omega, \omega' : \Omega$ and $\eta : \omega \Leftrightarrow \omega'$) is inductively defined as:*

$$\Gamma; \Delta, y : A \vdash P \approx_L Q :: T[\eta : \omega \Leftrightarrow \omega'] \text{ iff } \forall R_1, R_2. \text{ s.t. } R_1 \approx_L R_2 :: y{:}A[\eta : \omega \Leftrightarrow \omega'],$$
$$\Gamma; \Delta \vdash (\nu y)(\hat{\omega}(P) \mid \hat{\omega}(R_1)) \approx_L (\nu y)(\hat{\omega}'(Q) \mid \hat{\omega}'(R_2)) :: T[\eta : \omega \Leftrightarrow \omega']$$
$$\Gamma, u : A; \Delta \vdash P \approx_L Q :: T[\eta : \omega \Leftrightarrow \omega'] \text{ iff } \forall R_1, R_2. \text{ s.t. } R_1 \approx_L R_2 :: y{:}A[\eta : \omega \Leftrightarrow \omega'],$$
$$\Gamma; \Delta \vdash (\nu y)(\hat{\omega}(P) \mid !u(y).\hat{\omega}(R_1)) \approx_L (\nu y)(\hat{\omega}'(Q) \mid !u(y).\hat{\omega}'(R_2)) :: T[\eta : \omega \Leftrightarrow \omega']$$

This way, logical equivalence turns out to be a generalization of the logical predicate $\mathcal{T}_\eta^\omega[\Gamma; \Delta \vdash T]$ (Definition 7) to the binary setting. The key difference lies in the definition of candidate (here called equivalence candidate), which instead of guaranteeing termination, enforces closure under barbed congruence.

Theorem 6 below is the binary analog of Theorem 4 (Fundamental Theorem). Its proof is similar: we establish that logical equivalence is one of the equivalence candidates, and then show that well-typed processes are logically equivalent to themselves.

Theorem 6 (Logical Equivalence is an Equivalence Candidate). *The relation* $P \approx_L Q :: z{:}A[\eta : \omega \Leftrightarrow \omega']$ *is an equivalence candidate at* $z{:}\hat{\omega}(A)$ *and* $z{:}\hat{\omega}'(A)$.

The final ingredient for our desired parametricity result is the following theorem:

Theorem 7 (Compositionality). *Let B be any type. Also, let $\mathcal{R} :: -{:}\hat{\omega}(B) \Leftrightarrow \hat{\omega}'(B)$ stand for logical equivalence (cf. Definition 16).*
Then, $P \approx_L Q :: z{:}A\{B/X\}[\eta : \omega \Leftrightarrow \omega']$ if and only if

$$P \approx_L Q :: z{:}A[\eta[X \mapsto \mathcal{R}] : \omega[X \mapsto \hat{\omega}(B)] \Leftrightarrow \omega'[X \mapsto \hat{\omega}'(B)]]$$

We now state the main result of the section; its proof depends on a backward closure property, and on Theorems 6 and 7.

Theorem 8 (Relational Parametricity). *If $\Omega; \Gamma; \Delta \vdash P :: z{:}A$ then, for all $\omega, \omega' : \Omega$ and $\eta : \omega \Leftrightarrow \omega'$, we have $\Gamma; \Delta \vdash \hat{\omega}(P) \approx_L \hat{\omega}'(P) :: z{:}A[\eta : \omega \Leftrightarrow \omega']$.*

Remarkably, by appealing to parametricity and contextuality of logical equivalence, we can show that $\approx_L$ and $\cong$ coincide. This result establishes a definitive connection between the usual barb-based notion of observational equivalence from concurrency theory, and the logical equivalence induced by our logical relational semantics (see [5]).

Theorem 9 (Logical Equivalence and Barbed Congruence coincide). *Relations $\approx_L$ and $\cong$ coincide for well-typed processes. More precisely:*

1. *If $\Gamma; \Delta \vdash P \approx_L Q :: z{:}A[\eta : \omega \Leftrightarrow \omega']$ holds for any $\omega, \omega' : \Omega$ and $\eta : \omega \Leftrightarrow \omega'$, then $\Omega; \Gamma; \Delta \vdash P \cong Q :: z{:}A$*
2. *If $\Omega; \Gamma; \Delta \vdash P \cong Q :: z{:}A$ then $\Gamma; \Delta \vdash P \approx_L Q :: z{:}A[\eta : \omega \Leftrightarrow \omega']$ for some $\omega, \omega' : \Omega$ and $\eta : \omega \Leftrightarrow \omega'$.*

6 Using Parametricity to Reason about the Cloud Server

Here we illustrate a simple application of our parametricity result for reasoning about concurrent polymorphic processes. We are interested in studying a restaurant finding system; such an application is expected to rely on some maps application, to be uploaded to a cloud server. In our example, we would like to consider two different implementations of the system, each one relying on a different maps service. We assume that the two implementations will comply with the expected specification for the restaurant service, even if each one uses a different maps service (denoted by closed types AMaps and GMaps). This assumption may be precisely expressed by the judgment

$$s{:}!(\mathsf{api}{\multimap}X){\multimap}!X \vdash C_1 \approx_L C_2 :: z{:}\mathsf{rest}[\eta_r : \omega_1 \Leftrightarrow \omega_2] \tag{4}$$

where $\eta_r(X) = \mathcal{R}$, $\omega_1(X) = \mathsf{AMaps}$, and $\omega_2(X) = \mathsf{GMaps}$, where $\mathcal{R}$ is an equivalence candidate that relates AMaps and GMaps, i.e., $\mathcal{R} : \mathsf{AMaps} \Leftrightarrow \mathsf{GMaps}$. The type of the restaurant finding application is denoted rest; it does not involve type variable X. Also, we assume X does not occur in the implementations C_1, C_2. Intuitively, the above captures the fact that C_1 and C_2 are similar "up to" the relation $\mathcal{R}$.

By exploiting the shape of type CloudServer, we can ensure that *any* process S such that $\cdot \vdash S :: s$:CloudServer behaves uniformly, offering the same generic behavior to its clients. That is to say, once the server is instantiated with an uploaded application, the behavior of the resulting system will depend only on the type provided by the application. Recall the polymorphic type of our cloud server: $\mathsf{CloudServer} \triangleq \forall X.!(\mathsf{api} \multimap X) \multimap !X$. Based on the form of this type and combining inversion on typing and strong normalization (Theorem 5), there is a process $SBody$ such that

$$S \xrightarrow{\;s(X)\;} SBody \qquad X; \cdot; \cdot \vdash SBody :: s{:}!(\mathsf{api}{\multimap}X){\multimap}!X \qquad (5)$$

hold. By parametricity (Theorem 8) on (5), we obtain

$$\cdot \vdash \hat{\omega}(SBody) \approx_{\mathsf{L}} \hat{\omega}'(SBody) :: s{:}!(\mathsf{api}{\multimap}X){\multimap}!X[\eta : \omega \Leftrightarrow \omega']$$

for any ω, ω', and η. In particular, it holds for the η_r, ω_1 and ω_2 defined above:

$$\cdot \vdash \hat{\omega}_1(SBody) \approx_{\mathsf{L}} \hat{\omega}_2(SBody) :: s{:}!(\mathsf{api}{\multimap}X){\multimap}!X[\eta_r : \omega_1 \Leftrightarrow \omega_2] \qquad (6)$$

By Definition 17, the formal relationship between C_1 and C_2 given by (4) implies

$$\cdot \vdash (\nu s)(\hat{\omega}_1(R_1) \mid C_1) \approx_{\mathsf{L}} (\nu s)(\hat{\omega}_2(R_2) \mid C_2) :: z{:}\mathsf{rest}[\eta_r : \omega_1 \Leftrightarrow \omega_2]$$

for any R_1, R_2 such that $R_1 \approx_{\mathsf{L}} R_2 :: s{:}!(\mathsf{api}{\multimap}X){\multimap}!X[\eta_r : \omega_1 \Leftrightarrow \omega_2]$. In particular, it holds for the two processes related in (6) above. Combining these two facts, we have:

$$\cdot \vdash (\nu s)(\hat{\omega}_1(SBody) \mid C_1) \approx_{\mathsf{L}} (\nu s)(\hat{\omega}_2(SBody) \mid C_2) :: z{:}\mathsf{rest}[\eta_r : \omega_1 \Leftrightarrow \omega_2]$$

Since rest does not involve X, using Theorem 7 we actually have:

$$\cdot \vdash (\nu s)(\hat{\omega}_1(SBody) \mid C_1) \approx_{\mathsf{L}} (\nu s)(\hat{\omega}_2(SBody) \mid C_2) :: z{:}\mathsf{rest}[\emptyset : \emptyset \Leftrightarrow \emptyset] \qquad (7)$$

Now, given (7), and using backward closure of $\approx_{\mathsf{L}}$ under reductions (possible because of Theorem 6 and Definition 15), we obtain:

$$\cdot \vdash (\nu s)(S \mid \overline{s}\langle\mathsf{AMaps}\rangle.C_1) \approx_{\mathsf{L}} (\nu s)(S \mid \overline{s}\langle\mathsf{GMaps}\rangle.C_2) :: z{:}\mathsf{rest}[\emptyset : \emptyset \Leftrightarrow \emptyset]$$

Then, using Theorem 9, we finally have

$$\cdot \vdash (\nu s)(S \mid \overline{s}\langle\mathsf{AMaps}\rangle.C_1) \cong (\nu s)(S \mid \overline{s}\langle\mathsf{GMaps}\rangle.C_2) :: z{:}\mathsf{rest}$$

This simple, yet illustrative example shows how one may use our parametricity results to reason about the observable behavior of concurrent systems that interact under a polymorphic behavioral type discpline.

7 Related Work

To our knowledge, our work is the first to establish a relational parametricity principle (in the sense of Reynolds [24]) in the context of a rich behavioral type theory for concurrent processes. Combined with parametricity, our type preservation, progress, and strong normalization results therefore improve upon previous works on polymorphism for session types ([12,10,4,28,9,15], see below) by providing general, logic-based foundations for the analysis of behavioral genericity in structured communications.

By extending the notion of subtyping in [11], Gay [12] studied a form of bounded polymorphism associated to branch/choice types: each branch is quantified by a type variable with upper and lower bounds. Forms of unbounded polymorphism can be enabled via special types Bot and Top. Dezani et al. [10] studied bounded polymorphism for a session-typed, object-oriented language. Bono and Padovani [3,4] rely on unbounded polymorphism in a session types variant that is used to ensure correct (copyless) message-passing programs. Dardha et al. [9] develop an encoding of session types into linear/variant types; it can be extended to handle session types with existential parametric polymorphism (as in the π-calculus [25,27], see below) and bounded polymorphism (as in [12]). Goto et al. [15] develop a model of session polymorphism, in which session types are modeled as labeled transition systems which may incorporate deductive principles; polymorphism relies upon suitable deductions over transitions.

Most related to our developments are works by Berger et al. [1,2] and Wadler [28]. Berger et al. [1,2] proposed a polymorphically typed π-calculus with universal and existential quantification. Their system is not based on session types but results from combining so-called action types with linearity and duality principles. In their setting, enforcing resource usage disciplines entails a dedicated treatment for issues such as, e.g., sequentiality/causality in communications and type composition; in contrast, in the context of session-typed interactions, our logic-based approach offers general principles for handling such issues (e.g., typed process composition via cut). As in our case, they prove strong normalization of well-typed processes using reducibility candidates; however, due to the differences on typing, the proofs in [1,2] cannot be compared to our developments. In particular, our application of the reducibility candidates technique generalizes the linear logical relations we defined in [20]. While in [1] a parametricity result is stated, the journal paper [2] develops a behavioral theory based on generic transitions together with a fully abstract embedding of System F. Here again detailed comparisons with our proofs are difficult, because of the different typing disciplines considered in each case. Wadler [28] proposed an interpretation of session types as classical linear logic (along the lines of [7]). His system supports the kind of parametric polymorphism we develop here. However, the focus of [28] is not on the theory of parametric polymorphism. In particular, it does not address proof techniques for behavioral genericity nor establishes a relational parametricity principle, as we do here.

In a broader context—and loosely related to our work—Turner [27] studied impredicative, existential polymorphism for a simply-typed π-calculus (roughly, the discipline in which types describe the objects names can carry). In processes, polymorphism is expressed as explicit type parameters in input/output prefixes. Sangiorgi and Pierce [22] proposed a behavioral theory for Turner's framework. Neither of these works address strong normalization nor study relational parametricity. Building upon [22], Jeffrey and

Rathke [19] show that weak bisimulation is fully abstract for observational equivalence for an asynchronous polymorphic π-calculus. Recently, Zhao et al. [30] studied linearity and polymorphism for (variants of) System F. They prove relational parametricity via logical relations for open terms, but no concurrent interpretation is considered.

8   Concluding Remarks

In this paper, we have presented a systematic study of behavioral genericity for concurrent processes. Our study is in the context of session types—a rich behavioral type theory able to precisely describe complex communication protocols. Our work naturally generalizes recent discoveries on the correspondence between linear logic propositions and session types [6,7,20]. Previous works on genericity for concurrent processes appeal to various forms of polymorphism. In contrast to most of such works, and by developing a theory of impredicative, parametric polymorphism, we are able to formally connect the concept of behavioral parametricity with the well-known principle of relational parametricity, as introduced by Reynolds [24]. Since in our framework polymorphism accounts for the exchange of abstract protocols, relational parametricity enables us to effectively analyze concurrent systems which are parametric on arbitrarily complex communication disciplines. In addition to enjoying a relational parametricity principle, well-typed processes in our system respect session types in a deadlock-free way and are strongly normalizing. This unique combination of results confers very strong correctness guarantees for communicating systems. As a running example, we have illustrated how to specify and reason about a simple polymorphic cloud-based application server. In future work we would like to explore generalizations of our relational parametricity result so as to address security concerns (along the lines of [29]).

Acknowledgments. This research was supported by the Fundação para a Ciência e a Tecnologia (Portuguese Foundation for Science and Technology) through the Carnegie Mellon Portugal Program, under grants INTERFACES NGN-44 / 2009 and SFRH / BD / 33763 / 2009, and CITI; and by the Army Research Office under Award No. W911NF-09-1-0273. We thank the anonymous reviewers for their useful comments.

References

1. Berger, M., Honda, K., Yoshida, N.: Genericity and the π-Calculus. In: Gordon, A.D. (ed.) FOSSACS 2003. LNCS, vol. 2620, pp. 103–119. Springer, Heidelberg (2003)
2. Berger, M., Honda, K., Yoshida, N.: Genericity and the pi-calculus. Acta Inf. 42(2-3), 83–141 (2005)
3. Bono, V., Padovani, L.: Polymorphic endpoint types for copyless message passing. In: Proc. of ICE 2011. EPTCS, vol. 59, pp. 52–67 (2011)
4. Bono, V., Padovani, L.: Typing copyless message passing. Logical Methods in Computer Science 8(1) (2012)
5. Caires, L., Pérez, J.A., Pfenning, F., Toninho, B.: Relational parametricity for polymorphic session types. Tech. rep., CMU-CS-12-108, Carnegie Mellon Univ. (April 2012)
6. Caires, L., Pfenning, F.: Session Types as Intuitionistic Linear Propositions. In: Gastin, P., Laroussinie, F. (eds.) CONCUR 2010. LNCS, vol. 6269, pp. 222–236. Springer, Heidelberg (2010)
7. Caires, L., Pfenning, F., Toninho, B.: Linear logic propositions as session types (2012), under Revision - http://www.cs.cmu.edu/~fp/papers/sessions12.pdf

8. Caires, L., Pfenning, F., Toninho, B.: Towards concurrent type theory. In: TLDI 2012, pp. 1–12. ACM, New York (2012)
9. Dardha, O., Giachino, E., Sangiorgi, D.: Session Types Revisited. In: PPDP, pp. 139–150. ACM (2012)
10. Dezani-Ciancaglini, M., Giachino, E., Drossopoulou, S., Yoshida, N.: Bounded Session Types for Object Oriented Languages. In: de Boer, F.S., Bonsangue, M.M., Graf, S., de Roever, W.-P. (eds.) FMCO 2006. LNCS, vol. 4709, pp. 207–245. Springer, Heidelberg (2007)
11. Gay, S., Hole, M.: Subtyping for session types in the pi calculus. Acta Inf. 42, 191–225 (2005)
12. Gay, S.J.: Bounded polymorphism in session types. Math. Struc. in Comp. Sci. 18(5), 895–930 (2008)
13. Girard, J.Y.: Une extension de l'interprétation de Gödel à l'analyse, et son application à l'élimination de coupures dans l'analyse et la théorie des types. In: Proc. of the 2nd Scandinavian Logic Symposium, pp. 63–92. North-Holland Publishing Co. (1971)
14. Girard, J.Y., Lafont, Y., Taylor, P.: Proofs and Types. Cambridge Tracts in Theoretical Computer Science. Cambridge University Press (1989)
15. Goto, M., Jagadeesan, R., Jeffrey, A., Pitcher, C., Riely, J.: An Extensible Approach to Session Polymorphism (2012), http://fpl.cs.depaul.edu/projects/xpol/
16. Harper, R.: Practical Foundations for Programming Languages. Cambridge University Press (2012)
17. Honda, K.: Types for Dyadic Interaction. In: Best, E. (ed.) CONCUR 1993. LNCS, vol. 715, pp. 509–523. Springer, Heidelberg (1993)
18. Honda, K., Vasconcelos, V.T., Kubo, M.: Language Primitives and Type Discipline for Structured Communication-Based Programming. In: Hankin, C. (ed.) ESOP 1998. LNCS, vol. 1381, pp. 122–138. Springer, Heidelberg (1998)
19. Jeffrey, A., Rathke, J.: Full abstraction for polymorphic pi-calculus. Theor. Comput. Sci. 390(2-3), 171–196 (2008)
20. Pérez, J.A., Caires, L., Pfenning, F., Toninho, B.: Linear Logical Relations for Session-Based Concurrency. In: Seidl, H. (ed.) ESOP 2012. LNCS, vol. 7211, pp. 539–558. Springer, Heidelberg (2012)
21. Pfenning, F., Caires, L., Toninho, B.: Proof-Carrying Code in a Session-Typed Process Calculus. In: Jouannaud, J.-P., Shao, Z. (eds.) CPP 2011. LNCS, vol. 7086, pp. 21–36. Springer, Heidelberg (2011)
22. Pierce, B.C., Sangiorgi, D.: Behavioral equivalence in the polymorphic pi-calculus. J. ACM 47(3), 531–584 (2000)
23. Reynolds, J.C.: Towards a theory of type structure. In: Programming Symposium, Proceedings Colloque sur la Programmation, pp. 408–423. Springer, London (1974)
24. Reynolds, J.C.: Types, abstraction and parametric polymorphism. In: Mason, R.E.A. (ed.) Information Processing 1983, pp. 513–523. Elsevier Science Publishers B. V. (1983)
25. Sangiorgi, D., Walker, D.: The π-calculus: A Theory of Mobile Processes. Cambridge University Press, New York (2001)
26. Toninho, B., Caires, L., Pfenning, F.: Dependent session types via intuitionistic linear type theory. In: Proc. of PPDP 2011, pp. 161–172. ACM, New York (2011)
27. Turner, D.: The polymorphic pi-calculus: Theory and implementation. Tech. rep., ECS-LFCS-96-345, Univ. of Edinburgh (1996)
28. Wadler, P.: Propositions as sessions. In: Thiemann, P., Findler, R.B. (eds.) ICFP, pp. 273–286. ACM (2012)
29. Washburn, G., Weirich, S.: Generalizing parametricity using information-flow. In: LICS, pp. 62–71. IEEE Computer Society (2005)
30. Zhao, J., Zhang, Q., Zdancewic, S.: Relational Parametricity for a Polymorphic Linear Lambda Calculus. In: Ueda, K. (ed.) APLAS 2010. LNCS, vol. 6461, pp. 344–359. Springer, Heidelberg (2010)

Higher-Order Processes, Functions, and Sessions: A Monadic Integration

Bernardo Toninho[1,2], Luis Caires[2], and Frank Pfenning[1]

[1] Computer Science Department
Carnegie Mellon University
Pittsburgh, PA, USA
[2] CITI and Faculdade de Ciências e Tecnologia
Universidade Nova de Lisboa
Lisboa, Portugal

Abstract. In prior research we have developed a Curry-Howard interpretation of linear sequent calculus as session-typed processes. In this paper we uniformly integrate this computational interpretation in a functional language via a linear contextual monad that isolates session-based concurrency. Monadic values are open process expressions and are first class objects in the language, thus providing a logical foundation for higher-order session typed processes. We illustrate how the combined use of the monad and recursive types allows us to cleanly write a rich variety of concurrent programs, including higher-order programs that communicate processes. We show the standard metatheoretic result of type preservation, as well as a global progress theorem, which to the best of our knowledge, is new in the higher-order session typed setting.

1   Introduction

In prior work, we have developed a Curry-Howard interpretation of an intuitionistic linear sequent calculus, where linear propositions correspond to session types [11], sequent proofs to process expressions, and cut reduction to synchronous concurrent computation [4]. This π-calculus based system supports input and output of channels along channels, choice and selection, replicated input, generation of new channels, and message forwarding. Its logical origin led to straightforward generalizations to support data input and output [19] as well as polymorphism [20,6], incorporated as type input and output. This leaves open the question of how to fully and uniformly incorporate the system into a complete functional calculus to support higher-order, message-passing concurrent computation. In this paper we make a proposal for such an integration and explore its expressive power. We feel that the latter is particularly important, since it is not a priori clear how significantly our session-based (typed) communication restricts the π-calculus, or how easy it is to fully combine functional and concurrent computation while preserving the ability to reason about programs in the two paradigms.

Besides all the constructs of the π-calculus mentioned above, our language includes recursive types and, most importantly, a *contextual monad* to encapsulate

M. Felleisen and P. Gardner (Eds.): ESOP 2013, LNCS 7792, pp. 350–369, 2013.

open concurrent computations, which can be passed in functional computation but also *communicated* between processes in the style of *higher-order processes*, providing a uniform symmetric integration of both higher-order functions and processes. We allow the construction of recursive processes, which is a common motif in applications. As the examples demonstrate, the various features combine smoothly, allowing concise implementations of diverse examples such as streams and stream transducers, higher-order programs with process passing, polymorphic stacks and process networks for binary counting, among others we omit due to length constraints.

The rest of the paper is organized as follows: Section 2 sets up the necessary background for the presentation of our language. Sections 3.1 through 3.9 present the constructs of our language, intermixed with examples illustrating some of the key features of the constructs. Section 4 details two extended examples: a process implementation of stacks and a process network implementation of a binary counter. Section 5 discusses the metatheory of our language and we present some concluding remarks in Section 6.

2   Processes, Session Types and Functional Computation

In this section we introduce the preliminaries and notation necessary for the introduction of our language. We begin with the notion of session-typed process. We conceive of a process P as *offering* a specified service A along a channel c. The *session type* A prescribes the communication pattern along channel c. We have written this as $P :: c : A$. The process P may *use* services offered by other processes, each with their specified session types, leading to a *linear sequent*:

$$c_1{:}A_1, \ldots, c_n{:}A_n \vdash P :: c{:}A$$

where each of the channels c_i must be used linearly in P and in accordance with its session type A_i. We will abbreviate linear channel contexts with Δ. Note that the order in which the channels are listed is irrelevant, and they can be renamed consistently in the whole sequence as long as all channel names remain distinct. As we will see, to cover the full generality of our language, our typing judgment must account not only for linear channels Δ, but also shared channels which we maintain in a context Γ, and (functional) variables, which we maintain in a context Ψ, thus making our process typing judgment: $\Psi; \Gamma; \Delta \vdash P :: c{:}A$.

Our goal is to combine session typed processes and functional computation, to enable potentially sophisticated reasoning about concurrent programs by exploiting our Curry-Howard foundations. One of the first issues that arises is how to treat the channels c and c_i of the process typing judgment: One solution is to map channels to ordinary functional variables, forcing the entire language to be linear, which is a significant departure from typical approaches. Moreover, even if linear variables are supported, it is unclear how to restrict their occurrences so they are properly localized with respect to the structure of running processes.

Our solution is to encapsulate processes in a *contextual monad* so that each process is bundled with all channels (both linear and shared – the latter we cover in Section 3.9) it uses and the one that it offers. This is a linear counterpart to the contextual comonad presented in [15].

In our presentation in the following sections, we specify execution of concurrent programs in the form of a *substructural operational semantics* [17], for convenience of presentation. We rely on the following predicates: the linear proposition exec P denotes the state of a linear process expression P; !exec P denotes the state of a persistent process (which must always be a replicating input); and !eval $M\,V$ expresses that the functional term M evaluates to value V without using linear resources.

The rules that make up our substructural operational semantics, for those unfamiliar with this style, can be seen as a form of multiset rewrite rules [7] where the pattern to the left of the $\multimap$ arrow describes a state which is consumed and transformed into the one to the right. Existentials are used to generate names. Names or predicates marked with ! are not linear and thus not consumed as part of the rewrite (aptly modeling replication). The use of connectives from linear logic in this style of presentation, namely $\multimap$ to denote the state transformation, $\otimes$ to combine linear propositions from the context, and ! to denote persistence should not be confused with our session type constructors.

3   Combining Sessions and Functions

In this section we provide first an overview of the constructs of our language and then some details on each. The types of the language are separated into a functional part and a concurrent part, which are mutually dependent on each other. In types, we refer to functional type variables t, process type variables X, labels l_j, and channel names a. We briefly note the meaning of the each session type from the perspective of a provider.

$$\tau, \sigma ::= \tau \to \sigma \mid \ldots \mid \forall t.\, \tau \mid \mu t.\, \tau \mid t \qquad \text{(ordinary functional types)}$$
$$\mid \;\; \{a{:}A \leftarrow \overline{a_i{:}A_i}\} \qquad \text{process offering } A \text{ along channel } a,$$
$$\text{using channels } a_i \text{ offering } A_i$$

$A, B, C ::= \tau \supset A$	input value of type τ and continue as A
$\mid\;\; \tau \wedge A$	output value of type τ and continue as A
$\mid\;\; A \multimap B$	input channel of type A and continue as B
$\mid\;\; A \otimes B$	output fresh channel of type A and continue as B
$\mid\;\; 1$	terminate
$\mid\;\; \&\{\overline{l_j : A_j}\}$	offer choice between l_j and continue as A_j
$\mid\;\; \oplus\{\overline{l_j : A_j}\}$	provide one of the l_j and continue as A_j
$\mid\;\; !A$	provide replicable service A
$\mid\;\; \mu X.A \mid X$	recursive process type

$a \qquad ::= c \mid !u \qquad$ linear and shared channels

The functional types consist of functions types, polymorphic and recursive types and some additional standard constructs such as base types, products and sums that we have omitted for brevity. The novelty here is the contextual monadic type $\{a{:}A \leftarrow \overline{a_i{:}A_i}\}$, denoting the type of a process expression offering session A along channel a, using the channels a_i at types A_i. Channels a can either be linear (denoted by c or d) or shared (denoted by $!u$ or $!v$).

At the level of session types we have value input $\tau \supset A$ and value output $\tau \wedge A$, referring back to the functional layer. We also have recursive process types, absent from our prior work, which allows us to write some interesting concurrent programs. Next we summarize the terms M, N and process expressions P, Q of the language. Many of the process expressions have a continuation, which is separated from the first action by a semicolon (';'). To explicate the binding structure we have indicated the scope of variables that are bound using subscripts. An overlined expression abbreviates an indexed sequence.

$$
\begin{array}{llll}
M, N & ::= \lambda x{:}\tau.\, M_x \mid M\, N \mid \texttt{fix}\, x.\, M_x \mid \dots & \text{(usual functional constructs)} \\
& \mid \; a \leftarrow \{P_{a,\overline{a_i}}\} \leftarrow a_1,\dots,a_n & \text{process providing } a, \text{ using } a_1,\dots,a_n \\[4pt]
P, Q & ::= a \leftarrow M \leftarrow a_1,\dots,a_n; P_a & \text{compose process computed by } M \\
& & \text{in parallel with } P_a, \text{ communicating} \\
& & \text{along fresh channel } a \\[4pt]
& \mid \; x \leftarrow \texttt{input}\; c;\, Q_x & \text{input a value } x \text{ along channel } c \\
& \mid \; \_ \leftarrow \texttt{output}\; c\; M;\, P & \text{output value of } M \text{ along channel } c \\[4pt]
& \mid \; d \leftarrow \texttt{input}\; c;\, Q_d & \text{input channel } d \text{ along channel } c \\
& \mid \; \_ \leftarrow \texttt{output}\; c\; (d \leftarrow P_d);\, Q & \text{output a fresh channel } d \text{ along } c \\[4pt]
& \mid \; \texttt{close}\; c & \text{close channel } c \text{ and terminate} \\
& \mid \; \_ \leftarrow \texttt{wait}\; c;\, P & \text{wait for closure of } c \\[4pt]
& \mid \; \texttt{output}\; c\; !(d \leftarrow P_d) & \text{output a replicable } d \text{ along } c \text{ and terminate} \\
& \mid \; !u \leftarrow \texttt{input}\; c;\, Q_{!u} & \text{input shared channel } u \text{ along } c \\[4pt]
& \mid \; \texttt{case}\; c\; \texttt{of}\; \overline{l_j \Rightarrow P_j} & \text{branch on selection of } l_j \text{ along } c \\
& \mid \; \_ \leftarrow c.l_j;\, P & \text{select label } l_j \text{ along } c \\[4pt]
& \mid \; c \leftarrow \texttt{copy}\; !u;\, P_c & \text{spawn a copy of } !u \text{ along } c \\[4pt]
& \mid \; \texttt{fwd}\; c_1\; c_2 & \text{forward between } c_1 \text{ and } c_2
\end{array}
$$

The functional part of the language contains ordinary λ-abstraction, application, recursion, and the usual constructors for sum, product, and recursive types, omitted here for brevity. The main construct of interest is the internalization of process expressions through the contextual monadic construct $a \leftarrow \{P\} \leftarrow a_1,\dots a_n$, denoting a process P using channels a_i to provide along a.

Among the process expressions, the analogue of the monadic *bind* construct is $a \leftarrow M \leftarrow a_1,\dots,a_n; P_a$. It denotes the composition of the monadic object M (using channels a_i), spawning a new process that provides along a fresh channel for a, that will run in parallel with P_a. Typing enforces that if a is shared, all channels a_i must also be shared (otherwise we could violate linearity).

Using linear and persistent composition of monadic objects, we subsume direct process composition and provide a more uniform way of integrating composition of processes and functional computation. Monadic composition ultimately reduces to ordinary process composition during the computation.

Since we only provide a fixpoint operator at the functional level, writing recursive processes can only be done by writing a recursive function that returns an object of monadic type. We will see this pattern in our examples.

We write $\Psi = (x_1{:}\tau_1, \ldots, x_n{:}\tau_n)$ for the context declaring ordinary (functional) variables, $\Delta = (c_1{:}A_1, \ldots, c_n{:}A_n)$ and $\Gamma = (!u_1{:}B_1, \ldots, !u_n{:}B_n)$ for linear and shared channels, respectively. The order of declarations in all three forms of contexts is irrelevant, but all variables or channel names must be distinct.

$$\Psi \Vdash M : \tau \qquad \text{term } M \text{ has type } \tau$$
$$\Psi; \Gamma; \Delta \vdash P :: c{:}A \qquad \text{process } P \text{ offers } A \text{ along } c$$
$$\Delta = \mathsf{lin}(\overline{a_i{:}A_i}) \qquad \Delta \text{ consists of the linear channels } c_i{:}A_i \text{ in } \overline{a_i{:}A_i}$$
$$\Gamma = \mathsf{shd}(\overline{a_i{:}A_i}) \qquad \Gamma \text{ consists of the shared channels } !u_i{:}A_i \text{ in } \overline{a_i{:}A_i}$$

3.1   The Contextual Monad

We first detail our contextual monad, for now restricted to offering a service of type A along a *linear* channel c. It is embedded in the functional language with type $\{c{:}A \leftarrow \overline{a_i{:}A_i}\}$ and value constructor $c \leftarrow \{P_{c,\overline{a_i}}\} \leftarrow a_1, \ldots, a_n$.

A monadic value denotes a runnable process offering along channel c and using channels $a_1, \ldots, a_n$, serving both as a way of referring to processes in the functional layer and as a way of communicating processes in the process layer. The typing rule for the monad is:

$$\frac{\Delta = \mathsf{lin}(a_i{:}A_i) \quad \Gamma = \mathsf{shd}(a_i{:}A_i) \quad \Psi; \Gamma; \Delta \vdash P :: c{:}A}{\Psi \Vdash c \leftarrow \{P_{c,\overline{a_i}}\} \leftarrow \overline{a_i{:}A_i} : \{c : A \leftarrow \overline{a_i{:}A_i}\}} \ \{\}I$$

The monadic *bind* operation implements process composition. In the simplest case, $c \leftarrow M; Q_c$ composes the process underlying the monadic value M (which offers along c) with Q_c (which uses c and offers d). More generally, composition can refer to monadic values that use multiple channels: $c \leftarrow M \leftarrow a_1, \ldots, a_n; Q_c$. When writing code we often omit the semicolon, instead writing the continuation starting on the next line. The typing rule for the monadic bind is:

$$\frac{\Delta = \mathsf{lin}(\overline{a_i{:}A_i}) \quad \Gamma \supseteq \mathsf{shd}(\overline{a_i{:}A_i}) \quad \Psi \Vdash M : \{c{:}A \leftarrow \overline{a_i{:}A_i}\} \quad \Psi; \Gamma; \Delta', c{:}A \vdash Q_c :: d{:}D}{\Psi; \Gamma; \Delta, \Delta' \vdash c \leftarrow M \leftarrow \overline{a_i}; Q_c :: d{:}D} \ \{\}E$$

The shared channels need not all be used, because shared channels are not linear. On the other hand, linear names c_i must exactly match all names in Δ, enforcing linearity. The operational semantics for executing a monadic bind are:

$$\mathsf{exec}\,(c \leftarrow M \leftarrow \overline{a_i} \ ; \ Q_c) \otimes !\mathsf{eval}\, M \,(c \leftarrow \{P_{c,\overline{a_i}}\} \leftarrow \overline{a_i})$$
$$\multimap \{\exists c'.\, \mathsf{exec}\,(P_{c',\overline{a_i}}) \otimes \mathsf{exec}\,(Q_{c'})\}$$

Executing a bind evaluates M to a value of the appropriate form, which must contain a process expression P. We then create a fresh channel c' and execute of $P_{c',\overline{a_i}}$ itself, in parallel with $Q_{c'}$. In the value of M, the channels c and $\overline{a_i}$ are all bound names, so we rename them implicitly to match the interface of M in the monadic composition.

3.2 Value Communication ($\wedge$ and $\supset$)

Communicating a *value* of the functional language (as opposed to communicating a channel, which is slightly different, see Section 3.5) is expressed at the type level as $\tau \wedge A$ and $\tau \supset A$, corresponding to offering to send and receive values of type τ, respectively. Note that τ is not a session type, although we can communicate session-typed terms by using a monadic type. The language construct for such an output is $\_ \leftarrow \mathsf{output}\ c\ M; P$ with the typing rules:

$$\frac{\Psi \Vdash M : \tau \quad \Psi; \Gamma; \Delta \vdash P :: c : A}{\Psi; \Gamma; \Delta \vdash \_ \leftarrow \mathsf{output}\ c\ M\ ;\ P :: c : \tau \wedge A}\ \wedge R$$

$$\frac{\Psi \Vdash M : \tau \quad \Psi ; \Delta, c{:}A \vdash P :: d : D}{\Psi; \Gamma; \Delta, c{:}\tau \supset A \vdash \_ \leftarrow \mathsf{output}\ c\ M\ ;\ P :: d : D}\ \supset L$$

Theoretically, these are just trivial reformulations of the usual rules of the session-based process calculus, for example, as in [5]. We have therefore labeled them with their names from the linear sequent calculus.

When a process in the context provides a value output along a channel c, we can *input* it along c and bind a value variable x, written as $x \leftarrow \mathsf{input}\ c\ ; Q$. The same construct applies when we wish to define a session that offers to input a value. The typing rules are:

$$\frac{\Psi, x{:}\tau; \Gamma; \Delta, c{:}A \vdash Q_x :: d : D}{\Psi; \Gamma; \Delta, c{:}\tau \wedge A \vdash x \leftarrow \mathsf{input}\ c\ ; Q_x :: d : D}\ \wedge L$$

$$\frac{\Psi, x{:}\tau\ ; \Gamma; \Delta \vdash Q_x :: c : A}{\Psi\ ; \Gamma; \Delta \vdash x \leftarrow \mathsf{input}\ c\ ; Q_x :: c : \tau \supset A}\ \supset R$$

At this point we have *two* typing rules each for **input** and **output**. This is because $\mathsf{input}\ c$ either provides a service along $c : \tau \supset A$ or uses a service offered along $c : \tau \wedge A$, and dually for output. A type-checker can always tell whether a process provides or uses a channel, so there is no ambiguity. The rule that governs the semantics for these constructs is:

$$\begin{aligned} \mathsf{exec}\,(\_ \leftarrow \mathsf{output}\ c\ M\ ;\ P) \otimes \mathsf{exec}\,(x \leftarrow \mathsf{input}\ c\ ; Q_x) \otimes\ !\mathsf{eval}\ M\ V \\ \multimap \{\mathsf{exec}\,(P) \otimes \mathsf{exec}\,(Q_V)\} \end{aligned}$$

In accord with the call-by-value semantics of the functional language, the term that is to be output must be reduced to a value V, after which an input and an output can *synchronize*, both continuations proceed and the bound variable x is instantiated with the appropriate value.

3.3   Forwarding and Termination

In the underlying proof theory of the linear sequent calculus, we can satisfy an offer $c{:}A$ by using a channel $d{:}A$ of identical type through the identity rule:

$$\overline{\Psi;\Gamma;d{:}A \vdash \texttt{fwd}\,c\,d :: c{:}A}\;\; id$$

In the monadic formulation it is natural to write d (which is consumed) on the left, and c (which is provided) on the right. Operationally, the construct just forwards inputs or outputs along c to d and vice versa. Note that there is no process continuation here, since the offer of A along c has been satisfied in full by $d{:}A$. It therefore only appears as the last line in a monadic expression. The semantics of forwarding is:

$$\mathsf{exec}\,(\mathsf{fwd}\,c\,d) \multimap \{c = d\}$$

The rule applies a global substitution of d for c in the current context representing the state of all processes. In a spatially distributed situation, this cannot be directly implemented. One strategy is to send d along c, tagged as a forwarded channel. In essence, the process offering along c tells its client that it should now interact with the process offering d and then terminates. For this to work, the client must be able to discriminate such a message. Fortunately, since channels are session-typed and have only two endpoints, this does not require a broadcast or a complex protocol.

The process type **1**, the multiplicative unit of linear logic, maps to termination. The corresponding process constructor is close c with typing rule:

$$\overline{\Psi;\Gamma;\cdot \vdash \mathsf{close}\,c :: c : \mathbf{1}}\;\; 1R$$

According to the rules of linear logic, the linear channel context must be empty. Thus, communication along all channels that a process uses must be properly terminated before the process itself terminates. Conversely, if we are using a channel of type **1** we can *wait* for its underlying process to terminate with the *wait* construct: $\_ \leftarrow \texttt{wait}\,c\,;\,P$.

$$\dfrac{\Psi;\Gamma;\Delta \vdash P :: d : D}{\Psi;\Gamma;\Delta,c{:}\mathbf{1} \vdash \_ \leftarrow \texttt{wait}\,c\,;\,P :: d : D}\;\; 1L$$

The substructural operational semantics rule for these constructs is:

$$\mathsf{exec}\,(\mathsf{close}\,c) \otimes \mathsf{exec}\,(\_ \leftarrow \mathsf{wait}\,c\,;\,P) \multimap \{\mathsf{exec}\,(P)\}$$

Termination is straightforward. When we wait upon a channel that is being closed (as the name implies, `wait` is blocking – and so is `close`), the two operations are consumed and the continuation is executed.

3.4   Example: Streams

We want to produce an infinite stream of integers, starting at a given number n and counting up. This requires a coinductive type, defined as a recursive type (we distinguish between functional and session type definitions with type and stype, respectively).

```
stype intStream = int /\ intStream
```

In order to produce such a stream, we write a recursive function producing a process expression:

```
nats : int -> {c:intStream}
c <- nats x =
{ _ <- output c x
  c' <- nats (x+1)
  fwd c c' }
```

This an example of a function definition. We take some liberties with the syntax of these definitions for readability. In particular, we list interface channels on the left-hand side of the definition. In this formulation, every recursive call starts a new process with a new channel c'. Both for conciseness of notation and efficiency we provide a short-hand: if a tail-call of the recursive function provides a new channel which is then forwarded to the original offering channel, we can reuse the name directly, making the last line of the function above simply c <- nats (x+1).

It looks as if, for example, calling nats 0 might get into an infinite loop. However, communication in our language is synchronous, so the output will block until a matching consumer inputs the numbers.

We can now construct a stream transducer. As an example, we write a filter that takes a stream of integers and produces a stream of integers, retaining only those satisfying a given predicate $q : \text{int} \rightarrow \text{bool}$:

```
filter : (int -> bool) -> { d:intStream <- c:intStream }
d <- filter q <- c =
{ x <- input c
  case q x
    of true  => _ <- output d x
                d <- filter q <- c
     | false => d <- filter q <- c }
```

The filter function is recursive, but not a valid coinductive definition unless we can show that filter will be true for infinitely many elements of the stream.

3.5   Linear Channel Communication ($\otimes$ and $\multimap$)

An essential aspect of the π-calculus is the ability to pass channels among processes. This operation belongs to the process layer, since the functional layer can not track the proper linear use of such channels. In a session-typed system we enable processes to send and receive *fresh* communication channels, along which some particular session will be carried out. The types that capture this behavior are $A \otimes B$, denoting a channel which offers to output a fresh channel of type A and continue as B; and $A \multimap B$, which is the type for a channel that offers to input a fresh channel of type A in order to provide a continuation of type B (we will use $*$ for $\otimes$ when writing examples). The programming construct that achieves this is: $\_ \leftarrow \mathsf{output}\ c\ (d \leftarrow P)\ ;\ Q$ which outputs a fresh channel along c and spawns process P which offers some behavior along the fresh channel (bound in P as d). All available channels will be used in exactly one of the two processes P and Q. The typing rules are:

$$\frac{\Psi;\Gamma;\Delta \vdash P_d :: d : A \quad \Psi;\Gamma;\Delta' \vdash Q :: c : B}{\Psi;\Gamma;\Delta, \Delta' \vdash \_ \leftarrow \mathsf{output}\ c\ (d \leftarrow P_d)\ ;\ Q :: c : A \otimes B}\ \otimes R$$

$$\frac{\Psi;\Gamma;\Delta \vdash P_d :: d : A \quad \Psi;\Gamma;\Delta', c{:}B \vdash Q :: e : E}{\Psi;\Gamma;\Delta, \Delta', c{:}A \multimap B \vdash \_ \leftarrow \mathsf{output}\ c\ (d \leftarrow P_d)\ ;\ Q :: e : E}\ \multimap L$$

Two rules apply for this form of output: offering an output and interacting with the environment that contains a session of $\multimap$ type. Note how in both rules the left premise ensures that process P indeed provides A along d, whereas the right premise types the continuation, where c is now offered (resp. used) as B.

Correspondingly, the construct to input fresh channels is $d \leftarrow \mathsf{input}\ c\ ;\ R_d$.

$$\frac{\Psi;\Gamma;\Delta, d{:}A, c{:}B \vdash R_d :: e : E}{\Psi;\Gamma;\Delta, c{:}A \otimes B \vdash d \leftarrow \mathsf{input}\ c\ ;\ R_d :: e : E}\ \otimes L$$

$$\frac{\Psi;\Gamma;\Delta, d{:}A \vdash R_d :: c : B}{\Psi;\Gamma;\Delta \vdash d \leftarrow \mathsf{input}\ c\ ;\ R_d :: c : A \multimap B}\ \multimap R$$

The semantics for these constructions is defined as:

$$\mathsf{exec}\,(\_ \leftarrow \mathsf{output}\ c\ (d \leftarrow P_d)\ ;\ Q) \otimes \mathsf{exec}\,(d \leftarrow \mathsf{input}\ c\ ;\ R_d)$$
$$\multimap \{\exists d'.\ \mathsf{exec}\,(P_{d'}) \otimes \mathsf{exec}\,(Q) \otimes \mathsf{exec}\,(R_{d'})\}$$

When an input and an output along the same channel meet, a fresh channel d' is generated and passed to the continuation of the input and the process Q which is spawned and now offers along that channel, resulting in three parallel processes: the continuation of the input $R_{d'}$, the offering process $P_{d'}$ and the continuation of the output Q (where d' cannot occur by construction).

3.6 Choice and Branching ($\&$ and $\oplus$)

A common idiom when writing concurrent programs is to offer alternative behavior, where a client selects which behavior the server executes. In our system this is embodied by the labelled choice type $\&\{l_1{:}A_1, \ldots, l_k{:}A_k\}$, where the l_i are labels allowing other processes to select behaviors. Dually, it is also common for clients to be able to branch on alternative behavior, decided by the server.

From the server perspective, this is usually referred to as internal choice, in opposition to external choice which corresponds to choices made by the client, and is represented by the type $\oplus\{l_1:A_1,\ldots,l_k:A_k\}$.

To offer a choice to a client along a channel c we use a case construct: case c of $l_1 \Rightarrow P_1,\ldots,\Rightarrow l_k \Rightarrow P_k$ Such a construct waits for a selection of a label l_j on channel c, after which it will continue as the process P_j. Similarly, a client that is interacting with a server that offers an *internal* choice must branch on the possible outcomes of the server choice, which is also represented by the case construct. The typing rules are:

$$\frac{\Psi;\Gamma;\Delta \vdash P_1 :: c : A_1 \quad \ldots \quad \Psi;\Gamma;\Delta \vdash P_k :: c : A_k}{\Psi;\Gamma;\Delta \vdash \text{case } c \text{ of } \overline{l_j \Rightarrow P_j} :: c : \&\overline{\{l_j : A_j\}}} \&R$$

$$\frac{\Psi;\Gamma;\Delta, c{:}A_1 \vdash P_1 :: d : D \quad \ldots \quad \Psi;\Gamma;\Delta, c{:}A_k \vdash P_k :: d : D}{\Psi;\Gamma;\Delta, c: \oplus \overline{\{l_j : A_j\}} \vdash \text{case } c \text{ of } \overline{l_j \Rightarrow P_j} :: d : D} \oplus L$$

In linear logic terminology, the types $\&$ and $\oplus$ are additive. This means that the linear channels available to the processes in the premises are the same. Note how, in the first rule, the channel c to the right of the turnstyle arrow is the same in all the premises, denoting that after the selection takes place, the selected behavior will be carried out along the same channel. In the second rule, each branch is typed in a context where the channel c has committed to a choice.

To perform a selection of a label l_j on a channel, or to make a particular internal choice l_j along c, we use the process construct $\_ \leftarrow c.l_j \; ; \; P$. After performing such a selection, c will offer the behavior assigned to l_i. The typing rules for this construct are:

$$\frac{\Psi;\Gamma;\Delta, c{:}A_j \vdash P :: d : D}{\Psi;\Gamma;\Delta, c: \& \overline{\{l_j : A_j\}} \vdash \_ \leftarrow c.l_j \; ; \; P :: d : D} \&L$$

$$\frac{\Psi;\Gamma;\Delta \vdash P :: c : A_j}{\Psi;\Gamma;\Delta \vdash \_ \leftarrow c.l_j \; ; \; P :: c : \oplus\overline{\{l_j : A_j\}}} \oplus R$$

Finally, the operational semantics rule is:

$$\text{exec} (\_ \leftarrow c.l_j \; ; \; P) \otimes \text{exec} (\text{case } c \text{ of } \overline{l_j \Rightarrow Q_j}) \multimap \{\text{exec} (P) \otimes \text{exec} (Q_j)\}$$

Essentially, choices and selection block until both can be found along the same channel, after which the synchronization takes place and the continuation of the selection P and the corresponding selected process Q_i are executed concurrently.

3.7   Example: An App Store

Our contextual monad allows us to write functions that produce processes, but it also enables us to write process expressions that, through communication and composition of monadic values, communicate and execute actual processes. This contrasts with previous work where only purely functional values could be communicated in the functional layer [19] (also in the language of [20], while there is no distinction between functional and process expressions, it is not completely clear how one can in effect communicate suspended processes).

To clarify this, consider an App Store service that sells applications to its customers. These applications are not necessarily functional, in that they may communicate with the outside world. We can model such a service using monadic types as follows, using Choice {...} as our concrete syntax for &{...}:

```
stype AppStore = Choice {weather: {c:Weather <- d:API, e:GPS } /\ 1
                         travel: {c:Travel <- d:API } /\ 1
                         game: {c:Game <- d:API } /\ 1}
```

The type above describes a simplified App Store service, which offers three different applications to its customers (for simplicity, assume they are free): a weather forecast application, a travel information application, and a game. Upon selection from the client, the store will send to it the corresponding application. All the applications depend on a proprietary API that is not present locally in clients and is accessed remotely. Furthermore, the weather forecast application also makes use of a GPS connection to locate the user. These restrictions and dependencies are made precise by the contextual regions of the monadic types. The code for a client that downloads the weather application and runs it is:

```
ActivateGPS : unit -> {g:GPS}
WeatherClient : unit -> {c:Weather <- a:AppStore,d:API}
c <- WeatherClient() <- a:AppStore, d:API =
{ _ <- a.weather
  w <- input a
  _ <- wait a
  g <- ActivateGPS()
  c <- w <- d, g }
```

Note that unit -> t is isomorphic to t. The client requires an existing connection with the AppStore service and the connection with the API, which we assume is established by some other means. The client then performs the appropriate selection and download from the store. To run the application, it first makes use of a local function that activates its GPS module, supplying a channel handle g which is used to fulfill the required dependencies of the weather application. This simple example shows how we can cleanly integrate *communication* and *execution* of open process expressions into our functional language. It is straightforward to extend this example to more complex interfaces.

3.8   Example: A List Process

We exemplify the usage of branching by defining a type for a process implementation of a list. The process can either behave as the empty list (i.e. offer no behavior) or as a list with a head and a tail, modelled by the output of the head element of the list, followed by the output of a *fresh* channel consisting of the handle to the tail list process. The type employs data polymorphism in the elements of the list. We write Or {...} as concrete syntax for ⊕{...}.

```
stype List t = Or {nil: 1, cons: t /\ (List t * 1)}
```

maintained We can now define two functions, `Nil` and `Cons`: the first produces
a process that corresponds to the empty list and the second, given a value v of
type t will produce a process that expects to interact with a channel 1 denoting
a list of t's, such that it will implement, along channel c, a new list with v as
its head.

```
Nil : unit -> {c:List t}          Cons : t -> {c:List t <- l:List t}
c <- Nil () =                      c <- Cons v <- l =
{ _ <- c.nil                      { _ <- c.cons
   close c                           _ <- output c v
}                                     _ <- output c (l' <- fwd l l')
                                   close c }
```

Note that the `Cons` function, after sending the `cons` label along channel c and
outputting v, it will output a fresh channel l' that is meant to represent the
tail of the list, which is actually present along channel l. Thus, the function will
also spawn a process that will forward between l and l'.

3.9   Sharing and Replication (!)

All the process type constructors we have described thus far have been purely
linear, in the sense that they represent behavior that must take place exactly
once. *Shared channels* !u allow behavior to be replicated.

Shared channels appear in our language in two roles: we can *bind* a monadic
expression to a shared channel, provided the monadic expression does not depend
on linear channels; and we can *use* a channel of type !A, which we make precise
shortly. A monadic expression that does not depend on any linear channels can
be bound to a persistent channel $!u \leftarrow M \leftarrow !u_1, \ldots, !u_n$; P. where M is an
expression of monadic type, conforming to the linearity restriction mentioned
above. Type-theoretically, this is reminiscent of the cut[!] principle:

$$\frac{\Gamma \subseteq \overline{!u_i:B_i} \quad \Psi \Vdash M : \{!u:A \leftarrow \overline{!u_i:B_i}\} \quad \Psi ; \Gamma, u:A; \Delta \vdash Q_{!u} :: c : C}{\Psi; \Gamma; \Delta \vdash !u \leftarrow M \leftarrow \overline{!u_i} ; Q_{!u} :: c : C} \quad \{\}E^!$$

The idea is that the monadic process underlying M will be *replicated* as many
times as uses of u take place. The semantics for this form of bind are:

$$\text{exec}\,(!u \leftarrow M \leftarrow \overline{!u_i} ; Q_{!u}) \otimes \text{!eval}\, M\,(c \leftarrow \{P_{c,\overline{!u_i}}\} \leftarrow \overline{!u_i})$$
$$\multimap \{\exists u.\,\text{!exec}\,(c \leftarrow \text{input}\,!u ; P_{c,\overline{!u_i}}) \otimes \text{exec}\,(Q_{!u})\}$$

A persistent bind forces the evaluation of the monadic object and then spawns
a replicating process that will input on the generated (shared) channel u a fresh
channel c. Each such channel c will be used for communication between replicas
of P and its clients. This process is spawned in parallel with the continuation
$Q_{!u}$ which can trigger replications of P as needed.

Using a shared channel is accomplished by $c \leftarrow$ copy $!u$; P. The copy construct triggers the creation of a new process that implements the behavior ascribed to $!u$ along a fresh *linear* channel that is bound to c. The typing rule for copy explicates this concept:

$$\frac{\Psi; \Gamma, u{:}A; \Delta, c{:}A \vdash Q_c :: d : D}{\Psi; \Gamma, u{:}A; \Delta \vdash c \leftarrow \text{copy } !u \text{ ; } Q_c :: d : D} \text{ copy}$$

And the semantics are:

$$!\text{exec}\,(d \leftarrow \text{input}\,!u \text{ ; } P_d) \otimes \text{exec}\,(c \leftarrow \text{copy}\,!u \text{ ; } Q_c) \multimap \{\exists c'. \text{exec}(P_{c'}) \otimes \text{exec}(Q_{c'})\}$$

Note that the process performing an input along $!u$ persists, since the proposition !exec is persistent in the metalanguage of SSOS.

We internalize sharing at the process type level as $!A$, the type of a linear channel that can be promoted to a shared channel of type A. The constructs below may appear somewhat complex, but arise entirely from a Curry-Howard interpretation of intuitionistic linear logic. We provide a channel $c{:}!A$ of such a type with the construct output $c\,!(d \leftarrow P_d)$. Note that there is no continuation, and the subterm is preceded by a '!'. To use a channel of type $!A$, we input the fresh shared channel $!u \leftarrow$ input c ; Q_u.

The idea is that we will output along c a *fresh* channel $!u'$ which will be of a shared nature. It is along $!u'$ that subsequent interactions will take place, and thereafter all communication along c has terminated. The process expression P_d will then implement some behavior that will be *replicated* whenever (and only if) the fresh shared channel u' that was output is used. The typing rules, corresponding to the $!R$ and $!L$ from dual intuitionistic linear logic, are:

$$\frac{\Psi; \Gamma; \cdot \vdash P_d :: d : A}{\Psi; \Gamma; \cdot \vdash \text{output } c\,!(d \leftarrow P_d) :: c : !A} \text{ !R} \qquad \frac{\Gamma, u{:}A; \Delta \vdash Q_u :: d : D}{\Gamma; \Delta, c{:}!A \vdash !u \leftarrow \text{input } c \text{ ; } Q_u :: d : D} \text{ !L}$$

Note that P_d may not depend on any linear channels, so that it can be replicated as needed. The semantics for these forms of input and output are:

$$\text{exec}\,(\text{output}\,c\,!(d \leftarrow P_d)) \otimes \text{exec}\,(!u \leftarrow \text{input}\,c \text{ ; } Q_{!u})$$
$$\multimap \{\exists !u'. \,!\text{exec}\,(d \leftarrow \text{input}\,!u' \text{ ; } P_d) \otimes \text{exec}\,(Q_{!u'})\}$$

4   Extended Examples

In this section we cover two slightly larger examples that showcase some of the expressiveness of our language. We will first show how to define two different implementations of stacks using monadic processes and how our Curry-Howard basis allows for simple and elegant programs. Secondly, we will describe the implementation of a binary counter as a network of communicating processes.

Stacks. We begin by defining the stack session type. We write t => s as concrete syntax for $\tau \supset A$:

```
stype Stack t =  Choice {push: t => Stack t
                         pop: Or {none: unit /\ Stack t
                                  some:t /\ Stack t}
                         dealloc: 1}
```

The Stack recursive type denotes a channel along which a process offers the choice between three operations: push, which will then expect the input of an element that will be the new top of the stack; pop, which outputs either the top element or unit (if the stack is empty); and dealloc, which fully deallocates the stack and thus has type 1.

We present two distinct implementations of type Stack: stack1 makes use of functional lists to maintain the stack; the second implementation stack2, more interestingly, uses the list processes from Section 3.8 to implement the stack as a network of communicating processes.

```
stack1 : list t -> {c:Stack t}
c <- stack1 nil =                    | c <- stack1 (v::l) =
{ case c of                          { case c of
    push   => v <- input c               push   => v' <- input c
              c <- stack1 (v::nil)                   c  <- stack1 (v'::v::l)
    pop    => _ <- c.none                pop    => _  <- c.some
              _ <- output c ()                      _  <- output c v
              c <- stack1 nil                       c  <- stack1 l
    dealloc => close c }                 dealloc => close c }
```

The code above consists of a function, taking a list and producing a monadic object indexed by the given list. We define the function by branching on the structure of the list, as usual. We can, for instance, create an empty stack by calling stack1 with the empty list.

As mentioned above, our second implementation makes use of the list processes of Section 3.8. We begin by defining a function deallocList, whose purpose is to fully terminate a process network implementing a list. This means recursively consuming the list session and terminating it:

```
deallocList : unit -> {c:1 <- l:List t}
  c <- deallocList () <- l =
  { case l of
       nil  => _ <- wait l
               close c
       cons => v  <- input l
               l' <- input l
               _  <- wait l
               c  <- deallocList () <- l' }
```

We define our second stack implementation by making use of the Cons, Nil and deallocList functions. The function stack2 below produces a monadic stack process with an underlying process network implementing the list itself:

```
stack2 : unit -> {c:Stack t <- l:List t}
 c <- stack2 () <- l =
 { case c of
    push    => v  <- input c
               l' <- Cons v <- l
               c  <- stack2 <- l'
    pop     => case l of
               nil  => _  <- wait l
                       _  <- c.none
                       _  <- out c ()
                       l' <- Nil ()
                       c  <- stack2 () <- l'
              cons => v  <- input l
                      l' <- input l
                      _  <- wait l
                      _  <- c.some
                      _  <- out c v
                      c  <- stack2 () <- l'
  dealloc => c <- deallocList () <- l }
```

The monadic process specified above begins by offering the three stack operations: push, pop and dealloc. The first inputs along the stack channel the element that is to be pushed onto the stack and calls on the Cons function to produce a monadic process that appends to the list session l the new element, binding the resulting list process to l' and making a recursive call. The pop case needs to branch on whether or not the list session l encodes the empty list. If such is the case (nil), it waits for the termination of l, signals that the stack is empty and calls upon the Nil function to reconstruct an empty list for the recursive call; if not (cons), it inputs the element from the list session and the continuation list l'. It then outputs the received element and proceeds recursively. Finally, deallocList calls out to the list deallocation function.

Bit Counter Network As above, we begin with the interface type:

```
stype Counter = Choice {inc: Counter
                        val: nat /\ Counter
                        halt: 1}
```

The Counter session type provides three operations: an inc operation, which increments its internal state; a val operation, which just outputs the counter's current value and a halt operation which terminates the counter.

One way to implement such a counter is through a network of communicating processes, each storing a single bit of the bit string that encodes the value of the counter. We do this by defining two mutually recursive functions epsilon and bit. The former encodes the empty bit string, abiding to the counter interface. Notably, in the inc branch, a new bit process is spawned with value 1. To do this, we make a recursive call to the epsilon function, bound to channel d, and then simply call the bit function with argument 1, also providing it with the channel d. The bit function encodes an actual bit element of the bit string. It takes a number as an argument which is the 1 or 0 value of the bit and constructs a process expression that provides the counter interface along channel c by having access to the process encoding the previous bit in the string along channel d.

```
bit : nat -> {c:Counter <- d:Counter}     epsilon : unit -> {c:Counter}
  c <- bit b <- d =                         c <- epsilon () =
  { case c of                               { case c of
      inc  => case b of                         inc  => d <- epsilon ()
                0 => c <- bit 1 <- d                     c <- bit 1 <- d
                1 => _ <- d.inc
                     c <- bit 0 <- d
      val  => _ <- d.val                        val  => _ <- output c 0
              n <- input d                              c <- epsilon ()
              _ <- output c (2*n+b)
              c <- bit b <- d
      halt => _ <- d.halt                       halt => close c }
              _ <- wait d
              close c }
```

A bit b outputs the counter value by polling the previous bit for its counter value n and then outputting $2n + b$. This invariant ensures an adequate binary encoding of the counter. Termination triggers the cascade termination of all bits by sending a termination message to the previous bit, waiting on the channel and then terminating. The increment case simply recurses with value 1 if the bit is 0; otherwise it sends an increment message to the previous bit to encode the carry and recurses with value 0.

5   Metatheory

For the functional part of the language, we presuppose a standard call-by-value semantics. We could also use call-by-name, but for communication across channels, especially if distributed, one would not want to pass potentially large computations and the data structures they still rely on. If the functional language is overlaid with a termination checker (for examples, along the lines of Abel's proposal [1]), then the two should semantically coincide in any case. Since this is standard, we focus on the interesting new constructs: the monad, and the process expressions contained in them.

From the perspective of the functional language, an encapsulated process expression is a value and is not executed. Instead, functional programs can be used to construct concurrent programs which can be executed at the top-level, or with a special built-in construct such as *run*, which would have type

```
run : {c:1} -> unit
```

Not accidentally, this is analogous to Haskell's I/O monad [16], even if our language is call-by-value.

We now summarize the expected preservation and progress theorems. In order to state the type preservation theorem we must be able to talk about the types and channels during the execution of the processes, not just for a process expression P. An elegant way to accomplish this is to annotate each exec P with the channel c along which P offers its output and its type A. This exploits the observation that every process offers a service along exactly one channel, and for every channel there is exactly one process providing a service along it. This extended form is written exec $P\,c\,A$. The rules given above can be updated in a straightforward fashion, and the original rules can be recovered by erasure. The annotations fix the role of every channel in a communication as either offered or used, and we can check if the whole process state Ω is well-typed according to a signature of (linear and shared) channels Σ. We write $\models (\Sigma\,;\,\Omega) :: c_0 : 1$ if process state Ω uses channels in Σ accordingly and offers 1 along an initial channel c_0 that is offered but not used anywhere. Initially, we have a closed process expression P_0 and $\models (\cdot\,;\,\mathsf{exec}\,P_0\,c_0\,1) :: c_0 : 1$ (without loss of generality since using composition we can introduce well-typed processes offering an arbitrary type, regardless of the type of c_0). Overall, a pair consisting of the currently available channels and the process state evolves via multiset rewriting [7] to another pair, potentially containing new channels and the new process state.

Theorem 1 (Type Preservation).

(i) If $\cdot \Vdash M : \tau$ and !eval $M\,V$ then V is a value and $\cdot \Vdash V : \tau$.
(ii) If $\models (\Sigma\,;\,\Omega) :: c_0 : 1$ and $(\Sigma\,;\,\Omega) \longrightarrow^* (\Sigma'\,;\,\Omega')$ then $\models (\Sigma'\,;\,\Omega') :: c_0 : 1$.

Type preservation is fairly straightforward to prove, given the strong logical foundations of our language. We require the typical substitution property for the functional portion of the language. As for processes, the proof requires us to relate typing derivations of process expressions to typings of the global executing process state. This turns out to be easy, since substructural operational semantics breaks down the global state into its local process expressions.

Theorem 2 (Progress). *Assume for every term M such that $\cdot \Vdash M : \tau$ there exists a value V with !eval $M\,V$. Then for every well-typed process state $\models (\Sigma\,;\,\Omega) :: c_0 : 1$, either $\Omega = (!\Omega'', \mathsf{exec}\,(\mathsf{close}\,c_0)\,c_0\,1)$ where $!\Omega''$ consists of propositions of the form !exec P, or $(\Sigma\,;\,\Omega) \longrightarrow (\Sigma'\,;\,\Omega')$ for some Σ' and Ω'.*

Progress is, as usual, slightly harder to prove. Once we account for the internal transitions of processes and functional evaluation, we note that in a well-typed state Ω, persistent processes (which always perform a replicating input) can never block. Due to linear well-typing of the state, we can therefore restrict attention to the remaining $k+1$ processes that *offer* communication along $k+1$ channels, but *using* only k channels since c_0 does not have a match. Now we perform an induction on k. If P_0 is blocked on c_0, it must have the form stated in the theorem (by inversion on its typing) and we are done. If not, it must be blocked on some other channel, say, c_1. Now the process P_1 offering c_1 is either blocked on c_1, in which case it can communicate with P_0 and we can make a transition, or it must be blocked on some other c_2. We proceed in this way until we must come to P_k, which must be blocked on c_k and can communicate with P_{k-1} since no other linear channel c_{k+1} remains on which it could be blocked.

It is easy to modify the operational semantics to employ a small-step semantics for the functional layer, which ensures progress for the full language without relying on termination of functional computation.

We now return to consideration of what we have called the *linear contextual monad*. In general, a monad consists of a type constructor M supporting two operations usually called *return* and *bind*. The return operation allows for any value in the language to be made into a monadic object, whereas bind is a form of composition. These operations are expected to satisfy certain equational laws. Specifically, return is both a left and right unit for bind, and bind is associative.

Using our monadic introduction and composition constructs, we can reproduce similar laws. First, if we consider the process expression: $c \leftarrow \{c \leftarrow P_c\}; Q_c$, it is straightforward to see, using our semantics, that it behaves as just both P_c and Q_c executing in parallel. This is a form of left identity, and captures the computational effects of binding. Secondly, we can reconstruct a right identity law by observing that the term: $\{c \leftarrow (d \leftarrow M; \mathtt{fwd}\ c\ d)\}$ always behaves like M. This is reminiscent of an η-conversion law, but one must note that in the presence of non-termination, evaluating the expression M might not terminate, whereas the monadic expression is always a value. However, any context that uses both expressions will not be able to distinguish them, regardless of non-termination. Finally, it is easy to see that our composition construct is associative.

Taking the category theory perspective, these constructions are somewhat reminiscent of the work on Arrows [12], itself a special case of Relative Monads [2], which are monadic constructions for functors that are not endomorphic. A closer work, also rich in category theoretical foundations is that of Benton [3], where two functors F and G are defined, forming an adjunction between intuitionistic and linear functional calculi. Our construction is in essence a contextual variant of G, albeit with some slight differences, specifically the fact that we employ a let-style elimination and we bridge a functional and a process calculus, instead of two functional calculi.

6   Related Work and Conclusion

Our language is similar to the higher-order session typed calculi of [14]. However, our logical foundation makes the system substantially simpler, and the contextual monad allows for a cleaner integration of higher-order communication, which they accomplish by passing λ-abstractions. Furthermore, we obtain a global progress result, which is not present in [14].

A language with similar goals to ours is Wadler's GV [20], which is itself based on a session-typed functional language created by Gay and Vasconcelos [10]. GV is also a session-typed functional language, essentially consisting of a simply typed, linear λ-calculus extended with primitives for session-typed communication. A point of divergence of GV and our language is that GV is itself linear, whereas we base our functional language in a traditional λ-calculus equipped with a linear contextual monad that isolates communication and linear typing. Naturally, making the whole language linear avoids the need for the monad, since it becomes possible to write functions that, for instance, take a data value and a channel and send the piece of data along the channel (this is so because essentially all terms in GV can be translated to session-typed linear processes). On the other hand, the pervasively concurrent semantics means it is further from a practical integration of concurrency into an existing functional language. Another significant difference between the two approaches is that the underlying type theory of GV is classical, whereas ours is intuitionistic. Monads are intuitionistic in their logical form [9], which therefore makes the intuitionistic form of linear logic a particularly good candidate for a monadic integration of functional and concurrent computation based on a Curry-Howard correspondence. We believe our natural examples demonstrate this clearly. Prior work by Mazurak and Zdancewic [13] indicates that control operators may be a better candidate than a contextual monad for classical linear logic, if the functional character of the underlying language is to be fully preserved.

The language F* [18] shares similar goals and ideas, but it is aimed at security properties and distributed computation, while we aim at concurrency. Instead of linear types, F* uses affine types and its concurrency primitives are not based on a Curry-Howard correspondence. The various language levels, including communication, are separated not by a monad but through a complex kinding system that controls their interaction. Our language design aims to be a stepping stone towards full dependent verification (as traditional in type theory) and allowing for dynamic verification. F* makes several interesting contributions with respect to this tradeoff, in particular the use of value-dependent types.

Finally, there are a number of language features we have given short thrift here in order to concentrate on our essential contributions. One is the possibility of asynchronous communication. Work by DeYoung et al. [8] shows that this is consistent with a Curry-Howard approach although some programs we wrote here (like infinite stream producers) would have to be rewritten to account for the change in the operational semantics. Polymorphism [20,6] for process expressions is largely orthogonal and manageable as long as types are explicitly passed.

Future Work. Our main goal for future work is the generalization of the system we have presented here to a full dependent type theory that integrates reasoning about both functional and concurrent computation. Dependent types in the purely functional setting are a well understood concept, however the generalization to our language is far from straightforward since we move to a setting where session types can be indexed not only by purely functional terms, but also by session typed processes through the monadic type from the functional language. Similarly, dependent types in the functional layer share this feature. This means that type equality (crucial for type conversion in dependent type theories), which ultimately reduces to term equality, requires a suitable notion of *process equality*. While we obviously want a decidable equality, it is not clear what other criteria this notion of equality should obey. Moreover, reasoning about processes is typically done both inductively and coinductively, so to be able to internalize this reasoning in the language we require a primitive notion of coinductive reasoning, as well as a proper theory of inductive and coinductive definitions applied to our session typed setting. We plan to tackle these challenges in future work.

Acknowledgments. Support for this research was provided by the Fundação para a Ciência e a Tecnologia (Portuguese Foundation for Science and Technology) through the Carnegie Mellon Portugal Program, under grants SFRH / BD / 33763 / 2009 and INTERFACES NGN-44 / 2009, and CITI; and by the Army Research Office under Award No. W911NF-09-1-0273

References

1. Abel, A.: Type-based termination, inflationary fixed-points, and mixed inductive-coinductive types. In: Proceedings of FICS 2012, pp. 1–11 (2012)
2. Altenkirch, T., Chapman, J., Uustalu, T.: Monads Need Not Be Endofunctors. In: Ong, L. (ed.) FOSSACS 2010. LNCS, vol. 6014, pp. 297–311. Springer, Heidelberg (2010)
3. Benton, P.N.: A Mixed Linear and Non-Linear Logic: Proofs, Terms and Models (Extended Abstract). In: Pacholski, L., Tiuryn, J. (eds.) CSL 1994. LNCS, vol. 933, pp. 121–135. Springer, Heidelberg (1995)
4. Caires, L., Pfenning, F.: Session Types as Intuitionistic Linear Propositions. In: Gastin, P., Laroussinie, F. (eds.) CONCUR 2010. LNCS, vol. 6269, pp. 222–236. Springer, Heidelberg (2010)
5. Caires, L., Pfenning, F., Toninho, B.: Towards concurrent type theory. In: Types in Language Design and Implementation, pp. 1–12 (2012)
6. Caires, L., Pérez, J.A., Pfenning, F., Toninho, B.: Relational parametricity for polymorphic session types. Tech. Rep. CMU-CS-12-108, Carnegie Mellon Univ. (2012)
7. Cervesato, I., Scedrov, A.: Relating state-based and process-based concurrency through linear logic. Information and Computation 207(10), 1044–1077 (2009)
8. DeYoung, H., Caires, L., Pfenning, F., Toninho, B.: Cut reduction in linear logic as asynchronous session-typed communication. In: Computer Science Logic (2012)
9. Fairtlough, M., Mendler, M.: Propositional lax logic. Information and Computation 137(1), 1–33 (1997)
10. Gay, S., Vasconcelos, V.T.: Linear type theory for asynchronous session types. J. Funct. Programming 20(1), 19–50 (2010)
11. Honda, K.: Types for Dyadic Interaction. In: Best, E. (ed.) CONCUR 1993. LNCS, vol. 715, pp. 509–523. Springer, Heidelberg (1993)
12. Hughes, J.: Generalising monads to arrows. Sci. of Comp. Prog. 37, 67–111 (1998)
13. Mazurak, K., Zdancewic, S.: Lolliproc: to concurrency from classical linear logic via curry-howard and control. In: ICFP, pp. 39–50 (2010)
14. Mostrous, D., Yoshida, N.: Two Session Typing Systems for Higher-Order Mobile Processes. In: Della Rocca, S.R. (ed.) TLCA 2007. LNCS, vol. 4583, pp. 321–335. Springer, Heidelberg (2007)
15. Nanevski, A., Pfenning, F., Pientka, B.: Contextual modal type theory. Transactions on Computational Logic 9(3) (2008)
16. Peyton Jones, S.L., Wadler, P.: Imperative functional programming. In: Principles of Prog. Lang., POPL 1993, pp. 71–84 (1993)
17. Pfenning, F., Simmons, R.J.: Substructural operational semantics as ordered logic programming. In: Logic in Comp. Sci., pp. 101–110 (2009)
18. Swamy, N., Chen, J., Fournet, C., Strub, P.Y., Bhargavan, K., Yang, J.: Secure distributed programming with value-dependent types. In: ICFP, pp. 266–278 (2011)
19. Toninho, B., Caires, L., Pfenning, F.: Dependent session types via intuitionistic linear type theory. In: Prin. Pract. Decl. Program., pp. 161–172 (2011)
20. Wadler, P.: Propositions as sessions. In: ICFP, pp. 273–286 (2012)

Concurrent Flexible Reversibility*

Ivan Lanese[1], Michael Lienhardt[2], Claudio Antares Mezzina[3], Alan Schmitt[4], and Jean-Bernard Stefani[4]

[1] Focus Team, University of Bologna/Inria, Italy
[2] PPS Laboratory, Paris Diderot University, France
[3] SOA Unit, FBK, Trento, Italy
[4] Inria, France
{lanese,lienhard}@cs.unibo.it, mezzina@fbk.eu,
{alan.schmitt,jean-bernard.stefani}@inria.fr

Abstract. Concurrent reversibility has been studied in different areas, such as biological or dependable distributed systems. However, only "rigid" reversibility has been considered, allowing to go back to a past state and restart the exact same computation, possibly leading to divergence. In this paper, we present croll-π, a concurrent calculus featuring *flexible reversibility*, allowing the specification of alternatives to a computation to be used upon rollback. Alternatives in croll-π are attached to messages. We show the robustness of this mechanism by encoding more complex idioms for specifying flexible reversibility, and we illustrate the benefits of our approach by encoding a calculus of communicating transactions.

1 Introduction

Reversible programs can be executed both in the standard, forward direction as well as in the backward direction, to go back to past states. Reversible programming is attracting much interest for its potential in several areas. For instance, chemical and biological reactions are typically bidirectional, and the direction of execution is fixed by environmental conditions such as temperature. Similarly, quantum computations are reversible as long as they are not observed. Reversibility is also used for backtracking in the exploration of a program state-space toward a solution, either as part of the design of the programming language as in Prolog, or to implement transactions. We are particularly interested in the use of reversibility for modeling and programming concurrent reliable systems. In this setting, the main idea is that in case of an error the program backtracks to a past state where the decisions leading to the error have not been taken yet, so that a new forward execution may avoid repeating the (same) error.

Reversibility has a non trivial interplay with concurrency. Understanding this interplay is fundamental in many of the areas above, e.g., for biological or reliable distributed systems, which are naturally concurrent. In the spirit of concurrency,

---

* This work has been partially supported by the French National Research Agency (ANR), projects REVER ANR 11 INSE 007 and PiCoq ANR 10 BLAN 0305.

M. Felleisen and P. Gardner (Eds.): ESOP 2013, LNCS 7792, pp. 370–390, 2013.

independent threads of execution should be rolled-back independently, but causal dependencies between related threads should be taken into account.

This form of reversibility, termed *causal consistent*, was first introduced by RCCS [11], a reversible variant of CCS. RCCS paved the way to the definition of reversible variants of more expressive concurrent calculi [8, 18, 20, 22]. This line of research considered rigid, uncontrolled, step-by-step reversibility. *Step-by-step* means that each single step can be undone, as opposed, e.g., to checkpointing where many steps are undone at once. *Uncontrolled* means that there is no hint as to when to go forward and when to go backward, and up to where. *Rigid* means that the execution of a forward step followed by the corresponding backward step leads back to the starting state, where an identical computation can restart.

While these works have been useful to understand the basics of concurrent reversibility in different settings, some means to *control* reversibility are required in practice. In the literature four different forms of control have been proposed: relating the direction of execution to some energy parameter [2], introducing irreversible actions [12], using an explicit rollback primitive [17], and using a superposition operator to control forward and backward execution [24].

With the exception of [24], these works were based on causal consistent, rigid reversibility. However, rigid reversibility may not always be the best choice. In the setting of reliable systems, for instance, rigid reversibility means that to recover from an error a past state is reached. From this past state the computation that lead to the error is still possible. If the error was due to a transient fault, retrying the same computation may be enough to succeed. If the failure was permanent, the program may redo the same error again and again.

Our goal is to overcome this limitation by providing the programmer with suitable linguistic constructs to specify what to do after a causal consistent backward computation. Such constructs can be used to ensure that new forward computations explore new possibilities. To this end, we build on our previous work on roll-π [17], a calculus where concurrent reversibility is controlled by the roll γ operator. Executing it reverses the action referred by γ together with all the dependent actions. Here, we propose a new calculus called croll-π, for compensating roll-π, as a framework for *flexible reversibility*. We attempt to keep croll-π as close as possible to roll-π while enabling many new possible applications. We thus simply replace roll-π communication messages $a\langle P \rangle$ by *messages with alternative* $a\langle P \rangle \div c\langle Q \rangle$. In forward computation, a message $a\langle P \rangle \div c\langle Q \rangle$ behaves exactly as $a\langle P \rangle$. However, if the interaction consuming it is reversed, the original message is not recreated—as would be the case with rigid reversibility—but the alternative $c\langle Q \rangle$ is released instead. Our rollback and alternative message primitives provide a simple form of reversibility control, which always respects the causal consistency of reverse computation. It contrasts with the fine-grained control provided by the superposition constructs in [24], where the execution of a CCS process can be constrained by a controller, possibly reversing given past actions in a way that is non-causally consistent.

Our contributions are as follows. We show that the simple addition of alternatives to roll-π greatly extends its expressive power. We describe how messages with alternative allow for programming different patterns for flexible reversibility. Then, we show that croll-π can be used to model the communicating transactions of [13]. Notably, the tracking of causality of croll-π is more precise than the one in [13], thus allowing to improve on the original proposal by avoiding some spurious undo of actions. Additionally, we study some aspects of the behavioral theory of croll-π, including a context lemma for barbed congruence. This allows us to reason about croll-π programs, in particular to prove the correctness of the encodings of primitives for flexible reversibility and of the transactional calculus of [13]. Finally, we present an interpreter, written in Maude [10], for a small language based on croll-π.

Outline. Section 2 gives an informal introduction to croll-π. Section 3 defines the croll-π calculus, its reduction semantics, and it introduces the basics of its behavioral theory. Section 4 presents various croll-π idioms for flexible reversibility. Section 5 outlines the croll-π interpreter in Maude and a solution for the Eight Queens problem. Section 6 presents an encoding and an analysis of the Trans-CCS constructs from [13]. Section 7 concludes the paper with related work and a mention of future studies. The paper includes short proof sketches for the main results. We refer to the online technical report [16] for full proofs.

2   Informal Presentation

Rigid reversibility in roll-π. The croll-π calculus is a conservative extension of the roll-π calculus introduced in [17].[1] We briefly review the roll-π constructs before presenting the extension added by croll-π. Processes in roll-π are essentially processes of the asynchronous higher-order π-calculus [25], extended with a rollback primitive. Processes in roll-π cannot directly execute, only *configurations* can. A configuration is essentially a parallel composition of *tagged processes* along with *memories* tracking past interactions and *connectors* tracing causality information. In a tagged process of the form $k : P$, the tag k uniquely identifies the process P in a given configuration. We often use the term *key* instead of *tag*.

The uniqueness of tags in configurations is achieved thanks to the following reduction rule that defines how parallel processes are split.

$$k : P \mid Q \longrightarrow \nu k_1 \, k_2. \, k \prec (k_1, k_2) \mid k_1 : P \mid k_2 : Q$$

In the above reduction, $\mid$ is the parallel composition operator and ν is the restriction operator, both standard from the π-calculus. As usual, the scope of restriction extends as far to the right as possible. Connector $k \prec (k_1, k_2)$ is used to remember that the process tagged by k has been split into two sub-processes identified by the new keys k_1 and k_2. Thus complex processes can be split into *threads*, where a thread is either a *message*, of the form $a\langle P \rangle$ (where a is a channel name), a receiver process (also called a *trigger*), of the form $a(X) \triangleright_\gamma P$, or a *rollback* instruction of the form roll k, where k is a key.

---

[1] The version of roll-π presented here is slightly refined w.r.t. the one in [17].

A *forward* communication step occurs when a message on a channel can be received by a trigger on the same channel. It takes the following form (roll-π is an asynchronous higher-order calculus).

$$(k_1 : a\langle P \rangle) \mid (k_2 : a(X) \triangleright_\gamma Q) \longrightarrow \nu k. \, k : Q\{^{P,k}/_{X,\gamma}\} \mid [\mu; k]$$

In this forward step, keys k_1 and k_2 identify threads consisting respectively of a message $a\langle P \rangle$ on channel a and a trigger $a(X) \triangleright_\gamma Q$ expecting a message on channel a. The result of the message input yields, as in higher-order π, the body of the trigger Q with the formal parameter X instantiated by the received value, i.e., process P. Message input also has three side effects: (i) the tagging of the newly created process $Q\{^{P,k}/_{X,\gamma}\}$ by a fresh key k; (ii) the creation of a memory $[\mu; k]$, which records the original two threads,[2] $\mu = (k_1 : a\langle P \rangle) \mid (k_2 : a(X) \triangleright_\gamma Q)$, together with key k; and (iii) the instantiation of variable γ with the newly created key k (the trigger construct is a binder both for its process parameter and its key parameter).

In roll-π, a forward computation, i.e., a series of forward reduction steps as above, can be perfectly undone by backward reductions triggered by the occurrence of an instruction of the form roll k, where k refers to a previously instantiated memory. In roll-π, we have for instance the following forward and backward steps, where $M = (k_1 : a\langle Q \rangle) \mid (k_2 : a(X) \triangleright_\gamma X \mid \text{roll } \gamma)$:

$$M \longrightarrow \nu k. \, (k : Q \mid \text{roll } k) \mid [M; k] \longrightarrow$$
$$\nu k \, k_3 \, k_4. \, k \prec (k_3, k_4) \mid k_3 : Q \mid k_4 : \text{roll } k \mid [M; k] \longrightarrow M$$

The communication between threads k_1 and k_2 in the first step and the split of process k into k_3 and k_4 are perfectly undone by the third (backward) step.

More generally, the set of memories and connectors of a configuration M provides us with an ordering $<:$ between the keys of M that reflects their causal dependency: $k' <: k$ means that key k' has key k as *causal descendant*. Thus, the effects of a rollback can be characterized as follows. When a rollback takes place in a configuration M, triggered by an instruction $k_r : \text{roll } k$, it suppresses all threads and processes whose tag is a causal descendant of k, as well as all connectors $k' \prec (k_1, k_2)$ and memories $m = [k_1 : \tau_1 \mid k_2 : \tau_2; k']$ whose key k' is a causal descendant of k. When suppressing such a memory m, the rollback operation may release a thread $k_i : \tau_i$ if k_i is not a causal descendant of k (at least one of the threads of m must have k as causal antecedent if k' has k as causal antecedent). This is due to the fact that a thread that is not a causal descendant of k may be involved in a communication (and then captured into a memory) by a descendant of k. This thread can be seen as a resource that is taken from the environment through interaction, and it should be restored in case of rollback. Finally, rolling-back also releases the content μ of the memory $[\mu; k]$ targeted by the roll, reversing the corresponding communication step.

---

[2] Work can be done to store memories in a more efficient way. We will not consider this issue in the current paper; an approach can be found in [20].

Flexible reversibility in croll-π. In roll-π, a rollback perfectly undoes a computation originated by a specific message receipt. However, nothing prevents the same computation from taking place again and again (although not necessarily in the same context, as independent computations may have proceeded on their own in parallel). To allow for flexible reversibility, we extend roll-π with a single new construct, called a *message with alternative*. In croll-π, a message may now take the form $a\langle P\rangle \div C$, where alternative C may either be a message $c\langle Q\rangle \div \mathbf{0}$ with null alternative or the null process $\mathbf{0}$. When the message receipt of $k : a\langle P\rangle \div C$ is rolled-back, configuration $k : C$ is released instead of the original $k : a\langle P\rangle$, as would be the case in roll-π. (Only the alternative associated to the message in the memory $[\mu; k]$ targeted by the roll is released: other processes may be restored, but not modified.) For example, if $M = (k_1 : a\langle Q\rangle \div \mathbf{0}) \mid (k_2 : a(X) \triangleright_\gamma X \mid \mathsf{roll}\ \gamma)$ then we have the following computation, where the communication leading to the rollback becomes disabled.

$$M \longrightarrow \nu k.\,(k : Q \mid \mathsf{roll}\ k) \mid [M; k] \longrightarrow$$
$$\nu k\, k_3\, k_4.\, k \prec (k_3, k_4) \mid k_3 : Q \mid k_4 : \mathsf{roll}\ k \mid [M; k] \longrightarrow$$
$$k_1 : \mathbf{0} \mid (k_2 : a(X) \triangleright_\gamma X \mid \mathsf{roll}\ \gamma)$$

We will show that croll-π is powerful enough to devise various kinds of alternatives (see Section 4), whose implementation is not possible in roll-π (cf. Theorem 2). Also, thanks to the higher-order aspect of the calculus, the behavior of roll-π can still be programmed: rigid reversibility can be seen as a particular case of flexible reversibility. Thus, the introduction of messages with alternative has limited impact on the definition of the syntax and of the operational semantics, but it has a strong impact on what can actually be modeled in the calculus and on its theory.

3   The croll-π Calculus: Syntax and Semantics

3.1   Syntax

Names, keys, and variables. We assume the existence of the following denumerable infinite mutually-disjoint sets: the set $\mathcal{N}$ of *names*, the set $\mathcal{K}$ of *keys*, the set $\mathcal{V}_\mathcal{K}$ of *key variables*, and the set $\mathcal{V}_\mathcal{P}$ of *process variables*. $\mathbb{N}$ denotes the set of natural numbers. We let (together with their decorated variants): a, b, c range over $\mathcal{N}$; h, k, l range over $\mathcal{K}$; u, v, w range over $\mathcal{N} \cup \mathcal{K}$; γ range over $\mathcal{V}_\mathcal{K}$; X, Y, Z range over $\mathcal{V}_\mathcal{P}$. We denote by $\tilde{u}$ a finite set $u_1 \ldots u_n$.

Syntax. The syntax of the croll-π calculus is given in Figure 1. *Processes*, given by the P, Q productions, are the standard processes of the asynchronous higher-order π-calculus [25], except for the presence of the roll primitive, the extra bound tag variable in triggers, and messages with alternative that replace roll-π messages $a\langle P\rangle$. The alternative operator $\div$ binds more strongly than any other operator. *Configurations* in croll-π are given by the M, N productions. A configuration is built up from *tagged processes* $k : P$, *memories* $[\mu; k]$, and *connectors*

$$P, Q ::= \mathbf{0} \mid X \mid \nu a. P \mid (P \mid Q) \mid a(X) \triangleright_\gamma P \mid a\langle P \rangle \div C \mid \text{roll } k \mid \text{roll } \gamma$$
$$M, N ::= \mathbf{0} \mid \nu u. M \mid (M \mid N) \mid k : P \mid [\mu; k] \mid k \prec (k_1, k_2) \quad C ::= a\langle P \rangle \div \mathbf{0} \mid \mathbf{0}$$
$$\mu ::= (k_1 : a\langle P \rangle \div C) \mid (k_2 : a(X) \triangleright_\gamma Q)$$
$$a, b, c \in \mathcal{N} \quad X, Y, Z \in \mathcal{V}_P \quad \gamma \in \mathcal{V}_K \quad u, v, w \in \mathcal{N} \cup \mathcal{K} \quad h, k, l \in \mathcal{K}$$

Fig. 1. Syntax of croll-π

$k \prec (k_1, k_2)$. In a memory $[\mu; k]$, we call μ the *configuration part* of the memory and k its *key*. $\mathcal{P}$ denotes the set of croll-π processes and $\mathcal{C}$ the set of croll-π configurations. We let (together with their decorated variants) P, Q, R range over $\mathcal{P}$ and L, M, N range over $\mathcal{C}$. We call *thread* a process that is either a message with alternative $a\langle P \rangle \div C$, a trigger $a(X) \triangleright_\gamma P$, or a rollback instruction roll k. We let τ and its decorated variants range over threads. We write $\prod_{i \in I} M_i$ for the parallel composition of configurations M_i for each $i \in I$ (by convention $\prod_{i \in I} M_i = \mathbf{0}$ if $I = \emptyset$), and we abbreviate $a\langle \mathbf{0} \rangle$ to $\bar{a}$.

Free identifiers and free variables. Notions of free identifiers and free variables in croll-π are standard. Constructs with binders are of the following forms: $\nu a. P$ binds the name a with scope P; $\nu u. M$ binds the identifier u with scope M; and $a(X) \triangleright_\gamma P$ binds the process variable X and the key variable γ with scope P. We denote by $\mathtt{fn}(P)$ and $\mathtt{fn}(M)$ the set of free names and keys of process P and configuration M, respectively. Note in particular that $\mathtt{fn}(k : P) = \{k\} \cup \mathtt{fn}(P)$, $\mathtt{fn}(\text{roll } k) = \{k\}$. We say that a process P or a configuration M is *closed* if it has no free (process or key) variable. We denote by $\mathcal{P}_{cl}$ and $\mathcal{C}_{cl}$ the sets of closed processes and configurations, respectively. We abbreviate $a(X) \triangleright_\gamma P$, where X is not free in P, to $a \triangleright_\gamma P$; and $a(X) \triangleright_\gamma P$, where γ is not free in P, to $a(X) \triangleright P$.

Remark 1. We have no construct for replicated processes or internal choice in croll-π: as in the higher-order π-calculus, these can easily be encoded.

Remark 2. In the remainder of the paper, we adopt *Barendregt's Variable Convention*: if terms $t_1, \ldots, t_n$ occur in a certain context (e.g., definition, proof), then in these terms all bound identifiers and variables are chosen to be different from the free ones.

3.2   Reduction Semantics

The reduction semantics of croll-π is defined via a reduction relation $\longrightarrow$, which is a binary relation over closed configurations ($\longrightarrow \subset \mathcal{C}_{cl} \times \mathcal{C}_{cl}$), and a structural congruence relation $\equiv$, which is a binary relation over configurations ($\equiv \subset \mathcal{C} \times \mathcal{C}$). We define *configuration contexts* as "configurations with a hole $\bullet$", given by the grammar: $\mathbb{C} ::= \bullet \mid (M \mid \mathbb{C}) \mid \nu u. \mathbb{C}$. *General contexts* $\mathbb{G}$ are just configurations with a hole $\bullet$ in a place where an arbitrary process P can occur. A *congruence* on processes or configurations is an equivalence relation $\mathcal{R}$ that

(E.ParC) $M \mid N \equiv N \mid M$ (E.ParA) $M_1 \mid (M_2 \mid M_3) \equiv (M_1 \mid M_2) \mid M_3$

(E.NilM) $M \mid \mathbf{0} \equiv M$ (E.NewN) $\nu u.\,\mathbf{0} \equiv \mathbf{0}$

(E.NewC) $\nu u.\,\nu v.\,M \equiv \nu v.\,\nu u.\,M$ (E.NewP) $(\nu u.\,M) \mid N \equiv \nu u.\,(M \mid N)$

(E.α) $M =_\alpha N \implies M \equiv N$ (E.TagC) $k \prec (k_1, k_2) \equiv k \prec (k_2, k_1)$

(E.TagA) $\nu h.\,k \prec (h, k_3) \mid h \prec (k_1, k_2) \equiv \nu h.\,k \prec (k_1, h) \mid h \prec (k_2, k_3)$

Fig. 2. Structural congruence for croll-π

$$(\text{S.Com}) \quad \frac{\mu = (k_1 : a\langle P \rangle \div C) \mid (k_2 : a(X) \rhd_\gamma Q_2)}{(k_1 : a\langle P \rangle \div C) \mid (k_2 : a(X) \rhd_\gamma Q_2) \longrightarrow \nu k.\,(k : Q_2\{^{P,k}/_{X,\gamma}\}) \mid [\mu; k]}$$

$$(\text{S.TagN}) \; k : \nu a.\,P \longrightarrow \nu a.\,k : P$$

$$(\text{S.TagP}) \; k : P \mid Q \longrightarrow \nu k_1 k_2.\,k \prec (k_1, k_2) \mid k_1 : P \mid k_2 : Q$$

$$(\text{S.Roll}) \quad \frac{k <: N \quad \text{complete}(N \mid [\mu; k] \mid (k_r : \text{roll } k)) \quad \mu' = \text{xtr}(\mu)}{N \mid [\mu; k] \mid (k_r : \text{roll } k) \longrightarrow \mu' \mid N \!\,\rotatebox{180}{\$}\, k}$$

$$(\text{S.Ctx}) \; \frac{M \longrightarrow N}{\mathbb{C}[M] \longrightarrow \mathbb{C}[N]} \qquad (\text{S.Eqv}) \; \frac{M \equiv M' \quad M' \longrightarrow N' \quad N' \equiv N}{M \longrightarrow N}$$

Fig. 3. Reduction rules for croll-π

is closed for general or configuration contexts: $P \mathcal{R} Q \implies \mathbb{G}[P] \mathcal{R} \mathbb{G}[Q]$ and $M \mathcal{R} N \implies \mathbb{C}[M] \mathcal{R} \mathbb{C}[N]$.

Structural congruence $\equiv$ is defined as the smallest congruence on configurations that satisfies the axioms in Figure 2, where $t =_\alpha t'$ denotes equality of t and t' modulo α-conversion. Axioms E.ParC to E.α are standard from the π-calculus. Axioms E.TagC and E.TagA model commutativity and associativity of connectors, in order not to have a rigid tree structure. Thanks to axiom E.NewC, $\nu \tilde{u}.\,A$ stands for $\nu u_1 \ldots u_n.\,A$ if $\tilde{u} = u_1 \ldots u_n$.

Configurations can be written in normal form using structural congruence.

Lemma 1 (Normal form). *Given a configuration M, we have:*

$$M \equiv \nu \tilde{n}.\,\prod_i (k_i : P_i) \mid \prod_j [\mu_i; k_j] \mid \prod_l k_l \prec (k'_l, k''_l)$$

The reduction relation $\longrightarrow$ is defined as the smallest binary relation on closed configurations satisfying the rules of Figure 3. This extends the naïve semantics of roll-π introduced in [17],[3] and outlined here in Section 2, to manage alternatives. We denote by $\Longrightarrow$ the reflexive and transitive closure of $\longrightarrow$.

Reductions are either forward, given by rules S.Com, S.TagN, and S.TagP, or backward, defined by rule S.Roll. They are closed under configuration contexts (rule S.Ctx) and under structural congruence (rule S.Eqv). The rule for communication S.Com is the standard communication rule of the higher-order π-calculus with the side effects discussed in Section 2. Rule S.TagN allows restrictions in processes to be lifted at the configuration level. Rule S.TagP allows to split parallel processes. Rule S.Roll enacts rollback, canceling all the effects of the interaction identified by the unique key k, and releasing the initial configuration that gave rise to the interaction, where the alternative replaces the original message. This is the only difference between croll-π and roll-π: in the latter, the memory μ was directly released. However, this small modification yields significant changes to the expressive power of the calculus, as we will see later.

The rollback impacts only the causal descendants of k, defined as follows.

Definition 1 (Causal dependence). *Let M be a configuration and let $\mathcal{T}_M$ be the set of keys occurring in M. Causal dependence $<:_M$ is the reflexive and transitive closure of $<_M$, which is defined as the smallest binary relation on $\mathcal{T}_M$ satisfying the following clauses:*

- *$k <_M k'$ if $k \prec (k_1, k_2)$ occurs in M with $k' = k_1$ or $k' = k_2$;*
- *$k <_M k'$ if a thread $k : P$ occurs (inside μ) in a memory $[\mu; k']$ of M.*

If the configuration M is clear from the context, we write $k <: k'$ for $k <:_M k'$.

A backward reduction triggered by roll k involves *all* and *only* the descendants of key k. We ensure they are all selected by requiring that the configuration is *complete*, and that no other term is selected by requiring k-*dependence*.

Definition 2 (Complete configuration). *A configuration M is complete, denoted as $\mathsf{complete}(M)$, if, for each memory $[\mu; k]$ and each connector $k' \prec (k, k_1)$ or $k' \prec (k_1, k)$ that occurs in M there exists in M either a connector $k \prec (h_1, h_2)$ or a tagged process $k : P$ (possibly inside a memory).*

A configuration M is k-dependent if all its components depend on k.

Definition 3 (k-dependence). *Let M be a configuration such that:*

$$M \equiv \nu\tilde{u}. \ \prod_{i \in I}(k_i : P_i) \mid \prod_{j \in J}[\mu_j; k_j] \mid \prod_{l \in L} k_l \prec (k_l', k_l'') \ \text{with} \ k \notin \tilde{u}.$$

Configuration M is k-dependent, written $k <: M$ by overloading the notation for causal dependence among keys, if for every i in $I \cup J \cup L$, we have $k <:_M k_i$.

Rollback should release all the resources consumed by the computation to be rolled-back which were provided by other threads. They are computed as follows.

---

[3] We extend the naïve semantics instead of the high-level or the low-level semantics (also defined in [17]) for the sake of simplicity. However, reduction semantics corresponding to the high-level and low-level semantics of roll-π can similarly be specified.

Definition 4 (Projection). *Let M be a configuration such that:*
$M \equiv \nu\tilde{u}. \prod_{i \in I}(k_i : P_i) \mid \prod_{j \in J}[k_j' : R_j \mid k_j'' : T_j; k_j] \mid \prod_{l \in L} k_l \prec (k_l', k_l'')$ *with*
$k \notin \tilde{u}.$ *Then:*

$$M \wr_k = \nu\tilde{u}. \Big(\prod_{j' \in J'} k_{j'}' : R_{j'} \Big) \mid \Big(\prod_{j'' \in J''} k_{j''}'' : T_{j''} \Big)$$

where $J' = \{j \in J \mid k \nless: k_j'\}$ and $J'' = \{j \in J \mid k \nless: k_j''\}$.

Intuitively, $M \wr_k$ consists of the threads inside memories in M which are not dependent on k.

Finally, and this is the main novelty of croll-π, function xtr defined below replaces messages from the memory targeted by the roll by their alternatives.

Definition 5 (Extraction function).

$$\text{xtr}(M \mid N) = \text{xtr}(M) \mid \text{xtr}(N) \qquad\qquad \text{xtr}(k : a\langle P\rangle \div C) = k : C$$
$$\text{xtr}(k : a(X) \rhd_\gamma Q) = k : a(X) \rhd_\gamma Q$$

No other case needs to be taken into account as xtr is only called on the contents of memories.

Remark 3. Not all syntactically licit configurations make sense. In particular, we expect configurations to respect the causal information required for executing croll-π programs. We therefore work only with *coherent* configurations. A configuration is coherent if it is obtained by reduction starting from a configuration of the form $\nu k. k : P$ where P is closed and contains no roll h primitive (all the roll primitives should be of the form roll γ).

3.3   Barbed Congruence

We define notions of strong and weak barbed congruence to reason about croll-π processes and configurations. Name a is *observable* in configuration M, denoted as $M\downarrow_a$, if $M \equiv \nu\tilde{u}. (k : a\langle P\rangle \div C) \mid N$, with $a \notin \tilde{u}$. We write $M\mathcal{R}\downarrow_a$, where $\mathcal{R}$ is a binary relation on configurations, if there exists N such that $M\mathcal{R}N$ and $N\downarrow_a$. The following definitions are classical.

Definition 6 (Barbed congruences for configurations). *A relation $\mathcal{R} \subseteq \mathcal{C}_{cl} \times \mathcal{C}_{cl}$ on closed configurations is a* strong *(respectively* weak*) barbed simulation if whenever $M \, \mathcal{R} \, N$,*

  - *$M\downarrow_a$ implies $N\downarrow_a$ (respectively $N \Longrightarrow\downarrow_a$);*
  - *$M \longrightarrow M'$ implies $N \longrightarrow N'$ (respectively $N \Longrightarrow N'$) with $M'\mathcal{R}N'$.*

A relation $\mathcal{R} \subseteq \mathcal{C}_{cl} \times \mathcal{C}_{cl}$ is a strong (weak) barbed bisimulation *if $\mathcal{R}$ and $\mathcal{R}^{-1}$ are strong (weak) barbed simulations. We call* strong (weak) barbed bisimilarity *and denote by $\sim$ ($\approx$) the largest strong (weak) barbed bisimulation. The largest congruence for configuration contexts included in $\sim$ ($\approx$) is called* strong (weak) barbed congruence, *denoted by $\sim_c$ ($\approx_c$).*

The notion of strong and weak barbed congruence extends to closed and open processes, by considering general contexts that form closed configurations.

Definition 7 (Barbed congruences for processes). *A relation $\mathcal{R} \subseteq \mathcal{P}_{cl} \times \mathcal{P}_{cl}$ on closed processes is a* strong *(resp.* weak*) barbed congruence if whenever $P\mathcal{R}Q$, for all general contexts $\mathbb{G}$ such that $\mathbb{G}[P]$ and $\mathbb{G}[Q]$ are closed configurations, we have $\mathbb{G}[P] \sim_c \mathbb{G}[Q]$ (resp. $\mathbb{G}[P] \approx_c \mathbb{G}[Q]$).*

Two open processes P and Q are said to be strong *(resp.* weak*) barbed congruent, denoted by $P \sim_c^o Q$ (resp. $P \approx_c^o Q$) if for all substitutions σ such that $P\sigma$ and $Q\sigma$ are closed, we have $P\sigma \sim_c Q\sigma$ (resp. $P\sigma \approx_c Q\sigma$).*

Working with arbitrary contexts can quickly become unwieldy. We offer the following Context Lemma to simplify the proofs of congruence.

Theorem 1 (Context lemma). *Two processes P and Q are weak barbed congruent, $P \approx_c^o Q$, if and only if for all substitutions σ such that $P\sigma$ and $Q\sigma$ are closed, all closed configurations M, and all keys k, we have: $M \mid (k : P\sigma) \approx M \mid (k : Q\sigma)$.*

The proof of this Context Lemma is much more involved than the corresponding one in the π-calculus, notably because of the bookkeeping required in dealing with process and thread tags. It is obtained by composing the lemmas below.

The first lemma shows that the only relevant configuration contexts are parallel contexts.

Lemma 2 (Context lemma for closed configurations). *For any closed configurations M, N, $M \sim_c N$ if and only if, for all closed configurations L, $M \mid L \sim N \mid L$. Likewise, $M \approx_c N$ if and only if, for all L, $M \mid L \approx N \mid L$.*

Proof. The left to right implication is immediate, by definition of $\sim_c$. For the other direction, the proof consists in showing that $\mathcal{R} = \{\langle\mathbb{C}[M], \mathbb{C}[N]\rangle \mid \forall L, M \mid L \sim N \mid L\}$ is included in $\sim$. The weak case is identical to the strong one. $\square$

We can then prove the thesis on closed processes.

Lemma 3 (Context lemma for closed processes). *Let P and Q be closed processes. We have $P \approx_c Q$ if and only if, for all closed configuration contexts $\mathbb{C}$ and $k \notin \mathtt{fn}(P, Q)$, we have $\mathbb{C}[k : P] \approx \mathbb{C}[k : Q]$.*

Proof. The left to right implication is clear. One can prove the right to left direction by induction on the form of general contexts for processes, using Lemma 4 below for message contexts. $\square$

Lemma 4 (Factoring). *For all closed processes P, all closed configurations M such that $M\{^P/_X\}$ is closed, and all $c, t, k_0, k_0' \notin \mathtt{fn}(M, P)$, we have*

$$M\{^P/_X\} \approx_c \nu c, t, k_0, k_0'. M\{^{\bar{c}}/_X\} \mid k_0 : t\langle Y_P\rangle \mid k_0' : Y_P$$

where $Y_P = t(Y) \rhd (c \rhd P) \mid t\langle Y\rangle \mid Y$.

We then deal with open processes.

Lemma 5 (Context lemma for open processes). *Let P and Q be (possibly open) processes. We have $P \approx_c^o Q$ if and only if for all closed configuration contexts $\mathbb{C}$, all substitutions σ such that $P\sigma$ and $Q\sigma$ are closed, and all $k \notin \mathtt{fn}(P, Q)$, we have $\mathbb{C}[k : P\sigma] \approx \mathbb{C}[k : Q\sigma]$.*

Proof. For the only if part, one proceeds by induction on the number of bindings in σ. The case for zero bindings follows from Lemma 3. For the inductive case, we write $\mathbb{P}[\bullet]$ for a process where an occurrence of $\mathbf{0}$ has been replaced by $\bullet$, and we show that contexts of the form $\mathbb{P} = a\langle R \rangle \mid a(X) \triangleright \mathbb{P}'[\bullet]$ where a is fresh and $\mathbb{P} = a\langle R \rangle \mid a(X) \triangleright_\gamma \mathbb{P}'[\bullet]$ where a is fresh and X never occurs in the continuation actually enforce the desired binding.

For the if part, the proof is by induction on the number of triggers. If the number of triggers is 0 then the thesis follows from Lemma 3. The inductive case consists in showing that equivalence under substitutions ensures equivalence under a trigger context. □

Proof (of Theorem 1). A direct consequence of Lemma 5 and Lemma 2. □

4   croll-π Expressiveness

4.1   Alternative Idioms

The message with alternative $a\langle P \rangle \div C$ triggers alternative C upon rollback. We choose to restrict C to be either a message with $\mathbf{0}$ alternative or $\mathbf{0}$ itself in order to have a minimal extension of roll-π. However, this simple form of alternative is enough to encode far more complex alternative policies and constructs, as shown below. We define the semantics of the alternative idioms below by only changing function $\mathtt{xtr}$ in Definition 5. We then encode them in croll-π and prove the encoding correct w.r.t. weak barbed congruence. More precisely, for every extension below the notion of barbs is unchanged. The notion of barbed bisimulation thus relates processes with slightly different semantics (only $\mathtt{xtr}$ differs) but sharing the same notion of barbs. Since we consider extensions of croll-π, in weak barbed congruence we consider just closure under croll-π contexts. By showing that the extensions have the same expressive power of croll-π, we ensure that allowing them in contexts would not change the result. Every encoding maps unmentioned constructs homomorphically to themselves. After having defined each alternative idiom, we freely use it as an abbreviation.

Arbitrary alternatives. Messages with arbitrary alternative can be defined by allowing C to be any process Q. No changes are required to the definition of function $\mathtt{xtr}$. We can encode arbitrary alternatives as follows, where c is not free in P, Q.

$$(a\langle P \rangle \div Q)_{aa} = \nu c.\, a\langle (P)_{aa} \rangle \div c\langle (Q)_{aa} \rangle \div \mathbf{0} \mid c(X) \triangleright X$$

Proposition 1. $P \approx_c (P)_{aa}$ *for any closed process with arbitrary alternatives.*

$\mathcal{R} = \mathcal{R}_1 \cup \mathcal{R}_2 \cup \mathcal{R}_3 \cup \mathcal{R}_4 \cup \mathcal{R}_5 \cup Id$

$\mathcal{R}_1 = \{\langle k : a\langle P\rangle \div Q \mid L , k : (\nu c. \, a\langle P\rangle \div c\langle Q\rangle \div \mathbf{0} \mid c(X) \rhd X) \mid L\rangle\}$

$\mathcal{R}_2 = \{\langle k : a\langle P\rangle \div Q \mid L , \nu c\, k_1\, k_2. k \prec (k_1, k_2) \mid k_1 : a\langle P\rangle \div c\langle Q\rangle \div \mathbf{0} \mid k_2 : c(X) \rhd X \mid L\rangle\}$

$\mathcal{R}_3 = \{\langle \nu h. \, [k : a\langle P\rangle \div Q \mid k' : a(X) \rhd_\gamma R; h] \mid L'' ,$
$\qquad \nu c\, k_1\, k_2\, h. k \prec (k_1, k_2) \mid [k_1 : a\langle P\rangle \div c\langle Q\rangle \div \mathbf{0} \mid k' : a(X) \rhd_\gamma R; h] \mid k_2 : c(X) \rhd X \mid L''\rangle\}$

$\mathcal{R}_4 = \{\langle k : Q \mid L''' , \nu c\, k_1\, k_2. k \prec (k_1, k_2) \mid k_1 : c\langle Q\rangle \div \mathbf{0} \mid k_2 : c(X) \rhd X \mid L'''\rangle\}$

$\mathcal{R}_5 = \{\langle k : Q \mid L''' , \nu c\, k_1\, k_2\, h. k \prec (k_1, k_2) \mid [k_1 : c\langle Q\rangle \div \mathbf{0} \mid k_2 : c(X) \rhd X; h] \mid h : Q \mid L'''\rangle\}$

Fig. 4. Bisimulation relation for arbitrary alternatives

Proof. We consider just one instance of arbitrary alternative, the thesis will follow by transitivity.

Thanks to Lemma 5 and Lemma 2, we only need to prove that for all closed configurations L and $k \notin \mathtt{fn}(P)$, we have $k : a\langle P\rangle \div Q \mid L \approx k : (\nu c. \, a\langle P\rangle \div c\langle Q\rangle \div \mathbf{0} \mid c(X) \rhd X) \mid L$. We consider the relation $\mathcal{R}$ in Figure 4 and prove that it is a weak barbed bisimulation. In every relation, L is closed and $k \notin \mathtt{fn}(P)$.

In $\mathcal{R}_1$, the right configuration can reduce via rule S.TagN followed by S.TagP. These lead to $\mathcal{R}_2$. Performing these reductions is needed to match the barb and the relevant reductions of the left configuration, thus we consider directly $\mathcal{R}_2$. In $\mathcal{R}_2$ the barbs coincide. Rollbacks lead to the identity. The only possible communication is on a, and requires $L \equiv L' \mid k' : a(X) \rhd_\gamma R$. It leads to $\mathcal{R}_3$, where $L'' = L' \mid R\{^{P,h}/_{X,\gamma}\}$. In $\mathcal{R}_3$ the barbs coincide too. All the reductions can be matched by staying in $\mathcal{R}_3$ or going to the identity, but for executing a roll with key h. This leads to $\mathcal{R}_4$, where L''' is closed. From $\mathcal{R}_4$ we can always execute the internal communication at c leading to $\mathcal{R}_5$. The thesis follows from the result below, whose proof requires again to find a suitable bisimulation relation.

Lemma 6. *For each configuration M k-dependent and complete such that k', t, $k_1, k_2 \notin \mathtt{fn}(M)$ we have $M \approx_c \nu k'\, t\, k_1\, k_2. k \prec (k_1, k_2) \mid [k_1 : t\langle Q\rangle \div C \mid k_2 : t(X) \rhd R; k'] \mid M\{^{k'}/_k\}$.* $\qquad \square$

Proofs concerning other idioms follow similar lines, and can be found in the online technical report [16].

A particular case of arbitrary alternative $a\langle P\rangle \div Q$ is when Q is a message whose alternative is not $\mathbf{0}$. By applying this pattern recursively we can write $a_1\langle P_1\rangle \div \ldots \div a_n\langle P_n\rangle \div Q$. In particular, by choosing $a_1 = \cdots = a_n$ and $P_1 = \cdots = P_n$ we can try n times the alternative P before giving up by executing Q.

Endless retry. We can also retry the same alternative infinitely many times, thus obtaining the behavior of roll-π messages. These messages can be integrated into croll-π semantics by defining function $\mathtt{xtr}$ as the identity on them.

$$(\![a\langle P\rangle]\!)_{er} = \nu t. \, Y \mid a\langle(\![P]\!)_{er}\rangle \div t\langle Y\rangle \qquad Y = t(Z) \rhd Z \mid a\langle(\![P]\!)_{er}\rangle \div t\langle Z\rangle$$

Proposition 2. $P \approx_c (\!|P|\!)_{er}$ *for any closed process with* roll-π *messages.*

As corollary of Proposition 2 we thus have the following.

Corollary 1. croll-π *is a conservative extension of* roll-π.

Triggers with alternative. Until now we attached alternatives to messages. Symmetrically, one may attach alternatives to triggers. Thus, upon rollback, the message is released and the trigger is replaced by a new process.

The syntax for triggers with alternative is $(a(X) \rhd_\gamma Q) \div b\langle Q' \rangle \div \mathbf{0}$. As for messages, we use a single message as alternative, but one can use general processes as described earlier. Triggers with alternative are defined by the extract clause below.

$$\mathtt{xtr}(k : (a(X) \rhd_\gamma Q) \div b\langle Q' \rangle \div \mathbf{0}) = k : b\langle Q' \rangle \div \mathbf{0}$$

Interestingly, messages with alternative and triggers with alternative may coexist. The encoding of triggers with alternative is as follows.

$$(\!|(a(X) \rhd_\gamma Q) \div b\langle Q' \rangle \div \mathbf{0}|\!)_{at} = \nu c\, d.\, \overline{c} \div \overline{d} \div \mathbf{0} \mid (c \rhd_\gamma a(X) \rhd (\!|Q|\!)_{at}) \mid (d \rhd b\langle (\!|Q'|\!)_{at} \rangle \div \mathbf{0})$$

Proposition 3. $P \approx_c (\!|P|\!)_{at}$ *for any closed process with triggers with alternative.*

4.2   Comparing croll-π and roll-π

While Corollary 1 shows that croll-π is at least as expressive as roll-π, a natural question is whether croll-π is actually strictly more expressive than roll-π or not. The theorem below gives a positive answer to this question.

Theorem 2. *There is no encoding* $(\!|\bullet|\!)$ *from* croll-π *to* roll-π *such that for each* croll-π *configuration* M:

1. *if M has a computation including at least a backward step, then $(\!|M|\!)$ has a computation including at least a backward step;*
2. *if M has only finite computations, then $(\!|M|\!)$ has only finite computations.*

Proof. Consider configuration $M = \nu k.\, k : \overline{a} \div \overline{b} \div \mathbf{0} \mid a \rhd_\gamma \mathsf{roll}\ \gamma$. This configuration has a unique possible computation, composed by one forward step followed by one backward step. Assume towards a contradiction that an encoding exists and consider $(\!|M|\!)$. $(\!|M|\!)$ should have at least a computation including a backward step. From roll-π loop lemma [17, Theorem 1], if we have a backward step, we are able to go forward again, and then there is a looping computation. This is in contrast with the second condition of the encoding. The thesis follows.   □

The main point behind this result is that the Loop Lemma, a cornerstone of roll-π theory [17] capturing the essence of rigid rollback (and similar results in [8, 18, 20, 22]), does not hold in croll-π. Naturally, the result above does not imply that croll-π cannot be encoded in HOπ or in π-calculus. However, these calculi are too low level for us, as hinted at by the fact that the encoding of a simple reversible higher order calculus into HOπ is quite complex, as shown in [18].

$$Q_i \triangleq (act_i(Z) \triangleright p_i\langle i, 1\rangle \div \ldots \div p_i\langle i, 8\rangle \div f_i\langle \mathbf{0}\rangle \div \mathbf{0} \mid$$

$$(p_i(\mathbf{x_i}) \triangleright_{\gamma_i} !c_i\langle \mathbf{x_i}\rangle \div \mathbf{0} \mid act_{i+1}\langle \mathbf{0}\rangle \mid f_{i+1}(Y) \triangleright \mathsf{roll}\ \gamma_i \mid$$

$$\textstyle\prod_{j=1}^{i-1} c_j(\mathbf{y_j}) \triangleright \mathsf{if}\ err(\mathbf{x_i}, \mathbf{y_j})\ \mathsf{then}\ \mathsf{roll}\ \gamma_i))$$

$$err((x_1, x_2), (y_1, y_2)) \triangleq (x_1 = y_1 \vee x_2 = y_2 \vee |x_1 - y_1| = |x_2 - y_2|)$$

Fig. 5. The i-th queen

5   Programming in croll-π

A main goal of croll-π is to make reversibility techniques exploitable for application development. Even if croll-π is not yet a full-fledged language, we have developed a proof-of-concept interpreter for it. To the best of our knowledge, this is the first interpreter for a causal-consistent reversible language. We then put the interpreter at work on a few simple, yet interesting, programming problems. We detail below the algorithm we devised to solve the Eight Queens problem [3, p. 165]. The interpreter and the code for solving the Eight Queens problem are available at `http://proton.inrialpes.fr/~mlienhar/croll-pi/implem`, together with examples of encodings of primitives for error handling, and an implementation of the car repair scenario of the EU project Sensoria.

The interpreter for croll-π is written in Maude [10], a language based on both equational and rewriting logic that allows the programmer to define terms and reduction rules, e.g., to execute reduction semantics of process calculi. Most of croll-π's rules are straightforwardly interpreted, with the exception of rule S.ROLL. This rule is quite complex as it involves checks on an unbounded number of interacting components. Such an issue is already present in roll-π [17], where it is addressed by providing an easier to implement, yet equivalent, low-level semantics. This semantics replaces rule S.ROLL with a protocol that sends notifications to all the involved components to roll-back, then waits for them to do so. Extending the low-level semantics from roll-π to croll-π simply requires the application of function `xtr` to the memory targeted by the rollback. We do not detail the low-level semantics of croll-π here, and refer the reader to [17] for a detailed description in the setting of roll-π. Our Maude interpreter is based on this low-level semantics, extended with values (integers and pairs) and with the `if-then-else` construct. It is fairly concise (less than 350 lines of code).

The Eight Queens problem is a well-known constraint-programming problem which can be formulated as follows: how to place 8 queens on an 8×8 chess board so that no queen can directly capture another? We defined an algorithm in croll-π where queens are concurrent entities, numbered from 1 to 8, all executing the code schema shown in Figure 5. We use $\mathbf{x}$ to indicate a pair of integer variables (x_1, x_2), and replicated messages $!c_i\langle \mathbf{x}\rangle \div \mathbf{0}$ to denote the encoding of a parallel composition of an infinite number of messages $c_i\langle \mathbf{x}\rangle \div \mathbf{0}$ (cf. Remark 1).

The queens are activated in numeric order. The i-th queen is activated by a message on channel act_i from its predecessor (a message on act_1 is needed to start the whole computation). When a queen is activated it looks for its position by trying sequentially all the positions in the i-th row of the chess board. To try a position, it sends it over channel p_i. Then, the position is made available on channel c_i and the next queen is activated. Finally, the position is checked for compatibility with the positions of previous queens. This is done by computing (in parallel) $err(\mathsf{x_j}, \mathsf{x_i})$ for each $j < i$. If a check fails, roll γ_i rolls-back the choice of the position of queen i. The alternatives mechanism allows to try the next position. If no suitable position is available, the choice of position of queen $i - 1$ is rolled-back (possibly recursively) by the communication over f_i. Note that a roll-back of queen j makes all queens i with $i > j$ restart, since previously discarded positions may now be acceptable. This is obtained thanks to activation messages establishing the needed causal dependencies. When the computation ends, messages on c_i contain positions which are all compatible.

6   Asynchronous Interacting Transactions

This section shows how croll-π can model in a precise way interacting transactions with compensations as formalized in TransCCS [13]. Actually, the natural croll-π encoding improves on the semantics in [13], since croll-π causality tracking is more precise than the one in TransCCS, which is based on dynamic embedding of processes into transactions. Thus croll-π avoids some spurious undo of actions, as described below. Before entering the details of TransCCS, let us describe the general idea of transaction encoding.

We consider a very general notion of atomic (but not necessarily isolated) transaction, i.e., a process that executes completely or not at all. Informally, a transaction $[P, Q]_\gamma$ with name γ executing process P with compensation Q can be modeled by a process of the form:

$$[P, Q]_\gamma = \nu a\, c.\, \overline{a} \div \overline{c} \div \mathbf{0} \mid (a \rhd_\gamma P) \mid (c \rhd Q)$$

Intuitively, when $[P, Q]_\gamma$ is executed, it first starts process P under the rollback scope γ. Abortion of the transaction can be triggered in P by executing a roll γ. Whenever P is rolled-back, the rollback does not restart P (since the message on a is substituted by the alternative on c), but instead starts the compensation process Q. In this approach commit is implicit: when there is no reachable roll γ, the transaction is committed. From the explanation above, it should be clear that in the execution of $[P, Q]_\gamma$, either P executes completely, i.e., until it reaches a commit, or not at all, in the sense that it is perfectly rolled-back. If P is ever rolled-back, its failed execution can be compensated by that of process Q. Interestingly, and in contrast with irreversible actions used in [12], our rollback scopes can be nested without compromising this all-or-nothing semantics.

Let us now consider an asynchronous fragment of TransCCS [13], removing choice and recursion. Dealing with the whole calculus would not add new difficulties related to rollback, but only related to the encoding of such operators in

$$(\text{R-COMM}) \quad \overline{a} \mid a.P \longrightarrow P \qquad (\text{R-EMB}) \quad \frac{k \notin \text{fn}(R)}{[\![P \rhd_k Q]\!] \mid R \longrightarrow [\![P \mid R \rhd_k Q \mid R]\!]}$$

$$(\text{R-CO}) \quad [\![P \mid \text{co } k \rhd_k Q]\!] \longrightarrow P \qquad\qquad (\text{R-AB}) \quad [\![P \rhd_k Q]\!] \longrightarrow Q$$

and is closed under active contexts $\nu a. \bullet$, $\bullet \mid Q$ and $[\![\bullet \rhd_k Q]\!]$, and structural congruence.

Fig. 6. Reduction rules for TransCCS

higher-order π. The syntax of the fragment of TransCCS we consider is:

$$P ::= \mathbf{0} \mid \nu a.\, P \mid (P \mid Q) \mid \overline{a} \mid a.P \mid \text{co } k \mid [\![P \rhd_k Q]\!]$$

Essentially, it extends CCS with a transactional construct $[\![P \rhd_k Q]\!]$, executing a transaction with body P, name k and compensation Q, and a commit operator co k.

The rules defining the semantics of TransCCS are given in Figure 6. Structural congruence contains the usual rules for parallel composition and restriction. Keep in mind that transaction scope is a binder for its name k, thus k does not occur outside the transaction, and there is no name capture in rules R-Co and R-Emb.

A croll-π transaction $[P, Q]_\gamma$ as above has explicit abort, specified by roll γ, where γ is used as the transaction name, and implicit commit. TransCCS takes different design choices, using non-deterministic abort and programmable commit. Thus we have to instantiate the encoding above.

Definition 8 (TransCCS encoding). *Let P be a TransCCS process. Its encoding $(\!| \bullet |\!)_t$ in croll-π is defined as:*

$$(\!| \nu a.\, P |\!)_t = \nu a.\, (\!| P |\!)_t \qquad (\!| P \mid Q |\!)_t = (\!| P |\!)_t \mid (\!| Q |\!)_t \qquad (\!| \overline{a} |\!)_t = \overline{a}$$
$$(\!| a.P |\!)_t = a \rhd (\!| P |\!)_t \qquad (\!| \text{co } l |\!)_t = l(X) \rhd \mathbf{0} \qquad (\!| \mathbf{0} |\!)_t = \mathbf{0}$$

$$(\!| [\![P \rhd_l Q]\!] |\!)_t = [\nu l.\, (\!| P |\!)_t \mid l\langle \text{roll } \gamma \rangle \mid l(X) \rhd X, (\!| Q |\!)_t]_\gamma$$

Since in croll-π only configurations can execute, the behavior of P should be compared with $\nu k.\, k : (\!| P |\!)_t$.

In the encoding, abort is always possible since at any time the only occurrence of the roll in the transaction can be activated by a communication on l. On the other hand, executing the encoding of a TransCCS commit disables the roll related to the transaction. This allows to garbage collect the compensation, and thus corresponds to an actual commit. Note, however, that in croll-π the abort operation is not atomic as in TransCCS since the roll related to a transaction first has to be enabled through a communication on l, disabling in this way any possibility to commit, and then it can be executed. Clearly, until the roll is executed, the body of the transaction can continue its execution. To make abort atomic one would need the ability to disable an active roll, as could be done using a (mixed) choice such as $(\text{roll } k) + (l \rhd \mathbf{0})$. In this setting an output on l would commit the transaction. Adding choice would not make the reduction semantics more difficult, but its impact on behavioral equivalence has not been studied yet.

The relation between the behavior of a TransCCS process P and of its translation $(\!|P|\!)_t$ is not immediate, not only because of the comment above on atomicity, but also because of the approximate tracking of causality provided by TransCCS. TransCCS tracks interacting processes using rule (R-EMB): only processes inside the same transaction may interact, and when a process enters the transaction it is saved in the compensation, so that it can be restored in case of abort. However, no check is performed to ensure that the process actually interacts with the transaction code. For instance, a process $\bar{a} \mid a.P$ may enter a transaction $[\![Q \rhd_k R]\!]$ and then perform the communication at a. Such a communication would be undone in case of abort. This is a spurious undo, since the communication at a is not related to the transaction code. Actually, the same communication could have been performed outside the transaction, and in this case it would not have been undone.

In croll-π encoding, a process is "inside" the transaction with key k if and only if its tag is causally dependent on k. Thus a process enters a transaction only by interacting with a process inside it. For this reason, there is no reduction in croll-π corresponding to rule (R-EMB), and since no process inside the transaction is involved in the reduction at a above, the reduction would not be undone in case of abort, since it actually happens "outside" the transaction. Thus our encoding avoids spurious undo, and computations in croll-π correspond to computations in TransCCS with minimal applications of rule (R-EMB). These computations are however very difficult to characterize because of syntactic constraints. In fact, for two processes inside two parallel transactions k_1 and k_2 to interact, either k_1 should move inside k_2 or vice versa, but in both the cases not only the interacting processes move, as minimality would require, but also all the other processes inside the same transactions have to move. Intuitively, TransCCS approximates the causality relation, which is a dag, using the tree defined by containment. The spurious reductions undone in TransCCS can always be redone so to reach a state corresponding to the croll-π one. In this sense croll-π minimizes the set of interactions undone.

We define a notion of weak barbed bisimilarity $_t\approx_{c\pi}$ relating a TransCCS process P and a croll-π configuration M. First, we define barbs in TransCCS by the predicate $P\!\downarrow_a$, which is true in the cases below, false otherwise.

$$\bar{a}\!\downarrow_a \qquad\qquad \nu b.\, P\!\downarrow_a \ \text{if } P\!\downarrow_a \wedge a \neq b$$
$$P \mid P'\!\downarrow_a \ \text{if } P\!\downarrow_a \vee P'\!\downarrow_a \qquad\qquad [\![P \rhd_k Q]\!]\!\downarrow_a \ \text{if } P\!\downarrow_a \wedge a \neq k$$

Here, differently from [13], we observe barbs inside the transaction body, to have a natural correspondence with croll-π barbs.

Definition 9. *A relation $\mathcal{R}$ relating TransCCS processes P and croll-π configurations M is a weak barbed bisimulation if and only if for each $(P, M) \in \mathcal{R}$:*

1. if $P\downarrow_a$ then $M \Longrightarrow\downarrow_a$;
2. if $M\downarrow_a$ then $P \Longrightarrow\downarrow_a$;
3. if $P \longrightarrow P_1$ is derived using rule (R-AB) then $M \Longrightarrow M'$, $P_1 \Longrightarrow P_2$ and $P_2\mathcal{R}M'$;
4. if $P \longrightarrow P_1$ is derived without using rule (R-AB) then $M \Longrightarrow M'$ and $P_1\mathcal{R}M'$;
5. if $M \longrightarrow M'$ then either: (i) $P\mathcal{R}M'$ or (ii) $P \longrightarrow P_1$ and $P_1\mathcal{R}M'$ or (iii) $M' \longrightarrow M''$, $P \longrightarrow P_1$ and $P_1\mathcal{R}M''$.

Weak barbed bisimilarity $_t\approx_{c\pi}$ *is the largest weak barbed bisimulation.*

The main peculiarities of the definition above are in condition 3, which captures the need of redoing some reductions that are unduly rolled-back in TransCCS, and in case (iii) of condition 5, which forces atomic abort.

Theorem 3. *For each TransCCS process P, $P\ _t\approx_{c\pi} \nu k.\, k : (\!|P|\!)_t$.*

Proof. The proof has to take into account the fact that different croll-π configurations may correspond to the same TransCCS process. In particular, a TransCCS transaction $[\![P\triangleright_k Q]\!]$ is matched in different ways if Q is the original compensation or if part of it is the result of an application of rule (R-EMB).

Thus, in the proof, we give a syntactic characterization of the set of croll-π configurations $(\!|P|\!)^p$ matching a TransCCS process P. Then we show that $\nu k.\, k : (\!|P|\!)_t \in (\!|P|\!)^p$, and that there is a match between reductions of P and the weak reductions of each configuration in $(\!|P|\!)^p$. The proof, in the two directions, is by induction on the rule applied to derive a single step. □

7   Related Work and Conclusion

We have presented a concurrent process calculus with explicit rollback and minimal facilities for alternatives built on a reversible substrate analogous to a Lévy labeling [4] for concurrent computations. We have shown by way of examples how to build more complex alternative idioms and how to use rollback and alternatives in conjunction to encode transactional constructs. In particular, we have developed an analysis of communicating transactions proposed in TransCCS [13]. We also developed a proof-of-concept interpreter of our language and used it to give a concurrent solution of the Eight Queens problem.

Undo or rollback capabilities in sequential languages have a long history (see [19] for an early survey). In a concurrent setting, interest has developed more recently. Works such as [9] introduce logging and process group primitives as a basis for defining fault-tolerant abstractions, including transactions. Ziarek et al. [26] introduce a checkpoint abstraction for concurrent ML programs. Field et al. [15] extend the actor model with checkpointing constructs. Most of the approaches relying instead on a fully reversible concurrent language have already been discussed in the introduction. Here we just recall that models of reversible computation have also been studied in the context of computational biology, e.g., [8]. Also, the effect of reversibility on Hennessy-Milner logic has been studied in [23]. Several recent works have proposed a formal analysis of transactions, including [13] studied in this paper, as well as several other works such as [21, 5, 7] (see [1] for numerous references to the line of work concentrating on software transactional memories). Note that although reversible calculi can be used to implement transactions, they offer more flexibility. For instance, transactional events [14] only allow an all-or-nothing execution of transactions. Moreover, no visible side-effect is allowed during the transaction, as there is no way to specify how to compensate the side-effects of a failed transaction. A reversible calculus with alternatives allows the encoding of such compensations.

With the exception of the seminal work by Danos and Krivine [12] on RCCS, we are not aware of other work exploiting precise causal information as provided by our reversible machinery to analyze recovery-oriented constructs. Yet this precision seems important: as we have seen in Section 6, it allows us to weed out spurious undo of actions that appear in an approach that relies on a cruder transaction "embedding" mechanism. Although we have not developed a formal analysis yet, it seems this precision would be equally important, e.g., to avoid uncontrolled cascading rollbacks (domino effect) in [26] or to ensure that, in contrast to [15], rollback is always possible in failure-free computations. Although [9] introduces primitives able to track down causality information among groups of processes, called conclaves, it does not provide automatic support for undoing the effects of aborted conclaves, while our calculus directly provides a primitive to undo all the effects of a communication.

While encouraging, our results in Section 6 are only preliminary. Our concurrent rollback and minimal facilities for alternatives provide a good basis for understanding the "all-or-nothing" property of transactions. To this end it would be interesting to understand whether we are able to support both strong and weak atomicity of [21]. How to support isolation properties found, e.g., in software transactional memory models, in a way that combines well with these facilities remains to be seen. Further, we would like to study the exact relationships that exist between these facilities and the different notions of compensation that have appeared in formal models of computation for service-oriented computing, such as [5, 7]. It is also interesting to compare with zero-safe Petri nets [6], since tokens in zero places dynamically define transaction scopes as done by communications in croll-π.

From a practical point of view, we want both to refine the interpreter, and to test it against a wider range of more complex case studies. Concerning the interpreter, a main point is to allow for garbage collection of memories which cannot be restored any more, so to improve space efficiency.

References

[1] Abadi, M., Harris, T.: Perspectives on Transactional Memory. In: Bravetti, M., Zavattaro, G. (eds.) CONCUR 2009. LNCS, vol. 5710, pp. 1–14. Springer, Heidelberg (2009)

[2] Bacci, G., Danos, V., Kammar, O.: On the Statistical Thermodynamics of Reversible Communicating Processes. In: Corradini, A., Klin, B., Cîrstea, C. (eds.) CALCO 2011. LNCS, vol. 6859, pp. 1–18. Springer, Heidelberg (2011)

[3] Rouse Ball, W.W.: Mathematical Recreations and Essays, 12th edn. Macmillan, New York (1947)

[4] Berry, G., Lévy, J.-J.: Minimal and optimal computations of recursive programs. J. ACM 26(1) (1979)

[5] Bruni, R., Melgratti, H.C., Montanari, U.: Theoretical foundations for compensations in flow composition languages. In: POPL 2005. ACM (2005)

[6] Bruni, R., Montanari, U.: Zero-safe nets: Comparing the collective and individual token approaches. Information and Computation 156(1-2) (2000)

[7] Butler, M., Hoare, T., Ferreira, C.: A Trace Semantics for Long-Running Transactions. In: Abdallah, A.E., Jones, C.B., Sanders, J.W. (eds.) CSP25. LNCS, vol. 3525, pp. 133–150. Springer, Heidelberg (2005)

[8] Cardelli, L., Laneve, C.: Reversible structures. In: CMSB 2011. ACM (2011)

[9] Chothia, T., Duggan, D.: Abstractions for fault-tolerant global computing. Theor. Comput. Sci. 322(3) (2004)

[10] Clavel, M., Durán, F., Eker, S., Lincoln, P., Martí-Oliet, N., Meseguer, J., Quesada, J.F.: Maude: specification and programming in rewriting logic. Theor. Comp. Sci. 285(2) (2002)

[11] Danos, V., Krivine, J.: Reversible Communicating Systems. In: Gardner, P., Yoshida, N. (eds.) CONCUR 2004. LNCS, vol. 3170, pp. 292–307. Springer, Heidelberg (2004)

[12] Danos, V., Krivine, J.: Transactions in RCCS. In: Abadi, M., de Alfaro, L. (eds.) CONCUR 2005. LNCS, vol. 3653, pp. 398–412. Springer, Heidelberg (2005)

[13] de Vries, E., Koutavas, V., Hennessy, M.: Communicating Transactions. In: Gastin, P., Laroussinie, F. (eds.) CONCUR 2010. LNCS, vol. 6269, pp. 569–583. Springer, Heidelberg (2010)

[14] Donnelly, K., Fluet, M.: Transactional events. Journal of Functional Programming 18(5-6) (2008)

[15] Field, J., Varela, C.A.: Transactors: a programming model for maintaining globally consistent distributed state in unreliable environments. In: POPL 2005. ACM (2005)

[16] Lanese, I., Lienhardt, M., Mezzina, C.A., Schmitt, A., Stefani, J.-B.: Concurrent flexible reversibility (TR) (2012),
http://www.cs.unibo.it/~lanese/publications/
%20fulltext/TR-crollpi.pdf.gz

[17] Lanese, I., Mezzina, C.A., Schmitt, A., Stefani, J.-B.: Controlling Reversibility in Higher-Order Pi. In: Katoen, J.-P., König, B. (eds.) CONCUR 2011. LNCS, vol. 6901, pp. 297–311. Springer, Heidelberg (2011)

[18] Lanese, I., Mezzina, C.A., Stefani, J.-B.: Reversing Higher-Order Pi. In: Gastin, P., Laroussinie, F. (eds.) CONCUR 2010. LNCS, vol. 6269, pp. 478–493. Springer, Heidelberg (2010)

[19] Leeman, G.B.: A formal approach to undo operations in programming languages. ACM Trans. Program. Lang. Syst. 8(1) (1986)

[20] Lienhardt, M., Lanese, I., Mezzina, C.A., Stefani, J.-B.: A Reversible Abstract Machine and Its Space Overhead. In: Giese, H., Rosu, G. (eds.) FMOODS/FORTE 2012. LNCS, vol. 7273, pp. 1–17. Springer, Heidelberg (2012)

[21] Moore, K.F., Grossman, D.: High-level small-step operational semantics for transactions. In: POPL 2008. ACM (2008)

[22] Phillips, I., Ulidowski, I.: Reversing algebraic process calculi. J. Log. Algebr. Program. 73(1-2) (2007)

[23] Phillips, I., Ulidowski, I.: A logic with reverse modalities for history-preserving bisimulations. In: EXPRESS 2011. EPTCS, vol. 64 (2011)

[24] Phillips, I., Ulidowski, I., Yuen, S.: A Reversible Process Calculus and the Modelling of the ERK Signalling Pathway. In: Glück, R., Yokoyama, T. (eds.) RC 2012. LNCS, vol. 7581, pp. 218–232. Springer, Heidelberg (2013)

[25] Sangiorgi, D., Walker, D.: The π-calculus: A Theory of Mobile Processes. Cambridge University Press (2001)

[26] Ziarek, L., Jagannathan, S.: Lightweight checkpointing for concurrent ML. J. Funct. Program. 20(2) (2010)

Structural Lock Correlation
with Ownership Types

Yi Lu, John Potter, and Jingling Xue

Programming Languages and Compilers Group
School of Computer Science and Engineering
University of New South Wales, Sydney, NSW 2052, Australia
{ylu,potter,jingling}@cse.unsw.edu.au

Abstract. Concurrent object-oriented programming languages coordinate conflicting memory accesses through locking, which relies on programmer discipline and suffers from a lack of modularity and compile-time support. Programmers typically work with large libraries of code whose locking behaviours are not formally and precisely specified; thus understanding and writing concurrent programs is notoriously difficult and error-prone. This paper proposes *structural lock correlation*, a new model for establishing structural connections between locks and the memory locations they protect, in an ownership-based type and effect system. Structural lock correlation enables modular specification of locking. It offers a compiler-checkable lock abstraction with an enforceable contract at interface boundaries, leading to improved safety, understandability and composability of concurrent program components.

1 Introduction

Despite the progress in modern multicore architectures, it remains a challenge to develop better programming languages for concurrent programming. This is especially so for concurrent object oriented programming, where the combination of shared object memory and the endemic use of object aliasing pose special challenges. Data races are a common problem, which occur when two concurrent computations can access the same memory location without synchronisation and one of those accesses is a write. Races often imply violations of program invariants; achieving race freedom is crucial for the safety of concurrent programs.

Most concurrent object-oriented languages use mutual exclusion locks to synchronise concurrent memory accesses to avoid data races. But programming with locks is not easy: too little locking may not preserve program safety, while too much locking compromises concurrency and increases the chances of deadlock. A fundamental difficulty is that locking is a whole program requirement, which is hard to localise to a single class or module. All code that accesses shared memory, regardless of who developed it or where it is deployed, must be coordinated. Unfortunately the programmer typically works with large libraries whose locking behaviours are not precisely specified and checked. Understanding and writing properly synchronised code is notoriously difficult and error-prone.

M. Felleisen and P. Gardner (Eds.): ESOP 2013, LNCS 7792, pp. 391–410, 2013.
© Springer-Verlag Berlin Heidelberg 2013

Type systems for safe locking [9,10,3,2,8] (sometimes called *lock types*) have been used to enforce a fixed locking discipline across all code—all accesses to a shared object (or its fields) must hold a programmer-specified lock—this "memory guarded-by lock" relationship is called *lock correlation*. While quite useful, fixed lock correlations are often less flexible. For example, in lock type systems, once lock correlations are specified, those locks must be acquired even in sequential code where they are clearly unnecessary. This highlights the lack of context sensitivity in lock types. Moreover, as part of interface specification, locks required in lock correlations must be published unnecessarily; this tends to break the abstraction and information hiding principles underlying good software design, or may inhibit the use of fine-grained locks.

In this paper we present an effect-based approach for modular reasoning about locking behaviours, by specifying lock correlations as computational effects, called *lock effects*, or simply *effects*. Furthermore, by adopting an effect system based on *ownership types* [23,7,5], we are able to exploit the ownership tree structure to track lock correlations, even when we hide details of the locks and effects in lock effect abstractions. Memory side-effects are modelled as collections of subtrees in the object ownership tree. For every computation, we capture an approximation of the actual memory side-effects together with any locks that may be held while those effects are occurring. Ownership permits precise local descriptions of effects, which may depend on localised, private data. We can also easily abstract the details of effects, by approximating the actual effect using owners of the objects involved. This allows coarser, but still potentially useful information about local computations to be exported to a broader setting.

Lock effects help programmers choose locks as needed, depending on context. But modular specification of lock correlations is not easy: previous approaches are either not modular or encourage the breakdown of program abstractions. The problem of how to abstract lock details remains. Our solution is a new concept, *structural lock correlation*, where the side-effects are entirely within the ownership subtree rooted at the lock. In structural lock correlation, *the lock owns the correlated side-effects*. The major benefit of this concept is that it allows lock abstraction that preserves structural lock correlation. To reason about conflicting effects, the only detail about the lock that needs to be preserved is its ownership depth, or *rank* as we call it.

A trivial example illustrates some of these ideas; we also highlight another benefit of structural lock correlations in checking race freedom for concurrent computations. For simplicity, we use par as a lexically scoped parallel task construct [12,1] to introduce concurrency, and a sync expression analogous to Java's synchronised statements, typical of related work in this area:

```
par {
    sync (l1) { o1.f = ... };
    sync (l2) { o2.f = ... };
}
```

Each of the two tasks synchronises on a lock before updating an object. The two lock correlations are: <l1::o1> and <l2::o2>. To show that the tasks cannot conflict (race), it is sufficient to know either (i) o1 and o2 *must not alias*, implying that they are distinct objects, or (ii) l1 and l2 *must alias*, implying that the two object accesses are made mutually exclusive by a common lock.

With ownership there is a third way to show safety of the two tasks. Suppose we know that l1 owns o1 and l2 owns o2. Then we can conclude that this code is safe: if l1 and l2 are not aliases, then o1 and o2 are not, because they are in distinct ownership subtrees. if l1 and l2 are aliases, then two tasks are correctly synchronised. Essentially this just relies on the ownership structure; we do not need object encapsulation or reference confinement, often enforced in ownership type systems. This third way of showing safety is why structural lock correlation is useful, especially when we combine it with a form of lock abstraction.

Such lock abstraction enables better support for modular specification of lock correlations, facilitating understanding about locking requirements. Programmers, or compilers, can reason about where locking is needed or not. Lock effects provide an enforceable contract at interface boundaries, contributing to improved safety and composability for concurrent program components, at least for those which admit a structural locking policy.

The paper is organised as follows. Section 2 discusses background and informally introduces our model. Section 3 explains the model with examples. Section 4 formally presents a core language and associated type and effect system. Section 5 presents a dynamic semantics and some properties of the type system. Section 6 discusses related work. Section 7 concludes the paper.

2   A Model of Structural Lock Correlation

We briefly review relevant concepts from ownership types and effects, before we introduce our model for structural lock correlation.

2.1   Ownership-Based Effects

Ownership types provide static information about object structures. Effect systems provide various kinds of behavioural abstractions, most commonly dealing with memory access. Ownership-based effects use ownership trees to specify the extent of effects. Considerable work has been published on ownership-based effects with various applications, for example [23,7,5,20,3,6,4,16,15,17,1]. Unlike early papers on ownership types [23,7,5,20], we do not use ownership to encapsulate objects, with owners as access monitors for the objects they own. Rather, we use ownership here purely to establish structural relationships between objects; every object has a fixed owner, being another object or world, the top of the ownership tree. As usual for ownership type systems, object types specify their ownership context k which may be world, a class owner parameter p or a final expression including this (later, we provide a detailed syntax in the formal system of Section 4). Direct ownership is the covering relation for object containment: we write $k_1 \preceq k_2$ to say that k_1 is inside k_2, so that $\preceq$ is the reflexive, transitive closure of the (acyclic) ownership relation.

We adopt simple defaults to reduce annotation requirements. Class definitions with a single ownership parameter may omit the parameter and use the keyword owner within the class in its place. In type declarations, omitted owners default to owner; thus, by default, objects refer to other objects as peers, having the same owner. So, by default, we attain relatively flat ownership structures, with explicit use of this as owner to specify containment.

Side-effects ε are similar to those in JOE [6]; they are *writes* by default, with *reads* optional. Side-effects are expressed as regions π which are levelled forests of ownership trees. Used as a region, the ownership context k denotes the whole subtree of objects (reflexively) owned by k. Similarly, the region $k+n$ denotes the levelled forest of all ownership trees at depth n below k, that is, the set of all objects whose n'th owner is inside k. For convenience, we use the keyword peer to abbreviate region owner+1, which contains all objects with the same owner as this. Intuitively, based on the underlying object sets, we have the following subregion relations: this $\sqsubseteq$ peer $\sqsubseteq$ owner as illustrated on the left of Fig. 1.

Ownership allows us to summarise effects that occur inside an object using a single identifier k to denote the whole set of objects which would not otherwise be statically expressible (conventional region-based effect systems use regions for the same purpose). When we cannot name an ownership context because it is out of scope, we do not want to lose any effects specified with it. The role of $k+n$ is to provide ownership abstraction so that we can lift effect specifications to a wider scope, basing the specification on a context higher up in the ownership tree. Regions are just sets of objects, so the notion of subregion follows naturally, which then leads to a standard notion of side-effect abstraction.

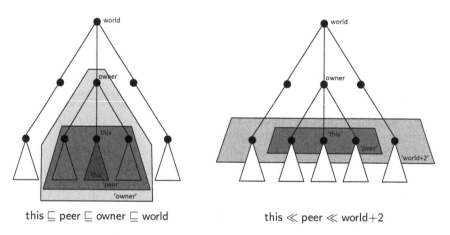

this $\sqsubseteq$ peer $\sqsubseteq$ owner $\sqsubseteq$ world   this $\ll$ peer $\ll$ world+2

Fig. 1. Comparison of ownership effect abstraction and lock abstraction. Nodes are objects; upward edges link objects to their owners in the ownership tree. On the left, shaded polygons are side-effect regions named in quotation marks. On the right, shaded polygons are lock contexts that bound an existentially abstracted lock.

2.2   Structural Lock Correlation

Our lock effects $L::\varepsilon$ denote lock correlations where the lockset L guards the side-effect ε. We have two kinds of lock correlations: *arbitrary* and *structural*. *Arbitrary lock correlations* are conventional, being analogous to lock correlations used in lock types. They require a fixed, concrete lock or lockset to guard the effect. They can be abstracted by taking a subset of the lockset and/or an abstracted side-effect. To maintain useful information about the lock guards, we do not want to remove them from the specification, but that is the only way locks can be abstracted for arbitrary lock correlations. This is the problem with the conventional kind of lock correlation: locks cannot (usefully) be abstracted.

In *structural lock correlations* the lock must own all of the associated side-effects. A structural lock is bracketed to distinguish it from an arbitrary lock. For example, the lock effect $[\omega]::\varepsilon$ indicates that the structural lock ω is held when side-effect ε occurs, where ω contains ε. Two structural lock correlations with structural locks at the same rank (depth in the ownership tree) are guaranteed to be correctly synchronised. Two locks at the same rank in the ownership tree are either aliased, in which case, mutual exclusion is provided, or not, in which case, the objects they own cannot be aliased.

It follows that it is safe to abstract structural locks to a superset of locks at the same level. We overload the $k+n$ syntax to denote a lock context comprising all locks (objects) whose n'th owner is k. The right-hand part of Fig. 1 illustrates structural lock abstraction, $\ll$, capturing the nesting of lock contexts at the same rank; it is defined formally in Section 4. Recall that peer abbreviates owner+1.

Structural lock correlations allow knowledge of the fixed correlation between the lockset and side-effect to be retained when structural locks and side-effects are abstracted. This allows us to lift lock effects to scopes where we cannot precisely name the actual locks or side-effects. It is the key to achieving modularity in our specifications of lock effects.

3   Examples

We illustrate structural lock correlation with a simple bank account with a balance field and customers with a collection of accounts in Fig. 2 (see also [10,3]). Customers can deposit given amounts into an account with a given index. We provide a variety of deposit methods to illustrate varying granularities of locking: the depositA method provides no synchronisation, depositB synchronises on this, and depositC synchronises on the account to be modified.

The Customer class has different locking policies for its different methods. We would like to specify lock effects so that clients will know how to use the different methods safely. In this paper we focus on lock effects rather than the underlying concurrency model. In order to demonstrate concurrent executions in the client code above, we use a simple par construct, which supports fork-join style parallelism [12,1]. In each of the par blocks above, the two customers, c and d, attempt to deposit concurrently.

```
class Account { int balance = 0; }      // CLIENT CODE
                                        Customer c, d; int i, j, x, y;
class Customer {                        ...
  private final Account[] accounts;     // case SeqA
  ...                                   c.depositA(i, x);  d.depositA(j, y);
  void depositA(int i, int x) {
    Account acct = account[i];          // case ParA
    acct.balance += x;                  par { c.depositA(i, x);
  }                                            d.depositA(j, y); }
  void depositB(int i, int x) {
    Account acct = account[i];          // case ParB
    sync (this) acct.balance += x;      par { c.depositB(i, x);
  }                                            d.depositB(j, y); }
  void depositC(int i, int x) {
    final Account acct = account[i];    // case ParC
    sync (acct) acct.balance += x;      par { c.depositC(i, x);
} }                                            d.depositC(j, y); }
```

Fig. 2. A bank accounts example with different granularities of locking

Note that the client code in case ParA is unsafe, because the operation += is not atomic and there is no synchronisation. If c and d are aliased, referring to the same customer, and if the account indices i and j are the same, then there is a possible data race on the account balance. Any attempt to check correct synchronisation should be able to detect this error.

In lock types, all shared variables must be guarded by a specified lock, which yields a fixed lock correlation. Case SeqA may be erroneously flagged as an error even if it is single threaded, because the balance is not guarded. This highlights the lack of context sensitivity in lock types. Either ParB or ParC may be accepted by lock types when a corresponding lock (either the customer or the account) is specified to guard balance. But the lock correlation specification is fixed, so lock types cannot accept both ParB and ParC simultaneously. We demonstrate how lock effects with structural lock correlation can deal with all these cases.

Structural Lock Correlation without Ownership We first illustrate our lock effects without any real ownership structure, where (by default), all objects are owned by world. The method effects for the three methods are:

```
depositA has effect <peer>
depositB has effect <this::peer>
depositC has effect <[peer]::peer>
```

Note that we do not consider the read effect on field accounts in method effects because the field is read-only and causes no conflict.

The effect for depositA indicates no lockset. The actual effect of the method could be expressed more precisely, within the method, as <acct>, but such an effect is not visible outside the method, as the local variable is out of scope. To export the effect from the method body, we abstract it to <peer>, since both the customer and the account objects are owned by the same (default) owner.

The effect for `depositB` indicates we are locking this, and the side-effect is the same as for `depositA`. When a client makes a call on a customer's `depositB` method, this is replaced by the actual customer, so the client knows that the call will acquire a lock on the customer object to guard its effect. This demonstrates the use of an arbitrary lock; there is no structural correlation, because the effect on the account is not contained within the lock of the customer.

The effect of `depositC` demonstrates a structural lock correlation. Inside the body of `depositC`, the lock effect is simply `<acct::acct>`. Because `acct` is inside `acct` ($\preceq$ is reflexive), we are permitted to abstract the arbitrary lock `acct` to a structural lock `[acct]`. So, by the same effect abstraction as above, the method effect becomes `<[peer]::peer>`. Despite the fact that the lock effects are no longer precise, the structural lock correlation is preserved. This abstract form of specification states that a method call will protect any of its effects (which must be within the peer forest) by acquiring some lock within the band of peers.

For the client, case SeqA is accepted, because the calls are made sequentially. Case ParA is rejected as it should be, because the side effects of the calls may conflict. In case ParB, `c` and `d` are the actual locks that are acquired. We also see that the effects of the two calls are the same, so they may conflict. Unfortunately the customers `c` and `d` may be different, this case must be rejected conservatively.

Case ParC is OK, perhaps surprisingly at the first glance. The reason is simple: we know both calls acquire a lock within the band of peers—the locks may be the same, or not. But we also know that the effect of each call is contained within the respective locks (that's the structural correlation at work). With the flat ownership of this example, that actually implies that the effect is the same as the lock (as we saw before we abstracted the method body effect above). There are two cases. If the locks are the same object, then they prevent the two calls from running concurrently—so there's no conflict. On the other hand, if the locks are not the same, then the effects are not the same—so no conflict.

For simplicity, when the structural lock is the same as the side-effect in a lock effect, we often omit the side-effect. For example, we write `<[peer]>` as a shorthand for `<[peer]::peer>`.

Structural Lock Correlation with Ownership. Now we can fix case ParB by using ownership types to establish a structural correlation between a lock (the customer) and its effects (the customer's accounts). Within the `Customer` class, we declare that all the accounts are owned by this customer:

```
private final Account<this>[] accounts;
```

The new method effects for the three methods are:

```
depositA has effect <this+1>
depositB has effect <[this]::this+1>
depositC has effect <[this+1]>
```

The effect for `depositA` indicates the account object is owned by the customer. For the same reason, the effect for `depositB` can now be written as a structural

Programs	$P ::= \overline{C}\, e$
Classes	$C ::= \text{class } c\langle \overline{p}\rangle \ [\text{extends } t]_{opt} \ \{[\text{final}]_{opt} \ t \ f; \ \overline{M}\}$
Types	$t ::= c\langle \overline{k}\rangle$
Methods	$M ::= t \ m(t \ x) \ \varphi \ \{e\}$
Expressions	$e ::= z \mid \text{new } t \mid e.f \mid e.f = e \mid e.m(e) \mid \text{sync } e\ e \mid \text{par } e\ e$
Variables	$z ::= x \mid \text{this}$
Effects	$\varphi ::= \emptyset \mid \varepsilon \mid L{::}\varphi \mid \varphi \cup \varphi$
Side-effects	$\varepsilon ::= \text{rd } \pi \mid \pi$
Regions	$\pi ::= k \mid k{+}n \mid e{\rightarrow}f$
Owner contexts	$k ::= \text{world} \mid p \mid e$
Locksets	$L ::= \emptyset \mid e \mid [\omega] \mid L \cup L$
Lock contexts	$\omega ::= k \mid k{+}n$
Environments	$\Gamma ::= \emptyset \mid \Gamma, p \mid \Gamma, z : t$
Identifiers	c, p, f, m, x
Ownership depth	$n \in \mathbb{N}$

$$k{+}0 \equiv k \qquad \emptyset{::}\varphi \equiv \varphi \qquad L{::}\emptyset \equiv \emptyset$$
$$L{::}L'{::}\varphi \equiv (L \cup L'){::}\varphi \qquad L{::}(\varphi \cup \varphi') \equiv L{::}\varphi \cup L{::}\varphi'$$

Fig. 3. Abstract syntax, with syntactic equivalences ($\equiv$).

lock correlation `<[this]::this+1>`. Similarly, the effect of `depositC` can be written as `<[this+1]::this+1>` or the shorthand `<[this+1]>`.

The same analysis results for SeqA and ParA are obtained as before. However, both ParB and Par C are now accepted as being correctly synchronised. In ParB, we know that the calls will acquire `c` and `d` as locks; they may or may not be aliased. If they are aliased, then both calls attempt to acquire the same lock. Now if they are not aliased, the two calls may run concurrently. The effect of each call is contained within the associated lock. We know that both customers are at the same ownership rank, and so, because they are distinct, the structure of ownership effects ensures that the two effects do not overlap, as required for safety. ParC can be argued similarly, but now the lock is some account object inside the customer, its owner. In brief, our motto is: *each lock protects its own*.

4   The Type System for Structural Lock Correlation

We present a small Java-like language, similar to those used in other ownership type systems [23,7,6,4,16,15,17], and incorporate lock effects.

The syntax for the core language is given is in Fig. 3. The identifiers name classes, ownership parameters, fields, methods and formal arguments of methods respectively. A program is a collection of classes with a main expression. Each class has a list of ownership parameters, an optional super type, and a list of field declarations and method definitions. Fields may be optionally declared final, as in Java. Types are simply classes with actual ownership bindings. Methods declare a return type and a single argument (for simplicity) and a lock effect corresponding to the method body. Expressions are straightforward, with reading of variables and fields, field assignments and method calls. There is no explicit sequential construct $(e; e)$—assignment and method calls already demonstrate sequential evaluation of subexpressions. For simplicity, like most formal type and effect systems, we omit conditionals and loops. The parallel construct is used to present formal properties about data races in a concurrent setting; formally it is simpler to illustrate soundness for our techniques using lexically scoped parallelism as provided by par, but this choice is not fundamental to our approach. A sync $e_1 e_2$ expression synchronises on the object referenced by e_1 to guard against other concurrent execution while evaluating e_2.

The lock effects φ record the correlation $L{::}\epsilon$ between the possible side-effects on memory and the set of locks (if any) guarding those memory accesses. The syntactic equivalences defined in Fig. 3 ensure that lock effects can always be normalised as a set of $L{::}\epsilon$ lockset/side-effect correlations. In the lockset syntax L, e is an arbitrary lock, while $[\omega]$ is the existential abstraction of a lock participating in a structural lock correlation. Side-effects are captured as read or write effects on a region of memory. A region π is an ownership subtree k, a levelled forest $k{+}n$, or a named object field $e{\to}f$. Named object fields allow fine-grained effects to be identified; as a side-effect they represent access to a single named field. Ownership contexts k have an ownership relation; they are either object-valued expressions, ownership parameters, or the fixed ownership root world. Every expression/object/type has an associated owner. The ownership-based region k denotes the tree of objects owned by the context k, directly or indirectly. The forest $k{+}n$ denotes all trees rooted at ownership depth n inside k, which we can describe in terms of iterated ownership, as $\{e \mid owner^i_\Gamma(e) = k \text{ for } i \geq n\}$. The *owner* of e is formally defined in the next section, and is dependent on the typing environment Γ for e. We merge cases, by noting that ownership trees $k{+}0$ and k are identical regions.

The ownership type system is largely standard, except that we do not enforce encapsulation[23,7,5,20,3,6]. Alternatively, existential ownership, based on our earlier scheme [16,15] could provide for more liberal reference to owned objects. We could also extend our system with constraints for disjointness and rank equivalence on ownership parameters for extra expressiveness. We omit such extensions in this paper to focus on the key novelty: structural lock correlation.

Well-formed Program, Class and Method $\vdash P$ $\vdash C$ $\Gamma \vdash M$

$$
\frac{\begin{array}{c} \vdash \overline{C} \\ \emptyset \vdash e : t\,!\,\varphi \end{array}}{\vdash \overline{C}\ e} \text{[PROGRAM]}
\qquad
\frac{\Gamma = \overline{p}, \text{this} : c\langle\overline{p}\rangle \qquad \Gamma \vdash \overline{M} \\ \Gamma \vdash t, \overline{t} \qquad owner(c\langle\overline{p}\rangle) = owner(t)}{\vdash \text{class } c\langle\overline{p}\rangle \ [\text{extends } t]_{opt} \ \{[\text{final}]_{opt}\ t\ f;\ \overline{M}\}} \text{[CLASS]}
$$

$$
\frac{\Gamma \vdash t, t' \quad \Gamma, x : t' \vdash e : t\,!\,\varphi \quad defin(\Gamma(\text{this}), \text{this}) = ... \ [\text{extends } t'']_{opt} \\ method(m, t'', \text{this}, x) = t_0\ t'_0\ \varphi' ... \quad t \leq t_0 \quad t'_0 \leq t' \quad \Gamma \vdash \varphi \sqsubseteq \varphi'}{\Gamma \vdash t\ m(t'\ x)\ \varphi\ \{e\}} \text{[METHOD]}
$$

Our type and effects system starts with top-level constructs. The judgements are given for a fixed program P. By [PROGRAM], a well-formed program has well-formed classes and a well-typed main expression. In [CLASS], a class checks its supertype, method definitions and field types in an environment containing the class's ownership parameters and a self-type binding for this. As is standard in ownership types, the owner of the class is the same as in its supertype; this prevents ownership information from being lost in type subsumption. With a slight abuse of notation, we omit those parts of the rule's antecedent that rely on the optional supertype when it is not present. Rule [METHOD] uses the auxiliary definitions to look up method definitions with appropriate bindings. The rule checks that a method body has the declared return type and effect, given the argument type declarations. A method is covariant in its return type and effect, and contravariant in its arguments; this is checked relative to the inherited version of the method, if any, instantiated with the self-type and method arguments.

$$\frac{[\text{LOOKUP-DEFIN}]}{defin(c\langle \overline{k}\rangle, e) = [\overline{k}/p, e/\text{this}]L} \qquad L = \text{class } c\langle\overline{p}\rangle \dots$$

$$\frac{[\text{LOOKUP-FIELDS}]}{fields(t,e) = \overline{[\text{final}]_{opt}\ t\ f}, fields(t',e)} \qquad defin(t,e) = \dots \text{ extends } t'\ \{\overline{[\text{final}]_{opt}\ t\ f} \dots \}$$

$$\frac{[\text{LOOKUP-METHOD}]}{method(m,t,e,e') = t'\ t''\ [e'/x]\varphi\ [e'/x]e''} \qquad defin(t,e) = \dots\ t'\ m(t''\ x)\ \varphi\ \{e''\} \dots$$

$$\frac{[\text{LOOKUP-OWNER}]}{owner_\Gamma(e) = owner(t)} \qquad \Gamma \vdash e : t\ !\ \varphi$$

$$\frac{[\text{LOOKUP-METHOD-EXT}]}{method(m,t,e,e') = method(m,t',e,e')} \qquad defin(t,e) = \dots \text{ extends } t'\ \{\ \dots\ ;\overline{M}\}\quad (\dots\ m(\dots)\ \dots) \notin \overline{M}$$

$$\frac{[\text{LOOKUP-OWNER-TYPE}]}{owner(c\langle k\ \dots\rangle) = k}$$

The auxiliary lookup functions resolve type instances for fields and methods selected in a target application, by binding this and its type appropriately. The recursive definition [LOOKUP-FIELDS] unwinds inherited field definitions, terminating when a top-level class with no supertype is reached. Method lookup is split into separate recursive and base cases. The first context parameter of a type is its owner [LOOKUP-OWNER-TYPE]; the owner of an object denoted by an arbitrary expression is determined from the type of the expression [LOOKUP-OWNER].

Expression Typing $\Gamma \vdash e : t\ !\ \varphi$

$$\frac{[\text{SELECTION}]}{\Gamma \vdash e : t\ !\ \varphi \quad (t'\ f) \in fields(t,e)}{\Gamma \vdash e.f : t'\ !\ \varphi \cup \text{rd } e{\to}f}$$

$$\frac{[\text{UPDATE}]}{\Gamma \vdash e : t\ !\ \varphi \quad \Gamma \vdash e' : t'\ !\ \varphi' \quad (t'\ f) \in fields(t,e) \quad \Gamma \vdash t'}{\Gamma \vdash e.f = e' : t'\ !\ \varphi \cup \varphi' \cup e{\to}f}$$

$$\frac{[\text{FINAL}]}{\Gamma \vdash e : t\ !\ \varphi \quad (\text{final } t'\ f) \in fields(t,e)}{\Gamma \vdash e.f : t'\ !\ \varphi}$$

$$\frac{[\text{CALL}]}{\Gamma \vdash e : t\ !\ \varphi \quad \Gamma \vdash e' : t'\ !\ \varphi' \quad \Gamma \vdash t' \quad method(m,t,e,e') = t''\ t'\ \varphi'' \dots}{\Gamma \vdash e.m(e') : t''\ !\ \varphi \cup \varphi' \cup \varphi''}$$

$$\frac{[\text{VARIABLE}]}{\Gamma \vdash z : t\ !\ \emptyset} \qquad z : t \in \Gamma$$

$$\frac{[\text{NEW}]}{\Gamma \vdash \text{new } t : t\ !\ \emptyset} \qquad \Gamma \vdash t$$

$$\frac{[\text{PARALLEL}]}{\Gamma \vdash e : t\ !\ \varphi \quad \Gamma \vdash e' : t'\ !\ \varphi' \quad \Gamma \vdash \varphi\ \#\ \varphi'}{\Gamma \vdash \text{par } e\ e' : t'\ !\ \varphi \cup \varphi'}$$

$$\frac{[\text{SYNCHRONISATION}]}{\Gamma \vdash e \quad \Gamma \vdash e' : t\ !\ \varphi}{\Gamma \vdash \text{sync } e\ e' : t\ !\ e::\varphi}$$

$$\frac{[\text{SUBSUMPTION}]}{\Gamma \vdash e : t'\ !\ \varphi' \quad \vdash t' \leq t \quad \Gamma \vdash \varphi' \sqsubseteq \varphi}{\Gamma \vdash e : t\ !\ \varphi}$$

The form of judgment for expressions is more or less standard for effect systems, where each rule checks both the type and the behavioural effect for expressions. The type judgements are unsurprising. [SYNCHRONISATION] states that the type of sync $e\ e'$ is the same as e', its guard (lock) expression e must be final thus having no effect itself, and the lock e is correlated with the effect of e'. [SYNCHRONISATION] is the only rule that affects the lock part of an effect. [PARALLEL] also yields the type of the second expression, in line with our (arbitrary) choice of the value of a par pair.

In general, the effect of an expression takes the union of its subexpression effects, with any additional effect of the particular kind of expression. Only object field access yields a side-effect: a read effect on the field in [SELECTION] and a write in [UPDATE]; these are the most specific side-effects, and can be abstracted via [SUBSUMPTION] which allows a subeffect to be replaced by a super effect in a judgment, thus losing precision, but possibly extending the visibility of the effect to a broader scope. In [CALL] the target binding of the method definition determines the additional lock effect φ'' of the call execution. Finally [PARALLEL] asserts that a par effect is simply the union of the subeffects of the parallel subexpressions. However, this judgment is only valid if the two subeffects do not conflict: $\varphi \# \varphi'$, as discussed in the next section.

Well-formed Types and Subtyping $\quad \Gamma \vdash t \quad \vdash t \leq t$

[TYPE]
$$\frac{\Gamma \vdash \overline{k}}{\Gamma \vdash c\langle \overline{k} \rangle}$$

[SUBTYPE-EXT]
$$\frac{\mathit{defin}(c\langle \overline{k} \rangle, \_) = \ldots \text{extends } t}{\vdash c\langle \overline{k} \rangle \leq t}$$

[SUBTYPE-REFL]
$$\frac{}{\vdash t \leq t}$$

[SUBTYPE-TRANS]
$$\frac{\vdash t \leq t'' \quad \vdash t'' \leq t'}{\vdash t \leq t'}$$

The rules for well-formed types and subtypes are standard for ownership types. Types can only be formed from well-formed contexts, and class inheritance and parameter substitution provides the base for the subtype relation. Well-formedness of types is checked wherever type declarations are explicit (in [CLASS] and [METHOD]) and wherever object references are created or bound (in [NEW], [UPDATE] and [CALL]).

Well-formed Contexts and Final Expressions $\quad \Gamma \vdash k \quad \Gamma \vdash_{\mathsf{final}} e : t$

[CONTEXT-FORMAL]
$$\frac{p \in \Gamma}{\Gamma \vdash p}$$

[CONTEXT-WORLD]
$$\frac{}{\Gamma \vdash \text{world}}$$

[CONTEXT-FINAL]
$$\frac{\Gamma \vdash_{\mathsf{final}} e : t}{\Gamma \vdash e}$$

[FINAL-VARIABLE]
$$\frac{z : t \in \Gamma}{\Gamma \vdash_{\mathsf{final}} z : t}$$

[FINAL-FIELD]
$$\frac{\Gamma \vdash_{\mathsf{final}} e : t \quad (\text{final } t' \; f) \in \mathit{fields}(t, e)}{\Gamma \vdash_{\mathsf{final}} e.f : t'}$$

Only final expressions are allowed as well-formed contexts by [CONTEXT-FINAL]. Variables (read-only method parameters and this) are final, as are final field expressions, where the target object is accessed via another final expression.

Nonconflict $\quad \Gamma \vdash \varphi \# \varphi$

[NONCONF-SIDEEFF]
$$\frac{\Gamma \vdash \varepsilon \# \varepsilon'}{\Gamma \vdash L{::}\varepsilon \# L'{::}\varepsilon'}$$

[NONCONF-ARBITRARY]
$$\frac{\Gamma \vdash e}{\Gamma \vdash e{::}\varepsilon \# e{::}\varepsilon'}$$

[NONCONF-STRUCTURAL]
$$\frac{\Gamma \vdash \omega \approx \omega'}{\Gamma \vdash [\omega]{::}\varepsilon \# [\omega']{::}\varepsilon'}$$

[NONCONF-LOCKSET]
$$\frac{\Gamma \vdash L'{::}\varepsilon \# \varphi \quad L' \subseteq L}{\Gamma \vdash L{::}\varepsilon \# \varphi}$$

[NONCONF-∅]
$$\frac{}{\Gamma \vdash \emptyset \# \varphi}$$

[NONCONF-UNION]
$$\frac{\Gamma \vdash \varphi \# \varphi' \quad \Gamma \vdash \varphi \# \varphi''}{\Gamma \vdash \varphi \# \varphi' \cup \varphi''}$$

[NONCONF-SYM]
$$\frac{\Gamma \vdash \varphi' \# \varphi}{\Gamma \vdash \varphi \# \varphi'}$$

Nonconflicting lock effects offer race-free concurrency. We presume that lock effects have been normalised to a set of lockset/side-effect correlations. The first three rules handle base cases, dealing with nonconflict between a pair of correlations, in three distinct ways: (i) by [NONCONF-SIDEEFF], if the side-effects are nonconflicting; (ii) by [NONCONF-ARBITRARY], if the same arbitrary lock exists in the lockset; and (iii) by [NONCONF-STRUCTURAL], if there are two structural locks with the same rank. Case (i) lifts nonconflict for side-effects to nonconflict for lock effects. Case (ii) is the standard notion that concurrent memory access must be protected by a common lock. Case (iii) is the key novelty. The structural lock correlation tells us that both side-effects are each protected by their own lock at the same ownership rank. There are two possibilities: either both existential locks are the same, in which case we are back to case (ii), or the two existential locks are distinct, in which case the corresponding ownership trees do not overlap. But being structural locks, each tree contains their respective side-effects, and so we are back to case (i). So there are no conflicts for both possibilities. By [NONCONF-UNION], all correlation pairs in the cross product of two lock effects must be nonconflicting in order for the two effects to be nonconflicting.

Subeffecting $\Gamma \vdash \varphi \sqsubseteq \varphi$

$$[\text{SUBEFF-STRUCTURAL}]$$
$$\frac{\Gamma \vdash \varepsilon \sqsubseteq e}{\Gamma \vdash e{::}\varepsilon \sqsubseteq [e]{::}\varepsilon}$$

$$[\text{SUBEFF-ABSTRACT}]$$
$$\frac{\Gamma \vdash \omega \ll \omega'}{\Gamma \vdash [\omega]{::}\varepsilon \sqsubseteq [\omega']{::}\varepsilon}$$

$$[\text{SUBEFF-LOCKSET}]$$
$$\frac{L' \subseteq L \quad \Gamma \vdash \varepsilon \sqsubseteq \varepsilon'}{\Gamma \vdash L{::}\varepsilon \sqsubseteq L'{::}\varepsilon'}$$

$$[\text{SUBEFF-TRANS}]$$
$$\frac{\Gamma \vdash \varphi \sqsubseteq \varphi'' \quad \Gamma \vdash \varphi'' \sqsubseteq \varphi'}{\Gamma \vdash \varphi \sqsubseteq \varphi'}$$

$$[\text{SUBEFF-UNION}]$$
$$\frac{\Gamma \vdash \varphi \sqsubseteq \varphi'' \quad \Gamma \vdash \varphi' \sqsubseteq \varphi'''}{\Gamma \vdash \varphi \cup \varphi' \sqsubseteq \varphi'' \cup \varphi'''}$$

The rule [SUBEFF-STRUCTURAL] asserts that e is acting as a structural lock in the lock effect: it owns its correlated effect. Such a lock can be replaced by the existential form $[e]$. Of itself, this is of little use, but by [SUBEFF-ABSTRACT] these structural locks may be abstracted, by moving up the ownership tree (see [RANK-OWNER] as discussed below), while preserving the rank where the actual lock exists; again, this abstraction increases the scope where the effects are visible. These two rules are the only means by which abstract structural correlations are introduced. Such abstraction preserves lock correlation and rank equivalence of the locks in a structural lock (see Lemmas 2 and 3 in Section 5). By [SUBEFF-LOCKSET] we can move to a supereffect by removing parts of the lock (because it is safe to lose locking information in supereffects), or by abstracting the side-effect.

Lock Abstraction and Rank Equivalence $\Gamma \vdash \omega \ll \omega$ $\Gamma \vdash \omega \approx \omega$

$$[\text{LOCK-ABSTRACT}]$$
$$\frac{owner_\Gamma^{n-m}(k) = k' \quad m \le n}{\Gamma \vdash k{+}m \ll k'{+}n}$$

$$[\text{RANK-OWNER}]$$
$$\frac{\exists i \cdot owner_\Gamma^{i-m}(k) = owner_\Gamma^{i-n}(k')}{\Gamma \vdash k{+}m \approx k'{+}n}$$

Recall that when $k{+}n$ is a region π, it denotes the forest of subtrees at ownership rank n below k. However, when $k{+}n$ is a lock context ω, it is used to assert that a structural lock exists at a rank n below k. In other words, allowed contexts for the lock are the roots of the region's forest. That is, the ω interpretation of $k+n$ is $\{e \mid owner_\Gamma^n(e) = k\}$.

The [RANK-OWNER] rule asserts that two lock contexts are at the same rank, if they are at the same rank below a common owner. Intuitively, we can abstract a structural lock to another lock context which contains all of the possible contexts of the original lock context. This loses precision about the possible values, by allowing extra contexts. However, in order to be able to reason about nonconflict of structural locks, we must ensure that all of the contexts are at the same rank. Hence [LOCK-ABSTRACT] defines $\Gamma \vdash k+m \ll k'+n$ for $m \leq n$ so that k' is the owner of k at the rank that ensures that both lock contexts appear at rank n below k'. Because k' owns k, $k'+n$ contains all of $k+m$, as required.

Structural lock abstraction preserves structural lock correlation, as already noted. It is worth noting that lock abstraction is only possible for locksets comprising a singleton (structural) lock. Any other (arbitrary) locks must be elided before the abstraction is allowed; if those locks are actually needed to demonstrate nonconflict for lock effects, then it is pointless to elide them, and hence pointless to aim for structural lock abstraction. This impacts on the design of synchronisation policies: to achieve abstraction of the locks, it is necessary, at least in our model, to focus on the use of ownership for structural locking, and avoid mixing structural and arbitrary locking.

Side-Effects Disjointness and Subsumption $\quad \Gamma \vdash \varepsilon \sqsubseteq \varepsilon \quad \Gamma \vdash \varepsilon \mathrel{\#} \varepsilon$

[SUB-SIDE-EFF-RD]	[SUB-SIDE-EFF-RD-WR]	[SIDE-EFF-RD]	[SIDE-EFF-RD-WR]
$\dfrac{\Gamma \vdash \pi \sqsubseteq \pi'}{\Gamma \vdash \mathsf{rd}\ \pi \sqsubseteq \mathsf{rd}\ \pi'}$	$\dfrac{\Gamma \vdash \pi \sqsubseteq \pi'}{\Gamma \vdash \mathsf{rd}\ \pi \sqsubseteq \pi'}$	$\dfrac{}{\Gamma \vdash \mathsf{rd}\ \pi \mathrel{\#} \mathsf{rd}\ \pi'}$	$\dfrac{\Gamma \vdash \pi \mathrel{\#} \pi'}{\Gamma \vdash \mathsf{rd}\ \pi \mathrel{\#} \pi'}$

Read side-effects may be subsumed by default (write) side-effects. Read side-effects do not conflict with each other. A read (or write) side-effect will not conflict with another write side-effect if their corresponding regions are disjoint.

Region Disjointness and Subsumption $\quad \Gamma \vdash \pi \sqsubseteq \pi \quad \Gamma \vdash \pi \mathrel{\#} \pi$

[SUBREG-FOREST]	[SUBREG-FIELD]	[SUBREG-WORLD]	[DISJOINT-FIELD]
$\dfrac{\exists i \cdot i + m \geq n \quad owner_\Gamma^i(k) = k'}{\Gamma \vdash k+m \sqsubseteq k'+n}$	$\dfrac{\Gamma \vdash e}{\Gamma \vdash e{\rightarrow}f \sqsubseteq e}$	$\dfrac{}{\Gamma \vdash \pi \sqsubseteq \mathsf{world}}$	$\dfrac{f \neq f'}{\Gamma \vdash e{\rightarrow}f \mathrel{\#} e'{\rightarrow}f'}$

[DISJOINT-FIELD-ALIAS]	[DISJOINT-RANK-EQ]	[DISJOINT-SUBREGION]
$\dfrac{\Gamma \vdash e \otimes e'}{\Gamma \vdash e{\rightarrow}f \mathrel{\#} e'{\rightarrow}f'}$	$\dfrac{\Gamma \vdash k \approx k' \quad \Gamma \vdash k \otimes k'}{\Gamma \vdash k \mathrel{\#} k'}$	$\dfrac{\Gamma \vdash \pi \sqsubseteq \pi'' \quad \Gamma \vdash \pi' \sqsubseteq \pi''' \quad \Gamma \vdash \pi'' \mathrel{\#} \pi'''}{\Gamma \vdash \pi \mathrel{\#} \pi'}$

By [SUBREG-FOREST], $\Gamma \vdash k+m \sqsubseteq k'+n$ just when k is owned by k', ensuring that the k region (subtree) is a subset of the k' subtree. The rank inequality ensures that $k+m$ has a deeper ownership rank than $k'+n$, thus ensuring that $k+m$'s region (forest) is a subset of $k'+n$'s. [LOCK-ABSTRACT] is a special case of

[SUBREG-FOREST] with $i = n - m$. [SUBREG-FIELD] deals with a special case where the named field is subsumed by the target expression/context it belongs to.

Two named fields are disjoint as regions just when they have distinct names, or they belong to two objects accessed via expressions which must not be aliased. The rule [DISJOINT-SUBREGION] asserts that subregions are disjoint if corresponding super regions are (that is, disjointness is preserved by forming subregions). Intuitively this matches the ownership tree model with subregions corresponding to subsetting of subtrees. To show disjointness we can apply this rule to lift one or both subregions to super regions k and k' at the same rank. This is clearly possible for regions of the form $k+m$ and $e{\to}f$. Then we test for disjointness by testing for non-aliasing of the two region roots k and k', according to [DISJOINT-RANK-EQ].

Nonaliasing $\Gamma \vdash k \otimes k$ $\Gamma \vdash t \otimes t$

[NONALIAS-OWNER-LEFT]
$$\frac{owner_\Gamma(k) = k'}{\Gamma \vdash k \otimes k'}$$

[NONALIAS-OWNER-RIGHT]
$$\frac{owner_\Gamma(k') = k}{\Gamma \vdash k \otimes k'}$$

[NONALIAS-CONTEXT]
$$\frac{\exists i \in 1..n \quad \cdot \quad \Gamma \vdash k_i \otimes k'_i}{\Gamma \vdash c\langle k_{1..n}\rangle \otimes c\langle k'_{1..n}\rangle}$$

[NONALIAS-CLASS]
$$\frac{c \neq c' \quad \text{class } c \text{ ... [extends } c''\langle...\rangle]_{opt} \text{ ...} \quad \text{class } c' \text{ ... [extends } c''\langle...\rangle]_{opt} \text{ ...}}{\Gamma \vdash c\langle \overline{k}\rangle \otimes c'\langle \overline{k'}\rangle}$$

[NONALIAS-TYPE]
$$\frac{\Gamma \vdash e : t \mathbin{!} \varepsilon \quad \Gamma \vdash e' : t' \mathbin{!} \varepsilon' \quad \Gamma \vdash t \otimes t'}{\Gamma \vdash e \otimes e'}$$

[NONALIAS-SUBTYPE]
$$\frac{\vdash t \leq t'' \quad \vdash t' \leq t''' \quad \Gamma \vdash t'' \otimes t'''}{\Gamma \vdash t \otimes t'}$$

We provide an ad hoc collection of rules that use a variety of simple techniques to show that two expressions must not alias the same object context. More advanced types for reasoning about nonaliasing exist (e.g. linearity or uniqueness), but we omit them to keep our model simpler for both formalism and programmers. An object cannot alias the objects it owns. Types cannot be aliased if any of their context parameters cannot alias, or if they have distinct class names and a common superclass, or are both top level classes, so that one cannot be a subtype of the other. [NONALIAS-CLASS] should be understood to mean the optional superclass is the same for both classes (that is, both are present and the same, or both are absent).

We show how to type check `ParB` in the bank example with structural lock correlation and ownership in Section 3, where we already know the method `depositB` has lock effect `<[this]::this+1>`. Because `c` and `d` are owned by the same (default) owner, they have the same type `Customer<owner>`. By [LOOKUP-OWNER], we have $owner(c) = owner(d)$. Then by [RANK-OWNER], we have `c` $\approx$ `d`. When `depositB` is called in `ParB`, by [LOOKUP-METHOD], the two calls have the lock effects `<[c]::c+1>` and `<[d]::d+1>`. By [NONCONF-STRUCTURAL], we have `<[c]::c+1>` `#` `<[d]::d+1>`. Finally by [PARALLEL], we find `par c.depositB() d.depositB()` is well-typed. Note that, our type system allows non-final expressions in types and effects via substitution (e.g. `c` and `d`), but they are only used to look up their static types at compile time, and do not depend on runtime identities.

5   Dynamic Semantics

In this section, we define the dynamic behaviour of our language, and demonstrate that a well-typed program cannot exhibit data races.

Locations	l		
Variables	$z ::= \dots \mid l$	Objects	$o ::= \overline{f \mapsto l}$
Expressions	$e ::= \dots \mid \mathsf{synced}\ l\ e$	Heaps	$H ::= \overline{l \mapsto o_t}$

Fig. 4. Extended syntax for dynamic semantics

The extended syntax which includes features required for the dynamic semantics is defined in Fig. 4. The syntax of variables is extended with runtime locations l. Since variables may appear in the syntax of expressions, contexts and environments (which may contain location typing), we do not define additional typing rules for locations except [NONALIAS-LOCATION]. Synchronised state $\mathsf{synced}\ l\ e$ indicates the lock l has been acquired when evaluating e. A heap H is a mapping from locations to objects with their types; an object o maps its fields to locations. In order to formalise the key properties of the type system, we establish a connection between the static and dynamic semantics by including ownership in the dynamic semantics (preserved in the types of objects in the heap). But the ownership information does not affect how expressions are evaluated so it does not have to be available at runtime.

Additional auxiliary definitions for dynamic semantics and properties are given below. [STATE] defines the consistency between type environments and runtime heaps; location typing provided in the type environment must match locations and their types in the heap which are well-formed by [OBJECT].

[NONALIAS-LOCATION]

$$\frac{l \neq l'}{\Gamma \vdash l \otimes l'}$$

[SYNCHRONISED]

$$\frac{\Gamma \vdash e : t\ !\ \varphi}{\Gamma \vdash \mathsf{synced}\ l\ e : t\ !\ l{::}\varphi}$$

[STATE]

$$\frac{\Gamma \vdash e : t\ !\ \varphi \qquad H = \overline{l \mapsto o_t} \qquad \Gamma \vdash \overline{l \mapsto o_t}}{\Gamma \vdash (H; L; e) : t\ !\ \varphi}$$

[OBJECT]

$$\frac{\Gamma \vdash l : t\ !\ \emptyset \qquad \Gamma \vdash t \qquad \Gamma \vdash \overline{l : t\ !\ \emptyset} \qquad fields(t, l) = \overline{\dots\ t\ f}}{\Gamma \vdash l \mapsto (\overline{f \mapsto l})_t}$$

We present a small step operational semantics in Fig. 5 where each reduction step is considered atomic. Evaluation states contain a heap, a lock store and an expression to be evaluated. The lock store records all locks that are currently held. Like in the formalism of lock types [9], locks are not reentrant; that is, an expression cannot reacquire a lock that it already holds. The evaluation of a program starts in an initial state, $\emptyset; \emptyset; e$, where e is the body of the main method with empty heap and lock store. Evaluation then takes place according to the rules which specify the behaviour of the various constructs in the language.

We use the conventional form of evaluation contexts to reduce the number of evaluation rules:

$$E ::= [\ ]\ \mid\ E.f\ \mid\ E.f = e\ \mid\ l.f = E\ \mid\ E.m(e)$$
$$\mid\ l.m(E)\ \mid\ \mathsf{sync}\ E\ e\ \mid\ \mathsf{par}\ E\ e\ \mid\ \mathsf{par}\ e\ E$$

which defines the order of evaluation of subexpressions in compound terms, except for parallel expressions which evaluate nondeterministically via their choice of subexpression—this is a standard way to model concurrency [9,8,1].

$$\begin{array}{cc}
\text{[EVAL-SELECTION]} & \text{[EVAL-FINAL]} \\
\dfrac{H(l) = o_t \quad (t'\ f) \in \text{fields}(t,l)}{H; L; l.f \xrightarrow{\text{rd } l \to f} H; L; H(l)(f)} & \dfrac{H(l) = o_t \quad (\text{final } t'\ f) \in \text{fields}(t,l)}{H; L; l.f \longrightarrow H; L; H(l)(f)}
\end{array}$$

$$\begin{array}{cc}
\text{[EVAL-UPDATE]} & \text{[EVAL-CALL]} \\
\dfrac{H' = H[l \mapsto H(l)[f \mapsto l']]}{H; L; l.f = l' \xrightarrow{l \to f} H'; L; l'} & \dfrac{H(l) = o_t \quad \text{method}(m,t,l,l') = \dots e}{H; L; l.m(l') \longrightarrow H; L; e}
\end{array}$$

$$\text{[EVAL-NEW]}$$
$$\dfrac{l \notin \text{dom}(H) \quad H_1 = H, l \mapsto \emptyset_t \quad \overline{[\text{final}]_{opt}\ t\ f} = \text{fields}(t,l) \\ \forall i \in 1..|\overline{f}| \quad \cdot \quad H_i; L; \text{new } t_i \longrightarrow H_{i+1}; L; l_i \quad H' = H_{|\overline{f}|+1}}{H; L; \text{new } t \longrightarrow H'[l \mapsto (\overline{f \mapsto l})_t]; L; l}$$

$$\begin{array}{cc}
\text{[EVAL-ACQUISITION]} & \text{[EVAL-SYNCED]} \\
\dfrac{l \notin L}{H; L; \text{sync } l\ e \longrightarrow H; L \cup l; \text{synced } l\ e} & \dfrac{H; L; e \xrightarrow{\varphi} H; L'; e'}{H; L; \text{synced } l\ e \xrightarrow{l :: \varphi} H; L'; \text{synced } l\ e'}
\end{array}$$

$$\begin{array}{ccc}
\text{[EVAL-RELEASE]} & \text{[EVAL-JOIN]} & \text{[EVAL-CONTEXT]} \\
\dfrac{L' = L \setminus l}{H; L; \text{synced } l\ l' \longrightarrow H; L'; l'} & \dfrac{}{H; L; \text{par } l\ l' \longrightarrow H; L; l'} & \dfrac{H; L; e \xrightarrow{\varphi} H'; L'; e'}{H; L; E[e] \xrightarrow{\varphi} H'; L'; E[e']}
\end{array}$$

Fig. 5. Small step operational semantics: $H; L; e \xrightarrow{\varphi} H; L; e$

The label φ on the transition is the effect that takes place during the transition (when $\emptyset$, it may be omitted). For simplicity, in [EVAL-NEW], we adopt the object creation semantics from [4] where all fields are initialised with new objects. This may not be the case in practice, but it does not affect our results because it has no side-effect. In [EVAL-ACQUISITION], the premise blocks unless the lock to be acquired is not held (i.e. not in the lock store); after the lock is acquired (recorded in synced l) the expression e becomes active and may progress by [EVAL-SYNCED]. Note [EVAL-SYNCED] yields an effect guarded by the acquired lock l; this corresponds to [SYNCHRONISATION] in the static semantics. [EVAL-RELEASE] removes a lock from the held lockset. [EVAL-JOIN] ensures the order of sequential execution. The reduction rules for other expressions are standard.

Finally, we formalise some of the key properties of the type system and sketch their proofs. Theorem 1 asserts preservation of types and effects over the reduction of well-typed expressions.

Theorem 1 (Preservation)

If $\Gamma \vdash (H; L; e) : t\ !\ \varphi$ and $H; L; e \xrightarrow{\varphi'} H'; L'; e'$, then $\Gamma \vdash (H'; L'; e') : t\ !\ \varphi$ and $\Gamma \vdash \varphi' \sqsubseteq \varphi$.

Proof. The proof proceeds by structural induction on the derivation of term evaluation with a set of substitution lemmas, which is largely standard as seen in [5,6,14].

Theorem 2 states that parallel expressions have no conflict effects during their execution. Since parallel expressions are lexically structured, this theorem applies to any possible interleaves.

Theorem 2 (Nonconflict)

If $\Gamma \vdash (H; L; \mathsf{par}\ e_1\ e_2) : t\ !\ \varphi$, $H; L; e_1 \xrightarrow{\varphi_1} H_1; L_1; e_1'$ and $H; L; e_2 \xrightarrow{\varphi_2} H_2; L_2; e_2'$, then $\Gamma \vdash \varphi_1\ \#\ \varphi_2$.

Proof. By [STATE], we have $\Gamma \vdash \mathsf{par}\ e_1\ e_2 : t\ !\ \varphi$. By [PARALLEL], we have $\Gamma \vdash e_1 : t_1\ !\ \varphi_1'$, $\Gamma \vdash e_2 : t_2\ !\ \varphi_2'$ and $\Gamma \vdash \varphi_1'\ \#\ \varphi_2'$. From [STATE], we know $\Gamma \vdash (H; L; e_1) : t_1\ !\ \varphi_1'$ and $\Gamma \vdash (H; L; e_2) : t_2\ !\ \varphi_2'$. By Theorem 1, we can have $\Gamma \vdash \varphi_1 \sqsubseteq \varphi_1'$ and $\Gamma \vdash \varphi_2 \sqsubseteq \varphi_2'$. Finally, by Lemma 1, we have the result.

Lemma 1 (Subeffects preserve nonconflict)

If $\Gamma \vdash \varphi_1 \sqsubseteq \varphi_1'$, $\Gamma \vdash \varphi_2 \sqsubseteq \varphi_2'$ and $\Gamma \vdash \varphi_1'\ \#\ \varphi_2'$, then $\Gamma \vdash \varphi_1\ \#\ \varphi_2$.

Proof. By induction on the derivations of $\Gamma \vdash \varphi\ \#\ \varphi$. Case [NONCONF-STRUCTURAL] uses Lemmas 2 and 3. Other cases are straightforward.

Lemma 2 (Lock abstraction preserves subeffects and rank)

If $\Gamma \vdash \omega \ll \omega'$, then $\Gamma \vdash \omega \sqsubseteq \omega'$ and $\Gamma \vdash \omega \approx \omega'$.

Proof. By [LOCK-ABSTRACT], $\omega = k + m$ and $\omega' = k' + n$ hold, where $owner_{\Gamma}^{n-m}(k) = k'$ and $0 \le m \le n$. Choosing $i = n$ in [RANK-OWNER] shows $\Gamma \vdash \omega \approx \omega'$. Finally, choosing $i = n - m$ in [SUBREG-FOREST] shows $\Gamma \vdash \omega \sqsubseteq \omega'$.

Lemma 3 (Lock abstraction preserves structural correlation)

If $\Gamma \vdash \omega \ll \omega'$ and $\Gamma \vdash \varepsilon \sqsubseteq \omega$, then $\Gamma \vdash \varepsilon \sqsubseteq \omega'$.

Proof. By Lemma 2 and [SUBEFF-TRANS].

Lemma 4 (Sub-side-effects preserve disjointness)

If $\Gamma \vdash \varepsilon_1 \sqsubseteq \varepsilon_1'$, $\Gamma \vdash \varepsilon_2 \sqsubseteq \varepsilon_2'$ and $\Gamma \vdash \varepsilon_1'\ \#\ \varepsilon_2'$, then $\Gamma \vdash \varepsilon_1\ \#\ \varepsilon_2$.

Proof. Easy induction on the derivations of $\Gamma \vdash \varepsilon\ \#\ \varepsilon$.

Data race freedom means that parallel expressions cannot cause conflicting side-effects without synchronisation. We formalise race freedom to show that arbitrary interleaves of evaluations do not cause conflicting side-effects [8]. To facilitate the proofs, we introduce a lockset lookup function $locks(e)$ which simply extracts all the locks currently held by e (i.e. all synced l in e).

Theorem 3 (Race freedom)

Given $H; L; \mathsf{par}\ e_1\ e_2$ is reachable from the initial state and $\Gamma \vdash (H; L; \mathsf{par}\ e_1\ e_2) : t\ !\ \varphi$, if $H; L; e_1 \xrightarrow{L_1::\varepsilon_1} H_1; L_1; e_1'$ and $H; L; e_2 \xrightarrow{L_2::\varepsilon_2} H_2; L_2; e_2'$, then $\Gamma \vdash \varepsilon_1\ \#\ \varepsilon_2$.

Proof. By Lemma 5, we have $locks(e_1) \cap locks(e_2) = \emptyset$. By Lemma 6, we have $L_1 \subseteq locks(e_1)$ and $L_2 \subseteq locks(e_2)$. By set disjointness, we have $L_1 \cap L_2 = \emptyset$. By Theorem 2, we have $\Gamma \vdash L_1::\varepsilon_1\ \#\ L_2::\varepsilon_2$. By [NONCONF-SIDEEFF], we have the result.

Lemma 5 (Mutual exclusion)
If $H; L;$ par e_1 e_2 is reachable from the initial state, then $locks(e_1) \cap locks(e_2) = \emptyset$.

Proof. Easy induction on the derivation of term evaluation. The only interesting case is [EVAL-ACQUISITION], which ensures at any time a lock can only be acquired at most once.

Lemma 6 (Lockset)
If $H; L_0; e \xrightarrow{L::\varepsilon} H'; L_0'; e'$, then $L \subseteq locks(e)$.

Proof. Let $L = l::L'$, we need to show $(l \cup L') \subseteq locks(e)$. We have $l \subseteq locks(e)$ by [EVAL-SYNCED] and $L' \subseteq locks(e)$ by induction.

6   Related Work

In earlier type systems for safe locking [9,10], shared fields are *guarded by* a fixed lock. This follows the recommended programming practice, where program annotations are added to data declarations, to document which locks are intended to guard which data. Any code accessing a field must hold the specified lock, regardless of its context. Requiring a fixed lock to protect certain data is inflexible as it does not allow clients to devise their own synchronisation policies. For modularity, lock type systems ask the programmer to annotate a method declaration with a *requires* clause to specify the locks that must be held at each call-site of the method. The specified locks are then used to check to see if the method body is race-free or not. This requires effects to set up a precondition for the method, thereby placing a restriction on where this method can be used. In contrast, lock effects describe the computational behaviour of a method body.

Instead of associating locks with fields, [11] associates locks with hierarchical regions, protecting state across many objects. A lock object can be the object itself or one of its final fields; it may also be renamed to hide its representation from clients. Method effects can be specified as annotations in terms of *requires* clauses or side effects. Like lock types, it does not offer lock abstraction and is not context sensitive in checking unsynchronised access to state.

SafeJava [3,2] relies on the object encapsulation enforced by an owners-as-dominators type system to provide a clear point for access control for safe locking. SafeJava is an extension to the lock types model, where the guarded-by requirement is specified implicitly for every field: the required lock is always the root of the ownership tree that the field belongs to. Only access to the root objects' fields and methods needs to be directly synchronised. Using universes types, [8] follows a fine-grained ownership-based locking convention, where an object's corresponding lock is its direct owner rather than any transitive root owner. But different levels of object access do not rely on higher-level locks, and must be separately synchronised. In general, these approaches rely on encapsulation, while our effect-based approach simply describes the effects of code and places no restriction on references. Our own work in [18] explores how to use ownership types to infer synchronisation requirement for structured parallelism. It does not consider explicit locks and does not use lock effects.

Locksmith [24] is a static race checker for C programs. It performs a whole-program analysis, based on an effect system, to accumulate lock correlation constraints, which are then resolved to ensure that all memory accesses are consistently protected by a common lock. Locksmith's lock correlations are intended to be inferred by a static analysis tool—they are not geared towards modular specification of locking requirements, but rely on a global program analysis.

Chord [22] is a static race checker for Java programs, based on a context-sensitive may alias analysis. Unlike Locksmith, Chord omits linearity checking, and unsoundly assumes must-aliasing of locks at the same allocation site in order to reduce the number of false positives produced. The later work [21] adds a *disjoint reachability analysis* to distinguish correlated lock/object pairs allocated at the same allocation site but in different iterations of a loop. Intuitively, if a lock reaches (via one or more field dereferences) an object and they were allocated in the same iteration, then locks allocated in different iterations must reach different objects at the same allocation site. This introduces a form of *conditional must-not aliasing* relation: two objects are not aliased under the assumption that their respective protecting locks are not aliased. The structural lock correlation we propose in this paper achieves a form of conditional must-not aliasing relation by exploiting ownership structure, and establishes such a relation in terms of modular specifications enabled by ownership-based lock effects.

7 Conclusion

Concurrent programs are difficult to reason about. Usually their behaviours are only informally and imprecisely specified. Our effect-based model supports modular checking of lock usage. Programmers must express their high-level design intentions via effect contracts on methods, thus helping to avoid intention-related bugs—the most dominant bug category in real-world applications [13]. We rely on lock correlations where structural locks protect data they own. Structural lock correlation is preserved through abstraction, as checked by the ownership-based type and effect system. Our approach is flexible, allowing locking requirements to be satisfied differently in different contexts. Lock effects also serve as an enforceable contact at interface boundaries, contributing to safety and composability of program components.

This paper does not consider unstructured threads. Our paper [19] explored reasoning about threads in order to track what side-effects may occur in parallel. We capture the effects of active threads in a form that mimics the tree structure of thread creation; it then compares these effects with those of any subsequent expressions to detect potential interference in a flow-sensitive manner. Such a technique can be adapted to the ownership-based effects described in this paper to detect data races between threads, but we leave that for future work.

Acknowledgements. This research is supported by Australian Research Grants, DP0987236 and DP130101970.

References

1. Bocchino Jr., R.L., Adve, V.S., Dig, D., Adve, S.V., Heumann, S., Komuravelli, R., Overbey, J., Simmons, P., Sung, H., Vakilian, M.: A type and effect system for Deterministic Parallel Java. In: OOPSLA (2009)
2. Boyapati, C., Lee, R., Rinard, M.: Ownership types for safe programming: Preventing data races and deadlocks. In: OOPSLA (2002)
3. Boyapati, C., Rinard, M.: A parameterized type system for race-free Java programs. In: OOPSLA (2001)
4. Cameron, N., Drossopoulou, S., Noble, J., Smith, M.: Multiple Ownership. In: OOPSLA (2007)
5. Clarke, D.: Object Ownership and Containment. PhD thesis, The University of New South Wales, Sydney, Australia (2001)
6. Clarke, D., Drossopoulou, S.: Ownership, encapsulation and disjointness of type and effect. In: OOPSLA (2002)
7. Clarke, D., Potter, J., Noble, J.: Ownership types for flexible alias protection. In: OOPSLA (1998)
8. Cunningham, D., Drossopoulou, S., Eisenbach, S.: Universe Types for Race Safety. In: VAMP (2007)
9. Flanagan, C., Abadi, M.: Types for Safe Locking. In: Swierstra, S.D. (ed.) ESOP 1999. LNCS, vol. 1576, pp. 91–108. Springer, Heidelberg (1999)
10. Flanagan, C., Freund, S.N.: Type-based race detection for Java. In: PLDI (2000)
11. Greenhouse, A., Scherlis, W.L.: Assuring and evolving concurrent programs: annotations and policy. In: ICSE (2002)
12. Lea, D.: A Java fork/join framework. In: Java Grande (2000)
13. Lu, S., Park, S., Seo, E., Zhou, Y.: Learning from mistakes - a comprehensive study on real world concurrency bug characteristics. In: ASPLOS (2008)
14. Lu, Y.: Object Validity, Effects and Accessibility with Ownership. PhD thesis, The University of New South Wales, Sydney, Australia (2008)
15. Lu, Y., Potter, J.: On Ownership and Accessibility. In: Thomas, D. (ed.) ECOOP 2006. LNCS, vol. 4067, pp. 99–123. Springer, Heidelberg (2006)
16. Lu, Y., Potter, J.: Protecting representation with effect encapsulation. In: POPL (2006)
17. Lu, Y., Potter, J., Xue, J.: Validity Invariants and Effects. In: Ernst, E. (ed.) ECOOP 2007. LNCS, vol. 4609, pp. 202–226. Springer, Heidelberg (2007)
18. Lu, Y., Potter, J., Xue, J.: Ownership Types for Object Synchronisation. In: Jhala, R., Igarashi, A. (eds.) APLAS 2012. LNCS, vol. 7705, pp. 18–33. Springer, Heidelberg (2012)
19. Lu, Y., Potter, J., Zhang, C., Xue, J.: A Type and Effect System for Determinism in Multithreaded Programs. In: Seidl, H. (ed.) ESOP 2012. LNCS, vol. 7211, pp. 518–538. Springer, Heidelberg (2012)
20. Müller, P., Poetzsch-Heffter, A.: Universes: A type system for controlling representation exposure. In: PLFP (1999)
21. Naik, M., Aiken, A.: Conditional must not aliasing for static race detection. In: POPL (2007)
22. Naik, M., Aiken, A., Whaley, J.: Effective static race detection for java. In: PLDI (2006)
23. Noble, J., Vitek, J., Potter, J.: Flexible Alias Protection. In: Jul, E. (ed.) ECOOP 1998. LNCS, vol. 1445, pp. 158–185. Springer, Heidelberg (1998)
24. Pratikakis, P., Foster, J.S., Hicks, M.: Locksmith: context-sensitive correlation analysis for race detection. In: PLDI (2006)

Taming Confusion for Modeling and Implementing Probabilistic Concurrent Systems*

Joost-Peter Katoen[1,2] and Doron Peled[3]

[1] Software Modeling and Verification Group
RWTH Aachen University
D-52056 Aachen, Germany
[2] Formal Methods and Tools Group
University of Twente
P.O. Box 217, 7500 AE Enschede, The Netherlands
[3] Department of Computer Science
Bar Ilan University
Ramat Gan 52900, Israel

Abstract. In concurrent systems, the choice of executing the next transition depends both on the timing between the agents that make independent or collaborative interactions available, and on the conflicts (nondeterministic choices) with other transitions. This creates a challenging modeling and implementation problem. When the system needs to make also probabilistic choices, the situation becomes even more complicated. We use the model of Petri nets to demonstrate the modeling and implementation problem. The proposed solution involves adding sequential observers called *agents* to the Petri net structure. Distributed probabilistic choices are facilitated in the presence of concurrency and nondeterminism, by selecting agents that make the choices, while guaranteeing that their view is temporarily stable. We provide a distributed scheduling algorithm for implementing a system that allows distributed probabilistic choice.

1 Introduction

Adding probabilities in the presence of concurrency and nondeterminism is challenging. Autonomous models in which branching probabilities and nondeterminism coexist are well understood. A prominent example is Markov decision processes (MDPs) [21]. Probabilistic automata (PAs) [23], a slight generalization of MDPs, have been equipped with parallel composition in a CSP-like fashion. They constitute a framework for concurrent systems that exhibit both nondeterministic and probabilistic behavior. Examples of such systems are randomized

---

* The first author is supported by the FP7 MEALS and SENSATION projects. The second author is supported by ISF grant 126/12 "Efficient Synthesis of Control for Concurrent Systems".

M. Felleisen and P. Gardner (Eds.): ESOP 2013, LNCS 7792, pp. 411–430, 2013.

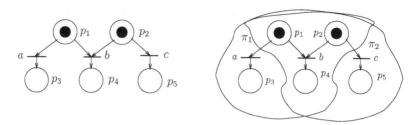

Fig. 1. A Petri net (left) covered by agents (right)

distributed algorithms and network security protocols. There is however a serious anomaly [17]: for concurrent PAs, a global scheduler may establish strong correlations between the behavior of system components and, e.g., resolve choices in one PA based on the outcome of a coin flip in the other.

An example illustrates the issue. Assume two scientists want to write a paper for a forthcoming important conference. Given the deadline, each can be involved in only one paper. Each scientist has his own idea that can be materialized into a single-authored paper a or c. They also have a joint idea for a paper b. The Petri net in Figure 1(left) depicts this situation. As they face a tough choice, they want to use some probabilistic measures to make the decision, e.g., a fair coin. The difficulty in modeling is that the available choices for such a decision may differ depending on the concurrent scheduling. If, say, the outcome of the flipped coin by the first author yields paper a, the selection of the other author is no more probabilistic; he has no choice but to write his own paper c. While writing two independent papers is concurrent, the selection by one author affects (e.g., removes) the alternative(s) for the other; this phenomenon is called *confusion* in Petri nets.

Such a subtle interplay between concurrency and probabilistic choices has recently led to various proposals to remedy or control this phenomenon, e.g., token-based schemes [7] and distributed schedulers [11], with impacts in the context of quantitative security [3] and testing theory [10]. In this paper, we start from an expressive concurrency model—Petri nets—and equip them with branching probabilities. An important advantage of Petri nets is that the artifacts that affect the aforementioned problem such as independence, conflict (or confusion), and concurrency are well studied. (Our concepts can be however also demonstrated similarly with other models.) The challenge with Petri nets is to deal with *confusion*. Indeed, various earlier proposals for probabilistic Petri nets restrict the semantics and/or their analysis to confusion-free nets [2,18,25]. Confusion describes a situation where a nondeterministic choice between transitions is affected (i.e., possibilities are added or removed) by firing an independent transition. This situation is problematic as, e.g., a probabilistic decision can be altered potentially without being observed.

Our proposal is to add information about the structure of a net, by defining what we call *agents*. The transitions of a net are covered by a set of (possibly intersecting) agents. Agents represent processes, observers, or component automata, which can make both nondeterministic and probabilistic decisions based on their "local" information. The selection of the next agent that can resolve a choice is done nondeterministically, and is supposed to be done by a scheduler. Adding agents to Petri nets yields, what we refer to as, *covered* nets. In Figure 1(right), the two agents π_1 and π_2, indicated by contours that encapsulate their transitions and places, model the two scientists. The selection between which scientist may decide first, say π_1, is done globally and nondeterministically. Agent π_1 can control transitions a and b and observe all places except p_5, i.e., all the input and output places related to its transitions.

Contributions of this paper. The technical contributions of this paper are:

- An extension of Petri nets with *agents*. Agents resolve choices based on a local state of the net, as opposed to resolving choices based on global state information (as is usual in net theory).
- A *semantics* for these nets with a two-level control mechanism: a (global) selection of an agent followed by a (local) choice by this agent. Under this semantics, concurrency occurs when an agent's transition does not affect the choices available to another agent. In contrast with standard net semantics, it identifies confusion as an additional source of dependency.
- The applicability of this framework to a novel notion of *probabilistic* Petri nets where agents are responsible to resolve probabilistic choices locally. This provides a novel and clean treatment of concurrency in the presence of branching probabilities, and naturally yields an MDP.
- A *distributed algorithm* for selecting a set of agents that can resolve their choices in an independent, concurrent fashion. The algorithm is based on a structural analysis of the net (thus is efficient), is deadlock free, and relies on low-level atomicity assumptions. To the best of our knowledge, this is the first algorithm that implements distributed scheduling of concurrent probabilistic systems.

2   Preliminaries

Petri nets. We start by introducing some basic concepts and notations of Petri nets; for more details, see e.g., [22].

Definition 1 (Syntax). *A 1-safe Petri net N is a tuple (P, T, E, s_0) where*

- *P is a finite set of places. The states of N are defined as $S = 2^P$.*
- *T is a finite set of transitions.*
- *$E \subseteq (P \times T) \cup (T \times P)$ is a bipartite relation between places and transitions.*
- *$s_0 \in S$ (i.e., $s_0 \subseteq P$) is the initial state.*

For a transition $t \in T$, let the set $\bullet t$ of input places be $\{p \in P \mid (p, t) \in E\}$, and the set $t^\bullet$ of output places be $\{p \in P \mid (t, p) \in E\}$. Similarly, for a place $p \in P$, we denote by $p^\bullet$ the transitions $\{t \in T \mid (p, t) \in E\}$, and by $\bullet p$ the transitions $\{t \in T \mid (t, p) \in E\}$.

Definition 2 (Enabled Transition). *A transition $t \in T$ is enabled in a state s, denoted $s[t\rangle$, if $^\bullet t \subseteq s$ and $t^\bullet \cap s \subseteq {}^\bullet t$. The set of enabled transitions in a state s is denoted $en(s)$. A state s is in* deadlock *if $en(s) = \emptyset$.*

Definition 3 (Fired Transition). *A transition $t \in en(s)$, i.e., $s[t\rangle$, can* fire *(or* execute*) from state s to state s', denoted by $s[t\rangle s'$, if $s' = (s \setminus {}^\bullet t) \cup t^\bullet$.*

Transitions are visualized as lines, places as circles, and the relation E is represented using arrows. The net in Figure 3 has places $p_1, p_2, \ldots, p_9$ and transitions $a, b, c, d, e,$ and f. We depict a state by putting a full circle, called a *token*, inside each place of that state, leaving the other places empty. The net in Figure 3 has the initial state $s_0 = \{p_1, p_2, p_9\}$. The transitions that are enabled in s_0 are a and b. If we fire transition a from that state, the token from place p_1 will be removed, and a token will be placed in p_3. All other tokens reside in their places.

Definition 4 (Execution). *An* execution *of a Petri net N is a maximal (i.e., it cannot be extended) alternating sequence of states and transitions $s_0 t_1 s_1 t_2 s_2 \ldots$, where s_0 is the initial state of N and for all $i \geq 0$, $s_i[t_{i+1}\rangle s_{i+1}$ holds.*

If it is clear from the context, we sometimes use just the sequence of states as executions. A state is *reachable* in a Petri net N if it occurs in at least one of its executions. The *state graph* of N is a digraph where the nodes represent reachable states of N and the edges represent the firing relation. Figure 4 depicts the state graph for the Petri net in Figure 3.

Decomposition into disjoint places. A composition of Petri nets, see Figure 2 (which can also be seen as a decomposition), was given, e.g., by Mazurkiewicz [19]. It combines different Petri nets by unifying their components. This can be seen as synchronizing the executions of transitions of the components that have the same name. The places of the components are disjoint, but this condition can be relaxed (e.g., when modeling systems with shared variables).

Definition 5 (Composition). *Let $N^1, N^2, \ldots, N^n$ be Petri nets, where $N^i = (P^i, T^i, E^i, s_0^i)$. Then the Mazurkiewicz composition of these nets is the net*

$$N = \left(\bigcup_{1 \leq i \leq n} P^i, \ \bigcup_{1 \leq i \leq n} T^i, \ \bigcup_{1 \leq i \leq n} E^i, \ \bigcup_{1 \leq i \leq n} s_0^i \right)$$

This kind of decomposition is also present in the component-based platform BIP (Behavior, Interaction, Priority) [6]. There, the finite state components may be engaged in internal or collaborative transitions. For a distributed implementation, a synchronization algorithm is required for selecting an interaction among several choices, dealing with the complication of guaranteeing a consistent interaction in the presence of different choices by the different participants. Specifically, it is essential to prevent the situation where a component is committed to an interaction, while another participant has meanwhile selected a conflicting interaction. A scheduler such as α-core [20] (that algorithm contains a small

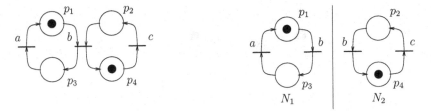

Fig. 2. Petri net composition/decomposition

error, which is corrected in [13]) provides such a guarantee by performing a two-phase exchange of messages for requesting an interaction and committing to it by all participants. In the next section, we propose another perspective on decomposing nets. The key to this decomposition is the concept of an *agent*.

3   Covering Petri Nets by Agents

This section introduces *covered* Petri nets, i.e., nets whose transitions are completely covered by agents. Agents act as entities that resolve nondeterministic (and later in Section 4, probabilistic) choices in a net. They do so on the basis of their local view of the state of the net. Executions of covered nets include in each step an agent that selects one of its enabled transition. It is nondeterministically determined when an agent (which has an enabled transition) gets its turn.

Covered Petri Nets. We first recapitulate some standard notions on transitions.

Definition 6 (Dependent, Conflicting Transition). *Transitions $t_1, t_2 \in T$ are* dependent *(see [19]) if $({}^\bullet t_1 \cup t_1{}^\bullet) \cap ({}^\bullet t_2 \cup t_2{}^\bullet) \neq \emptyset$. Let $D \subseteq T \times T$ be the* dependence *relation. Transitions $t_1, t_2 \in T$ are* independent *if $(t_1, t_2) \notin D$. Let $I = (T \times T) \setminus D$.*

Dependent transitions t_1 and t_2 are conflicting *if $({}^\bullet t_1 \cap {}^\bullet t_2) \cup (t_1{}^\bullet \cap t_2{}^\bullet) \neq \emptyset$. (We often call the transitions that are dependent but not conflicting* sequential.*)*

Dependent transitions have some common place. They are conflicting if they share some input or some output place. For example, the transitions a and b in Figure 1(left) are dependent (and conflicting), and so are transitions b and c. The transitions a and c are independent.

In order to facilitate probabilistic choices in Petri nets (see Section 4), we extend nets with agents that make decisions based on a partial view of the state of the net. This yields covered Petri nets.

Definition 7 (Covered Petri Net). *A* covered Petri net *(in short CPN)* $C = (N, \Pi)$ *is a net* $N = (P, T, E, s_0)$ *and a set* $\Pi \subset 2^T$ *of nonempty sets of transitions with* $T = \bigcup_{\pi \in \Pi} \pi$ *satisfying:*

1. *If $t, t' \in \pi$ and $(t, t') \in I$, then for no reachable state s of N, $t, t' \in en(s)$.*

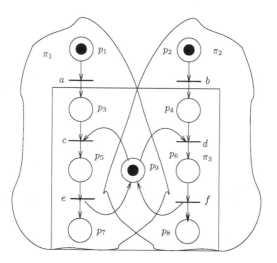

Fig. 3. A Petri net for mutual exclusion

2. *For each $p \in P$, there is a $\pi \in \Pi$ such that $^\bullet p \subseteq \pi$, and for any other $\pi' \in \Pi$, $|^\bullet p \cap \pi'| \leq 1$. The same holds when replacing $^\bullet p$ by $p^\bullet$.*

The sets of transitions in Π satisfying the above constraints are called agents.

Covering of Petri nets appears in [14]. Agents are nonempty and together cover all transitions of the net. A transition can belong to several agents, e.g., when it models a synchronization between agents. For instance, in Figure 1, transition b belongs to both agents π_1 and π_2. Let us explain the above definition in some more detail. The first constraint asserts that no two independent transitions in agent π can ever be executed from the same state[1]. Stated differently, transitions of an agent that can be simultaneously enabled are dependent. The second constraint requires that all input transitions of a place are captured by an agent; the same holds for all its output transitions. In addition, any other agent in Π contains at most one input transition (and similarly, for output transitions).

Example 1. The net in Figure 3 is covered by $\Pi = \{\pi_1, \pi_2, \pi_3\}$ with the *left* agent $\pi_1 = \{a, c, e\}$, the *right* agent $\pi_2 = \{b, d, f\}$, and the third agent $\pi_3 = \{c, d, e, f\}$. Remark that all transitions of agent π_3 are shared with some other agent. The set of agents $\Pi' = \{\pi_1, \pi_2\}$ does not cover the net as $^\bullet p_9 = \{e, f\}$ is not captured by a single agent, i.e., there is no single agent π with $^\bullet p_9 \subseteq \pi$.

The constraint on the places of the CPN reflects the goal of agents to resolve a choice. Only if $p^\bullet \subseteq \pi$ ($^\bullet p \subseteq \pi$, respectively), agent π can resolve the choice between transitions that require p to have (not have, respectively) a token. This

---

[1] This restriction, which we find natural, can be alleviated, but this requires a change in the algorithm presented in Section 5.

explains the choice of agents in Figure 1: $\pi_1 = p_1^\bullet = \{a, b\}$, and $\pi_2 = p_2^\bullet = \{b, c\}$. In Figure 5, $\pi_1 = \{b, c\}$ can execute c, while $\pi_2 = p_1^\bullet = \{a, b\}$ makes the choice between a and b.

Definition 8 (Neighborhood). *The neighborhood* $\mathsf{ngb}(T')$ *of a set* $T' \subseteq T$ *of transitions is the set of places* $\bigcup_{t \in T'}(^\bullet t \cup t^\bullet)$.

We will visually represent the separation of transitions of a Petri net into agents using a contour line that encapsulates the neighborhood of its agents. The neighborhood of agent π_1 in Figure 3 is $\{p_1, p_3, p_5, p_7, p_9\}$. Place p_9 belongs to the neighborhood of all indicated agents (i.e., π_1, π_2 and π_3), and acts as a semaphore.

Definition 9 (Local Information). *The local information of agent* $\pi \in \Pi$ *of a CPN* $C = (N, \Pi)$ *in state* s *of* N, *denoted* $s\lceil_\pi$, *is defined by* $s\lceil_\pi = s \cap \mathsf{ngb}(\pi)$.

In the net in Figure 3, the local information of π_1 in any state s equals $s \cap \{p_1, p_3, p_5, p_7, p_9\}$. In the initial state s_0, $s_0\lceil_{\pi_1}$ equals $\{p_1, p_9\}$. After executing transition b, the local information of π_1 does not change. The subsequent execution of transition d removes p_9 from the local information of π_1. The local information of an agent represents the limited view it has regarding the state of the system. This is formalized in the following lemma:

Lemma 1. *Let CPN* $C = (N, \Pi)$. *For states* s *and* s' *of* N, *and* $\pi \in \Pi$ *we have:*

1. *If* $s\lceil_\pi = s'\lceil_\pi$, *then* $en(s) = en(s')$.
2. *If* $s[t\rangle s'$ *for transition* $t \in \pi$, *then* $s \setminus \mathsf{ngb}(\pi) = s' \setminus \mathsf{ngb}(\pi)$.

CPN Executions. We now define the concept of executions for CPNs. A CPN execution involves not only the states and the enabled transitions fired from them (as for an execution of a Petri net, cf. Definition 4), but also the agents that are selected to decide which of their enabled transition will be fired. We call such a scheduling *agent centric* and in Section 5 provide an algorithm for implementing such scheduling. The basic principle of selecting agents is to give priority to agents that have a more complete view of a nondeterministic choice in the net. This is formalized by the notion of subsumption. Let CPN $C = (N, \Pi)$ with $\pi, \pi' \in \Pi$.

Definition 10 (Subsumption). *An agent* π *subsumes an agent* π' *over transition* $t \in \pi \cap \pi'$, *denoted* $\pi \gg_t \pi'$, *if the following conditions hold:*

1. *For each state* s *such that* $t \in en(s)$, $|en(s) \cap \pi'| = 1$, *i.e., there is no alternative choice for* π' *in* s *besides* t, *and*
2. *There is at least one state* s *such that* $t \in en(s)$ *and* $|en(s) \cap \pi| > 1$, *i.e.,* π *has a nondeterministic choice in* s *that includes* t.

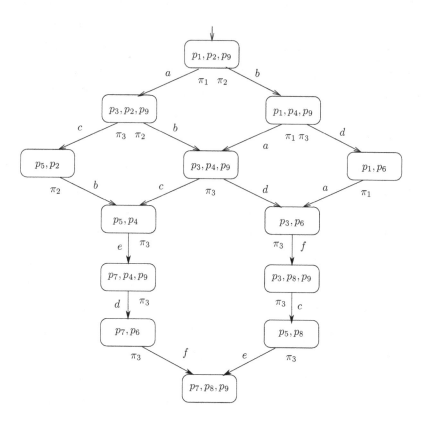

Fig. 4. State graph for the net (mutual exclusion) in Figure 3

In the following definition, an execution of a CPN only allows a transition t to be fired by an agent π' if there is no other agent π that subsumes π' over t. That is to say, if $\pi \gg_t \pi'$, agent π' will never be selected to make a decision to fire transition t. The justification for this notion is that its view is more restricted than that of agent π, which observes more alternatives to t.

In Figure 3, we have that $\pi_3 \gg_c \pi_1$ and (by symmetry) $\pi_3 \gg_d \pi_2$. In the notion of CPN execution defined below, agent π_3 resolves the nondeterministic choice between c and d, rather than agents π_1 or π_2. In a sense, we can remove the transitions c and d from the scope of agent π_1 and π_2, respectively. However, this will create a hole in the structure of the agent π_1 and π_2. (The same applies to the choice between the transitions e and f, although in this case the choice is somewhat fake as it is clear from the structure of the net that only one of these transitions can be enabled in all states.)

Definition 11 (CPN Execution). *An execution of a CPN $C = (N, \Pi)$ is a maximal sequence $s_0[\pi_1|t_1\rangle s_1[\pi_2|t_2\rangle s_2 \dots$ where s_0 is the initial state of N, for all $i \geq 0$, $s_i[t_{i+1}\rangle s_{i+1}$, $\pi_i \in \Pi$, $t_i \in \pi_i$ and there is no $\pi \in \Pi$ such that $\pi \gg_{t_i} \pi_i$.*

The choice between admissible agents (agents that currently have an enabled transition t and that are not subsumed by another one over t) is performed in a nondeterministic way.

The subsumption relation $\pi \gg_t \pi'$ is static: it does not depend on the current state. For simplicity of the presentation, we will remove henceforth from the description of an agent the transitions that it cannot execute due to subsumption. Thus, this leaves, for the CPN in Figure 3, $\pi_1 = \{a\}$ and $\pi_2 = \{b\}$.

Confusion and Weak Places. In the sequel of this section, we recall some standard notions from Petri net theory (such as confusion and concurrency), and introduce some new notions that become relevant for the scheduling algorithm in Section 5.

Definition 12 (Confusion). *The quadruple (t_1, t_2, t_3, s) is a confusion occurrence in state s if transitions t_1 and t_2 are conflicting, $(t_1, t_3) \in I$, $t_1, t_3 \in en(s)$, and the execution of t_3 (from s) changes the enabledness of t_2.[2] The pair $(t, t') \in T \times T$ is a confusion if there exists some transition $t'' \in T$ and a state s where (t, t'', t', s) is a confusion occurrence.*

Confusion appears in the nets in Figures 1 and 5. These are two classical examples of confusion, where the first one is symmetric and the second one is asymmetric. In Figure 1, (a, b, c, s_0) and (c, b, a, s_0) are confusion occurrences for the initial state $s_0 = \{p_1, p_2\}$. The former is due to the fact that a and b are conflicting and the firing of c disables b; the second is due to the conflict between c and b and firing a disables b. This gives (a, c) and (c, a) as (symmetric) confusions, respectively. In Figure 5, (a, b, c, s_0) is a confusion occurrence for the initial state $s_0 = \{p_1, p_2\}$ as firing c enables b. Thus, (a, c) is a confusion. Since (c, a) is not a confusion, this confusion is asymmetric. A confusion occurrence may not be detectable by considering the local information of an agent; e.g., in the net of Figure 5, neither agent π_1 nor agent π_2 can locally detect that the current (initial) state is a confusion occurrence.

Definition 13 (Confusion Pivot). *A place $p \in P$ is pivotal for a confusion (t, t'), if there is a confusion occurrence $(t, \hat{t}, t', s)$ such that firing t' from s changes the value of a place $p \in {}^\bullet\hat{t} \cup \hat{t}^\bullet$. We denote the pivotal places for a confusion (t, t') by $\mathsf{pivotal}(t, t')$. For $T' \subseteq T$, let $\mathsf{pivot}(T') = \bigcup_{t' \in T', t \in T} \mathsf{pivotal}(t', t)$.*

Intuitively, the pivot places are the places that are changing during the occurrence of the confusion, to create or to eliminate some choice, by the firing of an independent transition. In Figure 1, $\mathsf{pivot}(\pi_1) = \{p_2\}$ and $\mathsf{pivot}(\pi_2) = \{p_1\}$. In Figure 5, p_5 is pivotal for the confusion (a, c), resulting in $\mathsf{pivot}(\pi_2) = \{p_5\}$.

Definition 14 (Concurrent Transitions). *Independent transitions t and t' are concurrent if neither (t, t') nor (t', t) is a confusion. Let $C \subseteq T \times T$ be the symmetric and irreflexive concurrency relation.*

---

[2] That is, $t_2 \in en(s)$ and $t_2 \notin en(s')$, or $t_2 \notin en(s)$ and $t_2 \in en(s')$, where $s[t_3\rangle s'$.

The notion of concurrent transitions is pessimistic: two transitions t and t' may be in confusion, yet t' can execute independently of t without affecting its conflicts.

Definition 15 (Weak Places). *For CPN $\mathcal{C} = (N, \Pi)$ and $\pi \in \Pi$, let* $\mathsf{weak}(\pi) = \mathsf{ngb}(\pi) \cap \bigcup_{\pi' \in \Pi \setminus \{\pi\}} \mathsf{ngb}(\pi')$.

Thus, the places in $\mathsf{weak}(\pi)$ are in the part of the neighborhood of an agent π that can be changed by transitions fired by agents other than π. For example, in Figure 1, $\mathsf{weak}(\pi_1) = \{p_1, p_2, p_4\}$, and in Figure 5, $\mathsf{weak}(\pi_1) = \{p_5\}$.

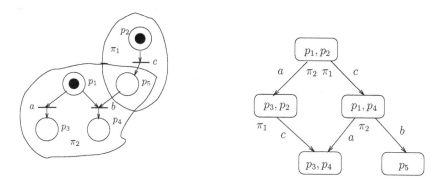

Fig. 5. A Petri net with confusion and its state graph

4   Probabilistic Covered Petri Nets

In this section, we extend the notion of covered Petri nets with branching probabilities. This naturally gives rise to a Petri net model that can be used to describe Markov decision processes [21] at a high level of abstraction. The nondeterministic choices in the MDPs correspond to the selection of (enabled) agents whereas the agents are responsible for resolving the probabilistic choices (based on their local view).

Probabilistic CPNs. In the sequel, for countable set T, let $Dist(T)$ be the set of probability distributions over T, and $Dist_\perp(T)$ be the set of distribution functions that for some elements in T may be undefined, i.e., yield the value $\perp$. Functions $\mu \in Dist_\perp(T)$ thus are of type $T \mapsto [0,1] \cup \{\perp\}$ and satisfy $\sum_{t \in T, \mu(t) \neq \perp} \mu(t) = 1$.

Definition 16 (Probabilistic CPN). *A probabilistic CPN $\mathcal{D} = (N, \Pi, f)$ is a CPN (N, Π) equipped with a function $f : \Pi \times S \to Dist_\perp(T)$ satisfying for all $\pi \in \Pi$ and $s \in S$:*

1. $f(\pi, s)(t) = \perp$ iff $t \notin en(s) \cap \pi$.
2. For each $s' \in S$, $f(\pi, s) = f(\pi, s')$ whenever $s\lceil_\pi = s'\lceil_\pi$.

Intuitively speaking, the function f assigns to a pair (π, s) a probability distribution over the enabled transitions in state s (of N) that are "visible" by the agent π. The first clause asserts that f is undefined only for transitions that are disabled for agent π. The second clause requires that an agent π, whose local views in states s and s' coincide, chooses a given transition in these states with equal probability. That is to say, the probability distribution over the enabled transitions only depends on the local information of the agent.

Example 2. Consider the CPN in Figure 1(right) and agent π_1 with $\mathsf{ngb}(\pi_1) = P \setminus \{p_5\}$ and let state $s = \{p_1, p_2\}$. Assume π_1 has a fair coin, yielding $f(\pi_1, s)(a) = f(\pi_1, s)(b) = \frac{1}{2}$. The same distribution for π_1 applies to the state $s' = \{p_1, p_2, p_5\}$, since $s\lceil_{\pi_1} = s'\lceil_{\pi_1}$. Now, consider agent π_2 with $\mathsf{ngb}(\pi_2) = P \setminus \{p_3\}$. Agent π_2 may select an enabled transition in s by flipping a biased coin, say, $f(\pi_2, s)(b) = \frac{1}{3}$ and $f(\pi_2, s)(c) = \frac{2}{3}$. Note that the transition b is common to the two agents, but its firing probabilities may differ, depending on which agent selects b. If π_1 is selected first to resolve the choice between a and b, and it selects to fire a, subsequently, we obtain the state $s'' = \{p_2, p_3\}$ and π_2 has a new local information view, namely $\{p_2\}$. Thus, it now only has the possibility to choose c, yielding $f(\pi_2, s'')(c) = 1$.

Example 3. Figure 3 represents a simple randomized mutual exclusion algorithm [4] where access to the critical section is arranged by an arbiter. In the initial state, agent π_1 can decide to fire transition a. By symmetry, agent π_2 can do the same for b. However, to fire transition c or d—acquiring access to the critical section—we use a third agent π_3 that acts as arbiter. If only c (or only d) is enabled, then π_3 decides to fire this transition. In case both c and d are enabled, i.e., in the state $\{p_3, p_4, p_9\}$, the agent π_3 flips a fair coin (say) yielding probability $\frac{1}{2}$ for transition c and d.

From probabilistic CPNs to MDPs. In the following, we show that probabilistic CPNs naturally give rise to MDPs (Markov Decision Processes [21]). In the sequel we also show that there is a one-to-one relationship between probabilistic CPN adversaries and (traditional) adversaries for MDPs. Let us start by recalling the notion of MDPs [21]. As we consider 1-safe Petri nets, it suffices to consider finite-state MDPs.

Definition 17 (Markov Decision Process). *A* Markov decision process (MDP) *is a tuple* $(Q, Act, \mathbb{P}, q_0)$ *where*

- *Q is a finite set of* states *with initial state* $q_0 \in Q$.
- *Act is a finite set of* actions.
- *$\mathbb{P} : Q \times Act \times Q \mapsto [0, 1]$ with for each* $q \in Q, \alpha \in Act, \displaystyle\sum_{q' \in Q} \mathbb{P}(q, \alpha, q') \in \{0, 1\}$.

An action α *is* enabled *in state* q *iff* $\mathbb{P}(q, \alpha, q') > 0$ *for some* $q' \in Q$.

The intuitive semantics of an MDP is as follows. In state q, one of its enabled actions is selected nondeterministically. As usual, we assume that for every state this set is nonempty. After having selected action α, say, in state q, the next state is randomly determined. More precisely, the probability of moving to state q' (which may equal q) is $\mathbb{P}(q, \alpha, q')$. An MDP execution is thus an alternating sequence of states and actions $q_0 \alpha_1 q_1 \alpha_2 \ldots$ such that α_{i+1} is enabled in state q_i. Probabilistic CPNs can be viewed as a modeling formalism for MDPs in the following way.

Definition 18 (The MDP of a probabilistic CPN). *Let $\mathcal{D} = (N, \Pi, f)$ be a probabilistic CPN with $N = (P, T, E, s_0)$. The MDP of $\mathcal{D}$, denoted $\mathsf{mdp}(\mathcal{D})$, is the tuple $(S, Act, \mathbb{P}, s_0)$, where $S = 2^P$, $Act = \Pi$, and*

$$\mathbb{P}(s, \pi, s') = \sum \{ f(\pi, s)(t) \mid t \in \pi, s[t\rangle s' \text{ and for no } \pi' \in \Pi, \pi' \gg_t \pi \}.$$

Stated in words, the states of $\mathsf{mdp}(\mathcal{D})$ are the states of the net N. Its actions are the agents. This corresponds to the intuition that an agent is selected nondeterministically, which resolves the probabilistic choice. The transition probabilities in $\mathsf{mdp}(\mathcal{D})$ correspond to the function f, provided the selected agent has the privilege to resolve the probabilistic choice. As several transitions in a given state of the net may result in the same target state, we take the sum over all individual probabilities of these transitions.

Adversaries. As the former of the previous examples showed, the probability of a transition occurrence may depend on the agent that has been selected. This suggests to define a probability measure over the behaviours of a probabilistic CPN that is subject to a given selection of agents. In order to do so, we resort to the standard notion of an adversary [21] (sometimes also called scheduler or strategy) and adapt this to our setting.

Definition 19 (MDP Adversary). *An adversary (strategy) for an MDP is a function A that maps execution fragments $q_0 \, q_1 \ldots q_n$ of the MDP such that the action $A(q_0 \, q_1 \ldots q_n)$ is enabled in q_n.*

An adversary thus selects an enabled action in the final state of a given execution fragment of the MDP.[3] The basic idea of an adversary for a probabilistic CPN is that it takes as argument a prefix of an execution and maps this onto an agent that can extend this prefix.

Definition 20 (Adversary for a probabilistic CPN). *An adversary A for a probabilistic CPN $\mathcal{C} = (N, \Pi, f)$ is a function that maps a prefix $\rho = s_0[\pi_1|t_1\rangle s_1 \ldots s_{n-1}[\pi_n|t_n\rangle s_n$ of an execution of $\mathcal{C}$ onto an agent $\pi_{n+1} \in \Pi$ such that $\rho[\pi_{n+1}|t_{n+1}\rangle s_{n+1}$ is a prefix of an execution of $\mathcal{C}$ for some $t_{n+1} \in \pi_{n+1}$.*

An adversary thus selects after a finite execution fragment of the covered net which agent is to resolve the next probabilistic choice. (The random choice,

---

[3] These are also called deterministic adversaries [21]. Our setting can easily be generalized to randomized adversaries that select agents according to a probability distribution. This falls however outside the scope of this paper.

i.e., the selection of transition t_{n+1} is done by the selected agent, not by the adversary.) An *A-execution* is an execution $s_0[\pi_1|t_1\rangle s_1[\pi_2|t_2\rangle s_2 \ldots$ of the probabilistic CPN such that for all $i \geq 0$, $\pi_{i+1} = A\left(s_0[\pi_1|t_1\rangle s_1 \ldots s_{i-1}[\pi_i|t_i\rangle s_i\right)$. That is to say, an *A*-execution is the execution fragment of the probabilistic CPN in which adversary A decides on every step which agent is to make a selection. A probability measure can now be defined on *A*-executions in the following way. The probability of the execution fragment s_0 is one, and the probability of $s_0[\pi_1|t_1\rangle s_1 \ldots s_{n-1}[\pi_n|t_n\rangle s_n$ is defined as the product $f(s_0, \pi_1)(t_1) \cdot \ldots \cdot f(s_{n-1}, \pi_n)(t_n)$. An alternative way of looking at this, is that an adversary A imposed on a probabilistic CPN yields an infinite Markov chain in which states correspond to finite execution fragments and transition probabilities are determined by the agent selected by adversary A in the current state.

Example 4. Consider the CPN of Figure 3 and let $s_0 = \{p_1, p_2, p_9\}$ with $A(s_0) = \pi_1$. As π_1 can only select transition a, this yields the execution fragment $\rho_1 = s_0[\pi_1|a\rangle s_1$ with $s_1 = s_0 \setminus \{p_1\} \cup \{p_3\}$. Let $A(\rho_1) = \pi_2$. As π_2 has a single choice, it selects transition b yielding $\rho_2 = s_0[\pi_1|a\rangle s_1[\pi_2|b\rangle s_2$ with $s_2 = \{p_3, p_4, p_9\}$. Now only π_3 has a choice between enabled transitions. If π_3 randomly selects c we obtain $\rho_3 = s_0[\pi_1|a\rangle s_1[\pi_2|b\rangle s_2[\pi_3|c\rangle s_3$. Assuming as before that π_3 flips a fair coin to resolve the choice between c and d, we obtain that the probability of execution fragment $\rho_3 = f(s_0, \pi_1)(a) \cdot f(s_1, \pi_2)(b) \cdot f(s_2, \pi_3)(c)$ which equals $1 \cdot 1 \cdot \frac{1}{2}$.

It is not difficult to see that an adversary of a probabilistic CPN corresponds directly to an adversary for its MDP. This immediately yields:

Lemma 2. *The Markov chain induced by adversary A on probabilistic CPN $\mathcal{D}$ is isomorphic to the Markov chain induced by A on the MDP $\mathsf{mdp}(\mathcal{D})$.*

A probabilistic CPN can thus be considered as a high-level (and possibly succinct) representation of an MDP. The MDP loses the structural information of the CPN, much as the state graph of a net. A measure over sets of infinite *A*-executions can be defined in the standard way using a cylinder set construction, see, e.g., [4, Ch. 10]. A measurable set of *A*-executions of a probabilistic CPN for a given adversary A is called an *event*. Based on the probability measure over *A*-executions one can now define the maximal, and dually the minimal, probability of certain events of interest. For instance, for set $G \subseteq S$ of states, let $\lozenge G$ denote the set of executions of a CPN that at some point reach some state in G. The set $\lozenge G$ is measurable (and thus an event). The maximal probability of $\lozenge G$ stands for the supremum over all possible agent selections (by any kind of adversary defined above) of eventually reaching G. In a similar way, the minimal probability is defined as the infimum over all possible agent selections to reach G. This can be generalized towards arbitrary LTL-formulas rather than simply reachability properties. Due to the above lemma, there is a direct relation between the occurrence probabilities in a probabilistic CPN to those in its MDP. Model-checking algorithms for MDPs [4, Ch. 10] can thus be exploited to calculate quantitative bounds such as the minimal and maximal probability of a reachability property $\lozenge G$, or of a temporal logic formula in LTL (or probabilistic CTL). The details of these algorithms fall outside the scope of this paper; it suffices here that the key numerical component is solving a system of linear inequations, whereas for LTL model checking of MDPs the construction of an automaton on infinite words is an additional important ingredient.

5   A Distributed Scheduling Algorithm for Making Probabilistic Choices

We described in this paper a Petri net based model that allows concurrency, non deterministic choice (among agents) and probabilistic choices. In order to show how distributed scheduling of probabilistic choices, as required by our model, can be achieved, we provide now an algorithm for implementing systems based on CPNs. The algorithm concretizes the possible schedulers of Def. 20.

Our algorithm is by no means the only possible way of implementing a system described as a probabilistic CPN, or the most efficient one. As identified in [7], it is important to provide a temporarily stable view for an agent that makes a probabilistic decision; the choices that this agent has must not change *after* the agent has finished collecting the information about its choices and *before* a probabilistic choice is made. In component-based systems [6,20] there is a similar difficulty in synchronization algorithms that guarantee a selection of an interaction. However, here the problem is to stabilize the interaction in which agents participate, rather than selecting a single interaction. Thus the approach is *agent centric* instead of *interaction centric*.

Requirements. We impose the following requirements on the distributed scheduling algorithm.

Concurrency. The algorithm allows concurrent probabilistic choices. (The algorithm in [7] allows only a single agent to make a choice; this is established by passing a token among the agents.)

Semaphores. The scheduling is implemented using semaphores. Only standard lock and free operators of semaphores are allowed. If needed, semaphore operations can be imitated by message passing.

Efficiency. A simple analysis of the structure of the Petri net, i.e., the graph between transition and places, and the partitioning into agents, in time quadratic in the size of the net, is performed once. This establishes the interactions that will be needed at run time.

Fine granularity. Atomicity is not assumed at a coarse granularity. Realistically we cannot assume that the local information of an agent needs to be examined atomically. While gathering this information, some of the checked places may have gained or lost a token. Thus, several actions may be needed in setting up the conditions for the correct firing of a transition according to the semantics of the CPN.

Liveness. No deadlock is introduced. In fact, the algorithm does not limit the executions and admits exactly the set of executions of the CPN.

Finite memory. The scheduling decisions for agents are based only on the current state of the execution and the value of the semaphores.

Partial view. The scheduling is based on the local information of agents and not on the global states [8].

The scheduling algorithm. The idea is to assign a semaphore to certain places of the net. We will henceforth relate interchangeably in notation, when clear from context, semaphores and the places they are associated with. Prior to firing a transition, a phase of locking semaphores associated with a set of places is carried out. This set is precisely defined below. The capturing of semaphores provides a temporarily stable view of an agent regarding the (probabilistic) choices that it needs to make. When an agent π makes a probabilistic decision, it needs to stabilize some tokens of weak(π) (this subset is defined precisely below), as the value of these places can affect π's set of choices. For the scheduling algorithm, we use a set of semaphores related to the weak places:

$$\mathsf{sem}(\Pi) = \bigcup_{\pi \in \Pi} \mathsf{weak}(\pi).$$

It is of course important to minimize the number of semaphores an agent is required to lock. Capturing weak(π) before firing a transition by π would indeed guarantee a stable environment for a probabilistic choice, but may incur needless overhead and severely restricts the concurrency by locking semaphores that are not relevant in the current state. We therefore propose a smaller subset of semaphores needed to be locked by agent π in state s so as for π to make a (probabilistic) choice:

$$\mathsf{capture}(\pi, s) = \mathsf{weak}(\pi) \cap (\mathsf{ngb}(en(s) \cap \pi) \cup \mathsf{pivot}(en(s) \cap \pi)).$$

Thus, capture(π, s) includes two sets of places:

weak(π) $\cap$ ngb($en(s) \cap \pi$) are the places that π may change by firing the next transition and can affect other agents; also, changing these places by firing a transition by another agent would affect their enabledness for π, and

weak(π) $\cap$ pivot($en(s) \cap \pi$) are the places that other agents can change and may alter the choices available to π.

For our algorithm we assume the existence of a partial order, denoted $\prec$, on the set of semaphores sem(Π) such that no two semaphores that are in weak(π) for some $\pi \in \Pi$ are unordered. We do neither assume that an agent collects its local information or acquires all needed semaphores atomically, nor that it changes all places involved in firing a transition atomically. However, we assume the existence of a mechanism by which an agent π can set an interrupt that informs it if a place was changed after its value has been inspected. By requiring that changing the value of a (weak) place p is done only after p's semaphore is acquired, we can safely assume that an agent knows the correct value of p when it holds its semaphore. Our algorithm now proceeds in two phases:

Phase 1. Each agent checks which of its transitions are enabled. It is not necessary that this is done atomically; rather, a lookup through the places (represented by variables, message queues, etc.) is performed. An interrupt that reports a change in the value of a place that has been already checked in this phase, causes a restart of this phase.

Phase 2. Agent π locks the semaphores $\mathsf{capture}(\pi, s)$ in an ascending order according to the partial order $\prec$. If there is an interrupt announcing a change in the value of a place p that was checked in Phase 1 before p's semaphore is locked, all the semaphores locked by π so far are released in descending order (according to $\prec$), and Phase 1 is restarted.

If agent π has acquired all semaphores in $\mathsf{capture}(\pi, s)$, it randomly selects one of its enabled transition. It is important to note that $\mathsf{capture}(\pi, s) = \mathsf{capture}(\pi, s')$ when $s\lceil_\pi = s'\lceil_\pi$. That is, $\mathsf{capture}(\pi, s)$ depends only on the local information of π. This allows calculating $\mathsf{capture}(\pi, s)$ during the execution of the algorithm locally by π.

Example 5. Consider the net in Figure 5. Agent π_2 has one weak place: p_5. In the initial state $s_0 = \{p_1, p_2\}$, $\mathsf{weak}(\pi_2)\cap\mathsf{ngb}(en(s_0)\cap\pi_2) = \emptyset$ because the places $\mathsf{ngb}(en(s_0) \cap \pi_2) = \mathsf{ngb}(\{a\}) = \{p_1, p_3\}$ are not weak (as they belong only to π_2). However, as p_5 is pivotal to the confusion (a, c), $\mathsf{capture}(\pi_2, s_0)$ is in this case $\mathsf{weak}(\pi_2) \cap \mathsf{pivot}(en(s_0) \cap \pi_2) = \{p_5\}$. Thus, in order for π_2 to maintain a stable situation with respect to the choices it can make (in this case, just firing a), π_2 must lock the semaphore for place p_5. Now agent π_1 cannot fire transition c: in order to do that from s_0, it needs to lock $\mathsf{capture}(\pi_1, s_0)$, which is, in this case, $\mathsf{weak}(\pi_1) \cap \mathsf{ngb}(en(s_0)\cap\pi_1) = \{p_5\}$. Note that π_2 needs to lock p_5 because it is pivotal to a confusion with transition a, whereas π_1 needs to lock p_5 because it may want to change it by firing c. The set of semaphores that an agent needs to lock is dependent on its local information; when p_1 does not have a token, agent π_2 does not need to lock the semaphore for p_5.

Lemma 3. *An agent π cannot change a place by firing a transition without capturing the corresponding semaphore for that place.*

Proof. Follows immediately from the need for an agent to lock, before firing the next transition, the semaphores for $\mathsf{capture}(\pi, s)$. This set includes $\mathsf{weak}(\pi) \cap \mathsf{ngb}(en(s) \cap \pi)$. $\qquad\square$

While no change occurs to the semaphores in $\mathsf{capture}(\pi, s)$, agent π has a stable set of choices, as proved by the following result.

Lemma 4. *A change to the set of currently enabled transitions of an agent π in a state s, i.e., $en(s)\cap\pi$, by firing a transition t by another agent π' (possibly $t \in \pi \cap \pi'$) in state s involves a change to some place in $\mathsf{capture}(\pi, s)$.*

Proof. Distinguish two cases.

1. t depends on some transition $t' \in en(s) \cap \pi$. By Def. 6, a state-change by t implies a change of a common place with $\mathsf{ngb}(t') \subseteq \mathsf{ngb}(en(s) \cap \pi)$. As t is executed by agent $\pi' \neq \pi$, this place also belongs to $\mathsf{weak}(\pi)$.

2. t is independent of all the transitions in $en(s) \cap \pi$. As (by assumption) t changes the enabled transitions of π in $en(s) \cap \pi$ while being independent of (all of) them, firing t enables some new transition of π, which, by the definition of agents, depends on some already enabled transition of π. Thus, by Def. 12, (t', t) is a confusion for some $t' \in en(s) \cap \pi$. By Def. 13, some place $p \in \mathsf{pivot}(en(s) \cap \pi)$ is altered by t to cause the enabledness of a transition of π in conflict with t'. As $t \notin \pi$, p is in $\mathsf{weak}(\pi)$.   □

Note how the need to lock a semaphore associated with a pivotal place due to a confusion can reduce concurrency between independent transitions. This is in accordance with Definition 14.

Lemma 5. *The scheduling algorithm does not introduce a deadlock.*

Proof. Capturing semaphores in ascending order and releasing them in descending order is a solution for a generalized mutual exclusion problem, suggested originally by Dijkstra for the dining philosophers problem. See [24] for its correctness, including deadlock freeness. Note that if Phase 1 restarts, some progress must have occurred, as a place was changed by firing some transition.   □

Lemma 6. *The scheduling algorithm admits exactly the set of CPN executions.*

Proof. Clearly, any execution of the net under the obtained scheduler must conform to the semantics of execution of the Petri nets. Conversely, for each execution of the CPN, we have a behavior of the scheduling algorithm in which the two phases related to the firing of each transition are clearly separated, where the capturing of the semaphores and the firing of a transition do not interleave (although the scheduling algorithm also allows interleaving of semaphore capturing, checking places and firing transitions in other ways).   □

The above algorithm determines a possible schedule of the agents to fire enabled transitions: any agent that has acquired the necessary semaphores can randomly choose one of its enabled transitions. Note that it is possible that several agents are in a position to carry out a random selection, in case they all acquired their semaphores. In this case, an agent can be picked nondeterministically. That is to say, the algorithm determines a possible adversary (scheduler) A for the probabilistic CPN at hand. The following result asserts that the computed schedule yields indeed probabilities (for LTL formulas) that fall inside the scope of the minimal and maximal probabilities that are typically determined by model-checking algorithms for MDPs.

Theorem 1. *For probabilistic CPN $\mathcal{D}$ and LTL formula φ, the probability of satisfying φ for any obtained schedule by our tho-phase algorithm is within the probability bounds of the MDP $\mathsf{mdp}(\mathcal{D})$ satisfying φ.*

Proof. Based on Lemmas 3, 4 and 5, the obtained adversaries for $\mathcal{D}$ by our algorithm correspond to a subset of the adversaries of the MDP $\mathsf{mdp}(\mathcal{D})$.   □

For various events of interest, such as the earlier mentioned reachability events of the form $\Diamond G$, the minimal and maximal probabilities are attained by a simple class of adversaries, the so-called *memoryless* adversaries. An adversary A

of a probabilistic CPN is memoryless whenever its decision for execution fragment $s_0[\pi_1|t_1\rangle \ldots [\pi_n|t_n\rangle s_n$ only depends on s_n. That is, a memoryless adversary selects for every visit to state s_n the same action regardless of the execution fragment before reaching s_n.

Theorem 2. *Our scheduling algorithm admits any memoryless adversary.*

Proof (sketch). An agent can only get its turn whenever it has acquired all semaphores. Acquiring the semaphores is based on the local information of an agent in a given state of the net. The decision whether an agent can perform a transition or not is memoryless. In case several agents can perform a transition (i.e., they have all acquired their necessary semaphores), the order between these agents is to be determined by the adversary. Our algorithm does not restrict this ordering: any memoryless order of admissible agents is allowed. A selected enabled agent then performs a (local) probabilistic choice.   □

6   Related Work

The most well known extensions of Petri nets with randomness are (generalized) stochastic Petri nets (GSPNs) [18]. There, transitions are equipped with rates, i.e., parameters of exponential distributions. In stochastic Petri nets (SPNs) all transitions have a rate—concurrency becomes a random phenomenon and confusion is absent. Due to immediate transitions in GSPNs, confusion re-appears. This is partially tackled using weights (resolving choices probabilistically based on a global state), but the analysis of GSPNs is basically restricted to confusion-free nets. Recently, a semantics of GSPNs with confusion has been proposed using stochastic real-time games [9,12].

The few works on probabilistic Petri nets treat probabilistic branching quite differently. In [2], probabilities are attached to outgoing edges of places. Alternatively, weights are assigned to edges [25]; here, choices are resolved in a probabilistic way whereas independent transitions fire in any order. A relation is shown between confusion-free weighted nets and Mazurkiewicz equivalence. Kudlek [15] focuses, instead, on the expressive power of the formalism, whereas [1] proposes truly concurrent probabilistic Petri nets. Here, the likelihood of processes is defined on partial orders, not on firing sequences. An MDP interpretation to nets is given in [5]. There, an extended Petri net model includes explicit transitions that indicate where a nondeterministic choice and where a probabilistic choice starts. Processes subscribe to such a choice, and the choice is made globally. To our knowledge, the treatment of probabilities in nets using the concept of agents—resolving probabilistic choices locally—is new.

The fact that global schedulers establish strong correlations between the behavior of system components (i.e., agents) has been observed earlier in [7,17]. To get around this problem [7] proposes *switched* probabilistic I/O automata. By passing a token between agents, one of the agents may make a probabilistic decision. This token-based scheme however restricts concurrency. In our model, concurrent nondeterministic and probabilistic decisions are possible. Concurrency is restricted only by confusions, which correspond to potential changes to the available choices. Also in testing theory and security analysis, it has been recognized that the resolution of local choices within a component using global knowledge yields undesirable and counterintuitive behavior. Our two-level scheduling mechanism in which agents are selected based on global state information, whereas agents select based on their local perspective, is closely related to that of *distributed* schedulers [11]. In contrast to our case, the selection of components there can be probabilistic. (As mentioned earlier, our framework can be easily extended to random agent selection.) Agent scheduling is also a principle used in the setting of quantitative security [3]. We are unaware of any concrete distributed algorithms realizing this kind of scheduling. In our case, we complement the theoretical setting with such algorithm.

7   Epilogue

In this paper, we enhanced Petri nets with agents covering the net transitions. The local view of an agent in a covered net consists of the neighborhood (input and output places) of its transitions. In a step of a net execution, an agent is nondeterministically selected which—based on its local view—resolves a (probabilistic) decision. This provides an elegant and robust basis for resolving probabilistic choices in a nondeterministic setting. It is shown that probabilistic covered nets can be viewed as high-level descriptions of MDPs. Finally, we presented a distributed scheduling algorithm (based on semaphores) for implementing such nets. Our algorithm is obtained by a simple structural analysis of net. Confusions, in our view, are no longer an obstacle for implementing Petri nets. Rather, they are an artifact reducing concurrency, similar to the notion of dependency in trace theory [19]. In fact, the identification and analysis of confusions provides a basis for our algorithm.

We used in this paper Petri nets to demonstrate the main concepts involved in modeling and implementing distributed probabilistic scheduling. In particular, confusion was originally observed in Petri nets and has a simple and clean formal presentation within this model. Nevertheless, our modeling concepts and scheduling algorithm can be easily adapted to other models that include concurrency and probabilistic choice.

Acknowledgments. The authors thank Barbara Jobstmann and Gadi Taubenfeld for valuable discussions.

References

1. Abbes, S.: The (True) Concurrent Markov Property and Some Applications to Markov Nets. In: Ciardo, G., Darondeau, P. (eds.) ICATPN 2005. LNCS, vol. 3536, pp. 70–89. Springer, Heidelberg (2005)
2. Albanese, M.: A constrained probabilistic Petri net framework for human activity detection in video. IEEE Trans. on Multimedia 10(6), 982–996 (2008)

3. Andrés, M.E., Palamidessi, C., van Rossum, P., Sokolova, A.: Information hiding in probabilistic concurrent systems. TCS 412(28), 3072–3089 (2011)
4. Baier, C., Katoen, J.-P.: Principles of Model Checking. MIT Press (2008)
5. Beccuti, M., Franceschinis, G., Haddad, S.: Markov Decision Petri Net and Markov Decision Well-Formed Net Formalisms. In: Kleijn, J., Yakovlev, A. (eds.) ICATPN 2007. LNCS, vol. 4546, pp. 43–62. Springer, Heidelberg (2007)
6. Bliudze, S., Sifakis, J.: The algebra of connectors - structuring interaction in BIP. IEEE Trans. Computers 57(10), 1315–1330 (2008)
7. Cheung, L., Lynch, N.A., Segala, R., Vaandrager, F.W.: Switched PIOA: Parallel composition via distributed scheduling. TCS 365(1-2), 83–108 (2006)
8. de Alfaro, L.: The verification of probabilistic systems under memoryless partial-information policies is hard. In: PROBMIV, pp. 19–32 (1999)
9. Eisentraut, C., Hermanns, H., Zhang, L.: Concurrency and Composition in a Stochastic World. In: Gastin, P., Laroussinie, F. (eds.) CONCUR 2010. LNCS, vol. 6269, pp. 21–39. Springer, Heidelberg (2010)
10. Georgievska, S., Andova, S.: Probabilistic may/must testing: retaining probabilities by restricted schedulers. Formal Asp. Comput. 24(4-6), 727–748 (2012)
11. Giro, S., D'Argenio, P.R.: On the expressive power of schedulers in distributed probabilistic systems. ENTCS 253(3), 45–71 (2009)
12. Katoen, J.-P.: GSPNs revisited: Simple semantics and new analysis algorithms. In: Application of Concurrency to System Design, pp. 6–11 (2012)
13. Katz, G., Peled, D.: Code Mutation in Verification and Automatic Code Correction. In: Esparza, J., Majumdar, R. (eds.) TACAS 2010. LNCS, vol. 6015, pp. 435–450. Springer, Heidelberg (2010)
14. Katz, G., Peled, D., Schewe, S.: Synthesis of Distributed Control through Knowledge Accumulation. In: Gopalakrishnan, G., Qadeer, S. (eds.) CAV 2011. LNCS, vol. 6806, pp. 510–525. Springer, Heidelberg (2011)
15. Kudlek, M.: Probability in Petri nets. Fund. Inf. 67(1-3), 121–130 (2005)
16. Lehmann, D.J., Rabin, M.O.: On the advantages of free choice: A symmetric and fully distributed solution to the dining philosophers problem. In: POPL, pp. 133–138 (1981)
17. Lynch, N.A., Segala, R., Vaandrager, F.W.: Observing branching structure through probabilistic contexts. SIAM J. Comp. 37(4), 977–1013 (2007)
18. Ajmone Marsan, M., Balbo, G., Conte, G., Donatelli, S., Franceschinis, G.: Modelling with Generalized Stochastic Petri Nets. Wiley (1995)
19. Mazurkiewicz, A.: Introduction to trace theory. In: Diekert, V., Rozenberg, G. (eds.) The Book of Traces. World Scientific (1995)
20. Pérez, J.A., Corchuelo, R., Toro, M.: An order-based algorithm for multiparty synchronization. Concurrency - Practice and Experience 16(12), 1173–1206 (2004)
21. Puterman, M.L.: Markov Decision Processes: Discrete Stochastic Dynamic Programming. Wiley (2005)
22. Rozenberg, G., Thiagarajan, P.S.: Petri Nets: Basic Notions, Structure, Behaviour. In: Rozenberg, G., de Bakker, J.W., de Roever, W.-P. (eds.) Current Trends in Concurrency. LNCS, vol. 224, pp. 585–668. Springer, Heidelberg (1986)
23. Segala, R., Lynch, N.A.: Probabilistic simulations for probabilistic processes. Nord. J. Comput. 2(2), 250–273 (1995)
24. Taubenfeld, G.: Synchronization Algorithms for Concurrent Programming. Prentice Hall (2006)
25. Varacca, D., Nielsen, M.: Probabilistic Petri nets and Mazurkiewicz equivalence (2003) (unpublished manuscript)

Model-Checking Higher-Order Programs
with Recursive Types

Naoki Kobayashi[1] and Atsushi Igarashi[2]

[1] The University of Tokyo
[2] Kyoto Univeristy

Abstract. Model checking of higher-order recursion schemes (HORS, for short) has been recently studied as a new promising technique for automated verification of higher-order programs. The previous HORS model checking could however deal with only *simply-typed* programs, so that its application was limited to functional programs. To deal with a broader range of programs such as object-oriented programs and multi-threaded programs, we extend HORS model checking to check properties of programs with *recursive* types. Although the extended model checking problem is undecidable, we develop a sound model-checking algorithm that is relatively complete with respect to a recursive intersection type system and prove its correctness. Preliminary results on the implementation and applications to verification of object-oriented programs and multi-threaded programs are also reported.

1   Introduction

The model checking of higher-order recursion schemes (HORS for short) [15] has been recently studied as a new technique for automated verification of higher-order functional programs [9,14,16,13]. HORS is essentially a simply-typed higher-order functional program with recursion for generating (possibly infinite) trees, and the goal of HORS model checking is to decide whether the tree generated by a given HORS satisfies a given property. The idea of applying the HORS model checking is to transform a given functional program M to a HORS $\mathcal{G}$ that generates a tree describing possible outputs or event sequences of the program [9]; verification of the program is then reduced to HORS model checking, to decide whether the tree generated by $\mathcal{G}$ represents valid outputs or event sequences. Based on this idea, various verification problems for functional programs have been reduced to it [9,14,16]. By combining it with predicate abstraction, a software model checker for functional programs can be constructed [16,13].

The above approach to automated verification of functional programs, however, cannot be smoothly extended to support other important programming language features, such as objects and concurrency. Object-oriented programs often use (mutually) recursive interfaces, which cannot be naturally modeled by HORS (which are *simply-typed* functional programs). In fact, even Featherweight Java (FJ) [5] (with only objects as primitive data) is Turing complete [22].

M. Felleisen and P. Gardner (Eds.): ESOP 2013, LNCS 7792, pp. 431–450, 2013.

As for concurrency, the model checking of concurrent pushdown systems [20] is undecidable. These imply that there cannot be a sound and complete reduction from verification problems for object-oriented or recursive concurrent programs to HORS model checking. These situations are in sharp contrast to the case for functional programs, for which we have a sound and complete reduction to HORS model checking, as long as the programs use only finite base types (such as booleans, but not unbounded integers) [9].

The present paper aims to overcome the above limitations by introducing an extension of HORS model checking, where models, i.e., higher-order recursion schemes, are extended with recursive types. The extended higher-order recursion schemes, called $\mu HORS$, are essentially the simply-typed λ-calculus extended with tree constructors, (term-level) recursion, and recursive types, which is Turing complete. The model checking of μHORS (μHORS model checking for short) is undecidable, but we can develop a sound (but incomplete) model checking procedure. The procedure uses the result that HORS model checking can be reduced to a type checking problem in an intersection type system [9,11,24], and solves the type checking problem. Although the procedure is incomplete (as μHORS model checking is undecidable) and may not terminate, it is relatively complete with respect to a certain recursive intersection type system: any program that is typable in the type system is eventually proved correct. The procedure incorporates a novel reduction of the intersection type checking to SAT solving, which may be of independent interest and applicable to ordinary HORS checking.

Being armed with μHORS model checking, we can construct a fully automated verification tool (or so called a "software model checker") for various programming languages. Given a program, we first apply a kind of program transformation to get a μHORS that generates a tree describing all the possible program behaviors of interest, and then use μHORS model checking to check that the tree describes only valid behaviors. As a proof of concept, we have implemented a prototype of the μHORS model checker and a translator from Featherweight Java (FJ) programs [5] to μHORS. Preliminary experiments show that we can indeed use the μHORS model checker to verify small but non-trivial object-oriented programs.

For the space restriction, we omit some examples and proofs, which are found in an extended version [10].

2   Preliminaries

This section introduces μHORS, defines model checking problems for them, and reduces it to a type-checking problem in a recursive intersection type system.

2.1   Recursive Intersection Types

Before introducing μHORS model checking, we first formalize recursive intersection types. We fix a finite set Q of base types below, and use the meta-variable q for its elements. We use the meta-variable α for type variables.

Definition 1. *A (recursive intersection) type is a pair (E, α), where E is a finite set of equations of the form $\alpha_i = \sigma_1 \to \cdots \to \sigma_m \to q$, and σ is of the form $\bigwedge\{\alpha_1, \ldots, \alpha_k\}$. Here m and k may be 0. We use the meta-variable τ for recursive intersection types. We write $\mathbf{Tv}(\tau)$ for the set of type variables occurring in τ. A recursive intersection type $\tau = (E, \alpha)$ is closed if, for every $\alpha \in \mathbf{Tv}(\tau)$, $(\alpha = \theta) \in E$ for some θ. When $(\alpha = \theta) \in E$, we write $E(\alpha)$ for θ.*

We identify types up to renaming of type variables. For example, $(\{\alpha = q\}, \alpha)$ is the same as $(\{\beta = q\}, \beta)$. Thus, for two closed types τ_0 and τ_1, we always assume that $\mathbf{Tv}(\tau_0) \cap \mathbf{Tv}(\tau_1) = \emptyset$. We often write $\alpha_1 \wedge \cdots \wedge \alpha_k$ or $\bigwedge_{i \in \{1,\ldots,k\}} \alpha_i$ for $\bigwedge\{\alpha_1, \ldots, \alpha_k\}$ and write $\top$ for $\bigwedge \emptyset$. Intuitively, (E, α) denotes the (recursive) type α that satisfies the equations in E. For example, $(\{\alpha = \alpha \to q\}, \alpha)$ represents the recursive type $\mu\alpha.(\alpha \to q)$ in the usual notation. We often use this term notation for recursive intersection types. By abuse of notation, when $E(\alpha) = \bigwedge_{i \in I_1} \alpha_i \to \cdots \to \bigwedge_{i \in I_k} \alpha_i \to q$, we write $\bigwedge_{i \in I_1}(E, \alpha_i) \to \cdots \to \bigwedge_{i \in I_k}(E, \alpha_i) \to q$ for (E, α). For example, when $E = \{\alpha_0 = \alpha_1 \to q_0, \alpha_1 = q_1\}$, (E, α_0) is also written as $(E, \alpha_1) \to q_0$ or $q_1 \to q_0$. The type $\sigma_1 \to \cdots \to \sigma_m \to q$ describes functions that take m arguments of types $\sigma_1, \ldots, \sigma_m$, and return a value of type q. The type $\alpha_1 \wedge \cdots \wedge \alpha_k$ describes values that have all of the types $\alpha_1, \ldots, \alpha_k$. For example, if $Q = \{q_1, q_2\}$, the identity function on base values ($\lambda x.x$ in the λ-calculus notation) would have types $(q_1 \to q_1) \wedge (q_2 \to q_2)$.

We define the subtyping relation $\tau_0 \leq \tau_1$, which intuitively means, as usual, that any value of type τ_0 can be used as a value of type τ_1.

Definition 2 (subtyping). *Let $\tau = (E'', \alpha)$ and $\tau' = (E', \alpha')$ be closed types, and let $E = E'' \cup E'$. The type τ is a subtype of τ', written $\tau \leq \tau'$, if there exists a binary relation $\mathcal{R}$ on $\mathbf{Tv}(\tau) \cup \mathbf{Tv}(\tau')$ such that (i) $(\alpha, \alpha') \in \mathcal{R}$ and (ii) for every $(\alpha_0, \alpha'_0) \in \mathcal{R}$, there exist $\sigma_1, \ldots, \sigma_m, \sigma'_1, \ldots, \sigma'_m, q$ such that $E(\alpha_0) = \sigma_1 \to \cdots \to \sigma_m \to q$ and $E(\alpha'_0) = \sigma'_1 \to \cdots \to \sigma'_m \to q$, with $(\sigma'_1, \sigma_1), \ldots, (\sigma'_m, \sigma_m) \in \mathcal{R}^\wedge$. Here, $\mathcal{R}^\wedge$ is:*
$$\{(\bigwedge\{\alpha'_1, \ldots, \alpha'_{k'}\}, \bigwedge\{\alpha_1, \ldots, \alpha_k\}) \mid \forall i \in \{1, \ldots, k\}. \exists j \in \{1, \ldots, k'\}. \alpha'_j \mathcal{R} \alpha_i\}.$$
We write $\tau \cong \tau'$ if $\tau \leq \tau'$ and $\tau' \leq \tau$.

Example 1. Let $\tau_0 = (\{\alpha_0 = \alpha_0 \to q\}, \alpha_0)$ and $\tau_1 = (\{\alpha_1 = \alpha_2 \to q, \alpha_2 = \alpha_1 \wedge \alpha_3 \to q, \alpha_3 = q\}, \alpha_1)$. $\tau_1 \leq \tau_0$ holds, with the relation $\{(\alpha_1, \alpha_0), (\alpha_0, \alpha_2)\}$ as a witness.

2.2 μHORS

We introduce below μHORS and its model checking problem, and reduce the latter to a type checking problem. To our knowledge, the notion of μHORS is new, but it is a subclass of the untyped HORS studied by Tsukada and Kobayashi [24], and the reduction from μHORS model checking to type checking (Theorem 1) is a corollary of the result of [24]. We shall therefore quickly go through the definitions and results; more formal definitions (apart from recursive types) and intuitions are found in [15,9,24].

μHORS and Model Checking Problems. The set of basic types (called *sorts*) is the subset of recursive intersection types, where Q is a singleton set $\{o\}$ (where o is the type of trees) and there is no intersection: in $\sigma = \bigwedge \{\alpha_1, \ldots, \alpha_k\}$, k is always 1. Below we often use the following term representation of sorts:

$$\kappa ::= \alpha \mid \kappa_1 \to \cdots \to \kappa_\ell \to o \mid \mu\alpha.\kappa.$$

Let Σ be a ranked alphabet, i.e., a map from symbols to their arities. An element of $dom(\Sigma)$ is used as a tree constructor. A *sort environment* is a map from variables to sorts. The set of *applicative terms* of type κ under a sort environment $\mathcal{K}$ is inductively defined by the following rules:

$$\mathcal{K}, x : \kappa \vdash x : \kappa \qquad\qquad \mathcal{K} \vdash a : \underbrace{o \to \cdots \to o}_{\Sigma(a)} \to o$$

$$\frac{\mathcal{K} \vdash t_1 : \kappa_1 \qquad \mathcal{K} \vdash t_2 : \kappa_2 \qquad \kappa_1 \cong (\kappa_2 \to \kappa)}{\mathcal{K} \vdash t_1\, t_2 : \kappa}$$

As usual, applications are left-associative, so that $t_1\, t_2\, t_3$ means $(t_1\, t_2)\, t_3$.

A μHORS $\mathcal{G}$ is a quadruple $(\mathcal{N}, \Sigma, \mathcal{R}, S)$ where: (i) $\mathcal{N}$ is a map from variables (called *non-terminals*) to sorts; (ii) Σ is a ranked alphabet, where $dom(\mathcal{N}) \cap dom(\Sigma) = \emptyset$; (iii) $\mathcal{R}$ is a map from non-terminals to a λ-term of the form $\lambda x_1. \cdots \lambda x_\ell.t$ where t is an applicative term; (iv) S, called the *start symbol*, is a non-terminal such that $\mathcal{N}(S) = o$. If $\mathcal{N}(F) = \kappa_1 \to \cdots \to \kappa_k \to o$ and $\mathcal{R}(F) = \lambda x_1. \cdots \lambda x_\ell.t$, then it must be the case that $k = \ell$ and $\mathcal{N}, x_1:\kappa_1, \ldots, x_\ell:\kappa_\ell \vdash t : o$.

The (possibly infinite) tree generated by $\mathcal{G}$, written by $Tree(\mathcal{G})$, is defined as the limit of infinite fair reductions of S [15] where the reduction relation $\longrightarrow$ is defined by: (i) $F\, t_1 \cdots t_\ell \longrightarrow [t_1/x_1, \ldots, t_\ell/x_\ell]t$ if $\mathcal{R}(F) = \lambda x_1. \cdots \lambda x_\ell.t$; and (ii) $a\, t_1 \cdots t_\ell \longrightarrow a\, t_1 \cdots t_{i-1}\, t_i'\, t_{i+1} \cdots t_\ell$ if $t_i \longrightarrow t_i'$ for some $i \in \{1, \ldots, \ell\}$. See [15] for the formal definition of $Tree(\mathcal{G})$.

Notation 1 *We write $\widetilde{u}$ for a sequence $u_1 \cdots u_\ell$. $\lambda\widetilde{x}.t$ stands for $\lambda x_1. \cdots \lambda x_\ell.t$, and $[\widetilde{s}/\widetilde{x}]t$ for $[s_1/x_1, \ldots, s_\ell/x_\ell]t$ (with the understanding that $\widetilde{s}$ and $\widetilde{x}$ have the same length ℓ). We often write the four components of $\mathcal{G}$ as $\mathcal{N}_\mathcal{G}, \Sigma_\mathcal{G}, \mathcal{R}_\mathcal{G}, S_\mathcal{G}$, and omit the subscript if it is clear from context. We often write $\mathcal{R}$ as a set of rewriting rules $\{F_1\, x_1 \cdots x_{\ell_1} \to t_1, \ldots, F_m\, x_1 \cdots x_{\ell_m} \to t_m\}$ if $\mathcal{R}(F_i) = \lambda x_1. \cdots \lambda x_{\ell_i}.t_i$ for each $i \in \{1, \ldots, m\}$.*

Example 2. Consider μHORS $\mathcal{G}_1 = (\mathcal{N}_1, \Sigma_1, \mathcal{R}_1, S)$ where $\mathcal{N}_1 = \{S \mapsto o, F \mapsto (o \to o)\}$, $\Sigma_1 = \{a \mapsto 2, b \mapsto 1, c \mapsto 0\}$, and $\mathcal{R}_1 = \{S \to F\, c, \quad F\, x \to a\, x\, (F\, (b\, x))\}$. S is rewritten as follows, and the tree in Figure 1 is generated:
$S \longrightarrow F\, c \longrightarrow a\, c\, (F\, (b\, c)) \longrightarrow a\, c\, (a\, (b\, c)\, (F\, (b\, (b\, c)))) \longrightarrow \cdots$.

Example 3. Consider μHORS $\mathcal{G}_2 = (\mathcal{N}_2, \Sigma_1, \mathcal{R}_2, S)$ where Σ_1 is as given in Example 2, and: $\mathcal{N}_2 = \{S \mapsto o, F \mapsto (o \to o), G \mapsto \mu\alpha.(\alpha \to o \to o)\}$ and $\mathcal{R}_2 = \{S \to F\, c, \quad F\, x \to G\, G\, x, \quad G\, g\, x \to a\, x\, (g\, g\, (b\, x))\}$. This is the same as $\mathcal{G}_1$ except that recursive types are used instead of term-level recursion. S is reduced as below, and the same tree as $Tree(\mathcal{G}_1)$ is generated.

$S \longrightarrow F\, c \longrightarrow G\, G\, c \longrightarrow a\, c\, (G\, G\, (b\, c)) \longrightarrow a\, c\, (a\, (b\, c)\, (G\, G\, (b\, (b\, c)))) \longrightarrow \cdots$

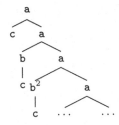

Fig. 1. The tree generated by $\mathcal{G}_1$ of Example 2

Remark 1. A tree node that is never instantiated to a terminal symbol is expressed by the special terminal symbol $\perp$ (with arity 0). For example, for μHORS $\mathcal{G}_3 = (\mathcal{N}_3, \Sigma_1, \mathcal{R}_3, S)$ where $\mathcal{N}_3 = \{S \mapsto \mathsf{o}, F \mapsto \mu\alpha.(\alpha \to \mathsf{o})\}$ and $\mathcal{R}_3 = \{S \to FF, Fx \to xx\}$, *Tree*$(\mathcal{G}_3)$ is a singleton tree $\perp$. □

As usual [15,9], we use (top-down) tree automata to express properties of the tree generated by higher-order recursion schemes. For a ranked alphabet Σ, a Σ-*labeled tree* T is a map from sequences of natural numbers (which represent paths of the tree) to $dom(\Sigma)$, such that (i) its domain $dom(T)$ is nonempty and closed under the prefix operation, and (ii) if $\pi \in dom(T)$ then $\{j \mid \pi j \in dom(T)\} = \{1, \ldots, \Sigma(T(\pi))\}$. A (deterministic) *trivial automaton* $\mathcal{B}$ is a quadruple (Σ, Q, δ, q_0), where Σ is a ranked alphabet, Q is a finite set of states, δ, called a transition function, is a partial map from $Q \times dom(\Sigma)$ to Q^* such that $|\delta(q, a)| = \Sigma(a)$, and q_0 is the initial state. A Σ-labeled tree T is *accepted* by $\mathcal{B}$ if there is a Q-labeled tree R (called a *run tree*) such that: (i) $dom(T) = dom(R)$; (ii) $R(\epsilon) = q_0$; and (iii) for every $\pi \in dom(R)$, $\delta(R(\pi), T(\pi)) = R(\pi 1) \cdots R(\pi \Sigma(T(\pi)))$. For a trivial automaton $\mathcal{B} = (\Sigma, Q, \delta, q_0)$ (with $\perp \notin dom(\Sigma)$), we write $\mathcal{B}^{\perp}$ for the trivial automaton $(\Sigma \cup \{\perp \mapsto 0\}, Q, \delta \cup \{(q, \perp) \mapsto \epsilon) \mid q \in Q\}, q_0)$. We often write $\Sigma_{\mathcal{B}}, Q_{\mathcal{B}}, \delta_{\mathcal{B}}, q_{\mathcal{B},0}$ for the four components of $\mathcal{B}$, and omit the subscript if it is clear from context. Trivial automata are sufficient for describing safety properties: see [12] for the logical characterization.

Example 4. Let $\mathcal{B}_1 = (\Sigma_1, \{q_0, q_1\}, \delta, q_0)$ where Σ_1 is as given in Example 2 and δ is given by: $\delta(q_0, \mathsf{a}) = q_0 q_0$, $\delta(q_0, \mathsf{b}) = \delta(q_1, \mathsf{b}) = q_1$, and $\delta(q_0, \mathsf{c}) = \delta(q_1, \mathsf{c}) = \epsilon$. It accepts a Σ_1-labeled (ranked) tree T if and only if a does not occur below b. In particular, $\mathcal{B}_1$ accepts the tree shown in Figure 1. □

The μHORS *model checking* is the problem of checking whether *Tree*$(\mathcal{G})$ is accepted by $\mathcal{B}^{\perp}$, given a μHORS $\mathcal{G}$ and a trivial automaton $\mathcal{B}$. The problem is in general undecidable [24]. We give a sound type system for checking that *Tree*$(\mathcal{G})$ is accepted by $\mathcal{B}^{\perp}$. The set of recursive intersection types is as given in Section 2.1, where the set Q of base types is the set of states of $\mathcal{B}$. Intuitively, a state q is regarded as the type of trees accepted by $\mathcal{B}^{\perp}$ from the state q [9].

The type judgment relations $\Gamma \vdash_{\mathcal{B}} t : \tau$ and $\Gamma \vdash_{\mathcal{B}} (\mathcal{G}, t) : \tau$ (where Γ, called a type environment, is a set of type bindings of the form $x : \tau$) are defined by:

$$\frac{\tau \leq \tau'}{\Gamma, x : \tau \vdash_{\mathcal{B}} x : \tau'} \qquad \frac{\delta_{\mathcal{B}}(q, a) = q_1 \cdots q_k \qquad q_1 \to \cdots \to q_k \to q \leq \tau}{\Gamma \vdash_{\mathcal{B}} a : \tau}$$

$$\frac{\Gamma \vdash_{\mathcal{B}} t_1 : \bigwedge_{i \in I} \tau_i \to \tau}{\Gamma \vdash_{\mathcal{B}} t_2 : \tau_i' \text{ and } \tau_i' \leq \tau_i \text{ (for every } i \in I)} \qquad \frac{\Gamma, x : \tau_1, \ldots, x : \tau_\ell \vdash_{\mathcal{B}} t : \tau}{x \text{ does not occur in } \Gamma}$$
$$\frac{}{\Gamma \vdash_{\mathcal{B}} t_1 t_2 : \tau} \qquad \frac{}{\Gamma \vdash_{\mathcal{B}} \lambda x.t : \bigwedge_{i \in \{1, \ldots, \ell\}} \tau_i \to \tau}$$

$$\frac{\forall (F : \tau) \in \Gamma. (\Gamma \vdash_{\mathcal{B}} \mathcal{R}(F) : \tau)}{\vdash_{\mathcal{B}} \mathcal{R} : \Gamma} \qquad \frac{\vdash_{\mathcal{B}} \mathcal{R}_{\mathcal{G}} : \Gamma \qquad \Gamma \vdash_{\mathcal{B}} t : \tau}{\Gamma \vdash_{\mathcal{B}} (\mathcal{G}, t) : \tau}$$

The following theorem is a special case of the soundness of Tsukada and Kobayashi's infinite intersection type system for untyped HORS [24].

Theorem 1 (soundness). *Let $\mathcal{B}$ be a trivial automaton $(\Sigma, Q, \delta, q_{\mathcal{B},0})$ and $\mathcal{G}$ be a μHORS. If $\Gamma \vdash_{\mathcal{B}} (\mathcal{G}, S_{\mathcal{G}}) : q_{\mathcal{B},0}$, then $Tree(\mathcal{G})$ is accepted by $\mathcal{B}^\perp$.*

Example 5. Recall $\mathcal{G}_1$ and $\mathcal{G}_2$ in Examples 2 and 3, and $\mathcal{B}_1$ in Example 4. $\Gamma_1 \vdash_{\mathcal{B}_1} (\mathcal{G}_1, S) : q_0$ and $\Gamma_2 \vdash_{\mathcal{B}_1} (\mathcal{G}_2, S) : q_0$ hold for $\Gamma_1 = \{S : q_0, F : (q_0 \wedge q_1) \to q_0\}$ and $\Gamma_2 = \Gamma_1 \cup \{G : \mu\alpha.(\alpha \to (q_0 \wedge q_1) \to q_0)\}$.   □

Given a type environment Γ, a μHORS $\mathcal{G}$, and an automaton $\mathcal{B}$, it is decidable whether $\Gamma \vdash_{\mathcal{B}} (\mathcal{G}, S_{\mathcal{G}}) : q_{\mathcal{B},0}$ holds. Thus, Γ can be used as a certificate for $Tree(\mathcal{G})$ being accepted by $\mathcal{B}$. The converse of the theorem above does not hold, i.e., there is a μHORS $\mathcal{G}$ such that $Tree(\mathcal{G})$ is accepted by $\mathcal{B}^\perp$ but $Tree(\mathcal{G})$ is not well-typed. We have the following properties on the (un)decidability of type checking. See [10] for a proof.

Theorem 2.   1. *Given a type environment Γ, a μHORS $\mathcal{G}$, and a trivial automaton $\mathcal{B}$, it is decidable whether $\Gamma \vdash_{\mathcal{B}} (\mathcal{G}, S_{\mathcal{G}}) : q_{\mathcal{B},0}$ holds.*
   2. *Given a μHORS $\mathcal{G}$ and a trivial automaton $\mathcal{B}$, it is undecidable whether there exists Γ such that $\Gamma \vdash_{\mathcal{B}} (\mathcal{G}, S_{\mathcal{G}}) : q_{\mathcal{B},0}$ holds.*

3   Model Checking μHORS

We now describe the main result of this paper: a model checking procedure for μHORS. We shall develop a procedure CHECK that satisfies:

$$\text{CHECK}(\mathcal{G}, \mathcal{B}) = \begin{cases} \Gamma' \text{ such that } \Gamma' \vdash_{\mathcal{B}} (\mathcal{G}, S_{\mathcal{G}}) : q_{\mathcal{B},0} \text{ if } \exists \Gamma.\Gamma \vdash_{\mathcal{B}} (\mathcal{G}, S_{\mathcal{G}}) : q_{\mathcal{B},0} \\ \text{No (with a counterexample) if } Tree(\mathcal{G}) \text{ is not accepted by } \mathcal{B}^\perp \end{cases}$$

By Theorem 2, the procedure CHECK can only be a semi-algorithm: it may not terminate if $Tree(\mathcal{G})$ is accepted by $\mathcal{B}^\perp$ but $\exists \Gamma.\Gamma \vdash_{\mathcal{B}} (\mathcal{G}, S_{\mathcal{G}}) : q_{\mathcal{B},0}$ does not hold.

An obvious approach would be to run (i) a sub-procedure FINDCERT$(\mathcal{G}, \mathcal{B})$ to enumerate all the finite type environments Γ and output Γ if $\Gamma \vdash_{\mathcal{B}} (\mathcal{G}, S_{\mathcal{G}}) : q_{\mathcal{B},0}$ holds, and in parallel, (ii) a sub-procedure FINDCE$(\mathcal{G}, \mathcal{B})$ to reduce $\mathcal{G}$ in a fair manner and output No if a partially generated tree is not accepted by $\mathcal{B}^\perp$. The first sub-procedure FINDCERT is, however, too non-deterministic to be used in practice.

We describe below a more realistic procedure for $\text{FINDCERT}(\mathcal{G}, \mathcal{B})$ that outputs Γ such that $\Gamma \vdash_\mathcal{B} (\mathcal{G}, S_\mathcal{G}) : q_{\mathcal{B},0}$ if there is any, and may diverge otherwise. As FINDCERT can incrementally find the types of non-terminals, we can use them to improve FINDCE as well, by removing well-typed terms from the search space. As such interaction between FINDCERT and FINDCE is the same as the case without recursive types [8], we focus on the discussion of FINDCERT below.

3.1 Type Inference Procedure

We first give an informal overview of the idea of FINDCERT. Since it is easy to check whether a given Γ is a valid certificate (i.e. whether $\Gamma \vdash_\mathcal{B} (\mathcal{G}, S_\mathcal{G}) : q_{\mathcal{B},0}$ holds), the main issue is how to find candidates for Γ. As in the algorithm for HORS without recursive types [8], the idea of finding Γ is to extract type information by partially reducing a given recursion scheme, and observing how each non-terminal symbol is used. For example, suppose that S is reduced as follows. $S : q_0 \longrightarrow^* C_1[F\,G : q_1] \longrightarrow^* C_2[G\,t : q_2] \longrightarrow^* C_3[t : q_1]$. Here, we have annotated each term with a state of the property automaton; $t : q$ means that the tree generated by t should be accepted from q. From the reduction sequence, we know t should have type q_1, from which we can guess that G should have type $q_1 \to q_2$, and we can further guess that F should have type $(q_1 \to q_2) \to q_1$. This way of guessing types is complete for HORS (without recursive types) [8]. In the presence of recursive types, however, we need a further twist, to obtain (relative) completeness. For example, suppose S is reduced as follows. $S : q_0 \longrightarrow^* C_1[F\,t_1 : q_1] \longrightarrow^* C_2[t_1\,t_2 : q_0] \longrightarrow^* C_3[t_2\,t_3 : q_1] \longrightarrow^* C_4[t_3\,t_4 : q_0] \longrightarrow^* \cdots$. This kind of calling chain terminates for ordinary HORS (since the terms are simply-typed), but may not terminate for μHORS because of recursive types. (For example, consider a variation of $\mathcal{G}_3$ in Remark 1, where the rule for F is replaced by $F\,x \to x\,(I\,x)$, with the new rule $I\,x \to x$. Then, we have an infinite calling chain: $S \longrightarrow^* F\,(I\,F) \longrightarrow^* (I\,F)\,(I\,(I\,F)) \longrightarrow^* (I\,(I\,F))\,(I\,(I\,(I\,F))) \longrightarrow^* \cdots$.) Thus, we would obtain an infinite set of type equations:

$$\alpha_F = \alpha_{t_1} \to q_1 \quad \alpha_{t_1} = \alpha_{t_2} \to q_0 \quad \alpha_{t_2} = \alpha_{t_3} \to q_1 \quad \alpha_{t_3} = \alpha_{t_4} \to q_0 \quad \cdots$$

(where α_t represents the type of term t). To address this problem, we introduce an equivalence relation $\sim$ on terms, and consider reductions modulo $\sim$. In the example above, if we choose $\sim$ so that $t_{2n-1} \sim t_{2n+1}$ and $F \sim t_{2n} \sim t_{2n+2}$, then we would have finite equations $\alpha_{[F]} = \alpha_{[t_1]} \to q_1$ and $\alpha_{[t_1]} = \alpha_{[F]} \to q_0$ (where $[t]$ is the equivalence class containing t), from which we can infer $\mu\alpha.(\alpha \to q_0) \to q_1$ as the type of F. As we show in Theorem 3 later, this way of type inference is complete *if a proper equivalence relation $\sim$ is given as an oracle*. It is not complete in general, but Theorem 4 ensures that no matter how $\sim$ is chosen, we can "amend" the inferred type environment to obtain a correct type environment. Based on the theorem, we can develop a complete procedure for FINDCERT.

We now turn to describe the idea more formally. Let $\mathbf{Tm}$ be the set of (well-sorted) closed terms constructed from non-terminals and terminals of $\mathcal{G}$, and $\sim$ be an equivalence relation on $\mathbf{Tm}$ that induces a *finite* set of equivalence classes. We write $[t]_\sim$ for the equivalence class containing t, i.e., $\{t' \mid t \sim t'\}$, and omit the subscript if clear from context. Intuitively, the equivalence relation $t_1 \sim t_2$

means that t_1 and t_2 behave similarly with respect to the given automaton $\mathcal{B}$. For the moment, we assume that $\sim$ is given as an oracle. Throughout the paper, we consider only equivalence relations that equate terms of the same sort, i.e., $t \sim t'$ implies $\mathcal{N} \vdash t : \kappa \Longleftrightarrow \mathcal{N} \vdash t' : \kappa$ for every κ.

We define the extended reduction relation $(\mathcal{X}, \mathcal{U}) \longrightarrow_\sim (\mathcal{X}', \mathcal{U}')$ as the least relation closed under the rules below, where $\mathcal{X}$ is a set of terms and $\mathcal{U}$ is a set of pairs consisting of a term and an automaton state or a special element $\texttt{fail}$. In rule R-NT, $\mathbf{STm}(t)$ denotes the set of all subterms of t.

$$\frac{(a\, t_1 \cdots t_\ell, q) \in \mathcal{U} \qquad \delta(q, a) = q_1 \cdots q_\ell}{(\mathcal{X}, \mathcal{U}) \longrightarrow_\sim (\mathcal{X}, \mathcal{U} \cup \{(t_1, q_1), \ldots, (t_\ell, q_\ell)\})} \qquad \text{(R-CONST)}$$

$$\frac{(a\, t_1 \cdots t_\ell, q) \in \mathcal{U} \qquad \delta(q, a) \text{ is undef. or } |\delta(q, a)| \neq \ell}{(\mathcal{X}, \mathcal{U}) \longrightarrow_\sim (\mathcal{X}, \mathcal{U} \cup \{\texttt{fail}\})} \qquad \text{(R-F)}$$

$$\frac{(F\, \widetilde{t}, q) \in \mathcal{U} \qquad \mathcal{R}(F) = \lambda\widetilde{x}.u}{(\mathcal{X}, \mathcal{U}) \longrightarrow_\sim (\mathcal{X} \cup \mathbf{STm}([\widetilde{t}/\widetilde{x}]u), \mathcal{U} \cup \{([\widetilde{t}/\widetilde{x}]u, q)\})} \qquad \text{(R-NT)}$$

$$\frac{(t\, t_1 \cdots t_k, q) \in \mathcal{U} \qquad t \sim t' \qquad t' \in \mathcal{X}}{(\mathcal{X}, \mathcal{U}) \longrightarrow_\sim (\mathcal{X}, \mathcal{U} \cup \{(t'\, t_1 \cdots t_k, q)\})} \qquad \text{(R-EQ)}$$

The main differences from the reduction relation $t \longrightarrow t'$ in Section 2.2 are: (i) each term t (of sort o) is coupled with its expected type, (ii) such pairs are kept in the $\mathcal{U}$ component after reductions (in other words, $(t, q) \in \mathcal{U}$ means that t should generate a tree accepted by $\mathcal{B}$ from state q), (iii) the $\mathcal{X}$ component keeps all the sub-terms that have occurred so far, and (iv) a subterm in a head position can be replaced by another term belonging to the same equivalence class (see rule R-EQ above). In rule R-CONST, $(a\, t_1 \cdots t_\ell, q)$ being an element of $\mathcal{U}$ means that $a\, t_1 \cdots t_\ell$ should generate a tree of type q (i.e., should be accepted by $\mathcal{B}$ from the state q). The premise $\delta(q, a) = q_1 \cdots q_\ell$ means that the i-th subtree should have type q_i, so that we add (t_i, q_i) to the second component. Rule R-F is applied when $(a\, t_1 \cdots t_\ell, q)$ is in the second set but no tree having a as its root can be accepted from the state q. The condition $|\delta(q, a)| \neq \ell$ actually never holds, by the assumption that $\sim$ equates only terms of the same sort. R-NT is the rule for reducing non-terminals. As mentioned above, rule R-EQ is used to replace a head of a term with an equivalent term with respect to $\sim$. Extended reduction sequences are in general infinite, and non-deterministic.

Example 6. Recall $\mathcal{G}_2$ in Example 3. Let $\sim^{(1)}$ be the least congruence relation that satisfies $\mathtt{b(c)} \sim \mathtt{c}$. Then, by using $\sim^{(1)}$ as $\sim$, we can reduce $(\{S\}, \{(S, q_0)\})$ as follows:

$$(S, q_0) \to (F\, c, q_0) \to (G\, G\, c, q_0) \to (a\, c\, (G\, G\, (b\, c)), q_0) \to (G\, G\, (b\, c), q_0)$$
$$(c, q_0) \quad (c, q_1) \leftarrow (b\, c, q_0) \leftarrow (a\, (b\, c)\, (G\, G\, (b\, (b\, c))), q_0) \to \cdots$$

Here, we have omitted the $\mathcal{X}$-component, and shown only elements relevant to reductions instead of the whole $\mathcal{U}$-component. In the figure, dashed arrows represent reductions by using rule R-EQ, and solid arrows represent reductions obtained by the other rules. From an infinite fair reduction sequence, we obtain the following set as $\mathcal{U}$:

$$\{(F\,(\mathrm{b}^k\,\mathrm{c}), q_0), (G\,G\,(\mathrm{b}^k\,\mathrm{c}), q_0), (\mathrm{b}^k\,\mathrm{c}, q_0), (\mathrm{b}^k\,\mathrm{c}, q_1) \mid k \geq 0\}$$
$$\cup\{(S, q_0)\} \cup \{(\mathrm{a}\,(\mathrm{b}^k\,\mathrm{c})\,(G\,G\,(\mathrm{b}^\ell\,\mathrm{c})), q_0) \mid k, \ell \geq 0\} \qquad \square$$

The goal below is to construct a candidate of type environment Γ that satisfies $\Gamma \vdash_B \mathcal{G} : q_0$, from a fair reduction sequence (where a reduction sequence is fair if every enabled reduction is eventually reduced). The idea of the construction of Γ is similar to the case for ordinary HORS [8]. For example, in Example 6 above, from the pairs (c, q_0) and (c, q_1), we can guess that the type of c is $q_0 \wedge q_1$. From the pair $(F\,\mathrm{c}, q_0)$, we guess that the return type of F is q_0, so that the type of F is $q_0 \wedge q_1 \to q_0$. The actual construction is, however, more involved than [8] because of the presence of recursive types and the term equivalence relation $\sim$.

Let $(\mathcal{X}_0, \mathcal{U}_0) \longrightarrow_\sim (\mathcal{X}_1, \mathcal{U}_1) \longrightarrow_\sim \cdots$ be a fair reduction sequence where $\mathcal{X}_0 = \{S\}$ and $\mathcal{U}_0 = \{(S, q_0)\}$, and let $\mathcal{X}$ and $\mathcal{U}$ be $\bigcup_{i\in\omega} \mathcal{X}_i$ and $\bigcup_{i\in\omega} \mathcal{U}_i$ respectively. We prepare a type variable $\alpha_{[t_0],\ldots,[t_k],q}$ for each $(t_0 t_1 \cdots t_k, q) \in \mathcal{U}$. Intuitively, $\alpha_{[t_0],\ldots,[t_k],q}$ is the type of t_0 in $t_0 t_1 \cdots t_k : q$. Let E be:

$$\{\alpha_{[t_0],[t_1],\ldots,[t_k],q} = \sigma_{[t_1]} \to \cdots \to \sigma_{[t_k]} \to q \mid (t_0 t_1 \cdots t_k, q) \in \mathcal{U}\},$$

where $\sigma_{[t]} = \bigwedge\{\alpha_{[t],[t_1'],\ldots,[t_\ell'],q'} \mid (t\,t_1' \cdots t_\ell', q') \in \mathcal{U}\}$. We define the type environment $\Gamma_{\mathcal{X},\mathcal{U},\sim}$ as $\{F : (E, \alpha_{[F],[t_1],\ldots,[t_k],q}) \mid (F\,t_1 \cdots t_k, q) \in \mathcal{U}\}$. By the condition that $\sim$ induces a *finite* number of equivalence classes, $\Gamma_{\mathcal{X},\mathcal{U},\sim}$ is finite.

Example 7. From the reductions in Example 6, we get the following type equations:

$$\alpha_{S,q_0} = q_0 \qquad \alpha_{F,\mathrm{c},q_0} = \alpha_{\mathrm{c},q_0} \wedge \alpha_{\mathrm{c},q_1} \to q_0 \qquad \alpha_{\mathrm{c},q_0} = q_0 \qquad \alpha_{\mathrm{c},q_1} = q_1$$
$$\alpha_{G,G,\mathrm{c},q_0} = \alpha_{G,G,\mathrm{c},q_0} \to \alpha_{\mathrm{c},q_0} \wedge \alpha_{\mathrm{c},q_1} \to q_0$$

Thus, the extracted type environment (in the usual term representation) is:

$$\{S : q_0, F : (q_0 \wedge q_1) \to q_0, G : \mu\alpha.(\alpha \to (q_0 \wedge q_1) \to q_0)\}. \qquad \square$$

The theorem below (see [10] for a proof) ensures that if $\mathcal{G}$ is typable and if $\sim$ is properly chosen, $\Gamma_{\mathcal{X},\mathcal{U},\sim}$ is a proper witness. For a type environment Γ, we define the equivalence relation $\sim_\Gamma$ by: $\sim_\Gamma = \{(t_1, t_2) \mid \forall \tau.(\Gamma \vdash t_1 : \tau \iff \Gamma \vdash t_2 : \tau)\}$.

Theorem 3. *If* $\Gamma \vdash_B (\mathcal{G}, S_{\mathcal{G}}) : q_{B,0}$ *and* $\sim \subseteq \sim_\Gamma$*, then* $\Gamma_{\mathcal{X},\mathcal{U},\sim} \vdash_B (\mathcal{G}, S_{\mathcal{G}}) : q_{B,0}$.

Example 8. Recall $\mathcal{G}_2$ in Example 3, and $\Gamma_2 = \{S : q_0, F : (q_0 \wedge q_1) \to q_0, G : \mu\alpha.(\alpha \to (q_0 \wedge q_1) \to q_0)\}$ in Example 5. The relation $\sim$ in Example 6 satisfies the assumption $\sim \subseteq \sim_{\Gamma_2}$ of Theorem 3, and $\Gamma_{\mathcal{X},\mathcal{U},\sim} \vdash_{B_1} (\mathcal{G}_2, S) : q_0$ holds indeed.

Theorem 3 cannot be directly used for type inference, since we do not know $\sim_\Gamma$ in advance. We shall prove below (in Theorem 4) that even if $\sim$ is not a subset of $\sim_\Gamma$, we can "amend" the type environment to get a valid one, by using the refinement relation $\sqsubseteq$ below. Intuitively, $\tau_1 \sqsubseteq \tau_2$ means that τ_1 is obtained from τ_2 by removing some intersection types. Note that unlike subtyping, the refinement relation is co-variant in the function type constructor ($\to$).

Definition 3 (refinement). *Let* $\tau_0 = (E_0, \alpha_0)$ *and* $\tau_1 = (E_1, \alpha_1)$ *be closed types, and let* $E = E_0 \cup E_1$. *The type* τ_0 *is a* refinement *of* τ_1, *written* $\tau_0 \sqsubseteq \tau_1$, *if there exists a binary relation* $\mathcal{R}$ *on* $\mathbf{Tv}(\tau_1) \cup \mathbf{Tv}(\tau_2)$ *such that (i)* $(\tau_0, \tau_1) \in \mathcal{R}$ *and (ii) for every* $(\tau_0', \tau_1') \in \mathcal{R}$, *there exist* $\sigma_1, \ldots, \sigma_m, \sigma_1', \ldots, \sigma_m', q$ *such that* $E(\alpha_0') = \sigma_1 \to \cdots \to \sigma_m \to q$ *and* $E(\alpha_1') = \sigma_1' \to \cdots \to \sigma_m' \to q$, *with* $(\sigma_1, \sigma_1'), \ldots, (\sigma_m, \sigma_m') \in \mathcal{R}^{\sqsubseteq}$. *Here,* $\mathcal{R}^{\sqsubseteq}$ *is defined as:*
$$\{(\bigwedge\{\alpha_1, \ldots, \alpha_k\}, \bigwedge\{\alpha_1', \ldots, \alpha_{k'}'\}) \mid \forall i \in \{1, \ldots, k\}.\exists j \in \{1, \ldots, k'\}.\alpha_i \mathcal{R} \alpha_j'\}.$$

We write $\Gamma_1 \sqsubseteq \Gamma_2$ if $dom(\Gamma_1) \subseteq dom(\Gamma_2)$ and for every $x : \tau_1 \in \Gamma_1$, there exists τ_2 such that $x : \tau_2 \in \Gamma_2$ and $\tau_1 \sqsubseteq \tau_2$.

Example 9. Let τ_1 be $q_1 \to q_2$ and τ_2 be $(q_1 \wedge q_0) \to q_2$. Then $\tau_1 \sqsubseteq \tau_2$ and $\tau_1 \to q_0 \sqsubseteq \tau_2 \to q_0$ hold. Note that $\tau_1 \leq \tau_2$ but $\tau_1 \to q_0 \not\leq \tau_2 \to q_0$.   □

Theorem 4. *Suppose* $\Gamma \vdash_\mathcal{B} (\mathcal{G}, S_\mathcal{G}) : q_{\mathcal{B},0}$. *Let* $\sim$ *be an equivalence relation on* $\mathbf{Tm}$ *and* $(\mathcal{X}_0, \mathcal{U}_0) \longrightarrow_\sim (\mathcal{X}_1, \mathcal{U}_1) \longrightarrow_\sim (\mathcal{X}_2, \mathcal{U}_2) \longrightarrow_\sim \cdots$ *be a fair reduction sequence, with* $(\mathcal{X}_0, \mathcal{U}_0) = (\{S\}, \{(S, q_{\mathcal{B},0})\})$. *Let* $\mathcal{U} = \bigcup_i \mathcal{U}_i$ *and* $\mathcal{X} = \bigcup_i \mathcal{X}_i$. *Then, there exists* Γ' *such that* $\Gamma' \sqsubseteq \Gamma_{\mathcal{X},\mathcal{U},\sim}$ *and* $\Gamma' \vdash (\mathcal{G}, S) : q_{\mathcal{B},0}$,

The proof is given in the extended version [10]. Intuitively, Theorem 4 holds because, if $\sim$ is not a subset of $\sim_\Gamma$, we only get extra reduction sequences, whose effect is only to add extra type bindings and elements in intersections. Thus, by removing the extra nodes and edges (using the refinement relation from right to left), we can obtain a proper type environment.

Example 10. Recall Example 6. Let $\sim^{(2)}$ be $\sim^{(1)} \cup \{(GG, \mathbf{b}), (\mathbf{b}, GG)\}$. In addition to the reductions in Example 6, we obtain the extra reduction sequence: $(\mathbf{b}\,\mathbf{c}, q_1) \to (GG\,\mathbf{c}, q_1) \to (\mathbf{a}\,\mathbf{c}\,(GG\,(\mathbf{b}\,\mathbf{c})), q_1) \to \mathtt{fail}$. From the reductions, we obtain the following type equations:

$$\alpha_{S,q_0} = q_0 \qquad \alpha_{F,\mathbf{c},q_0} = \alpha_{\mathbf{c},q_0} \wedge \alpha_{\mathbf{c},q_1} \to q_0 \qquad \alpha_{\mathbf{c},q_0} = q_0 \qquad \alpha_{\mathbf{c},q_1} = q_1$$
$$\alpha_{G,G,\mathbf{c},q_0} = \alpha_{G,G,\mathbf{c},q_0} \underline{\wedge \alpha_{G,G,\mathbf{c},q_1}} \to \alpha_{\mathbf{c},q_0} \wedge \alpha_{\mathbf{c},q_1} \to q_0$$
$$\underline{\alpha_{G,G,\mathbf{c},q_1} = \alpha_{G,G,\mathbf{c},q_1} \wedge \alpha_{G,G,\mathbf{c},q_1} \to \alpha_{\mathbf{c},q_0} \wedge \alpha_{\mathbf{c},q_1} \to q_1}$$

The part obtained from the extra reduction sequence is underlined. By ignoring that part, we get the same equations as Example 7, hence obtaining the correct type environment: $\{S : q_0, F : (q_0 \wedge q_1) \to q_0, G : \mu\alpha.(\alpha \to (q_0 \wedge q_1) \to q_0)\}$.   □

Theorem 4 yields the procedure FINDCERT in Figure 2. The condition $\exists \Gamma'.\Gamma' \vdash_\mathcal{B} (\mathcal{G}, S) : q_{\mathcal{B},0} \wedge \Gamma' \sqsubseteq \Gamma$ is in general undecidable because of the presence of recursive types. Thus, we bound the size (i.e., the number of type constructors) of Γ' by v, and gradually increase the bound. An algorithm to check whether there exists Γ' such that $|\Gamma'| < v$ and $\Gamma' \vdash_\mathcal{B} (\mathcal{G}, S) : q_{\mathcal{B},0} \wedge \Gamma' \sqsubseteq \Gamma$ is discussed in Section 3.2. By Theorem 4, we have:

Theorem 5 (relative completeness). *If* $\Gamma \vdash_\mathcal{B} (\mathcal{G}, S) : q_{\mathcal{B},0}$ *for some finite recursive type environment* Γ, *then* FINDCERT$(\mathcal{G}, S, q_{\mathcal{B},0})$ *eventually terminates and outputs* Γ' *such that* $\Gamma' \vdash_\mathcal{B} (\mathcal{G}, S) : q_{\mathcal{B},0}$.

To see the termination, notice that by the condition that $\sim$ induces a finite number of equivalence classes, there exists m such that $\Gamma_{\mathcal{X},\mathcal{U},\sim} = \Gamma_{\mathcal{X}_m,\mathcal{U}_m,\sim}$ in Theorem 4.

FINDCERT$(\mathcal{G}, \mathcal{B})$ = Rep$(\mathcal{G}, \mathcal{B}, \{S\}, \{(S, q_{\mathcal{B},0})\}, \{(S, S)\}, 1)$
Rep$(\mathcal{G}, \mathcal{B}, \mathcal{X}, \mathcal{U}, \sim, v)$ =
    let $(\mathcal{X}, \mathcal{U}) \longrightarrow^\ell_{\sim} (\mathcal{X}', \mathcal{U}')$ in let $\sim'$ = expandEq$(\sim, \mathcal{X}')$ in
    if $\Gamma' \vdash_{\mathcal{B}} (\mathcal{G}, S) : q_{\mathcal{B},0}$ for some $\Gamma' \sqsubseteq \Gamma_{\mathcal{X}',\mathcal{U}',\sim'}$ and $|\Gamma'| \le v$ then return Γ'
    else Rep$(\mathcal{G}, \mathcal{B}, \mathcal{X}', \mathcal{U}', \sim', v+1)$

Fig. 2. A type inference procedure. ($|\Gamma|$ denotes the largest type size in Γ.)

3.2 Type Checking by SAT Solving

We now discuss the sub-algorithm for FINDCERT, to check whether there exists
Γ' such that $|\Gamma'| \le v$ and $\Gamma' \vdash_{\mathcal{B}} (\mathcal{G}, S) : q_{\mathcal{B},0} \wedge \Gamma' \sqsubseteq \Gamma$.
We first rephrase the condition $|\Gamma'| \le v \wedge \Gamma' \sqsubseteq \Gamma$. For a set $E = \{\alpha_1 = \sigma_{1,1} \to$
$\cdots \sigma_{1,m_1} \to q_1, \dots, \alpha_n = \sigma_{n,1} \to \cdots \sigma_{n,m_n} \to q_n\}$, we write $E^{(k)}$ for:

$$\{\alpha_1^{(1)} = \sigma_{1,1}^{(k)} \to \cdots \sigma_{1,m_1}^{(k)} \to q_1, \dots, \alpha_n^{(1)} = \sigma_{n,1}^{(k)} \to \cdots \sigma_{n,m_n}^{(k)} \to q_n, \dots,$$
$$\alpha_1^{(k)} = \sigma_{1,1}^{(k)} \to \cdots \sigma_{1,m_1}^{(k)} \to q_1, \dots, \alpha_n^{(k)} = \sigma_{n,1}^{(k)} \to \cdots \sigma_{n,m_n}^{(k)} \to q_n, \},$$

obtained by preparing k copies for each type variable. Here, for $\sigma = \bigwedge\{\alpha_1, \dots, \alpha_\ell\}$,
$\sigma^{(k)}$ represents $\bigwedge\{\alpha_1^{(1)}, \dots, \alpha_\ell^{(1)}, \dots, \alpha_1^{(k)}, \dots, \alpha_\ell^{(k)}\}$. Clearly, $(E, \alpha_i) \cong (E^{(k)}, \alpha_i^{(1)})$.
We write $\Gamma^{(k)}$ for $\{x : (E^{(k)}, \alpha^{(i)}) \mid x : (E, \alpha) \in \Gamma, 1 \le i \le k\}$.
    We write $E \sqsubseteq_{\mathbf{s}} E'$ if E is obtained from E' by removing some elements from
intersections, i.e., if $E = \{\alpha_1 = \bigwedge S_{1,1} \to \cdots \bigwedge S_{1,m_1} \to q_1, \dots, \alpha_n = \bigwedge S_{n,1} \to$
$\cdots \bigwedge S_{n,m_n} \to q_n\}$ and $E' = \{\alpha_1 = \bigwedge S'_{1,1} \to \cdots \bigwedge S'_{1,m_1} \to q_1, \dots \alpha_n =$
$\bigwedge S'_{n,1} \to \cdots \bigwedge S'_{n,m_n} \to q_n\}$ with $S_{i,j} \subseteq S'_{i,j}$ for every i,j. It is pointwise
extended to $\Gamma \sqsubseteq_{\mathbf{s}} \Gamma'$ by: $\Gamma \sqsubseteq_{\mathbf{s}} \Gamma' \iff \forall x : (E, \alpha) \in \Gamma, \exists x : (E', \alpha) \in \Gamma'.E \sqsubseteq_{\mathbf{s}} E'$.
Then, $\Gamma' \sqsubseteq \Gamma$ is equivalent to $\exists k.\Gamma' \sqsubseteq_{\mathbf{s}} \Gamma^{(k)}$ (up to renaming of type variables).
Thus, the condition $|\Gamma'| \le v \wedge \Gamma' \sqsubseteq \Gamma$ in the algorithm can be replaced by
$\Gamma' \sqsubseteq_{\mathbf{s}} \Gamma^{(v)}$ without losing completeness.
    To check whether there exists Γ' such that $\Gamma' \vdash_{\mathcal{B}} (\mathcal{G}, S) : q_{\mathcal{B},0}$ and $\Gamma' \sqsubseteq_{\mathbf{s}}$
$\Gamma^{(k)}$, we attach a boolean variable to each type binding and each element of
an intersection in $\Gamma^{(k)}$, to express whether Γ' has the corresponding binding or
element. Thus, an annotated type environment is of the form $\{x_1 :^{b_1} \tau_1, \dots, x_m :^{b_m}$
$\tau_m\}$, where each type equation in $\tau_1, \dots, \tau_m$ is now of the form:
$\alpha = \bigwedge_{i \in I_1} b_{1,i} \alpha_{1,i} \to \cdots \to \bigwedge_{k \in I_k} b_{k,i} \alpha_{k,i} \to q$.
Given an assignment function f for boolean variables, the type environment
$f(\Delta)$ is given by:

$$f(\Delta) = \{x_i : f(\rho_i) \mid x_i :^{b_i} \rho_i \in \Delta \wedge f(b_i) = \mathbf{true}\}$$
$$f(E, \alpha) = (\{\alpha = f(\xi_1) \to \cdots \to f(\xi_k) \to q \mid (\alpha = \xi_1 \to \cdots \to \xi_k \to q) \in E\}, \alpha)$$
$$f(\bigwedge_{i \in I} b_i \alpha_i) = \bigwedge\{\alpha_i \mid i \in I, f(b_i) = \mathbf{true}\}$$

Let Δ be the type environment obtained by attaching boolean variables to $\Gamma^{(k)}$.
Then, the condition $\Gamma' \sqsubseteq_{\mathbf{s}} \Gamma^{(k)} \wedge \Gamma' \vdash_{\mathcal{B}} (\mathcal{G}, S) : q_{\mathcal{B},0}$ is reduced to: "Is there a
boolean assignment f such that $f(\Delta) \vdash_{\mathcal{B}} (\mathcal{G}, S) : q_{\mathcal{B},0}$?" It can be expressed as a
SAT problem as follows. We first introduce additional boolean variables: (i) For

each rule $F \mapsto \lambda x_1. \cdots \lambda x_k.t \in \mathcal{R}$, a subterm s of t, a type binding $F :^b \xi_1 \to \cdots \to \xi_k \to q \in \Delta$, and a type ρ in Δ, we prepare a variable $b_{\Delta, x_1 : \xi_1, \ldots, x_k : \xi_k \vdash s : \rho}$, which expresses whether $f(\Delta, x_1 : \xi_1, \ldots, x_k : \xi_k) \vdash_\mathcal{B} s : f(\rho)$ should hold. (ii) For each pair (ρ_1, ρ_2) of types occurring in Δ, we introduce $b_{\rho_1 \le \rho_2}$, which expresses whether $f(\rho_1) \le f(\rho_2)$ should hold. Now, the existence of a boolean assignment function f such that $f(\Delta) \vdash_\mathcal{B} (\mathcal{G}, S) : q_{\mathcal{B},0}$ is reduced to the satisfiability of the conjunction of all the following boolean formulas. We write $F : \bigwedge_{j \in \{1..n\}} b_j \rho_j \in \Delta$ for $F :^{b_1} \rho_1, \ldots, F :^{b_n} \rho_n \in \Delta$ below. For simplicity, we omit type equations E and identify α and $E(\alpha)$ below.

(i) $\bigvee \{b_i \mid S :^{b_i} q_{\mathcal{B},0} \in \Delta\}$.

(ii) $b \Rightarrow b_{\Delta, x_1 : \xi_1, \ldots, x_k : \xi_k \vdash t : q}$
for each $F :^b \xi_1 \to \cdots \to \xi_k \to q \in \Delta$ such that $\mathcal{R}(F) = \lambda x_1, \ldots, x_k.t$.

(iii) $b_{\Delta', x : \bigwedge_{j \in J} b_j \rho_j \vdash x : \rho} \Rightarrow \bigvee_{j \in J}(b_j \wedge b_{\rho_j \le \rho})$, for each $b_{\Delta', x : \bigwedge_{j \in J} b_j \rho_j \vdash x : \rho}$.

(iv) $b_{\Delta' \vdash a : \rho} \Rightarrow \bigvee \{b_{q_1 \to \cdots \to q_k \to q \le \rho} \mid \delta(a, q) = q_1 \cdots q_k\}$, for each $b_{\Delta' \vdash a : \rho}$.

(v) $b_{\Delta' \vdash t_1 t_2 : \rho} \Rightarrow \bigvee(b_{\Delta' \vdash t_1 : (\bigwedge_{j \in J} b_j \rho_j) \to \rho} \wedge (\bigwedge_{j \in J}(b_j \Rightarrow \bigvee(b_{\Delta' \vdash t_2 : \rho'} \wedge b_{\rho' \le \rho_j}))))$, for each $b_{\Delta' \vdash t_1 t_2 : \rho}$.

(vi) $b_{(\bigwedge_{i \in I} b_i \rho_i) \le (\bigwedge_{j \in J} b_j \rho'_j)} \Rightarrow \bigwedge_{j \in J}(b_j \Rightarrow \bigvee_{i \in I}(b_i \wedge b_{\rho_i \le \rho'_j}))$, for each $b_{(\bigwedge_{i \in I} b_i \rho_i) \le (\bigwedge_{j \in J} b_j \rho'_j)}$.

(vii) $b_{\xi_1 \to \cdots \to \xi_k \to q \le \xi'_1 \to \cdots \to \xi'_m \to q'} \Rightarrow k = m \wedge q = q' \wedge \bigwedge_{i \in \{1, \ldots, k\}} b_{\xi'_i \le \xi_i}$, for each $b_{\xi_1 \to \cdots \to \xi_k \to q \le \xi'_1 \to \cdots \to \xi'_m \to q'}$.

The first condition (i) ensures that $S : q_{\mathcal{B},0} \in f(\Delta)$. The condition (ii) ensures that each type binding in $f(\Delta)$ is valid (i.e., $\vdash_\mathcal{B} \mathcal{R} : f(\Delta)$). The next three conditions (iii)-(v) express the validity of a type judgment $f(\Delta, x_1 : \xi_1, \ldots, x_k : \xi_k) \vdash_\mathcal{B} t : f(\rho)$, corresponding to the typing rules for variables, constants, and applications. The last two conditions express the validity of a subtype relation.

By the above construction, there exists a boolean assignment function f such that $f(\Delta) \vdash (\mathcal{G}, S) : q_{\mathcal{B},0}$ if and only if the conjunction of the above boolean formulas is satisfiable. The latter can be solved by using a SAT solver.

Example 11. Recall $\Gamma_{\mathcal{X}^{(2)}, \mathcal{U}^{(2)}, \sim^{(2)}}$ in Example 10. By adding it with boolean variables, we obtain $\Delta = \{S : q_0, F : (q_0 \wedge q_1) \to q_0, G :^{b_0} \tau_0, G :^{b_1} \tau_1)\}$, where $\tau_i = (b_2 \tau_0 \wedge b_3 \tau_1) \to (q_0 \wedge q_1) \to q_i$ for $i \in \{0, 1\}$. (Here, for the sake of simplicity, we have added boolean variables only to critical parts.) From the typing of G, we get the following boolean constraints:

$b_i \Rightarrow b_{\Delta' \vdash a\,x\,(g\,g\,(b\,x)) : q_i}$ (for $i \in \{0, 1\}$) $b_{\Delta' \vdash a\,x\,(g\,g\,(b\,x)) : q_0} \Rightarrow b_{\Delta' \vdash g : q_0 \wedge q_1 \to q_0}$
$b_{\Delta' \vdash a\,x\,(g\,g\,(b\,x)) : q_1} \Rightarrow \text{false}$ $b_{\Delta' \vdash g : \tau_0} \Rightarrow b_2$ $b_{\Delta' \vdash g : \tau_1} \Rightarrow b_3$
$b_{\Delta' \vdash g : q_0 \wedge q_1 \to q_0} \Rightarrow (b_{\Delta' \vdash g : \tau_0} \wedge (b_2 \Rightarrow b_{\Delta' \vdash g : \tau_0}) \wedge (b_3 \Rightarrow b_{\Delta' \vdash g : \tau_1}))$

Here, $\Delta' = \Delta \cup \{g :^{b_2} \tau_0, g :^{b_3} \tau_1, x : q_0, x : q_1\}$. The above conditions are satisfied by f such that $f(b_0) = f(b_2) = \text{true}$ and $f(b_1) = f(b_3) = \text{false}$. Thus, we get $\Gamma' = f(\Delta) = \{S : q_0, F : (q_0 \wedge q_1) \to q_0, G : \tau_0\}$ where $\tau_0 = \tau_0 \to (q_0 \wedge q_1) \to q_0$. We have $\Gamma' \vdash_{\mathcal{B}_1} (\mathcal{G}_2, S) : q_0$ as required.   □

4   Applications

This section discusses two applications of μHORS model checking: verification of (functional) object-oriented programs and that of higher-order multi-threaded programs. Those programs can be verified via reduction to μHORS model checking. In both applications, the translation from a source program to μHORS is just like giving the semantics of the source program (in terms of the λ-calculus). This comes from the expressive power of the model of μHORS model checking (i.e., μHORS), which is the main advantage of our approach.

4.1   Model-Checking Functional Objects

In this section, we discuss how to reduce verification problems for (functional) object-oriented programs. The idea is to transform a program into μHORS that generates a tree representing all the possible action sequences[1] of the source program. The translation is sound *and complete* in the sense that all *and only* action sequences that occur are represented in the tree. Properties that can be checked include: reachability (i.e., whether program execution reaches certain program points), order of method invocations, and whether downcasts may fail. In a full version [10], we give a formal translation from (a call-by-value variant of) Featherweight Java (FJ) [5] to μHORS.

We use the following classes that represent natural numbers with methods for addition (**add**) and predecessors (**pred**) as a running example. The statement **fail;** signals a global action that denotes a failure. Method **rand** non-deterministically returns a natural number that is equal to or greater than the argument; $\square$ denotes a non-deterministic choice operator. The main expression to be executed takes a predecessor of a (non-deterministically chosen) non-zero natural number.

```
class Nat extends Object {
  Nat add(Nat n) { fail; }
  Nat pred() { fail; }
  Nat rand(Nat n) { return n□new S(this.rand(n)); } }
class Z extends Nat { Nat add(Nat n) { return n; } }
class S extends Nat {
  Nat p;
  Nat add(Nat n) { Nat p' = this.p.add(n);  return new S(p'); }
  Nat pred() { return this.p; } }
// main expression
new Z().rand(new Z()).add(new S(new Z())).pred();
```

To verify program execution does not **fail**, we translate the program to a μHORS that generates the tree representing all the possible global events, like: **br e (br e** $\cdots$ **)**. Here, **br** and **e** represent non-deterministic branch (caused by

---

[1] The source language has a construct to signal a global action, as well as a non-deterministic choice operator.

$\Box$) and program termination, respectively. Then, it suffices to check that the tree does not contain `fail` by using μHORS model checking.

Translation to μHORS. The main ideas of translation are: (i) to express an object as a record (or tuple) of functions that represent methods [2], and (ii) to represent each method in the continuation passing style (CPS) in order to correctly reflect the evaluation order and action sequences to μHORS. For example, an object of class S is expressed by a tuple $\langle S\_add, S\_pred, S\_rand \rangle$ of functions S_add, S_pred and S_rand that represent methods add, pred, and rand defined or inherited in class S, respectively.[2] A function that represents a method takes an argument that represents "self" and a continuation argument, as well as ordinary arguments of the method. In general, a method of the form

```
C₀ m(C₁ x₁, ..., Cₙ xₙ) { return e; }
```

is represented by the λ-term $\lambda x_1. \cdots \lambda x_n. \lambda this. \lambda k. [\![e]\!]_k$ where k is the continuation parameter and $[\![e]\!]_k$ denotes the translation of e, which passes the result of method execution to k. For example, method add in class S is represented by non-terminal S_add, whose body is

$$\lambda n. \lambda this. \lambda k. [\![\texttt{Nat p' = ...; return new S(p');}]\!]_k$$

Then, method invocation is expressed as self-application [7]. For example, invocation of add on an S object with a Z object as an argument is expressed by

$$S\_add \ \langle Z\_add, Z\_pred, Z\_rand \rangle \ \langle S\_add, S\_pred, S\_rand \rangle \ k$$

where k is the current continuation. Note that S_add is applied to a tuple that contains itself.

To deal with fields, each method is further abstracted by values of fields of this. So, the body of S_add is in fact

$$\lambda p. \lambda n. \lambda this. \lambda k. [\![\texttt{Nat p' = ...; return new S(p');}]\!]_k,$$

where p stands for this.p inside the method body. Although this scheme only supports field access of the form this.f, field access to any expressions other than this can be expressed by using "getter" methods. A non-terminal representing a method will be applied to initial field values when an object is instantiated. For example, object instantiation new S(p') is represented by $\langle S\_add \ p', S\_pred \ p', S\_rand \ p' \rangle$. By using pattern-matching for λ, method add in class S is expressed by the following two rules:

$$S\_add \mapsto \lambda\langle p_a, p_p, p_r \rangle. \lambda\langle n_a, n_p, n_r \rangle. \lambda\langle this_a, this_p, this_r \rangle. \lambda k.$$
$$\qquad\qquad p_a \ \langle n_a, n_p, n_r \rangle \ \langle p_a, p_p, p_r \rangle \ (F \ k),$$
$$F \qquad \mapsto \lambda k'. \lambda\langle p'_a, p'_p, p'_r \rangle.$$
$$\qquad\qquad k' \ \langle S\_add \ \langle p'_a, p'_p, p'_r \rangle, S\_pred \ \langle p'_a, p'_p, p'_r \rangle, S\_rand \ \langle p'_a, p'_p, p'_r \rangle \rangle$$

where F stands for the continuation of the variable definition `Nat p' = ...;`.

---

[2] μHORS does not have tuples as primitives but all the tuples can be eliminated. Tuples as function arguments can be eliminated by currying and there is no function that returns tuples, thanks to the CPS representation. See the full version for details.

A global action a such as fail is represented by a tree node a; non-deterministic choice is by the node br of arity 2. The (translation of the) main expression is given as the initial continuation a constant function that returns the tree node e of arity 0. So, in order to verify that the program does not fail, it suffices to verify that the generated tree consists only of nodes br and e.

We address the problem of the lack of subtyping in μHORS as follows. We represent every object as a tuple of the *same length* ℓ, where ℓ is the number of the methods defined in the whole program. If a certain method is undefined, we just insert a dummy function $\lambda \tilde{x}.\lambda k.\text{fail}$ in the corresponding position of the tuple. The dummy function just outputs fail to signal NoSuchMethodError whenever it is called.

The resulting encoding of an object is well-typed. Let $\{m_1, \ldots, m_\ell\}$ be all the method names in the program, and $\{n_1, \ldots, n_\ell\}$ be their arities. Then, the encoding of every object would have the same recursive sort κ_o, given by:

$$\kappa_o = \kappa_{m_1} \times \cdots \times \kappa_{m_\ell} \qquad \kappa_{m_i} = \underbrace{\kappa_o \to \cdots \kappa_o}_{n_i} \to \kappa_o \to \underbrace{(\kappa_o \to \mathsf{o})}_{\text{type of continuation}} \to \mathsf{o}$$

The source program execution yields a sequence of global actions $a_1 a_2 \cdots a_n$ if and only if the tree generated by the translation has a path labeled with $a_1 a_2 \cdots a_n$ (ignoring br). Thus safety property verification of FJ programs is reduced to μHORS model checking.

4.2 Model-Checking Higher-Order Multi-threaded Programs

This section discusses how to apply the extended HO model checking to verification of multi-threaded programs, where each thread may use higher-order functions and recursion. For the sake of simplicity, we discuss only programs consisting of two threads, whose syntax is given by:

$$P \text{ (programs)} ::= M_1 \parallel M_2$$
$$M \text{ (threads)} ::= ( ) \mid a \mid x \mid \mathbf{fun}(f, x, M) \mid M_1 M_2 \mid M_1 \square M_2$$

A program $P = M_1 \parallel M_2$ executes two threads M_1 and M_2 concurrently, where M_1 and M_2 are (call-by-value) higher-order functional programs with side effects. The expression a performs a global action a, and evaluates to the unit value ( ). We keep global actions abstract, so that various synchronization primitives and shared memory can be modeled. The expression $\mathbf{fun}(f, x, M)$ describes a recursive function f such that $f(x) = M$. When f does not occur in M, we write $\lambda x.M$ for $\mathbf{fun}(f, x, M)$. We also write let $x = M_1$ in M_2 for $(\lambda x.M_2)M_1$, and further abbreviate it to $M_1; M_2$ when x does not occur in M_2. $M_1 \square M_2$ evaluates M_1 or M_2 non-deterministically. The formal semantics is given in [10]. The goal of verification is, given a program M and a property ψ on global action sequences, to check whether all the possible action sequences of M satisfy ψ.

Example 12. Let M be the following thread:

let *sync* $f = $ lock; $f()$; unlock; *sync* f in let *cr* $x = $ enter; exit in *sync cr*, which models a thread acquiring a global lock before entering a critical section. We may then wish to verify that the global actions enter and exit can occur only alternately, as long as lock and unlock occur alternately. □

We can reduce verification problems for multi-threads to extended HO model checking problems by transforming a given program to a μHORS that generates a tree describing all the possible global action sequences. The ideas of the transformation are: (i) transform each thread to CPS (continuation-passing style) to correctly model the order of actions, as in [9], and (ii) apply each thread to a scheduler, and let a thread pass the control to the scheduler non-deterministically after each global action. The translation from programs to μHORS is:

$$(M_1 \parallel M_2)^\dagger = \texttt{br} \; (Sched \; (M_1{}^\dagger \; \lambda x.\texttt{e}) \; (M_2{}^\dagger \; \lambda x.\texttt{e})) \; (Sched \; (M_2{}^\dagger \; \lambda x.\texttt{e}) \; (M_1{}^\dagger \; \lambda x.\texttt{e}))$$
$$()^\dagger = \lambda k.\lambda g.k \, \texttt{e} \, g \quad x^\dagger = \lambda k.\lambda g.k \, x \, g \quad \texttt{fun}(f,x,M)^\dagger = \lambda k.\lambda g.k \, \texttt{fun}(f,x,M^\dagger) \, g$$
$$(M_1 \, M_2)^\dagger = \lambda k.\lambda g.M_1{}^\dagger \; (\lambda f.M_2{}^\dagger \lambda x.f \, x \, k) \, g$$
$$(M_1 \square M_2)^\dagger = \lambda k.\lambda g.\texttt{br} \; (M_1{}^\dagger \, k \, g) \; (M_2{}^\dagger \, k \, g) \quad a^\dagger = \lambda k.\lambda g.a \; (\texttt{br} \; (k \, \texttt{e} \, g) \; (g \, (k \, \texttt{e})))$$

Here, the non-terminal $Sched$ is defined by the rule $Sched \; x \; y \to x \; (Sched \; y)$, which schedules x first, passing to it the global continuation $Sched \; y$ (which will schedule y next). The terminal symbol $\texttt{br}$ represents a non-deterministic branch. On the righthand side of the last translation rule, a and $\texttt{e}$ are terminal symbols of arity 1 and 0 respectively. The program $M_1 \parallel M_2$ is translated to a tree-generating program, which either schedules M_1 then M_2, or M_2 then M_1. Apart from the global action (the last rule), the translation of a thread is essentially the standard call-by-value CPS transformation except that a global continuation is passed as an additional parameter. The global action a is transformed to a tree node a, followed by a non-deterministic branch (expressed by $\texttt{br}$). The first branch evaluates the local continuation, while the second branch yields the control to the other thread by invoking the global continuation g.

By the definition of the transformation above, it should be clear that (i) if P is simply-typed, then $P^\dagger$ is a well-typed μHORS, and (ii) P has a sequence of global actions $a_1 a_2 \cdots a_n$ if and only if the tree generated by $P^\dagger$ has a path labeled with $a_1 a_2 \cdots a_n$ (with $\texttt{br}$ ignored). Thus, verification of multi-threaded programs has been reduced to μHORS model checking; see [10] for more details.

Context-bounded model checking Qadeer and Rehof [19] showed that model checking of concurrent pushdown systems (or multi-threaded programs with *first-order* recursion) is decidable *if the number of context switches is bounded by a constant*. Our translation given above yields a generalization of the result: context-bounded model checking of multi-threaded, *higher-order* recursive programs is decidable. To obtain the result, it suffices to replace the scheduler $Sched$ with $Sched_\ell$ given below, which allows only ℓ context switches:

$$Sched_0 \; x \; y \to \texttt{e} \qquad Sched_{i+1} \; x \; y \to x \; (Sched_i \; y)$$

Then $Sched_i$'s have the following *non-recursive* types:

$$Sched_{2m} : \sigma_m \to \sigma_m \to \texttt{o} \qquad Sched_{2m+1} : \sigma_{m+1} \to \sigma_m \to \texttt{o}$$

where $\sigma_0 = \top$ and $\sigma_{i+1} = (\sigma_i \to o) \to o$. Thus, for the modified encoding $P^{\dagger \ell}$, we have: (i) If P is simply-typed, then $P^{\dagger \ell}$ is a well-typed μHORS *without recursive types*, and (ii) P with context-bound ℓ has a sequence of global actions $a_1 a_2 \cdots a_n$ if and only if the tree generated by $P^{\dagger \ell}$ has a path labeled with $a_1 a_2 \cdots a_n$ (with br ignored). As an immediate corollary of the above properties and the decidability of HORS model checking [15], we obtain that context-bounded model checking of multi-threaded higher-order programs is decidable.[3]

5 Implementation and Experiments

We have implemented a prototype model checker RTRecS for μHORS based on the procedure FindCert described in Section 3. As the underlying SAT solver, we have used MiniSat 2.2 (http://minisat.se/MiniSat.html). We have also implemented a translator from FJ programs to μHORS based on Section 4.1.

The implementation is based on the procedure FindCert in Figure 2, except for the following points. RTRecS first performs an equality-based flow analysis [17] before model checking, and uses it as the equivalence relation $\sim$. $\mathcal{U}$ is also over-approximated by using the result of the flow analysis; thus, in the current implementation, the reductions of terms (3rd line in Figure 2) are performed only for finding a counter-example, without using the rule R-Eq.

Table 1 summarizes the result of preliminary experiments. (For space restriction, we omit some results, which are found in [10].) The programs used for the experiments and the web interface for our prototype are available at http://www-kb.is.s.u-tokyo.ac.jp/~koba/fjmc/. The columns "#lines" and "#rules" show the number of lines of the source FJ program (if applicable) and the number of the rules of μHORS. The column "#states" shows the numer of states of the property automaton. The column "k" shows k of $\Gamma' \sqsubseteq_s \Gamma^{(k)}$ in Section 3.2. The column "#sat" shows the number of sat clauses (i.e., the number of disjunctive formulas in conjunctive normal form) for the final call of the SAT solver. The column "time" shows the running time (excluding the time for translation from FJ to μHORS, which is anyway quite small).

$\mathcal{G}_1$ and $\mathcal{G}_2$ are from Examples 2 and 3, where the checked property is expressed by $\mathcal{B}_1$ in Example 4. Thread is the μHORS obtained from Example 12. The other programs were obtained from FJ programs, based on the translation discussed in Section 4.1, and except for Twofiles, we verified that the programs do not fail (where the meaning of "failure" depends on each program, as explained below). Pred is the running example in Section 4. The next six are list-manipulating programs (implemented as objects), which are small but non-trivial programs. (In fact, L-filter and L-risers are object-oriented versions of benchmark programs of the PMRS verification tool [16].) For example, L-filter creates a list of natural numbers in a non-deterministic manner, filters out 0, and checks that the resulting list consists only of non-zero elements (and fails if it does not hold). See [10] for more details.

---

[3] We have considered only programs with two threads, but this restriction can be easily relaxed by using the same technique as Qadeer and Rehof [19].

Table 1. Experimental Results (CPU: Intel(R) Xeon(R) 3GHz, Memory: 8GB). Times are in seconds.

programs	#lines	#rules	#states	k	#sat	time
$\mathcal{G}_1$	–	2	2	1	27	0.001
$\mathcal{G}_2$	–	3	2	1	49	0.002
Thread	–	9	5	1	38,171	0.580
Pred	21	15	1	1	157	0.005
L-append	20	30	1	1	165	0.006
L-map	43	182	1	1	738	0.235
L-app-map	43	212	1	1	1,546	0.391
L-even	25	87	1	1	249	0.025
L-filter	59	122	1	2	5,964	0.491
L-risers	73	64	1	2	17,419	0.445
Twofiles	28	21	5	2	739,867	13.86

Twofiles was prepared as an example of verification of temporal properties. It is an object-oriented version of the program that accesses two files: one for read-only, and the other for write-only [9]. We verify that the read-only (write-only, resp.) file is closed after some reads (writes, resp.).

Our model checker RTRECS could successfully verify all the programs. The verification time and the size of SAT formulas were significantly larger for Twofiles compared with other programs. The explosion of the size of SAT formulas for Twofiles is due to the size of the automaton for describing the temporal property, which blows up the number of candidates of types to be considered. More optimizations are necessary for avoiding this problem. The number k was surprisingly small for all the benchmark programs; this indicates that our choice of $\sim$ based on the equality-based flow analysis provided a good approximation of types. Overall, the experimental results above are encouraging; we are not aware of other fully-automated (i.e. requiring no annotations), sound (i.e. no false negatives) verification tools that can verify all the programs above.

6   Related Work

The model checking of HORS has recently emerged as a new technique for verification of higher-order programs [15,9,14,16,13]. Except Tsukada and Kobayashi's work [24], however, all the previous studies dealt with *simply-typed* recursion schemes, which are not suitable for modeling objects. Tsukada and Kobayashi [24] studied model checking of *untyped* HORS and reduced it to a type checking problem for an infinite intersection type system. The latter problem is however undecidable and they did not provide any realistic procedure for model checking.

Several methods for model-checking functional programs have been proposed recently [21,9,14,16,25], and some of them [21,14,16] support recursive data structures (like lists). However, it is not clear how to extend them to support general recursive types (including negative occurrences of recursive type variables). Furthermore, many of them require annotations [21,25] and are less precise.

There are previous studies on model checking of object-oriented programs [3,4]. To our knowledge, however, they are based on finite state model checking; Java programs are either (i) abstracted to finite state models and then finite state model checkers are used to verify the abstract models, or (ii) directly model checked, but with an incomplete state exploration. In the former case, because of the huge semantic gap between object-oriented programs and finite state systems, a lot of information is lost by the translation from Java programs to models. In the latter case, a "model checker" is used mainly as a bug detection tool, instead of a verification tool. In contrast, our method uses μHORS as models, which are as expressive as source programs. No information is lost by the translation from FJ to μHORS, and no false alarms can be generated (although the model checker may not terminate for some valid programs). There are also other methods for verification or static analysis of object-oriented programs [1,18,23]. In general, they either require human intervention [1] or are fully automated but less precise than model checking. See [10] for more detailed discussion. Rowe and Bakel [22] proposed an intersection type system for reasoning about object-oriented programs, but did not give an automated verification algorithm.

There are many studies on model checking of recursive parallel programs [19,6], which obtain decidable fragments by restricting synchronization primitives or applying approximations. It is interesting to see whether each result can be extended to higher-order, recursive parallel programs (besides context-bounded model checking discussed in Section 4.2).

Acknowledgments. We thank Noriaki Nakano and anonymous reviewers for useful comments. This work is partially supported by Kakenhi 23220001.

References

1. Barnett, M., DeLine, R., Fähndrich, M., Jacobs, B., Leino, K.R.M., Schulte, W., Venter, H.: The Spec# Programming System: Challenges and Directions. In: Meyer, B., Woodcock, J. (eds.) VSTTE 2005. LNCS, vol. 4171, pp. 144–152. Springer, Heidelberg (2008)
2. Cardelli, L.: A semantics of multiple inheritance. Info. Comput. 76(2/3), 138–164 (1988)
3. Corbett, J.C., Dwyer, M.B., Hatcliff, J., Laubach, S., Pasareanu, C.S., Robby, Zheng, H.: Bandera: extracting finite-state models from Java source code. In: ICSE, pp. 439–448 (2000)
4. Havelund, K., Pressburger, T.: Model checking JAVA programs using JAVA pathfinder. STTT 2(4), 366–381 (2000)
5. Igarashi, A., Pierce, B.C., Wadler, P.: Featherweight Java: a minimal core calculus for Java and GJ. ACM Trans. Prog. Lang. Syst. 23(3), 396–450 (2001)
6. Kahlon, V.: Reasoning about Threads with Bounded Lock Chains. In: Katoen, J.-P., König, B. (eds.) CONCUR 2011. LNCS, vol. 6901, pp. 450–465. Springer, Heidelberg (2011)
7. Kamin, S.N., Reddy, U.S.: Two semantic models of object-oriented languages. In: Gunter, C.A., Mitchell, J.C. (eds.) Theoretical Aspects of Object-Oriented Programming, ch. 13, pp. 463–496. The MIT Press (1993)

8. Kobayashi, N.: Model-checking higher-order functions. In: Proceedings of PPDP 2009, pp. 25–36. ACM Press (2009)
9. Kobayashi, N.: Types and higher-order recursion schemes for verification of higher-order programs. In: Proc. of POPL, pp. 416–428 (2009)
10. Kobayashi, N., Igarashi, A.: Model-checking higher-order programs with recursive types (2012), An extended version available from http://www-kb.is.s.u-tokyo.ac.jp/~koba/fjmc/
11. Kobayashi, N., Ong, C.-H.L.: A type system equivalent to the modal mu-calculus model checking of higher-order recursion schemes. In: Proceedings of LICS 2009, pp. 179–188 (2009)
12. Kobayashi, N., Ong, C.-H.L.: Complexity of model checking recursion schemes for fragments of the modal mu-calculus. Logical Methods in Computer Science 7(4) (2011)
13. Kobayashi, N., Sato, R., Unno, H.: Predicate abstraction and cegar for higher-order model checking. In: Proc. of PLDI (2011)
14. Kobayashi, N., Tabuchi, N., Unno, H.: Higher-order multi-parameter tree transducers and recursion schemes for program verification. In: Proc. of POPL, pp. 495–508 (2010)
15. Ong, C.-H.L.: On model-checking trees generated by higher-order recursion schemes. In: LICS 2006, pp. 81–90 (2006)
16. Ong, C.-H.L., Ramsay, S.: Verifying higher-order programs with pattern-matching algebraic data types. In: Proc. of POPL, pp. 587–598 (2011)
17. Palsberg, J.: Equality-based flow analysis versus recursive types. ACM Trans. Prog. Lang. Syst. 20(6), 1251–1264 (1998)
18. Parkinson, M.J., Bierman, G.M.: Separation logic, abstraction and inheritance. In: Proc. of POPL, pp. 75–86 (2008)
19. Qadeer, S., Rehof, J.: Context-Bounded Model Checking of Concurrent Software. In: Halbwachs, N., Zuck, L.D. (eds.) TACAS 2005. LNCS, vol. 3440, pp. 93–107. Springer, Heidelberg (2005)
20. Ramalingam, G.: Context-sensitive synchronization-sensitive analysis is undecidable. ACM Trans. Prog. Lang. Syst. 22(2), 416–430 (2000)
21. Rondon, P.M., Kawaguchi, M., Jhala, R.: Liquid types. In: PLDI 2008, pp. 159–169 (2008)
22. Rowe, R., Van Bakel, S.: Approximation Semantics and Expressive Predicate Assignment for Object-Oriented Programming (Extended Abstract). In: Ong, L. (ed.) TLCA 2011. LNCS, vol. 6690, pp. 229–244. Springer, Heidelberg (2011)
23. Skalka, C.: Types and trace effects for object orientation. Higher-Order and Symbolic Computation 21(3), 239–282 (2008)
24. Tsukada, T., Kobayashi, N.: Untyped Recursion Schemes and Infinite Intersection Types. In: Ong, L. (ed.) FOSSACS 2010. LNCS, vol. 6014, pp. 343–357. Springer, Heidelberg (2010)
25. Unno, H., Tabuchi, N., Kobayashi, N.: Verification of Tree-Processing Programs via Higher-Order Model Checking. In: Ueda, K. (ed.) APLAS 2010. LNCS, vol. 6461, pp. 312–327. Springer, Heidelberg (2010)

Counterexample-Guided Precondition Inference*

Mohamed Nassim Seghir and Daniel Kroening

Computer Science Department, University of Oxford

Abstract. The precondition for an assertion inside a procedure is useful for understanding, verifying and debugging programs. As the procedure might be used in multiple calling-contexts within a program, the precondition should be sufficiently general to enable re-use. We present an extension of counterexample-guided abstraction refinement (CEGAR) for automated precondition inference. Starting with an over-approximation of both the set of safe and unsafe states, we iteratively refine them until they become disjoint. The resulting precondition is then necessary and sufficient for the validity of the assertion, which prevents false alarms. We have implemented our approach in a tool called P-Gen. We present experimental results on string and array-manipulating programs.

1   Introduction

Software model checking is a popular technique for program verification. A diverse range of tools based on this approach have been developed (e.g., SLAM [1], BLAST [20], MAGIC [7], SATABS [8] and TERMINATOR [11]) and successfully applied to real-world software. The key to effectiveness of these tools is *abstraction*, and predicate abstraction [16] is a well-established instance. The predicate discovery in tools implementing it is driven by *counterexample-guided abstraction refinement* [9], commonly known as CEGAR.

Most of the tools above answer the usual verification question: "given an assertion at some program location, is this assertion always valid?" When considering just a fragment of a program containing an assertion, we can ask a slightly different question: "In which context is the assertion valid?" The code fragment might be a procedure that is called at different program locations, hence the computed context should be as general as possible to be reusable at the different call sites. A simple and straightforward way to infer a precondition is to compute a conservative abstraction of the set of unsafe states, i.e., those states that can reach an error, and using its complement as precondition. The problem with this approach is that an over-approximation of the set of unsafe states might include safe states as well, resulting in an over-conservative precondition. The abstraction must then be refined by removing some of the safe states. This cannot always be performed in an enumerative fashion, as the set of safe states is often infinite.

* Supported by ERC project 280053, EPSRC project EP/H017585/1, the EU FP7 STREP PINCETTE and the ARTEMIS VETESS project.

M. Felleisen and P. Gardner (Eds.): ESOP 2013, LNCS 7792, pp. 451–471, 2013.

We propose a solution to this problem based on the abstraction (and thus generalization) of both the set of safe and unsafe states. Our approach is based on the CEGAR paradigm: starting with an over-approximation of both sets, we iteratively refine them until they become disjoint. Thus, the resulting precondition is sufficient and also necessary for the validity of the assertion. This guarantees the absence of false alarms, as the violation of the precondition by some calling context entails the violation of the assertion within the procedure. Our contributions are summarized as follows:

- A novel approach to generate *exact* preconditions, i.e., necessary and sufficient. Thus, the precondition is independent from the calling context. Most of the approaches in the literature generate preconditions that are only sufficient, thus the precondition often has to be re-adjusted if it is not satisfied by some calling context. In our case, a violation of the precondition will result in a real error, and we thus avoid false alarms.
- An implementation of the approach using ingredients that are common to most CEGAR-based verification tools. Thus, our technique represents a generic scheme for extending other tools to infer preconditions.
- A simple predicate inference mechanism for algorithms that manipulate arrays used on top of the standard predicate refinement procedure. This simple technique generates predicates that are often adequate to obtain the right program invariant and subsequently obtain the desired precondition.

The remainder of this paper is organized as follows: Section 2 illustrates our approach by means of examples. Section 3 introduces background material. Section 4 describes our approach for precondition inference and the refinement technique used in the CEGAR loop. Section 5 presents experimental results and Section 6 discusses related work.

2   Examples

Consider the program copy given in Figure 1(a). It takes as parameters two arrays a and b and the length b_l of array b. The program copies the elements of array b in the range $\{0, \ldots, b\_l - 1\}$ to the corresponding range in array a. The access to array a is safe if the index expression is in the range $\{0, \ldots, a\_l - 1\}$, where a_l is the length of array a. It is trivial to see that the lower bound is not violated. Let us then focus on the upper bound. The safety condition with regards to the upper bound is expressed by the assertion at location ℓ_2. Our goal is to find a precondition for procedure copy that guarantees that this assertion is never violated. The precondition must be expressed only using program elements visible at the entry-point of the procedure, i.e., it must be a predicate over the procedure parameters and the global variables. The precondition should also be *exact*, i.e., it should neither be too strong nor too weak.

Transformation to reachability. We will now illustrate our approach to precondition inference. We use standard notation and formally represent programs in

```
void copy(int a[], int b [], int b_1)          void copy_2(int a[], int b [])
{                                              {
    int i;                                         int i;
ℓ_0 : i = 0;                                    ℓ_0 : i = 0;
ℓ_1 : while(i < b_1)                            ℓ_1 : while(b[i] != 0)
    {                                              {
ℓ_2 :    assert(i < a_1);                       ℓ_2 :    assert(i < a_1);
         a[i] = b[i];                                    a[i] = b[i];
         i++;                                            i++;
    }                                              }
}                                              }

                (a)                                            (b)
```

Fig. 1. Two simple programs that copy a range of elements from array b to array a. In procedure copy, the limit of the range to be copied is explicitly given via b_1. In copy_2, the range is implicitly delimited via the sentinel value 0.

terms of transition constraints over primed and unprimed program variables. The set of transition constraints corresponding to program copy (Figure 1(a)) is given in Figure 2(a) and the associated control flow graph is given in Figure 2(b). The program counter is modeled explicitly using the variable pc, which ranges over the set of control locations. The assertion in the original program is replaced with a conditional branch whose condition is the negation of the assertion and whose target is the error location ℓ_E. The special location ℓ_F is the *final location*, and has no successor.

Observe that the error location is only reachable if $i \geq a\_1$ evaluates to true at location ℓ_2. The final location ℓ_F is reached in paths without error. The transition τ_0 corresponds to the initialization of variable i. The transition τ_1 represents the entrance to the loop and τ_2 the exit from the loop. The assertion is modeled via the transition τ_3, which conditionally alters the control flow to the error location. Finally, the transition τ_4 models the remainder of the loop body after the assert statement. Arrays a and b are represented by uninterpreted function symbols, and $a[x := e]$ denotes function update (the expression is equal to a where the xth element has been replaced by e).

Over-approximating the unsafe states. It is in general not possible to enumerate all the traces of a program. In our example, the program contains a cycle $\langle \tau_1; \tau_4 \rangle$ (Figure 2(b)) that can be unfolded an indefinite number of times, leading to an infinite number of traces. A solution to this problem is to provide a *backwards inductive invariant*: an invariant that includes all error states and which is inductive under the application of wp[1]. Predicate abstraction [16] is a suitable

---

[1] $\text{wp}(\tau, \varphi)$ is the weakest precondition for the formula φ with respect to statement (transition constraint) τ. It extends to a sequence of statements (trace) π.

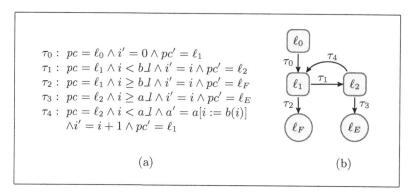

Fig. 2. Transition constraints for program copy (a) and the corresponding graphical representation (b) or the control flow graph

technique for building such an invariant. The key challenge when applying predicate abstraction is the choice of predicates.

Naive approaches for inferring predicates, e.g., based on weakest preconditions, often diverge [22]. In our example, suppose that we first obtain the error path $\tau_0; \tau_1; \tau_3$ from the abstract model. The analysis of this path via wp, i.e., $\mathsf{wp}(\tau_0; \tau_1; \tau_3, pc = \ell_E)$, gives us the formula $0 < b\_l \wedge 0 \geq a\_l$. We add the predicates $0 < b\_l$ and $0 \geq a\_l$ and set the precondition φ to be $0 \geq b\_l \vee 0 < a\_l$. If we unfold the loop once more we obtain the error trace $\tau_0; \tau_1; \tau_4; \tau_1; \tau_3$. We have $\mathsf{wp}(\tau_0; \tau_1; \tau_4; \tau_1; \tau_3, pc = \ell_E) \equiv 1 < b\_l \wedge 1 \geq a\_l$. This new trace is not covered by the previous one, as it is still feasible under our precondition φ. We then update φ to rule out the new trace to obtain $(0 \geq b\_l \vee 0 < a\_l) \wedge (1 \geq b\_l \vee 1 < a\_l)$. After unfolding the loop j times, we obtain $\mathsf{wp}(\tau_0; \langle \tau_1; \tau_4 \rangle^j; \tau_1; \tau_3, pc = \ell_E) \equiv j < b\_l \wedge j \geq a\_l$ and the precondition

$$\varphi \equiv \bigwedge_{j>0} j \geq b\_l \vee j < a\_l \, .$$

We can continue to unfold the loop, every time generating a new trace that is not covered by the previous ones. To address this divergence, we go beyond the syntactic approach to predicate discovery and use techniques to infer more general facts. For example, by linearly combining the predicates $0 < b\_l$ and $0 \geq a\_l$ (from the first iteration) we deduce $a\_l < b\_l$. This new predicate is a backwards invariant at location ℓ_0 with respect to the program, i.e.,

$$(\bigvee_{j>0} \mathsf{wp}(\pi_j, pc = \ell_E)) \Rightarrow (pc = \ell_0 \Rightarrow a\_l < b\_l) \, .$$

Thus, the predicate $a\_l < b\_l$ over-approximates the set of states that reach the error location. The precondition φ is then simply chosen to be $a\_l \geq b\_l$, i.e., the complement of that set.

Over-approximating the Safe States. When over-approximating the set of states that reach the error location, we always include all error states but may include some safe entry states as well. It means that the precondition, which is the complement of the computed set, may exclude safe traces and is thus unnecessarily strong. To tune the precision of the abstracted set of error states, our new algorithm also over-approximates the set of entry states that reach the final location ℓ_F (the safe states). We then check the intersection of this set with the (over-approximation of the) states that reach the error location. If the intersection is empty, we conclude that our current set of unsafe states does not include any safe state.

As we did for the error location, we obtain the over-approximation of the set of states reaching the final location given as the state formula $a\_l \geq b\_l \vee 0 \geq b\_l$. The intersection of this set with the set of unsafe states ($a\_l < b\_l$) is obtained by forming the conjunction:

$$(a\_l \geq b\_l \vee 0 \geq b\_l) \wedge (a\_l < b\_l) .$$

The formula above has satisfying assignments, which means that the two sets are not disjoint. As $a\_l \geq b\_l$ and $a\_l < b\_l$ are inconsistent, the intersection can only be in $0 \geq b\_l$. Thus, from $0 \geq b\_l$ we can reach both the error and final location. This outcome is caused by insufficient precision of the abstraction. Let us consider two traces, $\pi_E = \tau_0; \tau_1; \tau_3$ leading to the error location, and $\pi_F = \tau_0; \tau_2$ leading to the final location. We have $\mathsf{wp}(\pi_E, pc = \ell_E) \equiv 0 < b\_l \wedge 0 \geq a\_l$ and $\mathsf{wp}(\pi_F, pc = \ell_F) \equiv 0 \geq b\_l$. Thus, π_E is not feasible from states with $0 \geq b\_l$, which means that the set of unsafe states is not precise enough. It is then refined by adding the predicate $b\_l > 0$, which makes the two sets disjoint. The final precondition φ is given by

$$0 \geq b\_l \vee a\_l \geq b\_l .$$

The precondition φ is now necessary and sufficient, meaning that it does not allow any state to reach the error location and does not exclude any state that reaches the final location.

Inferring quantified preconditions. Let us consider a slightly modified version of the previous program copy, which is given in Figure 1(b). In this example, the range of elements to be copied from array b to a is not explicit, as it is indicated via a sentinel value (0 in the example). After going through the different steps described for the previous example, our method succeeds in inferring the precondition

$$(b[0] = 0) \vee (\exists x \in \{0, \ldots, a\_l\}. \, b[x] = 0) .$$

Observe that the precondition inferred by the algorithm is not equivalent to $\exists x \in \{0, \ldots, a\_l\}. \, b[x] = 0$; it is weaker. This is due the possibility of skipping the loop when $b[i] \neq 0$ is false, regardless of the value of a_l. This implies that runs from states in which $b[0] = 0$ are safe. This case is expressed via the first disjunct of the precondition above. We will re-visit the second example in Section 4 to illustrate our refinement procedure.

3   Preliminaries

In this section, we provide background on counterexample-guided abstraction refinement for predicate abstraction.

Program. To aid the formal presentation, we assume that a program is given as a set $\mathcal{TC}$ of transition constraints τ. A transition constraint τ is a formula of the form

$$g(X) \wedge x'_1 = e_1(X) \wedge \ldots \wedge x'_n = e_n(X) \tag{1}$$

where $X = \langle x_1, \ldots, x_n \rangle$ is a tuple (vector) of program variables, which include the program counter pc. In (1), unprimed variables refer to the program state before performing the transition and primed ones represent the program state after performing the transition. Formula $g(X)$ is called the *guard* and the remaining conjuncts of τ are the *update* or *assignment*.

Representing States Symbolically. Let us write $V = \{x_1, \ldots, x_n\}$ for the set of variables of the program (including the program counter pc). For a variable $x \in V$, $Type(x)$ is the type (range) of x and $\sigma(x)$ is a valuation of x such that $\sigma(x) \in Type(x)$. The variable pc ranges over the set of all program locations. Given X (a tuple of the variables), a program state is the valuation $\sigma(X) = \langle \sigma(x_1), \ldots, \sigma(x_n) \rangle$.

A set of program states S is represented symbolically by means of the *characteristic function* of S. The formula φ represents the set of all those states that correspond to a satisfying assignment of φ, i.e., $\{\sigma(X) \mid \varphi[\sigma(X)/X]\}^2$. We will use sets and their characteristic functions interchangeably. Symbolic states (formulas) are partially ordered via the implication operator $\Rightarrow$, i.e., $\varphi' \leq \varphi$ means $\varphi' \Rightarrow \varphi$.

State transformer. For a formula φ, the application of the operator pre with respect to the transition constraint τ returns a formula representing the set of all predecessor states of φ under the transition constraint τ, formally

$$\mathsf{pre}(\tau, \varphi(X)) \equiv g(X) \wedge \varphi[\langle e_1(X), \ldots, e_n(X) \rangle / X] .$$

For the whole program $\mathcal{TC}$, pre is given by

$$\mathsf{pre}(\varphi(X)) \equiv \bigvee_{\tau \in \mathcal{TC}} \mathsf{pre}(\tau, \varphi(X)) .$$

For a trace $\pi = \tau_1; \ldots; \tau_n$, we have

$$\mathsf{pre}(\tau_1; \ldots; \tau_n, \varphi) = \mathsf{pre}(\tau_1, \ldots \mathsf{pre}(\tau_{n-1}, \mathsf{pre}(\tau_n, \varphi))) .$$

If $\mathsf{pre}(\pi, \varphi)$ is not equivalent to false, then the trace π is *feasible*.

---

[2] The notation $f[Y/X]$ represents the expression obtained by replacing all occurrences of every variable from the vector X in f with the corresponding variable (value) from Y. It naturally extends to a collection (set or list) of expressions.

(Un)Safe states To ease the presentation, let us assume that the program contains a single error location ℓ_E and a single final location ℓ_F ($\ell_E \neq \ell_F$).[3] We denote by bad the set of *error states*, which is simply given by $pc = \ell_E$. Similarly, we call final the set of *final states*, which is represented by $pc = \ell_F$.

The set of safe states safe contains all states from which a final state is reachable. Formally,

$$\mathsf{safe} \equiv \mathsf{lfp}(\mathsf{pre}, \mathsf{final}) \tag{2}$$

where $\mathsf{lfp}(\mathsf{pre}, \varphi)$ denotes the least fixpoint of the operator pre above φ. Similarly, unsafe is the set of all states from which an error (bad) state is reachable:

$$\mathsf{unsafe} \equiv \mathsf{lfp}(\mathsf{pre}, \mathsf{bad}) \ . \tag{3}$$

The least fixpoints represent inductive backwards invariants, which we denote by ψ_{bad} and ψ_{final}, respectively. The invariants are inductive under pre, i.e.,

- $\mathsf{bad} \leq \psi_{\mathsf{bad}}$ and $\mathsf{final} \leq \psi_{\mathsf{final}}$
- $\mathsf{pre}(\psi_{\mathsf{bad}}) \leq \psi_{\mathsf{bad}}$ and $\mathsf{pre}(\psi_{\mathsf{final}}) \leq \psi_{\mathsf{final}}$

In the absence of non-determinism in the program, the sets of unsafe and safe states are disjoint, and we have

$$\mathsf{unsafe} \wedge \mathsf{safe} \equiv \mathsf{false} \ .$$

Predicate Abstraction. Predicate abstraction consists of approximating a state φ with a formula φ' constructed as a Boolean combination of predicates taken from a set P. Here, the term approximation means that any model that satisfies φ must satisfy φ'. Thus, a suitable approximation is obtained via the logical implication "$\Rightarrow$", i.e., φ' is the strongest Boolean combination built up from predicates taken from the finite set P such that $\varphi \Rightarrow \varphi'$.

Defining the abstraction function α as being the strongest Boolean combination of predicates in P is not practical because of the exponential complexity of the problem. Therefore, we use a lightweight version of α that consists of building the strongest conjunction of predicates in P:

$$\alpha(\varphi) \equiv \bigwedge p \ \mid \ p \in P \wedge \varphi \Rightarrow p \ .$$

Let us have $\mathcal{D}^{\sharp}$ the domain of formulas built up from the finite set of predicates P. The domain $\mathcal{D}^{\sharp}$ is not closed under pre, therefore, we define $\mathsf{pre}^{\sharp}$ under which $\mathcal{D}^{\sharp}$ is closed. Let us associate the concretization function $\gamma : \mathcal{D}^{\sharp} \to \mathcal{D}$ to α, we simply choose γ to be the identity function. Functions α and γ form a *Galois connection* with respect to $\geq$ ($\Leftarrow$) being the partial order relation for both $\mathcal{D}$ and $\mathcal{D}^{\sharp}$. Formally speaking

$$\forall x \in \mathcal{D} \ \forall y \in \mathcal{D}^{\sharp}. \ \alpha(x) \geq y \Leftrightarrow x \geq \gamma(y) \ .$$

---

[3] In case of multiple assertions, we add an edge from each assertion (guarded with the negation of the assertion) to ℓ_E. Similar treatment can be applied in the case of multiple return locations.

Hence, we define $\mathsf{pre}^\sharp : \mathcal{D}^\sharp \to \mathcal{D}^\sharp$, the abstract version of pre, as follows:

$$\mathsf{pre}^\sharp(\varphi) \equiv \alpha(\mathsf{pre}(\gamma(\varphi))) \,,$$

and thus

$$\mathsf{pre}^\sharp(\tau, \varphi) = \alpha(\mathsf{pre}(\tau, \varphi)) = \bigwedge p \ \mid \ p \in P \wedge \mathsf{pre}(\tau, \varphi) \Rightarrow p \,.$$

As seen for pre, the operator $\mathsf{pre}^\sharp$ also extends to traces. Henceforth, whenever we write $\mathsf{pre}^\sharp_P$ we mean that the abstraction (image) is computed by considering predicates from the set P.

The lattice of abstract states $(\mathcal{L}, \Rightarrow)$ is finite as the set of predicates is finite. Therefore, $\mathsf{lfp}(\mathsf{pre}^\sharp, \mathsf{bad})$ ($\mathsf{lfp}(\mathsf{pre}^\sharp, \mathsf{final})$), the least fixpoint for $\mathsf{pre}^\sharp$ above bad (final) in $\mathcal{L}$, is computable.

4   Precondition Inference

The precondition inference problem can be described as the computation of a formula φ such that:

$$\mathsf{lfp}(\mathsf{pre}, \mathsf{bad}) \wedge \varphi \equiv \mathsf{false} \tag{4}$$

The fixpoint for the preimage-operator pre is in general not computable, we thus compute the least fixpoint for $\mathsf{pre}^\sharp$. As we have $\mathsf{lfp}(\mathsf{pre}, \mathsf{bad}) \leq \mathsf{lfp}(\mathsf{pre}^\sharp, \mathsf{bad})$, it is sufficient to show that

$$\mathsf{lfp}(\mathsf{pre}^\sharp, \mathsf{bad}) \wedge \varphi \equiv \mathsf{false}$$

to conclude the validity of (4). The precondition φ can then be simply chosen as the negation of $\mathsf{lfp}(\mathsf{pre}^\sharp, \mathsf{bad})$ projected on the entry location. One problem with this approach is that due to the abstraction we may exclude some of the safe, terminating runs. A second challenge is the choice of predicates. We have seen in the illustrative example that a bad choice of predicates can lead to divergence. In what follows, we present a new CEGAR-based algorithm for precondition inference that guarantees that all safe executions are included in the precondition. We also propose a predicate discovery mechanism that goes beyond the approach based on weakest precondition.

4.1   Counterexample-Guided Precondition Inference

Our goal is to increase the precision of the set of unsafe states $\mathsf{unsafe}^\sharp$, making it free of safe states. This is non-trivial, since we cannot enumerate safe states, as there are in general infinitely many. Hence, we need to construct the set of safe states by over-approximating them as well. Our idea consists of building abstractions of increasing precision of both the set of safe and unsafe states until they become disjoint. We propose an implementation of this idea by extending the classical CEGAR paradigm, where its main ingredients are instantiated in our setting with the following:

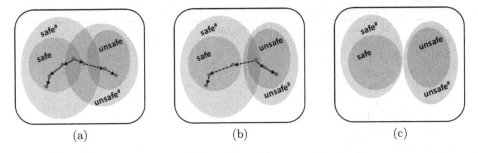

Fig. 3. Illustration of the main phases of algorithm InferPrecond. Dashed arrows indicate that the trace is spurious.

- **Abstraction**: we abstract both the set of safe and unsafe states.
- **Counterexample**: in our context, a counterexample is *two* abstract traces, a safe one and an unsafe one, beginning with a common initial state.
- **Counterexample simulation**: checks if the two traces can be concretized to effectively share a common concrete initial state. This is only possible in the presence of non-determinism in the program. The check is carried out by computing the weakest precondition for each trace. Hence, the counterexample is spurious if the two preconditions are disjoint.
- **Refinement**: the spurious counterexample is ruled out by adding predicates that refine the abstraction such that the two traces cannot share their initial state.
- **Termination criterion**: the iterative process stops when the two abstractions (of safe and unsafe states) are disjoint.

We present algorithm InferPrecond (Algorithm 1), which implements a counterexample-guided abstraction refinement loop for precondition inference. The algorithm starts with an over-approximation of both the set of safe and unsafe states (lines 5 and 6), denoted by $\mathsf{safe}^\sharp$ and $\mathsf{unsafe}^\sharp$, respectively. It iteratively refines them until their projections onto the initial location become disjoint, i.e., $(\mathsf{safe}^\sharp \wedge \mathsf{unsafe}^\sharp \wedge pc = \ell_0) \equiv \mathsf{false}$ (Figure 3(c)). The computed precondition is then the set of safe states projected onto the initial location ℓ_0 (line 8 of the algorithm).

The refinement process is applied whenever $\mathsf{safe}^\sharp$ and $\mathsf{unsafe}^\sharp$ intersect, i.e., when we have a bad trace and a safe one sharing their initial state. In Figure 3(a), $\mathsf{safe}^\sharp$ and $\mathsf{unsafe}^\sharp$ intersect, but the analysis reveals that the initial state is in reality in safe, thus the (dashed) trace in $\mathsf{unsafe}^\sharp$ is the one that is spurious. After refining $\mathsf{unsafe}^\sharp$, we obtain the abstraction in Figure 3(b). The two sets still intersect, however this time the spurious trace is in $\mathsf{safe}^\sharp$, as the initial state belongs to unsafe. The refinement process is carried out by calling the procedure Refine at line 14. This procedure takes as parameters two traces, one leading to the error location and another one leading to the final location, and returns a new set of predicates. We describe this procedure in detail in the next section.

Algorithm 1. InferPrecond

Input: set of transition constraints (program) $\mathcal{TC}$
Output: formula (precondition)

1 **Var** P: set of predicates;
2 **Var** safe$^\sharp$, unsafe$^\sharp$: formula;
3 $P := \emptyset$;
4 **while** true **do**
5   unsafe$^\sharp$:= lfp(pre$^\sharp_P$, bad);
6   safe$^\sharp$:= lfp(pre$^\sharp_P$, final);
7   **if** (safe$^\sharp \wedge$ unsafe$^\sharp \wedge pc = \ell_0) \equiv$ false **then**
8   **return** (safe$^\sharp \wedge pc = \ell_0$);
9   Let π_E and π_F two traces s.t. pre$^\sharp_P(\pi_E,$ bad$) \wedge$ pre$^\sharp_P(\pi_F,$ final$) \not\equiv$ false;
10   **if** pre$(\pi_E,$ bad$) \wedge$ pre$(\pi_F,$ final$) \not\equiv$ false **then**
11   print("warning: non-determinism in program");
12   **exit**;
13   **else**
14          $P := P \cup$ Refine(π_E, π_F);

Proposition 1. *The precondition* φ *computed by algorithm* InferPrecond *(a) guarantees the non-reachability of bad states and (b) the non-exclusion of safe terminating traces.*

Proof. **(a)** φ *guarantees non-reachability of bad states.* As computed by algorithm InferPrecond, $\varphi \equiv$ safe$^\sharp \wedge pc = \ell_0$. Let us assume that there are states in φ from which a bad state can be reached. Thus, there is an error trace π_E such that

$$\mathsf{pre}(\pi_E, \mathsf{bad}) \wedge \mathsf{safe}^\sharp \wedge pc = \ell_0 \not\equiv \mathsf{false} \tag{5}$$

We also know that

$$\mathsf{pre}(\pi_E, \mathsf{bad}) \Rightarrow \mathsf{unsafe}^\sharp , \tag{6}$$

as lfp(pre, bad) $\leq$ lfp(pre$^\sharp$, bad). From (5) and (6) we obtain

$$\mathsf{unsafe}^\sharp \wedge \mathsf{safe}^\sharp \wedge pc = \ell_0 \not\equiv \mathsf{false} ,$$

which contradicts the return condition at line 7 of algorithm InferPrecond.

(b) φ *does not exclude safe terminating traces.* Let us assume that φ excludes a given safe terminating trace π_F from ℓ_0 to ℓ_F, which means that

$$\mathsf{pre}(\pi_F, \mathsf{final}) \wedge \mathsf{safe}^\sharp \equiv \mathsf{false}$$

or

$$\mathsf{pre}(\pi_F, \mathsf{final}) \Rightarrow \neg\mathsf{safe}^\sharp . \tag{7}$$

We also have

$$\mathsf{pre}(\pi_F, \mathsf{final}) \Rightarrow \mathsf{safe}^\sharp , \tag{8}$$

as $\mathsf{lfp}(\mathsf{pre}, \mathsf{final}) \leq \mathsf{lfp}(\mathsf{pre}^\sharp, \mathsf{final})$. From (7) and (8) we conclude $\mathsf{pre}(\pi_F, \mathsf{final}) \equiv$ false, which means that such a trace π_F is not feasible.   □

As program model checking is not decidable, we have no guarantee for termination of algorithm InferPrecond. However, whenever it terminates, the previous proposition holds.

4.2   Refinement for Precondition Inference

The main goal of refinement is to generate the minimal possible set of predicates that rule out a maximum number of spurious traces. Hence, the generated predicates must be as general as possible. We present procedure Refine, which takes as parameters two traces, one trace π_E leading to the error location, and another one π_F leading to the final location. The returned result is a set of predicates P that enables the verifier to show the following:

$$\mathsf{pre}_P^\sharp(\pi_E, \mathsf{bad}) \wedge \mathsf{pre}_P^\sharp(\pi_F, \mathsf{final}) \equiv \mathsf{false} \ .$$

The procedure Refine relies on several other procedures: atoms, MinCorePrio and ExtractNewPreds. The procedure atoms is simply defined as

$$\mathsf{atoms}(\varphi_1 \wedge \ldots \wedge \varphi_n) = \{\varphi_1, \ldots, \varphi_n\} \ .$$

It takes a conjunction φ and returns the set of its conjuncts.

The procedure MinCorePrio takes three arguments. The first one is a conjunction φ, the second one is an arbitrary formula φ' and the third one is a list L of formulas. As precondition, φ and φ' must be inconsistent. The procedure computes a minimal core of the conjunction φ that is inconsistent with the second argument φ'. There is usually more than one core that can be returned. This choice can be controlled by means of L, the third argument. MinCorePrio gives priority to the set of formulas in L to appear in the resulting minimal core, as illustrated by Algorithm 3. The list L is sorted in ascending order according the priority of its elements. The algorithm proceeds by eliminating irrelevant predicates (conjuncts) of lesser priority (front) first. A predicate is irrelevant if its removal does not have an impact on the inconsistency of the new conjunction with φ'. The lowest priority is given to basic predicates in φ by storing them in the front of the list L (line 6). The consistency test at line 12 of the algorithm is carried out by calling a theorem prover.

Finally, procedure ExtractNewPreds implements a heuristic for predicate inference. It takes a conjunction as argument and returns a list of predicates sorted in ascending order of their likely importance to the convergence of the main CE-GAR loop. We will describe this procedure in more details later in this section.

Back to the main procedure Refine, we see that it first computes the weakest precondition (pre) for each of the two traces taken as parameters (lines 4 and 5) to obtain formulas ψ_E and ψ_F. It then applies ExtractNewPreds to augment ψ_E and ψ_F with new facts induced by the two formulas (lines 6, 7, 9, 10). Finally, the minimal unsatisfiabile cores of ψ_E and of ψ_F are computed (lines 8 and 11)

Algorithm 2. Refine

Input: two traces π_E and π_F
Output: set of predicates P

1 **Var** P (initially empty), S_E, S_F: set of formulas;
2 **Var** P_{new}: list of formulas;
3 **Var** ψ_E, ψ_F: formula;
4 $\psi_E := \mathsf{pre}(\pi_E, \mathsf{bad})$;
5 $\psi_F := \mathsf{pre}(\pi_F, \mathsf{final})$;
6 $P_{new} := \mathsf{ExtractNewPreds}(\psi_E)$;
7 $\psi_E := \psi_E \wedge (\bigwedge_{p \in P_{new}} p)$;
8 $\psi_E := \mathsf{MinCorePrio}(\psi_E, \psi_F, P_{new})$;
9 $P_{new} := \mathsf{ExtractNewPreds}(\psi_F)$;
10 $\psi_F := \psi_F \wedge (\bigwedge_{p \in P_{new}} p)$;
11 $\psi_F := \mathsf{MinCorePrio}(\psi_F, \psi_E, P_{new})$;
12 $P := P \cup \mathsf{atoms}(\psi_E) \cup \mathsf{atoms}(\psi_F)$;
13 **Let** $\pi_E = \tau_1; \ldots; \tau_i$;
14 **Let** $\pi_F = \tau'_1; \ldots; \tau'_j$;
15 **Let** $S_E = \bigcup_{k=1}^{i} \{\varphi_k\}$ s.t. $\varphi_k \equiv \mathsf{pre}(\tau_k; \ldots; \tau_i, \mathsf{bad})$;
16 **Let** $S_F = \bigcup_{k=1}^{j} \{\varphi'_k\}$ s.t. $\varphi'_k \equiv \mathsf{pre}(\tau'_k; \ldots; \tau'_j, \mathsf{final})$;
17 **foreach** k *in range* $\{1, \ldots, i-1\}$ **do**
18 $\quad$ $P_{new} := \mathsf{ExtractNewPreds}(\varphi_{k+1})$;
19 $\quad$ $\varphi_{k+1} := \varphi_{k+1} \wedge (\bigwedge_{p \in P_{new}} p)$;
20 $\quad$ $\psi_E := \mathsf{MinCorePrio}(\varphi_{k+1}[X'/X], \tau_k \wedge \neg\psi_E, P_{new}[X'/X])$;
21 $\quad$ $P := P \cup \mathsf{atoms}(\psi_E[X/X'])$;
22 **foreach** k *in range* $\{1, \ldots, j-1\}$ **do**
23 $\quad$ $P_{new} := \mathsf{ExtractNewPreds}(\varphi'_{k+1})$;
24 $\quad$ $\varphi'_{k+1} := \varphi'_{k+1} \wedge (\bigwedge_{p \in P_{new}} p)$;
25 $\quad$ $\psi_F := \mathsf{MinCorePrio}(\varphi'_{k+1}[X'/X], \tau'_k \wedge \neg\psi_F, P_{new}[X'/X])$;
26 $\quad$ $P := P \cup \mathsf{atoms}(\psi_F[X/X'])$;
27 **return** P;

---

and conjuncts appearing in either of them are added to the set of predicates (line 12).

In the next phase of the algorithm, the two formulas ψ_E and ψ_F are used to guide the inference of new predicates from states (φ_k's and φ'_k's) belonging to the error trace π_E (first loop, lines 17–21) and to the safe one π_F (second loop, lines 22–26). Along each trace and for each triple of pre-state ψ, transition τ and post-state φ, we want to compute the minimal core φ_m of φ augmented with facts inferred via $\mathsf{ExtractNewPreds}$ such that $\mathsf{pre}(\tau, \varphi_m) \Rightarrow \psi$, i.e., $\varphi_m[X'/X] \wedge \tau \wedge \neg\psi \equiv$ false. This amounts to computing the minimal core of $\varphi_m[X'/X]$ with respect to $\tau \wedge \neg\psi$, as performed in lines 20 and 25 of the algorithm.

The procedure $\mathsf{ExtractNewPreds}$ is applied to the states of π_E and π_F, i.e., the φ_k's and φ'_k's of each trace. These states are obtained via a backward analysis of π_E and π_F during the initial phase of the algorithm (lines 4 and 5). As mentioned earlier, the operator pre (also wp in our case) is limited in inferring

---

Algorithm 3. MinCorePrio

    Input: φ a conjunction of formulas, φ' a formula, L a list of formulas
    Output: a conjunction of formulas
1 **Var** φ'': formula;
2 **Var** S: set of formulas;
3 **Var** L, L': list of formulas;
4 $S := \mathsf{atoms}(\varphi)$;
5 $L' := L$;
6 add elements of S to L' in the front;
7 add elements of L to S;
8 **foreach** *formula* $\varphi_L \in L'$ **do**
9   **if** $S - \{\varphi_L\} = \emptyset$ **then**
10   **return** φ_L;
11     $\varphi'' := \bigwedge \varphi \mid \varphi \in S - \{\varphi_L\}$;
12   **if** $\varphi'' \wedge \varphi' \equiv \mathsf{false}$ **then**
13        $S := S - \{\varphi_L\}$;
14 $\varphi'' := \bigwedge \varphi \mid \varphi \in S$;
15 **return** φ'';

---

relevant predicates, as it fails to generalize. Therefore, procedure MinCorePrio biases the computation of the minimal core by giving priority to predicates found via ExtractNewPreds, which are more likely to be general.

4.3 Predicate Inference

The procedure ExtractNewPreds plays a key role in our approach. It is based on a system of inference rules in the spirit of [23], where an interpolation procedure [19] is used to find predicates, followed by the application of a system of inference rules to deduce *range predicates*. In [23], the interpolant provides a concise description of the cause of infeasibility of traces, thus the base formula is already minimal. However, the application of the inference rules may introduce redundancies. In our case, MinCorePrio is applied after inferring the new facts, hence, it prevents the inundation of the system with irrelevant predicates. This is not just an optimization: during our experiments, this step has often made the difference between termination and divergence. The system of inference rules that we are using is given in Figure 4.

Predicate inference system. Divergence of the refinement process is often caused by predicates over variables that are increasing or decreasing (counters). This leads to the generation of sequences of constants when loops are effectively unfolded. Another cause of divergence are arrays with counter variables in their index expressions. A simple solution, advocated by [22], is to (initially) discard such predicates.

$$\frac{c_1.e + e_1 \geq 0 \ , \ -c_2.e + e_2 \geq 0}{c_2.e_1 + c_1.e_2 \geq 0} \ (\text{ELIM})$$
$$(c_1, c_2 > 0)$$

$$\frac{x - e \geq 0 \ , \ -x + e \geq 0}{x = e} \ (\text{EQ})$$

$$\frac{\varphi(x) \ , \ x = e}{\varphi(e)} \ (\text{SUB})$$

$$\frac{\varphi(i), \ \neg\varphi(j) \ (i < j)}{\exists x \in \{i, \dots, j\}. \ \varphi(x), \ \exists x \in \{i, \dots, j\}. \ \neg\varphi(x)} \ (\text{EXIST})$$

$$\frac{\exists x \in \{i, \dots, j\}. \ \varphi(x), \ j \leq k}{\exists x \in \{i, \dots, k\}. \ \varphi(x)} \ (\text{EXT\_R})$$

$$\frac{\exists x \in \{i, \dots, j\}. \ \varphi(x), \ k \leq i}{\exists x \in \{k, \dots, j\}. \ \varphi(x)} \ (\text{EXT\_L})$$

$$\frac{\varphi(i)}{\forall x \in \{i\}. \ \varphi(x)} \ (\text{UNIV})$$

$$\frac{\forall x \in \{j, \dots, i\}. \ \varphi(x) \ , \ \forall x \in \{i+1, \dots, k\}. \ \varphi(x)}{\forall x \in \{j, \dots, k\}. \ \varphi(x)} \ (\text{LINK})$$

i and j are integer variables appearing
in a linear index expression in φ ($\neg\varphi$).

Fig. 4. Rules for predicate inference

The aim of the system of rules of Figure 4 is to eliminate likely diverging sequences of predicates whenever possible by inferring new predicates that are more general. Among the symbols used in the system, e refers to linear terms, x is a variable and φ is a formula. The rule ELIM linearly combines two constraints to eliminate common variables. Rule EQ infers equality constraints, which might be used by rule SUB to substitute occurrences of variables with equal terms. The rule UNIV builds a quantified formula and LINK bridges the intervals of two quantified formulas. Finally, the rule EXIST produces two existentially quantified formulas and the rules EXT_R and EXT_L extend the interval of an existentially quantified formula from the right and the left, respectively.

The procedure ExtractNewPreds (Algorithm 4) applies the rules of the inference system to the conjuncts of the formula given as argument and returns a list of predicates sorted in ascending order of priority. A predicate p_1 has higher priority than predicate p_2 if p_1 is produced by a rule where p_2 appears as one of its antecedents. The procedure starts with the list of basic predicates that are extracted from the formula given as argument. These predicates have the lowest priority. It then keeps applying the rules to predicates in the list until saturation, i.e., until no new predicates are produced. The code fragment from line 13 to 17 stores the new predicates according to their priority, i.e., in a position of the list that is beyond the positions of the associated antecedents.

The algorithm terminates as the two rules ELIM and EQ are only applied to basic predicates (condition at line 12). Thus, they will be called a finite number of times generating a finite number of linear constraints. All other rules will generate a finite number of predicates, as they all depend on linear constraints. We furthermore do not consider nested array expressions. The order in which the rules are applied does not matter.

Illustration. Let us illustrate the application of procedure Refine to program copy_2 of Figure 1(b). We call Refine with the error trace $\langle \ell_0, \ell_1, \ell_2, \ell_1, \ell_2, \ell_E \rangle$ and the safe trace $\langle \ell_0, \ell_1, \ell_2, \ell_1, \ell_F \rangle$, which both enter the loop in program copy_2

Algorithm 4. ExtractNewPreds

Input: formula φ
Output: list of formulas
1 **Var** S, S_b: set of formulas;
2 **Var** L, L': list of formulas;
3 **Var** R: list of inference rules;
4 $S_b := \mathsf{atoms}(\varphi)$;
5 insert elements of S_b in L';
6 $R := \{\mathsf{ELIM, EQ, UNIV, SUB, LINK, EXIST, EXT\_L, EXT\_R}\}$;
7 **repeat**
8    $L := L'$;
9   **foreach** *rule* $r \in R$ **do**
10   Let k be the number of premises of r;
11   **foreach** *tuple* $t \in L^k$ **do**
12   **if** $(r \notin \{\mathsf{ELIM, EQ}\}) \vee (\forall i \in \{1, \ldots, k\}.\ t_i \in S_b)$ **then**
13             $S := r(t)$;
14   Let $pos = \max\{pos_j \mid j \in \{1, \ldots, k\} \wedge L[pos_j] = t_j\}$;
15   **foreach** *predicate* $p \in S$ **do**
16   **if** $p \notin L'$ **then**
17   insert p after position *pos* in L';
18 **until** $L = L'$;
19 **return** L;

---

once. The analysis of these two traces is illustrated in Figure 5. The upper table shows results for the error trace and the lower one for the safe trace. In both tables, the first column contains the suffix of the trace that is analyzed backwards using the weakest precondition. The result is shown in the second column. Finally, the third column shows the new predicates that are inferred using the information from the second column. The superscript associated with each predicate is its priority. At the initial location, which corresponds to the second line in both tables, the predicate $\forall x \in \{0, \ldots, a\_l\}.\ b[x] \neq 0$ is the one with the highest priority for the error trace. It is inferred via the application of the rule UNIV followed by SUB.

For the safe trace, we have two predicates of the highest priority, namely $\exists x \in \{0, \ldots, a\_l\}.\ b[x] \neq 0$ and $\exists x \in \{0, \ldots, a\_l\}.\ b[x] = 0$. They are both generated by applying rules EXIST and EXT_R successively. The refinement procedure selects the second predicate as it is the one which separates the two initial states. The selected predicates are underlined in both tables. Going one step backward from the initial location ℓ_0 to location ℓ_1 in both traces, the selected predicates are $\forall x \in \{i, \ldots, a\_l\}.\ b[x] \neq 0$ and $\exists x \in \{i, \ldots, a\_l\}.\ b[x] = 0$ for the error and safe trace, respectively. These are the predicates on which the ones selected at the initial location ℓ_0 depend. One can assert that these two predicates are backwards invariants with respect to the cycle $\langle \ell_1, \ell_2, \ell_1 \rangle$. They thus cover an infinite number of traces.

Error trace	WP	New predicates
$\ell_1, \ell_2, \ell_1, \ell_2, \ell_E$	$i + 1 \geq a\_l, b[i+1] \neq 0, i < a\_l$ $b[i] \neq 0$	$a\_l = i + 1^{(1)}, \forall x \in [i, i+1]. b[x] \neq 0^{(1)}$ $\forall x \in [i, a\_l]. b[x] \neq 0^{(2)}$
$\ell_0, \ell_1, \ell_2, \ell_1, \ell_2, \ell_E$	$1 \geq a\_l, b[1] \neq 0, 0 < a\_l$ $b[0] \neq 0$	$a\_l = 1^{(1)}, \forall x \in [0, 1]. b[x] \neq 0^{(1)}$ $\forall x \in [0, a\_l]. b[x] \neq 0^{(2)}$

Safe trace	WP	New predicates
$\ell_1, \ell_2, \ell_1, \ell_F$	$b[i] \neq 0, i+1 \leq a\_l, b[i+1] = 0$	$\exists x \in [i, i+1]. b[x] \neq 0^{(1)}, \exists x \in [i, i+1]. b[x] = 0^{(1)}$ $\exists x \in [i, a\_l]. b[x] \neq 0^{(2)}, \exists x \in [i, a\_l]. b[x] = 0^{(2)}$
$\ell_0, \ell_1, \ell_2, \ell_1, \ell_F$	$b[0] \neq 0, 1 \leq a\_l, b[1] = 0$	$\exists x \in [0, 1]. b[x] \neq 0^{(1)}, \exists x \in [0, 1]. b[x] = 0^{(1)}$ $\exists x \in [0, a\_l]. b[x] \neq 0^{(2)}, \exists x \in [0, a\_l]. b[x] = 0^{(2)}$

Fig. 5. Illustration of algorithm Refine on program copy_2. The underlined predicates are selected by the refinement process. The superscript is the priority of each predicate.

5   Experimental Results

Implementation. We have implemented our precondition inference technique in the P-Gen[4] tool. P-Gen takes as input a C program containing a procedure annotated with an assertion to be verified. As output, it returns a formula that represents the set of pre-states from which the specified assertion holds for any execution.

Experiments. We performed experiments using a desktop computer with 3.7 GB of RAM and a quad-core processor with 2.83 GHz, running Linux. P-Gen uses several theorem provers to compute the abstraction and analyze counterexamples. We have initially used Yices [15] and Simplify [14], but observed limitations when handling quantified formulas. These limitations often lead to the divergence of CEGAR, as the refinement procedure picks up a set of quantifier-free predicates instead of a quantified predicate, and thus fails to generalize. We have subsequently integrated Z3 [13] and used it running as a standalone process communicating with P-Gen through pipes. The Z3 theorem prover was able to decide many queries that were not handled by the two other theorem provers.

The results of our experiments are summarized in Table 1. The column "Precond." shows the type of precondition inferred ("Q" stands for quantified and "S" stands for simple, i.e., quantifier-free). The column "Iter.U." ("Iter.S.") gives the number of iterations performed by CEGAR to compute the set of unsafe (safe) states and column "Pred.U." ("Pred.S.") gives the number of predicates inferred to abstract the set of unsafe (safe) states. Our tool is based on lazy abstraction [20], we therefore provide the average number of predicates per location instead of the total number of predicates. This number is an indicator for memory consumption, as predicates are encoding program states. Finally, column "Alt." refers to the number of alternations between the two abstractions

---

[4] http://www.cs.ox.ac.uk/people/nassim.seghir/pgen-web-page

Table 1. Experimental results for routines taken from the C string library (upper part) and from real-world programs (lower part)

Program	Precond.	Iter.U.	Pred.U.	Iter.S.	Pred.S.	Alt.	Time (s)
memcmp	Q + S	5	5	8	3	2	23.64
strcat	Q	4	4	4	3	2	0.77
memchr	Q + S	5	4	8	3	2	77.30
strlen	Q	4	4	4	3	2	0.80
memcpy	S	3	2	3	2	1	0.17
memmove	S	5	4	9	2	2	0.91
strchr	Q	5	7	7	4	2	1.92
r_strcat	Q	5	2	3	2	2	9.02
strcspn	Q	5	6	7	4	2	7.30
strspn	Q	5	6	7	4	2	7.05
my_strcmp	Q	5	7	7	4	2	2.70
my_strcpy	Q	4	4	4	3	2	1.41
AllNotNull	Q + S	6	5	5	3	2	2.07
perfc_copy_info	S	7	2	13	2	2	1.94
bitmap_shift_right	S	15	13	26	5	2	41.60
mvswap	S	7	5	8	4	3	0.70
BZ2_hbAssignCodes	S	8	4	6	4	2	0.73

(i.e., the number of times the procedure switches between the abstraction of unsafe states and the abstraction of safe states).

The upper part of the table relates to implementations of routines from the C string library[5]. The last two procedures, my_strcmp and my_strcpy, are modified versions of the original strcmp and strcpy. In the lower part of the table, we have AllNotNull, which was used by Cousot et al. as illustration [12]. Our tool infers a precondition equivalent to the one proposed in their paper. The procedures mvswap and BZ2_hbAssignCodes are taken from the source code of the compression program Bzip2[6]. The procedures perfc_copy_info and bitmap_shift_right belong to the Xen Hypervisor[7].

Although the refinement heuristic performs well in most of the cases, sometimes it does not select adequate predicates in early stages of the iterative process (as for memchr, memcmp and bitmap_shift_right), resulting in high time consumption. However, due to the precision of the precondition, this cost can often be amortised when checking code that uses the functions.

6   Related Work

The work presented in this paper is linked to several topics: predicate abstraction, invariant generation, counterexample-guided refinement, modular verification and

---

[5] http://en.wikibooks.org/wiki/C_Programming/Strings.

[6] http://www.bzip.org/

[7] http://www.xen.org/products/xenhyp.html

precondition inference. Along these axes, we elaborate on some related work from the literature.

The combination of predicate abstraction [16] with counterexample-guided abstraction refinement [9] has been pioneered by the SLAM [1] tool at Microsoft, and has subsequently been implemented in many other tools, including BLAST [20], MAGIC [7], ARMC [25], F-SOFT [21] and SATABS [8]. The DASH [2] and SYNERGY [17] algorithms are variants of this approach, as they are based on program testing to refine abstractions. Even closer to our approach, the tool YASM [18] combines over- and under-approximations to prove or refute program properties. However, all these tools and methods aim at checking the validity of a given assertion. In contrast, we use CEGAR to compute a precondition under which the assertion is valid. Our technique represents a general scheme for extending the previously mentioned tools to infer preconditions, as it uses ingredients that are common to all of them.

Moy proposed a technique to infer preconditions [24] using a combination of state-of-the-art techniques such as abstract interpretation, weakest preconditions and quantifier elimination. While his technique is stronger than many existing ones, it is unable to infer quantified preconditions. Our technique is able to infer universally- as well as existentially-quantified preconditions. Blanc and Kroening proposed a technique to optimize the simulation of SystemC code [3]. It consists of inferring conditions that are sufficient for the commutativity of pairs of processes. Like our algorithm, theirs also is based on CEGAR. However, they have no guarantee that the inferred precondition is exact. Our method does provide this guarantee.

Taghdiri proposed an approach for generating approximations of relations (over pre- and post-states) induced by functions [28]. A function specification (relation) is computed with respect to a context that includes the property to be verified, thus the specification may lack generality. Moreover, the number of times loops are unrolled is bounded, making the approach unsuitable for proving the absence of bugs. Our technique over-approximates the set of all behaviors. Thus, the preconditions computed by our method guarantee safety.

Sankaranarayanan et al. presented a technique that combines test and machine learning to infer likely data preconditions over a set of predicates [27]. In many cases, they were able to learn preconditions that ensure safe executions. However, as their technique is based on testing, it can only suggest preconditions, but does not guarantee their soundness.

In the context of abstract interpretation, Cousot et al. formulated the contract inference problem for intermittent assertions precisely [12]. The precondition extracted by their method does not exclude safe runs even when a non-deterministic choice could lead to bad ones. Our treatment of non-determinism is different, as we report a warning to the user. The method described in [12] as well as [4] and [26] rely on some predefined abstract domains. In our approach, the precision of the abstraction is automatically tuned as required by means of CEGAR. We can also enhance the refinement process by introducing new inference rules, without having to implement new transformers.

Calcagno et al. presented a technique based on Bi-Abduction to infer pre- and post-specifications of the heap [6]. One of the major advantages of their approach is scalability. Similar to their approach, we intend to complete the picture by integrating our method into an inter-procedural reasoning framework. Although we can deal with pointers, the properties handled by their technique are out of the scope for our tool as we do not have a theory to reason about heap properties. On the other side, contrary to our approach, the preconditions they compute are not exact, meaning that they might have to be refined. In the context of termination, Bozga et al. [5], proposed a method to generate exact preconditions for a restricted class of programs. Other techniques for inferring preconditions for termination are applicable to a larger set of programs [10], however they only generate sufficient preconditions.

7 Conclusion

We have presented a new method for precondition inference based on counter-example-guided abstraction refinement. Given a procedure containing an assertion, our method infers a formula that is sufficient for the validity of the specified assertion and exclusively refers to state variables visible at the entry point of the procedure. The inferred precondition is independent of the context, making it reusable. The computed precondition is also necessary for the validity of the assertion, i.e., it does not exclude any safe runs of the procedure. Hence, we avoid false alarms, as the violation of the precondition corresponds to a real error.

Our technique is based on ingredients commonly used in CEGAR-based assertion checkers, and it thus represents a general scheme for extending other verification tools to infer preconditions. Moreover, we believe that we can take advantage of components from other tools, such as advanced refinement mechanisms, which can be integrated seamlessly into our algorithm. Preliminary experimental results are encouraging, as we are able to generate exact preconditions (quantified as well as quantifier-free) for string- and array-manipulating programs.

References

1. Ball, T., Rajamani, S.K.: The SLAM project: debugging system software via static analysis. In: POPL, pp. 1–3 (2002)
2. Beckman, N.E., Nori, A.V., Rajamani, S.K., Simmons, R.J.: Proofs from tests. In: ISSTA, pp. 3–14 (2008)
3. Blanc, N., Kroening, D.: Race analysis for SystemC using model checking. In: Proceedings of ICCAD 2008, pp. 356–363. IEEE (2008)
4. Bourdoncle, F.: Abstract debugging of higher-order imperative languages. In: PLDI, pp. 46–55 (1993)
5. Bozga, M., Iosif, R., Konečný, F.: Deciding Conditional Termination. In: Flanagan, C., König, B. (eds.) TACAS 2012. LNCS, vol. 7214, pp. 252–266. Springer, Heidelberg (2012)

6. Calcagno, C., Distefano, D., O'Hearn, P.W., Yang, H.: Compositional shape analysis by means of bi-abduction. In: POPL, pp. 289–300 (2009)
7. Chaki, S., Clarke, E.M., Groce, A., Jha, S., Veith, H.: Modular verification of software components in C. In: ICSE, pp. 385–395 (2003)
8. Clarke, E., Kroening, D., Sharygina, N., Yorav, K.: Predicate abstraction of ANSI–C programs using SAT. Formal Methods in System Design (FMSD) 25, 105–127 (2004)
9. Clarke, E., Grumberg, O., Jha, S., Lu, Y., Veith, H.: Counterexample-Guided Abstraction Refinement. In: Emerson, E.A., Sistla, A.P. (eds.) CAV 2000. LNCS, vol. 1855, pp. 154–169. Springer, Heidelberg (2000)
10. Cook, B., Gulwani, S., Lev-Ami, T., Rybalchenko, A., Sagiv, M.: Proving Conditional Termination. In: Gupta, A., Malik, S. (eds.) CAV 2008. LNCS, vol. 5123, pp. 328–340. Springer, Heidelberg (2008)
11. Cook, B., Podelski, A., Rybalchenko, A.: TERMINATOR: Beyond Safety. In: Ball, T., Jones, R.B. (eds.) CAV 2006. LNCS, vol. 4144, pp. 415–418. Springer, Heidelberg (2006)
12. Cousot, P., Cousot, R., Logozzo, F.: Precondition Inference from Intermittent Assertions and Application to Contracts on Collections. In: Jhala, R., Schmidt, D. (eds.) VMCAI 2011. LNCS, vol. 6538, pp. 150–168. Springer, Heidelberg (2011)
13. de Moura, L., Bjørner, N.: Z3: An Efficient SMT Solver. In: Ramakrishnan, C.R., Rehof, J. (eds.) TACAS 2008. LNCS, vol. 4963, pp. 337–340. Springer, Heidelberg (2008)
14. Detlefs, D., Nelson, G., Saxe, J.B.: Simplify: A theorem prover for program checking. Technical Report HPL-2003-148, HP Lab. (2003)
15. Dutertre, B., de Moura, L.: A Fast Linear-Arithmetic Solver for DPLL(T). In: Ball, T., Jones, R.B. (eds.) CAV 2006. LNCS, vol. 4144, pp. 81–94. Springer, Heidelberg (2006)
16. Graf, S., Saïdi, H.: Construction of Abstract State Graphs with PVS. In: Grumberg, O. (ed.) CAV 1997. LNCS, vol. 1254, pp. 72–83. Springer, Heidelberg (1997)
17. Gulavani, B.S., Henzinger, T.A., Kannan, Y., Nori, A.V., Rajamani, S.K.: SYNERGY: a new algorithm for property checking. In: SIGSOFT FSE, pp. 117–127 (2006)
18. Gurfinkel, A., Wei, O., Chechik, M.: YASM: A Software Model-Checker for Verification and Refutation. In: Ball, T., Jones, R.B. (eds.) CAV 2006. LNCS, vol. 4144, pp. 170–174. Springer, Heidelberg (2006)
19. Henzinger, T.A., Jhala, R., Majumdar, R., McMillan, K.L.: Abstractions from proofs. In: POPL, pp. 232–244 (2004)
20. Henzinger, T.A., Jhala, R., Majumdar, R., Sutre, G.: Lazy abstraction. In: POPL, pp. 58–70 (2002)
21. Ivancic, F., Shlyakhter, I., Gupta, A., Ganai, M.K.: Model checking C programs using F-SOFT. In: ICCD, pp. 297–308 (2005)
22. Jhala, R., McMillan, K.L.: A Practical and Complete Approach to Predicate Refinement. In: Hermanns, H., Palsberg, J. (eds.) TACAS 2006. LNCS, vol. 3920, pp. 459–473. Springer, Heidelberg (2006)
23. Jhala, R., McMillan, K.L.: Array Abstractions from Proofs. In: Damm, W., Hermanns, H. (eds.) CAV 2007. LNCS, vol. 4590, pp. 193–206. Springer, Heidelberg (2007)

24. Moy, Y.: Sufficient Preconditions for Modular Assertion Checking. In: Logozzo, F., Peled, D.A., Zuck, L.D. (eds.) VMCAI 2008. LNCS, vol. 4905, pp. 188–202. Springer, Heidelberg (2008)

25. Podelski, A., Rybalchenko, A.: ARMC: The Logical Choice for Software Model Checking with Abstraction Refinement. In: Hanus, M. (ed.) PADL 2007. LNCS, vol. 4354, pp. 245–259. Springer, Heidelberg (2007)

26. Rival, X.: Understanding the Origin of Alarms in ASTRÉE. In: Hankin, C., Siveroni, I. (eds.) SAS 2005. LNCS, vol. 3672, pp. 303–319. Springer, Heidelberg (2005)

27. Sankaranarayanan, S., Chaudhuri, S., Ivancic, F., Gupta, A.: Dynamic inference of likely data preconditions over predicates by tree learning. In: ISSTA, pp. 295–306 (2008)

28. Taghdiri, M.: Inferring specifications to detect errors in code. In: ASE, pp. 144–153 (2004)

Information Reuse
for Multi-goal Reachability Analyses[*]

Dirk Beyer[1], Andreas Holzer[2], Michael Tautschnig[3,4], and Helmut Veith[2]

[1] University of Passau, Germany
[2] Vienna University of Technology, Austria
[3] University of Oxford, UK
[4] Queen Mary, University of London, UK

Abstract. It is known that model checkers can generate test inputs as witnesses for reachability specifications (or, equivalently, as counterexamples for safety properties). While this use of model checkers for testing yields a theoretically sound test-generation procedure, it scales poorly for computing complex test suites for large sets of test goals, because each test goal requires an expensive run of the model checker. We represent test goals as automata and exploit relations between automata in order to reuse existing reachability information for the analysis of subsequent test goals. Exploiting the sharing of sub-automata in a series of reachability queries, we achieve considerable performance improvements over the standard approach. We show the practical use of our multi-goal reachability analysis in a predicate-abstraction-based test-input generator for the test-specification language FQL.

1 Introduction

Consider the problem of performing many reachability queries on a program that is given as source code. This problem is common in white-box test generation [3, 12, 13], where the goal is to obtain inputs for different paths in a given program. If, for instance, we want to achieve basic-block coverage, we will for each basic block b generate a test-goal that asks if there is a program execution that reaches b and, ultimately, the program exit. In previous work, we designed the coverage-specification language FQL [20, 22], which provides a concise specification of complex coverage criteria. Such a coverage criterion is then translated into a (possibly huge) set of test goals (cf. Table 2). Each such test goal is represented as a finite automaton, called *test-goal automaton*, and specifies a reachability query. Test-goal automata often have overlapping parts, i.e., identical parts of the automata, which let us reuse analysis results across several queries. In this paper, we present an approach that exploits the automaton structure of reachability queries to efficiently reuse information when solving multiple queries. In order to define the potentially shared behavior of two automata A and A', we introduce the notion of *similarity of A and A' modulo a set X of transitions*, where X is a subset of the transitions

---

[*] This work was supported by the Canadian NSERC grant RGPIN 341819-07, by the Austrian National Research Network S11403-N23 (RiSE) of the Austrian Science Fund (FWF), by the Vienna Science and Technology Fund (WWTF) grant PROSEED, and by the EPSRC project EP/H017585/1.

M. Felleisen and P. Gardner (Eds.): ESOP 2013, LNCS 7792, pp. 472–491, 2013.

of A'. If A *simulates* A' *modulo* X, then we also have trace containment modulo X. That is, each sequence of transitions starting in an initial state of A' and not including a transition from X is also a sequence of transitions in A. This enables us to reason about reachability of program executions in A' based on the reachability results for A as long as we are investigating transition sequences shared by both automata. Using this notion of similarity, we face two challenges: *(i) how can we maximize the overlapping parts of automata* (for two automata we can always achieve similarity modulo X by choosing a sufficiently large X, but the bigger X is, the less information we can reuse), and *(ii) in which order shall we process the automata to achieve a minimal number of reachability analysis runs?*

The alphabet of a test-goal automaton is a finite set of observations of a program execution. An observation can be, for example, a specific code location that is visited during the execution or a predicate over program states. Each (partial) program execution can be mapped to a word over these observations and for each test-goal automaton we want to determine whether it describes a (partial) execution in the given program. Figure 2 shows a symbolic representation of the state space of program P given in Figure 1. Each node consists of a program location and a description of the heap and the stack when entering that program location. The edges correspond to the execution of program statements and each target node represents the strongest postcondition of the respective statement when applied to the source node. For the moment, we restrict ourselves to observe only code locations (for simplicity, represented by line numbers). Then, the observable sequences of P are $\langle 1,2,5,7,10\rangle$, $\langle 1,2,5,6,7,10\rangle$, and $\langle 1,4,5,7,8\rangle$. P satisfies test-goal automaton A_1 (cf. Figure 3) but not test-goal automata A_2 and A_3 (cf. Figure 4).

Due to recursion and loops it is generally undecidable whether a test goal is satisfiable on an arbitrary program. We use reachability analyses, e.g., CEGAR-based predicate abstraction [7, 17], to approximate the set of executions of a program until we either (i) have found a partial program execution that is described by a word in the language of the test-goal *or* (ii) we have shown that there is no such execution. The test-goal automaton guides the reachability analysis, i.e., the analysis tracks program and automaton states simultaneously

```
1  if (x > 10)
2     f1 = false ;
3  else
4     f1 = true;
5  if (x == 100)
6     f2 = false ;
7  if (f1)
8     s = f2;
9  else
10    s = f1;
```

Fig. 1. Example program P

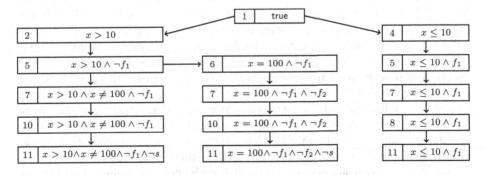

Fig. 2. Reachable state space of P (cf. Figure 1)

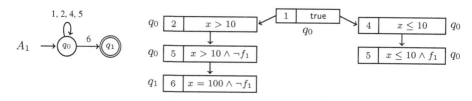

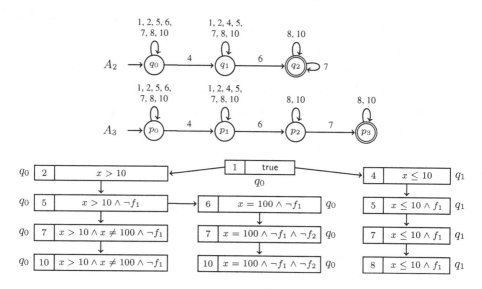

Fig. 3. State space of P restricted by A_1

Fig. 4. State space of P restricted by automaton A_2

and stops exploring the state space if there is no possible transition in the program state space or no possible next automaton transition (cf. the reduced state space in Fig. 3).

First, let us consider the case where the set X of excluded automaton transitions is empty, i.e., $X = \emptyset$. Then simulation modulo X amounts to the standard definition of simulation [25]. Let $H \subseteq Q' \times Q$ be a relation between the set of states Q' of an automaton A' and the set of states Q of an automaton A such that for each $(p, q) \in H$ there is for each outgoing transition (p, a, p') an outgoing transition (q, a, q') such that $(p', q') \in H$. We call H a *simulation relation*. We say that q *simulates* p if $(p, q) \in H$ and we say that A *simulates* A' if for each initial state p of A', there is an initial state q of A such that q simulates p. For example, in Fig. 4, automaton A_2 simulates automaton A_3. The simulation relation $H = \{(p_0, q_0), (p_1, q_1), (p_2, q_2), (p_2, q_3)\}$ witnesses this fact. The fact that A_2 simulates A_3 implies that each finite sequence of transitions starting in an initial state of A_3 corresponds to an equivalent sequence of transitions starting in an initial state of A_2. From the state space given in Fig. 4, we know that state q_2 is not reachable in A_2 and since H relates p_3 only to q_2, we can conclude that p_3 is not reachable as well and that therefore no accepting trace in A_3 exists.

In general, test-goal automata do not simulate each other. For example, consider the situation where a reachability analysis involving A_3 is performed. Then, each node in

Fig. 4 labeled with q_0 would be labeled with p_0 and each node labeled with q_1 would be labeled with p_1. The automaton A_3 does not simulate A_2 (e.g., A_2 accepts a word $\langle 4, 6, 7, 7 \rangle$ which is not accepted by A_3). Nevertheless, we can still reuse the reachability information obtained for A_3 when solving A_2: Let A_2' be the automaton A_2 where the transition $(q_2, 7, q_2)$ is removed. Then, A_3 simulates A_2', witnessed by the relation $H' = \{(q_0, p_0), (q_1, p_1), (q_2, p_2)\}$, and we say that A_3 *simulates A_2 modulo the transition set* $\{(q_2, 7, q_2)\}$. From the fact that state p_2 is not reachable we can conclude that q_2 is not reachable and that therefore A_2 is unsatisfiable. Based on the set of excluded transitions one skips parts of the already analyzed state space (those parts which involve these transitions) or continues state-space exploration at points that have been skipped during the previous state space exploration.

In Sect. 4, we combine automaton-based reasoning techniques as introduced above into an approach for multi-goal reachability analysis. Before that, we will formally introduce the automata that we use for representing reachability queries (cf. Sect. 2) and discuss our automaton-based reasoning techniques individually (cf. Sect. 3). We implemented the test-input generator CPA/TIGER, which is based on predicate-abstraction. We show in our experiments (cf. Sect. 5) that we significantly improve over a naive approach to multi-goal reachability analysis by applying our information reuse techniques. Furthermore, we compare our implementation with existing test generation tools. In Sect. 6 we discuss related work and show how our approach can be integrated into other test generation methods. Finally, we conclude and discuss future work in Sect. 7.

2 Test-Goal Automata

We first introduce our program representation, then define test-goal automata, and finally discuss how we represent information gathered by a reachability analysis.

Programs. We represent a program as a *control-flow automaton* (CFA) [5]. A CFA (L, E) is a directed, labeled graph, that consists of a finite set L of nodes and a finite set $E \subseteq L \times Ops \times L$ of edges. A node $\ell \in L$ models a program location (program counter valuation) and an edge $(\ell, op, \ell') \in E$ models a program transfer (control flows from location ℓ to ℓ', while performing program operation op). A program operation $op \in Ops$ is either an assignment or an assume operation[1]. Program operations can read from, and write to, a finite set of integer and Boolean variables. Figure 5 shows the CFA representing the source code shown in Fig. 1.

A *program state* c is a mapping from program counter and program variables to values. We denote the

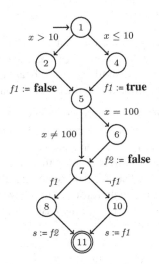

Fig. 5. CFA P_0 for code in Fig. 1

---

[1] Our implementation performs an interprocedural analysis (i.e., handles function call and function return), but for simplicity of presentation we limit the formalization to flat programs over integer and Boolean variables.

set of all program states by C. A set of program states is represented by a *state predicate* φ over the program counter and program variables. We denote the set of state predicates by Φ. We write $c \models \varphi$ (and say, c satisfies state predicate φ) if program state $c \in C$ is in the state set represented by $\varphi \in \Phi$, and we write $\llbracket \varphi \rrbracket = \{ c \in C \mid c \models \varphi \}$ for the set of concrete states represented by φ. The *concrete semantics* of a program operation $op \in Ops$ is given by the strongest postcondition SP_{op}, i.e., for a set of states represented by φ, the set of successor states is represented by $\varphi' = SP_{op}(\llbracket \varphi \rrbracket)$. A *program execution* is a sequence $c_0 \xrightarrow{e_0} c_1 \ldots c_i \xrightarrow{e_i} c_{i+1} \ldots$ of program states c_i, for $i \geq 0$, and consecutive CFA edges $e_i = (\ell_i, op_i, \ell_{i+1})$, for $i \geq 0$, such that $c_{i+1} \in SP_{op_i}(c_i)$ holds for each $c_i \xrightarrow{e_i} c_{i+1}$. We call a program execution *complete* if either the program location of the last state of the execution coincides with the program exit or the execution is infinite. Otherwise, we call the program execution *partial*.

Test-Goal Automata. A *test goal* describes a set of program traces. Test goals refer to the syntactic structure and semantics of a program. We characterize program traces syntactically by referring to CFA edges, and semantically by using state predicates. For example, a test goal can require to find a program execution (identified by an input assignment) to a particular program location (specified by a CFA edge), or to evaluate a certain expression to a specific value (specified by a CFA edge and a state predicate). We represent a test goal by a test-goal automaton:

A *test-goal automaton (TGA)* $A = (Q, \Sigma, \Delta, I, F)$ is a nondeterministic finite automaton, with a finite set Q of states, an alphabet $\Sigma \subseteq E \times \Phi$ consisting of pairs of CFA edges and state predicates, a transition relation $\Delta \subseteq Q \times \Sigma \times Q$, a set $I \subseteq Q$ of initial states, and a set $F \subseteq Q$ of accepting states. We write $q \xrightarrow{a} q'$ in case $(q, a, q') \in \Delta$. We say that A *accepts* a program execution $c_0 \xrightarrow{e_0} c_1 \cdots \xrightarrow{e_{n-1}} c_n$ if there is a sequence $q_0 \xrightarrow{(e_0, \psi_0)} q_1 \cdots \xrightarrow{(e_{n-1}, \psi_{n-1})} q_n$ of TGA transitions starting in an initial state $q_0 \in I$ and ending in a final state $q_n \in F$ such that $c_{i+1} \models \psi_i$ holds for each $q_i \xrightarrow{(e_i, \psi_i)} q_{i+1}$. The last condition $c_{i+1} \models \psi_i$ means that if there is a program transition from state c_i to state c_{i+1}, then the state predicate ψ_i is evaluated on the successor state c_{i+1}. By adding an additional initial CFA edge, one can also restrict the initial program state.

Example. Figure 6 shows a TGA with initial state q and final state p. The automaton requires that Line 11 (represented by CFA edge $(8, s{:=}f2, 11)$) is visited during a program execution and that flag s is true after executing the statement $s := f2$. Due to the self-loops at q and p there are no restrictions to a program execution other than the one stated above. An execution satisfying this test goal has to make both variables $f1$ and $f2$ true and therefore x can't have the value 100 in that execution. Figure 7 shows the set of TGAs representing basic-block coverage on program P_0 given in Fig. 5. For simplicity,

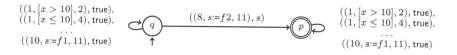

$\begin{aligned} &((1, [x > 10], 2), \text{true}), \\ &((1, [x \leq 10], 4), \text{true}), \\ &\qquad \ldots \\ &((10, s{:=}f1, 11), \text{true}) \end{aligned}$ $((8, s{:=}f2, 11), s)$ $\begin{aligned} &((1, [x > 10], 2), \text{true}), \\ &((1, [x \leq 10], 4), \text{true}), \\ &\qquad \ldots \\ &((10, s{:=}f1, 11), \text{true}) \end{aligned}$

Fig. 6. Example test-goal automaton A_{10}

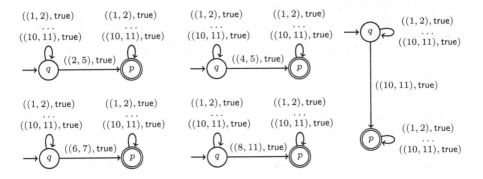

Fig. 7. Example test-goal automata for basic-block coverage

we omitted the operations labeling the CFA edges. For each entry of a basic block, i.e., CFA edges $(2, 5)$, $(4, 5)$, $(6, 7)$, $(8, 11)$, and $(10, 11)$, there is a respective automaton.

Representing Reachability Information. For our approach we consider reachability analyses that represent the reachable state space of a program by an *abstract reachability graph (ARG)* as it is done for example in predicate-abstraction-based model checkers [5, 6]. Let $P = (L, E)$ be a CFA and let $A = (Q, \Sigma, \delta, q_0, F)$ be a test-goal automaton. An abstract reachability graph $G_{P,A} = (S, T, s_0)$ consists of a finite set $S \subseteq ID \times L \times Q \times D$ of *abstract states*, where ID is a set of identifiers and D is an abstract data domain whose elements describe the heap and stack, finitely many transitions $T \subseteq S \times (E \times \Phi) \times S$ between these abstract states, and an *initial abstract state* s_0. The identifier is required to distinguish abstract states with otherwise equal values, which may be produced, e.g., by the ARG transformations of Sect. 3. To simplify the presentation, however, we omit the identifier in the remainder of this paper. An abstract state $s \in S$ induces a state predicate φ_s over the same program location and a heap and stack described by the valuation in the abstract domain. Via φ_s we obtain a set $[\![s]\!]$ of concrete program states. Given an abstract state s, all concrete states in $[\![s]\!]$ share the same program location, denoted by $\ell(s)$, and test-goal automaton state, denoted by $q(s)$. For the initial state it holds that $q(s_0) = q_0$. Let $t \in T$ be the transition $(s, (e, \varphi), s')$, then t has a corresponding CFA edge, i.e., $(\ell(s), e, \ell(s')) \in E$, and t has a corresponding TGA transition $(q(s), (e, \varphi), q(s')) \in \delta$. We denote $(\ell(s), e, \ell(s'))$ by t_P and denote $(q(s), (e, \varphi), q(s'))$ by t_A. Then, each sequence $t_1 t_2 \dots t_n$ of transitions in G corresponds to a sequence $\langle t_{P1}, t_{P2}, \dots, t_{Pn} \rangle$ of CFA edges and to a sequence $\langle t_{A1}, t_{A2}, \dots, t_{An} \rangle$ of TGA transitions. Note, the reverse direction does not necessarily hold since a reachability analysis might terminate its state space exploration without explicitly enumerating all sequences of CFA edges or TGA transitions.

Figure 8 shows an example of an ARG G obtained by a reachability analysis for the CFA depicted in Figure 5 and the TGA depicted in Figure 6. An ARG is a finite unwinding of the reachable state space. The unwinding stops in case no new behavior can be observed. In order to obtain a finite unwinding, abstraction might be applied. Paths through the ARG might be merged at points with the same program location and automaton state (cf. [6] for a detailed elaboration and formalization of merge and stop operators).

In the given example, the ARG G contains the accepting state $(11, p, s)$ (with s abstracting from $f1$ and $f2$ of a concrete execution of the program). We denote the directed acyclic graph reaching this state as the *witness of reachability* of $(11, p, s)$. A witness is *feasible* if there exists a real program execution encoded in the witness and *infeasible* otherwise. The witness given in Figure 8 (enclosed in a dotted line) is feasible, e.g., the input $x = 10, f2 = \text{true}$ causes an execution following the program path $\langle 1, 4, 5, 7, 8, 11 \rangle$ which is accepted by the TGA given in Figure 6.

In Section 3, we discuss how to turn an ARG G_{P,A_1} obtained for a TGA A_1 into an ARG G_{P,A_2} for a TGA A_2.

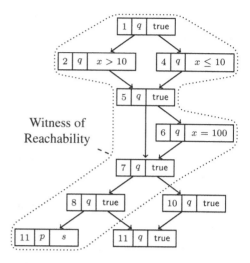

Fig. 8. Example ARG $G_{P_0,A_{10}}$ for CFA P_0 (see Figure 5) and TGA A_{10} (see Figure 6)

3   Reasoning on Test Goals

As input to a multi-goal reachability analysis we are given a CFA (L, E) and a set $\{A_1, A_2, \ldots, A_n\}$ of test-goal automata A_i. One way to tackle this problem is to invoke a reachability analysis for each test-goal automaton A_i individually. This approach would have to rediscover lots of information again and again when analysing the program with respect to different test-goal automata. Therefore, we will now discuss a notion of simulation that enables us to identify information that is reusable across reachability analyses for different test-goal automata.

Relating Test-Goal Automata. We relate test-goal automata by adapting the notion of similarity [25] to identify the transitions that violate the similarity of two automata:

Definition 1 (Similarity modulo X). *Given two TGA $A_1 = (Q_1, \Sigma, \delta_1, q_0, F_1)$ and $A_2 = (Q_2, \Sigma, \delta_2, p_0, F_2)$ and a set $X \subseteq \delta_2$ of automaton transitions in A_2, we call a relation $H \subseteq Q_2 \times Q_1$ a simulation relation modulo X from A_1 to A_2 if H is a simulation relation from A_1 to $\bar{A}_2 = (Q_2, \Sigma, \delta_2 \setminus X, p_0, F_2)$. This means that for each $(p, q) \in H$ and for each transition $(p, a, p') \in (\delta_2 \setminus X)$ there is a transition $(q, a, q') \in \delta_1$ s.t. $(p', q') \in H$.*

Example. Figure 9 shows two test goal automata A_1 and A_2. There, the relation $H = \{(p_0, q_0), (p_1, q_1), (p_2, q_2)\}$ is a simulation relation modulo $X = \{(p_1, c, p_2)\}$ from A_1 to A_2. Each sequence of transitions contained in the automaton $\bar{A}_2$, as defined above, is also reflected by a corresponding sequence in A_1. Note, sets other then the chosen X could be used to establish similarity from A_1 to A_2, e.g., by adding more transitions of A_2 to X. However, in order to increase the reuse of gathered reachability information small X are preferable.

Fig. 9. $\{(p_0, q_0), (p_1, q_1), (p_2, q_2)\}$ is a simulation relation modulo $\{(p_1, c, p_2)\}$ from A_1 to A_2

Algorithm 3.1. transform — Transform an ARG into another ARG

Input: TGA $A_1 = (Q_1, \Sigma, \delta_1, q_0, F_1)$ and $A_2 = (Q_2, \Sigma, \delta_2, p_0, F_2)$, initial abstract state $\bar{s}_0$, automaton transition $(p_0, ((\ell, op, \ell'), \varphi), p') \in \delta_2$ (where $q(\bar{s}_0) = p_0$ and $\ell(\bar{s}_0) = \ell$), simulation relation H modulo set of transitions X, ARG G_{P,A_1}, worklist W_{A_1}.

Output: Transformed ARG and worklist for further state-space exploration.

 1: $S' \leftarrow \bigcup_{s \in S} H(s)$
 2: $T' \leftarrow \bigcup_{t \in T} H(t)$
 3: **if** there is an abstract state $s'_0 \in S'$ such that $q(s') = p_0$ and $[\![s'_0]\!] \supseteq [\![\bar{s}_0]\!]$ **then**
 4:     **choose** such an s'_0
 5:     $S' \leftarrow \{s' \in S' \mid s' \text{ is reachable from } s'_0 \text{ via } T'\}$
 6:     $T' \leftarrow \{t \in T' \mid t \text{ is reachable from } s'_0 \text{ via } T'\}$
 7:     $W \leftarrow \{\langle \underbrace{(\ell, q, \psi)}_{=s'} \in S', \underbrace{(q, ((\ell, op, \ell'), \varphi), q')}_{=d} \in X\}$
 8:     $W \leftarrow W \cup \bigcup_{\langle \hat{s}, \hat{d}\rangle \in W_{A_1}} \left((H(\hat{s}) \cap S') \times H(\hat{d}) \right)$
 9:     **return** $\langle (S', T', s'_0), W \rangle$
10: **else**
11:     **return** $\langle (\{\bar{s}_0\}, \emptyset, \bar{s}_0), \{(p_0, ((\ell, op, \ell'), \varphi), p')\} \rangle$

Reusing Reachability Information. Using simulation relations, we can transform a given ARG G_{P,A_1} for a TGA A_1 into an ARG G_{P,A_2} for a TGA A_2. We first describe the general principle of this transformation and then point out how to efficiently apply it when analysing multiple automata in a row.

Algorithm 3.1 takes an ARG $G_{P,A_1} = (S, T, s_0)$ and transforms it into an ARG G_{P,A_2} based on a simulation relation H from a TGA A_1 to TGA A_2 modulo a set of transitions X. To compute the transformation we furthermore need the two TGA $A_1 = (Q_1, \Sigma, \delta_1, q_0, F_1)$ and $A_2 = (Q_2, \Sigma, \delta_2, p_0, F_2)$, the abstract state $\bar{s}_0$ (with $q(\bar{s}_0) = p_0$ and $\ell(\bar{s}_0) = \ell$), where we will start with the information reuse, and a TGA transition $(p_0, ((\ell, op, \ell'), \varphi), p') \in \delta_2$ whose role we will discuss later in the context of Algorithm 4.3. For the moment, omitting it does not affect the overall understanding of the transformation process. Given these inputs, we will obtain an ARG $G_{P,A_2} = (S', T', s'_0)$. Before we discuss the algorithm, we will first define the sets $H(s)$ and $H(t)$, for $s \in S$ and $t \in T$, by

$$H(s) = \{s' \mid (p, q(s)) \in H \text{ and } s' \text{ coincides with } s \text{ except that } q(s') = p\}$$

and, for $t = (s_1, (e, \varphi), s'_1)$,

$$H(t) = \{(s_2, (e, \varphi), s'_2) \mid s_2 \in H(s_1), s'_2 \in H(s'_1), (q(s_2), (e, \varphi), q(s'_2)) \in \delta_2 \setminus X\}.$$

The set X controls how many transitions from T can be reused, i.e., the larger X is, the less reachability information can be reused. In Lines 1 and 2 of the algorithm we define

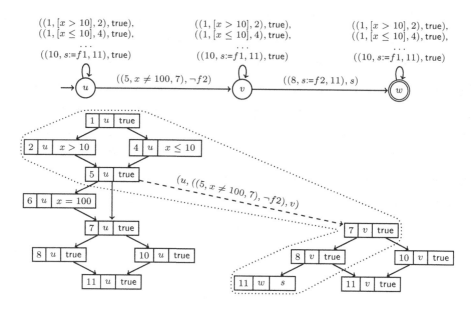

Fig. 10. ARG $G_{P_0,A_{11}}$ obtained from $G_{P_0,A_{10}}$ (cf. Figure 8) using the simulation relation $H = \{(u,q),(v,q),(w,p)\}$ modulo $X = \{(u,((5,x \neq 100, 7), \neg f2), v)\}$

the set of transformed abstract states $S' = \bigcup_{s \in S} H(s)$ and the set of transformed ARG transitions $T' = \bigcup_{t \in T} H(t)$ by simply translating all abstract states and all transitions of G_{P,A_1}. This might lead to many subparts of the resulting ARG not being connected to the initial abstract state. In Lines 5 and 6 we will restrict these two sets to the reachable part only (in the implementation the transformation is only done for the reachable part of the new ARG). But, in order to determine the reachable part of the newly generated ARG, we first have to determine what the initial abstract state will be. We do this based on the given abstract state $\bar{s}_0$. We describe our algorithms from the point of view of an overapproximating reachability analysis, which leads to the condition that an initial abstract state s'_0 has to contain all concrete states of $\bar{s}_0$, i.e., $[\![s'_0]\!] \supseteq [\![\bar{s}_0]\!]$. The concepts behind the algorithms given in this paper also work for an underapproximating analysis, but one has to use a dual reasoning, e.g., we would need the condition $[\![s'_0]\!] \subseteq [\![\bar{s}_0]\!]$ instead. In case there is no such abstract state s'_0, then we can't reuse any information and we return the ARG $(\{\bar{s}_0\}, \emptyset, \bar{s}_0)$. The role of the transition $(p_0, ((\ell, op, \ell'), \varphi), p')$ is explained in the discussion of Algorithm 4.3 and we therefore skip it for the moment. Assume there is a suitable abstract state s'_0, then we restrict S' and T', as discussed above, to the part reachable from s'_0. Lines 7 and 8 create a worklist W which contains abstract states and TGA transitions which have to be further explored. The transformation of these worklists will be explained in the discussion of Algorithm 4.3.

Figure 10 shows the ARG $G_{P_0,A_{11}}$ obtained from ARG $G_{P_0,A_{10}}$ by using the simulation relation $\{(u,q),(v,q),(w,p)\}$ modulo $\{(u,((5,x \neq 100,7), \neg f2), v)\}$. The resulting worklist is $\{\langle (5,u,\text{true}),(u,((5,x \neq 100,7), \neg f2),v)\rangle\}$. First, the left part of ARG $G_{P_0,A_{11}}$ is computed, and then, a reachability analysis determines the

---

Algorithm 3.2. Compute H, X

Input: $A = (Q, \Sigma, \Delta, q_0, F)$, $A' = (Q', \Sigma, \Delta', p_0, F')$.
Output: H and X such that A simulates A' modulo X.

1: $H \leftarrow \{(p_0, q_0)\}$, $H' \leftarrow \emptyset$
2: $X \leftarrow \emptyset$, $X' \leftarrow \emptyset$
3: **while** $H \neq H'$ or $X \neq X'$ **do**
4:     $H' \leftarrow H$
5:     $X' \leftarrow X$
6:     **if** there is a $(p, q) \in H$ s.t. there is a $(p, a, p') \in \Delta' \setminus X$ but no $(q, a, q') \in \Delta$ **then**
7:         $X \leftarrow X \cup \{(p, a, p')\}$
8:     **if** there is a $(p, q) \in H$ s.t. there is a $(p, a, p') \in \Delta' \setminus X$ but $(p', q') \notin H$ for all $(q, a, q') \in \Delta$ **then**
9:         **choose** a subset $U \subseteq \{q' \mid (q, a, q') \in \Delta\}$
10:        **if** $U \neq \emptyset$ **then**
11:            $H \leftarrow H \cup \{(p', q') \mid q' \in U\}$
12:        **else**
13:            $X \leftarrow X \cup \{(p, a, p')\}$
14: **return** (H, X)

---

abstract state $(7, v, \text{true})$ as successor of $(5, u, \text{true})$ along TGA transition $(u, ((5, x \neq 100, 7), \neg f2), v)$. Then we again use reachability information from ARG $G_{P_0, A_{10}}$ this time starting in abstract state $(7, v, \text{true})$. The DAG enclosed in the dotted line describes the witness after these three steps 'information reuse' — 'reachability analysis' — 'information reuse'. In Section 4 we describe how to combine these steps in an algorithm for multi-goal reachability analysis.

Computing Simulation-Modulo-X Relations. The amount of possible information reuse is determined by (i) the set X of transitions and (ii) the relation H. The bigger X is, the bigger H can be chosen, but at the same time the number of reusable transitions in an ARG decreases. Since the transitions encode the actual reachability information we have to find a balance between the size of X and the size of H.

Algorithm 3.2 computes, given two TGA A and A', a set X of transitions of A' such that A simulates A' modulo X. Furthermore, it computes a corresponding relation H. The algorithm starts in the initial states p_0 and q_0 of A' and A, respectively. Initially, the relation H only contains the tuple (p_0, q_0). Then, for each transition (p_0, a, p') outgoing from p_0 we check whether we can find a transition (q_0, a, q') outgoing from q_0 labeled with a as well. If there is no such transition, then A can't simulate A' wrt. to this transition and we have to add (p_0, a, p') to X. Algorithm 3.2 is parametric wrt. its behavior if there are such transitions: If (p', q') is not contained in H yet, the algorithm can decide whether it wants to add it to H at all. A bigger relation H might blow up the resulting translated state space. If the algorithm decides not to add any possible (p', q') to H, then the transition (p, a, p') has to be excluded, i.e., it has to be added to X. Otherwise, at least one of the (p', q') are added to H. Depending on which (p', q') are added to H the final H and X can vary. In our implementation (cf. Section 5) we have implemented a breadth-first search which adds all possible (p', q') to H. The automata we consider in our experiments have a tree-like structure and the different (p', q') do

---

Algorithm 4.1. Multi-Goal Reachability Analysis

Input: Program P, a sequence of TGA $A_1, A_2, \ldots, A_i, \ldots, A_n$ (see Section 4), an initial program location ℓ_0, and an initial data state d_0.

Output: Determines for each $1 \le i \le n$ whether P satisfies A_i and, if so, computes inputs.

  1: **for** $i = 1 \to n$ **do**
  2:    $s_0 \leftarrow (\ell_0, q_0, d_0)$ where q_0 is the initial state of A_i
  3:    **if** A_i is covered by an existing test input contained in the test suite **then**
  4:        **continue**
  5:    determine-feasibility(P, A_i, s_0)   *// Algorithm 4.2*

---

not interfere with each other in the later exploration. The algorithm then continues with the elements added newly to H.

Note that the symbols in Σ are actually interdependent, because they are tuples of CFA edges and state predicates. In case there is a transition (p, a, p') and a transition (q, b, q') for $(p, q) \in H$ and $a \ne b$ we might still have a simulation in case the CFA edges of a and b are the same and the state predicate of b is weaker than the state predicate of a. For simplicity of presentation, we omitted this case. In case of using an underapproximating reachability analysis one would dually require that the state predicate of b is stronger than the state predicate of a.

4   Multi-goal Reachability Analysis

In Section 3, we discussed how we can identify shared behavior of two TGA by simulation relations and how we can translate reachability information of one TGA into reachability information for another one. Now, we will use simulation relations as foundation for a reasoning engine that reuses already obtained reachability information. The input to our multi-goal reachability analysis is a sequence of TGA $A_1, A_2, \ldots, A_n$. At the end of this section, we will discuss how to exploit concise specifications of sets of TGA and how to obtain an order on these sets.

Algorithm 4.1 shows the main loop of our multi-goal reachability analysis. Its input is a program P, a sequence of TGA $A_1, \ldots, A_n$, the initial program location ℓ_0, and an initial abstract data state d_0 describing the heap and stack at program entry. For each test-goal automaton A_i, we first check whether we already have inputs inducing a program execution that satisfies A_i and, if so, we skip A_i from further analysis and we continue with A_{i+1}. We do this check by simply executing the program simultaneously with the TGA A_i with given inputs. If the execution reaches an accepting state of A_i, then, the inputs cover A_i. If A_i is not covered, we will perform a feasibility check.

Feasibility Check. Algorithm 4.2 realizes the feasiblity check of a TGA. For storing already gathered reachability information we assume a database that stores quadruples $\langle A, G_{P,A}, W_A, isFeasible \rangle$ where A is a TGA, $G_{P,A}$ is the ARG obtained for A, and W_A is a worklist containing the abstract states of $G_{P,A}$ where state-space exploration has to continue in order to exhaustively investigate the state space, and *isFeasible* is either FEASIBLE or INFEASIBLE, depending on whether P satisfies A or not. If $W_A \ne \emptyset$ then the state space didn't have to be exhaustively explored to determine the value of

---

Algorithm 4.2. determine-feasibility — Determine Feasibility of TGA

Input: CFA P, TGA $A = (Q, \Sigma, \Delta, q(s_0), F)$, initial abstract state s_0
Output: Computes whether A is feasible on P and, if so, determines inputs.
1: $W \leftarrow \{\langle s_0, (q(s_0), ((\ell(s_0), op, \ell'), \varphi), q') \rangle \mid (q(s_0), ((\ell(s_0), op, \ell'), \varphi), q') \in \Delta\}$
2: $G_{P,A} \leftarrow (\{s_0\}, \emptyset, s_0)$
3: **while** $W \neq \emptyset$ **do**
4:      pick $\langle s, (q, ((\ell, op, \ell'), \varphi), q') \rangle \in W$ and remove it from W
5:      $\langle G'_{P,A}, W' \rangle \leftarrow reuse(s, (q, ((\ell, op, \ell'), \varphi), q'), A)$ // Algorithm 4.3
6:      insert $G'_{P,A}$ into $G_{P,A}$ at s
7:      $\langle G_{P,A}, W' \rangle \leftarrow reach(W', A, G_{P,A})$
8:      $W \leftarrow W \cup W'$
9:      **if** there is an $s' \in G_{P,A}$ such that $q(s') \in F$ **then**
10:        $wit \leftarrow witness(s', G_{P,A})$
11:        **if** wit is feasible **then**
12:            derive inputs from wit and store them in test suite
13:            store $\langle A, G_{P,A}, W, \text{FEASIBLE} \rangle$ in reachability database
14:            **return** FEASIBLE
15:        **else**
16:            $\langle G_{P,A}, W \rangle \leftarrow refine(G_{P,A}, wit, W)$
17: store $\langle A, G_{P,A}, \emptyset, \text{INFEASIBLE} \rangle$ in reachability database
18: **return** INFEASIBLE

---

isFeasible. A worklist is a set of tuples of abstract states and TGA transitions. A tuple $\langle s, (q, ((\ell, op, \ell'), \varphi), q') \rangle$ requires a state-space exploration starting in abstract state s, where $q(s) = q$ and $\ell(s) = \ell$ holds, and performed along CFA edge (ℓ, op, ℓ') (the postcondition φ has to be considered by the reachability analysis as well).

The algorithm maintains a worklist W and an ARG $G_{P,A}$. Worklist W is initialized with all transitions potentially leaving the initial abstract state. At the beginning, $G_{P,A}$ only consists of the initial abstract state s_0. As long as W is not empty, the algorithm picks an element from the worklist and performs a state-space exploration. Before applying a reachability analysis the algorithm tries to reuse already computed reachability information. We call Algorithm 4.3 with the chosen abstract state and transition as well as the current TGA. The algorithm returns an ARG $G'_{P,A}$ and a worklist W'. $G'_{P,A}$ represents the reachability information reusable at abstract state s and W' contains the exploration points where reachability information is missing. In case no reuse is possible, the ARG containing only state s is returned and the worklist contains the tuple which was initially picked at Line 4. After calling Algorithm 4.3, the returned sub-ARG is inserted into $G_{P,A}$ at abstract state s. As already mentioned, W' contains the tuples where state-space exploration has to continue, therefore a reachability analysis is called with the task of exploring all points in W'. The reachability analysis might decide to return before having explored all tuples (or none at all) in W'. It returns an updated ARG and an updated worklist. The worklist W' might be non-empty if the reachability analysis found a witness for the feasibility of A or if we first want to check whether we can reuse some reachability information for the tuples in W'. We therefore add W' to W for later processing.

Algorithm 4.3. reuse — Reuse Stored Reachability Information

Input: Abs. state s, TGA $A = (Q, \Sigma, \Delta, q, F)$, transition $(q, ((\ell, op, \ell'), \varphi), q') \in \Delta$.
Output: ARG and worklist
1: let $\hat{q}$ be a new state, i.e., $\hat{q} \notin Q$
2: **if** $q \in F$ **then**
3:     $F' \leftarrow F \uplus \{\hat{q}\}$
4: **else**
5:     $F' \leftarrow F$
6: $A' \leftarrow (Q \uplus \{\hat{q}\}, \Sigma, \Delta \uplus \{(\hat{q}, ((\ell, op, \ell'), \varphi), q')\}, \hat{q}, F')$
7: **choose** a tuple $\langle \bar{A}, G_{P, \bar{A}}, W, f \rangle$ from the database
8: **if** $\langle \bar{A}, G_{P, \bar{A}}, W, f \rangle$ exists **then**
9:     compute H, X such that $\bar{A}$ simulates A' modulo X // Algorithm 3.2
10:     **if** $(q, ((\ell, op, \ell'), \varphi), q') \notin X$ **then**
11:        $\langle G_{P, A'}, W \rangle \leftarrow transform(\bar{A}, A', s, (\hat{q}, ((\ell, op, \ell'), \varphi), q'), H, X, G_{P, \bar{A}}, W)$
                                                                // Algorithm 3.1
12:        replace each occurrence of $\hat{q}$ in $G_{P, A'}$ and W by q
13:        **return** $\langle G_{P, A'}, W \rangle$
14: **return** $\langle (\{s\}, \emptyset, s), \{\langle s, (q, ((\ell, op, \ell'), \varphi), q') \rangle\} \rangle$

Lines 10 to 16 deal with the case where an abstract state with an accepting automaton state is found. Then, a witness is extracted and its feasibility is checked (the ARG encodes all information necessary to exactly represent the program paths in the witness as a formula ψ). If the witness is feasible we derive inputs from the model of ψ and store these inputs in the test suite. Furthermore, we extend our reachability information database by the tuple $\langle A, G_{P, A}, W, \text{FEASIBLE} \rangle$. Then, we return to the main multi-goal reachability analysis algorithm. If the witness is infeasible it means the reachability analysis was not precise enough during state-space exploration and we therefore refine the precision of the analysis based on the infeasible witness. This may result in a change in the ARG as well as in the worklist. In our implementation we use a reachability analysis based on predicate abstraction and CEGAR [7, 17].

After all elements in W are finally processed, we know that P does not satisfy A and store the according information in the database (cf. Line 17).

Reusing Stored Reachability Information. In order to determine reusable stored information, we first transform the given TGA A into a TGA A' which is the same as A except that a new state $\hat{q}$ and a transition $(\hat{q}, ((\ell, op, \ell'), \varphi), q')$ is added. By doing this, we ensure that the resulting reused ARG starts with the automaton transition passed to Algorithm 4.3. In case q is an accepting state we also make $\hat{q}$ an accepting state. In Line 7, a quadruple $\langle \bar{A}, G_{P, \bar{A}}, W, f \rangle$ is chosen from the reachability information database. The choice is parametric, i.e., one can use different strategies to select a quadruple, e.g., one can actually compute the maximal possible reuse for each stored quadruple and select the optimal one, or one can apply computationally cheaper heuristics based on the structure of the TGA stored in the quadruples. In case a strategy would decide not to reuse any information, it can just select some entry in the database and choose X such that no information reuse will happen. If the database is empty, the algorithm returns the ARG containing only the passed abstract state s and adds the tuple $\langle s, (q, ((\ell, op, \ell'), \varphi), q') \rangle$ to the worklist again.

Enumerating Test-Goal Automata. Algorithm 4.1 assumes a fixed order on the sequence of TGA. This is not a requirement for our approach. Actually, one of the central features of our multi-goal reachability analysis approach is not having all TGA available in advance in contrast to our previous test input generator FSHELL, where initially all TGA are encoded into the program. Depending on the nature of the TGA, this can drastically reduce the scalability of FSHELL, e.g., TGA encoding specific subpaths of the program decrease the performance considerably (cf. Table 1 in Section 5). FSHELL and CPA/TIGER derive their TGA from concise coverage specifications given in FQL. Concise means, the size of the specification might be logarithmic in the number of resulting TGA. But, the more concise the specification is, the more sharing the TGA have. This enables us to skip whole sets of TGA where we can infer infeasibility from other TGA (because the reason of infeasibility is in the shared part of these TGA).

In general, we could compare all TGA with each other and order the queries corresponding to the size of the resulting sets X. One can use computationally cheaper heuristics based on structural properties of the TGA and the program, e.g., an analysis of program dominators can exploit hidden connections between TGA. In Algorithm 4.2, the call to Algorithm 4.3 is interleaved with a reachability analysis. The degree of information reuse greatly varies based on the precision the analysis provides and the strategies that are used for computing simulation relations. Therefore, the order of TGA might be dynamically changed based on the results of the reachability analysis. In our implementation, we used a fixed order based on similarity of TGA and the structure of the CFA (see discussion of Table 5 in Sect. 5). We leave a systematic investigation of dynamic orders as future work.

5   Experiments

We implemented the tool CPA/TIGER to evaluate the performance of our approach. We use the Java-based verification framework CPACHECKER in order to reuse standard model-checking technology, and integrate our concepts as configurable program analyses. To demonstrate the capabilities of the new implementation, we compare it to the existing FQL backends FSHELL 1 [19] and FSHELL 2 [21]. Both versions are based on the C bounded model checker CBMC [9] and were implemented in C++. FSHELL takes as input a C program and an FQL query. FSHELL 1 instruments a C program with automata derived from an FQL query, whereas FSHELL 2 encodes these automata directly into the SAT-formula representing the C program under scrutiny. Since FSHELL 1 and 2 are based on bounded model checking (BMC), they require an explicit specification of loop bounds for programs with unbounded loops. For a fair comparison one has to consider that FSHELL 2 is written in C++ whereas CPA/TIGER is written in Java and additionally proves infeasibility of test goals.

Path Coverage in Programs with Unbounded Loops. To compare the scalability of the three tools in the context of different path lengths, we studied a small (26 lines of code) locking/unlocking example. The lock/unlock happens inside a loop that is

Table 1. n-bounded path coverage on `locks_1`

n	Nr. of test goals	Loop bound	FSHELL 1 t[s]	FSHELL 2 t[s]	CPA/TIGER t[s]
1	7	2	.6	.8	2.8
2	31	3	11.	.3	2.1
3	127	4	390.	.6	3.3
4	511	5	-	1.4	5.1
5	2047	6	-	15.	9.6
6	8191	7	-	230.	24.
7	32767	8	-	4600.	94.

only bounded by an input parameter, hence unwinding limits had to be specified for FSHELL 1 and 2, as stated in the loop-bound column in Table 1. We use FQL queries `cover PATHS(ID, n)`, where n ranges from 1 to 8, to specify n-bounded path coverage, i.e., these queries require test suites that cover each path in the program that repeats a CFA edge at most n times. The test-goal automata that are generated from these queries are mostly deterministic. Consequently, the guidance by test-goal automata yields very efficient analyses, which makes CPA/TIGER scale much better than FSHELL 2, which cannot exploit the fact of a highly deterministic guidance. FSHELL 1 cannot complete the experiments for $n > 3$ within a time limit of 15 minutes. CPA/TIGER scales sublinearly with the number of test goals, whereas the BMC-based approaches of FSHELL 1 and 2 are not well-suited for such programs and queries.

(Basic Block)^2 Coverage in Programs with Unbounded Loops. (Basic block)^2 coverage requires every pair of basic blocks to be covered by some test case and thereby is a better approximation of (unbounded) path coverage than simple basic-block coverage. Table 2 compares FSHELL 2 and CPA/TIGER with respect to (basic block)^2 coverage and (basic block)^3 coverage. In both cases, for loop bounds of 20, CPA/TIGER outperforms FSHELL 2. The FQL query `cover @BASICBLOCKENTRY->@BASICBLOCKENTRY` expresses this coverage criterion.

NT-Drivers. Table 3 summarizes the comparison of FSHELL 2 and CPA/TIGER with respect to simplified NT-drivers and basic block, (basic block)^2, and nodes-(basic block)^2 coverage. Nodes-(basic block)^2 coverage is similar to (basic block)^2 cover-

Table 2. (Basic block)^2 and (basic block)^3 coverage

Source	LOC	Nr. of test goals		FSHELL 2 (LB 20) t[s]		CPA/TIGER t[s]	
		BB^2	BB^3	BB^2	BB^3	BB^2	BB^3
`locks_5`	70	961	29791	22.	720.	7.2	120.
`locks_6`	81	1296	46656	31.	2100.	8.6	280.
`locks_7`	92	1681	68921	38.	3300.	12.	540.
`locks_8`	103	2116	97336	57.	3800.	14.	1200.
`locks_9`	114	2601	132651	64.	6700.	20.	1300.

Table 3. Basic block, (basic block)^2, and nodes-(basic block)^2 coverage on NT-Drivers

Source	LOC	Nr. of Test Goals			FSHELL 2 (LB 3) t[s]			CPA/TIGER t[s]		
		BB	BB^2	NBB^2	BB	BB^2	NBB^2	BB	BB^2	NBB^2
kbfilter1	771	118	13924	33124	2.9	7.3	1500.	7.9	36.	200.
kbfilter2	1352	203	41209	100489	5.2	24.	2700.	14.	97.	770.
kbfilter3	1349	202	40804	99856	5.1	19.	2500.	18.	95.	770.
floppy1	1510	209	43681	123904	3.5	21.	8600.	25.	140.	1100.
floppy2	1529	209	43681	124609	3.8	20.	11000.	23.	130.	1200.
floppy3	2198	291	84681	237169	12.	58.	10000.	46.	310.	3300.
floppy4	2198	291	84681	238144	13.	59.	11000.	41.	270.	3300.
cdaudio1	2997	420	176400	499849	48.	100.	11000.	95.	740.	11000.
cdaudio2	2992	417	173889	495616	26.	110.	9600.	100.	770.	12000.
diskperf	1477	202	40804	114244	4.7	27.	15000.	45.	280.	2000.

Table 4. Achieved line coverage

Source	CPA/TIGER		FSHELL 2	
	Line Coverage [%]	Test Cases	Line Coverage [%]	Test Cases
kbfilter1	88.46	26	88.85	25
kbfilter2	90.83	48	90.83	49
kbfilter3	90.36	48	90.36	48
floppy1	91.37	26	91.37	21
floppy2	89.40	28	89.81	22
floppy3	93.52	61	93.94	51
floppy4	93.67	60	93.67	51
cdaudio1	86.65	77	87.28	69
cdaudio2	86.42	75	87.04	69
diskperf	86.49	27	83.66	21

age but only requires one CFA node of each basic block. For basic block and (basic block)^2 coverage FSHELL 2 performs better, but, for nodes-(basic block)^2 coverage CPA/TIGER performs better. CPA/TIGER does not implement some optimizations for coverage criteria involving nodes which are already implemented for coverage criteria involving CFA edges. Preliminary experiments showed that we can expect a speed-up factor between 2 and 3 for NBB^2 coverage.

Achieved Coverage. Table 4 compares the coverage achieved by the test generators CPA/TIGER and FSHELL 2. Due to overapproximation by predicate abstraction (no bit-precision) there are cases in which CPA/TIGER misses a test case and does not achieve the same coverage as FSHELL 2. On the other hand there is also the last case in Table 4 where CPA/TIGER achieves a higher coverage than FSHELL 2 because of insufficient loop unwindings.

Effects of Information Reuse. In Table 5 we show the effects of the information reuse approach described in this paper. Column A gives the runtime of CPA/TIGER

Table 5. Effects of CPA/TIGER Optimizations exemplified on BB^2 Coverage

Source	A t[s]	B t[s]	C t[s]	D t[s]	E t[s]	F t[s]
kbfilter1	36.	34.	60.	72.	800.	48.
kbfilter2	97.	110.	230.	300.	3700.	170.
kbfilter3	95.	110.	230.	350.	3800.	160.
floppy1	140.	160.	300.	290.	14000.	390.
floppy2	130.	140.	310.	300.	13000.	360.
floppy3	310.	380.	920.	1200.	>15000.	670.
floppy4	270.	350.	920.	1100.	>15000.	610.
cdaudio1	740.	1100.	2400.	3000.	>15000.	2300.
cdaudio2	770.	1100.	2400.	2900.	>15000.	2300.
diskperf	280.	260.	470.	550.	>15000.	1700.

A: all optimizations enabled, **B**: without automaton optimization, **C**: without infeasibility propagation, **D**: inverted order of test goals, **E**: without ARG reuse, **F**: without predicate reuse

with all optimizations enabled. Besides the described reachability information reuse, CPA/TIGER also performs several other optimizations. Column B shows the runtime without a TGA minimization step, in column C, the runtime for a fast infeasibility propagation technique is given. By infeasibility propagation we mean that we can infer from the infeasibility of a TGA the infeasibility of other TGA in case we can show that the feasibility of these automata would imply the feasibility of the infeasible automaton (e.g., by exploiting domination information). Column D shows the effect of different enumeration orders for test-goal automata. The default enumeration strategy for test-goal automata is based on a breadth-first search of the underlying CFA – column D shows the runtime when inverting the order. We also did experiments using a depth-first enumeration of test goals but this strategy was not beneficial. The reuse of parts of the ARG causes the biggest impact in the performance of CPA/TIGER (column E). The last column (F) shows the runtime when not reusing predicates from earlier runs.

Availability. CPA/TIGER is free software and available from the CPACHECKER^2 web page. FSHELL^3 is available as binary for several platforms. The experimental data that are discussed in this article are available on the supplementary webpage http://cpachecker.sosy-lab.org/cpa-tiger.

6   Related Work

In our multi-goal reachability analysis approach we unify query-driven program testing (e.g., [20]) with monitor-based safety checking (e.g., [4, 26]). An extension of BLAST embeds path automata in a relational querying language, for specifying safety

---

^{2} http://cpachecker.sosy-lab.org
^{3} http://code.forsyte.de/fshell

verification problems [4, 5], but not test coverage, as a set of single-goal reachability queries. In a model-based setting, automata-based specifications of coverage were presented by Blom et al. [8] for test-case generation using the model checker UPPAAL [23]. In contrast to directed testing [12] —where 'directed' means directed by branching conditions and randomization— the directedness in our approach stems from user-defined coverage specifications which separate the control from algorithmic issues.

The test-input generator FSHELL [19,20] encodes many TGA into a formula describing a finite unrolling of a program and tries to determine which of the TGA are feasible. Due to the underlying BMC engine of FSHELL, FSHELL can not determine whether a TGA is infeasible (it can only achieve that for a specific unrolling), while CPA/TIGER is able to infer infeasibility as well. Furthermore, the architecture of CPA/TIGER enables the combination of different kinds of reachability analysis (under- and overapproximation as well as different abstraction techniques). We see FSHELL as an complementary test input generation technique which we plan to integrate into the CPA/TIGER architecture.

Our approach generalizes the concepts of summaries where usually pre- and postconditions for specific code parts are encoded. In principle, the summarized code part can be arbitrary, but so far summaries were usually generated at function level [1,2,11]. In this work, we propose the shared behavior of automata as criterion for summarizing and storing reachability information. Albarghouthi et al. [1] divide a reachability query into subqueries in order to parallelize the computation of *one* reachability analysis whereas our approach enables a parallelized analysis of different TGA as well. At the moment CPA/TIGER supports a very simple parallelization strategy: it splits the sets of test goals and performs separate multi-goal reachability analyses for these subsets of TGA. But, except for test inputs, we do not exchange any information between these analysis runs at the moment. Our approach has one potential benefit: the single reachability analyses do not have to finish in order to make reachability information available to other queries. We consider [1, 2, 11] as orthogonal work which is relevant in the context of the reachability analysis we perform. Their summarization and parallelization approach is only of limited use when we want to reason about information reuse across different reachability queries.

Extreme model checking [16] investigates the possible information reuse across different versions of a program. They reexplore a subtree of an abstract reachability tree at abstract states where their abstraction was affected by code changes. In constrast to our approach, they fix the specification across different analysis runs. In multi-goal reachability analysis the specification changes but the code remains the same. In their approach, only the prefix of an abstract reachability tree can be reused. We can reuse more than a prefix of an abstract reachability graph since we do not deal with code changes but changes in the specifications. As soon as the specifications behave the same for some part of the program, we can reuse the respective reachability information.

Different notions of simulation are used in work minimizing specifications given as Büchi automata [10, 27]. The simulation relations are formulated between the original automaton and a minimized version of it. In simulation modulo transition sets, we capture the situation that only parts of a specification are simulated by another automaton. Furthermore, we deal with automata over finite words instead of the infinite word automata used in the above mentioned work. We use simulation relations to identify shared parts of two automata and not to minimize an automaton. CPA/TIGER nevertheless performs some simple minimization steps in order to speed-up the reachability analysis process and increase the precision of the simulation relation computation.

Existing model-checking technology has been applied to test-case generation in a number of other projects, such as Java PathFinder [28] or SAL2 [15]. Recently, model checking and testing were given a more uniform view, combining over-approximating and under-approximating analyses [14] and using interpolation [24]. For hardware designs, [18] presented a coverage-driven test generation approach. As in our approach they reason about reachability as well as unreachability of coverage states (for a fixed coverage criterion) but use different techniques to achieve that: they use BDDs for encoding the state space and underapproximate the set of unreachable coverage states.

7 Conclusion and Future Work

This paper presents an approach for reusing reachability information based on the automaton structure of reachability queries. We introduced simulation modulo a transition set as central concept for identifying shared information of queries. This notion enables us to dynamically query for reachability information in a way similar to databases.

Future research on multi-goal reachability analysis based on our approach of information reuse has a theoretical and a practical side: on the theory side, a deeper investigation of how temporal logics and automata can be used to infer more facts from existing reachability information is of interest; on the practical side, our approach enables the parallelization of the reachability-analysis step and the information-reuse reasoning step which we have not investigated in depth yet. Furthermore, our approach enables the use of offline storage of reachability information which we want to investigate to improve scalability to large programs. At the moment, CPA/TIGER integrates over- and underapproximation in a very simplistic way. Since FSHELL 2 and CPA/TIGER showed complementary strengths in the experiments, a deeper investigation on how to combine over- and underapproximations in reachability analyses is needed.

References

1. Albarghouthi, A., Kumar, R., Nori, A.V., Rajamani, S.K.: Parallelizing Top-down Interprocedural Analyses. In: Proc. PLDI, pp. 217–228. ACM (2012)
2. Anand, S., Godefroid, P., Tillmann, N.: Demand-Driven Compositional Symbolic Execution. In: Ramakrishnan, C.R., Rehof, J. (eds.) TACAS 2008. LNCS, vol. 4963, pp. 367–381. Springer, Heidelberg (2008)
3. Beyer, D., Chlipala, A.J., Henzinger, T.A., Jhala, R., Majumdar, R.: Generating Tests from Counterexamples. In: Proc. ICSE, pp. 326–335. IEEE (2004)
4. Beyer, D., Chlipala, A.J., Henzinger, T.A., Jhala, R., Majumdar, R.: The BLAST Query Language for Software Verification. In: Giacobazzi, R. (ed.) SAS 2004. LNCS, vol. 3148, pp. 2–18. Springer, Heidelberg (2004)
5. Beyer, D., Henzinger, T.A., Jhala, R., Majumdar, R.: The Software Model Checker BLAST. Int. J. Softw. Tools Technol. Transfer 9(5-6), 505–525 (2007)
6. Beyer, D., Henzinger, T.A., Théoduloz, G.: Program Analysis with Dynamic Precision Adjustment. In: Proc. ASE, pp. 29–38. IEEE (2008)

7. Beyer, D., Keremoglu, M.E., Wendler, P.: Predicate Abstraction with Adjustable-block Encoding. In: Proc. FMCAD 2010, pp. 189–198. FMCAD Inc. (2010)
8. Blom, J., Hessel, A., Jonsson, B., Pettersson, P.: Specifying and Generating Test Cases Using Observer Automata. In: Grabowski, J., Nielsen, B. (eds.) FATES 2004. LNCS, vol. 3395, pp. 125–139. Springer, Heidelberg (2005)
9. Clarke, E., Kröning, D., Lerda, F.: A Tool for Checking ANSI-C Programs. In: Jensen, K., Podelski, A. (eds.) TACAS 2004. LNCS, vol. 2988, pp. 168–176. Springer, Heidelberg (2004)
10. Etessami, K., Wilke, T., Schuller, R.A.: Fair Simulation Relations, Parity Games, and State Space Reduction for Büchi Automata. SIAM J. Comput. 34(5), 1159–1175 (2005)
11. Godefroid, P.: Compositional Dynamic Test Generation. In: Proc. POPL, pp. 47–54. ACM (2007)
12. Godefroid, P., Klarlund, N., Sen, K.: DART: Directed Automated Random Testing. In: Proc. PLDI, pp. 213–223. ACM (2005)
13. Godefroid, P., Levin, M.Y., Molnar, D.A.: Automated Whitebox Fuzz Testing. In: Proc. NDSS, pp. 151–166. The Internet Society (2008)
14. Godefroid, P., Nori, A.V., Rajamani, S.K., Tetali, S.: Compositional May-must Program Analysis: Unleashing the Power of Alternation. In: Proc. POPL, pp. 43–56. ACM (2010)
15. Hamon, G., de Moura, L.M., Rushby, J.M.: Generating Efficient Test Sets with a Model Checker. In: Proc. SEFM, pp. 261–270. IEEE (2004)
16. Henzinger, T.A., Jhala, R., Majumdar, R., Sanvido, M.A.A.: Extreme Model Checking. In: Dershowitz, N. (ed.) Verification: Theory and Practice. LNCS, vol. 2772, pp. 332–358. Springer, Heidelberg (2004)
17. Henzinger, T.A., Jhala, R., Majumdar, R., Sutre, G.: Lazy Abstraction. In: Proc. POPL, pp. 58–70. ACM (2002)
18. Ho, P.H., Shiple, T., Harer, K., Kukula, J., Damiano, R., Bertacco, V., Taylor, J., Long, J.: Smart Simulation using Collaborative Formal and Simulation Engines. In: Proc. ICCAD, pp. 120–126. IEEE Press (2000)
19. Holzer, A., Schallhart, C., Tautschnig, M., Veith, H.: FSHELL: Systematic Test Case Generation for Dynamic Analysis and Measurement. In: Gupta, A., Malik, S. (eds.) CAV 2008. LNCS, vol. 5123, pp. 209–213. Springer, Heidelberg (2008)
20. Holzer, A., Schallhart, C., Tautschnig, M., Veith, H.: Query-Driven Program Testing. In: Jones, N.D., Müller-Olm, M. (eds.) VMCAI 2009. LNCS, vol. 5403, pp. 151–166. Springer, Heidelberg (2009)
21. Holzer, A., Schallhart, C., Tautschnig, M., Veith, H.: How Did You Specify Your Test Suite. In: Proc. ASE, pp. 407–416. ACM (2010)
22. Holzer, A., Tautschnig, M., Schallhart, C., Veith, H.: An Introduction to Test Specification in FQL. In: Barner, S., Kröning, D., Raz, O. (eds.) HVC 2010. LNCS, vol. 6504, pp. 9–22. Springer, Heidelberg (2010)
23. Larsen, K.G., Pettersson, P., Yi, W.: UPPAAL in a Nutshell. Int. J. Softw. Tools Technol. Transfer 1(1-2), 134–152 (1997)
24. McMillan, K.L.: Lazy Annotation for Program Testing and Verification. In: Touili, T., Cook, B., Jackson, P. (eds.) CAV 2010. LNCS, vol. 6174, pp. 104–118. Springer, Heidelberg (2010)
25. Milner, R.: An Algebraic Definition of Simulation Between Programs. In: Proc. IJCAI 1971, pp. 481–489. Morgan Kaufmann Publishers Inc. (1971)
26. Serý, O.: Enhanced Property Specification and Verification in BLAST. In: Chechik, M., Wirsing, M. (eds.) FASE 2009. LNCS, vol. 5503, pp. 456–469. Springer, Heidelberg (2009)
27. Somenzi, F., Bloem, R.: Efficient Büchi Automata from LTL Formulae. In: Emerson, E.A., Sistla, A.P. (eds.) CAV 2000. LNCS, vol. 1855, pp. 248–263. Springer, Heidelberg (2000)
28. Visser, W., Pasareanu, C.S., Khurshid, S.: Test Input Generation with Java PathFinder. In: Proc. ISSTA, pp. 97–107. ACM (2004)

Quarantining Weakness*
Compositional Reasoning under Relaxed Memory Models
(Extended Abstract)

Radha Jagadeesan[1], Gustavo Petri[2], Corin Pitcher[1], and James Riely[1]

[1] DePaul University
[2] Purdue University

1 Introduction

In sequential computing, every method of an object can be described in isolation via preconditions and postconditions. However, reasoning in a concurrent setting requires a characterization of all possible interactions across method invocations. Herlihy and Wing [1990]'s notion of linearizability simplifies such reasoning by intuitively ensuring that each method invocation "takes effect" between its invocation and response events.

This approach had two basic shortcomings. Firstly, in Herlihy and Wing's definition of linearizability, the interfaces are not expressive enough to codify external calls emanating from the component. Thus, objects are closed and passive.

Secondly, the definitions are for a memory model with a global total order on memory operations, thus satisfying *sequential consistency* (SC). SC is not realized by all architectures or runtime systems [Adve and Gharachorloo 1996; Adve and Boehm 2010], motivating models of relaxed memory in hardware, such as TSO [Sewell et al. 2010], PSO [SPARC, Inc. 1994], Power [Sarkar et al. 2011], and runtime systems, such as Java [Manson et al. 2005; Sevcík 2008] and C++ [Boehm and Adve 2008; Batty et al. 2011]. This has motivated recent definitions of linearizability specific to the TSO [Burckhardt et al. 2012; Gotsman et al. 2012] and C11 [Batty et al. 2013] memory models.

We propose new definitions to address both of these limitations. Our methodology aims to keep the interfaces free of the intricacies of particular relaxed memory models. Our approach has the following characteristics.

(1) We model calls to component functions process-algebraically. This allows us to treat callbacks and to give a symmetric definition of composition between clients and libraries. Thus, our definitions encompass active components (that can evolve autonomously even without input from the environment) and open components (that invoke methods on components provided by the environment) and environment assumptions (pre/postconditions and the permitted sequences of method calls to a component).

(2) Our definitions are not specific to a particular memory model. Rather, we identify the criteria that a relaxed memory model needs to satisfy in order to fit into our framework: the examples that satisfy our criteria include SC, TSO, PSO and a variant of the Java Memory Model (JMM).

---

* Research supported by NSF 0916741.

M. Felleisen and P. Gardner (Eds.): ESOP 2013, LNCS 7792, pp. 492–511, 2013.

We establish an abstraction theorem: a component can safely be substituted for its interface in a non-interfering program. Moreover, for special classes of programs, we simplify the reasoning further by quarantining the effects of relaxed memory, allowing programmers to program to sequential interfaces, even when the code has data races. Recall the definition of data race free (DRF) models: Informally, a program is DRF if no SC execution of the program leads to a state in which a write happens concurrently with another operation on the same location. A *DRF model* requires that the programmer's view of relaxed computation coincides with SC computations for programs that are DRF. TSO, PSO and the JMM are all DRF models. We establish the following.

(1) If a stateful component is DRF and the underlying memory model satisfies the DRF requirement, our notion of linearizability usually coincides with that of Herlihy and Wing, so classical techniques to verify linearizability can be used directly. Thus, in many cases, our definitions permit the use of standard proof techniques.

(2) If a client is DRF, and the underlying memory model satisfies the DRF requirement, the client can ignore all memory model subtleties when using a library that is linearizable as per our definitions, even if the library itself is *racy*. More precisely, it is sound for the client to reason solely with the sequential interface of the component, as in [Herlihy and Wing 1990].

Rest of the paper. In Section 2, we describe background material on linearizability in order to clarify the difficulties caused by relaxed memory. We discuss related work in Section 3 and develop our semantic framework in Sections 4–6. We define linearizability in Section 7 and provide several examples. In Section 8, we turn to techniques for establishing linearizability under relaxed memory using techniques developed for sequential consistency. In Section 9–10, we establish the basic properties of linearizability. Many definitions and all proofs are elided in this extended abstract.

2   Background: Linearizability

To illustrate the issues that arise when reasoning compositionally, we describe the specification and implementation of a lock and a one-place buffer implemented using the lock.

Specifying the lock. To begin, we give the specification of a lock using an regular expression. We use regular expressions informally; the actual specifications are sets of traces. Let s and t be thread identifiers. Because we are interested in overlapping executions, we separate call and return into separate actions: $\langle s?\text{call } f\ u\rangle$ represents a call by s to function f with argument u, and $\langle s!\text{ret } f\ v\rangle$ represents the corresponding return with result v. (The ? and ! indicate that these are calls *in* to the lock and returns *out*; we shall see the symmetric case shortly.)

$$(\ (\ \langle s?\text{call rl}\rangle\langle s!\text{ret rl}\rangle \ )^+ \langle t?\text{call aq}\rangle\langle t!\text{ret aq}\rangle \ )^*$$

According to the specification, the lock is initially in its "acquired" state. Only after one or more calls to the "release" method rl, can the lock be "reacquired" using aq. This regular expression is not meant to refer to specific concrete thread names s and t. Rather, it is meant to convey the idea that calls and returns have matching thread names.

Let Ψ_{lock} be the prefix-closed set of traces that satisfy this regular expression. This is a "sequential" specification of the lock, in that no two function calls overlap.

We now turn to implementation of the lock. Here we use an *atomic* variable, which we define to be similar to volatile variables in Java, with an additional compare-and-set (cas): w.cas(u,v) returns false if $w \neq u$, otherwise it returns true and sets w to v.

$$\text{atomic } w=1; \text{ fun } rl() \{ w=0; \} \qquad \text{(Lock)}$$
$$\text{fun } aq() \{ \text{ do skip until } w.cas(0,1); \}$$

Initially, calls to aq will spin, only returning after another thread calls rl. In the vocabulary of [Lamport 1979], a call to rl *happens-before* the return from aq. The happens-before relation allows a partial order to be recovered from the total order prescribed by a trace: actions of a single thread are ordered sequentially, but actions of different threads are unordered. Inter-thread order requires *synchronization*, which is we implement using atomic variables, such as w.

Every write to an atomic variable happens-before every subsequent read of the same atomic. An unsuccessful cas acts like a read, whereas a successful cas acts like both a read and a write. In traces, atomics produce three types of action: writes produce $\langle s \text{ rel } w \rangle$ actions, reads produce $\langle s \text{ acq } w \rangle$ actions, and successful cas produce $\langle s \text{ cas } w \rangle$ actions; unsuccessful cas produce nothing. The happens-before relation orders every $\langle \text{rel } w \rangle$ and $\langle \text{cas } w \rangle$ with every subsequent $\langle \text{acq } w \rangle$ and $\langle \text{cas } w \rangle$. These relations are based on the identity, w, of the atomic.

Let Φ_{lock} be the set of implementation traces generated by the implementation code above. These include traces of the form

$$((\langle s?\text{call } rl \rangle \langle s \text{ rel } w \rangle \langle s!\text{ret } rl \rangle)^+ \langle t?\text{call } aq \rangle \langle t \text{ cas } w \rangle \langle t!\text{ret } aq \rangle)^*.$$

(This regular expression is not exhaustive, since the implementation also generates overlapping function calls; however, it is sufficient for the discussion at hand.)

Herlihy and Wing [1990] propose linearizability as a way to relate the implementation of a concurrent component to its specification. An implementation is *linearizable* if for every trace of the implementation, there exists a trace in the specification such that (1) each thread makes the same method invocations in the same order, and (2) the order of non-overlapping invocations is preserved. We write $\Phi_{\text{lock}} \vDash \Psi_{\text{lock}}$ to indicate that Φ_{lock} is a valid implementation of Ψ_{lock} in this sense.

Specifying the buffer. We now give the specification and implementation of a one-place buffer using Lock. The buffer's sequential specification can be given as follows.

$$(\langle s?\text{call put } v \rangle \langle s!\text{ret put} \rangle \langle t?\text{call get} \rangle \langle t!\text{ret get } v \rangle)^*$$

As before, let Ψ_{buf} be the prefix-closed set of traces that satisfy this regular expression.

The implementation of the one place buffer uses two locks. We use subscripts to distinguish them. One of the locks has interface $\text{acq}_{\text{empty}}/\text{rel}_{\text{empty}}$ (initially "released", with w==0) and the other has interface $\text{acq}_{\text{full}}/\text{rel}_{\text{full}}$ (initially "acquired" with w==1). Thus, the buffer is initially empty. (Note that two "instances of a class" are represented here as two separate components.)

$$\text{var } x=0; \text{ fun put}(z) \{ \text{acq}_{\text{empty}}(); x=z; \text{rel}_{\text{full}}(); \} \qquad \text{(Buffer)}$$
$$\text{fun get}() \{ \text{acq}_{\text{full}}(); \text{ let } z=x; \text{rel}_{\text{empty}}(); \text{ return } z; \}$$

Let Φ_{buf} be the set of traces derived from this implementation, including traces such as

$$
\begin{aligned}
(\ &\langle\mathsf{s?call\ put\ v}\rangle \\
&\langle\mathsf{s!call\ acq_{empty}}\rangle\langle\mathsf{s?ret\ acq_{empty}}\rangle\langle\mathsf{s\ wr\ x\ v}\rangle\langle\mathsf{s!call\ rel_{full}}\rangle\langle\mathsf{s?ret\ rel_{full}}\rangle \\
&\langle\mathsf{s!ret\ put}\rangle\langle\mathsf{t?call\ get}\rangle \\
&\langle\mathsf{t!call\ acq_{full}}\rangle\langle\mathsf{t?ret\ acq_{full}}\rangle\langle\mathsf{t\ rd\ x\ v}\rangle\langle\mathsf{t!call\ rel_{empty}}\rangle\langle\mathsf{t?ret\ rel_{empty}}\rangle \\
&\langle\mathsf{t!ret\ put\ v}\rangle\ )^*.
\end{aligned}
$$

This trace contains actions of the form $\langle\mathsf{s!call\ f\ u}\rangle$ which represent a call out to another component; likewise, $\langle\mathsf{s?ret\ f\ v}\rangle$ represents the corresponding return. In this case, the implementation is using services provided by other components.

We would like to be able to verify the correctness of Buffer using the sequential specification of Lock. That is, conclude $\Phi_{\mathsf{buf}} \otimes \Phi_{\mathsf{lock}} \vDash \Psi_{\mathsf{buf}}$ from $\Phi_{\mathsf{buf}} \otimes \Psi_{\mathsf{lock}} \vDash \Psi_{\mathsf{buf}}$, where $\otimes$ is a suitable notion of composition. Herlihy and Wing validate this approach under SC semantics. Burckhardt, Gotsman, Musuvathi, and Yang [2012] show that Herlihy and Wing's results fail for relaxed memory models and adapt them to TSO. Here we provide a different solution to that problem.

Traditional linearizability fails here, because it is impossible to establish the premise $\Phi_{\mathsf{buf}} \otimes \Psi_{\mathsf{lock}} \vDash \Psi_{\mathsf{buf}}$. To see why, observe that any reasonable definition $\Phi_{\mathsf{buf}} \otimes \Psi_{\mathsf{lock}}$ admits the following trace under relaxed memory. (For brevity, the calls to the locks are shown as elipses.)

$$
\begin{aligned}
&\langle\mathsf{s?call\ put\ 1}\rangle\cdots\langle\mathsf{s\ wr\ x\ 1}\rangle\cdots\langle\mathsf{s!ret\ put}\rangle\langle\mathsf{t?call\ get}\rangle\cdots\langle\mathsf{t\ rd\ x\ 1}\rangle\cdots\langle\mathsf{t!ret\ get\ 1}\rangle \\
&\langle\mathsf{r?call\ put\ 2}\rangle\cdots\langle\mathsf{r\ wr\ x\ 2}\rangle\cdots\langle\mathsf{r!ret\ put}\rangle\langle\mathsf{t?call\ get}\rangle\cdots\langle\mathsf{t\ rd\ x\ 1}\rangle\cdots\langle\mathsf{t!ret\ get\ 1}\rangle
\end{aligned}
\qquad (\dagger)
$$

The final call to get returns a stale value. The race on variable x is not resolved, and thus the earlier write on x remains visible.

Of course, if one looks at the specification of Lock, the problem is immediately apparent: it's too weak! In relaxed models, data structures have memory effects which are not captured by their functional interface. Indeed, the documentation in APIs such as java.util.concurrent [Sun Microsystems 2004] pays significant attention to exactly this fact. These APIs detail the happens-before behavior of the methods using happens-before edges that go from the beginning of one method activation to the end of another (or a set of others); that is, from call to return.

We allow happens-before to be captured in specifications by introducing names, a, on actions. Each $\langle\mathsf{?call}\rangle$ gets a unique name, and each $\langle\mathsf{!ret}\rangle$ gets a set of names. The interpretation is that $\langle\mathsf{s?call\ f\ \vec{u}\ a}\rangle$ happens-before $\langle\mathsf{t!ret\ f\ \vec{v}\ A}\rangle$ if $a \in A$.

With this addition, Lock can be specified as follows

$$
(\ (\ \langle\mathsf{r?call\ rl}\rangle\langle\mathsf{r!ret\ rl}\rangle\ )^*\ \langle\mathsf{s?call\ rl\ a}\rangle\langle\mathsf{s!ret\ rl}\rangle\langle\mathsf{t?call\ aq}\rangle\langle\mathsf{t!ret\ aq\ \{a\}}\rangle\ )^*
$$

This specification is now strong enough to deduce happens-before edges from each put to get that it enables, and vice versa. Thus, in trace $(\dagger)$ above, the write to x in the first put is no longer visible to the second get. More generally, we are able to establish $\Phi_{\mathsf{buf}} \otimes \Psi_{\mathsf{lock}} \vDash \Psi_{\mathsf{buf}}$.

3   Related Work

We discuss the most closely related papers here, referring to others in context. Herlihy and Wing [1990] defined linearizability. From a client perspective, the set of linearizations of a linearizable object is an operational refinement of the object [Filipovic, O'Hearn, Rinetzky, and Yang 2010], i.e. the client is unable to distinguish the implementation from the specification. Thus, a client of a linearizable object can take an atomic view of method invocations. The verification method for object linearizability relies on finding linearization points for methods. For each function call, the linearization point is the moment at which the function appears to execute atomically. Composition of non-interfering objects preserves linearizability. Gotsman and Yang [2012] mitigate the stricture of interference-freedom in this framework using ownership ideas.

The papers cited above make a sharp distinction between clients and libraries; clients are permitted to make method invocations and libraries accept method invocations. Thus, they are unable to describe the interface of open components such as a thread pool that relies on an external bounded buffer library. In contrast, our enhanced notion of interfaces is able to describe such components. In terms of implementations, our library can both make and receive method invocations in external interactions, in addition to also being able to invoke internal library methods. Indeed, we stop short of adding full objects, as suggested by Filipovic, O'Hearn, Rinetzky, and Yang [2010], only to avoid cluttering the presentation with heavy syntactic machinery.

The definition of linearizability relies on an SC view of shared memory. Batty, Dodds, and Gotsman [2013] address linearizability in the context of the C/C++ memory models. When specialized to SC, their definition of linearizability is stricter than that of Herlihy and Wing. In contrast, when specialized to SC, our definitions are *not* stricter.

In TSO, an update to a variable might be buffered and may not be seen by a reader in a different thread until the update is committed to the main memory. Burckhardt et al. [2012] address linearizability for the TSO memory model. In contrast both to Herlihy and Wing and to our definitions, their paper incorporates two extra actions for each method invocation in the sequential specification of an object: one to record when buffer updates made by the client are seen by the library, and the other to record when the updates made by library are committed to main memory. In our work we maintain the atomicity of methods of Herlihy and Wing by only associating call and return actions with each method invocation.

More generally, our methodology keeps the interface of a component free of the intricacies of the particular relaxed memory model under consideration. In this paper, we are thus able to address SC, TSO, PSO and a JMM variant. In particular, our analysis of TSO is subtle enough to address all the examples of Burckhardt et al. [2012], even though, from a purely formal TSO perspective, there is clearly greater expressiveness in their definition. Consequently, any data race free client can work precisely against a SC interface in our setting, whereas Gotsman, Musuvathi, and Yang [2012] explore the conditions on compilation necessary to validate the use of SC interfaces under TSO.

4   Traces

The semantics of a component is given by a set of *traces*, defined below. We build the syntax from the following disjoint sets. Let $u, v \in \mathbb{Z}$ range over values, $a, b \in Act$ over action names, $A, B \subseteq Act$ over sets of action names, $f, g \in Fun$ over function names, $F \subseteq Fun$ over sets of function names, $s, t \in Thrd$ over thread names (including the reserved thread names "tinit" and "tcom") and $S, T \subseteq Thrd$ over sets thread names. Let $\eta \in Fun \uplus Thrd$ range over names, which include both function and thread names, and H, G over sets of names.

Traces are strings of *actions*. These are divided into *communication actions*, described below, and *memory actions*, described in Section 5. For now, let *Mem* be the set of all memory actions.

$$\alpha, \gamma ::= \langle s\,! \text{call } f\,\vec{u}\,a\,A \rangle \mid \langle s? \text{call } f\,\vec{u}\,a\,A \rangle \mid \langle s\,.\,\text{call } f\,\vec{u}\,a\,A \rangle$$
$$\mid \langle s? \text{ret } f\,\vec{u}\,a\,A \rangle \mid \langle s\,! \text{ret } f\,\vec{u}\,a\,A \rangle \mid \langle s\,.\,\text{ret } f\,\vec{u}\,a\,A \rangle \mid \cdots$$

Communication actions include seven components, discussed below: thread identifier s, polarity in $\{!, ?, .\}$, action type in $\{\text{call}, \text{ret}\}$, function name f, vector of arguments or return values $\vec{u}$, definition a, and use set A.

We typically elide the uninteresting parts of an action; missing parts are existentially quantified. For example, we write $\langle ! \text{call } f\,\vec{u}\,a\,A \rangle$ to abbreviate $(\exists s)\langle s\,! \text{call } f\,\vec{u}\,a\,A \rangle$, and similarly for other abbreviations such as $\langle s\,! \text{call} \rangle$, $\langle \text{call } f \rangle$, $\langle s\,! f \rangle$ and $\langle ! \rangle$.

The thread identifier identifies the thread that performed the action.

As in Jeffrey and Rathke [2005], call and return actions include a *polarity*. Actions containing a "?" are *input*; those containing "!" are *output*; actions containing "." are *internal*, as are memory actions. Input actions are offered by *quiescent* threads, whereas all others are initiated by *active* threads. Two actions are *complementary* if one is an input, the other an output and they are identical when action names and "?" and "!" are ignored. If $\alpha \in \{\langle ! \rangle, \langle ? \rangle\}$, we say α *is I/O*.

Actions $\langle ! \text{call } f \rangle$ and $\langle ? \text{ret } f \rangle$ occur in the traces of components that do *not* define f; whereas $\langle ? \text{call } f \rangle$, $\langle ! \text{ret } f \rangle$, $\langle . \text{call } f \rangle$ and $\langle . \text{ret } f \rangle$ occur those that *do*. Action $\langle ? \text{call} \rangle$ represents a call from outside the component, whereas $\langle . \text{call} \rangle$ represents a call from the component to itself. Thus, input and output actions cause a shift across the boundary of the component for that thread, whereas the internal actions do not.

Call actions include the vector of actual parameters. Return actions include a vector of return values. Several examples require multiple return values. An obvious generalization would be to support first-class tuples, but this would complicate the presentation.

The action names decorating actions are used to specify ordering properties (Section 5). Each action *defines* a unique action name a. For the purposes of defining traces and trace composition, these names are mere decorations: we identify traces up to the renaming of action names. In $\langle ? A \rangle$, the set A contains names defined by "!" actions and represents an order relied upon by the component. In $\langle ! A \rangle$, the set A contains names defined by "?" actions and represents an order guaranteed the component. In $\langle . A \rangle$, the set A contains names defined by "." actions and represent the interaction of two components, one which relies upon A and one which guarantees it. In operationally generated traces, A is empty for any $\langle ! A \rangle$ or $\langle . A \rangle$; these sets or nonempty when working with specification interfaces.

Definition 4.1 (Trace). For any given thread, define a *single-threaded balanced trace* to be one generated by the following grammar.

$$B ::= A \mid Q \qquad\qquad\qquad\qquad \text{(Single-threaded balanced trace)}$$
$$A ::= \langle .\text{call } f \rangle\, A\, \langle .\text{ret } f \rangle \mid A\, A \mid \varepsilon \qquad\qquad \text{(Active trace)}$$
$$\mid \langle !\text{call } f \rangle\, Q\, \langle ?\text{ret } f \rangle \mid M$$
$$Q ::= \langle ?\text{call } f \rangle\, A\, \langle !\text{ret } f \rangle \mid Q\, Q \mid \varepsilon \qquad\qquad \text{(Quiescent trace)}$$
$$M \in \textit{Mem} \qquad\qquad\qquad\qquad\qquad \text{(Memory action)}$$

(We elide uninteresting metavariables within actions. Because they are single-threaded, all actions have the same thread name.)

A *balanced trace* is any interleaving of single-threaded balanced traces with distinct thread names. A *trace* is a trace of actions that is well-formed and is also a prefix of a balanced trace. Let σ, ρ, π range over traces.   □

We give an inductive characterization of traces in the full version of this paper.

We expose, and nest, calls and returns as with VPLs [Alur and Madhusudan 2009]. As seen from the grammar, prefixes of single-threaded balanced trace are divided into two *polarities*: quiescent and active. By convention, ε is quiescent. For all other traces, the polarity is determined by the first action of the trace: if it is $\langle ?\text{call} \rangle$, then the trace is quiescent; otherwise the polarity is active.

Traces have three forms of bracketing, indexed by thread: call/return, input/output and output/input. (Internal actions provide no interesting bracketing other than call/return.) In the trace $\langle s?\text{call } f \rangle\langle s!\text{call } g \rangle\langle s?\text{ret } g \rangle\langle s!\text{ret } f \rangle$, the call/return matches are $\langle s?\text{call } f \rangle/\langle s!\text{ret } f \rangle$ and $\langle s!\text{call } g \rangle/\langle s?\text{ret } g \rangle$; the input/output matches are $\langle s?\text{call } f \rangle/\langle s!\text{call } g \rangle$ and $\langle s?\text{ret } g \rangle/\langle s!\text{ret } f \rangle$; the output/input match is $\langle s!\text{call } g \rangle/\langle s?\text{ret } g \rangle$.

Here are some further examples: $\langle s! \rangle\langle s? \rangle$ is a trace, but $\langle s! \rangle\langle s! \rangle$ is not. $\langle s! \rangle\langle t? \rangle\langle s? \rangle$ is a trace, but $\langle s! \rangle\langle s? \rangle\langle s? \rangle$ is not. $\langle s? \rangle\langle s. \rangle$ is a trace, but $\langle s! \rangle\langle s. \rangle$ is not.

Definition 4.2. Define the function *thrd* to return the thread name occurring inside an action and *thrds* to return the set of threads in a sequence of actions. Similarly, define the partial functions *fun* and *funs* to return the function name. For example, if $\alpha = \langle s!\text{call } f\ \vec{u}\ a\ A \rangle$, then $\textit{thrd}(\alpha) = s$ and $\textit{fun}(\alpha) = f$.

Given a trace σ, define the *thread projection* $\sigma|_s$ of that trace, which includes only the actions attributed to thread s; this is always a prefix of a single-threaded balanced trace. Define the following functions over traces.

$$\textit{intern}(\alpha_1 \cdots \alpha_n) \triangleq \{f \mid \exists i.\ \alpha_i = \langle ?\text{call } f \rangle \text{ or } \alpha_i = \langle .\text{call } f \rangle\}$$
$$\cup\, \{s \mid (\sigma|_s) \neq \varepsilon \text{ is an active trace}\} \setminus \{\text{tinit, tcom}\}$$
$$\textit{extern}(\alpha_1 \cdots \alpha_n) \triangleq \{f \mid \exists i.\ \alpha_i = \langle !\text{call } f \rangle\}$$
$$\cup\, \{s \mid (\sigma|_s) \neq \varepsilon \text{ is an quiescent trace}\}$$

These definitions lift to trace sets via set union. When interpreted over trace sets, *intern* identifies the functions and threads defined by the component, whereas *extern* identifies the functions and threads mentioned in a component, but not defined by it.

A trace σ is *coherent* if $intern(\sigma) \cap extern(\sigma) = \emptyset$. We assume that all traces are coherent. We also assume other well-formedness criteria, detailed in the full version of this paper.

A set Σ of traces is *coherent* if $intern(\Sigma) \cap extern(\Sigma) = \emptyset$. Note that this is stronger than requiring only that each individual trace be coherent. Let Φ, Ψ range over coherent sets of traces.

A trace is *sequential* if it can be extended in such a way that every $\langle s? \rangle$ is followed by actions exclusively by s, up to a terminating $\langle s! \rangle$. A trace set is *sequential* if it contains only sequential traces.

A trace set is an *interface* if it contains only I/O actions.   □

5   Memory Actions and Memory Orders

Our approach is parametric with respect to the specific memory model considered. For concreteness, we will consider four models here: seq, hb, tso and pso. To keep the formalism simple, we assume that (1) memory stores only integers, (2) atomics provide the only form of synchronization and (3) components are specified as sets of functions, variables and threads.

Let $z \in Reg$ range over registers (local variables), $x, y \in DataVar$ over data variables and $w \in SyncVar$ over synchronization variables. We use the general term *variable* to include data variables and synchronization variables, but not registers. Memory actions are as follows.

$$\alpha, \gamma ::= \cdots \mid \langle s \text{ wr } x\, u\, a \rangle \mid \langle s \text{ rd } x\, u\, a \rangle \mid \langle \text{com } s\, x\, a \rangle$$
$$\mid \langle s \text{ rel } w \rangle \quad \mid \langle s \text{ acq } w \rangle \quad \mid \langle s \text{ cas } w \rangle$$

For data variables, the actions record writes, reads and commits. For synchronization variables, the actions record releases, acquires and compare-and-sets. Action names (metavariable a, as before) are used to record relations between data actions. Commit actions are used by buffering models, such as tso and pso, to indicate the point at which a write is moved from the local buffer to main memory. Non-buffering models, such as seq and hb, have no commit actions.

Neither initializations nor commits are performed by the program, but by the underlying operational machinery. Initialization actions are normal writes attributed to the reserved pseudo-thread "tinit". Commit actions are only performed by the reserved pseudo-thread "tcom"; thus we simply define $thrd(\langle \text{com } s\, x\, a \rangle) = \text{tcom}$. In $\langle \text{com } s\, x\, a \rangle$, the identifiers s and x are redundant with the corresponding $\langle s \text{ wr } x\, u\, a \rangle$.

Synchronization variables carry memory effects whereas data variables do not. Registers are used to write programs, but are not shared between threads; thus, we do not require actions relating to registers.

The name a is *defined* in $\langle \text{wr } a \rangle$ and *used* in $\langle \text{rd } a \rangle$ and $\langle \text{com } a \rangle$. We expect that every write action is committed at most once and that the redundant information in read and commit actions should match the corresponding write. In addition, initialization writes by thread "tinit" must appear at the beginning of a trace. These bookkeeping requirements are included in the notion of *well-formed* trace, formalized in the full version of this paper. Most of the requirements are unsurprising. We note only that well-formedness does *not* require that a read be proceeded by the matching write, since this is not true under all of the models we consider.

Example 5.1. Consider the following traces, each containing actions from three different threads (eliding initialization and commit actions).

$$\langle s \, wr \, x \, a \rangle \langle t \, wr \, x \, b \rangle \langle r \, rd \, x \, b \rangle \tag{a}$$

$$\langle t \, wr \, x \, b \rangle \langle s \, wr \, x \, a \rangle \langle r \, rd \, x \, b \rangle \tag{b}$$

$$\langle s \, wr \, x \, a \rangle \langle r \, rd \, x \, b \rangle \langle t \, wr \, x \, b \rangle \tag{c}$$

$$\langle s \, wr \, x \, a \rangle \langle s \, wr \, y \, b \rangle \langle t \, wr \, x \, c \rangle \langle t \, wr \, y \, d \rangle \langle r \, rd \, y \, d \rangle \langle r \, rd \, x \, a \rangle \tag{d}$$

- Under seq, reads and writes are atomic; thus, a read must be fulfilled by the previous write. Only trace (a) is allowable; the others require that a read see a stale write.
- Under tso, writes are placed in a buffer which is not visible to other threads; for any given thread, the buffered writes are committed to main memory in FIFO order, but the order between threads is nondeterministic. Thus, traces (a) and (b) are allowable.
- pso is similar to tso, except that each thread has a separate buffer for each variable. Thus, traces (a), (b) and (d) are allowable.
- Under hb, a write may be seen by a reader even before it is generated by the writer. Thus, all four executions are allowable.   □

Example 5.2. Consider the following unsynchronized implementation of a one place buffer (on the left) and client (on the right).

```
var y=0                           var x=0
fun put (z) {y=z}                 thrd s {x=1; put(3); wait(4); let z'=x}
fun wait (z) {do skip until y==z} thrd t {wait(3); x=2; put(4)}
```

Ignoring initialization and commits, here is a single trace of the library and of the client, each in isolation. (The label sets decorating return actions are specification elements. Those on the library output actions are *guarantees*, whereas those on client input actions are *relies*.)

$$\langle s?call \, put \, 3 \, a \rangle \langle s \, wr \, y \, 3 \rangle \langle s!ret \, \emptyset \rangle \qquad \langle s \, wr \, x \, 1 \rangle \langle s!call \, put \, 3 \, a \rangle \langle s?ret \, \emptyset \rangle$$
$$\langle t?call \, wait \, 3 \, b \rangle \langle t \, rd \, y \, 3 \rangle \langle t!ret \, \{a\} \rangle \qquad \langle t!call \, wait \, 3 \, b \rangle \langle t?ret \, \{a\} \rangle \langle t \, wr \, x \, 2 \rangle$$
$$\langle t?call \, put \, 4 \, c \rangle \langle t \, wr \, y \, 4 \rangle \langle t!ret \, \emptyset \rangle \qquad \langle t!call \, put \, 4 \, c \rangle \langle t?ret \, \emptyset \rangle$$
$$\langle s?call \, wait \, 4 \, d \rangle \langle s \, rd \, y \, 4 \rangle \langle s!ret \, \{c\} \rangle \qquad \langle s!call \, wait \, 4 \, d \rangle \langle s?ret \, \{c\} \rangle \langle s \, rd \, x \, 1 \rangle$$

Composing the traces, we have the following trace (on the left), which, if we elide "." actions, is equivalent to the trace on the right.

$$\langle s \, wr \, x \, 1 \rangle \langle s.call \, put \, 3 \, a \rangle \langle s \, wr \, y \, 3 \rangle \langle s.ret \, \emptyset \rangle \qquad \langle s \, wr \, x \, 1 \rangle \langle s \, wr \, y \, 3 \rangle$$
$$\langle t.call \, wait \, 3 \, b \rangle \langle t \, rd \, y \, 3 \rangle \langle t.ret \, \{a\} \rangle \langle t \, wr \, x \, 2 \rangle \qquad \langle t \, rd \, y \, 3 \rangle \langle t \, wr \, x \, 2 \rangle$$
$$\langle t.call \, put \, 4 \, c \rangle \langle t \, wr \, y \, 4 \rangle \langle t.ret \, \emptyset \rangle \qquad \langle t \, wr \, y \, 4 \rangle \langle s \, rd \, y \, 4 \rangle$$
$$\langle s.call \, wait \, 4 \, d \rangle \langle s \, rd \, y \, 4 \rangle \langle s.ret \, \{c\} \rangle \langle s \, rd \, x \, 1 \rangle \qquad \langle s \, rd \, x \, 1 \rangle$$

Ignoring calls and returns, under what circumstances should such a trace be allowed?

On the one hand, it is clearly *not* allowed under sequential semantics, since $\langle s \, rd \, x \, 1 \rangle$ does not see the most recent write. On the other hand, it is clearly *allowed* under a happens-before semantics, since there is no synchronization between thread s and t.

For tso and pso, the situation is less obvious. In fact, pso will allow the trace, but tso will not. The difference is that tso enforces an ordering between $\langle t \text{ wr } x\ 2\rangle$ and $\langle t \text{ wr } y\ 4\rangle$, whereas pso does not.

Moving from the combined trace back to the trace of the library in isolation, for each memory model, we may ask "does the library implementation meets its specification?" In this case, the answer is positive for seq and tso, and negative for pso and hb.

Similarly, moving from the combined trace back to the trace of the client in isolation, for each memory model, we may ask "is the final client read valid?" For this question, the answers are reversed: valid for pso and hb, and invalid for seq and tso.   □

To formalize these properties, we introduce a notion of memory ordering, which is derivable from a trace. Recall that tinit is a reserved name.

Definition 5.3. The partial function *var* is undefined for commit and nonmemory actions and otherwise returns the variable mentioned: $var(\alpha) \stackrel{\Delta}{=} x$ if $\alpha \in \{\langle \text{wr } x\rangle, \langle \text{rd } x\rangle\}$; $var(\alpha) \stackrel{\Delta}{=} w$ if $\alpha \in \{\langle \text{rel } w\rangle, \langle \text{acq } w\rangle, \langle \text{cas } w\rangle\}$; and $var(\alpha)$ is undefined otherwise.

From a trace $\sigma = \alpha_1 \cdots \alpha_n$, we derive several relations.

- $i <^\sigma_{\text{rf}} j$ if $\alpha_i = \langle \text{wr } a\rangle$, $\alpha_j = \langle \text{rd } a\rangle$ *(reads-from relation)*
- $i <^\sigma_{\text{cb}} j$ if $\alpha_i = \langle \text{wr } a\rangle$, $\exists \ell < j.\ \alpha_\ell = \langle \text{com } a\rangle$ *(committed-before relation)*
- $i <^\sigma_{\text{rely}} j$ if $\alpha_i = \langle !\ a\rangle$, $\alpha_j = \langle ?\ A \cup \{a\}\rangle$ or $\alpha_i = \langle .\ a\rangle$, $\alpha_j = \langle .\ A \cup \{a\}\rangle$ *(rely order)*
- $i <^\sigma_{\text{guar}} j$ if $\alpha_i = \langle ?\ a\rangle$, $\alpha_j = \langle !\ A \cup \{a\}\rangle$ or $\alpha_i = \langle .\ a\rangle$, $\alpha_j = \langle .\ A \cup \{a\}\rangle$ *(guarantee)*
- $i <^\sigma_{\text{init}} j$ if $i < j$, $\text{thrd}(\alpha_i) = \text{tinit} \neq \text{thrd}(\alpha_j)$ *(init order)*
- $i <^\sigma_{\text{thrd}} j$ if $i < j$, $\text{thrd}(\alpha_i) = \text{thrd}(\alpha_j) \notin \{\text{tinit}, \text{tcom}\}$ *(thread order)*
- $i <^\sigma_{\text{var}} j$ if $i < j$, $var(\alpha_i) = var(\alpha_j)$ *(variable order)*
- $i <^\sigma_{\text{sync}} j$ if $i < j$, $\alpha_i \in \{\langle \text{rel } w\rangle, \langle \text{cas } w\rangle\}$, $\alpha_j \in \{\langle \text{acq } w\rangle, \langle \text{cas } w\rangle\}$
- $i <^\sigma_{\text{wr}} j$ if $i' < j'$, $\alpha_{i'} = \langle \text{com } a\rangle$, $\alpha_{j'} = \langle \text{com } b\rangle$, $\alpha_i = \langle \text{wr } x\ a\rangle$, $\alpha_j = \langle \text{wr } x\ b\rangle$

Here, $<_{\text{sync}}$ is *synchronization order* and $<_{\text{wr}}$ is *(unbuffered) write order*.
Using these relations, we define four *memory* orders and two *commit* orders.

- Define $<^\sigma_{\text{seq}}$ to be the transitive closure of $(<^\sigma_{\text{thrd}} \cup <^\sigma_{\text{rely}} \cup <^\sigma_{\text{init}} \cup <^\sigma_{\text{var}})$.
- Define $<^\sigma_{\text{hb}}$ to be the transitive closure of $(<^\sigma_{\text{thrd}} \cup <^\sigma_{\text{rely}} \cup <^\sigma_{\text{init}} \cup <^\sigma_{\text{sync}})$.
- Define $<^\sigma_{\text{tso}}$ to be the least transitive relation that includes $(<^\sigma_{\text{rely}} \cup <^\sigma_{\text{init}} \cup <^\sigma_{\text{sync}})$ and satisfies the following, where $\sigma = \alpha_1 \cdots \alpha_n$.
  (1) If $\text{thrd}(\alpha_i) \neq \text{thrd}(\alpha_j)$ then $i <^\sigma_{\text{tso}} j$ whenever $i <^\sigma_{\text{rf}} j$ or $i <^\sigma_{\text{wr}} j$.
  (2) If $\text{thrd}(\alpha_i) = \text{thrd}(\alpha_j)$ then $i <^\sigma_{\text{tso}} j$ whenever $i < j$, $\alpha_i \neq \langle \text{com}\rangle$, $\alpha_j \neq \langle \text{com}\rangle$, and either (a) $\alpha_i \neq \langle \text{wr}\rangle$, (b) $\alpha_j \neq \langle \text{rd}\rangle$, or (c) $\alpha_i = \langle \text{wr } a\rangle$, $\alpha_j = \langle \text{rd } a\rangle$ and $i <^\sigma_{\text{cb}} j$.
- Define $<^\sigma_{\text{pso}}$ similarly to $<^\sigma_{\text{tso}}$, replacing clause (b) with (b') and adding (d):
  (b') $\alpha_j \notin \{\langle \text{rd}\rangle, \langle \text{wr}\rangle\}$, (d) $\alpha_j = \langle \text{wr } x\rangle$ and $\alpha_i \in \{\langle \text{rd}\rangle, \langle \text{wr } x\rangle\}$.
- Define $i <^\sigma_{\text{compso}} j$ whenever $i < j$ and one of the following holds.
  (1) $\exists a.\ \alpha_i = \langle \text{wr } a\rangle$ and $\alpha_j = \langle \text{com } a\rangle$. (2) $\exists a, s, t.\ s \neq t$, $\alpha_i = \langle \text{com } s\ a\rangle$ and $\alpha_j = \langle t \text{ rd } a\rangle$. (3) $\exists s.\ \alpha_i = \langle \text{com } s\rangle$ and $\alpha_j \in \{\langle s \text{ rel}\rangle, \langle s \text{ cas}\rangle\}$. (4) $\exists i' < j' < i.\ \exists a, b.\ \alpha_{i'} = \langle \text{wr } a\rangle$, $\alpha_{j'} = \langle s! \text{call } b\rangle$, $\alpha_i = \langle \text{com } a\rangle$, $\alpha_j = \langle ?\text{ret } B\rangle$ and $b \in B$. (5) $\exists x.\ \alpha_i = \langle \text{com } x\rangle$ and $\alpha_j = \langle \text{com } x\rangle$.
- Define $<^\sigma_{\text{comtso}}$ similarly to $<^\sigma_{\text{compso}}$, adding (6) $\exists s.\ \alpha_i = \langle \text{com } s\rangle$ and $\alpha_j = \langle \text{com } s\rangle$.

Let $\mathcal{W}$ range over the memory orders in $\{\text{seq}, \text{hb}, \text{tso}, \text{pso}\}$.
For each $\mathcal{W}$, define $\lhd^\sigma_{\mathcal{W}}$ similarly to $<^\sigma_{\mathcal{W}}$, simply replacing $<^\sigma_{\text{rely}}$ with $<^\sigma_{\text{guar}}$.   □

The memory orders relate actions that affect the visibility of values. The (nontransitive) commit orders, $<^\sigma_{\text{comtso}}$ and $<^\sigma_{\text{compso}}$, relate commit actions to conflicting actions.

All four memory orders include $<_{\text{rely}}$, which specifies orderings guaranteed by the environment, and $<_{\text{init}}$, which specifies initialization. Initial writes are performed by the reserved thread "tinit". For traces of interfaces (which include only I/O actions), the four memory orders coincide.

The definitions of $<_{\text{seq}}$ and $<_{\text{hb}}$ are standard. Relative to hb, clause (1) of the definition of $<_{\text{tso}}$ captures tso's stronger inter-thread dependencies, and clause (2) captures tso's weaker intra-thread dependencies. Two actions of the same thread are ordered unless the first is a write and the second is a read; in this case, they are ordered if the write is committed before the read. With respect to tso, the definition of $<_{\text{pso}}$ removes the ordering between writes of different variables by the same thread.

For each $\mathcal{W}$, we define an operational semantics. The order-theoretic properties that require are $\mathcal{W}$-consistency (no stale reads) and $\mathcal{W}$-closure (no stalled threads).

A trace is $\mathcal{W}$-consistent if none of its read actions are matched with stale writes.

Definition 5.4. Trace $\sigma = \alpha_1 \cdots \alpha_n$ is $\mathcal{W}$-consistent if $<^\sigma_{\mathcal{W}}$ is antisymmetric and $\forall i, j \in [1, n]$. $\alpha_j = \langle \text{rd } x \rangle$ and $i <^\sigma_{\text{rf}} j$ imply $j \not<^\sigma_{\mathcal{W}} i$ and ($\not\exists k.\ \alpha_k = \langle \text{wr } x \rangle$ and $i <^\sigma_{\mathcal{W}} k <^\sigma_{\mathcal{W}} j$). A semantic function is $\mathcal{W}$-consistent if every trace it produces is $\mathcal{W}$-consistent. □

A trace set is $\mathcal{W}$-closed if, whenever σ is an allowed trace, then any interleaving consistent with $<^\sigma_{\mathcal{W}}$ is also allowed. For example, the following trace is seq-closed, but not tso-, pso- or hb-closed: $\langle \text{tinit wr x} \rangle \langle \text{s wr y} \rangle \langle \text{t wr y} \rangle$.

Definition 5.5. Trace $\rho = \gamma_1 \cdots \gamma_n$ is a $\mathcal{W}$-permutation of $\sigma = \alpha_1 \cdots \alpha_n$ via δ, if δ is an injective total function in $[1, n] \to [1, n]$ such that $\forall i, j \in [1, n]$. we have that (1) $\alpha_i \neq \langle ? \rangle$ implies $\gamma_{\delta(i)} = \alpha_i$, (2) $\alpha_i = \langle ? A \rangle$ implies $\gamma_{\delta(i)} = \alpha_i \{\!\!\{ ^B/_A \}\!\!\}$ and $B \subseteq A$, (3) $thrd(\alpha_i) = \text{tinit}$ implies $\delta(i) = i$, (4) $i <^\sigma_{\text{thrd}} j$ iff $\delta(i) <^\rho_{\text{thrd}} \delta(j)$, (5) $i <^\sigma_{\mathcal{W}} j$ iff $\delta(i) <^\rho_{\mathcal{W}} \delta(j)$, and (6) $i < j$ iff $\delta(i) < \delta(j)$ whenever $\exists w.\ w = var(\alpha_i) = var(\alpha_j)$. When $\mathcal{W} = \text{tso}$, we additionally require (7) $i <^\sigma_{\text{comtso}} j$ iff $\delta(i) <^\rho_{\text{comtso}} \delta(j)$, and similarly for pso. □

Definition 5.6. Trace set Φ is $\mathcal{W}$-closed if whenever $\sigma \in \Phi$ and ρ is an $\mathcal{W}$-permutation of σ, then $\rho \in \Phi$. A semantic function is $\mathcal{W}$-closed if every set it produces is $\mathcal{W}$-closed.□

6 Components

Components, M, N, are built using abstractions, Λ, and expressions, C, D. A component declares variables (with an initial value), threads (with an initial expression) and functions (with an abstraction). In addition to base components, there are component constructors for composition and restriction.

$$\Lambda ::= (\vec{z})\{C\}$$
$$C, D ::= u \mid z \mid x \mid w \mid x = C \mid w = C \mid w.\text{cas}(C, D) \mid \text{let } \vec{z} = C; D \mid \cdots$$
$$M, N ::= M \parallel N \mid M \setminus f \mid \text{var } x_1 = u_1; \cdots \text{var } x_\ell = u_\ell; \text{ atomic } w_1 = v_1; \cdots \text{atomic } w_m = v_m;$$
$$\text{thrd } s_1\ C_1; \cdots \text{thrd } s_n\ C_n; \text{ fun } f_1\ \Lambda_1 \cdots \text{fun } f_j\ \Lambda_j$$

Data variables are introduced by the keyword var; synchronization variables are introduced by the keyword atomic; registers are introduced by abstractions and let;-expressions. When unspecified, variables initially hold 0. It is important to note that the formal parameters to a function are registers, not shared variables. We require that each component uniquely declare every function and thread name that occurs within it. Variables that are declared in more than one subcomponent are shared, allowing the possibility of interference.

Definition 6.1. A component is *well formed* if (1) it contains at most one declaration for each thread and function name, and (2) all declarations of a variable agree on the initial value. Two components are *compatible* if their composition is well formed.   □

Henceforth we consider only well formed components.

For a base component $M = $ "var $\vec{x}=\vec{u}$; atomic $\vec{w}=\vec{v}$; thrd $\vec{s}\ \vec{C}$; fun $\vec{f}\ \vec{A}$", define *funs* $(M) \triangleq \vec{f}$ and *thrds*$(M) \triangleq \vec{s}$. For aggregate components, define *funs*$(M \parallel N) = funs$ $(M)\cup funs(N)$ and *funs*$(M \setminus f) = funs(M)$, and similarly for *thrds*. Note that *funs* returns the set of functions defined by a component, regardless of whether those functions are restricted. For a well formed component $M \parallel N$, we have that *funs*$(M) \cap funs(N) = \emptyset$.

Definition 6.2. For each memory order $<_{\mathcal{W}}$, the full version of this paper provides a corresponding operational semantics, defined as a partial function $\mathcal{O}_{\mathcal{W}}$. If *thrds*$(M) \cap S$ $= \emptyset$ then $\mathcal{O}_{\mathcal{W}}[\![M]\!](S)$ returns a set traces that is coherent, $\mathcal{W}$-consistent and $\mathcal{W}$-closed. □

In $\mathcal{O}_{\mathcal{W}}[\![M]\!](S)$, the threads of *thrds*$(M)$ are initially active in the component (and quiescent in the environment) whereas the threads of S are initially active in the environment (and quiescent in the component). The operational semantics are unsurprising. We comment only on the role of commit actions. These have a clear operational interpretation under tso and pso; however, both seq- and hb-consistency ignore commit actions. Both $\mathcal{O}_{seq}$ and $\mathcal{O}_{hb}$ generate a commit action immediately after each write. This ensures that $\mathcal{O}_{seq}$ traces are tso-consistent; we do not attempt to interpret $\mathcal{O}_{hb}$ traces under tso.

To understand the examples, it is important to understand how the operational semantics generates actions from expressions involving memory. (1) Register writes do not create actions; neither do reads. (2) Data variable writes create ⟨wr⟩ actions; reads create ⟨rd⟩ actions. ⟨com⟩ actions are generated immediately after a write in seq and hb; they are generated nondeterministically by tso and pso. (3) Synchronization variable writes create ⟨rel⟩ actions; reads create ⟨acq⟩ actions. Successful cas operations create ⟨cas⟩ actions; unsuccessful cas operations do not create actions.

7   Linearizability

Linearizability is defined in terms of I/O permutations.

Definition 7.1. Write $\alpha \approx \gamma$ if either $\alpha = \gamma$ or $\alpha = \langle ! A \rangle$ and $\gamma = \alpha\{\!\!\{^{B}\!/_{A}\}\!\!\}$.

Trace $\sigma = \alpha_1 \cdots \alpha_n$ has *I/O-permutation* $\rho = \gamma_1 \cdots \gamma_m$ via δ, if δ is an injective partial function over $[1, n] \rightarrow [1, m]$ such that

- $\forall i \in [1, n]$. if α_i is I/O then $\exists k \in [1, m]$. $\alpha_i \approx \gamma_k$ and $\delta(i) = k$, and
- $\forall k \in [1, m]$. if γ_k is I/O then $\exists i \in [1, n]$. $\alpha_i \approx \gamma_k$ and $\delta(i) = k$.   □

Definition 7.2 (Linearizability). Define $\Phi \vDash_{\mathcal{W}} \Psi$ if every $\sigma = \alpha_1 \cdots \alpha_n \in \Phi$ has an I/O permutation $\rho = \gamma_1 \cdots \gamma_m \in \Psi$ via δ, such that

- $\forall i, j \in [1, n]$. if α_i, α_j are I/O and $\delta(i) \triangleleft_{\mathcal{W}}^{\rho} \delta(j)$ then either $i <_{\mathcal{W}}^{\sigma} j$ or $i \triangleleft_{\mathcal{W}}^{\sigma} j$, and
- $\forall i, j \in [1, n]$. if α_i, α_j are I/O and $i <_{\mathcal{W}}^{\sigma} j$ then $\delta(i) < \delta(j)$. □

The first condition ensures that the orderings required by the specification are preserved in the implementation. The last condition ensures that the ordering on I/O actions in the implementation is reflected in the specification. As the next example illustrates, this is different from the traditional requirement that the ordering on non-overlapping I/O actions be reflected in the specification.

Example 7.3. As a simple example, consider the following unsynchronized counter.

```
var x;
fun inc() { let tmp=x; tmp=tmp+1; x=tmp; return tmp }
```
(Inc)

At first glance, we might expect this implementation to satisfy a specification which requires that the return values be non-decreasing; that is, we expect traces of form

$$\langle s?\text{call inc}\rangle\langle s!\text{ret } u_0\rangle \langle t?\text{call inc}\rangle\langle t!\text{ret } u_1\rangle \langle r?\text{call inc}\rangle\langle r!\text{ret } u_2\rangle \cdots$$

where $u_i \geq u_{i-1}$. Although this specification contains no ordering on actions, the implementation does not satisfy it, for seq, tso or pso, due to the lack of synchronization. To see this, consider a call by one thread with overlapping and following calls by another.

Our results allow us to consider whether the implementation satisfies the specification if clients are constrained so that each thread may call inc() at most once. In this case, we can answer affirmatively for all four models.

To illuminate the definition of linearizability, consider the following traces. (We elide the commit actions that immediately follow each write.) Inc generates the first trace under all memory models, but the second, only under hb.

$$\langle t?\text{call inc}\rangle\langle s?\text{call inc}\rangle\langle s \text{ rd } x \text{ 0 init}\rangle\langle s \text{ wr } x \text{ a}\rangle\langle s!\text{ret } 1\rangle\langle t \text{ rd } x \text{ 1 a}\rangle\langle t \text{ wr } x \text{ 2 b}\rangle\langle t!\text{ret } 2\rangle$$
$$\langle t?\text{call inc}\rangle\langle t \text{ rd } x \text{ 1 a}\rangle\langle t \text{ wr } x \text{ 2 b}\rangle\langle t!\text{ret } 2\rangle \langle s?\text{call inc}\rangle\langle s \text{ rd } x \text{ 0 init}\rangle\langle s \text{ wr } x \text{ 1 a}\rangle\langle s!\text{ret } 1\rangle$$

For each $\mathcal{W} \in \{\text{seq}, \text{tso}, \text{pso}\}$, the first trace is linearizable under $\vDash_{\mathcal{W}}$, whereas the second trace is not. The write and subsequent read of the shared variable creates order between threads (condition (2c) and (2d) for tso and pso) and thus we have $\langle t?\text{call inc}\rangle <_{\mathcal{W}}$ $\langle s!\text{ret } 1\rangle$ in the second trace. This causes the last clause of Definition 7.2 to fail.

Touching a shared data variable creates no ordering under hb, and therefore both traces are linearizable under $\vDash_{\text{hb}}$. This would not be the case if we were to adopt the traditional requirement for linearizability: that the order of non-overlapping method calls be respected. This would also not be the case if the last clause of Definition 7.2 required $\delta(i) <_{\mathcal{W}}^{\rho} \delta(j)$ rather than $\delta(i) < \delta(j)$, since $(<_{\mathcal{W}}^{\rho})$ is the empty relation for every specification trace ρ. □

Example 7.4. Suppose we have an implementation trace of the form

$$\langle s?\text{call inc}\rangle\langle s!\text{ret } u_0 \text{ a } \emptyset\rangle \langle t?\text{call inc } \{a\}\rangle\langle t!\text{ret } u_1 \text{ b}\rangle \langle r?\text{call inc } \{b\}\rangle\langle r!\text{ret } u_2\rangle \cdots$$

where the client has imposed ordering between each method return and the subsequent call. The definition of linearizability requires that the specification have exactly the same use sets, and thus the same client ordering. In this case, the specification may be more constrained. For example, it might require that $u_i > u_{i-1}$. □

Example 7.5. The following example is drawn from java.lang.String.hashCode. The specification requires that every call to hashCode return the same value. The implementation has a benign write-write data race.

```
var hash;
fun hashCode() { let h=hash;                                          (Hash)
    if h!=0 then { return h } else { let h=42; hash=h; return h } }
```

Here, we set hash to 42; in a real implementation, the value is derived from immutable fields of the object. hash is always set to the same value, regardless of the number of threads that call hashCode simultaneously. The intended sequential interface specification for Hash is:

$$(\langle s?\text{call hashCode}\rangle \langle s!\text{ret hashCode 42}\rangle)^*$$

Hash satisfies its sequential specification under all memory models.   □

We consider two implementations of an atomic pair, inspired by an example in [Burckhardt et al. 2012]. The specification requires that the get return the pair of values specified by the preceding set:

$$(\langle s?\text{call set } (u, v) \text{ a}\rangle \langle s!\text{ret}\rangle (\langle t?\text{call get}\rangle \langle t!\text{ret } (u, v) \{a\}\rangle)^*)^*$$

Example 7.6. The first implementation is fully synchronized using locks.

```
var x1; var x2; atomic lock;
fun set(z1,z2) { do skip until lock.cas(0,1); x1=z1; x2=z2; lock=0 }       (Pair1)
fun get() { do skip until lock.cas(0,1); let z1=x1; let z2=x2; lock=0; return z1,z2 }
```

Pair1 is linearizable under all memory models. The cas on the atomic variable provides the required order relation. The linearization point can be chosen to be the successful cas operation in both the methods. The specification also requires an order relationship from the call of set to the return of get as seen in the subsequence $\langle s?\text{call set } (v_1, v_2) \text{ a}\rangle$ $\cdots \langle t!\text{ret get } (v_1, v_2) \{a\}\rangle$. The order from the write of the atomic variable lock in set to the successful cas on lock in get establishes this relationship in the implementation.   □

Example 7.7. The second implementation uses locking for set, but not get. The version variable i is odd if and only if there is a write in progress.

```
var x1; var x2; var i; atomic lock;
fun set(z1,z2) { do skip until lock.cas(0,1); i++; x1=z1; x2=z2; i++; lock=0 }  (Pair2)
fun get() { while (1){ let j=i; if even(j) then let z1=x1; let z2=x2;
                                if j==i then return z1,z2 } }
```

Pair2 exemplifies a publication idiom characteristic of tso, allowing data races between writes and reads. Pair2 is also not linearizable under pso or hb.

Pair2 is linearizable under tso. A candidate linearization point for set is the first increment of i. The linearization point for get is the successful check of the counter i. Pair1 and Pair2 share the same specification, so the specification requires the same order relationship from the call of set to the return from get. The second condition of the definition of $<_{tso}$ on the counter i, from the write in set to the read in get, yields the required order. Neither pso nor hb provide this ordering.   □

Example 7.8. The next example is an "active" component, which implements an asynchronous function handler. This can be seen as a simplified thread pool, with a single, one-shot thread. Let v' be the result of performing the operation *op* on v.

$$\langle s?\text{call send } v\ a\rangle\langle s!\text{ret true}\rangle\ (\ (\ \langle t?\text{call get}\rangle\langle t!\text{ret } v'\ \{a\}\rangle\ )\ )\ |\ \langle r?\text{call send } u\rangle\langle r?\text{ret false}\rangle\ )^*$$

The first call to send succeeds, and calls to get return a value derived from its parameter. Subsequent calls to send return false.

```
var x; var y; atomic lock; atomic start; atomic stop;
fun send(z){ do { if (start==1) then return false } until lock.cas(0,1);
              x=z; start=1; return true }                              (Async)
fun get()   { do skip until stop==1; return y }
thread wrk  { do skip until start==1; y=op(x); stop=1 }
```

Async satisfies its sequential specification for all four memory models.

A candidate linearization point for send is the successful cas or reading start==1, depending on which path is taken. The linearization point for the worker thread wrk and get is the point of exit from the loops, via the variables start and stop, respectively. The specification requires an order relationship as seen in the subsequence $\langle s?\text{call send } v\ a\rangle$ $\cdots \langle t!\text{ret } v'\ \{a\}\rangle$. The implementation establishes this by combining two order relations yielded by atomic variables: start links send to wrk and stop links wrk to get.   □

Example 7.9. Async can be generalized to a thread pool which satisfies interface traces such as the following, where let v' be the result of performing some computation on v and j is a job identifier.

$$\langle s?\text{call send } v\ a\rangle\langle s!\text{ret } j\rangle\langle r?\text{call get } j\rangle\langle r!\text{ret } v'\ \{a\}\rangle$$

If the thread pool generates unique job identifiers, then it should be able to guarantee the happens-before relation given in the specification.

We describe an implementation parameterized on a bounded buffer and map. The bounded buffer holds waiting jobs and the map holds waiting results. Due to the complexity of the possible interleavings, we give exemplary traces rather than complete specifications. The implementation is straightforward.

The bounded buffer is an adaption of Buffer given in the introduction. To accomodate the example, the buffer holds pairs of values. If the buffer is FILO, then the sequential interface will include traces such as the following.

$$\langle s?\text{call bput } (1, 10)\ a\rangle\langle s!\text{ret}\rangle\ \langle t?\text{call bput } (1, 10)\ b\rangle\langle t!\text{ret}\rangle$$
$$\langle r?\text{call bget}\rangle\langle r!\text{ret } (1, 10)\ \{b\}\rangle\ \langle q?\text{call bget}\rangle\langle q!\text{ret } (1, 10)\ \{a\}\rangle$$

Note that the same value is put twice, by different threads. The use sets in the get actions indicate the FILO order, even though the values do not.

The map is similar. Here is an example showing a value that is retrieved twice.

$$\langle s?\text{call mput } (1, 10)\ a\rangle\langle s!\text{ret}\rangle\ \langle t?\text{call mput } (1, 10)\ b\rangle\langle t!\text{ret}\rangle$$
$$\langle r?\text{call mget } 1\rangle\langle r!\text{ret } 10\ \{b\}\rangle\ \langle q?\text{call mget } 1\rangle\langle q!\text{ret } 10\ \{b\}\rangle$$

Assuming a bounded buffer and map, the general thread pool has traces such as the following. For clarity, we show the function name on return actions.

$$\langle s?\text{call send } v\ a\rangle\ \langle s!\text{call bput } (v, j)\ b\rangle\langle s?\text{ret bput}\rangle\ \langle s!\text{ret send } j\rangle$$
$$\langle\text{wrk!call bget}\rangle\langle\text{wrk?ret bget } (v, j)\ \{b\}\rangle\ \langle\text{wrk!call mput } (j, v')\ c\rangle\langle\text{wrk?ret mput}\rangle$$
$$\langle r?\text{call get } j\rangle\ \langle r!\text{call mget } j\rangle\langle r?\text{ret mget } v'\ \{c\}\rangle\ \langle r!\text{ret get } v'\ \{a\}\rangle$$

The first line shows a client calling send with argument v. The thread pool creates a new job id j, stores the job in the buffer and returns j. Subsequently, the second line show a worker thread retrieving the job from the buffer, computing v', and storing the result in the map. Finally, the third line shows a client thread retrieving the result using a call to get j; in response, the thread pool retrieves j from the map and returns the corresponding value. In $\langle$!ret $\{a\}\rangle$, the decoration is a guarantee, similar to the decorations in previous examples: the thread pool guarantees that there will be memory effects between the call and corresponding return.

Consider the projection of this trace of the thread pool on the methods of the bounded buffer. We get:

$$\langle s!\text{call bput } (v, j)\ b\rangle \langle s?\text{ret bput}\rangle\ \langle wrk!\text{call bget}\rangle \langle wrk?\text{ret bget } (v, j)\ \{b\}\rangle$$

The sequence of calls to the buffer methods, and the values returned by them, line up with the trace of the buffer presented above. Furthermore, so do the label sets. In $\langle s!\text{call bput } (v, j)\ b\rangle$ and $\langle wrk?\text{ret bget } (v; j)\ \{b\}\rangle$, the label b indicates an assumption made by the thread pool on the bounded buffer. In the matching actions, $\langle s?\text{call bput } (v, j)\ b\rangle$ and $\langle wrk!\text{ret bget } (v, j)\ \{b\}\rangle)$, the label b indicates a guarantee provided by the bounded buffer interface to the thread pool. Here one can recognize the semantic ingredients necessary for a full higher-order multiplicative linear logic of interfaces, perhaps in the style of Interaction Categories [Abramsky et al. 1996]. In this paper, however, we do not pursue this further.　　　　　　　　　　　　　　　　　　　□

8   Proving Linearizability

We explore methods to quarantine data race free programs from the subtleties of relaxed memory models. First, we define a component to be *locally sequential consistent* when its SC traces provide a complete description of all its traces—or in the terminology of [Filipovic et al. 2010], when the set of its SC traces is an operational refinement of all of its traces.

Definition 8.1. Define $\sigma \sim_{\mathcal{W}} \rho$ when (1) $\sigma = \sigma_0 \gamma_1 \sigma_1 \cdots \gamma_n \sigma_n$ and $\rho = \rho_0 \gamma_1 \rho_1 \cdots \gamma_n \rho_n$ for some $\vec{\sigma}, \vec{\rho}, \vec{\gamma}$ such that each $\vec{\sigma}$ and $\vec{\rho}$ contains only write and commit actions, and (2) for every read action α, $\sigma\alpha$ is $\mathcal{W}$-consistent if and only if $\rho\alpha$ is $\mathcal{W}$-consistent.

A set of traces Φ is *locally sequentially consistent (LSC)* for $\mathcal{W}$ if

$$\forall \sigma \in \Phi.\ \exists \sigma' \in \Phi.\ \sigma \sim_{\mathcal{W}} \sigma' \text{ and } \sigma' \text{ is seq-consistent.}　　　□$$

Intuitively, a set is LSC if every trace can be matched by a seq-consistent trace in the set, where all non-write/non-commit actions must match exactly and in the same order (condition 1), and the reads available at the end are the same (condition 2).

Example 8.2. Inc is not LSC for any of the weak models. Hash is LSC for all four memory models. This demonstrates that LSC does not require the absence of data races.

Pair1 and Async are LSC for all four memory models; however, Pair2 is not LSC under any of the relaxed models. To see this, consider traces in which there is a completed call to set with parameters $(1,1)$ and a subsequent call to get returning $(1,1)$.

In every such trace, the write actions must occur before the call to get. Of these traces, choose one in which the loop in get initially fails because $i \neq j$. This trace will not be equivalent to any SC trace, since it must see a stale value.   □

We describe a sufficient condition to establish that a set is LSC.

Definition 8.3. Actions *conflict* if one is a write to a data variable and the other is a read or write to the same variable. Trace $\sigma = \alpha_1 \alpha_1 \cdots \alpha_n$ is *locally data race free (LDRF)* if whenever α_i and α_j conflict then either $i <^{\sigma}_{\mathsf{hb}} j$ or $j <^{\sigma}_{\mathsf{hb}} i$. A set of traces is LDRF if every member is LDRF.   □

Example 8.4. All of the examples from Section 7 are LDRF for all four memory models, with the exception of Inc, Hash and Pair2, which are not LDRF for any model.   □

Proposition 8.5. Any trace that is LDRF and $\mathcal{W}$-consistent is also seq-*consistent.*   □

Proposition 8.5 demonstrates that to establish that a component is LSC, it suffices to show that all of its traces are LDRF. This, in turn, can be established by various standard techniques for detecting data races. For tso, there is a weaker condition, "triangular race freedom", that suffices to establish that a component is LSC [Owens 2010].

In order to reason about a program using the SC semantics, we must ensure that the weak semantics is consistent with $\mathcal{O}_{\mathsf{seq}}$, in the sense that any seq-consistent trace generated by the weak semantics can also be generated by $\mathcal{O}_{\mathsf{seq}}$. All of the semantic functions we consider have this property.

Definition 8.6. A semantic function $\mathcal{S}$ is *consistent with* $\mathcal{O}_{\mathsf{seq}}$ if whenever $\sigma \in \mathcal{S}[\![M]\!]$ (S) and σ is seq-consistent then $\sigma \in \mathcal{O}_{\mathsf{seq}}[\![M]\!](S)$.   □

LSC components can be quarantined. For LSC programs, it is sometimes possible to use traditional SC techniques to reason about linearizability, even in a relaxed setting. The restrictions should be unsurprising to readers familiar with [Filipovic et al. 2010], which states that "OSC observationally refines OSA iff OSC is linearizable with respect to OSA, assuming that client operations may use at *least one shared global variable*." For such programs, our results allow proof techniques developed in the SC setting to apply to relaxed models.

A trace is *I/O-ordered for $\mathcal{W}$* if there is a $<_{\mathcal{W}}$ order between every input and output. Formally, $\sigma = \alpha_1 \cdots \alpha_n$ is I/O-ordered for $\mathcal{W}$ if whenever α_i and α_j are input/output bracketed (Section 4) then $i <^{\sigma}_{\mathcal{W}} j$. Let $erase(\sigma)$ be the trace derived from σ by replacing every name set occurring in return actions by the empty set; this has the effect of removing all of the happens-before relations from an interface.

Proposition 8.7.   Let $\mathcal{S}$ be a semantic function that is $\mathcal{W}$-consistent and consistent with $\mathcal{O}_{\mathsf{seq}}$. Let Ψ be a sequential interface. Let $\mathcal{S}[\![M]\!](S)$ be I/O-ordered and LSC for $\mathcal{W}$. Then $\mathcal{O}_{\mathsf{seq}}[\![M]\!](S) \vDash_{\mathsf{seq}} erase(\Psi)$ implies $\mathcal{S}[\![M]\!](S) \vDash_{\mathcal{W}} \Psi$.   □

Here $\mathcal{O}_{\mathsf{seq}}[\![M]\!](S) \vDash_{\mathsf{seq}} erase(\Psi)$ is similar to traditional linearizability. The use of *erase* (Ψ) ensures that the proof obligation is indeed the traditional one: ordering requirements are removed. Touchiness of the implementation and sequentiality of the specification are required to ensure that the order can be recovered.

In Corollary 10.4, we show that LSC clients can be isolated from the subtleties of relaxed memory used in the implementations of (even racy) libraries.

9   Composition

In order to state properties of linearizability, we must first define semantic versions of restriction and composition. Restriction is straightforward.

Definition 9.1. Let $incalls(\alpha_1 \cdots \alpha_n) \triangleq \{f \mid \exists i.\ \alpha = \langle \text{?call } f \rangle\}$.
Then $\Phi \setminus F \triangleq \{\sigma \in \Phi \mid incalls(\sigma) \cap F = \emptyset\}$.   □

Definition 9.2. An action sequence π is a *collapsed interleaving* of σ and ρ if there exists a π' such that (1) all actions of tinit occur at the beginning of π', (2) π' is an interleaving of σ and ρ, and (3) π is derived from π' by (3a) replacing every subsequence $\langle s\,!\text{call } f\ \bar{u}\ a\ A \rangle \langle s\,?\text{call } f\ \bar{u}\ a\ A \rangle$ by $\langle s\,.\text{call } f\ \bar{u}\ a\ A \rangle$, and (3b) replacing every subsequence $\langle s\,!\text{ret } \bar{u}\ a\ A \rangle \langle s\,?\text{ret } \bar{u}\ a\ A \rangle$ by $\langle s\,.\text{ret } \bar{u}\ a\ A \rangle$.   □

Definition 9.3 (Composition). Let $intern(\Phi) = H$ and $intern(\Psi) = G$. If $H \cap G = \emptyset$, then define $\Phi \otimes \Psi$ to be the set of traces, π, such that $extern(\pi) \cap (H \cup G) = \emptyset$, and π is a collapsed interleaving of some $\sigma \in \Phi$ and $\rho \in \Psi$.   □

In the full version of this paper, we provide an inductive characterization of composition and discuss its properties.

Example 9.4. Here are some single threaded examples to illustrate the definition. We elide the thread identifier. $\{\langle \text{?call } f \rangle\} \otimes \{\langle \text{?call } f \rangle\}$ and $\{\langle \text{wr} \rangle\} \otimes \{\langle \text{wr} \rangle\}$ are undefined because their *intern* overlap; the first pair on f, the second, on the thread identifier.

Composition forces complete synchronization on invocations of functions that are defined in either component, but permits interleaving of invocations of functions that are undefined in both components. Let $\mathscr{C}$ perform prefix closure.

$$\mathscr{C}\{\langle \text{?call f } 0 \rangle \langle !\text{ret} \rangle\} \otimes \mathscr{C}\{\langle \text{wr} \rangle\} \qquad = \mathscr{C}\{\langle \text{wr} \rangle\}$$
$$\mathscr{C}\{\langle \text{?call f } 0 \rangle \langle !\text{ret} \rangle\} \otimes \mathscr{C}\{\langle !\text{call f } 1 \rangle\} \qquad = \mathscr{C}\{\varepsilon\}$$
$$\mathscr{C}\{\langle \text{?call f } 0 \rangle \langle !\text{ret} \rangle\} \otimes \mathscr{C}\{\langle !\text{call f } 0 \rangle \langle \text{?ret} \rangle\} = \mathscr{C}\{\langle .\text{call f } 0 \rangle \langle .\text{ret} \rangle\}$$
$$\mathscr{C}\{\langle \text{?call f } 0 \rangle \langle !\text{ret} \rangle\} \otimes \mathscr{C}\{\langle \text{?call g } 0 \rangle \langle !\text{ret} \rangle\} = \mathscr{C}\{\langle \text{?call g} \rangle \langle !\text{ret } 0 \rangle \langle \text{?call f} \rangle \langle !\text{ret } 0 \rangle,$$
$$\langle \text{?call f} \rangle \langle !\text{ret } 0 \rangle \langle \text{?call g} \rangle \langle !\text{ret } 0 \rangle\}$$

Consider the following traces, where α_{11}–α_{32} are arbitrary memory actions. Both the first and second traces include calls to f, which is defined by third trace. The first trace also includes a call to g, which is defined by the second trace.

$$\alpha_{11} \langle !\text{call g} \rangle \langle \text{?ret} \rangle \alpha_{12} \langle !\text{call f} \rangle \langle \text{?ret} \rangle$$
$$\langle \text{?call g} \rangle \alpha_{21} \langle !\text{call f} \rangle \langle \text{?ret} \rangle \alpha_{22} \langle !\text{ret} \rangle$$
$$\langle \text{?call f} \rangle \alpha_{31} \langle !\text{ret} \rangle \langle \text{?call f} \rangle \alpha_{32} \langle !\text{ret} \rangle$$

The first two compose to $\alpha_{11} \langle .\text{call g} \rangle \alpha_{21} \langle !\text{call f} \rangle \langle \text{?ret} \rangle \alpha_{22} \langle .\text{ret} \rangle \alpha_{12} \langle !\text{call f} \rangle \langle \text{?ret} \rangle$. Composing the second and third gives $\langle \text{?call f} \rangle \alpha_{31} \langle !\text{ret} \rangle \langle \text{?call g} \rangle \alpha_{21} \langle .\text{call f} \rangle \alpha_{32} \langle .\text{ret} \rangle$ $\alpha_{22} \langle !\text{ret} \rangle$ and $\langle \text{?call g} \rangle \alpha_{21} \langle .\text{call f} \rangle \alpha_{31} \langle .\text{ret} \rangle \alpha_{22} \langle !\text{ret} \rangle \langle \text{?call f} \rangle \alpha_{32} \langle !\text{ret} \rangle$. Composing the first and third gives $\alpha_{11} \langle !\text{call g} \rangle \langle \text{?call f} \rangle \alpha_{31} \langle !\text{ret} \rangle \langle \text{?ret} \rangle \alpha_{12} \langle .\text{call f} \rangle \alpha_{32}$ $\langle .\text{ret} \rangle$. Composing all three gives

$$\alpha_{11} \langle .\text{call g} \rangle \alpha_{21} \langle .\text{call f} \rangle \alpha_{31} \langle .\text{ret} \rangle \alpha_{22} \langle .\text{ret} \rangle \alpha_{12} \langle .\text{call f} \rangle \alpha_{32} \langle .\text{ret} \rangle.$$ □

Example 9.5. For any single trace, the order of cross-thread actions is fixed. Thus, composing $\langle s?call\ f\rangle\langle t\ wr\rangle$ and $\langle s!call\ f\rangle$ produces only $\langle s.call\ f\rangle\langle t\ wr\rangle$. □

10 Properties of Linearizability

We present the results using the most general client. More general results can be found in the appendix.

Definition 10.1 (Interference freedom). Two components are *interference free* if they are compatible (Definition 6.1) and declare disjoint variables. □

Definition 10.2 (Compositionality). A semantic function $\mathscr{S}$ is *compositional* if
(1) $\mathscr{S}[\![M \setminus F]\!](S) = \mathscr{S}[\![M]\!](S) \setminus F$ and,
(2) $\mathscr{S}[\![M \parallel N]\!](S) \subseteq \mathscr{S}[\![M]\!](S) \otimes \mathscr{S}[\![N]\!](S)$, whenever M and N are interference free.□

Proposition 10.3 (Abstraction). Let $\mathscr{S}$ be coherent, compositional and $\mathscr{W}$-closed. Let M_L and M_C be interference free. If $\mathscr{S}[\![M_L]\!](S) \vDash_{\mathscr{W}} \Psi_L$ and $\mathscr{S}[\![M_C]\!](S) \otimes \Psi_L \vDash_{\mathscr{W}} \Psi_C$ then $\mathscr{S}[\![M_C \parallel M_L]\!](S) \vDash_{\mathscr{W}} \Psi_C$. □

Consider the Lock discussed in the introduction. If we are given that (1) the lock implements its specification (that is, $\mathscr{S}[\![Lock]\!](S) \vDash_{\mathscr{W}} \Psi_{lock}$) and (2) the one place buffers implements its specification when it uses the lock specification (that is, $\mathscr{S}[\![Buffer]\!]$ $(S) \otimes \Psi_{lock} \vDash_{\mathscr{W}} \Psi_{buf}$), then the theorem allows us to deduce that the implementation of the buffer realizes its specification ($\mathscr{S}[\![Buffer \parallel Lock]\!](S) \vDash_{\mathscr{W}} \Psi_{buf}$).

Corollary 10.4 (Quarantining weakness). Let $\mathscr{S}$ be coherent, compositional and $\mathscr{W}$-closed. Let M_L and M_C be interference free. Let Ψ_L and Ψ_C be sequential interfaces. Suppose $\Psi_L = erase(\Psi_L)$, $\mathscr{S}[\![M_C]\!](S)$ is LSC and either (1) $erase(\Psi_C) = \Psi_C$ or (2) $\mathscr{S}$ $[\![M_C]\!](S)$ is I/O-ordered. If $\mathscr{S}[\![M_L]\!](S) \vDash_{\mathscr{W}} \Psi_L$ and $\mathscr{S}[\![M_C]\!](S) \otimes \Psi_L \vDash_{seq} \Psi_C$ then $\mathscr{S}$ $[\![M_C \parallel M_L]\!](S) \vDash_{\mathscr{W}} \Psi_C$. □

Corollary 10.4 demonstrates that well-synchronized clients (that do not depend on the library for synchronization), are not affected by data races in the library. Consider the unsynchronized counter Inc from Examples 7.3-7.4. A fully-synchronized client can safely use the library without regard to its data races; for example, a fully-synchronized counter can be built using the unsynchronized one.

11 Conclusion

This paper investigates reasoning about concurrent data structures, with a special focus on isolating the complexity wrought by relaxed memory models. We have presented an adaptation of linearizability that accounts for relaxed memory and provided ways to reason compositionally. Our treatment is parametric with respect to the memory model, with the required properties of the memory model confined to a couple of key properties. We have been able to address SC, TSO, PSO and (a variant of) the JMM in this style.

References

Abramsky, S., Gay, S.J., Nagarajan, R.: Interaction categories and the foundations of typed concurrent programming. In: NATO ASI DPD, pp. 35–113 (1996)

Adve, S.V., Boehm, H.-J.: Memory models: a case for rethinking parallel languages and hardware. Commun. ACM 53, 90–101 (2010)

Adve, S.V., Gharachorloo, K.: Shared memory consistency models: A tutorial. Computer 29(12), 66–76 (1996)

Alur, R., Madhusudan, P.: Adding nesting structure to words. J. ACM 56(3) (2009)

Batty, M., Owens, S., Sarkar, S., Sewell, P., Weber, T.: Mathematizing C++ concurrency. In: POPL, pp. 55–66. ACM (2011)

Batty, M., Dodds, M., Gotsman, A.: Library abstraction for C/C++ concurrency. In: POPL (2013) (to appear)

Boehm, H.-J., Adve, S.V.: Foundations of the C++ concurrency memory model. In: PLDI, pp. 68–78. ACM (2008)

Burckhardt, S., Gotsman, A., Musuvathi, M., Yang, H.: Concurrent Library Correctness on the TSO Memory Model. In: Seidl, H. (ed.) ESOP 2012. LNCS, vol. 7211, pp. 87–107. Springer, Heidelberg (2012)

Demange, D., Laporte, V., Zhao, L., Jagannathan, S., Pichardie, D., Vitek, J.: Plan B: A buffered memory model for Java. In: POPL (2013) (to appear)

Ferreira, R., Feng, X., Shao, Z.: Parameterized Memory Models and Concurrent Separation Logic. In: Gordon, A.D. (ed.) ESOP 2010. LNCS, vol. 6012, pp. 267–286. Springer, Heidelberg (2010)

Filipovic, I., O'Hearn, P., Rinetzky, N., Yang, H.: Abstraction for concurrent objects. Theoretical Comp. Sci. 411, 4379–4398 (2010)

Gotsman, A., Yang, H.: Linearizability with Ownership Transfer. In: Koutny, M., Ulidowski, I. (eds.) CONCUR 2012. LNCS, vol. 7454, pp. 256–271. Springer, Heidelberg (2012)

Gotsman, A., Musuvathi, M., Yang, H.: Show No Weakness: Sequentially Consistent Specifications of TSO Libraries. In: Aguilera, M.K. (ed.) DISC 2012. LNCS, vol. 7611, pp. 31–45. Springer, Heidelberg (2012)

Herlihy, M., Wing, J.M.: Linearizability: A correctness condition for concurrent objects. ACM Trans. Program. Lang. Syst. 12(3), 463–492 (1990)

Jagadeesan, R., Pitcher, C., Riely, J.: Generative Operational Semantics for Relaxed Memory Models. In: Gordon, A.D. (ed.) ESOP 2010. LNCS, vol. 6012, pp. 307–326. Springer, Heidelberg (2010)

Jeffrey, A., Rathke, J.: A fully abstract testing semantics for concurrent objects. Theoretical Comp. Sci. 338, 17–63 (2005)

Lamport, L.: How to make a multiprocessor computer that correctly executes multiprocess program. IEEE Trans. Comput. 28(9), 690–691 (1979)

Manson, J., Pugh, W., Adve, S.V.: The Java memory model. In: POPL, pp. 378–391 (2005)

Owens, S.: Reasoning about the Implementation of Concurrency Abstractions on x86-TSO. In: D'Hondt, T. (ed.) ECOOP 2010. LNCS, vol. 6183, pp. 478–503. Springer, Heidelberg (2010)

Sarkar, S., Sewell, P., Alglave, J., Maranget, L., Williams, D.: Understanding power multiprocessors. In: PLDI, pp. 175–186. ACM (2011)

Sevcík, J.: Program Transformations in Weak Memory Models. PhD thesis, Laboratory for Foundations of Computer Science, University of Edinburgh (2008)

Sewell, P., Sarkar, S., Owens, S., Nardelli, F.Z., Myreen, M.O.: x86-TSO: a rigorous and usable programmer's model for x86 multiprocessors. Commun. ACM 53(7), 89–97 (2010)

SPARC, Inc.: The SPARC Architecture Manual (version 9). Prentice-Hall, Inc., Upper Saddle River (1994)

Sun Microsystems (2004), http://docs.oracle.com/javase/1.5.0/docs/api/java/util/concurrent/atomic/package-summary.html

Software Verification for Weak Memory via Program Transformation*

Jade Alglave[1,2], Daniel Kroening[2], Vincent Nimal[2], and Michael Tautschnig[2,3]

[1] University College London
[2] University of Oxford
[3] Queen Mary, University of London

dedicated to the memory of Kohei Honda

Abstract Multiprocessors implement weak memory models, but program verifiers often assume *Sequential Consistency* (SC), and thus may miss bugs due to weak memory. We propose a sound transformation of the program to verify, enabling SC tools to perform verification w.r.t. weak memory. We present experiments for a broad variety of models (from x86-TSO to Power) and a vast range of verification tools, quantify the additional cost of the transformation and highlight the cases when we can drastically reduce it. Our benchmarks include work-queue management code from PostgreSQL.

1 Introduction

Current multi-core architectures such as Intel's x86, IBM's Power or ARM implement *weak memory models* for performance reasons, allowing optimisations such as *instruction reordering*, *store buffering* or *write atomicity relaxation* [3]. These models make concurrent programming and debugging extremely challenging, because the execution of a concurrent program might not be an interleaving of its instructions, as would be the case on a Sequentially Consistent (SC) architecture [21]. As an instance, the lock-free signalling code in the open-source database PostgreSQL failed regression tests on a PowerPC cluster, due to the memory model. We study this bug in detail in Sec. 5.

This observation highlights the crucial need for weak memory aware verification. Yet, most existing work assume SC, hence might miss bugs specific to weak memory. Recent work addresses the design or the adaptation of existing methods and tools to weak memory [25,29,17,13,23,11,2], but often focuses on one specific model or cannot handle the write atomicity relaxation of Power/ARM: generality remains a challenge.

Since we want to avoid writing one tool per architecture of interest, we propose a unified method. Given a program analyser handling SC concurrency for C programs, we *transform its input* to simulate the possible non-SC behaviours of the program whilst executing the program on SC. Essentially, we augment our programs with arrays to simulate (on SC) the buffering and caching scenarios due to weak memory.

---

* Supported by ERC project 280053, EPSRC project EP/G026254/1 and the Semiconductor Research Coroporation (SRC) under task 2269.002.

M. Felleisen and P. Gardner (Eds.): ESOP 2013, LNCS 7792, pp. 512–532, 2013.

The verification problem for weak memory models is known to be hard (e.g. non-primitive recursive for TSO), if not undecidable (e.g. for RMO-like models) [9]. This means that we cannot design a *complete* verification method. Yet, we can achieve *soundness*, by implementing our tools in tandem with the design of a proof, and by stressing our tools with test cases reflecting subtle points of the proof.

We also aim for an effective and unified verification setup, where one can easily plug a tool of choice. This paper meets these objectives by making three new contributions:

1. To design our transformation, we define in Sec. 3 an abstract state machine that we prove (in the Coq proof assistant) equivalent to the framework of [8] (recalled in Sec. 2). We also explain how this equivalence proof allows us to design a drastically improved transformation with a speed-up of more than two orders of magnitude.
2. Sec. 4 describes our implementation, highlighting the generality of our approach: we support a broad variety of models (x86/TSO, PSO, RMO and Power) and all concurrency-aware program analysers for C programs (cf. experiments below).
3. Sec. 5 details our experiments. i) We systematically validate our implementation w.r.t. our theoretical study with 555 *litmus tests* exercising weak memory artefacts. We study the overhead and validate the viability of our transformation using Blender [20], CheckFence [13], ESBMC [14], MMChecker [17], Poirot [1], SatAbs [15], and Threader [16]. ii) We verify an excerpt of the relational database software PostgreSQL, which has a bug specific to Power. iii) Our transformation easily scales to systems code from the Linux kernel or the Apache HTTP server, and also industrial code.

We provide the source and documentation of our tools, our benchmarks, experimental reports, Coq proofs and their typeset sketches online: www.cprover.org/wmm/

Related Work. We focus here on the *verification* problem, i.e., detecting the behaviours that are buggy, not all the non-SC ones. This problem is non-primitive recursive for TSO [9]. It is undecidable if read/write or read/read pairs can be reordered, as in RMO-like models [9]. Forbidding *causal loops* restores decidability; relaxing write atomicity makes the problem undecidable again [10].

Existing solutions use various bounds over the objects of the model [11,19], over-approximate the possible program behaviours [20,18], or relinquish termination [22]. For TSO, [2] presents a sound and complete solution. We present a provably sound method that allows to lift any SC method or tool to a large spectrum of weak memory models, ranging from x86 to Power. We build an operational model; [24] presented such a model, but theirs is restricted to TSO. Given the undecidability of the problem, we cannot provide completeness, as we focus on soundness. We do not use any bound in our theoretical model (Sec. 3), but our implementation uses finite buffers (Sec. 4).

Our approach also reduces the amount of instrumentation in a provably sound manner. Unlike [11], we only instrument selected shared memory accesses. For TSO this would follow immediately from [12], but we generalise to models such as Power.

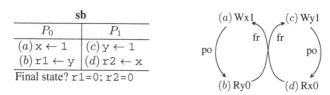

sb	
P_0	P_1
$(a)\, x \leftarrow 1$	$(c)\, y \leftarrow 1$
$(b)\, r1 \leftarrow y$	$(d)\, r2 \leftarrow x$
Final state? $r1=0$; $r2=0$	

Fig. 1. Store Buffering (**sb**)

iriw			
P_0	P_1	P_2	P_3
$(a)\, r1 \leftarrow x$	$(c)\, r3 \leftarrow y$	$(e)\, x \leftarrow 1$	$(f)\, y \leftarrow 1$
$(b)\, r2 \leftarrow y$	$(d)\, r4 \leftarrow x$		
Final state? $r1=1$; $r2=0$; $r3=1$; $r4=0$;			

Fig. 2. Independent Reads of Independent Writes (**iriw**)

2   Context: Axiomatic Memory Model

In an operational view, weak memory effects occur as follows: A processor can commit a write first to a store buffer, then to a cache, and finally to memory. When a write hits the memory, all the processors agree on its value. But while the write is in transit through store buffers and caches, a read can occur before the value is actually available to all processors from the memory.

To describe such scenarios, we use the framework of [8], which provably embraces several *(weak) architectures*: SC [21], Sun TSO (i.e. the x86 model [24]), PSO and RMO, Alpha, and a fragment of Power. At the core of this framework we use *relations* over *read and write memory events*. We introduce this framework on *litmus tests*, as shown in Fig. 1. The left-hand side of the figure shows a multi-threaded program. The shared variables x and y are initialised to zero. A store instruction (e.g. $x \leftarrow 1$ on P_0) gives rise to a write event ((a)Wx1), and a load (e.g. $r1 \leftarrow y$ on P_0) to a read event ((b)Ry0). The property of interest is whether there exists an execution of the program such that the final state is $r1=0$ and $r2=0$. To determine this, we study the *event graph*, given on the right-hand side of the figure. An architecture allows an execution when it represents a *global happens-before* order over all processors. A cycle in an event graph is a violation of global happens before, unless the architecture relaxes any of the relations contributing to this cycle. Thus, if the graph has a cycle, we check if the architecture *may relax* some relations. Such a relaxation makes the graph acyclic, which implies that the architecture allows the final state.

In SC, nothing is be relaxed, thus the cycle in Fig. 1 forbids the execution. On the other hand, x86 relaxes the program order (po in Fig. 1) between writes and reads, thus the forbidding cycle no longer exists, and the given final state can be observed.

Formalisation. An *event* is a read or a write memory access, composed of a unique identifier, a direction R for read or W for write, a memory address, and a value. We represent each instruction by the events it issues. In Fig. 2, we associate the store $x \leftarrow 1$ on processor P_2 with the event (e)Wx1. We define two utility functions on events:

$\mathrm{proc}(e)$ returns the processor executing the event e, and $\mathrm{addr}(e)$ yields the address of a read or write event e.

A set of events $\mathbb{E}$ and their program order po form an *event structure* $E \triangleq (\mathbb{E}, \mathsf{po})$. po is a per-processor total order over the events of $\mathbb{E}$. We write $\mathsf{dp} \subseteq \mathsf{po}$ for the relation that models the *dependencies* between instructions, e.g. an *address dependency* occurs when computing the address of a load or store from the value of a preceding load.

We represent the *communication* between processors leading to the final state via an *execution witness* $X \triangleq (\mathsf{ws}, \mathsf{rf})$, which consists of two relations over the events. First, the *write serialisation* ws is a per-address total order on writes which models the *memory coherence* widely assumed by modern architectures. It links a write w to any write w' to the same address that hits the memory after w. Second, the *read-from* relation rf links a write w to a read r such that r reads the value written by w.

Given a pair of writes $(w', w) \in \mathsf{ws}$ and a read-from pair $(w', r) \in \mathsf{rf}$, we are to complete global happens before: w' happens before w by ws and r reads from w' by rf. Thus r is to happen before w, as otherwise it would have to read from w. To that aim, we derive the *from-read* relation fr from ws and rf. A read r is in fr with a write w when the write w' from which r reads hit the memory before w did. Formally, we have: $(r, w) \in \mathsf{fr} \triangleq \exists w', (w', r) \in \mathsf{rf} \wedge (w', w) \in \mathsf{ws}$.

In Fig. 2, the specified outcome corresponds to the execution on the right if each memory location initially holds 0. If r1=1 in the end, the read (a) obtained its value from the write (e) on P_2, hence $(e, a) \in \mathsf{rf}$. If r2=0 in the end, the read (b) obtained its value from the initial state, thus before the write (f) on P_3, hence $(b, f) \in \mathsf{fr}$. Similarly, we have $(f, c) \in \mathsf{rf}$ from r3=1, and $(d, e) \in \mathsf{fr}$ from r4=0.

Relaxed or safe. We model the scenario of reads to occur in advance, as described at the beginning of this section, by some subrelation of the read-from rf being *relaxed*, i.e. not included in global happens before. When a processor can read from its own store buffer [3] (the typical TSO/x86 scenario), we relax the internal read-from rfi. When two processors P_0 and P_1 can communicate privately via a cache (a case of *write atomicity* relaxation [3]), we relax the external read-from rfe, and call the corresponding write *non-atomic*. This is the main particularity of Power or ARM, and cannot happen on TSO/x86. Some program-order pairs may be relaxed (e.g. write-read pairs on x86, and all but dp ones on Power), i.e. only a subset of po is guaranteed to occur in this order. This subset constitutes *preserved program order*, ppo.

When a relation may not be relaxed, we call it *safe*. Architectures provide special *fence* (or *barrier*) instructions to prevent weak behaviours. Following [8], the relation fence $\subseteq$ po induced by a fence is *non-cumulative* when it only orders certain pairs of events surrounding the fence, i.e. fence is safe. The relation fence is *cumulative* when it additionally makes writes atomic, e.g. by flushing caches. In our axiomatic model, this amounts to making sequences of external read-from and fences (rfe; fence or fence; rfe) safe, even though rfe alone would not be safe for the architecture. We denote the union of fence and the additional cumulativity by ab.

Architectures. An *architecture* A determines the set safe_A of the relations safe on A, i.e. the relations embedded in global happens before. Following [8], we always consider the write serialisation ws and the from-read relation fr safe. SC relaxes nothing, i.e. rf and po are safe. TSO authorises the reordering of write-read pairs and store buffering but nothing else. Fences are safe by design, thus $\mathsf{ab} \subseteq \mathsf{safe}_A$.

Finally, an execution (E, X) is *valid* on A when the three following conditions hold. 1. SC holds per address, i.e. the communication and the program order for accesses with same address po-loc are compatible: $\mathrm{uniproc}(E, X) \triangleq \mathrm{acyclic}(\mathsf{ws} \cup \mathsf{rf} \cup \mathsf{fr} \cup \mathsf{po\text{-}loc})$. 2. Values do not come out of thin air, i.e. there is no causal loop: $\mathrm{thin}(E, X) \triangleq \mathrm{acyclic}(\mathsf{rf} \cup \mathsf{dp})$. 3. There exists a linearisation of events in global happens before, i.e. the safe relations do not form a cycle: $\mathrm{ghb}(E, X) \triangleq \mathrm{acyclic}((\mathsf{ws} \cup \mathsf{rf} \cup \mathsf{fr} \cup \mathsf{po}) \cap \mathsf{safe}_A)$. Formally:

$$\mathrm{valid}_A(E, X) \triangleq \mathrm{uniproc}(E, X) \wedge \mathrm{thin}(E, X) \wedge \mathrm{ghb}(E, X)$$

3   Simulating Weak Behaviours on SC

We develop a provably correct instrumentation strategy for programs. To this end, we first give an operational description of memory models in terms of an *abstract state machine* (Sec. 3.1). We then show in Sec. 3.3 the equivalence of the axiomatic model of Sec. 2 and the abstract machine. We explain in Sec. 3.4 how this equivalence proof guides our instrumentation strategy.

3.1   Abstract Machine

We define a non-deterministic state machine that reads a sequence of *labels*. The machine has a designated bad state $\perp$, and all other states of the machine represent system configurations, i.e. the memory, write buffers, and the set of pending reads. We write addr, evt, and rln for the types of memory addresses, events and relations, respectively.

Definition 1 (State). *A state of the machine is either $\perp$ or a triple* (m, b, rs), *where*

- *the memory $(m : addr \rightarrow evt)$ maps a memory address ℓ to a write to ℓ;*
- *the write buffer $(b : rln\ evt)$ is a total order over writes to the same address; the buffer has a special symbol $\perp_b$, placed before all events in the buffer;*
- *the read set $(rs : set\ evt)$ is a set of read events.*

We have a single set of reads, but one totally ordered buffer per address. Existing formalisations [24,11] use per-thread buffers, whereas our buffers are solely per-address objects. This allows us to model not only store buffering (which per-thread objects would allow), but also caching scenarios (fully non-atomic stores) as exhibited by **iriw+dps**, i.e. the **iriw** test of Fig. 2 with dependencies between the reads on P_0 and P_1 to prevent their reordering.

The machine performs transitions depending on *delay* and *flush* labels. Intuitively, a delay label pushes an object in the write buffer or read set. A flush label makes it exit the write buffer or read set. The details of transitions are described below.

Definition 2 (Label). *For a write event w, $d(w(w))$ denotes its delay label, and $f(w(w))$ its flush label. For a read event r, its delay label (with direction r, read) is denoted by $d(r(w, r))$, and its flush is denoted by $f(r(w, r))$.*

$\text{updm}(\mathsf{m}, w) \triangleq x \mapsto \text{if } \text{addr}(x) = \text{addr}(w) \text{ then } w \text{ else } x$

$\text{updb}(\mathsf{b}, w) \triangleq \mathsf{b} \cup \{(w_1, w_2) \mid w_1 = \bot_\mathsf{b} \vee ((\bot_\mathsf{b}, w_1) \in \mathsf{b} \wedge \text{addr}(w_1) = \text{addr}(w)) \wedge$
$\qquad\qquad\qquad w_2 = w\}$

$\text{updrs}(\mathsf{rs}, r) \triangleq \mathsf{rs} \cup \{r\}$

$\text{delb}(\mathsf{b}, w) \triangleq \{(w_1, w_2) \mid (w_1, w_2) \in \mathsf{b} \wedge w_1 \neq w \wedge w_2 \neq w\}$

$\text{delrs}(\mathsf{rs}, r) \triangleq \{e \mid e \in \mathsf{rs} \wedge e \neq r\}$

$\text{last}(\mathsf{b}, w) \triangleq (\neg(\exists w', (\bot_\mathsf{b}, w') \in \mathsf{b}) \wedge w = \bot_\mathsf{b}) \vee$
$\qquad\qquad\qquad ((\exists w', (\bot_\mathsf{b}, w') \in \mathsf{b}) \wedge (\bot_\mathsf{b}, w) \in \mathsf{b} \wedge \neg(\exists w', (w', w) \in \mathsf{b}))$

$\text{rfm}(\mathsf{m}, \mathsf{b}, w) \triangleq w = \mathsf{m}(\text{addr}(r)) \wedge \text{rr}(\mathsf{b}, \{w \mid (w, r) \in \text{po-loc}\}) = \emptyset$

WRITE TO BUFFER
$$\top$$
$$\frac{}{s \xrightarrow{\;\text{d}(\text{w}(w))\;} (\mathsf{m}, \text{updb}(\mathsf{b}, w), \mathsf{rs})}$$

DELAY READ
$$\top$$
$$\frac{}{s \xrightarrow{\;\text{d}(\text{r}(w,r))\;} (\mathsf{m}, \mathsf{b}, \text{updrs}(\mathsf{rs}, r))}$$

READ FROM SET

WRITE FROM BUFFER TO MEMORY

$\text{rr}(\mathsf{b}, \{e \mid (e, w) \in \text{ppo} \cup \text{ab}\}) = \emptyset \wedge$	(W1)	
$\mathsf{rs} \cap \{e \mid (e, w) \in \text{ppo} \cup \text{ab}\} = \emptyset \wedge$	(W2)	
$\mathsf{rs} \cap \{r \mid (r, w) \in \text{po-loc}\} = \emptyset \wedge$	(W3)	
$\text{last}(\text{rr}(\mathsf{b}, \{e \mid \text{addr}(e) = \ell\}), w)$	(W4)	

$$\frac{}{s \xrightarrow{\;\text{f}(\text{w}(w))\;} (\text{updm}(\mathsf{m}, w), \text{delb}(\mathsf{b}, w), \mathsf{rs})}$$

$r \in \mathsf{rs} \wedge$	(R1)
$\mathsf{rs} \cap \{r \mid (r, w) \in \text{dp}\} = \emptyset \wedge$	(R2)
$\text{rr}(\mathsf{b}, \{e \mid (e, r) \in \text{ppo} \cup \text{ab}\}) = \emptyset \wedge$	(R3)
$\mathsf{rs} \cap \{e \mid (e, w) \in \text{ppo} \cup \text{ab}\} = \emptyset \wedge$	(R4)
$[\text{rfm}(\mathsf{m}, \mathsf{b}, w) \vee$	(R5)
$(w \neq \mathsf{m}(\text{addr}(r)) \wedge w \in \mathsf{b} \wedge \text{visible}(w, r))]$	(R6)

$$\frac{}{s \xrightarrow{\;\text{f}(\text{r}(w,r))\;} (\mathsf{m}, \mathsf{b}, \text{delrs}(\mathsf{rs}, r))}$$

Fig. 3. The abstract machine

A set L of labels is well-formed w.r.t. an event structure E when: in $\text{d}(\text{w}(w))$ or $\text{f}(\text{w}(w))$, w is a write of E; in $\text{d}(\text{r}(w,r))$ or $\text{f}(\text{r}(w,r))$, w is a write of E and r a read of E, both with the same address; any event of E has a unique corresponding flush label in L; when a flush label belongs to L, so does its delay counterpart.

Transitions. We write $s \xrightarrow{l} s'$ to denote that the machine can make a transition from state s to state s' reading label l. Let the machine be in a state $(\mathsf{m}, \mathsf{b}, \mathsf{rs})$. Given a label, the machine performs transitions from one state to another if the conditions described below are fulfilled. Otherwise, the machine transitions to $\bot$ (it gets stuck).

In Fig. 3, we give the formal definition of the transitions of our machine. We need to define a few auxiliary functions, also formally defined in Fig. 3. We update the memory with a write w via $\text{updm}(\mathsf{m}, w)$, a buffer with a write w via $\text{updb}(\mathsf{b}, w)$, and a set with a read r via $\text{updrs}(\mathsf{rs}, r)$. We delete a write w from a buffer via $\text{delb}(\mathsf{b}, w)$ and we delete a read r from a set via $\text{delrs}(\mathsf{rs}, r)$. We write $\text{rr}(R, S)$ for the restriction of a relation R to a set S, i.e. $\{(x, y) \mid (x, y) \in R \wedge x \in S \wedge y \in S\}$. We pick the last write to an address ℓ of a buffer via $\text{last}(\mathsf{b}, w)$. In prose, the transitions are as follows. To avoid ambiguity in wording, we write "r-before" or "r-after" to express before or after w.r.t. the relation r.

- *Write to buffer*: a write $\mathrm{d}(\mathrm{w}(w))$ to address ℓ can always enter the buffer b, taking its place b-after all the writes to ℓ that are already in b.
- *Delay read*: a read $\mathrm{d}(\mathrm{r}(w, r))$ can always enter the read set rs.
- *Write from buffer to memory*: a write $\mathrm{f}(\mathrm{w}(w))$ to address ℓ exits the buffer b and updates the memory at ℓ if:
  - there is no event e in the buffer nor in the read set which is ppo $\cup$ ab-before w (Conditions (W1) and (W2));
  - *and* there is no read from ℓ in the buffer which is po-before w (Cond. (W3));
  - *and* there is no write to ℓ in the buffer which is b-before w (Condition (W4)).

- *Read from set*: a read $\mathrm{f}(\mathrm{r}(w, r))$ from ℓ (Condition (R1)) exits the read set if:
  - there is no read in the read set that is dp-before w (Condition (R2));
  - *and* there is no event in the buffer or in the read set that is ppo $\cup$ ab-before r (Conditions (R3) and (R4));
  - *and either* w is in memory, and there is no write to ℓ in the buffer that is po-before r (Condition (R5));
  - *or* if w is not in memory, w is in the buffer and is *visible to* r (a notion defined below) (Condition (R6)).

To define a write w as *visible to a read* r, we need a few auxiliary functions. We define the part of the buffer visible to a read r as follows: $\mathsf{b}_r \triangleq \{w \mid (\perp_{\mathsf{b}}, w) \in \mathsf{b} \wedge ((\mathsf{rfi} \subseteq \mathrm{safe}_A) \Rightarrow \mathrm{proc}(w) = \mathrm{proc}(r)) \wedge ((\mathsf{rfe} \subseteq \mathrm{safe}_A) \Rightarrow \mathrm{proc}(w) \neq \mathrm{proc}(r))))\}$. Now, w is visible to r when:

w and r share the same address ℓ;

w is in the part of the buffer visible to r, namely if rfi (resp. rfe) is safe then w cannot be on the same (resp. a different) thread as r ($w \in \mathsf{b}_r$);

w is b-before the first write w_a to ℓ that is po-after r;

w is equal to, or b-after, the last write w_b to ℓ that is po-before r.

All states except $\perp$ are accepting states. Thus, the abstract machine accepts a sequence p of labels $l_0, l_1, \ldots$ if there is a sequence of states $s_0, s_1, \ldots$ such that $s_i \xrightarrow{l_i} s_{i+1}$ and $s_i \neq \perp$ for all i.

Definition 3 (Accepting sequence). *A sequence p is a total order over L compatible with the program order, i.e. for two events $(x, y) \in$ po, their delay labels appear in the same order in p. It is* accepting *iff the sequence p is accepted by the abstract machine.*

3.2 Illustration Using Examples

We illustrate the machine by revisiting the **sb** test of Fig. 1 for TSO and the **iriw** test of Fig. 2 for Power. Fig. 4 and 5 reproduce on the left the event graphs from Fig. 1 and 2. On the right, they show the counterparts in the abstract machine. We explain the labels on the arrows in the next section (§"From the axiomatic model to the machine"). We use the following graphical conventions. In the axiomatic world (i.e. on the left of our figures), we reflect a pair that an architecture relaxes by a dashed arrow. For example, in the **sb** test of Fig. 4 on TSO, the write-read pairs (a, b) and (d, c) can be relaxed.

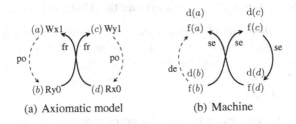

Fig. 4. Revisiting **sb** on TSO with our machine

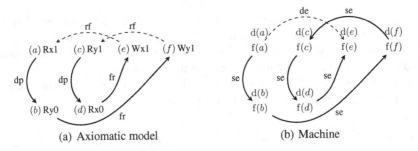

Fig. 5. Revisiting **iriw+dps** on Power with our machine

Likewise, in the **iriw+dps** test of Fig. 5 on Power, the read-from pairs (e, a) and (f, c) can be relaxed (as opposed to the read-read pairs (a, b) on P_0 and (c, d) on P_1, which are safe because of dependencies).

In any given execution, the abstract machine may choose to relax any pair that is not safe. Such pairs are depicted with a dashed arrow. Pairs that the machine does not relax are depicted with a thick arrow.

In Fig. 1, the pairs (a, b) on P_0 and (c, d) on P_1 are relaxed on TSO. Our machine may simulate the behaviour permitted on TSO by following the scenario in Fig. 4(b), which corresponds to the path $d(a) \to d(b) \to d(c) \to d(d) \to f(b) \to f(c) \to f(d) \to f(a)$. In the figure, the label "se" corresponds to a safe exit, and "de" to a delay exit, which are formalised below. The machine delays all events w.r.t. program order. In this scenario, the machine chooses to relax the pairs (a, b) by flushing the read b before the write a, ensuring that the registers r1 and r2 hold 0 in the end.

In Fig. 2, assume dependencies between the reads on P_0 and P_1, so that (a, b) on P_0 and (c, d) on P_1 are safe on Power. Yet (e, a) and (f, c) may be relaxed on Power, because Power has non-atomic writes. Our machine may simulate the weak behaviour exhibited on Power by following Fig. 5(b), which corresponds to the path $d(e) \to d(a) \to f(a) \to d(b) \to f(b) \to d(f) \to f(f) \to d(c) \to f(c) \to d(d) \to f(d) \to f(e)$. Since (a, b) and (c, d) are safe on Power, our machine flushes a before b (resp. c before d). Since $(b, f) \in$ fr (resp. $(d, e) \in$ fr), which is always safe, the machine flushes b before f (resp. d before e), ensuring that b and d read from memory, thus r2 and r4 hold 0 in the end. Finally, in this scenario, the machine chooses to relax the pairs (e, a) by flushing a before e, ensuring that r1 and r3 hold the value 1 in the end.

3.3 Equivalence of the Axiomatic Model and the Abstract Machine

We now prove the equivalence of the axiomatic model of Sec. 2 and the machine defined in Sec. 3.1. We first show that we can build an execution valid in the axiomatic model from any path of labels accepted by the machine (Thm. 1). We then show that we can build a path of labels accepted by the machine from any execution that is valid in axiomatic model (Thm. 2).

Theorem 1 (From the machine to the axiomatic model). *Let E be an event structure and L be a set of labels well-formed w.r.t. E. Then there exists an execution witness valid for E, if there is an accepting sequence p over L.*

Let $\mathrm{ptoX}(p, L)$ denote the execution witness of Thm. 1. Recall from Sec. 2 that an execution witness is a pair of write serialisation and read-from map. Intuitively, we build these as follows. The write serialisation gathers the pairs of writes to the same address according to the order of their flushed parts in the accepting sequence p: $\{(w_1, w_2) \mid \mathrm{addr}(w_1) = \mathrm{addr}(w_2) \wedge (\mathrm{f}(\mathrm{w}(w_1)), \mathrm{f}(\mathrm{w}(w_2))) \in p\}$. For the read-from map, we simply gather the pairs given by the labels of L: $\{(w, r) \mid \mathrm{addr}(w) = \mathrm{addr}(r) \wedge \mathrm{f}(\mathrm{r}(w, r)) \in L\}$.

Proof (Thm. 1). We need to show that $(E, \mathrm{ptoX}(p, L))$ passes the uniproc, thin and ghb checks. The three proofs follow the same lines, thus we focus on the first for brevity.

The execution passes the uniproc check iff for all $(x, y) \in$ po-loc, we do not have $(y, x) \in$ rf$\cup$fr$\cup$ws$\cup$(ws; rf)$\cup$(fr; rf) [4, App. A]. By contradiction take $(x, y) \in$ po-loc and $(y, x) \in$ rf $\cup$ fr $\cup$ rf. We proceed by case disjunction over $(y, x) \in$ rf $\cup$ fr $\cup$ ws $\cup$ (ws; rf) $\cup$ (fr; rf). We write ℓ for the address shared by x and y.

If $(y, x) \in$ rf, $\mathrm{f}(\mathrm{r}(y, x))$ is in L. Since p is accepting, the Read from set transition on $\mathrm{f}(\mathrm{r}(y, x))$ does not block. Hence y is in memory, or y is in the buffer and visible to x. If y is in memory, y has been flushed, i.e. the Write from buffer to memory transition on $\mathrm{f}(\mathrm{w}(y))$ did not block. Hence there is no read from ℓ po-before y in the set. Yet $(x, y) \in$ po-loc, and x is still in the set when y is in memory, a contradiction. If y is in the buffer and visible to x, y is in the buffer before the first write to ℓ po-after x. Yet, $(x, y) \in$ po-loc, a contradiction.

For brevity, we present only the rf case; all the other cases are similar, using the premises of the rules of the machine. For example the $(y, x) \in$ ws case uses the Write from buffer to memory rule, in particular the fact that y exits the buffer if there is no write to ℓ before it in the buffer; yet x is still in there. The $(y, x) \in$ fr case uses the Read from set rule, in particular the fact that if the write w from which x reads is in memory, then there is no write to ℓ po-before y in the buffer; yet x is in there. If w is in the buffer, we use the fact that w is equal to, or in the buffer after, the last write to ℓ po-before x, which will block the flush of w, a contradiction. $\square$

For the other direction, we first build labels from the events of E. We augment our events with directions: a write w becomes $\mathrm{w}(w)$ and r becomes $\mathrm{r}(w, r)$, where $(w, r) \in$ rf. Then we *split* an augmented event e into its delayed part $\mathrm{d}(e)$, and its flushed part $\mathrm{f}(e)$. We write $\mathrm{labels}(E, X)$ for the labels built from the events of E.

Then we form the *delay pairs* of (E, X), as follows. We build the relation ndelay over the events of E, such that: $((\text{ws} \cup \text{rf} \cup \text{fr}) \cap \text{safe}_A) \subseteq$ ndelay; ndelay is transitive;

ndelay is irreflexive; if $(x, y) \notin$ ndelay then $(y, x) \in$ ndelay. The delay pairs are the pairs (x, y) of events of E that are not in ndelay.

Given (E, X) and a choice of delay pairs, we build an accepting path p as follows, with e, e_1, and e_2 denoting augmented events:

Delay before flush we always delay an event e before we flush it, i.e. $(d(e), f(e)) \in p$;
Enter $(e_1, e_2) \in$ po enter the buffer or set in this order, i.e. $(d(e_1), d(e_2)) \in p$;
Rf a write enters before we flush a read from it, i.e. $(d(e_1), f(e_2)) \in p$ if $(e_1, e_2) \in$ rf;
Safe Exit $(e_1, e_2) \in$ ndelay are flushed in the same order, i.e. $(f(e_1), f(e_2)) \in p$.
Delay Exit $(e_1, e_2) \notin$ ndelay are flushed in the opposite order, i.e. $(f(e_2), f(e_1)) \in p$.

Reconsider Fig. 4(b) and 5(b). We omit the arrows corresponding to the first three cases to ease the reading of the figures. In Fig. 4(b), we chose (a, b) to be a delay pair, hence we flush them b before a, following the delay exit rule. On the contrary, (b, c), (c, d) and (d, a) are not delay pairs, hence we flush b before c, c before d and d before a, following the safe exit rule. The same explanation applies in Fig. 5 to the pair (e, a) being delayed, and (a, b), (f, c), (c, d) and (d, e) being safe.

We build $\text{Xtop}(E, X, \text{ndelay})$ as above. As ndelay is transitive and irreflexive, $\text{Xtop}(E, X, \text{ndelay})$ is acyclic. Hence the transitive closure $(\text{Xtop}(E, X, \text{ndelay}))^+$ is a partial order of the labels. Any linearisation $\text{lin}((\text{Xtop}(E, X, \text{ndelay}))^+)$ of this transitive closure forms an actual path, which we show accepting when 1. X is valid 2. this linearisation has finite prefixes, in which case we say that (E, X) has finite prefixes:

Theorem 2 (From the axiomatic model to the machine). *For any valid execution (E, X) with finite prefixes, there is an accepting path p over labels L well-formed w.r.t. E.*

Proof. We need to show that no transition can block the machine. The Write to buffer and Delay read transitions are trivial since they can never block.

For the Write from buffer to memory case, suppose as a contradiction that the transition blocks on a write w to an address ℓ. If there is e ppo $\cup$ ab-before w in the buffer or the set, (e, w) cannot be a delay pair (because ppo and ab are safe), i.e. should be flushed in order, contradicting the presence of e in the buffer or the set. Otherwise, there is in the set a read r from ℓ po-before w. Therefore (r, w) is in fr, thus safe, hence cannot be a delay pair, and the same argument applies. Finally, if there is a write w' to ℓ before w in the buffer; one can show that (w', w) is in ws, hence w' should be flushed before w, a contradiction.

For the Read from set case, suppose as a contradiction that the transition blocks on a read (w, r) with address ℓ. If there is a read r' dp-before w in the set, one can show that r' should be flushed before r, and r should be flushed before r' (i.e. a thin-air cycle in X), a contradiction. If there is an event ppo $\cup$ ab-before r in the buffer or the set, the reasoning is the same as above in the write case. If w is in memory and there is a write to ℓ po-before r in the buffer, we create a uniproc cycle, a contradiction. If w is in the buffer and not visible to r, there are two cases. Either w is not on a thread whose buffer r can read w.r.t. A, in which case (w, r) do not form a delay pair and should be flushed in this order, contradicting the presence of w in the buffer. Or w is in the buffer after the first write to ℓ po-after r (or before the last write to ℓ po-before r), in which case we create a uniproc cycle. $\square$

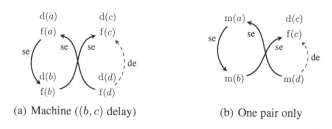

(a) Machine ((b, c) delay)   (b) One pair only

Fig. 6. Choices for instrumenting **sb** for TSO

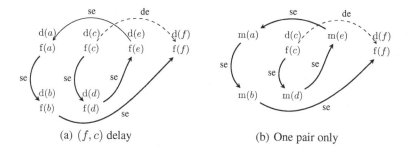

(a) (f, c) delay   (b) One pair only

Fig. 7. Choices for instrumenting **iriw+dps** for Power

3.4   Instrumentation

Thm. 2 leaves freedom in the instrumentation strategy. We can exploit the choice of delay pairs and the choice of the linearisation of $\mathrm{Xtop}(E, X)$ in order to reduce the overhead of running or verifying an instrumented program.

Choice of delay pairs. The conditions on the ndelay relation restrict the choice of delay pairs. We have to put at least all the safe pairs into ndelay, by the first condition.

Since ndelay is transitive and irreflexive, it is acyclic. An execution (E, X) presents a cycle iff it is not SC (if it is SC, all pairs are safe and there is no cycle). [7, Thm.1] shows that an execution is valid on A but not on SC iff it contains *critical cycles*[1]. Thus we can put all pairs in ndelay, except one unsafe pair per critical cycle, which corresponds to the last condition over ndelay.

In Fig. 4(b), we build an accepting path corresponding to the axiomatic execution of Fig. 4(a) by choosing the unsafe pair (a, b) on the cycle to be a delay. In Fig. 6(a), we choose the unsafe pair (c, d). Similarly for Fig. 5(a), we can build an accepting path

---

[1] We recall here the definition of [7]. Two events (x, y) are *competing*, written $(x, y) \in$ cmp, if they are from distinct processors, to the same address, and at least one of them is a write (e.g. in Fig. 2, the read (a) from x on P_0 and the write (e) to x on P_2). A cycle $\sigma \subseteq$ cmp $\cup$ po is critical when it is not a cycle in $(\mathsf{cmp} \cup (\mathsf{ppo} \cap \mathsf{safe}_A)^+)$ and it satisfies the two following properties: **(i)** Per processor, there are at most two memory accesses (x, y) on this processor and $\mathrm{addr}(x) \neq \mathrm{addr}(y)$. **(ii)** For a given memory address x, there are at most three accesses relative to x, and these accesses are from distinct processors $((w, w') \in$ cmp, $(w, r) \in$ cmp, $(r, w) \in$ cmp or $\{(r, w), (w, r')\} \subseteq$ cmp). Fig. 2, shows a critical cycle of **iriw** on Power.

corresponding to the axiomatic execution of Fig. 5(a) by choosing e.g. (e, a) as delay (cf. Fig. 5(b)). In Fig. 7(a), we choose (f, c) as delay.

Our examples are symmetric, thus the choice of which pair to delay should not make a difference. In Fig. 1, (a, b) and (c, d) are write-read pairs. Similarly in Fig. 2, (e, a) and (f, c) are of the same nature, namely rfe pairs. For asymmetric examples, the chosen delayed pair can make a crucial difference (cf. Sec. 5), if the instrumentation of one pair causes more execution or verification time overhead than the other.

Choice of the linearisation. Thm. 2 accepts any linearisation of $(\text{Xtop}(E, X, \text{ndelay}))^+$. Yet, some require less instrumentation than others. Consider Fig. 6(a) and (b): in both we choose to delay the pair (c, d). On the left, we can pick any interleaving (compatible with Xtop) of the delayed and flushed events to instantiate Thm. 2, e.g. $\text{d}(a) \to \text{d}(b) \to \text{d}(c) \to \text{d}(d) \to \text{f}(b) \to \text{f}(d) \to \text{f}(c) \to \text{f}(a)$.

On the right, we write $\text{m}(e)$ when the delayed and flushed part of an event happen without intervening events in between. Observe that in this case, the event e occurs w.r.t. memory: if it is a read, it reads from the memory; if it is a write, it writes to memory. In Fig. 6(b), we pick a particular interleaving, namely the one where all events are w.r.t. memory, except for the event c. This interleaving requires to instrument only one instruction, as opposed to all of them on the left.

Similarly in Fig. 7(a) and (b), we choose in both cases to delay the pair (f, c). On the left, we instrument all instructions. On the right, we instrument only the pair (f, c).

4   Implementation

4.1   Overview

We implemented the transformation technique of Sec. 3. Our tool reads a concurrent C program, possibly with inline assembly `mfence`, `sync`, or `lwsync` instructions (cf. Sec. 2). It generates a new concurrent C program augmented with C equivalents of write buffers and read sets of Sec. 3.1. The transformation proceeds in three main steps:

1. We devise an *abstract event structure*, as defined below, the concretisation of which amounts to all event structures (cf. Sec. 2) of the program.
2. Given an architecture, we identify potential critical cycles in this structure.
3. We instrument unsafe pairs in the cycle, as described in Sec. 3.4.

The resulting program is then passed to any SC program analyser.

The first two steps guide the program transformation of the third step, in order to reduce the overhead for subsequent verification. As our experiments confirm (Sec. 5), we drastically improve verification performance over instrumenting all instructions.

4.2   Abstract Event Structures

As described in Sec. 3, we can choose to delay only one pair per critical cycle. To do so, all critical cycles need to be identified first. Sec. 2 defines cycles over events and event structures, which use concrete addresses and values, and thus correspond to concrete execution traces. As the enumeration of all traces is infeasible, we compute a conservative, over-approximate set of possible cycles using static analysis. In this program analysis we introduce *abstract events*, which summarise all concrete events that have the same process identifier, program counter, direction and memory address. We extend the definition of event structure to *abstract event structures*, which are identical except that they use abstract events.

Statements to abstract events. The derivation of an abstract event structure from a non-branching multi-threaded program is straight-forward. For each thread, decompose each statement into abstract events, extracting all writes or reads of shared memory. For an assignment to a location designated by a pointer variable, consider the example `*(&x+z) = y;`, where `&x` denotes the address of x and `*p` the value held at address p. We first read y, then read z and finally we write to the object pointed to by `&x+z`, which is determined using an alias analysis[2]. If the precision of the alias analysis is insufficient to determine the object, we assume that this write can target any of the objects in the program.

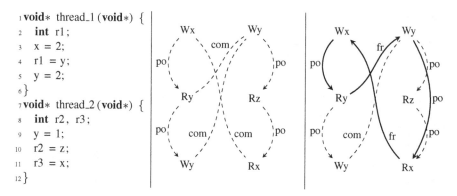

```
1 void* thread_1 (void*) {
2   int r1;
3   x = 2;
4   r1 = y;
5   y = 2;
6 }
7 void* thread_2 (void*) {
8   int r2, r3;
9   y = 1;
10  r2 = z;
11  r3 = x;
12 }
```

Fig. 8. The program on the left contains an **sb** cycle (cf. Fig. 1). We build the abstract event graph in the middle, and indeed detect the cycle in the graph, on the right.

Abstract event graph. In order to devise SC cycles that become critical cycles on a weaker architecture, we look for cycles in ws ∪ fr ∪ rf ∪ po (definition of SC, [5, Thm. 3]). Abstract events in each thread are ordered by program order, po, which we derive as described below. As we do not use concrete values, we compute over-approximations of the relations ws, rf and fr. We further abstract from directed edges and use undirected edges in these over-approximations. We call the abstract event structure equipped with over-approximations of ws, rf and fr an *abstract event graph*. We compute the over-approximations as follows:

- the internal rf, fr and ws pairs (relating two events on the same thread) are already covered by po edges;

---

[2] The alias analysis we use is known to be sound for the weak architectures we consider [6].

- the external rf, fr and ws pairs (relating two events from different threads) are abstracted by undirected external communications, denoted by com, and relate any pair of write-read, read-write or write-write between two distinct threads.

Fig. 8 depicts this first step in the middle, which is the resulting abstract event graph of the program shown on the left-hand side. A concretisation of the abstract event graph may yield critical cycles. Fig. 8 shows an example of a critical cycle on the right-hand side. Whether this cycle can be fully concretised to an execution witness, filling in concrete values in all abstract events, is left as task to a verification back end.

Control flow. To build an abstract event graph for branching programs, we consider the if-then-else branches, loops and function calls. Functions are analysed as if they were inlined, thus recursion is not handled. For if-then-else, po in the abstract event graph follows both of the branches separately, and then joins at the end of the condition. For loops or backward jumps and given a pair $(x, y) \in$ po, the back-edge may render x reachable from y as well. We thus include copies of x and y in the abstract event graph, such that (y, x) in po if such a back-edge exists. By [7] it suffices to use a single copy, as a critical cycle does not require more than two events in program order per thread.

The analysis proceeds in a forward manner along the control-flow graph of a given program. For each statement recorded in a node of the control-flow graph, the abstract events are computed. When preserved program order is defined via dp (cf. Sec. 2), possible dependencies between abstract events are recorded as well.

4.3   Detecting Critical Cycles

Given the abstract event graph of a program, we need to compute an over-approximate set of critical cycles. To increase scalability of this procedure, we first identify all strongly connected components (SCCs) in the graph using Tarjan's 1972 algorithm [27], which is linear in the size of the abstract event graph. The detection of critical cycles can then be performed in parallel and independently for each SCC, as no cycle can span multiple SCCs. The SCCs also offer first insights about the program under test: two distinct SCCs will refer to two parts of the code that are independently accessing and updating shared memory.

Detecting all the critical cycles in an SCC. Our cycle computation is based on Tarjan's 1973 algorithm [28]. The abstract event graph, however, does not encode the transitive closure of po. Thus, we first extract *candidate cycles* by picking at most two abstract events per thread, which are guaranteed to be (transitively) linked by program order. For each candidate cycle we then perform additional filtering, as such a cycle need not be critical: a candidate is guaranteed to be *not* critical if it does not contain any *unsafe pair* for the given architecture, or is a cycle in *uniproc* or *thin-air*. All of these checks need to be performed a-posteriori for a complete cycle.

Tarjan's original algorithm is worst-case exponential in the number of vertices (abstract events), and our subsequent filtering adds additional complexity. To deal with this complexity, we soundly limit the exploration using properties of critical cycles, such as all program-order pairs per address in a critical cycle being one of write-write, read-write, write-read or read-write-read [4].

4.4   Selecting and Instrumenting Delay Pairs

The above cycle detection yields candidates for unsafe pairs of abstract events to be delayed in each cycle. Following Sec. 3.4, we instrument one pair to delay per cycle. We may select these pairs arbitrarily, but we describe below a weighted instrumentation that decidedly reduces verification time, as we show in Sec. 5.

We first normalise the program such that all shared memory accesses appear in assignments only; any reads in branching conditions or function call parameters are moved to temporary variables as follows: **if** $(\phi(x))$ ...; $\longmapsto$ tmp = $\phi(x)$; **if**(tmp) ...; for an expression ϕ over a shared memory address x. In the following, we thus restrict ourselves to assignment statements.

For each memory address x of events in unsafe pairs we introduce an array $b(x)$. In addition to the properties described in Sec. 3.1, we also keep track of the originating thread of the write to x. We introduce an additional pointer for each local variable reading from a shared memory address, i.e. an r such that $r = x$;. In a pair to delay, in one of the critical cycles or after, we equip r with a pointer $rs(r)$, which implements the read set of Sec. 3.1. We now describe the instrumentation of writes, then reads. To soundly over-approximate all possible behaviours, all instrumented operations are guarded by **if**(*), expressing non-deterministic choice.

Instrumenting writes. We implement here the two operations associated to the weak-memory effects of a write w, as defined in Sec. 3.1: (1) delaying a write, $d(w(w))$, by appending to the buffer, and (2) flushing a write, $f(w(w))$, removing it from the buffer. A delayed write amounts to appending an element to the array:

x = smthg; $\longmapsto$ **if**(*) $b(x)$.push(smthg,thread.number); **else** x = smthg;

According to Sec. 3.1, each delay is accompanied by a flush. Yet the point in time when the flush happens is not determined. We would thus need to add non-deterministic flush instructions at each statement in the program. This transformation would make the program highly non-deterministic, and very hard for a model checker to analyse. Therefore, we insert flushes only where they might have an effect, i.e. before each potential read from the address that was written to, and make them flush a non-deterministic number of writes in FIFO-manner. The function *take* implements the semantics of "write from buffer to memory" of Fig. 3 on C arrays for a non-deterministic number of elements, and returns the resulting in-memory value at address x.

smthg = x; $\longmapsto$ **if**(*) x = $b(x)$.take(thread.number); smthg = x;

Instrumenting reads. Here we are to implement the two operations for reads: delaying a read $d(r(w,r))$ and reading from the set, $f(r(w,r))$. We delay a read by recording the memory address to be read from. Note that, given our program normalisation, our reads manifest as assignments to local variables. For a local variable r1, we delay the read of x as follows:

r1 = x; $\longmapsto$ **if**(*) $rs(r1)$ = &x; **else** r1 = x;

Input: the edges to instrument E, the cycles C_j
Problem: minimise $\sum_{e_i \in E} \mathbf{d}(e_i) * x_i$
s.t. $\forall j, \sum_{e_i \in C_j \cap E} x_i >= 1$ (ensures soundness)
where
  e_i is a pair to potentially instrument,
  x_i is a Boolean variable stating whether we instrument e_i,
  and $\mathbf{d}()$ is the cost of an instrumentation.
Output: the x_i, stating which pairs to instrument

Fig. 9. Mixed integer programming problem to choose the pairs to instrument

For flushing the read, considerations analogous to the write case are made: we flush non-deterministically upon an actual read (then of r1) only, instead of every program point. The flush dereferences the address previously recorded:

r2 = r1; $\longmapsto$ **if**(rs($r1$) != 0 && *) { r1 = *rs($r1$); rs($r1$) = 0;} r2 = r1;

4.5 Weighted Selection of Unsafe Pairs

Above, we selected an arbitrary unsafe pair per cycle, as this suffices to reveal all weak-memory effects (cf. Sec. 3). We do observe, however, that the choice of pairs has a strong effect on verification time. We thus assign an empirically devised cost **d** to candidate pairs. With our implementation, we chose **d**(poW*)=1 (pairs in program order where the first event is a write), **d**(poRW)=2 (read-write pairs in program order), **d**(rfe)=2 (write-read pairs on different threads), **d**(poRR)=3 (read-read pairs in program order). Given a set E of pairs to delay in the graph with critical cycles C_j, we solve the mixed integer programming problem of Fig. 9. Our experiments show that this encoding yields a speedup of 26% over all architectures with an SC bounded model-checker.

5 Experimental Results

We exercised our method and measured its cost using 8 tools. We considered 5 ANSI-C model checkers: a bounded model checker based on CBMC; SatAbs, a verifier based on predicate abstraction, using Boom as the model checker for the Boolean program; ES-BMC, a bounded model checker; Threader, a thread-modular verifier; and Poirot, which implements a context-bounded translation to sequential programs. These tools cover a broad spectrum of symbolic algorithms for verifying SC programs. We also experimented with Blender, CheckFence, and MMChecker. We ran our experiments on Linux 2.6.32 64-bit machines with 3.07 GHz (only Poirot was run on a Windows system). Further details on the results are available on our web page.

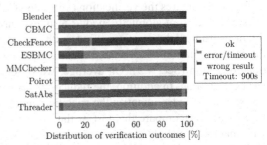

Fig. 10. All tools on all litmus tests and models

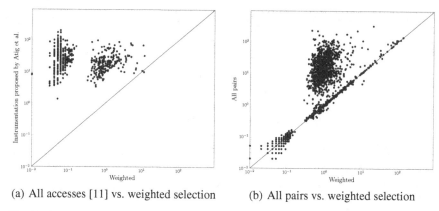

(a) All accesses [11] vs. weighted selection   (b) All pairs vs. weighted selection

Fig. 11. Comparison of verification times of CBMC (seconds) for different instrumentations

Validation. First, we systematically validate our setup using 555 litmus tests exposing weak memory artefacts (e.g. instruction reordering, store buffering, write atomicity relaxation) in isolation. The diy tool automatically generates x86, Power and ARM assembly programs implementing an idiom that cannot be reached on SC, but can be reached on a given model. For example, **sb** (Fig. 1) exhibits store buffering, thus the final state can be reached on any weak model, from TSO to Power.

Each litmus test comes with an assertion that models the SC violation exercised by the test, e.g. the outcomes of Fig. 1 and 2. Thus, verifying a litmus test amounts to checking whether the model under scrutiny can reach the specified outcome. We then convert these tests automatically into C code, leading to programs of 48 lines on average, involving 2 to 4 threads.

These examples provide assurance that we soundly implement the theory of Sec. 3: we verify each test w.r.t. SC, i.e. without transformation, then w.r.t. TSO, PSO, RMO, and Power. Despite the tests being small, they provide challenging concurrent idioms to verify. Fig. 10 compares the tools on all tests and models. Most tools, with the exception of Blender, CBMC and SatAbs, time out or give wrong results on a vast majority of tests. Blender only expectedly fails on tests involving lwsync fences; CBMC and SatAbs return spurious results in 1.5% of the tests, caused by the over-approximation in the implementation of our instrumentation.

Fig. 11 compares the verification time using CBMC over all litmus families (e.g. rfe tests exercise store atomicity, podwr tests exercise the write-read reordering) for different instrumentation options. First, with the restriction to TSO, Fig. 11(a) compares the instrumentation of all shared memory accesses proposed in [11] to the weighted transformation (Sec. 4.5). On average, we observe a more than 300-fold speedup in verification time. In addition, the reduced instrumentation also yields 246 fewer spurious results. We also quantify the specific benefit of the weighted selection of pairs in Fig. 11(b). We compare the cost of the instrumentation of all pairs on critical cycles with that of the weighted transformation (Sec. 4.5) for all models, tools and tests. The average speedup over all models and tests is still more than one order of magnitude. We give the detailed results for all experiments online.

We also verified several TSO examples that have been used in the literature (details are online). Note that these examples in fact only exhibit idioms already covered by our litmus tests (e.g. Dekker corresponds to the **sb** test of Fig. 1). Furthermore, we applied the instrumentation to code taken from the Read-Copy-Update algorithm in the Linux kernel and scheduling code in the Apache HTTP server, as well as industrial code from IBM. We observe that the instrumentation tool completes even on such code of up to 28,000 lines in less than 1 second, and in 32 seconds on IBM's code. We now study one real-life example in detail, an excerpt of the relational database software PostgreSQL.

Worker Synchronization in PostgreSQL. Mid 2011, PostgreSQL developers observed that a regression test occasionally failed on a multi-core PowerPC system.[3] The test implements a protocol passing a token in a ring of processes. Further analysis drew the attention to an interprocess signalling mechanism. It turned out that the code had already been subject to an inconclusive discussion in late 2010.[4]

The code in Listing 1 is an inlined version of the problematic code, with an additional assertion in line 7. Each element of the array "latch" is a Boolean variable stored in shared memory to facilitate interprocess communication. Each working process waits to have its latch set and then expects to have work to do (from line 9 onwards). Here, the work consists of passing around a token via the array "flag". Once the process is done with its work, it passes the token on (line 11), and sets the latch of the process the token was passed to (line 12).

```
1 #define WORKERS 2
2 volatile _Bool latch [WORKERS];
3 volatile _Bool flag [WORKERS];
4 void worker(int i )
5 { while(! latch [ i ]);
6   for (;;)
7   { assert (! latch [ i ]  ||  flag [ i ]);
8     latch [ i ] = 0;
9     if ( flag [ i ])
10    { flag [ i ] = 0;
11      flag [( i+1)%WORKERS] = 1;
12      latch [( i+1)%WORKERS] = 1; }
13    while(! latch [ i ]);   } }
```

Listing 1. Token passing in pgsql.c

Starvation seemingly cannot occur: when a process is woken up, it has work to do (has the token). Yet, the PostgreSQL developers observed that the wait in line 13 (which in the original code is bounded in time) would time out, thus signalling starvation of the ring of processes. The developers identified the memory model of the platform as possible culprit: it was assumed that the processor would at times delay the write in line 11 until after the latch had been set.

We transform the code of Listing 1 for two workers under Power. The event graphs show two idioms: **lb** (load buffering) and **mp** (message passing), in Fig. 12 and 13. The code fragments on the left-hand side give the corresponding line numbers in Listing 1.

The **lb** idiom contains the two *if* statements controlling the access to both critical sections. Since the **lb** idiom is yet unimplemented by Power machines (despite being allowed by the architecture [26]), we believe that this is not the bug observed by the PostgreSQL developers. Yet, it might lead to actual bugs on future machines.

In contrast, the **mp** case is commonly observed on Power machines (e.g. 1.7G/167G on Power 7 [26]). The **mp** case arises in the PostgreSQL code by the combination

---

[3] http://archives.postgresql.org/pgsql-hackers/
   2011-08/msg00330.php

[4] http://archives.postgresql.org/
   pgsql-hackers/2010-11/msg01575.php

pgsql (lb)	
Worker 0	Worker 1
(9) if (flag[0])	(9) if (flag[1])
(11) flag[1]=1;	(11) flag[0]=1;
Observed: flag[0]=1; flag[1]=1	

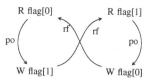

Fig. 12. An **lb** idiom detected in `pgsql.c`

pgsql (mp)	
Worker 0	Worker 1
(11) flag[1]=1;	(5) while (!latch[1]);
(12) latch[1]=1;	(9) if (flag[1])
Observed: latch[1]=1; flag[1]=0	

Fig. 13. An **mp** idiom detected in `pgsql.c`

of some writes in the critical section of the first worker, and the access to the critical section of the second worker; the relevant code lines are in Fig. 13.

We first check the fully transformed code with SatAbs. After 21.34 seconds, SatAbs provides a counterexample (given online), where we first execute the first worker up to line 13. All accesses are w.r.t. memory, except at lines 11 and 12, where the values 0 and 1 are stored into the buffers of flag[0] and flag[1]. Then the second worker starts, reading the updated value 1 of latch[1]. It exits the blocking while (line 5) and reaches the assertion. Here, latch[1] still holds 1, and flag[1] still holds 0, as Worker 0 has not yet flushed the write waiting in its buffer. Thus, the condition of the *if* is not true, the critical section is skipped, and the program arrives at line 13, without having authorised the next worker to enter the critical section, and loops forever.

As **mp** can arise on Power e.g. because of non-atomic writes, we know by Sec. 3.4 that we only need to transform one **rfe** pair of the cycle, and relaunch the verification. SatAbs spends 1.29 seconds to check it (and finds a counterexample, as previously).

PostgreSQL developers discussed fixes, but only committed comments to the code base, as it remained unclear whether the intended fixes were appropriate. We proposed a provably correct patch solving both **lb** and **mp**. After discussion with the developers[5], we improved it to meet the developers' desire to maintain the current API. The final patch introduces two `lwsync` barriers: after line 8 and before line 12.

6   Conclusion

We have presented a provably sound method to verify concurrent software w.r.t. weak memory. Our contribution allows to lift SC methods and tools to a wide range of weak memory models (from x86 to Power), by means of program transformation.

---

[5] `http://archives.postgresql.org/`
`pgsql-hackers/2012-03/msg01506.php`

Our approach crucially relies on the definition of a generic operational model equivalent to the axiomatic one of [8]. We do not favour any style of model in particular, but we highlight the importance of the availability of several equivalent mathematical styles to model semantics as intricate as weak memory. In addition, operational models are often the style of choice in the verification community; we contribute here to the vocabulary to tackle the verification problem w.r.t. weak memory.

Our extensive experiments and in particular the PostgreSQL bug demonstrate the practicability of our approach from several different perspectives. First, we confirmed a known bug (**mp**), and validated the fix proposed by the developers, including an evaluation of different synchronisation options. Second, we found an additional idiom (**lb**), which will cause a bug on future Power machines; our fix repairs it already.

References

1. http://research.microsoft.com/en-us/projects/poirot/
2. Abdulla, P.A., Atig, M.F., Chen, Y.-F., Leonardsson, C., Rezine, A.: Counter-Example Guided Fence Insertion under TSO. In: Flanagan, C., König, B. (eds.) TACAS 2012. LNCS, vol. 7214, pp. 204–219. Springer, Heidelberg (2012)
3. Adve, S.V., Gharachorloo, K.: Shared Memory Consistency Models: A Tutorial. IEEE Computer 29, 66–76 (1995)
4. Alglave, J.: A Shared Memory Poetics. Ph.D. thesis, Université Paris 7 and INRIA (2010)
5. Alglave, J.: A Formal Hierarchy of Weak Memory Models. In: FMSD (2012)
6. Alglave, J., Kroening, D., Lugton, J., Nimal, V., Tautschnig, M.: Soundness of Data Flow Analyses for Weak Memory Models. In: Yang, H. (ed.) APLAS 2011. LNCS, vol. 7078, pp. 272–288. Springer, Heidelberg (2011)
7. Alglave, J., Maranget, L.: Stability in Weak Memory Models. In: Gopalakrishnan, G., Qadeer, S. (eds.) CAV 2011. LNCS, vol. 6806, pp. 50–66. Springer, Heidelberg (2011)
8. Alglave, J., Maranget, L., Sarkar, S., Sewell, P.: Fences in Weak Memory Models. In: Touili, T., Cook, B., Jackson, P. (eds.) CAV 2010. LNCS, vol. 6174, pp. 258–272. Springer, Heidelberg (2010)
9. Atig, M.F., Bouajjani, A., Burckhardt, S., Musuvathi, M.: On the verification problem for weak memory models. In: POPL (2010)
10. Atig, M.F., Bouajjani, A., Burckhardt, S., Musuvathi, M.: What's Decidable about Weak Memory Models? In: Seidl, H. (ed.) ESOP 2012. LNCS, vol. 7211, pp. 26–46. Springer, Heidelberg (2012)
11. Atig, M.F., Bouajjani, A., Parlato, G.: Getting Rid of Store-Buffers in TSO Analysis. In: Gopalakrishnan, G., Qadeer, S. (eds.) CAV 2011. LNCS, vol. 6806, pp. 99–115. Springer, Heidelberg (2011)
12. Bouajjani, A., Meyer, R., Möhlmann, E.: Deciding Robustness against Total Store Ordering. In: Aceto, L., Henzinger, M., Sgall, J. (eds.) ICALP 2011, Part II. LNCS, vol. 6756, pp. 428–440. Springer, Heidelberg (2011)
13. Burckhardt, S., Alur, R., Martin, M.K.: Checkfence: Checking consistency of concurrent data types on relaxed memory models. In: PLDI (2007)
14. Cordeiro, L., Fischer, B.: Verifying multi-threaded software using SMT-based context-bounded model checking. In: ICSE. pp. 331–340. ACM (2011)
15. Donaldson, A., Kaiser, A., Kroening, D., Wahl, T.: Symmetry-Aware Predicate Abstraction for Shared-Variable Concurrent Programs. In: Gopalakrishnan, G., Qadeer, S. (eds.) CAV 2011. LNCS, vol. 6806, pp. 356–371. Springer, Heidelberg (2011)

16. Gupta, A., Popeea, C., Rybalchenko, A.: Threader: A Constraint-Based Verifier for Multi-threaded Programs. In: Gopalakrishnan, G., Qadeer, S. (eds.) CAV 2011. LNCS, vol. 6806, pp. 412–417. Springer, Heidelberg (2011)
17. Huynh, T.Q., Roychoudhury, A.: A Memory Model Sensitive Checker for C#. In: Misra, J., Nipkow, T., Sekerinski, E. (eds.) FM 2006. LNCS, vol. 4085, pp. 476–491. Springer, Heidelberg (2006)
18. Jin, H., Yavuz-Kahveci, T., Sanders, B.A.: Java Memory Model-Aware Model Checking. In: Flanagan, C., König, B. (eds.) TACAS 2012. LNCS, vol. 7214, pp. 220–236. Springer, Heidelberg (2012)
19. Kuperstein, M., Vechev, M., Yahav, E.: Automatic inference of memory fences. In: FMCAD (2010)
20. Kuperstein, M., Vechev, M., Yahav, E.: Partial-Coherence Abstractions for Relaxed Memory Models. In: PLDI (2011)
21. Lamport, L.: How to Make a Correct Multiprocess Program Execute Correctly on a Multiprocessor. IEEE Trans. Comput. 46(7), 779–782 (1979)
22. Linden, A., Wolper, P.: A Verification-Based Approach to Memory Fence Insertion in Relaxed Memory Systems. In: Groce, A., Musuvathi, M. (eds.) SPIN 2011. LNCS, vol. 6823, pp. 144–160. Springer, Heidelberg (2011)
23. Owens, S.: Reasoning about the Implementation of Concurrency Abstractions on x86-TSO. In: D'Hondt, T. (ed.) ECOOP 2010. LNCS, vol. 6183, pp. 478–503. Springer, Heidelberg (2010)
24. Owens, S., Sarkar, S., Sewell, P.: A Better x86 Memory Model: x86-TSO. In: Berghofer, S., Nipkow, T., Urban, C., Wenzel, M. (eds.) TPHOLs 2009. LNCS, vol. 5674, pp. 391–407. Springer, Heidelberg (2009)
25. Park, S., Dill, D.: An executable specification, analyzer and verifier for RMO. In: SPAA (1995)
26. Sarkar, S., Sewell, P., Alglave, J., Maranget, L., Williams, D.: Understanding Power multiprocessors. In: PLDI (2011)
27. Tarjan, R.: Depth-first search and linear graph algorithms. SIAM J. Comput. (1972)
28. Tarjan, R.: Enumeration of the elementary circuits of a directed graph. SIAM J. Comput. (1973)
29. Yang, Y., Gopalakrishnan, G., Lindstrom, G.: Memory-Model-Sensitive Data Race Analysis. In: Davies, J., Schulte, W., Barnett, M. (eds.) ICFEM 2004. LNCS, vol. 3308, pp. 30–45. Springer, Heidelberg (2004)

Checking and Enforcing Robustness against TSO

Ahmed Bouajjani[1], Egor Derevenetc[2,3], and Roland Meyer[3]

[1] LIAFA, University Paris 7
[2] Fraunhofer ITWM
[3] University of Kaiserslautern
abou@liafa.univ-paris-diderot.fr,
{derevenetc,meyer}@cs.uni-kl.de

Abstract. We present algorithms for checking and enforcing robustness of concurrent programs against the Total Store Ordering (TSO) memory model. A program is robust if all its TSO computations correspond to computations under the Sequential Consistency (SC) semantics.

We provide a complete characterization of non-robustness in terms of so-called attacks: a restricted form of (harmful) out-of-program-order executions. Then, we show that detecting attacks can be parallelized, and can be solved using state reachability queries under the SC semantics in a suitably instrumented program obtained by a linear size source-to-source translation. Importantly, the construction is valid for an unbounded number of memory addresses and an arbitrary number of parallel threads. It is independent from the data domain and from the size of store buffers in the TSO semantics. In particular, when the data domain is finite and the number of addresses is fixed, we obtain decidability and complexity results for robustness, even for a parametric number of threads.

As a second contribution, we provide an algorithm for computing an optimal set of fences that enforce robustness. We consider two criteria of optimality: minimization of program size and maximization of its performance. The algorithms we define are implemented, and we successfully applied them to analyzing and correcting several concurrent algorithms.

1 Introduction

Sequential Consistency (SC) [21] is a natural shared-memory model where the actions of different threads are interleaved while the program order between actions of each thread is preserved. For performance reasons, however, modern multiprocessors implement weaker memory models relaxing program order. For instance, the common store-to-load relaxation, which allows loads to overtake earlier stores, reflects the use of *store buffers*. It is actually the main feature of the TSO (Total Store Ordering) model adopted, e.g., in x86 machines [28].

Nonetheless, programmers often assume that memory accesses are performed according to SC, where they are instantaneous and atomic. This assumption is safe for *data-race-free* programs [3], but in many situations data-race-freedom does not apply. This is, for instance, the case of programs implementing synchronization operations, concurrency libraries, and other performance-critical system services employing lock-free synchronization. These programs are designed to be

M. Felleisen and P. Gardner (Eds.): ESOP 2013, LNCS 7792, pp. 533–553, 2013.

robust against relaxations, i.e., relaxations should not introduce behaviors that are impossible under SC. Memory fences must be included appropriately in programs to prevent non-SC behaviors. Getting such programs right is a notoriously difficult and error-prone task. Therefore, important issues in this context are (1) checking robustness of a program against the relaxations of a memory model, and (2) identifying a set of program locations where it is *necessary* to insert fences to ensure robustness.

In this paper we address these two issues in the case of TSO. We consider a general setting without any bounds on the shared-memory size, nor on the size of the store buffers in the TSO semantics, nor on the number of threads. This allows us to reason about robustness of general algorithms without assuming any fixed values for these parameters that depend on the actual machine's implementation. Moreover, we tackle these issues for general programs, independently from the domain of data they manipulate.

Robustness against memory models has been addressed first by Burckhardt and Musuvathi in [10] (actually, for TSO only), and subsequently by Burnim et al. in [11]. Alglave and Maranget developed a general framework for reasoning about robustness against memory models in [4,5] (where the term *stability* is used instead of robustness). Roughly, these works are based on characterizing robustness in terms of acyclicity of a suitable happens-before relation. In that, they follow Shasha and Snir [29] who introduced a notion of *trace* that captures the control and data dependencies between events of an SC computation, and established that computations that are not SC have a cyclic happens-before relation. We adopt here the same notion of (trace-)robustness, i.e., a program is robust if every TSO computation has the same trace as some SC computation.

From an algorithmic point of view, the existing works mentioned above *do not provide decision procedures* for robustness. [10,11] provide testing procedures based on enumerating TSO runs and checking that they do not produce happens-before cycles. Clearly, while these procedures can establish non-robustness, they can never prove a program robust. On the other hand, [5] provides a sound over-approximate static analysis that allows for proving robustness, but may also inaccurately conclude to non-robustness and insert fences unnecessarily. We are interested here in developing an approach that allows for precise checking of trace-robustness, and for optimal fence insertion (in a sense defined later).

In our previous work [9], trace-robustness against TSO has been proven to be decidable and PSPACE-complete, even for unbounded store buffers, in the case of a fixed number of threads and assuming a fixed number of shared variables, ranging over a finite data domain. The method that shows this decidability and complexity result does not provide a practical algorithm: it is based on a non-deterministic, bounded enumeration of computations. Moreover, it does not carry over to the general setting we consider here. Therefore, in this paper we propose a novel approach to checking robustness that is fundamentally different from [9]. We provide a general, source-to-source reduction of the trace-robustness problem against TSO to the *state reachability problem under the SC semantics*. In other words, we show that trace-robustness is not more expensive than SC state reachability, which is the unavoidable problem to be solved by any precise decision algorithm for concurrent programs. This is the *key contribution of the paper* from which we derive other results, such as decidability results in particular cases, as well as an algorithm for efficient fence insertion.

To establish our reduction, we first provide a complete characterization of non-robustness in terms of so-called *feasible attacks*. An attack is a pair of load and store instructions of a thread, called the attacker, whose reordering may lead to a non-SC computation. In that case we say the attack is feasible, because it has a (TSO) witness computation. The special form of witness computations allows us to detect them by solving an SC state reachability query in an *instrumented program*. The fact that *only the SC semantics* (of the instrumented program) needs to be considered for detecting non-SC behaviors (of the original program) is important: it relieves us of examining TSO computations, which obliges one to encode (somehow) the contents of store buffers (as in, e.g., [10,11]). Interestingly, the feasibility checks for different attacks can be parallelized, which speeds up the decision procedure. Overall, we provide a reduction of the TSO robustness problem to a quadratic number (in the size of the program) of state reachability queries under the SC semantics in linear-size instrumented programs of the same type as the original one. Our construction is source-to-source and is valid for (1) an unbounded number of memory addresses/variables, (2) an arbitrary data domain, (3) an arbitrary number of threads, and (4) unbounded store buffers.

With this reduction, we can harness all techniques and tools that are available for solving SC reachability queries (either exactly, or approximately) in various classes of concurrent programs, regardless of decidability and complexity issues. It also yields decision algorithms for significant classes of programs. Assume we have a finite number of memory addresses, and the data domain is finite. Then, for a fixed number of threads, a direct consequence of our reduction is that the robustness problem is decidable and in PSPACE since it is polynomially reducible to state reachability in finite-state concurrent programs. Therefore, we obtain in this case a *simple* robustness checking algorithm which matches the complexity upper bound proven in [9]. Our construction also provides an effective decision algorithm for the up to now open case where the *number of threads is parametric*. In this case, SC state reachability queries can be solved in vector addition systems with states (VASS), or equivalently as coverability in Petri nets, which is known to be decidable [27] and EXPSPACE-hard [24]. In both cases (fixed and parametric number of threads) the decision algorithms do not assume bounded store buffers.

As last contribution, we address the issue of enforcing robustness by fence insertion. Obviously, inserting a fence after each store ensures robustness, but it also ruins all performance benefits that a relaxed memory model brings. A natural requirement on the set of fences is irreducibility, i.e., minimality wrt. set inclusion. Since there may be several irreducible sets enforcing robustness, it is natural to ask for a set that optimizes some notion of cost. We assume that we have a *cost function* that defines the cost of inserting a fence at each program location. For instance, by assuming cost 1 for all locations, we optimize the size of the fence set. Other cost functions reflect the performance of the resulting program. We propose an algorithm which, given a cost function, computes an optimal set of fences. The algorithm is based on 0/1-integer linear programming and exploits the notion of attacks to guide the selection of fences.

We implemented the algorithms (using SPIN as a back-end SC reachability checker), and applied them successfully to checking and correcting a number of examples, including mutual exclusion protocols and concurrent data structures. The experiments we have carried out show that our approach is quite effective: (1) many of the attacks to be examined can be discarded by simple syntactic checks (e.g., the presence of a fence between the store and load instructions), and those that require solving reachability queries are handled in few seconds, (2) the fence insertion procedure finds efficiently optimal sets of fences, in particular, it can handle the version of the Non-Blocking Write protocol [18] described in [25] (where the write is guarded by a Linux x86 spinlock) for which Owens' method based on so-called *triangular data races* (see below) inserts unnecessary fences.

Related Work. There are only few results on decidability and complexity of relaxed memory models. Reachability under TSO has been shown to be decidable but non-primitive recursive [7] in the case of a finite number of threads and a finite data domain. In the same setting, trace-robustness has been shown to be PSPACE-complete [9] using a combinatorial approach.

Alur et al. have shown that checking sequential consistency of a concurrent implementation wrt. a specification is undecidable in general [6]. This result does not contradict our findings: we consider here the special case where the implementation is the TSO semantics and the specification is the SC semantics of the same program. In [15], the problem of deciding whether a given computation is SC feasible has been proven NP-complete. Robustness is concerned with all TSO computations, instead.

As mentioned above, the problem of checking and enforcing trace-robustness against weak memory models has been addressed in [10,11,5], but none of these works provide (sound and complete) decision procedures. Owens proposes in [25] a notion of robustness that is *stronger* than trace-robustness, based on detecting triangular data races. This allows for sound trace-robustness checking but, as Owens shows in his paper, in some cases leads to unnecessary fences which can be harmful for performance. Moreover, the notion of triangular data races comes without an algorithm for checking it[1]. Complexity considerations (using the techniques in [9]) show that detecting triangular data races requires solving state reachability queries under SC. Therefore, as we show here, checking trace-robustness is not more expensive than detecting triangular data races.

State-based robustness (which preserves the reachable states) is a weaker robustness criterion, but does not preserve path properties in contrast to trace-robustness, and is of significantly higher complexity (non-primitive recursive as it can be deduced from [7], instead of PSPACE). It has been addressed in a

---

[1] Citation from [25]: "... *formal reasoning directly on traces can be tedious, so a program logic or sound static analyzer specialized to proving triangular-race freedom might make the application of TRF more convenient.*"

precise manner in [2,23], where symbolic decision procedures together with fence insertion algorithms are provided. The same issue is addressed in [19,20] using over-approximate reachability analysis based on abstractions of the store buffers.

Finally, let us mention work that considers the dual approach: starting from a robust program, remove unnecessary fences [30]. This work is aimed at compiler optimizations and does not provide a decision procedure for robustness. It can also not find an optimal set of fences that enforce trace-robustness.

2   Parallel Programs

Syntax. We consider parallel programs with shared memory as defined by the grammar in Figure 1. Programs have a name and consist of a finite number of threads. Each thread has an identifier and a list of local registers it operates on. The thread's source code is given as a finite sequence of labelled instructions. More than one instruction can be marked by the same label; this allows us to implement conditional branching, iteration, and non-determinism in a lightweight syntax. The instruction set includes loads from memory to a local register, stores to memory, memory fences to control the TSO store buffers, local computations, and assertions. Figure 2 provides a sample program.

$$\begin{aligned}
\langle prog \rangle &::= \textbf{program } \langle pid \rangle \, \langle thrd \rangle^* \\
\langle thrd \rangle &::= \textbf{thread } \langle tid \rangle \\
&\quad \textbf{regs } \langle reg \rangle^* \\
&\quad \textbf{init } \langle label \rangle \\
&\quad \textbf{begin } \langle linst \rangle^* \textbf{ end} \\
\langle linst \rangle &::= \langle label \rangle \colon \langle inst \rangle ; \textbf{ goto } \langle label \rangle ; \\
\langle inst \rangle &::= \langle reg \rangle \leftarrow \texttt{mem}[\langle expr \rangle] \\
&\quad | \;\; \texttt{mem}[\langle expr \rangle] \leftarrow \langle expr \rangle \\
&\quad | \;\; \texttt{mfence} \\
&\quad | \;\; \langle reg \rangle \leftarrow \langle expr \rangle \\
&\quad | \;\; \textbf{assert } \langle expr \rangle \\
\langle expr \rangle &::= \langle fun \rangle (\langle reg \rangle^*)
\end{aligned}$$

Fig. 1. Syntax of parallel programs

```
program Dekker
    thread t₁ regs r₁ init l₀ begin
        l₀: mem[x] ← 1; goto l₁;
        l₁: r₁ ← mem[y]; goto l₂;
    end
    thread t₂ regs r₂ init l'₀ begin
        l'₀: mem[y] ← 1; goto l'₁;
        l'₁: r₂ ← mem[x]; goto l'₂;
    end
```

Fig. 2. Simplified version of Dekker's mutex algorithm. Under SC, it is impossible that $r_1 = r_2 = 0$ when both threads reach l_2 and l'_2.

We assume a program comes with two sets: a *data domain* DOM and a *function domain* FUN. The data domain should contain value zero: $0 \in$ DOM. Moreover, we assume that all values from DOM can be used as addresses. Each memory location accessed by loads and stores is identified by such an address, and memory locations identified by different addresses do not overlap. The set FUN contains functions that are defined on the data domain and can be used in the program. Note that we do not make any finiteness assumptions.

TSO Semantics. Fix a program $\mathcal{P}$ with threads THRD $:= \{t_1, \ldots, t_n\}$. Let each thread t_i have the initial label $l_{0,i}$ and declare registers $\overline{r_i}$. We define the set of variables as the union of addresses and registers: VAR $:=$ DOM $\cup \cup_{i \in [1,n]} \overline{r_i}$. We denote the set of all instruction labels that occur in threads by LAB.

The TSO semantics we define is operational, in terms of labelled transitions between states. On the x86 TSO architecture, each thread effectively has a local FIFO buffer that keeps stores for later execution [26,28,10,11]. Therefore, a *state* is a triple $s = (pc, val, buf)$ where the program counter $pc: THRD \to LAB$ holds, for each thread, the label of the instruction(s) to be executed next. The valuation $val: VAR \to DOM$ gives the values of registers and memory locations. The third component $buf: THRD \to (DOM \times DOM)^*$ is the (per thread) buffer content: a sequence of address-value pairs $a \leftarrow v$.

In the *initial state* $s_0 := (pc_0, val_0, buf_0)$ the program counter is set to the initial labels, $pc_0(t_i) := l_{0,i}$ for all $t_i \in THRD$, registers and addresses hold value zero, $val_0(x) := 0$ for all $x \in VAR$, and all buffers are empty, $buf_0(t) := \varepsilon$ for all $t \in THRD$. Here, ε denotes the empty sequence.

Instructions yield transitions between states that are labelled by *actions* from $ACT := THRD \times (\{isu, loc\} \cup (\{ld, st\} \times DOM \times DOM))$. An action consists of the thread id and the actual arguments of the executed instruction. We use loc to abstract assignments and asserts that are local to a thread. An issue action isu indicates that a store was executed by a thread. The store action (t, st, a, v) gives the moment when the store becomes visible in memory.

The *TSO transition relation* $\to_{TSO}$ is the smallest relation between TSO states that is defined by the rules in Table 1. The rules repeat, up to notation and support for locked instructions, Figure 1 from [26]. The first two rules implement loads from the buffer and from the memory, respectively. By the third rule, store instructions enqueue write operations to the buffer. The fourth rule non-deterministically dequeues and executes them on memory. The fifth rule defines that memory fences can only be executed when the buffer is empty. The last two rules refer to local assignments and assertions. We omit locked instructions to keep things simple. Introducing them is straightforward and does not affect the results. Indeed, our implementation supports them [1].

The set of *TSO computations* contains all sequences of actions that lead from the initial TSO state to a state where all buffers are empty:

$$C_{TSO}(\mathcal{P}) := \{\tau \in ACT^* \mid s_0 \xrightarrow{\tau}_{TSO} s \text{ for some TSO state}$$
$$s = (pc, val, buf) \text{ with } buf(t) = \varepsilon \text{ for all } t \in THRD\}.$$

The requirement of empty buffers is not important for our results but rather a modelling choice. Figure 3 presents a TSO computation of Dekker's program where the store of the first thread is delayed past the load.

$$\tau = (t_1, isu)\,(t_1, ld, y, 0)\,(t_2, isu)\,(t_2, st, y, 1)\,(t_2, ld, x, 0)\,(t_1, st, x, 1)$$

Fig. 3. A TSO computation of Dekker's algorithm. The arc connects the issue action with the corresponding delayed store action of the first thread.

SC Semantics. Under SC [21], stores are not buffered and hence states are pairs (pc, val). The rules for SC transitions are appropriately simplified TSO rules. To avoid case distinctions between TSO and SC in the definition of traces, a store

Table 1. TSO transition rules, assuming $pc(t) = l$, an instruction $\langle instr \rangle$ at label l with destination l', and $pc' := pc[t := l']$. We use $\downarrow$ to denote projection and $*$ for any value, i.e., $buf(t) \downarrow (a \leftarrow *)$ is the list of address-value pairs in the buffer of thread t that have address a.

$$\frac{\langle instr \rangle = r \leftarrow \texttt{mem}[f_a(\overline{r_a})],\ a = f_a(val(\overline{r_a})),\ buf(t) \downarrow (a \leftarrow *) = \beta \cdot (a \leftarrow v)}{(pc, val, buf) \xrightarrow{(t,\, \mathsf{ld},\, a,\, v)}_{\mathsf{TSO}} (pc', val[r := v], buf)}$$

$$\frac{\langle instr \rangle = r \leftarrow \texttt{mem}[f_a(\overline{r_a})],\ a = f_a(val(\overline{r_a})),\ buf(t) \downarrow (a \leftarrow *) = \varepsilon,\ v = val(a)}{(pc, val, buf) \xrightarrow{(t,\, \mathsf{ld},\, a,\, v)}_{\mathsf{TSO}} (pc', val[r := v], buf)}$$

$$\frac{\langle instr \rangle = \texttt{mem}[f_a(\overline{r_a})] \leftarrow f_v(\overline{r_v}),\ a = f_a(val(\overline{r_a})),\ v = f_v(val(\overline{r_v}))}{(pc, val, buf) \xrightarrow{(t,\, \mathsf{isu})}_{\mathsf{TSO}} (pc', val, buf[t := buf(t) \cdot (a \leftarrow v)])}$$

$$\frac{buf(t) = (a \leftarrow v) \cdot \beta}{(pc, val, buf) \xrightarrow{(t,\, \mathsf{st},\, a,\, v)}_{\mathsf{TSO}} (pc, val[a := v], buf[t := \beta])}$$

$$\frac{\langle instr \rangle = \texttt{mfence},\ buf(t) = \varepsilon}{(pc, val, buf) \xrightarrow{(t,\, \mathsf{loc})}_{\mathsf{TSO}} (pc', val, buf)}$$

$$\frac{\langle instr \rangle = r \leftarrow f(\overline{r})}{(pc, val, buf) \xrightarrow{(t,\, \mathsf{loc})}_{\mathsf{TSO}} (pc', val[r := f(val(\overline{r}))], buf)}$$

$$\frac{\langle instr \rangle = \texttt{assert}\ f(\overline{r}),\ f(val(\overline{r})) \neq 0}{(pc, val, buf) \xrightarrow{(t,\, \mathsf{loc})}_{\mathsf{TSO}} (pc', val, buf)}$$

instruction generates two actions: an issue followed by the store. Memory fences have no effect under SC. We denote the set of all SC computations of $\mathcal{P}$ by

$$C_{\mathsf{SC}}(\mathcal{P}) := \{\sigma \in \mathsf{ACT}^* \mid s_0 \xrightarrow{\sigma}_{\mathsf{SC}} s \text{ for some SC state } s\}.$$

3   TSO Robustness

Robustness ensures that the behaviour of a program does not change when it is run on TSO hardware as compared to SC. We study trace-based robustness as in [29,10,11,5,9]. Traces capture the essence of a computation: the control and data dependencies among actions. More formally, consider some computation $\alpha \in C_{\mathsf{SC}}(\mathcal{P}) \cup C_{\mathsf{TSO}}(\mathcal{P})$. The *trace* $\mathsf{Tr}(\alpha)$ is a graph where the nodes are labelled by the actions in α (stores and issue yield one node). The arcs are defined by the following relations. We have a per thread $t \in \mathsf{THRD}$ total order $\rightarrow_{\mathsf{po}}^t$ that gives the order in which the actions of t where issued. Similarly, we have a per address $a \in \mathsf{DOM}$ total order $\rightarrow_{\mathsf{st}}^a$ that gives the ordering of all stores to a. We call the unions $\rightarrow_{\mathsf{po}} := \cup_{t \in \mathsf{THRD}} \rightarrow_{\mathsf{po}}^t$ and $\rightarrow_{\mathsf{st}} := \cup_{a \in \mathsf{DOM}} \rightarrow_{\mathsf{st}}^a$ the *program order* and the *store order* of the trace. Finally, there is a *source relation* $\rightarrow_{\mathsf{src}}$ that determines the store from which a load receives its value. By $\mathsf{Tr}_{\mathsf{mm}}(\mathcal{P}) := \mathsf{Tr}(C_{\mathsf{mm}}(\mathcal{P}))$ with $\mathsf{mm} \in \{\mathsf{SC}, \mathsf{TSO}\}$ we denote the set of all *SC/TSO traces* of program $\mathcal{P}$. The *TSO robustness problem* checks whether the sets coincide.

Given: A parallel program $\mathcal{P}$.

Problem: Does $\mathsf{Tr_{TSO}}(\mathcal{P}) = \mathsf{Tr_{SC}}(\mathcal{P})$ hold?

Since inclusion $\mathsf{Tr_{SC}}(\mathcal{P}) \subseteq \mathsf{Tr_{TSO}}(\mathcal{P})$ always holds, we only have to check the reverse inclusion. We call a computation $\tau \in \mathsf{C_{TSO}}(\mathcal{P})$ *violating* if its trace is not among the SC traces of the program, i.e., $\mathsf{Tr}(\tau) \notin \mathsf{Tr_{SC}}(\mathcal{P})$. Violating TSO-computations employ cyclic accesses to addresses that SC is unable to serialize [29]. These cyclic accesses are made visible using a *conflict relation* from loads to stores. Intuitively, $\mathsf{ld} \to_{\mathsf{cf}} \mathsf{st}$ means that st overwrites the value that ld reads. The union of all four relations is commonly called *happens-before relation* of the trace, $\to_{\mathsf{hb}} := \to_{\mathsf{po}} \cup \to_{\mathsf{st}} \cup \to_{\mathsf{src}} \cup \to_{\mathsf{cf}}$.

Lemma 1 ([29]). *Consider TSO trace $\mathsf{Tr}(\tau) \in \mathsf{Tr_{TSO}}(\mathcal{P})$. Then $\mathsf{Tr}(\tau) \in \mathsf{Tr_{SC}}(\mathcal{P})$ iff $\to_{\mathsf{hb}}$ is acyclic.*

Consider computation τ in Figure 3. The load from thread t_1 conflicts with the store from t_2 because the load reads the initial value of y while the store overwrites it. The situation with the load from t_2 and the store from t_1 is symmetric. Together with the program order, the conflict relations produce a cycle:

$$\mathsf{Tr}(\tau): \quad \begin{array}{ccc} (t_1, \mathsf{st}, \mathsf{x}, 1) & \xleftarrow{\quad cf \quad} & (t_2, \mathsf{ld}, \mathsf{x}, 0) \\ \scriptstyle po \big\uparrow & & \big\downarrow \scriptstyle po \\ (t_1, \mathsf{ld}, \mathsf{y}, 0) & \xrightarrow[\quad cf \quad]{} & (t_2, \mathsf{st}, \mathsf{y}, 1) \end{array}$$

Indeed, there is no SC computation with this trace, as predicted by Lemma 1.

Lemma 1 does not provide a method for finding cyclic traces. We have recently shown that TSO robustness is decidable, in fact, PSPACE-complete [9]. The algorithm underlying this result, however, is based on enumeration and not meant to be implemented. The main contribution of the present work is a novel and practical approach to checking robustness.

The only concept we keep from our earlier work are minimal violations. A *minimal violation* is a violating computation that uses a minimal total number of delays. Interestingly, for minimal violations the following holds.

Lemma 2 (Locality [9,8]). *In a minimal violation, only one thread delays stores.*

Consider the computation in Figure 3. It relies on a single delay in thread t_1 and, indeed, is a minimal violation. As predicted by the lemma, the second thread writes to its buffer and immediately flushes it.

4   Attacks on TSO Robustness

Our approach to checking TSO robustness combines two insights. We first rephrase robustness in terms of a simpler problem: the absence of feasible attacks. We then devise an algorithm that checks attacks for feasibility. Interestingly, SC reachability techniques are sufficient for this purpose. Together, this yields a sound and complete reduction of TSO robustness to SC reachability.

The notion of attacks is inspired by the shape of minimal violations. We show that if a program is not robust, then there are violations of the form shown in

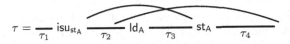

$$\tau = \underbrace{\quad}_{\tau_1} \text{isu}_{\text{st}_A} \underbrace{\quad}_{\tau_2} \text{ld}_A \underbrace{\quad}_{\tau_3} \text{st}_A \underbrace{\quad}_{\tau_4}$$

Fig. 4. TSO witness for the attack $(t_A, \text{stinst}, \text{ldinst})$. It satisfies the following constraints. **(W1)** Only the attacker delays stores. **(W2)** Store st_A is an instance of stinst. It is the first store of the attacker that is delayed. Load ld_A is an instance of ldinst. It is the last action of the attacker that is overstepped by st_A. So τ_2 contains loads, assignments, asserts, and issues, but no fences and stores of the attacker. It may contain arbitrary helper actions. **(W3)** We require $\text{ld}_A \to_{\text{hb}}^+ \text{act}$ for every action act in $\text{ld}_A \cdot \tau_3 \cdot \text{st}_A$. An issue + store of a helper is counted as one action act. **(W4)** Sequence τ_4 only consists of stores of the attacker that were issued before ld_A and that have been delayed. **(W5)** All these stores st satisfy $addr(\text{st}) \neq addr(\text{ld}_A)$, i.e., ld_A has not read its value early.

Figure 4: one thread, the *attacker*, delays a store action st_A past a later load action ld_A in order to break robustness. The remaining threads become *helpers* and provide a happens-before path from ld_A to st_A. This yields a happens-before cycle and shows non-robustness.

Thread, store instruction stinst of st_A, and load instruction ldinst of ld_A are syntactic objects. The idea of our approach is to fix these three parameters, the *attack*, prior to the analysis. The algorithm then tries to find a witness computation that proves the attack feasible.

Definition 1. *An attack* $A = (t_A, \text{stinst}, \text{ldinst})$ *consists of a thread* $t_A \in \text{THRD}$ *called* attacker, *a store instruction* stinst *and a load instruction* ldinst. *A TSO witness for* A *is a computation of the form in Figure 4, i.e., it satisfies* **(W1)** *to* **(W5)**. *If a TSO witness exists, the attack is called* feasible.

In Dekker's algorithm, there is an attack $A = (t_A, \text{stinst}, \text{ldinst})$ with $t_A = t_1$, stinst the store at l_0, and ldinst the load at l_1. A TSO witness for this attack is the computation τ from Figure 3. With reference to Figure 4, we have $\tau_1 = \varepsilon$, $\text{isu}_{\text{st}_A} = (t_1, \text{isu})$, $\tau_2 = \varepsilon$, $\text{ld}_A = (t_1, \text{ld}, \text{y}, 0)$, $\tau_3 = (t_2, \text{isu}) \cdot (t_2, \text{st}, \text{y}, 1) \cdot (t_2, \text{ld}, \text{x}, 0)$, $\text{st}_A = (t_1, \text{st}, \text{x}, 1)$, $\tau_4 = \varepsilon$. The program also contains a symmetric attack A' with t_2 as the attacker.

Although TSO witnesses are quite restrictive computations, robustness can be reduced to verifying that no attack has a TSO witness.

Theorem 1 (Complete Characterization of Robustness with Attacks). *Program* $\mathcal{P}$ *is robust iff no attack is feasible, i.e., no attack admits a TSO witness.*

Proof. The existence of a TSO witness implies non-robustness of the program. Indeed, a TSO witness comes with a happens-before cycle $\text{st}_A \to_{\text{po}}^+ \text{ld}_A \to_{\text{hb}}^+ \text{st}_A$. We argue that also the reverse holds: if a program is not robust, there is a feasible attack. Assume $\mathcal{P}$ is not robust. We construct a TSO witness computation. Among the violating computations, we select $\tau \in \text{C}_{\text{TSO}}(\mathcal{P})$ where the number of delays is minimal. The computation need not be unique. By Lemma 2, in τ only one thread t_A uses its buffer and **(W1)** holds. We elaborate on the shape of τ.

Initially, the attacker executes under SC so that stores immediately follow their issues. This computation is embedded into τ_1 in Figure 4. Eventually, the attacker starts delaying stores. Let st_A be the first store that is delayed. It gets reordered past several loads, the last of which being ld_A. This shows (**W2**).

Consider the helper actions in τ_3. To see that we can assume (**W3**), first note that $ld_A \rightarrow^+_{hb} st_A$ holds. If there was no such path, st_A could be placed before ld_A without changing the trace. This would save a delay, in contradiction to minimality of τ. Assume $\tau_3 = \tau_3' \cdot act \cdot \tau_3''$ where act is the first action so that $ld_A \not\rightarrow^+_{hb} act$. Then act is independent from all actions in $ld_A \cdot \tau_3'$. We find a computation with the same trace where act is placed before ld_A.

With cycle $st_A \rightarrow^+_{po} ld_A \rightarrow^+_{hb} st_A$, computation τ_4 only needs to contain the stores of the attacker that have been delayed past ld_A. Since these stores are non-blocking, the helpers can stop with the last action in τ_3. We can moreover assume ld_A to be the program order last action of the attacker. (**W4**) holds.

We now argue that ld_A has not read its value early from any of the delayed stores, (**W5**). Towards a contradiction, assume ld_A obtained its value from st in $\tau_4 = \tau_{41} \cdot st \cdot \tau_{42}$. There is a computation τ' where we avoid the early read: it replaces τ_4 by $\tau_{41} \cdot st \cdot ld_A \cdot \tau_{42}$. The traces of τ and τ' coincide, but τ' saves the delay of st past ld_A. A contradiction to minimality.

It is readily checked that τ is a TSO witness for the attack $(t_A, stinst, ldinst)$ where $stinst$ and $ldinst$ are the instructions that st_A and ld_A are derived from. □

Since the number of attacks is only quadratic in the size of the program, we can just enumerate them and check whether one admits a TSO witness. To check whether a witness exists, we employ the instrumentation described in the following section.

5   Instrumentation

Consider program $\mathcal{P}$ with attack $A = (t_A, stinst, ldinst)$. TSO witnesses for A only make limited use of the store buffers, to an extent that allows us to characterize them by SC computations in a program $\mathcal{P}_A$ that is *instrumented for attack A*. By instrumentation we mean that $\mathcal{P}_A$ replaces every thread by a modified version. Capturing TSO witnesses with a program that runs under SC is difficult for two reasons. First, TSO has unbounded store buffers which can delay arbitrarily many stores. Second, the happens-before dependence that the helpers create may involve an arbitrary number of actions. Our instrumentation copes with both problems, using the following tricks.

To handle store buffering, we instrument the attacker thread (Section 5.1). Essentially, we emulate store buffering under SC using auxiliary addresses. To explain the idea, consider the TSO witness in Figure 4. When the instrumented attacker executes the delayed stores $st_A \cdot \tau_4$ under SC, they occur right behind their issue actions. To mimic store buffering, these stores now access auxiliary addresses that the other threads do not load. As a result, the stores remain invisible to the helpers. This is as intended: the delayed stores $st_A \cdot \tau_4$ in Figure 4 are also never accessed by helper threads. But how many auxiliary addresses do we need to faithfully simulate buffers? It is sufficient to have *a single auxiliary address* per address in the program. The reason is that a load always reads the most recent store to its address that is held in the buffer.

To build up a happens-before path from ld_A to st_A, we instrument the helper threads (Section 5.2). The question is how to decide whether a new action act is in happens-before relation with an earlier action act′ so that $\mathsf{ld}_A \to_{\mathsf{hb}}^* \mathsf{act}' \to_{\mathsf{hb}}^* \mathsf{act}$. What is the information we need about the earlier actions in order to append act? It is sufficient to know two facts. Has the thread already contributed an action act′? This information ensures $\mathsf{act}' \to_{\mathsf{po}}^* \mathsf{act}$, and can be kept in the control flow of the thread. Moreover, we keep track of whether the path contains a load or store access to the address $addr(\mathsf{act})$. If there was a load access act′ = ld, we can add a store act = st and get $\mathsf{ld} \to_{\mathsf{hb}}^* \mathsf{st}$. If there was a store, we are free to add a load or a store. Hence, we need *one auxiliary address* per address in the program for this access information: no access, load access, store access.

Consider the TSO witness for Dekker given in Figure 3. Instead of buffering $(t_1, \mathsf{st}, \mathsf{x}, 1)$, the instrumentation immediately executes the store after its issue action. But instead of address x, the action accesses the auxiliary address (x, d) that is invisible to the other threads. So, the SC computation of the instrumented program roughly looks like this:

$$(t_1, \mathsf{isu}) \cdot (t_1, \mathsf{st}, (\mathsf{x}, \mathsf{d}), 1) \cdot (t_1, \mathsf{ld}, \mathsf{y}, 0) \overset{(1)}{\cdot} (t_2, \mathsf{isu})(t_2, \mathsf{st}, \mathsf{y}, 1) \overset{(2)}{\cdot} (t_2, \mathsf{ld}, \mathsf{x}, 0).$$

At moment (1), we know that there has been a load access to address y. At moment (2), address y has even seen a store. At the end of the computation, address y has seen a store and address x has seen a load.

The store of t_2 can be appended since it is in happens-before relation with the attacker's load. The following load can be added as t_2 has contributed the previous store. The search terminates here since the helper's load accesses address x that was used by the store from the attack.

5.1   Instrumentation of the Attacker

The instrumentation emulates the buffering of stores in a TSO witness (Figure 4). Starting from st_A, the stores are replaced by stores $\mathsf{st}_A^{\mathsf{aux}}$ to auxiliary addresses (a, d) that are only visible to the attacker. As long as a has not been written, (a, d) holds the initial value 0. Once the attacker stores v into a, we set $\mathsf{mem}[(a, \mathsf{d})] = (v, \mathsf{d})$. In this way, (a, d) always holds the most recent store. A load $r \leftarrow \mathsf{mem}[a]$ of the attacker reads a value v from the buffer whenever $\mathsf{mem}[(a, \mathsf{d})] = (v, \mathsf{d})$; otherwise $\mathsf{mem}[(a, \mathsf{d})] = 0$ and the load obtains the value $v = \mathsf{mem}[a]$ from memory. We turn to the translation.

Let t_A declare registers r^*, have initial location l_0, and define instructions $\langle linst \rangle^*$ that contain stinst and ldinst from the attack. The instrumentation is

$$[\mathsf{t}_A] := \mathbf{thread}\ \tilde{\mathsf{t}}_A\ \mathbf{regs}\ r^*\ \mathbf{init}\ \mathsf{l}_0$$
$$\mathbf{begin}\ \langle linst \rangle^*\ [\mathsf{stinst}]_{\mathsf{A1}}\ [\mathsf{ldinst}]_{\mathsf{A1}}\ [\langle linst \rangle]_{\mathsf{A2}}^*\ \mathbf{end}.$$

It introduces a copy of the source code $[\langle linst \rangle]_{\mathsf{A2}}^*$ where the stores are replaced by accesses to the auxiliary addresses. To move to the code copy, the attacker uses an instrumented version $[\mathsf{stinst}]_{\mathsf{A1}}$ of stinst.

$$[\![l_1 : \mathtt{mem}[e_1] \leftarrow e_2; \ \mathtt{goto}\ l_2;]\!]_{A1} := l_1 : \mathtt{mem}[(e_1,\mathsf{d})] \leftarrow (e_2,\mathsf{d}); \ \mathtt{goto}\ \tilde{l}_x; \tag{1}$$
$$\tilde{l}_x : \mathtt{mem}[a_{\mathsf{st_A}}] \leftarrow e_1; \ \mathtt{goto}\ \tilde{l}_2;$$

$$[\![l_1 : r \leftarrow \mathtt{mem}[e]; \ \mathtt{goto}\ l_2;]\!]_{A1} := \tilde{l}_1 : \mathtt{assert}\ \mathtt{mem}[(e,\mathsf{d})] = 0; \ \mathtt{goto}\ \tilde{l}_{x1}; \tag{2}$$
$$\tilde{l}_{x1} : \mathtt{mem}[\mathtt{hb}] \leftarrow \mathtt{true}; \ \mathtt{goto}\ \tilde{l}_{x2};$$
$$\tilde{l}_{x2} : \mathtt{mem}[(e,\mathtt{hb})] \leftarrow \mathsf{lda}; \ \mathtt{goto}\ \tilde{l}_{x3};$$

$$[\![l_1 : \mathtt{mem}[e_1] \leftarrow e_2; \ \mathtt{goto}\ l_2;]\!]_{A2} := \tilde{l}_1 : \mathtt{mem}[(e_1,\mathsf{d})] \leftarrow (e_2,\mathsf{d}); \ \mathtt{goto}\ \tilde{l}_2; \tag{3}$$

$$[\![l_1 : r \leftarrow \mathtt{mem}[e]; \ \mathtt{goto}\ l_2;]\!]_{A2} := \tilde{l}_1 : \mathtt{assert}\ \mathtt{mem}[(e,\mathsf{d})] = 0; \ \mathtt{goto}\ \tilde{l}_{x1}; \tag{4}$$
$$\tilde{l}_{x1} : r \leftarrow \mathtt{mem}[e]; \ \mathtt{goto}\ \tilde{l}_2;$$
$$\tilde{l}_1 : \mathtt{assert}\ \mathtt{mem}[(e,\mathsf{d})] \neq 0; \ \mathtt{goto}\ \tilde{l}_{x2};$$
$$\tilde{l}_{x2} : (r,\mathsf{d}) \leftarrow \mathtt{mem}[(e,\mathsf{d})]; \ \mathtt{goto}\ \tilde{l}_2;$$

$$[\![l_1 : local; \ \mathtt{goto}\ l_2;]\!]_{A2} := \tilde{l}_1 : local; \ \mathtt{goto}\ \tilde{l}_2; \tag{5}$$

$$[\![l_1 : \mathtt{mfence}; \ \mathtt{goto}\ l_2;]\!]_{A2} := \tag{6}$$

Fig. 5. Instrumentation of the attacker

The translation of instructions is defined in Figure 5. We make a few remarks. The instrumentation (1) of stinst saves the address used in the store in a fresh address $a_{\mathsf{st_A}}$. For the sake of readability, Equation (4) uses memory accesses in asserts. Equation (6) deletes fences, as they forbid to delay $\mathsf{st_A}$ over $\mathsf{ld_A}$. Equation (2) checks that the load used in the attack has not read its value early, sets an auxiliary happens-before address (e, hb) to access level load, lda, and halts the attacker. We postpone the definition of access levels until the translation of helpers. The equation also sets a flag hb that forbids helpers to execute actions not contributing to the happens-before path. Figure 6 illustrates the instrumentation on our running example.

5.2   Instrumentation of Helpers

In TSO witnesses, all helper actions after $\mathsf{ld_A}$ are in happens-before relation with $\mathsf{ld_A}$, by **(W3)**. To ensure this, we use Lemma 3. The proof from left to right is by definition of happens-before. For the reverse direction, note that happens-before is *stable under insertion*. Consider $\mathsf{st} \to_{\mathsf{src}} \mathsf{ld}$. A happens-before relation remains valid in any computation that places actions between st and ld.

Lemma 3. *Consider* $\tau = \tau_1 \cdot act_1 \cdot \tau_2 \in C_{SC}(\mathcal{P})$ *where for all* act_2 *in* τ_2 *we have* $act_1 \to_{\mathsf{hb}}^* act_2$. *Computation* $\tau \cdot act$ *satisfies* $act_1 \to_{\mathsf{hb}}^* act$ *iff*
(i) *there is an action* act_2 *in* $act_1 \cdot \tau_2$ *with* $thread(act_2) = thread(act)$ *or*
(ii) *act is a load whose address is stored in* $act_1 \cdot \tau_2$ *or*
(iii) *act is a store (with issue) whose address is loaded or stored in* $act_1 \cdot \tau_2$.

The lemma suggests the following instrumentation. For every helper t, we track whether it has executed an action that depends on $\mathsf{ld_A}$. The idea is to use the control flow. Upon detection of this first action, the thread moves to a copy of its code. All actions from this copy stay in happens-before relation with $\mathsf{ld_A}$.

```
thread t̃₁ regs r₁ init l₀ begin
/* Original code */
l₀: mem[x] ← 1; goto l₁;
l₁: r₁ ← mem[y]; goto l₂;


/* Instrumented stinst */
l₀: mem[(x,d)] ← (1,d); goto l̃ₓ;
l̃ₓ: mem[aₛₜₐ] ← x; goto l̃₁;


/* Instrumented ldinst */
l̃₁: assert mem[(y,d)] = 0; goto l̃ₓ₁;
l̃ₓ₁: mem[hb] ← true; goto l̃ₓ₂;
l̃ₓ₂: mem[(y,hb)] ← lda; goto l̃ₓ₃;
end
```

```
/* Instrumented copy of the store */
l̃₀: mem[(x,d)] ← (1,d); goto l̃₁;

/* Instrumented copy of the load */
l̃₁: assert mem[(y,d)] = 0; goto l̃ₓ₄;
l̃ₓ₄: r₁ ← mem[y]; goto l̃₂;
l̃₁: assert mem[(y,d)] ≠ 0; goto l̃ₓ₅;
l̃ₓ₅: (r₁,d) ← mem[(y,d)]; goto l̃₂;
```

Fig. 6. Attacker instrumentation of thread t_1 in Dekker from Figure 2. The attack's store is the store at label l_0, the load is the load at label l_1.

It remains to decide whether an action act allows a thread to move to the code copy. According to Lemma 3, this depends on the earlier accesses to the address $a = addr(\text{act})$. We introduce auxiliary *happens-before addresses* (a, hb) that provide this access information. The addresses (a, hb) range over the domain $\{0, \text{lda}, \text{sta}\}$ of *access types*. It is sufficient to keep track of the *maximal* access type wrt. the ordering 0 (no access) $<$ lda (load access) $<$ sta (store access).

For the definition, consider a helper thread t that declares registers r^*, has initial label l_0, and defines instructions $\langle linst \rangle^*$. The instrumented thread is

$$[\![t]\!] := \text{thread } \tilde{t} \text{ regs } \tilde{r}, r^* \text{ init } l_0$$
$$\text{begin } [\![\langle linst \rangle]\!]^*_{\text{H0}} \; [\![\langle ldstinst \rangle]\!]^*_{\text{H1}} \; [\![\langle linst \rangle]\!]^*_{\text{H2}} \; [\![\langle l \rangle]\!]^*_{\text{H3}} \text{ end.}$$

The instrumentation of the original code $[\![\langle linst \rangle]\!]_{\text{H0}}$ forces helpers to either enter the code copy or stop when the hb flag is raised. To move to the code copy, we instrument the subsequence $\langle ldstinst \rangle^*$ of all load and store instructions in $\langle linst \rangle^*$. The code copy is $[\![\langle linst \rangle]\!]^*_{\text{H2}}$. Let $\langle l \rangle^*$ be all labels used by the thread. The additional instructions $[\![\langle l \rangle]\!]^*_{\text{H3}}$ raise a success flag when a TSO witness has been found.

The translation of instructions is given in Figure 7. We make some remarks. Transitions to the code copy check the auxiliary addresses for whether the current action is in happens-before relation with lda_A. Loads in Equation (8) check for an earlier store access to their address, Lemma 3(ii). Stores in Equation (9) require that the address has seen at least a load, Lemma 3(iii). They set the access level to sta. Loads and stores in the code copy maintain the auxiliary addresses to contain the maximal access types, Equations (12) and (11). Note the auxiliary register $\tilde{r}$ that ensures we do not overwrite the address. At every label of the code copy we add a check, Equation (13), whether the address used in the attack's store has been accessed in the code copy. If so, a success flag is raised.

$$[\![l_1 : \mathit{instr};\ \mathrm{goto}\ l_2;]\!]_{H0} := l_1 : \mathrm{assert}\ \mathrm{mem[hb]} = 0;\ \mathrm{goto}\ l_x; \tag{7}$$
$$l_x : \mathit{instr};\ \mathrm{goto}\ l_2;$$

$$[\![l_1 : r \leftarrow \mathrm{mem}[e];\ \mathrm{goto}\ l_2;]\!]_{H1} := l_1 : \mathrm{assert}\ \mathrm{mem}[(e, \mathrm{hb})] = \mathrm{sta};\ \mathrm{goto}\ \tilde{l}_x; \tag{8}$$
$$\tilde{l}_x : r \leftarrow \mathrm{mem}[e];\ \mathrm{goto}\ \tilde{l}_2;$$

$$[\![l_1 : \mathrm{mem}[e_1] \leftarrow e_2;\ \mathrm{goto}\ l_2;]\!]_{H1} := l_1 : \mathrm{assert}\ \mathrm{mem}[(e_1, \mathrm{hb})] \geq \mathrm{lda};\ \mathrm{goto}\ \tilde{l}_{x1}; \tag{9}$$
$$\tilde{l}_{x1} : \mathrm{mem}[e_1] \leftarrow e_2;\ \mathrm{goto}\ \tilde{l}_{x2};$$
$$\tilde{l}_{x2} : \mathrm{mem}[(e_1, \mathrm{hb})] \leftarrow \mathrm{sta};\ \mathrm{goto}\ \tilde{l}_2;$$

$$[\![l_1 : \mathit{local/mfence};\ \mathrm{goto}\ l_2;]\!]_{H2} := \tilde{l}_1 : \mathit{local/mfence};\ \mathrm{goto}\ \tilde{l}_2; \tag{10}$$

$$[\![l_1 : \mathrm{mem}[e_1] \leftarrow e_2;\ \mathrm{goto}\ l_2;]\!]_{H2} := \tilde{l}_1 : \mathrm{mem}[e_1] \leftarrow e_2;\ \mathrm{goto}\ \tilde{l}_x; \tag{11}$$
$$\tilde{l}_x : \mathrm{mem}[(e_1, \mathrm{hb})] \leftarrow \mathrm{sta};\ \mathrm{goto}\ \tilde{l}_2;$$

$$[\![l_1 : r \leftarrow \mathrm{mem}[e];\ \mathrm{goto}\ l_2;]\!]_{H2} := \tilde{l}_1 : \tilde{r} \leftarrow e;\ \mathrm{goto}\ \tilde{l}_{x1}; \tag{12}$$
$$\tilde{l}_{x1} : r \leftarrow \mathrm{mem}[\tilde{r}];\ \mathrm{goto}\ \tilde{l}_{x2};$$
$$\tilde{l}_{x2} : \mathrm{mem}[(\tilde{r}, \mathrm{hb})] \leftarrow \max\{\mathrm{lda}, \mathrm{mem}[(\tilde{r}, \mathrm{hb})]\};\ \mathrm{goto}\ \tilde{l}_2;$$

$$[\![l]\!]_{H3} := \tilde{l} : \tilde{r} \leftarrow \mathrm{mem}[a_{\mathrm{st_A}}];\ \mathrm{goto}\ \tilde{l}_{x1}; \tag{13}$$
$$\tilde{l}_{x1} : \tilde{r} \leftarrow \mathrm{mem}[(\tilde{r}, \mathrm{hb})];\ \mathrm{goto}\ \tilde{l}_{x2};$$
$$\tilde{l}_{x2} : \mathrm{assert}\ \tilde{r} \neq 0;\ \mathrm{goto}\ \tilde{l}_{x3};$$
$$\tilde{l}_{x3} : \mathrm{mem[suc]} \leftarrow \mathrm{true};\ \mathrm{goto}\ \tilde{l}_{x4};$$

Fig. 7. Instrumentation of helpers

5.3 Soundness and Completeness

The flag indicates that the SC computation corresponds to a TSO witness, and we call (pc, val) with val(suc) = true a *goal configuration*. The instrumentation thus reduces feasibility of attack A to SC reachability of a goal configuration in program $\mathcal{P}_A$. The instrumentation is sound and complete. If a goal configuration is reachable, we can reconstruct a TSO witness for the attack. In turn, every TSO witness ensures the goal configuration is reachable.

Theorem 2 (Soundness and Completeness [8]). *Attack A is feasible in program $\mathcal{P}$ iff program $\mathcal{P}_A$ reaches a goal configuration under SC.*

In combination with Theorem 1, we can check robustness by inspecting all $\mathcal{P}_A$.

Theorem 3 (From TSO Robustness to SC Reachability). *Program $\mathcal{P}$ is robust iff no instrumentation $\mathcal{P}_A$ reaches a goal configuration under SC.*

The instrumentation we provide is linear in size. Then, it follows from Theorem 3 that checking robustness for programs over finite data domains is in PSPACE. The problem is actually PSPACE-complete due to the lower bound in [9].

6 TSO Robustness for Parameterized Programs

We extend the study of robustness to *parameterized programs*. A parameterized program represents an infinite family of instance programs that replicate the threads multiple times. Syntactically, parameterized programs coincide with the parallel programs we introduced in Section 2: they have a name and declare a finite set of threads $t_1, \ldots, t_k$. The difference is in the semantics. A parameterized program defines, for every vector $I = (n_1, \ldots, n_k) \in \mathbb{N}^k$, an *instance program* $\mathcal{P}(I)$ that declares n_i copies of thread t_i.

In the parameterized setting, the robustness problem asks for whether all instances of a given program are robust:

Given: A parameterized program $\mathcal{P}$.
Problem: Does $\mathsf{Tr}_{\mathsf{TSO}}(\mathcal{P}(I)) = \mathsf{Tr}_{\mathsf{SC}}(\mathcal{P}(I))$ hold for all instances $\mathcal{P}(I)$ of $\mathcal{P}$?

The problem is interesting because libraries usually cannot make assumptions on the number of threads that use their functions. They have to guarantee proper functioning for any number.

We reduce robustness for parameterized programs to a parameterized version of reachability, based on the following insight. A parameterized program is not robust if and only if there is an instance $\mathcal{P}(I)$ that is not robust. With Theorem 1, instance $\mathcal{P}(I)$ is not robust if and only if there is an attack A that is feasible. With the instrumentation from Section 5 and Theorem 2, this feasibility can be checked as reachability of a goal configuration in $\mathcal{P}(I)_\mathsf{A}$.

Algorithmically, it is impossible to instrument all (infinitely many) instance programs. Instead, the idea is to instrument directly the parameterized program $\mathcal{P}$ towards the attack A. Using the constructions from Section 5, we modify every thread and again obtain program $\mathcal{P}_\mathsf{A}$, which is now parameterized.

Actually, for the attacker we have to be slightly more careful. In an instance program, only one copy of the thread should act as the attacker, the remaining copies must behave like helpers. Therefore, we instrument the thread not only as an attacker, but also as a helper. To ensure that only one copy of the attacker delays stores, we add an additional flag variable. Before starting an attack, the thread checks this variable. If it contains the initial value, the thread sets the flag and starts delaying stores. If it has a different value, the thread continues to run sequentially. This check requires an atomic test-and-set operation which can be implemented on x86 by the `lock cmpxchg` instruction. Support for locked instructions is immediate to add to our programming model.

Modulo these two changes, the instances $\mathcal{P}_\mathsf{A}(I)$ coincide with the instrumentations $\mathcal{P}(I)_\mathsf{A}$. Together with the previous argumentation this justifies the following theorem.

Theorem 4. *A parameterized program $\mathcal{P}$ is not robust iff there is an attack A so that an instance $\mathcal{P}_\mathsf{A}(I)$ of program $\mathcal{P}_\mathsf{A}$ reaches a goal configuration under SC.*

Reachability of a goal configuration in one instance of $\mathcal{P}_\mathsf{A}$ can be reformulated as a coverability problem for Petri nets, which is known to be decidable [27]. The key observation in the reduction to Petri nets is that threads in instance programs never use their identifiers, simply because they are copies of the same source code. This means there is no need to track the identity of threads, it is sufficient to count how many instances of a thread are in each state — a technique known as counter abstraction [14].

Theorem 5 ([8]). *Robustness for parameterized programs over finite data domains is decidable and* EXPSPACE-*hard — already for Boolean programs.*

For the lower bound, we in turn encode the coverability problem for Petri nets into robustness for parameterized programs [24].

7   Fence Insertion

To ease the presentation, we return to parallel programs. Since the algorithm only relies on a robustness checker, it carries over to the parametric setting.

Our goal is to insert a set of fences that ensure robustness of the resulting program. By *inserting a fence at label* l we mean the following modification of the program. Introduce a fresh label l_f. Then, translate each instruction l: inst; goto l'; into l_f: inst; goto l';. Finally, add an instruction l: mfence; goto l_f;.

We call a set of labels $\mathcal{F}$ in program $\mathcal{P}$ a *valid fence set* if inserting fences at these labels yields a robust program. We say that $\mathcal{F}$ is *irreducible* if no strict subset is a valid fence set. In general, however, we look for a valid fence set which is *optimal* in some sense, and pose the *fence computation problem* as follows:

Given: A program $\mathcal{P}$ and a strictly positive *cost function* $\mathcal{C}\colon \mathsf{LAB} \to \mathbb{R}^+$.
Problem: Compute a valid fence set $\mathcal{F}$ with $\Sigma_{l \in \mathcal{F}} \mathcal{C}(l)$ minimal.

Since we assume $\mathcal{C}$ to be strictly positive, every optimal fence set is irreducible.

We consider two criteria of optimality: minimization of program size and maximization of program performance. By solving the problem for $\mathcal{C} \equiv 1$ we compute a fence set of minimal size, thus minimizing the code size of the fenced program. Maximization of program performance requires minimizing the number of times memory fence instructions are executed: practical measurements [1] show that it is impossible to save CPU cycles by executing more fences, but with less stores in the TSO buffer. For this, $\mathcal{C}(l)$ is defined as the frequency at which instructions labeled by l occur in executions of the original program $\mathcal{P}$. Concrete values of $\mathcal{C}$ can be either estimated by profiling or computed by mathematical reasoning about the program.

From a complexity point of view, fence computation is at least as hard as robustness. Indeed, robustness holds if and only if the optimal valid fence set is $\mathcal{F} = \emptyset$. Actually, since fence sets can be enumerated, computing an optimal valid fence set does not require more space than checking robustness. Notice that this also holds in the parameterized case.

Theorem 6. *For programs over finite domains, fence computation is* PSPACE-*complete. In the parameterized case, it is decidable and* EXPSPACE-*hard.*

In the remainder of the section, we give a practical algorithm for computing optimal valid fence sets.

7.1   Fence Sets for Attacks

We say that a label l is *involved in the attack* $\mathsf{A} = (t_\mathsf{A}, \mathsf{stinst}, \mathsf{ldinst})$ if it belongs to some path in the control flow graph of t_A from the destination label of stinst to the source label of ldinst. We denote the set of all such labels by $\mathcal{L}_\mathsf{A}$.

We call a set of labels $\mathcal{F}_A$ *an eliminating fence set for attack A* if adding fences at all labels in $\mathcal{F}_A$ eliminates the attack. Dekker's algorithm has two eliminating fence sets: $\mathcal{F}_A = \{l_1\}$ eliminates the only attack by t_1, and $\mathcal{F}_{A'} = \{l_1'\}$ eliminates the only attack by t_2. Actually, the sets are *irreducible*: no strict subset eliminates the attack. Note that any irreducible eliminating set $\mathcal{F}_A$ satisfies $\mathcal{F}_A \subseteq \mathcal{L}_A$.

Lemma 4. *Every irreducible valid fence set $\mathcal{F}$ can be represented as a union of irreducible eliminating fence sets for all feasible attacks.*

Proof. By Theorem 1, fence set $\mathcal{F}$ eliminates all feasible attacks. Therefore, it includes some irreducible eliminating fence set $\mathcal{F}_A$ for every feasible attack A. By irreducibility, $\mathcal{F}$ cannot contain labels outside the union of these $\mathcal{F}_A$ sets. $\square$

In compliance with the lemma, in Dekker's program $\mathcal{F} = \mathcal{F}_A \cup \mathcal{F}_{A'}$.

Lemma 4 is useful for fence computation since optimal fence sets are always irreducible. All irreducible eliminating fence sets for attacks can be constructed by an exhaustive search through all selections of labels involved in the attack.

Note that this search may raise an exponential number of reachability queries. In practice this rarely constitutes a problem. First, attacks seldom involve a large number of labels, so the number of candidates is small. Second, the reachability checks can be avoided if a candidate fence set covers all the ways in the control flow graph from stinst to ldinst.

7.2   Computing an Optimal Valid Fence Set

To choose among the sets $\mathcal{F}_A$, we set up a 0/1-integer linear programming (ILP) problem $M_P \cdot x_P \geq b_P$. The optimal solutions $f(x_P) \to \min$ correspond to optimal fence sets. Here, 0/1 means the variables are Boolean.

We define inequalities that encode the feasible attacks with their corrections. Consider attack A for which we have determined the irreducible eliminating fence sets $\mathcal{F}_1, \ldots, \mathcal{F}_n$. For each set, we introduce a variable $x_{\mathcal{F}_i}$ and set up Inequality (14)(left). It selects a fence set to eliminate the attack.

$$\sum_{1 \leq i \leq n} x_{\mathcal{F}_i} \geq 1 \qquad \sum_{l \in \mathcal{F}_i} x_l \geq |\mathcal{F}_i| x_{\mathcal{F}_i} \qquad f(x_P) := \sum_{l \in \mathsf{LAB}} \mathcal{C}(l) x_l. \qquad (14)$$

When $\mathcal{F}_i$ has been chosen, we insert a fence at each of its labels l. We add further variables x_l, and encode this insertion by Inequality (14)(center). By definition of the ILP, the variables $x_{\mathcal{F}_i}$ and x_l will only take Boolean values 0 or 1. So if $x_{\mathcal{F}_i}$ is set to 1, the inequality requires that all x_l with $l \in \mathcal{F}_i$ are set to 1.

Our goal is to select fences with minimal costs. We encode this into the objective function (14)(right). An optimal solution x^* of the resulting 0/1-ILP denotes the fence set $\mathcal{F}(x^*) := \{l \in \mathsf{LAB} \mid x_l^* = 1\}$.

Theorem 7. $\mathcal{F}(x^*)$ *is valid and optimal, and thus solves fence computation.*

8 Experimental Evaluation

We implemented our algorithms in a prototype called TRENCHER [1]. The tool performs the reduction of robustness to SC reachability given in Section 5 and computes a minimal fence set as described in Section 7. TRENCHER executes independent reachability queries in parallel and uses SPIN [17] as back-end model checker. With TRENCHER, we have performed a series of experiments.

8.1 Examples

The first class of examples are mutual exclusion protocols that are implemented via shared variables. These protocols are typically not robust under TSO and require additional fences after stores to synchronization variables. We studied robust and non-robust instances of Dekker and Peterson for two threads, as well as Lamport's fast mutex [22] for three threads. Moreover, we checked the CLH and MCS locks: robust list-based queue locks that use compare-and-set [16].

As second class of examples, we considered concurrent data structures. The Lock-Free Stack is a concurrent stack implementation using compare-and-swap [16]. Cilk's THE WSQ is a work stealing queue from the implementation of the Cilk-5 programming language [13].

Finally, we considered miscellaneous concurrent algorithms that are known to be sensitive to program order relaxations. We analysed several instances of the Non-Blocking Write protocol [18]. NBWL is the spinlock + non-blocking write example considered by Owens in Section 8 of [25]. Finally, our tool discovered the known bug in Java's Parker implementation that is due to TSO relaxations [12].

8.2 Benchmarking

We executed TRENCHER on the examples, using a machine with Intel(R) Core(TM) i5 CPU M 560 @ 2.67GHz (4 cores) running GNU/Linux. Table 2 summarizes the results. The columns T, L, and I give the numbers of threads, labels, and instructions in the examples. RQ is the number of reachability queries raised by TRENCHER. Provided the example is robust, this number is equal to the number of attacks $(t_A, \text{stinst}, \text{ldinst})$. NR1 is the number of verification queries that were answered negatively by TRENCHER itself, without running SPIN. Such queries correspond to attacks where stinst cannot be delayed past ldinst because of memory fences or locked instructions in between. NR2 and R are the numbers of queries that are answered negatively/positively by the external model checker. Hence, RQ = NR1 + NR2 + R. F is the number of fences inserted.

The column Spin gives the total CPU time taken by SPIN and Clang, the C compiler, to produce a verifier executable (pan). The column Ver provides the total CPU time taken by TRENCHER and the external verifier. Real is the wall-clock time in seconds of processing an example. All times are given in seconds.

Table 2. Benchmarking results. The test inputs are available online [1].

Program	T	L	I	RQ	NR1	NR2	R	F	Spin	Ver	Real
Peterson (non-robust)	2	14	18	23	2	12	9	2	7.7	0.5	2.9
Peterson (robust)	2	16	20	12	12	0	0	0	0.0	0.0	0.0
Dekker (non-robust)	2	24	30	95	12	28	55	4	31.7	2.1	14.2
Dekker (robust)	2	32	38	30	30	0	0	0	0.0	0.0	0.0
Lamport (non-robust)	3	33	36	36	9	15	12	6	14.4	6.0	5.9
Lamport (robust)	3	39	42	27	27	0	0	0	0.0	0.0	0.0
CLH Lock (robust)	7	62	58	54	48	6	0	0	4.9	0.2	1.6
MCS Lock (robust)	4	52	50	30	26	4	0	0	2.9	0.4	0.9
Lock-Free Stack (robust)	4	46	50	14	14	0	0	0	0.0	0.0	0.0
Cilk's THE WSQ (non-robust)	5	86	79	152	141	8	3	3	10.0	18.0	7.4
NBW2 (non-robust)	2	21	19	15	9	5	1	1	2.5	0.2	0.8
NBW3 (robust)	2	22	20	15	15	0	0	0	0.0	0.0	0.0
NBW4 (robust)	3	25	22	9	7	2	0	0	0.7	0.1	0.4
NBWL (robust)	4	45	45	30	26	4	0	0	2.7	0.2	0.7
Parker (non-robust)	2	9	8	2	0	1	1	1	0.5	0.0	0.3
Parker (robust)	2	10	9	2	2	0	0	0	0.0	0.0	0.0

8.3 Discussion

The analysis of robust algorithms is particularly fast. They typically only have a small number of attacks that have to be checked by a model checker. The robust versions of Dekker and Peterson do not have such attacks at all. In the CLH and MCS locks, their number is less than 20%.

In some examples (non-robust Dekker, CLH Lock, NBW2, NBW4), up to 94% of the CPU time was spent on generating verifiers. This leaves room for improvement by switching to a model checker without compilation phase. For some examples (LamNR, CLH Lock), the wall-clock time constitutes 1/3 to 1/4 of the CPU time (4-cores). This confirms good parallelizability of the approach.

Remarkably, our trace-based analysis can establish robustness of the NBWL example, as opposed to the earlier analysis via triangular data races which has to place a fence [25].

We note that there is a reduction of TSO robustness to a *single* SC reachability query, again in an instrumented program of linear size. The idea is to let each thread act as an attacker and as a helper, and to apply $[\![-]\!]_{A1}$ to all loads and stores rather than to a single attack. This alternative reduction is implemented in TRENCHER, but it performed worse in our experiments because of a higher degree of non-determinism and the lack of parallelization options.

Acknowledgements. The second author was granted by the Competence Center High Performance Computing and Visualization (CC-HPC) of the Fraunhofer Institute for Industrial Mathematics (ITWM). The work was partially supported by the PROCOPE project ROIS: Robustness under Realistic Instruction Sets.

References

1. Trencher: a tool for checking and enforcing robustness against TSO,
   http://concurrency.cs.uni-kl.de/trencher.html
2. Abdulla, P.A., Atig, M.F., Chen, Y.-F., Leonardsson, C., Rezine, A.: Counter-Example Guided Fence Insertion under TSO. In: Flanagan, C., König, B. (eds.) TACAS 2012. LNCS, vol. 7214, pp. 204–219. Springer, Heidelberg (2012)
3. Adve, S.V., Hill, M.D.: A unified formalization of four shared-memory models. IEEE Trans. Parallel Distrib. Syst. 4(6), 613–624 (1993)
4. Alglave, J.: A Shared Memory Poetics. PhD thesis, University Paris 7 (2010)
5. Alglave, J., Maranget, L.: Stability in Weak Memory Models. In: Gopalakrishnan, G., Qadeer, S. (eds.) CAV 2011. LNCS, vol. 6806, pp. 50–66. Springer, Heidelberg (2011)
6. Alur, R., McMillan, K., Peled, D.: Model-Checking of Correctness Conditions for Concurrent Objects. In: LICS, pp. 219–228. IEEE Computer Society Press (1996)
7. Atig, M.F., Bouajjani, A., Burckhardt, S., Musuvathi, M.: On the Verification Problem for Weak Memory Models. In: POPL, pp. 7–18. ACM (2010)
8. Bouajjani, A., Derevenetc, E., Meyer, R.: Checking and enforcing robustness against TSO. CoRR, abs/1208.6152 (2012), http://arxiv.org/abs/1208.6152
9. Bouajjani, A., Meyer, R., Möhlmann, E.: Deciding Robustness against Total Store Ordering. In: Aceto, L., Henzinger, M., Sgall, J. (eds.) ICALP 2011, Part II. LNCS, vol. 6756, pp. 428–440. Springer, Heidelberg (2011)
10. Burckhardt, S., Musuvathi, M.: Effective Program Verification for Relaxed Memory Models. In: Gupta, A., Malik, S. (eds.) CAV 2008. LNCS, vol. 5123, pp. 107–120. Springer, Heidelberg (2008)
11. Burnim, J., Sen, K., Stergiou, C.: Sound and Complete Monitoring of Sequential Consistency for Relaxed Memory Models. In: Abdulla, P.A., Leino, K.R.M. (eds.) TACAS 2011. LNCS, vol. 6605, pp. 11–25. Springer, Heidelberg (2011)
12. Dice, D.: A race in locksupport park() arising from weak memory models (November 2009),
    https://blogs.oracle.com/dave/entry/a_race_in_locksupport_park
13. Frigo, M., Leiserson, C.E., Randall, K.H.: The implementation of the Cilk-5 multithreaded language. SIGPLAN Not. 33(5), 212–223 (1998)
14. German, S.M., Sistla, P.A.: Reasoning about systems with many processes. JACM 39, 675–735 (1992)
15. Gibbons, P.B., Korach, E.: Testing shared memories. SIAM J. Comp. 26(4), 1208–1244 (1997)
16. Herlihy, M., Shavit, N.: The Art of Multiprocessor Programming. MKP (2008)
17. Holzmann, G.J.: The model checker SPIN. IEEE Tr. Soft. Eng. 23, 279–295 (1997)
18. Kopetz, H., Reisinger, J.: The Non-Blocking Write Protocol NBW: A Solution to a Real-Time Synchronisation Problem. In: IEEE Real-Time Systems Symposium, pp. 131–137. IEEE Computer Society Press (1993)
19. Kuperstein, M., Vechev, M.T., Yahav, E.: Partial-Coherence Abstractions for Relaxed Memory Models. In: PLDI, pp. 187–198. ACM (2011)
20. Kuperstein, M., Vechev, M.T., Yahav, E.: Automatic inference of memory fences. SIGACT News 43(2), 108–123 (2012)
21. Lamport, L.: How to make a multiprocessor computer that correctly executes multiprocess programs. IEEE Trans. Comp. 28(9), 690–691 (1979)
22. Lamport, L.: A fast mutual exclusion algorithm. ACM Tr. Comp. Sys. 5(1) (1987)

23. Linden, A., Wolper, P.: A Verification-Based Approach to Memory Fence Insertion in Relaxed Memory Systems. In: Groce, A., Musuvathi, M. (eds.) SPIN 2011. LNCS, vol. 6823, pp. 144–160. Springer, Heidelberg (2011)
24. Lipton, R.: The reachability problem requires exponential space. Technical Report 62, Yale University (1976)
25. Owens, S.: Reasoning about the Implementation of Concurrency Abstractions on x86-TSO. In: D'Hondt, T. (ed.) ECOOP 2010. LNCS, vol. 6183, pp. 478–503. Springer, Heidelberg (2010)
26. Owens, S., Sarkar, S., Sewell, P.: A better x86 memory model: x86-TSO (extended version). Technical Report CL-TR-745, University of Cambridge (2009)
27. Rackoff, C.: The covering and boundedness problems for vector addition systems. Theor. Comp. Sci. 6, 223–231 (1978)
28. Sewell, P., Sarkar, S., Owens, S., Nardelli, F.Z., Myreen, M.O.: x86-TSO: a rigorous and usable programmer's model for x86 multiprocessors. CACM 53, 89–97 (2010)
29. Shasha, D., Snir, M.: Efficient and correct execution of parallel programs that share memory. ACM TOPLAS 10(2), 282–312 (1988)
30. Vafeiadis, V., Zappa Nardelli, F.: Verifying Fence Elimination Optimisations. In: Yahav, E. (ed.) SAS 2011. LNCS, vol. 6887, pp. 146–162. Springer, Heidelberg (2011)

GADTs Meet Subtyping*

Gabriel Scherer and Didier Rémy

INRIA, Rocquencourt

Abstract. While generalized algebraic datatypes (GADTs) are now considered well-understood, adding them to a language with a notion of subtyping comes with a few surprises. What does it mean for a GADT parameter to be covariant? The answer turns out to be quite subtle. It involves fine-grained properties of the subtyping relation that raise interesting design questions. We allow variance annotations in GADT definitions, study their soundness, and present a sound and complete algorithm to check them. Our work may be applied to real-world ML-like languages with explicit subtyping such as OCaml, or to languages with general subtyping constraints.

1 Introduction

In languages that have a notion of subtyping, the interface of parametrized types usually specifies a *variance*. It defines the subtyping relation between two instances of a parametrized type from the subtyping relations that hold between their parameters. For example, the type α list of immutable lists is expected to be *covariant*: we wish σ list $\leq \sigma'$ list as soon as $\sigma \leq \sigma'$.

Variance is essential in languages with parametric polymorphism whose programming idioms rely on subtyping, in particular object-oriented languages, or languages with structural datatypes such as extensible records and variants, dependently typed languages with inductive types (to represent positivity requirements), or additional information in types such as permissions, effects, *etc.* A last reason to care about variance is its use in the *relaxed value restriction* [Gar04]: while a possibly-effectful expression, also called an *expansive expression*, cannot be soundly generalized in ML—unless some sophisticated enhancement of the type system keeps track of effectful expressions—it is always sound to generalize type variables that only appear in covariant positions, as they may not classify mutable data. Therefore, it is important for extensions of type definitions, such as generalized algebraic datatypes (GADTs), to support it as well through a clear and expressive definition of parameter covariance.

For example, consider the following GADT of well-typed expressions:

```
type +α exp =
  | Val  : α → α exp
  | Int  : int → int exp
  | Thunk : ∀β. β exp * (β → α) → α exp
  | Prod : ∀βγ. β exp * γ exp → (β * γ) exp
```

---

* Part of this work has been done at IRILL.

M. Felleisen and P. Gardner (Eds.): ESOP 2013, LNCS 7792, pp. 554–573, 2013.

Is it safe to say that `exp` is covariant in its type parameter? It turns out that, using the subtyping relation of the OCaml type system, the answer is "yes". But, surprisingly to us, in a type system with a top type $\top$, the answer would be "no". We introduce this example in details in §2—and present some interesting counter-examples of incorrect variance annotations.

Verifying variance annotations for simple algebraic datatypes is straightforward: it suffices to check that covariant type variables appear only positively and contravariant variables only negatively in the types of the arguments of the datatype constructors. GADTs can be formalized as extensions of datatypes where constructors have typed arguments, but also a set of existential variables and equality constraints. Then, the simple check of algebraic datatypes apparently becomes a searching problem: witnesses for existentials must be found so as to satisfy the equality constraints. That is, there is a natural correctness criterion (already present in previous work); however, it is expressed in a "semantic" form that is not suitable for a simple implementation in a type checker. We present this semantic criterion in §3 after reviewing the formal framework of variance-based subtyping.

The main contribution of our work, described in §4, is to develop a syntactic criterion that ensures the semantics criterion. Our solution extends the simple check of algebraic datatypes in a non-obvious way by introducing two new notions. First, *upward and downward-closure* of type constructors explains how to check that a single equality constraint is still satisfiable in presence of variance (but also raises interesting design issues for the subtyping relation). Second, *zipping* explains when witnesses exist for existential variables, that is, when multiple constraints using the same existential may soundly be used without interfering with each other. These two properties are combined into a new syntactic judgment of *decomposability* that is central to our syntactic criterion. We prove that our syntactic criterion is sound and complete with respect to the semantic criterion. The proof of soundness is relatively direct, but completeness is much harder.

We discuss the implication of our results in §5, in particular the notion of upward and downward-closure properties of type constructors, on the design of a subtyping relation. We also contrast this approach, motivated by the needs of a language of a ML family, with a different and mostly orthogonal approach taken by existing object-oriented languages, namely C♯ and Scala, where a natural notion of GADTs involves subtyping constraints, rather than equality constraints. We can re-evaluate our syntactic criterion in this setting: it is still sound, but the question of completeness is left open.

In summary, we propose a syntactic criterion for checking the soundness of variance annotations of GADTs with equality constraints in a language with subtyping. Our work is directly applicable to the OCaml language, but our approach can also be transposed to languages with general subtyping constraints, and raises interesting design questions. A long version of the present article, containing the detailed proofs and additional details and discussion, is available online [SR].

2   Examples

Let us first explain why it is reasonable to say that α exp is covariant. Informally, if we are able to coerce a value of type α into one of type α' (we write $(v :> \alpha')$ to explicitly cast a value v of type α to a value of type α'), then we are also able to transform a value of type α exp into one of type α' exp. Here is some pseudo-code[1] for the coercion function:

```
let coerce :  α exp → α′ exp = function
  | Val (v : α) -> Val (v :> α′)
  | Int n -> Int n
  | Thunk β (b : β exp) (f : β → α) ->
    Thunk β b (fun x -> (f x :> α′))
  | Prod β γ ((b, c) : β exp ∗ γ exp) ->
    (∗ if β ∗ γ ≤ α′, then α′ is of the form β′ ∗ γ′
        with β ≤ β′ and γ ≤ γ′ ∗)
    Prod β′ γ′ ((b :> β′ exp), (c :> γ′ exp))
```

In the `Prod` case, we make an informal use of something we know about the OCaml type system: the supertypes of a tuple are all tuples. By entering the branch, we gain the knowledge that α must be equal to some type of the form $\beta * \gamma$. So from $\alpha \le \alpha'$ we know that $\beta * \gamma \le \alpha'$. Therefore, α' must itself be a pair of the form $\beta' * \gamma'$. By covariance of the product, we deduce that $\beta \le \beta'$ and $\gamma \le \gamma'$. We may thus conclude by casting at types β' exp and γ' exp, recursively.

Similarly, in the `Int` case, we know that α must be an `int` and therefore an `int exp` is returned. This is because we know that, in OCaml, no type is above `int`: if `int` $\le \tau$, then τ must be `int`.

What we use in both cases is reasoning of the form[2]: "if $T[\overline{\beta}] \le \alpha'$, then I know that α' is of the form $T[\overline{\beta'}]$ for some $\overline{\beta}'$". We call this an *upward closure* property: when we "go up" from a $T[\overline{\beta}]$, we only find types that also have the structure of T. Similarly, for contravariant parameters, we would need a *downward closure* property: T is downward-closed if $T[\overline{\beta}] \ge \alpha'$ entails that α' is of the form $T[\overline{\beta'}]$.

Before studying a more troubling example, we define the classic equality type (α, β) eq and the corresponding casting function cast $: \forall\alpha\beta.(\alpha, \beta)$ eq $\to \alpha \to \beta$:

```
type (α, β) eq =            let cast r =
  | Refl : ∀γ. (γ, γ) eq       match r with Refl -> (fun x -> x)
```

Notice that it would be unsound[3] to define `eq` as covariant, even in only one parameter. For example, if we had `type (+α, =β) eq`, from any $\sigma \le \tau$, we could subtype (σ, σ) eq into (τ, σ) eq, allowing a cast from any value of type τ back into one of type σ, which is unsound in general.

---

[1] The variables β' and γ' of the `Prod` case are never really defined, only justified at the meta-level, making this code only an informal sketch.

[2] We write $T[\overline{\beta}]$ for a type expression T that may contain free occurrences of variables $\overline{\beta}$ and $T[\overline{\sigma}]$ for the simultaneous substitution of $\overline{\sigma}$ for $\overline{\beta}$ in T.

[3] This counterexample is due to Jeremy Yallop.

As a counter-example, the following declaration is incorrect: the type α bad cannot be declared covariant.

```
type +α bad =
  | K : < m : int > → < m : int > bad
let v = (K (object method m = 1 end) :> < > bad)
```

This declaration uses the OCaml object type < m : int >, which qualifies objects having a method m returning an integer. It is a subtype of object types with fewer methods, in this case the empty object type < >, so the alleged covariance of bad, if accepted by the compiler, would allow us to cast a value of type < m : int > bad into one of type < > bad and thus have the above value v of type <> bad. However, if such a value v existed, we could produce an equality witness (< >, <m : int>) eq that allows to cast any empty object of type < > into an object of type < m : int >, but this is unsound, of course!

```
let get_eq : α bad → (α, < m : int >) eq = function
  | K _ -> Refl      (* locally α = < m : int > *)
let wrong : < > -> < m : int > =
  let eq : (< >, < m : int >) eq = get_eq v in cast eq
```

It is possible to reproduce this example using a different feature of the OCaml type system named *private type abbreviation*[4]: a module using a type type s = τ *internally* may describe its interface as type s = private τ. This is a compromise between a type abbreviation and an abstract type: it is possible to cast a value of type s into one of type τ, but not, conversely, to construct a value of type s from one of type τ. In other words, s is a strict subtype of τ: we have s $\leq$ τ but not s $\geq$ τ. Take for example type file_descr = private int: this semi-abstraction is useful to enforce invariants by restricting the construction of values of type file_descr, while allowing users to conveniently and efficiently destruct them for inspection at type int. Using an unsound but quite innocent-looking covariant GADT datatype, one is able to construct a function to cast any integer into a file_descr, which defeats the purpose of this abstraction—see the extended version of this article for the full example.

The difference between the former, correct Prod case and those two latter situations with unsound variance is the notion of upward closure. The types $\alpha * \beta$ and int used in the correct example were upward-closed. On the contrary, the private type file_descr has a distinct supertype int, and similarly, the object type < m:int > has a supertype < > with a different structure (no method m).

Finally, the need for covariance of α exp can be justified either by applications using subtyping on data (for example object types or polymorphic variants), or by the relaxed value restriction. If we used the Thunk constructor to delay a computation returning an object of type < m : int >, that is itself of type < m : int > exp, we may need to see it as a computation returning the empty object < >. We could also wish to define an abstract interface through a module boundary that would not expose any implementation detail about the datatype; for example, using Product to implement a list interface.

---

[4] This counterexample is due to Jacques Garrigue.

```
module Exp : sig
  type α exp
  val inj : α -> α exp
  val pair : α exp -> β exp -> (α * β) exp
  val fst : (α * β) exp -> α exp
end
```

What would then be the type of `Exp.inj` `[]`? In presence of the value restriction, this application cannot be generalized, and we get a weak polymorphic type $?\alpha$ `list Exp.exp` for some non-generalized inference variable $?\alpha$. If we change the interface to express that `Exp.exp` is covariant, then we get the expected polymorphic type $\forall\alpha.\alpha$ `list Exp.exp`.

3   A Formal Setting

3.1   The Subtyping Relation

Ground types consist of base type q, types τ p, function types $\tau_1 \to \tau_2$, product types $\tau_1 * \tau_2$, and a set of algebraic datatypes $\overline{\sigma}$ t. We also write σ and ρ for types, $\overline{\sigma}$ for a sequence of types $(\sigma_i)_{i \in I}$, and we use prefix notation for datatype parameters, as is the usage in ML. Datatypes may be user-defined by toplevel declarations of the form:

$$\text{type } \overline{v\alpha} \text{ t} = \text{K}_1 \text{ of } \tau^1[\overline{\alpha}] \mid \dots \text{K}_n \text{ of } \tau^n[\overline{\alpha}]$$

This is a disjoint sum: the constructors K_c represent all possible cases and each type $\tau^c[\overline{\alpha}]$ is the domain of the constructor K_c. Applying K_c to an argument e of a corresponding ground type $\tau[\overline{\sigma}]$ constructs a term of type $\overline{\sigma}$ t. Values of this type are deconstructed using pattern matching clauses of the form $\text{K}_c \ x \to e$, one for each constructor.

The sequence $\overline{v\alpha}$ is a binding list of type variables α_i along with their *variance annotation* v_i. Variances range in the set $\{+, -, =, \bowtie\}$. We may associate a relation $(\prec_v)$ between types to each variance v:

- $\prec_+$ is the *covariant* relation $(\leq)$;
- $\prec_-$ is the *contravariant* relation $(\geq)$, the symmetric of $(\leq)$;
- $\prec_=$ is the *invariant* relation $(=)$ defined as the intersection of $(\leq)$ and $(\geq)$;
- $\prec_\bowtie$ is the *irrelevant* relation $(\bowtie)$, *i.e.* the full relation such that $\sigma \bowtie \tau$ holds for all types σ and τ.

Given a reflexive transitive relation $(\leqslant)$ on base types, the subtyping relation on ground types $(\leq)$ is defined by the inference rules of Figure 1, which, in particular, give their meaning to the variance annotations $\overline{v\alpha}$. The judgment type $\overline{v\alpha}$ t simply means that the type constructor t has been previously defined with the variance annotation $\overline{v\alpha}$. Notice that the rules for arrow and product types, SUB-FUN and SUB-PROD, can be subsumed by the rule for datatypes SUB-CONSTR. Indeed, one can consider them as special datatypes (with a specific

$$\text{SUB-REFL} \quad \frac{}{\sigma \leq \sigma}$$

$$\text{SUB-TRANS} \quad \frac{\sigma_1 \leq \sigma_2 \quad \sigma_2 \leq \sigma_3}{\sigma_1 \leq \sigma_3}$$

$$\text{SUB-FUN} \quad \frac{\sigma \geq \sigma' \quad \tau \leq \tau'}{\sigma \to \tau \leq \sigma' \to \tau'}$$

$$\text{SUB-PROD} \quad \frac{\sigma \leq \sigma' \quad \tau \leq \tau'}{\sigma * \tau \leq \sigma' * \tau'}$$

$$\text{SUB-CONSTR} \quad \frac{\text{type } \overline{v\alpha} \text{ t} \quad \forall i, \sigma_i \prec_{v_i} \sigma'_i}{\overline{\sigma} \text{ t} \leq \overline{\sigma}' \text{ t}}$$

$$\text{SUB-P} \quad \frac{\sigma \leq \sigma'}{\sigma \text{ p} \leq \sigma' \text{ p}}$$

$$\text{SUB-PQ} \quad \frac{}{\sigma \text{ p} \leq \text{q}}$$

Fig. 1. Subtyping relation

dynamic semantics) of variance $(-, +)$ and $(+, +)$, respectively. For this reason, the following definitions will not explicitly detail the cases for arrows and products.

The rules SUB-P and SUB-PQ were added for the explicit purpose of introducing some amount of non-atomic subtyping in our relation. For two fixed type constructors p (unary) and q (nullary), we have $\sigma \text{ p} \leq \text{q}$ for any σ. Note that q is not a top type as it is not above all types, only above the σ p. Of course, we could add other such type constructors, but those are enough to make the system interesting and representative of complex subtype relation.

As usual in subtyping systems, we could reformulate our judgment in a syntax-directed way, to prove that it admits good inversion properties: if $\overline{\sigma} \text{ t} \leq \overline{\sigma}' \text{ t}$ and type $\overline{v\alpha} \text{ t}$, then one can deduce that for each i, $\sigma_i \prec_{v_i} \sigma'_i$.

The non-atomic rule SUB-PQ ensures that our subtyping relation is not "too structured" and is a meaningful choice for a formal study applicable to real-world languages with possibly top or bottom types, private types, record width subtyping, etc. In particular, the type constructor p is *not* upward-closed (and conversely q is not downward-closed), as used informally in the examples and defined for arbitrary variances in the following way:

Definition 1 (Constructor closure). *A type constructor $\overline{\alpha}$ t is v-closed if, for any type sequence $\overline{\sigma}$ and type τ such that $\overline{\sigma} \text{ t} \prec_v \tau$ hold, then τ is necessarily equal to $\overline{\sigma}' \text{ t}$ for some $\overline{\sigma}'$.*

3.2 The Algebra of Variances

If we know that $\overline{\sigma} \text{ t} \leq \overline{\sigma}' \text{ t}$, that is $\overline{\sigma} \text{ t} \prec_+ \overline{\sigma}' \text{ t}$, and the constructor t has variable $\overline{v\alpha}$, an inversion principle tells us that $\sigma_i \prec_{v_i} \sigma'_i$ for each i. But what if we only know $\overline{\sigma} \text{ t} \prec_u \overline{\sigma}' \text{ t}$ for some variance u different from $(+)$? If u is $(-)$, we get the reverse relation $\sigma_i \succ_{v_i} \sigma'_i$. If u is $(\bowtie)$, we get $\sigma_i \bowtie \sigma'_i$, that is, nothing. This outlines a *composition* operation on variances $u.v_i$, such that if $\overline{\sigma} \text{ t} \prec_u \overline{\sigma}' \text{ t}$ then $\sigma_i \prec_{u.v_i} \sigma'_i$ holds. It is defined by the table in figure 3.2.

This operation is associative and commutative. Such an operator, and the algebraic properties of variances explained below, have already been used by other authors, for example [Abe06].

There is a natural order relation between *variances*, which is the *coarser-than* order between the corresponding relations: $v \leq w$ if and only if $(\prec_v) \supseteq (\prec_w)$;

i.e. if and only if, for all σ and τ, $\sigma \prec_w \tau$ implies $\sigma \prec_v \tau$.[5] This reflexive, partial order is described by the lattice diagram in figure 3.2. All variances are smaller than $=$ and bigger than $\bowtie$.

Fig. 2. Variance composition table   **Fig. 3.** Variance order diagram

From the order lattice on variances we can define join $\vee$ and meet $\wedge$ of variances: $v \vee w$ is the biggest variance such that $v \vee w \leq v$ and $v \vee w \leq w$; conversely, $v \wedge w$ is the lowest variance such that $v \leq v \wedge w$ and $w \leq v \wedge w$. Finally, the composition operation is monotone: if $v \leq v'$ then $w.v \leq w.v'$ and $v.w \leq v'.w$.

We often manipulate vectors $\overline{v\alpha}$ of variable associated with variances, which correpond to the "context" Γ of a type declaration. We extend our operation pairwise on those contexts: $\Gamma \vee \Gamma'$ and $\Gamma \wedge \Gamma'$, and the ordering between contexts $\Gamma \leq \Gamma'$. We also extend the variance-dependent subtyping relation ($\prec_v$), which becomes an order ($\prec_\Gamma$) between vectors of type of the same length: $\overline{\sigma} \prec_{\overline{v\alpha}} \overline{\sigma}'$ holds when we have $\sigma_i \prec_{v_i} \sigma_i'$ for all i.

3.3 A Judgment for Variance of Type Expressions

We define a judgment to check the variance of a type expression. Given a context Γ of the form $\overline{v\alpha}$, that is, where each variable is annotated with a variance, the judgment $\Gamma \vdash \tau : v$ checks that the expression τ varies along v when the variables of τ vary along their variance in Γ. For example, $(+\alpha) \vdash \tau[\alpha] : +$ holds when $\tau[\alpha]$ is covariant in its variable α. The inference rules for the judgment $\Gamma \vdash \tau : v$ are defined on Figure 4.

The parameter v evolves when going into subderivations: when checking $\Gamma \vdash \tau_1 \to \tau_2 : v$, contravariance is expressed by checking $\Gamma \vdash \tau_1 : (v.-)$. Previous work (on variance as [Abe06] and [EKRY06], but also on irrelevance as in [Pfe01]) used no such parameter, but modified the context instead, checking $\Gamma/- \vdash \tau_1$ for some "variance cancellation" operation $vw/$ (see [Abe06] for a principled presentation). Our own inference rules preserve the same context in the whole derivation and can be more easily adapted to the decomposability judgment $\Gamma \vdash \tau : v \Rightarrow v'$ that we introduce in §4.4.

---

[5] The reason for this order reversal is that the relations occur as hypotheses, in negative position, in definition of subtyping: if we have $v \leq w$ and **type** $v\alpha$ **t**, it is safe to assume **type** $w\alpha$ **t**, since $\sigma \prec_w \sigma'$ implies $\sigma \prec_v \sigma'$, which implies σ **t** $\leq \sigma'$ **t**. One may also see it, as Abel notes, as an "information order": knowing that $\sigma \prec_+ \tau$ "gives you more information" than knowing that $\sigma \prec_\bowtie \tau$, therefore $\bowtie \leq +$.

$$\frac{\text{VC-VAR}}{w\alpha \in \Gamma \qquad w \geq v}{\Gamma \vdash \alpha : v}$$

$$\frac{\text{VC-CONSTR}}{\Gamma \vdash \text{type } \overline{w\alpha} \text{ t} \qquad \forall i, \ \Gamma \vdash \sigma_i : v.w_i}{\Gamma \vdash \overline{\sigma} \text{ t} : v}$$

Fig. 4. Variance assignment

A semantics for variance assignment. This syntactic judgment $\Gamma \vdash \tau : v$ corresponds to a semantic property about the types and context involved, which formalizes our intuition of "when the variables vary along Γ, the expression τ varies along v". We also give a few formal results about this judgment.

Definition 2 (Interpretation of the variance checking judgment)
We write $[\![\Gamma \vdash \tau : v]\!]$ *for the property:* $\forall \overline{\sigma}, \overline{\sigma}', \ \overline{\sigma} \prec_\Gamma \overline{\sigma}' \implies \tau[\overline{\sigma}] \prec_v \tau[\overline{\sigma}']$.

Lemma 1 (Correctness of variance checking)
$\Gamma \vdash \tau : v$ *is provable if and only if* $[\![\Gamma \vdash \tau : v]\!]$ *holds.*

Lemma 2 (Monotonicity)
If $\Gamma \vdash \tau : v$ *is provable and* $\Gamma \leq \Gamma'$ *then* $\Gamma' \vdash \tau : v$ *is provable.*

Lemma 3 (Principality). *For any type* τ *and any variance* v, *there exists a minimal context* Δ *such that* $\Delta \vdash \tau : v$ *holds. That is, for any other context* Γ *such that* $\Gamma \vdash \tau : v$, *we have* $\Delta \leq \Gamma$.

We can generalize inversion of head type constructors (§3.1) to whole type expressions. The most general inversion is given by the principal context.

Theorem 1 (Inversion). *For any type* $\tau[\overline{\alpha}]$, *variance* v, *and type sequences* $\overline{\sigma}$ *and* $\overline{\sigma}'$, *the subtyping relation* $\tau[\overline{\sigma}] \prec_v \tau[\overline{\sigma}']$ *holds if and only if the judgment* $\Gamma \vdash \tau : v$ *holds for some context* Γ *such that* $\overline{\sigma} \prec_\Gamma \overline{\sigma}'$. *Furthermore, if* $\tau[\overline{\sigma}] \prec_v \tau[\overline{\sigma}']$ *holds, then* $\overline{\sigma} \prec_\Delta \overline{\sigma}'$ *holds, where* Δ *is the minimal context such that* $\Delta \vdash \tau : v$.

3.4   Variance Annotations in ADTs

As a preparation for the difficult case of GADTs, we first present our approach in the well-understood case of algebraic datatypes. We exhibit a semantic criterion that justifies the correctness of a variance annotation; then, we propose an equivalent syntactic judgment. Of course, we recover the usual criterion that covariant variables should only occur positively.

In general, an ADT definition of the form

$$\text{type } \overline{v\alpha} \text{ t} = \big|_{c \in C} \text{ K}_c \text{ of } \tau^c[\overline{\alpha}]$$

cannot be accepted with any variance $\overline{v\alpha}$ t. For example, the declaration (type $v\alpha$ inv = Fun of $\alpha \to \alpha$) is only sound when v is invariant. Accepting a variance assignment $\overline{v\alpha}$ determines the relations between closed types $\overline{\sigma}$ and $\overline{\sigma}'$ under which the relation $\overline{\sigma}$ t $\leq \overline{\sigma}'$ t is correct.

In the definition of $+\alpha$ exp we justified the covariance of exp by the existence of a coercion function. We now formalize this idea for the general case. To check the correctness of $\overline{\sigma}$ t $\leq \overline{\sigma}'$ t we check the existence of a coercion term that turns a closed value q of type $\overline{\sigma}$ t into one of type $\overline{\sigma}'$ t that is equal to q up to type information. We actually search for coercions of the form:

$$\texttt{match } (q : \overline{\sigma} \texttt{ t}) \texttt{ with } |_{c \in C} \texttt{ K}_c(x : \tau^c[\overline{\sigma}]) \to \texttt{K}_c(x :> \tau^c[\overline{\sigma}'])$$

Note that erasing types gives an η-expansion of the sum type, *i.e.* this is really a coercion. Hence, such a coercion exists if and only if it is well-typed, that is, each cast of the form $(x : \tau^c[\overline{\sigma}] :> \tau^c[\overline{\sigma}'])$ is itself well-typed. This gives our semantic criterion for ADTs.

Definition 3 (Semantic soundness criterion for ADTs)
We accept the ADT definition of $\overline{v\alpha}$t with constructors $(K_c \text{ of } \tau^c[\overline{\alpha}])_{c \in C}$ if

$$\forall c \in C, \forall \overline{\sigma}, \forall \overline{\sigma}', \quad \overline{\sigma} \texttt{ t} \leq \overline{\sigma}' \texttt{ t} \implies \tau^c[\overline{\sigma}] \leq \tau^c[\overline{\sigma}']$$

The syntactic criterion for ADTs. We notice that this criterion is exactly the semantic interpretation of the variance checking judgment (Definition 2): the type type $\overline{v\alpha}$ t is accepted if and only if the judgment $\overline{v\alpha} \vdash \tau^c : (+)$ is derivable for each constructor type $\tau^c[\overline{\alpha}]$.

This syntactic criterion coincides with the well-known alogrithm implemented in type checkers[6]: checking positive occurences of a variable α corresponds to a proof obligation of the form $\overline{v\alpha} \vdash \alpha : +$, which is valid only when α has variance $(+)$ or $(=)$ in Γ; checking negative occurences correspond to a proof obligation $\overline{v\alpha} \vdash \alpha : -$, *etc.* This extends seamlessly to irrelevant variables, which must appear only under irrelevant context $\overline{v\alpha} \vdash \alpha : \bowtie$—or not at all.

3.5   Variance Annotations in GADTs

A general description of GADTs. When used to build terms of type $\overline{\alpha}$ t, a constructor K of τ behaves like a function of type $\forall \overline{\alpha}.(\tau \to \overline{\alpha} \texttt{ t})$. Notice that the codomain is exactly $\overline{\alpha}$ t, the type t instantiated with parametric variables. GADTs arise by relaxing this restriction, allowing constructors with richer types of the form $\forall \overline{\alpha}.(\tau \to \overline{\sigma} \texttt{ t})$. See for example the declaration of constructor Prod in the introduction:

$$| \texttt{ Prod } : \forall \beta\gamma. \; \beta \texttt{ exp} * \gamma \texttt{ exp} \to (\beta * \gamma) \texttt{ exp}$$

Instead of being just α exp, the codomain is now $(\beta * \gamma)$ exp. We moved from simple algebraic datatypes to so-called *generalized* algebraic datatypes. This approach is natural and convenient for the users, so it is exactly the syntax chosen in languages with explicit GADTs support, such as Haskell and OCaml,

---

[6] One should keep in mind that this criterion suffers the usual bane of static typing, it can reject programs that do not go wrong: type $-\alpha$ weird = K of $\alpha * \bot$. For more details, see the beginning of the §4 in the long version of this article.

and is reminiscent of the inductive datatype definitions of dependently typed languages.

However, for the formal study of GADTs, a different formulation based on equality constraints is preferred. We use the following equivalent presentation, already present in previous works [SP07]. We force the codomain of the constructor Prod to be α t again, instead of $(\beta * \gamma)$ t, by adding an explicit equality constraint $\alpha = \beta * \gamma$.

```
type α exp =
  | Val of ∃β[α = β]. β
  | Int of [α = int]. int
  | Thunk of ∃βγ[α = γ]. β exp * (β → γ)
  | Prod of ∃βγ[α = β * γ]. β exp * γ exp
```

In the rest of the paper, we extend our former core language with such definitions. This does not impact the notion of subtyping, which is defined on GADT type constructors with variance type $\overline{v\alpha}$ t just as it previously was on simple ADT type constructors. What needs to be changed, however, is the soundness criterion for checking the variance of type definitions

The correctness criterion. We must adapt our semantic criterion for datatype declarations (Definition 3) from simple ADTs to GADTs. Again, we check under which relations between $\overline{\sigma}$ and $\overline{\sigma}'$ the subtyping relation $\overline{\sigma}$ t $\leq \overline{\sigma}'$ t holds for some GADT definition $\overline{v\alpha}$ t.

The difference is that a constructor K_c that had an argument of type $\tau^c[\overline{\alpha}]$ in the simple ADT case, now has the more complex type $\exists \overline{\beta}[D[\overline{\alpha}, \overline{\beta}]].\tau^c[\overline{\beta}]$, for a set of existential variables $\overline{\beta}$ and a set of equality constraints D—of the form $(\alpha_i = T_i[\overline{\beta}])_{i \in I}$ for a family of type expressions $(T_i[\overline{\beta}])_{i \in I}$. Given a closed value q of type $\overline{\sigma}$ t, the coercion term is:

$$\text{match } (q : \overline{\sigma} \text{ t}) \text{ with } |_{c \in C} \; K_c(x : \tau^c[\overline{\rho}_c]) \to K_c(x :> \tau^c[\overline{\rho}'_c])$$

We do not need to consider the dead cases: we only match on the constructors for which there exists an instantiation $\overline{\rho}_c$ of the existential variables $\overline{\beta}$ such that the constraint $D[\overline{\sigma}, \overline{\rho}]$, *i.e.* $\bigwedge_{i \in I} \sigma_i = T_i[\overline{\rho}_c]$, holds. To type-check this term, we need to find another instantiation $\overline{\rho}'_c$ that verifies the constraints $D[\overline{\sigma}', \overline{\rho}']$. This coercion type-checks only when $\tau^c[\overline{\rho}_c] \leq \tau^c[\overline{\rho}'_c]$ holds. This gives our semantic criterion for GADTs:

Definition 4 (Semantic soundness criterion for GADTs). *We accept the GADT definition of* **type** $\overline{v\alpha}$ t *with constructors* $(K_c \text{ of } \exists\overline{\beta}[D[\overline{\alpha}, \overline{\beta}]].\tau^c[\overline{\alpha}])_{c \in C}$, *if for all c in C we have:*

$$\forall \overline{\sigma}, \overline{\sigma}', \overline{\rho}, \; (\overline{\sigma} \text{ t} \leq \overline{\sigma}' \text{ t} \wedge D[\overline{\sigma}, \overline{\rho}] \implies \exists \overline{\rho}', \; D[\overline{\sigma}', \overline{\rho}'] \wedge \tau[\overline{\rho}] \leq \tau[\overline{\rho}']) \qquad \text{(REQ)}$$

As for ADTs, this criterion ensures soundness: if, under some variance annotation, a datatype declaration satisfies it, then the implied subtyping relations are all expressible as coercions in the language, and therefore correct. Whereas the simpler ADT criterion was already widely present in the literature, this one is less known; it is however present in the previous work of Simonet and Pottier [SP07] (presented as a constraint entailment problem).

Another way to understand this criterion would be to define constrained existential types of the form $\exists\overline{\beta}[D[\overline{\alpha},\overline{\beta}]].\tau[\overline{\beta}]$ as first-class types and, with the right notion of subtyping for those, require that $\overline{\sigma}\ t \leq \overline{\sigma}'\ t$ imply $(\exists\overline{\beta}[D[\overline{\sigma},\overline{\beta}]].\tau[\overline{\beta}]) \leq (\exists\overline{\beta}[D[\overline{\sigma}',\overline{\beta}]].\tau[\overline{\beta}])$. The (easy) equivalence between those two presentations is detailed in the work of Simonet and Pottier [SP07].

4   Checking Variances of GADT

4.1   Expressing Decomposability

If we specialize REQ to the Prod constructor of the α exp example datatype, $i.e.$ Prod of $\exists\beta\gamma[\alpha = \beta * \gamma]\beta$ exp $* \gamma$ exp, we get:

$$\forall\sigma,\sigma',\rho_1,\rho_2,$$
$$\big(\sigma\ \mathrm{exp} \leq \sigma'\ \mathrm{exp} \wedge \sigma = \rho_1 * \rho_2 \implies \exists\rho_1',\rho_2',(\sigma' = \rho_1' * \rho_2' \wedge \rho_1 * \rho_2 \leq \rho_1' * \rho_2')\big)$$

We can substitute equalities and use the (user-defined) covariance to simplify the subtyping constraint $\sigma\ \mathrm{exp} \leq \sigma'\ \mathrm{exp}$ into $\sigma \leq \sigma'$:

$$\forall\sigma',\rho_1,\rho_2,\ \big(\rho_1 * \rho_2 \leq \sigma' \implies \exists\rho_1',\rho_2',(\sigma' = \rho_1' * \rho_2' \wedge \rho_1 \leq \rho_1' \wedge \rho_2 \leq \rho_2')\big) \quad (1)$$

This is the $upward\ closure$ property mentioned in the introduction. The preceeding transformation is safe only if any supertype σ' of a product $\rho_1 * \rho_2$ is itself a product, $i.e.$ is of the form $\rho_1' * \rho_2'$ for some ρ_1' and ρ_2'.

More generally, for a type $\Gamma \vdash \sigma$ and a variance v, we are interested in a closure property of the following form, where the notation $(\overline{\rho} : \Gamma)$ simply classifies type vectors $\overline{\rho}$ that have exactly one type ρ_i for each variable in Γ:

$$\forall(\overline{\rho} : \Gamma),\sigma',\quad \sigma[\overline{\rho}] \prec_v \sigma' \implies \exists(\overline{\rho}' : \Gamma),\ \sigma' = \sigma[\overline{\rho}']$$

Here, the context Γ represents the set of existential variables of the constructor (β and γ in our example). We can easily express the condition $\rho_1 \leq \rho_1'$ and $\rho_2 \leq \rho_2'$ on the right-hand side of the implication by considering a context Γ annotated with variances $(+\beta, +\gamma)$, and using the context ordering $(\prec_\Gamma)$. Then, (1) is equivalent to:

$$\forall(\overline{\rho} : \Gamma),\sigma',\quad \sigma[\overline{\rho}] \prec_v \sigma' \implies \exists(\overline{\rho}' : \Gamma),\ \overline{\rho} \prec_\Gamma \overline{\rho}' \wedge \sigma' = \sigma[\overline{\rho}']$$

Our aim is now to find a set of inference rules to check decomposability; we will later reconnect it to REQ. In fact, we study a slightly more general relation, where the equality $\sigma[\overline{\rho}'] = \sigma'$ on the right-hand side is relaxed to an arbitrary relation $\sigma[\overline{\rho}'] \prec_{v'} \sigma'$:

Definition 5 (Decomposability). *Given a context Γ, a type expression $\sigma[\overline{\beta}]$ and two variances v and v', we say that σ is decomposable under Γ from variance v to variance v', which we write $\Gamma \Vdash \sigma : v \rightsquigarrow v'$, if the following property holds:*

$$\forall(\overline{\rho}:\Gamma), \sigma', \; \sigma[\overline{\rho}] \prec_v \sigma' \implies \exists(\overline{\rho}':\Gamma), \; \overline{\rho} \prec_\Gamma \overline{\rho}' \wedge \sigma[\overline{\rho}'] \prec_{v'} \sigma'$$

We use the symbol $\Vdash$ rather than $\vdash$ to highlight the fact that this is just a logic formula, not the semantic interpretation of a syntactic judgment—we will introduce one later in section 4.4.

Remark that, due to the *positive* occurrence of the relation $\prec_\Gamma$ in the proposition $\Gamma \Vdash \tau : v \rightsquigarrow v'$ and the anti-monotonicity of $\prec_\Gamma$, this formula is "anti-monotone" with respect to the context ordering $\Gamma \leq \Gamma'$. This corresponds to saying that we can still decompose, but with less information on the existential witness $\overline{\rho}'$.

Lemma 4 (Anti-monotonicity)
If $\Gamma \Vdash \tau : v \rightsquigarrow v'$ holds and $\Gamma' \leq \Gamma$, then $\Gamma' \Vdash \tau : v \rightsquigarrow v'$ also holds.

4.2   Variable Occurrences

In the `Prod` case, the type whose decomposability was considered is $\beta * \gamma$ (in the context β, γ). In this very simple case, decomposability depends only on the type constructor for the product. In the present type system, with very strong invertibility principles on the subtyping relation, both upward and downward closures hold for products. In the general case, we require that this specific type constructor be upward-closed.

In general, the closure of the head type constructor alone is not enough to ensure decomposability of the whole type. For example, in a complex type expression with subterms, we should consider the closure of the type constructors appearing in the subterms as well. Besides, there are subtleties when a variable occurs several times.

For example, while $\beta * \gamma$ is decomposable from $(+)$ to $(=)$, $\beta * \beta$ is not: $\bot * \bot$ is an instantiation of $\beta * \beta$, and a subtype of, *e.g.*, `int` $*$ `bool`, which is not an instance[7] of $\beta * \beta$. The same variable occurring twice in covariant position (or having one covariant and one invariant or contravariant occurence) breaks decomposability.

On the other hand, two invariant occurrences are possible: β `ref` $*$ β `ref` is upward-closed (assuming the type constructor `ref` is invariant and upward-closed): if $(\sigma$ `ref` $* \sigma$ `ref`$) \leq \sigma'$, then by upward closure of the product, σ' is of the form $\sigma_1' * \sigma_2'$, and by its covariance σ `ref` $\leq \sigma_1'$ and σ `ref` $\leq \sigma_2'$. Now by invariance of `ref` we have $\sigma_1' = \sigma$ `ref` $= \sigma_2'$, and therefore σ' is equal to σ `ref` $* \sigma$ `ref`, which is an instance of β `ref` $* \beta$ `ref`.

---

[7] We use the term *instance* to denote the replacement of all the free variables of a type expression under context by closed types—not the specialization of an ML type scheme.

Finally, a variable may appear in irrelevant positions without affecting closure properties; $\beta * (\beta \text{ irr})$ (where irr is an upward-closed irrelevant type, defined for example as $\text{type } \alpha \text{ irr} = \text{int}$) is upward closed: if $\sigma * (\sigma \text{ irr}) \leq \sigma'$, then σ' is of the form $\sigma_1' * (\sigma_2' \text{ irr})$ with $\sigma \leq \sigma_1'$ and $\sigma \bowtie \sigma_2'$, which is equiconvertible to $\sigma_1' * (\sigma_1' \text{ irr})$ by irrelevance, an instance of $\beta * (\beta \text{ irr})$.

4.3   Context Zipping

The intuition to think about these different cases is to consider that, for any σ', we are looking for a way to construct a "witness" $\overline{\sigma}'$ such that $\tau[\overline{\sigma}'] = \sigma'$ from the hypothesis $\tau[\overline{\sigma}] \prec_v \sigma'$. When a type variable appears only once, its witness can be determined by inspecting the corresponding position in the type σ'. For example, in $\alpha * \beta \leq \text{bool} * \text{int}$, the mapping $\alpha \mapsto \text{bool}, \beta \mapsto \text{int}$ gives the witness pair bool, int.

However, when a variable appears twice, the two witnesses corresponding to the two occurrences may not coincide. (Consider for example $\beta * \beta \leq \text{bool} * \text{int}$.) If a variable β_i appears in several *invariant* occurrences, the witness of each occurrence is forced to be equal to the corresponding subterm of $\tau[\overline{\sigma}]$, that is σ_i, and therefore the various witnesses are themselves equal, hence compatible. On the contrary, for two covariant occurrences (as in the $\beta * \beta$ case), it is possible to pick a σ' such that the two witnesses are incompatible—and similarly for one covariant and one invariant occurrence. Finally, an irrelevant occurrence will never break closure properties, as all witnesses (forced by another occurrence) are compatible.

To express these merging properties, we define a *zip* operation $v_1 \curlywedge v_2$, that formally expresses which combinations of variances are possible for several occurrences of the same variable; it is a partial operation (for example, it is not defined in the covariant-covariant case, which breaks the closure properties) with the following table:

$v \curlywedge w$	$=$	$+$	$-$	$\bowtie$ w
$=$	$=$			$=$
$+$				$+$
$-$				$-$
$\bowtie$	$=$	$+$	$-$	$\bowtie$
v				

4.4   Syntactic Decomposability

Equipped with the zipping operation, we introduce a judgment $\Gamma \vdash \tau : v \Rightarrow v'$ to express decomposability, syntactically, defined by the inference rules on Figure 5. We also define its semantic interpretation $[\![\Gamma \vdash \tau : v \Rightarrow v']\!]$. The judgment and its interpretation were co-designed, so keeping the interpretation in mind is the best way to understand the subtleties of the inference rules. We use zipping, which requires correct variances, to merge sub-derivations into larger ones, so, in addition to decomposability, the interpretation also ensures that v is a correct

$$\frac{\text{SC-TRIV}}{v \geq v' \qquad \Gamma \vdash \tau : v}{\Gamma \vdash \tau : v \Rightarrow v'} \qquad \frac{\text{SC-VAR}}{w\alpha \in \Gamma \qquad w = v}{\Gamma \vdash \alpha : v \Rightarrow v'}$$

$$\frac{\text{SC-CONSTR}}{\Gamma \vdash \text{type } \overline{w\alpha}\ t : v\text{-closed} \qquad \Gamma = \lambda_i\, \Gamma_i \qquad \forall i,\ \Gamma_i \vdash \sigma_i : v.w_i \Rightarrow v'.w_i}{\Gamma \vdash \overline{\sigma}\, t : v \Rightarrow v'}$$

Fig. 5. Syntactic decomposablity

variance for τ under Γ. This subtlety is why we have two different properties for decomposability, $\Gamma \Vdash \tau : v \rightsquigarrow v'$ and $[\![\Gamma \vdash \tau : v \Rightarrow v']\!]$.

Definition 6 (Interpretation of syntactic decomposability)
We write $[\![\Gamma \vdash \tau : v \Rightarrow v']\!]$ for the conjunction of properties $[\![\Gamma \vdash \tau : v]\!]$ and $\Gamma \Vdash \tau : v \rightsquigarrow v'$.

To understand the inference rules, the first thing to notice is that the present rules are not completely syntax-directed: we first check whether $v \geq v'$ holds, and if not, we apply syntax-directed inference rules; existence of derivations is still easily decidable. If $v \geq v'$ holds, satisfying $\Gamma \Vdash \tau : v \rightsquigarrow v'$ (Definition 5) is trivial: $\tau[\overline{\sigma}] \prec_v \tau'$ implies $\tau[\overline{\sigma}] \prec_{v'} \tau'$, so taking $\overline{\sigma}$ for $\overline{\sigma}'$ is always a correct witness, which is represented by Rule SC-TRIV. The other rules then follow the same structure as the variance-checking judgment.

Rule SC-VAR is very similar to VC-VAR, except that the condition $w \geq v$ is replaced by a stronger equality $w = v$. This difference comes from the fact that the semantic condition for closure checking (Definition 2) includes both a variance check, which is monotonic in the context (Lemma 2) and the decomposability property, which is anti-monotonic (Lemma 4), so the present judgment must be invariant with respect to the context.

The most interesting rule is SC-CONSTR. It checks first that the head type constructor is v-closed (according to Definition 1); then, it checks that each subtype is decomposable from v to v', *with compatible witnesses*, that is, in an environment family $(\Gamma_i)_{i \in I}$ that can be zipped into a unique environment Γ.

Lemma 5 (Soundness of syntactic decomposability)
If the judgment $\Gamma \vdash \tau : v \Rightarrow v'$ holds, then $[\![\Gamma \vdash \tau : v \Rightarrow v']\!]$ holds.

Completeness is the general case is however much more difficult and we only prove it when the right-hand side variance v' is $(=)$. In other words, we take back the generality that we have introduced in §4.1 when defining decomposability.

Lemma 6 (Completeness of syntactic decomposability)
If $[\![\Gamma \vdash \tau : v \Rightarrow v']\!]$ holds for $v' \in \{=, \bowtie\}$, then $\Gamma \vdash \tau : v \Rightarrow v'$ is provable.

Lemma 6 is an essential piece to finally turn the semantic criterion REQ into a purely syntactic form.

Theorem 2 (Algorithmic criterion). *Given a variance annotation* $(v_i \alpha_i)_{i \in I}$ *and a constructor declaration of type* $(\exists \overline{\beta} \left[\bigwedge_{i \in I} \alpha_i = T_i[\overline{\beta}] \right] . \tau[\overline{\beta}])$, *the soundness criterion* REQ *for this constructor is equivalent to*

$$\exists \Gamma, (\Gamma_i)_{i \in I}, \quad \Gamma \vdash \tau : (+) \quad \wedge \quad \Gamma = \bigwedge_{i \in I} \Gamma_i \quad \wedge \quad \forall i \in I, \Gamma_i \vdash T_i : v_i \Rightarrow (=)$$

The three parts of this formula can be explained to a user, as soon as the underlying semantic phenomenons (variable interference through zipping, and upward- and downward-closure) have been understood—there is no way to get around that. They are best read from right to left. The last part on the $(T_i)_{i \in I}$ is the decomposability requirement that failed in our example with `< m : int >`: the type expressions equated with a covariant variable should be upward-closed, and those equated with a contravariant one downward-closed. The zipping part checks that the equations do not create interference through shared existential variables, as in `type (+α, =β) eq = Refl of` $\exists \gamma [\alpha = \gamma, \beta = \gamma]$. Finally, the variance check corresponds to the classic variance check on argument types of ADTs. One can verify that in presence of a simple ADT, this new criterion reduces to the simple syntactic criterion.

This presentation of the correctness criterion only relies on syntactic judgments. It is pragmatic in the sense that it suggests a simple and direct implementation, as a generalization of the check currently implemented in type system engines—which corresponds to the $\Gamma \vdash \tau : (+)$ part.

To compute the contexts Γ and $(\Gamma_i)_{i \in I}$ existentially quantified in this formula, one can use a variant of our syntactic judgments where the environment Γ is not an input, but an output of the judgment; in fact, one should return for each variable α the *set* of possible variances for this judgment to hold. For example, the query $(? \vdash \alpha * \beta \; \text{ref} : +)$ should return $(\alpha \mapsto \{+, =\}; \beta \mapsto \{=\})$. Defining those algorithmic variants of the judgments is routine. The sets of variances corresponding to the decomposability of the $(T_i)_{i \in I}$ $(? \vdash T_i : v_i \Rightarrow (=))$ should be zipped together and intersected with the possible variances for τ, returned by $(? \vdash \tau : +)$. The algorithmic criterion is satisfied if and only if the intersection is not empty; this can be decided in a simple and efficient way.

5 Discussion

5.1 Upward and Downward Closure in a ML Type System

In the type system we have used so far, all type constructors but p and q are both upward and downward-closed. This simple situation, however, does not hold in general: richer subtyping relations will have weaker invertibility properties. As soon as a bottom type $\perp$ is introduced, for example, such that that for all type σ we have $\perp \leq \sigma$, downward-closure fails for all types – but $\perp$ itself. For example, products are no longer downward-closed: $\Gamma \vdash \sigma * \tau \geq \perp$ does not implies that $\perp$ is equal to some $\sigma' * \tau'$. Conversely, if one adds a top type $\top$, bigger than all other types, then most type are not upward-closed anymore.

In OCaml, there is no $\bot$ or $\top$ type[8]. However, object types and polymorphic variants have subtyping, so they are, in general, neither upward nor downward-closed. Finally, subtyping is also used in private type definitions, which were demonstrated in the example. Our closure-checking relation therefore degenerates into the following, quite unsatisfying, picture:

- no type is downward-closed because of the existence of private types;
- no object type but the empty object type is upward-closed;
- no arrow type is upward-closed because its left-hand-side would need to be downward-closed;
- datatypes are upward-closed if their components types are.

From a pragmatic point of view, the situation is not so bad; as our main practical motivation for finer variance checks is the relaxed value restriction, we care about upward-closure (covariance) more than downward-closure (contravariance). This criterion tells us that covariant parameters can be instantiated with covariant datatypes defined from sum and product types (but no arrow), which would satisfy a reasonable set of use cases.

5.2 A Better Control on Upward and Downward-Closure

There is a subtle design question here. Decomposability is fundamentally a `negative` statement on the subtyping relation, guaranteeing that some types have no supertypes of a different structure. It is therefore not necessarily preserved by addition to the subtyping relation – our system, informally, is `non--monotone` in the subtyping relation.

This means that if we adopt the correctness criterion above, we must be careful in the future not to enrich the subtyping relation too much. Consider `private` types for example: one could imagine a symmetric concept of a type that would be strictly *above* a given type τ; we will name those types `invisible` types (they can be constructed, but not observed). Invisible types and GADT covariance seem to be working against each other: if the designer adds one, adding the other later will be difficult.

A solution to this tension is to allow the user to *locally* guarantee negative properties about subtyping (what is *not* a subtype), at the cost of selectively abandoning the corresponding flexibility. Just as object-oriented languages have `final` classes that cannot be extended any more, we would like to be able to define some types as `downward-closed` (respectively `upward-closed`), that cannot later be made `private` (resp. `invisible`). Such declarations would be rejected if the defining type, for example an object type, already has subtypes (resp. supertypes), and would forbid further declarations of types below (resp. above) the defined type, effectively guaranteeing downward (resp. upward) closure.

---

[8] A bottom type would be admissible, but a top type would be unsound in OCaml, as different types may have different runtime representations. Existential types, that may mix values of different types, are constructed explicitly through a boxing step.

Finally, upward or downward closure is a semantic aspect of a type that we must have the freedom to publish through an interface: abstract types could optionally be declared `upward-closed` or `downward-closed`.

5.3   Subtyping Constraints and Variance Assignment

We will now revisit our example of strongly typed expressions in the introduction. A simple way to get such a type to be covariant would be, instead of proving delicate, non-monotonic upward-closure properties on the tuple type involved in the equation $\alpha = \beta * \gamma$, to *change* this definition so that the resulting type is obviously covariant:

```
type +α exp =
  | Val of ∃β[α ≥ β].β
  | Int of [α ≥ int].int
  | Thunk of ∃βγ[α ≥ γ].β exp * (β → γ)
  | Prod of ∃βγ[α ≥ β * γ].β exp * γ exp
```

We have turned each equality constraint $\alpha = T[\overline{\beta}]$ into a subtyping constraint $\alpha \geq T[\overline{\beta}]$. For a type α' such that $\alpha \leq \alpha'$, we get by transitivity that $\alpha' \geq T[\overline{\beta}]$. This means that α exp trivially satisfies the correctness criterion REQ. Formally, instead of checking $\Gamma \vdash T_i : v_i \Rightarrow (=)$, we are now checking $\Gamma \vdash T_i : v_i \Rightarrow (+)$, which is significantly easier to satisfy: when v_i is itself $+$ we can directly apply the SC-TRIV rule. Note that this only works in the easy direction: while $\Gamma \vdash T_i : (+) \Rightarrow (+)$ is easy to check, $\Gamma \vdash T_i : (+) \Rightarrow (-)$ is just as hard as $\Gamma \vdash T_i : (+) \Rightarrow (=)$. In particular, an equality $(\sigma = \sigma')$ is already equivalent to a pair of inequalities $(\sigma \leq \sigma' \wedge \sigma \geq \sigma')$.

While this different datatype gives us a weaker subtyping assumption when pattern-matching, we are still able to write the classic function eval : α exp $\to \alpha$, because the constraints $\alpha \geq \tau$ are in the right direction to get an α as a result.

```
let rec eval : α exp → α = function
  | Val β (v : β) -> (v :> α)
  | Int (n : int) -> (n :> α)
  | Thunk β γ ((v : β exp), (f : β → γ)) ->
    (f (eval v) :> α)
  | Prod β γ ((b : β exp), (c : γ exp)) ->
    ((eval b, eval c) :> α)
```

This variation on GADTs, using subtyping instead of equality constraints, has been studied by Emir *et al* [EKRY06] in the context of the C♯ programming language—it is also expressible in Scala. However, using subtyping constraints in GADTs has important practical drawbacks in a ML-like language. While typed object-oriented programming languages tend to use explicit polymorphism and implicit subtyping, ML uses implicit polymorphism and explicit subtyping (when present). Thus in ML, equality constraints can be implicitly used while subtyping constraints must be explicitly used: unification-based inference favors bidirectional equality over unidirectional subtyping. This makes GADT definitions based on single subtyping constraints less convenient to use, because of the corresponding syntactic burden, and this is probably the reason why the notion of GADTs found in functional languages use only equality constraints. Subtyping constraints need also be explicit in the type declaration, forcing the user out of the convenient "generalized codomain type" syntax.

Finally, weakening equality constraints into a subtyping constraint in one direction is not always possible; sometimes the strictly weaker expressivity of the type forbids important uses. One must then use an equality constraint, and use our decomposability-based reasoning to justify the variance annotation. Consider the following example:

```
type +α tree =
  | Node of ∃β[α = β list]. (β tree) list
let append : α tree * α tree → α tree = function
  | Node β₁ (l1 : β₁ tree list), Node β₂ (l2 : β₂ tree list) ->
      Node (List.append l1 l2)
```

We know that the two arguments of `append` have the same type α `tree`. When matching on the `Node` constructors, we learn that α is equal to both β_1 `list` and β_2 `list`, from which we can deduce that β_1 is equal to β_2 by non-irrelevance of `list`. The concatenation of the lists `l1` and `l2` type-checks because this equality holds. If we used a type system without the decomposability criterion, we would need to turn the constructor constraint into $\exists\beta[\alpha \geq \beta$ `list`$]$ to preserve covariance of α `tree`. We wouldn't necessarily have β_1 and β_2 equal anymore, so (`List.append l1 l2`), hence the definition of `append` would not type-check. We would need decomposability-based reasoning to deduce, from $\alpha \geq \beta$ `list` and the fact that `list` is upward-closed, that in fact $\alpha = \beta'$ `list` for some β'.

This demonstrates that single subtyping constraints and our novel decomposability check on equality constraints are of incomparable expressivity: each setting handles programs that the other cannot type-check. From a theoretical standpoint, we think there is value in exploring the combination of both systems: using subtyping constraints rather than equalities, but also using decomposability to deduce stronger equalities when possible.

Note that while our soundness result directly transposes to a type-system with decomposability conditions on subtyping rather than equality constraints, our completeness result is special-cased on equality constraints. Completeness in the case of subtyping constraints is an open question.

6   Related Work

Simonet and Pottier [SP07] have studied GADTs in a general framework HMG(X), inspired by HM(X). They were interested in type inference using constraints, so considered GADTs with arbitrary constraints rather than type equalities, and considered the case of subtyping with applications to information flow security in mind. Their formulation of the checking problem for datatype declarations, as a constraint-solving problem, is exactly our semantic criterion and is not amenable to a direct implementation. Correspondingly, they did not encounter any of the new notions of upward and downward-closure and variable interference (zipping) discussed in the present work. They define a dynamic semantics and prove that this semantic criterion implies subject reduction and progress. However, we cannot directly reuse their soundness result as they work in a setting where all constructors are upward- and downward-closed (their subtyping relation is atomic). We believe this is only an artifact of their presentation and their proof should be easily extensible to our setting.

Emir, Kennedy, Russo and Yu [EKRY06] studied the soundness of an object-oriented calculus with subtyping constraints on classes and methods. Previous work [KR05] had established the correspondence between equality constraints on methods in an object-oriented style and GADT constraints on type constructors in functional style. Through this surprisingly non-obvious correspondence, their system matches our presentation of GADTs with subtyping constraints and easier variance assignment, detailed in §5.3. They provide several usage examples and a full soundness proof using a classic syntactic argument. However, they do not consider the more delicate notions of decomposability, and their system therefore cannot handle some of the examples presented here.

7   Future Work

Experiments with v-closure of type constructors as a new semantic property. In a language with non-atomic subtyping such as OCaml, we need to distinguish v-closed and non-v-closed type constructors. This is a new semantic property that, in particular, must be reflected through abstraction boundaries: we should be able to say about an abstract type that it is v-closed, or not say anything.

How inconvenient in practice is the need to expose those properties to have good variance for GADTs? Will the users be able to determine whether they want to enforce v-closure for a particular type they are defining?

Completeness of variance annotations with domain information. The way we present GADTs using equality constraints instead of the codomain syntax is well-known to practictioners, under the form of a "factoring" transformation where an arbitrary GADT is expressed as a simple ADT, using the equality GADT (α, β) eq as part of the constructor arguments to reify equality information.

This transformation does not work anymore with our current notion of GADTs in presence of subtyping. Indeed, all we can soundly say about the equality type (α, β) eq is that it must be invariant in both its parameters; using $(\alpha, T_i[\overline{\beta}])$ eq as part of a constructor type would force the paramter α to be invariant.

We think it would possible to re-enable factoring by eq by considering *domain information*, that is, information on constraints that must hold for the type to be inhabited. If we restricted the subtyping rule with conclusion $\overline{\sigma}\ t \leq \overline{\sigma}'\ t$ to only cases where $\overline{\sigma}\ t$ and $\overline{\sigma}'\ t$ are inhabited—with a separate rule to conclude subtyping in the non-inhabited case—we could have a finer variance check, as we would only need to show that the criterion SEQ holds between two instances of the inhabited domain, and not any instance. If we stated that the domain of the type (α, β) eq is restricted by the constraint $\alpha = \beta$, we could soundly declare the variance $(\bowtie\alpha, \bowtie\beta)$ eq on this domain—which no longer prevents from factoring out GADTs by equality types.

8 Conclusion

Checking the variance of GADTs is surprisingly more difficult (and interesting) than we initially thought. We have studied a novel criterion of upward and downward closure of type expressions and proposed a corresponding syntactic judgment that is easily implementable. We presented a core formal framework to prove both its correctness and its completeness with respect to a natural semantic criterion.

This closure criterion exposes important tensions in the design of a subtyping relation, for which we previously knew of no convincing example in the context of ML-derived programming languages. We have suggested new language features to help alleviate these tensions, whose convenience and practicality is yet to be assessed by real-world usage.

Considering extensions of GADTs in a rich type system is useful in practice; it is also an interesting and demanding test of one's type system design.

References

Abe06.   Abel, A.: Polarized subtyping for sized types. Mathematical Structures in Computer Science (2006); Goguen, H., Compagnoni, A. (eds.) Special issue on subtyping

EKRY06. Emir, B., Kennedy, A., Russo, C.V., Yu, D.: Variance and Generalized Constraints for C# Generics. In: Thomas, D. (ed.) ECOOP 2006. LNCS, vol. 4067, pp. 279–303. Springer, Heidelberg (2006)

Gar04.   Garrigue, J.: Relaxing the Value Restriction. In: Kameyama, Y., Stuckey, P.J. (eds.) FLOPS 2004. LNCS, vol. 2998, pp. 196–213. Springer, Heidelberg (2004)

KR05.   Kennedy, A., Russo, C.V.: Generalized algebraic data types and object-oriented programming. In: Proceedings of the 20th Annual ACM SIGPLAN Conference on Object-Oriented Programming, Systems, Languages, and Applications (2005), http://research.microsoft.com/pubs/64040/gadtoop.pdf

Pfe01.   Pfenning, F.: Intensionality, extensionality, and proof irrelevance in modal type theory. In: Proceedings of the 16th IEEE Symposium on Logic in Computer Science, LICS 2001, June 16-19, Boston University, USA (2001)

SP07.   Simonet, V., Pottier, F.: A constraint-based approach to guarded algebraic data types. ACM Transactions on Programming Languages and Systems 29(1) (January 2007)

SR.   Scherer, G., Rémy, D.: GADTs meet subtyping. Long version, available electronically, http://gallium.inria.fr/~remy/gadts/

A Data Driven Approach for Algebraic Loop Invariants*

Rahul Sharma[1], Saurabh Gupta[2], Bharath Hariharan[2],
Alex Aiken[1], Percy Liang[1], and Aditya V. Nori[3]

[1] Stanford University
{sharmar,aiken,pliang}@cs.stanford.edu
[2] University of California at Berkeley
{sgupta,bharath2}@eecs.berkeley.edu
[3] Microsoft Research India
adityan@microsoft.com

Abstract. We describe a GUESS-AND-CHECK algorithm for computing algebraic equation invariants of the form $\wedge_i f_i(x_1, \ldots, x_n) = 0$, where each f_i is a polynomial over the variables $x_1, \ldots, x_n$ of the program. The "guess" phase is data driven and derives a candidate invariant from data generated from concrete executions of the program. This candidate invariant is subsequently validated in a "check" phase by an off-the-shelf SMT solver. Iterating between the two phases leads to a sound algorithm. Moreover, we are able to prove a bound on the number of decision procedure queries which GUESS-AND-CHECK requires to obtain a sound invariant. We show how GUESS-AND-CHECK can be extended to generate arbitrary boolean combinations of linear equalities as invariants, which enables us to generate expressive invariants to be consumed by tools that cannot handle non-linear arithmetic. We have evaluated our technique on a number of benchmark programs from recent papers on invariant generation. Our results are encouraging – we are able to efficiently compute algebraic invariants in all cases, with only a few tests.

Keywords: Non-linear, loop invariants, SMT.

1 Introduction

The task of generating loop invariants lies at the heart of any program verification technique. A wide variety of techniques have been developed for generating linear invariants, including methods based on abstract interpretation [8,13] and constraint solving [7,11], among others.

Recently, researchers have also applied these techniques to the generation of non-linear loop invariants [23,17,21,22,18]. These techniques discover *algebraic invariants*, that is, invariants of the form

$$\wedge_i f_i(x_1, \ldots, x_n) = 0$$

---

* This work was supported by NSF grant CCF-0915766.

M. Felleisen and P. Gardner (Eds.): ESOP 2013, LNCS 7792, pp. 574–592, 2013.
© Springer-Verlag Berlin Heidelberg 2013

where each f_i is a polynomial defined over the variables $x_1, \ldots, x_n$ of the program. Note that algebraic invariants implicitly handle disjunctions: if $f_1 = 0 \vee f_2 = 0$ is an invariant then $f_1 = 0 \vee f_2 = 0 \Leftrightarrow f_1 f_2 = 0$. Thus, algebraic invariants are as expressive as arbitrary boolean combinations of algebraic equations.

Most previous techniques for algebraic loop invariants are based on Gröbner bases computations, which cause a considerable slowdown [4]. Therefore, there has been recent interest in techniques for generating algebraic invariants that do not use Gröbner bases [4,18] (see Section 7). In this paper, we address the problem of invariant generation from a data driven perspective. In particular, we use techniques from linear algebra to analyze data generated from executions of a program in order to efficiently "guess" a candidate invariant. This phase can leverage test suites of programs for data generation. This guessed invariant is subsequently checked for validity via a decision procedure. Our algorithm GUESS-AND-CHECK for generating algebraic invariants calls these guess and check phases iteratively until it finds the desired invariant. Failure to prove that a candidate is an invariant results in counterexamples or more data that are used to refine the guess in the next iteration. Furthermore, we are also able to prove a bound on the number of iterations of GUESS-AND-CHECK.

Our guess and check data driven approach for computing invariants has a number of advantages:

- Checking whether the candidate invariant is an invariant is done via a decision procedure. Our belief is that using a decision procedure to check the validity of a candidate invariant can be much more efficient than using it to infer an actual invariant.
- Since the guess phase operates over data, its complexity is largely independent of the complexity or size of the program (the amount of data depends on the number of variables in scope). This is in contrast to approaches based on static analysis, and therefore it is at least plausible that a data driven approach may work well even in situations that are difficult for static analysis. Moreover, the guess step just involves basic matrix manipulations, for which very efficient implementations exist.

There are major drawbacks, both theoretical and practical, with most previous techniques for algebraic invariants. First, these techniques either restrict predicates on branches to either equalities or dis-equalities [6,17], or cannot handle nested loops [15,22], or interpret program variables as real numbers [23,4,21]. It is well known that the semantics of a program assuming integer variables, in the presence of division and modulo operators, is not over-approximated by the semantics of the program assuming real variables. Therefore, these approaches may not produce correct invariants in cases where the program variables are actually integers. Our technique does not suffer from these drawbacks: our check phase can consume a rich syntax and answer queries over both integers and reals (see Section 4.2). Moreover, since these techniques can find algebraic invariants, they can find non-linear invariants representing boolean combinations of linear equalities. If a loop has the invariant $y = x \vee y = -x$ then these techniques can find the invariant $x^2 = y^2$ that is semantically equivalent to the linear invariant:

$$x = y \vee x = -y \Leftrightarrow (x + y)(x - y) = 0 \Leftrightarrow x^2 = y^2$$

But if the invariant is to be consumed by a verification tool that works over linear arithmetic (as most tools do), then $x^2 = y^2$ is not useful. A simple extension to our technique allows us to extract an equivalent (disjunctive) linear invariant from an algebraic invariant when such a linear invariant exists. This extension is possible as our technique is data driven (see Section 5.1).

It is also interesting to note that our algorithm is an iterative refinement procedure similar to the counterexample-guided abstraction refinement (CEGAR) [5] technique used in software model checking. In CEGAR, we start with an over-approximation of program behaviors and perform iterative refinement until we have either found a proof of correctness or a bug. GUESS-AND-CHECK is dual to CEGAR – we start with an under-approximation of program behaviors and add more behaviors until we are done. Most techniques for invariant discovery using CEGAR-like techniques have no termination guarantees. Since we focus on the language of polynomial equalities for invariants, we are able to give a termination guarantee for our technique.

Our main contribution is a new sound data driven algorithm for computing algebraic invariants. Specifically:

- We provide a data driven algorithm for generation of invariants restricted to conjunctions of algebraic equations. We observe that a known algorithm [18] is a suitable fit for our guess step. We formally prove that this algorithm computes an under-approximation of the algebraic loop invariant. That is, if G is the guess or candidate invariant, and I is an invariant then $G \Rightarrow I$. This guess will contain all algebraic equations constituting the invariants and possibly more spurious equations.
- We augment our guessing procedure with a decision procedure to obtain a sound algorithm. If the decision procedure successfully answers the queries made, then the output is an invariant and we do generate all valid invariants up to a given degree d. Moreover we are able to prove a bound on the number of decision procedure queries.
- Using the observation that a boolean combination of linear equalities with d disjunctions (in DNF form) is equivalent to an algebraic invariant of degree d [17,26], we describe an algorithm to generate an equivalent linear invariant from an algebraic invariant.
- We evaluate our technique on benchmark programs from various papers on generation of algebraic loop invariants and our results are encouraging—starting with a small amount of data, GUESS-AND-CHECK terminates on all benchmarks in one iteration, that is, our first guess is an actual invariant.

The remainder of the paper is organized as follows. Section 2 motivates and informally illustrates the GUESS-AND-CHECK algorithm over an example program. Section 3 introduces the background for the technical material in the paper. Section 4 presents the GUESS-AND-CHECK algorithm for algebraic invariants and also proves its correctness and termination. Section 5 describes some extensions: our technique for obtaining disjunctive linear invariants from algebraic invariants and a discussion about richer theories such as arrays. Section 6 evaluates our implementation of the GUESS-AND-CHECK algorithm on several benchmarks for algebraic loop invariants. Section 7 surveys related work and, finally, Section 8 concludes the paper.

2 Overview of the Technique

We will illustrate our technique over the example program shown in Figure 1. Our objective is to compute the loop invariant for the loop in this program. Informally, a loop invariant over-approximates the set of all possible program states that are possible at a loop head. This method can be generalized to obtain invariants at any program point. This program has a loop (lines 3 – 6) that is non-deterministic. In line 2 and 6, we have instrumentation code that writes the program state (the values of the variables x and y) to a log file. The loop invariant for this program is $I \equiv y + y^2 = 2x$. Since our approach is data driven, the starting point is to run the program with test inputs and accumulate the resulting data (in other words, the resulting program states) in a log. Assume that the program execution exercises the loop once. On such an execution, we obtain program states $x = y = 0$ and $x = y = 1$.

```
1:   assume(x=0 && y=0);
2:   writelog(x, y);
3:   while (nondet()) do
4:      y := y+1;
5:      x := x+y;
6:      writelog(x, y);
```

```
1:   if (x >= 0) then y := x
2:   else y := -x;
3:   writelog(x, y);
4:   while (y>=0 && nondet()) do
5:      if(x >= y) then
6:              y := y+1; x := x+1;
7:      else y := y+1; x := x-1;
8:      writelog(x, y);
```

Fig. 1. Example for algebraic invariants.   **Fig. 2.** Example for (disjunctive) linear invariants.

It turns out that for our technique to work, we need to assume an upper bound d on the degree of the polynomials that constitute the invariant. For this example, we assume that $d = 2$, which allows us to exhaustively enumerate all the monomials over the program variables up to the chosen degree. For our example, $\vec{\alpha} = \{1, x, y, y^2, x^2, xy\}$ is the set of all monomials over the variables x and y with degree less than or equal to 2. The number of monomials of degree d in n variables is large: $\binom{n+d-1}{d}$. Heuristics exist to discard the monomials that are unlikely to be a part of an invariant [24].

Using $\vec{\alpha}$ and the program states, we construct a *data matrix* A that is a 2×6 matrix with one row corresponding to each program state and six columns, one for each monomial in $\vec{\alpha}$. Every entry in j^{th} column of A represents the value of the jth monomial over the program execution. Therefore,

$$A = \begin{array}{|c|c|c|c|c|c|} \hline 1 & x & y & y^2 & x^2 & xy \\ \hline 1 & 0 & 0 & 0 & 0 & 0 \\ \hline 1 & 1 & 1 & 1 & 1 & 1 \\ \hline \end{array} \qquad (1)$$

As we will see in Section 4.1, we can employ the null space of A to compute a candidate invariant I as follows. If $\{b_1, b_2, \ldots, b_k\}$ is a basis for the null space of the data matrix A, then

$$I \equiv \bigwedge_{i=1}^{k} ([1, x, y, y^2, x^2, xy]b_i = 0) \qquad (2)$$

is a candidate invariant that is logically stronger than the strongest algebraic invariant. The null space of A is defined by four basis vectors, representing four algebraic equations:

$$I \equiv x = y \wedge x = y^2 \wedge x = x^2 \wedge x = xy \qquad (3)$$

Next, in the check phase, we check whether I as specified by Equation 3 is actually an invariant. Abstractly, if $L \equiv$ while B do S is a loop, then to check if I is a loop invariant, we need to establish the following conditions:

1. If φ is a precondition at the beginning of L, then $\varphi \Rightarrow I$.
2. Furthermore, executing the loop body S with a state satisfying $I \wedge B$, always results in a state satisfying the invariant I.

The above checks for validating I are performed by an off-the-shelf decision procedure [16]. For our example, we first check whether the precondition at the beginning of the loop implies I:

$$(x = 0 \wedge y = 0) \Rightarrow (x = y = x^2 = y^2 = xy)$$

This condition is indeed valid, and therefore we check whether I is inductive (we obtain the predicate representing the loop body via symbolic execution [14]):

$$((x = y = x^2 = y^2 = xy) \wedge y' = y + 1 \wedge x' = x + y') \Rightarrow (x' = y' = x'^2 = y'^2 = x'y')$$

This predicate is not valid, and we obtain a counterexample $x' = 3$, $y' = 2$ at line 3 of the program. Let us assume that we generate more program states by executing the loop for three iterations and starting with $x = 3$ and $y = 2$. As a result, we get a data matrix (that also includes the rows from the previous data matrix) as shown:

$$A = \begin{array}{|c|c|c|c|c|c|} \hline 1 & x & y & y^2 & x^2 & xy \\ \hline 1 & 0 & 0 & 0 & 0 & 0 \\ \hline 1 & 1 & 1 & 1 & 1 & 1 \\ \hline 1 & 3 & 2 & 4 & 9 & 8 \\ \hline 1 & 6 & 3 & 9 & 36 & 18 \\ \hline 1 & 10 & 4 & 16 & 100 & 40 \\ \hline \end{array} \qquad (4)$$

As with the earlier iteration, we require the basis of the null space of A and this is defined by the single vector: $[0, 2, -1, -1, 0, 0]$. Therefore, from Equation 2, it follows that the candidate invariant is $I \equiv 2x - y - y^2 = 0$.

Now, the conditions that must hold for I to be a loop invariant are:

1. $(x = 0 \land y = 0) \Rightarrow y + y^2 = 2x$, and
2. $(y + y^2 = 2x \land y' = y + 1 \land x' = x + y') \Rightarrow (y' + y'^2 = 2x')$

both of which are deemed to be valid by the check phase, and therefore $I \equiv y + y^2 = 2x$ is the desired loop invariant.

Following a similar approach, we can infer the algebraic invariant $x^2 = y^2$ for Figure 2. In Section 5.1, we show a data-driven procedure to generate equivalent linear invariants from algebraic invariants and use the same to infer the linear invariant $y = x \lor y = -x$ for Figure 2.

3   Preliminaries

We consider programs belonging to the following language of *while programs*:

$$S ::= x{:}{=}M \mid S; S \mid \text{if } B \text{ then } S \text{ else } S \mid \text{while } B \text{ do } S$$

where x is a variable over a countably infinite sort *loc* of memory locations, M is an expression, and B is a boolean expression. Expressions in this language are either of type `int` or `bool`.

A *monomial* α over the variables $\vec{x} = x_1, \ldots x_n$ is a term of the form $\alpha(\vec{x}) = x_1^{k_1} x_2^{k_2} \ldots x_n^{k_n}$. The *degree* of a monomial is $\sum_{i=1}^{n} k_i$. A *polynomial* $f(x_1, \ldots, x_n)$ defined over n variables $\vec{x} = x_1, \ldots, x_n$ is a weighted sum of monomials and has the following form.

$$f(\vec{x}) = \sum_k w_k x_1^{k_1} x_2^{k_2} \ldots x_n^{k_n} = \sum_k w_k \alpha_k \tag{5}$$

where $\alpha_k = x_1^{k_1} x_2^{k_2} \ldots x_n^{k_n}$ is a monomial. We are interested in polynomials over rationals, that is, $\forall k \; . \; w_k \in \mathbb{Q}$. The *degree* of a polynomial is the maximum degree over its constituent monomials: $max_k \{ degree(\alpha_k) \mid w_k \neq 0 \}$.

An *algebraic equation* is of the form $f(\vec{x}) = 0$, where f is a polynomial. Given a loop $L = \text{while } B \text{ do } S$ defined over variables $\vec{x} = x_1, \ldots, x_n$ together with a precondition φ, a *loop invariant* I is the strongest predicate such that $\varphi \Rightarrow I$ and $\{I \land B\}S\{I\}$. Any predicate I satisfying these two conditions is an invariant for L. If we do not impose the condition that we need the strongest invariant, then the trivial predicate $I = true$ is a valid invariant. In this section, we will focus on *algebraic invariants* for a loop. An algebraic invariant $\mathcal{I}$ is of the form $\wedge_i f_i(\vec{x}) = 0$, where each f_i is a polynomial over the variables $\vec{x}$ of the loop.

3.1   Matrix Algebra

This section reviews basic linear algebra. Readers familiar with matrix algebra may safely skip this section.

The *span* of a set of vectors $\{x_1, x_2, \ldots, x_n\}$, $x_i \in \mathbb{Q}^m$, is the set of all vectors that can be expressed as a linear combination of $\{x_1, x_2, \ldots, x_n\}$. Therefore,

$$span(\{x_1, x_2, \ldots, x_n\}) = \{v \mid v = \sum_{i=1}^{n} \alpha_i x_i, \alpha_i \in \mathbb{Q}\} \qquad (6)$$

For any $P = span(x_1, \ldots, x_n) \subseteq \mathbb{Q}^m$, if every vector $v \in P$ can be written as a linear combination of vectors from a linearly independent set $B = \{b_1, b_2, \ldots, b_k\}$, and B is minimal, then B forms a *basis* of P, and k is called the *dimension* of the set P.

The *range* of a matrix $A \in \mathbb{Q}^{m \times n}$ is the span of the columns of A. That is,

$$range(A) = \{v \in \mathbb{Q}^m \mid v = Ax, x \in \mathbb{Q}^n\} \qquad (7)$$

The dimension of $range(A)$ is called $rank(A)$. The *null space* of a matrix $A \in \mathbb{Q}^{m \times n}$ is the set of all vectors that equal to 0 when multiplied by A. More precisely,

$$NullSpace(A) = \{x \in \mathbb{Q}^n \mid Ax = 0\} \qquad (8)$$

The dimension of $NullSpace(A)$ is called its *nullity*. For instance, the matrix

$$A = \begin{bmatrix} 1 & 2 & -3 \\ 3 & 5 & 9 \\ 5 & 9 & 3 \end{bmatrix} \text{ has a null space spanned by } \left\{ \begin{bmatrix} -33 \\ 18 \\ 1 \end{bmatrix} \right\} \text{ with } nullity(A) = 1.$$

A basis for the null space of a $m \times n$ matrix can be computed in time $O(m^2 n)$. A *subspace* of $\mathbb{Q}^n$, spanned by a basis B, are the vectors x that satisfy $Ax = 0$, where A is a basis for the null space of B. From the fundamental theorem of linear algebra, for any matrix $A \in \mathbb{Q}^{m \times n}$, we know

$$rank(A) + nullity(A) = n \qquad (9)$$

4   The Guess-and-Check Algorithm

The GUESS-AND-CHECK algorithm is described in Figure 3. The algorithm takes as input a while program L, a precondition φ on the inputs to L, and an upper bound d on the degree of the desired invariant, and returns an algebraic loop invariant $\mathcal{I}$. If $L = \texttt{while } B \texttt{ do } S$, then recall that $\mathcal{I}$ is the strongest predicate such that

$$\varphi \Rightarrow \mathcal{I} \text{ and } \{\mathcal{I} \wedge B\}S\{\mathcal{I}\} \qquad (10)$$

As the name suggests, GUESS-AND-CHECK consists of two phases.

1. *Guess phase* : this phase processes the data in the form of concrete program states at the loop head to compute a data matrix, and uses linear algebra techniques to compute a candidate invariant.

GUESS-AND-CHECK(L,φ,d)
Returns: A loop invariant $\mathcal{I}$ for L.

1: $\vec{x} := vars(L)$
2: $Tests := TestGen(\varphi, L)$
3: $logfile := \langle\rangle$
4: **for** $\vec{t} \in Tests$ **do**
5:    $logfile := logfile :: Execute(L, \vec{x} = \vec{t})$
6: **end for**
7: **repeat**
8:    $\mathcal{I} := Guess(logfile, d)$
9:    $(done, \vec{t}) := Check(\mathcal{I}, L, \varphi)$
10:    **if** $\neg done$ **then**
11:       $logfile := logfile :: t$
12:    **end if**
13: **until** $done$
14: **return** $\mathcal{I}$

$Guess(logfile, d)$
Returns: A candidate invariant

1: **if** $logfile = \langle\rangle$ **then**
2:    **return** $false$
3: **end if**
4: $A := DataMatrix(logfile, d)$
5: $\mathcal{B} := Basis(NullSpace(A))$
6: **if** $\mathcal{B} = \emptyset$ **then**
7:    // No non-trivial invariant
8:    **return** $true$
9: **end if**
10: **return** $CandidateInvariant(\mathcal{B})$

Fig. 3. GUESS-AND-CHECK computes an algebraic invariant of degree d for an input while program L with a precondition φ

2. *Check phase* (line 9): this phase uses an off-the-shelf decision procedure for checking if the candidate invariant computed in the guess phase is indeed a true invariant (using the conditions in Equation 10) [16].

The GUESS-AND-CHECK algorithm works as follows. In line 1, $\vec{x}$ represents the input variables of the while program L. The procedure *TestGen* is any test generation technique that generates a set of test inputs *Tests* that satisfy the precondition φ. Alternatively, our technique could also employ an existing test suite for *Tests*. The variable *logfile* maintains a sequence of concrete program states at the loop head of L. Line 3 initializes *logfile* to the empty sequence. Lines 4–13 perform the main computation of the algorithm. First, the program L is executed over every test $\vec{t} \in Tests$ via the call to *Execute* in line 5. *Execute* runs a loop till termination (or for a timeout to avoid non-terminating executions) on a test input and generates a sequence of states at the loop head. E.g., *Execute*(`while`($x! = 0$) `do` $x--, x = 2$) will generate states $\{x = 2, x = 1, x = 0\}$ for the data matrix. Note that this sequence also include the states that violate the loop guard. The call to *Guess* (line 8) constructs a matrix A with one row for every program state in *logfile* and one column for every monomial from the set of all monomials over $\vec{x}$ whose degree is bounded above by d (as informally illustrated in Section 2). The $(i, j)^{th}$ entry of A is the value of the jth monomial evaluated over the program state represented by the ith row.

Next, using off-the-shelf linear algebra solvers, we compute the basis for the null space of A. If $\mathcal{B}$ is empty, then this means that there is no algebraic equation, of given degree d, that the data satisfies and we return *true*. Otherwise, the candidate invariant represented by $\mathcal{B}$ is given to the checking procedure *Check* in

line 9. The procedure *Check* uses off-the-shelf SMT solvers [16] to check whether
the candidate invariant $\mathcal{I}$ satisfies the conditions in Equation 10. If so, then $\mathcal{I}$
is an invariant and the procedure terminates by returning $\mathcal{I}$. Otherwise, *Check*
returns a counter-example in the form of a test input $\vec{t}$ that explains why $\mathcal{I}$ is not
an invariant – the computation is repeated with this new test input $\vec{t}$, and the
process continues until we have found an invariant. Note that, as in Section 2, we
can also add the states generated by $Execute(L, \vec{x} = \vec{t})$ to *logfile* (instead of just
adding $\vec{t}$). In either case, the size of *logfile* strictly increases in every iteration.

In summary, the guess and check phases of GUESS-AND-CHECK operate iteratively, and in each iteration if the actual invariant cannot be derived, then the
algorithm automatically figures out the reason for this and corrective measures
are taken in the form of generating more test inputs (this corresponds to the case
where the data generated is insufficient for guessing a sound invariant). In the
next section, we will formally show the correctness of the GUESS-AND-CHECK
algorithm – we prove that it is a sound and we bound the number of iterations
of GUESS-AND-CHECK (the loop consisting of lines 7 to 13 of Figure 3).

4.1   Connections between Null Spaces and Invariants

In the previous section, we have seen how GUESS-AND-CHECK computes an
algebraic invariant over monomials $\vec{\alpha}$ that consist of all monomials over the
variables of the input while program with degree bounded above by d. The
starting point for proving correctness of GUESS-AND-CHECK is the data matrix
A as computed in line 1 of *Guess* procedure of Figure 3.

An invariant $\mathcal{I} \equiv \wedge_i^k (w_i^T \vec{\alpha} = 0)$ has the property that for each w_i, $1 \leq i \leq k$,
$w_i^T a_j = 0$ for each row $a_j \in \mathbb{Q}^n$ of A – in other words, $Aw_i = 0$. This shows that
each w_i is a vector in the null space of the data matrix A. Conversely, any vector
in $NullSpace(A)$ is a reasonable candidate for being a part of an invariant.

We make the observation that a candidate invariant will be a true invariant if
the dimension of the space spanned by the set $\{w_i\}_{1 \leq i \leq k}$ equals $nullity(A)$. We
will assume, without loss of generality, that $\{w_i\}_{1 \leq i \leq k}$ is a linearly independent
set. Then, by definition, the dimension of the space spanned by $\{w_i\}_{1 \leq i \leq k}$ is k.

Consider an n-dimensional space where each axis corresponds to a monomial
of $\vec{\alpha}$. Then the rows of the matrix A are points in this n-dimensional space. Now
assume that $w^T \vec{\alpha} = 0$ is an invariant, that is, $k = 1$. This means that all rows a_j
of A satisfy $w^T a_j = 0$. In particular, the points corresponding to the rows of A
lie on an $n-1$ dimensional subspace defined by $w^T \vec{\alpha} = 0$. If the data or program
states generated by the test inputs *Tests* (line 2 in Figure 3) is insufficient, then A
might not have rows spanning the $n-1$ dimensions. Therefore, from Equation 9,
we have $n - rank(A) = nullity(A) \geq 1$ if the invariant is a single algebraic
equation. Generalizing this, we can say that $nullity(A)$ is an upper bound on
the number of algebraic equations in the invariant. The following lemma and
theorem formalize this intuition.

Lemma 1 (Invariant is in null space). *If $\wedge_i^k w_i^T \vec{\alpha} = 0$ is an invariant, and
A is the data matrix, then all w_i lie in $NullSpace(A)$.*

Proof. This follows from the fact that for every w_i, $1 \leq i \leq k$, $Aw_i = 0$.

Therefore, the null space of the data matrix A gives us the subspace in which the invariants lie. In particular, if we arrange the vectors that form the basis for *NullSpace*(A) as columns in a matrix V, then *range*(V) defines the space of candidate invariants.

Theorem 1. *If $\wedge_{i=1}^{k} w_i^T \vec{\alpha} = 0$ is an invariant with the set $\{w_1, w_2, \ldots, w_k\}$ forming a linearly independent set, A is the data matrix and nullity$(A) = k$, then any basis for NullSpace(A) forms an invariant.*

Proof. Let $B = [v_1 \cdots v_k]$ be a matrix with each v_i, $1 \leq i \leq k$ being a column vector, and with *span*$(\{v_1, \ldots, v_k\})$ equal to *NullSpace*(A). That is, $\{v_1, \ldots, v_k\}$ is a basis for *NullSpace*(A). From Lemma 1, we know that every w_i, $1 \leq i \leq k$, lies in *span*$(\{v_1, \ldots, v_k\})$. This means that every w_i, $1 \leq i \leq k$, can be written as $w_i = Bu_i$ for some vector $u_i \in \mathbb{Q}^k$. Therefore, if $B^T \vec{\alpha} = 0$ then $u_i^T B^T \vec{\alpha} = 0$, which implies that $w_i^T \vec{\alpha} = 0$, $1 \leq i \leq k$.

Observe that $\{w_1, w_2, \ldots, w_k\}$ form a basis for *NullSpace*(A), and therefore every v_j, $1 \leq j \leq k$, can be written as a linear combination of vectors from $\{w_1, w_2, \ldots, w_k\}$. From this, it follows that $\wedge_{i=1}^{k} w_i^T \vec{\alpha} = 0 \implies v_j^T \vec{\alpha} = 0$ for all $1 \leq j \leq k$. Thus, $\wedge_{i=1}^{k} w_i^T \vec{\alpha} = 0 \Leftrightarrow \wedge_{j=1}^{k} v_j^T \vec{\alpha} = 0$.

Theorem 1 precisely defines the implementation of the "guess" step. Furthermore, Theorem 1 also states that we need to have enough data represented by the data matrix A so that *nullity*(A) equals k, the dimension of the space spanned by $\{w_i\}_{1 \leq i \leq k}$. If this is indeed the case, then $\mathcal{I} \equiv \wedge_{j=1}^{k} v_j^T \vec{\alpha} = 0$ will be an invariant. On the other hand, if the data is not enough, then Lemma 1 guarantees that the candidate invariant $\mathcal{I}$ is a sound under-approximation of the loop invariant. If the null space is zero-dimensional, then only the trivial invariant *true* constitutes an invariant over conjunction of polynomial equations that has degree less than or equal to d.

The question of how much data must be generated in order to attain *nullity*$(A) = k$ is an empirical one. In our experiments, we were able to generate invariants using a relatively small data matrix for various benchmarks from the literature.

4.2   Check Candidate Invariants

Computing the null space of the data matrix provides us a way for proposing candidate invariants. The candidates are complete; they do not miss any algebraic equations. But they might be unsound. They might contain spurious equations. To obtain soundness, we will use a decision procedure analogous to the technique proposed in [25].

Theorem 2 (Soundness). *If the algorithm* GUESS-AND-CHECK *terminates and the underlying decision procedure for checking candidate invariants (Check) is sound, then it returns an invariant.*

Next, we prove that the algorithm GUESS-AND-CHECK terminates.

Theorem 3 (Termination). *If the underlying decision procedure Check is sound and complete, then the algorithm* GUESS-AND-CHECK *will terminate after at most n iterations, where n is the total number of monomials whose degree is bounded by d.*

Proof. Let $A \in \mathbb{Q}^{m \times n}$ be the data matrix computed in line 4 in the *Guess* procedure of Figure 3. If the candidate invariant $\mathcal{I}$ computed in line 8 of GUESS-AND-CHECK is an invariant (that is, *done = true*), then GUESS-AND-CHECK terminates.

Therefore, let us assume that $\mathcal{I}$ is not an invariant, and let $\vec{t}$ be the test or counterexample that violates the candidate invariant as computed in line 9 of the algorithm. As a result, GUESS-AND-CHECK adds $\vec{t}$ to A – call the resulting matrix $\hat{A}$. By construction, we also know that $\vec{t} \notin range(A^T)$. Therefore, it follows that $rank(\hat{A}) = rank(A) + 1$. More generally, adding a counter-example to the data matrix A necessarily increases its rank by 1. From Equation 9, we know that the rank of A is bounded above by n, which implies that GUESS-AND-CHECK will terminate in at most n iterations.

Note that since we are concerned with integer manipulating programs, a sound and complete decision procedure for *Check* cannot exist: the queries are in Peano arithmetic which is undecidable. However, for our experiments, we found that the Z3 [16] SMT solver sufficed (see Section 6). Z3 has limited support for non-linear integer arithmetic: It combines extensions on top of simplex and reduction to SAT (after bounding) for these queries. One might try to achieve completeness for GUESS-AND-CHECK by giving up soundness. Just as [23,4,21], if we interpret program variables as real numbers then Z3 does have a sound and complete decision procedure for non-linear real arithmetic [12] that has been demonstrated to be practical. Since Z3 supports both non-linear integer and real arithmetic, we can easily combine or switch between the two, if desired (see Section 6).

4.3   Nested Loops

GUESS-AND-CHECK easily extends to nested loops, while maintaining soundness and termination properties. Given a program with M loops, we construct data matrices for each loop. Let the number of columns of the data matrix of ith loop be denoted by n_i. We run tests and generate candidate invariants $\vec{I}$ at all loop heads. Next, the candidate invariants are checked simultaneously. For checking the candidate invariant of an outer loop, the inner loop is replaced by its candidate invariant and a constraint is generated. For checking the inner loop, the candidate invariant of the outer loop is used to compute a pre-condition. If a counter-example is obtained then it generates more data and invariant computation is repeated. We continue these guess and check iterations until the check phase passes for all the loops; thus, on termination the output consists of sound invariants for all loops. Also, the initial candidate invariants $\vec{I}$ are under-approximations of the actual invariants by Lemma 1, a property that is maintained throughout the procedure and allows us to conclude that when the procedure terminates the output invariants are the strongest possible over algebraic equations. To prove termination, note that each failed decision procedure query increases the rank of some data matrix for some loop, which implies that the number of decision procedure queries which can fail is bounded by $\sum_{i=1}^{M} n_i$. Hence, if $N = max \; n_i$ then the total number of decision procedure queries is bounded by $M^2 N$.

5   Extensions

In this section we discuss two extensions of our technique. We first discuss how algebraic invariants can be converted to equivalent linear invariants. Then we discuss how our approach can be extended to compute invariants over more expressive theories, such as the theory of arrays.

5.1   From Algebraic to Linear Invariants

Conventional invariant generation techniques for linear equalities [13] do not handle disjunctions. Using disjunctive completion to obtain disjunctions of equalities entails a careful design of the widening operator. Techniques for generation of non-linear invariants can generate algebraic invariants that are equivalent to a boolean combination of linear equalities. But if these invariants are to be consumed by a tool that understands only linear arithmetic, it is important to obtain the original linear invariant from the algebraic invariant. For example, verification engines like [10] are based on linear arithmetic and cannot use non-linear predicates for predicate abstraction. It is not obvious how this step can be performed since the discovered polynomials might not factor into linear factors.

Since our approach is data driven, we can solve this problem using standard machine learning techniques. Here is another perspective on converting algebraic to linear invariants. Assume that the algebraic invariant is equivalent to a boolean combination of linear equalities. Express this linear invariant in DNF form. For instance, for the program in Figure 2, we have the DNF formula $y = -x \lor y = x$. The rows of the data matrix A are satisfying assignments of this DNF formula. Hence, each row satisfies some disjunct: each row of A satisfies $y = -x$ or $y = x$. If we create partitions of our data such that the states in each partition satisfy the same disjunct, then all the states of a single partition will lie on a subspace: they will satisfy some conjunction of linear equalities. The aim is to find the subspaces in which the states lie. Since a subspace represents a conjunction of linear equalities, a disjunction of all such subspaces can represent an invariant that is a boolean combination of linear equalities.

The problem of obtaining boolean combinations of linear equalities that a given data matrix satisfies is called subspace segmentation in the machine learning community. This problem arises in applications such as face clustering, video segmentation, motion segmentation, and several algorithms have been proposed over the years. In this section we will apply the algorithm of Vidal, Ma, and

Sastry [26] to obtain linear invariants from algebraic invariants. The main insight is that the derivative of the polynomials constituting the algebraic invariant evaluated at a program state characterizes the subspace in which the state lies.

The derivative of the polynomial corresponding to the algebraic invariant for Figure 2, that is, $x^2 - y^2$ is $[2x, -2y]$: the first entry is partial derivative w.r.t. x and the second entry is the partial derivative w.r.t. y. Running the program with test input $x \in \{-1, 1\}$ for say 4 iterations each will results in a data matrix A with 10 rows. The first and last rows are shown:

$$A = \begin{array}{|c|c|c|c|c|c|} \hline 1 & x & y & y^2 & x^2 & xy \\ \hline 1 & -1 & 1 & 1 & 1 & -1 \\ \hline 1 & 5 & 5 & 25 & 25 & 25 \\ \hline \end{array} \tag{11}$$

Evaluating the derivative at first state of A gives us $[-2, -2]$. This shows that the first state belongs to $-2x - 2y = 0$ i.e. $x = -y$. Evaluating at the last state gives us $[10, -10]$, which shows that the last state belongs to $10x - 10y = 0$ or $x = y$. The other 8 states of A (not shown in Equation 11) also belong to $x = y$ or $x = -y$ and we return the disjunction of these two predicates as the candidate invariant. The relationship between the boolean structure of a linear invariant and its equivalent algebraic invariant can be described as follows: the number of conjunctions in the linear invariant (in CNF form) corresponds to the number of conjunctions in the algebraic invariant, and the number of disjunctions in the linear invariant (in DNF form) corresponds to the degree of the algebraic invariant.

Now we explain why this approach works. We sketch the proof from [26] for the case when there is a single algebraic equation $f(\vec{x}) = 0$, that is, the invariant is a disjunction of linear equalities. The case of multiple algebraic equations is similar. Say the invariant is $\vee_i w_i^T \vec{x} = 0 \Leftrightarrow \left(\prod_i w_i^T \vec{x}\right) = 0 \equiv f(\vec{x}) = 0$. The derivative of $f(\vec{x})$, denoted by $\nabla f(\vec{x})$, is a vector of $|\vec{x}|$ elements where the lth element of the vector is a partial derivative with respect to the lth variable:

$$(\nabla f(\vec{x}))_l = \frac{\partial f(\vec{x})}{\partial x_l}.$$

Now using,

$$\nabla (f(\vec{x})g(\vec{x})) = (\nabla f(\vec{x})) \, g(\vec{x}) + f(\vec{x}) \, (\nabla g(\vec{x}))$$

and

$$\nabla w^T \vec{x} = \left[\frac{\partial w_1 x_1}{\partial x_1}, \dots, \frac{\partial w_n x_n}{\partial x_n} \right]^T = w \text{ where } |\vec{x}| = n$$

we obtain:

$$\nabla f(\vec{x}) = \nabla \left(\prod_i w_i^T \vec{x} \right) = \sum_i w_i \prod_{j \neq i} (w_j^T \vec{x})$$

Say a program state a satisfies $w_k^T a = 0$. Then $(\nabla f)(a)$ is a scalar multiple of w_k because $\prod_{j \neq i} w_j^T a = 0$ for $i \neq k$. Hence evaluating the derivative at a program state provides the subspace in which the state lies. For more details see [26].

Next we remove from A the states that lie in the same subspace. Next, if A still contains a program state then we can repeat by finding the derivative at that state. In the end we get a collection of subspaces that contain every state of the original data-matrix. A union of these subspaces gives us a boolean combination of linear equalities.

Theorem 4. *Given an algebraic invariant $\mathcal{I} = NullSpace(A)$ equivalent to a linear invariant, the procedure of [26] finds a linear invariant equivalent to $\mathcal{I}$.*

Note that this conversion is unsound if no equivalent linear invariant exists. Hence the linear predicate should be checked for equivalence with the algebraic invariant; this check can be performed using a decision procedure. Note that we are able to easily incorporate the technique of [26] with GUESS-AND-CHECK as our technique is data driven. Also, this conversion just requires differentiating polynomials symbolically, that can be performed linearly in the size of the invariant, and evaluating the derivative at all points in the data matrix. The latter operation is just a matrix multiplication. Hence this algorithm is quite efficient.

5.2   Richer Theories

An interesting question is whether the algorithm GUESS-AND-CHECK generalizes to richer theories beyond polynomial arithmetic. It is indeed possible and requires careful design of the representation of data. For instance, if we want to infer invariants in the theory of linear arithmetic and arrays, we can have an additional column in the data matrix for values obtained from arrays. Similarly, we can have a variable that stores the value returned from an uninterpreted function and assign it a column in the data matrix. Hence it is possible to use our technique to infer conjunctions of equalities in richer theories too if we know the constituents of the invariants, analogous to invariant generation techniques based on templates.

In order to illustrate how the GUESS-AND-CHECK technique would work for programs with arrays, consider the example program shown in Figure 4. We want to prove that the assertion in line 6 holds for all inputs to the program. Assume that we log the values of $a[i]$ and i after every iteration and that the degree bound is $d = 1$. The data matrix that GUESS-AND-CHECK constructs has three columns and let us assume that we run a single test with input $n = 1$ resulting in rows corresponding to program states induced by this input at the loop head. The data matrix A is shown in Figure 5. The null space of A is defined by the basis vector $B = [0, 1, -1]^T$, and therefore we obtain the invariant $a[i] = i$ that is sufficient to prove that the assertion holds.

Our approach of using a dynamic analysis technique to generate data in the form of concrete program states and augmenting it with a decision procedure to obtain a sound technique is a general one. Similar ideas have been used for computing interpolants [25]. We can also take the method for discovering array invariants or polynomial inequalities of [18] and extend it to a sound procedure in a similar fashion.

```
1:   (i,a[0]) = (0,0);
2:   assume (n > 0);
3:   while (i != n) do
4:      i := i+1;
5:      a[i] := a[i-1]+1;
6:   done
7:   assert(a[n] == n);
```

Fig. 4. Example with arrays

$$A = \begin{array}{|c|c|c|} \hline 1 & i & a[i] \\ \hline 1 & 0 & 0 \\ \hline 1 & 1 & 1 \\ \hline \end{array}$$

Fig. 5. Data for n=1

Table 1. Name is the name of the benchmark; #vars is the number of variables in the benchmark; deg is the user specified maximum possible degree of the discovered invariant; Data is the number of times the loop under consideration is executed over all tests; #and is the number of algebraic equalities in the discovered invariant; Guess is the time taken by the guess phase of GUESS-AND-CHECK in seconds. Check is the time in seconds taken by the check phase of GUESS-AND-CHECK to verify that the candidate invariant is actually an invariant. The last column represents the total time.

Name	#vars	deg	Data	#and	Guess (s)	Check (s)	Total (s)
Mul2 [23]	4	2	75	1	0.0007	0.010	0.0107
LCM/GCD [23]	6	2	329	1	0.004	0.012	0.016
Div [23]	6	2	343	3	0.454	0.134	0.588
Bezout [21]	8	2	362	5	0.765	0.149	0.914
Factor [21]	5	3	100	1	0.002	0.010	0.012
Prod [22]	5	2	84	1	0.0007	0.011	0.0117
Petter [22]	2	6	10	1	0.0003	0.012	0.0123
Dijkstra [22]	6	2	362	1	0.003	0.015	0.018
Cubes [20].	4	3	31	10	0.014	0.062	0.076
geoReihe1 [20]	3	2	25	1	0.0003	0.010	0.0103
geoReihe2 [20]	3	2	25	1	0.0004	0.017	0.0174
geoReihe3 [20]	4	3	125	1	0.001	0.010	0.011
potSumm1 [20]	2	1	10	1	0.0002	0.011	0.0112
potSumm2 [20]	2	2	10	1	0.0002	0.009	0.0092
potSumm3 [20]	2	3	10	1	0.0002	0.012	0.0122
potSumm4 [20]	2	4	10	1	0.0002	0.010	0.0102

6   Experimental Evaluation

We evaluate the GUESS-AND-CHECK algorithm on a number of benchmarks from the literature. All experiments were performed on a 2.5GHz Intel i5 processor system with 4 GB RAM running Ubuntu 10.04 LTS.

Benchmarks. The benchmarks over which we evaluated the GUESS-AND-CHECK algorithm are from a number of recent research papers on inferring algebraic invariants [21,22,23]. These are shown in the first column of Table 1. These programs were implemented in C for data generation.

Evaluation. We now describe our implementation and our experimental results of Table 1. For a detailed description of the implementation please see [24]. The second column of Table 1 shows the number of variables in each benchmark program. The third column shows the given upper bound for the degree of the polynomials in the inferred invariant.

The fourth column shows the number of rows of the data matrix. The data or tests are generated naively; each input variable is allowed to take values from 1 to N where N is between 5 and 20 for the experiments. Hence if there are two input variables we have N^2 tests. These tests are executed till termination to generate data. While it is possible to generate tests more intelligently, using inputs from a very small bounding box demonstrates the generality of our technique by not tying it to any symbolic execution engine. Note that including all the states reaching the loop head, over all tests, can include redundant states that do not affect the output. Since the algorithms for null space computation are quite efficient, we do not attempt to identify and remove redundant states. If needed, heuristics like considering a random subset of the states [18] can be employed to keep the size of data matrices small. The fifth column shows the number of algebraic equations in the discovered loop invariant. For most of the programs, a single algebraic equation was sufficient. The null space and the basis computations were performed using off-the-shelf linear algebra algorithms in MATLAB. GUESS-AND-CHECK finds invariants equivalent to those reported in the earlier papers [20,21,22,23]. The time (in seconds) taken by the guess phase of GUESS-AND-CHECK is reported in the sixth column of Table 1.

We use Z3 [16] for checking that the proposed invariants are actually invariants (implementation of *Check* procedure in the GUESS-AND-CHECK algorithm). Theorem prover Z3 was able to easily handle the simple queries made by GUESS-AND-CHECK, because once an invariant has been obtained, the constraint encoding that the invariant is inductive is quite a simple constraint to solve and our naively generated tests were sufficient to generate an actual invariant. For all programs, except Div, we declare the variables as integers. So even though these queries are in Peano arithmetic, and can contain integer division and modulo operators, the decision procedure is able to discharge them. For Div the invariant that [23] finds is inductive only if the variables are over reals. When we execute GUESS-AND-CHECK on Div, where the queries are in Peano arithmetic, we obtain the trivial invariant *true* after three guess-and-check iterations. Next, we lift the variables to reals when querying Z3. Now, we discover the invariant found by [23] in one guess-and-check iteration and this is the result shown in Table 1. By the soundness of our approach, we conclude that an approach producing a non-trivial algebraic invariant for this benchmark can be unsound for integer manipulating programs containing division or modulo operators.

Finally, the time taken by GUESS-AND-CHECK on these benchmarks is comparable to the state-of-the-art correct-by-construction invariant generation techniques [4]. Since these benchmarks are small and the time taken by both our technique and [4] is less than a second on these programs, a comparison of run times may not be indicative of performance of either approach on larger loops.

For these benchmarks, our algorithm is significantly faster than any algorithm using Gröbner bases. For instance, on the benchmark `factor`, [22] takes 55.4 seconds, while [21] takes 2.61 seconds. We discover the same invariant in 0.012 seconds. However, the exact timings must be taken with a grain of salt (we are running on a newer generation of hardware). See Section 7 for a more detailed comparison with the previous work. We leave the collection of a hard benchmark suite for algebraic invariant generation tools as future work.

7 Related Work

We now place the GUESS-AND-CHECK algorithm in the context of existing work on discovering algebraic loop invariants. Major benefits of our data driven approach include finding sound invariants for integer manipulating programs, consuming a rich syntax (depends only on the decision procedure), and extracting linear invariants from algebraic invariants in time linear in the data, that increases the applicability of our algorithm. Sankaranarayanan et al. [23] describe a constraint based technique that uses user-defined templates for computing algebraic invariants. Their objective is to find an instantiation of these templates that satisfies the constraints and results in an invariant. The constraints they use contain quantifiers and therefore the cost of solving them is quite high.

Abstract interpretation based techniques either ignore [15,22] or restrict conditions on branches to equalities or dis-equalities [17,6,21,4]. The techniques of [6,21,22,15] use Gröbner bases computations and [17] has no upper complexity bound. Cachera et al. [4] provide an algorithm that does not use Gröbner bases but interprets variables as taking values over the real numbers. In contrast, we handle programs with division and modulo operations soundly. Bagnara et al. [3] introduce new variables for monomials and generate linear invariants over them by abstract interpretation. Amato et al. [2] analyze data from program executions to tune their abstract interpretation.

Nguyen et al. [18] have proposed a dynamic analysis for inference of candidate invariants. They do not provide any formal characterization of the output of their algorithm and do not prove any soundness and completeness theorems. The Daikon tool [9] generates likely invariants from tests and templates. Our approach is similar in that it is also based on analyzing data from tests. Daikon does not provide any formal guarantees such as soundness and completeness over the invariants it generates. In the context of Daikon, it is interesting to note from [19] that very few test cases suffice for invariant generation. Indeed, this has been our experience with GUESS-AND-CHECK as well.

8 Conclusion

We have presented a sound data driven algorithm for discovering algebraic equation invariants. We use linear algebra techniques to guess an invariant from the data generated from program runs, and use decision procedures for non-linear arithmetic to validate these candidate invariants.

We are able to formally prove that the guessed invariant under-approximates the actual invariant, as well as bound the number of iterations of GUESS-AND-CHECK. Thus, the key novelty of the GUESS-AND-CHECK approach is the data driven analysis together with formal guarantees of soundness and termination. Our guarantees are stronger than some of the previous techniques, since we do not lift integral variables of programs to reals. Moreover, the data driven approach facilitates transformation of algebraic invariants to linear invariants. We have also informally shown how our approach can be extended to more expressive theories such as arrays.

We have implemented the GUESS-AND-CHECK algorithm and evaluated it on a number of benchmarks from recent papers on invariant generation and our results are encouraging. Future work includes incorporating the GUESS-AND-CHECK algorithm into a mainstream program verification engine [10] that can consume the candidate invariants as relevant predicates for proofs and a bug-finding engine [1] that can use the candidate invariants to abstract loops by their sound under-approximations and obtain better coverage. Since these tools generally work over linear arithmetic, the transformation from algebraic to linear invariants will play a critical role.

Acknowledgements. We thank the anonymous reviewers for their constructive comments. We thank Divya Gupta and Hristo Paskov for helpful discussions.

References

1. Aiken, A., Bugrara, S., Dillig, I., Dillig, T., Hackett, B., Hawkins, P.: An overview of the saturn project. In: PASTE, pp. 43–48 (2007)
2. Amato, G., Parton, M., Scozzari, F.: Discovering invariants via simple component analysis. J. Symb. Comput. 47(12), 1533–1560 (2012)
3. Bagnara, R., Rodríguez-Carbonell, E., Zaffanella, E.: Generation of Basic Semialgebraic Invariants Using Convex Polyhedra. In: Hankin, C., Siveroni, I. (eds.) SAS 2005. LNCS, vol. 3672, pp. 19–34. Springer, Heidelberg (2005)
4. Cachera, D., Jensen, T., Jobin, A., Kirchner, F.: Inference of Polynomial Invariants for Imperative Programs: A Farewell to Gröbner Bases. In: Miné, A., Schmidt, D. (eds.) SAS 2012. LNCS, vol. 7460, pp. 58–74. Springer, Heidelberg (2012)
5. Clarke, E., Grumberg, O., Jha, S., Lu, Y., Veith, H.: Counterexample-Guided Abstraction Refinement. In: Emerson, E.A., Sistla, A.P. (eds.) CAV 2000. LNCS, vol. 1855, pp. 154–169. Springer, Heidelberg (2000)
6. Colón, M.A.: Approximating the Algebraic Relational Semantics of Imperative Programs. In: Giacobazzi, R. (ed.) SAS 2004. LNCS, vol. 3148, pp. 296–311. Springer, Heidelberg (2004)
7. Colón, M.A., Sankaranarayanan, S., Sipma, H.B.: Linear Invariant Generation Using Non-linear Constraint Solving. In: Hunt Jr., W.A., Somenzi, F. (eds.) CAV 2003. LNCS, vol. 2725, pp. 420–432. Springer, Heidelberg (2003)
8. Cousot, P., Halbwachs, N.: Automatic discovery of linear restraints among variables of a program. In: POPL, pp. 84–96 (1978)
9. Ernst, M.D., Perkins, J.H., Guo, P.J., McCamant, S., Pacheco, C., Tschantz, M.S., Xiao, C.: The daikon system for dynamic detection of likely invariants. Sci. Comput. Program. 69(1-3), 35–45 (2007)

10. Gulavani, B.S., Henzinger, T.A., Kannan, Y., Nori, A.V., Rajamani, S.K.: Synergy: a new algorithm for property checking. In: SIGSOFT FSE, pp. 117–127 (2006)
11. Gupta, A., Majumdar, R., Rybalchenko, A.: From Tests to Proofs. In: Kowalewski, S., Philippou, A. (eds.) TACAS 2009. LNCS, vol. 5505, pp. 262–276. Springer, Heidelberg (2009)
12. Jovanović, D., de Moura, L.: Solving Non-linear Arithmetic. In: Gramlich, B., Miller, D., Sattler, U. (eds.) IJCAR 2012. LNCS, vol. 7364, pp. 339–354. Springer, Heidelberg (2012)
13. Karr, M.: Affine relationships among variables of a program. Acta Inf. 6, 133–151 (1976)
14. King, J.C.: Symbolic execution and program testing. Commun. ACM 19(7), 385–394 (1976)
15. Kovács, L.: A Complete Invariant Generation Approach for P-solvable Loops. In: Pnueli, A., Virbitskaite, I., Voronkov, A. (eds.) PSI 2009. LNCS, vol. 5947, pp. 242–256. Springer, Heidelberg (2010)
16. de Moura, L., Bjørner, N.: Z3: An Efficient SMT Solver. In: Ramakrishnan, C.R., Rehof, J. (eds.) TACAS 2008. LNCS, vol. 4963, pp. 337–340. Springer, Heidelberg (2008)
17. Müller-Olm, M., Seidl, H.: Computing polynomial program invariants. Inf. Process. Lett. 91(5), 233–244 (2004)
18. Nguyen, T., Kapur, D., Weimer, W., Forrest, S.: Using dynamic analysis to discover polynomial and array invariants. In: ICSE, pp. 683–693 (2012)
19. Nimmer, J.W., Ernst, M.D.: Automatic generation of program specifications. In: ISSTA, pp. 229–239 (2002)
20. Petter, M.: Berechnung von polynomiellen invarianten. Master's thesis, Fakultät für Informatik, Technische Universität München (2004)
21. Rodríguez-Carbonell, E., Kapur, D.: Automatic generation of polynomial invariants of bounded degree using abstract interpretation. Science of Computer Programming 64(1), 54–75 (2007)
22. Rodríguez-Carbonell, E., Kapur, D.: Generating all polynomial invariants in simple loops. Journal of Symbolic Computation 42(4), 443–476 (2007)
23. Sankaranarayanan, S., Sipma, H., Manna, Z.: Non-linear loop invariant generation using Gröbner bases. In: POPL, pp. 318–329 (2004)
24. Sharma, R., Gupta, S., Hariharan, B., Aiken, A., Nori, A.V.: A data driven approach for algebraic loop invariants. Tech. Report MSR-TR-2012-97, Microsoft Research (2012)
25. Sharma, R., Nori, A.V., Aiken, A.: Interpolants as Classifiers. In: Madhusudan, P., Seshia, S.A. (eds.) CAV 2012. LNCS, vol. 7358, pp. 71–87. Springer, Heidelberg (2012)
26. Vidal, R., Ma, Y., Sastry, S.: Generalized principal component analysis (GPCA). IEEE Trans. Pattern Anal. Mach. Intell. 27(12), 1945–1959 (2005)

Automatic Type Inference for Amortised Heap-Space Analysis

Martin Hofmann and Dulma Rodriguez

[1] University of Munich
`martin.hofmann@ifi.lmu.de`
[2] Monoidics Ltd
`dulma.rodriguez@monoidics.com`

Abstract. We present a fully automatic, sound and modular heap-space analysis for object-oriented programs. In particular, we provide type inference for the system of refinement types RAJA, which checks upper bounds of heap-space usage based on amortised analysis. Until now, the refined RAJA types had to be manually specified. Our type inference increases the usability of the system, as no user-defined annotations are required.

The type inference consists of constraint generation and solving. First, we present a system for generating subtyping and arithmetic constraints based on the RAJA typing rules. Second, we reduce the subtyping constraints to inequalities over infinite trees, which can be solved using an algorithm that we have described in previous work. This paper also enriches the original type system by introducing polymorphic method types, enabling a modular analysis.

Keywords: Type systems, resource analysis, memory management.

1 Introduction

We study the problem of predicting the dynamic memory allocation of an object-oriented program in a freelist-based memory model. In short, we compute a number N such that at any point in the execution of the program the number of "new" instructions executed thus far minus the number of "free" instructions executed thus far does not exceed N. This (perhaps) seemingly simple task is complicated by the following factors:

- The computed bound N should be symbolic, i.e. a closed form expression in the size of the input which is provided, e.g., as a list of strings;
- The control flow of the program depends on the input and on the shape of intermediate data structures like lists or trees;
- The control flow strongly depends on dynamic class tags as is common in class-based object-oriented programming.

We remark that there is nothing special about "new" and "free"; one can in just the same way count the number of "tick" instructions and in this way obtain upper bounds on execution time, or indeed on the expenditure of any other quantifiable resource (number of open connections, text messages sent, real money spent, etc.).

M. Felleisen and P. Gardner (Eds.): ESOP 2013, LNCS 7792, pp. 593–613, 2013.

The need for resource prediction has been widely recognised [1–3] and is also intuitively plausible. Just think of software running on small, resource-constrained devices such as smart cards, microcontrollers, phones, or software running on large servers shared between many users as in cloud computing. While there is still some way to go until we can serve these applications at industrial level, there has been considerable progress in the last years.

Approaches based on recurrence solving [1, 4, 5] or on abstract interpretation [6, 2, 3] have matured to a point where programs of several hundred lines of code can be automatically analysed. These techniques work under the assumption that control-flow is either fixed or determined by some easily obtainable numeric parameters such as length or size of input or linear arithmetic functions thereof. Other dependencies of the control flow are over-approximated by simply taking the maximum over all possible runs. This works well for programs which use arrays that are allocated at the beginning with a given size and processed with a simple iteration pattern. This is very useful in embedded systems or scientific computing where most programs have such a shape. It does not work well with object-oriented programs where resource behaviour depends on the dynamic class tags of objects, such as when functional data structures such as lists or trees are implemented using the Composite pattern.

In previous work [7–10] we and others argued that the method of amortised analysis [11, 12] might be of help here. Therein, data structures are assigned non-negative numbers, called *potential*, in an *a priori* arbitrary fashion. If done cleverly, it then becomes possible to obtain *constant* bounds on the "amortised cost" of an individual operation, that is, its actual resource usage plus the difference in potential of the data structure before and after performing the operation. This makes it possible to take into account the effect that an operation might have on the resource usage of subsequent operations and also to merely add up amortised costs without having to explicitly track size and shape of intermediate data structures.

In traditional amortised analysis [11] where the emphasis lies on the manual analysis of algorithms, the potentials were ascribed to particular data structures such as union-find trees by some formula that must be manually provided. When amortised analysis is used for automatic resource analysis one uses refined types to define the potentials — typing rules then ensure that potential and actual resource usage is accounted for correctly. Combined with type inference, it then allows for an automatic inference of the potential functions.

In amortised resource analysis for statically typed functional programs the data structures remain fixed (e.g. lists or trees) and only the potential functions must be found. In the object-oriented case, even the data structures themselves must be discovered by the analysis because objects can be used for just anything be it lists, trees, graphs, etc. As a result, automatic inference becomes considerably more challenging unless one is willing to accept user annotations specifying the way in which objects are to be used, for instance in the form of separation logic annotations [13].

Here, we investigate how far we can go without requiring any such annotations. We build upon a system of refinement types for amortised analysis for a Java-like language called Resource Aware JAva (RAJA) [7]. This is a powerful type system that can capture the heap-space requirements of many programs. Moreover, the type system takes aliasing into account, which means that the resource analysis based on this system is sound for programs which contain shared or even cyclic data structures. In previous work [8], we have described a type checking algorithm for RAJA and an implementation capable of checking user supplied typing annotations which were still quite cumbersome and difficult to come up with and this hindered practical use.

In this paper, we remove this obstacle and show how the refinement types can be inferred, so as to make the analysis fully automatic and eliminate the burden of manual annotations from the programmer. The main contributions of this paper are as follows:

1. We provide for the first time fully automatic amortised resource inference for object-oriented programs, which is sound and modular.
2. We reduce the problem of type inference for RAJA to the problem of satisfiability of inequalities over infinite trees labelled with non-negative real numbers.
3. We validate the type system RAJA and the type inference algorithm with a publicly available implementation and experimental evaluation.

In previous work [14] we presented the novel problem of satisfiability of arithmetic constraints over infinite labelled trees. Moreover, we provided a heuristic algorithm for constraint solving, which consists of reducing the constraints to an equivalent finite set of linear arithmetic constraints. This was possible in many cases when the solutions were regular trees.

The fact that we can only solve constraints when their solutions are regular trees implies that our analysis is restricted to linear bounds. We shall explain this connection later when we describe how we obtain the bounds from the infinite trees. Since this problem has only been described recently, it is still unknown whether it is decidable. If it is decidable and an algorithm for solving the constraints was found, we would be able to compute non-linear bounds with the same method.

The type system that we present in this paper is a slightly modified version of the original type system from [7]: we present syntax-directed typing rules that make the system more suitable for automatic type inference. We also introduce polymorphic method types that enable a modular analysis. However, we do not allow polymorphic recursion since it would cause many difficulties to the type inference and we have not found useful examples where it is required.

This paper is organised as follows. In the next section we give an informal presentation of the system and show its use in some examples. In Section 3 we describe briefly our target language FJEU and we introduce formally the typing system RAJA. Section 4 describes the type inference algorithm. In Section 5 we show experimental results. Finally we review related work and conclude in Section 6.

```
1    abstract class List {
2        abstract List copy();abstract DList toDList(DList prev);}
3    class Nil extends List {
4        List copy() { return this; }
5        DList toDList(DList prev) {return new DNil();}}
6    class Cons extends List  { List next; int elem;
7        List copy() {
8            Cons res = new Cons();
9            res.elem = this.elem;
10           res.next = this.next.copy(); return res; }
11       DList toDList(DList prev) {
12           DCons res = new DCons();
13           res.elem = this.elem;
14           res.next = this.next.toDList(res);
15           res.prev = prev; return res; }}
16   abstract class DList   { }
17   class DNil extends DList   { }
18   class DCons extends DList { int elem; DList next; DList prev;}
19   class Main {
20       List main_copy(List list) {return list.copy();}
21       DList main_dlist(List list) {return list.toDList(new DNil());} }
```

Fig. 1. Example program

2   Informal Presentation and Examples

We aim to statically analyse the heap-space consumption of class-based object-oriented programs. Since we wish to abstract from concrete memory models, we assume a simple freelist based model where we maintain a set of free memory units, the freelist. When creating an object, a heap unit required to store it is taken from the freelist, provided it contains enough units. When deallocating an object, the unit returns to the freelist. We remark that we deallocate objects explicitly by means of a free expression, since we assume no garbage collection. We also assume that any attempt to access a previously deallocated object leads to immediate abortion of the program and all resource predictions are on condition that no such abortion takes place. Static analysis for preventing such illicit accesses is an orthogonal problem and not addressed in this paper.

We also note that we can treat free-instructions as no-ops and use a garbage collector. Assuming that the garbage collector discovers all deallocation opportunities and that it is invoked whenever the freelist becomes short then our inferred bounds are also valid in the presence of garbage collection. We have not explored this avenue in detail, however.

We then demonstrate the front end of our method with a couple of small examples. Fig. 1 shows a method for copying a singly-linked-list and a method for converting a singly-linked-list into a doubly-linked-list. Here we use Java syntax to simplify the understanding of the programs; the syntax of our target language FJEU is slightly different. Consider the method main_copy. Running the analysis yields the following results; no annotations by the programmer are required. The length of the input refers to the length of the list given as argument to the method.

```
Program will execute successfully with a free-list >= |input|
```

It is clear that the heap-space consumption of this program is exactly the length of the list. When we analyse the method main_dlist we obtain the following:

`Program will execute successfully with a free-list >= 2 + |input|`

Here the heap-space consumption is the length of the list plus the two DNil objects that represent the two ends of the doubly-linked list.

Our goal is to find (statically) an upper bound on the initial size of the freelist so that the given program can be executed without running out of memory. We seek to assign data structures a potential that can be used to pay for any object creation. Then, the potential of the data structures in their initial state will represent an upper bound on the total heap consumption of the program.

We wish to assign different objects of the same class different potentials, thus, we need to *refine* the notion of classes. We introduce the *views*, a set of names, which, together with the classes, build the appropriate refined types to which we will assign potential. Moreover, since classes are compound types consisting of fields and methods, we need to give refined types for these also. A refined type consist of a class C and a view r, written C^r. The potential function $\Diamond(.)$ assigns each refined type a potential, which is a non-negative real number. The functions $\mathsf{A}^{\mathsf{get}}(\cdot,\cdot)$ and $\mathsf{A}^{\mathsf{set}}(\cdot,\cdot)$ assign views to the fields, where $\mathsf{A}^{\mathsf{get}}(C^r,a)$ represents the view used when reading the field a of class C under the view r, and $\mathsf{A}^{\mathsf{set}}(C^r,a)$ is the view used when writing a.

Thus, views consist of a set of names, together with maps $\Diamond(\cdot)$, $\mathsf{A}^{\mathsf{get}}(\cdot,\cdot)$ and $\mathsf{A}^{\mathsf{set}}(\cdot,\cdot)$. Alternatively, we can see them as infinite trees, where nodes are labelled by a tuple of non-negative real numbers (one number for each class in the given program), and edges are labelled with elements of the set

$$\{C.a.\mathsf{get}, C.a.\mathsf{set} \mid C \text{ is a class and } a \text{ is a field of } C\}$$

For instance, if we assume that the only class in the program is Cons and g denotes Cons.next.get and s denotes Cons.next.set, then the following tree represents a view:

This view is regular, because it contains only finitely many different subtrees. We define an inequality relation $\sqsubseteq$ on views, which is covariant in the get subtrees and contravariant in the set subtrees. We also define subtyping over refined types: C^r is a subtype of D^s iff C is a subclass of D and $r \sqsubseteq s$.

A monomorphic method type for a method m consists of views for the method's arguments, a view for its result and two numbers representing the potential consumed and released by the method respectively. More concretely, if a method m has a type $C^{r_0}; E_1^{r_1}, \ldots, E_j^{r_j} \xrightarrow{n/n'} H^{r_{j+1}}$, this means that it is defined in the

$$\text{Nil.copy()} \quad = \text{Nil}^{v_{self}} \xrightarrow{q_1/q_2} \text{List}^{v_{res}} \ \& \ v_{self} \sqsubseteq v_{res}$$

$$\text{Cons.copy()} \quad = \text{Cons}^{v_{self}} \xrightarrow{q_1/q_2} \text{List}^{v_{res}} \ \& $$
$$A^{get}(\text{Cons}^{v_{self}}, \text{next}) \sqsubseteq v_{self} \ \wedge \ \Diamond(\text{Cons}^{v_{self}}) \geq \Diamond(\text{Cons}^{v_{res}}) + 1$$

$$\text{Main.main\_copy()} = \text{Main}^{v_{self}}; \text{List}^{v_l} \xrightarrow{q_1/q_2} \text{List}^{v_{res}} \ \& \ v_l \sqsubseteq v_{res}$$
$$A^{get}(\text{Cons}^{v_l}, \text{next}) \sqsubseteq v_l \ \wedge \ \Diamond(\text{Cons}^{v_l}) \geq \Diamond(\text{Cons}^{v_{res}}) + 1$$

$\Diamond(\cdot)$	rich	poor
List, Nil, Main	0	0
Cons	1	0

	Cons^{rich}	Cons^{poor}
$A^{get}(\cdot, \text{next})$	rich	poor
$A^{set}(\cdot, \text{next})$	rich	poor

Fig. 2. RAJA types for the copy example

refined type C^{r_0} and may be called with arguments $v_1 : E_1^{r_1}, \ldots, v_j : E_j^{r_j}$, whose associated potential will be consumed as well as an additional potential of n. The return value will be of type $H^{r_{j+1}}$, carrying an according potential. In addition to this, a potential of n' units will be returned.

Polymorphic method types are like monomorphic RAJA method types, but views and numbers replaced by variables and constraints upon them. A polymorphic method type consists of view variables for its arguments, a view variable for its result and two number variables. Moreover, it contains a conjunction of subtyping and linear arithmetic constraints that capture the resource consumption of the method. The subtyping constraints show how the views for the arguments and result relate. For instance, the constraint $A^{get}(C^v, a) \sqsubseteq w$ means that given a valuation π that maps view variables to views $\pi = \{v \mapsto r, w \mapsto s\}$, the get view of the field a of class C under the view r must be a subtype of s.

One run-time object can have several refined types at once, since it can be regarded through different views at the same time. The overall potential of a run-time configuration is the (possibly infinite) sum over all access paths in scope that lead to an actual object. Thus, if an object has several access paths leading to it (aliasing), it may make several contributions to the total potential. Our type system has an explicit contraction rule: If a variable is used more than once, the associated potential is split by assigning different views to each use.

Analysis of List Copy. In the following, we wish to illustrate the system by showing the details of the analysis of main_copy from Fig. 1. We shall explain a simplified form of the constraints obtained by analysing the program. We assume that for each method, we assign the view variable v_{self} to the variable this and the view variable v_{res} to the result of the function. When analysing the body of Nil.copy, we obtain the constraint $v_{self} \sqsubseteq v_{res}$ (line 4). Further, in the method Cons.copy, line 8 produces the constraint $\Diamond(\text{Cons}^{v_{self}}) \geq \Diamond(\text{Cons}^{v_{res}}) + 1$, because the current object needs to pay for the creation of the new Cons object and also for its potential. Moreover, since the method is called recursively with the next item in the list (line 10), the refined type of the next node must be a subtype of the refined type of the current node, which is expressed in the constraint $A^{get}(\text{Cons}^{v_{self}}, \text{next}) \sqsubseteq v_{self}$. The method List.copy is abstract, so we obtain no constraints. However, a virtual call to it may be resolved to a call to Nil.copy() or to Cons.copy(). Thus, to ensure soundness, we need to add the constraints of Cons.copy() and Nil.copy() to List.copy(). Then, when we call the method List.copy() in main_copy, we obtain the appropriate constraints after variable substitution (see Fig. 2).

The valuation $\pi = (\{v_{self} \mapsto rich, v_{res} \mapsto poor\}, \{q_1 \mapsto 0, q_2 \mapsto 0\})$ builds the best possible solution for the constraints. Our algorithm infers the following monomorphic method type for main_copy: $\mathsf{Main}^{rich}; \mathsf{List}^{rich} \xrightarrow{0/0} \mathsf{List}^{poor}$. This type says that the heap consumption of main_copy is bounded by the potential of the list l. The potential of l is calculated as the sum over all access paths starting from l and not leading to null. Each of these has a dynamic type: Cons, or Nil for the end of the list. Each also has a view that can be computed by chaining the view of l along the get views, which is the view rich in each case. For each access path, we look up the potential annotation of its dynamic type under its view. Given $\Diamond(\mathsf{Cons}^{rich}) = 1$ and $\Diamond(\mathsf{Nil}^{rich}) = 0$, this is 1 in every case except for the path leading to Nil. The resulting sum is the length of the list $|l|$.

Now, imagine that the view rich was defined differently, as the first element of the following family of views:

$$\Diamond(\mathsf{Cons}^{rich_i}) = 2^i, \mathsf{A}^{get}(\mathsf{Cons}^{rich_i}; next) = rich_{i+1}, \mathsf{A}^{set}(\mathsf{Cons}^{rich_i}; next) = rich_{i+1}, i \geq 0$$

Then, the potential of the list l would be $2^{|l|} - 1$, thus we could obtain an exponential bound for the heap requirements of the method. Also notice that the view rich would not be regular. Therefore, we cannot compute such bounds at the moment, because of the restrictions of our constraint solver.

To conclude this example, we wish to give an intuition for the need for refined types. Imagine that we could give potential only to the class Cons. Line 8 would then produce the constraint $\Diamond(\mathsf{Cons}) \geq \Diamond(\mathsf{Cons}) + 1$, which is unsatisfiable. We require more sophisticated types to achieve a more refined behaviour: a Cons object with potential 1 can be copied, but the result is a Cons object with potential 0, which cannot.

3   System RAJA

FJ with Update. Our formal model of Java, FJEU, is an extension of Featherweight Java (FJ) [15] with attribute update, conditional and explicit deallocation. An FJEU program $\mathcal{P} = (\mathscr{C}, main)$ consists of a partial finite map from class names to class definitions $\mathscr{C}$, and a distinguished method main to be executed when running the program. We write $\mathsf{S}(C)$ to denote the *super-class* D of C, provided that C has a super-class. We write $\mathsf{A}(C)$ to denote the ordered set of fields of C, including inherited ones. We write $C.a$ to denote the class type of each field a of class C. Similarly we write $\mathsf{Meth}(C)$ to denote the set of all defined method names of C, including inherited ones. For a method name m of class C we write $\mathsf{M}_{body}(C, m)$ to denote the term that comprises the *method body* of method m and $C.m$ to denote the *method type* of m in class C. If otherwise m is not defined in C, then $\mathsf{M}_{body}(C, m) = \mathsf{M}_{body}(D, m)$ and $C.m = D.m$, provided that D is the super class of C. Each class has only one implicit constructor, which sets all class attributes to a null value.

We now extend FJEU to an annotated version, Resource Aware JAva (RAJA). We set $\mathbb{D} = \mathbb{R}_0^+ \cup \{\infty\}$, i.e., the set of non-negative real numbers together with an element ∞. Ordering and addition on $\mathbb{R}_0^+$ extend to $\mathbb{D}$ by $\infty + x = x + \infty = \infty$ and $x \leq \infty$.

Definition 1. *We define the set $\mathcal{V}$ of* views *coinductively by*

- $\Diamond(\cdot)$ *assigns to each view $r \in \mathcal{V}$ and class $C \in \mathcal{C}$ a number $\Diamond(C^r)$.*
- $\mathsf{A}^{\mathrm{get}}(\cdot, \cdot)$ *assigns to each view $r \in \mathcal{V}$ and class $C \in \mathcal{C}$ and field $a \in \mathsf{A}(C)$ a view $s = \mathsf{A}^{\mathrm{get}}(C^r, a)$.*
- $\mathsf{A}^{\mathrm{set}}(\cdot, \cdot)$ *assigns to each view $r \in \mathcal{V}$ and class $C \in \mathcal{C}$ and field $a \in \mathsf{A}(C)$ a view $s' = \mathsf{A}^{\mathrm{set}}(C^r, a)$.*

The following inequality relation $\sqsubseteq$ is covariant in the get views and contravariant in the set views.

Definition 2 ($\mathbf{r \sqsubseteq s}$). *Let $r, s \in \mathcal{V}$. We define $r \sqsubseteq s$ coinductively by*

$$\forall C \in \mathcal{C} \,.\, \Diamond(C^r) \geq \Diamond(C^s)$$
$$\forall C \in \mathcal{C} \,\forall a \in \mathsf{A}(C) \,.\, \mathsf{A}^{\mathrm{get}}(C^r, a) \sqsubseteq \mathsf{A}^{\mathrm{get}}(C^s, a)$$
$$\forall C \in \mathcal{C} \,\forall a \in \mathsf{A}(C) \,.\, \mathsf{A}^{\mathrm{set}}(C^s, a) \sqsubseteq \mathsf{A}^{\mathrm{set}}(C^r, a)$$

We define the operations on views $\oplus : \mathcal{V} \times \mathcal{V} \to \mathcal{V}$ and $\boxplus : \mathcal{V} \times \mathcal{V} \to \mathcal{V}$ simultaneously as follows. Let $s_1, s_2 \in \mathcal{V}$ then, for each $C \in \mathcal{C}$, $a \in \mathsf{A}(C)$ we set:

$$\Diamond(C^{s_1 \oplus s_2}) = \Diamond(C^{s_1}) + \Diamond(C^{s_2}) \qquad \Diamond(C^{s_1 \boxplus s_2}) = \min(\Diamond(C^{s_1}), \Diamond(C^{s_2}))$$
$$\mathsf{A}^{\mathrm{get}}(C^{s_1 \oplus s_2}, a) = \mathsf{A}^{\mathrm{get}}(C^{s_1}, a) \oplus \mathsf{A}^{\mathrm{get}}(C^{s_2}, a) \quad \mathsf{A}^{\mathrm{get}}(C^{s_1 \boxplus s_2}, a) = \mathsf{A}^{\mathrm{get}}(C^{s_1}, a) \boxplus \mathsf{A}^{\mathrm{get}}(C^{s_2}, a)$$
$$\mathsf{A}^{\mathrm{set}}(C^{s_1 \oplus s_2}, a) = \mathsf{A}^{\mathrm{set}}(C^{s_1}, a) \boxplus \mathsf{A}^{\mathrm{set}}(C^{s_2}, a) \quad \mathsf{A}^{\mathrm{set}}(C^{s_1 \boxplus s_2}, a) = \mathsf{A}^{\mathrm{set}}(C^{s_1}, a) \oplus \mathsf{A}^{\mathrm{set}}(C^{s_2}, a)$$

Let $\dot{-} : \mathbb{D} \times \mathbb{D} \to \mathbb{D}$ be defined by: $n \dot{-} m = \begin{cases} n - m & \text{if } n - m \geq 0 \\ 0 & \text{otherwise} \end{cases}$.

We define an operation $(s \dot{-} n)_D : \mathcal{V} \times \mathbb{D} \times \mathcal{C} \to \mathcal{V}$ that takes a view s and a number $n \in \mathbb{D}$ and class D and returns another view that is just like s, except for the potential of D^s, which is $\Diamond(D^s) \dot{-} n$. We set for each $C \in \mathcal{C}$ and each $a \in \mathsf{A}(C)$:

$$\Diamond(C^{(s \dot{-} n)_D}) = \begin{cases} \Diamond(C^s) \dot{-} n & \text{if } C = D \\ \Diamond(C^s) & \text{otherwise} \end{cases} \qquad \mathsf{A}^{\mathrm{get}}(C^{(s \dot{-} n)_D}, a) = \mathsf{A}^{\mathrm{get}}(C^s, a)$$
$$\mathsf{A}^{\mathrm{set}}(C^{(s \dot{-} n)_D}, a) = \mathsf{A}^{\mathrm{set}}(C^s, a)$$

A refined type consists of a class C and a view r and is written C^r. We extend the subtyping of FJEU classes to refined types as follows. Since both $\sqsubseteq$ and $<:$ on FJEU are reflexive and transitive so is $<:$ on RAJA.

Definition 3 ($\mathbf{C^r <: D^s}$). *We extend subtyping to refined types by $C^r <: D^s$ iff $C <: D$ and $r \sqsubseteq s$.*

In the following grammar, we define subtyping and arithmetic constraints. tt is the empty constraint, i.e. a constraint that is always satisfied. Moreover, $n \in \mathbb{D}$, v ranges over view variables and p over arithmetic variables.

$$\mathsf{vexp} ::= v \mid \mathsf{A}^{\mathrm{get}}(C_i^v, a) \mid \mathsf{A}^{\mathrm{set}}(C_i^v, a) \mid v \oplus v$$
$$\mathsf{ae} \ ::= n \mid p \mid \Diamond(C^v) \mid \mathsf{ae} + \mathsf{ae}$$

$$\mathcal{TC} ::= C^{\mathsf{vexp}} <: D^{\mathsf{vexp}}$$
$$\mathcal{AC} ::= \mathsf{ae}_1 \geq \mathsf{ae}_2 \mid \mathsf{ae}_1 \leq \mathsf{ae}_2$$
$$\mathcal{C} \ ::= \mathcal{AC} \mid \mathcal{TC} \mid \mathcal{C} \wedge \mathcal{C} \mid \mathsf{tt}$$

Let $\pi = (\pi_v, \pi_a)$ be a pair of maps: π_v is map from view variables to views and π_a is a map from number variables to numbers. We then define *the meaning of arithmetic expressions* $\pi(\mathsf{ae})$ in the obvious way, e.g. $\pi(\Diamond(C^v)) = \Diamond(C^{\pi_v(v)})$. *The meaning of view expressions* $\pi(\mathsf{vexp})$ is defined as one might expect, e.g. $\pi(\mathsf{A}^{\mathrm{get}}(C_i^v, a)) = \mathsf{A}^{\mathrm{get}}(C_i^{\pi(v)}, a)$. We say that π satisfies a conjunction of constraints $\mathcal{C}$, written $\pi \models \mathcal{C}$, if π satisfies each constraint in $\mathcal{C}$.

If $v = v_0, \dots, v_{n+1}$ is a vector of length $n + 2$, with $n \geq 0$, we write $\mathfrak{v}$ for meaning the (possibly empty) vector $v_1, \dots, v_n$.

Definition 4 (An *n-ary monomorphic RAJA method type*)
An n-ary monomorphic RAJA method type T consists of $n + 2$ views s and two numbers m_1, m_2 written $T = s_0; \mathfrak{s} \xrightarrow{m_1/m_2} s_{n+1}$.

We also write $C^{s_0}; E^{\mathfrak{s}} \xrightarrow{m_1/m_2} H^{s_{n+1}}$ to denote an FJEU method type combined with a corresponding monomorphic RAJA method type.

Definition 5 (An *n-ary polymorphic RAJA method type*)
An n-ary polymorphic RAJA method type ϕ consists of $n + 2$ view variables v and two arithmetic variables $q = q_1, q_2$ and existentially quantified (view and arithmetic) variables w, t and a conjunction of subtyping and arithmetic constraints on them written $\phi = \forall v, q \; \exists w, t . v_0; \mathfrak{v} \xrightarrow{q_1/q_2} v_{n+1} \; \& \; \mathcal{C}(v, q, w, t)$.

We often write $\forall v, q \; \exists w, t . C^{v_0}; E^{\mathfrak{v}} \xrightarrow{q_1/q_2} H^{v_{n+1}} \; \& \; \mathcal{C}(v, q, w, t)$ to denote an FJEU method type combined with a corresponding polymorphic RAJA method type. A polymorphic method type stands for the set of all monomorphic types that satisfy its constraints. Because this type does not depend on the method's callers, the type inference for the method can be performed modularly.

Definition 6 (Instance of a polymorphic method type).
Let $T = C^{s_0}; E^{\mathfrak{s}} \xrightarrow{m_1/m_2} H^{s_{n+1}}$ be a monomorphic RAJA method type and $\phi = \forall v, q \; \exists w, t . C^{v_0}; E^{\mathfrak{v}} \xrightarrow{q_1/q_2} H^{v_{n+1}} \; \& \; \mathcal{C}(v, q, w, t)$ a polymorphic RAJA method type. We say that T is an instance of ϕ, written: "T instanceof ϕ" iff there exists a valuation π with $\pi \models \mathcal{C}$ such that $\pi(v_i) = s_i$ for $i \in \{0, \dots, n+1\}$ and $\pi(q_j) = m_j$ for $j \in \{1, 2\}$.

We define trivial polymorphic RAJA method types with no constraints for a given class C and method m, by: $\top^{(C,m)} = \forall v, q . v_0; \mathfrak{v} \xrightarrow{q_1/q_2} v_{n+1} \; \& \; \mathsf{tt}$.

Definition 7 (Subtyping of monomorphic method types)
If $T = r \xrightarrow{n_1/n_2} r_{n+1}$ and $T' = s \xrightarrow{m_1/m_2} s_{n+1}$ then $T <: T'$ is defined as $n_1 \leq m_1$ and $n_2 \geq m_2$ and $r_0 = s_0$ and $s_i \sqsubseteq r_i$ for $i = 1, \dots, n$ and $r_{n+1} \sqsubseteq s_{n+1}$.

Definition 8 (Subtyping of polymorphic method types)
Let $\mathscr{C} \models C <: D$ *and let* ϕ *and* ψ *be polymorphic RAJA method types refining a FJEU method type of method m in class C and D, respectively. Then* $\phi <: \psi$ *iff:* $\forall T'$ *with* T' instanceof ψ . $\exists T$ *with* T instanceof ϕ *such that* $T <: T'$.

We call a polymorphic RAJA method type *empty* if its constraints are unsatisfiable and *nonempty* if they can be satisfied.

Definition 9 (RAJA program)
A RAJA program is an annotation of an FJEU program $\mathcal{P} = (\mathscr{C}, \mathsf{main})$ *in the form of a tuple* $\mathscr{R} = (\mathscr{C}, \mathsf{main}, \mathsf{M})$ *where* M *assigns to each class C and method* $m \in \mathsf{Meth}(C)$ *with n arguments an n-ary polymorphic RAJA method type* $\mathsf{M}(C, m)$.

3.1 Typing RAJA

The RAJA-typing judgement is formally defined by the rules in Figure 3. The type system allows us to derive assertions of the form $\mathsf{M}; \varXi; \varGamma \vdash^{n}_{n'} e : C^r$ where e is an expression or program phrase, C is an FJEU class, r is a view (so C^r is a refined type). Moreover, $\varXi$ is a map from classes and methods to monomorphic RAJA method types. Finally n, n' are non-negative numbers. The meaning of such a judgement is as follows. If e terminates successfully in some environment η and heap σ with unbounded memory resources available then it will also terminate successfully with a bounded freelist of size at least n plus the potential ascribed to η, σ with respect to the typing in $\varGamma$.

We present here a syntax-directed version of the original typing system from [7], which contains the following rule ($\lozenge Share$) to ensure that a variable can be used more than once without duplication of potential.

$$\frac{\mathsf{Y}(s\,|\,s_1,\ldots,s_j) \qquad \varGamma, \boldsymbol{y}\!:\!\boldsymbol{D^s} \vdash^{n}_{n'} e : C^r}{\varGamma, x\!:\!D^s \vdash^{n}_{n'} e[x/y_1,\ldots,x/y_j] : C^r} \; (\lozenge Share)$$

Here we integrate the rule ($\lozenge Share$) into the rule ($\lozenge Let$) using the fact that $\mathsf{Y}(r\,|\,s_1, s_2)$ is equivalent to $r \sqsubseteq s_1 \oplus s_2$. This result has been omitted in this paper for lack of space; details can be found in [16]. We do not integrate ($\lozenge Share$) in other rules such as ($\lozenge Invocation$) or ($\lozenge Update$) because, for simplicity, we require that in those expressions a variable appears only once.

Monomorphic vs. Polymorphic Recursion. In type systems with polymorphic types and recursion, polymorphic recursion is possible. Polymorphic recursion means that, in recursive calls, any instance of the polymorphic type can be used, whereas in monomorphic recursion only one instance can be used: the same instance that the polymorphic type is being type-checked with.

Here we allow only monomorphic recursion. The reason for not treating polymorphic recursion is that type inference in the presence of polymorphic recursion is difficult, in particular we would need to compute a fixpoint when generating constraints for recursive functions. We decided to develop a simpler type

$$RAJA\ Typing \qquad \boxed{\mathsf{M}; \Xi; \Gamma \vdash^{n}_{n'} e : C^r}$$

$$\frac{\forall a \in A(D)\,.\,A^{set}(D^r, a) \sqsubseteq A^{get}(D^r, a) \quad D <: C \quad n \geq \Diamond(D^r) + 1 \quad n' \leq n - \Diamond(D^r) - 1}{\mathsf{M}; \Xi; \Gamma \vdash^{n}_{n'} \ new\ D : C^r}$$

$$\frac{n' \leq n + \min\{\Diamond(D^r) \mid D <: C\} + 1}{\mathsf{M}; \Xi; \Gamma, x : C^r \vdash^{n}_{n'} \ free\,(x) : E^s} \ (\Diamond Free) \qquad \frac{D <: E \quad D^r <: C^s \quad n' \leq n}{\mathsf{M}; \Gamma, x : E^r \vdash^{n}_{n'} (D)x : C^s} \ (\Diamond Cast)$$

$$\frac{n' \leq n}{\mathsf{M}; \Xi; \Gamma \vdash^{n}_{n'} \ null : C^s} \ (\Diamond Null) \qquad \frac{E^r <: C^s \quad n' \leq n}{\mathsf{M}; \Xi; \Gamma, x : E^r \vdash^{n}_{n'} x : C^s} \ (\Diamond Var)$$

$$\frac{\forall F <: C\,.\,A^{get}(F^r, a) \sqsubseteq s \quad C.a <: D \quad n' \leq n}{\mathsf{M}; \Xi; \Gamma, x : C^r \vdash^{n}_{n'} x.a : D^s} \ (\Diamond Access)$$

$$\frac{\forall G <: E\,.\,s \sqsubseteq A^{set}(G^r, a) \quad F <: E.a \quad E^r <: C^q \quad n' \leq n}{\mathsf{M}; \Xi; \Gamma, x : E^r, y : F^s \vdash^{n}_{n'} x.a \leftarrow y : C^q} \ (\Diamond Upd.)$$

$$\frac{x \in \Gamma \quad \mathsf{M}; \Xi; \Gamma \vdash^{n}_{n'} e_1 : C^r \quad \mathsf{M}; \Xi; \Gamma \vdash^{n}_{n'} e_2 : C^r}{\mathsf{M}; \Xi; \Gamma \vdash^{n}_{n'} \ if\ x\ instanceof\ E\ then\ e_1\ else\ e_2 : C^r} \ (\Diamond Cond.)$$

$$\frac{\mathsf{M}; \Xi; \boldsymbol{y} : \boldsymbol{F^p} \vdash^{n}_{n'} e_1 : D^s \quad \mathsf{M}; \Xi; \boldsymbol{y} : \boldsymbol{F^q}, x : D^s \vdash^{n'}_{n''} e_2 : C^r \quad r_i \sqsubseteq p_i \oplus q_i}{\mathsf{M}; \Xi; \boldsymbol{y} : \boldsymbol{F^r} \vdash^{n}_{n''} \ let\ D\,x = e_1\ in\ e_2 : C^r} \ (\Diamond Let)$$

$$(G^{s_0}; \boldsymbol{E^s} \xrightarrow{t/t'} H^{s'}) \ instanceof\ \mathsf{M}(G, m)$$

$$\frac{G^{r_0} <: G^{s_0} \quad F_i^{r_i} <: E_i^{s_i} \quad H^{s'} <: C^{r'} \quad n \geq t \quad n' \leq t' + n - t}{\mathsf{M}; \Xi; \Gamma, x : G^{r_0}, \boldsymbol{y} : \boldsymbol{F^r} \vdash^{n}_{n'} x.m\,(y_1, \ldots, y_j) : C^{r'}} \ (\Diamond PInv.)$$

$$(G^{s_0}; \boldsymbol{E^s} \xrightarrow{t/t'} H^{s'}) \in \Xi(G, m)$$

$$\frac{G^{r_0} <: G^{s_0} \quad F_i^{r_i} <: E_i^{s_i} \quad H^{s'} <: C^{r'} \quad n \geq t \quad n' \leq t' + n - t}{\mathsf{M}; \Xi; x : G^{r_0}, \boldsymbol{y} : \boldsymbol{F^r} \vdash^{n}_{n'} x.m\,(y_1, \ldots, y_j) : C^{r'}} \ (\Diamond MInv.)$$

$$RAJA\ Method\ Typing \qquad \boxed{\vdash_{\mathsf{m}} \mathsf{M}\ ok}$$

$$\vdash_{\mathsf{m}} \mathsf{M'}\ ok \quad dom(\Xi) = dom(\mathsf{M''}) \quad \forall (C, m) \in \mathsf{M''} \quad \Xi(C, m) = T$$

$$\forall T = (C^{r_0}; \boldsymbol{E^t} \xrightarrow{n/n'} H^{r_{n+1}}) \ instanceof\ \mathsf{M''}(C, m) \quad (r_0 \dotminus \mathsf{p})_C \sqsubseteq s_0$$

$$\frac{\mathsf{M'}; \Xi; this : C^{s_0}, x_1 : E_1^{s_1}, \ldots, x_j : E_j^{s_j} \vdash^{n+p}_{n'} e : H^{r_{j+1}} \quad r_i \sqsubseteq s_i \quad \Diamond(C^{r_0}) \geq p}{\vdash_{\mathsf{m}} \mathsf{M'} \uplus \mathsf{M''}\ ok}$$

Fig. 3. RAJA Typing

inference algorithm, that does not require a fixpoint computation, because we did not find useful examples where the polymorphic recursion is required.

We need to distinguish between recursive and non-recursive method calls. With non-recursive methods calls, we can use any instance of the polymorphic type of the called method. That is why there are two rules for method invocation: ($\Diamond PInv.$) for polymorphic method invocation and ($\Diamond MInv.$) for monomorphic method invocation. In the rule ($\Diamond PInv.$) we assume that the called method is not mutually recursive with the method we are currently analysing, and consequently, we can use any instance of its polymorphic type. On the other hand, we apply the rule ($\Diamond MInv.$) when the called method appears in the map $\Xi : \forall C \in \mathscr{C} . \mathsf{Meth}(C) \rightarrow \mathsf{MonoType}$ which means that this method and the method whose body we are analysing are mutually recursive.

The judgement for typing the body of a method ($\vdash_m$ M ok of Fig. 3) shall mean that all the methods in the domain of the map M are well-typed.

Also notice in the judgement $\vdash_m$ M ok the number p. It represents the amount of items of potential that we take from the potential of the refined type of this in the type T for using in the method's body. Thus, we need to check that the potential of the refined type of this is at least p.

Definition 10 (Well-typed RAJA-program)
A RAJA-program $\mathscr{R} = (\mathscr{C}, \mathsf{main}, \mathsf{M})$ is well-typed *if the following conditions are satisfied:*

1. $\vdash_m$ M ok
2. $\forall C \in \mathscr{C}, m \in \mathsf{Meth}(C) . \mathsf{M}(C, m)$ *is nonempty.*
3. $\forall C, D \in \mathscr{C}$ *with* $S(C) = D \Rightarrow \mathsf{M}(C, m) <: \mathsf{M}(D, m)$.

A full soundness proof for this system is given in [16]. It consists of a small modification of the soundness proof for the original RAJA system [7].

4   Type Inference for RAJA

4.1   Constraint Generation

In the following we present rules for generating subtyping and arithmetic constraints from FJEU programs. The rules (Fig. 4) describe a constraint generation judgement $\mathsf{M}; \Xi; \Gamma \vdash_{p'}^{p} e : C^v \,\&\, \mathcal{C}$ where e is an expression, Γ maps variables to FJEU types refined with view variables, C^v is an FJEU type refined with a view variable, p and p' are arithmetic variables and $\mathcal{C}$ is a conjunction of subtyping and arithmetic constraints. Further, Ξ is a map from classes and methods with n arguments to $n + 2$ view variables and two arithmetic variables.

We write $\pi(\Xi)$ to mean the map from classes and methods to monomorphic RAJA method types that is obtained after substituting every view and arithmetic variable in Ξ with its value in the valuation π. Similarly, $\pi(\Gamma)$ means the context that we obtain after substituting the view variables in Γ with their values in π. In addition, we use the notations $|\Xi|$ and $|\Gamma|$ for meaning the following. If Ξ is a map from classes and method names to monomorphic RAJA types,

$$\boxed{\mathsf{M}; \Xi; \Gamma \vdash^{p}_{p'} e : C^v \ \& \ \mathcal{C}}$$

$$\frac{\mathcal{C} = (E^v <: C^u \ \wedge \ p' \leq p)}{\mathsf{M}; \Xi; \Gamma, x{:}E^v \vdash^{p}_{p'} x : C^u \ \& \ \mathcal{C}} \qquad \frac{\mathcal{C} = (p' \leq p)}{\mathsf{M}; \Xi; \Gamma \vdash^{p}_{p'} \mathsf{null} : C^v \ \& \ \mathcal{C}} \qquad \frac{\mathcal{C} = \bigwedge_{D<:C} p' \leq p + \Diamond(D^v) + 1}{\mathsf{M}; \Xi; \Gamma, x{:}C^v \vdash^{p}_{p'} \mathsf{free}\,(x) : E^u \ \& \ \mathcal{C}}$$

$$\frac{\mathcal{E} = D^v <: C^v \qquad \mathcal{AC} = p \geq \Diamond(D^v) + 1 \ \wedge \ p' \leq p - \Diamond(D^v) - 1}{\mathsf{M}; \Xi; \Gamma \vdash^{p}_{p'} \mathsf{new}\ D : C^v \ \& \ \mathcal{E} \ \wedge \ \mathcal{AC} \ \wedge \ \bigwedge_{a \in A(D)} \mathsf{A}^{\mathrm{set}}(D^v, a) \sqsubseteq \mathsf{A}^{\mathrm{get}}(D^v, a)} \ (\vdash New)$$

$$\frac{\mathcal{C} = (D^v <: E^v \ \wedge \ D^v <: C^u \ \wedge \ p' \leq p)}{\mathsf{M}; \Xi; \Gamma, x{:}E^v \vdash^{p}_{p'} (D)\,x : C^u \ \& \ \mathcal{C}} \ (\vdash Cast) \qquad \frac{\mathcal{C} = \bigwedge_{E<:C} (C.a)^{\mathsf{A}^{\mathrm{get}}(E^v, a)} <: D^u \ \wedge \ p' \leq p)}{\mathsf{M}; \Xi; \Gamma, x{:}C^v \vdash^{p}_{p'} x.a : D^u \ \& \ \mathcal{C}}$$

$$\frac{\mathcal{C} = (\bigwedge_{E<:C} F^w <: (C.a)^{\mathsf{A}^{\mathrm{set}}(E^v, a)} \ \wedge \ C^v <: D^u)}{\mathsf{M}; \Xi; \Gamma, x{:}C^v, y{:}F^w \vdash^{p}_{p'} x.a \leftarrow y : D^u \ \& \ \mathcal{C} \ \wedge \ p' \leq p} \ (\vdash Update)$$

$$\frac{\mathsf{M}; \Xi; \Gamma \vdash^{p}_{p'} e_1 : C^v \ \& \ \mathcal{C}_1 \qquad \mathsf{M}; \Xi; \Gamma \vdash^{p}_{p'} e_2 : C^v \ \& \ \mathcal{C}_2 \qquad \mathcal{C} = (\mathcal{C}_1 \ \wedge \ \mathcal{C}_2)}{\mathsf{M}; \Xi; \Gamma \vdash^{p}_{p'} \mathsf{if}\ x\ \mathsf{instanceof}\ E\ \mathsf{then}\ e_1\ \mathsf{else}\ e_2 : C^v \ \& \ \mathcal{C}} \ (\vdash Cond.)$$

$$\frac{\mathsf{M}; \Xi; \boldsymbol{y}{:}\boldsymbol{F}^v \vdash^{p}_{p'} e_1 : D^u \ \& \ \mathcal{C}_1 \qquad \mathsf{M}; \Xi; \boldsymbol{y}{:}\boldsymbol{F}^w, x{:}D^u \vdash^{p'}_{p''} e_2 : C^v \ \& \ \mathcal{C}_2}{\mathsf{M}; \Xi; \boldsymbol{y}{:}\boldsymbol{F}^u \vdash^{p}_{p''} \mathsf{let}\ D\,x = e_1\ \mathsf{in}\ e_2 : C^v \ \& \ (\mathcal{C}_1 \ \wedge \ \mathcal{C}_2 \ \wedge \ \bigwedge_i u_i \sqsubseteq v_i \oplus w_i)} \ (\vdash Let)$$

$$\frac{\Xi(G,m) = G^{v_0}; \boldsymbol{E}^{\boldsymbol{v}} \ \xrightarrow{q_1/q_2}\ H^{v_{n+1}}}{\mathcal{TC} = G^u <: G^{v_0} \ \wedge \ F_i^{u_i} <: E_i^{v_i} \ \wedge \ H^{v_{n+1}} <: C^{u'} \ \wedge \ p \geq q_1 \ \wedge \ p' \leq q_2 + p - q_1}{\mathsf{M}; \Xi; \Gamma, x{:}G^u, \boldsymbol{y}{:}\boldsymbol{F}^u \vdash^{p}_{p'} x.m\,(y_1, \dots, y_j) : C^{u'} \ \& \ \mathcal{TC}} \ (\vdash MInv)$$

$$\frac{\mathsf{M}(G,m) = \forall \boldsymbol{v}, \boldsymbol{q}\ \exists \boldsymbol{v'}, \boldsymbol{q'}\ .\ G^{v_0}; \boldsymbol{E}^{\boldsymbol{v}} \ \xrightarrow{q_1/q_2}\ H^{v_{n+1}} \ \& \ \mathcal{D} \qquad \mathcal{D}' = \mathcal{D}[\boldsymbol{w}/\boldsymbol{v}, \boldsymbol{w'}/\boldsymbol{v'}, \boldsymbol{t}/\boldsymbol{q}, \boldsymbol{t'}/\boldsymbol{q'}]}{\mathcal{TC} = G^u <: G^{w_0} \ \wedge \ F_i^{u_i} <: E_i^{w_i} \ \wedge \ H^{w_{n+1}} <: C^{u'} \ \wedge \ p \geq t_1 \ \wedge \ p' \leq t_2 + p - t_1}{\mathsf{M}; \Xi; \Gamma, x{:}G^u, \boldsymbol{y}{:}\boldsymbol{F}^u \vdash^{p}_{p'} x.m\,(y_1, \dots, y_j) : C^{u'} \ \& \ \mathcal{TC} \ \wedge \ \mathcal{D}'} \ (\vdash PInv)$$

$$\boxed{\vdash_{\mathsf{mc}} \mathsf{M}\ \mathsf{ok}}$$

$$\vdash_{\mathsf{mc}} \mathsf{M}'\ \mathsf{ok} \qquad \forall i = 1\,..\,k \quad (C_i, m_i) \in \mathrm{dom}(\mathsf{M}'') \qquad \Xi(C_i, m_i) = C_i^{v_0}; \boldsymbol{E}^{\boldsymbol{v}} \ \xrightarrow{p_1/p_2}\ H^{v_{n+1}}$$

$$\mathsf{M}'; \Xi; \mathsf{this}{:}C_i^{\bar{v}_0}, \boldsymbol{x}{:}\boldsymbol{E}^v \vdash^{\bar{p}_1}_{p_2} \mathsf{M}_{\mathsf{body}}(C, m) : H^{v_{n+1}} \ \& \ \mathcal{C}^{(i)}$$

$$\psi^{(i)} = \forall \boldsymbol{v}, \boldsymbol{p}.\ C^{v_0}; \boldsymbol{E}^{\boldsymbol{v}} \ \xrightarrow{p_1/p_2}\ H^{v_{n+1}} \ \& \ (\mathcal{C}^{(i)} \ \wedge \ v_0 \sqsubseteq \bar{v}_0 \ \wedge \ \Diamond(C_i^{v_0}) + p_1 \geq \Diamond\big(C_i^{\bar{v}_0}\big) + \bar{p}_1)$$

$$\mathsf{S}(D_j) = C_i \qquad \lambda_j = \begin{cases} \mathsf{M}'(D_j, m_i) & \text{if } (D_j, m_i) \in \mathrm{dom}(\mathsf{M}') \\ \top^{(D_j, m_i)} & \text{if } (D_j, m_i) \in \mathrm{dom}(\mathsf{M}'') \end{cases} \qquad \phi^{(i)} = \psi^{(i)} \vee \bigvee_j \lambda_j$$

$$\frac{\mathsf{M}''(C_i, m_i) = \forall \boldsymbol{v}, \boldsymbol{p}.\ C_i^{v_0}; \boldsymbol{E}^{\boldsymbol{v}} \ \xrightarrow{p_1/p_2}\ H^{v_{n+1}} \ \& \ \mathcal{D}^{(i)} \qquad \mathcal{D}^{(i)} = \bigwedge_{l \in \{1, \dots, k\}} \mathsf{constr}(\phi^{(l)})}{\vdash_{\mathsf{mc}} \mathsf{M}' \uplus \mathsf{M}''\ \mathsf{ok}}$$

Fig. 4. Generation of RAJA polymorphic types

then $|\Xi|$ denotes a map from classes and method names to view and arithmetic variables with $\mathrm{dom}(|\Xi|) = \mathrm{dom}(\Xi)$. Similarly, if Γ is an FJEU context, then $|\Gamma|$ is a context from program variables to FJEU types refined with view variables with the same domain as Γ. The judgement reads: expression e has type C^v in the context Γ, subject to the constraints $\mathcal{C}$. Moreover, the judgement defines a *total* function generateConstraints that generates constraints for an expression:

$$\mathsf{generateConstraints}(\mathsf{M}, \Xi, \Gamma, p, p', e, C^v) = \mathcal{C} \ \mathrm{if} \ \mathsf{M}; \Xi; \Gamma \vdash^{p}_{p'} e : C^v \ \& \ \mathcal{C}$$

The subtyping constraints are of the form $C^v <: D^u$ where C and D are classes and v and u are view variables. We also create constraints of the form $u \sqsubseteq v \oplus w$ in the rule ($\vdash Let$), where $v \oplus w$ is a view expression.

There are two rules for method invocation: ($\vdash PInv$) for polymorphic method invocation and ($\vdash MInv$) for monomorphic method invocation. In ($\vdash PInv$) we assume that the called method has already been analysed and so its polymorphic RAJA method type is available. The constraints generated by this rule consist of the method's constraints, where we substitute the view and arithmetic variables with fresh ones, in conjunction with standard subtyping and arithmetic constraints. We apply the rule ($\Diamond MInv.$) when the called method appears in the map Ξ, which means, as we discussed earlier, that the method and the method whose body we are analysing are mutually recursive. In that case the constraints for the method are not yet available. Thus, we only generate the standard subtyping and arithmetic constraints.

The judgement $\vdash_{\mathsf{mc}} \mathsf{M} \ \mathsf{ok}$ returns RAJA polymorphic method types for the methods in M by generating the constraints for the methods' bodies. We perform the analysis on the basis of the call graph of the program, which we modify slightly by adding the inheritance relations to it. For example, the graph corresponding to the program for copying lists defined in Fig. 1, can be represented as follows:

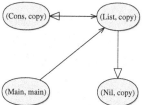

After we have built the graph, we decompose it in its strongly connected components to obtain the acyclic component graph G^{SCC}. Afterwards, we sort the obtained dag G^{SCC} topologically and call the constraint generation algorithm in that order, with the strongly connected components being analysed together. When applied to the graph above, we obtain the following order where (Cons, copy) and (List, copy) are analysed together.

$$(\mathsf{Nil}, \mathsf{copy}), [(\mathsf{Cons}, \mathsf{copy}), (\mathsf{List}, \mathsf{copy})], (\mathsf{Main}, \mathsf{main})$$

Now, why do we need to extend the call graph with inheritance relations? The reason for this is that, before we analyse a method m in a class C, we would like to analyse the same method m in each subclass D of C. For proving soundness of the constraint generation algorithm we need to show $M(D, m) <: M(C, m)$, and this follows trivially when we add the constraints of $D.m$ to the polymorphic type of $C.m$. For example, the method List.copy should contain the constraints of the methods Cons.copy and Nil.copy, as explained earlier.

In the following we prove that, if the constraints generated for the expression e are satisfiable, then the expression is typeable in the RAJA system with the result type, context and effect given by the solution to the constraints.

Lemma 1 (Soundness of constraint generation)
If $\mathcal{E} :: M; \Xi; \Gamma \vdash_{q_2}^{q_1} e : C^v$ & C and $\pi \models C$ then $M; \pi(\Xi); \pi(\Gamma) \vdash_{\pi(q_2)}^{\pi(q_1)} e : C^{\pi(v)}$.

Proof. By induction on $\mathcal{E}$.

Lemma 2 (Soundness of constraint generation for methods)
Let $\mathcal{P} = (\mathscr{C}, \text{main})$ be an FJEU program and let $\mathcal{E} :: \vdash_{mc} M$ ok and let $M(C, m)$ be non-empty for each $(C, m) \in \text{dom}(M)$. Then:

1. $\vdash_m M$ ok.
2. $S(D) = C$ implies $M(D, m) <: M(C, m)$.

Proof. 1. By induction on $\mathcal{E}$.
2. Follows by the design of the judgement $\vdash_{mc} M$ ok, as discussed earlier.

Next, we show that, when applied to a typeable expression, the constraint generation rules emit a satisfiable constraint set.

Lemma 3 (Completeness of constraint generation)
If $\mathcal{E} :: M; \Xi; \Gamma \vdash_{n_2}^{n_1} e : C^r$ and $M; |\Xi|; |\Gamma| \vdash_{p_2}^{p_1} e : C^v$ & C then there exists π with $\pi(p_i) = n_i$, $\pi(v) = r$, $\pi(|\Gamma|) = \Gamma$, $\pi(|\Xi|) = \Xi$ such that $\pi \models C$.

Proof. By induction on $\mathcal{E}$.

Lemma 4 (Completeness of constraint generation for methods)
Let $\mathscr{R} = (\mathscr{C}, \text{main}, M)$ be a well-typed RAJA program and let $\mathcal{N}$ be a map with $\text{dom}(\mathcal{N}) = \text{dom}(M)$ and $\mathcal{E} :: \vdash_{mc} \mathcal{N}$ ok. Then for all $(C, m) \in M$ holds $\mathcal{N}(C, m) <: M(C, m)$.

Proof. By induction on $\mathcal{E}$.

4.2   Constraint Solving

In this section we shall see how to apply RAJA types to the analysis of the heap-space requirements of methods. Currently, our tool is not capable of computing bounds for arbitrary methods, but only for the method main. This is because translating refined types to closed-form upper bounds is challenging and requires further research. We wish to compute an upper bound on the number of heap cells needed for executing main as a function of main's arguments, which follows from the potential given to its arguments by its RAJA type. We have seen in the previous section how to obtain a polymorphic RAJA type for main, but, for being able to read off the potential from that type, we need a concrete instance of the type, which we can obtain by solving the type's constraints.

Whereas solving linear arithmetic constraints is easily achieved by an LP-Solver, solving subtyping constraints is more challenging. The task of solving a constraint $C^u <: D^v$ can be reduced to the tasks of solving $C <: D$ and $u \sqsubseteq v$, by the definition of subtyping. $C <: D$ can be checked easily by analysing the inheritance relations in the program. Thus, the real challenge is solving $u \sqsubseteq v$. Solving these kind of constraints is difficult for various reasons.

First, views are infinite objects, and the inequality relation over views is defined coinductively. Thus, unfolding the definition of inequality; that is, trying to solve the constraints $\Diamond(C^u) \geq \Diamond(C^v)$ for each $C \in \mathcal{C}$ and $\mathsf{A}^{\mathsf{get}}(C^u, a) \sqsubseteq \mathsf{A}^{\mathsf{get}}(C^v, a)$ and $\mathsf{A}^{\mathsf{set}}(C^v, a) \sqsubseteq \mathsf{A}^{\mathsf{set}}(C^u, a)$ for each $a \in \mathsf{A}(C)$ would lead to more unfolding steps and this process would not terminate.

Second, subtyping over views is covariant in the get views and contravariant in the set views. The contravariance also brings difficulties. For this reason, we studied in previous work [14] a simpler type of infinite trees than views. We fix a finite set $\mathcal{L} = \{l_1, \ldots, l_n\}$ of labels to address the children of a node, e.g. $\mathcal{L} = \{L, R\}$ for infinite binary trees and $\mathcal{L} = \{tl\}$ for infinite lists. Such trees can be added, scaled, and compared componentwise; furthermore, we have an operation $\Diamond(.)$ that extracts the root label of a tree, thus if t is a tree then $\Diamond(t)$ is an element of $\mathbb{D}$. Finally, if t is a tree and $l \in \mathcal{L}$ then $l(t)$ is the l-labelled immediate subtree of t. We define a preorder $\sqsubseteq$ between trees as follows:

Definition 11. *Let* $t, t' \in \mathsf{T}_{\mathbb{D}}^{\mathcal{L}}$. *We define* $t \sqsubseteq t'$ *coinductively by* $t \sqsubseteq t' \iff \Diamond(t) \leq \Diamond(t')$ *and* $l_i(t) \sqsubseteq l_i(t')$ *for all* $l_i \in \mathcal{L}$.

This inequality relation is covariant in all cases. Because these trees are simpler objects, solving constraints over them is simpler than solving constraints over views. Thus, we solve the inequalities over views by reducing them to inequalities over infinite trees. For solving constraints over infinite trees, we still have the problem that unfolding the inequality relation would not terminate. This is why, to ensure termination of unfolding, we developed a heuristic algorithm for solving these constraints that assumes that the solutions to the constraints are regular infinite trees. This implies, however, that the algorithm is not able to solve all the constraints but only a subset of them that admit regular solutions. Therefore, when using this algorithm, we can solve only subtyping constraints that admit regular views as a solution, which correspond to programs whose heap-space consumption is a linear function of its input. Hence, the algorithm that we present in this paper can compute only linear bounds on the heap-space requirements of programs. However, we remark that this is because no better algorithm for solving the constraints over infinite trees is known at the moment.

We present here a reduction from views to infinite trees. The idea of the reduction is to separate the "positive parts" and "negative parts" of a view, to build infinite trees. To reduce a view $r \in \mathcal{V}$, we define, for each class $C_i \in \mathscr{C}$, the infinite trees $r_i^+, r_i^- \in \mathsf{T}_{\mathbb{D}}^{\mathcal{L}}$, where $\mathcal{L} = \mathcal{L}^+ \cup \mathcal{L}^-$ and $L^+ = \{l_{kj}^+ \mid C_k \in$

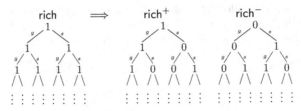

Fig. 5. View rich reduced to rich$^+$ and rich$^-$, assuming that $\mathcal{C} = \{\,\mathsf{Cons}\,\}$

$\mathcal{C}, a_j \in A(C_k)\}$ and $L^- = \{l_{kj}^- \mid C_k \in \mathcal{C}, a_j \in A(C_k)\}$ such that we can reduce inequalities between views to inequalities between infinite trees. More exactly, we want to prove: $r \sqsubseteq s \Rightarrow \bigwedge_{C_i \in \mathcal{C}} s_i^+ \sqsubseteq r_i^+ \wedge r_i^- \sqsubseteq s_i^-$. Fig. 5 shows a representation of the reduction applied to the view rich.

Definition 12. *Let* $r \in \mathcal{V}$. *We define* $\mathsf{expand}(r) = (r^+, r^-)$, *where* r_i^+ *and* r_i^- *are defined coinductively as follows. Let* $C_i \in \mathcal{C}$ *and* $C_k \in \mathcal{C}$ *and* $a_j \in A(C_k)$.

$$
\begin{aligned}
&\Diamond(r_i^+) \ = \Diamond(C_i^r) && \Diamond(r_i^-) \ = 0 \\
&l_{kj}^+(r_i^+) = A^{\mathsf{get}}(C_k^r, a_j)_i^+ && l_{kj}^+(r_i^-) = A^{\mathsf{get}}(C_k^r, a_j)_i^- \\
&l_{kj}^-(r_i^+) = A^{\mathsf{set}}(C_k^r, a_j)_i^- && l_{kj}^-(r_i^-) = A^{\mathsf{set}}(C_k^r, a_j)_i^+
\end{aligned}
$$

Lemma 5. *Let* $r \sqsubseteq s$ *and let* $(r^+, r^-) = \mathsf{expand}(r)$ *and* $(s^+, s^-) = \mathsf{expand}(s)$.

1. $s_i^+ \sqsubseteq r_i^+$ *for all* i.
2. $r_i^- \sqsubseteq s_i^-$ *for all* i.

Proof. Simultaneously by coinduction.

Next, we build a view from two vectors of trees t and t', with $|t| = |t'| = |\mathcal{C}|$.

Definition 13. *We define the function* $\mathsf{reduce}(t, t') = r$, *where* $r \in \mathcal{V}$, *coinductively as follows.*

$$
\begin{aligned}
\Diamond(C_i^r) \ &= \Diamond(t_i) \dot{-} \Diamond(t_i') \\
A^{\mathsf{get}}(C_k^r, a_j) &= \mathsf{reduce}(\overrightarrow{l_{kj}^+(t_i)}, \overrightarrow{l_{kj}^+(t_i')}) \\
A^{\mathsf{set}}(C_k^r, a_j) &= \mathsf{reduce}(\overrightarrow{l_{kj}^-(t_i')}, \overrightarrow{l_{kj}^-(t_i)})
\end{aligned}
$$

First, we notice that reduce is the left inverse of expand.

Lemma 6. *Let* $r \in \mathcal{V}$. *Then* $\mathsf{reduce}(\mathsf{expand}(r)) = r$.

Proof. By coinduction.

Lemma 7. *Let* t, t', p, p' *be vectors of infinite trees. Then, if* $t_i' \sqsubseteq p_i'$ *and* $p_i \sqsubseteq t_i$ *for each* i, *then* $\mathsf{reduce}(t, t') \sqsubseteq \mathsf{reduce}(p, p')$.

Proof. By coinduction.

Now we can reduce inequalities over views to inequalities of infinite trees, based on the reduction from views to infinite trees. When we obtain a solution for the set of constraints over infinite trees, we can build a solution for the original set of inequalities over views, based on the reduction from infinite trees to views. The details are omitted for lack of space, and can be found in [16].

Table 1. Experimental results. The column **Heap space** shows the prediction of the required size of the free-list which in each case was equal to the actual heap-space requirements of the program and **Run time** represents the run time of the analysis.

Program	LoC	Heap space	Run time	Program	LoC	Heap space	Run time
Copy	37	n	0.2s	CAppend	60	$2 + 2n$	0.7s
CircList	56	$1 + n$	1.6s	MergeSort	127	1	10.3s
InsSort	66	$2 + n$	1.9s	BankAcc	200	$2 + 8n$	6.3s
DList	70	$3 + n$	1.2s	Bank	908	$11 + 6n$	9.8 min
Append	80	$2 + n$	3s				

5   Experimental Results

We have implemented a tool in OCaml for type checking, evaluating and analysing the heap-space requirements of FJEU programs, based on the algorithm presented in this paper. The tool uses the result of the analysis for building an optimised heap for evaluating the programs; that is, it creates a heap with a size equal to the size predicted by the analysis. The tool assumes that each FJEU program contains a main method which has one parameter of type List. Further, the tool assumes that it is given an input file for the program execution. The interpreter then creates a singly linked list (one node for each row of the input file) and saves it in the heap before it starts executing the program.

The analyser component of the tool can analyse methods whose heap-space consumption is a linear function on the size of its arguments. When it analyses the main method of a program, it delivers two non-negative real numbers a and b, which shall mean that the program can be evaluated with no memory errors with a heap of size at least $a \cdot |$input file$| + b$.

Table 1 shows some programs that we could analyse with our tool. For each example, we could solve the constraints and resultantly provide a (linear) upper bound for its heap-space requirements. The experiments were performed on a 2.20GHz Intel(R) Core(TM)2 Duo CPU laptop with 2GB RAM. The run-time of the analysis varied from 0.2s to about 10 minutes on a program of 908 LoC. Being able to analyse 908 LoC may seem rather modest, but one should note that nearly all these LoC contribute to the analysis. A typical real program will contain large portions that look like white space to the analysis, e.g. numerical computations, I/O, etc. and resource-wise independent parts of a larger program could be analysed separately.

All bounds are exact in the above experiments, although our soundness result only ensures an upper bound. There is a demo website where the examples can be analysed and downloaded, and the user can perform the analysis on their own programs[1].

---

[1] http://raja.tcs.ifi.lmu.de

6 Conclusions and Related Work

We have presented a type-based analysis of the heap-space requirements of object-oriented programs. The soundness of each step of the analysis has been rigorously proved. Moreover, the analysis was modular, enabled by the use of polymorphic types. Thus, in principle, the analysis is capable of scaling to large programs, although there is plenty of room for improvement. Polymorphic types also enable an incremental analysis because they can be saved after the analysis, and in most cases they do not need to be re-generated when more classes and methods are added to the programs.

Related Work. Constraint-based type reconstruction for numerically refinement types has been introduced in [17] and been further developed in [18] under the name "liquid types" which further introduces techniques from predicate abstraction and model checking.

Our method for the generation of view constraints is directly inspired by those works, in particular [17]; however, the view constraints thus gleaned are not directly amenable to algorithmic solution. The main conceptual contribution of the present work is thus not so much the RAJA type system which has already been presented elsewhere, albeit in slightly different and less general form, but rather the solution of the generated typing or view constraints by translation to tree constraints and iterated elimination.

Looking at the black-box front end of our contribution—the fully automatic inference of symbolic resource bounds for object-oriented programs, we can place our contribution in the following perspective. The topic has been researched intensively in the past years and many different approaches to it have been proposed.

In a series of papers [2, 13, 19] Chin and his collaborators have used sized types and separation logic for the generation of symbolic resource bounds for object-oriented programs. Presently, the method is not fully automatic because the user must provide aliasing and shape information. Furthermore, in the functional realm, the amortised approach has proved superior to related methods in the case of algorithms that heavily use intermediate data structures whose size is difficult to describe [10]. However, it might very well be possible to combine our approach with the generic system "HIP and SLEEK" [19] that maintains and propagates separation logic assertions for an object-oriented language.

In the recurrence-based approach COSTA [4, 1], one introduces an unknown resource bounding function for each method and then derives recurrence constraints for those by going over the control-flow graph. The main methodological innovation lies not so much in the analysis which uses mainly standard techniques, but in the development of improved solvers for these recurrences. As discussed above the amortised approach is superior when resource usage is intertwined with size and layout of intermediate data structures. The path-length analysis performed by COSTA to infer size-relations is sound with the condition that there is no aliasing and cyclic data, whereas the analysis performed by RAJA is sound for all programs and we do not require an extra cyclicity analysis. Nevertheless, we hope that the advanced recurrence-solving technology developed by the COSTA team could allow us to go beyond linear arithmetic constraints and bounds.

For imperative non-object-oriented programs several other fully- or semi-automatic analyses have been developed, notably SPEED [3] which is based on the inference of linear arithmetic relationships between manually added counter variables. Here, the performance in the presence of dynamically allocated data structures strongly depends on the instrumentation. SPEED also uses user-defined quantitative functions that are associated with abstract data-structures. In contrary, RAJA is fully automatic and does not require any user-input.

Atkey [20] combined amortised analysis and separation logic to analyse imperative programs. Like RAJA, Atkey's system can compute only linear bounds. On the other hand, the user needs to provide complex annotations.

Acknowledgements. We acknowledge support by the DFG Graduiertenkolleg 1480 Programm- und Modell-Analyse (PUMA).

References

1. Albert, E., Arenas, P., Genaim, S., Puebla, G.: Closed-Form Upper Bounds in Static Cost Analysis. Journal of Automated Reasoning (2010)
2. Chin, W.-N., Nguyen, H.H., Qin, S.C., Rinard, M.: Memory Usage Verification for OO Programs. In: Hankin, C., Siveroni, I. (eds.) SAS 2005. LNCS, vol. 3672, pp. 70–86. Springer, Heidelberg (2005)
3. Gulwani, S., Mehra, K.K., Chilimbi, T.M.: SPEED: precise and efficient static estimation of program computational complexity. In: POPL. ACM (2009)
4. Albert, E., Arenas, P., Genaim, S., Puebla, G., Zanardini, D.: COSTA: Design and Implementation of a Cost and Termination Analyzer for Java Bytecode. In: de Boer, F.S., Bonsangue, M.M., Graf, S., de Roever, W.-P. (eds.) FMCO 2007. LNCS, vol. 5382, pp. 113–132. Springer, Heidelberg (2008)
5. Grobauer, B.: Topics in Semantics-based Program Manipulation. PhD thesis, BRICS Aarhus (2001)
6. Gomez, G., Liu, Y.A.: Automatic time-bound analysis for a higher-order language. In: PEPM (2002)
7. Hofmann, M., Jost, S.: Type-Based Amortised Heap-Space Analysis. In: Sestoft, P. (ed.) ESOP 2006. LNCS, vol. 3924, pp. 22–37. Springer, Heidelberg (2006)
8. Hofmann, M., Rodriguez, D.: Efficient Type-Checking for Amortised Heap-Space Analysis. In: Grädel, E., Kahle, R. (eds.) CSL 2009. LNCS, vol. 5771, pp. 317–331. Springer, Heidelberg (2009)
9. Jost, S., Loid, H.W., Hammond, K., Hofmann, M.: Static determination of quantitative resource usage for higher-order programs. In: POPL (January 2010)
10. Hoffmann, J., Aehlig, K., Hofmann, M.: Multivariate amortized resource analysis. In: POPL (2011)
11. Tarjan, R.E.: Amortized computational complexity. SIAM Journal on Algebraic and Discrete Methods 6(2), 306–318 (1985)
12. Okasaki, C.: Purely Functional Data Structures. Cambridge University Press (1998)

13. He, G., Qin, S., Luo, C., Chin, W.-N.: Memory Usage Verification Using Hip/Sleek. In: Liu, Z., Ravn, A.P. (eds.) ATVA 2009. LNCS, vol. 5799, pp. 166–181. Springer, Heidelberg (2009)
14. Hofmann, M., Rodriguez, D.: Linear Constraints over Infinite Trees. In: Bjørner, N., Voronkov, A. (eds.) LPAR-18 2012. LNCS, vol. 7180, pp. 343–358. Springer, Heidelberg (2012)
15. Igarashi, A., Pierce, B., Wadler, P.: Featherweight Java: A minimal core calculus for Java and GJ. In: OOPSLA (1999)
16. Rodriguez, D.: Amortised Resource Analysis for Object Oriented Programs. PhD thesis, Ludwig-Maximilians-Universität München (2012)
17. Knowles, K., Flanagan, C.: Type Reconstruction for General Refinement Types. In: De Nicola, R. (ed.) ESOP 2007. LNCS, vol. 4421, pp. 505–519. Springer, Heidelberg (2007)
18. Rondon, P.M., Kawaguci, M., Jhala, R.: Liquid types. ACM SIGPLAN Notices 43(6), 159–169 (2008)
19. Chin, W.N., David, C., Gherghina, C.: A hip and sleek verification system. In: OOPSLA Companion (2011)
20. Atkey, R.: Amortised resource analysis with separation logic. Logical Methods in Computer Science 7(2) (2011)

Keyword Index

Author Index